# FORD | TAURUS/SABLE
## 1986-95 REPAIR MANUAL

CHILTON'S

P9-DCI-922

| | |
|---|---|
| **CEO** | Rick Van Dalen |
| **President** | Dean F. Morgantini, S.A.E. |
| **Vice President–Finance** | Barry L. Beck |
| **Vice President–Sales** | Glenn D. Potere |
| **Executive Editor** | Kevin M. G. Maher, A.S.E. |
| **Manager–Consumer Automotive** | Richard Schwartz, A.S.E. |
| **Manager–Professional Automotive** | Richard J. Rivele |
| **Manager–Marine/Recreation** | James R. Marotta, A.S.E. |
| **Production Specialists** | Brian Hollingsworth, Melinda Possinger |
| **Project Managers** | Thomas A. Mellon, A.S.E., S.A.E., Eric Michael Mihalyi, A.S.E., S.T.S., S.A.E., Christine L. Sheeky, S.A.E., Richard T. Smith, Ron Webb |
| **Schematics Editors** | Christopher G. Ritchie, A.S.E., S.A.E., S.T.S., Stephanie A. Spunt |
| **Editor** | Christine L. Sheeky, S.A.E. |

**CHILTON** *Automotive Books*

PUBLISHED BY **W. G. NICHOLS, INC.**

Manufactured in USA
© 1995 W. G. Nichols, Inc.
1025 Andrew Drive
West Chester, PA 19380
ISBN 0-8019-8687-7
Library of Congress Catalog Card No. 94-069430
11 12 13 14 15  9876543210

# Contents

# Contents

## 7 DRIVE TRAIN

## 8 SUSPENSION AND STEERING

## 9 BRAKES

## 10 BODY

## GLOSSARY

## MASTER INDEX

## SAFETY NOTICE

Proper service and repair procedures are vital to the safe, reliable operation of all motor vehicles, as well as the personal safety of those performing repairs. This manual outlines procedures for servicing and repairing vehicles using safe, effective methods. The procedures contain many NOTES, CAUTIONS and WARNINGS which should be followed, along with standard procedures to eliminate the possibility of personal injury or improper service which could damage the vehicle or compromise its safety.

It is important to note that repair procedures and techniques, tools and parts for servicing motor vehicles, as well as the skill and experience of the individual performing the work vary widely. It is not possible to anticipate all of the conceivable ways or conditions under which vehicles may be serviced, or to provide cautions as to all possible hazards that may result. Standard and accepted safety precautions and equipment should be used when handling toxic or flammable fluids, and safety goggles or other protection should be used during cutting, grinding, chiseling, prying, or any other process that can cause material removal or projectiles.

Some procedures require the use of tools specially designed for a specific purpose. Before substituting another tool or procedure, you must be completely satisfied that neither your personal safety, nor the performance of the vehicle will be endangered.

Although information in this manual is based on industry sources and is complete as possible at the time of publication, the possibility exists that some car manufacturers made later changes which could not be included here. While striving for total accuracy, Nichols Publishing cannot assume responsibility for any errors, changes or omissions that may occur in the compilation of this data.

## PART NUMBERS

Part numbers listed in this reference are not recommendations by Nichols Publishing for any product brand name. They are references that can be used with interchange manuals and aftermarket supplier catalogs to locate each brand supplier's discrete part number.

## SPECIAL TOOLS

Special tools are recommended by the vehicle manufacturer to perform their specific job. Use has been kept to a minimum, but where absolutely necessary, they are referred to in the text by the part number of the tool manufacturer. These tools can be purchased, under the appropriate part number, from your local dealer or regional distributor, or an equivalent tool can be purchased locally from a tool supplier or parts outlet. Before substituting any tool for the one recommended, read the SAFETY NOTICE at the top of this page.

## ACKNOWLEDGMENTS

This publication contains material that is reproduced and distributed under a license from Ford Motor Company. No further reproduction or distribution of the Ford Motor Company material is allowed without the express written permission from Ford Motor Company.

Nichols Publishing would like to express thanks to all of the fine companies who participate in the production of our books:
- Hand tools supplied by Craftsman are used during all phases of our vehicle teardown and photography.
- Many of the fine specialty tools used in our procedures were provided courtesy of Lisle Corporation.
- Lincoln Automotive Products (1 Lincoln Way, St. Louis, MO 63120) has provided their industrial shop equipment, including jacks (engine, transmission and floor), engine stands, fluid and lubrication tools, as well as shop presses.
- Rotary Lifts (1-800-640-5438 or www.Rotary-Lift.com), the largest automobile lift manufacturer in the world, offering the biggest variety of surface and in-ground lifts available, has fulfilled our shop's lift needs.
- Much of our shop's electronic testing equipment was supplied by Universal Enterprises Inc. (UEI).
- Safety-Kleen Systems Inc. has provided parts cleaning stations and assistance with environmentally sound disposal of residual wastes.
- United Gilsonite Laboratories (UGL), manufacturer of Drylok® concrete floor paint, has provided materials and expertise for the coating and protection of our shop floor.

## HOW TO USE THIS BOOK

Chilton's Total Car Care manual for Ford Taurus and Mercury Sable is intended to help you learn more about the inner workings of your car and save you money on its upkeep and operation. The first two sections will be used the most, since they contain maintenance and tune-up information and procedures. Studies have shown that a properly tuned and maintained car can get better gas mileage than an out-of-tune car. The other sections deal with the more complex systems of your vehicle. Operating systems from engine through brakes are covered to the extent that we feel the average do-it-yourselfer becomes mechanically involved, as well as more complex procedures that will benefit both the advanced do-it-yourselfer mechanic as well as the professional.

A secondary purpose of this book is as a reference for owners who want to understand their car and/or their mechanics better. In this case, no tools at all are required.

Before attempting any repairs or service on your car, read through the entire procedure outlined in the appropriate section. This will give you the overall view of what tools and supplies will be required. There is nothing more frustrating than having to walk to the bus stop on Monday morning because you were short one gasket on Sunday afternoon. So read ahead and plan ahead. Each operation should be approached logically and all procedures thoroughly understood before attempting any work. Some special tools that may be required can often be rented from local automotive jobbers or places specializing in renting tools and equipment. Check the yellow pages of your phone book.

Sections contain adjustments, maintenance, removal and installation procedures, and repair or overhaul procedures. When repair is not considered practical, we tell you how to remove the failed part and then how to install the new or rebuilt replacement. In this way, you at least save the labor costs. Backyard overhaul of some components is just not practical, but the removal and installation procedure is often simple and well within the capabilities of the average car owner.

Two basic mechanic's rules should be mentioned here. First, whenever the left side of the car or engine is referred to, it is meant to specify the driver's side of the car. Conversely, the right side of the car means the passenger's side. Second, all screws and bolts are removed by turning counterclockwise, and tightened by turning clockwise, unless otherwise noted.

Safety is always the most important rule. Constantly be aware of the dangers involved in working on or around an automobile and take proper precautions to avoid the risk of personal injury or damage to the vehicle. See the procedure in this section, Servicing Your Vehicle Safely, and the SAFETY NOTICE on the acknowledgment page before attempting any service procedures.

Pay attention to the instructions provided. There are 3 common mistakes in mechanical work:

1. Incorrect order of assembly, disassembly or adjustment. When taking something apart or putting it together, doing things in the wrong order usually just costs you extra time; however it CAN break something. Read the entire procedure before beginning disassembly. Do everything in the order in which the instructions say you should do it, even if you can't immediately see a reason for it. When you're taking apart something that is very intricate, you might want to draw a picture of how it looks when assembled at one point in order to make sure you get everything back in its proper position. We will supply exploded views whenever possible, but sometimes the job requires more attention to detail than an illustration provides. When making adjustments (especially tune-up adjustments), do them in order. One adjustment often affects another and you cannot expect satisfactory results unless each adjustment is made only when it cannot be changed by any other.

2. Overtightening (or undertightening) nuts and bolts. While it is more common for overtorquing to cause damage, undertorquing can cause a fastener to vibrate loose and cause serious damage. Especially when dealing with aluminum parts, pay attention to torque specifications and utilize a torque wrench during assembly. If a torque figure is not available, remember that if you are using the right tool to do the job, you will probably not have to strain yourself to get a fastener tight enough. The pitch of most threads is so slight that the tension you put on the wrench will be multiplied many, many times in actual force on what you are tightening. A good example of how critical torque is can be seen in the case of spark plug installation, especially when you are putting the plug into an aluminum cylinder head. Too little torque can fail to crush the gasket, causing leakage of combustion gases and consequent overheating of the plug and engine parts. Too much torque can damage the threads or distort the plug, which changes the spark gap.

**➡There are many commercial chemical products available for ensuring that fasteners won't come loose, even if they are not torqued just right (a very common brand is Loctite®). If you're worried about getting something together tight enough to hold, but loose enough to avoid mechanical damage during assembly, one of these products might offer substantial insurance. Read the label on the package and make sure the product is compatible with the materials, fluids, etc. involved before choosing one.**

3. Crossthreading. This occurs when a part such as a bolt is screwed into a nut or casting at the wrong angle and forced, causing the threads to become damaged. Crossthreading is more likely to occur if access is difficult. It helps to clean and lubricate fasteners, and to start threading with the part to be installed going straight in, using your fingers. If you encounter resistance, unscrew the part and start over again at a different angle until it can be inserted and turned several times without much effort. Keep in mind that many parts, especially spark plugs, use tapered threads so that gentle turning will automatically bring the part you're threading to the proper angle if you don't force it or resist a change in angle. Don't put a wrench on the part until it's been turned in a couple of times by hand. If you suddenly encounter resistance and the part has not seated fully, don't force it. Pull it back out and make sure it's clean and threading properly.

Always take your time and be patient; once you have some experience, working on your car will become an enjoyable hobby.

## TOOLS AND EQUIPMENT

**➧ See Figures 1 thru 12**

Naturally, without the proper tools and equipment it is impossible to properly service your vehicle. It would be impossible to catalog each tool that you would need to perform each or every operation in this book. It would also be unwise for the amateur to rush out and buy an expensive set of tools on the theory that he may need one or more of them at sometime.

The best approach is to proceed slowly, gathering a good quality set of those tools that are used most frequently. Don't be misled by the low cost of bargain tools. It is far better to spend a little more for better quality. Forged wrenches, 6 or 12-point sockets and fine tooth ratchets are by far preferable to their less expensive counterparts. As any good mechanic can tell you, there are few worse experiences than trying to work on a car with bad tools. Your monetary savings will be far outweighed by frustration and mangled knuckles.

Certain tools, plus a basic ability to handle tools, are required to get started. A basic mechanics tool set, a torque wrench, and a Torx bits set. Torx bits are hexlobular drivers which fit both inside and outside on special Torx head fasteners used in various places on your vehicle.

Begin accumulating those tools that are used most frequently; those associated with routine maintenance and tune-up.

In addition to the normal assortment of screwdrivers and pliers you should have the following tools for routine maintenance jobs (your vehicle, depending on the model year, uses both SAE and metric fasteners):

- SAE/Metric wrenches, sockets and combination open end/box end wrenches in sizes from 1/8 in. (3mm) to 3/4 in. (19mm); and a spark plug socket 13/16 in. (21mm). If possible, buy various length socket drive extensions. One break in this department is that the metric sockets available in the U.S. will all fit the ratchet handles and extensions you may already have (1/4 in., 3/8 in., and 1/2 in. drive).

- Jackstands for support.
- Oil filter wrench.
- Oil filter spout for pouring oil.
- Grease gun for chassis lubrication.
- Hydrometer for checking the battery.
- A container for draining oil.
- Many rags for wiping up the inevitable mess.

In addition to the above items, there are several others that are not absolutely necessary, but handy to have around. These include oil-dry (cat box litter works just as well and may be cheaper), a transmission funnel and the usual supply of lubricants, antifreeze and fluids, although these can be purchased as needed. This is a basic list for routine maintenance, but only your personal needs and desires can accurately determine your list of necessary tools.

The second list of tools is for tune-ups. While the tools involved here are slightly more sophisticated, they need not be outrageously expensive. There are several inexpensive tach/dwell meters on the market that are every bit as good for the average mechanic as a professional model. Just be sure that it goes to at least 1200–1500 rpm on the tach scale and that it works on 4 and 6 cylinder engines. A basic list of tune-up equipment could include:

- Tach-dwell meter.
- Spark plug wrench.

Fig. 3 A hydraulic floor jack and a set of jackstands are essential for lifting and supporting the vehicle

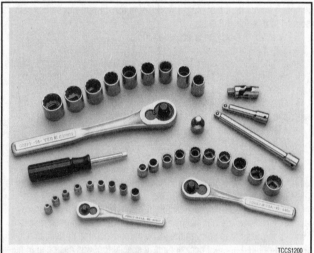

Fig. 1 All but the most basic procedure will require an assortment of ratchets and sockets

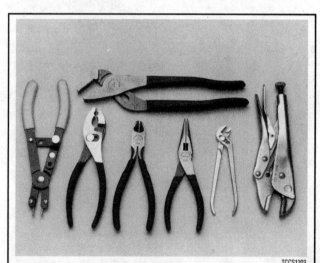

Fig. 4 An assortment of pliers will be handy, especially for old rusted parts and stripped bolt heads

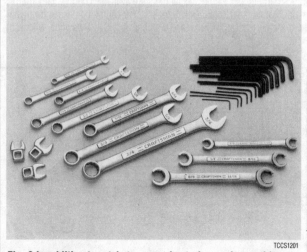

Fig. 2 In addition to ratchets, a good set of wrenches and hex keys will be necessary

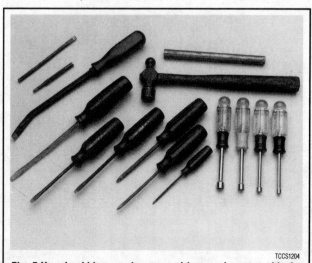

Fig. 5 You should have various screwdrivers, a hammer, chisels and prybars in your toolbox

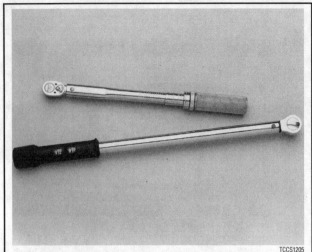

Fig. 6 Many repairs will require the use of torque wrench to assure the components are properly fastened

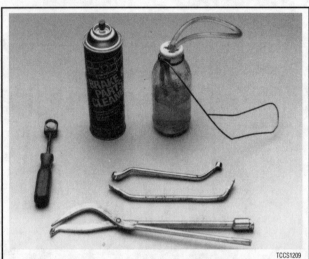

Fig. 7 Although not always necessary, using specialized brake tools will save time

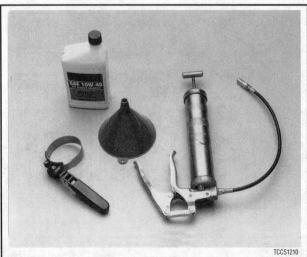

Fig. 8 A few inexpensive lubrication tools will make regular service easier

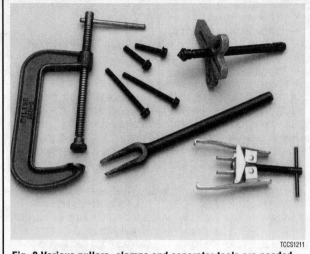

Fig. 9 Various pullers, clamps and separator tools are needed for the repair of many components

• Timing light (a DC light that works from the vehicle's battery is best, although an AC light that plugs into 110V house current will suffice with some sacrifice in brightness).
• Wire spark plug gauge/adjusting tools.
• Set of feeler gauges.

In addition to these basic tools, there are several other tools and gauges you may find useful. In fact, some of these you may come to decide you can't live without. These include:

• Compression gauge. The screw-in type is slower to use, but eliminates the possibility of a faulty reading due to escaping pressure.
• Manifold vacuum gauge.
• A test light.
• Volt/ohmmeter (or multimeter).
• Induction meter. This is used for determining whether or not there is current in a wire, and may come in handy if a wire is broken somewhere in a wiring harness.

Normally, the use of special factory tools is avoided for repair procedures, since these are not readily available for the do-it-yourself mechanic. When it is possible to perform the job with more commonly available tools, it will be pointed out, but occasionally, a special tool was designed to perform a specific function and should be used. Before substituting another tool, you should be convinced that neither your safety nor the performance of the vehicle will be compromised.

When a special tool is indicated, it will be referred to by the manufacturer's part number. Some special tools are available commercially from major tool manufacturers. Others for your car can be purchased from your Ford/Mercury dealer or from the Owatonna Tool Co., Owatonna, Minnesota 55060.

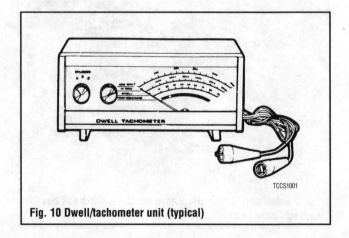

Fig. 10 Dwell/tachometer unit (typical)

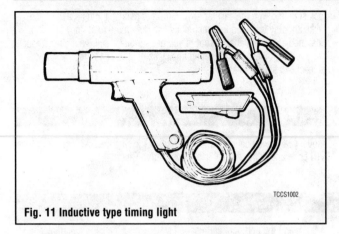

**Fig. 11 Inductive type timing light**

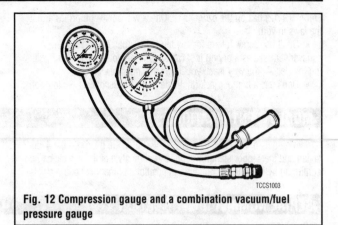

**Fig. 12 Compression gauge and a combination vacuum/fuel pressure gauge**

As a final note, you will probably find a torque wrench necessary for all but the most basic work. The beam type models are perfectly adequate, although the newer click types are more precise.

Torque specification for each fastener will be given in the procedure in any case that a specific torque value is required. If no torque specifications are given, use the following values as a guide, based upon fastener size:

**Bolts marked 6T**
- 6mm bolt/nut—5–7 ft. lbs. (7–9 Nm)
- 8mm bolt/nut—12–17 ft. lbs. (16–23 Nm)

- 10mm bolt/nut—23–34 ft. lbs. (31–46 Nm)
- 12mm bolt/nut—41–59 ft. lbs. (56–80 Nm)
- 14mm bolt/nut—56–76 ft. lbs. (76–103 Nm)

**Bolts marked 8T**
- 6mm bolt/nut—6–9 ft. lbs. (8–12 Nm)
- 8mm bolt/nut—13–20 ft. lbs. (18–27 Nm)
- 10mm bolt/nut—27–40 ft. lbs. (37–54 Nm)
- 12mm bolt/nut—46–69 ft. lbs. (62–93 Nm)
- 14mm bolt/nut—75–101 ft. lbs. (102–137 Nm)

## SERVICING YOUR VEHICLE SAFELY

It is virtually impossible to anticipate all of the hazards involved with automotive maintenance and service but care and common sense will prevent most accidents.

The rules of safety for mechanics range from "don't smoke around gasoline," to "use the proper tool for the job." The trick to avoiding injuries is to develop safe work habits and take every possible precaution.

### Do's

- Do keep a fire extinguisher and first aid kit within easy reach.
- Do wear safety glasses or goggles when cutting, drilling, grinding or prying. If you wear glasses for the sake of vision, wear safety goggles over your regular glasses.
- Do shield your eyes whenever you work around the battery. Batteries contain sulfuric acid. In case of contact with the eyes or skin, flush the area with water or a mixture of water and baking soda, and get medical attention immediately.
- Do use safety stands for any under car service. Jacks are for raising vehicles; safety stands are for making sure the vehicle stays raised until you want it to come down. Whenever the vehicle is raised, block the wheels remaining on the ground and set the parking brake.
- Do use adequate ventilation when working with any chemicals or hazardous materials. Like carbon monoxide, the asbestos dust resulting from brake lining wear can be poisonous in sufficient quantities.
- Do disconnect the negative battery cable when working on the electrical system. The secondary ignition system can contain up to 40,000 volts.
- Do follow manufacturer's directions whenever working with potentially hazardous materials. Both brake fluid and antifreeze are poisonous if taken internally.
- Do properly maintain your tools. Loose hammerheads, mushroomed punches and chisels, frayed or poorly grounded electrical cords, excessively worn screwdrivers, spread wrenches (open end), and cracked sockets can cause accidents.
- Do use the proper size and type of tool for the job being done.
- Do, when possible, pull on a wrench handle rather than push on it, and adjust your stance to prevent a fall.
- Do be sure that adjustable wrenches are tightly adjusted on the nut or bolt and pulled so that the fastener's face is on the side of the fixed jaw.

- Do select a wrench or socket that fits the nut or bolt. The wrench or socket should sit straight, not cocked.
- Do strike squarely with a hammer to avoid glancing blows.
- Do set the parking brake and block the drive wheels if the work requires that the engine is running.

### Don'ts

- Don't run an engine in a garage or anywhere else without proper ventilation—EVER! Carbon monoxide is poisonous. It is absorbed by the body 400 times faster than oxygen. It takes a long time to leave the human body and you can build up a deadly supply of it in your system by simply breathing in a little every day. You may not realize you are slowly poisoning yourself. Always use power vents, windows, fans or open the garage doors.
- Don't work around moving parts while wearing a necktie or other loose clothing. Short sleeves are much safer than long, loose sleeves. Hard-toed shoes with neoprene soles protect your toes and give a better grip on slippery surfaces. Jewelry such as watches, fancy belt buckles, beads or body adornment of any kind is not safe working around a car. Long hair should be hidden under a hat or cap.
- Don't use pockets for tool boxes. A fall or bump can drive a screwdriver deep into your body. Even a wiping cloth hanging from your back pocket can wrap around a spinning shaft or fan.
- Don't smoke when working around gasoline, cleaning solvent or other flammable material.
- Don't smoke when working around the battery. When the battery is being charged, it gives off explosive hydrogen gas.
- Don't use gasoline to wash your hands. There are excellent soaps available. Gasoline removes all the natural oils from the skin so that bone dry hands will suck up oil and grease.
- Don't service the air conditioning system unless you are equipped with the necessary tools and training. The refrigerant, R-12 or 134a, extremely cold when compressed, and when released into the air will instantly freeze any surface it contacts, including your eyes. Although the refrigerant is normally non-toxic, R-12 becomes a deadly poisonous gas in the presence of an open flame. One good whiff of the vapors from burning refrigerant can be fatal.
- Don't release refrigerant into the atmosphere. In most states it is now illegal to discharge refrigerant into the atmosphere due to harmful effects

Freon® (R-12) has on the ozone layer. Check with local authorities about the laws in your state.

• Don't use screwdrivers for anything other than driving screws! A screwdriver used as a prying tool can snap when you least expect it, causing injuries. At the very least, you'll ruin a good screwdriver.

• Don't use a bumper jack (that little ratchet, scissors, or pantograph jack supplied with the car) for anything other than changing a flat! These jacks are only intended for emergency use out on the road; they are NOT designed as a maintenance tool. If you are serious about maintaining your car yourself, invest in a hydraulic floor jack of at least 1½ ton capacity, and at least two sturdy jackstands.

## MODEL IDENTIFICATION

Two models of the Ford Taurus/Mercury Sable are offered—the 4-door sedan and the 4-door station wagon. The body style of the vehicle can be confirmed by locating the 6th and 7th positions of the VIN code. Vehicle model year identification can be verified by locating the 10th position of the VIN code and using the Vehicle Identification Chart.

## SERIAL NUMBER IDENTIFICATION

### Vehicle

▶ **See Figure 13**

The official vehicle identification (serial) number (used for title and registration purposes) is stamped on a metal tab fastened to the instrument panel and visible through the driver's side of the windshield from the outside. The vehicle identification (serial) number contains a 17-digit number. The number is used for warranty identification of the vehicle and indicates: manufacturer, type of restraint system, line, series, body type, engine, model year, and consecutive unit number.

weight, and the pertinent certification statements. The certification also repeats the VIN number, and gives the color code and accessories found on the car.

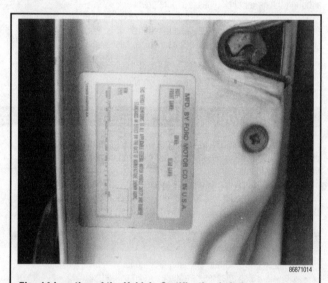

Fig. 14 Location of the Vehicle Certification Label

Fig. 13 Location of the Vehicle Identification Number (VIN) visible through the windshield

### Certification Label

▶ **See Figure 14**

The Vehicle Certification Label is found on the left door lock face panel or door pillar. The upper half of the label contains the name of the manufacturer, month and year of manufacture, gross weight rating, gross axle

### Engine

The vehicle's engine identification is located in the 8th position of the VIN code.

### Transaxle

The transaxle code is located on the bottom edge of the Vehicle Certification Label for vehicles equipped with the manual transaxle. The identification tag for vehicles equipped with the ATX automatic transaxle is located under one of the valve body cover retaining bolts. The identification tag for vehicles equipped with the AXOD, AXOD-E, AX4S and AX4N automatic transaxles is located on top of the converter housing.

## ENGINE IDENTIFICATION

| Year | Model | Engine Displacement Liters (cc) | Engine Series (ID/VIN) | Fuel System | No. of Cylinders | Engine Type |
|---|---|---|---|---|---|---|
| 1986 | Taurus | 2.5 (2524) | D | CFI | 4 | OHV |
| | Taurus | 3.0 (2971) | U | EFI | 6 | OHV |
| | Sable | 2.5 (2524) | D | CFI | 4 | OHV |
| | Sable | 3.0 (2971) | U | EFI | 6 | OHV |
| 1987 | Taurus | 2.5 (2524) | D | CFI | 4 | OHV |
| | Taurus | 3.0 (2971) | U | EFI | 6 | OHV |
| | Sable | 2.5 (2524) | D | CFI | 4 | OHV |
| | Sable | 3.0 (2971) | U | EFI | 6 | OHV |
| 1988 | Taurus | 2.5 (2524) | D | CFI | 4 | OHV |
| | Taurus | 3.0 (2971) | U | EFI | 6 | OHV |
| | Taurus | 3.8 (3802) | 4 | EFI | 6 | OHV |
| | Sable | 3.0 (2971) | U | EFI | 6 | OHV |
| | Sable | 3.8 (3802) | 4 | EFI | 6 | OHV |
| 1989 | Taurus | 2.5 (2524) | D | CFI | 4 | OHV |
| | Taurus | 3.0 (2971) | U | EFI | 6 | OHV |
| | Taurus | 3.8 (3802) | 4 | EFI | 6 | OHV |
| | Taurus SHO | 3.0 (2980) | Y | SFI | 6 | DOHC |
| | Sable | 3.0 (2971) | U | EFI | 6 | OHV |
| | Sable | 3.8 (3802) | 4 | EFI | 6 | OHV |
| 1990 | Taurus | 2.5 (2524) | D | CFI | 4 | OHV |
| | Taurus | 3.0 (2971) | U | EFI | 6 | OHV |
| | Taurus | 3.8 (3802) | 4 | EFI | 6 | OHV |
| | Taurus SHO | 3.0 (2980) | Y | SFI | 6 | DOHC |
| | Sable | 3.0 (2971) | U | EFI | 6 | OHV |
| | Sable | 3.8 (3802) | 4 | EFI | 6 | OHV |
| 1991 | Taurus | 2.5 (2524) | D | CFI | 4 | OHV |
| | Taurus | 3.0 (2971) | U | EFI | 6 | OHV |
| | Taurus | 3.8 (3802) | 4 | EFI | 6 | OHV |
| | Taurus SHO | 3.0 (2980) | Y | SFI | 6 | DOHC |
| | Sable | 3.0 (2971) | U | EFI | 6 | OHV |
| | Sable | 3.8 (3802) | 4 | EFI | 6 | OHV |
| 1992 | Taurus | 3.0 (2971) | U | EFI | 6 | OHV |
| | Taurus | 3.8 (3802) | 4 | EFI | 6 | OHV |
| | Taurus SHO | 3.0 (2980) | Y | SFI | 6 | DOHC |
| | Sable | 3.0 (2971) | U | EFI | 6 | OHV |
| | Sable | 3.8 (3802) | 4 | EFI | 6 | OHV |
| 1993 | Taurus | 3.0 (2971) | U | SFI | 6 | OHV |
| | Taurus | 3.8 (3802) | 4 | SFI | 6 | OHV |
| | Taurus SHO | 3.0 (2980) | Y | SFI | 6 | DOHC |
| | Taurus SHO | 3.2 (3191) | P | SFI | 6 | DOHC |
| | Sable | 3.0 (2971) | U | SFI | 6 | OHV |
| | Sable | 3.8 (3802) | 4 | SFI | 6 | OHV |
| 1994 | Taurus | 3.0 (2971) | U | SFI | 6 | OHV |
| | Taurus SHO | 3.0 (2980) | Y | SFI | 6 | DOHC |
| | Taurus SHO | 3.2 (3191) | P | SFI | 6 | DOHC |
| | Sable | 3.0 (2971) | U | SFI | 6 | OHV |
| | Sable | 3.8 (3802) | 4 | SFI | 6 | OHV |

86871501

## ENGINE IDENTIFICATION

| Year | Model | Engine Displacement Liters (cc) | Engine Series (ID/VIN) | Fuel System | No. of Cylinders | Engine Type |
|---|---|---|---|---|---|---|
| 1995 | Taurus | 3.0 (2980) | U | SFI | 6 | OHV |
| | Taurus | 3.8 (3802) | 4 | SFI | 6 | OHV |
| | Taurus SHO | 3.0 (2980) | Y | SFI | 6 | DOHC |
| | Taurus SHO | 3.2 (3191) | P | SFI | 6 | DOHC |
| | Sable | 3.0 (2971) | U | SFI | 6 | OHV |

EFI - Electronic fuel injection
CFI - Central fuel injection
SFI - Sequential fuel injection
OHV - Overhead valve
DOHC - Double overhead camshaft

86871502

## VEHICLE IDENTIFICATION CHART

| Engine Code | | | | | | Model Year | |
|---|---|---|---|---|---|---|---|
| Code | Liters | Cu. In. (cc) | Cyl. | Fuel Sys. | Eng. Mfg. | Code | Year |
| D (86-90) | 2.5 | 154 (2524) | 4 | CFI | Ford | G | 1986 |
| D (1991) | 2.5 | 154 (2524) | 4 | MFI | Ford | H | 1987 |
| U (86-92) | 3.0 | 181 (2971) | 6 | MFI | Ford | J | 1988 |
| U (93-95) | 3.0 | 181 (2971) | 6 | SFI | Ford | K | 1989 |
| 4 (88-92) | 3.8 | 232 (3802) | 6 | MFI | Ford | L | 1990 |
| 4 (93-95) | 3.8 | 232 (3802) | 6 | SFI | Ford | M | 1991 |
| Y (89-95) | 3.0 | 182 (2980) | 6 | SFI | Yamaha | N | 1992 |
| P (93-95) | 3.2 | 195 (3191) | 6 | SFI | Yamaha | P | 1993 |
| | | | | | | R | 1994 |
| | | | | | | S | 1995 |

CFI - Central fuel injection
MFI - Multiport fuel injection
SFI - Sequential fuel injection

86871500

## ROUTINE MAINTENANCE

### Air Cleaner

The air cleaner element should be replaced every 30 months or 30,000 miles (48,000 km). More frequent changes are necessary if the car is operated in dusty conditions.

#### REMOVAL & INSTALLATION

♦ **See Figures 15 thru 20**

#### Except 1994–95 Vehicles

1. Loosen the air cleaner outlet tube clamps at both ends, then remove the tube. For the 2.5L and 3.0L engines, loosen the clamp at the throttle body only, and leave the tube connected to the cover.
2. On the 3.0L and the 3.0L SHO, disengage the airflow sensor electrical connector.
3. Release the air cleaner upper cover retaining clips or remove the retaining bolts.
4. Remove the air cleaner cover, then remove the air cleaner element.

**To install:**

5. Clean the inside surfaces of the air cleaner body, then install the new filter element.
6. Install the air cleaner upper cover, then install the bolts or fasten the retaining clips.
7. If removed, engage the airflow sensor electrical connector.
8. Install the air cleaner outlet tube.

#### 1994–95 Vehicles

1. Loosen the clamp securing the air cleaner outlet tube to the mass air flow sensor, then disconnect the air cleaner outlet tube.
2. If equipped, disconnect the engine control sensor wiring from the mass air flow sensor and the intake air temperature sensor.
3. On all engines except for the 3.8L engine, release the retaining clips to remove the air cleaner cover.
4. For the 3.8L engine, loosen the air cleaner cover retaining bolts until the cover is free from the air cleaner body, but DO NOT remove the screws.

5. Position the air cleaner cover aside, then remove the air cleaner element.

**To install:**

6. Clean all inside surfaces of the air cleaner and cover, then install the air cleaner element.
7. Position the air cleaner cover, then install the retaining clips or fasten the bolts, as applicable. If equipped, tighten the bolts to 20–30 inch lbs. (2.5–3.5 Nm).
8. If equipped, connect the engine control sensor wiring to the mass air flow sensor and the intake air temperature sensor.
9. Install the air cleaner outlet tube. On 3.0L engines, tighten the clamp to 24–48 inch lbs. (2.7–5.4 Nm). For all other engines, tighten the clamp to 12–22 inch lbs. (1.4–2.5 Nm).

### Fuel Filter

#### RELIEVING FUEL SYSTEM PRESSURE

#### Except 2.5L CFI Engine

The pressure in the fuel system must be relieved before attempting to disconnect any fuel lines. A special valve is incorporated on the fuel rail assembly for the purpose of relieving the pressure in the fuel system.

1. Remove the fuel tank cap.
2. Remove the cap from the pressure relief Schrader valve on the fuel rail.
3. Attach pressure gauge tool T80L-9974-A or equivalent, to the fuel pressure relief valve.
4. Release the pressure from the system into a suitable container.
5. Remove the pressure gauge tool, then install the cap on the pressure relief valve. Install the fuel tank cap.

#### 2.5L CFI Engine

1. Disengage the electrical connector from the inertia switch, located on the left side of the luggage compartment.
2. Crank the engine for 15 seconds to relieve the fuel system pressure.
3. Connect the inertia switch.

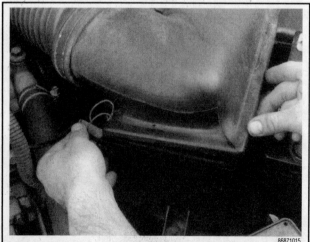

**Fig. 15 Unfastening the air cleaner cover retaining clips—early model 2.5L engine shown**

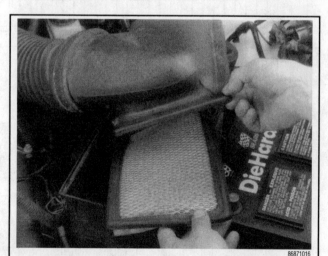

**Fig. 16 Removing the air cleaner element—early model 2.5L engine shown**

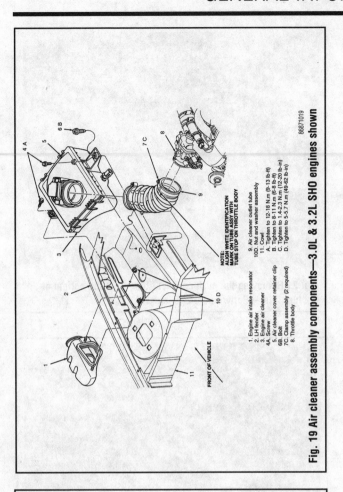

NOTE: WHITE IDENTIFICATION
MARK MUST BE BETWEEN
TUBE STOP ON THROTTLE BODY

1. Engine air intake resonator
2. LH fender
3. Engine air cleaner
4A. Screw
6B. Bolt
7C. Air cleaner cover retainer clip
7C. Clamp assembly (2 required)
8. Throttle body

9. Air cleaner outlet tube
10D. Nut and washer assembly
11. Cowl
A. Tighten to 12-18 N·m (9-13 lb-ft)
B. Tighten to 8-11 N·m (6-8 lb-in)
C. Tighten to 1.4-2.3 N·m (12-20 lb-in)
D. Tighten to 5-5.7 N·m (49-62 lb-in)

**Fig. 19 Air cleaner assembly components—3.0L & 3.2L SHO engines shown**

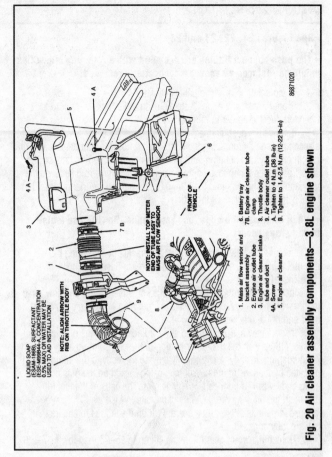

LIQUID SOAP, SURFACTANT
(ESAM-188B), CONCENTRATION
(ESE-M99B44-A CONCENTRATION
0.5% MAX OF WATER MAY BE
USED TO AID INSTALLATION

NOTE: INSTALL TOP METER
END OF TUBE ASSY TO
MASS AIR FLOW SENSOR

NOTE: ALIGN ARROW WITH
RIB ON THROTTLE BODY

1. Mass air flow sensor and
   bracket assembly
2. Engine air outlet tube
3. Engine air cleaner intake
   tube and duct
4A. Screw
5. Engine air cleaner

6. Battery tray
7B. Engine air cleaner tube
   clamp
8. Throttle body
9. Air cleaner outlet tube
A. Tighten to 1.4-2.5 N·m (36 lb-in)
B. Tighten to 1.4-2.5 N·m (12-22 lb-in)

**Fig. 20 Air cleaner assembly components—3.8L engine shown**

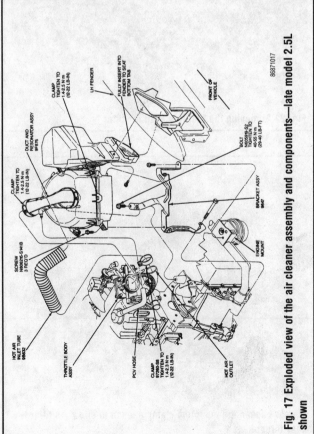

HOT AIR
INLET TUBE
ASSY

THROTTLE BODY
ASSY

PCV HOSE

CLAMP
9772ND-S8
TIGHTEN TO
1.4-2.3 N·m
(12-22 LB-IN)

HOT AIR
OUTLET

SCREW
N606125-S41B
3 REQ'D

CLAMP
TIGHTEN TO
1.4-2.5 N·m
(12-22 LB-IN)

DUCT AND
RESONATOR ASSY
9F876

LH FENDER

FULLY INSERT INTO
FENDER TO SEAT
BOTTOM TAB

BOLT
N805899-S2
TIGHTEN TO
40-55 N·m
(29-40 LB-FT)

BRACKET ASSY
9647

ENGINE
MOUNT

FRONT OF
VEHICLE

**Fig. 17 Exploded view of the air cleaner assembly and components—late model 2.5L shown**

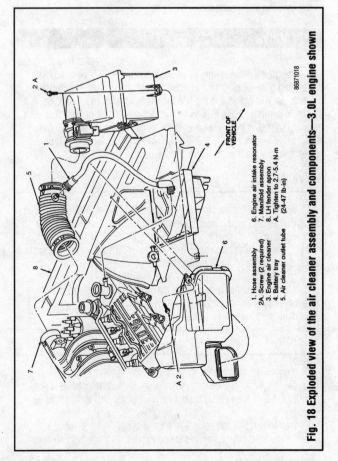

FRONT OF
VEHICLE

1. Hose assembly
2A. Screw (2 required)
3. Engine air cleaner
4. Battery tray
5. Air cleaner outlet tube

6. Engine air intake resonator
7. Manifold assembly
8. LH fender apron
A. Tighten to 2.7-5.4 N·m
   (24-47 lb-in)

**Fig. 18 Exploded view of the air cleaner assembly and components—3.0L engine shown**

## REMOVAL & INSTALLATION

▶ **See Figures 21, 22, 23 and 24**

➡ **The push connect fittings are designed with a retaining clip. Clips should be replaced whenever a connector is removed.**

1. Disconnect the negative battery cable.
2. Properly relieve the fuel system pressure. For details, refer to the procedure located earlier in this section.
3. Remove the push connect fittings at both ends of the fuel filter. This is accomplished by removing the hairpin clips from the fittings. Remove the hairpin clips by first bending, and then breaking the shipping tabs on the clips. Spread the 2 clip legs approximately ⅛ in. (3mm) to disengage the body and push the legs into the fitting. Gently pull on the triangular end of the clip and work it clear of the fitting.

➡ **When removing the clips, use your hands. Do NOT use tools, as damage may occur.**

4. Remove the filter from the mounting bracket by loosening the worm gear mounting clamp enough to allow the filter to pass through.

**To install:**

5. Install the filter in the mounting bracket, ensuring that the flow direction arrow is pointing forward. Locate the fuel filter against the tab at the lower end of the bracket.
6. Insert a new hairpin clip into any 2 adjacent openings on each push connect fitting, with the triangular portion of the clip pointing away from the fitting opening. Install the clip to fully engage the body of the fitting. This is indicated by the legs of the hairpin clip being locked on the outside of the fitting body. Apply a light coat of engine oil to the ends of the fuel filter, then push the fittings onto the ends of the filter. When the fittings are engaged, a definite click will be heard. Pull on the fittings to ensure that they are fully engaged.
7. Tighten the worm gear mounting clamp to 15–25 inch lbs. (1.7–2.8 Nm).
8. Start the engine and check for leaks.

## PCV Valve

The Positive Crankcase Ventilation (PCV) system cycles crankcase gases back through the engine, where they are burned. The PCV valve regulates the amount of ventilating air and blow-by gas to the intake manifold and prevents backfire from traveling into the crankcase. For most vehicles, this system is comprised of a PCV valve connected to a tube or hose that goes from a grommet in the valve cover to the throttle body. On some engines, such as the 3.0L and 3.2L SHO, the system simply consists of a tube routed from the valve cover to the throttle body.

## SERVICING

1. Visually inspect the components of the PCV system. Check for rough idle, slow starting, high oil consumption and loose, leaking, clogged or damaged hoses.
2. Check the fresh air supply hose and the PCV hose for air leakage or flow restriction due to loose engagement, hose splitting, cracking or kinking, nipple damage, rubber grommet fit or any other damage.
3. If a component is suspected as the obvious cause of a malfunction, correct the cause before proceeding to the next step.
4. If all checks are okay, proceed to the pinpoint tests.

## PINPOINT TESTS

1. If equipped, remove the PCV valve from the valve cover grommet and shake the valve. If the valve rattles when shaken, reinstall and proceed to Step 2. If the valve does not rattle, it is sticking and should be replaced.
2. Start the engine and bring it to normal operating temperature.
3. On the 2.5L engine, remove the corrugated hose from the oil separa-

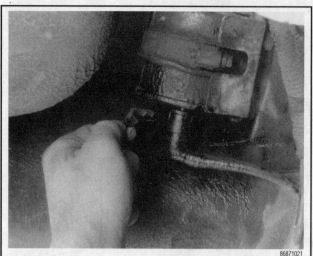

**Fig. 21 Removing the push connect fitting from the bottom of the fuel filter—Early model 2.5L shown**

**Fig. 22 Removing the fuel line from the filter**

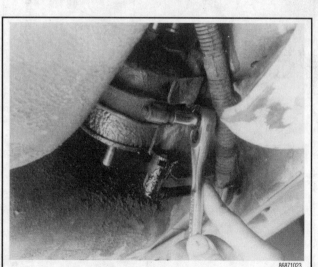

**Fig. 23 Loosen the mounting clamp enough to allow the filter to pass through**

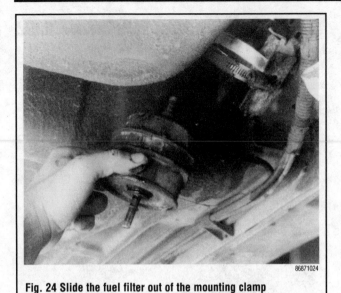

**Fig. 24 Slide the fuel filter out of the mounting clamp**

tor nipple. On all other engines, disconnect the hose from the remote air cleaner or air outlet tube.

4. Place a stiff piece of paper over the nipple or hose end and wait 1 minute. If vacuum holds the paper in place, the system is okay; reconnect the hose. If the paper is not held in place, the system is plugged or the evaporative emission valve (if equipped) is leaking. If the evaporative emission valve is suspected of leaking, proceed to Step 5.

5. If equipped, disconnect the evaporative hose, and cap the connector.

6. Place a stiff piece of paper over the hose/nipple, as in Step 4, and wait 1 minute. If vacuum holds the paper in place, proceed to evaporative emission system testing. If the paper is not held in place, check for vacuum leaks/obstruction in the oil cap, PCV valve and hoses, or for split grommets. Also check the oil separator on the 2.5L engine and valve cover for a gasket lead or incorrect bolt torque.

## REMOVAL & INSTALLATION

### 2.5 and 3.0L Engines—Except SHO

▶ **See Figures 25 and 26**

1. Remove the fuel vapor hose and the crankcase ventilation hose from the PCV valve.

**Fig. 25 PCV system—early model 2.5L engine shown**

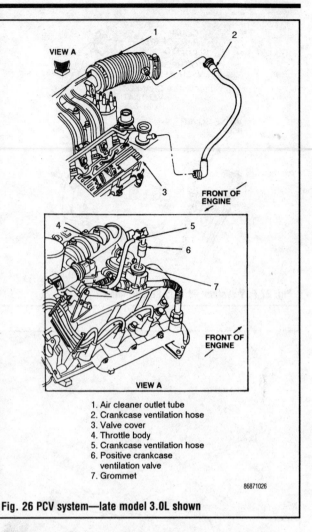

1. Air cleaner outlet tube
2. Crankcase ventilation hose
3. Valve cover
4. Throttle body
5. Crankcase ventilation hose
6. Positive crankcase ventilation valve
7. Grommet

**Fig. 26 PCV system—late model 3.0L shown**

2. Remove the PCV valve from the PCV valve grommet.

**To install:**

3. Inspect the valve and grommet for deterioration, and replace if necessary.

4. Install the PCV valve into the valve grommet, then connect the fuel vapor and crankcase ventilation hoses.

### 3.0L and 3.2L SHO Engines

▶ **See Figure 27**

1. Loosen the crankcase ventilation tube clamps.

2. Carefully disconnect the tube from the left-hand side valve cover fitting and the throttle body.

**To install:**

3. Inspect the crankcase ventilation tube for deterioration and replace if necessary.

4. Connect the tube to the valve cover fitting and the throttle body, then secure with the retaining clamps.

### 3.8L Engine

▶ **See Figure 28**

1. Disconnect the crankcase ventilation tube from the PCV valve.

2. Remove the valve from the PCV valve grommet.

**To install:**

3. Inspect the PCV valve and grommet for deterioration, and replace if necessary.

4. Install the PCV valve into the valve grommet, then connect the crankcase ventilation tube.

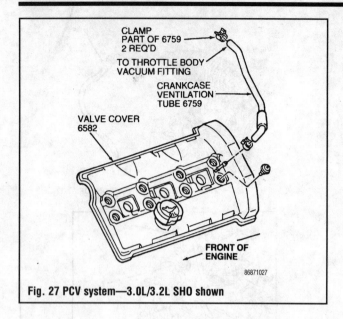

Fig. 27 PCV system—3.0L/3.2L SHO shown

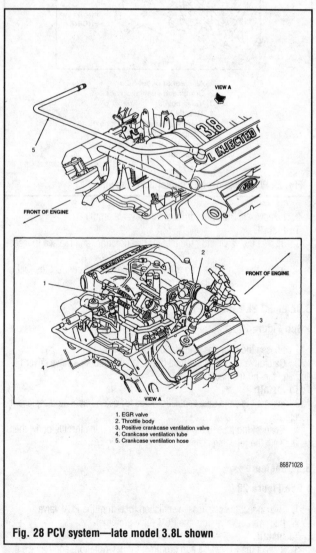

1. EGR valve
2. Throttle body
3. Positive crankcase ventilation valve
4. Crankcase ventilation tube
5. Crankcase ventilation hose

Fig. 28 PCV system—late model 3.8L shown

## Evaporative Canister

♦ See Figures 29 thru 34

To prevent gasoline vapors from being vented into the atmosphere, an evaporative emission system captures the vapors and stores them in a carbon-filled canister. The 3.0L Flexible Fuel (FF) vehicles utilize 4 separate canisters for this purpose.

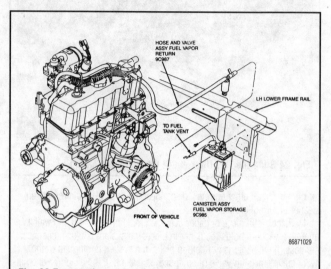

Fig. 29 Evaporative emission control system and related components—2.5L engine

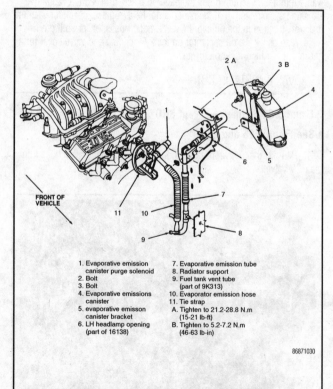

1. Evaporative emission canister purge solenoid
2. Bolt
3. Bolt
4. Evaporative emissions canister
5. evaporative emission canister bracket
6. LH headlamp opening (part of 16138)
7. Evaporative emission tube
8. Radiator support
9. Fuel tank vent tube (part of 9K313)
10. Evaporator emission hose
11. Tie strap
A. Tighten to 21.2-28.8 N.m (15-21 lb-ft)
B. Tighten to 5.2-7.2 N.m (46-63 lb-in)

Fig. 30 Evaporative emission control system and related components—3.0L engine (Except Flexible Fuel)

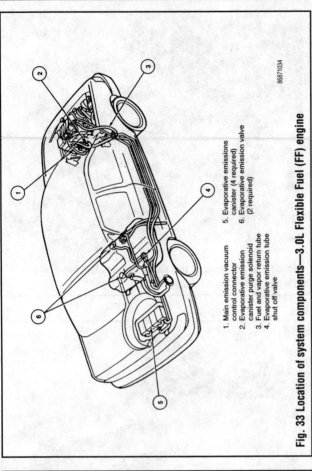

1. Main emission vacuum control connector
2. Evaporative emission canister purge solenoid
3. Fuel and vapor return tube
4. Evaporative emission tube shut off valve
5. Evaporative emissions canister (4 required)
6. Evaporative emission valve (2 required)

Fig. 33 Location of system components—3.0L Flexible Fuel (FF) engine

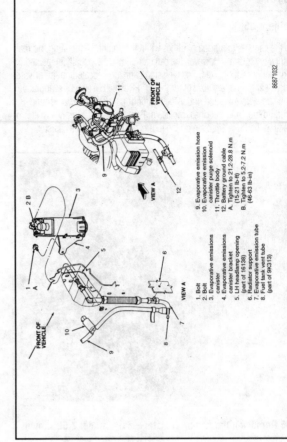

2 B. Bolt
3. Evaporative emissions canister
4. Evaporative emissions canister bracket
5. LH headlamp opening (part of 16138)
6. Radiator support
7. Evaporative emission tube (part of 9K313)

1. Bolt
2. Bolt
3. Evaporative emissions canister
9. Evaporative emission hose
10. Evaporative emission canister purge solenoid
11. Throttle body
12. Battery ground cable
A. Tighten to 21.2-28.8 N·m (15-21 lb-ft)
B. Tighten to 5.2-7.2 N·m (46-63 lb-in)

Fig. 34 Evaporative emission control system and related components—3.0L SHO shown; 3.2L SHO similar

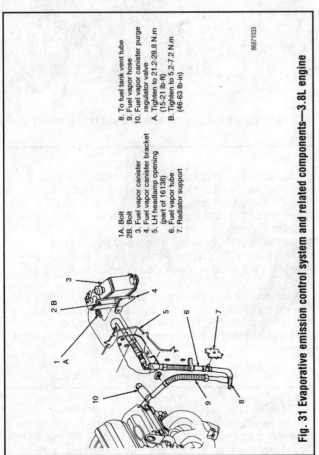

1A. Bolt
2B. Bolt
3. Fuel vapor canister
4. Fuel vapor canister bracket
5. LH headlamp opening (part of 16138)
6. Fuel vapor tube
7. Radiator support
8. To fuel tank vent tube
9. Fuel vapor hose
10. Fuel vapor canister purge regulator valve
A. Tighten to 21.2-28.8 N·m (15-21 lb-ft)
B. Tighten to 5.2-7.2 N·m (46-63 lb-in)

Fig. 31 Evaporative emission control system and related components—3.8L engine

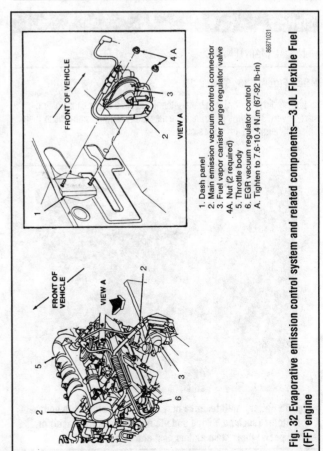

1. Dash panel
2. Main emission vacuum control connector
3. Fuel vapor canister purge regulator valve
4A. Nut (2 required)
5. Throttle body
6. EGR vacuum regulator control
A. Tighten to 7.6-10.4 N·m (67-92 lb-in)

Fig. 32 Evaporative emission control system and related components—3.0L Flexible Fuel (FF) engine

## SERVICING

▶ **See Figure 35**

Since the canister is purged of fumes when the engine is operating, no real maintenance is required. However, the canister should be visually inspected for cracks, loose connections, etc. The emission canister is located on the driver's side fender near the battery, except for the 3.0 FF, which uses four evaporative emissions canisters mounted under the rear floor pan. The canister should have no liquid fuel in it; if it does, replace it. Replacement is simply a matter of disconnecting the hoses, loosening the mount and replacing the canister.

Fig. 35 Removing the carbon canister—Early model 2.5L shown

## Battery

### GENERAL MAINTENANCE

▶ **See Figures 36, 37 and 38**

Loose, dirty, or corroded battery terminals are a major cause of "no-start." Every 3 months or so, remove the battery terminals and clean them. This will help to retard corrosion.

Fig. 36 Battery maintenance may be accomplished with household items (such as baking soda to neutralize spilled acid) or with special tools such as this post and terminal cleaner

Fig. 37 The underside of this special battery tool has a wire brush to clean post terminals

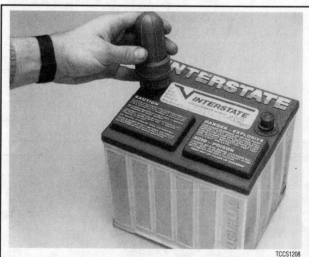

Fig. 38 Place the tool over the terminals and twist to clean the post

Check the battery cables for signs of wear or chafing and replace any cable or terminal that looks marginal. Battery terminals can be easily cleaned and inexpensive terminal cleaning tools are an excellent investment that will pay for themselves many times over. They can usually be purchased from any well-equipped auto store or parts department. Side terminal batteries require a different tool to clean the threads in the battery case. The accumulated white powder and corrosion can be cleaned from the top of the battery with an old toothbrush and a solution of baking soda and water.

Unless you have a maintenance-free battery, check the electrolyte level and the specific gravity of each cell. Be sure that the vent holes in each cell cap are not blocked by grease or dirt. The vent holes allow hydrogen gas, formed by the chemical reaction in the battery, to escape safely.

### FLUID LEVEL (EXCEPT MAINTENANCE-FREE BATTERIES)

▶ **See Figure 39**

Check the battery electrolyte level at least once a month, or more often in hot weather or during periods of extended car operation. The level can be checked through the case on translucent polypropylene batteries; the cell

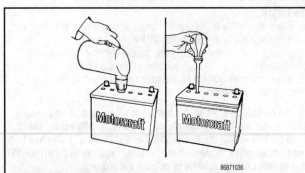

**Fig. 39 Two devices used to maintain electrolyte level: A self-leveling filler which fills to a predetermined level and a syringe-type filler**

caps must be removed on other models. The electrolyte level in each cell should be kept filled to the split ring inside, or the line marked on the outside of the case.

If the level is low, add only distilled water, or colorless, odorless drinking water, through the opening until the level is correct. Each cell is completely separate from the others, so each must be checked and filled individually.

If water is added in freezing weather, the car should be driven several miles to allow the water to mix with the electrolyte. Otherwise, the battery could freeze.

## SPECIFIC GRAVITY (EXCEPT MAINTENANCE-FREE BATTERIES)

At least once a year, check the specific gravity of the battery using a hydrometer.

A hydrometer, is an inexpensive instrument available from many sources, including auto parts stores. The hydrometer has a squeeze bulb at one end and a nozzle at the other. Battery electrolyte is sucked into the hydrometer until the float is lifted from its seat. The specific gravity is then read by noting the position of the float. Generally, if after charging, the specific gravity between any two cells varies more than 50 points (0.50), the battery is bad and should be replaced.

It is not possible to check the specific gravity in this manner on sealed (maintenance-free) batteries. Instead, the indicator built into the top of the case must be relied on to display any signs of battery deterioration. If the indicator is dark, the battery can be assumed to be OK. If the indicator is light, the specific gravity is low, and the battery should be charged or replaced.

## CABLES

Once every 6 months, the battery terminals and the cable clamps should be cleaned. Loosen the clamps and remove the cables, negative cable first. On batteries with posts on top, the use of a puller specially made for this purpose is recommended. Damage may occur to the battery if proper terminal pullers are not used. These are inexpensive, and available in auto parts stores. Side terminal battery cables are secured with a bolt, and do not require a puller.

Clean the cable clamps and the battery terminal with a wire brush, until all corrosion, grease, etc. is removed and the metal is shiny. It is especially important to clean the inside of the clamp thoroughly, since a small deposit of foreign material or oxidation there can prevent a sound electrical connection and inhibit starting and/or charging. Special tools are available for cleaning these parts, one type for conventional batteries and another type for side terminal batteries.

Before installing the cable, loosen the battery hold-down clamp or strap, remove the battery and check the battery tray. Clear it of any debris, and check it for soundness. Rust should be wire brushed away, and the metal given a coat of anti-rust paint. Before replacing the battery, wash it with soap and water to remove any dirt. Replace the battery and tighten the hold-

down clamp or strap securely, but be careful not to overtighten, which will crack the battery case.

After the clamps and terminals are clean, reinstall the cables, negative cable last; do not hammer on the clamps to install. Tighten the clamps securely, but do not distort them. Give the clamps and terminals a thin external coat of grease after installation, to retard corrosion.

Check the cables at the same time that the terminals are cleaned. If the cable insulation is cracked or broken, or if the ends are frayed, the cable should be replaced with a new cable of the same length and gauge.

➡**Keep flames and sparks away from the battery; it gives off explosive hydrogen gas. Battery electrolyte contains sulfuric acid. If you should splash any on your skin or in your eyes, flush the affected areas with plenty of clear water; if it lands in your eyes, get medical help immediately.**

## CHARGING

Before recharging a battery, see if any of the following problems exist:
- Loose alternator belt
- Pinched or grounded alternator/voltage regulator wiring harness
- Loose wiring connection at the alternator and/or voltage regulator
- Loose or corroded connections at the battery and/or the engine ground
- Excessive battery drain due to any accessories or lighting left on.

If any of these exist, remedy the problem, then check to see if the battery still needs to be charged. Cold batteries will not readily accept a charge. Therefore, batteries should be allowed to warm up to approximately 41°F (5°C) before charging. This may require allowing the battery to warm up at room temperature for four to eight hours, depending on the initial temperature and the size of the battery. A battery which has been completely discharged may be slow to accept a charge initially, and in some cases may not accept a charge at the normal charger setting. When batteries are in this condition, charging can be started by using a dead battery switch, on chargers equipped with one.

Completely discharged batteries, which have been discharged for a prolonged period of time (over one month) or which have an open circuit voltage of less than two volts, may not indicate accepting a charge even when the dead battery switch is used. The initial charge rate accepted by batteries in this condition is so low, that the ammeter on some charges will not show any indication of charge for up to 10 minutes. To determine whether a battery is accepting a charge, follow the charger manufacturer's instructions for the use of the dead battery switch. If the dead battery switch is the spring-loaded type, it should be held in the ON position for up to three minutes.

After releasing the dead battery switch and with the charger still on, measure the battery voltage. If it shows 12 volts or higher, the battery is accepting a charge and is capable of being recharged. But, it may require up to two hours of charging on batteries colder than 41°F (5°C) before the charge rate is high enough to register on the charger ammeter. If a battery cannot be charged by this procedure, it should be replaced.

Once the battery has begun to accept a charge, it can be charge to serviceable state or full charge by one of two methods:
- Use the AUTOMATIC setting on chargers so equipped. This setting maintains the charging rate within safe limits by adjusting the voltage and the current to prevent excessive gassing and the spewing of electrolyte. About two to four hours is needed to charge a completely discharged battery to a serviceable state. If a full state of charge is desired, the charge can be completed by a low current rate of 3–5 amps for several hours.
- The second method is to use the MANUAL or constant current setting on the charger. Initially set the charging rate for 30–40 amps and maintain this setting for about 30 minutes or as long as there is not excessive gassing and electrolyte spewing. If gassing results, the charge rate must be reduced to a level where gassing will stop. This is especially true for maintenance-free batteries, in which excessive gassing will result in non-replaceable loss of electrolyte, shortening the battery life.

The total charge necessary will vary with battery size and its initial state of charge. In general, to bring a discharged battery to a serviceable state of charge, the amount of charging current multiplied by the charging time should equal the battery amp-hour capacity. For example, a 45 AH battery will need 15 amps of charge for three hours, or 9 amps of charge for five hours. If a full state of charge is desired, the charge can be completed by a low constant current of 3–5 amps for several hours.

## REPLACEMENT

▶ See Figure 40

The cold power rating of a battery measures battery starting performance and provides an approximate relationship between battery size and engine size. As a general rule, the cold power rating of a replacement battery should match or exceed your engine size in cubic inches.

### ✱✱ CAUTION

**Batteries normally produce explosive gases which can cause personal injury. DO NOT allow flames, sparks or lighted substances to come near the battery. When charging or working near a battery, always shield your face and protect your eyes. Also, always provide adequate ventilation.**

1. Carefully disconnect the negative battery cable from the battery terminal, and position it aside.
2. Carefully disconnect the positive cable from the battery terminal, and position it aside.
3. Clean the cable terminals using an acid neutralizing solution and a terminal cleaning brush.
4. Remove the battery hold-down clamp(s) by disconnecting the retaining nut(s) and bolt(s).
5. Remove the battery.

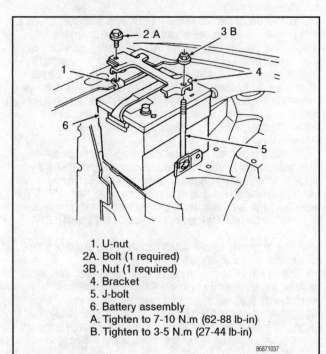

1. U-nut
2A. Bolt (1 required)
3B. Nut (1 required)
4. Bracket
5. J-bolt
6. Battery assembly
A. Tighten to 7-10 N.m (62-88 lb-in)
B. Tighten to 3-5 N.m (27-44 lb-in)

86871037

**Fig. 40 Common battery hold-down assembly**

**To install:**
6. Clean the battery tray and hold-down clamp(s) with a wire brush and scraper. Replace any components that are worn.
7. Place the battery in the battery tray making sure that the positive and negative terminals are in the same position as they were previous to removal.
8. Assemble and tighten the hold-down hardware so that the battery is secure. Do not overtighten.

➡**For some vehicles, when the battery is disconnected and reconnected, abnormal driving symptoms may temporarily occur. The reason for this is that the Powertrain Control Module (PCM) has to relearn its adaptive strategy. Your vehicle may have to be driven 10 miles or more for the module to relearn the strategy.**

9. Secure the positive, then the negative battery cables to the proper terminals. Do not overtighten.

### Belts

All vehicles are equipped with V-ribbed drive belts. Replacement belts should be of the same type as originally installed. Loose belts will result in slippage and cause improper operation of the driven accessory, power steering, air conditioning, etc. Overtightened belts will put a severe load on accessory bearings and will almost certainly cause them to self-destruct. Some systems are equipped with an automatic belt tensioner, and will not require any tension adjustments. The drive belt condition should be inspected at 60,000 miles (96,000 km), then at every 15,000 miles (24,000 km) thereafter.

## INSPECTION

Inspect all drive belts for excessive wear, cracks, glazed condition, and frayed or broken cords. Replace any drive belt showing one or more of the above conditions.

➡**If a drive belt continually gets cut, the crankshaft pulley might have a sharp projection on it. Have the pulley replaced if this condition continues.**

## ADJUSTMENT

**Alternator Belt**

*2.5L, 3.2L SHO, 3.8L AND SOME 3.0L ENGINES*

The V-ribbed belts used on these engines, utilize an automatic belt tensioner which maintains proper belt tension for the life of the belt. The automatic belt tensioner has a belt wear indicator mark, as well as **MIN** and **MAX** marks. If the indicator mark is not between the **MIN** and **MAX** marks, the belt is worn or an incorrect belt is installed.

*3.0L ENGINE WITHOUT AUTOMATIC TENSIONER— EXCEPT SHO*

1. Disconnect the negative battery cable.
2. Loosen the alternator adjustment and pivot bolts.
3. Apply tension to the belt using the adjusting screw.
4. Using a belt tension gauge, set the belt to the proper tension. The tension should be 140–160 lbs. (533–711 N) for a new belt or 110–130 lbs. (356–445 N) for a used belt on vehicles through 1991. On 1992 vehicles, tighten to 190–210 lbs. (845–935 N) for a new belt and 140–160 lbs. (622–712 N) for a used belt.
5. When the belt is properly tensioned, tighten the alternator adjustment bolt to 27 ft. lbs. (37 Nm).

6. Remove the tension gauge and run the engine for 5 minutes.

7. With the engine **OFF** and the belt tension gauge in place, check that the adjusting screw is in contact with the bracket before loosening the alternator adjustment bolt. Rotate the adjustment screw until the belt is tensioned to 110–130 lbs. (356–445 N) for vehicles through 1991 or 140–160 lbs. (622–712 N) for 1992 vehicles.

8. Tighten the alternator adjustment bolt to 27 ft. lbs. (37 Nm) and the pivot bolt to 43 ft. lbs. (58 Nm).

### *3.0L SHO ENGINE*

1. Disconnect the negative battery cable.
2. Loosen the idler/tensioner pulley nut.
3. Turn the adjusting bolt until the belt is adjusted properly.

➡**Turning the wrench to the right tightens the belt adjustment; turning the wrench to the left loosens the belt tension.**

4. Tighten the idler/tensioner pulley nut to 25–37 ft. lbs. (34–50 Nm) and check the belt tension.

### REMOVAL & INSTALLATION

➡**When installing belts on the pulley, ensure that all of the V-grooves are making contact with the pulleys.**

### 2.5L Engine

### *ALTERNATOR, POWER STEERING AND AIR CONDITIONING BELT*

▶ **See Figure 41**

1. Insert a ½ in. breaker bar into the square hole in the tensioner, then rotate the tensioner counterclockwise and remove the belt from the pulleys.

➡**Be careful when removing or installing belts that the tool doesn't slip!**

**To install:**

2. Install the belt over all pulleys except the alternator pulley.
3. Rotate the tensioner as described in Step 1 and install the belt over the alternator pulley. Check that all the V-grooves make proper contact with the pulleys.

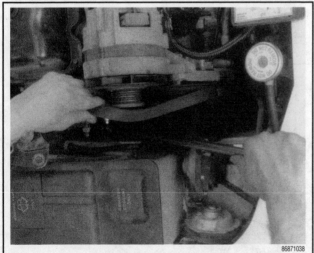

**Fig. 41 Removing the belt from the pulleys—early 2.5L engine shown**

### 3.0L Engine—Except SHO

### *ALTERNATOR BELT WITHOUT AUTOMATIC TENSIONER*

1. Loosen the adjusting arm and pivot bolts.
2. Turn the alternator belt adjusting screw counterclockwise until the old belt can be removed.
3. Remove the belt.

**To install:**

4. Install the new belt over the pulleys. Check that all the V-grooves make proper contact with the pulleys.
5. Adjust the belt tension, then tighten the adjusting arm and pivot bolts.

### 3.0L SHO Engine

### *ALTERNATOR BELT*

▶ **See Figure 42**

1. Loosen the nut in the center of the idler pulley.
2. Loosen the idler adjusting screw until the old belt can be removed, then remove the belt.

**To install:**

3. Install the new belt over the pulleys in proper contact with the pulleys.
4. Adjust the new belt to specifications as follows: Turn the idler pulley nut to the right to tighten the belt to a specification of 220–265 lbs. (980–1180 N). Torque the idler pulley nut to 25–37 ft. lbs. (34–50 Nm).

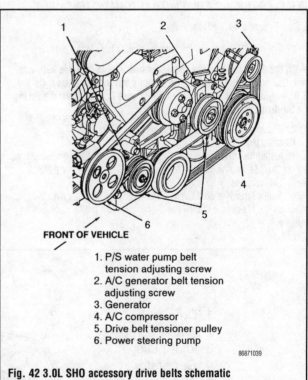

**FRONT OF VEHICLE**

1. P/S water pump belt tension adjusting screw
2. A/C generator belt tension adjusting screw
3. Generator
4. A/C compressor
5. Drive belt tensioner pulley
6. Power steering pump

**Fig. 42 3.0L SHO accessory drive belts schematic**

### *POWER STEERING AND AIR CONDITIONING BELT*

▶ **See Figure 42**

1. Remove the alternator belt.
2. Loosen the nut on the tensioner pulley.

3.  Turn the belt adjusting screw on the tensioner counterclockwise until the belt can be removed, then remove the belt.
**To install:**
4.  Position the new belt over the proper pulleys, making sure the V-grooves are properly seated.
5.  Install the alternator belt.
6.  Adjust the power steering and air conditioning belt to a specification of 154–198 lbs. (690–980 N) with a belt tension gauge.
7.  Adjust the alternator belt.

### 3.2L SHO Engine

#### *WITH AUTOMATIC TENSIONER*

▶ See Figure 43

1.  Place a 14mm socket over the bolt on the drive belt tensioner and rotate it clockwise (downward) to release belt tension.
2.  Remove the drive belt from the pulleys.
**To install:**
3.  Install the drive belt over all the pulleys except for the power steering pump pulley. Make sure that all the V-grooves make proper contact with the pulleys.
4.  Place a 14mm socket over the bolt on the drive belt tensioner pulley and rotate it clockwise (downward), then install the drive belt over the power steering pump pulley.

### 3.0L Engine (Except SHO) and 3.8L Engine

#### *VEHICLES THROUGH 1993 WITH AUTOMATIC TENSIONER*

▶ See Figures 44 and 45

1.  Insert a ½ in. breaker bar into the square hole in the tensioner.

➡On the 3.8L engine, the tensioner has a ½ in. square hole cast into the rear of the tension arm directly behind the pulley. On the 3.0L engine, the ½ in. square hole is cast into the spring housing on the front of the tensioner.

2.  Rotate the tensioner clockwise and remove the belt.
**To install:**
3.  Install the drive belt over all the pulleys, except for the alternator pulley on the 3.0L engine for vehicles through 1992, or the idler pulley for 1993 3.0L vehicles.
4.  Rotate tensioner counterclockwise and install the belt over the alternator pulley. Make sure that all the V-grooves make proper contact with the pulleys.

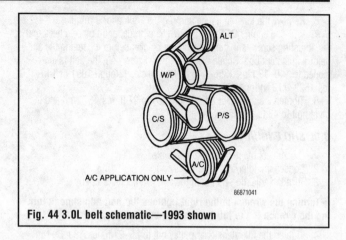

**Fig. 44 3.0L belt schematic—1993 shown**

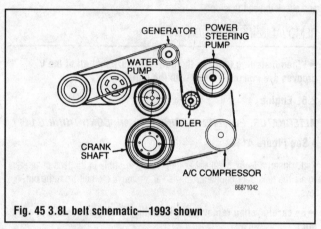

**Fig. 45 3.8L belt schematic—1993 shown**

5.  On the 3.0L engine, install the alternator belt for vehicles through 1992.
6.  For 1993 3.0L vehicles, install the drive belt over the idler pulley.

#### *1994–95 VEHICLES WITH AUTOMATIC TENSIONER*

▶ See Figures 46 and 47

1.  Using a 15mm socket or wrench on the attaching bolt, rotate the drive belt tensioner pulley clockwise to relieve the tension.

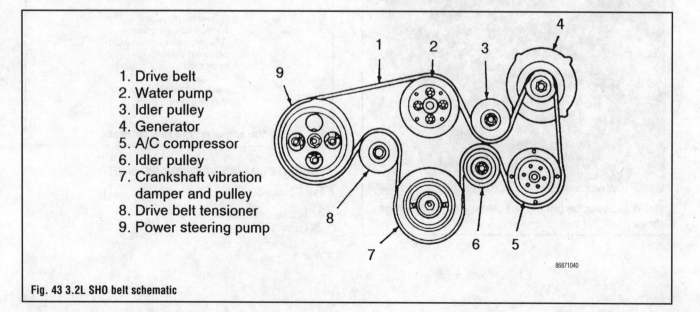

1. Drive belt
2. Water pump
3. Idler pulley
4. Generator
5. A/C compressor
6. Idler pulley
7. Crankshaft vibration damper and pulley
8. Drive belt tensioner
9. Power steering pump

**Fig. 43 3.2L SHO belt schematic**

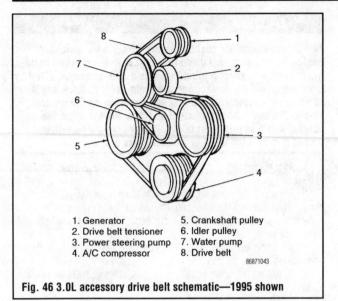

1. Generator
2. Drive belt tensioner
3. Power steering pump
4. A/C compressor
5. Crankshaft pulley
6. Idler pulley
7. Water pump
8. Drive belt

86871043

**Fig. 46 3.0L accessory drive belt schematic—1995 shown**

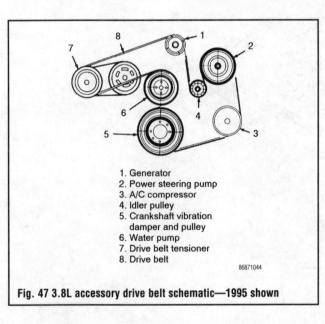

1. Generator
2. Power steering pump
3. A/C compressor
4. Idler pulley
5. Crankshaft vibration damper and pulley
6. Water pump
7. Drive belt tensioner
8. Drive belt

86871044

**Fig. 47 3.8L accessory drive belt schematic—1995 shown**

2. Remove the drive belt.

**To install:**

3. Install the drive belt over all the pulleys, other than the drive belt tensioner.

4. Rotate the drive belt tensioner clockwise, using a 15mm socket or wrench, then install the belt over the drive belt tensioner pulley.

5. Make sure that all of the V-grooves make proper contact with the pulleys.

## Timing Belt

### INSPECTION

Vehicles equipped with the 3.0L and 3.2L SHO engines are the only vehicles covered by this manual which utilize timing belts. The timing belt should be inspected for cracks, wear, or other damage, and should be replaced every 100,000 miles (160,000 km). For timing belt removal and installation procedures, please refer to Section 3 of this manual.

## Hoses

### INSPECTION

Upper and lower radiator hoses, along with the heater hoses, should be inspected for deterioration, leaks and loose hose clamps at least every 15,000 miles (24,000 km). It is also wise to check the hoses periodically in early spring and at the beginning of the fall or winter when you are performing other maintenance. A quick visual inspection may discover a weakened hose which could have left you stranded had it remained unrepaired.

Whenever you are checking the hoses, make sure the engine and cooling system are cold. Visually inspect for cracking, rotting or collapsed hoses, and replace as necessary. Run your hand along the length of the hose. If a weak or swollen spot is noted when squeezing the hose wall, the hose should be replaced.

### REMOVAL & INSTALLATION

▶ **See Figures 48 thru 56**

1. Disconnect the negative battery cable, then place protective covers over the fenders.

2. Place a suitable drain pan under the radiator.

### ✷✷ CAUTION

**Never remove the pressure cap while the engine is running, or personal injury from scalding hot coolant or steam may result. If possible, wait until the engine has cooled to remove the pressure cap. If this is not possible, wrap a thick cloth around the pressure cap, then depress and turn it slowly to the stop. Step back while pressure is released from the cooling system. When you are sure all the pressure has been released, turn and remove the cap.**

➡ **If only the upper hose is to be replaced, you need only drain off enough coolant so that the level is below the hose.**

3. Remove the radiator pressure cap. Attach a ⅜ in. (9.5mm) diameter hose to the radiator draincock, then open the draincock and drain the radiator.

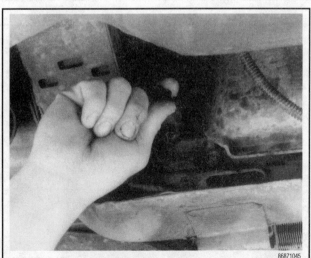

86871045

**Fig. 48 Opening the radiator draincock located at the lower rear corner of the radiator**

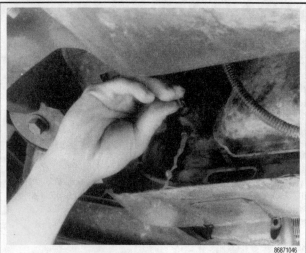

**Fig. 49 Attaching a small hose to the draincock will help direct the flow of coolant into the drainpan, thereby reducing the mess**

## ❋❋ CAUTION

The engine should be cool before any hoses are replaced. If engine is hot, let it cool down for at least an hour. When draining the coolant, keep in mind that cats and dogs are attracted by ethylene glycol antifreeze, and are quite likely to drink any that is left in an uncovered container or in puddles on the ground. This will prove fatal in sufficient quantity. Always drain the coolant into a sealable container. Coolant should be reused unless it is contaminated or several years old.

4. After the radiator has drained, position the drain pan under the hose to be removed.

5. To remove the lower hose, loosen the lower hose clamps, then disconnect the hose from the water pump or radiator lower hose tube, and allow it to drain. Disconnect the other end of the hose from the radiator and remove the hose.

6. To remove the upper hose, loosen the retaining clamps, then disconnect and remove the hose.

7. To remove the heater hose(s), loosen the clamps, then remove the hose(s).

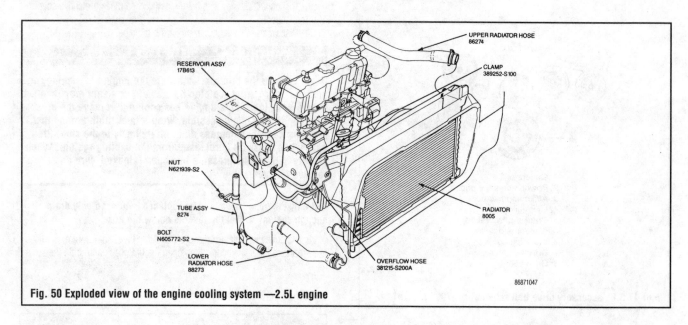

**Fig. 50 Exploded view of the engine cooling system —2.5L engine**

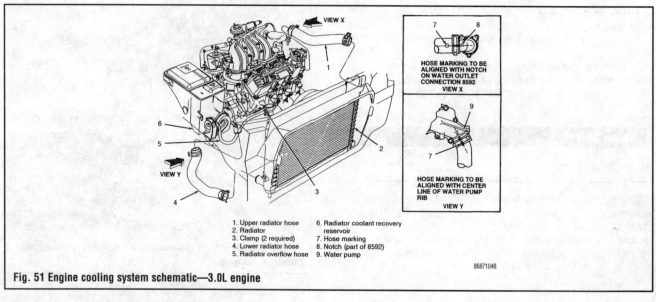

1. Upper radiator hose
2. Radiator
3. Clamp (2 required)
4. Lower radiator hose
5. Radiator overflow hose
6. Radiator coolant recovery reservoir
7. Hose marking
8. Notch (part of 8592)
9. Water pump

**Fig. 51 Engine cooling system schematic—3.0L engine**

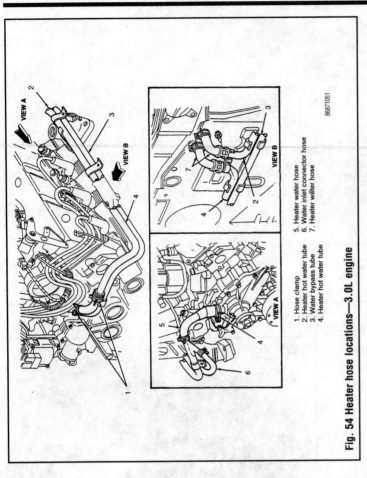

86871051

1. Hose clamp
2. Heater hot water tube
3. Water bypass tube
4. Heater hot water tube
5. Heater water hose
6. Water inlet connector hose
7. Heater water hose

**Fig. 54 Heater hose locations—3.0L engine**

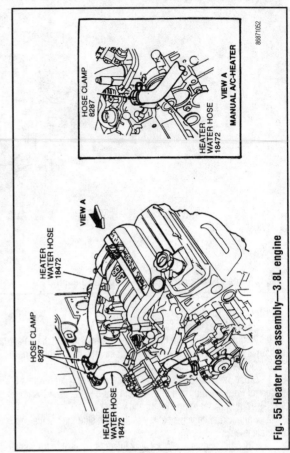

86871052

HOSE CLAMP
8287

HEATER
WATER HOSE
18472

VIEW A
MANUAL A/C-HEATER

HEATER
WATER HOSE
18472

VIEW A

HOSE CLAMP
8287

HEATER
WATER HOSE
18472

**Fig. 55 Heater hose assembly—3.8L engine**

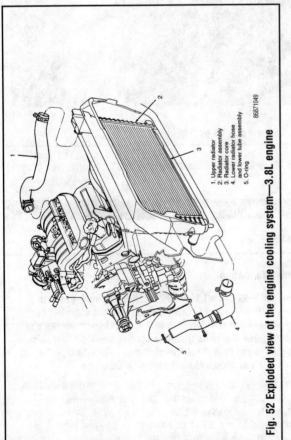

86871049

1. Upper radiator
2. Radiator assembly
3. Radiator core
4. Lower radiator hose and lower tube assembly
5. O-ring

**Fig. 52 Exploded view of the engine cooling system—3.8L engine**

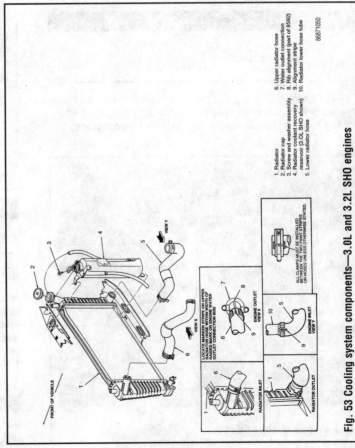

86871050

1. Radiator
2. Radiator cap
3. Screw and washer assembly
4. Radiator coolant recovery reservoir (3.0L SHO shown)
5. Lower radiator hose
6. Upper radiator hose
7. Water outlet connection
8. Rib alignment (part of 8592)
9. Alignment stripe
10. Radiator lower hose tube

FRONT OF VEHICLE

VIEW X

VIEW Y

ENGINE OUTLET
VIEW Y

ENGINE INLET
VIEW Y

RADIATOR INLET

RADIATOR OUTLET

ALL CLAMPS MUST BE INSTALLED BETWEEN THE TWO PAINT STRIPES ON HOSES UNLESS OTHERWISE STATED

LOCATE MARKER STRIPE ON UPPER RADIATOR HOSE WITHIN WIDTH OF RADIATOR STRIPE AT RADIATOR OUTLET CONNECTION 8592

**Fig. 53 Cooling system components—3.0L and 3.2L SHO engines**

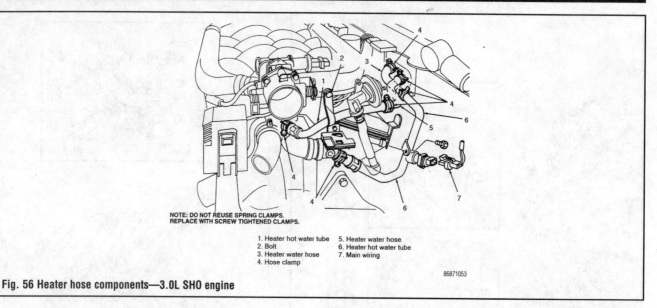

NOTE: DO NOT REUSE SPRING CLAMPS.
REPLACE WITH SCREW TIGHTENED CLAMPS.

1. Heater hot water tube
2. Bolt
3. Heater water hose
4. Hose clamp
5. Heater water hose
6. Heater hot water tube
7. Main wiring

86871053

**Fig. 56 Heater hose components—3.0L SHO engine**

**To install:**

8. Position the hose(s) to the appropriate connection(s).

9. If applicable, position the hose clamps between the alignment marks on both ends of the hose, then slide the hose onto the connections.

10. Tighten the hose clamps to 20–30 inch lbs. (2.2–3.4 Nm).

11. Close the radiator draincock. Fill the cooling system with a 50/50 mixture of Ford Premium Cooling System Fluid E2FZ-19549-AA or B (CXC-8-B in Canada) or equivalent and water.

12. Connect the negative battery cable, then start the engine and check for coolant leaks.

13. When the engine cools, recheck the coolant level in the radiator, or reservoir container, then remove the fender covers.

## CV Boot

▶ See Figures 57 and 58

### INSPECTION

CV joint boots should be periodically inspected. It would be a wise idea to examine the boot every time your vehicle is raised and supported. Check the boot for signs of cracks, tears or splits and repair/replace as necessary.

TCCS1010

**Fig. 57 View of a torn CV boot**

TCCS1011

**Fig. 58 View of a CV boot in good condition**

For CV boot and joint repair, as well as overhaul procedures, please refer to Section 7 of this manual.

## Air Conditioning

### R-134A SYSTEMS

**General Information**

➡ **Some 1992–93 and all 1994–95 vehicles are equipped with a refrigerant (R-134a) that is incompatible with the older R-12 or Freon®. This newer refrigerant is NOT available commercially in most areas, and it may be illegal to service a vehicle with this refrigerant. If you have a vehicle equipped with R-134a, it should be taken to a qualified technician for all A/C service.**

Some 1992–93 vehicles equipped with the 3.0L engine, and all 1994–95 vehicles are using R-134a refrigerant, rather than the conventional R-12 refrigerant. The new R-134a refrigerant is not harmful to the ozone layer of the atmosphere. It has many of the same properties as the old type of refrigerant and is similar in both form and function. These two refrigerants are not interchangeable with one another. Therefore, do not mix the two types of refrigerant, the tools used in servicing the air conditioning system, or component replacement parts from these two types of air conditioning systems. Failure to follow these guidelines will result in damage to the vehicle air conditioning system, and may also result in personal injury to the individual.

## System Identification

In order to determine which type of system your vehicle has, an identification data plate is located on the major system components. If the system components have YELLOW R-134a non-cfc tags, then the system requires R-134a refrigerant. These systems can also be identified by a gold-colored air conditioning compressor clutch and green-colored O-rings used throughout the system.

## GENERAL SERVICING PROCEDURES

➡**It is recommended, and possibly required by law, that a qualified technician perform the following services.**

The most important aspect of air conditioning service is the maintenance of a pure and adequate charge of refrigerant in the system. A refrigeration system cannot function properly if a significant percentage of the charge is lost. Leaks are common because the severe vibration encountered under-hood in an automobile can easily cause a sufficient cracking or loosening of the air conditioning fittings. As a result, the extreme operating pressures of the system force refrigerant out.

The problem can be understood by considering what happens to the system as it is operated with a continuous leak. Because the expansion valve regulates the flow of refrigerant to the evaporator, the level of refrigerant there is fairly constant. The receiver/drier stores any excess refrigerant, so a loss will first appear as a reduction in the level of liquid. As this level nears the bottom of the vessel, some refrigerant vapor bubbles will begin to appear in the stream of liquid supplied to the expansion valve. This vapor decreases the capacity of the expansion valve very little as the valve opens to compensate for its presence. As the quantity of liquid in the condenser decreases, the operating pressure will drop there and throughout the high side of the system. As the refrigerant continues to be expelled, the pressure available to force the liquid through the expansion valve will continue to decrease, and, eventually, the valve's orifice will prove to be too much of a restriction for adequate flow, even with the needle fully withdrawn.

At this point, low side pressure will start to drop, and severe reduction in cooling capacity, marked by freeze-up of the evaporator coil, will result. Eventually, the operating pressure of the evaporator will be lower than the pressure of the atmosphere surrounding it, and air will be drawn into the system wherever there are leaks in the low side.

Because all atmospheric air contains at least some moisture, water will enter the system and mix with the refrigerant and oil. Trace amounts of moisture will cause sludging of the oil, and corrosion of the system. Saturation and clogging of the filter/drier, and freezing of the expansion valve orifice will eventually result. As air fills the system to a greater and greater extent, it will interfere more and more with the normal flows of refrigerant and heat.

From this description, it should be obvious that much of the technician's time will be spent detecting leaks, repairing them, and then restoring the purity and quantity of the refrigerant charge. A list of general rules should be followed in addition to all safety precautions:
- Keep all tools as clean and dry as possible.
- Thoroughly purge the service gauges and hoses of air and moisture before connecting them to the system. Keep them capped when not in use.
- Thoroughly clean any refrigerant fitting before disconnecting it, in order to minimize the entrance of dirt into the system.
- Plan any operation that requires opening the system beforehand in order to minimize the length of time it will be exposed to open air. Cap or seal the open ends to minimize the entrance of foreign material.
- When adding oil, pour it through an extremely clean and dry tube or funnel. Keep the oil capped whenever possible. Do not use oil that has not been kept tightly sealed.

- Use only the appropriate refrigerant. Although you are unlikely to find it for sale, DO NOT use old containers of R-12 which were intended for cleaning or powering air horns.
- Completely evacuate any system that has been opened to replace a component, other than when isolating the compressor, or that has leaked sufficiently to draw in moisture and air. This requires evacuating air and moisture with a good vacuum pump for at least one hour. If a system has been open for a considerable length of time, it may be advisable to evacuate the system for up to 12 hours (overnight).
- Use a wrench on both halves of a fitting that is to be disconnected, so as to avoid placing torque on any of the refrigerant lines.
- When overhauling a compressor, pour some oil into a clean glass and inspect it. If there is evidence of dirt or metal particles, or both, flush all refrigerant components with clean refrigerant before evacuating and recharging the system. In addition, if metal particles are present, the compressor should be replaced.
- Schrader valves may leak only when under full operating pressure. Therefore, if leakage is suspected, but cannot be located, operate the system with a full charge of refrigerant and look for leaks from all Schrader valves. Replace any faulty valves.

## SAFETY WARNINGS

Because of the inherent dangers involved with working on air conditioning systems and R-12 refrigerant, the following safety precautions must be strictly adhered to in order to service the system safely:

➡**Some vehicles covered by this manual are equipped with R-134a, NOT R-12 refrigerant. These 2 refrigerants are NOT compatible. Using the incorrect refrigerant in an R-134a system will lead to compressor failure, refrigerant oil sludge and/or poor air conditioning system performance.**

- Avoid contact with a charged refrigeration system, even when working on another part of the air conditioning system or vehicle. If a heavy tool comes into contact with a section of copper tubing or a heat exchanger, it can easily cause the relatively soft material to rupture.
- When it is necessary to apply force to a fitting which contains refrigerant, as when checking that all system couplings are securely tightened, use a wrench on both parts of the fitting involved, if possible. This will avoid putting torque on the refrigerant tubing. (It is advisable, when possible, to use tubing or line wrenches when tightening these flare nut fittings.

➡**R-12 refrigerant is a chlorofluorocarbon which, when released into the atmosphere, can contribute to the depletion of the ozone layer in the upper atmosphere. Ozone filters out harmful radiation from the sun.**

- Do not attempt to discharge the system by merely loosening a fitting, or removing the service valve caps and cracking these valves. Precise control is possible only when using the service gauges. Wear protective gloves when connecting or disconnecting service gauge hoses.

➡**Be sure to consult the laws in your area before servicing the air conditioning system. In some cases, it is illegal to perform repairs involving refrigerant unless the work is done by a certified technician.**

- Discharge the system using the proper discharge equipment, as high concentrations of the gas can exclude oxygen and act as an anesthetic. When leak testing or soldering this is particularly important, as toxic gas is formed when the R-12 contacts any flame.
- Never start a system without first verifying that both service valves (if equipped) are backseated, and that all fittings throughout the system are snugly connected.
- Always wear goggles when working on a system to protect the eyes. If refrigerant contacts the eye, it is advisable in all cases to see a physician as soon as possible.
- Frostbite from liquid refrigerant should be treated by first gradually warming the area with cool water, and then gently applying petroleum jelly. A physician should be consulted.

• Always completely discharge the system into a suitable recovery system before painting the vehicle (if the paint is to be baked on), or before welding anywhere near the refrigerant lines.

• When servicing the system, minimize the time that any refrigerant line or fitting is open to the air in order to prevent moisture or dirt from entering the system. Contaminants such as moisture or dirt can damage internal system components. Always replace O-rings on lines or fittings which are disconnected. Prior to installation, coat, but do not soak, replacement O-rings with suitable compressor oil.

➡**Most repair work on an air conditioning system should be left to a certified professional. DO NOT, under any circumstances, attempt to loosen or tighten any fittings or perform any work other than that outlined here.**

## SYSTEM INSPECTION

It is possible to detect possible air conditioning system problems by a visual inspection. Check for a broken air conditioning belt, dirt blocking the condenser, disconnected wires, a loose compressor clutch, and oily residue around the air conditioning hose fittings. Missing service gauge port caps may also cause a leak to develop.

## REFRIGERANT LEVEL CHECKS

The only way to accurately check the refrigerant level is to measure the system evaporator pressures with a manifold gauge set, although rapid on/off cycling of the compressor clutch indicates that the air conditioning system is low on refrigerant. The normal refrigerant capacity is 39–41 oz. (1106–1162 grams).

## GAUGE SETS

The following procedure is for the attachment of a manifold gauge set to the service gauge port valves. If charging station equipment is used, follow the equipment manufacturer's instructions.

### ✳✳ CAUTION

**The air conditioning system is under high pressure when the engine is running. When connecting and disconnecting the manifold gauge set, make sure the engine is not running.**

1. Turn both manifold gauge set valves fully clockwise to close the high and low pressure hoses at the gauge set refrigerant center outlet.

➡**Rotunda high side adapter set D81L-19703-A or Motorcraft Tool YT-354/355 (or equivalent) is required to connect the manifold gauge set or a charging station to the high pressure service access gauge port valve.**

2. Remove the caps from the high and low pressure service gauge port valves.

3. If the manifold gauge set hoses do not have the valve depressing pins in them, install fitting adapters T71P-19703-S and R containing the pins on the manifold gauge hoses.

4. Connect the high and low pressure refrigerant hoses to their respective service ports, making sure they are hooked up correctly and fully seated. Tighten the fittings by hand, making sure they are not cross-threaded. Remember that an adapter is necessary to connect the manifold gauge hose to the high pressure fitting.

## DISCHARGING THE SYSTEM

➡**Air conditioning system R-12 refrigerant is a chlorofluorocarbon which, when released into the atmosphere, can contribute to the depletion of the ozone layer in the upper atmosphere. Ozone filters out harmful radiation from the sun. ALWAYS use an approved recovery/recycling machine that meets SAE standards when discharging**

the air conditioning system. Follow the operating instructions provided with the approved equipment exactly to properly discharge the air conditioning system.

### ✳✳ WARNING

**Some 1992 and later vehicles use R-134a refrigerant in place of the conventional R-12 refrigerant. Refer to the information on R-134a refrigerant systems in this Section. Also, any air conditioning equipment used to service the conventional R-12 refrigerant systems CANNOT be used to service the R-134a refrigerant systems.**

The use of refrigerant recovery systems and recycling stations makes possible the recovery and reuse of refrigerant after contaminants and moisture have been removed. If a recovery system or recycling station is used, the following general procedures should be followed, in addition to the operating instructions provided by the equipment manufacturer.

1. Connect the refrigerant recycling station hose(s) to the vehicle air conditioning service ports and the recovery station inlet fitting.

➡**Hoses should have shut off devices or check valves within 12 in. (305mm) of the hose end to minimize the introduction of air into the recycling station and to minimize the amount of refrigerant released when the hoses are disconnected.**

2. Turn the power to the recycling station **ON** to start the recovery process. Allow the recycling station to pump the refrigerant from the system until the station pressure goes into a vacuum. On some stations, the pump will be shut off automatically by a low pressure switch in the electrical system. On other units it may be necessary to manually turn off the pump.

3. Once the recycling station has evacuated the vehicle air conditioning system, close the station inlet valve, if equipped. Then, switch **OFF** the electrical power.

4. Allow the vehicle air conditioning system to remain closed for about 2 minutes. Observe the system vacuum level as shown on the gauge. If the pressure does not rise, disconnect the recycling station hose(s).

5. If the system pressure rises, repeat Steps 2, 3 and 4 until the vacuum level remains stable for 2 minutes.

## EVACUATING THE SYSTEM

➡**Some 1992 and later vehicles use R-134a refrigerant in place of the conventional R-12 refrigerant. Refer to the information on R-134a refrigerant systems in this Section. Also, any air conditioning equipment used to service R-12 refrigerant systems CANNOT be used to service R-134a refrigerant systems.**

1. Connect a manifold gauge set as follows:
    a. Turn both manifold gauge set valves fully to the right, to close the high and low pressure hoses to the center manifold and hose.
    b. Remove the caps from the high and low pressure service gauge port valves.
    c. If the manifold gauge set hoses do not have valve depressing pins in them, install fitting adapters T71P19703S and R or equivalent, which have pins, on the low and high pressure hoses.
    d. Connect the high and low pressure hoses, or adapters, to the respective high and low pressure service gauge port valves. High side adapter set D81L-19703-A or tool YT-354/355 or equivalent is required to connect a manifold gauge set or charging station to the high pressure gauge port valve.

➡**Service tee fitting D87P-19703-A, which may be mounted on the clutch cycling pressure switch fitting, is available for use in the low pressure side of fixed orifice tube systems, to be used in place of the low pressure gauge port valve.**

2. Leak test all connections and components with flame-type leak detector 023-00006 or equivalent, or electronic leak detector 055-00014, 055-00015 or equivalent.

## ✳✳ CAUTION

**Fumes from flame-type leak detectors are noxious; avoid inhaling fumes or personal injury may result.**

➡**Good ventilation is necessary in the area where air conditioning leak testing is to be done. If the surrounding air is contaminated with refrigerant gas, the leak detector will indicate this gas all the time. Odors from other chemicals such as antifreeze, diesel fuel, disc brake cleaner or other cleaning solvents can cause the same problem. A fan, even in a well ventilated area, is very helpful in removing small traces of air contamination that might affect the leak detector.**

3. Using an approved recovery/recycling station, properly discharge the refrigerant system.

4. Make sure both manifold gauge valves are turned fully clockwise. Make sure the center hose connection at the manifold gauge is tight.

5. Connect the manifold gauge set center hose to a vacuum pump.

6. Open the manifold gauge set valves and start the vacuum pump.

7. Evacuate the system with the vacuum pump until the low pressure gauge reads at least 25 in. Hg (84 kPa) or as close to 30 in. Hg (101 kPa) as possible. Continue to operate the vacuum pump for 15 minutes. If a part of the system has been replaced, continue to operate the vacuum pump for another 20–30 minutes.

8. When evacuation of the system is complete, close the manifold gauge set valves and turn the vacuum pump **OFF**.

9. Observe the low pressure gauge for 5 minutes to ensure that system vacuum is held. If vacuum is held, charge the system. If vacuum is not held for 5 minutes, leak test the system, service the leaks and evacuate the system again.

### CHARGING THE SYSTEM

➡**Some 1992 and later vehicles use R-134a refrigerant in place of the conventional type R-12 refrigerant. Refer to the information on R-134a refrigerant systems in this section. Also any air conditioning equipment used to service R-12 refrigerant systems CANNOT be used to service R-134a refrigerant systems.**

1. Connect a manifold gauge set according to the proper procedure. Properly discharge and evacuate the system.

2. With the manifold gauge set valves closed to the center hose, disconnect the vacuum pump from the manifold gauge set.

3. Connect the center hose of the manifold gauge set to a refrigerant drum.

➡**Use only a safety type dispensing valve.**

4. Loosen the center hose at the manifold gauge set and open the refrigerant drum valve. Purge air and moisture from the center hose, then tighten the center hose connection at the manifold gauge set.

5. Detach the wire harness snap lock connector from the clutch cycling or low pressure switch and install a jumper wire across the 2 terminals of the connector.

6. Open the manifold gauge set low side valve to allow refrigerant to enter the system. Keep the refrigerant container in an upright position.

7. When no more refrigerant is being drawn into the system, start the engine and set the control assembly to the MAX cold and HI blower positions to draw the remaining refrigerant into the system. If equipped, press the air conditioning switch. Continue to add refrigerant to the system until the specified weight of the refrigerant is in the system. Then close the manifold gauge set low pressure valve and the refrigerant supply valve.

8. Remove the jumper wire from the clutch cycling or low pressure switch snap lock connector. Attach the connector to the pressure switch.

9. Operate the system until pressures stabilize to verify normal operation and system pressures.

10. In high ambient temperatures, it may be necessary to operate a high volume fan positioned to blow air through the radiator and condenser to aid in cooling the engine and prevent excessive refrigerant system pressures.

11. When charging is completed and system operating pressures are normal, disconnect the manifold gauge set from the vehicle. Install the protective caps on the service gauge port valves.

### LEAK TESTING THE SYSTEM

Connect the manifold gauge set. Be sure that both valves are closed. Both gauges should read about 122–163 in. Hg (413–551 kPa) with the engine not running. If very little or no pressure is indicated, leave the vacuum pump valve closed. Open the refrigerant tank valve and set the low pressure gauge valve to the counterclockwise position. This will open the system to tank pressure. Check all system connections, the compressor head gasket and shaft seal for leaks using a leak detector tool.

## Windshield Wipers

For maximum effectiveness and longest element (refill) life, the windshield and wiper blades should be kept clean. Dirt, tree sap, road tar and so on, will cause streaking, smearing and blade deterioration if left on the glass. It is advisable to wash the windshield carefully with a commercial glass cleaner at least once a month. Clean off the wiper blades with the wet rag afterwards. Do not attempt to move the wipers by hand; damage to the motor and drive mechanism could result.

To inspect and/or remove the wiper refills, place the wiper switch in the **LOW** speed position and the ignition switch in the **ACC** position. When the wiper blades are approximately vertical on the windshield, turn the ignition switch to **OFF**.

Examine the wiper refills. If they are cracked, broken or torn, they should be replaced immediately. Replacement intervals will vary with usage, although ozone deterioration usually limits refill life to about one year. If the wiper pattern is smeared or streaked, or if the blade chatters across the glass, the refills should be replaced. It is easiest and most sensible to replace the refills in pairs.

### REMOVAL & INSTALLATION

▶ **See Figures 59, 60 and 61**

Normally, if the wipers are not cleaning the windshield properly, only the refill has to be replaced. The blade and arm usually require replacement only in the event of damage. It is not necessary (except on new Tridon® refills) to remove the arm or the blade to replace the refill (rubber part), though you may have to position the arm higher on the glass. You can do this by turning the ignition switch **ON** and operating the wipers. When they are positioned where they are accessible, turn the ignition switch **OFF**.

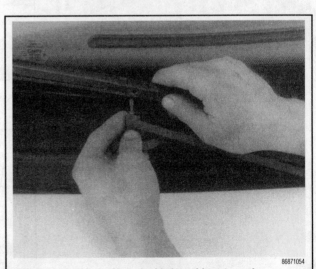

86871054

**Fig. 59 If necessary, the entire blade and insert may be removed from the end of the arm**

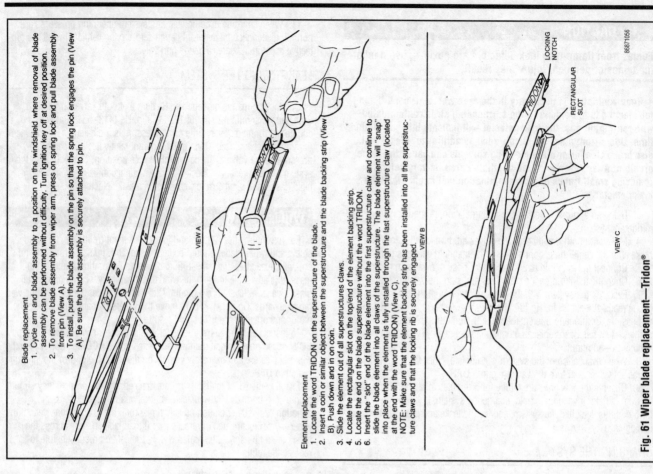

**Blade replacement**

1. Cycle arm and blade assembly to a position on the windshield where removal of blade assembly can be performed without difficulty. Turn ignition key off at desired position.
2. To remove blade assembly from wiper arm, press on spring lock and pull blade assembly from pin (View A).
3. To install, push the blade assembly on the pin so that the spring lock engages the pin (View A). Be sure the blade assembly is securely attached to pin.

VIEW A

**Element replacement**

1. Locate the word TRIDON on the superstructure of the blade.
2. Insert a coin or similar object between the superstructure and the blade backing strip (View B). Push down and in on coin.
3. Slide the element out of all superstructures claws.
4. Locate the rectangular slot on the top/end of the element backing strip.
5. Locate the end on the blade superstructure without the word TRIDON.
6. Insert the "slot" end of the blade element into the first superstructure claw and continue to slide the blade element into all claws of the superstructure. The blade element will "snap" into place when the element is fully installed through the last superstructure claw (located at the end with the word TRIDON) (View C).
   NOTE: Make sure that the element backing strip has been installed into all the superstructure claws and that the locking rib is securely engaged.

VIEW B

LOCKING NOTCH

RECTANGULAR SLOT

VIEW C

**Fig. 61 Wiper blade replacement—Tridon®**

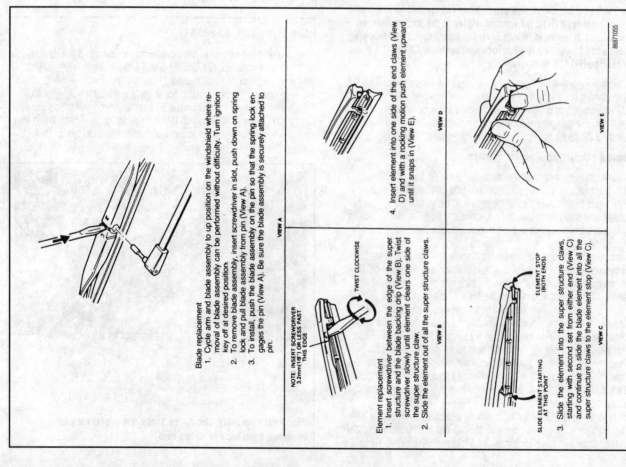

**Blade replacement**

1. Cycle arm and blade assembly to up position on the windshield where removal of blade assembly can be performed without difficulty. Turn ignition key off at desired position.
2. To remove blade assembly, insert screwdriver in slot, push down on spring lock and pull blade assembly from pin (View A).
3. To install, push the blade assembly on the pin so that the spring lock engages the pin (View A). Be sure the blade assembly is securely attached to pin.

VIEW A

NOTE: INSERT SCREWDRIVER 3.2mm(1/8") OR LESS PAST THIS EDGE

TWIST CLOCKWISE

VIEW B

**Element replacement**

1. Insert screwdriver between the edge of the super structure and the blade backing drip (View B). Twist screwdriver slowly until element clears one side of the super structure claw.
2. Slide the element out of all the super structure claws.

SLIDE ELEMENT STARTING AT THIS POINT

ELEMENT STOP (BOTH ENDS)

VIEW C

3. Slide the element into the super structure claws, starting with second set from either end (View C) and continue to slide the blade element into all the super structure claws to the element stop (View C).

4. Insert element into one side of the end claws (View D) and with a rocking motion push element upward until it snaps in (View E).

VIEW D

VIEW E

**Fig. 60 Wiper blade replacement—Trico®**

If your vehicle is equipped with aftermarket blades, there are several different possible types of refills. Aftermarket wipers frequently use a different type blade or refill than the original. Here are some common aftermarket blades, though not all may be available for your car.

Most Anco® styles use a release button that is pushed down to allow the refill to slide out of the yoke jaws. The new refill slides back into the frame and locks in place.

Some Trico® refills are removed by locating where the metal backing strip or the refill is wider. Insert a small prybar between the frame and metal backing strip. Press down to release the refill from the retaining tab.

Other types of Trico® refills have two metal tabs which are unlocked by squeezing them together. The rubber filler can then be withdrawn from the frame jaws. A new refill is installed by inserting the refill into the front frame jaws and sliding it rearward to engage the remaining frame jaws. There are usually four jaws; be certain when installing, that the refill is engaged in all of them. At the end of its travel, the tabs will lock into place on the front jaws of the wiper blade frame.

Another type of refill is made from polycarbonate. The refill has a simple locking device at one end which flexes downward out of the groove into which the jaws of the holder fit, allowing easy release. By sliding the new refill through all the jaws and pushing through the slight resistance when it reaches the end of its travel, the refill will lock into position.

To replace the Tridon® refill, it is necessary to remove the wiper arm or blade. This refill has a plastic backing strip with a notch about 1 in. (25mm) from the end. Hold the blade (frame) on a hard surface so the frame is tightly bowed. Grip the tip of the backing strip and pull up while twisting counterclockwise. The backing strip will snap out of the retaining tab. Do this for the remaining tabs until the refill is free of the arm. The length of these refills is molded into the end and they should be replaced with identical types.

Regardless of the type of refill used, make sure that all of the frame jaws are engaged as the refill is pushed into place and locked. If the metal blade holder and frame are allowed to touch the glass during wiper operation, the glass will be scratched.

## Tires and Wheels

### TIRE ROTATION

▶ **See Figure 62**

Tire wear can be equalized by switching the position of the tires about every 7,500 miles (12,000 km). Including a conventional spare tire in the rotation pattern can give up to 20% more tread life. Do not include a SpaceSaver® or other temporary spare tire in the rotation pattern.

### TIRE DESIGN

▶ **See Figures 63, 64, 65 and 66**

All tires made since 1968 have 8 built-in tread wear indicator bars that show up as ½ in. (13mm) wide smooth bands across the tire when 1/16 in. (1.6mm) of tread remains. The appearance of tread wear indicators means that the tires should be replaced. In fact, many states have laws prohibiting the use of tires with less than 1/16 in. (1.6mm) of tread remaining. Tread thickness under 1/16 in. (1.6mm) is very dangerous on wet roads due to hydroplaning.

You can check your own tread depth with an inexpensive gauge or by using a Lincoln head penny. Slip the Lincoln penny into several tread grooves. If you can see the top of Lincoln's head in 2 adjacent grooves, the tires have less than

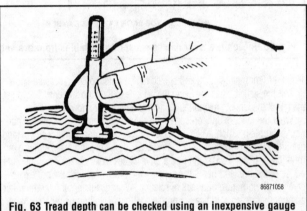

**Fig. 63 Tread depth can be checked using an inexpensive gauge**

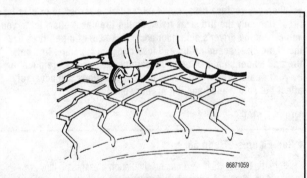

**Fig. 64 If a gauge is not available, a penny may be used to check for tire tread depth; when the top of Lincoln's head is visible, it is probably time for a new tire**

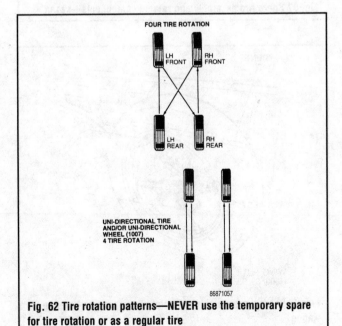

**Fig. 62 Tire rotation patterns—NEVER use the temporary spare for tire rotation or as a regular tire**

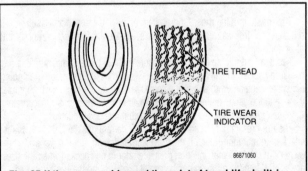

**Fig. 65 If tires are used beyond the point of tread life, built-in wear indicators will begin to appear as lines perpendicular to the tread**

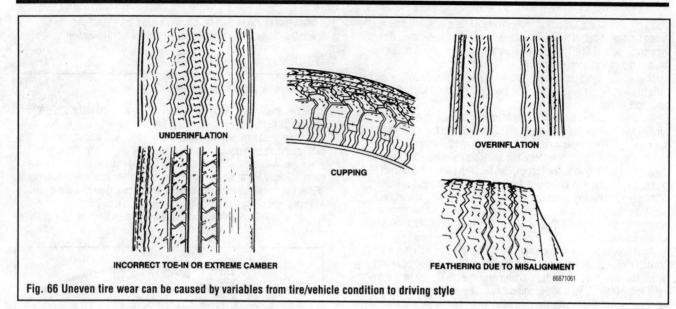

Fig. 66 Uneven tire wear can be caused by variables from tire/vehicle condition to driving style

¹⁄₁₆ in. (1.6mm) of tread left and should be replaced. You can measure snow tires in the same manner by using the tail side of the Lincoln penny. If you see the top of the Lincoln memorial, it's time to replace the snow tires.

Wear that occurs only on certain portions of the tire may indicate a particular problem which, when corrected or avoided, may significantly extend tire life. Wear that occurs only in the center of the tire indicates either over-inflation or heavy acceleration on a drive wheel. Wear occurring at the outer edges of the tire, and not at the center may indicate underinflation, excessively hard cornering or a lack of rotation. Wear occurring at only the outer edge of the tire, may indicate a problem with wheel alignment or, perhaps, a non-uniformity defect in the tire.

➡When you replace tires, never mix radial, bias-belted or bias type tires. Use only the tire sizes listed on the tire decal attached to your vehicle on the driver's side door post. Make sure that all tires are the same size, speed rating and load carrying capacity. Use only tire and wheel combinations as recommended on the tire decal or by your dealer. Failure to follow these precautions can adversely affect the safety and handling of your vehicle.

### TIRE STORAGE

♦ See Figures 67 and 68

Store the tires at their recommended inflation pressures if they are mounted on wheels. All tires should be kept in a cool, dry place. If they are stored in the garage or basement, do not let them stand on a concrete floor; set them on strips of wood.

### TIRE INFLATION

Tire inflation is the most ignored item of auto maintenance. Gasoline mileage can drop as much as 0.8% for every 1 pound per square inch (psi) of underinflation.

Two items should be a permanent fixture in every glove compartment: a tire pressure gauge and a tread depth gauge. Check the tire air pressure (including the spare) regularly with a pocket type gauge. Kicking the tires won't tell you a thing, and the gauge on the service station air hose is notoriously inaccurate. Also, just looking at the tire does not indicate if it is underinflated.

The tire pressures recommended for your car are usually found on a label attached to the door pillar, on the glove compartment's inner cover and in the owner's manual. Ideally, inflation pressure should be checked when the tires are cool. When the air becomes heated; it expands and the pressure increases. Every 10°F (-12°C) rise (or drop) in temperature means a difference of 1 psi (7 kPa), which also explains why the tire appears to lose air on a very cold night. When it is impossible to check the tires cold, allow for

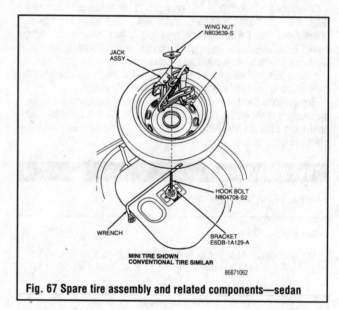

Fig. 67 Spare tire assembly and related components—sedan

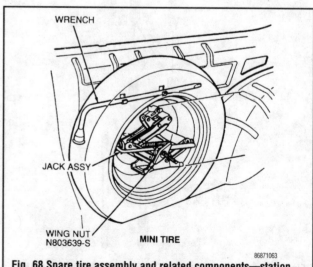

Fig. 68 Spare tire assembly and related components—station wagon

pressure build-up due to heat. If the hot pressure exceeds the cold pressure by more than 15 psi (103 kPa), reduce your speed. Otherwise internal heat is created in the tire. When the heat approaches the temperature at which the tire was cured during manufacture, the tread can separate from the body.

### ✳✳ WARNING

**Never counteract excessive pressure build-up by bleeding off air pressure (letting some air out). This will only further raise the tire operating temperature.**

## FLUIDS AND LUBRICANTS

Used fluids such as engine oil, transmission fluid, antifreeze and brake fluid are hazardous wastes and must be disposed of properly. Before draining any fluid, consult your local authorities; in many areas, waste oil, etc. is being accepted as a part of recycling programs. A number of service stations and auto parts stores are also accepting waste fluids for recycling.

Be sure of the recycling center's policies before draining any fluids, as many will not accept different fluids that have been mixed together, such as oil and antifreeze.

## Fuel and Engine Oil Recommendations

### FUEL RECOMMENDATIONS

➡️**Some fuel additives contain chemicals that can damage the catalytic converter and/or oxygen sensor. Read all of the labels carefully before using any additive in the engine or fuel system.**

All vehicles covered by this manual are designed to run on unleaded fuel. The used of a leaded fuel in a car requiring unleaded fuel will plug the catalytic converter and render it inoperative. It will also increase exhaust backpressure to the point where engine output will be severely reduced. The minimum octane rating of the unleaded fuel being used must be at least 87, which usually means regular unleaded, but some high performance engines may require higher ratings. Fuel should be selected for the brand and octane which performs best with your engine. Judge a gasoline by its ability to prevent pinging, its engine starting capabilities (cold and hot) and general all-weather performance.

➡️**For information regarding vehicles equipped with the Flexible Fuel (FF) system, refer to your owner's manual for fuel recommendations.**

As far as the octane rating is concerned, refer to the General Engine Specifications Chart in Section 3 of this manual to find your engine and its compression ratio. If the compression ration is 9.0:1 or lower, in most cases a regular unleaded grade of gasoline can be used. If the compression ratio is 9.0:1-9.3:1, use a premium grade of unleaded fuel.

The use of a fuel too low in octane (a measurement of antiknock quality) will result in spark knock. Since many factors such as altitude, terrain, air temperature and humidity affect operating efficiency, knocking may result even though the recommended fuel is being used. If persistent knocking occurs, it may be necessary to switch to a higher grade of fuel. Continuous or heavy knocking may result in engine damage.

➡️**Your engine's fuel requirement can change with time, mainly due to carbon buildup, which will in turn change the compression ratio. If your engine pings, knocks, or diesels (runs with the ignition off) switch to a higher grade of fuel. Sometimes just changing brands will cure the problem. If it becomes necessary to retard the timing from the specifications, don't change it more than a few degrees. Retarded timing will reduce power output and fuel mileage, in addition to making the engine run hotter.**

## CARE OF WHEEL COVERS AND ALUMINUM WHEELS

To clean the wheels, wheel covers and wheel ornamentation, use a mild soap solution and thoroughly rinse with clean water. Do not use steel wool, abrasive type cleaner or strong detergents containing high alkaline or caustic agents, as damage to the protective coating and discoloration may result.

### OIL RECOMMENDATIONS

▶ **See Figure 69**

The SAE (Society of Automotive Engineers) grade number indicates the viscosity of the engine oil and, thus, its ability to lubricate at a given temperature. The lower the SAE grade number, the lighter the oil; the lower the viscosity, the easier it is to crank the engine in cold weather. Oil viscosities should be chosen from those oils recommended for the lowest anticipated temperatures during the oil change interval. With the proper viscosity you will be assured of easy cold starting and sufficient engine protection.

Multi-viscosity oils (5W-30, 10W-30, etc.) offer the important advantage of being adaptable to temperature extremes. They allow easy starting at low temperatures, yet they give good protection at high speeds and engine temperatures. This is a decided advantage in changeable climates or in long distance driving.

The API (American Petroleum Institute) designation indicates the classification of engine oil used under certain given operating conditions. Only oils designated for use Service SG, or the latest superceding oil grade, should be used. Oils of the SG type perform a variety of functions inside the engine in addition to their basic function as a lubricant. Through a balanced system of metallic detergents and polymeric dispersants, the oil prevents the formation of high and low temperature deposits and also keeps sludge and dirt particles in suspension. Acids, particularly sulfuric acid, as well as other byproducts of combustion, are neutralized. Both the SAE grade number and the API designation can be found of the side of the oil bottle. Oil meeting API classification SG, SG/CC or SG/CD is recommended for use in your vehicle. Ford has filled your crankcase with SAE 5W-30 and recommends that you continue to use this as long as the outside temperatures don't exceed 100°F (38°C). There are other options, however, such as SAE 10W-30; refer to the accompanying oil viscosity/ambient temperature chart.

### Synthetic Oil

There are excellent synthetic and fuel-efficient oils available that, under the right circumstances, can help provide better fuel mileage and better

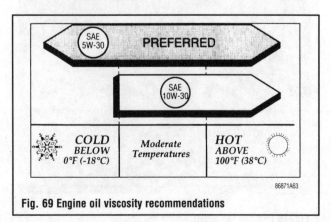

Fig. 69 Engine oil viscosity recommendations

engine protection. However, these advantages come at a price, which can be three or four times the price per quart of conventional motor oils.

Before pouring any synthetic oils into your car's engine, you should consider the condition of the engine and the type of driving you do. It is also wise to check the vehicle manufacturer's position on synthetic oils.

Generally, it is best to avoid the use of synthetic oil in both brand new and older, high mileage engines. New engines require a proper break-in, and the synthetics are so slippery that they can impede this; most manufacturers recommend that you wait at least 5,000 miles (8,000 km) before switching to a synthetic oil. Conversely, older engines are looser and tend to use more oil; synthetics will slip past worn parts more readily than regular oil, and will be used up faster. If your car already leaks and/or uses oil (due to worn parts or bad seals/gaskets), it may leak and use more with a synthetic inside.

Consider your type of driving. If most of your accumulated mileage is on the highway at higher, steadier speed, a synthetic oil will reduce friction and probably help deliver better fuel mileage. If you choose to use synthetic oil in this case, synthetic oils which are certified and have the preferred viscosity may be used in your engine; however, the oil and filter must still be changed according to the maintenance schedule. Cars used under harder, stop-and-go, short hop circumstances should always be serviced more frequently, and for these cars, synthetic oil may not be a wise investment.

## Engine

### OIL LEVEL CHECK

▶ **See Figures 70 and 71**

Every time you stop for fuel, check the engine oil, making sure the engine has fully warmed and the vehicle is parked on a level surface. Because it takes a few minutes for all the oil to drain back to the oil pan, you should wait a few minutes before checking your oil. If you are doing this at a fuel stop, first fill the fuel tank, then open the hood and check the oil, (but don't get so carried away as to forget to pay for the fuel. Most station attendants won't believe that you forgot.)

1. Be sure your car is parked on level ground.
2. Shut off the engine. When checking the oil level, it is best for the engine to be at normal operating temperature, although checking the oil immediately after stopping will lead to a false reading. Wait a few minutes after turning off the engine to allow the oil to drain back into the crankcase.
3. Open the hood and locate the dipstick in a guide tube at the left-center, front of the engine. Pull the dipstick from its tube, wipe it clean with a lint-free rag, then reinsert it. Push it down firmly to assure that it is firmly seated in the tube.

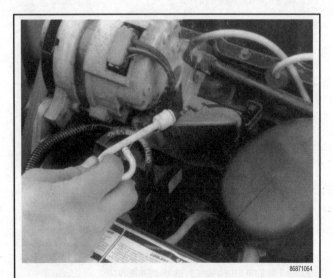

**Fig. 70 Remove the dipstick from the engine**

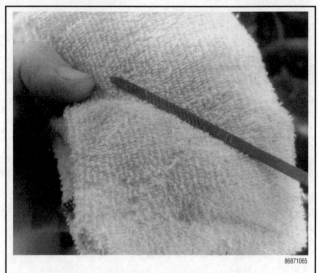

**Fig. 71 Wipe the dipstick with a clean, lint-free rag**

4. Pull the dipstick out again and, holding it horizontally, read the oil level. The oil should be between the MAX and ADD marks on the dipstick. If the oil is below the ADD mark, add oil of the proper viscosity through the capped opening in the top of the cylinder head cover or filler tube, as applicable.
5. Reinsert the dipstick and check the oil level again after adding any oil. Approximately one quart of oil will raise the level from the ADD mark to the MAX mark. Be sure not to overfill the crankcase and waste the oil. Excess oil will generally be consumed at an accelerated rate.

### OIL AND FILTER CHANGE

▶ **See Figures 72, 73, 74, 75 and 76**

Change the engine oil and oil filter every 6 months or 5,000 miles (8,000 km). If the car is used in severe service or dusty conditions, change the engine oil and oil filter every 3 months or 3,000 miles (4,800 km). Following these recommended intervals will help keep you car engine in good condition. Dirty oil loses its lubricating qualities and can cause premature wear in your engine.

1. Make sure the engine is at normal operating temperature (this promotes complete draining of the old oil).
2. Apply the parking brake and block the wheels, or raise and safely support the car evenly on jackstands.
3. Place a drain pan of about 6 quart capacity under the engine oil pan drain plug. Wipe the drain plug and surrounding area clean using an old rag.

### ❊❊ CAUTION

**The EPA warns that prolonged contact with used engine oil may cause a number of skin disorders, including cancer! You should make every effort to minimize your exposure to used engine oil. Protective gloves should be worn when changing the oil. Wash your hands and any other exposed skin areas as soon as possible after exposure to used engine oil. Soap and water, or waterless hand cleaner should be used.**

4. Loosen the drain plug using the proper size box or socket wrench. Turn the plug out by hand, using a rag to shield your fingers from the hot oil. By keeping an inward pressure on the plug as you unscrew it, oil won't escape past the threads and you can remove it without being burned by the hot oil.
5. Quickly withdraw the plug and move your hands out of the way, but be careful not to drop the plug into the drain pan, as fishing it out can be an unpleasant mess. Allow all the old oil to drain completely into the pan, then inspect the drain plug gasket and replace it if necessary.

Fig. 72 Loosen and remove the oil drain plug

Fig. 75 Remove the oil filler cap located on the valve cover

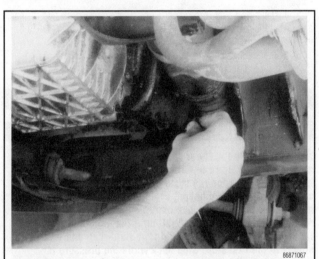

Fig. 73 Having the engine at normal operating temperature will promote complete draining of the engine oil

Fig. 76 Refill the crankcase with the proper grade and capacity of engine oil

6. Install and carefully tighten the drain plug. Be careful not to over-tighten the drain plug, otherwise you'll be buying a new pan or a trick replacement plug for stripped threads.

7. Move the drain pan under the engine oil filter. Use a strap-type or cap-type filter wrench to loosen the oil filter. Cover your hand with a rag and spin the filter off by hand; turn it slowly. Keep in mind that it's holding about one quart of dirty, hot oil.

8. Empty the oil filter into the drain pan and properly dispose of the filter.

9. Wipe the engine filter mount clean with a lint-free rag. Coat the rubber gasket on the new oil filter with clean engine oil, applying it with a finger. Carefully start the filter onto the threaded engine mount, by hand. When the filter touches the adapter surface, give it another ½–1 turn (no more, or you'll squash the gasket and it will leak).

10. Lower the vehicle to the ground. Refill the crankcase to specification with the proper grade and type motor oil. Install the filler cap and start the engine. Allow the engine to idle and check for oil leaks. Shut off the engine, wait several minutes, then check the oil level with the dipstick. The oil level will drop as the filter fills up with oil. Add oil to the proper dipstick level.

When you have finished this job, you will notice that you now possess four or five quarts of dirty oil. Pour it into plastic jugs, such as clean milk or antifreeze containers. Then, locate a service station or automotive parts store where you can pour it into their used oil tank for recycling.

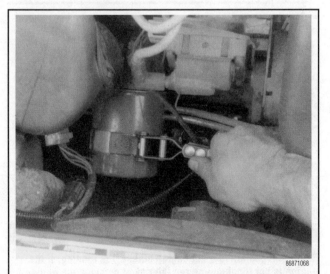

Fig. 74 Remove the oil filter using a strap-type filter wrench

### ☀ WARNING

**Pouring used motor oil into a storm drain not only pollutes the environment, it violates Federal law. Dispose of waste oil properly.**

## Manual Transaxle

### FLUID RECOMMENDATIONS AND LEVEL CHECK

▶ **See Figure 77**

Each time the engine oil is changed, the fluid level of the transaxle should be checked. The car must be resting on level ground or supported on jackstands (front and back) evenly. To check the fluid, remove the filler plug, located on the upper front (driver's side) of the transaxle with a ⅜ in. (10mm) extension and ratchet.

The filler plug has a hex head; do not mistake any other bolts for the filler plug. Do not overfill the transaxle. The oil level should be even with the edge of the filler hole or within ¼ in. (6mm) of the hole. If the oil is low, add Motorcraft Type F or Dexron®II automatic transmission fluid.

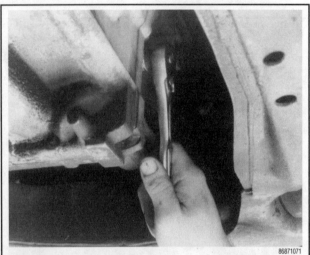

**Fig. 77 Checking the manual transaxle fluid—early model 2.5L shown**

86871071

## Automatic Transaxle

### FLUID RECOMMENDATIONS AND LEVEL CHECK

A dipstick is provided in the engine compartment to check the level of the automatic transaxle. Check the Maintenance Component Location charts at the end of this section for the dipstick location on your vehicle. Be sure the car is on level ground and that the car's engine and transaxle have reached normal operating temperatures.

1. Start the engine, set the parking brake, and put the transaxle selector lever in the PARK position.

2. Move the selector lever through all the positions and return to the PARK position. DO NOT TURN OFF THE ENGINE DURING THE FLUID LEVEL CHECK.

3. Clean all dirt from the dipstick cap before removing the dipstick. Remove the dipstick and wipe clean.

4. Reinsert the dipstick making sure it is fully seated. Pull the dipstick out of the tube and check the fluid level. The fluid level should be between the FULL and ADD marks.

5. If necessary, add enough fluid through the dipstick tube/filler to bring the level to the FULL mark on the dipstick. Use Dexron®II or Mercon® fluid in the ATX 3-speed transaxle, AXOD and AXOD-E overdrive transaxles.

Do not overfill the transaxle. Doing so can cause damage to the transaxle. Make sure the dipstick is fully seated. If by chance you overfill the transaxle, thread a small piece of rubber vacuum hose into the dipstick tube until it hits the bottom, then withdraw the excess fluid using a large, clean turkey baster or equivalent.

### DRAIN AND REFILL

In normal service it should not be necessary or required to drain and refill the automatic transaxle. However, under severe operation or dusty conditions, the fluid should be changed every 20 months or 20,000 miles (32,000 km).

1. Raise the car and safely support it on jackstands. If the pan is equipped with a drain plug, drain the fluid into a suitable container.

2. If the pan does not have a drain plug, place a suitable drain pan underneath the transaxle oil pan. Loosen the oil pan mounting bolts and allow the fluid to drain until it reaches the level of the pan flange. Remove the attaching bolts, leaving one end attached so that the pan will tip and the rest of the fluid will drain.

3. Remove the oil pan and thoroughly clean it. Remove the old gasket. Make sure that the gasket mounting surfaces are clean.

4. Unfasten the transaxle filter screen retaining bolt and remove the screen.

5. Install a new filter screen and O-ring. Place a new gasket on the pan and install the pan to the transaxle. Torque the transaxle pan to 15–19 ft. lbs. (20–26 Nm).

6. Fill the transaxle to the correct level. Remove the jackstands and lower the car to the ground.

## Cooling System

### ☀ CAUTION

**Never remove the radiator cap under any conditions while the engine is hot! Failure to follow these instructions could result in damage to the cooling system and engine, as well as personal injury. To avoid having scalding hot coolant or steam blow out of the radiator, use extreme care whenever you are removing the radiator cap. Wait until the engine has cooled, then wrap a thick cloth around the radiator cap and turn it slowly to the first stop. Step back while the pressure is released from the cooling system. When you are sure the pressure has been released, press down on the radiator cap (still holding the cloth in position), then turn and remove the radiator cap.**

➡ **On vehicles equipped with a coolant recovery reservoir, removal of the radiator cap is normally not required, except for when draining the system or inspecting the radiator and cap.**

Servicing the cooling system can be a dangerous matter unless the proper precautions are observed. It is best to check the coolant level in the radiator when the engine is cold. All vehicles covered by this manual should be equipped with a coolant recovery reservoir. If the coolant level is at or near the FULL COLD line (engine cold) or the FULL HOT line (engine hot), the level is satisfactory. Always be certain that the filler caps on both the radiator and the recovery reservoir are closed tightly.

If the coolant level is found to be low, add a 50/50 mixture of coolant that meets Ford specifications, such as Ford Cooling System Fluid, Prestone® II or other approved coolant and clean water. Coolant may be added either through the filler neck on the radiator or directly into the recovery reservoir.

### ☀ CAUTION

**Never add coolant to a hot engine unless it is running. If the engine is not running, you run the risk of cracking the engine block.**

It is wise to pressure check the cooling system at least once a year. If the coolant level is chronically low or rusty, the system should be thoroughly checked for leaks.

At least once every two years or 30,000 miles (48,000 km), the engine and radiator should be inspected, flushed and refilled with fresh coolant. If the coolant is left in the system too long, it loses its ability to prevent rust corrosion. If the coolant has too much water, it won't protect against freezing.

The pressure cap should be examined for signs of age or deterioration. The fan belt and other drive belts should be inspected and adjusted to the proper tension.

Hose clamps should be tightened, and soft or cracked hoses replaced. Damp spots, or accumulations of rust or dye near the hoses, water pump or other areas indicate possible leakage, which must be corrected before filling the system with fresh coolant.

## FLUID RECOMMENDATIONS

This engine has an aluminum cylinder head and requires a corrosion inhibiting coolant formulation to avoid radiator damage. Use only a permanent type coolant that meets Ford Specifications such as Ford Cooling System Fluid, Prestone® II, or other approved coolants. Mix the coolant with clean water until a 50/50 solution is attained.

## LEVEL CHECK

The cooling system of your car contains, among other items, a radiator and an expansion tank/recovery reservoir. When the engine is running heat is generated. The rise in temperature causes the coolant, in the radiator, to expand and builds up internal pressure. When a certain pressure is reached, a pressure relief valve in the radiator filler cap (pressure cap) is lifted from its seat and allows coolant to flow through the radiator filler neck, down a hose, and into the expansion reservoir.

When the system temperature and pressure are reduced in the radiator, the water in the expansion reservoir is siphoned back into the radiator.

On systems with a coolant recovery tank, maintain the coolant level between the marks on the recovery reservoir.

➡**If, for some reason, the vehicle does not have a coolant recovery tank, maintain the coolant level 1–2 in. (25–51mm) below the bottom of the radiator filler neck when the engine is cold and 1 in. (25mm) below the bottom of the filler neck when the engine is hot.**

## DRAIN AND REFILL

For best protection against freezing and overheating, maintain an approximate 50% water and 50% ethylene glycol (or other suitable) antifreeze mixture in the cooling system. Do not mix different brands of antifreeze to avoid possible chemical damage to the cooling system.

Avoid using water that is known to have a high alkaline content or is very hard, except in emergency situations. Drain and flush the cooling system as soon as possible after using such water.

### ✳✳ CAUTION

**Cover the radiator cap with a thick cloth before removing it from a radiator in a vehicle that is hot. Turn the cap counterclockwise slowly until pressure can be heard escaping. Allow all pressure to escape from the radiator before completely removing the radiator cap. It is best to allow the engine to cool, if possible, before removing the radiator cap.**

➡**Never add cold water to an overheated engine while the engine is not running.**

After filling the radiator, run the engine until it reaches normal operating temperature, to make sure that the thermostat has opened and all the air is bled from the system.

### ✳✳ CAUTION

**The cooling fan motor is controlled by a temperature switch. The fan may come on and run even when the engine is off and will continue to run until the engine has cooled to a predetermined level. Take care not to get your fingers, etc. close to the fan blades.**

**Draining Coolant**

▶ **See Figures 78 and 79**

### ✳✳ CAUTION

**When draining the coolant, keep in mind that cats and dogs are attracted by ethylene glycol antifreeze, and are quite likely to drink any that is left in an uncovered container or in puddles on the ground. This will prove fatal in sufficient quantity. Always drain the coolant into a sealable container. Coolant should be reused unless it is contaminated or several years old.**

To drain the coolant, connect a hose approximately 18 in. (46cm) long, with an inside diameter of ⅜ in. (9.5mm), to the nipple on the drain valve

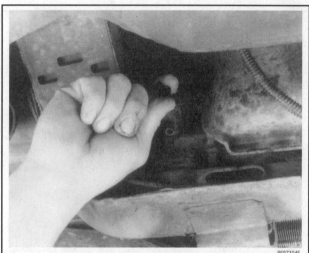
Fig. 78 Open the drain valve located on the bottom of the radiator

Fig. 79 Attaching a small hose to the draincock will help direct the flow of coolant into the drain pan, thereby reducing the mess

located on the bottom of the radiator. With the engine cool, set the heater control to the maximum heat position. Remove the radiator cap and open the drain valve or loosen the Allen head plug ³⁄₁₆ in. (5mm), allowing the coolant to drain into a suitable container. When all of the coolant is drained, remove the hose and close the drain valve or Allen head plug.

### Replacing Coolant

**▶ See Figures 80, 81 and 82**

If there is any evidence of rust or scaling in the cooling system, the system should be flushed thoroughly before refilling. Refer to the flushing/cleaning procedure, later in this section. With the engine OFF and COOL:

1. Using a funnel, add the designated quantity of a 50% coolant and 50% water solution to the radiator.

2. Reinstall the radiator cap to the fully installed position, then back it off to the first stop.

3. Start and idle the engine until the upper radiator hose is warm.

4. Immediately shut off the engine. Cautiously remove the radiator cap and add water until the radiator is full. Reinstall the radiator cap securely.

5. Add coolant to the ADD mark on the reservoir, then fill to the FULL HOT mark with water.

6. Check the system for leaks and return the heater temperature control to its normal position.

**Fig. 80 All vehicles covered by this manual should be equipped with a coolant reservoir**

**Fig. 81 Add coolant to the correct marks on the reservoir**

**Fig. 82 Check the coolant level to make sure it is sufficient**

## RADIATOR CAP INSPECTION

**▶ See Figures 83 and 84**

Allow the engine to cool sufficiently before attempting to remove the radiator cap. Use a rag to cover the cap, then remove by pressing down and turning counterclockwise to the first stop. If any hissing is noted (indicating the release of pressure), wait until the hissing stops completely, then press down again and turn counterclockwise until the cap can be removed.

**✳✳ CAUTION**

**DO NOT attempt to remove the radiator cap while the engine is hot. Severe personal injury from steam burns can result.**

Check the condition of the radiator cap gasket and seal inside the cap. The radiator cap is designed to seal the cooling system under normal operating conditions which allow the buildup of a certain amount of pressure (this pressure rating is stamped or printed on the cap). The pressure in the system raises the boiling point of the coolant to help prevent overheating. If the radiator cap does not seal properly, the boiling point of the coolant is lowered and overheating will likely occur. If the cap must be replaced, purchase a new cap according to the pressure rating which is specified for your vehicle.

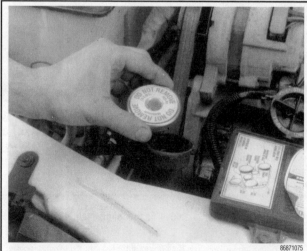

**Fig. 83 Allow the engine to cool before attempting to remove the radiator cap. DO NOT remove the cap while the engine is hot!**

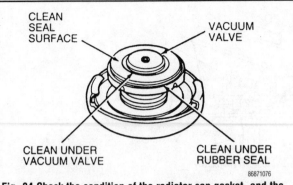

**Fig. 84 Check the condition of the radiator cap gasket, and the seal inside of the cap**

Prior to installing the radiator cap, inspect and clean the filler neck. If you are reusing the old cap, clean it thoroughly with clear water. After installing the cap, make sure the arrows align with the overflow hose.

## FLUSHING AND CLEANING THE SYSTEM

1. Drain the cooling system, including the radiator and engine block. Close the drain valve/plugs, then refill the system with water at the radiator fill neck.
2. Allow the engine to idle for about 5 minutes. Turn the engine off. Drain the cooling system again.
3. Repeat the above steps until nearly clear water is drained from the radiator. Allow the remaining water to drain and then close the draincock.
4. Disconnect the overflow hose from the radiator filler neck. Remove the coolant recovery reservoir from the fender apron and empty the fluid.
5. Flush the reservoir with clean water. Reinstall the reservoir.
6. Fill the radiator and cooling system with the proper concentration of coolant and water. Don't forget to also fill the reservoir to its proper level.

## Brake Master Cylinder

▶ **See Figures 85 and 86**

### FLUID RECOMMENDATIONS

When adding to or refilling the master cylinder, be sure to use Heavy Duty (H. D.) brake fluid that meets or exceeds Ford Motor Company specification ESA-M6C25-A, such as Motorcraft C6AZ-19542-AA or BA or equivalent.

**✳✳ CAUTION**

**Brake fluid damages paint. It also absorbs moisture from the air; never leave a container or the master cylinder uncovered any longer than necessary. All parts in contact with the brake fluid (master cylinder, hoses, plunger assemblies, etc.) must be kept clean, since any contamination of the brake fluid can adversely affect braking performance.**

### LEVEL CHECK

▶ **See Figures 87 and 88**

It should be obvious how important the brake system is to the safe operation of your vehicle. Maintaining the correct level of clean brake fluid is critical for the proper operation of your vehicle. A low fluid level indicates a need for service (there may be a leak in the system or the brake pads may just be worn and in need of replacement). In any case, the brake fluid level should be inspected at least during every oil change, but more often is desirable. Every time you open the hood is a good time to glance at the master cylinder reservoir.

The brake master cylinder is located under the hood, on the left side (driver's side) of the firewall. Check the Maintenance Component Location charts, at the end of this section, for the exact location on your vehicle. Before removing the master cylinder reservoir cap, make sure the vehicle is resting on level ground and clean all the dirt away from the top of the master cylinder. Remove the master cylinder cap.

Some vehicles covered by this manual are equipped with and Anti-lock Brake System (ABS). To check the fluid level in the master cylinder reservoir of a vehicle equipped with ABS:

1. Turn the ignition **OFF**.
2. Pump the brake pedal at least 20 times or until the pedal feel becomes hard, then turn the ignition key to the **ON** position.
3. Wait at least 60 seconds to be sure that the fluid level is stabilized.
4. The fluid level should be at the MAX line as indicated on the side of the reservoir.

➡ **The fluid level will lower somewhat due to normal brake lining wear. However, if the level is less than half the volume of the reservoir, check the brake system for leaks. Leaks in the brake hydraulic system most commonly occur at the rear wheel cylinders or at the front calipers. Leaks at the brake lines or the master cylinder can also be the cause of lost brake fluid. If a leak is detected, repair it and bleed the system, as described in Section 9.**

5. If the level is low, remove the cap and add Heavy Duty Brake Fluid (Dot 3) until the MAX line is reached. The level of the brake fluid should be at the **MAX** line embossed on the translucent plastic reservoir of the master cylinder.

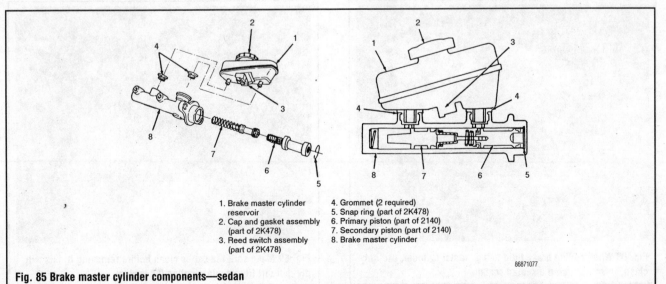

1. Brake master cylinder reservoir
2. Cap and gasket assembly (part of 2K478)
3. Reed switch assembly (part of 2K478)
4. Grommet (2 required)
5. Snap ring (part of 2K478)
6. Primary piston (part of 2140)
7. Secondary piston (part of 2140)
8. Brake master cylinder

**Fig. 85 Brake master cylinder components—sedan**

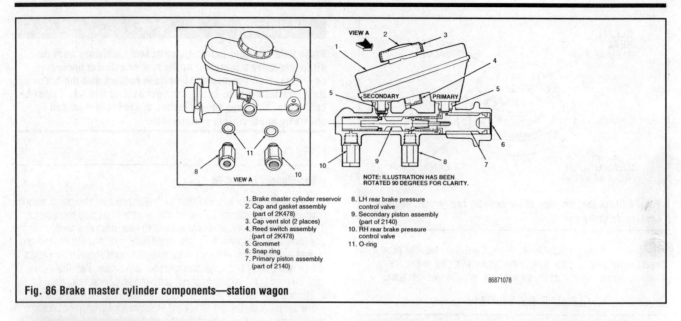

1. Brake master cylinder reservoir
2. Cap and gasket assembly (part of 2K478)
3. Cap vent slot (2 places)
4. Reed switch assembly (part of 2K478)
5. Grommet
6. Snap ring
7. Primary piston assembly (part of 2140)
8. LH rear brake pressure control valve
9. Secondary piston assembly (part of 2140)
10. RH rear brake pressure control valve
11. O-ring

NOTE: ILLUSTRATION HAS BEEN ROTATED 90 DEGREES FOR CLARITY.

Fig. 86 Brake master cylinder components—station wagon

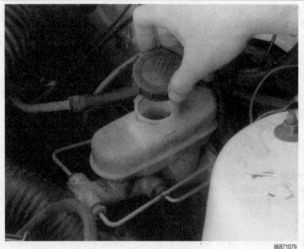

Fig. 87 Before taking the cap off of the master cylinder, make sure all dirt and/or debris is cleaned off

➡If the master cylinder reservoir has a cap with an expanding rubber diaphragm, be sure to push the diaphragm up into the cap before installing the cap.

## Power Steering Pump

### FLUID RECOMMENDATIONS

Use Ford Motor Company's premium power steering fluid E6AZ-19582-AA (ESW-M2C33-F) or equivalent.

### LEVEL CHECK

◆ **See Figures 89, 90, 91 and 92**

You should check the level of the power steering fluid at least twice a year. You may check the fluid when the engine is either hot or cold.

To check the fluid when the engine is hot:

1. Start the engine and let it run until it reaches normal operating temperature.

2. While the engine is idling, turn the steering wheel all the way to the right and then to the left several times. Turn the engine **OFF**.

Fig. 88 When adding brake fluid to the master cylinder, use only clean, fresh fluid from a sealed container

Fig. 89 Make sure the cap is clean before removing it; this will prevent dirt from contaminating the system

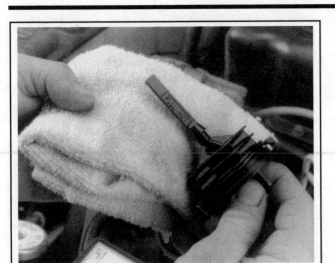

**Fig. 90 If checking the fluid when the engine is hot, it should be within the proper marks of the FULL HOT side of the dipstick**

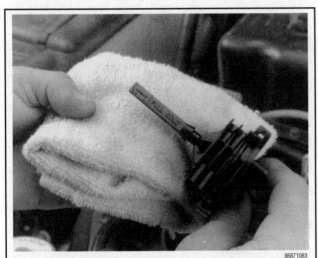

**Fig. 91 Power steering dipstick fluid level marks for checking the fluid when the engine is cold**

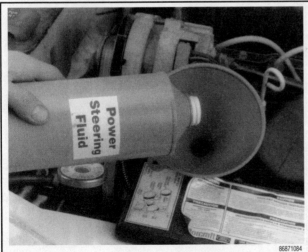

**Fig. 92 Add power steering fluid in small amounts, but do not overfill**

3. Open the hood and remove the power steering pump dipstick located on the right side (passenger side) near the front of the engine.

4. Wipe the dipstick clean and reinsert it into the pump reservoir. Withdraw the dipstick and note the fluid level. The level must show in the FULL HOT range on the dipstick.

5. If the power steering fluid is low, add the proper fluid in small amounts, continuously checking the level, until you reach the FULL HOT range, but do not overfill. Remove any excess fluid with a clean suction bulb or equivalent.

➡If you check the power steering fluid when the engine is cold, make sure that the fluid level reaches the FULL COLD range on the dipstick. However, the reading will only be accurate if the fluid temperature is approximately 50–85°F (10–30°C).

## Steering Rack

### FLUID RECOMMENDATIONS

Use Ford Motor Company's premium power steering fluid E6AZ-19582-AA (ESW-M2C33-F) or equivalent.

## Body Maintenance

Regular body maintenance preserves the vehicle's appearance during the life of the vehicle. When washing or waxing the exterior of the vehicle, be sure to use products that meet or exceed Ford Motor Company's specifications. Replace all damaged weatherstrips as needed. Replace all chipped or cracked glass as needed. Drain holes are located under each rocker panel, quarter panel and door; these holes should be kept open to allow water to drain.

## Rear Wheel Bearings

▶ See Figure 95

➡These procedures are for rear wheel bearings only. For information regarding front wheel bearings, please refer to Section 7 of this manual.

### ✳✳ CAUTION

When servicing the rear wheel bearings, use caution because brake shoes may contain asbestos, which has been determined to be a cancer causing agent. Never clean the brake surfaces with compressed air! Avoid inhaling any dust from any brake surface! When cleaning brake surfaces, use a commercially available brake cleaning fluid.

Once every 30,000 miles (48,000 km), clean and repack the rear wheel bearings using Long-Life Lubricant, Ford part no. C1AZ-19590-B, or equivalent.

➡Sodium-based grease is not compatible with lithium-based grease. Read the package labels and be careful not to mix the two types. If there is any doubt as to the type of grease used, completely clean the old grease from the bearing and hub before repacking.

Before handling the bearings, there are a few things that you should remember to do and not to do.

**Remember to DO the following:**
• Remove all outside dirt from the housing before exposing the bearing.
• Treat a used bearing as gently as you would a new one.
• Work with clean tools in clean surroundings.
• Use clean, dry canvas gloves, or at least clean, dry hands.
• Use clean solvents and flushing fluids.
• Use clean paper when laying out the bearings to dry.
• Protect disassembled bearings from rust and dirt by covering them up.
• Use clean rags to wipe bearings.
• Keep the bearings in oil-proof paper when they are to be stored or are not in use.
• Clean the inside of the housing before replacing the bearing.

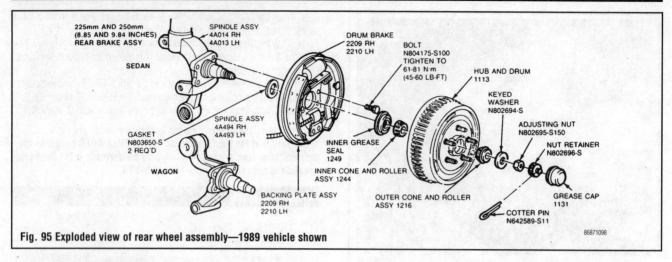

Fig. 95 Exploded view of rear wheel assembly—1989 vehicle shown

**Also observe the following:**
- Do not work in dirty surroundings.
- Do not use dirty, chipped or damaged tools.
- Do not work on wooden work benches or use wooden mallets.
- Do not handle bearings with dirty or moist hands.
- Do not use gasoline for cleaning; use a safe solvent.
- Do not spin-dry bearings with compressed air as they will be damaged.
- Do not spin dirty bearings.
- Do not use cotton waste or dirty cloths to wipe bearings.
- Do not scratch or nick bearing surfaces.
- Do not allow the bearing to come in contact with dirt or rust at any time.

## ADJUSTMENT

▶ See Figure 96

The following procedure applies only to 1986–89 vehicles. Adjustment is not possible on 1990–95 vehicles. This procedure should be performed whenever the wheel is excessively loose on the spindle or it does not rotate freely.

➡ **The rear wheel uses a tapered roller bearing which may feel loose when properly adjusted; this condition should be considered normal.**

1. Remove the wheel cover or ornament/nut cover. Loosen the lug nuts if the wheel must be removed.

➡ **If the vehicle is equipped with styled steel or aluminum wheels, the wheel/tire assembly must be removed to access the dust cover for removal.**

2. Raise and safely support the rear of the vehicle until the tires clear the floor.
3. If necessary, remove the wheel.
4. Remove the hub grease cap, taking care not to damage it.
5. Remove the cotter pin and the nut retainer. Discard the cotter pin.
6. Back off the hub nut one full turn.
7. Tighten the adjusting nut to 17–25 ft. lbs. (23–24 Nm) while rotating the hub and drum assembly to seat the bearings. Back off the adjusting nut ½ turn, then retighten it to 24–28 inch lbs. (2.7–3.2 Nm).
8. Position the nut retainer over the adjusting nut so the slots are in line with the cotter pin hole, without rotating the adjusting nut.
9. Install a new cotter pin and bend the ends around the retainer flange.
10. Check the hub rotation. If the hub rotates freely, install the grease cap. If not, check the bearings for damage and replace, as necessary.
11. If applicable, install the wheel and tire assembly, as well as the wheel cover/ornament, then lower the vehicle.

## REMOVAL, PACKING & INSTALLATION

**With Drum Brakes**

*1986–89 VEHICLES*

▶ See Figures 97 thru 106

1. Raise the vehicle and support it safely on jackstands. Remove the wheel from the hub and drum.

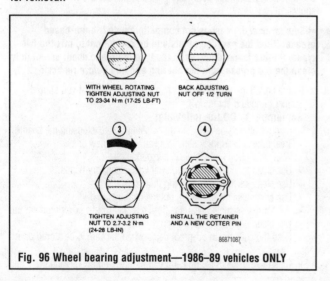

Fig. 96 Wheel bearing adjustment—1986–89 vehicles ONLY

Fig. 97 Pry the grease cap from the hub. Be careful not to distort or damage the flange

Fig. 98 After removing the grease cap, unbend the cotter pin

Fig. 101 Remove the keyed washer from the spindle

Fig. 99 Grasp the cotter pin with needle-nose pliers and pull or pry it free of the spindle. Discard the cotter pin and replace it with a new one during installation

Fig. 102 Remove the outer bearing assembly. Note that this can be done with the hub and drum on or off the vehicle

Fig. 100 Remove the adjusting nut from the spindle

Fig. 103 Remove the hub and drum assembly from the spindle

Fig. 104 Removing the grease seal; discard the seal after removing. Note that the preferred method for removing the seal is with a proper seal remover tool

Fig. 106 This is NOT the proper method for installing the grease seal, refer to the procedure for the proper tool to use when installing the seal

Fig. 105 With the seal removed, the inner bearing may be removed from the hub

2. Remove the grease cap from the hub. Remove the cotter pin, nut retainer, adjusting nut and keyed flat washer from the spindle. Discard the cotter pin.

3. Pull the hub and drum assembly off the spindle, being careful not to drop the outer bearing assembly.

4. Remove the outer bearing assembly.

5. Using seal remover tool 1175-AC or equivalent, remove and discard the grease seal. Remove the inner bearing assembly from the hub.

6. Wipe all the lubricant from the spindle and inside of the hub. Cover the spindle with a clean cloth, then vacuum all loose dust and dirt from the brake assembly. Carefully remove the cloth to prevent dirt from falling on the spindle.

7. Clean both bearing assemblies and cups using a suitable solvent. Inspect the bearing assemblies and cups for excessive wear, scratches, pits or other damage and replace as necessary.

8. If the cups are to be replaced, remove them with impact slide hammer T50T-100-A and bearing cup puller T77F-1102-A, or equivalent.

**To install:**

9. If the inner and outer bearing cups were removed, install the replacement cups using driver handle T80T-4000-W as well as bearing cup replacers T73T-1217-A and T77F-1217-A, or equivalent. Support the drum

hub on a block of wood to prevent damage. Make sure the cups are properly seated in the hub.

➡**Do not use the cone and roller assembly to install the cups. This will result in damage to the bearing cup as well as the cone and roller assembly.**

10. Make sure all of the spindle and bearing surfaces are clean.

11. Using a bearing packer, pack the bearing assemblies with a suitable wheel bearing grease. If a packer is not available, work in as much grease as possible between the rollers and cages with your hands; also grease the cup surfaces.

➡**Allow all of the cleaning solvent to dry before repacking the bearings. Do not spin-dry the bearings with air pressure.**

12. Install the inner bearing cone and roller assembly in the inner cup. Apply a light film of grease to the lips of a new grease seal and install the seal with rear hub seal replacer T56T-4676-B or equivalent. Make sure the retainer flange is seated all around.

13. Apply a light film of grease on the spindle shaft bearing surfaces. Install the hub and drum assembly on the spindle. Keep the hub centered on the spindle to prevent damage to the grease seal and spindle threads.

14. Install the outer bearing assembly and the keyed flat washer on the spindle.

15. Install the adjusting nut and adjust the wheel bearings, as previously described.

16. Install a new cotter pin, then install the grease cap.

➡**Replace the grease cap if there is corrosion on the inner surface of the cap.**

17. Place the wheel and tire on the drum, then install the lug nuts and tighten them alternately to draw the wheel evenly against the hub and drum.

18. Carefully lower the vehicle, then tighten the lug nuts (with a hand tool) to 85–105 ft. lbs. (115–142 Nm). Do not use power tools to tighten the lug nuts. Install the wheelcover.

### 1990–95 VEHICLES

▸ **See Figure 107**

1. Loosen the rear wheel lug nuts.
2. Raise and safely support the vehicle on jackstands.
3. Remove the rear wheel and tire assembly.
4. Remove the two pushnuts retaining the brake drum to the hub, then remove the drum.
5. Remove and discard the hub cap grease seal from the rear hub assembly.
6. Remove the rear axle hub retaining nut, then discard the nut.

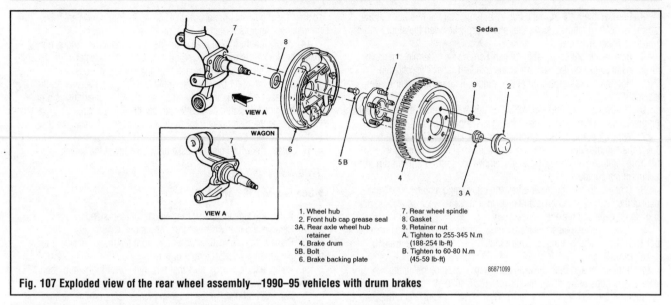

Sedan

WAGON

VIEW A

1. Wheel hub
2. Front hub cap grease seal
3A. Rear axle wheel hub retainer
4. Brake drum
5B. Bolt
6. Brake backing plate
7. Rear wheel spindle
8. Gasket
9. Retainer nut
A. Tighten to 255-345 N.m (188-254 lb-ft)
B. Tighten to 60-80 N.m (45-59 lb-ft)

86871099

**Fig. 107 Exploded view of the rear wheel assembly—1990–95 vehicles with drum brakes**

7. Remove the bearing and hub assembly from the rear wheel spindle.

**To install:**

8. Position the bearing and hub assembly onto the spindle.

9. Install a new rear axle wheel hub retaining nut, then tighten the nut to 188–254 ft. lbs. (255–345 Nm).

10. Using Coil Remover T89P-19623 or equivalent, install a new hub cap grease seal. Lightly tap on the tool until the seal is fully seated.

11. Install the brake drum onto the rear hub, then attach the two push-nuts that retain the brake drum.

12. Install the wheel and tire assembly, then carefully lower the vehicle.

## With Disc Brakes

### 1989 SHO

♦ See Figure 108

1. Raise the vehicle and support it safely on jackstands. Remove the tire and wheel assembly from the hub.

2. Remove the brake caliper after removing the 2 bolts that attach the caliper support to the cast iron brake adapter. Do not remove the caliper pins from the caliper assembly. Lift the caliper off of the rotor and support it with a length of wire. Do not allow the caliper assembly to hang from the brake hose.

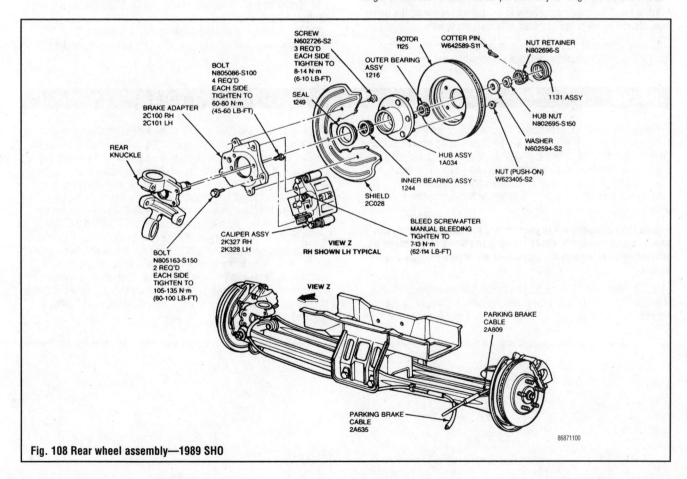

SCREW
N602726-S2
3 REQ'D
EACH SIDE
TIGHTEN TO
8-14 N·m
(6-10 LB-FT)

ROTOR
1125

COTTER PIN
W642589-S11

NUT RETAINER
N802696-S

BOLT
N805086-S100
4 REQ'D
EACH SIDE
TIGHTEN TO
60-80 N·m
(45-60 LB-FT)

OUTER BEARING
ASSY
1216

BRAKE ADAPTER
2C100 RH
2C101 LH

SEAL
1249

1131 ASSY

HUB NUT
N802695-S150

REAR
KNUCKLE

WASHER
N602594-S2

HUB ASSY
1A034

NUT (PUSH-ON)
W623405-S2

INNER BEARING ASSY
1244

SHIELD
2C028

CALIPER ASSY
2K327 RH
2K328 LH

VIEW Z
RH SHOWN LH TYPICAL

BLEED SCREW-AFTER
MANUAL BLEEDING
TIGHTEN TO
7-13 N·m
(62-114 LB-FT)

BOLT
N805163-S150
2 REQ'D
EACH SIDE
TIGHTEN TO
105-135 N·m
(80-100 LB-FT)

VIEW Z

PARKING BRAKE
CABLE
2A809

PARKING BRAKE
CABLE
2A635

86871100

**Fig. 108 Rear wheel assembly—1989 SHO**

3. Remove the rotor from the hub by pulling it off the hub bolts. If the rotor is difficult to remove, strike the rotor sharply between the studs with a rubber or plastic hammer.

4. Remove the grease cap from the hub. Remove the cotter pin, nut retainer, adjusting nut and keyed flat washer from the spindle. Discard the cotter pin.

5. Pull the hub assembly off of the spindle. Remove the outer bearing assembly.

6. Using seal remover tool 1175AC or equivalent, remove and discard the grease seal. Remove the inner bearing assembly from the hub.

7. Wipe all of the lubricant from the spindle and inside of the hub. Cover the spindle with a clean cloth and vacuum all of the loose dust and dirt from the brake assembly. Carefully remove the cloth to prevent dirt from falling on the spindle.

8. Clean both bearing assemblies and cups using a suitable solvent. Inspect the bearing assemblies and cups for excessive wear, scratches, pits or other damage and replace as necessary.

9. If the cups are being replaced, remove them with impact slide hammer tool T50T-100-A and bearing cup puller tool T77F-1102-A, or equivalent.

**To install:**

10. If the inner and outer bearing cups were removed, install the replacement cups using driver handle tool T80T-4000-W as well as bearing cup replacer tools T73F-1217-A and T77F-1217-B, or equivalent. Support the hub on a block of wood to prevent damage. Make sure the cups are properly seated in the hub.

➡ **Do not use the cone and roller assembly to install the cups. This will result in damage to the bearing cup, as well as the cone and roller assembly.**

11. Make sure all of the spindle and bearing surfaces are clean.

12. Pack the bearing assemblies with suitable wheel bearing grease using a bearing packer. If a packer is not available, work in as much grease as possible between the rollers and the cages with your hands. Grease the cup surfaces.

➡ **Allow all of the cleaning solvent to dry before repacking the bearings. Do not spin-dry the bearings with compressed air.**

13. Place the inner bearing cone and roller assembly in the inner cup. Apply a light film of grease to the lips of a new grease seal and install the seal with rear hub seal replacer tool T56T-4676-B or equivalent. Make sure the retainer flange is seated all around.

14. Apply a light film of grease on the spindle shaft bearing surfaces. Install the hub assembly on the spindle. Keep the hub centered on the spindle to prevent damage to the grease seal and spindle threads.

15. Install the outer bearing assembly and keyed flat washer on the spindle. Install the adjusting nut and adjust the wheel bearings as previously described. Install a new cotter pin and the grease cap.

16. Install the disc brake rotor to the hub assembly. Install the disc brake caliper over the rotor.

17. Install the wheel and tire assembly, then lower the vehicle.

### 1990–95 VEHICLES

▶ **See Figures 109 and 110**

1. Raise and safely support the vehicle with jackstands.
2. Remove the rear wheel and tire assembly.
3. Remove the rear caliper assembly from the brake adapter. Support the caliper assembly with a length of wire.
4. Remove the push-on nuts that retain the rotor to the hub, then remove the rotor.
5. Remove and discard the hub cap grease seal from the bearing and hub assembly.
6. Remove and discard the rear axle bearing and hub assembly retainer.
7. Remove the rear wheel hub from the rear wheel spindle.

**To install:**

8. Position the rear hub on the rear wheel spindle.
9. Install a new rear axle wheel hub retainer. Tighten the retainer to 188–254 ft. lbs. (255–345 Nm).
10. Using Coil Remover T89P-19623-FH or equivalent, install a new rear hub cap grease seal. Gently tap on the tool until the rear hub cap grease seal is fully seated.
11. Install the rear disc brake rotor on the hub. Install the two push-on nuts that retain the rotor.
12. Install the rear disc brake caliper to the brake adapter.
13. Install the wheel and tire assembly, then carefully lower the vehicle.

## JACKING

The service jack that is provided with your vehicle is designed for changing tires. It should NOT, under any circumstances be used to support the car while you crawl under it and work. To do so is to recklessly jeopardize your life. Whenever it is necessary to get under a car to perform service operations, always be sure that it is adequately supported using jackstands at the proper points. Also, be sure to always block the wheels when changing tires.

➡ **Once the jackstands are in position and the vehicle's weight has been lowered onto them, shake the car a few times before crawling underneath to make sure the jackstands are securely supporting the weight.**

Service operations in this book often require that one end or both ends of the car be raised and safely supported. The ideal method, of course, would be to use a grease pit or a hydraulic hoist. Since this is beyond both the resources and requirements of the do-it-yourselfer, consider more practical equipment. A small hydraulic, screw or scissors jack; or else a floor jack will raise the vehicle sufficiently for almost all the procedures in this guide. The rolling floor jack is probably the easiest and most convenient of these to use. But the vehicle must still be supported by at least two sturdy jackstands, if you intend to work under the car at any time. When using a floor jack, raise the front of the vehicle by positioning the floor jack under either the subframe or body side rail behind the engine support bracket. The rear may be lifted by positioning a floor jack under either rear suspension body bracket. Under no circumstances should the vehicle ever be lifted by the front or rear control arms, halfshafts or CV joints. Severe damage to the vehicle could result. An alternate method of raising the car would be drive-on ramps. Be sure to block the wheels when using ramps. Spend a little extra time to ensure that your car is lifted and supported safely.

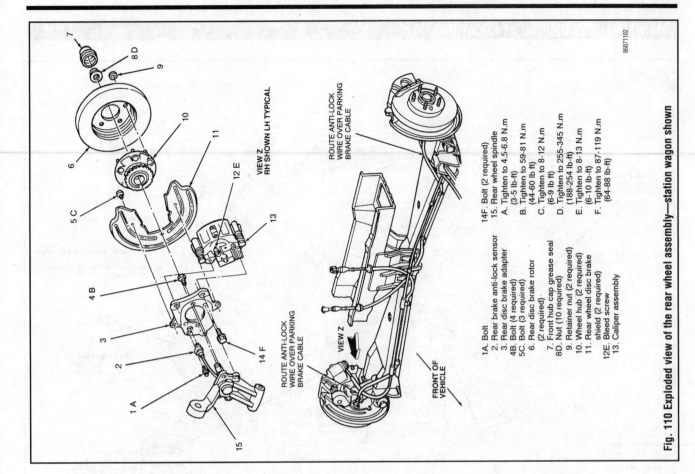

VIEW Z
RH SHOWN LH TYPICAL

ROUTE ANTI-LOCK
WIRE OVER PARKING
BRAKE CABLE

ROUTE ANTI-LOCK WIRE OVER PARKING
BRAKE CABLE

VIEW Z

FRONT OF
VEHICLE

1A. Bolt
2. Rear brake anti-lock sensor
3. Rear disc brake adapter
4B. Bolt (4 required)
5C. Bolt (3 required)
6. Rear disc brake rotor
7. Front hub cap grease seal
(2 required)
8D. Nut (10 required)
9. Retainer nut (2 required)
10. Wheel hub (2 required)
11. Rear wheel disc brake
shield (2 required)
12E. Bleed screw
13. Caliper assembly

14F. Bolt (2 required)
15. Rear wheel spindle
A. Tighten to 4.5-6.8 N.m
(3-5 lb-ft)
B. Tighten to 59-81 N.m
(44-60 lb ft)
C. Tighten to 8-12 N.m
(6-9 lb ft)
D. Tighten to 255-345 N.m
(188-254 lb-ft)
E. Tighten to 8-13 N.m
(6-10 lb-ft)
F. Tighten to 87-119 N.m
(64-88 lb-ft)

**Fig. 110 Exploded view of the rear wheel assembly—station wagon shown**

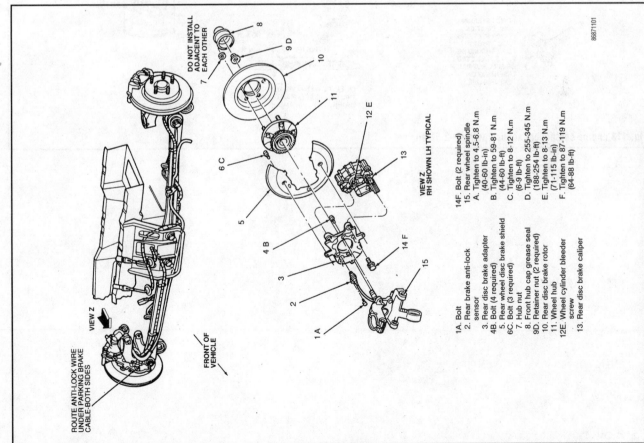

DO NOT INSTALL
ADJACENT TO
EACH OTHER

VIEW Z
RH SHOWN LH TYPICAL

ROUTE ANTI-LOCK WIRE
UNDER PARKING BRAKE
CABLE-BOTH SIDES

VIEW Z

FRONT OF
VEHICLE

1A. Bolt
2. Rear brake anti-lock
sensor
3. Rear disc brake adapter
4B. Bolt (4 required)
5. Rear wheel disc brake shield
6C. Bolt (3 required)
7. Hub nut
8. Front hub cap grease seal
9D. Retainer nut (2 required)
10. Rear disc brake rotor
11. Wheel hub
12E. Wheel cylinder bleeder
screw
13. Rear disc brake caliper

14F. Bolt (2 required)
15. Rear wheel spindle
A. Tighten to 4.5-6.8 N.m
(40-60 lb-in)
B. Tighten to 59-81 N.m
(44-60 lb-ft)
C. Tighten to 8-12 N.m
(6-9 lb-ft)
D. Tighten to 255-345 N.m
(188-254 lb-ft)
E. Tighten to 8-13 N.m
(71-115 lb-in)
F. Tighten to 87-119 N.m
(64-88 lb-ft)

**Fig. 109 Exploded view of the rear wheel assembly—sedan shown**

## MAINTENANCE COMPONENT LOCATIONS

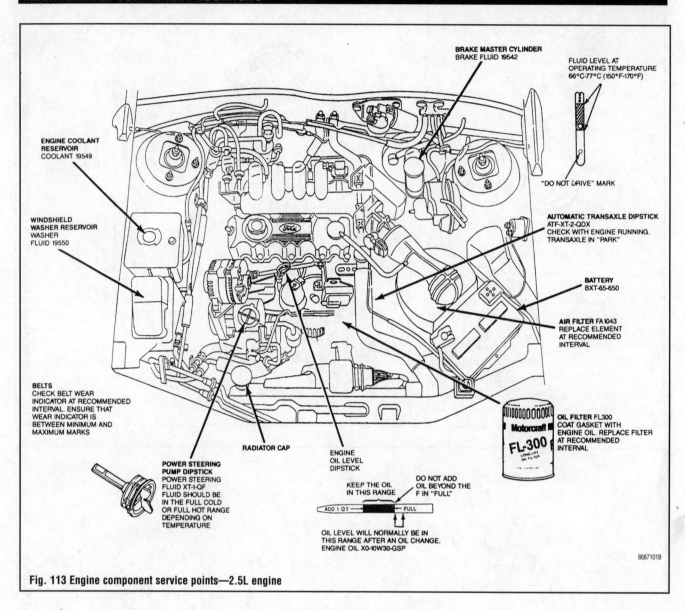

ENGINE COOLANT
RESERVOIR
COOLANT 19549

WINDSHIELD
WASHER RESERVOIR
WASHER
FLUID 19550

BELTS
CHECK BELT WEAR
INDICATOR AT RECOMMENDED
INTERVAL. ENSURE THAT
WEAR INDICATOR IS
BETWEEN MINIMUM AND
MAXIMUM MARKS

POWER STEERING
PUMP DIPSTICK
POWER STEERING
FLUID XT-1-QF
FLUID SHOULD BE
IN THE FULL COLD
OR FULL HOT RANGE
DEPENDING ON
TEMPERATURE

RADIATOR CAP

ENGINE
OIL LEVEL
DIPSTICK

BRAKE MASTER CYLINDER
BRAKE FLUID 19542

FLUID LEVEL AT
OPERATING TEMPERATURE
66°C-77°C (150°F-170°F)

"DO NOT DRIVE" MARK

AUTOMATIC TRANSAXLE DIPSTICK
ATF-XT-2-QDX
CHECK WITH ENGINE RUNNING.
TRANSAXLE IN "PARK"

BATTERY
BXT-65-650

AIR FILTER FA1043
REPLACE ELEMENT
AT RECOMMENDED
INTERVAL

OIL FILTER FL300
COAT GASKET WITH
ENGINE OIL. REPLACE FILTER
AT RECOMMENDED
INTERVAL

Motorcraft
FL-300
LONG LIFE
OIL FILTER

KEEP THE OIL
IN THIS RANGE

DO NOT ADD
OIL BEYOND THE
F IN "FULL"

ADD 1 QT          FULL

OIL LEVEL WILL NORMALLY BE IN
THIS RANGE AFTER AN OIL CHANGE.
ENGINE OIL X0-10W30-GSP

8687101B

**Fig. 113 Engine component service points—2.5L engine**

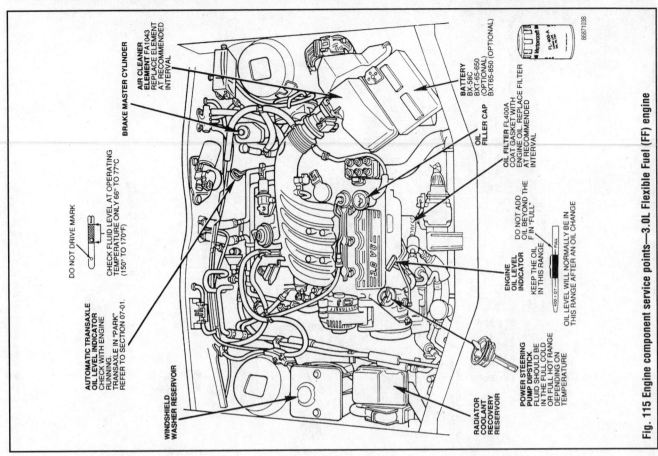

**Fig. 115 Engine component service points—3.0L Flexible Fuel (FF) engine**

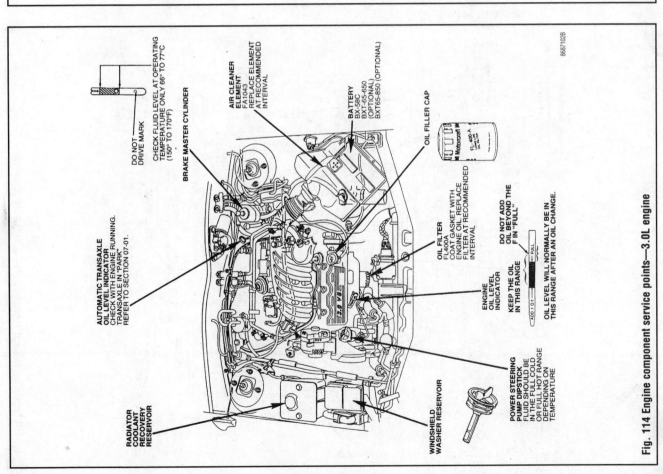

**Fig. 114 Engine component service points—3.0L engine**

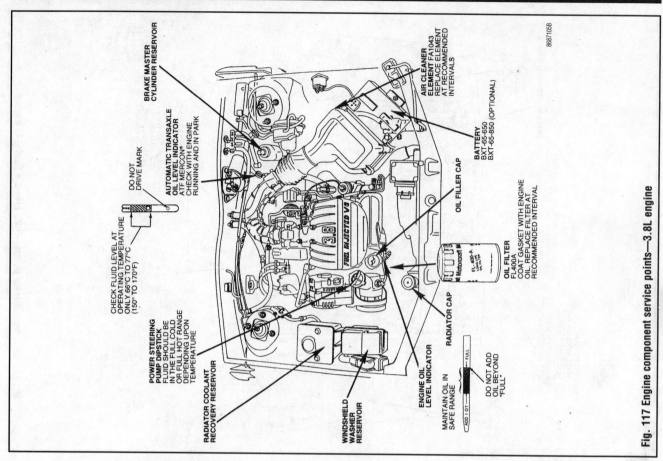

Fig. 117 Engine component service points—3.8L engine

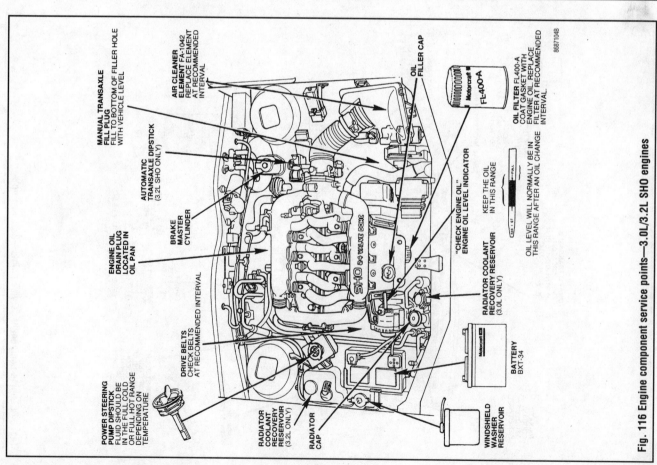

Fig. 116 Engine component service points—3.0L/3.2L SHO engines

## CAPACITIES

| Year | Model | Engine ID/VIN | Engine Displacement Liters (cc) | Engine Oil with Filter | Transmission (pts.) 4-Spd | 5-Spd | Auto. | Drive Axle Front (pts.) | Rear (pts.) | Fuel Tank (gal.) | Cooling System (qts.) |
|---|---|---|---|---|---|---|---|---|---|---|---|
| 1995 | Sable | U | 3.0 (2980) | 4.5 | - | - | 24.5 | 1 | - | 3 | 11.0 |
| | Sable | 4 | 3.8 (3801) | 4.5 | - | - | 24.5 | 1 | - | 3 | 12 |
| | Taurus | U | 3.0 (2980) | 4.5 | - | - | 28.0 | 1 | - | 3 | 11.0 |
| | Taurus | 4 | 3.8 (3801) | 4.5 | - | - | 24.5 | 1 | - | 3 | 12.1 |
| | Taurus SHO | Y | 3.0 (2980) | 5.0 | - | 6.2 | - | 1 | - | 18.4 | 11.6 |
| | Taurus SHO | P | 3.2 (3191) | 5.0 | - | - | 24.5 | 1 | - | 18.4 | 11.4 |
| | Sable | U | 3.0 (2980) | 4.5 | - | - | 28.0 | 1 | - | 3 | 11.0 |
| | Sable | 4 | 3.8 (3802) | 4.5 | - | - | 24.5 | 1 | - | 3 | 12.1 |

1 Included in transaxle capacity
2 Standard Tank: 16.0 Gals.
 Optional Extended Range Tank: 18.6 Gals.
3 Standard Tank: 16.0 Gals.
 Optional Extended Range Tank: 18.4 Gals.
4 All except wagon w/ A/C: 11.0 qts.
 Wagon w/ A/C: 11.8 qts.

86871401

## CAPACITIES

| Year | Model | Engine ID/VIN | Engine Displacement Liters (cc) | Engine Oil with Filter | Transmission (pts.) 4-Spd | 5-Spd | Auto. | Drive Axle Front (pts.) | Rear (pts.) | Fuel Tank (gal.) | Cooling System (qts.) |
|---|---|---|---|---|---|---|---|---|---|---|---|
| 1986 | Taurus | D | 2.5 (2501) | 5.0 | 6.2 | - | 16.6 | 1 | - | 2 | 8.3 |
| | Taurus | U | 3.0 (2980) | 4.5 | - | - | 21.8 | 1 | - | 2 | 4 |
| | Sable | D | 2.5 (2501) | 5.0 | 6.2 | - | 16.6 | 1 | - | 2 | 4 |
| | Sable | U | 3.0 (2980) | 4.5 | - | - | 21.8 | 1 | - | 2 | 4 |
| 1987 | Taurus | D | 2.5 (2501) | 5.0 | 6.2 | - | 16.8 | 1 | - | 2 | 8.3 |
| | Taurus | U | 3.0 (2980) | 4.5 | - | - | 26.2 | 1 | - | 2 | 12.1 |
| | Sable | D | 2.5 (2501) | 5.0 | 6.2 | - | 16.8 | 1 | - | 2 | 4 |
| | Sable | U | 3.0 (2980) | 4.5 | - | - | 26.2 | 1 | - | 2 | 12.1 |
| 1988 | Taurus | D | 2.5 (2501) | 5.0 | 6.1 | - | 16.8 | 1 | - | 2 | 8.3 |
| | Taurus | U | 3.0 (2980) | 4.5 | - | - | 26.2 | 1 | - | 2 | 12.1 |
| | Taurus | 4 | 3.8 (3802) | 4.5 | - | - | 26.2 | 1 | - | 2 | 12.1 |
| | Sable | 4 | 3.8 (3802) | 4.5 | - | - | 26.8 | 1 | - | 2 | 12.1 |
| 1989 | Taurus | D | 2.5 (2501) | 5.0 | 6.1 | - | 16.8 | 1 | - | 2 | 8.3 |
| | Taurus | U | 3.0 (2980) | 4.5 | - | - | 25.6 | 1 | - | 2 | 12.1 |
| | Taurus SHO | Y | 3.0 (2980) | 5.0 | - | 6.1 | - | 1 | - | 18.6 | 11.6 |
| | Sable | U | 3.0 (2980) | 4.5 | - | - | 16.8 | 1 | - | 2 | 12.1 |
| | Sable | 4 | 3.8 (3802) | 4.5 | - | - | 25.6 | 1 | - | 2 | 12.1 |
| 1990 | Taurus | D | 2.5 (2501) | 5.0 | - | - | 16.8 | 1 | - | 2 | 8.3 |
| | Taurus | U | 3.0 (2980) | 4.5 | - | - | 25.6 | 1 | - | 2 | 12.1 |
| | Taurus | 4 | 3.8 (3801) | 4.5 | - | - | 25.6 | 1 | - | 2 | 12.1 |
| | Taurus SHO | Y | 3.0 (2980) | 5.0 | - | 6.1 | - | 1 | - | 18.6 | 11.6 |
| | Sable | U | 3.0 (2980) | 4.5 | - | - | 25.6 | 1 | - | 2 | 12.1 |
| 1991 | Sable | 4 | 3.8 (3801) | 4.5 | - | - | 25.6 | 1 | - | 2 | 12.1 |
| | Taurus | D | 2.5 (2501) | 5.0 | - | - | 25.6 | 1 | - | 3 | 8.3 |
| | Taurus | U | 3.0 (2980) | 4.5 | - | - | 25.6 | 1 | - | 3 | 12.1 |
| 1992 | Taurus | 4 | 3.8 (3801) | 4.5 | - | - | 25.6 | 1 | - | 3 | 12.1 |
| | Taurus | U | 3.0 (2980) | 4.5 | - | - | 25.6 | 1 | - | 3 | 11.6 |
| | Taurus SHO | Y | 3.0 (2980) | 5.0 | - | 6.2 | - | 1 | - | 18.4 | 11.6 |
| | Sable | 4 | 3.8 (3801) | 4.5 | - | - | 25.6 | 1 | - | 3 | 12.1 |
| 1993 | Taurus | U | 3.0 (2980) | 4.5 | - | - | 25.6 | 1 | - | 3 | 12.1 |
| | Taurus SHO | Y | 3.0 (2980) | 5.0 | - | 6.1 | - | 1 | - | 18.4 | 11.6 |
| | Sable | P | 3.2 (3191) | 5.0 | - | - | 25.6 | 1 | - | 3 | 11.4 |
| | Taurus SHO | U | 3.0 (2980) | 4.5 | - | - | 25.6 | 1 | - | 3 | 12.1 |
| 1994 | Sable | 4 | 3.8 (3801) | 4.5 | - | - | 24.5 | 1 | - | 3 | 11.0 |
| | Taurus | U | 3.0 (2980) | 4.5 | - | - | 24.5 | 1 | - | 3 | 12.1 |
| | Taurus SHO | Y | 3.0 (2980) | 5.0 | 6.2 | - | - | 1 | - | 18.4 | 11.6 |
| | Taurus SHO | P | 3.2 (3191) | 5.0 | - | - | 24.5 | 1 | - | - | - |

86871400

**Follow Maintenance Schedule A if your driving habits MAINLY include one or more of the following conditions:**

1. Short trips of less than 10 miles, when outside temperatures remain below freezing.
2. Operating the vehicle during hot weather in stop-and-go "rush hour" traffic.
3. Towing a trailer or using a car-top carrier.
4. Operating in severe dust conditions.
5. Extensive idling, such as police, taxi or door-to-door delivery service.

**MAINTENANCE INTERVAL SCHEDULE A**

The services shown in this schedule up to 60,000 miles are to be performed after 60,000 miles at the same intervals

Mileage intervals (×1000): 3  6  9  12  15  18  21  24  27  30  33  36  39  42  45  48  51  54  57  60

| Item No. | To Be Serviced | Minimum Time Interval |
|---|---|---|
| | EMISSION CONTROL SERVICE | |
| 1 | Replace engine oil & filter | Every 3 months |
| 2 | Spark plugs – 2.5L, 3.0L, 3.8L | |
| 3 | Spark plugs – 3.0L SHO, 3.2L SHO | |
| 4 | Inspect accessory drive belt(s) | |
| 5 | Replace air cleaner filter (1) | |
| 6 | Replace PCV valve | |
| 7 | Replace cam belt – 3.0/3.2L SHO only | |
| 8 | Adjust valve lash – 3.0/3.2L SHO only | |
| 9 | Replace engine coolant | Every 36 months |
| 10 | Check coolant protection, hoses, & clamps | Every 12 months |
| | GENERAL MAINTENANCE | |
| 11 | Inspect exhaust shields | |
| 12 | Change A/T fluid (2.5L, 3.0L, 3.8L) (3) | |
| 13 | Inspect disc brake pads & rotors (2) | |
| 14 | Inspect brake lining & drums (2) | |
| 15 | Inspect battery fluid level (SHO only) (2) | |
| 16 | Inspect & repack rear wheel bearings | |
| 17 | Rotate tires | |
| 18 | Check supercharger fluid level (SHO only) | |

(1) If operating in severe dust conditions, more frequent intervals may be required. Consult your dealer.
(2) If your driving includes continuous stop-and-go driving or driving in mountainous areas, more frequent intervals may be required.
(3) Change the automatic transaxle fluid if your driving habits frequently include one or more of the following conditions: Operation during hot weather (above 90 degrees F, 32 degrees C), carrying heavy loads and in hilly terrain. Towing a trailer or using a car-to carrier. Police, taxi or door-to-door delivery service.

86871300

**Follow Maintenance Schedule B if, generally, you drive your vehicle on a daily basis for more than 10 miles and NONE of the conditions for Schedule A apply.**

### 1986-93 MAINTENANCE INTERVAL SCHEDULE B

| Item No | To Be Serviced | Minimum Time Interval | The services shown in this schedule up to 60,000 miles are to be performed after 60,000 miles at the same intervals | | | | | | | |
|---|---|---|---|---|---|---|---|---|---|---|
| | | | 7.5 | 15 | 22.5 | 30 | 37.5 | 45 | 52.5 | 60 |
| **EMISSION CONTROL SERVICE** | | | | | | | | | | |
| 1 | Replace engine oil & filter | Every 3 months | ■ | ■ | ■ | ■ | ■ | ■ | ■ | ■ |
| 2 | Spark plugs - 2.5L, 3.0L, 3.8L | | | | | ■ | | | | ■ |
| 3 | Spark plugs - 3.0L SHO, 3.2L SHO | | | | | | | | | ■ |
| 4 | Inspect accessory drive belt(s) | | | | | ■ | | | | ■ |
| 5 | Replace air cleaner filter (1) | | | | | ■ | | | | ■ |
| 6 | Replace PCV valve | | | | | | | | | ■ |
| 7 | Replace cam belt - 3.0/3.2L SHO only | | | | | | | | | ■ |
| 8 | Adjust valve lash - 3.0/3.2L SHO only | | | | | | | | | ■ |
| 9 | Replace engine coolant | Every 36 months | | | | ■ | | | | ■ |
| 10 | Check coolant protection, hoses, & clamps | Every 12 months | | ■ | | | | ■ | | ■ |
| **GENERAL MAINTENANCE** | | | | | | | | | | |
| 11 | Inspect exhaust shields | | | | | ■ | | | | ■ |
| 12 | Change A/T fluid (2.5L, 3.0L, 3.8L) (3) | | | | | ■ | | | | ■ |
| 13 | Inspect disc brake pads & rotors (2) | | | | | ■ | | | | ■ |
| 14 | Inspect brake lining & drums (2) | | | | | ■ | | | | ■ |
| 15 | Inspect battery fluid level (SHO only) (2) | Every 24 months | | | ■ | | | ■ | | |
| 16 | Inspect & repack rear wheel bearings | | | | | ■ | | | | ■ |
| 17 | Rotate tires | | ■ | | ■ | | ■ | | ■ | |
| 18 | Check supercharger fluid level (SHO only) | | | | | ■ | | | | ■ |

(1) If operating in severe dust conditions, more frequent intervals may be required. Consult your dealer.

(2) If your driving includes continuous stop-and-go driving or driving in mountainous areas, more frequent intervals may be required.

(3) Change automatic transaxle fluid it your driving habits frequently include one or more of the following conditions: Operation during hot weather (above 90 degrees F, 32 degrees C), carrying heavy loads and in hilly terrain. Towing a trailer or using a car-to carrier. Police, taxi or door-to-door delivery service.

86871301

**Follow Maintenance Schedule B if, generally, you drive your vehicle on a daily basis for more than 10 miles and NONE of the conditions for Schedule A apply.**

### 1994-95 MAINTENANCE INTERVAL SCHEDULE B

| Item No | To Be Serviced | Minimum Time Interval | The services shown in this schedule up to 60,000 miles are to be performed after 60,000 miles at the same intervals | | | | | | | | | | | |
|---|---|---|---|---|---|---|---|---|---|---|---|---|---|---|
| | | | 5 | 10 | 15 | 20 | 25 | 30 | 35 | 40 | 45 | 50 | 55 | 60 |
| **EMISSION CONTROL SERVICE** | | | | | | | | | | | | | | |
| 1 | Change engine oil and replace filter | Every 3 months | ■ | ■ | ■ | ■ | ■ | ■ | ■ | ■ | ■ | ■ | ■ | ■ |
| 2 | Spark plugs - 2.5L, 3.0L, 3.8L | | | | | | | ■ | | | | | | ■ |
| 3 | Spark plugs - 3.0L SHO, 3.2L SHO | | | | | | | | | | | | | ■ |
| 4 | Inspect accessory drive belt(s) | | | | | | | ■ | | | | | | ■ |
| 5 | Replace air cleaner filter (1) | | | | | | | ■ | | | | | | ■ |
| 6 | Replace PCV valve | | | | | | | | | | | | | ■ |
| 7 | Replace cam belt - 3.0/3.2L SHO only | | | | | | | | | | | | | ■ |
| 8 | Adjust valve lash - 3.0/3.2L SHO only | | | | | | | | | | | | | ■ |
| 9 | Replace engine coolant (4) | Every 36 months | | | | | | | | | | ■ | | |
| 10 | Check coolant protection, hoses, & clamps | Every 12 months | | | ■ | | | | | | ■ | | | ■ |
| **GENERAL MAINTENANCE** | | | | | | | | | | | | | | |
| 11 | Inspect exhaust shields | | | | | | | ■ | | | | | | ■ |
| 12 | Change A/T fluid (2.5L, 3.0L, 3.8L) (3) | | | | | | | ■ | | | | | | ■ |
| 13 | Inspect disc brake pads & rotors (2) | | | | | | | ■ | | | | | | ■ |
| 14 | Inspect brake lining & drums (2) | | | | | | | ■ | | | | | | ■ |
| 15 | Inspect battery fluid level (SHO only) (2) | Every 24 months | | | | | ■ | | | | | ■ | | |
| 16 | Inspect & repack rear wheel bearings | | | | | | | ■ | | | | | | ■ |
| 17 | Rotate tires & adjust air pressure | | ■ | | ■ | | ■ | | ■ | | ■ | | ■ | |
| 18 | Check supercharger fluid level (SHO only) | | | | | | | ■ | | | | | | ■ |

(1) If operating in severe dust conditions, more frequent intervals may be required. Consult your dealer.

(2) If your driving includes continuous stop-and-go driving or driving in mountainous areas, more frequent intervals may be required.

(3) Change automatic transaxle fluid it your driving habits frequently include one or more of the following conditions: Operation during hot weather (above 90 degrees F, 32 degrees C), carrying heavy loads and in hilly terrain. Towing a trailer or using a car-to carrier. Police, taxi or door-to-door delivery service.

(4) Change the engine coolant initially at 50,000 miles or 48 months. Thereafter, change the coolant every 30,000 miles or 36 months.

86871302

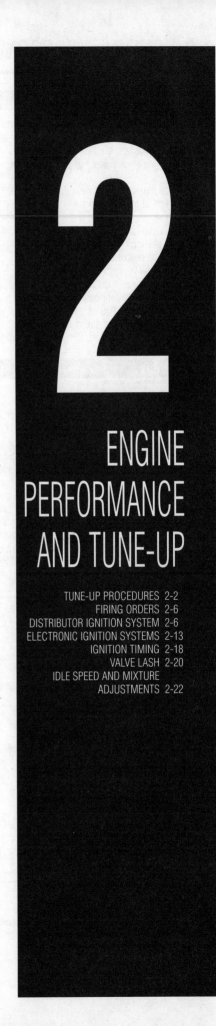

# 2

# ENGINE PERFORMANCE AND TUNE-UP

## TUNE-UP PROCEDURES

In order to extract the full measure of performance and economy from your engine, it is essential that it be properly tuned at regular intervals. A regular tune-up will keep your car's engine running smoothly and will prevent the annoying breakdowns and poor performance associated with an untuned engine.

A complete tune-up should be performed at least every 12,000 miles (19,200 km) or 12 months, whichever comes first. The interval should be halved if the vehicle is operated under severe conditions such as trailer towing, prolonged idling, start-and-stop driving, or if a driveability problem such as hard starting or poor running is noticed. It is assumed that the routine maintenance described in Section 1 has been kept up, as this will have a decided effect on the results of a tune-up.

If the specifications on the underhood tune-up sticker (located in the engine compartment of your car) disagree with the tune-up specifications chart in this section, the figures on the sticker must be used. The sticker often reflects changes made during the production run or revised information that applies to the particular systems in that vehicle.

## Spark Plugs

▶ **See Figures 1, 2 and 3**

A typical spark plug consists of a metal shell surrounding a ceramic insulator. A metal electrode extends downward through the center of the insulator and protrudes a small distance. Located at the end of the plug and attached to the side of the outer metal shell is the side electrode. The side electrode bends in at a 90° angle so that its tip is even with, and parallel to, the tip of the center electrode. The distance between these two electrodes (measured in thousandths of an inch) is called the spark plug gap. The spark plug in no way produces a spark, but merely provides a gap across which the current can arc. The coil produces anywhere from 20,000–40,000 volts which travels to the distributor, where it is transmitted through the spark plug wires to the spark plugs. The current passes along the center electrode, and, in doing so, ignites the air/fuel mixture in the combustion chamber.

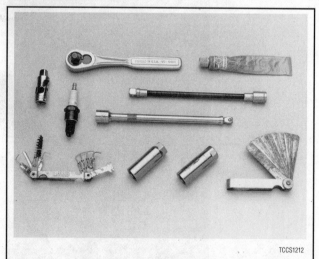

TCCS1212

**Fig. 1 A variety of tools and gauges are needed for spark plug service**

Spark plugs ignite the air and fuel mixture in the cylinder as the piston reaches the top of the compression stroke. The controlled explosion that results forces the piston down, turning the crankshaft and the rest of the drive train.

The average life of a spark plug is dependent on a number of factors; the mechanical condition of the engine, the type of fuel, driving conditions and driving style.

Ford recommends that spark plugs be changed every 30,000 miles (48,000 km). Under severe driving conditions, those intervals should be halved. Severe driving conditions are:
- Extended periods of idling or low speed operation, such as off-road or door-to-door delivery.
- Driving short distances (less than 10 miles/16 km) when the average temperature is below 10°F (12°C) for 60 days or more.
- Excessive dust or blowing dirt conditions.

When you remove the spark plugs, check their condition. They are a good indicator of the condition of the engine. It is a good idea to remove the spark plugs at regular intervals, such as every 6,000 or so miles (9,600 km), just so you can keep an eye on the mechanical state of the engine.

A small deposit of light tan or gray material on a spark plug that has been used for any period of time is considered normal. Any other color, or abnormal amounts of deposit, indicate that there is something amiss in the engine.

The gap between the center electrode and the side or ground electrode can be expected to increase not more than 0.001 in. (0.025mm) every 1,000 miles (1,600 km) under normal conditions. When, and if, a plug fouls and begins to misfire, you will have to investigate, correct the cause of the fouling and either clean or replace the plug.

There are several reasons why a spark plug will foul and you can learn which reason is at fault by just looking at the plug. A few of the most common reasons for plug fouling and a description of fouled plug appearance are shown in the corresponding chart.

### SPARK PLUG HEAT RANGE

Spark plug heat range is the ability of the plug to dissipate heat. The longer the insulator (or the farther it extends into the engine), the hotter the plug will operate; the shorter the insulator, the cooler it will operate. A plug that absorbs little heat and remains too cool will quickly accumulate deposits of oil and carbon since it is not hot enough to burn them off. This leads to plug fouling and consequently to misfiring. A plug that absorbs too much heat will have no deposits, but, due to the excessive heat, the electrodes will burn away quickly and in some instances, preignition may result. Preignition takes place when plug tips get so hot that they glow sufficiently to ignite the fuel/air mixture before the actual spark occurs. This early ignition will usually cause a pinging during low speeds and heavy loads.

The general rule of thumb for choosing the correct heat range when selecting a spark plug is: if most of your driving is long distance, high speed travel, use a cooler plug; if most of your driving is stop and go, use a hotter plug. Original equipment plugs are compromise plugs, but most people never have occasion to change their plugs from the factory recommended heat range.

### REPLACING SPARK PLUGS

A set of spark plugs usually requires replacement every 30,000 miles (48,000 km), depending on your style of driving. In normal operation, plug gap increases about 0.001 in. (0.025mm) for every 1,000–2,500 miles (1,600–4,000 km). As the gap increases, the plug's voltage requirement also increases. It requires greater voltage to jump the wider gap and about two-to-three times as much voltage to fire a plug at higher speeds than at idle.

The spark plugs used in your car require a deep spark plug socket for removal and installation. A specially designed pair of wire removal pliers, Spark Plug Wire Remover T74P-6666-A or equivalent, is also a good tool to have for vehicles other than the 3.0L/3.2L SHO. The special pliers have cupped jaws that grip the plug wire boot and make the job of twisting and pulling the wire from the plug easier.

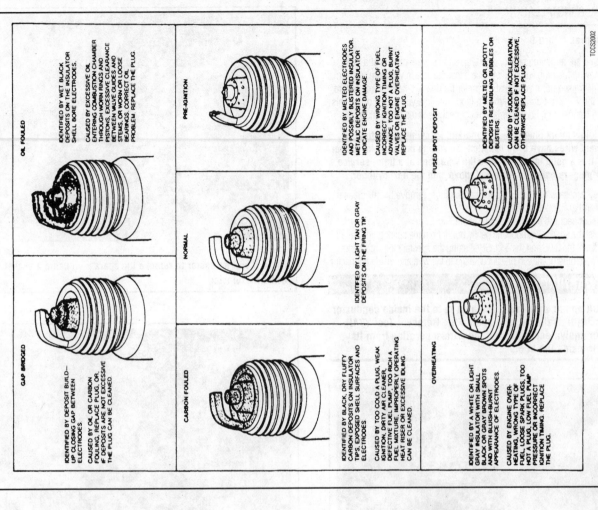

**Fig. 3 Inspect the spark plug to determine engine running conditions**

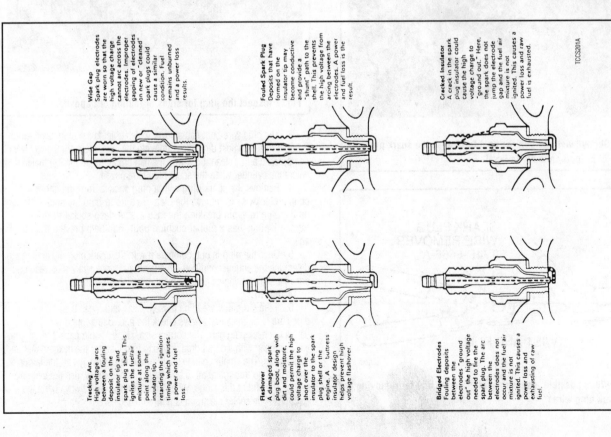

**Fig. 2 Used spark plugs which show damage may indicate engine problems**

REMOVAL & INSTALLATION

♦ **See Figures 4 thru 9**

When you are removing spark plugs, you should work on one at a time. Avoid removing the plug wires all at once because, unless you number them, they may get mixed up; if you must (or prefer to) do so, take a minute before removing the wires to number them with tape. The time you spend doing this will pay off later when it comes time to reconnect the wires to the plugs.

➡ **The original spark plug wires are marked for cylinder location. If replacement wires have been installed, be sure to tag them for proper location. It is a good idea to remove the wires one at a time, service the spark plug, reinstall the wire and move onto the next cylinder.**

For easy access when servicing the spark plugs, remove the air cleaner assembly and air intake tube.
1. Disconnect the negative battery cable.
2. Twist the spark plug boot and gently pull it from the spark plug. For all vehicles except the 3.0L and the 3.2L SHO, using the special plug wire pliers will aid in ease of removal and prevent damage to the wire and inside connector.

**✷✷ WARNING**

**Never pull on the wire itself, as damage to the inside conductor could occur! If available, use Spark Plug Remover Tool Y74P-6666-A or equivalent to prevent the wire separating from its connector inside the boot.**

Fig. 4 Gently twist and pull the boot to remove the spark plug wire; NEVER pull on the wire itself

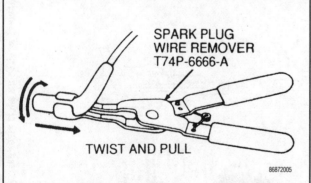

SPARK PLUG WIRE REMOVER T74P-6666-A

TWIST AND PULL

Fig. 5 When possible, use a special grasping tool for removing the spark plug wires

Fig. 6 It will be easier to remove the spark plug using a socket with an extension

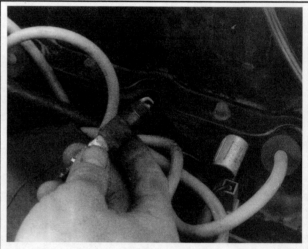

Fig. 7 Inspect the plug for signs of fouling or deposits

3. The plug wire boot has a cover which shields the plug cavity (in the cylinder head) against dirt. After removing the wire, blow out the cavity with compressed air or clean it out with a small brush, so no foreign material enters the cylinder when the spark plug is removed.
4. Remove the spark plug with a plug socket. Turn the socket counterclockwise to remove the plug. Be sure to hold the socket straight on the plug to avoid breaking the insulator. A deep socket designed for spark plugs has a rubber cushion built-in to help prevent plug breakage.
5. Once the plug is out, compare it with the spark plug illustrations to determine the engine condition. This is crucial since spark plug readings are vital signs of engine condition and pending problems.

**To install:**

6. If the old plugs are to be reused, clean and regap them. If new spark plugs are to be installed, always check the gap. Use a round wire feeler gauge to check plug gap. The correct size gauge should pass through the electrode gap with a slight drag. If you're in doubt, try the next smaller and larger sizes. The smaller gauge should go through easily and the larger should not go through at all. If adjustment is necessary, use the bending tool on the end of the gauge. When adjusting the gap, always bend the side electrode. The center electrode is non-adjustable.

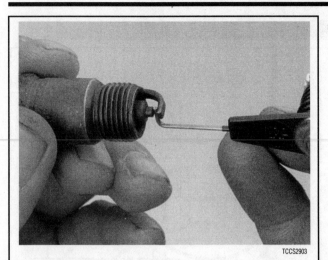

**Fig. 8 Always use a wire gauge to check the electrode gap on used plugs**

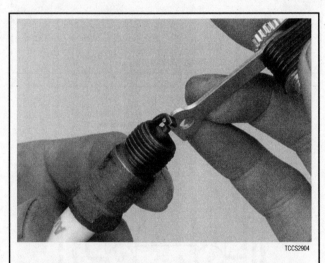

**Fig. 9 Adjust the gap by bending the side electrode very slightly towards or away from the center electrode**

7. Squirt a drop of penetrating oil on the threads of the spark plug and install it. Don't oil the threads heavily. Turn the plug in clockwise by hand until it is snug.

### ❋❋ CAUTION

**Do not use the spark plug socket to thread the plugs. Always thread the plug by hand to prevent the possibility of cross-threading and damaging the cylinder head.**

8. After the the plug is finger-tight, torque it to 17–22 ft. lbs. (23–30 Nm). DO NOT OVERTIGHTEN!

9. Thinly coat the inside of the boot and terminal with silicone dielectric compound (Motorcraft D7AZ-19A331-A or equivalent).

10. Install the plug wire boot firmly over the spark plug. Push the boot until it clicks into place. The click may be felt or heard, then gently pull back on the boot to assure proper contact.

11. Connect the negative battery cable.

## Spark Plug Wires

### CHECKING AND REPLACING SPARK PLUG WIRES

#### ▶ See Figures 5 and 10

Your car is equipped with an electronic ignition system which utilizes 8mm wires to conduct the hotter spark produced. The boots on these wires are designed to cover the spark plug cavities on the cylinder head.

Inspect the wires without removing them from the spark plugs, distributor cap or coil. Look for visible damage such as cuts, pinches, cracks or torn boots. Replace any wires that show damage. If the boot is damaged, it may be replaced by itself. It is not necessary to replace the complete wire just for the boot.

To remove the wire, grasp and twist the boot back and forth while pulling away from the spark plug. Use the specialized pliers mentioned earlier in this section, if available. For 3.0L and 3.2L SHO vehicles, in order to remove the wires from the ignition coil, squeeze the locking tabs of the ignition wire retainer and use a gentle twisting/pulling motion.

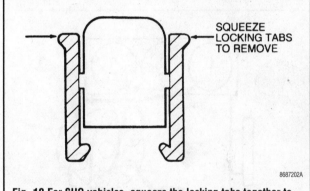

**Fig. 10 For SHO vehicles, squeeze the locking tabs together to remove the wires from the ignition coil**

➡**Always coat the terminals of any wire that is removed or replaced with a thin layer of silicone dielectric compound (D7AZ-19A331-A or equivalent).**

When installing a wire, be sure it is firmly mounted over or on the plug, distributor cap connector or coil terminal.

Every 30,000–45,000 miles (48,000–72,000 km), the resistance of the wires should be checked using an ohmmeter. Wires with excessive resistance will cause misfiring and may make the engine difficult to start in damp weather.

To check resistance, remove the distributor cap, leaving the wires in place. Connect one lead of an ohmmeter to an electrode within the cap; connect the other lead to the corresponding spark plug terminal (remove it from the spark plug for this test). Any wire with a resistance over 7,000 ohms per foot of wire should be replaced.

## FIRING ORDERS

▶ **See Figures 11, 12, 13 and 14**

➡ To aid in installation and avoid confusion, remove and tag the spark plug wires one at a time.Fig. 13 3.8L Engine

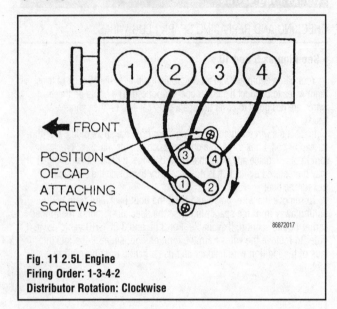

**Fig. 11 2.5L Engine**
**Firing Order: 1-3-4-2**
**Distributor Rotation: Clockwise**

86872017

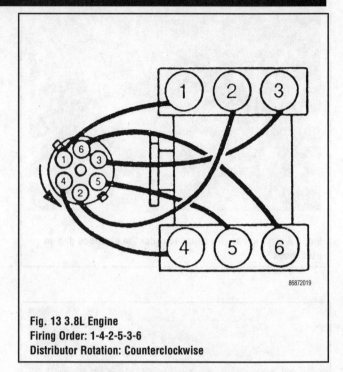

**Fig. 13 3.8L Engine**
**Firing Order: 1-4-2-5-3-6**
**Distributor Rotation: Counterclockwise**

86872019

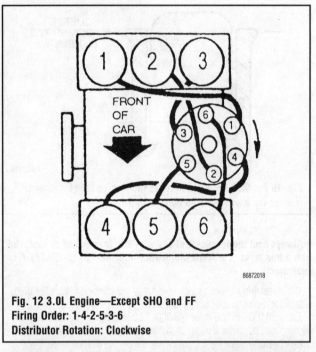

**Fig. 12 3.0L Engine—Except SHO and FF**
**Firing Order: 1-4-2-5-3-6**
**Distributor Rotation: Clockwise**

86872018

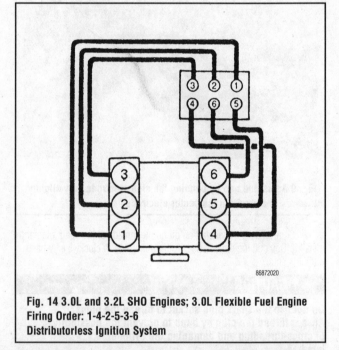

**Fig. 14 3.0L and 3.2L SHO Engines; 3.0L Flexible Fuel Engine**
**Firing Order: 1-4-2-5-3-6**
**Distributorless Ignition System**

86872020

## DISTRIBUTOR IGNITION SYSTEM

Your car uses one of three different electronic ignition systems. The 2.5L, 3.0L and 3.8L engines utilize the standard Distributor Ignition (DI) system. The 3.0L/3.2L SHO and the 3.0L Flexible Fuel (FF) engines use two different Electronic Ignition (EI) systems, formerly known as Distributorless Ignition (DIS). The purpose of using an electronic ignition system is to eliminate the deterioration of spark quality which occurred in the earlier breaker point ignition system as the breaker points wore, to extend maintenance intervals, and to provide a more intense and reliable spark at every firing impulse, in order to ignite the leaner gas mixtures necessary to control emissions.

## Description & Operation

▶ **See Figures 15 and 16**

Taurus and Sable models equipped with the 2.5L, 3.0L, and 3.8L engines incorporate an ignition system using a Universal Distributor. The ignition system includes:

• A universal distributor that has a diecast housing with a Hall effect distributor stator.

• An "E" type ignition coil which transforms battery voltage on the primary circuit, into about 28,000 volts on the secondary circuit each time the ignition coil receives a signal from the Ignition Control Module (ICM).

• An ignition control module which features EEC-IV or PCM-controlled ignition coil charge times.

Some of the earlier models are equipped with a TFI-IV module. TFI stands for Thick Film Integrated and incorporates a molded thermoplastic module mounted on the distributor base. In later systems, the TFI-IV module's functions are carried out by the ignition control module.

In this system, the distributor is driven off the camshaft and uses no centrifugal or vacuum advance. The distributor operates by using a Hall effect vane switch assembly, causing the ignition coil to be switched on and off by the EEC-IV and TFI-IV modules on earlier vehicles, or the Powertrain Control Module (PCM) and the Ignition Control Module (ICM) on later vehicles.

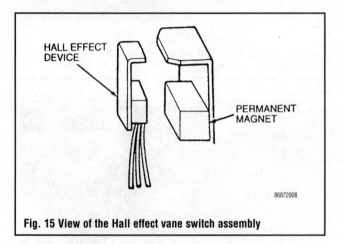

**Fig. 15 View of the Hall effect vane switch assembly**

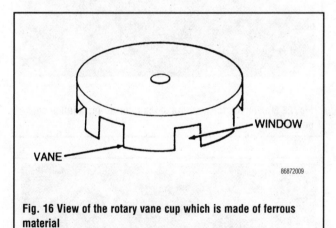

**Fig. 16 View of the rotary vane cup which is made of ferrous material**

The vane switch is an encapsulated package consisting of a Hall sensor on one side and a permanent magnet on the other side. A rotary vane cup, made of ferrous material, is used to trigger the signal OFF and ON. When the window of the vane cup is between the magnet and the Hall effect device, a magnetic flux field is completed from the magnet through the Hall effect device and back to the magnet. As the vane passes through this opening, the flux lines are shunted through the vane and back to the magnet. During this time, a voltage is produced as the vane passes through the opening. When the vane clears the opening, the window edge causes the signal to go to zero volts. The signal is then used by the EEC-IV or PCM (as applicable) for crankshaft position sensing and the computation of the desired spark advance based on engine demand and calibration. The voltage distribution is accomplished through a conventional rotor, cap and ignition wires.

## Component Testing

### IGNITION COIL

**♦ See Figures 17 and 18**

1. Follow the coil wire from the center terminal on the distributor cap to the end at the ignition coil. Make sure the transaxle is in Park (AT) or Neutral (MT) and that the ignition is turned **OFF**.

2. Separate the wiring harness connector from the ignition module at the distributor. Inspect for dirt, corrosion and damage. Reconnect the harness if no problems are found.

**➡Push the connector tabs together to separate.**

3. Attach a 12 volt DC test light between the coil Tach terminal and an engine ground, then crank the engine. If the light flashes or is continuous:

   a. Turn the ignition switch **OFF**.

   b. Disengage the ignition coil connector on top of the coil and inspect for dirt, corrosion and/or damage.

   c. Using an ohmmeter, measure the ignition coil primary resistance from the positive (+) to the negative (-) terminal of the ignition coil. See the corresponding figures for terminal locations.

   d. The ohmmeter reading should be 0.3–1.0 ohms. If the reading is less than 0.3 ohms or greater than 1.0 ohms, the ignition coil should be replaced.

   e. Using an ohmmeter, measure the coil secondary resistance; connect it to the negative (-) terminal and the high voltage terminal.

   f. The resistance should be 6,500–11,500 ohms with the ohmmeter set on ohms x 1000. If the reading is less than 6,500 ohms or greater than 11,500 ohms, replace the ignition coil.

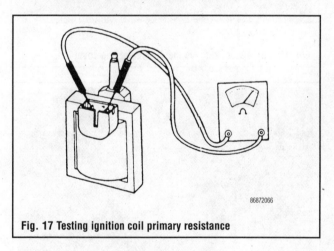

**Fig. 17 Testing ignition coil primary resistance**

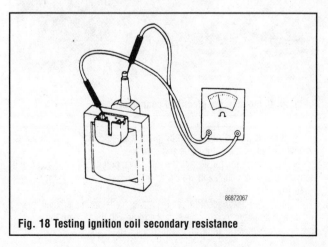

**Fig. 18 Testing ignition coil secondary resistance**

## Component Replacement

### REMOVAL & INSTALLATION

**Distributor Cap and Rotor**

▶ **See Figures 19 thru 25**

1. Disconnect the negative battery cable.
2. If equipped, remove the distributor cap cover, then disengage the electrical connector, if applicable.
3. If necessary, tag and remove the spark plug wires from the cap.
4. Loosen the distributor hold-down screws.

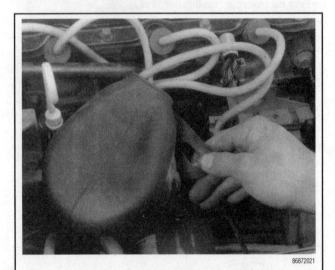

Fig. 19 If equipped, remove the distributor cap cover

Fig. 20 Disengage the electrical connector

5. Remove the distributor cap by lifting it straight off the distributor to prevent damage to the rotor blade and spring.
6. Matchmark the position of the rotor, then pull it upward to remove it from the distributor shaft and armature.

**To install:**

7. Install the rotor according to the marks made during removal, making sure to align the locating boss on the rotor with the hole on the armature, then fully seat the rotor on the distributor shaft.

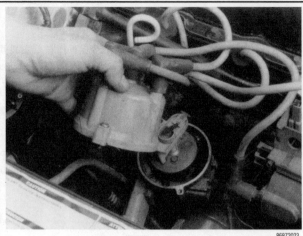

Fig. 21 Lift the distributor cap straight up to prevent damage to the rotor blade and spring

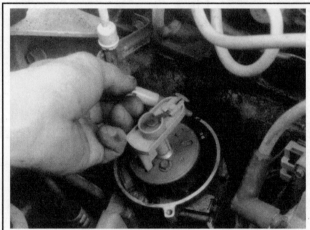

Fig. 22 Matchmark the position of the rotor for installation purposes

Fig. 23 Pull the rotor upward to remove it from the distributor shaft and armature

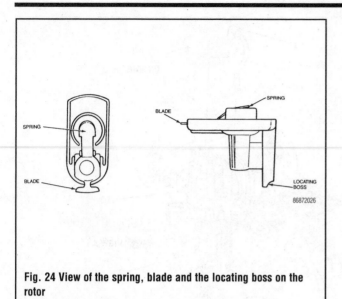

Fig. 24 View of the spring, blade and the locating boss on the rotor

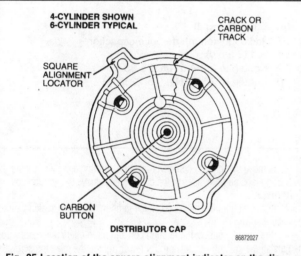

Fig. 25 Location of the square alignment indicator on the distributor cap

Fig. 26 Disconnect the distributor-to-ignition coil wire—early model 2.5L shown

Fig. 27 Disengage the engine wiring connector from the coil—early model 2.5L shown

Fig. 28 Remove the ignition coil retaining screws

8. Position the distributor cap on the housing, noting the square alignment locator, if equipped. Tighten the hold-down screws to 18–23 inch lbs. (2.0–2.6 Nm).

9. If removed, connect the spark plug wires to their correct location on the distributor cap as tagged during removal.

10. If equipped, install the distributor cap cover, then connect the negative battery cable.

## Ignition Coil

▶ See Figures 26, 27, 28, 29 and 30

1. Disconnect the negative battery cable.

2. Disconnect the distributor-to-ignition coil wire from the ignition coil.

3. Disengage the TFI-IV harness or the engine control sensor wiring connector from the ignition coil, as applicable.

4. On the 3.8L engine, disengage the engine control wiring connector from the radio ignition interference capacitor.

5. Remove the ignition coil retaining screws and the ignition coil and radio interference capacitor (if equipped) from the ignition coil mounting bracket.

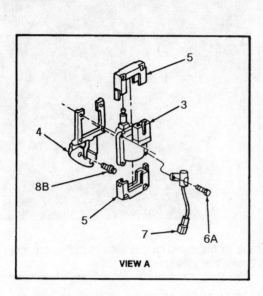
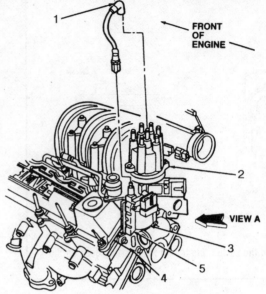

| | |
|---|---|
| 1 Ignition coil to distributor high tension wiring | 6A Screw (4 req'd) |
| 2 Distributor cap | 7 Radio ignition interference capacitor |
| 3 Ignition coil | 8B Bolt (2 req'd) |
| 4 Ignition coil mounting bracket | A Tighten to 2.8-4.0 Nm (25-35 lb.in.) |
| 5 Ignition coil cover | B Tighten to 20-30 Nm (15-22 lb.ft.) |

86872031

**Fig. 29 Ignition coil and related components—late model 3.0L shown**

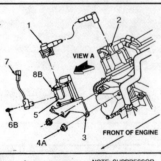

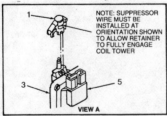

NOTE: SUPPRESSOR WIRE MUST BE INSTALLED AT ORIENTATION SHOWN TO ALLOW RETAINER TO FULLY ENGAGE COIL TOWER

1 Ignition coil to distributor high tension wiring
2 Distributor cap
3 Ignition coil mounting bracket
4A Nut (2 req'd)
5 Ignition coil
6B Screw
7 Radio ignition interference capacitor
8B Screw (4 req'd)
A Tighten to 40-50 Nm (30-41 lb.ft.)
B Tighten to 2.8-4.0 Nm (25-35 lb.in.)

86872032

**Fig. 30 Ignition coil and related components—late model 3.8L shown**

6. Remove the ignition coil cover from the ignition coil by releasing the locking tabs on both sides of the cover, then remove the ignition coil.

**To install:**

7. Install the ignition coil, then attach ignition coil cover, making sure the cover is firmly in place.

8. If removed, connect the ignition coil and radio interference capacitor, then install the ignition coil retaining screws. Tighten the retaining screws to 25–35 inch lbs. (2.8–4.0 Nm).

9. Connect the coil wire, then engage any electrical connectors that were removed.

10. Connect the negative battery cable.

**Ignition Control Module (ICM)**

➡**In earlier models, the ICM was referred to as the TFI-IV Ignition Module; the name was later changed to Ignition Control Module (ICM).**

### *2.5L AND 3.0L ENGINES*

◗ See Figure 31

1. Remove the distributor cap and position it away from the work area, with the wires still attached.

2. Disengage the engine control sensor wiring connector (late model vehicles) or the TFI-IV harness connector from the ignition control module.

3. Remove the distributor from the engine. For details, please refer to the procedure located later in this section.

4. Place the distributor on a work bench, then remove the two module retaining screws.

➡**Do NOT attempt to lift the module from the mounting surface before moving the entire module toward the distributor flange! This will cause the pins to break at the distributor/module connector.**

5. Pull the right-hand side of the module down toward the distributor mounting flange and back up to disengage the module terminals from the connector in the distributor housing. The module may then be pulled toward the flange and away from the distributor.

6. Remove the module from the distributor.

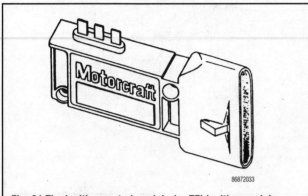

86872033

**Fig. 31 The ignition control module (or TFI ignition module, as applicable), is located on the distributor**

**To install:**

7. Coat the metal base of the module with Silicone Dielectric Compound D7AZ-19A331-A, or equivalent meeting Ford specifications, approximately 1/32 in. (0.79mm) thick.

8. Place the module on the distributor housing mounting flange.

9. Carefully position the module toward the distributor housing, then align the three distributor connecting pins.

10. Install the two module retaining screws, then starting with the upper right-hand screw, tighten the screws to 15–35 inch lbs. (1.7–4.0 Nm).

11. Install the distributor as explained later in this section.

12. Install the distributor cap, then tighten the mounting screws to 18–23 inch lbs. (2.0–2.6 Nm).

13. Engage the engine control sensor wiring connector or TFI-IV harness connector, as applicable, to the module.

14. Connect the negative battery cable.

15. Using an inductive timing light, check the timing and adjust as necessary. This procedure is covered later in this section.

### 3.8L ENGINE

▶ See Figure 32

1. Disconnect the negative battery cable.

2. Remove the screws attaching the cowl vent screen to the top of the cowl.

3. Separate the engine compartment cowl seal strip from the cowl vent screen and the cowl dash extension panel in the area of the ignition control module.

4. Lift the cowl vent screen off to allow access to the ignition control module/TFI module assembly.

➡**The connector latch is underneath the ICM/TFI shroud. Press upward to unlatch.**

5. Disengage the engine control sensor wiring connector from the ICM or TFI, as applicable.

➡**The ignition control module and heatsink are mounted with the heatsink fins pointed downward.**

6. Remove the two retaining nuts attaching the ICM/TFI and heatsink to the dash panel, then remove the ICM/TFI and the heatsink.

7. Remove the two module retaining screws, then remove the ICM or TFI from the heatsink.

8. While holding the module connector shroud with one hand, pull the seal off the other end of the module.

**To install:**

9. Coat the metal base of the ICM or TFI module uniformly with Silicone Dielectric Compound D7AZ-19A331-A or equivalent, about 1/32 in. (0.79mm) thick.

10. Place the module onto the heatsink. Install the retaining screws, then tighten them to 15–35 inch lbs. (1.7–4.0 Nm).

11. Push the seal over the module connector shroud and heatsink studs with the metal part toward the heatsink.

12. Insert the module and heatsink into the cowl dash extension panel enough to have the mounting studs protrude into the engine compartment side.

13. Hand-tighten the retaining nuts to 44–70 inch lbs. (5–8 Nm).

14. Engage the engine control sensor wiring connector to the module.

15. Install the cowl vent screen and retaining screws, then install the engine compartment cowl panel and seal strip.

16. Connect the negative battery cable.

### Distributor

▶ See Figures 33, 34, 35, 36 and 37

1. Disconnect the negative battery cable.

2. Disconnect the engine control sensor wiring from the distributor.

3. With a marker, chalk or crayon, mark the position of the No. 1 cylinder distributor cap wire tower on the distributor housing for installation reference.

4. Loosen the distributor cap hold-down screws, then pull the cap straight up and off the distributor to prevent damage to the distributor rotor blade and spring.

5. Position the distributor cap with the ignition wires intact, out of the way.

6. Matchmark the position of the rotor, then remove it by pulling it upward from the distributor shaft and armature.

7. Disconnect the hold-down clamp and distributor retaining bolt, then remove the distributor from the engine by pulling it upward.

8. Cover the distributor opening in the cylinder block or engine front cover, as applicable, with a clean rag to prevent any foreign material or debris from entering the engine.

**To install:**

⁂ **CAUTION**

**Before installing the distributor, you must coat the entire drive gear and the camshaft distributor gear through the distributor hole with Engine Assembly Lubricant D9AZ-19579-D or equivalent.**

➡**Inspect the distributor before installing it. Inspect the O-ring. It should fit tightly and NOT have any cuts. The distributor drive gear should be free of nicks, cracks and excessive wear. When rotated, the distributor should move freely, without binding.**

### TIMING NOT DISTURBED

This condition exists if the engine has not been rotated while the distributor was removed.

1. Install the distributor and the rotor, aligning the distributor housing and the rotor with the marks made during removal.

2. Install the distributor hold-down bolt and clamp. Only snug the bolt at this time.

3. Connect the wiring harness to the distributor.

4. Install the rotor and the distributor cap. Make sure the ignition wires are securely connected to the distributor cap and spark plugs. Tighten the distributor cap screws to 18–23 inch lbs. (2.0–2.6 Nm).

5. Connect a suitable timing light to the engine (following the manufacturer's instructions) and connect the negative battery cable, then start the

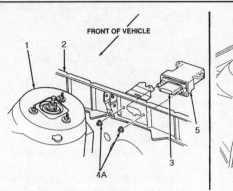
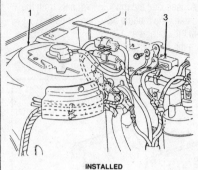

1 RH front fender apron
2 Dash panel
3 Ignition control module
4 Retaining nuts (2 req'd)
5 Ignition control module heat sink
A Tighten to 5-8 Nm (44-70 lb.in.)

86872034

**Fig. 32 Location of the ignition control module—3.8L engines only**

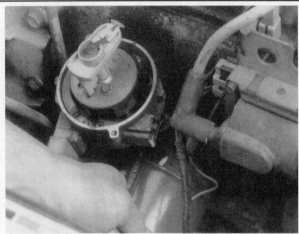

86872035

**Fig. 33 Position the cap with the wires intact out of the way for ease of removal**

86872036

**Fig. 34 Removing the distributor hold-down bolt. Note: The preferred method requires the removal of the rotor when removing the distributor.**

engine and set the initial timing. Timing procedures are located later in this section.

6. Turn the engine **OFF**, then tighten the distributor hold-down bolt to 17–25 ft. lbs. (23–34 Nm) on the 2.5L engine, 14–21 ft. lbs. (19–28 Nm) on the 3.0L engine, or 20–29 ft. lbs. (27–39 Nm) on the 3.8L engine.

7. Start the engine and recheck the timing to verify it did not change while tightening the hold-down bolt, then stop the engine and remove the timing light.

### TIMING DISTURBED

This condition exists if the engine has been rotated with the distributor removed. To correctly install the distributor, the No. 1 piston must be at TDC of the compression stroke.

1. Disconnect the spark plug wire and the spark plug from the No. 1 cylinder.

2. Place your finger over the spark plug hole, then rotate the engine clockwise (by turning the crankshaft pulley) until compression is felt at the spark plug hole.

3. With the No. 1 piston on the compression stroke, align the timing pointer with the TDC mark on the crankshaft damper.

86872037

**Fig. 35 Lift the distributor from the engine; once the distributor is lifted partly out it, may be tilted slightly and removed**

Fig. 36 If the O-ring is cracked or nicked, it must be replaced

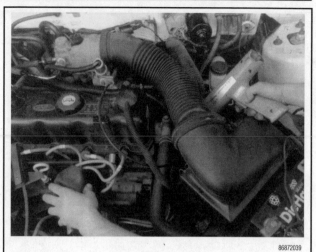

Fig. 37 After the distributor is installed, check the timing with a timing light

4. Align the locating boss on the rotor with the hole on the armature. Install the rotor on the distributor shaft, making sure it is fully seated on the distributor shaft. Rotate the shaft so the rotor tip is pointing toward the distributor cap's No. 1 spark plug tower position.

5. While installing the distributor, continue turning the rotor slightly, so the leading edge of the vane is centered in the distributor stator assembly.

6. Rotate the distributor in the block to align the leading edge of the vane and distributor stator assembly. Make sure the rotor is pointing toward the distributor cap No. 1 spark plug tower position.

➡If the vane and distributor stator cannot be aligned by rotating the distributor in the block, remove the distributor just enough to disengage the distributor gear from the camshaft gear. Turn the rotor enough to engage the distributor gear on another tooth of the camshaft gear. Repeat this procedure, if necessary.

7. Install the distributor hold-down bolt and clamp. Only snug the bolt at this time.

8. Connect the wiring harness to the distributor, then install the distributor cap. Tighten the distributor cap hold-down screws to 18–23 inch lbs. (2.0–2.6 Nm).

9. Install the No. 1 spark plug and wire.

10. Connect a suitable timing light (following the manufacturer's instructions) and connect the negative battery cable. Start the engine, then check and adjust the timing, as necessary.

11. Turn the engine **OFF**, then tighten the distributor hold-down bolt. Tighten the bolt to 17–25 ft. lbs. (23–34 Nm) on the 2.5L engine, 14–21 ft. lbs. (19–28 Nm) on the 3.0L engine, or 20–29 ft. lbs. (27–40 Nm) on the 3.8L engine.

12. Start the engine and recheck the timing to verify it did not change while tightening the hold-down bolt, then stop the engine and remove the timing light.

# ELECTRONIC IGNITION SYSTEMS

## Description & Operation

### 3.0L/3.2L SHO

◆ See Figures 38, 39, 40 and 41

Tauruses with 3.0L and 3.2L SHO engines are equipped with an Electronic Ignition (EI) system previously known as the Distributorless Ignition System (DIS). As the name implies, there is no conventional distributor assembly in the engine. This system consists of:

• A Crankshaft Position sensor (CKP sensor, formerly crankshaft timing sensor) that is a single Hall effect magnetic switch, which is activated by three vanes on the crankshaft timing pulley. The signal generated by this sensor is called Crankshaft Position (CKP). The CKP signal provides base timing and crankshaft speed (rpm) information to the Ignition Control Module (ICM) and the Powertrain Control Module (PCM).

• A Camshaft Position sensor (CMP sensor) that is a single Hall effect magnetic switch also, but is activated by a single vane driven by the camshaft. This sensor provides camshaft rotational location information to the PCM. The Ignition Control Module (ICM) uses a Camshaft Position (CMP) signal for ignition coil fire sequencing. The PCM also uses the CMP signal for fuel injector synchronization.

• An ignition coil that houses the spark plug wires like the convention distributor cap. The ignition "coil" actually contains three separate ignition coils. Each coil is controlled by the Ignition Control Module (ICM) through three coil leads. Each ignition coil activates two spark plugs simultaneously, one on the compression stroke (this uses the majority of the ignition coil's energy) and one on the exhaust stroke (this uses very little of the ignition coil's stored energy).

• An Ignition Control Module (ICM) which receives the CKP signal from the CKP sensor. During normal operation, the CKP signal is sent to the PCM from the CKP sensor and provides base ignition timing and RPM information. The ICM receives the CMP signal from CMP sensor, providing

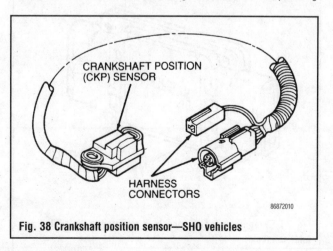

Fig. 38 Crankshaft position sensor—SHO vehicles

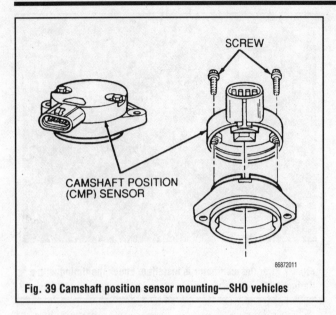

Fig. 39 Camshaft position sensor mounting—SHO vehicles

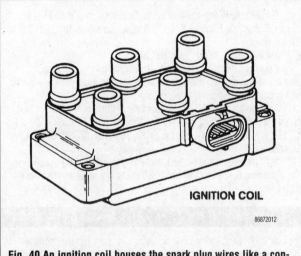

Fig. 40 An ignition coil houses the spark plug wires like a conventional distributor cap

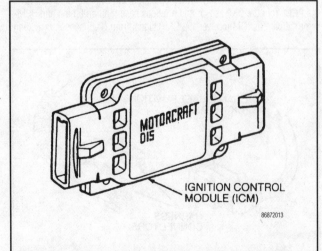

Fig. 41 The ignition control module is mounted to the engine air inlet connector

the ICM with the information required to synchronize the ignition coils in the proper sequence. It also receives the Spark Output (SPOUT) from the PCM. The SPOUT signal contains the optimum spark timing and dwell information.

## 3.0L FLEXIBLE FUEL (FF) VEHICLES

**♦ See Figures 42, 43 and 44**

The 3.0L Flexible Fuel Taurus is equipped with an ignition system that is very similar to that of the 3.0/3.2L SHO vehicles. The main difference is the crankshaft position sensor. The system includes:

• A Crankshaft Position sensor (CKP sensor) which is a variable reluctance sensor triggered by a "36-minus-1" tooth trigger wheel located on the crankshaft pulley and damper. The signal generated from the CKP sensor is called the Crankshaft Position signal (CKP signal). This signal provides base timing and crankshaft speed (rpm) information to the Ignition Control Module (ICM). The ICM uses this information with the spark advance information from the PCM to determine ignition coil ON and OFF time.

• An ignition "coil" which is mounted to the rear of the left-hand cylinder head. It actually contains three separate ignition coils. Each ignition coil is controlled by the ignition control module through three coil leads. Each igni-

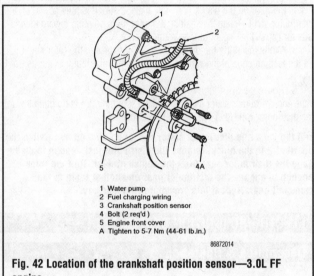

1 Water pump
2 Fuel charging wiring
3 Crankshaft position sensor
4 Bolt (2 req'd )
5 Engine front cover
A Tighten to 5-7 Nm (44-61 lb.in.)

Fig. 42 Location of the crankshaft position sensor—3.0L FF engine

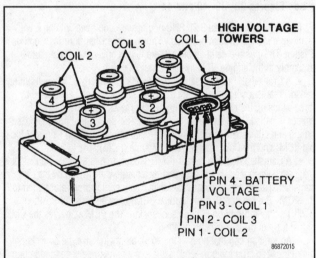

Fig. 43 The spark plug wire numbers are marked on the ignition coil towers

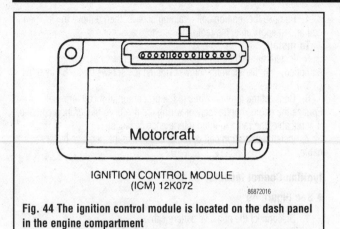

**Fig. 44 The ignition control module is located on the dash panel in the engine compartment**

tion coil activates two spark plugs simultaneously, one on the compression stroke (this plug uses the majority of the ignition coil's energy) and one on the exhaust stroke (this plug uses very little of the ignition coil's stored energy).

• An Ignition Coil Module (ICM) which is located on the dash panel in the engine compartment. It receives engine position and speed information from the CKP sensor, and desired spark advance information from the PCM. The ignition module uses this information to determine which ignition coil to fire, calculating the ON and OFF times of the ignition coils required to achieve the correct dwell and spark advance. It outputs a Profile Ignition Pickup (PIP) signal and an Ignition Diagnostic Monitor (IDM) signal for use by the PCM. It also sends information on system failures through the IDM signal to the PCM, stores information for use during diagnostic test mode, and provides the signal for the tachometer.

## Component Replacement

### 3.0L/3.2L SHO VEHICLES

#### Crankshaft Position (CKP) Sensor

▶ See Figures 45 and 46

1. Disconnect the negative battery cable.
2. Loosen the drive belt tensioner for the A/C compressor and power steering drive belts.
3. Remove the drive belts from the crankshaft vibration damper and pulley.
4. Disconnect the ignition control module, then remove the engine air inlet connector.
5. Remove the upper outer timing belt cover.
6. Disengage the crankshaft position sensor wiring harness at the con-

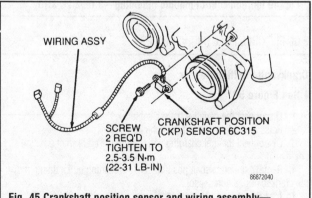

**Fig. 45 Crankshaft position sensor and wiring assembly—3.0L/3.2L SHO**

nector, then route the crankshaft position sensor harness through the outer timing belt cover.

7. Raise and safely support the vehicle, then remove the right front wheel and tire assembly.
8. Remove the crankshaft vibration damper and pulley using Steering Wheel Puller T67L-3600-A, or equivalent.
9. Remove the center and lower outer timing belt cover.
10. Rotate the crankshaft by hand to position the metal vane of the crankshaft sprocket outside of the crankshaft position sensor air gap.
11. Remove the two CKP sensor retaining screws, then remove the crankshaft position sensor from the engine.

**To install:**

12. Route the crankshaft position sensor wiring harness through the outer timing belt cover. Position the CKP sensor on the mounting pad and install the retaining screws loosely. Do not tighten the screws at this time.
13. Set the clearance between the CKP sensor assembly and one vane on the crankshaft sprocket with a 0.03 in. (0.8mm) feeler gauge, then tighten the retaining screws to 22–31 inch lbs. (2.5–3.5 Nm).

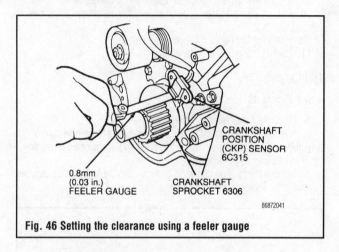

**Fig. 46 Setting the clearance using a feeler gauge**

➡Do NOT overtighten the CKP retaining screws! Damage to the crankshaft position sensor will result.

14. Install the lower outer timing belt cover. Make sure you don't damage the CKP sensor wiring harness. Install the crankshaft vibration damper and pulley using the Crank Gear and Damper Replacer T83T-6316-B, or equivalent. Tighten the pulley bolt to 112–127 ft. lbs. (152–172 Nm).
15. Install the center outer timing belt cover.
16. Install the wheel and tire assembly. Tighten the lug nuts to 85–105 ft. lbs. (115–142 Nm), then lower the vehicle.
17. Route and connect the crankshaft position sensor wiring harness.
18. Install the upper outer timing belt cover.
19. Install the engine air inlet connector, then engage the ignition control module.
20. Install the A/C compressor and power steering pump drive belts.
21. Connect the negative battery cable.

#### Camshaft Position (CMP) Sensor

▶ See Figure 47

1. Disconnect the negative battery cable.
2. Remove the front engine support damper.
3. Remove the power steering pump drive belt.
4. Remove the power steering pump pulley.
5. Disengage the Camshaft Position (CMP) sensor wiring connector.
6. Remove the CMP sensor retaining bolts, them remove the camshaft position sensor.

**To install:**

7. Install the camshaft position sensor and secure using the retaining bolts. Tighten the bolts to 22–31 inch lbs. (2.5–3.5 Nm).

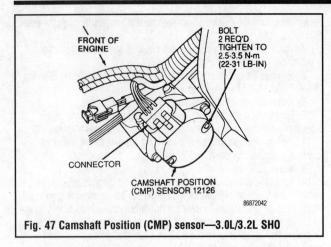

**Fig. 47 Camshaft Position (CMP) sensor—3.0L/3.2L SHO**

8. Engage the camshaft position sensor wiring connector.
9. Install the power steering pump pulley, then install the power steering belt.
10. Install the front engine support damper.
11. Connect the negative battery cable.

### Ignition Coil

▶ **See Figure 48**

1. Disconnect the negative battery cable.
2. Remove the ignition coil cover, then disengage the engine control sensor wiring connector from the ignition coil and, if equipped, the radio ignition interference capacitor.
3. Remove the ignition coil wires by squeezing the locking tabs together to release the ignition coil boot retainers.

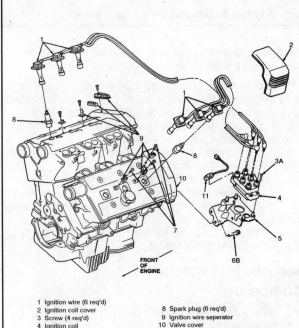

1 Ignition wire (6 req'd)
2 Ignition coil cover
3 Screw (4 req'd)
4 Ignition coil
5 Ignition coil bracket
6 Bolt (2 req'd)
7 Screw (3 req'd each side)
8 Spark plug (6 req'd)
9 Ignition wire seperator
10 Valve cover
11 Radio ignition interference capacitor
A Tighten to 4.5–7.0 Nm (40–62 lb.in.)
B Tighten to 28–42 Nm (21–31 lb.ft.)

**Fig. 48 Ignition coil and related system components—3.0L/3.2L SHO**

4. Remove the ignition coil retaining screws, then remove the ignition coil and, if applicable, the radio interference capacitor.
**To install:**
5. Install the ignition coil, radio ignition interference capacitor (if equipped) and the retaining screws. Tighten the screws to 40–62 inch lbs. (4.5–7.0 Nm).
6. Connect the ignition wires to the proper ignition coil terminals. Engage the engine control sensor wiring connector to the ignition coil and, if applicable, the radio ignition interference capacitor.
7. Install the ignition coil cover, then connect the negative battery cable.

### Ignition Control Module

▶ **See Figure 49**

1. Disconnect the negative battery cable.
2. Disengage both engine control sensor wiring connectors at the Ignition Control Module (ICM), by pressing down on the locking tabs stamped "PUSH", then remove the wiring connector.
3. Unfasten the retaining bolts, then remove the ICM.
**To install:**
4. Apply an even coat of about 1/32 in. (0.8mm) of Silicone Dielectric Compound D7AZ-19A331-A, or equivalent, to the mounting surface of the ignition control module.
5. Install the ICM and secure using the retaining bolts. Tighten the bolts to 22–31 inch lbs. (2.5–3.5 Nm).
6. Engage both engine control sensor wiring connectors to the ignition control module.
7. Connect the negative battery cable.

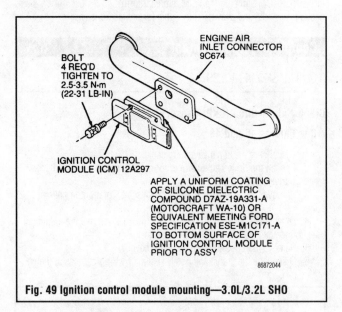

**Fig. 49 Ignition control module mounting—3.0L/3.2L SHO**

## 3.0L FLEXIBLE FUEL (FF) VEHICLES

### Crankshaft Position Sensor

▶ **See Figure 50**

1. Disconnect the negative battery cable.
2. Raise and safely support the vehicle.
3. Disconnect the fuel charging wiring from the crankshaft position sensor.
4. Remove the crankshaft position sensor retaining bolts, then remove the crankshaft position sensor.
**To install:**
5. Position the crankshaft position sensor and secure using the retaining bolts. Tighten the retaining bolts to 44–61 inch lbs. (5–7 Nm).

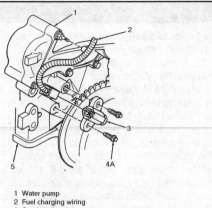

1 Water pump
2 Fuel charging wiring
3 Crankshaft position sensor
4 Bolt (2 req'd)
5 Engine front cover
A Tighten to 5-7 Nm (44-61 lb.in.)

86872045

**Fig. 50 Crankshaft position sensor—3.0L Flexible Fuel (FF)**

➡**Do NOT overtighten the retaining bolts or damage to the crankshaft position sensor may result!**

6. Properly route the fuel charging wiring, then connect it to the crankshaft position sensor.
7. Lower the vehicle, then connect the negative battery cable.

## Ignition Coil

◆ **See Figure 51**

1. Disconnect the negative battery cable.

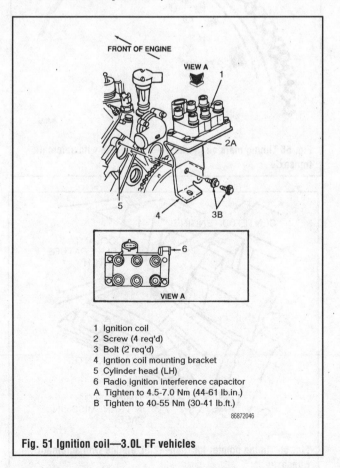

1 Ignition coil
2 Screw (4 req'd)
3 Bolt (2 req'd)
4 Ignition coil mounting bracket
5 Cylinder head (LH)
6 Radio ignition interference capacitor
A Tighten to 4.5-7.0 Nm (44-61 lb.in.)
B Tighten to 40-55 Nm (30-41 lb.ft.)

86872046

**Fig. 51 Ignition coil—3.0L FF vehicles**

2. Disengage the fuel charging wiring connectors from the ignition coil and the radio ignition interference capacitor.
3. Disconnect the ignition wires by squeezing the locking tabs together and twisting while pulling upward.
4. Remove the four ignition coil retaining screws, then remove the ignition coil and radio interference capacitor from the ignition coil bracket. Save the capacitor for installation with the ignition coil.

**To install:**

5. Position the ignition coil and radio ignition interference capacitor to the ignition coil bracket and secure with the retaining screws. Tighten the retaining screws to 44–61 inch lbs. (5–7 Nm).
6. Apply Silicone Dielectric Compound D7AZ-19A331-A, or equivalent, to all ignition wire boots.
7. Install each ignition wire connector to the proper terminal on the ignition coil, making sure all of the boots are fully seated.
8. Connect the fuel charging wiring to the ignition coil and radio ignition interference capacitor, then connect the negative battery cable.

## Ignition Control Module

◆ **See Figure 52**

1. Disconnect the negative battery cable.
2. Disengage the engine control sensor wiring connector from the ignition control module by carefully lifting upwards on the locking tabs while grasping the connector body and pulling away from the ignition control module.
3. Remove the two ignition control module retaining screws, then remove the ignition control module.

4. Position the ignition control module to the ignition control bracket and secure using the retaining screws. Tighten the screws to 24–32 inch lbs. (2.7–3.6 Nm).
5. Engage the ignition control module connector by pushing until the connector fingers are positioned over the locking wedge feature on the ICM.

➡**Locking the connector is important to ensure sealing of the connector and ignition control module interface.**

6. Connect the negative battery cable.

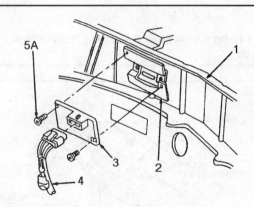

1 Dash panel
2 Ignition control module bracket
3 Ignition control module
4 Engine control sensor wiring
5 Screw (2 req'd)
A Tighten to 2.7-3.7 Nm (24-32 lb.in.)

86872047

**Fig. 52 Ignition control module location—3.0L FF vehicle**

## IGNITION TIMING

▶ **See Figures 53 thru 58**

Ignition timing is the measurement, in degrees of crankshaft rotation, of the point at which the spark plugs fire in each of the cylinders. It is measured in degrees before or after Top Dead Center (TDC) of the compression stroke.

Because it takes a fraction of a second for the spark plug to ignite the mixture in the cylinder, the spark plug must fire a little before the piston reaches TDC. Otherwise, the mixture will not be completely ignited as the piston passes TDC and the full power of the explosion will not be used by the engine.

The timing measurement is given in degrees of crankshaft rotation BEFORE the piston reaches TDC (BTDC). If the setting for the ignition timing is 10° BTDC, the spark plug must fire 10° before each piston reaches TDC. This only holds true, however, when the engine is at idle speed.

As the engine speed increases, the pistons go faster. The spark plugs have to ignite the fuel even sooner if it is to be completely ignited when the piston reaches TDC. To do this, distributors have various means of advancing the spark timing as the engine speed increases. On some earlier model vehicles, this is accomplished by centrifugal weights within the distributor along with a vacuum diaphragm mounted on the side of the distributor. Models covered by this manual use signals from various sensors, making all timing changes electronically, and no vacuum or mechanical advance is used. The 3.0L and 3.2L SHO engines and the 3.0L Flexible Fuel engines

use a distributorless electronic ignition system. Operation of this system allows for full electronic control of the timing.

If the ignition is set too far advanced (BTDC), the ignition and expansion of the fuel in the cylinder will occur too soon and tend to force the piston down while it is still traveling up. This causes engine ping. If the ignition spark is set too far retarded, After TDC (ATDC), the piston will have already passed TDC and started on its way down when the fuel is ignited. This will cause the piston to be forced down for only a portion of its travel, and will result in poor engine performance as well as a lack of power.

The timing marks on the 2.5L engine are visible through a hole in the top of the transaxle case. The 3.0L and 3.8L engines have the timing marks on the crankshaft pulley and a timing marker near the pulley. A stroboscopic (dynamic) timing light is used, which is hooked into the circuit of the No. 1 cylinder spark plug. Every time the spark plug fires, the timing light flashes. By aiming the timing light at the timing marks while the engine is running, the exact position of the piston within the cylinder can be easily read since the stroboscopic flash makes the mark on the pulley appear to be standing still. Proper timing is indicated when the notch is aligned with the correct number on the scale.

There are three basic types of timing lights available. The first is a simple neon bulb with two wire connections (one for the spark plug and one for the plug wire, to connect the light in series). This type of light is quite dim, and must be held closely to the marks to be seen, but it is quite inexpensive. The second type of light is powered by the car's battery. Two alli-

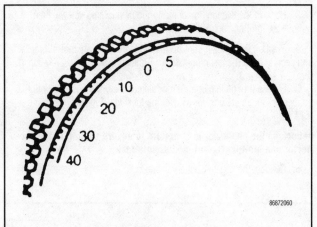

**Fig. 53 Timing mark on flywheel—2.5L engine with manual transaxle**

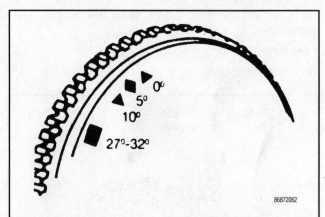

**Fig. 55 Timing mark on flywheel—2.5L engine with automatic transaxle**

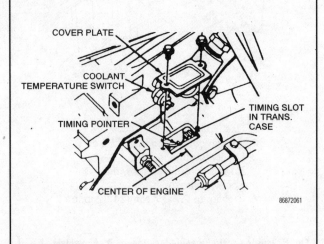

**Fig. 54 Timing pointer location—2.5L engine with manual transaxle**

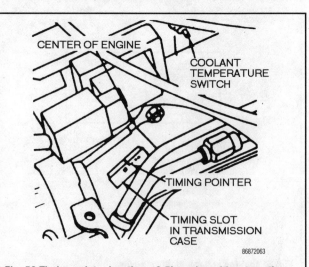

**Fig. 56 Timing pointer location—2.5L engine with automatic transaxle**

gator clips connect to the battery terminals, while a third wire connects to the spark plug with an adapter. This type of light is more expensive, but the xenon bulb provides a nice bright flash which can even be seen in sunlight. The third type replaces the battery source with 110 volt house current, but still attaches to the No. 1 spark plug wire in order to determine when the plug is fired. Some timing lights have other functions built into them, such as dwell meters, tachometers, or remote starting switches. These are convenient, in that they reduce the tangle of wires under the hood, but may duplicate the functions of tools you already have.

➡**Never pierce a spark plug wire in order to attach a timing light or perform tests. The pierced insulation will eventually lead to an electrical arc and related ignition troubles.**

Since your car has electronic ignition, you should use a timing light with an inductive pickup. This pickup simply clamps onto the No. 1 spark plug wire, eliminating the adapter. It is not susceptible to cross-firing or false triggering, which may occur with a conventional light, due to the greater voltages produced by electronic ignition.

## Timing

### INSPECTION & ADJUSTMENT

#### Except 3.0L Flexible Fuel (FF), 3.0L and 3.2L SHO Engines

The timing marks on the 2.5L engine are located on the flywheel and are visible through a hole in the transaxle case for manual transaxles. To view the timing marks, a cover plate on top of the transaxle must be removed. For 2.5L engines equipped with automatic transaxles, the timing marks are visible through a hole in the transaxle case.

The 3.0L and 3.8L engines have the timing marks on the crankshaft pulley and a timing pointer near the pulley. To check and adjust the ignition timing:

1. Place the transaxle in the **P** (AT) or **N** (MT) position. The air conditioner and heater must be in the **OFF** position.
2. Open the hood, locate the timing marks and clean them with a stiff brush or solvent. On vehicles equipped with a manual transaxle, it will be necessary to remove the transaxle cover plate which allows access to the timing marks.
3. Using a white chalk or paint, highlight the specified timing mark and pointer.
4. Near the distributor, detach the inline Spark Output (SPOUT) connector or remove the shorting bar from the double wire SPOUT connector. The spout connector is the center wire between the Electronic Control Assembly (ECA) connector and the Thick Film Integrated (TFI) or Ignition Control (ICM) module.

5. Connect an inductive-type timing light, Rotunda tool No. 059-00006 or equivalent, to the No. 1 spark plug wire. DO NOT puncture the ignition wire with any type of probing device.

➡**The high ignition coil voltage generated in the EEC-IV ignition system may falsely trigger the timing lights with capacitive or direct connect pick-ups. It is necessary that an inductive type timing light be used in this procedure.**

6. Connect a suitable tachometer, Rotunda tool No. 099-00003 or equivalent, to the engine. The ignition coil connector allows a test lead with an alligator clip to be connected to the Distributor Electronic Control (DEC) terminal without removing the connector.

➡**The ignition coil electrical connector allows a test lead with an alligator clip to be connected to its dark green/yellow dotted wire terminal without removing the connector. Be careful not to ground the alligator clip, for permanent damage to the ignition coil will result.**

7. Start the engine, using the ignition key, and allow it to run until it reaches normal operating temperature.

➡**Only use the ignition key to start the vehicle. Do NOT use a remote starter, as disconnecting the start wire at the starter relay will cause the TFI or ICM to revert back to the start mode timing, after the vehicle is started. Reconnecting the start wire after the vehicle is running will not correct the timing.**

8. Check the engine idle rpm; if it is not within specifications, adjust as necessary. Idle speed is not adjustable on 1991–95 vehicles. After the rpm has been adjusted or checked, aim the timing light at the timing marks. If they are not aligned, loosen the distributor clamp bolts slightly and rotate the distributor body until the marks are aligned under the timing light illumination.
9. Tighten the distributor clamp bolts and recheck the ignition timing. Readjust the idle speed, if necessary or possible.
10. Turn the engine **OFF**, remove all test equipment, reconnect the inline SPOUT connector to the distributor and, if necessary, reinstall the cover plate on manual transaxle vehicles.

#### 3.0L Flexible Fuel (FF), 3.0L and 3.2L SHO Engines

The base ignition timing is set at 10° Before Top Dead Center (BTDC) and is not adjustable.

### TACHOMETER HOOKUP

On distributor-equipped models with an "E" type ignition coil, the tachometer connection is made at the back of the wire harness connector. A cut-out is provided and the tachometer lead wire alligator clip can be connected to the dark green/yellow dotted wire of the electrical harness plug.

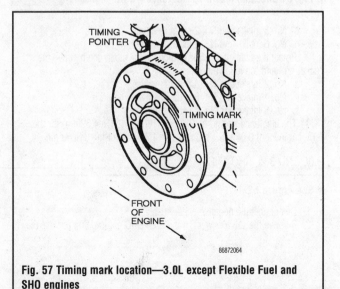

**Fig. 57 Timing mark location—3.0L except Flexible Fuel and SHO engines**

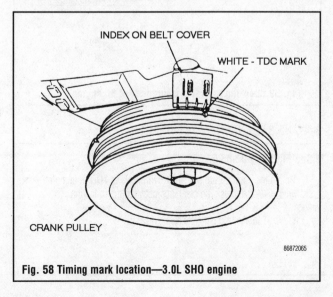

**Fig. 58 Timing mark location—3.0L SHO engine**

## VALVE LASH

Valve lash adjustment determines how far the valves enter the cylinder and how long they stay open and/or closed.

➡️ **While all valve adjustments must be made as accurately as possible, it is better to have the valve adjustment slightly loose than slightly tight, as a burned valve may result from overly tight adjustments.**

### Checking

The valve stem-to-rocker arm clearance for all engines except the 3.0L and the 3.2L SHO should be within specification with the valve lifter completely collapsed. To determine the rocker arm-to-valve lifter clearance, make the following checks:

#### 2.5L ENGINE

▶ **See Figure 59**

1. Set the No. 1 piston on TDC of the compression stroke. The timing marks on the camshaft and crankshaft gears will be together. Check the clearance in the No. 1 intake, No. 1 exhaust, No. 2 intake and No. 3 exhaust valves.

2. Rotate the crankshaft 1 complete turn (360°), or 180° for the camshaft gear. Check the clearance on the No. 2 exhaust, No. 3 intake, No. 4 intake and No. 4 exhaust valves.

3. The clearance between the rocker arm and the valve stem tip should be 0.071–0.170 in. (1.80–4.34mm) with the lifter on the base circle of the cam.

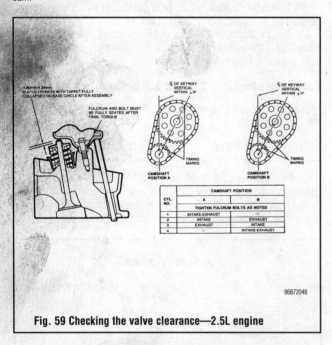

Fig. 59 Checking the valve clearance—2.5L engine

#### 3.0L AND 3.8L ENGINE—EXCEPT SHO

▶ **See Figures 60 and 61**

1. Rotate the engine until the No. 1 cylinder is at TDC of its compression stroke and check the clearance between the following valves:

  a. No. 1 intake and No. 1 exhaust valves

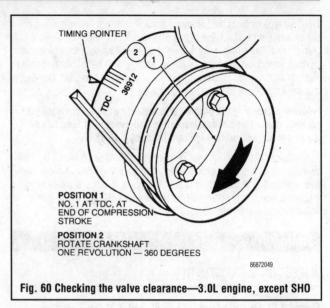

Fig. 60 Checking the valve clearance—3.0L engine, except SHO

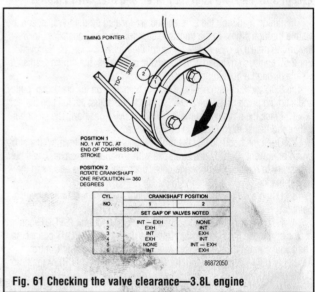

Fig. 61 Checking the valve clearance—3.8L engine

  b. No. 3 intake and No. 2 exhaust valves
  c. No. 6 intake and No. 4 exhaust valves

2. Rotate the crankshaft 360° and check the clearance between the rocker arm and the following valves:

  a. No. 2 intake and No. 3 exhaust valves
  b. No. 4 intake and No. 5 exhaust valves
  c. No. 5 intake and No. 6 exhaust valves

3. The clearance should be 0.085–0.185 in. (2.15–4.69mm) for the 3.0L engine and 0.089–0.189 in. (2.25–4.79mm) for the 3.8L engine.

#### 3.0L AND 3.2L SHO ENGINES

▶ **See Figure 62**

1. Disconnect the negative battery cable.
2. Remove the valve cover. For the 3.2L SHO engine, first remove the

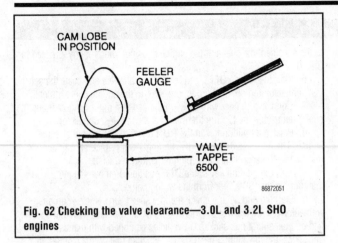

**Fig. 62 Checking the valve clearance—3.0L and 3.2L SHO engines**

EGR valve-to-exhaust manifold tube to gain access to the right-hand valve cover. For details regarding these procedures, please refer to

3. Remove the intake manifold assembly. For details regarding this procedure, please refer to Section 3 of this manual.

4. Insert a feeler gauge under the cam lob at a 90° angle to the camshaft. Clearance for the intake valves should be 0.006–0.010 in. (0.15–0.25mm). Clearance for the exhaust valves should be 0.010–0.014 in. (0.25–0.35mm).

➡The cam lobes must be directed 90° or more away from the valve lifters/tappets.

## Adjustment

For all engines covered by this manual, except the 3.0L and 3.2L SHO, the intake and exhaust valves are driven by the camshaft working through hydraulic lash adjusters. The lash adjusters eliminate the need for periodic valve lash adjustments.

### 3.0L AND 3.2L SHO ENGINES

◆ **See Figures 63, 64 and 65**

1. Disconnect the negative battery cable.
2. Remove the valve covers. For the 3.2L SHO engine, remove the EGR valve-to-exhaust manifold tube to gain access to the right-hand valve cover. For details regarding these procedures, please refer to Section 3 of this manual.
3. Remove the intake manifold assembly. For details regarding this procedure, please refer to Section 3 of this manual.

**Fig. 63 Install the compressor tool under the cam, next to the lobe, and rotate it down to depress the valve lifter/tappet**

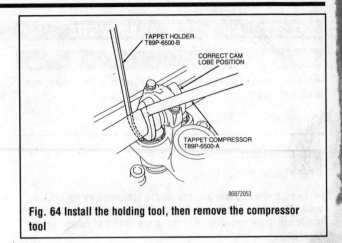

**Fig. 64 Install the holding tool, then remove the compressor tool**

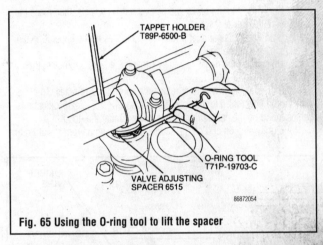

**Fig. 65 Using the O-ring tool to lift the spacer**

4. Install Lifter/Tappet Compressor T89P-6500-A or equivalent under the camshaft, next to the lobe, and rotate it downward to depress the valve lifter/tappet.
5. Install the valve lifter/tappet holding tool T89P-6500-B or equivalent, and remove the compressor tool.
6. Using O-ring tool T71P-19703-C or equivalent, lift the valve adjusting spacer and remove the spacer with a magnet.
7. Determine the size of the spacer by the numbers on the bottom face of the spacer, or by measuring it with a micrometer.
8. Install the replacement valve adjusting spacer that will permit the specified clearance. Be sure to install the spacer with the numbers down and make sure the spacer is properly seated.
9. Release the lifter/tappet holder by installing the compressor tool.
10. Repeat the procedure for each valve by rotating the crankshaft as necessary.
11. After all of the valve clearances are checked and/or adjusted, inspect all of the spacers to ensure that they are fully seated in their valve lifters/tappets.
12. Inspect the valve cover gaskets and replace, if necessary. For details regarding this procedure, please refer to Section 3 of this manual.
13. Install the intake manifold and the valve covers, as described in Section 3 of this manual
14. Connect the negative battery cable.

## IDLE SPEED AND MIXTURE ADJUSTMENTS

### Idle Speed Adjustment

➡The idle speed on 1991–95 vehicles is preset at the factory, and is not adjustable.

#### 2.5L ENGINE

**1986–90 Vehicles**

▸ See Figures 66 and 67

➡The curb idle and fast idle speeds are controlled by the EEC-IV computer and the Idle Speed Control (ISC) device. If the control system is operating correctly, the speeds are fixed and should not be changed.

1. Apply the parking brake and block the drive wheels, then place the vehicle in **P** (AT) or **N** (MT).
2. Start the engine and let it run until it reaches normal operating temperature, then turn the engine **OFF**.
3. Disconnect the negative battery cable for at least 5 minutes, then reconnect it.
4. Start the engine and let it run at idle speed for 2 minutes. The idle rpm should now return to the specified idle speed. The idle specifications can be found on the calibration sticker located under the hood.
5. Lightly step on and off the accelerator. The engine rpm should return

to the specified idle speed. If the engine does not idle properly, proceed to Step 6.

6. Shut the engine **OFF**, then remove the air cleaner. Locate the self-test connector and self-test input connector in the engine compartment.
7. Connect a jumper wire between the self-test input connector and the signal return pin, the top right terminal on the self-test connector.
8. Place the ignition key in the **RUN** position, but do not start the engine. The Idle Speed Control (ISC) plunger will retract, so wait approximately 10–15 seconds until the plunger is fully retracted.
9. Turn the ignition key to the **OFF** position. Remove the jumper wire, then unplug the ISC motor from the wiring harness.
10. Start the engine and check the idle speed. On vehicles equipped with automatic transaxles, the idle should be 50 rpm less than that specified on the calibrations sticker. On vehicles equipped with manual transaxles, the idle should be 100 rpm less than that on the calibration sticker. If not, proceed to Step 11.
11. Remove the throttle body from the vehicle. For details regarding this procedure, please refer to Section 5 of this manual.
12. Using a small punch, or equivalent, punch through and remove the aluminum plug which covers the throttle stop adjusting screw.
13. Remove and replace the throttle stop screw, then install the throttle body assembly onto the vehicle.
14. Start the engine and allow the idle to stabilize. Set the idle rpm to that specified in Step 10.
15. Turn the engine **OFF**. Reconnect the ISC motor wire harness, remove all test equipment, then reinstall the air cleaner assembly.

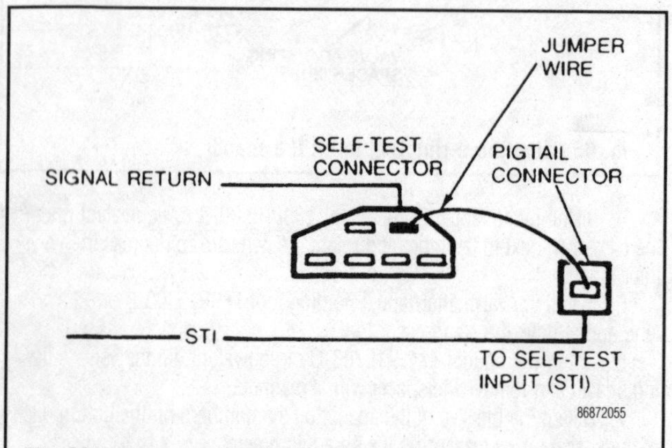

#### 3.0L ENGINE—EXCEPT SHO

**1986–90 Vehicles**

▸ See Figure 68

➡The curb idle speed rpm is controlled by the EEC-IV computer (ECM) and the Idle Speed Control (ISC) air bypass valve assembly. The throttle stop screw is factory set and does not directly control the idle speed. Adjustment of this setting should be performed only as part of a full EEC-IV diagnosis of irregular idle conditions or idle speeds. Failure to accurately set the throttle plate stop position as described in the following procedure could result in false idle speed control.

1. Apply the parking brake, turn the A/C control selector OFF and block the wheels.

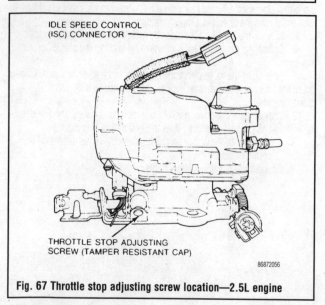

**Fig. 66 Jumper wire terminal connection points—2.5L engine**

**Fig. 67 Throttle stop adjusting screw location—2.5L engine**

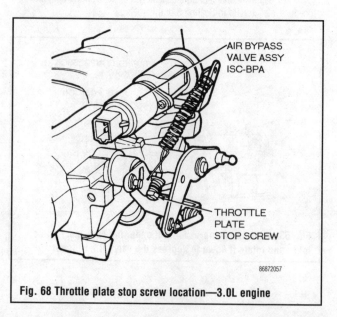

**Fig. 68 Throttle plate stop screw location—3.0L engine**

2. Connect a tachometer and an inductive timing light to the engine. Start the engine and allow it to reach normal operating temperatures.

3. Unplug the Spark Output (SPOUT) line at the distributor, then check and/or adjust the ignition timing to the specification listed on the underhood emission calibration decal.

4. Shut the engine **OFF** and remove the PCV hose from the PCV valve. Install a 0.20 in. (5mm) diameter orifice, tool T86P-9600-A or equivalent.

5. Disengage the electrical connector from the idle speed control/air bypass valve solenoid.

6. Start the engine and run it at 2,000 rpm for 30 seconds.

7. If equipped with an automatic transaxle, place the selector in **D**. If equipped with a manual transaxle, place the selector in Neutral.

8. Check and/or adjust (if necessary) the idle speed to 740–780 rpm by turning the throttle plate stop screw.

9. After adjusting the idle speed, stop the engine, then disconnect the battery for at least 5 minutes.

10. Start the engine and confirm that the idle speed is now adjusted to specifications; if not, readjust as necessary.

11. Turn the engine **OFF** and remove all test equipment. Reconnect the PCV entry line, the SPOUT line and the idle speed control/air bypass solenoid.

12. Make sure the throttle plate is not stuck in the bore and that the linkage is not preventing the throttle from closing.

## 3.0L SHO ENGINE

### 1989–90 Vehicles

▶ See Figure 69

1. Apply the parking brake, turn the A/C control selector OFF, then block the wheels.

2. Connect a tachometer and an inductive timing light to the engine. Start the engine and allow it to reach normal operating temperatures.

3. Unplug the Spark Output (SPOUT) line at the distributor, then check and/or adjust the ignition timing to the specification listed on the underhood emission calibration decal.

4. Stop the engine and disconnect the PCV hose at the intake manifold. Plug the PCV hose. Remove the Canister Purge Solenoid (CANP) hose from the intake manifold, then connect tool No. T89P-9600-AH or equivalent, between the PCV and CANP ports.

5. Disconnect the idle speed control/air bypass solenoid.

6. Start the engine and let it idle. Place the transaxle selector lever in **N**.

7. Check and/or adjust the idle speed to 770–830 rpm by turning the throttle plate stop screw.

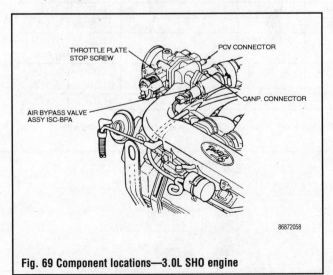

**Fig. 69 Component locations—3.0L SHO engine**

8. Turn the engine **OFF**, then repeat Steps 6 and 7.

9. Stop the engine and remove all test equipment. Remove tool T89P-9600-AH or equivalent, then unplug the PCV hose. Connect the PCV and CANP hoses. Reconnect the idle speed control/air bypass solenoid.

10. Make sure the throttle is not stuck in the bore and the linkage is not preventing the throttle from closing.

## 3.8L ENGINE

▶ See Figure 70

### 1988 Vehicles

1. Apply the parking brake, block the drive wheels and place the vehicle in **P** (AT) or **N** (MT).

2. Start the engine and let it run until it reaches normal operating temperature, then turn the engine **OFF**.

3. Connect an inductive tachometer, then start the engine and run it at 2,500 rpm for 30 seconds.

4. Allow the engine idle to stabilize, then place the automatic transaxle in **P** or the manual transaxle in neutral.

5. Adjust the engine idle rpm to the specification shown on the vehicle emission calibration label by turning the throttle stop screw.

6. After the idle speed is within specification, repeat Steps 3–6 to ensure that the adjustment is correct.

7. Turn the engine **OFF**, then disconnect the test equipment and unblock the wheels.

### 1989–90 Vehicles

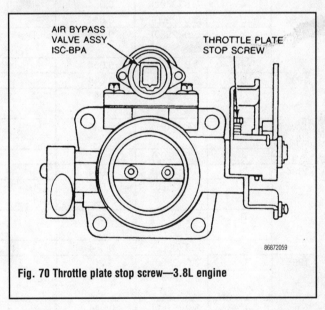

**Fig. 70 Throttle plate stop screw—3.8L engine**

1. Apply the parking brake, block the drive wheels, and place the vehicle in **P**.

2. Start the engine and let it run until it reaches normal operating temperature, then turn the engine **OFF**.

3. Back the throttle plate stop screw clear off the throttle lever pad.

4. Place a 0.010 in. (0.25mm) feeler gauge between the throttle plate stop screw and the throttle lever pad. Turn the screw in until contact is made, then turn it and additional 1½ turns. Remove the feeler gauge.

5. Start the engine and let the idle stabilize for 2 minutes. Lightly depress and release the accelerator, then let the engine idle.

## Idle Mixture Adjustment

Idle mixture is controlled by the electronic control unit. No adjustment is possible.

### GASOLINE ENGINE TUNE-UP SPECIFICATIONS

| Year | Engine ID/VIN | Engine Displacement Liters (cc) | Spark Plugs Gap (in.) | Ignition Timing (deg.) MT | Ignition Timing (deg.) AT | Fuel Pump (psi) | Idle Speed (rpm) MT | Idle Speed (rpm) AT | Valve Clearance In. | Valve Clearance Ex. |
|---|---|---|---|---|---|---|---|---|---|---|
| 1986 | D | 2.5 (2501) | 0.044 | 10B | 10B | 13-17 | 725 | 650 | HYD | HYD |
| | U | 3.0 (2980) | 0.044 | - | 10B | 35-45 | - | 625 | HYD | HYD |
| 1987 | D | 2.5 (2501) | 0.044 | 10B | 10B | 13-17 | 725 | 650 | HYD | HYD |
| | U | 3.0 (2980) | 0.044 | - | 10B | 35-45 | - | 625 | HYD | HYD |
| 1988 | D | 2.5 (2501) | 0.044 | 10B | 10B | 13-17 | 725 | 650 | HYD | HYD |
| | U | 3.0 (2971) | 0.044 | - | 10B | 35-45 | - | 625 | HYD | HYD |
| | 4 | 3.8 (3802) | 0.044 | - | 10B | 35-45 | - | 550 | HYD | HYD |
| 1989 | D | 2.5 (2501) | 0.044 | 10B | 10B | 35-45 | 725 | 650 | HYD | HYD |
| | U | 3.0 (2980) | 0.052 | - | 10B | 35-45 | - | 625 | HYD | HYD |
| | Y | 3.0 (2980) | 0.044 | 10B | - | 36-39 | 800 | - | 0.006-0.01 | 0.010-0.014 |
| | 4 | 3.8 (3802) | 0.054 | - | 10B | 35-45 | - | 550 | HYD | HYD |
| 1990 | D | 2.5 (2501) | 0.044 | 10B | 10B | 35-45 | 725 | 650 | HYD | HYD |
| | U | 3.0 (2980) | 0.044 | - | 10B | 35-45 | - | 625 | HYD | HYD |
| | Y | 3.0 (2980) | 0.044 | 10B | - | 36-39 | 800 | - | 0.006-0.010 | 0.010-0.014 |
| | 4 | 3.8 (3802) | 0.054 | - | 10B | 35-45 | - | 550 | HYD | HYD |
| 1991 | D | 2.5 (2501) | 0.044 | 10B | 10B | 45-60 | 725 | 650 | HYD | HYD |
| | U | 3.0 (2980) | 0.044 | - | 10B | 35-45 | - | 625 | HYD | HYD |
| | Y | 3.0 (2980) | 0.044 | 10B | - | 36-39 | 800 | - | 0.006-0.010 | 0.010-0.014 |
| | 4 | 3.8 (3802) | 0.054 | - | 10B | 35-45 | - | 550 | HYD | HYD |
| 1992 | U | 3.0 (2980) | 0.044 | - | 10B | 35-40 | - | 625 | HYD | HYD |
| | Y | 3.0 (2980) | 0.044 | 10B | - | 30-45 | 800 | - | 0.006-0.010 | 0.010-0.014 |
| | 4 | 3.8 (3802) | 0.054 | - | 10B | 35-40 | - | 550 | HYD | HYD |
| 1993 | U | 3.0 (2980) | 0.044 | - | 10B | 35-45 | - | 625 | HYD | HYD |
| | Y | 3.0 (2980) | 0.044 | 10B | - | 30-45 | 800 | - | 0.006-0.010 | 0.010-0.014 |
| | P | 3.2 (3191) | 0.044 | - | 10B | 30-45 | - | | 0.006-0.010 | 0.010-0.010 |
| | 4 | 3.8 (3802) | 0.054 | - | 10B | 35-45 | - | 550 | HYD | HYD |
| 1994 | U | 3.0 (2980) | 0.044 | - | 10B | 30-45 [2] | 1 | 1 | HYD | HYD |
| | Y | 3.0 (2980) | 0.044 | 10B | - | 28-33 [2] | 1 | - | 0.006-0.010 | 0.010-0.014 |
| | P | 3.2 (3191) | 0.044 | - | 10B | 28-33 [2] | - | 750 | 0.006-0.010 | 0.010-0.010 |
| | 4 | 3.8 (3802) | 0.054 | - | 10B | 30-45 [2] | 1 | 1 | HYD | HYD |
| 1995 | U | 3.0 (2980) | 0.044 | - | 10B | 30-45 [2] | - | 1 | HYD | HYD |
| | Y | 3.0 (2980) | 0.044 | 10B | - | 28-33 [2] | 1 | - | 0.006-0.010 | 0.010-0.014 |
| | P | 3.2 (3191) | 0.044 | - | 10B | 30-45 [2] | - | 800 | 0.006-0.010 | 0.010-0.014 |
| | 4 | 3.8 (3802) | 0.054 | - | 10B | 30-45 [2] | - | 1 | HYD | HYD |

NOTE: The Vehicle Emission Control Information label often reflects specification changes made during production. The label figures must be used if they differ from those in this chart.
B - Before top dead center
HYD - Hydraulic
1 Refer to the Vehicle Emission Control Label
2 Fuel Pressure with engine running, pressure regulator vacuum hose connected

86872100

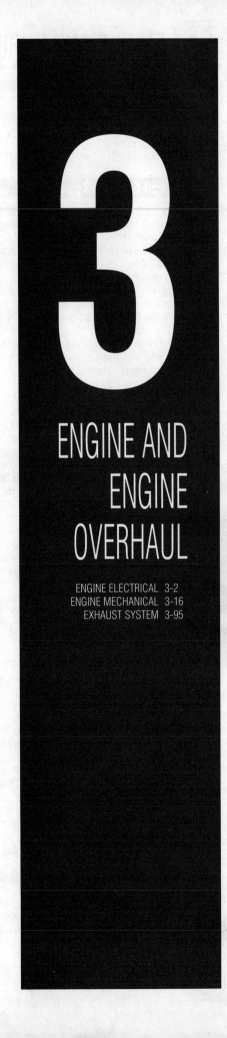

# 3

## ENGINE AND ENGINE OVERHAUL

## ENGINE ELECTRICAL

The engine electrical can be broken down into three distinct subsystems:
1. The starting system
2. The charging system
3. The ignition system

### Battery and Starting System

The battery is the first link in the chain of mechanisms which work together to provide cranking of the engine. In most modern cars, the battery is a lead-acid electrochemical device consisting of six 2 volt (2V) subsections connected in series so the unit is capable of producing approximately 12V of electrical current. Each subsection, or cell, consists of a series of positive and negative plates held a short distance apart in a solution of sulfuric acid and water. The two types of plates are of dissimilar metals. This causes a chemical reaction to be set up, and it is this reaction which produces current flow from the battery when its positive and negative terminals are connected to an electrical appliance such as a lamp or motor. The continued transfer of electrons would eventually convert the sulfuric acid in the electrolyte to water and make the two plates identical in chemical composition. As electrical energy is removed from the battery, its voltage output tends to drop. Thus, measuring battery voltage and battery electrolyte composition are two ways of checking the ability of the unit to supply power. During engine starting, electrical energy is removed from the battery. However, if the charging circuit is in good condition and the operating conditions are normal, the power removed from the battery will soon be replaced by the alternator which will force electrons back through the battery, reversing the normal flow, and restoring the battery to its original chemical state.

The battery and starting motor are linked by very heavy electrical cables designed to minimize resistance to the flow of current. Generally, the major power supply cable that leaves the battery goes directly to the starter, while other electrical system needs are supplied by a smaller cable. During starter operation, power flows from the battery to the starter and is grounded through the car's frame and the battery's negative ground strap.

The starting motor is a specially designed, direct current electric motor capable of producing a large amount of power for its size. One thing that allows the motor to produce a great deal of power is its tremendous rotating speed. It drives the engine through a tiny pinion gear (attached to the starter's armature), which drives the very large flywheel ring gear at a greatly reduced speed. Another factor allowing it to produce so much power is that only intermittent operation is required of it. Thus, little allowance for air circulation is required, and the windings can be built into a very small space.

The starter solenoid is a magnetic device which employs the small current supplied by the starting switch circuit of the ignition switch. This magnetic action moves a plunger which mechanically engages the starter and electrically closes the heavy switch which connects it to the battery. The starting switch circuit commonly consists of the starting switch contained within the ignition switch, a transmission neutral or clutch safety switch and the wiring necessary to connect these with the starter solenoid or relay.

A pinion, which is a small gear, is mounted to a one-way drive clutch. This clutch is splined to the starter armature shaft. When the ignition switch is moved to the start position, the solenoid plunger slides the pinion toward the flywheel ring gear via a collar and spring. If the teeth butt one another, the spring will be compressed and will force the gears to mesh as soon as the starter turns far enough to allow them to do so. As the solenoid plunger reaches the end of its travel, it closes the contacts that connect the battery and starter, then the engine is cranked.

As soon as the engine starts, the flywheel ring gear begins turning fast enough to drive the pinion at an extremely high rate of speed. At this point, the one-way clutch begins allowing the pinion to spin faster than the starter shaft so that the starter will not operate at excessive speed. When the ignition switch is released from the starter position, the solenoid is de-ener-

gized, and a spring contained within the solenoid assembly pulls the gear out of mesh and interrupts the current flow to the starter.

Many late model starters employ a separate relay, mounted away from the starter, to switch the motor and solenoid current on and off. The relay thus replaces the solenoid electrical switch, but does not eliminate the need for a solenoid mounted on the starter used to mechanically engage the starter drive gears. The relay is used to mechanically engage the starter drive gears. The relay is used to reduce the amount of current the starting switch must carry.

### Charging System

The automobile charging system provides electrical power for operation of the vehicle's ignition system, starting system and all of the electrical accessories. The battery serves as an electrical surge or storage tank, storing (in chemical form) the energy originally produced by the belt driven alternator. The system also provides a means of regulating alternator output to protect the battery from being overcharged and to avoid excessive voltage to the accessories.

The storage battery is a chemical device incorporating parallel lead plates in a tank containing a sulfuric acid/water solution. Adjacent plates are slightly dissimilar, and the chemical reaction of the two dissimilar places produces electrical energy when the battery is connected to a load such as the starter motor. The chemical reaction is reversible, so that when the alternator is producing a voltage grater than that produced by the battery, electricity is forced into the battery, and the battery is returned to its fully charged state.

The vehicle's alternator is driven mechanically, through a belt, by the engine crankshaft. The alternator consists of two coils of fine wire, one stationary (the stator), and one movable (the rotor). The rotor may also be known as the armature, and consists of fine wire wrapped around an iron core mounted on a shaft. The electricity which flows through the two coils of wire (provided initially by the battery) creates an intense magnetic field around both rotor and stator, and the interaction between the two fields creates voltage, allowing the alternator to power the accessories and charge the battery.

All vehicles covered in this manual are equipped with an alternating current generator or alternator. Such units are more efficient than the generators used in older vehicles, can be rotated at higher speeds, and have fewer brush problems. In an alternator, the field rotates while all the current produced passes only through the stator windings. The brushes bear against continuous slip rings rather than a commutator. This prevents the current from traveling in the wrong direction. A series of diodes is wired together to permit the alternating flow of the stator to be converted to a pulsating, but unidirectional, flow at the alternator output. The alternator's field is wired in series with the voltage regulator.

The regulator consists of several circuits. Each circuit has a core, or magnetic coil of wire, which operates a switch. Each switch is connected to ground through one or more resistors. The coil of wire responds directly to system voltage. When the voltage reaches the required level, the magnetic field created by the winding of the wire closes the switch and inserts a resistance into the generator field circuit, thus reducing the output. The contacts of the switch cycle open and close many times each second to precisely control voltage. Alternators are self-limiting as far as maximum current is concerned.

### Ignition System

There are two different types of ignition systems found on these vehicles. Most of the vehicles utilize a Distributor Ignition (DI) system which incorporates a conventional distributor. The SHO and the 3.0L Flexible Fuel (FF) vehicles utilize a distributorless ignition system known as Electronic Ignition (EI).

➡For more information, testing and removal/replacement procedures regarding the ignition systems, please refer to Section 2 of this manual.

## Safety Precautions

Observing these precautions will help avoid damage to the vehicle's electrical system and ensure safe handling of the system components:

- Be absolutely sure of the polarity of a booster battery before making connections. Connect the cables positive-to-positive, and negative-to-a good ground. Connect positive cables first and then make the last connection to an engine ground on the vehicle with the dead battery so that arcing cannot ignite hydrogen gas that may have accumulated near the battery. Even momentary connection of a booster battery with the polarity reversed will damage alternator diodes.
- Disconnect both vehicle battery cables before attempting to charge a battery.
- Never ground the alternator output or battery terminal. Be cautious when using metal tools around a battery to avoid creating a short circuit between the terminals.
- Never run an alternator without load unless the field circuit is disconnected.
- Never attempt to polarize an alternator.

## Alternator

### ALTERNATOR PRECAUTIONS

To prevent damage to the on-board computer, alternator and regulator, the following precautionary measures must be taken when working with the electrical system.

- If the battery is removed for any reason, make sure it is reconnected with the correct polarity. Reversing the battery connections may result in damage to the one-way rectifiers. Always check the battery polarity visually. This should be done before any connections are made to be sure that all of the connections correspond to the battery ground polarity.
- When utilizing a booster battery as a starting aid, always connect the positive to positive terminals and the negative terminal from the booster battery to a good engine ground on the vehicle being started.
- Never use a fast charger as a booster to start vehicles.
- Disconnect the battery cables when charging the battery with a fast charger; the charger has a tendency to force current through the diodes in the opposite direction for which they were designed. This burns out the diodes.
- Never attempt to polarize the alternator.
- Do not use test lights of more than 12 volts when checking diode continuity.
- Do not short across or ground any of the alternator terminals.
- The polarity of the battery, alternator and regulator must be matched and considered before making any electrical connections within the system.
- Never separate the alternator on an open circuit. Make sure all connections within the circuit are clean and tight.
- Disconnect the battery ground terminal when performing any service on electrical components.
- Disconnect the battery if arc welding is to be done on the vehicle.

### REMOVAL & INSTALLATION

The different engine applications that the Ford Taurus and Mercury Sable are equipped with utilize different types of alternators. The following is a list of vehicle applications.

**For 1986–90 vehicles:**
- The 3.0L and the 3.8L engines utilize a side terminal alternator.
- The 2.5L and the 3.8L (with Police Package only) engines utilize an alternator with an integral rear mount regulator and an internal fan.
- The 3.0L SHO engines utilize an alternator with an internal fan and regulator.

**For 1991–93 vehicles:**
- The 2.5L, 3.0L and 3.8L engines utilize an alternator with a rear mount regulator and an internal fan.
- The 3.0L and 3.2L SHO engines utilize an alternator with an internal regulator and fan.

**For 1994–95 vehicles:**
- The 3.0L, 3.8L and 3.0L SHO engines utilize an alternator with a rear mount regulator and an internal fan.
- The 3.2L SHO vehicles utilize an alternator with a internal regulator and fan.

### Side Terminal Alternator

### ▶ See Figure 1

1. Disconnect the negative battery cable.
2. Loosen the alternator pivot bolt, then remove the adjusting bolt.
3. Remove the alternator drive belt from the drive pulley.
4. Tag and disengage the wiring terminals from the back of the alternator. The stator and the field wiring are the push-on type of retainer. After depressing the lock tab, the connector should be pulled straight off of the terminal to prevent damage.
5. Remove the alternator pivot bolt, then remove the alternator from the engine.

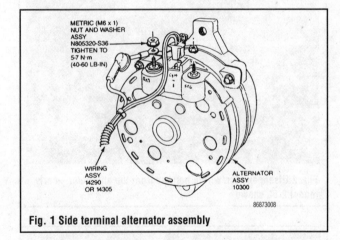

**Fig. 1 Side terminal alternator assembly**

### To install:
6. Position the alternator on the engine.
7. Install the alternator pivot bolt and the adjusting bolt, but do NOT tighten the bolts until the drive belt it tensioned.
8. Engage the wiring terminals to the alternator, as tagged during removal.
9. Install the drive belt over the alternator drive pulley, then adjust the belt tension using Belt Tension Gauge 023-00019, or equivalent.

➡When adjusting belt tension, apply pressure on the front housing only.

10. Tighten the adjusting bolt to 30–45 ft. lbs. (41–61 Nm), then tighten the pivot bolt to 50–70 ft. lbs. (68–94 Nm).
11. Connect the negative battery cable.

**Rear Mount Regulator With Internal Fan**

*EXCEPT 3.0L SHO ENGINE*

♦ See Figures 2 thru 7

1. Disconnect the negative battery cable.
2. Disengage the wiring harness electrical connectors from the alternator and the regulator.
3. Loosen the pivot bolt, then remove the mounting brace bolt from the alternator.
4. Remove the accessory drive belt from the alternator pulley.
5. If equipped, remove the alternator brace, then remove the alternator/voltage regulator assembly from the engine.

**To install:**

6. Position the alternator/regulator assembly on the engine, then install the pivot and mounting brace bolts, but do NOT tighten the bolts until the drive belt is tensioned.
7. If equipped, install the alternator brace. Tighten the retaining nut to 15–22 ft. lbs. (20–30 Nm). On the 3.0L engine, tighten the alternator brace bolts to 7–8 ft. lbs. (8.5–11 Nm).
8. Install the drive belt over the alternator pulley, then tighten the mounting brace bolt to 15–22 ft. lbs. (20–30 Nm) and the pivot bolt to 30–41 ft. lbs. (40–55 Nm).

Fig. 4 Loosen the mounting/pivot bolts—early model 2.5L shown

Fig. 2 Disengage the wiring harness from the alternator—early model 2.5L shown

Fig. 5 Remove the mounting/pivot bolts from the alternator—early model 2.5L shown

Fig. 3 Disengage the wiring harness from the voltage regulator—early model 2.5L shown

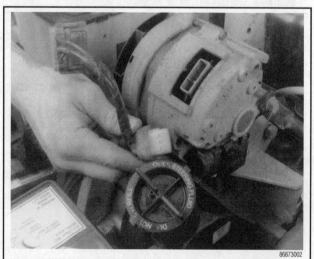

Fig. 6 Remove the alternator/regulator assembly from the vehicle—early model 2.5L shown

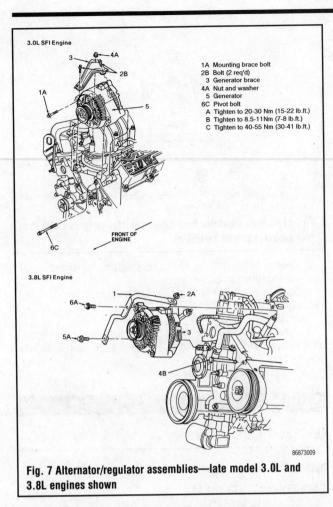

3.0L SFI Engine

1A Mounting brace bolt
2B Bolt (2 req'd)
 3 Generator brace
4A Nut and washer
 5 Generator
6C Pivot bolt
 A Tighten to 20-30 Nm (15-22 lb.ft.)
 B Tighten to 8.5-11Nm (7-8 lb.ft.)
 C Tighten to 40-55 Nm (30-41 lb.ft.)

3.8L SFI Engine

**Fig. 7 Alternator/regulator assemblies—late model 3.0L and 3.8L engines shown**

9. Engage the wiring harness connector(s) to the alternator/voltage regulator, as applicable. If equipped, tighten the output terminal nut to 80–97 inch lbs. (9–11 Nm).

10. Connect the negative battery cable.

### 3.0L SHO ENGINE

▶ **See Figure 8**

1. Disconnect the negative battery cable.
2. Remove the accessory drive belt from the alternator.

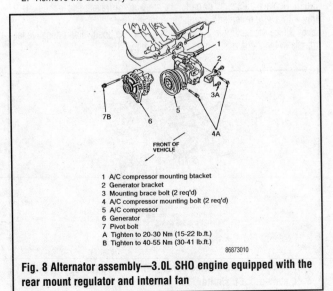

1 A/C compressor mounting bracket
2 Generator bracket
3 Mounting brace bolt (2 req'd)
4 A/C compressor mounting bolt (2 req'd)
5 A/C compressor
6 Generator
7 Pivot bolt
A Tighten to 20-30 Nm (15-22 lb.ft.)
B Tighten to 40-55 Nm (30-41 lb.ft.)

**Fig. 8 Alternator assembly—3.0L SHO engine equipped with the rear mount regulator and internal fan**

3. Disengage the electrical harness connector and the output terminal wiring.

4. Remove the mounting bolt at the front of the alternator, and the two bolts at the rear.

5. Remove the alternator from the engine.

**To install:**

6. Position the alternator on the engine and install the mounting bolts. Tighten the rear mounting bolts to 15–22 ft. lbs. (20–30 Nm) and the front bolt to 30–41 ft. lbs. (40–55 Nm).

7. Engage the electrical connector and the output terminal wiring. Tighten the output terminal nut to 80–97 inch lbs. (9–11 Nm).

8. Install the alternator drive belt on the alternator, then connect the negative battery cable.

### Internal Fan and Regulator

#### VEHICLES THROUGH 1993

▶ **See Figure 9**

For this procedure, you will need Belt Tension Gauge T63L-8620-A, Alternator Pulley Remover T65P-10300-B, and Rotunda Belt Tension Gauge 021-00019.

1. Disconnect the battery cables (negative, then positive), then remove the battery and battery tray. For details regarding this procedure, please refer to the procedure later in this section.

2. Tag and disengage the electrical wiring harness connector and the output terminal wiring from the alternator.

3. Loosen the belt tensioner, then remove the alternator belt from the pulley.

4. Remove the mounting bolt on the front of the alternator and the two bolts from the rear of the alternator, then remove the alternator from the vehicle.

**To install:**

5. Position the alternator in the vehicle, then install the three mounting bolts. Tighten the front bolt to 36–53 ft. lbs. (48–72 Nm) and the rear bolts to 26–36 ft. lbs. (34–50 Nm).

6. Install the alternator belt, then set the belt tension to 148–191 lbs. (658–854 N) for a used belt, or to 220–264 lbs. (978–1178 N) for a new belt, using the earlier specified tension gauge.

7. Engage the output terminal wire and the electrical harness connector to the alternator.

8. Install the battery tray and the battery, then connect the battery cables. For details regarding battery and tray installation, please refer to the procedure later in this section.

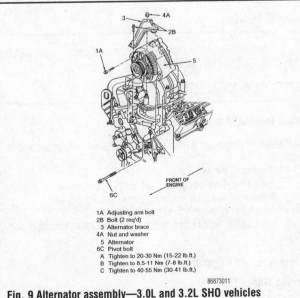

1A Adjusting arm bolt
2B Bolt (2 req'd)
 3 Alternator brace
4A Nut and washer
 5 Alternator
6C Pivot bolt
 A Tighten to 20-30 Nm (15-22 lb.ft.)
 B Tighten to 8.5-11 Nm (7-8 lb.ft.)
 C Tighten to 40-55 Nm (30-41 lb.ft.)

**Fig. 9 Alternator assembly—3.0L and 3.2L SHO vehicles through 1993**

*1994–95 VEHICLES*

▶ **See Figure 10**

Vehicles equipped with this alternator include the 1994 3.0L SHO and 1994–95 3.2L SHO.

1. Disconnect the negative battery cable.
2. Remove the drive belt from the alternator. For details regarding this procedure, please refer to Section 1 of this manual.
3. Disengage the electrical harness connector and the output terminal wiring.
4. Remove the bolt from the rear alternator bracket-to-alternator, then remove the two mounting brackets.
5. Remove the alternator from the vehicle.

**To install:**

6. Position the alternator in the vehicle, then install the two mounting brackets. Tighten the bracket retaining bolts to 15–22 ft. lbs. (20–30 Nm).

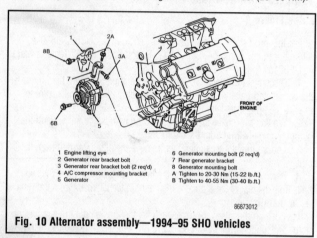

| | |
|---|---|
| 1 Engine lifting eye | 6 Generator mounting bolt (2 req'd) |
| 2 Generator rear bracket bolt | 7 Rear generator bracket |
| 3 Generator rear bracket bolt (2 req'd) | 8 Generator mounting bolt |
| 4 A/C compressor mounting bracket | A Tighten to 20-30 Nm (15-22 lb.ft.) |
| 5 Generator | B Tighten to 40-55 Nm (30-40 lb.ft.) |

86873012

**Fig. 10 Alternator assembly—1994–95 SHO vehicles**

7. Install the bolt to the rear bracket and tighten to 30–40 ft. lbs. (40–55 Nm).
8. Engage the output terminal wiring and the electrical harness connector.
9. Install the alternator belt, then connect the negative battery cable. For details regarding belt installation, please refer to Section 1 of this manual.

## Voltage Regulator

### ADJUSTMENT

The electronic voltage regulator is calibrated and preset by the manufacturer. No adjustment is required or possible.

### REMOVAL & INSTALLATION

#### Side Terminal Alternator

This voltage regulator is mounted on the right-hand fender apron of the vehicle.

1. Disconnect the negative battery cable.
2. Detach the electrical connectors from the wiring harness.
3. Remove the regulator mounting screws and the regulator.
4. Installation is the reverse of the removal procedure.
5. Connect the negative battery cable. Test the system for proper voltage regulation.

#### Rear Mounted Regulator

▶ **See Figure 11**

This voltage regulator is mounted on the rear of the alternator housing.

1. Disconnect the negative battery cable.

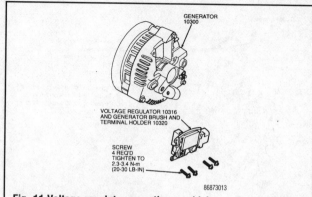

**Fig. 11 Voltage regulator mounting—vehicles equipped with the rear mount regulator alternator**

2. Remove the four retaining Torx® screws attaching the voltage regulator to the alternator rear housing.
3. Remove the regulator, with the alternator brush and terminal holder still attached, from the alternator.

**To install:**

4. Install the regulator to the rear of the alternator assembly and fasten using the four retaining screws. Tighten the screws to 20–30 inch lbs. (2.3–3.4 Nm).
5. Connect the negative battery cable.

## Battery

### REMOVAL & INSTALLATION

#### Battery

▶ **See Figures 12, 13 and 14**

1. Disconnect the negative battery cable, and then the positive battery cable.
2. Remove the battery hold-down bracket retaining bolt, then remove the hold-down bracket.

➡ **Before removing the battery from the vehicle, make sure to note the position of the positive and negative terminals.**

3. Carefully lift the battery from its mounting and remove it from the vehicle.

**To install:**

4. Clean the cable terminals and the hold-down clamp with a wire brush. Replace all cables or parts that are worn or frayed. Clean the battery tray with a wire brush and a suitable scraping tool.
5. Place the battery in the battery tray with the positive and negative terminals in the same position as prior to removal.

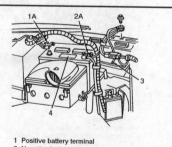

| | |
|---|---|
| 1 Positive battery terminal | |
| 2 Negative battery terminal | |
| 3 Anti-lock brake wiring | |
| 4 Front fender apron | |
| A Tighten to 6-10 Nm (60-90 lb.in.) | |

86873014

**Fig. 12 Battery and related components—3.0L (except SHO) and 3.8L shown, 2.5L similar**

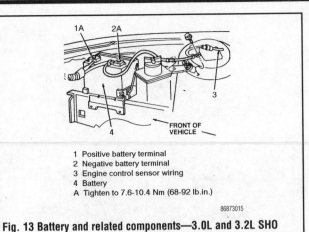

1 Positive battery terminal
2 Negative battery terminal
3 Engine control sensor wiring
4 Battery
A Tighten to 7.6-10.4 Nm (68-92 lb.in.)

**Fig. 13 Battery and related components—3.0L and 3.2L SHO**

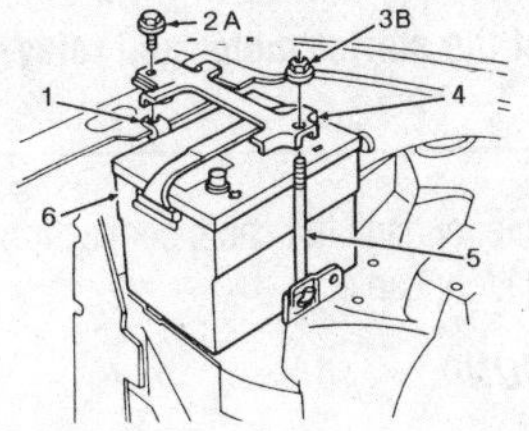

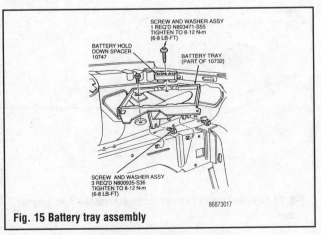

1 U-nut
2 Bolt (1 req'd)
3 Nut (1 req'd)
4 Battery hold down clamp
5 Battery mounting clamp bolt
6 Battery
A Tighten to 7-10 Nm (62-88 lb.in.)
B Tighten to 3-5 Nm (27-44 lb.in.)

**Fig. 14 View of the battery hold-down clamp assembly**

6. Assemble and tighten the hold-down hardware so the battery is secure. Do NOT overtighten.

➥**When the battery is disconnected and reconnected, some abnormal driving symptoms may occur while the Powertrain Control Module (PCM) relearns its adaptive strategy. The car may have to be driven 10 or more miles to relearn this strategy.**

7. Secure cables to the proper terminals, securing the positive cable first, but do NOT overtighten. Apply petroleum jelly to the battery terminals.

## Battery Tray

▶ **See Figure 15**

1. Remove the battery from the vehicle, as explained previously in this section.

2. Remove the retaining bolts, screws and washers from the battery tray, then remove the tray from the vehicle.

**To install:**

3. Position the battery tray to the front fender apron in the engine compartment.

4. Install the retaining bolts, screws and washers, then tighten each to 6–8 ft. lbs. (8–12 Nm).

5. Install the battery in the engine compartment as previously outlined in this section, then tighten the hold-down spacer bolt to 6–8 ft. lbs. (8–12 Nm).

## Starter

### TESTING

Before removing the starter for repair or replacement, check the condition of all circuit wiring for damage. Inspect all connections to the starter motor, relay, ignition switch, and battery, including all ground connections. Clean and tighten all connections as required.

### REMOVAL & INSTALLATION

#### 1986–91 Vehicles

##### *ALL 2.5L AND 3.0L MODELS; 3.8L SEDAN*

▶ **See Figures 16, 17, 18, 19 and 20**

1. Disconnect the negative battery cable and the cable connection at the starter.

2. Raise and safely support the vehicle.

3. Remove the cable support and ground cable connection from the upper starter stud bolt.

4. If equipped, remove the starter brace from the cylinder block and the starter.

5. On 2.5L engines, remove the three starter-to-bell housing bolts. On 3.0L engines, remove the two starter-to bell housing bolts.

6. On vehicles equipped with an automatic transaxle, remove the starter between the subframe and the radiator. For vehicles equipped with a manual transaxle, remove the starter between the subframe and the engine.

**To install:**

7. Position the starter, then secure using the retaining bolts. Tighten the bolts to 15–20 ft. lbs. (20–27 Nm).

8. If applicable, install the starter brace to the cylinder block and starter.

9. Engage the ground cable connection to the upper starter stud bolt, then install the cable support.

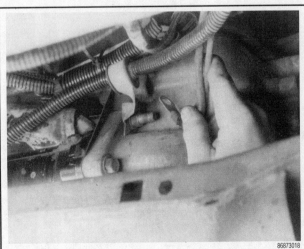

**Fig. 16 Disengage the connection from the upper starter stud bolt—early model 2.5L shown**

SCREW AND WASHER ASSY
1 REQ'D N803471-S55
TIGHTEN TO 8-12 N-m
(6-8 LB-FT)

BATTERY HOLD
DOWN SPACER
10747

BATTERY TRAY
(PART OF 10732)

SCREW AND WASHER ASSY
3 REQ'D N800935-S36
TIGHTEN TO 8-12 N-m
(6-8 LB-FT)

**Fig. 15 Battery tray assembly**

Fig. 17 Remove the starter retaining bolts—early model 2.5L shown

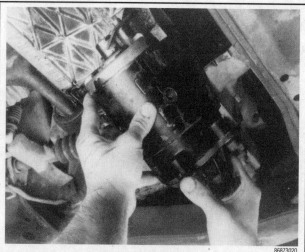

Fig. 18 Remove the starter motor from the vehicle—early model 2.5L shown

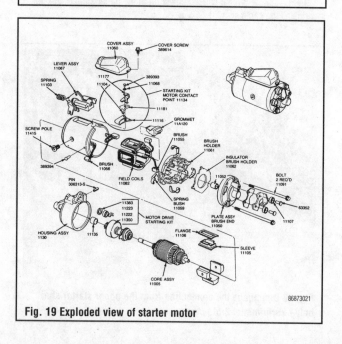

Fig. 19 Exploded view of starter motor

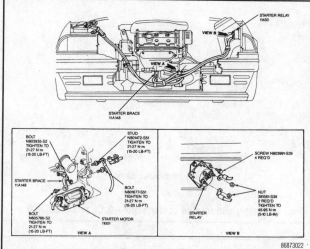

Fig. 20 Location of the starter motor and relay—1989 3.0L SHO shown

10. Lower the vehicle, engage the cable connection at the starter, then connect the negative battery cable.

### 3.8L STATION WAGON

▶ See Figure 21

1. Disconnect the negative battery cable, then raise and safely support the vehicle.

2. Disengage the the starter cable and the relay connector from the starter solenoid.

➡When disengaging the hardshell connector at the S-terminal, be sure to grasp the connector to pull it off. Do NOT pull on the wire!

3. Remove the starter retaining bolts, then remove the starter.
**To install:**

4. Position the starter motor to the engine, then finger-start the retaining bolts. Starting with the topmost bolt, tighten the bolts to 15–20 ft. lbs. (20–27 Nm).

5. Fasten the starter cable and the relay connector to the motor. Tighten the starter cable nut to 80–119 inch lbs. (9–13.5 Nm).

6. Lower the vehicle, then connect the negative battery cable.

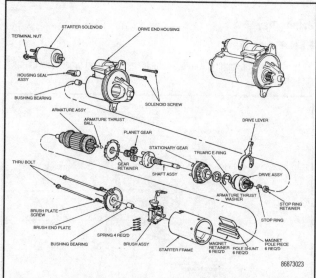

Fig. 21 Exploded view of starter motor assembly—3.8L wagon shown

**1992–95 Vehicles**

♦ **See Figure 22**

### ✳✳ CAUTION

**When performing any work on the starter, keep in mind that the heavy gauge input lead to the starter solenoid is hot at all times. To avoid, injury be sure that the protective cap is installed over the terminal and is replaced after any service.**

1. Disconnect the negative battery cable.

➡ **When the battery has been disconnected and reconnected, some abnormal driveability symptoms may occur while the PCM relearns its adaptive strategy. The vehicle may have to be driven 10 or more miles to relearn its strategy.**

2. Raise and safely support the vehicle.
3. Disengage the starter cable and the push-on connector from the starter solenoid.
4. Remove the upper and lower retaining bolts, then remove the starter motor from the vehicle.

**To install:**

5. Position the starter motor to the engine, then install the upper and lower retaining bolts finger-tight.
6. Tighten the retaining bolts to 15–20 ft. lbs. (20–27 Nm).
7. Engage the starter solenoid connector, making sure to push straight on until the connector locks in position. A noticeable click should be heard or detent felt.

8. Install the starter cable nut to the starter solenoid B terminal. Tighten the nut to 80–124 inch lbs. (9–14 Nm), then install the red starter solenoid safety cap.
9. Lower the vehicle, then connect the negative battery cable.

### STARTER RELAY REPLACEMENT

♦ **See Figures 23, 24 and 25**

1. Disconnect the negative battery cable.
2. Disengage the relay-to-ignition switch electrical connector.
3. Disconnect the nut retaining the relay-to-starter and relay-to-battery electrical connectors.
4. Disconnect the retaining screws, then remove the relay from the vehicle.

**To install:**

5. Position the relay in the vehicle, then install the retaining screws.
6. Fasten the nuts retaining the relay-to-starter and relay-to-battery electrical connectors. Tighten the nuts to 45–89 inch lbs. (5–10 Nm).
7. Engage the relay-to-ignition switch electrical connector.
8. Connect the negative battery cable.

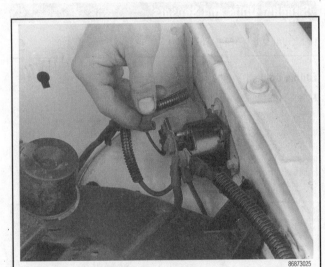

Fig. 23 Disengage the relay-to-ignition switch electrical connector—early model 2.5L shown

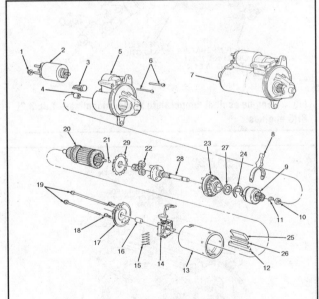

| | |
|---|---|
| 1 Terminal nut | 15 Brush spring |
| 2 Starter solenoid | 16 Bushing |
| 3 Housing seal | 17 Brush end plate and bushing |
| 4 Bushing | 18 Brush plate screw (2 req'd) |
| 5 Drive end housing | 19 Through-bolt (2 req'd) |
| 6 Solenoid screw (2 req'd) | 20 Starter motor armature |
| 7 Starter motor | 21 Armature thrust ball |
| 8 Drive lever and pin | 22 Planet gear |
| 9 Starter drive | 23 Stationary gear |
| 10 Stop ring retainer | 24 Truarc E-ring |
| 11 Starter drive stop ring | 25 Magnet pole piece (6 req'd) |
| 12 Magnet retainer (6 req'd) | 26 Pole shunt (6 req'd) |
| 13 Starter frame and magnet | 27 Pinion thrust washer |
| 14 Brush holder | 28 Output shaft |
| | 29 Planet gear retainer |

Fig. 22 Exploded view of the starter motor assembly—1992–95 vehicles

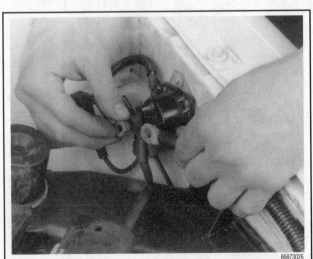

Fig. 24 Unfasten the nut retaining the starter and battery connections—early model 2.5L shown

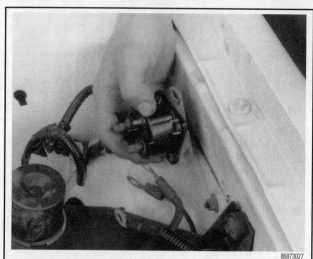

**Fig. 25 After disconnecting the retaining screws, remove the relay from the vehicle**

## Sending Units and Sensors

### REMOVAL & INSTALLATION

#### Engine Coolant Temperature (ECT) Sensor

▶ See Figures 26, 27 and 28

The engine coolant temperature sensor detects the temperature of the engine coolant and sends a signal, supplying this information to the Powertrain Control Module (PCM). It is located at the rear of the intake manifold for all engines except some 3.0L SHO engines and all 3.2L SHO engines. For the 3.0L and the 3.2L SHO engines, the sensor is located at the rear of

the right-hand side cylinder head, in the No. 1 water hose connection directly below the throttle body. The sensor signal is used to modify ignition timing, EGR flow and the air/fuel ratio as a function of the engine coolant temperature.

1. Disconnect the negative battery cable.
2. Drain the cooling system until its level is below that of the sensor. For information regarding this procedure, please refer to Section 1 of this manual.
3. Disengage the engine control sensor wiring from the coolant temperature sensor.
4. Remove the necessary components to gain access to the sensor assembly.
5. Using the proper size wrench or socket and ratchet, remove the sensor from its mounting.

**To install:**

6. Before installing, apply Pipe Sealant with Teflon®, D8AZ-19554-A or equivalent, on the sensor threads.
7. Install the sensor to the intake manifold or water hose connection as applicable. Tighten the sensor to 12–17 ft. lbs. (16–23 Nm).
8. Engage the electrical connector, then refill the cooling system to the correct level with a 50/50 mixture of Ford approved coolant and water.
9. Connect the negative battery cable, then start the engine and check the coolant level.

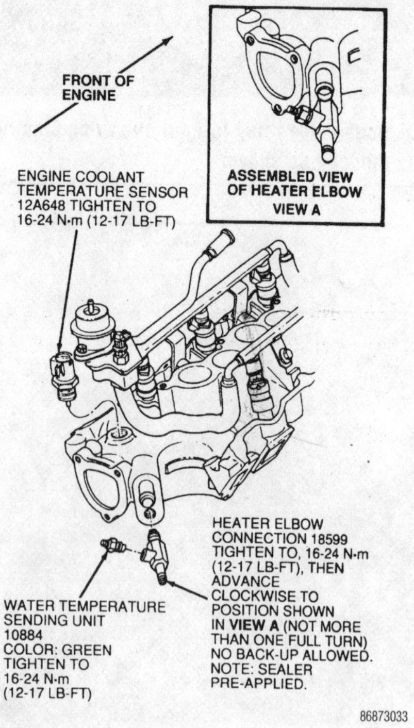

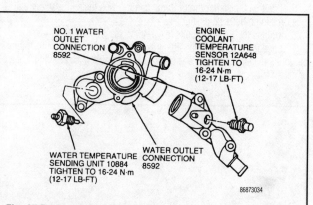

**Fig. 27 Engine coolant temperature sensor mounting—3.0L/3.2L SHO engines**

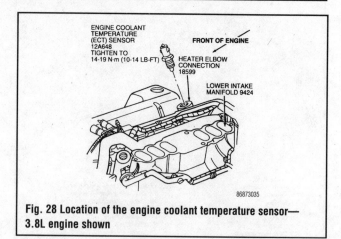

**Fig. 28 Location of the engine coolant temperature sensor— 3.8L engine shown**

#### Intake Air Temperature (IAT)/Air Charge Temperature (ACT) Sensor

▶ See Figures 29, 30, 31, 32 and 33

The intake air or air charge temperature sensor sends a signal to the PCM, indicating the temperature of air coming into the engine. It is located in the side of the throttle body or in the air cleaner assembly on late model vehicles. On early model vehicles, the sensor is located at the rear of the intake manifold, or on the side of the throttle body.

**Fig. 26 Location of the engine coolant temperature sensor— 3.0L engine shown, except SHO**

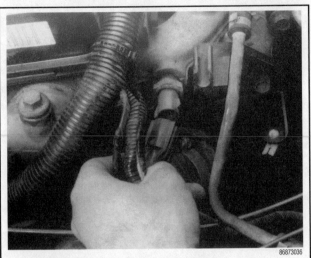

**Fig. 29 Disengage the IAT/ACT sensor electrical connector— early model 2.5L engine shown**

1. Disconnect the negative battery cable.
2. Disengage the electrical connector from the sensor.
3. To remove the sensor from the throttle body or intake manifold, unscrew the sensor, then remove it from the engine.
4. To remove the sensor from the air cleaner assembly, turn the sensor 90° counterclockwise, then remove it from the air cleaner cover or body, as applicable.

**To install:**

5. If applicable, install the sensor into the throttle body or intake manifold, then tighten it to 12–17 ft. lbs. (16–23 Nm).
6. If applicable, install the sensor into the air cleaner cover or body, being careful not to damage the plastic threads.
7. Engage the electrical connector, then connect the negative battery cable.

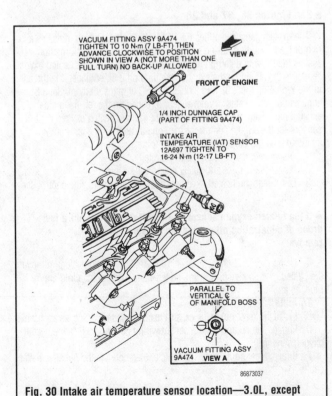

**Fig. 30 Intake air temperature sensor location—3.0L, except Flexible Fuel (FF) and SHO vehicles**

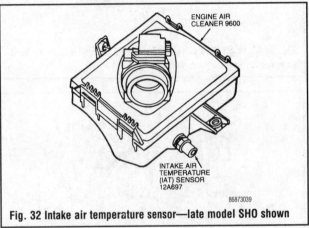

1 Engine air cleaner
2 LH front fender
3 Intake air temperature sensor
4 Air cleaner outlet tube
5 Throttle body

**Fig. 31 IAT sensor mounting—3.0L Flexible Fuel (FF) shown**

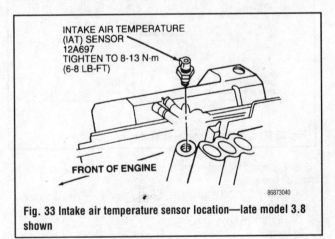

**Fig. 32 Intake air temperature sensor—late model SHO shown**

**Fig. 33 Intake air temperature sensor location—late model 3.8 shown**

## Mass Air Flow (MAF) Sensor

▶ **See Figures 34 and 35**

The mass air flow sensor sends a voltage signal to the PCM indicating the mass or amount of air coming into the engine. The PCM then uses this signal to calculate the fuel injector pulse time, to achieve the correct fuel/air mixture. The sensor is located between the engine air cleaner and the throttle body, or mounted on the top of the air cleaner assembly.

### 3.0L ENGINE—EXCEPT SHO

1. Disconnect the negative battery cable.
2. Remove the air cleaner outlet tube by loosening the retaining clamps, then tag and disconnect any hoses or tubes.

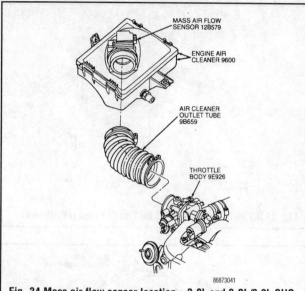

**Fig. 34 Mass air flow sensor location—3.0L and 3.0L/3.2L SHO engines**

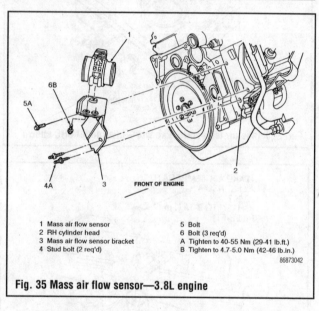

| | |
|---|---|
| 1 Mass air flow sensor | 5 Bolt |
| 2 RH cylinder head | 6 Bolt (3 req'd) |
| 3 Mass air flow sensor bracket | A Tighten to 40-55 Nm (29-41 lb.ft.) |
| 4 Stud bolt (2 req'd) | B Tighten to 4.7-5.0 Nm (42-46 lb.in.) |

86873042

**Fig. 35 Mass air flow sensor—3.8L engine**

3. Disengage the engine control sensor wiring connector from the mass air flow sensor.

4. Remove the four retaining bolts, then carefully remove the sensor from the vehicle.

5. Discard the mass air flow gasket.

**To install:**

6. Position the mass air flow sensor with a new gasket onto the air cleaner cover.

7. Install the four retaining bolts, then tighten them to 25 inch lbs. (3 Nm).

8. Install the air cleaner outlet tube by aligning the white identification mark on the tube with the tube stop on the throttle body, then tighten the retaining clamps to 24–48 inch lbs. (2.7–5.4 Nm).

9. Engage the engine control sensor wiring connector to the mass air flow sensor.

10. Connect the negative battery cable, then start the engine and check for vacuum leaks.

### 3.0L AND 3.2L SHO ENGINES

1. Disconnect the negative battery cable.

2. Remove the air cleaner outlet tube from the throttle body and the mass air flow sensor.

3. Disengage the engine control sensor wiring connector from the mass air flow sensor.

4. Remove the air cleaner cover from the air cleaner assembly.

5. Loosen the sensor-to-air cleaner cover seal clamp.

6. Remove the sensor retaining screws from the air cleaner cover, then remove the mass air flow sensor.

**To install:**

7. Install the mass air flow sensor and fasten using the retaining screws. Tighten the screws to 71–102 inch lbs. (8–11 Nm).

8. Secure the sensor-to-air cleaner cover seal clamp, then install the cover onto the air cleaner assembly.

9. Engage the engine control sensor wiring connector to the mass air flow sensor, then install the air cleaner outlet tube. Tighten the tube clamps to 12–18 inch lbs. (1.4–2.0 Nm).

10. Connect the negative battery cable.

### 3.8L ENGINE

1. Disconnect the negative battery cable.

2. Disengage the engine control sensor wiring connector from the mass air flow sensor.

3. Loosen the air cleaner tube clamps on the engine air outlet tube and the air cleaner outlet tube, then disconnect the tubes from the mass air flow sensor.

4. Remove the mass air flow sensor-to-mass air flow sensor bracket retaining bolt(s), then remove the sensor.

**To install:**

5. Install the sensor to the bracket and fasten using the retaining bolt(s). Tighten the bolt(s) to 42–46 inch lbs. (4.7–5.0 Nm).

6. Connect the air cleaner tubes to the mass air flow sensor, and tighten the clamps to 12–22 inch lbs. (1.4–2.5 Nm).

7. Engage the engine control sensor wiring connector to the mass air flow sensor.

8. Connect the negative battery cable.

### Heated Oxygen Sensor (HO$_2$S)

**♦ See Figures 36, 37 and 38**

The oxygen sensor supplies the PCM with a signal which indicates a rich or lean condition during engine operation. This input information assists the PCM in determining the proper air/fuel ratio. The heated oxygen sensor is threaded into the exhaust manifold on 2.5L engines. It is threaded in the Y-pipe on the 3.0L and 3.0L/3.2L SHO engines. Early model 3.8L engines utilize a heated oxygen sensor threaded on the left-hand side exhaust pipe. Later model 3.8L engines utilize two heated oxygen control sensors for the engine control system, one located on the left-hand exhaust manifold, and the other located on the Y-pipe.

1. Disconnect the negative battery cable.

2. If necessary, raise and safely support the vehicle.

3. Disengage the heated oxygen sensor(s) from the engine control sensor wiring.

➡**If the heated oxygen sensor is difficult to take off, put a few drops of penetrating oil around the sensor to aid in removal.**

4. Using Oxygen Sensor Wrench T94P-9472-A, or equivalent, remove the heated oxygen sensor(s) from the left-hand exhaust manifold and/or Y-pipe, as applicable.

**To install:**

5. Install the sensor(s) to the exhaust manifold and/or Y-pipe, as applicable.

6. Engage the engine control sensor wiring connector(s) to the heated oxygen sensor(s).

7. If raised, carefully lower the vehicle, then connect the negative battery cable.

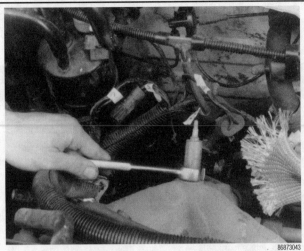

**Fig. 36 After disengaging the electrical connector, unscrew the heated oxygen sensor—2.5L engine shown**

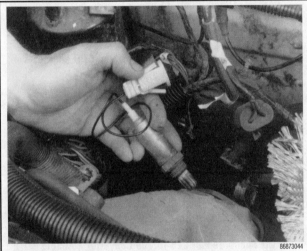

**Fig. 37 Remove the heated oxygen sensor from the vehicle—2.5L engine shown**

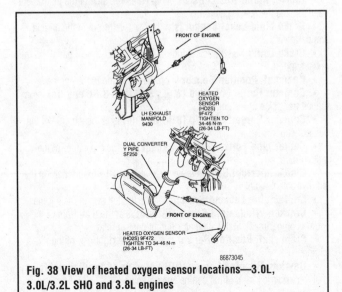

**Fig. 38 View of heated oxygen sensor locations—3.0L, 3.0L/3.2L SHO and 3.8L engines**

## Knock Sensor

### 3.0L AND 3.2L SHO ENGINES

♦ **See Figure 39**

The knock sensor detects spark knock or detonation, and if found, sends a signal to the PCM. After the PCM receives this signal, it will retard ignition timing as necessary to eliminate the knock/detonation. The knock sensor is located under the intake manifold and fuel injection rails.

1. Disconnect the negative battery cable.
2. Disengage the engine control sensor wiring connector from the knock sensor.
3. Carefully unthread the sensor, then remove it from the engine.

**To install:**

4. Install the sensor, then tighten it to 21–29 ft. lbs. (29–39 Nm).
5. Engage the electrical connector, then connect the negative battery cable.

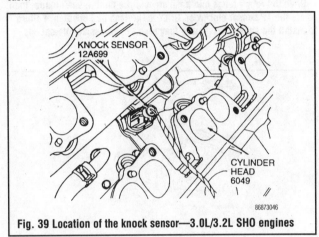

**Fig. 39 Location of the knock sensor—3.0L/3.2L SHO engines**

## Manifold Absolute Pressure (MAP) Sensor

♦ **See Figure 40**

The MAP sensor measures changes in manifold vacuum, resulting from changes in engine load and speed, then converts this to a voltage output. This gives the PCM information on engine load. It is used as a barometric sensor for altitude compensation, updating the PCM during key ON, engine OFF and every wide-open throttle. The PCM uses the MAP sensor for spark advance, EGR flow and air/fuel ratio.

1. Disconnect the negative battery cable.
2. Disengage the electrical connector and the vacuum line from the sensor.
3. Unfasten the sensor mounting bolts, then remove the sensor.

**To install:**

4. Install the MAP sensor using the retaining bolts.
5. Engage the vacuum line and the electrical connector to the sensor.
6. Connect the negative battery cable.

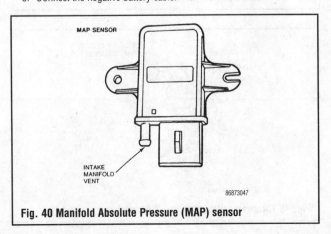

**Fig. 40 Manifold Absolute Pressure (MAP) sensor**

### Throttle Position (TP) Sensor

▶ **See Figures 41, 42 and 43**

The TP sensor is mounted to the throttle shaft and is used to supply a voltage output change proportional to the change in the throttle position. It is used by the ECU to determine engine operation mode: closed throttle, part throttle and wide-open throttle. The proper fuel mixture, spark and EGR will be output only when the operation mode has been determined correctly.

1. Disconnect the negative battery cable.
2. Make scribe marks on the throttle body and the throttle position sensor to indicated proper alignment during installation.
3. Disengage the electrical connector from the throttle position sensor.
4. Unfasten the mounting screws, then remove the sensor.

**To install:**

5. Install the throttle position sensor. Make sure that the rotary tangs on the sensor are in proper alignment and that the wires are pointing down.

➡**Slide the rotary tangs into position over the throttle shaft blade, then rotate the TP sensor clockwise ONLY to the installed position. Failure to install the sensor in this way may result in excessive idle speeds.**

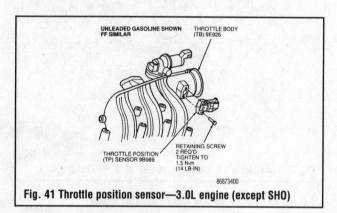

**Fig. 41 Throttle position sensor—3.0L engine (except SHO)**

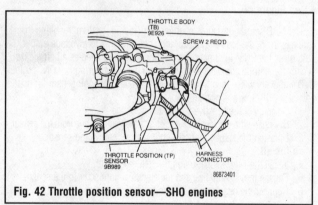

**Fig. 42 Throttle position sensor—SHO engines**

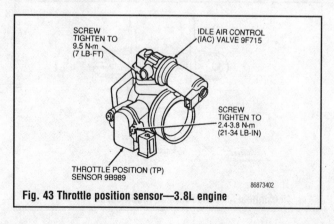

**Fig. 43 Throttle position sensor—3.8L engine**

6. Align the scribe marks on the throttle body and the TP sensor. Secure the sensor to the throttle body using the retaining screws.
7. Engage the throttle position sensor electrical connector.
8. Connect the negative battery cable.

## Relay, Sensor, Switch, Module and Computer Locations

• **A/C Clutch Cycling Pressure Switch (except SHO engine)** is at the right rear of the engine compartment, mounted on A/C accumulator.
• **A/C Clutch Cycling Pressure Switch (SHO engine)** is at the right front of the engine, mounted on the A/C accumulator.
• **Air Bag Backup Power Supply** is behind the right instrument panel, right side of the glove box.
• **Air Bag Diagnostic Module** is behind the center of the instrument panel.
• **Air Bag Rear Sensor** is inside the left kick panel.
• **Air Charge Temperature Sensor (2.5L engine)** is on the left rear of the intake manifold.
• **Air Charge Temperature Sensor (3.0L engine)** is on the top of the engine.
• **Air Charge Temperature Sensor (SHO engine)** is on the left side of the engine, in the air cleaner.
• **Alternator Output Control Relay** is between the right front inner fender and the fender splash shield.
• **Ambient Temperature Sensor** is at the left front of the engine compartment on the left side of the radiator.
• **Anti-Lock Brake Control Module (except SHO engine)** is at the right fender apron.
• **Anti-Lock Brake Control Module (SHO engine)** is at the lower left front of the engine compartment.
• **Anti-Lock Brake Diode** is on the left rear corner of the engine compartment, taped to the wiring harness.
• **Anti-Lock Motor Relay** is on the lower left front of the engine compartment.
• **Anti-Lock Power Relay** is at the left rear corner of the engine compartment.
• **Anti-Lock Test Connector** is at the left rear corner of the engine compartment.
• **Autolamp Dual Coil Relay** is behind the center of the instrument panel, mounted on a brace.
• **AXOD Speed Sensor and Torque Converter Solenoid** is at the lower left rear of the engine.
• **Barometric Absolute Pressure (BAP) Sensor** is on the right side of the firewall.
• **Blower Motor Resistors** are behind the right side of the instrument panel, inside the heater plenum.
• **Brake Fluid Level Sensor** is at the lower left front of the engine compartment.
• **Brake Lamp Switch** is behind the left-side instrument panel, on the pedal support.
• **Camshaft Position Sensor** is on the right side of the engine.
• **Canister Purge Solenoid (2.5L, 3.0L and 3.8L engine)** is on the left front side of the engine.
• **Canister Purge Solenoid (SHO engine)** is at the left side of the radiator support.
• **Center Line Forward Crash Sensor** is at the top center of the radiator support.
• **Clutch Interrupt Switch** is on the clutch pedal support, behind the left instrument panel.
• **Cold Engine Lockout Switch** is at the top left rear of the engine.
• **Cracked Windshield Sense Resistor** is at the right front of the engine compartment, at the alternator output control relay.
• **Crankshaft Position Sensor** is at the lower right rear of the engine.
• **Daytime Running Lamps (DRL) Module (Canadian vehicles)** is at the lower left front of the engine compartment.

- **Diagnostic Warning Module** is behind the right instrument panel, above the glove box.
- **Distributorless Ignition System (DIS) Module** is on the right side of the engine.
- **Door Ajar Switches** are at the door handle assemblies within the respective doors.
- **Driver's Seat Belt Switch** is within the left front seat belt assembly.
- **Dual Brake Warning Switch** is at the left rear of the engine compartment, within the brake master cylinder.
- **EGR Vacuum Regulator Solenoid (2.5L and 3.0L engine)** is at the right side of the engine compartment at the shock tower.
- **EGR Vacuum Regulator Solenoid (SHO engine)** is at the left rear of the engine compartment.
- **Electronic Automatic Temperature Control (EATC) Module** is behind the center of the instrument panel.
- **Electronic Engine Control (EEC) Module** is in the engine compartment, on the right side of the firewall.
- **Engine Coolant Temperature Sensor (2.5L engine)** is at the left rear of the engine, below the manifolds.
- **Engine Coolant Temperature Sensor (3.0L, 3.8L and SHO engine)** is at the top left side of the engine.
- **Fan Dropping Resistor (2.5L and 3.0L engine)** is at the left front of the engine.
- **Fan Dropping Resistor (SHO engine)** is at the center of the firewall.
- **Fog Light Relay** is behind the center of the instrument panel, mounted on a brace.
- **Fog Light Fuse** is behind the left side of the instrument panel, near the fuse panel.
- **Forward Crash Sensor** is inside the lower front of each front fender.
- **Fuel Pump** is inside the fuel tank.
- **Fuel Sender** is the inside fuel tank.
- **Fuse Panel** is behind the left lower instrument panel.
- **Heated Exhaust Gas Oxygen (HEGO) Sensor #1 (2.5L engine)** is at the center rear of the engine in the exhaust manifold.
- **Heated Exhaust Gas Oxygen (HEGO) Sensor #1 (3.0L engine)** is at the lower right front of the engine in the exhaust manifold.
- **Heated Exhaust Gas Oxygen (HEGO) Sensor #1 (3.8L engine)** is at the center rear of the engine in the exhaust manifold.
- **Heated Exhaust Gas Oxygen (HEGO) Sensor #1 (SHO engine)** is at the lower left rear of the engine in the exhaust manifold.
- **Heated Exhaust Gas Oxygen (HEGO) Sensor #2 (3.8L engine)** is at the lower right front of the engine in the exhaust manifold.
- **Heated Exhaust Gas Oxygen (HEGO) Sensor #2 (SHO engine)** is at the lower right front of the engine in the exhaust manifold.
- **Heated Windshield Control Module** is at the right side of the steering column, behind the instrument panel.
- **Heated Windshield Test Connector** is at the left rear of the engine compartment.
- **Horn Relay** is behind the center of the instrument panel, mounted on a brace.
- **Idle Air Control** is at the top rear of the engine.
- **Idle Speed Control (2.5L engine)** is at the top rear of the engine.
- **Ignition Suppressor Resistor (2.5L engine)** is on the left front of the engine, near the ignition coil.
- **Ignition Suppressor Resistor (3.0L and 3.8L engine)** is on the left side of the engine, near the ignition coil.
- **Illuminated Entry Module (Sedan)** is behind the rear seat, under the left side of the package tray.
- **Illuminated Entry Module (Wagon)** is inside the center of the left rear quarter panel.
- **In Car Temperature Sensor** is behind the top right side of the instrument panel.
- **Inertia Switch (Sedan)** is inside the front of the left rear quarter panel.
- **Inertia Switch (Wagon)** is inside the center of the rear quarter panel.

- **Integrated Control Module** is at the front of the engine compartment, on the radiator support.
- **Interval Wiper/Washer Module** is behind the center of the instrument panel, mounted on a brace.
- **Key Warning Switch** is contained within the ignition switch.
- **Keyless Entry Module (Sedan)** is behind the rear seat, under left side of the package tray.
- **Keyless Entry Module (Wagon)** is inside the center of the left rear quarter panel.
- **Knock Sensor (except SHO engine)** is at the center rear of the engine.
- **Knock Sensor (SHO engine)** is at the lower left front of the engine on the air cleaner assembly.
- **LCD Dimming Relay** is behind the center of the instrument panel, mounted on a brace.
- **Liftgate Ajar Switch** is at the lower center of the liftgate, part of the latch assembly.
- **Liftgate Mercury Switch** is inside the top of the liftgate.
- **Liftgate Release Relay** is at the right rear corner of the cargo area.
- **Liftgate Release Solenoid** is in the bottom of the liftgate.
- **Light Sensor/Amplifier** is attached to the underside of the right-side instrument panel.
- **Low Oil Level Relay** is behind the center of the instrument panel, mounted on a brace.
- **Low Oil Level Switch (2.5L engine)** is at the lower right rear of the engine.
- **Low Oil Level Switch (3.0L, 3.8L and SHO engine)** is at the lower center rear of the engine.
- **Low Washer Fluid Level Switch** is at the right front of the engine compartment, within the washer fluid reservoir.
- **Luggage Compartment Mercury Switch** is at the left front corner of the trunk lid, near the hinge.
- **Manifold Absolute Pressure (MAP) Sensor** is at the right side of the firewall.
- **Mass Air Flow Sensor** is on the top left side of the engine on the air cleaner assembly.
- **Moonroof Relay** is behind the right side of the instrument panel.
- **Neutral Safety Switch** is at the left side of the engine, on top of the transaxle.
- **Oil Pressure Switch (2.5L engine)** is at the center front of the engine, near the oil filter.
- **Oil Pressure Switch (3.0L engine)** is on the left side of the engine.
- **Oil Pressure Switch (3.8L engine)** is on the lower right side of the engine.
- **Oil Pressure Switch (SHO engine)** is at the lower left rear of the engine.
- **Pedal Position Switch** is behind the left side of the instrument panel, on the brake pedal support.
- **Police Accessory Circuit Breaker** is at the left side of the engine compartment, near the starter relay.
- **Police Accessory Relay** is behind the center of the instrument panel.
- **Power Steering Pressure Switch** is at the lower left rear of the engine.
- **Pressure Feedback EGR Sensor (2.5L engine)** is at the left rear of the engine.
- **Pressure Feedback EGR Sensor (3.0L engine)** is at the top right side of the engine.
- **Pressure Feedback EGR Sensor (3.8L and SHO engine)** is at the top left side of the engine.
- **Radiator Coolant Sensor** is at the right front of the engine compartment.
- **Radio Noise Capacitor (2.5L and 3.0L engine)** is at the left front of the engine, near the ignition coil.
- **Radio Noise Capacitor (3.8L engine)** is at the left rear of the engine, near the ignition coil.
- **Radio Noise Capacitor (SHO engine)** is at the top of the engine, at the left front.

- **Rear Courtesy Lamp Diode** is at the top left corner of the cargo compartment within the rear lamp harness.
- **Rear Defogger Relay and Timer** is inside the defogger switch housing.
- **Reverse Switch** is on the left side of the engine, on top of the transaxle.
- **Self Test Input Connector** is on the right rear of the engine compartment, near the EEC module.
- **Shorting Plug #1 (2.5L engine)** is at the center front of the engine.
- **Shorting Plug #1 (3.0L engine)** is at the left side of the engine.
- **Shorting Plug #1 (3.8L engine)** is at the right rear of the engine compartment.
- **Shorting Plug #1 (SHO engine)** is at the right rear side of the engine.
- **Shorting Plug #2 (SHO engine)** is at the center front of the engine compartment.
- **Solenoid Control Valve Body** is at the lower left front of the engine compartment.
- **Speed Control Servo** is on the left side of the engine compartment, on the shock tower.
- **Starter Relay** is on the left front fender apron, in front of the shock tower.
- **Stop Lamp Switch** is behind the left-side instrument panel, on the pedal support.
- **Sunload Sensor** is behind the top left side of the instrument panel.
- **TFI Ignition Module (2.5L engine)** is at the center front of the engine.
- **TFI Ignition Module (3.0L engine)** is at the top left side of the engine, connected to the distributor assembly.

- **TFI Ignition Module (3.8L engine)** is on the right side of the firewall.
- **Throttle Position Sensor (2.5L engine)** is at the rear center of the engine, on the right side of the injection assembly.
- **Throttle Position Sensor (3.0L engine)** is on the top left side of the engine.
- **Throttle Position Sensor (3.8L engine)** is on the top center of the engine.
- **Throttle Position Sensor (SHO engine)** is on the top left side of the engine compartment.
- **Trunk Release Solenoid** is at the right rear of the trunk lid, part of the trunk latch assembly.
- **Variable Assist Power Steering (VAPS) Module** is at the right side of the steering column, behind the instrument panel.
- **Variable Assist Power Steering (VAPS) Test Connector** is at the left rear of the engine compartment.
- **Variable Assist Stepper Motor** is at the lower left rear of the engine.
- **Vehicle Speed Sensor (2.5L engine)** is on the left rear of the transaxle.
- **Vehicle Speed Sensor (3.0L, 3.8L engine)** is at the center rear of the engine.
- **Vehicle Speed Sensor (SHO engine)** is at the lower left rear of the engine or mounted on the transaxle.
- **VIP Self-Test Output Connector** is at the right rear of the engine compartment, near the EEC module.
- **Voltage Regulator** is on the left front fender apron.
- **Warning Chime Module** is behind the lower left instrument panel.
- **Window Safety Relay** is behind the right kick panel.

## ENGINE MECHANICAL

### Engine Overhaul Tips

Most engine overhaul procedures are fairly standard. In addition to specific parts replacement procedures and specifications for your individual engine, this section is also a guide to acceptable rebuilding procedures. Examples of standard rebuilding practice are shown and should be used along with specific details concerning your particular engine.

Competent and accurate machine shop services will ensure maximum performance, reliability and engine life.

In most instances, it is more profitable for the do-it-yourself mechanic to remove, clean and inspect the component, buy the necessary parts and deliver these to a shop for actual machine work.

On the other hand, much of the rebuilding work (crankshaft, block, bearings, piston rods, and other components) is well within the scope of the do-it-yourself mechanic's tools and abilities. You will have to decide for yourself the depth of involvement you desire in an engine repair or rebuild.

### TOOLS

The tools required for an engine overhaul or parts replacement will depend on the depth of your involvement. With few exceptions, they will be the tools found in a mechanic's basic tool kit (see Section 1 of this manual). More in-depth work will require some or all of the following:
- a dial indicator (reading in thousandths) mounted on a universal base
- micrometers and telescoping gauges
- jaw and screw-type pullers
- scraper
- valve spring compressor
- ring groove cleaner
- piston ring expander and compressor
- ridge reamer
- cylinder hone or glaze breaker
- Plastigage®

- engine stand

The use of most of these tools is covered in this section. Many can be rented for a one-time use from a local parts jobber or tool supply house specializing in automotive work.

Occasionally, the use of special tools is called for. See the information on Special Tools and the Safety Notice in the front of this book before substituting another tool.

### INSPECTION TECHNIQUES

Procedures and specifications are given in this section for inspecting, cleaning and assessing the wear limits of most major components. Other procedures such as Magnaflux® and Zyglo® can be used to locate material flaws and stress cracks. Magnaflux® is a magnetic process applicable only to ferrous materials. The Zyglo® process coats the material with a fluorescent dye penetrant and can be used on any material. Checking for suspected surface cracks can be more readily made using spot check dye. The dye is sprayed onto the suspected area, wiped off and the area sprayed with a developer. Cracks will show up brightly.

### OVERHAUL TIPS

Aluminum has become extremely popular for use in engines, due to its low weight. Observe the following precautions when handling aluminum parts:
- Never hot tank aluminum part (the caustic hot tank solution will eat the aluminum).
- Remove all aluminum parts (identification tag, etc.) from engine parts prior to the tanking.
- Always coat threads lightly with engine oil or anti-seize compounds before installation, to prevent seizure.
- Never overtorque bolts or spark plugs, especially in aluminum threads.

When assembling the engine, any parts that will be exposed to frictional contact must be prelubed to provide lubrication at initial start-up. Any product specifically formulated for this purpose can be used, but engine oil is not recommended as a prelube in most cases.

When semi-permanent (locked, but removable) installation of bolts or nuts is desired, threads should be cleaned and coated with Loctite® or other similar, commercial non-hardening sealant.

## REPAIRING DAMAGED THREADS

▶ **See Figures 44, 45, 46, 47 and 48**

Several methods of repairing damaged threads are available. Heli-Coil® (shown here), Keenserts® and Microdot® are among the most widely used. All involve basically the same principle—drilling out stripped threads, tapping the hole and installing a prewound insert—making welding, plugging and oversize fasteners unnecessary.

Two types of thread repair inserts are usually supplied: a standard type for most Inch Coarse, Inch Fine, Metric Coarse and Metric Fine thread sizes, and a spark plug type to fit most spark plug port sizes. Consult the individual manufacturer's catalog to determine exact applications. Typical thread repair kits will contain a selection of prewound threaded inserts, a tap (corresponding to the outside diameter threads of the insert) and an installation tool. Spark plug inserts usually differ because they require a tap equipped with pilot threads and a combined reamer/tap section. Most manufacturers also supply blister-packed thread repair inserts separately, in addition to a master kit containing a variety of taps and inserts plus installation tools.

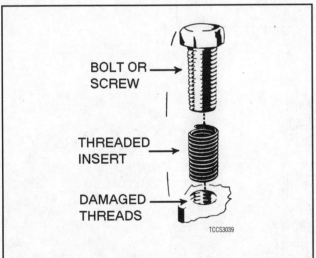

**Fig. 44 Damaged bolt hole threads can be replaced with thread repair inserts**

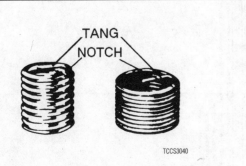

**Fig. 45 Standard thread repair insert (left), and spark plug thread insert**

Before effecting a repair to a threaded hole, remove any snapped, broken or damaged bolts or studs. Penetrating oil can be used to free frozen threads. The offending item can be removed with locking pliers or with a screw or stud extractor. After the hole is clear, the thread can be repaired, as shown in the series of accompanying illustrations and in the kit manufacturer's instructions.

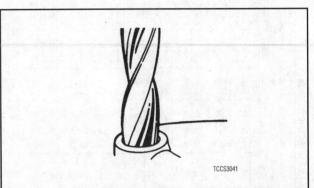

**Fig. 46 Drill out the damaged threads with the specified drill. Be sure to drill completely through the hole or to the bottom of a blind hole**

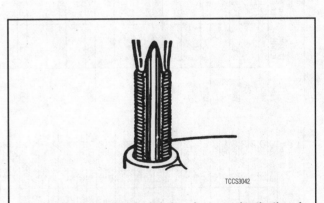

**Fig. 47 Using the kit, tap the hole in order to receive the thread insert. Keep the tap well oiled and back it out frequently to avoid clogging the threads**

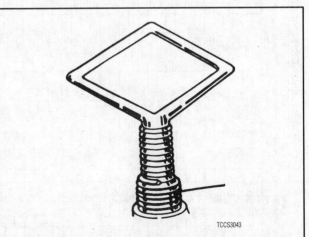

**Fig. 48 Screw the threaded insert onto the installer tool until the tang engages the slot. Thread the insert into the hole until it is ¼–½ turn below the top surface, then remove the tool and break off the tang using a punch**

## VALVE SPECIFICATIONS

| Year | Engine ID/VIN | Engine Displacement Liters (cc) | Seat Angle (deg.) | Face Angle (deg.) | Spring Test Pressure (lbs. @ in.) | Spring Installed Height (in.) | Stem-to-Guide Clearance (in.) Intake | Stem-to-Guide Clearance (in.) Exhaust | Stem Diameter (in.) Intake | Stem Diameter (in.) Exhaust |
|---|---|---|---|---|---|---|---|---|---|---|
| 1986 | D | 2.5 (2524) | 45 | 45 | 182 @ 1.13 | 1.490 | 0.0018 | 0.0023 | 0.3422 | 0.3418 |
|  | U | 3.0 (2971) | 45 | 44 | 185 @ 1.11 | 1.850 | 0.0001-0.0027 | 0.0015-0.0032 | 0.3126 | 0.3121 |
| 1987 | D | 2.5 (2524) | 45 | 45 | 182 @ 1.13 | 1.490 | 0.0018 | 0.0023 | 0.3422 | 0.3418 |
|  | U | 3.0 (2971) | 45 | 44 | 185 @ 1.11 | 1.580 | 0.0001-0.0027 | 0.0015-0.0032 | 0.3126 | 0.3121 |
| 1988 | D | 2.5 (2524) | 45 | 45 | 182 @ 1.13 | 1.490 | 0.0018 | 0.0023 | 0.3.422 | 0.3418 |
|  | U | 3.0 (2971) | 45 | 44 | 180 @ 1.16 | 1.580 | 0.0001-0.0027 | 0.0015-0.0032 | 0.3126 | 0.3121 |
|  | 4 | 3.8 (3802) | 44.5 | 45.8 | 190 @ 128 | 2.020 | 0.0010-0.0028 | 0.0015-0.0033 | 0.3415-0.3423 | 0.3410-0.3418 |
| 1989 | D | 2.5 (2524) | 45 | 45 | 182 @ 1.13 | 1.490 | 0.0018 | 0.0023 | 0.3422 | 0.3418 |
|  | U | 3.0 (2971) | 45 | 44 | 180 @ 1.16 | 1.580 | 0.0001-0.0028 | 0.0015-0.0033 | 0.3126 | 0.3121 |
|  | Y | 3.0 (2980) | 45 | 45.5 | 121 @ 1.19 | 1.760 [1] | 0.0010-0.0023 | 0.0012-0.0025 | 0.2346-0.2352 | 0.2344-0.2350 |
|  | 4 | 3.8 (3802) | 44.5 | 45.8 | 220 @ 118 | 1.970 | 0.0010-0.0028 | 0.0015-0.0033 | 0.3415-0.3423 | 0.3410-0.3418 |
| 1990 | D | 2.5 (2501) | 45 | 45 | 182 @ 1.13 | 1.490 | 0.0018 | 0.0023 | 0.3422 | 0.3418 |
|  | U | 3.0 (2971) | 45 | 44 | 180 @ 1.16 | 1.580 | 0.0001-0.0028 | 0.0015-0.0033 | 0.3126 | 0.3121 |
|  | Y | 3.0 (2980) | 45 | 45.5 | 121 @ 1.19 | 1.760 [1] | 0.0010-0.0023 | 0.0012-0.0025 | 0.2346-0.2352 | 0.2344-0.2350 |
|  | 4 | 3.8 (3802) | 44.5 | 45.8 | 220 @ 1.18 | 1.970 | 0.0010-0.0028 | 0.0015-0.0033 | 0.3415-0.3423 | 0.3410-0.3418 |
| 1991 | Y | 3.0 (2980) | 45 | 45.5 | 121 @ 1.19 | 1.760 [1] | 0.0010-0.0023 | 0.0012-0.0025 | 0.2346-0.2352 | 0.2344-0.2350 |
|  | 4 | 3.8 (3802) | 44.5 | 45.8 | 220 @ 1.18 | 1.970 | 0.0010-0.0028 | 0.0015-0.0033 | 0.3415-0.3423 | 0.3410-0.3418 |
| 1992 | U | 3.0 (2971) | 45 | 44 | 180 @ 1.16 | 1.580 | 0.0001-0.0028 | 0.0015-0.0033 | 0.3126 | 0.3121 |
|  | Y | 3.0 (2980) | 45 | 45.5 | 121 @ 1.19 | 1.520 | 0.0010-0.0023 | 0.0012-0.0025 | 0.2346-0.2352 | 0.2344-0.2350 |
| 1993 | P | 3.2 (3191) | 45 | 45.5 | 121 @ 1.19 | 1.520 | 0.0010-0.0023 | 0.0012-0.0025 | 0.2346-0.2352 | 0.2344-0.2350 |
|  | 4 | 3.8 (3802) | 44.5 | 45.8 | 220 @ 1.18 | 1.970 | 0.0010-0.0028 | 0.0015-0.0033 | 0.3415-0.3423 | 0.3410-0.3418 |

86873301

## GENERAL ENGINE SPECIFICATIONS

| Year | Engine ID/VIN | Engine Displacement Liters (cc) | Fuel System Type | Net Horsepower @ rpm | Net Torque @ rpm (ft. lbs.) | Bore x Stroke (in.) | Compression Ratio | Oil Pressure @ rpm |
|---|---|---|---|---|---|---|---|---|
| 1986 | D | 2.5 (2524) | CFI | 88@4600 | 130@2800 | 3.70 x 3.60 | 9.7:1 | 55-70@2000 |
|  | U | 3.0 (2971) | EFI | 140@4600 | 160@3000 | 3.50 x 3.10 | 9.3:1 | 55-70@2000 |
| 1987 | D | 2.5 (2524) | CFI | 88@4600 | 130@2800 | 3.70 x 3.60 | 9.7:1 | 55-70@2000 |
|  | U | 3.0 (2971) | EFI | 140@4600 | 160@2800 | 3.50 x 3.10 | 9.3:1 | 55-70@2000 |
| 1988 | D | 2.5 (2524) | EFI | 88@4600 | 130@2800 | 3.70 x 3.60 | 9.7:1 | 55-70@2000 |
|  | U | 3.0 (2971) | EFI | 140@4800 | 160@3000 | 3.50 x 3.10 | 9.3:1 | 55-70@2000 |
|  | 4 | 3.8 (3802) | EFI | 120@3600 | 205@1600 | 3.81 x 3.39 | 8.7:1 | 40-60@2000 |
| 1989 | D | 2.5 (2524) | CFI | 88@4600 | 130@2800 | 3.70 x 3.60 | 9.7:1 | 55-70@2000 |
|  | U | 3.0 (2971) | EFI | 140@4800 | 160@3000 | 3.50 x 3.10 | 9.3:1 | 55-70@2000 |
|  | Y | 3.0 (2971) | SFI | 220@6200 | 200@4800 | 3.50 x 3.15 | 9.8:1 | 40-60@2000 |
|  | 4 | 3.8 (3802) | EFI | 120@3600 | 205@1600 | 3.81 x 3.39 | 8.7:1 | 40-60@2000 |
| 1990 | D | 2.5 (2524) | CFI | 88@4600 | 130@2800 | 3.70 x 3.60 | 9.7:1 | 55-70@2000 |
|  | U | 3.0 (2971) | EFI | 140@4800 | 160@3000 | 3.50 x 3.15 | 9.8:1 | 40-65@2000 |
|  | Y | 3.0 (2971) | SFI | 220@6200 | 200@4800 | 3.50 x 3.15 | 9.8:1 | 40-60@2000 |
|  | 4 | 3.8 (3802) | EFI | 140@3800 | 215@2400 | 3.81 x 3.39 | 8.7:1 | 40-60@2000 |
| 1991 | U | 3.0 (2971) | EFI | 140@4800 | 160@3000 | 3.50 x 3.15 | 9.8:1 | 40-65@2000 |
|  | Y | 3.0 (2971) | SFI | 220@6200 | 200@4800 | 3.50 x 3.15 | 8.2:1 | 40-60@2000 |
|  | P | 3.2 (3191) | SFI | 140@3800 | 215@2400 | 3.62 x 3.15 | 9.8:1 | 40-60@2000 |
|  | 4 | 3.8 (3802) | SFI | 140@3800 | 215@2400 | 3.81 x 3.39 | 8.2:1 | 40-60@2000 |
| 1992 | U | 3.0 (2971) | EFI | 140@4800 | 160@3000 | 3.50 x 3.15 | 9.8:1 | 55-70@2500 |
|  | Y | 3.0 (2971) | SFI | 220@6200 | 200@4800 | 3.50 x 3.15 | 8.2:1 | 40-60@2000 |
|  | P | 3.2 (3191) | SFI | 140@3800 | 215@2400 | 3.62 x 3.15 | 9.3:2 | 40-60@2000 |
|  | 4 | 3.8 (3802) | SFI | 140@3800 | 215@2400 | 3.81 x 3.39 | 9.8:1 | 40-60@2000 |
| 1993 | U | 3.0 (2971) | EFI | 140@4800 | 160@3000 | 3.50 x 3.15 | 8.2:1 | 55-70@2000 |
|  | Y | 3.0 (2980) | SFI | 220@6200 | 200@4800 | 3.50 x 3.15 | 9.8:1 | 40-65@2000 |
|  | P | 3.2 (3191) | SFI | 140@3800 | 215@2400 | 3.62 x 3.15 | 9.3:2 | 40-60@2000 |
|  | 4 | 3.8 (3802) | SFI | 140@3800 | 215@2400 | 3.81 x 3.39 | 8.2:1 | 40-60@2000 |
| 1994 | U | 3.0 (2971) | SFI | 140@4800 | 160@3000 | 3.50 x 3.15 | 9.8:1 | 55-70@2500 |
|  | Y | 3.0 (2980) | SFI | 220@6200 | 200@4800 | 3.50 x 3.15 | 8.2:1 | 40-60@2500 |
|  | P | 3.2 (3191) | SFI | 140@3800 | 215@2400 | 3.62 x 3.15 | 9.3:2 | 40-60@2000 |
|  | 4 | 3.8 (3802) | SFI | 140@3800 | 215@2400 | 3.81 x 3.39 | 9.8:1 | 40-60@2000 |
| 1995 | U | 3.0 (2971) | SFI | 140@4800 | 160@3000 | 3.50 x 3.15 | 8.2:1 | 55-70@2500 |
|  | Y | 3.0 (2980) | SFI | 220@6200 | 200@4800 | 3.50 x 3.15 | 9.8:1 | 40-60@2000 |
|  | P | 3.2 (3191) | SFI | 140@3800 | 215@2400 | 3.62 x 3.15 | 9.8:1 | 40-60@2000 |
|  | 4 | 3.8 (3802) | SFI | 140@3800 | 215@2400 | 3.81 x 3.39 | 9.0:1 | 40-60@2500 |

NOTE: Horsepower and torque and SAE net figures. They are measured at the rear of the transmission with all accessories installed and operating. Since the figures vary when a given engine is installed in different models, some are representative rather than exact.

EFI - Electronic fuel injection
CFI - Central fuel injection
SFI - Sequential fuel injection

86873300

## CAMSHAFT SPECIFICATIONS

All measurements given in inches.

| Year | Engine ID/VIN | Engine Displacement Liters (cc) | Journal Diameter 1 | 2 | 3 | 4 | 5 | Elevation In. | Ex. | Bearing Clearance | Camshaft End Play |
|---|---|---|---|---|---|---|---|---|---|---|---|
| 1986 | D | 2.5 (2524) | 2.006-2.008 | 2.006-2.008 | 2.006-2.008 | 2.006-2.008 | 2.006-2.008 | 0.249 | 0.239 | 0.001-0.003 | 0.009 |
| | U | 3.0 (2980) | 2.0074-2.0084 | 2.0074-2.0084 | 2.0074-2.0084 | 2.0074-2.0084 | NA | 0.260 | 0.260 | 0.001-0.003 | [1] |
| 1987 | D | 2.5 (2524) | 2.006-2.008 | 2.006-2.008 | 2.006-2.008 | 2.006-2.008 | 2.006-2.008 | 0.249 | 0.239 | 0.001-0.003 | 0.009 |
| | U | 3.0 (2980) | 2.0074-2.0084 | 2.0074-2.0084 | 2.0074-2.0084 | 2.0074-2.0084 | NA | 0.260 | 0.260 | 0.001-0.003 | 0.005 |
| 1988 | D | 2.5 (2524) | 2.006-2.008 | 2.006-2.008 | 2.006-2.008 | 2.006-2.008 | 2.006-2.008 | 0.249 | 0.239 | 0.001-0.003 | 0.009 |
| | U | 3.0 (2980) | 2.0074-2.0084 | 2.0074-2.0084 | 2.0074-2.0084 | 2.0074-2.0084 | NA | 0.260 | 0.260 | 0.001-0.003 | 0.005 |
| | 4 | 3.8 (3802) | 2.0505-2.0515 | 2.0505-2.0515 | 2.0505-2.0515 | 2.0505-2.0515 | 2.0505-2.0515 | 0.240 | 0.241 | 0.001-0.003 | [1] |
| 1989 | D | 2.5 (2524) | 2.006-2.008 | 2.006-2.008 | 2.006-2.008 | 2.006-2.008 | 2.006-2.008 | 0.249 | 0.239 | 0.001-0.003 | 0.009 |
| | D | 3.0 (2980) | 2.0074-2.0084 | 2.0074-2.0084 | 2.0074-2.0084 | 2.0074-2.0084 | 2.0074-2.0084 | 0.260 | 0.260 | 0.001-0.003 | 0.005 |
| | Y | 3.0 (2980) | 1.2189-1.2195 | 1.2189-1.2195 | 1.2189-1.2195 | 1.2189-1.2195 | 1.2189-1.2195 | 0.335 | 0.315 | 0.0010-0.0026 | 0.012 |
| | 4 | 3.8 (3802) | 2.0505-2.0515 | 2.0505-2.0515 | 2.0505-2.0515 | 2.0505-2.0515 | 2.0505-2.0515 | 0.245 | 0.259 | 0.001-0.003 | 0.005 |
| 1990 | D | 2.5 (2524) | 2.006-2.008 | 2.006-2.008 | 2.006-2.008 | 2.006-2.008 | 2.006-2.008 | 0.249 | 0.239 | 0.001-0.003 | 0.009 |
| | Y | 3.0 (2971) | 1.2189-1.2195 | 1.2189-1.2195 | 1.2189-1.2195 | 1.2189-1.2195 | 1.2189-1.2195 | 0.335 | 0.315 | 0.0010-0.0026 | 0.012 |
| | U | 3.0 (2980) | 2.0074-2.0084 | 2.0074-2.0084 | 2.0074-2.0084 | 2.0074-2.0084 | NA | 0.260 | 0.260 | 0.001-0.003 | 0.005 |
| | 4 | 3.8 (3802) | 2.0505-2.0515 | 2.0505-2.0515 | 2.0505-2.0515 | 2.0505-2.0515 | 2.0505-2.0515 | 0.245 | 0.259 | 0.001-0.003 | 0.001-0.006 |
| 1991 | D | 2.5 (2524) | 2.006-2.008 | 2.006-2.008 | 2.006-2.008 | 2.006-2.008 | 2.006-2.008 | 0.249 | 0.239 | 0.001-0.003 | 0.009 |
| | Y | 3.0 (2980) | 1.2189-1.2195 | 1.2189-1.2195 | 1.2189-1.2195 | 1.2189-1.2195 | 1.2189-1.2195 | 0.335 | 0.315 | 0.0010-0.0026 | 0.012 |
| | U | 3.0 (2980) | 2.0074-2.0084 | 2.0074-2.0084 | 2.0074-2.0084 | 2.0074-2.0084 | NA | 0.260 | 0.260 | 0.001-0.003 | 0.005 |
| | 4 | 3.8 (3802) | 2.0505-2.0515 | 2.0505-2.0515 | 2.0505-2.0515 | 2.0505-2.0515 | 2.0505-2.0515 | 0.245 | 0.259 | 0.001-0.003 | 0.001-0.006 |
| 1992 | U | 3.0 (2980) | 2.0074-2.0084 | 2.0074-2.0084 | 2.0074-2.0084 | 2.0074-2.0084 | NA | 0.255-0.260 | 0.255-0.260 | 0.001-0.003 | [1] |
| | Y | 3.0 (2980) | 1.2189-1.2195 | 1.2189-1.2195 | 1.2189-1.2195 | 1.2189-1.2195 | 1.2189-1.2195 | 0.335 | 0.315 | 0.0010-0.0026 | 0.012 |
| | 4 | 3.8 (3802) | 2.0505-2.0515 | 2.0505-2.0515 | 2.0505-2.0515 | 2.0505-2.0515 | 2.0505-2.0515 | 0.245 | 0.259 | 0.001-0.003 | 0.001-0.006 |

86873303

## VALVE SPECIFICATIONS

| Year | Engine ID/VIN | Engine Displacement Liters (cc) | Seat Angle (deg.) | Face Angle (deg.) | Spring Test Pressure (lbs. @ in.) | Spring Installed Height (in.) | Stem-to-Guide Clearance (in.) Intake | Exhaust | Stem Diameter (in.) Intake | Exhaust |
|---|---|---|---|---|---|---|---|---|---|---|
| 1994 | U | 3.0 (2971) | 45 | 44 | 180 @ 1.16 | 1.580 | 0.0001-0.0028 | 0.0015-0.0033 | 0.3126-0.3134 | 0.3121-0.3129 |
| | Y | 3.0 (2980) | 45 | 45.5 | 121 @ 1.19 | 1.760 [1] | 0.0010-0.0023 | 0.0012-0.0025 | 0.2346-0.2352 | 0.2344-0.2350 |
| | P | 3.2 (3191) | 45 | 45.5 | 121 @ 1.19 | 1.760 [1] | 0.0010-0.0023 | 0.0012-0.0025 | 0.2346-0.2352 | 0.2344-0.2350 |
| | 4 | 3.8 (3802) | 44.5 | 45.8 | 220 @ 1.18 | 1.970 | 0.0010-0.0028 | 0.0015-0.0033 | 0.3415-0.3423 | 0.3410-0.3418 |
| 1995 | U | 3.0 (2980) | 45 | 44 | 180 @ 1.16 | 1.580 | 0.0001-0.0028 | 0.0015-0.0033 | 0.3126-0.3134 | 0.3121-0.3129 |
| | Y | 3.0 (2980) | 45 | 45.5 | 121 @ 1.19 | 1.760 [1] | 0.0010-0.0023 | 0.0012-0.0025 | 0.2346-0.2352 | 0.2344-0.2350 |
| | P | 3.2 (3191) | 45 | 45.5 | 121 @ 1.19 | 1.760 [1] | 0.0010-0.0023 | 0.0012-0.0025 | 0.2346-0.2352 | 0.2344-0.2350 |
| | 4 | 3.8 (3802) | 44.5 | 45.8 | 220 @ 1.18 | 1.970 | 0.0010-0.0028 | 0.0015-0.0033 | 0.3415-0.3423 | 0.3410-0.3418 |

1: Approximate Free Length

86873302

## CRANKSHAFT AND CONNECTING ROD SPECIFICATIONS

All measurements are given in inches.

| Year | Engine ID/VIN | Engine Displacement Liters (cc) | Main Brg. Journal Dia. | Crankshaft Main Brg. Oil Clearance | Crankshaft Shaft End-play | Crankshaft Thrust on No. | Connecting Rod Journal Diameter | Connecting Rod Oil Clearance | Connecting Rod Side Clearance |
|---|---|---|---|---|---|---|---|---|---|
| 1986 | D | 2.5 (2501) | 2.2489-2.2490 | 0.0008-0.0015 | 0.004-0.008 | 3 | 2.1232-2.1240 | 0.0008-0.0014 | 0.0035-0.0105 |
|  | U | 3.0 (2971) | 2.5190-2.5198 | 0.0010-0.0014 | 0.004-0.008 | 3 | 2.1240 | 0.0010-0.0014 | 0.006-0.014 |
| 1987 | D | 2.5 (2501) | 2.2489-2.2490 | 0.0008-0.0015 | 0.004-0.008 | 3 | 2.1232-2.1240 | 0.0008-0.0014 | 0.0035-0.0105 |
|  | U | 3.0 (2971) | 2.5190-2.5198 | 0.0010-0.0014 | 0.004-0.008 | 3 | 2.1240 | 0.0010-0.0014 | 0.006-0.014 |
| 1988 | D | 2.5 (2501) | 2.2489-2.2490 | 0.0008-0.0015 | 0.004-0.008 | 3 | 2.1232-2.1240 | 0.0008-0.0014 | 0.0035-0.0105 |
|  | U | 3.0 (2971) | 2.5190-2.5198 | 0.0010-0.0014 | 0.004-0.008 | 3 | 2.1253-2.1261 | 0.0010-0.0014 | 0.006-0.014 |
|  | 4 | 3.8 (3802) | 2.5190-2.5198 | 0.0010-0.0014 | 0.004-0.008 | 3 | 2.3103-2.3111 | 0.0010-0.0014 | 0.0047-0.0114 |
| 1989 | D | 2.5 (2501) | 2.2489-2.2490 | 0.0008-0.0015 | 0.004-0.008 | 3 | 2.1232-2.1240 | 0.0008-0.0014 | 0.0035-0.0105 |
|  | Y | 3.0 (2980) | 2.5187-2.5197 | 0.0011-0.0022 | 0.0008-0.0087 | 3 | 2.0463-2.0472 | 0.0009-0.0022 | 0.0063-0.0123 |
|  | U | 3.0 (1971) | 2.5190-2.5198 | 0.0010-0.0014 | 0.004-0.008 | 3 | 2.1253-2.1261 | 0.0010-0.0014 | 0.006-0.014 |
|  | 4 | 3.8 (3802) | 2.5190-2.5198 | 0.0010-0.0014 | 0.004-0.008 | 3 | 2.3103-2.3111 | 0.0010-0.0014 | 0.0047-0.0114 |
| 1990 | D | 2.5 (2501) | 2.2489-2.2490 | 0.0008-0.0015 | 0.004-0.008 | 3 | 2.1232-2.1240 | 0.0008-0.0014 | 0.0035-0.0105 |
|  | Y | 3.0 (2980) | 2.5187-2.5197 | 0.0011-0.0022 | 0.0008-0.0087 | 3 | 2.0463-2.0472 | 0.0009-0.0022 | 0.0063-0.0123 |
|  | U | 3.0 (2971) | 2.5190-2.5198 | 0.0010-0.0014 | 0.004-0.008 | 3 | 2.1253-2.1261 | 0.0010-0.0014 | 0.006-0.014 |
|  | 4 | 3.8 (3802) | 2.5189-2.5198 | 0.0010-0.0014 | 0.004-0.008 | 3 | 2.3103-2.3111 | 0.0010-0.0014 | 0.0047-0.0114 |
| 1991 | D | 2.5 (2501) | 2.2489-2.2490 | 0.0008-0.0015 | 0.004-0.008 | 3 | 2.1232-2.1240 | 0.0008-0.0014 | 0.0035-0.0105 |
|  | Y | 3.0 (2980) | 2.5187-2.5197 | 0.0011-0.0022 | 0.0008-0.0087 | 3 | 2.0463-2.0472 | 0.0009-0.0022 | 0.0063-0.0123 |
|  | U | 3.0 (2971) | 2.5190-2.5198 | 0.0010-0.0014 | 0.004-0.008 | 3 | 2.1253-2.1261 | 0.0010-0.0014 | 0.006-0.014 |
| 1992 | D | 2.5 (2501) | 2.2489-2.2490 | 0.0008-0.0015 | 0.004-0.008 | 3 | 2.1232-2.1240 | 0.0008-0.0014 | 0.0035-0.0105 |
|  | Y | 3.0 (2980) | 2.5187-2.5197 | 0.0011-0.0022 | 0.0008-0.0087 | 3 | 2.0463-2.0472 | 0.0009-0.0022 | 0.0063-0.0123 |
|  | 4 | 3.8 (3802) | 2.5190-2.5198 | 0.0010-0.0014 | 0.004-0.008 | 3 | 2.3103-2.3111 | 0.0010-0.0014 | 0.0047-0.0114 |
| 1993 | U | 3.0 (2971) | 2.5190-2.5198 | 0.0010-0.0014 | 0.004-0.008 | 3 | 2.1253-2.1261 | 0.0010-0.0014 | 0.006-0.014 |

86873305

## CAMSHAFT SPECIFICATIONS

All measurements given in inches.

| Year | Engine ID/VIN | Engine Displacement Liters (cc) | Journal Diameter 1 | 2 | 3 | 4 | 5 | Elevation In. | Elevation Ex. | Bearing Clearance | Camshaft End Play |
|---|---|---|---|---|---|---|---|---|---|---|---|
| 1993 | U | 3.0 (2980) | 2.0074-2.0084 | 2.0074-2.0084 | 2.0074-2.0084 | 2.0074-2.0084 | NA | 0.255-0.260 | 0.255-0.260 | 0.001-0.003 | 0.005 |
|  | Y | 3.0 (2980) | 1.2189-1.2195 | 1.2189-1.2195 | 1.2189-1.2195 | 1.2189-1.2195 | 1.2189-1.2195 | 0.335 | 0.315 | 0.0010-0.0026 | 0.012 |
|  | P | 3.2 (3191) | 1.2189-1.2195 | 1.2189-1.2195 | 1.2189-1.2195 | 1.2189-1.2195 | 1.2189-1.2195 | 0.315 | 0.315 | 0.0010-0.0026 | 0.012 |
|  | 4 | 3.8 (3802) | 2.0505-2.0515 | 2.0505-2.0515 | 2.0505-2.0515 | 2.0505-2.0515 | 2.0505-2.0515 | 0.245 | 0.259 | 0.001-0.003 | 0.001-0.006 |
| 1994 | U | 3.0 (2980) | 2.0074-2.0084 | 2.0074-2.0084 | 2.0074-2.0084 | 2.0074-2.0084 | 2.0074-2.0084 | 0.2550-0.2600 | 0.2550-0.2600 | 0.001-0.003 | 0.001-0.006 |
|  | Y | 3.0 (2980) | 1.2189-1.2195 | 1.2189-1.2195 | 1.2189-1.2195 | 1.2189-1.2195 | 1.2189-1.2195 | 0.3350 | 0.3150 | 0.0010-0.0026 | 0.001-0.005 |
|  | P | 3.2 (3191) | 1.2189-1.2195 | 1.2189-1.2195 | 1.2189-1.2195 | 1.2189-1.2195 | 1.2189-1.2195 | 0.3150 | 0.3150 | 0.0010-0.0030 | 0.0012 |
|  | 4 | 3.8 (3802) | 2.0505-2.0515 | 2.0505-2.0515 | 2.0505-2.0515 | 2.0505-2.0515 | 2.0505-2.0515 | 0.2400-0.2450 | 0.2540-0.2590 | 0.0010-0.0026 | 0.0012 |
| 1995 | U | 3.0 (2980) | 2.0074-2.0084 | 2.0074-2.0084 | 2.0074-2.0084 | 2.0074-2.0084 | 2.0074-2.0084 | 0.2550-0.2600 | 0.2550-0.2600 | 0.0010-0.0030 | 0.0010-0.0050 |
|  | Y | 3.0 (2980) | 1.2189-1.2195 | 1.2189-1.2195 | 1.2189-1.2195 | 1.2189-1.2195 | 1.2189-1.2195 | 0.3550 | 0.3150 | 0.0010-0.0030 | 0.0012 |
|  | P | 3.2 (3191) | 1.2189-1.2195 | 1.2189-1.2195 | 1.2189-1.2195 | 1.2189-1.2195 | 1.2189-1.2195 | 0.3150 | 0.3150 | 0.0010-0.0026 | 0.0012 |
|  | 4 | 3.8 (3802) | 2.0505-2.0515 | 2.0505-2.0515 | 2.0505-2.0515 | 2.0505-2.0515 | 2.0505-2.0515 | 0.2400-0.2450 | 0.2540-0.2590 | 0.0010-0.0030 | 0.0010-0.0060 |

NA - Not Available

1 Endplay is controlled by button and spring on camshaft end

86873304

## PISTON AND RING SPECIFICATIONS

All measurements are given in inches.

| Year | Engine ID/VIN | Engine Displacement Liters (cc) | Piston Clearance | Ring Gap Top Compression | Ring Gap Bottom Compression | Ring Gap Oil Control | Ring Side Clearance Top Compression | Ring Side Clearance Bottom Compression | Ring Side Clearance Oil Control |
|---|---|---|---|---|---|---|---|---|---|
| 1986 | D | 2.5 (2524) | 0.0012-0.0022 | 0.008-0.016 | 0.008-0.016 | 0.015-0.055 | 0.002-0.004 | 0.002-0.004 | SNUG |
|  | U | 3.0 (2971) | 0.0012-0.0023 | 0.010-0.020 | 0.010-0.020 | 0.010-0.049 | 0.0016-0.0037 | 0.0016-0.0037 | SNUG |
| 1987 | D | 2.5 (2524) | 0.0012-0.0022 | 0.008-0.016 | 0.008-0.016 | 0.015-0.055 | 0.002-0.004 | 0.002-0.004 | SNUG |
|  | U | 3.0 (2971) | 0.0014-0.0022 | 0.010-0.020 | 0.010-0.020 | 0.010-0.049 | 0.0012-0.0031 | 0.0012-0.0031 | SNUG |
| 1988 | D | 2.5 (2524) | 0.0012-0.0022 | 0.008-0.016 | 0.008-0.016 | 0.015-0.055 | 0.002-0.004 | 0.002-0.004 | SNUG |
|  | U | 3.0 (2971) | 0.0014-0.0022 | 0.010-0.020 | 0.010-0.020 | 0.010-0.049 | 0.0012-0.0031 | 0.0012-0.0031 | SNUG |
|  | 4 | 3.8 (3802) | 0.0014-0.0032 | 0.0200 | 0.0200 | 0.015-0.050 | 0.0016-0.0037 | 0.0016-0.0037 | SNUG |
| 1989 | D | 2.5 (2524) | 0.0012-0.0022 | 0.008-0.016 | 0.008-0.016 | 0.015-0.055 | 0.002-0.004 | 0.002-0.004 | SNUG |
|  | U | 3.0 (2971) | 0.0014-0.0022 | 0.010-0.020 | 0.010-0.020 | 0.010-0.049 | 0.0012-0.0031 | 0.0012-0.0031 | SNUG |
|  | Y | 3.0 (2980) | 0.0012-0.0020 | 0.012-0.018 | 0.012-0.018 | 0.008-0.020 | 0.0008-0.0024 | 0.0006-0.0022 | 0.0024-0.0059 |
|  | 4 | 3.8 (3802) | 0.0014-0.0032 | 0.011-0.012 | 0.010-0.020 | 0.015-0.058 | 0.0016-0.0034 | 0.0016-0.0034 | SNUG |
| 1990 | D | 2.5 (2524) | 0.0012-0.0022 | 0.008-0.016 | 0.008-0.016 | 0.015-0.055 | 0.002-0.004 | 0.002-0.004 | SNUG |
|  | U | 3.0 (2971) | 0.0014-0.0020 | 0.010-0.020 | 0.010-0.020 | 0.010-0.049 | 0.0012-0.0031 | 0.0012-0.0031 | SNUG |
|  | Y | 3.0 (2980) | 0.0012-0.0022 | 0.012-0.018 | 0.012-0.018 | 0.008-0.020 | 0.0008-0.0024 | 0.0006-0.0022 | 0.0024-0.0059 |
|  | 4 | 3.8 (3802) | 0.0014-0.0032 | 0.011-0.012 | 0.010-0.022 | 0.015-0.058 | 0.0016-0.0034 | 0.0016-0.0034 | SNUG |
| 1991 | D | 2.5 (2524) | 0.0012-0.0220 | 0.008-0.016 | 0.008-0.016 | 0.015-0.055 | 0.002-0.004 | 0.002-0.004 | SNUG |
|  | U | 3.0 (2971) | 0.0014-0.0020 | 0.010-0.020 | 0.010-0.020 | 0.010-0.049 | 0.0012-0.0031 | 0.0012-0.0031 | SNUG |
|  | Y | 3.0 (2980) | 0.022- | 0.012-0.018 | 0.012-0.018 | 0.008-0.020 | 0.0008-0.0024 | 0.0006-0.0022 | 0.0024-0.0059 |
|  | 4 | 3.8 (3802) | 0.0014-0.0032 | 0.011-0.012 | 0.010-0.020 | 0.015-0.058 | 0.0016-0.0034 | 0.0016-0.0034 | SNUG |
| 1992 | U | 3.0 (2971) | 0.0014-0.0022 | 0.010-0.020 | 0.010-0.020 | 0.010-0.049 | 0.0012-0.0031 | 0.0012-0.0031 | SNUG |
|  | Y | 3.0 (2980) | 0.0012-0.0020 | 0.012-0.018 | 0.012-0.018 | 0.008-0.020 | 0.0008-0.0024 | 0.0006-0.0022 | 0.0024-0.0059 |
|  | 4 | 3.8 (3802) | 0.0014-0.0032 | 0.012 | 0.010-0.022 | 0.015-0.058 | 0.0016-0.0034 | 0.0016-0.0034 | SNUG |

86873307

## CRANKSHAFT AND CONNECTING ROD SPECIFICATIONS

All measurements are given in inches.

| Year | Engine ID/VIN | Engine Displacement Liters (cc) | Crankshaft Main Brg. Journal Dia. | Crankshaft Main Brg. Oil Clearance | Crankshaft Shaft End-play | Crankshaft Thrust on No. | Connecting Rod Journal Diameter | Connecting Rod Oil Clearance | Connecting Rod Side Clearance |
|---|---|---|---|---|---|---|---|---|---|
|  | Y | 3.0 (2980) | 2.5187-2.5197 | 0.0011-0.0022 | 0.0008-0.0087 | 3 | 2.0463-2.0472 | 0.0009-0.0022 | 0.0063-0.0123 |
|  | P | 3.2 (3191) | 2.5187-2.5197 | 0.0011-0.0022 | 0.0008-0.0087 | 3 | 2.0463-2.0472 | 0.0009-0.0022 | 0.0063-0.0138 |
|  | 4 | 3.8 (3802) | 2.5190-2.5198 | 0.0010-0.0014 | 0.004-0.008 | 3 | 2.3103-2.3111 | 0.0010-0.0014 | 0.0047-0.0114 |
| 1994 | U | 3.0 (2971) | 2.5190-2.5198 | 0.0010-0.0014 | 0.004-0.008 | 3 | 2.1253-2.1261 | 0.0010-0.0014 | 0.006-0.014 |
|  | Y | 3.0 (2980) | 2.5187-2.5197 | 0.0011-0.0022 | 0.0008-0.0087 | 3 | 2.0463-2.0472 | 0.0009-0.0022 | 0.0063-0.0138 |
|  | P | 3.2 (3191) | 2.5187-2.5197 | 0.0011-0.0022 | 0.0008-0.0087 | 3 | 2.0463-2.0472 | 0.0009-0.0022 | 0.0063-0.0138 |
|  | 4 | 3.8 (3802) | 2.5190-2.5198 | 0.0010-0.0014 | 0.004-0.008 | 3 | 2.3103-2.3111 | 0.0010-0.0014 | 0.0047-0.0140 |
| 1995 | U | 3.0 (2980) | 2.5190-2.5198 | 0.0010-0.0014 | 0.0040-0.0080 | 3 | 2.1253-2.1261 | 0.0010-0.0014 | 0.0060-0.0140 |
|  | Y | 3.0 (2980) | 2.5190-2.5198 | 0.0010-0.0014 | 0.0008-0.0087 | 3 | 2.0463-2.0472 | 0.0009-0.0022 | 0.0063-0.0138 |
|  | P | 3.2 (3191) | 2.5187-2.5197 | 0.0011-0.0022 | 0.0008-0.0087 | 3 | 2.0463-2.0472 | 0.0009-0.0022 | 0.0063-0.0138 |
|  | 4 | 3.8 (3802) | 2.5190-2.5198 | 0.0010-0.0014 | 0.0040-0.0080 | 3 | 2.3103-2.3111 | 0.0010-0.0014 | 0.0047-0.0140 |

86873306

## PISTON AND RING SPECIFICATIONS

All measurements are given in inches.

| Year | Engine ID/VIN | Engine Displacement Liters (cc) | Piston Clearance | Ring Gap Top Compression | Ring Gap Bottom Compression | Ring Gap Oil Control | Ring Side Clearance Top Compression | Ring Side Clearance Bottom Compression | Ring Side Clearance Oil Control |
|---|---|---|---|---|---|---|---|---|---|
| 1993 | U | 3.0 (2971) | 0.0014-0.0022 | 0.010-0.020 | 0.010-0.020 | 0.010-0.049 | 0.0012-0.0031 | 0.0012-0.0031 | SNUG |
|  | Y | 3.0 (2980) | 0.0012-0.0020 | 0.012-0.018 | 0.012-0.018 | 0.008-0.020 | 0.0008-0.0022 | 0.0006-0.0022 | 0.0024-0.0059 |
|  | P | 3.2 (3191) | 0.0012-0.0020 | 0.012-0.018 | 0.018-0.024 | 0.008-0.020 | 0.0008-0.0031 | 0.0008-0.0024 | 0.0024-0.0059 |
|  | 4 | 3.8 (3802) | 0.0014-0.0032 | 0.011-0.012 | 0.010-0.020 | 0.015-0.058 | 0.0016-0.0034 | 0.0016-0.0034 | SNUG |
| 1994 | U | 3.0 (2971) | 0.0014-0.0022 | 0.010-0.020 | 0.010-0.020 | 0.010-0.049 | 0.0012-0.0031 | 0.0012-0.0031 | SNUG |
|  | Y | 3.0 (2980) | 0.0012-0.0020 | 0.012-0.018 | 0.012-0.018 | 0.008-0.020 | 0.0008-0.0024 | 0.0006-0.0022 | 0.0024-0.0059 |
|  | P | 3.2 (3191) | 0.0012-0.0020 | 0.012-0.018 | 0.018-0.024 | 0.008-0.020 | 0.0016-0.0031 | 0.0008-0.0024 | 0.0024-0.0059 |
|  | 4 | 3.8 (3802) | 0.0014-0.0032 | 0.011-0.012 | 0.010-0.020 | 0.015-0.058 | 0.0016-0.0034 | 0.0016-0.0034 | SNUG |
| 1995 | U | 3.0 (2971) | 0.0014-0.0022 | 0.010-0.020 | 0.010-0.020 | 0.010-0.049 | 0.0012-0.0031 | 0.0012-0.0031 | SNUG |
|  | Y | 3.0 (2980) | 0.0012-0.0020 | 0.012-0.018 | 0.012-0.018 | 0.008-0.020 | 0.0008-0.0024 | 0.0006-0.0022 | 0.0024-0.0059 |
|  | P | 3.2 (3191) | 0.0012-0.0020 | 0.012-0.018 | 0.018-0.024 | 0.008-0.020 | 0.0016-0.0031 | 0.0008-0.0024 | 0.0024-0.0059 |
|  | 4 | 3.8 (3802) | 0.0014-0.0032 | 0.011-0.012 | 0.010-0.020 | 0.015-0.058 | 0.0016-0.0034 | 0.0016-0.0034 | SNUG |

86873308

## TORQUE SPECIFICATIONS

All readings in ft. lbs.

| Year | Engine ID/VIN | Engine Displacement Liters (cc) | Cylinder Head Bolts | Main Bearing Bolts | Rod Bearing Bolts | Crankshaft Damper Bolts | Flywheel Bolts | Manifold Intake | Manifold Exhaust | Spark Plugs | Lug Nut |
|---|---|---|---|---|---|---|---|---|---|---|---|
| 1986 | D | 2.5 (2524) | ① | 51-66 | 21-26 | 140-170 | 54-64 | 15-23 | 15 | 5-10 | 95 |
|  | U | 3.0 (2971) | ② | 65-81 | ⑨ | 141-169 | 54-64 | ⑪ | 19 | 5-10 | 95 |
| 1987 | D | 2.5 (2524) | ① | 51-66 | 21-26 | 140-170 | 54-64 | 15-23 | 15 | 5-10 | 95 |
|  | U | 3.0 (2971) | ② | 65-81 | ⑨ | 141-170 | 54-64 | ⑪ | 15 | 5-10 | 95 |
| 1988 | D | 2.5 (2524) | ① | 51-66 | 21-26 | 140-170 | 54-64 | 15-23 | 15 | 5-10 | 95 |
|  | U | 3.0 (2971) | ③ | 65-81 | ⑨ | 141-169 | 54-64 | ⑪ | 15 | 5-11 | 95 |
|  | 4 | 3.8 (3802) | ③ | 65-81 | 31-36 | 75-85 | 75-85 | ⑫ | 15-22 | 5-10 | 95 |
| 1989 | D | 2.5 (2524) | ① | 51-66 | 21-26 | 140-170 | 54-64 | 15-23 | 15 | 5-10 | 95 |
|  | U | 3.0 (2971) | ② | 65-81 | ⑨ | 141-169 | 54-64 | ⑪ | 15 | 5-10 | 95 |
|  | Y | 3.0 (2980) | 61-69 | 58-65 | 33-36 | 112-127 | 51-58 | 12-17 | 26-38 | 16-20 | 95 |
|  | 4 | 3.8 (3802) | ① | 65-81 | 31-36 | 85-100 | 75-85 | ⑫ | 15-22 | 5-11 | 95 |
| 1990 | D | 2.5 (2524) | ① | 51-66 | 21-26 | 140-170 | 54-64 | 15-23 | 15 | 5-10 | 95 |
|  | U | 3.0 (2971) | ① | 65-81 | ⑩ | 141-169 | 54-64 | ⑫ | 15 | 5-10 | 95 |
|  | Y | 3.0 (2980) |  | 65-81 | 7 | 112-127 | 51-58 | 12-17 | 26-38 | 16-20 | 95 |
|  | 4 | 3.8 (3802) | ③ | 65-81 | 31-36 | 85-100 | 75-85 | ⑫ | 15-22 | 5-11 | 95 |
| 1991 | D | 2.5 (2524) | ③ | 65-81 | 21-26 | 140-170 | 54-64 | 15-23 | 15 | 5-10 | 95 |
|  | U | 3.0 (2971) | ② | 65-81 | ⑨ | 141-169 | 54-64 | ⑪ | 15 | 5-10 | 95 |
|  | Y | 3.0 (2980) | ④ | 65-81 | ⑩ | 112-127 | 51-58 | 12-17 | 26-38 | 16-20 | 95 |
|  | 4 | 3.8 (3802) | ③ | 65-81 | 31-36 | 85-100 | 75-85 | ⑫ | 15-22 | 5-11 | 95 |
| 1992 | 4 | 3.8 (3802) | ② | 65-81 | ⑨ | 141-169 | 54-64 | ⑪ | 15 | 5-10 | 95 |
|  | U | 3.0 (2971) | ② | 65-81 | ⑨ | 141-169 | 54-64 | ⑪ | 15 | 5-10 | 95 |
|  | Y | 3.0 (2980) | ④ | 65-81 | ⑩ | 112-127 | 51-58 | 12-17 | 26-38 | 16-20 | 95 |
|  | 4 | 3.8 (3802) | ③ | 65-81 | 31-36 | 85-100 | 75-85 | ⑫ | 15-22 | 5-11 | 95 |
| 1993 | U | 3.0 (2971) | ④ | 65-81 | ⑩ | 112-127 | 58-64 | 11-16 | 26-38 | 17-19 | 95 |
|  | Y | 3.0 (2980) | ④ | 65-81 | ⑩ | 113-126 | 58-64 | 11-17 | 26-38 | 16-20 | 95 |
|  | P | 3.2 (3191) | ⑤ | 55-63 | 8 | 112-127 | 75-85 | 11-17 | 15-22 | 5-11 | 95 |
|  | 4 | 3.8 (3802) | ⑥ | 65-81 | 31-36 | 85-100 | 54-64 | ⑬ | 15-22 | 7-15 | 95 |
| 1994 | U | 3.0 (2971) | ④ | 65-81 | ⑩ | 112-127 | 58-64 | 11-16 | 26-38 | 16-20 | 95 |
|  | Y | 3.0 (2980) | ④ | 65-81 | ⑩ | 113-126 | 58-64 | 11-17 | 26-38 | 15-22 | 95 |
|  | P | 3.2 (3191) | ⑤ | 55-63 | 26 | 112-127 | 75-85 | 11-17 | 15-22 | 7-15 | 95 |
|  | 4 | 3.8 (3802) | ⑥ | 65-81 | 31-36 | 103-132 | 54-64 | ⑭ | 15-22 | 7-15 | 95 |
| 1995 | U | 3.0 (2980) | ④ | 65-81 | ⑩ | 113-126 | 51-58 | 11-16 | 26-38 | 15-22 | 95 |
|  | Y | 3.2 (3191) | ⑤ | 55-63 | 8 | 112-127 | 51-58 | 11-17 | 15-22 | 7-15 | 95 |
|  | 4 | 3.8 (3802) | ⑥ | 65-81 | 31-36 | 103-132 | 54-64 | ⑭ | 15-22 | 7-15 | 95 |

86873309

① Step 1: 52-59 ft. lbs.
 Step 2: 70-76 ft. lbs.

② Step 1: 48-54 ft. lbs.
 Step 2: 63-80 ft. lbs.

③ Step 1: 37 ft. lbs.
 Step 2: 45 ft. lbs.
 Step 3: 52 ft. lbs.

④ Step 1: 37-50 ft. lbs.
 Step 2: 62-68 ft. lbs.

⑤ Step 1: 33-41 ft. lbs.
 Step 2: 63-73 ft. lbs.

⑥ Do not reuse cylinder head bolts.
 Step 1: 15 ft. lbs
 Step 2: 29 ft. lbs.
 Step 3: 37 ft. lbs.

Step 4: Back off bolts two or three times one at a time
Step 5: Long Bolts: 11-18 ft. lbs.
Step 6: Short Bolts: 7-15 ft. lbs.
Step 7: Rotate 85-95 degrees

⑦ Step 1: 37-50 ft. lbs.

⑧ Step 1: 34-41 ft. lbs.
 Step 2: 58-64 ft. lbs.
 Step 2: 58-65 ft. lbs.

⑨ Step 1: Tighten to 20-28 ft. lbs.
 Step 2: Back off the nuts a minimum of two revolutions
 Step 3: Apply final torque of 20-25 ft. lbs.

⑩ Step 1: 22-26 ft. lbs.
 Step 2: 33-36 ft. lbs.

⑪ Step 1: 11 ft. lbs
 Step 2: 18 ft. lbs.
 Step 3: 24 ft. lbs.

⑫ Step 1: 7 ft. lbs.
 Step 2: 15 ft. lbs.
 Step 3: 24 ft. lbs.

⑬ Step 1: 15-22 ft. lbs.
 Step 2: 19-24 ft. lbs.

⑭ Step 1: 13 ft. lbs.
 Step 2: 16 ft. lbs.

## Engine

### REMOVAL & INSTALLATION

### ✳✳ CAUTION

**When draining the coolant, keep in mind that cats and dogs are attracted by ethylene glycol antifreeze, and are quite likely to drink any that is left in an uncovered container or in puddles on the ground. This will prove fatal in sufficient quantity. Always drain the coolant into a sealable container. Coolant should be reused unless it is contaminated or several years old.**

The EPA warns that prolonged contact with used engine oil may cause a number of skin disorders, including cancer! You should make every effort to minimize your exposure to used engine oil. Protective gloves should be worn when changing the oil. Wash your hands and any other exposed skin areas as soon as possible after exposure to used engine oil. Soap and water, or waterless hand cleaner should be used.

### ✳✳ WARNING

**The manufacturer requires the discharge and recovery of the air conditioning system for these procedures. DO NOT attempt this without the proper equipment! Depending on your vehicle application, the air conditioning system may utilize R-12 or R-134a refrigerant. These two refrigerants should NOT be mixed, and depending on your local laws, attempting to service your A/C system could be illegal!**

### 2.5L Engine

1. Properly relieve the fuel system pressure. For fuel system relief procedures, please refer to Section 1 or 5 of this manual.
2. If equipped with an automatic transaxle, remove the transaxle timing window cover and rotate the engine until the flywheel timing marker is aligned with the timing pointer.
3. If equipped with an automatic transaxle, place a reference mark on the crankshaft pulley at the 12 o'clock position (TDC) then rotate the crankshaft pulley mark to the 6 o'clock position (BTDC).
4. Disconnect the negative battery cable.
5. Matchmark the hood hinges for installation reference, then remove the hood.
6. Remove the air cleaner assembly, then position a drain pan under the radiator and drain the cooling system. Close the drain valve.
7. Disconnect the upper radiator hose at the engine.
8. Identify, tag and disconnect all electrical wiring and vacuum hoses as required.
9. Disconnect the crankcase ventilation hose at the valve cover and the intake manifold.
10. Disconnect the fuel lines at the fuel rail, then disconnect the heater hoses at the water outlet connector and the water pump.
11. Disconnect the engine ground wire.
12. Disconnect the accelerator and throttle valve control cables at the throttle body.
13. If equipped, properly discharge the air conditioning system and remove the suction and discharge lines from the compressor.
14. On manual transaxle equipped vehicles, remove the engine damper brace.
15. Remove the driver belt and water pump pulley.
16. Remove the air cleaner-to-canister hose.
17. Raise and safely support the vehicle.
18. Drain the engine oil, then remove the oil filter.
19. Disconnect the starter cable, then remove the starter motor. For details regarding starter motor removal, please refer to the procedure earlier in this section.
20. On automatic transaxle equipped vehicles, remove the converter

nuts and align the previously made reference mark as close to the 6 o'clock (BTDC) position as possible with the converter stud visible.

➡**The flywheel timing marker must be in the 6 o'clock (BTDC) position for proper engine removal and installation.**

21. Disconnect the engine damper at the subframe bracket.
22. Remove the engine insulator nuts.
23. Disconnect the exhaust pipe from the manifold.
24. Disconnect the canister and halfshaft brackets from the engine.
25. Remove the lower engine-to-transaxle retaining bolts.
26. Disconnect the lower radiator hose.
27. Carefully lower the vehicle, then position a floor jack under the transaxle.
28. Disconnect the power steering lines from the power steering pump.
29. Install engine lifting eyes tool D81L-6001-D or equivalent and engine support tool T79P-6000-A or equivalent.
30. Connect suitable lifting equipment to support the engine, then remove the upper engine-to-transaxle retaining bolts.
31. Remove the engine from the vehicle and support on a suitable holding fixture, then remove the lifting equipment.

**To install:**

32. Install engine lifting eyes tool D81L-6001-D and engine support tool T79P-6000-A or equivalent, then attach the lifting equipment.

➡**Make sure the timing marker is in the 6 o'clock (BDC) position.**

33. Remove the engine from the stand and position it in the vehicle. Remove the lifting equipment.
34. Using a floor jack to aid in alignment, install the upper engine-to-transaxle bolts and tighten them to 26–34 ft. lbs. (35–46 Nm).
35. Connect the power steering lines to the pump.
36. Raise and safely support the vehicle.
37. Connect the lower radiator hose to the tube.
38. Install the lower engine-to-transaxle attaching bolts and tighten to 26–34 ft. lbs. (35–46 Nm).
39. Connect the halfshaft and canister brackets to the engine.
40. Connect the exhaust pipe to the manifold.
41. Install the engine insulator nuts and tighten them to 40–55 ft. lbs. (54–75 Nm).
42. Position the marks on the crankshaft pulley as close to 6 o'clock position (BTDC) as possible, and install the converter nuts. Tighten the nuts to 20–33 ft. lbs. (27–45 Nm).
43. Install the starter, then connect the starter cable. For details, please refer to the procedure earlier in this section.
44. Install the oil filter and make sure the oil drain plug is tight.
45. Connect the engine damper-to-subframe bracket.
46. Carefully lower the vehicle.
47. Install the air cleaner-to-canister hose, and the water pump pulley and drive belt.
48. If equipped with A/C, connect the pressure and suction lines to the air conditioning compressor.
49. Connect the accelerator cable and throttle valve control cable at the throttle body.
50. Connect the ground wire at the engine, then connect the heater hoses at the water outlet connector and the water pump.
51. Connect the fuel lines to the fuel rail.
52. Connect the crankcase ventilation hose at the valve cover and the intake manifold.
53. Connect the engine control sensor wiring assembly and vacuum lines.
54. Connect the upper radiator hose at the engine, then install the air cleaner assembly.
55. Connect the negative battery cable.
56. Rotate the engine until the flywheel timing marker is aligned with the timing pointer.
57. Install the timing window cover.
58. Engage the electrical connector at the inertia switch.

59. Fill the cooling system with the proper amount and type of coolant. Fill the crankcase with the proper engine oil to the required level.

60. Align and install the hood, using the marks made during removal.

61. Charge the air conditioning system, if equipped.

62. Check all fluid levels, the start the vehicle and check for leaks.

### 3.0L Engine

#### EXCEPT SHO ENGINES

▶ See Figures 49, 50, 51 and 52

1. Disconnect the battery cables, then properly drain the cooling system.

2. Matchmark the hood hinges for installation reference, then remove the hood.

3. Evacuate the air conditioning system safely and properly.

4. Relieve the fuel system pressure. For details regarding this procedure, please refer to Section 1 or 5 of this manual.

5. Remove the air cleaner assembly, then remove the battery and the battery tray.

6. Remove the integrated relay controller, cooling fan and radiator with fan shroud. Remove the engine bounce damper bracket on the shock tower.

7. Remove the evaporative emission line, upper radiator hose, starter brace and lower radiator hose.

8. Remove the exhaust pipes from both exhaust manifolds. Disconnect and plug the power steering pump lines.

9. Disconnect the fuel lines, then remove and tag all necessary vacuum lines.

10. Disconnect the ground strap, heater lines, accelerator cable linkage, throttle valve linkage and speed control cable.

11. For gasoline engines, tag and disengage the following wiring connectors; alternator, A/C clutch, heated oxygen sensor, ignition coil, radio frequency suppressor, cooling fan voltage resistor, engine coolant temperature sensor, ignition control module, injector wiring harness, ISC motor wire, throttle position sensor, oil pressure sending switch, ground wire, block heater (if equipped), knock sensor, EGR sensor and oil level sensor.

12. For Flexible Fuel (FF) engines, tag and disengage the following wiring connectors: alternator, A/C clutch, heated oxygen sensor, engine control sensor, injector wiring harness, IAT sensor, IAC sensor, throttle position sensor, oil pressure sending switch, engine ground wire, block heater (if equipped), low oil level sensor, and the water temperature indicator sender unit.

13. Raise the vehicle and support it safely. Remove the engine mount bolts and engine mounts. Remove the transaxle to engine mounting bolts and transaxle brace assembly.

14. Lower the vehicle. Install a suitable engine lifting plate onto the engine and use a suitable engine hoist to remove the engine from the vehicle. Remove the main wiring harness from the engine.

#### To install:

15. Install the main wiring harness on the engine. Position the engine in the vehicle and remove the engine lifting plate.

16. Raise the vehicle and support it safely. Install the engine mounts and bolts, and tighten to 40–55 ft. lbs. (54–75 Nm). Install the transaxle brace assembly and tighten the bolts to 40–55 ft. lbs. (54–75 Nm).

17. Attach all wiring connectors according to their labels.

18. Connect the ground strap, heater lines, accelerator cable linkage, throttle valve linkage and speed control cables.

19. Connect the power steering pump lines.

20. Fasten the exhaust pipes to the exhaust manifolds.

21. Connect the fuel lines and vacuum lines.

22. Install the evaporative emission line, upper radiator hose, starter brace and lower radiator hose.

23. Install the integrated relay controller, cooling fan and radiator with fan shroud. Install the engine bounce damper bracket on the shock tower.

24. Install the battery tray and the battery, then install the air cleaner assembly.

25. Charge the air conditioning system, using the correct equipment and precautions.

26. Fill the cooling system with the proper type and quantity of coolant. Fill the crankcase with the correct type of motor oil to the required level.

27. Install the hood according to the alignment marks made during removal.

28. Connect the negative battery cable, then start the engine and check for leaks.

### 3.0L and 3.2L SHO Engines

1. Properly drain the engine cooling system.

2. Disconnect the battery cables, then remove the battery and battery tray.

3. Properly relieve the fuel system pressure. For details, please refer to the procedure in Section 1 or 5 of this manual.

4. If equipped, disengage the wiring connector retaining the underhood light, then mark the position of the hood hinges and remove the hood.

5. Remove the oil level dipstick.

6. Disengage the alternator and voltage regulator wiring assembly.

7. Remove the radiator upper sight shield.

8. Properly discharge the air conditioning system, using suitable equipment.

9. Remove the radiator coolant recovery reservoir assembly.

10. Remove the computer control module, air cleaner outlet tube assembly, upper radiator hose, electric fan and shroud assembly.

11. Remove the lower radiator hose, then remove the radiator.

12. Disconnect the fuel supply hose and the fuel return hose from the fuel injection supply manifold.

13. Remove the Barometric Absolute Pressure (BAP) sensor.

14. Remove the engine vibration damper and bracket assembly from the right side of the engine.

15. Remove the engine mounting damper bracket.

16. Remove the retaining bolt from the power steering reservoir and place the reservoir aside. Disconnect and plug the hose to the power steering oil cooler at the power steering pump.

17. Disconnect the throttle linkage, then tag and disconnect the vacuum hoses.

18. Disconnect the heater hoses at the heater core.

19. Disengage the electrical connectors from the engine control sensor wiring on the rear of the engine.

20. On the 3.0L SHO engine only, loosen the accessory drive belt tensioner pulley, then remove the belt from the A/C compressor and the alternator.

21. On the 3.2L SHO engine only, loosen the accessory drive belt tensioner. Remove the single accessory drive belt, then remove the tensioner pulley.

22. On the 3.0L SHO only, loosen the accessory drive belt lower tensioner pulley, then remove the power steering pump belt, and the lower tensioner pulley.

23. Disconnect the A/C cycling switch on top of the suction accumulator/drier.

24. Disconnect the evaporator-to-compressor suction line at the dash panel, then remove the suction accumulator/drier and the A/C accumulator bracket.

25. Remove the alternator assembly. For details, please refer to the procedure located earlier in this section.

26. Disconnect the A/C manifold and tube, then remove the A/C compressor and bracket assembly.

27. Raise and safely support the vehicle.

28. Place a drain pan under the vehicle's oil pan, then drain the motor oil and remove the filter element. Move the drain pan away from the vehicle.

29. Remove the wheel and tire assemblies. Disengage the oil level sensor switch.

30. Disconnect the right-side lower ball joint, tie rod end and front stabilizer bar.

31. Remove the front axle bearing bracket from the cylinder block, then remove the right-side halfshaft from the transaxle.

32. Disconnect the heated oxygen sensor assembly.

33. Disconnect the 4 dual converter/Y pipe-to-exhaust manifold retaining bolts.

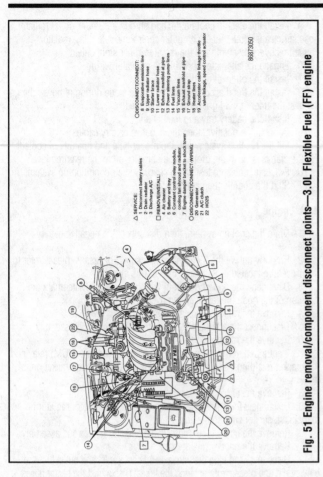

△ SERVICE:
1. Disconnect battery cables
2. Drain radiator
3. Discharge A/C

□ REMOVE/INSTALL:
4. Battery and tray
5. Battery and tray
6. Constant control relay module, cooling fan shroud and radiator
7. Engine door bracket to shock tower

○ DISCONNECT/CONNECT:-WIRING:
20. A/C clutch
21. A/C clutch
22. HO2S

○ DISCONNECT/CONNECT:
8. Evaporative emission line
9. Upper radiator hose
10. Starter brace
11. Lower radiator hose
12. Exhaust manifold at pipe
13. Power steering pump lines
14. Fuel lines
15. Vacuum lines
16. Exhaust manifold at pipe
17. Ground strap
18. Heater lines
19. Accelerator cable linkage throttle valve linkage, speed control actuator

Fig. 51 Engine removal/component disconnect points—3.0L Flexible Fuel (FF) engine

86873050

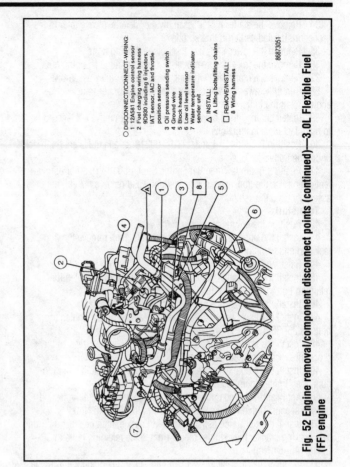

○ DISCONNECT/CONNECT:-WIRING:
1. 12A581 Engine control sensor
2. Fuel charging wiring harness 9D930 including 6 injectors, IAT sensor, IAC and throttle position sensor
3. Oil pressure sending switch
4. Ground wire
5. Block heater
6. Low oil level sensor
7. Water temperature indicator sender unit

△ INSTALL:
A. Lifting bolts/lifting chains

□ REMOVE/INSTALL:
8. Wiring harness

Fig. 52 Engine removal/component disconnect points (continued)—3.0L Flexible Fuel (FF) engine

86873051

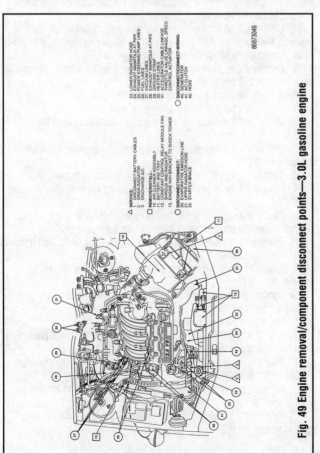

△ SERVICE:
1. DISCONNECT BATTERY CABLES
2. DRAIN RADIATOR
3. DISCHARGE A/C

□ REMOVE/INSTALL:
10. AIR CLEANER ASSEMBLY
11. 
12. CONSTANT CONTROL, RELAY MODULE COOLING FAN
13. ENGINE WH BRACKET TO SHOCK TOWER

○ DISCONNECT/CONNECT:
20. EVAPORATIVE EMISSION LINE
21. UPPER RADIATOR HOSE
22. STARTER BRACE

23. LOWER RADIATOR HOSE
24. EXHAUST MANIFOLD AT PIPE
25. POWER STEERING PUMP LINES
26. FUEL LINES
28. VACUUM LINES
29. EXHAUST MANIFOLD AT PIPE
30. GROUND STRAP
31. 
ACCELERATOR CABLE LINKAGE THROTTLE VALVE LINKAGE, SPEED CONTROL ACTUATOR

○ DISCONNECT/CONNECT:-WIRING:
40. GENERATOR
41. A/C CLUTCH
42. HO2S

Fig. 49 Engine removal/component disconnect points—3.0L gasoline engine

86873048

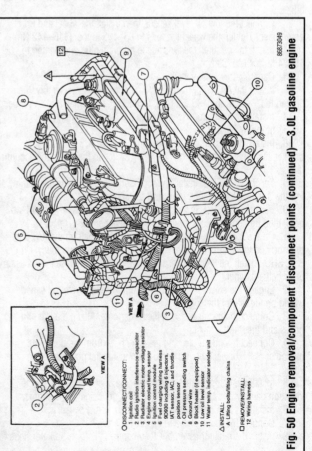

VIEW A

○ DISCONNECT/CONNECT:
1. Ignition coil
2. Radio ignition interference capacitor
3. Radiator electric motor voltage resistor
4. Engine coolant temp. sensor
5. Ignition control module
6. Fuel charging wiring harness 9D930 including 6 injectors, IAT sensor, IAC, and throttle position sensor
7. Oil pressure sending switch
8. Ground wire
9. Block heater (if equipped)
10. Low oil level sensor
11. Water temp. indicator sender unit

△ INSTALL:
A. Lifting bolts/lifting chains

□ REMOVE/INSTALL:
12. Wiring harness

Fig. 50 Engine removal/component disconnect points (continued)—3.0L gasoline engine

86873049

34. Remove the starter motor assembly. For details, please refer to the procedure located earlier in this section.

35. Remove the lower transaxle-to-engine retaining bolts.

36. Remove the front engine mount-to-front subframe retaining nuts.

37. Remove the crankshaft vibration damper and pulley assembly.

38. Carefully lower the vehicle, then remove the upper transaxle-to-engine retaining bolts.

39. Install engine lifting bracket D89L-6001-A or equivalent, according to manufacturer's instructions.

40. Position Rotunda Hi-Lift Jack 014-00210, or an equivalent floor jack under the transaxle.

41. Position Rotunda Three Bar Engine Support 014-00750 or equivalent, then raise the transaxle assembly slightly and remove the engine assembly from the vehicle.

**To install:**

42. Position the engine assembly in the vehicle.

43. Install the upper transaxle-to-engine bolts, then remove the floor jack and engine lifting equipment.

44. Raise and safely support the vehicle.

45. Install the crankshaft damper and pulley assembly. Tighten the retaining bolt to 112–127 ft. lbs. (152–172 Nm).

46. Install the front engine mount-to-front subframe nuts.

47. Install the lower transaxle-to-engine retaining bolts. Tighten the bolts to 25–35 ft. lbs. (34–47 Nm).

48. Install the starter motor assembly. For details, please refer to the procedure located earlier in this section.

49. Install the 4 dual converter Y pipe-to-exhaust manifold retaining nuts, then tighten them to 20–35 ft. lbs. (27–47 Nm).

50. Apply anti-seize compound to the threads, then install the heated oxygen sensor. Tighten the sensor to 27–33 ft. lbs. (37–45 Nm).

51. Install the right-side halfshaft to the transaxle, then connect the front axle bearing bracket the cylinder block. Tighten the retaining bolts to 30–47 ft. lbs. (40–64 Nm).

52. Connect the right-side lower ball joint, tie rod end and the front stabilizer bar.

53. Connect the low oil level sensor, then install the wheel and tire assemblies. Tighten the wheel lug nuts to 85–105 ft. lbs. (115–142 Nm).

54. Install the oil filter, then install the oil drain plug and tighten to 15–24 ft. lbs. (20–33 Nm).

55. Carefully lower the vehicle.

56. Install the A/C compressor and mounting bracket assembly, then tighten to 27–41 ft. lbs. (36–55 Nm). Connect the A/C manifold and tube.

57. Install the alternator assembly and tighten the retaining bolts to 36–53 ft. lbs. (49–72 Nm).

58. Install the suction accumulator/drier and the A/C accumulator bracket assembly, then connect the cycling switch to the top of the accumulator.

59. For the 3.2L SHO, install the accessory drive belt tensioner pulley. For the 3.0L SHO, install the lower belt tensioner.

60. For the 3.0L SHO, install the power steering accessory belt (4-rib belt), then tighten the accessory drive belt tensioner pulley.

61. On the 3.0L SHO, install the accessory drive belt on the A/C compressor, and the alternator pulley, then tighten the tensioner pulley. On the 3.2L SHO, install the single accessory drive belt, then release the accessory drive belt tensioner.

62. Engage the electrical connectors from the engine control sensor wiring on the rear of the engine.

63. Connect the heater hoses at the heater core. Attach the vacuum hoses and the throttle linkage.

64. Connect the power steering pressure hose from the power steering oil cooler at the power steering pump, then install the power steering reservoir.

65. Install the damper bracket to the engine, then install the engine vibration damper and bracket assembly to the right side of the engine.

66. Install the Barometric Absolute Pressure (BAP) sensor.

67. Connect the fuel return and supply hoses.

68. Install the radiator assembly, then connect the lower radiator hose.

69. Install the electric cooling fan and shroud assembly, upper radiator hose, air cleaner outlet tube, computer control module relay, radiator coolant recovery reservoir and the radiator upper sight shield.

70. Engage the alternator and voltage regulator wiring.

71. Install the oil level dipstick.

72. Install the hood according to the marks made during removal, then connect the underhood light wiring, if equipped.

73. Install the battery tray and the battery.

74. Connect the positive, then the negative battery cables.

75. Fill the cooling system with the proper type and quantity of coolant. Fill the crankcase with the proper type of motor oil to the required level.

76. Evacuate, pressure test and recharge the air conditioning system.

77. Start the engine, then check for leaks.

### 3.8L Engine

1. Drain the cooling system, then disconnect the negative battery cable.

2. Properly relieve the fuel system pressure. For details, please refer to the procedure located in Section 1 or 5 of this manual.

3. Disengage the underhood light wiring connector. Matchmark the position of the hood hinges, then remove the hood.

4. Remove the oil level indicator tube.

5. Disconnect the alternator-to-voltage regulator wiring assembly.

6. Remove the radiator upper sight shield.

7. If equipped, remove the Powertrain Control Module (PCM) relay and the bracket retaining bolts, then position the PCM relay and bracket out of the way.

8. Remove the air cleaner assembly.

9. Disconnect the cooling fan motor and the front center radiator primary crash sensor wire connectors.

10. Remove the cooling fan motor/fan blade and fan shroud assembly.

11. Remove the upper radiator hose.

12. Disconnect and plug the transaxle oil cooler inlet and outlet tubes to prevent dirt and grease from entering the tubes. Disconnect the heater hoses.

13. Disconnect the power steering pressure hose assembly.

14. Disconnect the engine control sensor wiring from the A/C clutch field coil. Discharge the A/C system using the proper equipment, then disconnect the compressor-to-condenser discharge line.

15. Remove the radiator coolant recovery reservoir assembly. Remove the wiring shield from the throttle body.

16. Remove the accelerator cable mounting bracket.

17. Disconnect the fuel supply and return lines.

18. Disconnect the power steering pump pressure hose from the bracket.

19. Disconnect the fuel charging wiring from the engine control sensor wiring assembly.

20. Identify, tag and disconnect all necessary vacuum hoses.

21. Disconnect the ground wire assembly. Remove the air cleaner outlet tube.

22. Disconnect one end of the throttle control valve cable. Detach the bulkhead electrical connector and transaxle pressure switches.

23. Remove the transaxle support assembly retaining bolts, then remove the transaxle support assembly from the vehicle.

24. Raise and safely support the vehicle. Remove the wheel and tire assemblies.

25. Position a drain pan under the car's oil pan, then drain the engine oil and remove the filter. Move the drain pan out of the way.

26. Disconnect the heated oxygen sensor.

27. Loosen and remove the drive belt. Remove the crankshaft pulley and drive belt tensioner assemblies.

28. Remove the starter motor. For details, please refer to the procedure located earlier in this section.

29. Remove the dual converter Y-pipe retaining bolts, then remove the Y-pipe.

30. Remove the left and right front engine support insulator-to-front subframe retaining nuts.

31. If equipped, remove the engine rear cover, then remove the converter-to-flywheel nuts.

32. Disconnect the engine control sensor wiring from the low oil level sensor. Remove the crankshaft pulley and damper assembly.

33. Disconnect the lower radiator hose.

34. Remove the engine-to-transaxle bolts and partially lower the vehicle. Remove the front wheel and tire assemblies.

35. Unfasten the water pump pulley retaining bolt, then remove the water pump pulley.

36. Remove the distributor cap and position aside, then pull out the distributor rotor.

37. Remove the radiator.

38. Unfasten the exhaust manifold bolt lock retaining bolts. Remove the thermactor air pump retaining bolts and the thermactor air pump.

39. Disconnect the engine control sensor wiring from the oil pressure sensor.

40. Install Engine Lifting Eyes D81L-6001-D, or equivalent, then position and install suitable engine lifting equipment.

41. Position a suitable jack under the transaxle and raise the transaxle slightly.

42. Carefully remove the engine from the vehicle.

**To install:**

➡ **Lightly oil all bolt and stud threads before installation, except those specifying special sealant.**

43. Position the engine assembly in the vehicle.

44. Install the engine-to-transaxle bolts, then remove the jack from under the transaxle and remove the engine lifting equipment. Remove the engine lifting eyes. Place all lifting equipment aside and out of the way.

45. Tighten the engine-to-transaxle bolts to 41–50 ft. lbs. (55–68 Nm).

46. Engage the engine control sensor wiring to the oil pressure sensor.

47. Install the air conditioning compressor and tighten the retaining bolts to 30–45 ft. lbs. (41–61 Nm). Connect the compressor-to-condenser discharge line.

48. Connect the A/C clutch field coil to the engine control sensor wiring.

49. Fasten the heater hoses and the fuel supply and return hoses, then connect the vacuum hoses.

50. Connect the engine control module wiring assembly.

51. Attach the transaxle oil cooler inlet and outlet tubes.

52. Install the radiator assembly.

53. Partially raise and safely support the vehicle.

54. Install the converter-to-flywheel nuts/bolts and tighten to 20–34 ft. lbs. (27–46 Nm).

55. Install the left and right front engine supports, then install the engine rear plate.

56. Install the starter motor. For details, please refer to the procedure located earlier in this section.

57. Connect the lower radiator hose.

58. Install the drive belt tensioner assembly and the crankshaft pulley and vibration damper assembly. Tighten the crankshaft pulley retaining bolts to 20–28 ft. lbs. (27–38 Nm).

59. Install the dual converter Y-pipe, then connect the engine control sensor wiring to the heated exhaust gas oxygen sensor.

60. Install the oil filter, then connect the engine control sensor wiring to the low oil level sensor.

61. Carefully lower the vehicle.

62. Position the thermactor air supply pump and install the retaining bolts.

63. Connect the vacuum pump and install the exhaust air supply pump pulley assembly.

64. Install the wiring shield.

65. Install the distributor cap and rotor.

66. Install the radiator coolant recovery reservoir assembly, upper radiator hose and water pump pulley.

67. Connect the alternator-to-voltage regulator wiring assembly, then fasten the fuel charging wiring to the engine control sensor wiring.

68. Connect the wiring assembly ground.

69. Install the accelerator cable mounting bracket.

70. Connect the power steering pressure hose assembly and the power steering return hose.

71. Install the cooling fan motor/fan blade and the fan shroud assembly.

72. Connect the cooling fan motor and the front center radiator primary crash sensor wire connectors.

73. Install the Powertrain Control Module (PCM) relay and bracket. Make sure to tighten the retainers securely.

74. Install the drive belts.

75. Position and install the engine and transaxle support assembly.

76. Install the radiator upper sight shield.

77. Partially raise and safely support the vehicle. Install the wheel and tire assemblies, then tighten the lug nuts to 85–105 ft. lbs. (115–142 Nm).

78. Carefully lower the vehicle.

79. Install the hood, using the aligning marks made during removal, and connect the negative battery cable.

80. Fill the cooling system with the proper type and quantity of coolant. Fill the crankcase with the proper type and viscosity of motor oil to the required level.

81. Evacuate, pressure test and recharge the A/C system, using the proper equipment.

82. Start the engine and check for leaks.

## Engine Mounts

### REMOVAL & INSTALLATION

#### 2.5L and 3.0L Engines

##### *RIGHT REAR ENGINE INSULATOR (NO. 3)*

1. Disconnect the negative battery cable. Remove the lower damper nut from the right side of the engine on manual transaxle equipped vehicles. Raise and support the vehicle safely.

2. Place a suitable jack and a block of wood beneath the engine block.

3. Remove the nut attaching the right front and rear insulators to the frame.

4. Raise the engine with the jack until enough of a load is taken off of the insulator.

5. Remove the insulator retaining bolts, then remove the insulator from the engine support bracket.

6. Installation is the reverse of the removal procedure. Tighten the insulator-to-engine support bracket to 40–55 ft. lbs. (54–75 Nm). Tighten the nut attaching the right, front and rear insulators to the frame to 55–75 ft. lbs. (75–102 Nm).

##### *LEFT ENGINE INSULATOR AND SUPPORT ASSEMBLY—AUTOMATIC TRANSAXLE*

1. Disconnect the negative battery cable. Raise and support the vehicle safely. Remove the wheel and tire assembly.

2. Place a suitable jack and a block of wood under the transaxle and support the transaxle.

3. Remove the nuts attaching the insulator to the support assembly. Remove the through-bolts attaching the insulator to the frame.

4. Raise the transaxle with the jack enough to relieve the weight on the insulator.

5. Remove the bolts attaching the support assembly to the transaxle. Remove the insulator and/or transaxle support assembly.

6. Installation is the reverse of the removal procedure. Tighten the support assembly retaining bolts to 40–55 ft. lbs. (54–75 Nm). Tighten the insulator-to-frame bolts to 60–86 ft. lbs. (81–116 Nm). Tighten the insulator-to-support assembly nuts to 55–75 ft. lbs. (74–102 Nm).

##### *LEFT ENGINE INSULATOR AND SUPPORT ASSEMBLY—MANUAL TRANSAXLE*

1. Disconnect the negative battery cable. Raise and support the vehicle safely. Remove the tire and wheel assembly.

2. Place a jack and a block of wood under the transaxle and support the transaxle.

3. Remove the bolts attaching the insulator to the frame.

4. Raise the transaxle with the jack enough to relieve the weight on the insulator.

5. Remove the bolts attaching the insulator to the transaxle. Remove the insulator.

6. Installation is the reverse of the removal procedure. Tighten the insulator-to-transaxle bolts to 60–86 ft. lbs. (81–116 Nm). Tighten the insulator-to-frame bolts to 60–86 ft. lbs. (81–116 Nm).

### RIGHT FRONT ENGINE INSULATOR (NO. 2)

1. Disconnect the negative battery cable. Remove the lower damper nut or bolt from the right side of the engine. Raise and support the vehicle safely.

2. Place a jack and a block of wood under the engine block.

3. Remove the nuts attaching the right front and rear insulators to the frame.

4. Raise the engine with the jack until enough of a load is taken off of the insulator.

5. Remove the bolt(s) and the insulator from the engine bracket.

6. Installation is the reverse of the removal procedure. Tighten the insulator-to-engine bracket bolt(s) to 40–55 ft. lbs. (54–75 Nm) on the 2.5L engine, or 71–95 ft. lbs. (96–129 Nm) on the 3.0L engine. Tighten the nut attaching the right front and right rear insulators to the frame to 55–75 ft. lbs. (75–102 Nm).

### 3.0L and 3.2L SHO Engines

### RIGHT FRONT (NO. 2) AND RIGHT REAR (NO. 3)

1. Remove the lower damper bolt from the right side of the engine.

2. Raise the vehicle and support it safely.

3. Place a jack and a wood block in a suitable place under the engine.

4. Remove the roll damper-to-engine retaining nuts and remove the roll damper.

5. Raise the engine enough to unload the insulator.

6. Remove the 2 through-bolts and remove the insulators from the engine bracket.

7. Installation is the reverse of the removal procedure. Tighten the insulator-to-engine bracket bolts to 40–55 ft. lbs. (54–75 Nm). Tighten the insulator-to-frame nuts to 50–70 ft. lbs. (68–95 Nm). Tighten the roll damper retaining nuts to 40–55 ft. lbs. (54–75 Nm). Tighten the engine damper-to-engine bolt to 40–55 ft. lbs. (54–75 Nm).

### LEFT ENGINE INSULATOR AND SUPPORT ASSEMBLY

1. Remove the bolt retaining the roll damper to the lower damper bracket and place the damper shaft aside.

2. Remove the back-up light switch and the energy management bracket.

3. Raise the vehicle and support it with jackstands under the vehicle body, allowing the subframe to hang.

4. Remove the left tire and wheel assembly.

5. Place a jack and wood block under the transaxle.

6. Remove the nuts retaining the lower damper bracket to the engine mount and the bolts retaining the insulator to the transaxle and subframe.

7. Raise the transaxle with the jack enough to unload the insulator.

8. Remove the insulator and lower damper bracket.

9. Installation is the reverse of the removal procedure. Tighten the damper bracket-to-insulator nuts to 40–55 ft. lbs. (54–75 Nm) and the insulator-to-transaxle bolts to 70–95 ft. lbs. (95–139 Nm). Tighten the insulator-to-frame bolts to 60–85 ft. lbs. (81–115 Nm) and the damper to damper bracket bolt to 40–55 ft. lbs. (54–75 Nm).

### 3.8L Engine

### RIGHT FRONT ENGINE INSULATOR

1. Disconnect the negative battery cable. Remove the air conditioning compressor-to-engine mounting bracket mounting bolts and position the compressor to the side. Do not discharge the air conditioning system.

2. Raise the vehicle and support safely.

3. Remove the nut attaching the engine mount to the air conditioning compressor bracket.

4. Temporarily attach the air conditioning compressor to the mounting bracket with the 2 lower bolts.

5. Position a jack and wood block in a convenient location under the engine block.

6. Remove the upper and lower nuts attaching the right front and left rear insulators to the frame.

7. Raise the engine with the jack enough to relieve the load on the insulator.

8. Remove the insulator assembly. Remove the heat shield from the insulator.

9. Installation is the reverse of the removal procedure. Tighten the upper insulator stud retaining nut to 40–55 ft. lbs. (54–75 Nm) and the lower retaining nut to 50–70 ft. lbs. (68–95 Nm).

### RIGHT REAR ENGINE INSULATOR (NO. 3)

1. Disconnect the negative battery cable and raise, then support the vehicle safely.

2. Remove the nuts retaining the right front and right rear engine mounts to the frame.

3. Lower the vehicle.

4. Using suitable engine lifting equipment, raise the engine approximately 1 in. (25mm).

5. Loosen the retaining nut on the right rear (No. 3) mount and heat shield assembly.

6. Raise and support the vehicle safely.

7. Remove the insulator retaining nut and the insulator and heat shield assembly.

8. Installation is the reverse of the removal procedure. Tighten the top retaining nut on the insulator to 40–55 ft. lbs. (54–75 Nm). Tighten the retaining nuts on the right front and right rear engine mounts to 55–75 ft. lbs. (75–102 Nm).

### LEFT ENGINE MOUNT AND SUPPORT ASSEMBLY

1. Raise the vehicle and support it safely.

2. Remove the tire and wheel assembly.

3. Place a jack and wood block under the transaxle and support the transaxle.

4. Remove the 2 bolts retaining the vertical restrictor assembly.

5. Remove the nut retaining the transaxle mount to the support assembly.

6. Remove the 2 through-bolts retaining the transaxle mount to the frame.

7. Raise the transaxle with the jack enough to unload the mount.

8. Remove the bolts retaining the support assembly to the transaxle and remove the mount and/or transaxle support assembly.

9. Installation is the reverse of the removal procedure. Tighten the support assembly-to-transaxle bolts to 35 ft. lbs. (48 Nm) and the mount-to-frame bolts to 60–86 ft. lbs. (81–116 Nm). Tighten the transaxle mount-to-support nut to 55–75 ft. lbs. (75–102 Nm) and the 2 bolts retaining the vertical restrictor assembly to 40–55 ft. lbs. (54–75 Nm).

## Rocker Arm (Valve) Cover

### REMOVAL & INSTALLATION

### 2.5L Engine

#### ▶ See Figures 53, 54, 55, 56 and 57

1. Disconnect the negative battery cable.

2. If necessary, remove the oil fill cap and rocker arm filter, and set aside.

3. Disconnect the PCV hose and set it aside.

Fig. 53 Disconnect the PCV hose, then set it aside—early model 2.5L shown

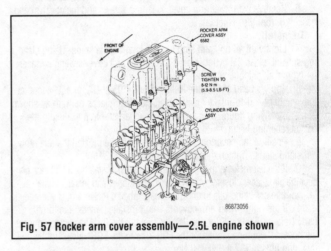

Fig. 56 Inspect the rocker arm cover gasket for damage—early model 2.5L shown

Fig. 54 Remove the rocker arm cover retaining bolts—early model 2.5L shown

Fig. 57 Rocker arm cover assembly—2.5L engine shown

4. Disconnect the throttle linkage cable from the top of the rocker arm cover. If equipped, disconnect the speed control cable from the top of the rocker arm cover.

5. Remove the rocker arm cover bolts. Remove the rocker cover and gasket assembly from the engine.

**To install:**

6. Clean the cylinder head and rocker arm cover mating surfaces.

➡**When using RTV sealant, install the rocker arm cover within five minutes to prevent the sealant from ``skinning'' over.**

7. If the gasket is damaged by a cut and/or nick of about ⅛ in. (3mm) (two cuts or nicks at the most), fill in the damaged area with RTV sealant E8AZ-19562-A or equivalent. If the gasket is damaged more than that, the entire rocker arm cover must be replaced.

8. If damaged, replace the rubber isolator(s), washer, or bolt and rubber isolator assembly.

➡**If reusing the old rocker arm cover bolts, always put a drop of adhesive threadlock (ESE-M2G260-AA) or equivalent on the threads of the bolt, prior to installation. Only new bolts are pre-applied with adhesive. Failure to do so may result in an oil leak.**

9. Install the rocker arm cover assembly, then tighten the retaining bolts to 6–9 ft. lbs. (8–12 Nm).

10. If equipped, connect the speed control cable and the throttle linkage cable to the top of the rocker arm cover.

11. Connect the PCV hose into the rocker arm cover, then install the rocker arm filter and the oil fill cap, if removed.

Fig. 55 Remove the rocker arm cover from the engine—early model 2.5L shown

➡**RTV must be cured completely before coming in contact with engine oil. Wait about one hour before starting the engine to allow the RTV to cure.**

12. Connect the negative battery cable, then start the engine and run it at a fast idle. Check for any oil leaks.

### 3.0L Engine

#### 1986–90 VEHICLES

▶ **See Figure 58**

1. Disconnect the negative battery cable.
2. Tag and disconnect the spark plug wires.
3. Remove the ignition wire/separator assembly from the rocker arm cover retaining studs, then move it out of the way.
4. If the left rocker arm cover is being removed: remove the oil fill cap, disconnect the air cleaner closure system hose and remove the fuel injector harness stand-offs from the inboard rocker arm cover, then move the harness out of the way.
5. If the right rocker arm cover is being removed: remove the PCV valve and, if equipped, loosen the lower EGR tube retaining nut and rotate the tube aside. Remove the throttle body and move the fuel injection harness aside.
6. Remove the rocker arm cover attaching screws and the cover(s) and gasket(s) from the vehicle.

**To install:**

7. Lightly oil all bolt and stud threads before installation. Using cleaning solvent, clean the cylinder head and rocker arm cover sealing surfaces to remove all silicone sealer and/or dirt.
8. Apply a bead of Silicone Rubber D6AZ-19562-BA, or equivalent, at the cylinder head-to-intake manifold rail step (two places per rail) as shown in accompanying figure, then position a new gasket into place using the gasket retaining features.
9. Position the cover onto the cylinder head, then install the retaining bolts and studs. Tighten the retainers to 9 ft. lbs. (12 Nm).
10. If the left rocker arm cover is being installed: install the oil fill cap, connect the air cleaner closure system hose to the nipple, and install the fuel injector harness stand-offs to the appropriate inboard rocker arm cover studs.
11. If the right rocker arm cover is being installed: install the throttle body (refer to Section 5 for details), then install the PCV valve and connect the hoses. If equipped, connect the EGR tube to the EGR valve. Tighten the retaining nuts to (37 ft. lbs. (50 Nm).
12. Connect the ignition wires to the spark plugs, as tagged during removal. Install the ignition wire separator stand-offs to the appropriate rocker arm cover studs.
13. Connect the negative battery cable, then start the engine and check for oil and/or vacuum leaks.

#### 1991–95 VEHICLES

▶ **See Figures 59 and 60**

➡**The rocker arm/valve covers on these vehicles have built-in gaskets which should last the life of the vehicle.**

1. Disconnect the negative battery cable.
2. Tag and disconnect the ignition wires from the spark plugs.
3. Remove the ignition wire(s) and bracket from the rocker arm/valve cover retaining studs, then move it out of the way.
4. If the left valve cover is being removed: disconnect the crankcase ventilation tube, remove the oil filler cap, and remove the the fuel charging wiring harness stand-offs from the inboard valve cover studs, then move the harness out of the way.
5. If the right valve cover is being removed, first remove the throttle body (refer to Section 5 for this procedure). Loosen the lower EGR valve-to-exhaust manifold tube retaining nut and rotate the EGR valve-to-exhaust manifold tube out of the way. Remove the PCV valve, then remove the fuel charging wiring stand-offs from the inboard valve cover studs and move the fuel charging wiring out of the way.
6. Loosen the valve cover retaining bolts and studs, then carefully slide a sharp, thin-bladed object between the cylinder head and the valve cover gasket where the intake manifold mates to the cylinder head. Be careful to cut only the sealer and not the valve cover gasket itself.
7. Remove the valve cover, making sure that the silicone sealer does not pull the integral valve cover gasket from the cover.

➡**If removing the gasket, make sure to note the bolt and stud locations before removing the valve cover gasket, as the fasteners are secured by the valve cover gasket.**

8. If necessary, remove the built-in (or integral) valve cover gasket by pulling it from the valve cover gasket channel.

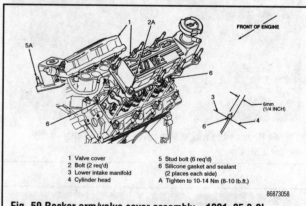

**Fig. 59 Rocker arm/valve cover assembly—1991–95 3.0L engines (except SHO)**

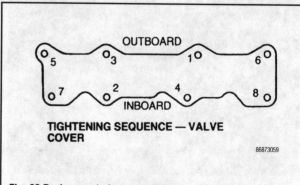

**Fig. 60 Rocker arm/valve cover tightening sequence—1991–95 3.0L vehicles (except SHO)**

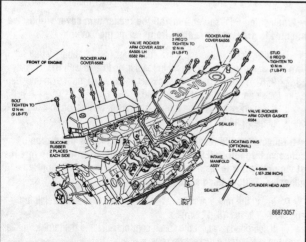

**Fig. 58 Rocker arm cover and related components—1990 3.0L engine shown**

**To install:**

9. Lightly oil all bolt and stud bolt threads before installation. Clean the gasket with a soft, clean cloth to remove any dirt, then using a suitable solvent, clean off any remaining silicone sealant.

➡**Check the valve cover gasket for correct installation. A new valve cover gasket will lay flat to the valve cover in both the channel and fastener areas. If the gasket is installed wrong, oil leakage will occur.**

10. If installing a new gasket, align the fastener holes, then lay the new gasket onto the channel.

11. Install the valve cover gasket to each fastener by securing the fastener head with a nut driver or socket. Seat the fastener against the valve cover and, at the same time, roll the gasket around the fastener collar. If it's installed correctly, all of the fasteners will be secured by the valve cover gasket and will not fall out.

12. Before applying sealer, clean all sealing surfaces with Metal Surface Cleaner F4AZ-19A536-RA or equivalent, to remove any residues that may interfere with the sealer's ability to adhere.

13. Apply a bead of Silicone Gasket and Sealant F1AZ-19562-A or equivalent, at the cylinder head-to-intake manifold step (two places per side) as shown in the accompanying figure.

➡**When installing the valve cover, use a "straight down" approach, to avoid smearing or smudging the sealant, which will cause leaks.**

14. Position the valve cover on the cylinder head and hand-tighten the retaining bolts and stud bolts, then tighten in sequence (see accompanying figure) to 8–10 ft. lbs. (10–14 Nm).

15. If the left cover is being installed: install the oil filler cap, fasten the crankcase ventilation tube to the connector, and install the fuel charging wiring stand-offs to the appropriate inboard valve cover stud bolts.

16. If the right cover is being installed: install the fuel charging wiring stand-offs to the appropriate inboard valve cover stud bolts, install the throttle body (see Section 5 of this manual for details), install the PCV valve, then connect the crankcase ventilation tube, and connect the EGR valve-to-exhaust manifold tube-to-EGR valve. Tighten both retaining nuts to 26–48 ft. lbs. (35–65 Nm).

17. Install the ignition wire(s) and bracket to the rocker arm/valve cover retaining studs, then connect the ignition wires to the spark plugs as tagged during removal.

18. Connect the negative battery cable.

### 3.0L and 3.2L SHO Engines

1. Disconnect the negative battery cable.
2. Properly relieve the fuel system pressure. For details, please refer to the procedure in Section 1 or 5 of this manual.
3. Tag and disengage all vacuum lines and electrical connectors from the intake manifold.
4. Remove the upper intake manifold assembly. For details, please refer to the procedure later in this section.
5. Tag and disconnect the spark plug wires.
6. If the left cover is being removed, remove the oil fill cap and the ignition coil plastic cover.
7. If the right cover is being removed, disconnect the fuel lines.
8. Remove the rocker arm/valve cover retaining bolts, then remove the cover.

**To install:**

➡**Lightly oil all bolt and stud threads before installation. Clean the cylinder head and valve cover sealing surfaces, using solvent, to remove all dirt.**

9. Inspect the gasket and the three spark plug holes for damage and replace, if necessary. Position the valve cover on the cylinder head and install the retaining bolts. Tighten the bolts to 7–12 ft. lbs. (9.5–16 Nm).

10. If the left valve cover is being installed, install the ignition coil plastic cover and the oil filler cap.

11. If the right valve cover is being installed, connect the fuel lines.

12. Connect the spark plug wires as tagged during removal.

13. Install the upper intake manifold. For details, please refer to the procedure located later in this section.

14. Engage all vacuum lines and electrical connectors, as tagged during removal, to the intake manifold.

15. Connect the negative battery cable, then start the engine and check for fuel, coolant, and/or oil leaks.

### 3.8L Engine

◆ **See Figure 61**

1. Disconnect the negative battery cable.
2. Tag and disconnect the ignition wires from the spark plugs.
3. Remove the ignition wire separators from the valve cover retaining bolt studs.
4. For 1993–95 vehicles, remove the upper intake manifold. For details, please refer to the procedure located later in this section.
5. If the left cover is being removed, remove the oil fill cap.
6. If the right cover is being removed, position the air cleaner assembly aside and remove the PCV valve.
7. Remove the rocker arm/valve cover mounting bolts, then remove the cover.

**To install:**

8. Lightly oil all bolt and stud bolt threads, then, using solvent, clean the cylinder head and valve cover sealing surface to remove all gasket material and dirt.

9. Position a new rocker arm/valve cover gasket on the cylinder head, then install the retaining bolts. Make sure to note the position of the ignition wire separator stud bolts, then tighten the retaining bolts to 80–106 inch lbs. (9–12 Nm).

10. If removed, install the upper intake manifold. For details, please refer to the procedure located later in this section.

11. If the left cover is being installed, install the oil filler cap.

12. If the right cover is being installed, install the PCV valve, then the air cleaner.

13. Install the ignition wire separators, then connect the ignition wires to the spark plugs as tagged during removal.

14. Connect the negative battery cable, then start the engine and check for oil leaks.

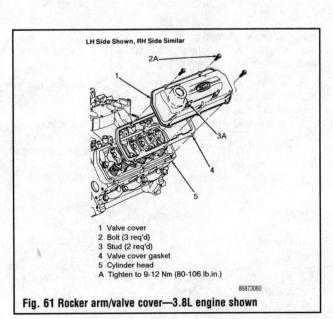

1 Valve cover
2 Bolt (3 req'd)
3 Stud (2 req'd)
4 Valve cover gasket
5 Cylinder head
A Tighten to 9-12 Nm (80-106 lb.in.)

86873060

**Fig. 61 Rocker arm/valve cover—3.8L engine shown**

## Rocker Arms

### REMOVAL & INSTALLATION

#### 2.5L Engine

▶ See Figures 62, 63 and 64

1. Disconnect the negative battery cable.
2. Remove the rocker arm cover. For details, please refer to the procedure located earlier in this section.
3. Remove the rocker arm bolts, fulcrums, rocker arms and fulcrum washers. Keep all parts in order so they can be reinstalled to their original position.

**To install:**

4. Clean the cylinder head and rocker arm cover mating surfaces.
5. Coat the valve tips, rocker arm and fulcrum contact areas with Lubricate® or equivalent.
6. For each valve, rotate the engine until the lifter is on the base circle of the cam (valve closed).
7. Install the rocker arm and components, then tighten the rocker arm bolts in 2 steps, first to 6–8 ft. lbs. (8–11 Nm) and second to 20–26 ft. lbs. (27–35 Nm). Be sure the lifter is on the base circle of the cam for each rocker arm as it is installed. For the final tightening, the camshaft may be in any position. Check the valve lash.
8. Install a new rocker arm cover gasket, using suitable sealer, unless the cover is equipped with a molded-in gasket, in which case no sealer should be used.
9. Install the rocker arm cover and tighten the bolts to 6–8 ft. lbs. (8–11 Nm), then install/connect the components to the rocker arm cover. For details, please refer to the rocker arm cover procedure located earlier in this section.
10. Connect the negative battery cable.

#### 3.0L Engine—Except SHO

1. Disconnect the negative battery cable. Tag and disconnect the ignition wires from the spark plugs.
2. Remove the rocker arm/valve covers from the cylinder head. For details, please refer to the procedure located earlier in this section.
3. Remove the rocker arm bolts, fulcrums, rocker arms and fulcrum washers. Keep all parts in order so they can be reinstalled to their original position.

**To install:**

4. Lightly oil all the bolt and stud threads before installation. Coat the valve tips, rocker arm and fulcrum contact areas with Engine Assembly Lubricant D9AZ-19579-D, or equivalent.

➡Rocker arm seats must be fully seated in the cylinder head, and the pushrod(s) must be fully seated in the rocker arm valve lifter sockets before final tightening.

5. Install the rocker arms into position with the pushrods, then snug the retaining bolt. Rotate the crankshaft to position the camshaft lobes straight down and away from the rocker arm.
6. Tighten the retaining bolts which secure the rocker arm seats into the cylinder head to 5–11 ft. lbs. (7–15 Nm), then final-tighten the retaining bolts to 19–28 ft. lbs. (26–38 Nm). Be sure the lifter is on the base circle of the cam for each rocker arm as it is installed.
7. Install the rocker arm/valve covers. For details, please refer to the procedure located earlier in this section.
8. Attach the ignition wires to the spark plugs as tagged during removal, then connect the negative battery cable.

#### 3.8L Engine

1. Disconnect the negative battery cable.
2. Remove the rocker arm/valve cover(s). For details, please refer to the procedure located earlier in this section.
3. Remove the rocker arm bolt, fulcrum and rocker arm. Keep all parts in order so they can be reinstalled in their original positions.

**Fig. 62 Loosen the rocker arm retaining bolts—early 2.5L engine shown**

**Fig. 63 Remove the rocker arm bolts—early 2.5L engine shown**

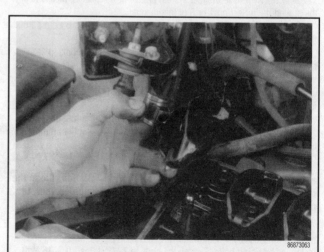

**Fig. 64 When removing the rocker arm and fulcrum, make sure to keep all parts in order so they can be installed in their original position**

**To install:**

4. Lubricated all rocker arms with Engine Assembly Lubricant D9AZ-19579-D or equivalent.

➡**Rocker arm seats must be fully seated in the cylinder head, and pushrods must be seated in the rocker arm sockets before final tightening, or engine damage may occur.**

5. For each valve, rotate the crankshaft until the valve lifter rests on the heel (base circle) of the camshaft lobe. Position the rocker arm(s) over the push rods, then install the rocker arm seats. Tighten the rocker arm seat retaining bolts to 44 inch lbs. (5 Nm).

6. Final-tighten the rocker arm retaining bolt(s) to 19–25 ft. lbs. (25–35 Nm). For final tightening, the camshaft may be in any position.

7. Clean the rocker arm cover and cylinder head mating surfaces of old gasket material and dirt.

8. Install the rocker arm/valve cover(s). For details, please refer to the procedure located earlier in this section.

9. Connect the negative battery cable.

## Thermostat

### REMOVAL & INSTALLATION

### ✳✳ CAUTION

**When draining the coolant, keep in mind that cats and dogs are attracted by ethylene glycol antifreeze, and are quite likely to drink any that is left in an uncovered container or in puddles on the ground. This will prove fatal in sufficient quantity. Always drain the coolant into a sealable container. Coolant should be reused unless it is contaminated or several years old.**

#### 2.5L Engine

▸ **See Figures 65, 66, 67 and 68**

1. Disconnect the negative battery cable.

2. Position a suitable drain pan below the radiator. Carefully remove the radiator cap, then attach a 0.4 in. (9.5mm) hose to the drain tube (to prevent a mess) and open the draincock. Drain the radiator to a corre-

sponding level below the water outlet connection, then close the drain-cock.

3. Remove the vent plug from the water outlet connection.

4. Loosen the top hose clamp at the radiator, then remove the water outlet connection retaining bolts and lift the outlet clear of the engine. Remove the thermostat by pulling it out of the water outlet connection.

➡**Do not pry the housing off.**

**To install:**

5. Make sure the water outlet connection and cylinder head mating surfaces are clean and free from gasket material. Make sure the water outlet connection pocket and air vent passage are clean and free from rust. Clean the vent plug and gasket.

6. Place the thermostat in position, fully inserted to compress the gasket and pressed into the water outlet connection to secure. Install the water outlet connection to the cylinder head using a new gasket. Tighten the bolts to 12–18 ft. lbs. (16–24 Nm). Position the top hose to the radiator and tighten the clamps.

7. Refill the cooling system. Connect the negative battery cable. Start the engine and check for leaks. Check the coolant level and add as required.

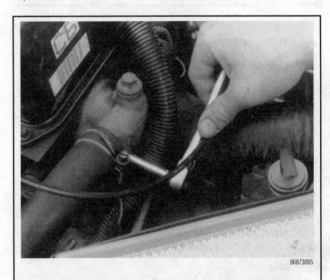

**Fig. 66 Remove the water outlet connection retaining bolts**

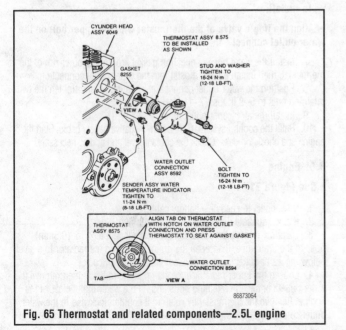

**Fig. 65 Thermostat and related components—2.5L engine**

**Fig. 67 Remove the thermostat by pulling it out of the water outlet connection**

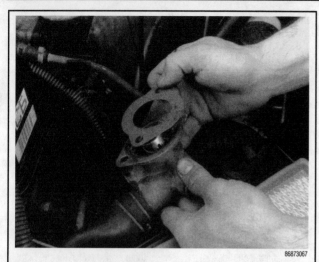

**Fig. 68 Use a new gasket when installing the water outlet connection**

### 3.0L Engine—Except SHO

▶ See Figure 69

1. Disconnect the negative battery cable.
2. Place a suitable drain pan under the radiator.
3. Carefully remove the radiator cap and open the draincock, then drain the cooling system.
4. Remove the upper radiator hose from the water outlet connection/thermostat housing.
5. Remove the three retaining bolts from the water outlet connection/thermostat housing.
6. Remove the housing and the thermostat as an assembly.
7. Remove the thermostat from the housing/water outlet connection, then discard the water outlet hose gasket and carefully clean the mating surfaces with a gasket scraper.

➡ **Be careful when scraping the gasket surfaces because aluminum gouges easily, forming leaks paths.**

**To install:**
8. Make sure all sealing surfaces are free of old gasket material.
9. Insert the thermostat into the water outlet connection/housing and rotate clockwise to lock it in. Note the location of the jiggle valve in relation to the water outlet connection.
10. Position a new gasket onto the water outlet connection/housing using the bolts as a holding device. Install the thermostat assembly, then tighten the retaining bolts to 8–10 ft. lbs. (10–14 Nm).

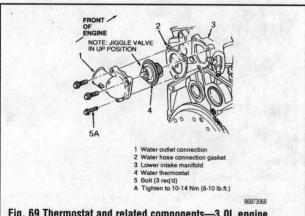

1 Water outlet connection
2 Water hose connection gasket
3 Lower intake manifold
4 Water thermostat
5 Bolt (3 req'd)
A Tighten to 10-14 Nm (8-10 lb.ft.)

**Fig. 69 Thermostat and related components—3.0L engine (except SHO)**

➡ **Make sure that the hose clamps are beyond the center of the clamping surface of the connection. Any used hose clamps must be replaced with new clamps to ensure proper sealing at the connection.**

11. Install the upper radiator hose and position the clamps between the alignment marks on both ends of the hose, then slide the hose on the connections. Tighten the screw clamps to 20–30 inch lbs. (2.2–3.4 Nm).
12. Fill and bleed the cooling system. Connect the negative battery cable, start the engine and check for coolant leaks. Check the coolant level and add as required.

### 3.0L and 3.2L SHO Engines

▶ See Figure 70

1. Disconnect the negative battery cable.
2. Place a suitable drain pan below the radiator. Remove the radiator cap and open the draincock. Partially drain the cooling system, then close the draincock.
3. Remove the air cleaner outlet tube.
4. Disconnect the upper radiator hose from the water outlet connection.
5. Remove the two retaining nuts, then remove the water outlet connection.
6. Remove the thermostat and the water hose connection gasket from the water outlet connection.

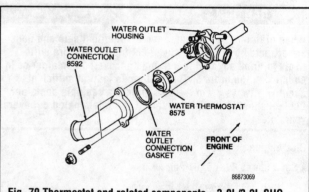

**Fig. 70 Thermostat and related components—3.0L/3.2L SHO engines**

**To install:**
➡ **Align the jiggle valve of the thermostat with the upper bolt on the water outlet connection.**

7. Install the water hose connection gasket around the outer rim of the thermostat, then install the thermostat into the water outlet connection.
8. Position the water outlet connection, then install and tighten the two retaining nuts to 5–8 ft. lbs. (7–11 Nm).
9. Install the air cleaner outlet tube.
10. Refill the cooling system. Connect the negative battery cable. Start the engine and check for leaks. Check the coolant level and add as necessary.

### 3.8L Engine

▶ See Figure 71

1. Disconnect the negative battery cable.
2. Place a suitable drain pan below the radiator.
3. Carefully remove the radiator cap, then connect a ⅜ in. (9.5mm) hose to the drain tube, then open the draincock. Drain the radiator to a level below the water outlet connection, then close the draincock.
4. Loosen the upper radiator hose clamp at the radiator, then remove the water outlet connection retaining bolts and lift the water outlet clear of the engine. Remove the thermostat by rotating it counterclockwise in the water outlet connection until the thermostat becomes free to remove.

➡ **Do not pry the water outlet connection off.**

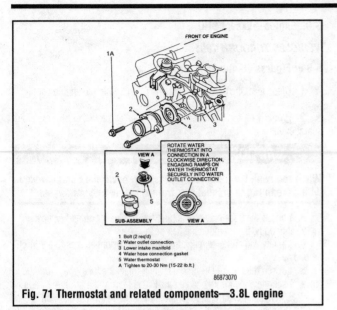

1  Bolt (2 req'd)
2  Water outlet connection
3  Lower intake manifold
4  Water hose connection gasket
5  Water thermostat
A  Tighten to 20-30 Nm (15-22 lb.ft.)

ROTATE WATER THERMOSTAT INTO CONNECTION IN A CLOCKWISE DIRECTION, ENGAGING RAMPS ON WATER THERMOSTAT SECURELY INTO WATER OUTLET CONNECTION

FRONT OF ENGINE

VIEW A

SUB-ASSEMBLY    VIEW A

86873070

**Fig. 71 Thermostat and related components—3.8L engine**

**To install:**

5.  Make sure the water outlet connection pocket and all mating surfaces are clean.

6.  Fully insert the thermostat and rotate it clockwise in the water outlet connection to secure.

7.  Position the water outlet connection to the intake manifold with a new gasket and secure the retaining bolts. Tighten the bolts to 15–22 ft. lbs. (20–30 Nm).

➡**Make sure the hose clamps are beyond the bead and placed in the center of the clamping surface of the connection. Any used hose clamps must be replaced with a new clamp to ensure proper sealing at the connection.**

8.  Position the upper radiator hose to the radiator. Position the clamps between the alignment marks on both ends of the upper radiator hose, then slide the hose on the connections. Tighten the screw clamps to 20–30 inch lbs. (2.2–3.4 Nm).

9.  Refill the cooling system. Connect the negative battery cable. Start the engine and check for leaks. Check the coolant level and add as required.

## Cooling System Bleeding

### ✳✳ CAUTION

**When draining the coolant, keep in mind that cats and dogs are attracted by ethylene glycol antifreeze, and are quite likely to drink any that is left in an uncovered container or in puddles on the ground. This will prove fatal in sufficient quantity. Always drain the coolant into a sealable container. Coolant should be reused unless it is contaminated or several years old.**

When the entire cooling system is drained, the following procedure should be used to ensure a complete fill.

1.  Install the block drain plug, if removed, and close the draincock. With the engine off, add antifreeze to the radiator to a level of 50 percent of the total cooling system capacity. Then add water until it reaches the radiator filler neck seat.

➡**On 2.5L engines, remove the vent plug on the water connection outlet. The vent plug must be removed before the radiator is filled or the engine may not fill completely. Do not turn the plastic cap under the vent plug or the gasket may be damaged. Do not try to add coolant through the vent plug hole. Install the vent plug after filling the radiator and before starting the engine.**

2.  Install the radiator cap to the first notch to keep spillage to a minimum.

3.  Start the engine and let it idle until the upper radiator hose is warm. This indicates that the thermostat is open and coolant is flowing through the entire system.

4.  Carefully remove the radiator cap and top off the radiator with water. Install the cap on the radiator securely.

5.  Fill the coolant recovery reservoir to the FULL COLD mark with antifreeze, then add water to the FULL HOT mark. This will ensure that a proper mixture is in the coolant recovery bottle.

6.  Check for leaks at the draincock, block plug and at the vent plug on 2.5L engine.

## Intake Manifold

### REMOVAL & INSTALLATION

#### 2.5L Engine

▶ **See Figures 72, 73 and 74**

1.  Open and secure the hood.

2.  Properly relieve the fuel system pressure, then disconnect the negative battery cable.

3.  Drain the cooling system.

4.  Remove accelerator cable and, if equipped, the cruise control cable.

5.  Remove the air cleaner assembly and the heat stove tube at the heat shield.

6.  Tag and disengage any required vacuum lines and electrical connections.

7.  As required on vehicles before 1990, disconnect the thermactor check valve hose at the tube assembly and remove the bracket-to-EGR valve attaching nuts.

8.  Disconnect the fuel supply and return lines.

9.  As required on vehicles before 1990, disconnect the water inlet tube at the intake manifold. On 1991 vehicles, remove the exhaust manifold heat shroud assembly.

10.  Disconnect the EGR tube at the EGR valve.

11.  Unfasten the intake manifold retaining bolts and remove the intake manifold. Remove the gasket and clean the gasket contact surfaces.

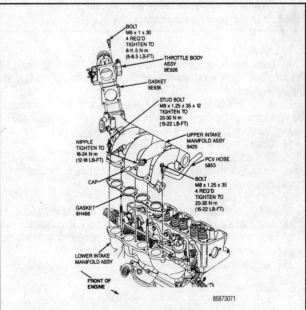

BOLT
M6 x 1 x 30
4 REQ'D
TIGHTEN TO
8-11.5 N·m
(6-8.5 LB-FT)

THROTTLE BODY
ASSY
9E926

GASKET
9E936

STUD BOLT
M8 x 1.25 x 35 x 12
TIGHTEN TO
20-30 N·m
(15-22 LB-FT)

UPPER INTAKE
MANIFOLD ASSY
9425

PCV HOSE
5853

NIPPLE
TIGHTEN TO
16-24 N·m
(12-18 LB-FT)

CAP

BOLT
M8 x 1.25 x 35
4 REQ'D
TIGHTEN TO
20-30 N·m
(15-22 LB-FT)

GASKET
9H486

LOWER INTAKE
MANIFOLD ASSY

FRONT OF
ENGINE

86873071

**Fig. 72 Common intake manifold assembly—late model 2.5L engine shown**

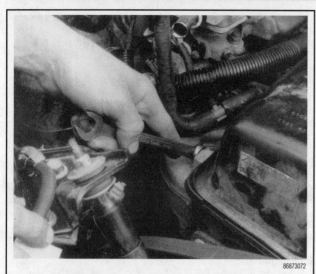

**Fig. 73 Remove the intake manifold retaining bolts**

**Fig. 74 After removing the intake manifold, remove the gasket and clean the gasket mating surfaces**

### To install:

12. Install the intake manifold using a new gasket, then secure using the retaining bolts. Tighten the retaining bolts to 15–22 ft. lbs. (20–30 Nm) in the proper sequence.

13. As required on vehicles before 1990, connect the water inlet tube at the intake manifold, connect the thermactor check valve hose at the tube assembly and install the bracket-to-EGR valve attaching nuts.

14. Connect the EGR tube to the EGR valve.

15. Connect the fuel supply and return lines.

16. Fasten any applicable vacuum lines and electrical connectors, as tagged during removal.

17. On 1991 vehicles, install the heat shroud.

18. Install the air cleaner assembly and the heat stove tube.

19. Install accelerator cable and cruise control cable, if equipped.

20. Connect the negative battery cable and fill the cooling system to the proper level with a 50/50 mixture of coolant and water.

21. Start the engine and check for leaks.

### 3.0L Engine—Except SHO

#### VEHICLES THROUGH 1991

♦ See Figures 75 and 76

1. Disconnect the negative battery cable and drain the engine cooling system.

2. Properly relieve the fuel system pressure at the fuel supply manifold schrader valve.

> ### ✳✳ CAUTION
>
> **When relieving the fuel system pressure, cover the Schrader valve with a clean rag to prevent fuel from spraying into your eyes!**

3. Loosen the hose clamp attaching the air cleaner outlet flex hose to the throttle body, then remove the flex hose.

4. Identify, tag and disengage and all vacuum connections to the throttle body.

5. Loosen the lower EGR tube nut, then rotate the tube away from the valve. Disconnect the throttle cable and TV cable from the throttle linkage.

6. Disengage the air charge temperature sensor, throttle position sensor, air-by-pass valve, and pressure feedback EGR electrical connectors.

7. Disconnect the throttle body retaining bolts, then remove the throttle body. For details regarding throttle body removal, please refer to the procedure in Section 5 of this manual.

8. Remove the fuel lines safety clips, then disconnect the fuel lines from the fuel supply manifold. Cover the ends of the fuel lines to prevent dirt and/or debris from entering the lines. Remove the fuel injector wiring harness stand-offs from the inboard rocker arm cover retaining studs and each injector from the engine.

➡ **Fuel injectors and the fuel supply manifold may be removed with the intake manifold as an assembly.**

9. Remove the ignition coil and bracket and set aside, out of the way.

10. Tag and disconnect the spark plug wires, then remove the rocker arm covers. For details regarding rocker arm cover removal, please refer to the procedure located earlier in this section.

11. Disconnect the upper radiator hose and heater hoses.

12. If equipped, remove the distributor cap rubber boot, then mark the position of the distributor housing to the engine block and remove the cap and note the rotor position.

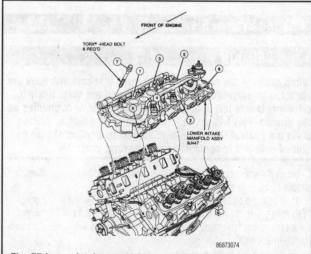

**Fig. 75 Lower intake manifold assembly—3.0L engine (except SHO)**

13. Disengage the distributor electrical connector, then remove the distributor assembly.

14. Disconnect the engine coolant temperature sensor and temperature sending unit connector.

15. Loosen the intake valve retaining nut from the No. 3 cylinder and rotate the rocker arm from the retainer, then remove the pushrod.

16. Using a Torx® head socket, remove the intake manifold attaching bolts, then place a suitable prybar between the intake manifold (near the thermostat) and the transmission. Use the prybar to carefully loosen the intake manifold from the sealing surfaces.

17. Lift the intake manifold away from the engine. Place clean rags in the lifter valley to catch any dirt or gasket materials. Remove the manifold side gaskets and seals and discard. Scrape the sealing surfaces to remove any trace of gasket material and rubber sealant.

➡ Be careful when scraping aluminum surfaces to prevent gouging which will cause leaking. To remove the old silicone rubber, use a suitable cleaning solvent.

### To install:

➡ Lightly oil all the attaching bolts and stud threads before installation. When using a silicone rubber sealer, assembly must occur within 15 minutes after the sealer has been applied. After this time, the sealer may start to set-up and its sealing quality may be reduced. In high temperature/humidity conditions, the sealant will start to set up in approximately 5 minutes.

18. The intake manifold, cylinder head and cylinder block mating surfaces should be clean and free of old silicone rubber sealer. Use a suitable solvent to clean these surfaces.

19. Apply a Silicone Rubber Sealer D6AZ-19562-AA, or equivalent, to the intersection of the cylinder block end rails and cylinder heads.

20. Install the front and rear intake manifold end seals in place and secure. Install the intake manifold gaskets.

➡ The gaskets are marked for correct installation.

21. Carefully lower the intake manifold into position on the cylinder block and cylinder heads to prevent smearing the silicone sealer and causing gasket voids.

22. Using a Torx® head socket, install the retaining bolts and tighten the bolts, in sequence, to 11 ft. lbs. (15 Nm), then retorque to 21 ft. lbs. (28 Nm).

23. Install the fuel supply manifold and injectors. Apply lubricant to the injector holes in the intake manifold and fuel supply manifold prior to injector installation. Install the fuel supply manifold retaining bolts and tighten to 7 ft. lbs. (10 Nm).

24. Install the thermostat housing and a new gasket, if removed. Tighten the retaining bolts to 9 ft. lbs. (12 Nm).

25. Install the No. 3 cylinder intake valve pushrod. Apply Lubricant ESE-M2C39 or equivalent to the pushrod and valve stem prior to installation. Position the lifter on the base circle of the camshaft and tighten the rocker arm bolt in 2 steps, first to 8 ft. lbs. (11 Nm) and then to 24 ft. lbs. (32 Nm).

26. Install the rocker arm covers. For information regarding rocker arm installation, please refer to the procedure located earlier in this section.

27. Install the fuel injector harness. Install the stand-offs to the inboard rocker arm retaining studs, then attach the connectors to the fuel injectors.

28. Install the throttle body using a new gaskets. For details, please refer to throttle body installation in Section 5 of this manual.

29. Connect the PCV hose to the PCV valve.

30. If equipped, install the EGR tube and nut, using a new gasket. Tighten the nut on both ends to 37 ft. lbs. (50 Nm). Install the EGR cover using a new gasket. Tighten the bolts to 18 ft. lbs. (25 Nm).

31. Engage any electrical connectors or vacuum lines as tagged during removal.

32. Connect the fuel lines, then install the fuel line safety clips.

33. Install the distributor assembly, aligning the marks that were made during the removal procedure, then engage the electrical connector. Install the distributor cap rubber boot, if equipped.

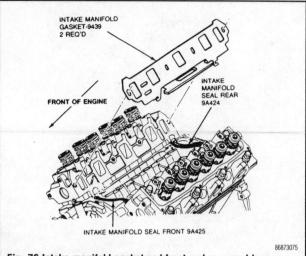

**Fig. 76 Intake manifold gasket and front and rear seal location—3.0L engine (except SHO)**

34. Install the spark plug wire harness to the plugs, using the retaining features attaching onto the rocker cover stud bolts.

35. Install the coil and bracket to the left hand front cylinder head. Tighten the retaining bolts to 35 ft. lbs. (48 Nm).

36. Engage the engine coolant temperature (ECT) sensor and the temperature sending unit electrical connectors.

37. Install the upper radiator and heater hose, making sure the clamp is fastened securely.

38. Install the air cleaner outlet flex tube to the throttle body, then tighten the clamp to 30 inch lbs. (4 Nm).

39. Fill and bleed the cooling system, then drain and replace the engine oil.

40. Reconnect the negative battery cable, start the engine and check for coolant, fuel, vacuum and oil leaks.

41. Check and if necessary, adjust the engine idle speed, transaxle throttle linkage and speed control.

### *1992–95 VEHICLES*

♦ **See Figures 77, 78 and 79**

1. Disconnect the negative battery cable, then properly drain the cooling system.

2. Remove the idle air control valve snow shield.

3. Remove the PCV tube from the rocker arm/valve cover and the air cleaner outlet tube.

4. Remove the aspirator hose from the air cleaner outlet tube. Remove the air cleaner from the throttle body and the air cleaner outlet tube.

➡ Before relieving the fuel pressure, cover the Schrader valve with a clean rag to prevent fuel from spraying into your eyes.

5. Carefully relieve the fuel system pressure at the fuel pressure relief Schrader valve. For details regarding this procedure, please refer to Section 1 of this manual.

6. Remove the fuel line clips, then disconnect the fuel lines.

7. Tag and disconnect vacuum lines from the throttle body.

8. For unleaded fuel vehicles only, disengage the intake air temperature and distributor electrical connector. For flexible fuel (FF) vehicles only, disengage the CSI and camshaft position sensor electrical connectors.

9. Disengage the throttle position sensor, the idle air control sensor, engine coolant temperature sensor, and the pressure feedback, or differential pressure feedback EGR sensor electrical connectors.

10. Disconnect the upper radiator hose from the thermostat housing. After loosening the retaining clamp, use a twisting motion on the hose to loosen it from the thermostat housing.

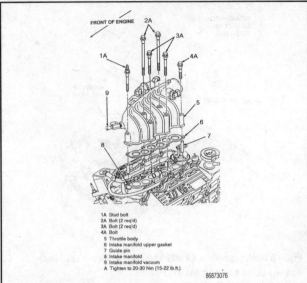

1A Stud bolt
2A Bolt (2 req'd)
3A Bolt (2 req'd)
4A Bolt
5 Throttle body
6 Intake manifold upper gasket
7 Guide pin
8 Intake manifold
9 Intake manifold vacuum
A Tighten to 20–30 Nm (15–22 lb.ft.)

86873076

**Fig. 77 Throttle body (upper intake manifold) removal—1994 3.0L unleaded gasoline engine shown**

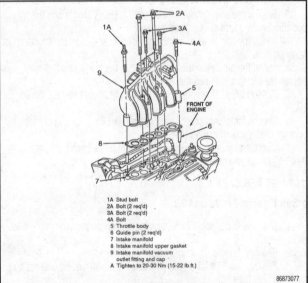

1A Stud bolt
2A Bolt (2 req'd)
3A Bolt (2 req'd)
4A Bolt
5 Throttle body
6 Guide pin (2 req'd)
7 Intake manifold
8 Intake manifold upper gasket
9 Intake manifold vacuum
   outlet fitting and cap
A Tighten to 20–30 Nm (15–22 lb.ft.)

86873077

**Fig. 78 Throttle body (upper intake manifold removal—1994 3.0L flexible fuel (FF) engine shown**

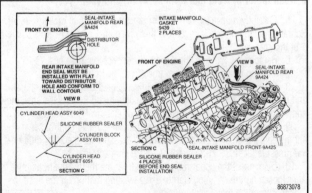

86873078

**Fig. 79 Intake manifold gasket and seal location—3.0L engine**

11. Remove the brace spanning from the alternator bracket to the throttle body stud.

12. Disconnect the throttle body retaining bolts, then remove the throttle body. For throttle body removal, please refer to the procedure in Section 5 of this manual.

13. Loosen the EGR retaining nut, them remove it from the EGR valve-to-exhaust manifold tube from the exhaust manifold.

14. Disconnect the fuel injector harness retaining stand-offs from the inboard rocker arm cover studs. Carefully disengage the electrical connections to each injector, then remove the fuel charging wiring from the engine.

➡**The intake manifold assembly may be removed with the fuel supply manifold and injectors in place.**

15. Disconnect the heater hoses.

16. Tag and remove the spark plug wires using a twisting motion on the plug rubber boot. Do NOT pull on the wire itself. Remove the harness retaining stand-offs from the rocker arm cover studs.

➡**Do NOT remove or disturb the camshaft position sensor during the disassembly process. On the 3.0L Flexible Fuel (FF) engine, the camshaft position sensor is NOT adjustable, and it requires a special tool to correctly index the camshaft position.**

17. On unleaded gasoline engines only, mark the distributor housing to engine block and note the rotor position. Remove the distributor retaining bolt and washer, then remove the distributor.

18. Remove the ignition coil from the rear of the left hand cylinder head.

19. Remove the rocker arm/valve covers. For details regarding rocker arm cover removal, please refer to the procedure located earlier in this section.

20. Loosen the cylinder No. 3 intake valve rocker arm retaining nut, then rotate the arm off the push rod and away from the top of the valve stem. Remove the push rod.

21. Using a Torx® head socket, remove the intake manifold retaining bolts. Before trying to take the intake manifold out of the engine, carefully wedge a suitable prybar between the intake manifold and the engine block and pry upward on the tool using the area between the thermostat and the transaxle as a leverage point to break the seal. Remove the intake manifold from the engine.

**To install:**

22. Lightly oil all retaining bolt and stud bolt threads before installation.

➡**Be careful when scraping aluminum gasket surfaces because aluminum gouges easily, and if scratched, may cause gasket leaks.**

23. Clean the mating surfaces of the intake manifold and cylinder head. Lay a clean cloth in the lifter valley to catch any gasket material. After scraping, carefully lift the cloth from the valley preventing any particles from entering the oil drain holes or cylinder head. Use a suitable solvent to remove old rubber sealant.

24. If installing a new intake manifold, transfer the engine coolant temperature (ECT) sensor, thermostat, gasket and housing, heater hose elbow and coolant temperature sending unit to the new manifold.

25. If removed, install the fuel supply manifold. Apply engine oil (10W30) or equivalent oil lightly to the fuel injector rubber O-rings before installation. Install the injectors into the fuel supply manifold. Carefully align the manifold assembly to the intake manifold and the injector holes. Push one side into place, one at a time until the manifold ``clicks'' into place. Install the fuel supply manifold retaining bolts and tighten them to 71–106 inch lbs. (8–12 Nm).

26. Apply a ¼ in. (5–6mm) drop of Silicone Rubber D6AZ-19562-AA or BA or equivalent, to the intersection of the cylinder block and the cylinder head assembly at the four corners shown.

27. Position the intake gaskets onto the cylinder heads. Align the intake gasket locking tabs to the provisions on the cylinder head gaskets.

28. Install the front and rear intake manifold seals and secure with the retainers.

29. Carefully lower the intake manifold into position, aligning the manifold bolts holes to those in the cylinder head. Use care to prevent disturbing the rubber sealer which can cause sealing voids. Install bolts No. 1, 2,3,4 and hand tighten. Tighten, in numerical sequence, to 15–22 ft. lbs. (20–30 Nm), then again in sequence to 19–24 ft. lbs. (26–32 Nm).

30. On unleaded gasoline engines only, coat the distributor gear teeth with Engine Assembly Lubricant D9AZ-19579-D or equivalent. Install the distributor, and align to premarked location on the cylinder block and rotor position. Install the retaining bolt and washer and hand tighten.

31. Apply engine oil (10W30) or equivalent, to the cylinder No. 3 intake valve push rod and rocker arm. Install the push rod. Move the rocker arm into position with the push rod, then snug the retaining bolt. Rotate the crankshaft to position the crankshaft lobe straight down and away from the valve lifter. Tighten the retaining bolt to 5–11 ft. lbs. (7–15 Nm) to seat the rocker arm fulcrum into the cylinder head. Final tighten the bolt to 19–28 ft. lbs. (26–38 Nm) in any position.

➡The fulcrum must be seated into the cylinder head and the push rod must be fully seated in the rocker arm and lifter sockets before final tightening.

32. Install the rocker arm cover. For details, please see the rocker arm cover procedure located earlier in this section.

33. Install the fuel charging wiring to each injector. Secure the wiring with the stand-offs to the inboard rocker arm cover studs.

34. Install the ignition coil to the rear of the left hand cylinder head, then tighten the retaining bolts to 29–41 ft. lbs. (40–55 Nm).

35. For unleaded gasoline engines only, install the distributor cap and ignition wires. Install the wire harness stand-offs to the rocker arm cover studs, then connect the ignition wires to the spark plugs and the ignition coil.

36. Using a new gasket, install the throttle body assembly.

37. Install the EGR valve-to-exhaust manifold tube from the exhaust manifold-to-EGR valve. Tighten the retaining nuts to 26–48 ft. lbs. (35–65 Nm).

38. Connect the fuel lines, then install the fuel lines safety clips.

39. Install the upper radiator hose and heater hoses. Make sure to tighten the retaining clamps securely.

40. Connect the vacuum lines as tagged during removal.

41. For unleaded fuel engines only, engage the electrical connectors to the intake air temperature, and the distributor. For flexible fuel engines only, engage the electrical connectors to the CSI and camshaft position sensor.

42. Engage the electrical connectors to the idle air control, throttle position, engine coolant temperature, pressure feedback or differential pressure feedback EGR sensors, the ignition coil and temperature sending unit.

43. Fill and bleed the cooling system with specified coolant and proper mixture.

➡Because engine coolant is corrosive to all engine bearing material, replacing the oil after the removal of a coolant carrying component prevents damage.

44. Fill the crankcase with the correct viscosity and amount of engine oil.

45. Install the air cleaner outlet tube to the throttle body and air cleaner. Tighten the retaining clamps to 24–48 inch lbs. (2.7–5.4 Nm).

46. Install the PCV tube to the rocker arm cover and the air cleaner outlet tube.

47. Connect the negative battery cable, then start the engine and check for coolant, oil, fuel, and/or vacuum leaks.

➡Flexible Fuel (FF) base initial engine timing is NOT adjustable.

48. Verify, and if necessary, correct the base initial engine timing to 10° BTDC (before top dead center), then tighten the distributor retaining bolt to 18 ft. lbs. (24 Nm).

49. Install the idle air control valve snowshield.

## 3.0L and 3.2L SHO Engines

▶ **See Figures 80 and 81**

1. Disconnect the negative battery cable.

2. Partially drain the cooling system to allow removal of the intake manifold.

3. Tag and disengage the electrical connectors and vacuum lines from the intake manifold.

4. Remove the air cleaner outlet tube.

5. Disconnect the coolant hoses, throttle position sensor wiring and cables from the throttle body.

6. Remove the four bolts retaining the upper intake manifold supports.

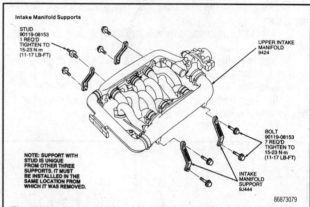

Fig. 80 Intake manifold and bracket assembly—3.0L and 3.2L SHO engines

7. Loosen the four lower bolts, then remove the intake manifold supports.

8. Remove the bolts retaining the intake manifold to the cylinder heads.

9. Remove the intake manifold and the intake manifold upper gaskets.

**To install:**

10. Lightly oil all of the retaining bolts and stud threads before installation.

➡If not damaged, the intake manifold upper gasket is reusable.

11. Position the intake manifold upper gasket on the cylinder head, then position the intake manifold on the cylinder heads.

12. Install the retaining bolts, then tighten the bolts to 11–17 ft. lbs. (15–23 Nm).

13. Install the intake manifold supports, then tighten the retaining bolts to 11–17 ft. lbs. (15–23 Nm).

14. Connect the coolant hoses, throttle position sensor wiring and cables to the throttle body.

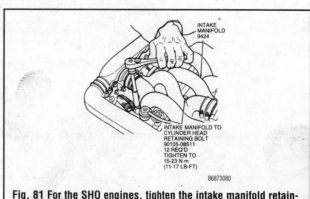

Fig. 81 For the SHO engines, tighten the intake manifold retaining bolts to 11–17 ft. lbs. (15–23 Nm).

15. Engage all electrical connectors and vacuum lines to the intake manifold.

16. Install the air cleaner outlet tube.

17. Fill the cooling system with the proper type and quantity of coolant.

18. Connect the negative battery, then start the engine and check for coolant leaks. Check that there is a proper level of coolant, and add coolant if necessary.

### 3.8L Engine

#### VEHICLES THROUGH 1993

♦ See Figures 82, 83 and 84

1. Disconnect the negative battery cable, then properly drain the cooling system.

2. Remove the air cleaner assembly including the air intake duct and heat tube.

3. Disconnect the accelerator cable at the throttle body assembly. If equipped, disconnect speed control cable

4. Disconnect the transaxle linkage at the upper intake manifold.

5. Remove the attaching bolts from the accelerator cable mounting bracket, then position the cables aside.

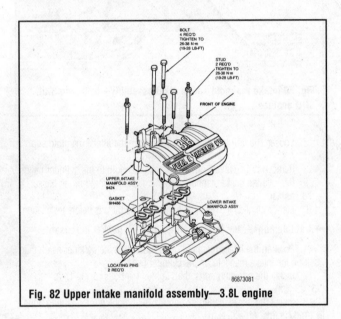

**Fig. 82 Upper intake manifold assembly—3.8L engine**

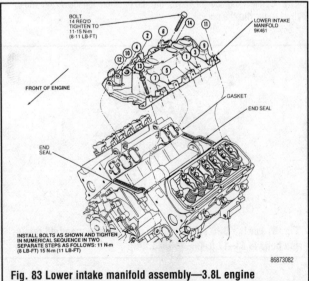

**Fig. 83 Lower intake manifold assembly—3.8L engine**

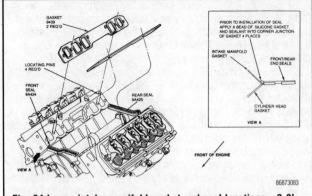

**Fig. 84 Lower intake manifold gasket and seal locations—3.8L engine**

6. Disconnect the Secondary Air Injection (AIR)/thermactor air supply hose at the check valve.

7. Disconnect the flexible fuel lines from steel lines over the rocker arm cover.

8. Disconnect the fuel lines at the injector fuel rail assembly.

9. Disconnect the radiator hose at the thermostat housing connection.

10. Disconnect the coolant bypass hose at the intake manifold connection.

11. Disconnect the heater tube at the intake manifold. Remove the heater tube support bracket attaching nut. Remove the heater hose at rear of heater tube. Loosen hose clamp at heater elbow, then remove the heater tube with the hose attached. Remove the heater tube with fuel lines attached and set the assembly aside.

12. Tag and disconnect the vacuum lines at the fuel rail assembly and the intake manifold.

13. Tag and disengage all necessary electrical connectors.

14. If equipped with A/C, remove the air compressor support bracket.

15. Disconnect the PCV lines. One is located on the upper intake manifold. The second is located at the left rocker cover and the lower intake stud.

16. Remove the throttle body assembly and remove the EGR valve assembly from the upper intake manifold. For details regarding throttle body removal, please refer to Section 5 of this manual.

17. Remove the attaching nut, then remove the wiring retainer bracket located at the left front of the intake manifold and set aside with the spark plug wires.

18. Remove the upper intake manifold attaching bolts/studs. Remove the upper intake manifold and gasket.

19. Remove the injectors and fuel injection supply manifold assembly.

20. Remove the heater water outlet hose.

➠When removing the intake manifold retainers keep them in order so they can be installed in their original positions.

21. Remove the lower intake manifold attaching bolts/studs, then remove the lower intake manifold. Remove the manifold side gaskets and end seals. Discard and replace with new gaskets and end seals.

➠The manifold is sealed at each end with RTV-type sealer. To break the seal, it may be necessary to pry on the front of the manifold with a small or medium pry bar. If it is necessary to pry on the manifold, use care to prevent damage to the machined surfaces.

To install:

22. Lightly oil all attaching bolt and stud threads before installation.

➠When using silicone rubber sealer, assembly must occur within 15 minutes after sealer application. After this time, the sealer may start to set-up and its sealing effectiveness may be reduced. The lower intake manifold, cylinder head and cylinder block mating surfaces should be clean and free of oil gasketing material. Use a suitable solvent to clean these surfaces.

23. Apply a dab of Gasket and Trim Adhesive D7AZ-19B508-B, or equivalent adhesive, to each cylinder head mating surface. Press the new intake manifold gaskets into place, using locating pins as necessary to aid in assembly alignment.

24. Apply a 1/8 in. (3–4mm) bead of silicone sealer at each corner where the cylinder head joins the cylinder block.

25. Install the front and rear intake manifold end seals.

26. Carefully lower the intake manifold into position on cylinder block and cylinder heads. Use locating pins as necessary to guide the manifold.

27. Install the retaining bolts and stud bolts in their original locations.

28. For vehicles through 1991, torque the retaining bolts in numerical sequence to the following specifications in 3 steps:
   a. Step 1: 8 ft. lbs. (11 Nm)
   b. Step 2: 15 ft. lbs. (20 Nm)
   c. Step 3: 24 ft. lbs. (32 Nm)

29. For 1992–93 vehicles torque the retaining bolts in numerical sequence to the following specifications in 2 steps:
   a. Step 1: 8 ft. lbs. (11 Nm)
   b. Step 2: 15 ft. lbs. (20 Nm)

30. Connect the rear PCV line to upper intake tube, then install the front PCV tube so the mounting bracket sits over the lower intake stud.

31. Install the injectors and fuel rail assembly. Tighten the screws to 6–8 ft. lbs. (8–11 Nm).

32. Position the upper intake gasket and manifold on top of the lower intake. Use locating pins to secure position of gasket between manifolds.

33. Install bolts and studs in their original locations. Tighten the 4 center bolts, then tighten the end bolts. Repeat Steps 28 or 29 depending on vehicle year application.

34. Install the EGR valve assembly on the manifold. Tighten the attaching bolt to 15–22 ft. lbs. (20–30 Nm).

35. Install the throttle body. Cross-tighten the retaining nuts to 15–22 ft. lbs. (20–30 Nm).

36. Connect the rear PCV line at PCV valve and upper intake manifold connections. If equipped with A/C, install the compressor support bracket. Tighten the retaining fasteners to 15–22 ft. lbs. (20–30 Nm).

37. Engage all electrical connectors and vacuum hoses.

38. Connect the heater tube hose to the heater elbow. Position the heater tube support bracket and tighten attaching nut to 15–22 ft. lbs. (20–30 Nm). Tighten the hose clamp at the heater elbow securely.

39. Connect the heater hose to the rear of the heater tube, then tighten the hose clamp.

40. Connect the coolant bypass and upper radiator hoses and tighten the hose clamps securely.

41. Connect the fuel line(s) at injector fuel rail assembly, then connect the flexible fuel lines to the steel lines.

42. Position the accelerator cable mounting bracket, then install and tighten the retaining bolts to 15–22 ft. lbs. (20–30 Nm).

43. Connect the speed control cable, if equipped. Connect the transaxle linkage at the upper intake manifold.

44. Fill the cooling system to the proper level with the specified coolant.

45. Connect the negative battery cable, then start the engine and check for coolant or fuel leaks.

46. Check and, if necessary, adjust engine idle speed, transaxle throttle linkage and speed control.

47. Install the air cleaner assembly and air intake duct.

### 1994–95 VEHICLES

▶ See Figures 85 and 86

1. Disconnect the negative battery cable, then properly drain the engine cooling system.

2. Remove the air cleaner outlet tube.

3. Disconnect the accelerator cable at the throttle body. If equipped, disconnect the cruise control actuator.

4. Remove the retaining bolts from the accelerator cable bracket, then position the cables aside.

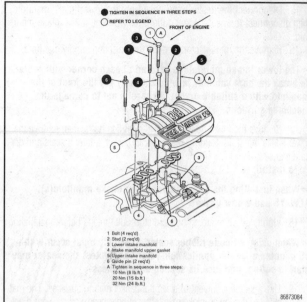

**Fig. 85 Upper intake manifold assembly—1995 3.8L engine shown**

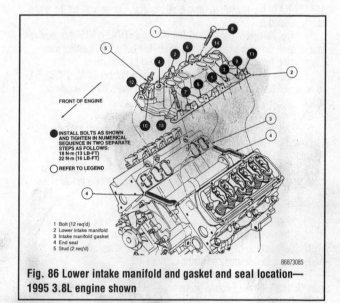

**Fig. 86 Lower intake manifold and gasket and seal location—1995 3.8L engine shown**

5. Tag and disconnect the vacuum lines from the fuel pressure regulator and the intake manifold.

6. Disengage any necessary electrical connectors.

7. Remove the drive belt. For details regarding this procedure, please refer to Section 1 of this manual.

8. Disconnect the crankcase ventilation hoses located on the upper intake manifold.

9. Remove the alternator mounting brace.

10. If necessary, disconnect the throttle body retaining bolts, then remove the throttle body.

11. If necessary remove the EGR valve from the upper intake manifold.

12. Remove the retaining nut, then remove the wiring retainer bracket located at the left hand front of the intake manifold, then set it aside with the ignition wires.

13. Remove the upper intake manifold upper gasket retaining bolts and stud bolt, then remove the intake manifold from the engine.

14. Disconnect the upper radiator hose from the water hose connection.

15. Disconnect the heater water hose from the lower intake manifold, then disconnect the heater water outlet tube from the lower intake manifold.

16. Remove the fuel injectors and the fuel injection supply manifold.

➡ **The lower intake manifold is secured at each corner with sealer. To break the seal you may have to carefully pry the front of the manifold with a suitable prybar. Be careful not to damage the machined surfaces.**

17. Remove the lower intake manifold retaining bolts, then remove the lower intake manifold. Remove the manifold gasket, and end seals and discard them.

**To install:**

➡ **When installing the upper and/or lower intake manifold(s), ALWAYS use a new gasket.**

18. Lightly oil all retaining bolt and stud bolt threads before installation.

➡ **When using silicone rubber sealer, assembly must occur within 15 minutes of sealer application. After 15 minutes, the sealer may start to set-up, and lose its sealing effectiveness.**

19. Use a suitable solvent to clean the gasket mating surfaces. The mating surfaces of the lower intake manifold, cylinder head and cylinder block should be clean and free of old gasketing material.

20. Before applying sealer, clean the sealing surfaces of the cylinder heads and the lower intake manifold with Metal Surface Cleaner F4AZ-19A536-RA or equivalent, to remove all residues that may affect the sealer's ability to adhere.

21. Apply a dab of Gasket and Trim Adhesive D7AZ-19B508 or equivalent, to each cylinder head mating surface. Press the new gaskets into place, using locating pins as necessary to aid in alignment.

22. Apply a ⅛ in. (3–4mm) bead of Silicone Rubber D6AZ-19562-BA or equivalent, at each corner where the cylinder head joins the cylinder block.

23. Install the front and rear intake manifold end seals.

24. Carefully install the intake manifold into position on the cylinder block and cylinder heads. Use locating pins, as necessary, to guide the intake manifold.

25. Install the retaining bolts in their original locations. Tighten the bolts in numerical sequence to the following specifications in two steps:
   a. Step 1: 13 ft. lbs. (18 Nm)
   b. Step 2: 16 ft. lbs. (22 Nm)

26. Install the fuel injectors and the fuel injection supply manifold. Tighten the retaining bolts to 6–8 ft. lbs. (8–11 Nm).

27. Connect the heater water outlet tube to the lower intake manifold. Make sure to fasten the hose clamp securely.

28. Connect the heater water hose to the lower intake manifold, making sure to fasten the hose clamp securely.

29. Connect the upper radiator hose to the water hose connection and tighten clamp securely.

30. Apply a light coat of Pipe Sealant with Teflon® or equivalent to the upper intake manifold retaining bolts and stud bolts.

31. Install the upper manifold retaining bolts and stud bolts in there original location, then tighten in numerical sequence in three steps:
   a. Step 1: 8 ft. lbs. (10 Nm)
   b. Step 2: 15 ft. lbs. (20 Nm)
   c. Step 3: 24 ft. lbs. (32 Nm)

32. If removed, install the EGR valve on the intake manifold, then tighten the retaining nuts to 15–22 ft. lbs. (20–30 Nm).

33. If removed, install the throttle body using the retaining nuts. Torque the nuts in a cross-tightening sequence to 15–22 ft. lbs. (20–30 Nm).

34. Connect the rear crankcase ventilation hoses at the PCV valve and the upper intake manifold.

35. Install the alternator mounting brace, then install the drive belt. For drive belt installation procedures, please refer to Section 1 of this manual.

36. Engage the necessary electrical connectors and vacuum hoses.

37. Position the accelerator cable bracket, then install and tighten the retaining bolts to 15–22 ft. lbs. (20–30 Nm).

38. If equipped, connect the cruise control actuator to the throttle body, then connect the accelerator cable to the throttle body.

39. Install the air cleaner and air cleaner outlet tube, then fill the cooling system with the proper type and quantity of coolant.

40. Connect the negative battery cable, then start the engine and check for oil, coolant or fuel leaks.

## Exhaust Manifold

### REMOVAL & INSTALLATION

#### 2.5L Engine

➡ **See Figure 87**

1. Disconnect the negative battery cable.
2. Drain the cooling system.
3. Remove the accelerator cable and, if equipped, the cruise control cable.
4. Remove air cleaner assembly and heat stove tube at the heat shield.
5. Identify, tag and disengage all necessary vacuum lines and electrical connections.
6. Disconnect the exhaust pipe-to-exhaust manifold retaining nuts.
7. Remove exhaust manifold heat shroud. Disengage the oxygen sensor wire at the connector.
8. Disconnect the fuel supply and return lines.
9. As required on vehicles before 1990, disconnect the thermactor check valve hose at tube assembly, remove bracket-to-EGR valve attaching nuts and disconnect water inlet tube at intake manifold.
10. Disconnect EGR tube from the EGR valve.
11. Remove the intake manifold. For details regarding intake manifold removal, please refer to the procedure located earlier in this section.
12. Remove the exhaust manifold retaining nuts, then remove the exhaust manifold from the vehicle.

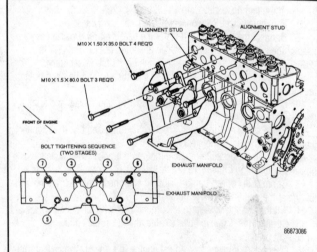

**Fig. 87 Exhaust manifold and bolt tightening sequence—2.5L engine**

**To install:**
13. Position the exhaust manifold to the cylinder head using guide bolts in holes 2 and 3.
14. Install the remaining attaching bolts.
15. Tighten the attaching bolts until snug, then remove guide bolts and install attaching bolts in holes 2 and 3.
16. Tighten all of the exhaust manifold bolts to specification using the following tightening procedure: torque retaining bolts, in sequence, to 5–7 ft. lbs. (7–10 Nm), then retorque, in sequence, to 20–30 ft. lbs. (27–41 Nm).

17. Install the intake manifold gasket and bolts. Tighten the intake manifold retaining bolts to 15–23 ft. lbs. (20–30 Nm).

18. As required on vehicles before 1990, connect the water inlet tube at intake manifold, connect thermactor check valve hose at tube assembly and install bracket to EGR valve attaching nuts.

19. Connect the oxygen sensor wire.

20. Connect the EGR tube to EGR valve.

21. Install exhaust manifold studs.

22. Connect exhaust pipe to the exhaust manifold.

23. Engage the vacuum lines and electrical connectors as tagged during removal.

24. Install the air cleaner assembly and heat stove tube.

25. Install accelerator cable and cruise control cable, if equipped.

26. Connect the negative battery cable, then fill the cooling system to the proper level.

27. Start engine and check for leaks, then check the coolant level, and add if necessary.

### 3.0L Engine

#### LEFT SIDE

▶ See Figure 88

1. Disconnect the negative battery cable. Remove the oil level indicator support bracket.

2. Remove the engine control sensor wiring from the oil level indicator tube bracket, then remove the oil dipstick and the oil level indicator tube.

3. On 1986–89 vehicles, remove the power steering pump pressure and return hoses.

4. Raise and safely support the vehicle.

5. Remove the exhaust manifold-to-dual converter Y-pipe retaining nuts.

6. Lower the vehicle. Remove the exhaust manifold attaching bolts, then remove the exhaust manifold.

#### To install:

7. Clean all exhaust manifold, cylinder head and Y-pipe mating surfaces, then lightly oil all bolt and stud threads.

8. Position the exhaust manifold on the cylinder head, then install the retaining bolts. Tighten the retaining bolts to 15–22 ft. lbs. (20–30 Nm).

9. Raise and safely support the vehicle, then connect the dual converter Y-pipe to the exhaust manifold. Tighten the retaining nuts to 25–34 ft. lbs. (34–47 Nm).

10. Install the oil level indicator tube bracket, then position the electrical harness. Tighten the retaining nut to 11–15 ft. lbs. (15–20 Nm).

11. If removed, connect the power steering pump pressure and return hoses.

12. Connect the negative battery cable, then start the engine and check for leaks.

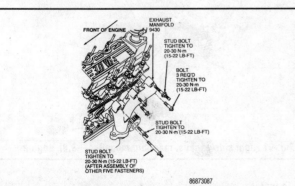

**Fig. 88 Left side exhaust manifold mounting—3.0L engine (except SHO)**

#### RIGHT SIDE

▶ See Figure 89

1. Disconnect the negative battery cable. Remove the heater hose support bracket.

2. Disconnect and plug the heater hoses.

3. Disconnect the pressure feedback (PFE) or differential pressure feedback (DPFE) hose(s) from the EGR valve-to-exhaust manifold tube.

4. Remove the EGR valve-to-exhaust manifold tube from the exhaust manifold. Use a backup wrench on the EGR valve tube-to-manifold connector.

5. If equipped, remove the water bypass tube.

6. Raise and safely support the vehicle. Remove the exhaust manifold-to-dual converter Y-pipe retaining nuts, then remove the pipe from the manifold.

7. Lower the vehicle. Remove the exhaust manifold retaining bolts, then remove the exhaust manifold from the vehicle.

#### To install:

8. Clean all exhaust manifold, cylinder head and Y-pipe mating surfaces, then lightly oil all bolt and stud threads.

9. If replacing the exhaust manifold, remove the EGR valve-to-exhaust manifold tube and install it on the new manifold.

10. Position the exhaust manifold on the cylinder head, then install the retaining bolts. Tighten the retaining bolts to 15–22 ft. lbs. (20–30 Nm).

11. Raise and safely support the vehicle.

12. Connect the dual converter Y-pipe to the exhaust manifold. Tighten the retaining nuts to 25–34 ft. lbs. (34–47Nm).

13. If removed, install the water bypass tube, then tighten the retaining nut to 15–22 ft. lbs. (20–30 Nm).

14. Connect the EGR valve-to-exhaust manifold tube to the exhaust manifold, then tighten to 26–48 ft. lbs. (35–65 Nm).

15. Connect the PFE or DPFE hose(s), then connect the negative battery cable.

16. Start the engine and check for exhaust and/or coolant leaks.

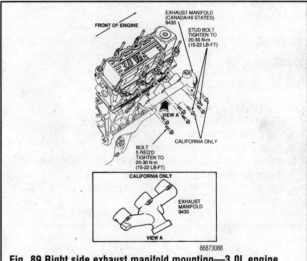

**Fig. 89 Right side exhaust manifold mounting—3.0L engine (except SHO)**

### 3.0L SHO Engine

➡**Always use new gaskets when installing the exhaust manifolds.**

#### LEFT SIDE

1. Disconnect the negative battery cable.

2. Remove the oil level indicator tube support bracket.

3. Remove the power steering pressure and return hoses.

4. Remove the exhaust manifold-to-dual converter Y-pipe retaining nuts.

5. Remove the heat shield retaining bolts.

6. Remove the exhaust manifold retaining nuts, then remove the exhaust manifold.

**To install:**

7. Clean all exhaust manifold, cylinder head and Y-pipe mating surfaces, then lightly oil all bolt and stud threads.

8. Position the exhaust manifold on the cylinder head, using a new gasket, then install the retaining nuts. Tighten the retaining nuts 26–38 ft. lbs. (35–52 Nm).

9. Install the heat shield retaining bolts, then tighten the bolts to 11–17 ft. lbs. (15–23 Nm).

10. Connect the dual converter Y-pipe to the exhaust manifold. Tighten the retaining nuts to 15–24 ft. lbs. (20–32 Nm).

11. Connect the power steering pressure and return hoses.

12. Install the oil level indicator tube support bracket.

13. Connect the negative battery cable.

### RIGHT SIDE

1. Disconnect the negative battery cable.

2. Remove the right hand cylinder head. For details regarding cylinder head removal, please see the procedure located later in this Section.

3. Remove the heat shield retaining bolts.

4. Remove the exhaust manifold retaining nuts, then remove the exhaust manifold.

**To install:**

5. Clean all of the cylinder head, exhaust manifold and Y-pipe mating surfaces, then lightly oil all bolt and stud threads.

6. Position the exhaust manifold on the cylinder head, a new gasket, then install the retaining nuts. Tighten the nuts to 15–24 ft. lbs. (20–32 Nm).

7. Install the heat shield retaining bolts. Tighten to 11–17 ft. lbs. (15–23 Nm).

8. Install the right hand cylinder head. For details regarding cylinder head installation, please refer to the procedure located later in this section.

9. Connect the negative battery cable, then start the engine and check for exhaust and/or coolant leaks.

### 3.8L Engine

#### LEFT SIDE

▶ See Figure 90

1. Disconnect the negative battery cable.

2. Remove the oil level dipstick tube support bracket.

3. Tag and disconnect the spark plug wires.

4. Raise and safely support the vehicle.

5. Remove the exhaust manifold-to-exhaust pipe attaching nuts.

6. Lower the vehicle.

7. Remove the exhaust manifold retaining bolts, then remove the exhaust manifold from the vehicle.

**To install:**

8. Lightly oil all bolt and stud threads before installation. Clean the exhaust manifold, cylinder head and Y-pipe mating surfaces.

9. Position the exhaust manifold on the cylinder head. Install the lower front bolt hole on the No. 5 cylinder as a pilot bolt.

➡**A slight warpage in the exhaust manifold may cause a misalignment between the bolt holes in the head and the manifold. Elongate the holes in the exhaust manifold as necessary to correct the misalignment, if apparent. Do not elongate the pilot hole, the lower front bolt on No. 5 cylinder.**

10. Install the remaining exhaust manifold retaining bolts, then tighten the bolts 15–22 ft. lbs. (20–30 Nm).

11. Raise and safely support the vehicle.

12. Connect the dual converter Y-pipe to the exhaust manifold. Tighten the attaching nuts to 16–24 ft. lbs. (21–32 Nm).

13. Carefully lower the vehicle.

14. Connect the spark plug wires as tagged during removal.

15. Install the oil level dipstick tube support bracket attaching nut. Tighten to 15–22 ft. lbs. (20–30 Nm).

16. Connect the negative battery cable, then start the engine and check for exhaust leaks.

### RIGHT SIDE

▶ See Figure 91

1. Disconnect the negative battery cable.

2. Remove the air cleaner and the air cleaner outlet tube assembly.

3. If equipped, disconnect the thermactor hose or the Secondary Air Injection (AIR) hose from the downstream air tube check valve.

4. Tag and disconnect the ignition wire from the ignition coil, then tag and disconnect the wires from the spark plugs. Remove the spark plugs.

5. Disconnect the EGR valve-to-exhaust manifold tube of the exhaust manifold.

6. Raise and safely support the vehicle.

7. Remove the transaxle dipstick tube.

8. For vehicles through 1990, remove the thermactor air tube by cutting the tube clamp at the underbody catalyst fitting with a suitable cutting tool.

9. Remove the exhaust manifold-to-exhaust pipe attaching nuts.

10. Carefully lower the vehicle.

11. Remove the exhaust manifold retaining bolts, them remove the exhaust manifold from the vehicle.

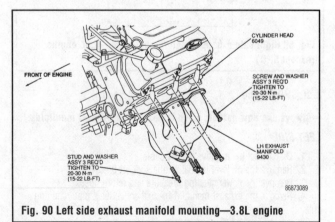

1 Cylinder head     5 Bolt (2 req'd)
2 Stud bolt (4 req'd)     6 Exhaust manifold
3 Wiring bracket (3 req'd)     A Tighten to 20-30 Nm (15-22 lb.ft.)
4 Nut (3 req'd)

86873090

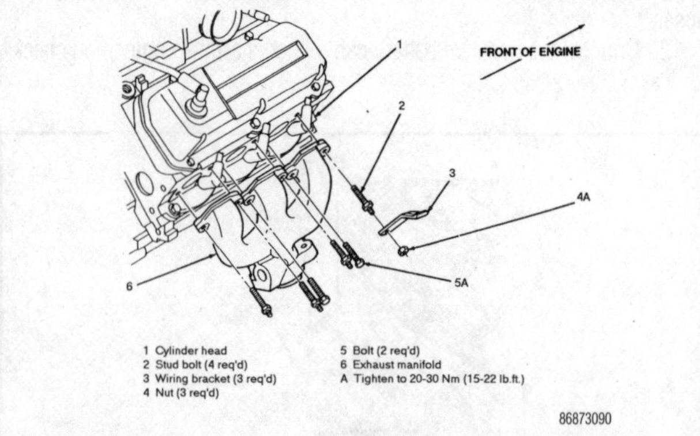

**Fig. 91 Right side exhaust manifold mounting—3.8L engine**

**To install:**

12. Lightly oil all bolt and stud threads before installation. Clean the exhaust manifold, cylinder head and Y-pipe mating surfaces.

13. Position the inner half of the heat shroud, if equipped, and exhaust manifold on cylinder head. Start two retaining bolts to align the manifold

CYLINDER HEAD 6049

SCREW AND WASHER ASSY 3 REQ'D TIGHTEN TO 20-30 N·m (15-22 LB-FT)

LH EXHAUST MANIFOLD 9430

STUD AND WASHER ASSY 3 REQ'D TIGHTEN TO 20-30 N·m (15-22 LB-FT)

FRONT OF ENGINE

86873089

**Fig. 90 Left side exhaust manifold mounting—3.8L engine**

with the cylinder head. Install the remaining retaining bolts and tighten to 15–22 ft. lbs. (20–30 Nm).

➡A slight warpage in the exhaust manifold may cause a misalignment between the bolt holes in the cylinder head and exhaust manifold. Elongate the holes in the exhaust manifold as necessary to to correct the misalignment. Do not elongate the pilot hole (the lower rear bolt hole on the No. 2 cylinder).

14. Raise and safely support the vehicle.

15. Connect the dual converter Y-pipe to the exhaust manifold. Tighten the retaining nuts to 16–24 ft. lbs. (22–33 Nm).

16. For vehicles through 1990, position the thermactor hose to the downstream air tube and clamp tube to the underbody catalyst fitting.

17. Install the transaxle dipstick tube, then carefully lower the vehicle.

18. If equipped, install the outer heat shroud, then tighten the retaining screws to 50–70 inch lbs. (6–8 Nm).

19. Install the spark plugs. Connect the ignition wires to their respective spark plugs, then connect the ignition wire to the coil.

20. Connect the EGR valve-to-exhaust manifold tube.

21. Connect the thermactor hose or the Secondary Air Injection (AIR) hose to the downstream air tube and secure with the retaining clamp.

22. Install the air cleaner and the air cleaner outlet tube assembly.

23. Connect the negative battery cable, then start the engine and check for exhaust leaks. Check the transaxle fluid.

## Radiator

### REMOVAL & INSTALLATION

♦ **See Figures 92 thru 102**

### ✳✳ CAUTION

**When draining the coolant, keep in mind that cats and dogs are attracted by ethylene glycol antifreeze, and are quite likely to drink any that is left in an uncovered container or in puddles on the ground. This will prove fatal in sufficient quantity. Always drain the coolant into a sealable container. Coolant should be reused unless it is contaminated or several years old.**

1. Disconnect the negative battery cable.

2. Drain the cooling system by removing the radiator cap and opening the draincock located at the lower rear corner of the radiator inlet tank.

3. Remove the rubber overflow tube from the coolant recovery bottle and detach it from the radiator. On the Taurus SHO, disconnect the tube from the radiator and remove the recovery bottle.

4. Remove 2 upper shroud retaining screws and lift the shroud out of the lower retaining clip(s).

5. Disconnect the electric cooling fan motor wires and remove the fan and shroud assembly.

6. Loosen the upper and lower hose clamps at the radiator and remove the hoses from the radiator tank connectors.

7. If equipped with an automatic transaxle, disconnect the transmission oil cooling lines from the transmission oil cooler radiator fittings using disconnect tool T82L-9500-AH or equivalent.

8. For vehicles through 1992, if equipped with 3.0L or SHO engines, remove the two radiator upper retaining screws. For vehicles through 1992, if equipped with the 3.8L engine, remove 2 hex nuts from the right radiator support bracket and 2 screws from the left radiator support bracket and remove the brackets.

9. For 1993–94 3.0L engines, remove the two radiator upper retaining screws. For 1993–94 3.8L and SHO engines, remove the two hex nuts from the right hand radiator support bracket, then remove the two retaining nuts from the left hand radiator support bracket, then remove both brackets.

10. For all 1995 vehicles, remove the two hex nuts from the right hand side radiator support bracket, then remove the bracket. Remove the two

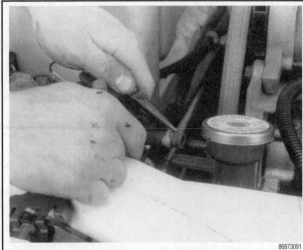

Fig. 92 Removing the coolant hoses—Early model 2.5L engine shown

Fig. 93 Remove the radiator retaining bolts/screws

Fig. 94 Lift the radiator upward, then remove it from the engine

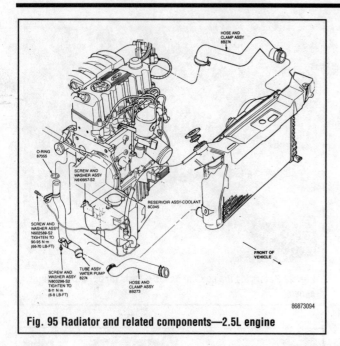

**Fig. 95 Radiator and related components—2.5L engine**

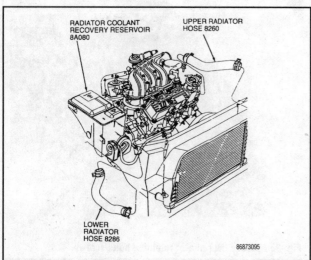

**Fig. 96 Radiator and related components—3.0L engine (except SHO)**

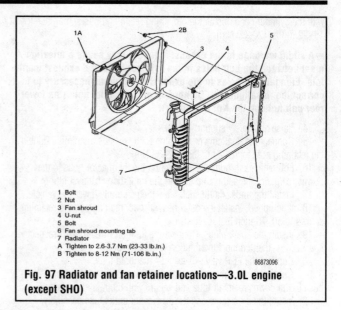

1 Bolt
2 Nut
3 Fan shroud
4 U-nut
5 Bolt
6 Fan shroud mounting tab
7 Radiator
A Tighten to 2.6–3.7 Nm (23–33 lb.in.)
B Tighten to 8–12 Nm (71–106 lb.in.)

**Fig. 97 Radiator and fan retainer locations—3.0L engine (except SHO)**

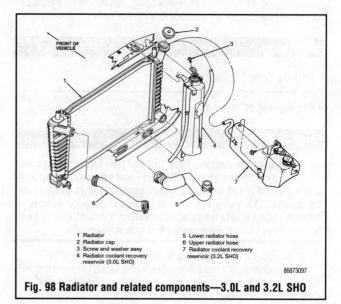

1 Radiator
2 Radiator cap
3 Screw and washer assy
4 Radiator coolant recovery reservoir (3.0L SHO)
5 Lower radiator hose
6 Upper radiator hose
7 Radiator coolant recovery reservoir (3.2L SHO)

**Fig. 98 Radiator and related components—3.0L and 3.2L SHO**

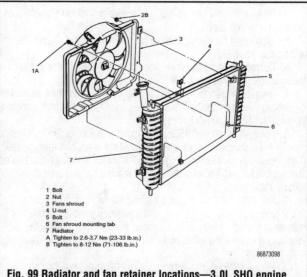

1 Bolt
2 Nut
3 Fans shroud
4 U-nut
5 Bolt
6 Fan shroud mounting tab
7 Radiator
A Tighten to 2.6–3.7 Nm (23–33 lb.in.)
B Tighten to 8–12 Nm (71–106 lb.in.)

**Fig. 99 Radiator and fan retainer locations—3.0L SHO engine**

screws from the left hand side radiator support bracket, then remove the bracket.

11. Tilt the radiator rearward approximately 1 in. (25mm) and lift it directly upward, clear of the radiator support.

12. If the lower or upper radiator hose it to be replaced, loosen the clamp at the engine end and, using a twisting motion, slip the hose off the connections.

13. Remove the radiator lower support rubber pads, if pad replacement is necessary.

**To install:**

14. Position the radiator lower support rubber pads to the lower support, if removed.

➡**Make sure the hose clamps are beyond the bead and placed in the center of the clamping surface of the connection. Any used clamps must be replaced with a new clamp to ensure proper sealing at the connection.**

15. If the lower or upper hose has been replaced, position the hose on the engine with the index arrow in-line with the mark on the fitting at the engine. Tighten the screw clamps to 20–30 inch lbs. (2.5–3.4 Nm). On

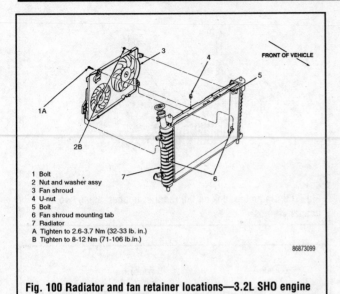

1  Bolt
2  Nut and washer assy
3  Fan shroud
4  U-nut
5  Bolt
6  Fan shroud mounting tab
7  Radiator
A  Tighten to 2.6-3.7 Nm (32-33 lb. in.)
B  Tighten to 8-12 Nm (71-106 lb.in.)

86873099

**Fig. 100 Radiator and fan retainer locations—3.2L SHO engine**

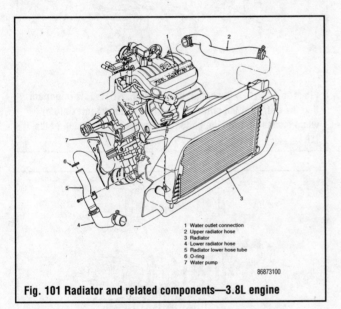

1  Water outlet connection
2  Upper radiator hose
3  Radiator
4  Lower radiator hose
5  Radiator lower hose tube
6  O-ring
7  Water pump

86873100

**Fig. 101 Radiator and related components—3.8L engine**

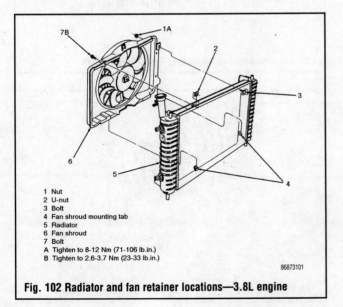

1  Nut
2  U-nut
3  Bolt
4  Fan shroud mounting tab
5  Radiator
6  Fan shroud
7  Bolt
A  Tighten to 8-12 Nm (71-106 lb.in.)
B  Tighten to 2.6-3.7 Nm (23-33 lb.in.)

86873101

**Fig. 102 Radiator and fan retainer locations—3.8L engine**

3.8L engines through 1992, install the constant tension hose hose clamp between the alignment marks on the hose.

16. Position the radiator into the engine compartment, and to the radiator support. Insert the moulded pins at the bottom of each tank through slotted holes in the lower support rubber pads.

17. Inspect the radiator nylon tank upper mounting bushings for damage. Replace if damaged.

18. On 3.8L engines through 1992, inspect the outer tank metallic pin bracket, and the left and right hand support brackets. Replace if necessary.

19. On 3.8L engines through 1992, if the outlet tank pin bracket must be replaced, remove the two retaining bolts. Position the bracket on the outlet tank, then install the two retaining bolts and tighten to 6.6–9.6 ft. lbs. (9–13 Nm).

20. For all engines through 1992 and 1993–94 3.0L engines, make sure that the plastic pads on the bottom of the radiator tanks are resting on the rubber pads. Install the two upper retaining bolts to attach the radiator to the radiator support. For all engines except the 3.8L, tighten the bolts to 46–60 inch lbs. (5–7 Nm). On the 3.8L engine through 1992, tighten the bolts to 13–20 ft. lbs. (17–27 Nm).

21. For vehicles through 1992, equipped with the 3.8L engine, position the right hand support bracket onto the radiator and over the two studs on the radiator support.

22. On the 3.8L engine through 1992, position the left hand support bracket over the radiator and the radiator support. Align the holes in the bracket with the corresponding holes in the radiator support and secure with the two retaining screws. Tighten the screws to 9–17 ft. lbs. (12–24 Nm).

23. On the 1993–94 3.8L and SHO engines and all 1995 engines, position the left and right hand support bracket over the radiator and radiator support. Align the holes in the bracket with the corresponding holes in the radiator support and secure with the two retaining screws. Tighten the screws to 9–17 ft. lbs. (12–24 Nm).

24. If applicable, secure the right hand support bracket to the radiator support with two hex nuts, then tighten the nuts to 8.7–17.7 ft. lbs. (11.8–24 Nm).

➡**Make sure that the hose clamps are beyond the bead and placed in the center of the clamping surface of the connection. Any used clamps must be replaced with new clamps to ensure proper sealing.**

25. Install the radiator upper and lower hoses to the radiator. Position the hose on the radiator connector so that the index arrow on the hose is in line with the mark on the connector. Position the clamps between the alignment marks on both ends of the hose, then slide the hose on the connections. Tighten the clamps to 20–30 inch lbs. (2.3–3.4 Nm). On 3.8L and 3.0L SHO engines through 1992, install the constant tension hose clamp between the alignment marks on the hoses.

26. On vehicles equipped with automatic transaxles, connect the oil cooler lines using Pipe Sealant with Teflon® D8AZ-19554-A or equivalent oil resistant sealer.

27. Install the fan and shroud assembly by connecting the motor wiring and positioning it on the lower retainer clips. Attach the top of the shroud to the radiator with the two screw and washer assemblies, and nuts. Tighten to 35 inch lbs. (4 Nm).

28. Attach the rubber overflow tube to the radiator filler neck overflow nipple and the coolant recovery bottle. On the SHO, install the coolant recovery bottle, then connect the overflow hose.

29. Connect the negative battery cable.

30. Install a 50/50 mixture of clean water and fresh antifreeze, then run the engine for 15 minutes. Check the coolant level and bring it to within 1½ in. (38mm) of the radiator filler neck.

## Engine Oil Cooler

### REMOVAL & INSTALLATION

▸ **See Figures 103 thru 108**

1. Disconnect the negative battery cable.

2. Remove the radiator outlet tank from the radiator. To remove the radiator outlet tank:

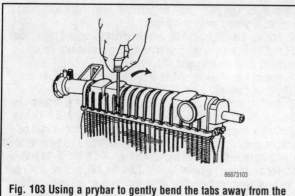

**Fig. 103 Using a prybar to gently bend the tabs away from the radiator tank**

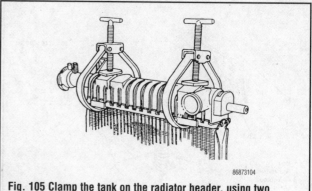

**Fig. 105 Clamp the tank on the radiator header, using two header clamps**

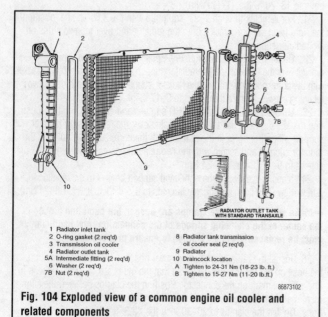

1 Radiator inlet tank
2 O-ring gasket (2 req'd)
3 Transmission oil cooler
4 Radiator outlet tank
5A Intermediate fitting (2 req'd)
6 Washer (2 req'd)
7B Nut (2 req'd)
8 Radiator tank transmission oil cooler seal (2 req'd)
9 Radiator
10 Draincock location
A Tighten to 24-31 Nm (18-23 lb. ft.)
B Tighten to 15-27 Nm (11-20 lb.ft.)

RADIATOR OUTLET TANK WITH STANDARD TRANSAXLE

**Fig. 104 Exploded view of a common engine oil cooler and related components**

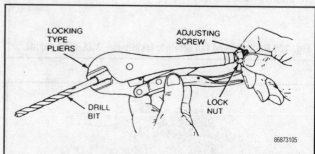

**Fig. 106 Adjusting the height of the crimp. NOTE: It is important that the height of the crimp be $^{27}/_{64}$ in. (10.9mm) (maximum) when measured from the bottom of the header to the top of the tab**

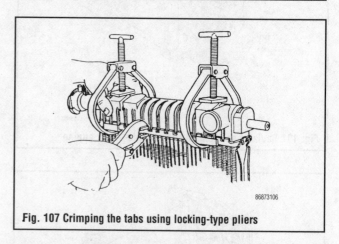

**Fig. 107 Crimping the tabs using locking-type pliers**

a. Remove the radiator from the vehicle as outlined earlier in this section.

b. Using Borroughs Tool BT-8260, or an equivalent prybar, insert the end of the tool between the header tab and the radiator tank and gently bend the tab away from the radiator tank. Repeat the procedure for each tab. Do NOT open the tabs more than is necessary to for tank removal.

c. Lift the radiator outlet tank from the radiator, then remove and discard the O-ring.

3. Remove the retaining nuts and washers from the oil cooler inlet and outlet connections, then lift the oil cooler from the radiator outlet tank.

4. Remove the radiator tank gasket from the oil cooler inlet and outlet connections, if the cooler is to be reused.

**To install:**

5. Position the transmission oil cooler to the radiator outlet tank, then insert the inlet and outlet oil tube connectors through the holes in the radiator outlet tank.

6. Install the flat washer and nut on each oil cooler connection to the retain the oil cooler in the radiator outlet tank.

7. Tighten the oil cooler retaining nuts to 12–14 ft. lbs. (15–19 Nm). Tighten the intermediate fitting to 18–23 ft. lbs. (24–31 Nm).

8. Install the radiator outlet tank on the radiator core header. To install the outlet tank:

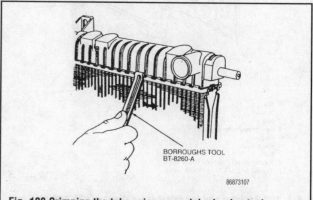

**Fig. 108 Crimping the tabs using a special crimping tool**

a. Inspect the seal surface of the radiator core header to ensure it is clean and undamaged. Check to be sure that the new O-ring to be installed, is not twisted.

b. Dip the new O-ring in coolant, then place it in the header groove.

c. Position the tank to the header, being careful not to scratch the radiator tank sealing surfaces with the tabs.

d. Clamp the radiator tank into position on the header using two header clamps, as shown in the accompanying figure, then tighten the clamps to compress the O-ring gasket.

e. If locking-type pliers will be used to squeeze the header tabs against the radiator tank, install a hex nut on the pliers adjusting screw. With the jaws of the pliers closed and locked, turn the adjusting screw to position the jaws against the shank of a $^{27}/_{64}$ in. (10.9mm) drill bit. Tighten the hex nut on the adjusting screw against the handle to lock the adjustment in place.

f. Using a special crimping tool or locking-type pliers, squeeze header tabs down against the lip of the radiator tank base, while rotating the pliers toward the radiator tank.

g. Remove the header clamps from the radiator and squeeze the tab(s) down that were behind the clamps.

h. Install the radiator as outlined earlier in this section.

9. Connect the negative battery cable, then start the engine and check for leaks.

## Engine Fan

### REMOVAL & INSTALLATION

♦ **See Figures 109 thru 119**

1. Disconnect the negative battery cable.
2. Remove the radiator upper sight shield.
3. Disengage the electrical connector, then remove the integrated relay control/constant control relay module assembly located on the radiator support.
4. Disconnect the fan electrical connector.
5. If necessary, remove the air bag crash sensor.
6. Unbolt the fan/shroud assembly from the radiator and remove.
7. Remove the retainer and the fan from the motor shaft and unbolt fan motor from the shroud.
8. Installation is the reverse of the removal procedures. Tighten the fan shroud retaining bolt to 23–33 inch lbs. (2.6–3.7 Nm). Tighten the fan shroud retaining nut to 71–106 inch lbs. (8–12 Nm).

Fig. 110 Remove the radiator upper sight shield

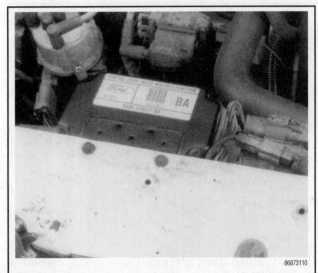

Fig. 111 Location of the relay module—Early model 2.5L engine

Fig. 109 Disconnect the radiator upper sight shield retaining bolts

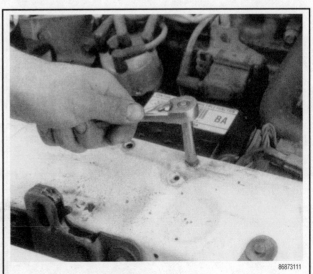

Fig. 112 Disconnect the relay retaining bolts

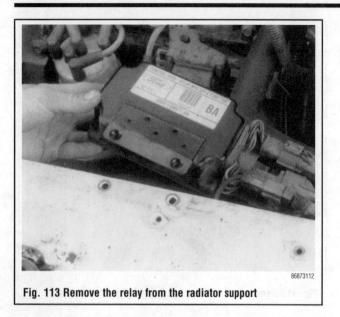

Fig. 113 Remove the relay from the radiator support

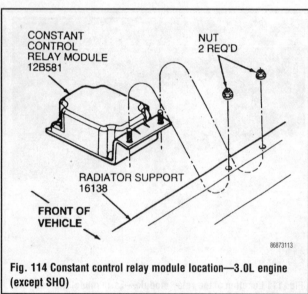

CONSTANT
CONTROL
RELAY MODULE
12B581

NUT
2 REQ'D

RADIATOR SUPPORT
16138

FRONT OF
VEHICLE

Fig. 114 Constant control relay module location—3.0L engine
(except SHO)

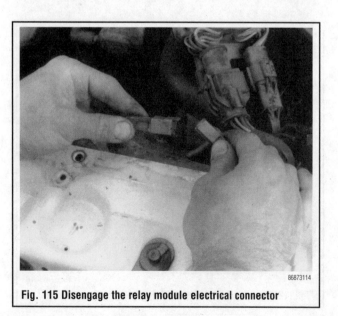

Fig. 115 Disengage the relay module electrical connector

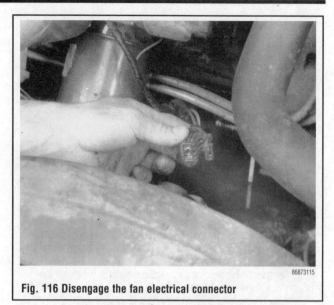

Fig. 116 Disengage the fan electrical connector

Fig. 117 Unbolt the fan assembly from the radiator

Fig. 118 Remove the fan from the engine

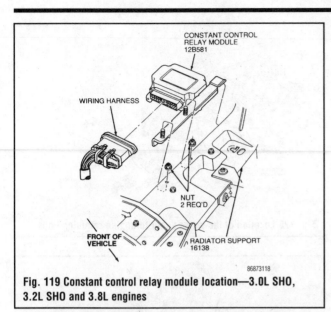

Fig. 119 Constant control relay module location—3.0L SHO, 3.2L SHO and 3.8L engines

## Water Pump

### REMOVAL & INSTALLATION

#### 2.5L Engine

▶ See Figures 120, 121, 122 and 123

1. Disconnect the negative battery cable.
2. Carefully remove the radiator cap, then position a drain pan under the bottom radiator hose.
3. Raise and safely support the vehicle. Remove the lower radiator hose from the radiator and drain the coolant into the drain pan.
4. Remove the water pump inlet tube.
5. Loosen the belt tensioner by inserting a ½ in. flex handle in the square hole of the tensioner, then rotate the tensioner counterclockwise and remove the belt from the pulleys.
6. Disconnect the heater hose from the water pump.
7. Remove the water pump retaining bolts, then remove the water pump assembly from the engine.

#### To install:

8. Using a gasket scraper, clean the water pump and cylinder block so that they are free of old gasket material.

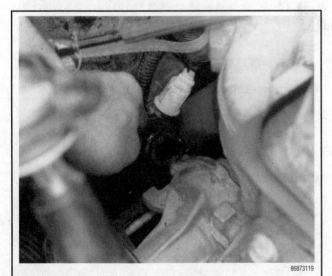

Fig. 120 Remove the water pump inlet tube

Fig. 121 After removing the retaining bolts, remove the water pump assembly from the engine

Fig. 122 If necessary, removing the water pump-to-pulley retaining bolts, then remove the pulley

Fig. 123 Remove all old gasket material from the water pump, then use a new gasket during installation

9. Apply Perfect Seal Sealing Compound B5A-19554-A or equivalent to the new water pump gasket, then place the water pump assembly and new gasket to the cylinder block.

10. Install the three water pump retaining bolts. Tighten the bolts to 15–22 ft. lbs. (20–30 Nm).

11. Connect the heater hose to the water pump.

12. Install the water pump belt on the pulley, then adjust the tension. For details, please refer to Section 1 of this manual.

13. Use a new O-ring for the water pump inlet, then install the water pump inlet. Tighten the retaining bolts to 7 ft. lbs. (10 Nm).

14. Close the radiator draincock. Install the drive belt on the water pump pulley, then adjust the tension. See Section 1 for details.

15. Connect the negative battery cable. Refill the cooling system to the specified level, then run the engine until it reaches normal operating temperatures. Check for leaks, then check the coolant level and add as necessary.

### 3.0L Engine—Except SHO

#### 1986–89 VEHICLES

▶ **See Figures 124, 125 and 126**

1. Disconnect the negative battery cable, then place a drain pan under the radiator draincock and properly drain the engine cooling system.

2. Loosen the accessory belt idle, then remove the drive belts.

3. Remove the two nuts and bolt retaining the idler bracket to the engine, then remove the bracket.

4. Disconnect the heater hose at the water pump.

5. Remove the four pulley-to-pump hub bolts. The pulley will remain loose on the hub because there is not enough clearance between the inner fender and the water pump, restricting removal from the vehicle.

6. Remove the eleven water pump-to-engine retaining bolts, then lift the water pump and pulley from the vehicle.

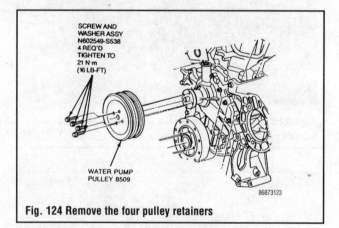

**Fig. 124 Remove the four pulley retainers**

**To install:**

➡ **Lightly oil all bolt and stud threads before installation except those specifying special sealant.**

7. Clean the water pump and engine front cover gasket mating surfaces.

8. Position a new gasket on the water pump sealing surface using Gasket and Trim Adhesive D7AZ-19B508-AA or equivalent.

9. With the pulley positioned on the water pump hub, position the water pump on the front cover, then install the retaining bolts. Tighten the retaining bolts, as specified on the accompanying figures.

➡ **Two different lengths of retaining bolts are used. Refer to the accompanying figure for specifications.**

10. Install the pulley-to-pump hob bolts. Tighten the bolts to 16 ft. lbs. (22 Nm).

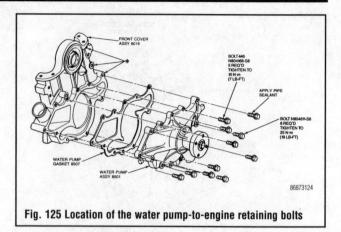

**Fig. 125 Location of the water pump-to-engine retaining bolts**

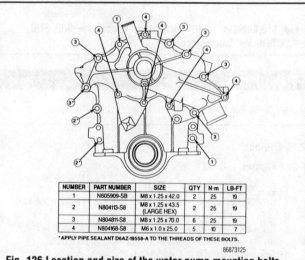

| NUMBER | PART NUMBER | SIZE | QTY | N·m | LB-FT |
|--------|-------------|------|-----|-----|-------|
| 1 | N605909-SB | M8 x 1.25 x 42.0 | 2 | 25 | 19 |
| 2 | N804113-S8 | M8 x 1.25 x 43.5 (LARGE HEX) | 2 | 25 | 19 |
| 3 | N804811-S8 | M8 x 1.25 x 70.0 | 6 | 25 | 19 |
| 4 | N804168-S8 | M6 x 1.0 x 25.0 | 5 | 10 | 7 |

*APPLY PIPE SEALANT D6AZ-19558-A TO THE THREADS OF THESE BOLTS.

**Fig. 126 Location and size of the water pump mounting bolts and torque specifications—1986–89 3.0L engine (except SHO)**

11. Connect the coolant bypass/heater hose to the water pump.

12. Install the idle bracket to the engine front cover.

13. Position the accessory drive belt over the pump pulley, then adjust the drive belt tension, if equipped with a manual tensioner. For details regarding belt tensioning, please refer to the procedure located in Section 1 of this manual.

14. Connect the negative battery cable, then fill the cooling system to the proper level with the correct mixture of coolant and water. Start the engine and let it run until it reaches normal operating temperatures, then check for leaks and check the coolant level.

#### 1990–95 VEHICLES

▶ **See Figures 127, 128 and 129**

1. Disconnect the negative battery cable, then place a drain pan under the radiator drain cock.

2. Carefully remove the radiator cap, then open the drain cock on the radiator and drain the cooling system.

3. Loosen the four water pump pulley retaining bolts while the accessory drive belts are still tight.

4. Loosen the alternator belt adjuster jack screw to provide enough clearance for the removal of the alternator belt.

5. Using a ½ in. breaker bar, rotate the automatic tensioner down and to the left. Remove the power steering/air conditioner belt.

6. Remove the two nuts and bolt retaining the drive belt automatic tensioner to the engine, then remove the tensioner.

7. Disconnect and remove the lower radiator and heater hose from the water pump.

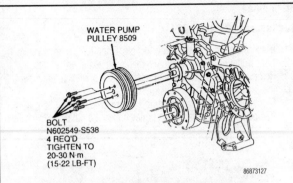

**Fig. 127 Location of the four water pump pulley retaining bolts—Late model 3.0L (except SHO)**

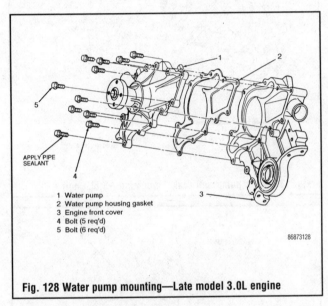

1 Water pump
2 Water pump housing gasket
3 Engine front cover
4 Bolt (5 req'd)
5 Bolt (6 req'd)

**Fig. 128 Water pump mounting—Late model 3.0L engine**

8. Remove the eleven water pump-to-engine retaining bolts, then lift the water pump and pulley up and out of the vehicle.

9. Remove the water pump pulley retaining bolts, them remove the pulley from the water pump.

**To install:**

➡**Be careful not to gouge the aluminum surfaces when scraping the old gasket material from the mating surfaces of the water pump and front cover.**

10. Clean the gasket surfaces on the water pump and front cover. Lightly oil all bolt and stud threads except those requiring special sealant.

11. Position a new water pump housing gasket on the water pump sealing surface using Gasket and Trim Adhesive D7AZ-19B508-B or equivalent, to hold the gasket in place.

➡**Apply Pipe Sealant with Teflon® D8AZ-19554-A or equivalent to bolt No. 3 (see fig.) before installation.**

12. With the water pump pulley and retaining bolts loosely installed on the water pump, align the water pump-to-engine front cover, then install the retaining bolts.

13. Tighten the bolts to the following specifications:
   a. Numbers 4, 5, 6, 7, 8, 9 and 10 to 15–22 ft. lbs. (20–30 Nm).
   b. Numbers 11, 12, 13, 14 and 15 to 71–106 inch lbs (8–12 Nm).

14. Hand-tighten the water pump pulley retaining bolts.

15. Install the automatic belt tensioner assembly. Tighten the two retaining nuts and bolt to 35 ft. lbs. (47 Nm).

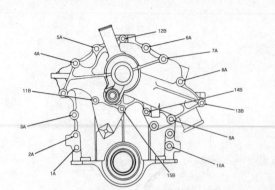

| Fasteners | | | | Fasteners | | | |
|---|---|---|---|---|---|---|---|
| Fastener And Hole Number | Part Number | Size | Fastener Application | Fastener And Hole Number | Part Number | Size | Fastener Application |
| 1A | N804113 | M8 x 1.25 x 43.5 | Engine Front Cover To Cylinder Block | 9A | N804811 | M8 x 1.25 x 70 | Water Pump And Engine Front Cover To Cylinder Block |
| 2A | N804113 | M8 x 1.25 x 43.5 | Engine Front Cover To Cylinder Block | 10A | N606543 | M8 x 1.25 x 52 | Engine Front Cover To Cylinder Block |
| 3A | N804811 | M8 x 1.25 x 70 | Water Pump And Engine Front Cover To Cylinder Block | 11B | N804576 | M6 x 1 x 28.5 | Water Pump to Engine Front Cover |
| 4A | N804811 | M8 x 1.25 x 70 | Water Pump And Engine Front Cover To Cylinder Block | 12B | N804576 | M6 x 1 x 28.5 | Water Pump to Engine Front Cover |
| 5A | N605909 | M8 x 1.25 x 42 | Engine Front Cover To Cylinder Block | 13B | N804576 | M6 x 1 x 28.5 | Water Pump to Engine Front Cover |
| 6A | N804811 | M8 x 1.25 x 70 | Water Pump And Engine Front Cover To Cylinder Block | 14B | N804576 | M6 x 1 x 28.5 | Water Pump to Engine Front Cover |
| 7A | N804811 | M8 x 1.25 x 70 | Water Pump And Engine Front Cover To Cylinder Block | 15B | N804576 | M6 x 1 x 28.5 | Water Pump to Engine Front Cover |

A. Tighten to 20-30 N·m (15-22 Lb-Ft)
B. Tighten to 8- 12 N·m (71-106 Lb-In)

**Fig. 129 Water pump retaining fastener locations, size and torque specification**

16. Install the alternator and power steering belts. Final tighten the water pump pulley retaining bolts to 15–22 ft. lbs. (22–30 Nm).

17. Position the hose clamps between the alignment marks on both ends of the hose, then slide the hose on the connection. Tighten the hose clamps to 20–30 inch lbs. (2.2–3.4 Nm).

18. Fill and bleed the cooling system with the appropriate quantity and coolant type.

19. Connect the negative battery cable. Start the engine and check for leaks.

### 3.0L and 3.2L SHO Engines

▶ **See Figure 130**

1. Disconnect the battery cables, then, if necessary for access, remove the battery and the battery tray. For details, please refer to the battery and battery tray removal procedures located earlier in this section.

2. Properly drain the cooling system.

3. Remove the accessory drive belts. For details regarding this procedure, please refer to Section 1 of this manual.

4. For the 3.0L SHO, remove the left-hand side drive belt tensioner pulley and bracket. For the 3.2L SHO remove the left-hand side drive belt pulleys.

5. Disengage the electrical connector from the ignition control module and the ground strap.

6. Loosen the four screw clamps on the upper intake/engine inlet connector tube, then remove the retaining bolts and remove the connector tube.

7. Remove the upper outer timing belt cover.

8. Raise and safely support the vehicle. Remove the right wheel and tire assembly.

9. Remove the splash guard/shield.

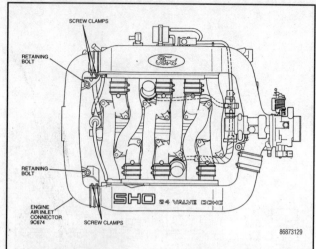

**Fig. 130 Engine air inlet connector location and mounting—3.0L and 3.2L SHO engines**

10. Using steering wheel puller T67L-3600-A, remove the crankshaft vibration damper and pulley.

11. Disconnect the crankshaft position (CKP) sensor wiring harness, then move it out of the way.

12. Disconnect the bolts from the center outer timing belt cover, then remove the cover.

13. On the 3.0L SHO, remove the right-hand side drive belt tensioner idler pulley and bracket. On the 3.2L SHO, remove the drive belt tensioner.

14. Remove the water pump attaching bolts, then remove the water pump and housing gasket.

**To install:**

➡**Lightly oil all bolt threads before installation.**

15. Clean the old gasket material from the water pump and cylinder block mating surfaces.

16. Position a new water pump housing gasket on the water pump sealing surface using Gasket and Trim Adhesive D7AZ-19B508-B or equivalent, to hold the gasket in position.

17. Install the water pump and retaining bolts to the cylinder block, then tighten the bolts to 12–17 ft. lbs. (16–23 Nm).

18. On the 3.0L SHO, install the right-hand drive belt tensioner idler pulley and bracket. On the 3.2L SHO install the drive belt tensioner.

19. Install the center outer timing cover.

20. Connect the crankshaft position (CKP) sensor wire harness.

21. Install the lower outer timing belt cover.

22. Using Screw and Washer Set T89P-6701-A and Step Plate D80L-630-3 or equivalent, install the crankshaft vibration damper and pulley. Install the retaining bolt, then tighten to 112–127 ft. lbs. (152–172 Nm).

23. Install the splash guard/shield.

24. Install the tire and wheel assembly. Tighten the lug nuts to 85–105 ft. lbs. (115–142 Nm).

25. Carefully lower the vehicle.

26. Install the upper outer timing belt cover.

27. On the 3.0L SHO, install the left-hand side drive belt tensioner idler pulley and bracket. On the 3.2L SHO, install the left-hand side drive belt idler pulleys.

28. Install the engine upper intake/air inlet connector tube.

29. Install the two retaining bolts on the upper intake/air inlet connector tube. Tighten the bolts to 11–17 ft. lbs. (15–23 Nm), then tighten the four screw clamps.

30. Engage the ignition control module electrical connector.

31. Install the accessory drive belts. For details please refer to the belt installation procedure in Section 1 of this manual.

32. Connect the negative battery cable, then fill the cooling system to the correct level with a 50/50 mixture of approved coolant and water. Start the engine and check for leaks. Add more coolant if necessary.

### 3.8L Engine

▶ **See Figures 131 and 132**

1. Disconnect the negative battery cable. Drain the cooling system.

2. Loosen the drive belt tensioner, then remove the drive belts.

3. Remove the two nuts and bolt retaining the drive belt tensioner to the engine.

4. Disconnect the heater hose at the water pump.

5. Remove the four water pump pulley bolts. The pulley will remain

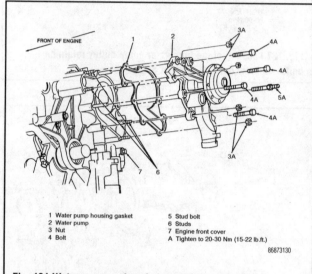

| 1 Water pump housing gasket | 5 Stud bolt |
| 2 Water pump | 6 Studs |
| 3 Nut | 7 Engine front cover |
| 4 Bolt | A Tighten to 20-30 Nm (15-22 lb.ft.) |

**Fig. 131 Water pump and gasket mounting—3.8L engine**

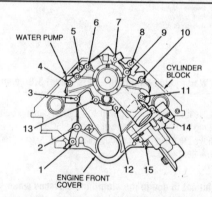

| Reference Number | Part Number | Size | Part Name |
|---|---|---|---|
| 1 | N805112 | M8 x 1.25 x 98.0 | Stud |
| 2 | N805112 | M8 x 1.25 x 98.0 | Stud |
| 3 | N805757 | M8 x 1.25 x 131.0 | Stud |
| 4 | N805757 | M8 x 1.25 x 131.0 | Stud |
| 5 | N605787 | M8 x 1.25 x 25.0 | Bolt |
| 6 | N605908 | M8 x 1.25 x 35.0 | Bolt |
| 7 | N605908 | M8 x 1.25 x 35.0 | Bolt |
| 8 | N605787 | M8 x 1.25 x 25.0 | Bolt |
| 9 | N804756 | M8 x 1.25 x 61.5 | Stud Bolt |
| 10 | N805275 | M8 x 1.25 x 141.0 | Stud |
| 11 | N804757 | M8 x 1.25 x 131.0 | Stud |
| 12 | N605908 | M8 x 1.25 x 35.0 | Bolt |
| 13 | N605908 | M8 x 1.25 x 35.0 | Bolt |
| 14 | N804839 | M8 x 1.25 x 105.0 | Bolt |
| 15 | N804841 | M8 x 1.25 x 20.0 | Cap Screw |

**Fig. 132 3.8L engine water pump retaining bolt locations. Since two bolt lengths are used, install the bolts as shown to prevent possible damage to the engine**

loose on the hub because there is insufficient room between the inner fender and the water pump, restricting removal from the vehicle.

6. Remove the water pump-to-engine retaining bolts, then lift the water pump and pulley assembly out of the vehicle.

**To install:**

7. Lightly oil all bolt and stud threads before installation except those that require sealant. Thoroughly clean the water pump and front cover gasket contact surfaces.

8. Position the new water pump gasket on the pump sealing surface using Gasket and Trim Adhesive D7AZ-19B508-B or equivalent.

9. With the water pump pulley positioned on the water pump hub, position the water pump on the engine front cover, then install the retaining bolts. Tighten the retaining bolts to 15–22 ft. lbs. (20–30 Nm).

➡There are two different length of bolts used to retain the water pump. Install the bolts as shown in the accompanying figure or damage to the engine may occur.

10. Install the water pump pulley bolts, then tighten the bolts to 16 ft. lbs. (21 Nm).

11. Connect the heater water hose to the water pump.

12. Install the drive belt tensioner to the engine front cover, then install the drive belt.

13. Connect the negative battery cable, then fill the cooling system with a 50/50 mixture of approved coolant and water. Start and run the engine until in reaches normal operating temperatures, then check for leaks and check the coolant level.

## Cylinder Head

### REMOVAL & INSTALLATION

#### 2.5L Engine

▶ **See Figures 133 thru 138**

1. Disconnect the negative battery cable. Drain the cooling system.

2. Remove the air cleaner assembly. Properly relieve the fuel system pressure.

3. As required on vehicles before 1990, disconnect the heater hose at the fitting located under the intake manifold. On 1991 vehicles, disconnect the heater hose at the heater inlet tube and disconnect the adapter hose at the water outlet connector.

4. Disconnect the upper radiator hose at the cylinder head, then disengage the electric cooling fan switch at the plastic connector.

Fig. 134 Removing the cylinder head bolts—2.5L engine

Fig. 135 An assistant is handy when removing the cylinder head from the engine

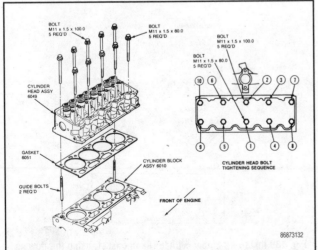

Fig. 133 Cylinder head assembly and head bolt tightening sequence—2.5L engine

Fig. 136 Remove the cylinder head gasket and replace with a new one when installing the head

Fig. 137 Clean the engine block mating surface with a gasket scraper to get rid of all of the old gasket material

Fig. 138 Torque the head bolts in sequence and to the correct specification

5. Disconnect the distributor cap and spark plug wires, then remove as an assembly.

6. If necessary, tag and disconnect the spark plugs.

7. Disconnect the EGR tube at the EGR valve.

8. Disconnect and tag the required vacuum hoses. Remove the accessory drive belts.

9. Disconnect the choke cap wire.

10. Remove rocker arm cover retaining bolts, then remove the cover.

11. Remove the rocker arm fulcrum bolts, the fulcrums, rocker arms and pushrods. Identify the location of each so they may be reinstalled in their original positions.

12. Disconnect the fuel supply and return lines at the rubber connections. Disconnect the accelerator cable and speed control cable, if equipped.

13. Raise and safely support the vehicle. Disconnect the exhaust system at the exhaust pipe, and hose at the tube. Lower the vehicle.

14. Remove the cylinder head bolts. Remove the cylinder head and gasket with the exhaust and intake manifolds attached.

**To install:**

15. Clean all gasket material from the mating surface of the cylinder head and block. Position the cylinder head gasket on the cylinder block, using a suitable sealer to retain the gasket.

16. Before installing the cylinder head, thread 2 Cylinder Head Alignment Studs T84P-6065-A through the head bolt holes in the gasket and into the block at opposite corners of the block.

17. Install the cylinder head and cylinder head bolts. Start and run down several head bolts and remove the 2 guide bolts. Replace them with the remaining head bolts. Tighten the bolts in sequence in 2 steps, first to 52–59 ft. lbs. (70–80 Nm) and then to 70–76 ft. lbs. (95–103 Nm).

18. Raise and safely support the vehicle. Connect the exhaust system at the exhaust pipe and hose to metal tube. Lower the vehicle.

19. Install the thermactor pump drive belt, if equipped.

20. Connect the accelerator cable and speed control cable, if equipped.

21. Connect the fuel supply and return lines. Connect the choke cap wire, if equipped.

22. Install the pushrods, rocker arms, fulcrums and fulcrum bolts in their original positions. Install the rocker arm cover.

23. Connect the EGR tube at the EGR valve. Install the distributor cap and spark plug wires as an assembly. If removed , install the spark plugs, as tagged during removal.

24. Install all accessory drive belts.

25. Connect the required vacuum hoses. Install the air cleaner assembly. Engage the electric cooling fan switch at the connector.

26. Connect the upper radiator hose and the heater hose. Fill the cooling system. Connect the negative battery cable.

27. Start the engine and check for leaks. After the engine has reached normal operating temperature, check and if necessary add coolant.

### 3.0L Engine—Except SHO

#### ♦ See Figures 139 and 140

1. For 1992–95 vehicles, rotate the crankshaft to 0° TDC on the compression stroke.

2. Disconnect the negative battery cable. Properly relieve the fuel system pressure, then drain the cooling system.

3. Remove the air cleaner outlet flex hose-to-throttle body.

4. Loosen the accessory drive belt idler pulley, remove the drive belt.

5. If the left cylinder head is being removed, perform the following:

   a. Disconnect the alternator electrical connectors.

   b. Rotate the tensioner clockwise and remove the accessory drive belt.

   c. Remove the automatic belt tensioner assembly.

   d. Remove the alternator.

   e. Remove the power steering mounting bracket retaining bolts. Leave the hoses connected and place the pump aside in a position to prevent fluid from leaking out.

   f. Remove the engine oil dipstick tube from the exhaust manifold.

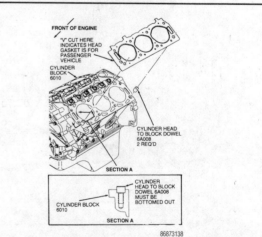

Fig. 139 Installing a new cylinder head gasket, using the dowels in the block for alignment. If the dowels are damaged, they must be replaced

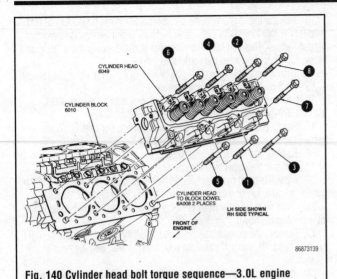

**Fig. 140 Cylinder head bolt torque sequence—3.0L engine (except SHO)**

6. If the right head is being removed, perform the following:

    a. Remove the alternator belt tensioner bracket.

    b. Remove the heater supply tube retaining brackets from the exhaust manifold.

    c. Remove the vehicle speed sensor cable retaining bolt and the EGR vacuum regulator sensor and bracket.

7. Remove the exhaust manifolds from both heads. Remove the PCV and the rocker arm covers. Loosen the rocker arm fulcrum attaching bolts enough to allow the rocker arm to be lifted off the pushrod and rotated to one side.

8. Remove the pushrods. Be sure to identify and label the position of each pushrod. The rods should be installed in their original position during reassembly.

9. Remove the intake manifold. For details, please refer to the procedure located earlier in this section.

10. Remove the cylinder head attaching bolts and remove the cylinder heads from the engine. Remove and discard the old cylinder head gaskets.

**To install:**

11. Lightly oil all bolt and stud bolt threads before installation. Clean the cylinder head, intake manifold, rocker arm cover and cylinder head gasket contact surfaces. If the cylinder head was removed for a cylinder head gasket replacement, check the flatness of the cylinder head and block gasket surfaces.

➡**If the flat surface of the cylinder head is warped, do not plane or grind off more than 0.010 in. (0.25mm). If the head is machined past its resurface limit, the head will have to be replaced with a new one.**

12. Position new head gaskets on the cylinder block, noting the UP position on the gasket face, using the dowels in the engine block for alignment. If the dowels are damaged, they must be replaced.

13. Position the cylinder head on the cylinder block. Tighten the cylinder head attaching bolts in 2 steps following the proper torque sequence. The first step is 37 ft. lbs. (50 Nm) and the second step is 68 ft. lbs. (92 Nm).

➡**When cylinder head attaching bolts have been tightened using the above procedure, it is not necessary to retighten the bolts after extended engine operation. The bolts can be rechecked for tightness if desired.**

14. Install the intake manifold. For details, please refer to the procedure located earlier in this section.

15. Engage the coolant temperature sending unit connectors.

16. Dip each pushrod end in oil conditioner or heavy engine oil. Install the pushrods in their original position.

17. Before installation, coat the valve tips, rocker arm and fulcrum contact areas with Lubricate® or equivalent. Lightly oil all the bolt and stud threads before installation.

18. Rotate the engine until the lifter is on the base circle of the cam (valve closed).

19. Install the rocker arm and components and torque the rocker arm fulcrum bolts to 24 ft. lbs. (32 Nm). Be sure the lifter is on the base circle of the cam for each rocker arm as it is installed.

➡**The fulcrums must be fully seated in the cylinder head and the pushrods must be seated in the rocker arm sockets prior to the final tightening.**

20. Install the exhaust manifold(s). For details, please refer to the procedure located earlier in this section.

21. Install the oil dipstick tube.

22. Install the remaining components by reversing the removal procedure.

23. Fill the cooling system with the proper type and quantity of approved coolant.

24. Connect the negative battery cable, then start the engine and check for leaks.

25. Check and if necessary, adjust the transaxle throttle linkage and speed control. Install the air cleaner outlet tube duct.

## 3.0L and 3.2L SHO Engines

▶ **See Figures 141, 142, 143 and 144**

1. Disconnect the negative battery cable.

2. Drain the cooling system, then properly relieve the fuel system pressure.

3. Remove the air cleaner outlet tube.

4. Remove the intake manifold. For detail, please refer to the procedure located earlier in this section.

5. Loosen the accessory drive belt tensioners, then remove the drive belts.

6. Remove the upper outer timing belt cover.

7. For the 3.0L SHO, Remove the left-hand side drive belt tensioner idler pulley and bracket assembly. For the 3.2L SHO engine, remove the left-hand drive belt idler pulleys.

8. Raise and safely support the vehicle.

9. Remove the right wheel and tire assembly, then remove the front fender splash shield.

10. Remove the crankshaft vibration damper and pulley.

11. Remove the lower timing belt cover.

12. Align both camshaft pulley timing marks with the index marks on the upper steel belt cover.

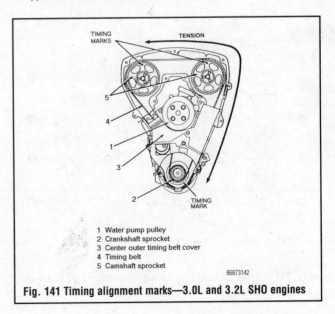

1 Water pump pulley
2 Crankshaft sprocket
3 Center outer timing belt cover
4 Timing belt
5 Camshaft sprocket

**Fig. 141 Timing alignment marks—3.0L and 3.2L SHO engines**

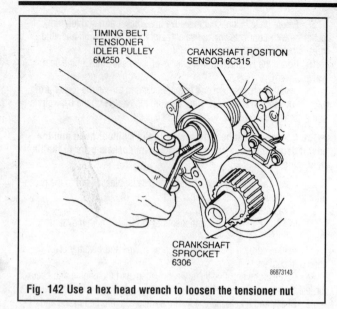

Fig. 142 Use a hex head wrench to loosen the tensioner nut

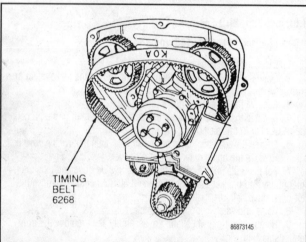

Fig. 143 When removing the timing belt, note the location of the letters KOA on the belt. The belt MUST be installed in the same direction

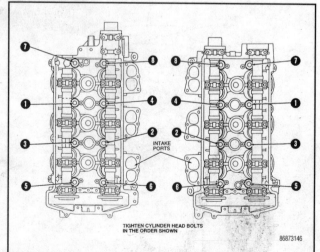

Fig. 144 Cylinder head bolt tightening sequence—3.0L and 3.2L SHO

13. Release the tension on the belt by loosening the tensioner nut and rotating the tensioner with a hex head wrench. When tension is released, tighten the nut. This will hold the tensioner in place. Lower the vehicle until the wheels touch but keep the vehicle supported.

14. Disconnect the crankshaft position (CKP) sensor wiring assembly.

15. Remove the center cover assembly.

16. Remove the timing belt, noting the location of the letters **KOA** on the belt. The belt must be installed in the same direction.

17. Remove the rocker arm/valve covers covers. For details, please refer to the procedure located earlier in this section.

18. Remove the camshaft sprockets.

19. Remove the upper and the center inner timing belt covers.

20. If the left-hand cylinder head is being removed, remove the ignition control module, ignition coil bracket and the oil level dipstick tube.

21. If the right cylinder head is being removed, remove the coolant outlet/water bypass hose.

22. Remove the exhaust manifold on the left cylinder head. On the right cylinder head, the exhaust manifold must be removed with the head as an assembly.

23. Remove the cylinder head-to-block retaining bolts and washers, then remove the cylinder head from the engine.

**To install:**

➡Lightly oil all bolt and stud bolt threads before installation except those specifying special sealant.

24. Remove any foreign material or oil from the top of the cylinder block and/or the lower surfaces of the cylinder head and clean the cylinder head and engine block mating surfaces of all old gasket material.

25. Position the cylinder head and gasket on the engine block and align with the cylinder head-to-block dowels.

26. Install the cylinder head bolts and tighten, in sequence, in 2 steps, the first to 36–51 ft. lbs. (49–69 Nm) and finally to 62–69 ft. lbs. (83–93 Nm).

27. When installing the left cylinder head, install the exhaust manifold, ignition control module, ignition coil bracket and the oil dipstick tube.

28. When installing the right cylinder head, install the coolant outlet/water bypass hose and connect the dual converter Y-pipe.

29. Install the upper and center inner timing belt covers.

30. Install the camshaft pulleys in the timed position.

31. Install the rocker arm/valve covers head covers. For details, please refer to the procedure located earlier in this section.

32. Install and adjust the timing belt.

33. Install the center timing belt cover.

34. Connect the crankshaft position (CKP) sensor wiring harness assembly.

35. Install the lower outer timing belt cover.

36. Raise and safely support the vehicle.

37. Install the front fender splash shield, then install the right wheel and tire assembly. Tighten the lug nuts to 85–105 ft. lbs. (115–142 Nm).

38. For the 3.0L SHO, install the left-hand idler pulley and bracket assembly. For the 3.2L SHO install the drive belt tensioner.

39. Install the upper outer timing belt cover.

40. Install the drive belts. For details, please refer to the belt installation procedure located in Section 1 of this manual.

41. Install the intake manifold. For details, please refer to the procedure located earlier in this section.

42. Install the air cleaner outlet tube.

43. Connect the negative battery cable.

44. Fill the engine cooling system with the proper type and quantity of coolant.

45. Start the engine and check for coolant, fuel or oil leaks.

### 3.8L Engine

◆ See Figures 145 and 146

1. Drain the cooling system, then disconnect the negative battery cable.

2. Properly relieve the fuel system pressure.

3. Remove the air cleaner assembly including air intake duct and heat tube.

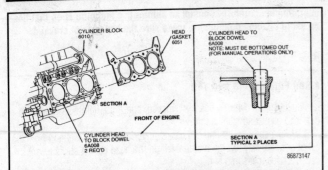

Fig. 145 When replacing or reinstalling the head, ALWAYS use new gasket(s) and bolts to avoid possible coolant and/or compression leaks which could result in engine damage

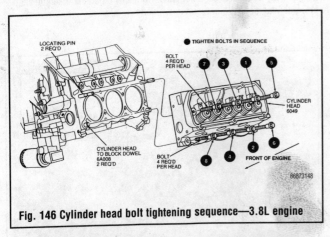

Fig. 146 Cylinder head bolt tightening sequence—3.8L engine

4. Loosen the accessory drive belt idler, then remove the drive belt.

5. If the left cylinder head is being removed, perform the following:

a. Remove the oil filler cap.

b. Remove the power steering pump. Leave the hoses connected and place the pump/bracket assembly aside in a position to prevent the fluid from leaking out.

c. If equipped with air conditioning, remove mounting bracket attaching bolts. Leaving the hoses connected, position the compressor aside.

d. Remove the alternator and bracket.

6. If the right cylinder head is being removed, perform the following:

a. Disconnect the thermactor air control valve or bypass valve hose assembly at the air pump.

b. If equipped, disconnect the thermactor tube support bracket from the rear of cylinder head.

c. Remove accessory drive idler.

d. Remove the thermactor pump pulley and thermactor pump.

e. Remove the PCV valve.

7. Remove the upper intake manifold. For details, please refer to the procedure located earlier in this section.

8. Remove the valve/rocker arm cover retaining bolts, then remove the covers.

9. Remove the injector fuel rail assembly.

10. Remove the lower intake manifold and the exhaust manifold(s). For details, please refer to the procedure located earlier in this section.

11. Loosen the rocker arm fulcrum attaching bolts enough to allow rocker arm to be lifted off the pushrod and rotate to one side. Remove the pushrods. Identify and label the position of each pushrod. Pushrods should be installed in their original position during assembly.

➡You must use new cylinder head retaining bolts and gaskets when replacing or reinstalling the cylinder head!

12. Remove the cylinder head attaching bolts and discard. Do NOT reuse the old bolts.

13. Remove the cylinder head(s). Remove and discard old cylinder head gasket(s).

**To install:**

14. Lightly oil all bolt threads before installation.

15. Clean cylinder head, intake manifold, valve rocker arm cover and cylinder head gasket contact surfaces. If cylinder head was removed for a cylinder head gasket replacement, check flatness of cylinder head and block gasket surfaces.

16. Position the new head gasket(s) onto cylinder block using dowels for alignment. Position cylinder head(s) onto block.

17. Apply a thin coating of pipe sealant with Teflon® to the threads of the short cylinder head bolts, nearest to the exhaust manifold. Do not apply sealant to the long bolts. Install the cylinder head bolts.

➡Always use new cylinder head bolts to ensure a leak-tight assembly. Torque retention with used bolts can vary, which may result in coolant or compression leakage at the cylinder head mating surface area.

18. For vehicles through 1994, tighten the cylinder head attaching bolts, in sequence, to the following specifications:

- Step 1:37 ft. lbs. (50 Nm)
- Step 2:45 ft. lbs. (60 Nm)
- Step 3:52 ft. lbs. (70 Nm)
- Step 4:59 ft. lbs. (80 Nm)

19. For 1995 vehicles, tighten the cylinder head attaching bolts, in sequence, to the following specifications:

- Step 1: 15 ft. lbs. (20 Nm)
- Step 2: 29 ft. lbs. (40 Nm)
- Step 3: 37 ft. lbs. (50 Nm)

20. For vehicles through 1992, retighten the cylinder head bolts, in sequence, one at a time in the following manner:

a. Long cylinder head bolts: Loosen the bolts and back them out 2–3 turns. Retighten to 11–18 ft. lbs. (15–25 Nm). Then tighten the bolt an additional 85–105° and go to the next bolt in sequence.

b. Short cylinder head bolts: Loosen the bolts and back them out 2–3 turns. Retighten to 11–18 ft. lbs. (15–25 Nm). Then tighten the bolt an additional 65–85°.

21. For 1993–95 vehicles, retighten the cylinder head bolts, in sequence, one at a time in the following manner:

a. Long cylinder head bolts: Loosen the bolts and back them out 2–3 turns. Retighten to 11–18 ft. lbs. (15–25 Nm). Then tighten the bolt an additional 85–95° and go to the next bolt in sequence.

b. Short cylinder head bolts: Loosen the bolt and back them out 2–3 turns. Retighten to 7–15 ft. lbs. (10–20 Nm). Then tighten the bolt an additional 85–95°.

➡When cylinder head attaching bolts have been tightened using the above procedures, it is not necessary to retighten bolts after extended engine operation. However, bolts can be checked for tightness if desired.

22. Dip each pushrod end in oil conditioner or heavy engine oil, then install the pushrods in their original position.

23. For each valve, rotate crankshaft until the tappet rests on the heel (base circle) of the camshaft lobe. Torque the fulcrum attaching bolts to 44 inch lbs. (5 Nm) maximum.

24. Lubricate all rocker arm assemblies with oil conditioner or heavy engine oil.

25. Tighten the fulcrum bolts a second time to 19–25 ft. lbs. (26–34 Nm). For final tightening, camshaft may be in any position.

➡If original valve train components are being installed, a valve clearance check is not required. If a component has been replaced, perform a valve clearance check.

26. Install the exhaust manifold(s) and the lower intake manifold. For details, please see these procedures located earlier in this section.

27. Install the injector fuel rail assembly. Tighten the retaining bolts to 71–97 inch lbs. (8–11 Nm).

28. Position the rocker arm/valve cover(s) and new gasket on cylinder

head and install attaching bolts. Note location of spark plug wire routing clip stud bolts. Tighten attaching bolts to 80–106 inch lbs. (9–12 Nm).

29. Install the upper intake manifold, then connect the ignition wires to the spark plugs.

30. If the left cylinder head is being installed, perform the following: install oil fill cap, compressor mounting and support brackets, power steering pump mounting and support brackets and the alternator/support bracket.

31. If the right cylinder head is being installed, perform the following: install the PCV valve, alternator bracket, thermactor pump and pump pulley, accessory drive idler, thermactor air control valve or air bypass valve hose.

32. Install the accessory drive belt. Attach the thermactor tube(s) support bracket to the rear of the cylinder head. Tighten the attaching bolts to 30–40 ft. lbs. (40–55 Nm).

33. Install the air cleaner assembly, including the air intake duct and heat tube.

34. Connect the negative battery cable and fill the cooling system.

35. Start the engine and check for leaks.

## CLEANING & INSPECTION

#### ▶ See Figure 147

1. With the valves installed to protect the valve seats, remove carbon deposits from the combustion chambers and valve heads with a drill-mounted wire brush. Be careful not to damage the cylinder head gasket surface. If the head is to be disassembled, proceed to Step 3. If the head is not to be disassembled, proceed to Step 2.

2. Remove all dirt, oil and old gasket material from the cylinder head with solvent. Clean the bolt holes and the oil passage. Be careful not to get solvent on the valve seals as the solvent may damage them. If available, dry the cylinder head with compressed air. Check the head for cracks or other damage, and check the gasket surface for burrs, nicks and flatness. If you are in doubt about the head's serviceability, consult a reputable automotive machine shop.

3. Remove the valves, springs and retainers, then clean the valve guide bores with a valve guide cleaning tool. Remove all dirt, oil and old gasket material from the cylinder head with solvent. Clean the bolt holes and the oil passage.

4. Remove all deposits from the valves with a wire brush or buffing wheel. Inspect the valves as described later in this section.

5. Check the head for cracks using a dye penetrant in the valve seat area and ports, head surface and top. Check the gasket surface for burrs, nicks and flatness. If you are in doubt about the head's serviceability, consult a reputable automotive machine shop.

➡ **If the cylinder head was removed due to an overheating condition and a crack is suspected, do not assume that the head is not cracked because a crack is not visually found. A crack can be so small that it cannot be seen by eye, but can pass coolant when the engine is at** operating temperature. Consult an automotive machine shop that has pressure testing equipment to make sure the head is not cracked.

## RESURFACING

#### ▶ See Figures 148 and 149

Whenever the cylinder head is removed, check the flatness of the cylinder head gasket surface as follows:

1. Make sure all dirt and old gasket material has been cleaned from the cylinder head. Any foreign material left on the head gasket surface can cause a false measurement.

2. Place a straightedge straight across and diagonally across the gasket surface of the cylinder head (in the positions shown in the figures). Using feeler gauges, determine the clearance at the center of the straightedge.

3. If warpage exceeds the 0.006 in. (0.15mm) then the cylinder head should likely be resurfaced or replaced. Contact a reputable machine shop for machining service and recommendations.

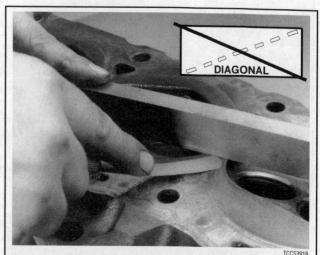

Fig. 148 Checking the cylinder head for flatness diagonally across the head surface

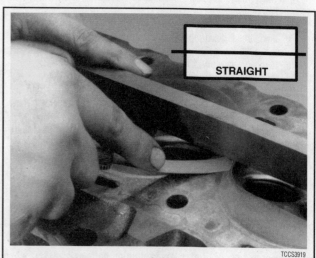

Fig. 149 Checking the cylinder head for flatness straight across the head surface

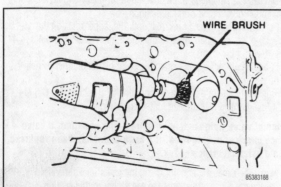

Fig. 147 Clean the combustion chamber using a drill-mounted wire brush

➡**When resurfacing the cylinder head(s), the intake manifold mounting position is altered and must be corrected by machining a proportionate amount from the intake manifold flange.**

## Valves

### REMOVAL & INSTALLATION

1. Remove the cylinder head(s) and place on a clean surface.
2. Block the head on its side, or install a pair of head-holding brackets made especially for valve removal.
3. Use a socket slightly larger than the valve stem and keepers, place the socket over the valve stem and gently hit the socket with a plastic hammer to break loose any varnish buildup.
4. Remove the valve keepers, retainer, spring shield and valve spring using a valve spring compressor (the locking C-clamp type is the easiest kind to use).
5. Put the parts in a separate container numbered for the cylinder being worked on. Do not mix them with other parts removed.
6. Remove and discard the valve stem oil seal, a new seal will be used at assembly time.
7. Remove the valve from the cylinder head and place, in order, through numbered holes punched in a stiff piece of cardboard or wooden valve holding stick.

➡**The exhaust valve stems, on some engines, are equipped with small metal caps. Take care not to lose the caps. Make sure to reinstall them at assembly time. Replace any caps that are worn.**

8. Use an electric drill and rotary wire brush to clean the intake and exhaust valve ports, combustion chamber and valve seats. In some cases, the carbon will need to be chipped away. Use a blunt pointed drift for carbon chipping, be careful around the valve seat areas.
9. Use a wire valve guide cleaning brush and safe solvent to clean the valve guides.
10. Clean the valves with a revolving wire brush. Heavy carbon deposits may be removed with the blunt drift.

➡**When using a wire brush to clean carbon from the valve ports, valves, etc., be sure that the deposits are actually removed, rather than burnished.**

11. Wash and clean all valve spring, keepers, retaining caps etc., in safe solvent.
12. Clean the head with a brush and some safe solvent and wipe dry.
13. Check the head for cracks. Cracks in the cylinder head usually start around an exhaust valve seat because it is the hottest part of the combustion chamber. If a crack is suspected but cannot be detected visually have the area checked with dye penetrant or other method by a machine shop.
14. After all cylinder head parts are reasonably clean, check the valve stem-to-guide clearance. If a dial indicator is not on hand, a visual inspection can give you a fairly good idea if the guide, valve stem or both are worn.
15. Insert the valve into the guide until slightly away from the valve seat. Wiggle the valve sideways. A small amount of wobble is normal, excessive wobble means a worn guide or valve stem. If a dial indicator is on hand, mount the indicator so that the stem of the valve is at 90° to the valve stem, as close to the valve guide as possible. Move the valve off the seat, and measure the valve guide-to-stem clearance by rocking the stem back and forth to actuate the dial indicator. Measure the valve stem using a micrometer and compare to specifications to determine whether stem or guide wear is causing excessive clearance.
16. The valve guide, if worn, must be repaired before the valve seats can be resurfaced. Ford supplies valves with oversize stems to fit valve guides that are reamed to oversize for repair. The machine shop will be able to handle the guide reaming for you. In some cases, if the guide is not too badly worn, knurling may be all that is required.
17. Reface, or have the valves and valve seats refaced. The valve seats should be a true 45° angle for the 2.5L and 3.0L engines, and 44.5° angle for the 3.8L engine. Remove only enough material to clean up any pits or grooves. Be sure the valve seat is not too wide or narrow. Use a 60° grinding wheel to remove material from the bottom of the seat for raising and a 30° grinding wheel to remove material from the top of the seat to narrow.
18. After the valves are refaced by machine, hand lap them to the valve seat. Clean the grinding compound off and check the position of face-to-seat contact. Contact should be close to the center of the valve face. If contact is close to the top edge of the valve, narrow the seat; if too close to the bottom edge, raise the seat.
19. Valves should be refaced to a true angle of 44° for the 2.5L and 3.0L engines, and 45.8° for the 3.8L engine. Remove only enough metal to clean up the valve face or to correct run-out. If the edge of the valve head, after machining, is 0.8mm or less replace the valve. The tip of the valve stem should also be dressed on the valve grinding machine, however, do not remove more than 0.010 in. (0.25mm).
20. After all valve and valve seats have been machined, check the remaining valve train parts (springs, retainers, keepers, etc.) for wear. Check the valve springs for straightness and tension.
21. Reassemble the head in the reverse order of disassembly using new valve guide seals and lubricating the valve stems. Check the valve spring installed height, shim or replace as necessary.

## Valve Stem Seals

### REPLACEMENT

Most engines are equipped with a positive valve stem seal using a Teflon® insert. Teflon® seals are available for other engines but usually require valve guide machining, consult your automotive machine shop for advice on having positive valve stem oil seals installed.

When installing valve stem oil seals, ensure that a small amount of oil is able to pass the seal to lubricate the valve stems and guide walls; otherwise, excessive wear will occur.

#### Head Off Vehicle

1. Remove the cylinder head from the vehicle. Position the assembly in a cylinder head holding fixture.
2. Using the proper valve stem seal removal tool, remove the valve keepers from the valve stem. Remove and discard the old valve stem seal.
3. As required, remove the valve from the cylinder head. Be sure to keep the valves in the proper order for reassembly.
4. Continue this process for the remaining valves.
5. Installation is the reverse of the removal procedure.

#### Head On Vehicle

1. Disconnect the negative battery cable. Remove the valve cover.
2. Remove the spark plug from the cylinder that you are working on.
3. Position the engine so that both the intake and exhaust valves are closed.
4. Screw the proper tool into the spark plug hole. Attach an air line to the tool and pressurize the cylinder with low pressure compressed air, just enough to hold the valves in the closed position.

➡**Failure to properly compress air into the cylinder will result in the valve falling into the cylinder bore which will necessitate disassembling the engine to retrieve them.**

5. Using the proper valve stem seal removal tool, remove the valve keepers from the valve stem. Remove and discard the old valve seal.
6. Installation is the reverse of the removal procedure.

## Valve Seats

If a valve seat is damaged or burnt and cannot be serviced by refacing, it may be possible to have the seat machined and an insert installed. Consult the automotive machine shop for their advice.

➡The aluminum heads on some engines are equipped with inserts.

## Valve Guides

Worn valve guides can, in most cases, be reamed to accept a valve with an oversized stem. Valve guides that are not excessively worn or distorted may, in some cases, be knurled rather than reamed. However, if the valve stem is worn reaming for an oversized valve stem is the answer since a new valve would be required.

Knurling is a process in which metal is displaced and raised, thereby reducing clearance. Knurling also produces excellent oil control. The possibility of knurling instead of reaming the valve guides should be discussed with a machinist.

## Valve Lifters

### REMOVAL & INSTALLATION

#### 2.5L Engine

1. Disconnect the negative battery cable. Remove the cylinder head.
2. Using a magnet, remove the lifters. Identify, tag and place the lifters in a rack so they can be installed in the original positions.
3. If the lifters are stuck in their bores by excessive varnish or gum, it may be necessary to use a hydraulic lifter puller tool to remove the lifters. Rotate the lifters back and forth to loosen any gum and varnish which may have formed. Keep the assemblies intact until the are to be cleaned.
4. Install the lifters through the pushrod openings with a magnet.
5. Install the cylinder head and related parts.

#### 3.0L Engine—Except SHO

1. Disconnect the negative battery cable.
2. Drain the cooling system and relieve the fuel system pressure.
3. Disconnect the fuel lines from the fuel supply manifold and remove the throttle body.
4. Disconnect the spark plug wires from the spark plugs. Remove the ignition wire/separator assembly from the rocker cover retaining studs.
5. Mark the position of the distributor housing and rotor and remove the distributor.
6. Remove the rocker arm covers. Loosen the No. 3 intake valve rocker arm retaining bolt to allow the rocker arm to be rotated to 1 side.
7. Remove the intake manifold assembly.
8. Loosen the rocker arm fulcrum retaining bolt enough to allow the rocker arm to be lifted off the pushrod and rotated to 1 side.
9. Remove the pushrod(s). If more than 1 is removed, identify each pushrods location. The pushrods should be installed in their original position during reassembly.
10. On 1992 engines equipped with roller lifters, loosen the two roller lifter guide plate retaining bolts. Remove the guide plate retainer assembly from the lifter valley. Remove the lifter guide plate from the lifter by lifting straight up. To remove, grasp the lifter and pull it in line with the bore.
11. Remove the lifter(s) using a magnet, as required.

➡If the lifter(s) are stuck in the bore(s) due to excessive varnish or gum deposits, it may be necessary to use a claw-type tool to aid removal. Rotate the lifter back and forth to loosen it from the gum or varnish that may have formed on the lifter.

#### To install:

12. Clean all gasket mating surfaces. Place a rag in the lifter valley to catch any stray gasket material.
13. Lubricate each lifter and bore with heavy engine oil. Install the lifter in the bore, checking for free fit.
14. If equipped with roller lifters align the lifter flat to the lifter guide plate. Install the plate with the word UP and or button visible. Install the guide retainer assembly over the guide plates. Tighten the bolts to 810 ft. lbs.

15. Install the intake manifold and new gaskets. Dip each pushrod end in oil conditioner and install in it's original position.
16. For each valve, rotate the crankshaft until the lifter rests on the base circle of the camshaft lobe. Position the rocker arms over the pushrod and valve. Tighten the retaining bolt to 8 ft. lbs. (11 Nm) to initially seat the fulcrum into the cylinder head and onto the pushrod. Final tighten the bolt to 24 ft. lbs. (32 Nm).
17. Install the rocker arm covers and the distributor.
18. Install the throttle body and connect the fuel lines to the fuel supply manifold. Install the safety clips.
19. Install the coolant hoses. Fill and bleed the cooling system. Drain and change the crankcase oil.
20. Connect the air cleaner hoses to the throttle body and rocker cover.
21. Connect the negative battery cable, start the engine and check for leaks. Check the ignition timing.

#### 3.8L Engine

1. Disconnect the negative battery cable. Disconnect the secondary ignition wires at the spark plugs.
2. Remove the plug wire routing clips from mounting studs on the rocker arm cover attaching bolts. Lay plug wires with routing clips toward the front of engine.
3. Remove the upper intake manifold, rocker arm covers and lower intake manifold.
4. Sufficiently loosen each rocker arm fulcrum attaching bolt to allow the rocker arm to be lifted off the pushrod and rotated to one side.
5. Remove the pushrods. The location of each pushrod should be identified and labeled. When engine is assembled, each rod should be installed in its original position.
6. If equipped with roller lifters, remove the 2 tappet guide plate retainers and 6 guide plates.
7. Remove the lifters using a magnet. The location of each lifters should be identified and labeled. When engine is assembled, each lifter should be installed in its original position.

➡If lifters are stuck in bores due to excessive varnish or gum deposits, it may be necessary to use a hydraulic lifter puller tool to aid removal. When using a remover tool, rotate lifter back and forth to loosen it from gum or varnish that may have formed on the lifter.

#### To install:

8. Lightly oil all bolt and stud threads before installation. Using solvent, clean the cylinder head and valve rocker arm cover sealing surfaces.
9. Lubricate each lifter and bore with oil conditioner or heavy engine oil.
10. Install each lifter in bore from which it was removed. If a new tappet(s) is being installed, check new lifter for a free fit in bore.
11. If equipped with roller lifters, align the flats on the sides of the lifters and install the 6 guide plates between the adjacent lifters. Make sure the word "up" and/or button is showing. Install the 3 guide plate retainers and tighten the 4 bolts to 6–10 ft. lbs. (8–14 Nm).
12. Dip each pushrod end in oil conditioner or heavy engine oil. Install pushrods in their original positions.
13. For each valve, rotate crankshaft until lifter rests onto heel (base circle) of camshaft lobe. Position rocker arms over pushrods and install the fulcrums. Initially tighten the fulcrum attaching bolts to 44 inch lbs. (5 Nm) maximum.
14. Lubricate all rocker arm assemblies with suitable heavy engine oil.
15. Finally tighten the fulcrum bolts to 19–25 ft. lbs. (26–34 Nm). For the final tightening, the camshaft may be in any position.

➡Fulcrums must be fully seated in the cylinder head and pushrods must be seated in rocker arm sockets prior to the final tightening.

16. Complete the installation of the lower intake manifold, valve rocker arm covers and the upper intake manifold by reversing the removal procedure.
17. Install the plug wire routing clips and connect wires to the spark plugs.
18. Start the engine and check for oil or coolant leaks.

## Oil Pan

### REMOVAL & INSTALLATION

### ✳✳ CAUTION

The EPA warns that prolonged contact with used engine oil may cause a number of skin disorders, including cancer! You should make every effort to minimize your exposure to used engine oil. Protective gloves should be worn when changing the oil. Wash your hands and any other exposed skin areas as soon as possible after exposure to used engine oil. Soap and water, or waterless hand cleaner should be used.

### 2.5L Engine

▶ **See Figures 150 thru 155**

1. Disconnect the negative battery cable. Raise and safely support the vehicle.
2. Drain the crankcase, then drain the cooling system by removing the lower radiator hose.
3. On vehicles equipped with a manual transaxle, remove the roll restrictor.
4. Disconnect the starter cable, then remove the starter.
5. Disconnect the exhaust pipe from oil pan.
6. Remove the engine coolant tube located at the lower radiator hose, at the water pump and at the tabs on the oil pan. Position air conditioner line off to the side.
7. Disconnect the retaining bolts, then remove the oil pan.

**To install:**

8. Clean both mating surfaces of oil pan and cylinder block, making certain all traces of RTV sealant are removed.
9. Remove and clean oil pump pick-up tube and screen assembly. After cleaning, install tube and screen assembly.
10. Fill the oil pan groove with RTV sealer; the bead should be approximately ⅛ in. (3mm) above the surface of the pan rail. Immediately (within 5 minutes) install the oil pan.
11. Install and tighten the 2 oil pan-to-transaxle bolts to 30–39 ft. lbs. (41–53 Nm) to align the pan with the transaxle then back off ½ turn.
12. Tighten the pan flange bolts to 6–8 ft. lbs. (8–11 Nm).
13. Tighten the 2 oil pan-to-transaxle bolts to 30–39 ft. lbs. (41–53 Nm).

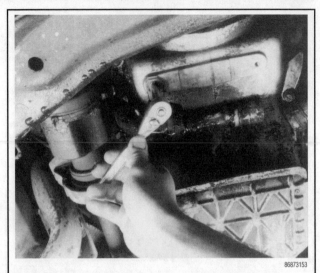

Fig. 151 Remove the coolant tube-to-oil pan retainers, then. . .

Fig. 152 . . . remove the coolant tube from the pan

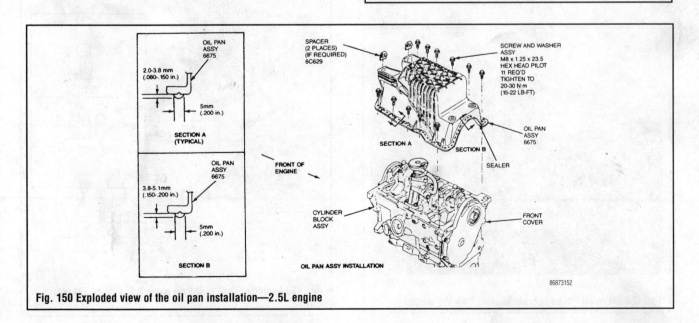

Fig. 150 Exploded view of the oil pan installation—2.5L engine

**Fig. 153 Remove the oil pan retaining bolts**

**Fig. 154 Carefully lower the oil pan from the engine**

**Fig. 155 Clean all traces of gasket/sealer from the oil pan**

14. Install the exhaust pipe bracket to the oil pan.
15. Install the engine coolant tube and the air conditioning line.
16. Install the starter, then connect the starter cable.
17. Carefully lower the vehicle, then fill the crankcase and cooling system to the proper level.
18. Start the engine and inspect for leaks.

### 3.0L ENGINE—EXCEPT SHO
▶ See Figure 156

1. Disconnect the negative battery cable and remove the oil level dipstick.
2. Raise and safely support the vehicle. If equipped with a low level sensor, remove the retainer clip at the sensor. Disengage the electrical connector from the sensor.
3. Drain the crankcase.
4. Remove the starter motor. For details, please refer to the procedure located earlier in this section.
5. Disengage the electrical connector from the oxygen sensor.
6. Remove the dual converter Y-pipe.
7. Remove the lower engine/flywheel dust cover from the torque converter housing.
8. Remove the oil pan attaching bolts, then slowly remove the oil pan, making sure the internal pan baffle does not snag the oil pump screen cover and tube. Remove the oil pan gasket.

**To install:**

9. Clean the gasket surfaces on the cylinder block and oil pan. Clean the sealing surface with Metal Surface Cleaner F4AZ-19A536-RA or equivalent. Apply a ¼ in. (6mm) bead of silicone sealer to the junction of the rear main bearing cap and cylinder block junction of the front cover assembly and cylinder block.

➡️**When using a silicone sealer, the assembly process should occur within 15 minutes after the sealer has been applied. After this time, the sealer may start to set-up and its sealing effectiveness may be affected.**

10. Position the oil pan gasket to the oil pan with sealing bends against the oil pan surface and secure with Gasket and Trim Adhesive D7AZ-19B508-B.
11. Position the oil pan on the engine block and install the oil pan attaching bolts. Torque the bolts to 8 ft. lbs. (10 Nm), then back off the all of the bolts and retighten them.

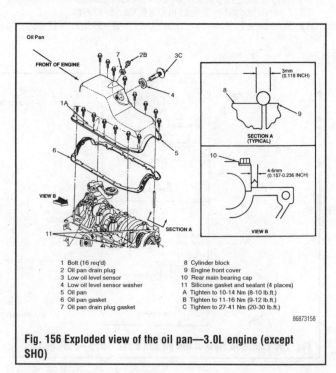

1 Bolt (16 req'd)
2 Oil pan drain plug
3 Low oil level sensor
4 Low oil level sensor washer
5 Oil pan
6 Oil pan gasket
7 Oil pan drain plug gasket
8 Cylinder block
9 Engine front cover
10 Rear main bearing cap
11 Silicone gasket and sealant (4 places)
A Tighten to 10-14 Nm (8-10 lb.ft.)
B Tighten to 11-16 Nm (9-12 lb.ft.)
C Tighten to 27-41 Nm (20-30 lb.ft.)

**Fig. 156 Exploded view of the oil pan—3.0L engine (except SHO)**

12. Install the lower engine/flywheel dust cover to the torque converter housing. Install the Y-pipe assembly.

13. Engage the oxygen sensor connector.

14. Install the starter motor. For installation details, please refer to the starter motor procedure located earlier in this section.

15. Fasten the low oil level sensor connector to the sensor and install the retainer clip. Lower the vehicle and replace the oil level dipstick.

16. Connect the negative battery cable. Fill the crankcase with the correct viscosity and amount of engine oil, then start the engine and check for oil and exhaust leaks.

### 3.0L and 3.2L SHO Engines

▶ **See Figures 157 and 158**

1. Disconnect the negative battery cable.
2. Remove the oil level dipstick.
3. Raise and safely support the vehicle.
4. If equipped with a low oil level sensor, remove the retainer clip, then disengage the electrical connector from the sensor.
5. Drain the engine oil.
6. Remove the starter motor. For details, please refer to the procedure located earlier in this section.
7. Disconnect the heated oxygen sensors.
8. Remove the dual converter Y-pipe assembly.
9. Remove the lower flywheel dust cover from the converter housing.
10. Remove the oil pan attaching bolts, then carefully remove the oil pan.
11. Remove the front oil pan seal and the oil pan rear seal.

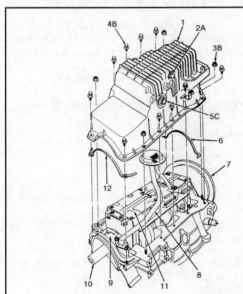

1 Oil pan
2 Oil pan drain plug
3 Nut (4 req'd)
4 Bolt (10 req'd)
5 Low oil level sensor
6 Oil pan rear seal
7 Flywheel
8 Oil pump screen cover and tube
9 Oil pump
10 Crankshaft
11 Oil pan baffle
12 Front oil pan seal
A Tighten to 20-33 Nm (15-24 lb.ft.)
B Tighten to 15-23 Nm (11-17 lb.ft.)
C Tighten to 21-33 Nm (15-24 lb.ft.)

86873159

**Fig. 157 Exploded view of the oil pan assembly—3.0L and 3.2L engine**

**To install:**

12. Clean the gasket surfaces of the cylinder block and the oil pan.

➡**When using silicone sealer, assembly should occur within 15 minutes of application or the sealer may start to seal up losing its effectiveness.**

13. Clean the oil pan sealing surfaces, then apply a 0.2 in. (5mm) continuous bead of silicone sealer to the oil pan sealing surfaces.

14. Install a new front and rear oil pan seal, then position the oil pan and tighten the retaining bolts, in sequence, to 11–17 ft. lbs. (15–23 Nm).

15. Install the lower flywheel dust cover to the converter housing.

16. Install the Y-pipe assembly, then connect the heated oxygen sensors.

17. Install the starter. For details, please refer to the procedure located earlier in this section.

18. Engage the low oil level sensor connector to the sensor. Install the retainer clip.

19. Carefully lower the vehicle.

20. Replace the oil level dipstick and connect the negative battery cable.

21. Fill the crankcase with the proper type and quantity of oil. Start the vehicle and check for leaks.

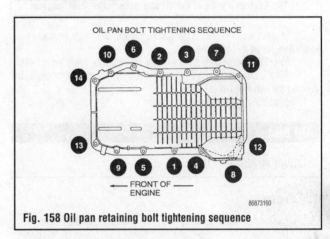

OIL PAN BOLT TIGHTENING SEQUENCE

← FRONT OF ENGINE →

86873160

**Fig. 158 Oil pan retaining bolt tightening sequence**

### 3.8L Engine

▶ **See Figure 159**

1. Disconnect the negative battery cable.
2. Raise and safely support the vehicle.
3. Drain the oil pan, then remove the oil filter. Position the drain pan out of the way.
4. Remove the dual converter Y-pipe assembly.
5. Remove the starter motor. For details, please refer to the procedure located earlier in this section.
6. Remove the engine rear plate/converter housing cover.
7. Remove the retaining bolts and remove the oil pan.

**To install:**

8. Clean the gasket surfaces on cylinder block and the oil pan.

9. Trial fit oil pan to cylinder block. Ensure that enough clearance has been provided to allow the oil pan to be installed without sealant being scraped off when pan is positioned under the engine.

10. Apply a bead of silicone sealer to the oil pan flange. Also apply a bead of sealer to the front cover/cylinder block joint and fill the grooves on both sides of the rear main seal cap.

➡**When using silicone rubber sealer, assembly must occur within 15 minutes after sealer application. After this time, the sealer may start to harden and its sealing effectiveness may be reduced.**

11. Install the oil pan and secure to the block with the attaching screws. Tighten the screws to 7–9 ft. lbs. (9–12 Nm).

12. Install a new oil filter.

13. Install the engine rear plate/converter housing cover.

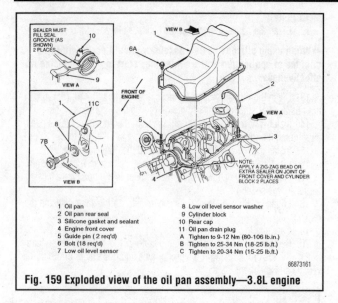

Fig. 159 Exploded view of the oil pan assembly—3.8L engine

1 Oil pan
2 Oil pan rear seal
3 Silicone gasket and sealant
4 Engine front cover
5 Guide pin ( 2 req'd)
6 Bolt (18 req'd)
7 Low oil level sensor
8 Low oil level sensor washer
9 Cylinder block
10 Rear cap
11 Oil pan drain plug
A Tighten to 9-12 Nm (80-106 lb.in.)
B Tighten to 25-34 Nm (18-25 lb.ft.)
C Tighten to 20-34 Nm (15-25 lb.ft.)

86873161

14. Install the starter motor. For details, please refer to the procedure located earlier in this section.

15. Install the Y-pipe converter assembly, then carefully lower the vehicle.

16. Fill the crankcase with the correct viscosity and amount of oil, then connect the negative battery cable.

17. Start the engine and check for leaks.

## Oil Pump

### REMOVAL & INSTALLATION

#### 2.5L Engine

1. Disconnect the negative battery cable, then remove the oil pan.

2. Disconnect the oil pump attaching bolts, then remove the oil pump and intermediate driveshaft.

**To install:**

3. Prime the oil pump by filling the inlet port with engine oil. Rotate the pump shaft until oil flows from the outlet port.

4. If the screen and cover assembly have been removed, replace the gasket. Clean and reinstall the screen and cover assembly, then tighten attaching bolts.

5. Position the intermediate driveshaft into the distributor socket.

6. Insert intermediate driveshaft into oil pump. Install pump and shaft as an assembly.

➥**Do not attempt to force the pump into position if it will not seat. The shaft hex may be misaligned with the distributor shaft. To align, remove the oil pump and rotate the intermediate driveshaft into a new position.**

7. Tighten the oil pump attaching bolts to 15–22 ft. lbs. (20–30 Nm).

8. Install the oil pan.

9. Fill the crankcase with the correct viscosity and amount of oil, then connect the negative battery cable. Start engine and check for leaks.

#### 3.0L Engine—Except SHO

▶ **See Figure 160**

1. Disconnect the negative battery cable.

2. Remove the oil pan.

3. Remove the oil pump attaching bolts. Lift the oil pump from the engine. If replacing the pump, withdraw the oil pump intermediate shaft.

**To install:**

4. Prime the oil pump by filling either the inlet or the outlet port with

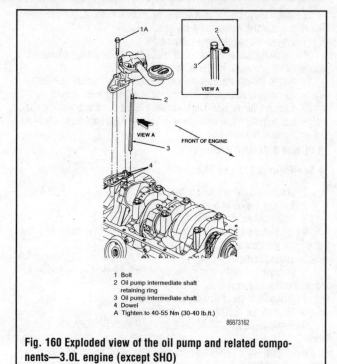

Fig. 160 Exploded view of the oil pump and related components—3.0L engine (except SHO)

1 Bolt
2 Oil pump intermediate shaft retaining ring
3 Oil pump intermediate shaft
4 Dowel
A Tighten to 40-55 Nm (30-40 lb.ft.)

86873162

engine oil. Rotate the pump shaft to distribute the oil within the oil pump body cavity.

5. Insert the oil pump intermediate shaft assembly into the hex drive hole in the oil pump assembly until the retainer "clicks" into place. Place the oil pump in the proper position with a new gasket and install the retaining bolt.

6. Torque the oil pump retaining bolt to 35 ft. lbs. (48 Nm).

7. Install the oil pan.

8. Fill the crankcase. Connect the negative battery cable, then start engine and check for leaks.

#### 3.0L and 3.2L SHO Engines

1. Disconnect the negative battery cable.

2. Remove the oil pan.

3. Remove the accessory drive belt.

4. Remove the timing belt. For details, please refer to the procedure located later in this section.

5. Remove the oil pump-to-cylinder block retaining bolts, them remove the oil pump.

**To install:**

6. Align the oil pump on the crankshaft and install the oil pump retaining bolts. Tighten the bolts to 11–17 ft. lbs. (15–23 Nm).

7. Install the timing belt.

8. Install the oil pan.

9. Fill the crankcase with the proper type and quantity of oil.

10. Start the engine and check for leaks.

#### 3.8L Engine

➥**The oil pump, oil pressure relief valve and drive intermediate shaft are contained in the front cover assembly.**

1. Disconnect the negative battery cable.

2. If necessary for access, remove the oil filter.

3. Remove the oil pump and filter body-to-engine front cover retaining bolts, them remove the oil pump and filter body from the engine front cover.

4. Inspect the oil pump body seal, oil pump and filter body, and engine front cover for distortion. Replace damaged components as necessary.

**To install:**

5. Position the oil pump and filter body on the engine front cover, then install the retaining bolts.

6. Tighten the four large engine front cover retaining bolts to 17–23 ft. lbs. (23–32 Nm), then tighten the remaining retaining bolts to 6–8 ft. lbs. (8–11 Nm).

7. If removed, install the oil filter, then connect the negative battery cable.

## INSPECTION AND OVERHAUL

### 2.5L and 3.0L Engines

1. Remove the oil pump from the vehicle.
2. Inspect the inside of the pump housing for damage or excessive wear.
3. Check the mating surface for wear. Minor scuff marks are normal but if the cover, gears or housing are excessively worn, scored or grooved, replace the pump.
4. Inspect the rotor for nicks, burrs, or score marks. Remove minor imperfections with an oil stone.
5. Measure the inner-to-outer rotor tip clearance. The clearance must not exceed 0.012 in. (0.30mm) with a feeler gauge inserted ½ in. (13mm) minimum with the rotors removed from the pump housing.
6. With the rotor assembly installed in the housing, place a straight edge across the rotor assembly and housing. Measure the clearance (rotor end-play) between the the inner and outer rotors. The clearance is 0.005 in. (0.13mm) maximum.
7. Check the relief valve spring tension. If the spring is worn or damaged, replace the pump. Check the relief valve piston for freedom of movement in the bore.

### 3.0L SHO Engine

1. Remove the oil pump from the vehicle.
2. Inspect the inside of the pump housing for damage or excessive wear.
3. Check the mating surface for wear. Minor scuff marks are normal but if the cover, gears or housing are excessively worn, scored or grooved, replace the pump.
4. Check the inner rotor tip-to-outer rotor tip clearance using a feeler gauge. The clearance must not exceed 0.0024–0.0071 in. (0.06–0.18mm) with the feeler gauge inserted ½ in. (13mm) minimum and the rotors removed from the pump housing.
5. With the rotor assembly installed in the pump housing, place a straight-edge over the rotor assembly and the housing. Measure the clearance (rotor end-play) between the straight-edge and the rotor and outer race. The clearance should be 0.0012–0.0035 in. (0.03–0.09mm).
6. Check the relief valve spring tension. If the spring is worn or damaged, replace the pump. Check the relief valve piston for freedom of movement in the bore.

### 3.8L Engine

#### PUMP GEAR END CLEARANCE

1. Inspect the pump cover mating surface on the front cover and pump body. Visually inspect the O-ring for any cuts and/or nicks and replace, if necessary. Remove any burrs or nicks.
2. Measure the thickness of the gear using a micrometer. The gear should measure 1.19–1.20 in. (30.226–30.480mm) thick.
3. If the gear is less than the specified minimum thickness, replace the gear. If the gear thickness is within specification, it may be necessary to replace the pump body. If the gear thickness is within the specified limits, proceed to Step 4.
4. Measure the depth of the gear pocket in the oil pump body. The depth should be 1.200–1.202 in. (30.48–30.53mm) thick.
5. If the depth is more than 1.202 in. (30.53mm), replace the oil pump body.

#### PUMP GEAR SIDE CLEARANCE

1. Measure the side clearance by inserting a feeler gauge between the gear tooth and the side wall of the gear pocket.
2. The clearance should be a maximum of 0.005 in. (0.13mm) and the gears should be free to turn. If the clearance is greater than 0.005 in. (0.13mm), proceed to Step 3.
3. Measure the diameter of the gear using a micrometer. The gear should be 1.505–1.509 in. (38.227–38.329mm) wide.
4. If the gear is less than 1.505 in. (38.227mm) in diameter, replace the gear and measure the clearance as in Step 1. If the diameter of the gear is within the specified limits, go to Step 5.
5. Measure the diameter of the gear pocket in the front cover. The diameter should be 1.504–1.507 in. (38.20–38.28mm). If the diameter is less than 1.504 in. (38.20mm), replace the front cover and measure the clearance as in Step 1.

## Timing Chain Cover

### REMOVAL & INSTALLATION

#### 2.5L Engine

▶ See Figures 161 and 162

1. Disconnect the negative battery cable.
2. Remove the engine and transaxle assembly from the vehicle and position in a suitable holding fixture. Remove the dipstick.
3. If equipped, remove the accessory drive pulley. Remove the crankshaft pulley attaching bolt and washer, then remove the pulley.
4. Using Front Seal Remover T74P-6700-A or equivalent, remove the timing/front cover oil seal.
5. Remove the front cover attaching bolts from front cover. Pry the top of the front cover away from the block.
6. Clean all dirt and old gasket material from all mating surfaces.
7. Remove the oil pan.

**To install:**

8. Clean and inspect all parts before installation. Make sure that the cylinder block and front cover are free of old gasket material and/or dirt.
9. Apply oil resistant sealer to a new front cover gasket, then position the gasket into front cover.
10. With the front oil seal removed, position the front cover on the engine.
11. Position front cover alignment tool T84P-6019-C or equivalent, onto the end of the crankshaft, ensuring the crank key is aligned with the keyway in the tool. Bolt the front cover to the engine and tighten the bolts to 6–8 ft. lbs. (8–11 Nm). Remove the front cover alignment tool.
12. Install a new front cover oil seal using Pinion Oil Seal Installer T83T-4676-A, or equivalent suitable seal installer. Lubricate the hub of the crankshaft pulley with polyethylene grease to prevent damage to the seal during installation and initial engine start.

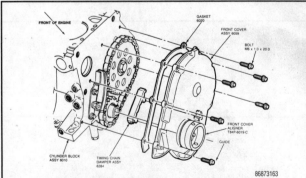

**Fig. 161 Exploded view of the timing chain/engine front cover—early model 2.5L engine shown**

13. Install the crankshaft pulley.

14. Install the oil pan.

15. If equipped, install the accessory drive pulley.

16. Install crankshaft pulley attaching bolt and washer. Tighten to 140–170 ft. lbs. (190–230 Nm).

17. Install the engine and transaxle assembly in the vehicle. Connect the negative battery cable.

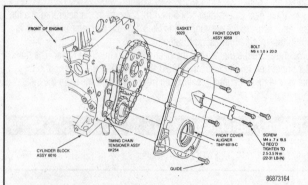

**Fig. 162 Exploded view of the timing chain/engine front cover—late model 2.5L engine shown**

### 3.0L Engine—Except SHO

♦ **See Figures 163, 164, 165, 166 and 167**

1. Disconnect the negative battery cable. Properly drain the engine cooling system.

2. Loosen the four water pump pulley bolts while the water pump drive belt is in place.

3. Loosen the alternator belt-adjuster jackscrew to provide enough slack in the alternator drive belt for removal.

4. Using a ½ in. drive breaker bar, rotate the automatic belt tensioner down and to the left or right (depending upon application) to remove the water pump drive belt.

5. Remove the lower radiator hose and the heater hose from the water pump.

6. Remove the crankshaft pulley and damper:

a. If necessary, raise and safely support the vehicle, then remove the right-hand front wheel and tire assembly.

b. Remove the four crankshaft pulley-to-damper retaining bolts, then remove the crankshaft pulley.

c. Remove the crankshaft damper retaining bolt and washer.

d. Remove the damper using Crankshaft Damper Remover T58P-6316-D and Vibration Damper Remover Adapter T82L-6316-B.

e. Remove the timing cover/crankshaft front seal from the engine front cover using Jet Plug Remover T77L-9533-B.

7. Disengage the engine control sensor wiring from the crankshaft position (CKP) sensor and locating stud bolt (Flexible Fuel (FF) only).

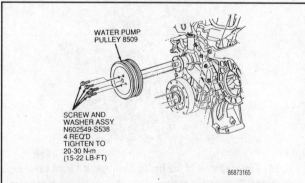

**Fig. 163 Remove the water pump retaining bolts, then remove the water pump pulley**

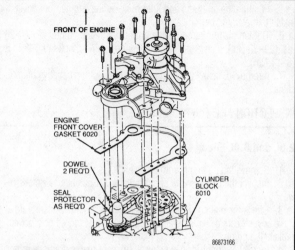

**Fig. 164 After removing the retaining bolts, remove the front cover from the engine**

8. Drain and remove the oil pan.

9. Remove the water pump pulley retaining bolts and water pump pulley.

10. Remove the retaining bolts from the timing cover to the block, then remove the timing cover.

➡ **The timing cover and water pump may be removed as an assembly by not removing bolts 11–15.**

**To install:**

11. Lightly oil all bolt and stud threads except those specifying special sealant.

➡ **Be careful when scraping the old gasket material from the timing/front cover because aluminum gouges easily, and if scratched, leakage may occur.**

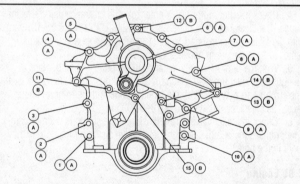

| FASTENER AND HOLE NO. | FASTENERS | | | TORQUE SPECIFICATIONS | |
|---|---|---|---|---|---|
| | PART NO. | SIZE | FASTENER APPLICATION | N·m | LB-FT |
| 1A | N804113 | M8 x 1.25 x 43.5 | F/C TO BLOCK | 20-30 | 15-22 |
| 2A | N804113 | M8 x 1.25 x 43.5 | F/C TO BLOCK | 20-30 | 15-22 |
| 3A | N804811 | M8 x 1.25 x 70 | W/P & F/C TO BLOCK | 20-30 | 15-22 |
| 4A | N804811 | M8 x 1.25 x 70 | W/P & F/C TO BLOCK | 20-30 | 15-22 |
| 5A | N605909 | M8 x 1.25 x 42 | F/C TO BLOCK | 20-30 | 15-22 |
| 6A | N804811 | M8 x 1.25 x 70 | W/P & F/C TO BLOCK | 20-30 | 15-22 |
| 7A | N804811 | M8 x 1.25 x 70 | W/P & F/C TO BLOCK | 20-30 | 15-22 |
| 8A | N804811 | M8 x 1.25 x 70 | W/P & F/C TO BLOCK | 20-30 | 15-22 |
| 9A | N804811 | M8 x 1.25 x 70 | W/P & F/C TO BLOCK | 20-30 | 15-22 |
| 10A | N606543 | M8 x 1.25 x 52 | F/C TO BLOCK | 20-30 | 15-22 |
| 11B | N804576 | M6 x 1 x 28.5 | W/P TO F/C | 8-12 | 71-106 (lb-in) |
| 12B | N804576 | M6 x 1 x 28.5 | W/P TO F/C | 8-12 | 71-106 (lb-in) |
| 13B | N804576 | M6 x 1 x 28.5 | W/P TO F/C | 8-12 | 71-106 (lb-in) |
| 14B | N804576 | M6 x 1 x 28.5 | W/P TO F/C | 8-12 | 71-106 (lb-in) |
| 15B | N804576 | M6 x 1 x 28.5 | W/P TO F/C | 8-12 | 71-106 (lb-in) |

W/P—Water Pump
F/C—Engine Front Cover

**Fig. 165 Cover mounting bolt location and torque specifications**

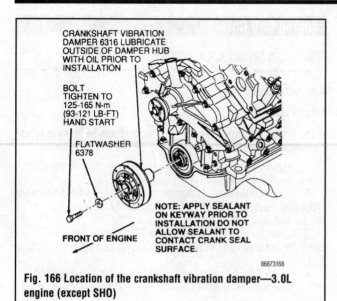

**Fig. 166 Location of the crankshaft vibration damper—3.0L engine (except SHO)**

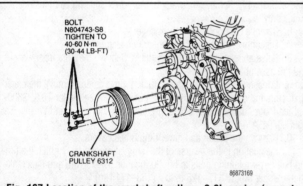

**Fig. 167 Location of the crankshaft pulley—3.0L engine (except SHO)**

12. Clean all old gasket material and sealer from the timing cover, oil pan and cylinder block.

13. Inspect the timing cover seal for wear or damage, and replace if necessary.

14. Align a new timing cover gasket over the cylinder block dowels.

15. Install the timing cover/water pump assembly onto the cylinder block with the water pump pulley loosely attached to the water pump hub.

16. Apply pipe sealant to bolt numbers 1, 2 and 3 and hand start them along with the rest of the cover retaining bolts. Tighten bolts 1–10 to 15–22 ft. lbs. (20–30 Nm) and 11–15 to 71–106 inch lbs. (8–12 Nm).

17. Install the oil pan and tighten the retaining bolts to 9 ft. lbs. (12 Nm).

18. Hand tighten the water pump pulley retaining bolts.

19. Install the crankshaft damper and pulley:

a. Lubricate the oil seal with clean oil, then install the seal suing Vibration Damper and Seal Replacer T82L-6316-A and Front Cover Replacer T70P.

b. Coat the crankshaft damper sealing surface with clean engine oil. Apply Silicone Rubber D6AZ-19562-AA or BA to the keyway of the damper before installation. Install the damper using Vibration Damper and Seal Replacer T82L-6316-A.

c. Install the damper retaining bolt and washer. Tighten to 93–121 ft. lbs. (125–165 Nm).

d. Install the crankshaft pulley, then install the four retaining bolts. Tighten the bolts to 30–44 ft. lbs. (40–60 Nm).

e. If removed, install the right-hand wheel and tire assembly, then carefully lower the vehicle.

20. Install the automatic belt tensioner. Tighten the two retaining nuts and bolt to 35 ft. lbs. (48 Nm).

21. Install the water pump and accessory drive belts. Torque the water pump pulley retaining bolts to 15–22 ft. lbs. (20–30 Nm).

22. Install the lower radiator hose and the heater hose and tighten the clamps.

23. Fill the crankcase with the correct amount and type of engine oil. Connect the negative battery cable. Fill and bleed the cooling system.

24. Start the engine and check for coolant and oil leaks.

## 3.8L Engine

### ♦ See Figure 168

1. Disconnect the negative battery cable. Properly drain the cooling system and the engine oil.

2. Remove the air cleaner assembly and air intake duct.

3. If necessary, remove the fan shroud attaching screws and bolts, then remove the fan/clutch assembly and shroud.

4. Loosen the accessory drive belt idler. Remove the drive belt and water pump pulley.

5. Remove the power steering pump mounting bracket attaching bolts. Leaving the hoses connected, place the pump/bracket assembly in a position that will prevent the loss of power steering fluid.

6. If equipped with air conditioning, remove the compressor front support bracket. Leave the compressor in place.

7. Disconnect coolant bypass and heater hoses at the water pump. Disconnect the radiator upper hose at the thermostat housing.

8. Disconnect the coil wire from the distributor cap, then remove the cap with the secondary wires still attached. Remove the distributor retaining clamp and lift distributor out of the front cover.

9. Raise and safely support the vehicle.

10. Remove the crankshaft damper and pulley.

➡**If the crankshaft pulley and vibration damper have to be separated, mark the damper and pulley so they may be reassembled in the same relative position. This is important as the damper and pulley are initially balanced as a unit. If the crankshaft damper is being replaced, check if the original damper has balance pins installed. If so, new balance pins (E0SZ-6A328-A or equivalent) must be installed on the new damper in the same position as the original damper. The crankshaft pulley must also be installed in the original installation position.**

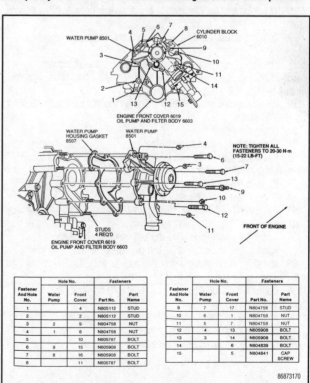

| Fastener And Hole No. | Hole No. | | Fasteners | |
| --- | --- | --- | --- | --- |
| | Water Pump | Front Cover | Part No. | Part Name |
| 1 | | 4 | N805112 | STUD |
| 2 | | 2 | N805112 | STUD |
| 3 | 2 | 9 | N804758 | NUT |
| 4 | 1 | 8 | N804758 | NUT |
| 5 | | 10 | N605787 | BOLT |
| 6 | 9 | 15 | N605908 | BOLT |
| 7 | 8 | 16 | N605908 | BOLT |
| 8 | | 11 | N605787 | BOLT |

| Fastener And Hole No. | Hole No. | | Fasteners | |
| --- | --- | --- | --- | --- |
| | Water Pump | Front Cover | Part No. | Part Name |
| 9 | 7 | 17 | N804756 | STUD |
| 10 | 6 | 1 | N804758 | NUT |
| 11 | 5 | 7 | N804758 | NUT |
| 12 | 4 | 13 | N605908 | BOLT |
| 13 | 3 | 14 | N605908 | BOLT |
| 14 | | 6 | N804839 | BOLT |
| 15 | | 5 | N804841 | CAP SCREW |

**Fig. 168 Timing/engine front cover mounting—3.8L engine**

11. Remove the oil filter, the disconnect the radiator lower hose at the water pump.

12. Remove the oil pan. For details, please refer to the procedure located earlier in this section.

13. Lower the vehicle.

14. Remove the front cover attaching bolts.

➡**Do not overlook the cover attaching bolt located behind the oil filter adapter. The front cover will break if pried upon and all of the attaching bolts are not removed.**

15. Remove the ignition timing indicator.

16. Remove the front cover and water pump as an assembly. Remove the cover gasket and discard.

➡**The front cover houses the oil pump. If a new front cover is to be installed, remove the water pump and oil pump from the old front cover.**

**To install:**

17. Lightly oil all bolt and stud threads before installation. Clean all gasket surfaces on the front cover, cylinder block and fuel pump. If reusing the front cover, replace crankshaft front oil seal.

18. If a new front cover is to be installed, complete the following:
    a. Install the oil pump gears.
    b. Clean the water pump gasket surface. Position a new water pump gasket on the front cover and install the water pump. Install the pump attaching bolts and tighten to 15–22 ft. lbs. (20–30 Nm).

19. Install the distributor drive gear.

20. Lubricate the crankshaft front oil seal with clean engine oil.

21. Position a new cover gasket on the cylinder block and install the front cover/water pump assembly using dowels for proper alignment. A suitable contact adhesive is recommended to hold the gasket in position while the front cover is installed.

22. Position and install the ignition timing indicator.

23. Install the front cover attaching bolts. Apply Loctite® or equivalent, to the threads of the bolt installed below the oil filter housing prior to installation. This bolt is to be installed and tightened last. Tighten all bolts to 15–22 ft. lbs. (20–30 Nm).

24. Raise the vehicle and support safely.

25. Install the oil pan. Connect the radiator lower hose. Install a new oil filter..

26. Coat the crankshaft damper sealing surface with clean engine oil.

27. Position the crankshaft pulley key in the crankshaft keyway.

28. Install the damper with damper washer and attaching bolt. Tighten the bolt to 103–132 ft. lbs. (140–179 Nm).

29. Install the crankshaft pulley and tighten the attaching bolts 19–28 ft. lbs. (26–38 Nm).

30. Lower the vehicle.

31. Connect the coolant bypass hose.

32. Install the distributor with rotor pointing at No. 1 distributor cap tower. Install the distributor cap and coil wire.

33. Connect the radiator upper hose at thermostat housing.

34. Connect the heater hose.

35. If equipped with air conditioning, install compressor and mounting brackets.

36. Install the power steering pump and mounting brackets.

37. Position the accessory drive belt over the pulleys.

38. Install the water pump pulley. Position the accessory drive belt over water pump pulley and tighten the belt.

39. Connect the negative battery cable. Fill the crankcase and cooling system to the proper level.

40. Install the air cleaner assembly and air intake duct.

41. Start the engine and check for leaks.

42. Check the ignition timing and adjust as required.

## Timing Belt Cover

### REMOVAL & INSTALLATION

#### 3.0L SHO Engine

▸ **See Figure 169**

➡**The timing belt/front cover on the 3.0L SHO engine is made up of 3 separate sections.**

1. Disconnect the battery cables and remove the battery. Remove the right engine roll damper.

2. Disconnect the wiring to the ignition module. Remove the engine air inlet/intake manifold crossover tube bolts, loosen the crossover tube clamps, then remove the crossover tube.

3. Loosen the alternator/air conditioner belt tensioner pulley and relieve the tension on the belt by backing out the adjustment screw. Remove the belt.

4. Loosen the water pump/power steering belt tensioner pulley and relieve the tension on the belt by backing out the adjustment screw. Remove the belt.

5. Remove the alternator/air conditioner belt tensioner pulley and bracket assembly. Remove the water pump/power steering belt tensioner pulley only.

6. Remove the upper timing belt cover.

7. Disconnect the crankshaft sensor connectors.

8. Raise and safely support the vehicle. Remove the right front wheel and tire assembly.

9. Loosen the fender splash shield and move aside. Remove the crankshaft vibration damper and pulley using Steering Wheel Puller T67L-3600-A, Step Plate Adapter D80L-630-3 or equivalent and Screw and Washer Set T89P-6701-A.

10. Remove the center and lower timing belt covers.

11. Installation is the reverse of the removal procedure. Tighten the timing belt cover retaining bolts to 60–90 inch lbs. (7–10 Nm) and the crankshaft damper bolt to 113–126 ft. lbs. (153–171 Nm).

#### 3.2L SHO Engine

▸ **See Figure 169**

➡**The front cover on the 3.2L SHO engine is made up of 3 separate sections.**

1. Disconnect the battery cables, then remove the battery from the engine.

2. Remove the right-hand engine roll damper.

3. Disconnect the wiring to the ignition control module. Remove the engine air inlet connector/intake manifold crossover tube bolts, loosen the crossover tube clamps, then remove the crossover tube.

4. Rotate the accessory drive belt tensioner clockwise to relieve the tension, then remove the belt.

5. Disconnect the surge tank fittings.

6. Remove the bolts retaining the upper and lower idler pulleys to the engine, then remove the pulleys.

7. Using strap wrench D85L-6000-A, or equivalent, to hold the power steering pump pulley, remove the nut, washer, then remove the power steering pulley.

8. Remove the retaining bolt from the belt tensioner, then remove the tensioner.

9. Remove the upper and center timing belt covers.

10. Disengage the crankshaft position (CKP) sensor electrical connectors.

11. Raise and safely support the vehicle, then remove the right front wheel and tire assembly.

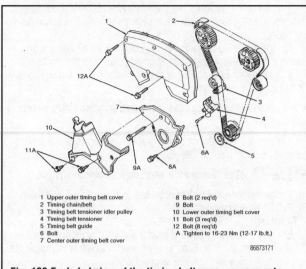

| | |
|---|---|
| 1 Upper outer timing belt cover | 8 Bolt (2 req'd) |
| 2 Timing chain/belt | 9 Bolt |
| 3 Timing belt tensioner idler pulley | 10 Lower outer timing belt cover |
| 4 Timing belt tensioner | 11 Bolt (3 req'd) |
| 5 Timing belt guide | 12 Bolt (8 req'd) |
| 6 Bolt | A Tighten to 16-23 Nm (12-17 lb.ft.) |
| 7 Center outer timing belt cover | |

86873171

**Fig. 169 Exploded view of the timing belt cover components— 3.0L and 3.2L SHO engines**

12. Loosen the fender splash shield and move it aside. Remove the crankshaft vibration damper and pulley using Puller T67L-3600-A, Step Plate Adapter D80L-630-3 and Screw Washer Set T89P-6701-A.

13. Remove the lower timing belt cover.

14. Installation is the reverse of the removal procedure. Tighten the timing belt cover retaining bolts to 12–17 ft. lbs. (16–23 Nm) and the crankshaft damper bolt to 112–127 ft. lbs. (152–172 Nm).

## Timing Chain Cover Oil Seal

### REPLACEMENT

#### 2.5L Engine

➡The removal and installation of the front cover oil seal on these engines can only be accomplished with the engine removed from the vehicle.

1. Remove the engine from the vehicle and position in a suitable holding fixture.

2. Remove the bolt and washer at the crankshaft pulley, then remove the crankshaft pulley.

3. Using Differential Side Bearing Puller T77F-4220-B1, remove the front cover oil seal.

**To install:**

4. Coat a new seal with Long Life Lubricant C1AZ-19590-BA, or equivalent grease. Using Pinion Oil Seal Installer T83T-4676-A or equivalent, install the seal into the cover. Make sure the seal is fully seated. Check the seal after installation to be sure the spring is properly positioned in the seal.

5. Install the crankshaft pulley, attaching bolt and washer. Tighten the crankshaft pulley bolt to 140–170 ft. lbs. (190–230 Nm).

#### 3.0L Engine—Except SHO

1. Disconnect the negative battery cable and remove the accessory drive belt(s).

2. Raise and safely support the vehicle. Remove the right front wheel and tire assembly.

3. Remove the pulley-to-damper attaching bolts, then remove the crankshaft pulley.

4. Remove the crankshaft damper retaining bolt and washer. Remove the damper from the crankshaft using Crankshaft Damper Remover T58P-6316-D and Vibration Damper Remover Adapter T82L-6316-B or equivalent damper removal tool.

5. Remove the front seal from the timing cover using Jet Plug Remover T77L-9533-B or equivalent tool and be careful not to damage the front cover and crankshaft.

**To install:**

➡Before installation, inspect the front cover and shaft seal surface of the crankshaft damper for damage, nicks, burrs or other roughness which may cause the new seal to fail. Service or replace components as necessary.

6. Lubricate the seal lip with clean engine oil and install the seal using Vibration Damper and Seal Replacer T82L-6316-A and Front Cover Seal Replacer T70P-6B070-A or equivalent seal installer tools.

7. Coat the crankshaft damper sealing surface with clean engine oil. Apply RTV to the keyway of the damper prior to installation. Install the damper using a damper seal installer tool. Install the damper retaining bolt and washer. Tighten to 93–121 ft. lbs. (125–165 Nm).

8. Position the crankshaft pulley and install the attaching bolts. Tighten the attaching bolts to 30–44 ft. lbs. (40–60 Nm).

9. Install the right front wheel and tire assembly, then carefully lower the vehicle.

10. Position the drive belt over the crankshaft pulley. Check the drive belt for proper routing and engagement in the pulleys.

11. Reconnect the negative battery cable and start the engine and check for oil leaks.

#### 3.8L Engine

1. Disconnect the negative battery cable.

2. Loosen the accessory drive belt idler.

3. Raise the vehicle and support safely.

4. Disengage the accessory drive belt and remove crankshaft pulley.

5. Remove the crankshaft/vibration damper using Crankshaft Damper Remover T58P-6316-D and Vibration Damper Remover Adapter T82L-6316-B or equivalent suitable removal tools.

6. Remove the seal from the front cover with a suitable prying tool. Use care to prevent damage to front cover and crankshaft.

**To install:**

➡Inspect the front cover and crankshaft damper for damage, nicks, burrs or other roughness which may cause the seal to fail. Service or replace components as necessary.

7. Lubricate the seal lip with clean engine oil and install the seal using Damper/Front Cover Seal Replacer T82L-6316-A and Front Cover Seal Replacer T70P-6B070-A or equivalent suitable seal installers.

8. Lubricate the seal surface on the damper with clean engine oil. Install damper and pulley assembly. Install the damper attaching bolt and tighten to 103–132 ft. lbs. (140–179 Nm).

9. Position the crankshaft pulley and install the retaining bolts. Tighten to 19–28 ft. lbs. (26–38 Nm).

10. Position accessory drive belt over crankshaft pulley.

11. Lower the vehicle.

12. Check accessory drive belt for proper routing and engagement in the pulleys. Adjust the drive belt tension.

13. Connect the negative battery cable. Start the engine and check for leaks.

## Timing Belt Cover Oil Seal

### REMOVAL & INSTALLATION

#### 3.0L and 3.2L SHO Engines

♦ **See Figures 170, 171, 172 and 173**

1. Loosen the accessory drive belts.

2. Raise and safely support the vehicle, then remove the right front wheel and tire assembly.

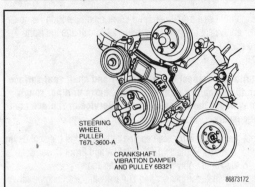

**Fig. 170 Using a suitable steering wheel puller to remove the crankshaft vibration damper and pulley**

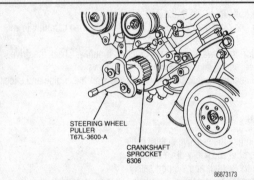

**Fig. 171 Using a suitable steering wheel puller to remove the crankshaft sprocket**

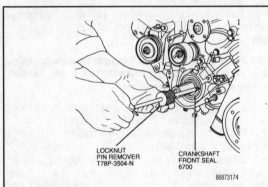

**Fig. 172 To remove the front oil seal, use a suitable locknut pin remover**

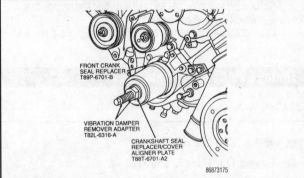

**Fig. 173 Installing the timing belt cover oil seal—3.0L and 3.2L SHO engines**

3. Remove the crankshaft vibration damper and pulley attaching bolt, then remove the accessory drive belts from the crankshaft vibration damper and pulley.

4. Using Steering Wheel Puller T67L-3600-A or equivalent puller, remove the crankshaft vibration damper and pulley from the crankshaft.

5. Remove the timing belt. For details, please refer to the procedure located later in this section.

➡**Be careful not to damage the crankshaft position (CKP) sensor or pulse wheel.**

6. Remove the crankshaft timing gear/sprocket using Steering Wheel Puller T67L-3600-A or suitable puller.

➡**Be careful not to damage the crankshaft sensor or shutter.**

7. Remove the crankshaft front oil seal using Locknut Pin Remover T87P-3504-N, or equivalent.

**To install:**

8. Inspect the front cover and shaft seal surface of the crankshaft damper for damage, nicks, burrs or other roughness which may cause the new seal to fail. Repair or replace as necessary.

9. Using Vibration Damper Remover Adapter T82L-6316-A, Crankshaft Seal Replacer/Cover Aligner Plate T88T-6701-A2 and Front Crank Replacer T89P-6701-B, install a new crankshaft front oil seal. Install Crankshaft Seal Replacer/Cover Aligner T88T-6701-A with forcing screw from Vibration Damper Remover Adapter T82L-6316-A to press the crankshaft front seal the rest of the way into the oil.

10. Install the crankshaft timing gear/sprocket onto the crankshaft.

11. Install the timing belt. For details, please refer to the procedure located later in this section.

12. Install the crankshaft vibration damper and pulley using Front Crank Seal Installer T89P-6701-B. Tighten the damper attaching bolt to 112–127 ft. lbs. (152–172 Nm).

13. Position the drive belts over the crankshaft vibration damper and pulley.

14. Install the front right side wheel and tire assembly. Tighten the lug nuts to 85–105 ft. lbs. (152–172 Nm).

15. Carefully lower the vehicle, the install the drive belts. Check the belts for proper routing and engagement in the pulleys and adjust belt tension to specification.

16. Connect the negative battery cable, then start the engine and check for oil leaks.

## Timing Chain

### REMOVAL & INSTALLATION

#### 2.5L Engine

♦ **See Figures 174 and 175**

1. Remove the engine and transaxle from the vehicle as an assembly and position in a suitable holding fixture. Remove the dipstick.

2. Remove accessory drive pulley, if equipped, Remove the crankshaft pulley attaching bolt and washer and remove pulley.

3. Remove front cover attaching bolts from front cover. Pry the top of the front cover away from the block.

4. Clean any gasket material from the surfaces.

5. Check timing chain and sprockets for excessive wear. If the timing chain and sprockets are worn, replace with new.

6. Check timing chain tensioner blade for wear depth. If the wear depth exceeds specification, replace tensioner.

7. Turn engine over until the timing marks are aligned. Remove camshaft sprocket attaching bolt and washer. Slide both sprockets and timing chain forward and remove as an assembly.

8. If equipped, check timing chain vibration damper for excessive wear. Replace if necessary; the damper is located inside the front cover.

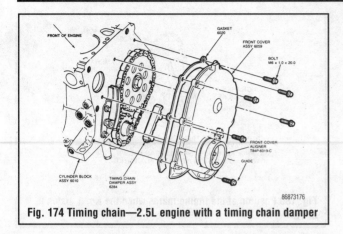

**Fig. 174 Timing chain—2.5L engine with a timing chain damper**

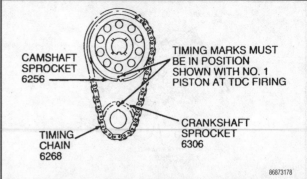

**Fig. 176 Rotate the crankshaft until the No. 1 piston is at the TDC of its compression stroke and the timing marks are aligned**

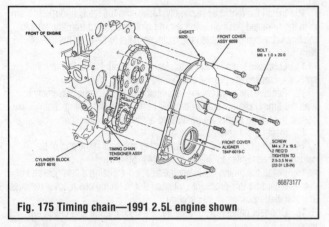

**Fig. 175 Timing chain—1991 2.5L engine shown**

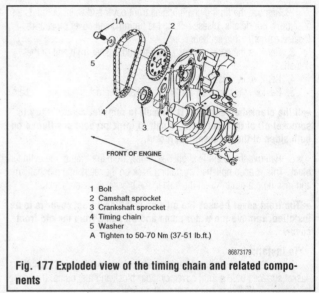

1 Bolt
2 Camshaft sprocket
3 Crankshaft sprocket
4 Timing chain
5 Washer
A Tighten to 50-70 Nm (37-51 lb.ft.)

**Fig. 177 Exploded view of the timing chain and related components**

9. Remove the oil pan. For details, please refer to the procedure regarding this procedure.

**To install:**

10. Clean and inspect all parts before installation. Clean the oil pan, cylinder block and front cover of gasket material and dirt.

11. Slide both sprockets and timing chain onto the camshaft and crankshaft with timing marks aligned. Install camshaft bolt and washer and tighten to 41–56 ft. lbs. (56–76 Nm). Oil timing chain, sprockets and tensioner after installation with clean engine oil.

12. Apply oil resistant sealer to a new front cover gasket and position gasket into front cover.

13. Remove the front cover oil seal and position the front cover on the engine.

14. Position front cover alignment tool T84P-6019-C or equivalent, onto the end of the crankshaft, ensuring the crank key is aligned with the keyway in the tool. Bolt the front cover to the engine and tighten the bolts to 6–8 ft. lbs. (8–11 Nm). Remove the front cover alignment tool.

15. Install a new front cover oil seal using a suitable seal installer. Lubricate the hub of the crankshaft pulley with polyethylene grease to prevent damage to the seal during installation and initial engine start. Install crankshaft pulley.

16. Install the oil pan.

17. Install the accessory drive pulley, if equipped.

18. Install crankshaft pulley attaching bolt and washer. Tighten to 140–170 ft. lbs. (190–230 Nm).

19. Remove engine from work stand and install in vehicle.

## 3.0L Engine Except SHO

### ◆ See Figures 176 and 177

1. Disconnect the negative battery cable. Drain the cooling system and crankcase. Remove the crankshaft pulley and front cover assemblies.

2. Rotate the crankshaft until the No. 1 piston is at the TDC on its compression stroke and the timing marks are aligned.

3. Remove the camshaft sprocket attaching bolt and washer. Slide both sprockets and timing chain forward and remove as an assembly.

4. Check the timing chain and sprockets for excessive wear. Replace if necessary.

**To install:**

➡ **Before installation, clean and inspect all parts. Clean the gasket material and dirt from the oil pan, cylinder block and front cover.**

5. Slide both sprockets and timing chain onto the camshaft and crankshaft with the timing marks aligned. Install the camshaft bolt and washer and torque to 37–51 ft. lbs. (50–70 Nm). Apply clean engine oil to the timing chain and sprockets after installation.

➡ **The camshaft bolt has a drilled oil passage in it for timing chain lubrication. If the bolt is damaged, do not replace it with a standard bolt.**

6. Install the timing cover and the crankshaft pulley and damper. Tighten the crankshaft damper bolt to 93–121 ft. lbs. (126–164 Nm) and the pulley bolts to 30–44 ft. lbs. (41–60 Nm).

7. Fill the crankcase with the proper type and quantity of oil. Fill and bleed the engine cooling system.

8. Connect the negative battery cable, then start the engine and check for coolant, oil and exhaust leaks.

## 3.8L Engine

### ◆ See Figures 178, 179 and 180

1. Disconnect the negative battery cable. Drain the cooling system and crankcase.

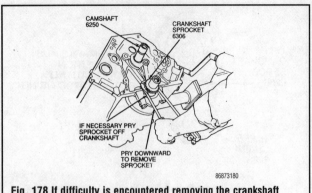

**Fig. 178 If difficulty is encountered removing the crankshaft sprocket, use 2 prybars to carefully pry if off the shaft**

2. Remove the timing chain/engine front cover and water pump as an assembly. For details, please refer to the timing chain cover procedure located earlier in this section.

3. Remove the camshaft sprocket bolt and washer from end of the camshaft.

4. Remove the distributor drive gear.

5. Remove the camshaft sprocket, crankshaft sprocket and timing chain.

➡**If the crankshaft sprocket is difficult to remove, carefully pry to sprocket off of the shaft using a pair of large prybars positioned on both sides of the crankshaft sprocket.**

6. Remove the chain tensioner assembly from the front of the cylinder block. This is accomplished by pulling back on the ratcheting mechanism and installing a pin through the hole in the bracket to relieve tension.

➡**The front cover houses the oil pump. If a new front cover is to be installed, remove the water pump and oil pump from the old front cover.**

**To install:**

7. Lightly oil all bolt and stud threads before installation. Clean all gasket surfaces on the front cover, cylinder block and fuel pump. If reusing the front cover, replace crankshaft front oil seal.

8. If a new front cover is to be installed, complete the following:

    a. Install the oil pump gears.

    b. Clean the water pump gasket surface. Position a new water pump gasket on the front cover and install water pump. Install the pump attaching bolts and tighten to 15–22 ft. lbs. (20–30 Nm).

9. Rotate the crankshaft as necessary to position piston No. 1 at TDC and the crankshaft keyway at the 12 o' clock position.

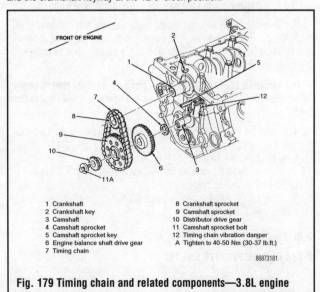

| | |
|---|---|
| 1 Crankshaft | 8 Crankshaft sprocket |
| 2 Crankshaft key | 9 Camshaft sprocket |
| 3 Camshaft | 10 Distributor drive gear |
| 4 Camshaft sprocket | 11 Camshaft sprocket bolt |
| 5 Camshaft sprocket key | 12 Timing chain vibration damper |
| 6 Engine balance shaft drive gear | A Tighten to 40-50 Nm (30-37 lb.ft.) |
| 7 Timing chain | |

**Fig. 179 Timing chain and related components—3.8L engine**

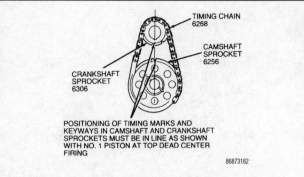

**Fig. 180 Position of the timing marks when the No. 1 piston is at TDC**

10. Install the tensioner assembly. Make sure the ratcheting mechanism is in the retracted position with the pin pointing outward from the hole in the bracket assembly. Tighten the retaining bolts to 6–10 ft. lbs. (8–14 Nm).

11. Lubricate timing chain with clean engine oil. Install the camshaft sprocket, crankshaft sprocket and timing chain.

12. Remove the pin from the tensioner/vibration damper assembly to load the timing chain vibration damper arm against the timing chain. Make certain the timing marks are positioned across from each other.

13. Install the distributor drive gear.

14. Install the camshaft sprocket washer and bolt at the end of the camshaft, then tighten to 30–37 ft. lbs. (41–50 Nm).

15. Install the timing chain/engine front cover, using a new gasket. For details regarding this procedure, please refer to timing chain cover removal and installation earlier in this section.

16. Connect battery ground cable. Start the engine and check for leaks.

## Timing Belt and Tensioner

### REMOVAL & INSTALLATION

#### 3.0L SHO Engine

▶ **See Figures 181 thru 186**

1. Disconnect the battery cables.

2. Remove the battery.

3. Remove the right engine roll damper/front engine support damper.

4. Disconnect the wiring to the ignition control module.

5. Remove the engine air inlet/intake manifold crossover tube bolts. Loosen the intake manifold tube hose clamps. Remove the engine air inlet/intake manifold crossover tube.

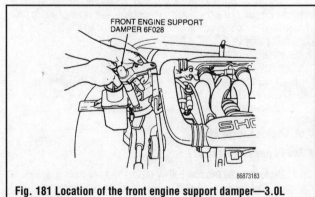

**Fig. 181 Location of the front engine support damper—3.0L SHO engine**

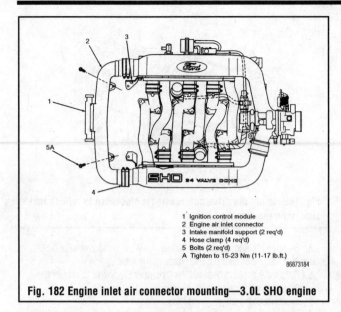

1 Ignition control module
2 Engine air inlet connector
3 Intake manifold support (2 req'd)
4 Hose clamp (4 req'd)
5 Bolts (2 req'd)
A Tighten to 15-23 Nm (11-17 lb.ft.)

86873184

**Fig. 182 Engine inlet air connector mounting—3.0L SHO engine**

6. Loosen the alternator/air conditioning belt tensioner pulley and relieve the tension on the belt by backing out the adjustment screw. Remove the alternator/air conditioning belt.

7. Loosen the water pump/power steering belt tensioner pulley and relieve the tension on the belt by backing out the adjustment screw. Remove the water pump/power steering belt.

8. Remove the alternator/air conditioning belt tensioner pulley and bracket assembly.

9. Remove the water pump/power steering belt tensioner pulley only.

10. Remove the upper timing belt cover.

11. Disengage the crankshaft position (CKP) sensor connectors.

12. Place the gear selector in **N** (neutral).

13. Set the engine to the TDC on No. 1 cylinder position. Make sure the white mark on the crankshaft damper aligns with the **0** degree index mark on the lower timing belt cover and that the marks on the intake camshaft pulleys align with the index marks on the metal timing belt cover.

14. Raise and safely support the vehicle.

15. Remove the right front wheel and tire assembly.

16. Loosen the fender splash shield and place it aside.

17. Using a suitable puller, remove the crankshaft damper.

18. Remove the lower timing belt cover.

19. Remove the center timing belt cover and disconnect the crankshaft sensor wire and grommet from the slot in the cover and the stud on the water pump.

20. Loosen the timing belt tensioner, rotate the pulley 180° (½ turn) clockwise and tighten the tensioner nut to hold the pulley in the unload position.

21. Carefully lower the vehicle, then remove the timing belt.

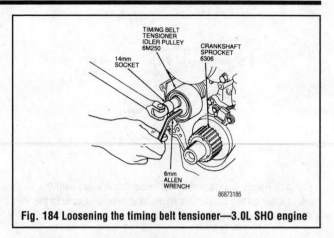

**Fig. 184 Loosening the timing belt tensioner—3.0L SHO engine**

**To install:**

➡**Before installing the timing belt, inspect it for cracks, wear or other damage and replace, if necessary. Do not allow the timing belt to come into contact with gasoline, oil, water, coolant or steam. Do not twist or turn the belt inside out.**

22. Make sure the engine is at TDC on the No. 1 cylinder. Check that the camshaft pulley marks line up with the index marks on the upper steel belt cover and that the crankshaft pulley aligns with the index mark on the oil pump housing. The timing belt has 3 yellow lines. Each line aligns with the index marks.

23. Install the timing belt over the crankshaft and camshaft pulleys. The lettering on the belt **KOA** should be readable from the rear of the engine; top of the lettering to the front of the engine. Make sure the yellow lines are aligned with the index marks on the pulleys.

24. Release the tensioner locknut and leave the nut loose.

25. Raise the vehicle and support safely.

26. Install the center timing belt cover. Make sure the crankshaft sensor wiring and grommet are installed and routed properly. Tighten the mounting bolts to 62–97 inch lbs. (7–11 Nm).

27. Install the lower timing belt cover. Tighten the bolts to 62–97 inch lbs. (7–11 Nm).

28. Using a suitable tool, install the crankshaft damper. Tighten the damper attaching bolt to 113–126 ft. lbs. (153–171 Nm).

29. Rotate the crankshaft 2 revolutions in the clockwise direction until the yellow mark on the damper aligns with the 0° mark on the lower timing belt cover.

30. Remove the plastic door in the lower timing belt cover. Tighten the tensioner locknut to 24–38 ft. lbs. (33–51 Nm) and install the plastic door.

31. Rotate the crankshaft 60° (⅙ turn) more in the clockwise direction until the white mark on the crankshaft vibration damper aligns with the 0° mark on the lower timing belt cover.

32. Lower the vehicle.

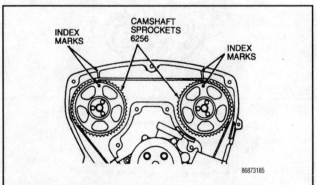

**Fig. 183 Alignment of marks with the engine set to TDC on the No. 1 cylinder position.**

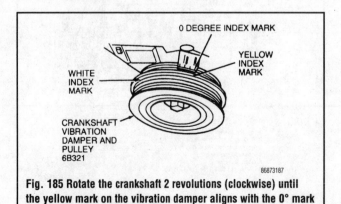

**Fig. 185 Rotate the crankshaft 2 revolutions (clockwise) until the yellow mark on the vibration damper aligns with the 0° mark on the lower timing belt cover**

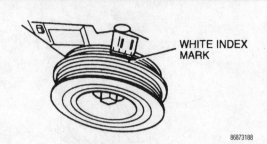

Fig. 186 Rotate the crankshaft 60° more (clockwise) until the white mark on the crankshaft vibration damper aligns with the 0° mark on the lower timing belt cover

33. Make sure the index marks on the camshaft pulleys align with the marks on the rear metal timing belt cover.

34. Route the crankshaft sensor wiring and connect with the engine wiring harness.

35. Install the upper timing belt cover. Tighten the bolts to 62–97 inch lbs. (7–11 Nm).

36. Install the water pump/power steering tensioner pulley. Tighten the nut to 11–17 ft. lbs. (15–23 Nm).

37. Install the alternator/air conditioning tensioner pulley and bracket assembly. Tighten the bolts to 11–17 ft. lbs. (15–23 Nm).

38. Install the water pump/power steering and alternator/air conditioning belts and set the tension. Tighten the idler pulley nut to 25–36 ft. lbs. (34–49 Nm).

39. Install the engine air inlet connector/intake manifold crossover tube. Tighten the bolts to 11–17 ft. lbs. (15–23 Nm).

40. Install the engine roll damper/engine front support damper.

41. Install the battery, then connect the battery cables.

42. Raise the vehicle and support safely.

43. Install the front fender splash shield.

44. Install the right front wheel and tire assembly. Tighten the lug nuts to 85–105 ft. lbs. (115–142 Nm).

45. Lower the vehicle.

### 3.2L SHO Engine

▶ See Figures 187 thru 198

1. Disconnect the battery cables, then remove the battery.
2. Remove the right-hand engine roll damper/engine support damper.
3. Disengage the wiring to the ignition control module.

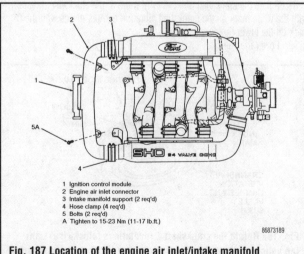

1 Ignition control module
2 Engine air inlet connector
3 Intake manifold support (2 req'd)
4 Hose clamp (4 req'd)
5 Bolts (2 req'd)
A Tighten to 15-23 Nm (11-17 lb.ft.)

Fig. 187 Location of the engine air inlet/intake manifold crossover tube

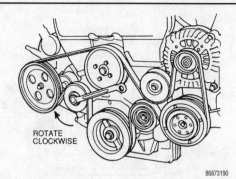

Fig. 188 Rotate the drive belt tensioner clockwise to relieve tension, then remove the belt

4. Remove the engine air inlet/intake manifold crossover tube bolts. Loosen the tube hose clamps, then remove the tube.

5. Rotate the accessory drive belt tensioner clockwise to relieve tension, then remove the belt.

6. Disconnect the surge tank fitting.

7. Remove the bolts retaining the upper and lower idler pulleys to the engine, then remove the pulleys.

8. Using Strap Wrench D85L-6000-A or equivalent, to hold the power steering pump pulley, remove the nut and the washer, then remove the power steering pulley.

9. Remove the retaining bolt from the belt tensioner, then remove the tensioner.

10. Remove the upper and center timing belt covers.

11. Disengage the crankshaft position (CKP) sensor electrical connectors.

12. Place the transaxle selector in **N** (neutral).

13. Rotate the crankshaft until the No. 1 cylinder piston is at TDC of the compression stroke. Make sure the white mark on the crankshaft damper aligns with the 0° index mark on the lower timing belt cover and the marks on the intake camshaft sprockets align with the index marks on the metal timing belt cover.

14. Raise and safely support the vehicle, then remove the right front wheel and tire assembly.

15. Loosen the fender splash shield and place it aside.

16. Using a suitable puller, remove the crankshaft vibration damper.

17. Remove the lower timing belt cover and belt guide.

18. Remove the upper timing belt tensioner bolt.

19. Slowly loosen the lower timing belt tension bolt, then remove the tensioner.

20. Carefully lower the vehicle, then remove the timing belt.

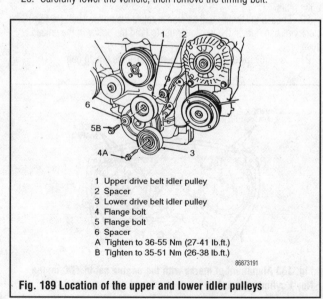

1 Upper drive belt idler pulley
2 Spacer
3 Lower drive belt idler pulley
4 Flange bolt
5 Flange bolt
6 Spacer
A Tighten to 36-55 Nm (27-41 lb.ft.)
B Tighten to 35-51 Nm (26-38 lb.ft.)

Fig. 189 Location of the upper and lower idler pulleys

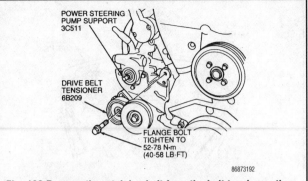

Fig. 190 Remove the retaining bolt from the belt tensioner, then remove the tensioner

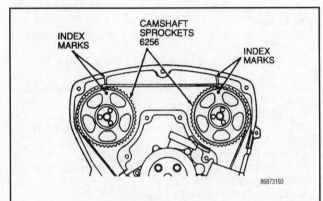

Fig. 191 Location of alignment marks on the camshaft sprockets

**To install:**

➡️Before installing the timing belt, inspect it for cracks, wear or other damage and replace, if necessary. Do not allow the timing belt to come into contact with gasoline, oil, water, coolant or steam. Do not twist or turn the belt inside out.

21. Slowly compress the timing belt tensioner in a soft jawed vice until the hole in the tensioner housing aligns with the hole in the tensioner rod.

### ✳✳ CAUTION

**Be careful when compressing the timing belt tensioner in the vice to ensure that the tensioner does not slip from the vice.**

22. Insert a ¹⁄₂₀ in. (1.27mm) hex wrench through the holes.
23. Release the timing belt tensioner from the vice.
24. If a new belt is being installed, loosen the timing belt idler bolt.

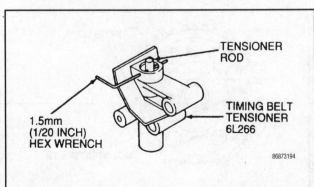

Fig. 192 Insert a ¹⁄₂₀ in. (1.5mm) hex wrench through the holes in the tensioner

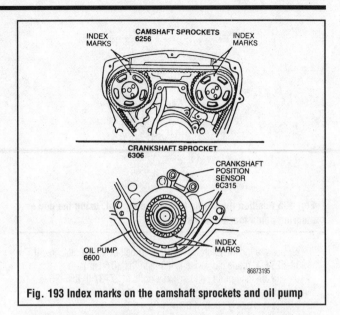

Fig. 193 Index marks on the camshaft sprockets and oil pump

25. Make sure the engine is at TDC on the No. 1 cylinder. Check that the camshaft sprocket marks line up with the index marks on the upper steel belt cover, and that the crankshaft sprocket aligns with the index mark on the oil pump housing.

➡️The timing belt has 3 yellow lines. Each line aligns with the index marks.

26. Install the timing belt over the crankshaft and camshaft sprockets. The lettering on the belt **KOB** should be readable from the rear of the engine; top of the lettering to the front of the engine. Make sure the yellow lines are aligned with the index marks on the sprockets.

### ✳✳ WARNING

**Do NOT install the timing belt tensioner with the rod extended.**

27. Install the timing belt tensioner on the cylinder block while pushing the timing belt idler toward the belt. Tighten the tensioner bolts to 12–17 ft. lbs. (16–23 Nm).
28. Install the grommets between the timing belt tensioner and the oil pump.
29. Remove the ¹⁄₂₀ in. (1.27mm) hex wrench from the timing belt tensioner.
30. If a new belt is being installed, perform the following steps:
    a. Position the timing belt tensioner tool T93P-6254-A or equivalent, using the power steering pump bracket holes.
    b. Hand tighten the timing belt idler bolt.

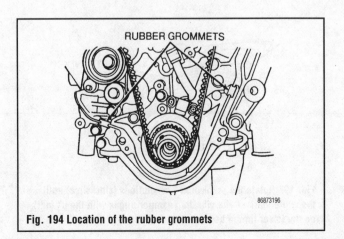

Fig. 194 Location of the rubber grommets

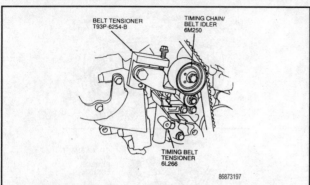

**Fig. 195 Position the timing belt tensioner tool, using the power steering pump bracket holes**

c. Using a inch lbs. torque wrench with belt tensioner attachment T93P-6254-A, rotate clockwise to 4.3 inch lbs. (0.5 Nm).

d. Tighten the timing belt tensioner bolts to 27–37 ft. lbs. (36–50 Nm), then remove the timing belt tensioning tool.

31. Raise and safely support the vehicle.

32. Install the belt guide and lower timing belt cover. Tighten the retaining bolts to 12–17 ft. lbs. (16–23 Nm).

33. Using a suitable tool, install the crankshaft vibration damper. Tighten the damper attaching bolt to 113–126 ft. lbs. (152–172 Nm).

34. Rotate the crankshaft 2 revolutions in the clockwise direction until the white mark on the vibration damper aligns with the 0° marks on the lower timing belt cover.

35. Carefully lower the vehicle.

36. Make sure the index marks on the camshaft sprockets align with the marks on the rear metal timing belt cover.

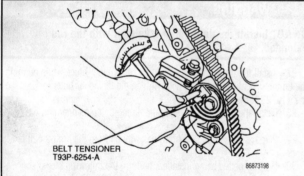

**Fig. 196 Using an inch lbs. torque wrench with a belt tensioner attachment, rotate clockwise to 4.3 inch lbs. (0.5 Nm)**

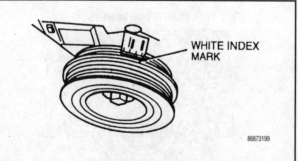

**Fig. 197 Rotate the crankshaft 2 revolutions (clockwise) until the white mark on the vibration damper aligns with the 0° mark on the lower timing belt cover**

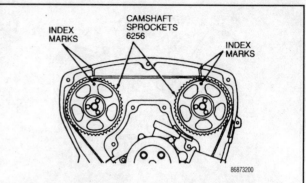

**Fig. 198 Make sure the index marks on the camshaft sprockets align with the marks on the rear metal timing belt cover**

37. Route the crankshaft position sensor wiring, then connect it with the wiring harness.

38. Install the center and upper timing belt covers. Tighten the bolts to 12–17 ft. lbs. (16–23 Nm).

39. Install the water pump pulley. Tighten the nut to 12–17 ft. lbs. (16–23 Nm).

40. Install the single accessory drive belt while rotating the accessory drive belt tensioner clockwise.

41. Install the surge tank fitting.

42. Install the engine air inlet connector/intake manifold crossover tube. Tighten the bolts to 11–17 ft. lbs. (15–23 Nm).

43. Install the engine roll damper/support damper.

44. Install the battery, then connect the wiring to the ignition control module, and connect the battery cable.

45. Raise and safely support the vehicle.

46. Install the fender splash shield, then install the right front wheel and tire assembly. Carefully lower the vehicle, then tighten the lug nuts to 85–105 ft. lbs. (115–142 Nm).

## Timing Sprockets

### REMOVAL & INSTALLATION

#### 3.0L and 3.2L SHO Engines

##### CAMSHAFT SPROCKETS

♦ See Figure 199

1. Disconnect the negative battery cable.

2. Position the engine to TDC at the No. 1 cylinder.

3. Remove the intake manifold. For details, please refer to the procedure located earlier in this section.

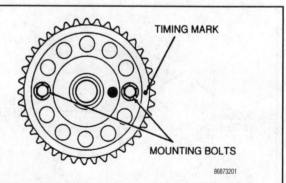

**Fig. 199 Location of the camshaft sprocket retaining bolts and timing mark—SHO engines**

4. Remove the timing belt. For details, please refer to the procedure located earlier in this section.

5. Remove the valve covers.

6. Remove the camshaft sprocket retaining bolts and camshaft sprockets, noting the position of the dowel pins.

**To install:**

7. Align the timing marks on the camshaft sprockets with the camshafts, then install the sprockets. Tighten the retaining bolts to 10–13 ft. lbs (14–18 Nm).

8. Install the valve covers.

9. Install the timing belt and the intake manifold. For details, please refer to the appropriate procedures located earlier in this section.

10. Connect the negative battery cable.

### CRANKSHAFT SPROCKETS

▶ See Figure 200

1. Disconnect the negative battery cable.

2. Remove the timing belt. For details, please refer to the procedure located earlier in this section.

➡ **Be careful not to damage the crankshaft position (CKP) sensor or the pulse wheel.**

3. Remove the crankshaft sprocket using Steering Wheel Puller T67L-3600-A or equivalent.

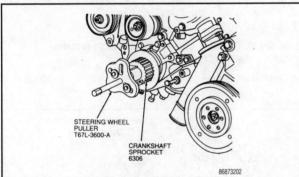

STEERING WHEEL
PULLER
T67L-3600-A

CRANKSHAFT
SPROCKET
6306

86873202

**Fig. 200 To remove the crankshaft sprocket use a steering wheel puller**

**To install:**

4. Install the crankshaft sprocket onto the crankshaft.

5. Install the timing belt. Please refer to the timing belt procedure, located earlier in this section, for details.

6. Connect the negative battery.

## Camshaft

### REMOVAL & INSTALLATION

#### 2.5L Engine

1. Drain the cooling system and the crankcase. Relieve the fuel system pressure.

2. Remove the engine from the vehicle and position in a suitable holding fixture. Remove the engine oil dipstick.

3. Remove necessary drive belts and pulleys.

4. Remove cylinder head. For details, please refer to the cylinder head procedure located earlier in this section.

5. Using a magnet, remove the hydraulic lifters and label them so they can be installed in their original positions. If the tappets are stuck in the bores by excessive varnish, etc., use a suitable claw-type puller to remove the tappets.

6. Loosen and remove the drive belt, fan and pulley.

7. Using Differential Side Bearing Puller T77F-4220-B1 or equivalent, remove the crankshaft pulley.

8. Remove the oil pan.

9. Remove the cylinder front cover and gasket.

10. Check the camshaft end-play as follows:

    a. Push the camshaft toward the rear of the engine and install a dial indicator tool, so the indicator point is on the camshaft sprocket attaching screw.

    b. Zero the dial indicator. Position a small prybar or equivalent, between the camshaft sprocket or gear and block.

    c. Pull the camshaft forward and release it. Compare the dial indicator reading with the camshaft end-play specification of 0.009 in. (0.23mm).

    d. If the camshaft end-play is over the amount specified, replace the thrust plate.

11. Remove the timing chain, sprockets and timing chain tensioner.

12. Remove camshaft thrust plate. Carefully remove the camshaft by pulling it toward the front of the engine. Use caution to avoid damaging bearings, journals and lobes.

**To install:**

13. Clean and inspect all parts before installation.

14. Lubricate camshaft lobes and journals with heavy engine oil. Carefully slide the camshaft through the bearings in the cylinder block.

15. Install the thrust plate. Tighten attaching bolts to 6–9 ft. lbs. (8–12 Nm).

16. Install the timing chain, sprockets and timing chain tensioner.

17. Install the cylinder front cover and crankshaft pulley.

18. Clean the oil pump inlet tube screen, oil pan and cylinder block gasket surfaces. Prime oil pump by filling the inlet opening with oil and rotate the pump shaft until oil emerges from the outlet tube. Install oil pump, oil pump inlet tube screen and oil pan.

19. Install the accessory drive belts and pulleys.

20. Lubricate the lifters and lifter bores with heavy engine oil. Install tappets into their original bores.

21. Install cylinder head.

22. Install the engine assembly.

23. Position No. 1 piston at TDC after the compression stroke. Position distributor in the block with the rotor at the No. 1 firing position. Install distributor retaining clamp.

24. Connect engine temperature sending unit wire. Connect coil primary wire. Install distributor cap. Connect spark plug wires and the coil high tension lead.

25. Fill the cooling system and crankcase to the proper levels. Connect the negative battery cable.

26. Start the engine. Check and adjust ignition timing, if necessary and check for coolant, oil, fuel and/or vacuum leaks.

#### 3.0L Engine—Except SHO

▶ See Figure 201

1. Drain the cooling system and crankcase. Relieve the fuel system pressure.

2. Remove the engine from the vehicle and position in a suitable holding fixture.

3. Remove the accessory drive components from the front of the engine to allow for camshaft removal.

4. Remove the throttle body and the fuel injector harness. For details, please refer to the procedures located in Section 5 of this manual.

5. On unleaded gasoline engines only, matchmark and remove the distributor assembly. For details, please refer to the procedure located earlier in this section.

6. Remove the ignition coil from the rear of the left-hand cylinder head.

7. Tag and disconnect the spark plug wires, then remove the rocker arm covers.

8. Loosen the cylinder No. 3 intake valve rocker arm seat retaining bolt and rotate the rocker arm off of the pushrod and away from the top of the valve stem, then remove the pushrod.

9. Remove the alternator, brackets, drive belt tensioner and drive belt.

10. Remove the intake manifold.

11. Loosen the rocker arm fulcrum nuts and position the rocker arms to the side for easy access to the pushrods. Remove the pushrods and label so they may be installed in their original positions.

12. Using a suitable magnet or lifter removal tool, remove the hydraulic lifters/tappets and keep them in order so they can be installed in their original positions. If the lifters/tappets are stuck in the bores by excessive varnish use a hydraulic lifter puller to remove the lifters/tappets.

13. Remove the crankshaft pulley and damper using a suitable removal tool.

14. Remove the oil pan assembly.

15. Remove the front cover assembly. Align the timing marks on the camshaft and crankshaft gears. Check the camshaft end-play as follows:

   a. Push the camshaft toward the rear of the engine and install a dial indicator tool, so the indicator point is on the camshaft sprocket attaching screw.

   b. Zero the dial indicator. Position a small prybar or equivalent, between the camshaft sprocket or gear and block.

   c. Pull the camshaft forward and release it. Compare the dial indicator reading with the camshaft end-play service limit specification of 0.005 in. (0.13mm).

   d. If the camshaft end-play is over the amount specified, replace the thrust plate.

16. Remove the timing chain and sprockets.

17. Remove the camshaft thrust plate. Carefully remove the camshaft by pulling it toward the front of the engine. Remove it slowly to avoid damaging the bearings, journals and lobes.

**To install:**

18. Clean and inspect all parts before installation.

19. Lubricate camshaft lobes and journals with heavy engine oil. Carefully insert the camshaft through the bearings in the cylinder block.

20. Lubricate the engine thrust plate with Engine Assembly Lubricant D9AZ-19579-D, then install the thrust plate. Tighten the retaining bolts to 7 ft. lbs. (10 Nm).

21. Install the timing chain and sprockets. Check the camshaft sprocket bolt for blockage of drilled oil passages prior to installation and clean, if necessary.

22. Install the front timing cover and crankshaft damper and pulley.

23. Lubricate the lifters/tappets and lifter bores with a heavy engine oil. Install the lifters/tappets into their original bores.

24. Install the intake manifold assembly.

25. For unleaded gasoline engines only, coat the distributor drive gear teeth with Engine Assembly Lubricant D9AZ-19579-D or equivalent, then install the distributor, aligning with the marks made during removal and hand tighten the retaining bolt.

26. Lubricate the pushrods and rocker arms with heavy engine oil. Install the pushrods and rocker arms into their original positions. Rotate the crankshaft to set each lifter on its base circle, then tighten the rocker arm bolt. Tighten the rocker arm bolts to 19–28 ft. lbs. (26–38 Nm).

27. Install the oil pan.

28. Install the rocker arm/valve covers.

29. Install the alternator, brackets, drive belt tensioner and the drive belt.

30. Install the fuel injector harness and the throttle body

31. Install the distributor cap, then connect the ignition wires to the spark plugs as tagged during removal.

32. Install the engine assembly into the vehicle. For details, please refer to the procedure located in this section.

33. Connect the negative battery cable. Start the engine and check for leaks. Check and adjust the ignition timing (unleaded gasoline engines only), then tighten the distributor mounting bolt to 15–22 ft. lbs. (20–30 Nm).

### 3.0L SHO Engine

#### ▶ See Figures 202 thru 209

1. Disconnect the negative battery cable. Properly relieve the fuel system pressure.

2. Set the engine on TDC on No. 1 cylinder.

3. Remove the intake manifold assembly.

4. Remove the timing cover and belt.

5. Remove the cylinder head covers.

6. Remove the camshaft pulleys, noting the location of the dowel pins.

7. Remove the upper rear timing belt cover.

8. Uniformly loosen the camshaft bearing caps.

**➡If the camshaft bearing caps are not uniformly loosened, camshaft damage may result.**

9. Remove the bearing caps and note their positions for installation.

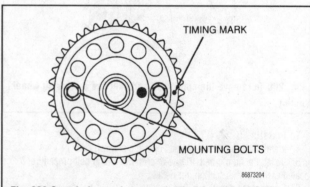

**Fig. 202 Camshaft sprocket mounting bolt locations—SHO engines**

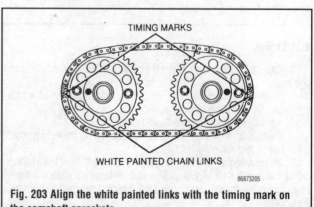

**Fig. 203 Align the white painted links with the timing mark on the camshaft sprockets**

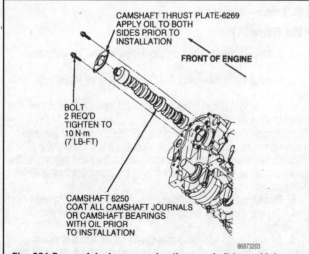

**Fig. 201 Be careful when removing the camshaft to avoid damaging the bearings, journals and lobes**

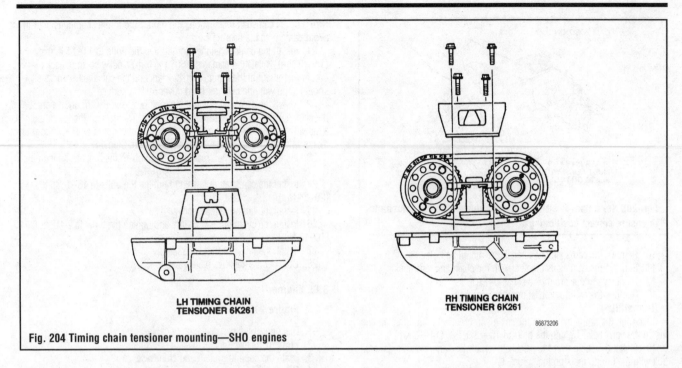

LH TIMING CHAIN
TENSIONER 6K261

RH TIMING CHAIN
TENSIONER 6K261

86873206

**Fig. 204 Timing chain tensioner mounting—SHO engines**

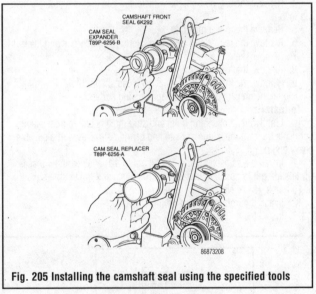

CAMSHAFT FRONT
SEAL 6K292

CAM SEAL
EXPANDER
T89P-6256-B

CAM SEAL REPLACER
T89P-6256-A

86873208

**Fig. 205 Installing the camshaft seal using the specified tools**

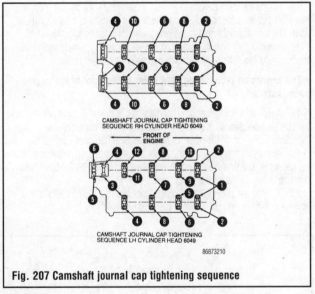

CAMSHAFT JOURNAL CAP TIGHTENING
SEQUENCE RH CYLINDER HEAD 6049

FRONT OF
ENGINE

CAMSHAFT JOURNAL CAP TIGHTENING
SEQUENCE LH CYLINDER HEAD 6049

86873210

**Fig. 207 Camshaft journal cap tightening sequence**

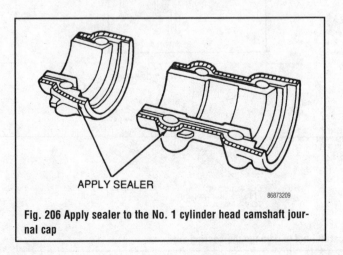

APPLY SEALER

86873209

**Fig. 206 Apply sealer to the No. 1 cylinder head camshaft journal cap**

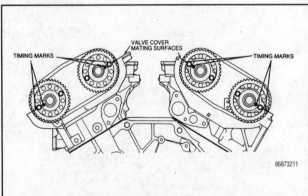

TIMING MARKS

VALVE COVER
MATING SURFACES

TIMING MARKS

86873211

**Fig. 208 Marks on the camshaft sprockets should align with the valve/head cover mating surface**

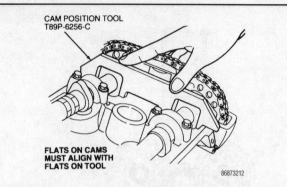

CAM POSITION TOOL
T89P-6256-C

FLATS ON CAMS
MUST ALIGN WITH
FLATS ON TOOL

86873212

**Fig. 209 Set a Cam Position Tool or equivalent on the camshafts to ensure correct positioning**

10. Remove the camshaft chain tensioner mounting bolts.
11. Remove the camshafts together with the chain and tensioner.
12. Remove and discard the camshaft oil seal.
13. Remove the chain sprocket from the camshaft.

**To install:**

14. Align the timing marks on the chain sprockets with the camshaft and install the sprockets. Tighten the bolts to 10–13 ft. lbs. (14–18 Nm).
15. Install the chain over the camshaft sprockets. Align the white painted link with the timing mark on the sprocket.
16. Rotate the camshafts 60° (1/6 turn) counterclockwise. Set the chain tensioner between the sprockets and install the camshafts on the cylinder head. The left and right chain tensioners are not interchangeable.
17. Apply a thin coat of engine oil to the camshaft journals and install bearing caps No. 2 through No. 5 and loosely install the bolts.

➡**The arrows on the bearing caps point to the front of the engine when installed.**

18. Apply silicone sealer to outer diameter of the new camshaft seal and the seal seating area on the cylinder head. Install the camshaft seal using Cam Seal Expander T89P-6256-B, and Cam Seal Replacer T89P-6256-A.
19. Apply silicone sealer to the No. 1 bearing cap, then install the bearing cap while holding the camshaft front seal in place with the Cam Seal Replacer. Loosely install the bolts.
20. Tighten the bearing caps in sequence using a 2 step method. Tighten to 6–9 ft. lbs. (8–12 Nm), then tighten to 12–16 ft. lbs. (16–22

Nm). For left camshaft installation, apply pressure to the chain tensioner to avoid damage to the bearing caps.
21. Install the chain tensioner and tighten the bolts to 11–14 ft. lbs. (15–19 Nm). Rotate the camshafts 60° (1/6 turn) clockwise and check for proper alignment of the timing marks. Marks on the camshaft sprockets should align with the cylinder head cover mating surface.
22. Install the camshaft positioning tool T89P-6256-C or equivalent, on the camshafts to check for correct positioning. The flats on the tool should align with the flats on the camshaft. If the tool does not fit and/or timing marks will not line up, repeat the procedure from Step 14.
23. Install the timing belt rear cover and tighten the bolts to 70 inch lbs. (7.8 Nm).
24. Install the camshaft pulleys and tighten the bolts to 15–18 ft. lbs. (20–24 Nm).
25. Install the timing belt and cover.
26. Install the cylinder head covers and tighten the bolts to 7–12 ft. lbs. (10–16 Nm).
27. Install the intake manifold assembly.
28. Connect the negative battery cable.

### 3.8L Engine

▶ **See Figure 210**

1. Disconnect the negative battery cable.
2. Properly relieve the fuel system pressure.
3. Drain the cooling system and crankcase.
4. Remove the engine from the vehicle and position in a suitable holding fixture.
5. Remove the intake manifold.
6. Remove the rocker arm covers, rocker arms, pushrods and lifters.
7. Remove the oil pan.
8. Remove the front cover and timing chain.
9. Remove the thrust plate. Remove the camshaft through the front of the engine, being careful not to damage bearing surfaces.

**To install:**

10. Lightly oil all attaching bolts and stud threads before installation. Lubricate the cam lobes, thrust plate and bearing surfaces with a suitable heavy engine oil.
11. Install the camshaft being careful not to damage bearing surfaces while sliding into position. Install the thrust plate and tighten the bolts to 6–10 ft. lbs. (8–14 Nm).
12. Install the front cover and timing chain.
13. Install the oil pan.

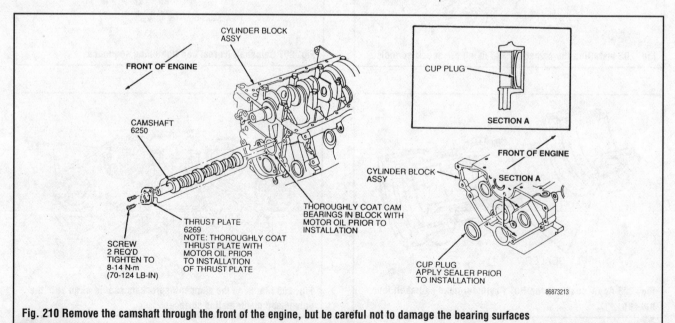

86873213

**Fig. 210 Remove the camshaft through the front of the engine, but be careful not to damage the bearing surfaces**

14. Install the lifters.
15. Install the upper and lower intake manifolds.
16. Install the engine assembly.
17. Fill the cooling system and crankcase to the proper level and connect the negative battery cable.
18. Start the engine. Check and adjust the ignition timing and engine idle speed as necessary. Check for leaks.

## INSPECTION

1. Remove the camshaft from the engine.
2. Check each lobe for excessive wear, flatness, pitting or other physical damage. Replace the camshaft as required.
3. Using a micrometer measure the lobes, if not within specification, replace the camshaft.
4. If replacing the camshaft be sure to check and replace the valve lifters.

## Balance Shaft

## REMOVAL & INSTALLATION

### 3.8L Engine

▶ See Figure 211

1. Remove the engine from the vehicle.
2. Remove the intake manifolds.
3. Remove the oil pan.
4. Remove the front cover and timing chain and camshaft sprocket.
5. Remove the balance shaft drive gear and spacer.
6. Remove the balance shaft gear, thrust plate and shaft assembly.

**To install:**

7. Thoroughly coat the balance shaft bearings in the block with engine oil.
8. Install the balance shaft gear.
9. Install the balance shaft, thrust plate and gear, then tighten the retaining bolts to 6–10 ft. lbs. (8–14 Nm).
10. Install the timing chain and camshaft sprocket.
11. Install the oil pan.
12. Install the timing cover.
13. Install the intake manifolds.
14. Install the engine in the vehicle.

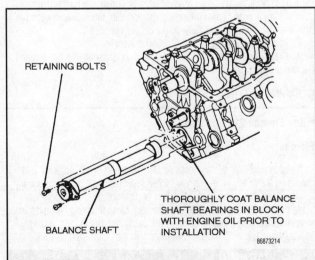

Fig. 211 Balance shaft assembly and related components—3.8L engine

## Pistons and Connecting Rods

### REMOVAL

▶ See Figures 212 thru 217

Although in some cases the pistons and connecting rods may be removed with the engine still in the vehicle, it is rarely worth the aggravation, especially when you are not working with a lift. On vehicles where this is possible (cylinder head and oil pan removal are both possible with the engine installed and there is sufficient working clearance) take EXTREME care to assure no dirt or contamination is allowed into the cylinders during assembly and installation.

Before removing the pistons, the top of the cylinder bore must be examined for a ridge. A ridge at the top of the bore is the result of normal cylinder wear, caused by the piston rings only traveling so far up the bore in the course of the piston stroke. If the ridge can be felt by hand; it must be removed before the pistons are removed.

A ridge reamer is necessary for this operation. Place the piston at the bottom of its stroke, and cover it with a rag. Cut the ridge away with the

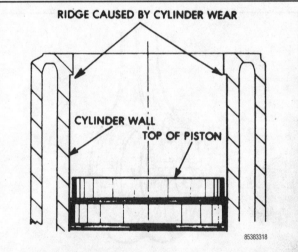

Fig. 212 If present, the cylinder ridge must be removed before the pistons are removed from the block

Fig. 213 Removing the ridge from the cylinder bore using a ridge cutter

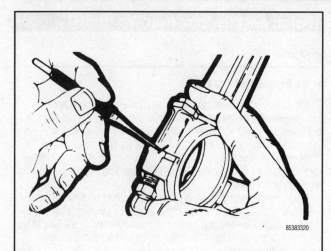

**Fig. 214 Match connecting rods to their caps using a scribe mark**

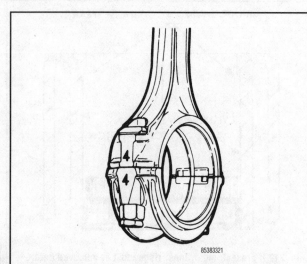

**Fig. 215 Match the connecting rods to their cylinders using a number stamp**

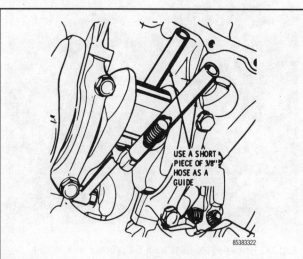

**Fig. 216 Cut lengths of rubber hose for connecting rod bolt guides**

USE A SHORT PIECE OF 3/8" HOSE AS A GUIDE

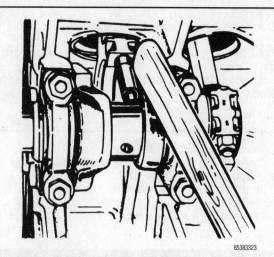

**Fig. 217 Carefully tap the piston and rod assembly out using a wooden hammer handle**

ridge reamer, using extreme care to avoid cutting too deeply. Remove the rag, and remove the cuttings that remain on the piston with a magnet and a rag soaked in clean oil. Make sure the piston top and cylinder bore are absolutely clean before moving the piston. For more details, refer to the ridge removal and honing procedures later in this section.

1. Remove cylinder head or heads.
2. Remove the oil pan.
3. If necessary, remove the oil pump assembly.
4. Matchmark the connecting rod cap to the connecting rod with a scribe; each cap must be reinstalled on its proper rod in the proper direction. Remove the connecting rod bearing cap and the rod bearing. Number the top of each piston with silver paint or a felt-tip pen for reference during assembly.
5. Cut lengths of ⅜ in. (10mm) diameter hose to use as rod bolt guides. Install the hose over the threads of the rod bolts, to prevent the bolt threads from damaging the crankshaft journals and cylinder walls when the piston is removed.
6. Squirt some clean engine oil onto the cylinder wall from above, until the wall is coated. Carefully push the piston and rod assembly up and out of the cylinder by tapping on the bottom of the connecting rod with a wooden hammer handle.
7. Place the rod bearing and cap back on the connecting rod, and install the nut temporarily. Using a number stamp or punch, stamp the cylinder number on the side of the connecting rod and cap; this will help keep the proper piston and rod assembly on the proper cylinder.
8. Remove remaining pistons in similar manner.
9. Clean and inspect the engine block, the crankshaft, the pistons and the connecting rods.

## CLEANING AND INSPECTION

▶ See Figures 218 thru 223

### Pistons

A piston ring expander is necessary for removing piston rings without damaging them; any other method (screwdriver blades, pliers, etc.) usually results in the ring being bent, scratched or distorted, or the piston itself being damaged. When the rings are removed, clean the piston grooves using an appropriate ring groove cleaning tool, using care not to cut too deeply. Thoroughly clean all carbon and varnish from the piston with solvent.

**✳✳ WARNING**

Do not use a wire brush or caustic solvent (acids, etc.) on pistons. Inspect the pistons for scuffing, scoring, cracks, pitting, or

Fig. 218 Use a ring expander tool to remove the piston rings

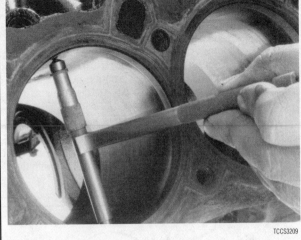

Fig. 220 A telescoping gauge may be used to measure the cylinder bore diameter

Fig. 219 Clean the piston grooves using a ring groove cleaner

Fig. 221 Measure the piston's outer diameter using a micrometer

**excessive ring groove wear. If these are evident, the piston must be replaced.**

Clean the varnish from the piston skirts and pins with a cleaning solvent. DO NOT WIRE BRUSH ANY PART OF THE PISTON. Clean the ring grooves with a groove cleaner and make sure that the oil ring holes and slots are clean.

Inspect the piston for cracked ring lands, scuffed or damaged skirts, eroded areas at the top of the piston. Replace the pistons that are damaged or show signs of excessive wear.

Inspect the grooves for nicks of burrs that might cause the rings to hang up.

Measure the piston in relation to cylinder diameter. Refer to the cylinder bore cleaning and inspection procedures later in this section.

### Connecting Rods

Wash the connecting rods in cleaning solvent and dry with compressed air. Check for twisted or bent rods and inspect for nicks or cracks. Replace connecting rods that are damaged.

### Cylinder Bores

The piston should also be checked in relation to the cylinder diameter. Using a telescoping gauge and micrometer, or a dial gauge, measure the

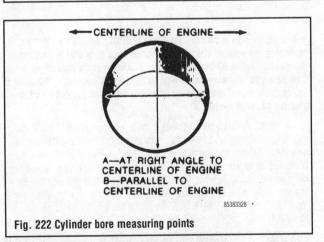

Fig. 222 Cylinder bore measuring points

cylinder bore diameter perpendicular (90 degrees) to the piston pin, about 1–2½ in. (25–64mm) below the cylinder block deck (surface where the block mates with the heads). Then, with the micrometer, measure the piston perpendicular to its wrist pin on the skirt. The difference between the two measurements is the piston clearance.

If the clearance is within specifications or slightly below (after the cylinders have been bored or honed), finish honing is all that is necessary, If the clearance is excessive, try to obtain a slightly larger piston to bring the clearance within specifications. If this is not possible obtain, the first oversize piston and hone the cylinder or (if necessary) bore the cylinder to size. Generally, if the cylinder bore is tapered more than 0.005 in. (0.127mm) or is out-of-round more than 0.003 in. (0.0762mm), it is advisable to rebore for the smallest possible oversize piston and rings. After measuring, mark the pistons with a felt-tip pen for reference and for assembly.

➡**Boring of the cylinder block should be performed by a reputable machine shop with the proper equipment. In some cases, clean-up honing can be done with the cylinder block in the vehicle, but most excessive honing and all cylinder boring MUST BE done with the block stripped and removed from the vehicle.**

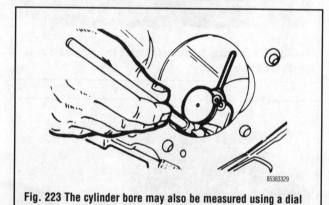
**Fig. 223 The cylinder bore may also be measured using a dial gauge**

## RIDGE REMOVAL & HONING

◆ **See Figures 224, 225 and 226**

1. Before the piston is removed from the cylinder, check for a ridge at the top of the cylinder bore. This ridge occurs because the piston ring does not travel all the way to the top of the bore, thereby leaving an unworn portion of the bore surface.

2. Clean away any carbon buildup at the top of the cylinder with sand paper, in order to see the extent of the ridge more clearly. If the ridge is slight, it will be safe to remove the pistons without damaging the rings or piston ring lands. If the ridge is severe, and easily catches your fingernail, it will have to be removed using a ridge reamer.

➡**A severe ridge is an indication of excessive bore wear. Before removing the piston, check the cylinder bore diameter with a bore gauge, as explained in the cleaning and inspection procedure. Compare your measurement with engine specification. If the bore is excessively worn, the cylinder will have to bored oversize and the piston and rings replaced.**

3. Install the ridge removal tool in the top of the cylinder bore. Carefully follow the manufacturers instructions for operation. Only remove the amount of material necessary to remove the ridge. Place the piston at the bottom of its stroke, and cover it with a rag. Cut the ridge away with the ridge reamer, using extreme care to avoid cutting too deeply. Remove the rag, and remove the cuttings that remain on the piston with a magnet and a rag soaked in clean oil. Make sure the piston top and cylinder bore are absolutely clean before moving the piston.

### ❊❊ WARNING

**Be very careful if you are unfamiliar with operating a ridge reamer. It is very easy to remove more cylinder bore material than you want, possibly requiring a cylinder overbore and piston replacement that may not have been necessary.**

**Fig. 224 Removing cylinder glazing using a flexible hone**

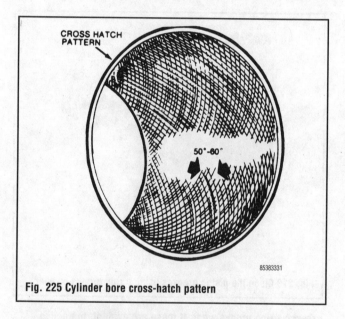
**Fig. 225 Cylinder bore cross-hatch pattern**

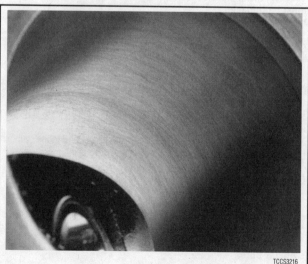
**Fig. 226 A properly cross-hatched cylinder bore**

4. After the piston and connecting rod assembly have been removed, check the clearances as explained earlier in this section under the cleaning and inspection procedure, to determine whether boring and honing or just light honing are required. If boring is necessary, consult an automotive machine shop. If light honing is all that is necessary, proceed with the next step.

5. Honing is best done with the crankshaft removed, to prevent damage to the crankshaft and to make the post-honing cleaning easier, as the honing process will scatter metal particles. However, if you do not want to remove the crankshaft, position the connecting rod journal for the cylinder being honed as far away from the bottom of the cylinder bore as possible, and wrap a shop cloth around the journal.

6. Honing can be done either with a flexible glaze breaker type hone or with a rigid hone that has honing stones and guide shoes. The flexible hone removes the least amount of metal, and is especially recommended if your piston-to-cylinder bore clearance is on the loose side. The flexible hone is useful to provide a finish on which the new piston rings will seat. A rigid hone will remove more material than the flexible hone and requires more operator skill.

7. Regardless of which type of hone you use, carefully follow the manufacturers instructions for operation.

8. The hone should be moved up and down the bore at sufficient speed to obtain a uniform finish. A rigid hone will provide a definite cross-hatch finish; operate the rigid hone at a speed to obtain a 45–65 degree included angle in the cross-hatch. The finish marks should be clean but not sharp, free from embedded particles and torn or folded metal.

9. Periodically during the honing procedure, thoroughly clean the cylinder bore and check the piston-to-bore clearance with the piston for that cylinder.

10. After honing is completed, thoroughly wash the cylinder bores and the rest of the engine with hot water and detergent. Scrub the bores well with a stiff bristle brush and rinse thoroughly with hot water. Thorough cleaning is essential, for if any abrasive material is left in the cylinder bore, it will rapidly wear the new rings and the cylinder bore. If any abrasive material is left in the rest of the engine, it will be picked up by the oil and carried throughout the engine, damaging bearings and other parts.

11. After the bores are cleaned, wipe them down with a clean cloth coated with light engine oil, to keep them from rusting.

**To install:**

12. Lubricate each piston, rod bearing, and cylinder wall with heavy weight engine oil.

13. Take the bearing nuts and cap off connecting rod. Install rubber hoses over the connecting rod bolts to protect the block and crankshaft journal.

14. Install a ring compressor over the piston, position piston with the mark toward front of engine and carefully install.

15. Position the connecting rod with bearing insert over the crank journal. Install the rod cap with bearing in proper position. Secure with rod nuts and torque to the proper specifications. Install all of the rod and piston assemblies.

## PISTON RING REPLACEMENT

1. Take the new piston rings and compress them, one at a time into the cylinder that they will be used in. Press the ring about 25mm below the top of the cylinder block using an inverted piston.

2. Use a feeler gauge and measure the distance between the ends of the ring. This is called measuring the ring end gap. Compare the reading to the one called for in the specifications table. If the measurement is too small, when the engine heats up the ring ends will butt together and cause damage. File the ends of the ring with a fine file to obtain necessary clearance.

➡**If inadequate ring end gap is utilized, ring breakage will result.**

3. Inspect the ring grooves on the piston for excessive wear or taper. If necessary, have the grooves recut for use with a standard ring and spacer. The machine shop can handle the job for you.

4. Check the ring grooves by rolling the new piston ring around the groove to check for burrs or carbon deposits. If any are found, remove with a fine file. Hold the ring in the groove and measure side clearance with a feeler gauge. If the clearance is excessive, spacer(s) will have to be added.

➡**Always add spacers above the piston ring.**

5. Install the ring on the piston, lower oil ring first. Use a ring installing tool (piston ring expander) on the compression rings. Consult the instruction sheet that comes with the rings to be sure they are installed with the correct side up. A mark on the ring usually faces upward.

6. When installing oil rings, first, install the expanding ring in the groove. Hold the ends of the ring butted together (they must not overlap) and install the bottom rail (scraper) with the end about 25mm away from the butted end of the control ring. Install the top rail about 25mm away from the butted end of the control but on the opposite side from the lower rail. Be careful not to scrap the piston when installing oil control rings.

7. Install the two compression rings. The lower ring first.

8. Consult the illustration for ring positioning, arrange the rings as shown, install a ring compressor and insert the piston and rod assembly into the engine.

## PISTON PIN REPLACEMENT

1. Matchmark the piston head and the connecting rod for reassembly.

2. Position the piston assembly in a piston pin removal tool.

3. Following the tool manufacturers instructions, press the piston pin from the piston.

4. Check the piston pin bore for damage, replace defective components as required. Check the piston pin for damage, replace as required.

5. Installation is the reverse of the removal procedure.

## ROD BEARING REPLACEMENT

1. Remove the engine from the vehicle. Position the engine assembly in a suitable holding fixture.

2. Remove the oil pan. Remove the oil pump, as required.

3. Rotate the crankshaft so that you can remove the rod bearing cap. Matchmark the rod bearing cap so that it can be reinstalled properly.

4. Remove the rod bearing cap. Remove the upper half of the bearing from its mounting.

5. Carefully remove the lower half of the bearing from its mounting. It may be necessary to push the piston down in the cylinder bore to to this.

6. Installation is the reverse of the removal procedure.

## Freeze Plugs

♦ **See Figures 227 and 228**

For the vehicles covered by this manual, one of two types of freeze plugs may be used: a cup-type plug or an expansion-type plug. They are removed in the same way, however two different kinds of tools are used to install them.

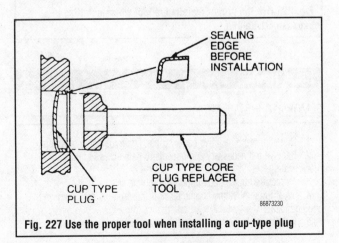

**Fig. 227 Use the proper tool when installing a cup-type plug**

## REMOVAL & INSTALLATION

1. Disconnect the negative battery cable. Drain the cooling system.
2. Remove the necessary components to gain access to the freeze plug.
3. As required, raise and support the vehicle safely.
4. Drill a ½ in. (12.7mm) hole in the center of the plug, then remove the plug using a Universal Impact Slide Hammer T59L-100-B or equivalent. Inspect the plug bore for damage that might interfere with the proper sealing of the plug. If the bore is damaged, you will have to bore the surface to accommodate the next specified oversize plug.

➡**Oversize plugs are identified by the "OS" stamped in the flat on the cup side of the plug.**

**To install:**

5. Lightly coat the plug and/or bore with an oil resistant Stud and Bearing Mount E0AZ-19554-BA or Threadlock 262 E2FZ-19554-B or equivalent.
6. Cup type core plugs are installed with the flanged edge outward. The maximum diameter of this plug is located at the outer edge of the flange. The flange on cup type plugs flares outward with the largest diameter at the outer sealing edge.
7. Expansion type core plugs are installed with the flanged edge inward. The maximum diameter of this plug is located at the base of the flange with the flange flaring inward.
8. For the cup-type plug, it is important to push or drive the plug into the machined bore by using the proper tool. Never drive the plug using a tool that contacts the crowned part of the plug. Damage to the plug and/or plug bore may result. When installed, the trailing (maximum) diameter must be below the the chamfered edge of the bore to effectively seal the plugged bore.
9. For the expansion-type plug, it is important to pull the plug into the machined bore by using a properly designed tool. Never drive the plug into the bore using a tool that contacts the flange. Leakage and/or plug blowout will result. the flanged (trailing) edge must be below the chamfered edge of the bore to effectively seal the plugged bore.
10. Install all the removed components. Lower the vehicle, as required.
11. Fill the cooling system and check for leaks.

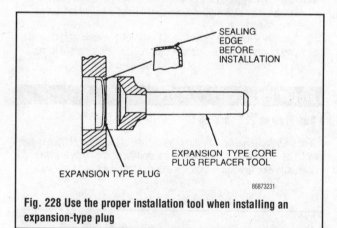

**Fig. 228 Use the proper installation tool when installing an expansion-type plug**

## Block Heater

### REMOVAL & INSTALLATION

1. Disconnect the negative battery cable. Drain the cooling system.
2. Remove the necessary components to gain access to the engine block heater.
3. As required, raise and support the vehicle safely.
4. Carefully remove the engine block heater from its mounting on the engine block.
5. Installation is the reverse of the removal procedure.

## Rear Main Seal

▸ **See Figures 229 thru 235**

### REMOVAL & INSTALLATION

1. Disconnect the negative battery cable.
2. Raise and safely support the vehicle.
3. Remove the transaxle. For details, please refer to the procedure located in Section 7 of this manual.
4. Remove the flywheel and the rear cover plate, if necessary.
5. Using a sharp awl, punch one hole into the crankshaft rear oil seal metal surface between the seal lip and the cylinder block.
6. On all engines except the SHO engines, screw in the threaded end of Jet Plug Remover T77L-9533-B or equivalent, then use the tool to remove the seal.
7. For the SHO engines, Locknut Pin Remover T78P-3504-N into the crankshaft rear oil seal, then remove the seal from the retainer.

➡**Use caution to avoid damaging the oil seal surface.**

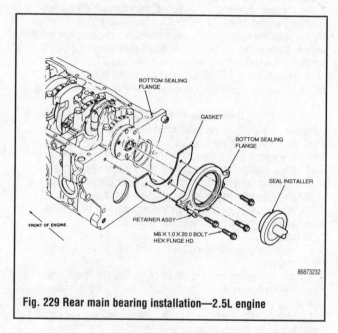

**Fig. 229 Rear main bearing installation—2.5L engine**

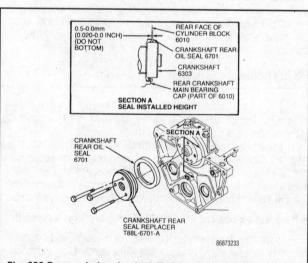

**Fig. 230 Rear main bearing installation—3.0L engine (except SHO)**

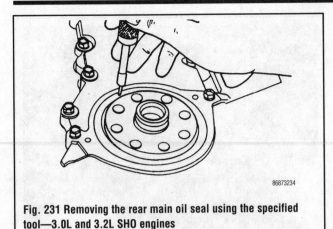

Fig. 231 Removing the rear main oil seal using the specified tool—3.0L and 3.2L SHO engines

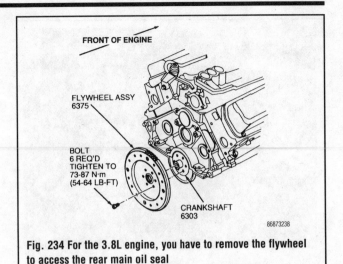

Fig. 234 For the 3.8L engine, you have to remove the flywheel to access the rear main oil seal

Fig. 232 Crankshaft rear main oil seal cover—3.0L and 3.2L SHO engines

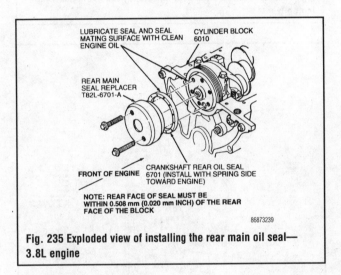

Fig. 235 Exploded view of installing the rear main oil seal—3.8L engine

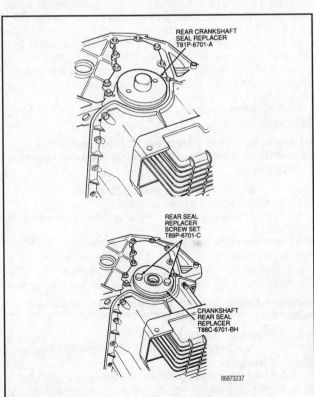

Fig. 233 Installing the rear main oil seal on the SHO engines using the required tools

## To install:

8. Inspect the crankshaft seal area for any damage which may cause the seal to leak. If damage is evident, service or replace the crankshaft as necessary.

9. Coat the crankshaft seal area and the lip with engine oil.

10. Using a Rear Crankshaft Seal Replacer T81P-6701-A seal installer tool, install the seal. Tighten the bolts of the seal installer tool evenly so the seal is straight and seats without misalignment.

11. Install the flywheel. Tighten attaching bolts to 54–64 ft. lbs. (73–87 Nm) on all except the SHO engines. On the SHO engines, tighten the bolts to 51–58 ft. lbs. (69–79 Nm).

12. Install rear cover plate, if necessary.

13. Install the transaxle and connect the negative battery cable.

## Crankshaft and Main Bearings

### REMOVAL & INSTALLATION

#### 2.5L Engine

▶ See Figures 236, 237 and 238

1. Disconnect the negative battery cable, then drain the engine oil.

2. Remove the engine from the vehicle, then place it on a work stand, then remove the oil level dipstick.

3. Remove the accessory drive pulley, if so equipped. Remove the crankshaft pulley attaching bolts and washer.

Fig. 236 Remove the main bearing caps by removing the retaining bolts

Fig. 238 Torque the main bearing cap bolts to specification

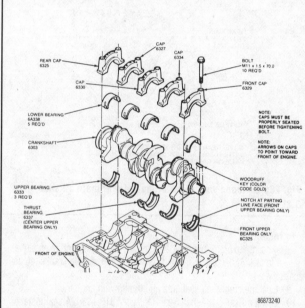

Fig. 237 Exploded view of the crankshaft and the related components—2.5L engine

4. Remove the cylinder front cover and the air conditioning idler pulley assembly, if so equipped. Remove cover assembly.

5. Check the timing chain deflection. Remove the timing chain and sprockets.

6. Invert the engine on the work stand. Remove the flywheel and the rear seal cover. Remove the oil pan and gasket. Remove the oil pump inlet and the oil pump assembly.

7. Ensure all bearing caps (main and connecting rod) are marked so they can be installed in their original positions. Turn the crankshaft until the connecting rod from which the cap is being removed is up. Remove the connecting rod cap. Install a rubber hose onto the connecting rod bolts to prevent journal damage. Push the connecting rod and piston assembly up in the cylinder, then install the cap and nuts in their original positions. Repeat the procedure for the remaining connecting rod assemblies.

8. Remove the main bearing caps.

9. Carefully lift crankshaft out of the block so the upper thrust bearing surfaces are not damaged. Reinstall the main bearing caps on the block.

➡Handle the crankshaft with care to avoid possible fracture or damage to the finished surfaces.

To install:

➡If the bearings are to be reused they should be identified to ensure that they are installed in their original position.

10. Remove the main bearing inserts from the block and bearing caps.

11. Remove the connecting rod bearing inserts from the connecting rods and caps.

12. Install a new rear oil seal in the rear seal cover.

13. Apply a thin coat of Ford Polyethylene Grease D0AZ-19584-A (ESR-M1C159-A or ESB-M1C93-A) or equivalent, to the rear crankshaft surface. Do not apply sealer to the area forward of oil sealer groove. Inspect all the machined surfaces on the crankshaft for nicks, scratches or scores which could cause premature bearing wear.

14. If the crankshaft main bearing journals have been refinished to a definite undersize, install the correct undersize bearings, usually 0.25mm, 0.50mm, 0.80mm undersize. Ensure the bearing inserts and bearing bores are clean. Foreign material under the inserts will distort the bearing and cause a failure.

15. Place the upper main bearing inserts in position in the bores with the tang fitted in the slot provided.

➡Lubricate the bearing surfaces with Oil Conditioner part No. D9AZ-19579-CF or equivalent. Conditioner is needed for lubrication at initial start up.

16. Install the lower main bearing inserts in the bearing caps.

17. Carefully lower the crankshaft into place.

18. Check the clearance of each main bearing. Select fit the bearings for proper clearance.

19. After the bearings have been fitted, apply a light coat of oil conditioner to journals and bearings. Install all the bearing caps and torque to proper specifications. Tighten the main bearing cap bolts to 52–66 ft. lbs. (70–90 Nm) and the connecting rod cap nuts to 21–26 ft. lbs. (28–35 Nm).

➡The main bearing caps must be installed in their original positions.

20. Align the upper thrust bearing.

21. Check the crankshaft end play, using a dial indicator mounted on the front of the engine.

22. If the end play exceeds specification, replace the upper thrust bearing. If the end play is less than the specification, inspect the thrust bearing faces for damage, dirt or improper alignment. Install the thrust bearing and align the faces. Check the end play.

23. Install the new bearing inserts in the connecting rods and caps.

Install rubber hoses on the rod bolts to prevent crankshaft journal damage. Check the clearance of each bearing using a piece of Plastigage®.

24. If the bearing clearances are to specification, apply a light coat of Oil Conditioner part No. D9AZ-19579-CF to the journals and bearings.

25. Turn the crankshaft throw to the bottom of the stroke. Push the piston all the way down until the rod bearings seat on the crankshaft journal.

26. Install the connecting rod cap and nuts. Torque the nuts to specifications

27. After the piston and connecting rod assemblies have been installed, check all the connecting-rod-crankshaft journal clearances using a piece of Plastigage®.

28. Turn the engine on the work stand so the front end is up. Install the timing chain, sprockets, timing chain tensioner, front cover, oil seal and the crankshaft pulley.

29. Clean the oil pan, oil pump and the oil pump screen assembly.

30. Prime the oil pump by filling the inlet opening with oil and rotating the pump shaft until oil emerges from the outlet opening. Install the oil pump. Install the oil pan.

31. Position the flywheel on the crankshaft. Apply Pipe Sealant with Teflon D8AZ-19554-A (ESG-M4G194-A and ESR-M18P7-A) or equivalent oil resistant sealer to the flywheel attaching bolts using a cross tightening sequence. Torque the bolts to 54–64 ft. lbs. (73–87 Nm).

➡ **On the flywheel, if equipped with manual transmission, locate clutch disc and install pressure plate.**

32. Turn the engine on the work stand so the engine is in the normal upright position. Install the oil level dipstick. Install the accessory drive pulley, if so equipped. Install and adjust the drive belt and the accessory belts to specification.

33. Remove the engine from work stand. Install the engine in the vehicle. Fill the crankcase with the correct amount and type of oil, then connect the negative battery cable.

### 3.0L Engine—Except SHO

▶ **See Figures 239 and 240**

1. With the engine removed from the vehicle and placed on a workstand, loosen the idler pulley and the alternator belt adjusting bolt.

2. Remove the oil pan and gasket.

3. Remove the front cover assembly.

4. Check the timing chain deflection. Remove the timing chain and sprockets.

5. Invert the engine on the workstand. For vehicles through 1993, remove the flywheel. For 1994–95 vehicles remove the pushrod. Remove the oil pump inlet and the oil pump assembly.

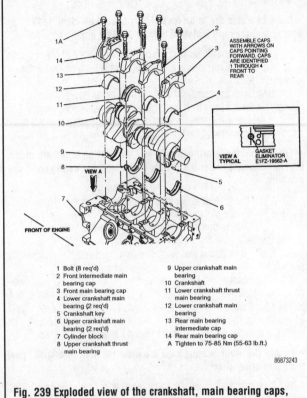

| | |
|---|---|
| 1 Bolt (8 req'd) | 9 Upper crankshaft main |
| 2 Front intermediate main | bearing |
|    bearing cap | 10 Crankshaft |
| 3 Front main bearing cap | 11 Lower crankshaft thrust |
| 4 Lower crankshaft main |    main bearing |
|    bearing (2 req'd) | 12 Lower crankshaft main |
| 5 Crankshaft key |    bearing |
| 6 Upper crankshaft main | 13 Rear main bearing |
|    bearing (2 req'd) |    intermediate cap |
| 7 Cylinder block | 14 Rear main bearing cap |
| 8 Upper crankshaft thrust | A Tighten to 75-85 Nm (55-63 lb.ft.) |
|    main bearing | |

**Fig. 239 Exploded view of the crankshaft, main bearing caps, and bearings—3.0L engine (except SHO)**

6. Ensure all bearing caps (main and connecting rod) are marked so that they can be installed in their original positions. Turn the crankshaft until the connecting rod from which the cap is being removed is up. Remove the connecting rod cap. Push the connecting rod and piston assembly up in the cylinder. Repeat the procedure for the remaining connecting rod assemblies.

7. Remove the main bearing caps.

➡**Handle the crankshaft with care to avoid possible damage to the finished surfaces or the engine.**

8. Carefully lift the crankshaft out of the block so that the upper thrust bearing surfaces are not damaged.

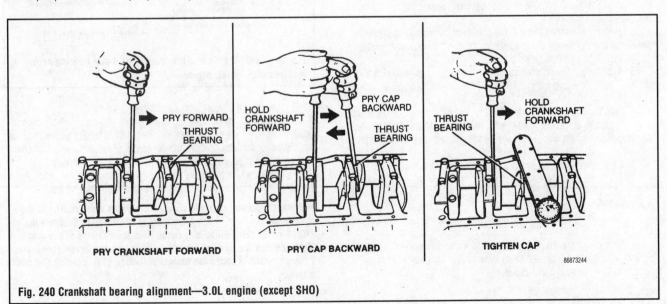

**Fig. 240 Crankshaft bearing alignment—3.0L engine (except SHO)**

**To install:**

➡**If the bearings are to be reused they should be identified to ensure that they are installed in their original positions.**

9. Remove the main bearing inserts from the block and bearing caps.

10. Remove the connecting rod bearing inserts from the connecting rods and caps.

11. Inspect all the machined surfaces on the crankshaft for nicks, scratches, scores, etc., which could cause premature bearing wear.

12. If the crankshaft main bearing journals have been refinished to a definite undersize, install the correct undersize bearings.

➡**Ensure that the bearing inserts and the bearing bores are clean. Foreign material under the inserts will distort the bearing and cause a failure.**

13. Place the upper main bearing inserts into position in the bores with the tang fitted in the slot provided.

14. Install the lower main bearing inserts in the bearing caps.

15. Carefully lower the crankshaft into place.

16. Check the clearance of each main bearing. Select fit the bearings for proper clearance.

17. After the bearings have been fitted, apply a light coat of Oil Conditioner part No. D9AZ-19578-CO or heavy engine oil, SAE 50 weight, to the journals bearings and rear seal surface. Install all the bearing caps. Apply RTV to the gap between the rear main bearing and the block. Take care to keep RTV from the parting surfaces between the block and the cap.

➡**Ensure the main bearing caps are installed in their original positions and orientation.**

18. Lubricate the journal with oil conditioner or heavy engine oil 50 SAE weight. Install the thrust bearing cap with the bolts finger-tight. Pry the crankshaft forward against the thrust surface of the upper half of the crankshaft thrust main bearing. Hold the crankshaft cap to the rear. This will align the thrust surfaces of both halves of the bearing to be positioned properly. Retain the forward pressure on the crankshaft. Tighten the cap bolts to 55–63 ft. lbs. (75–85 Nm).

19. Check the crankshaft end play with a dial indicator mounted on the front of the engine.

20. If the end play exceeds specification, replace the upper and lower thrust bearings. If the end play is less than specification, inspect the thrust bearing faces for damage, dirt or improper alignment. Install the thrust bearing and align the faces. Recheck the end play.

21. Install the new bearing inserts in the connecting rods and caps. Check the clearance of each bearing by using a piece of Plastigage®.

22. If the bearing clearances are to specification, apply a light coat of Oil Conditioner part No. D9AZ-19579-C or heavy engine oil, SAE 50 weight, to the journals and bearings.

23. Turn the crankshaft throw to the bottom of the stroke. Push the piston all the way down until the rod bearings seat on the crankshaft journal.

24. Install the connecting rod cap.

25. After the piston and connecting rod assemblies have been installed, check all the connecting rod crankshaft journal clearances using a piece of Plastigage®.

26. Turn the engine on the work stand so that the front end is up. Install the timing chain, sprockets, front cover, new oil seal and crankshaft pulley. Turn the engine on the work stand so that the rear end is up. Install the rear oil seal.

27. Clean the oil pan, oil pump and the oil pump screen assembly.

28. Prime the oil pump by filling the inlet opening with oil and rotating the pump shaft until the oil emerges from the outlet opening. Install the oil pump, baffle and oil pan.

29. Position the flywheel on the crankshaft. Tighten to 54-64 ft. lbs. (73–87 Nm).

30. Turn the engine on work stand so that the engine is in the normal upright position. Install the accessory drive pulley. Install and adjust the accessory drive belts to specification.

31. Install the torque converter, as required.

32. Remove the engine from the work stand. Install the engine in the vehicle.

**3.8L Engine**

◆ **See Figure 241**

➡**If the bearings are to be reused, they should be identified to ensure that they are installed in their original positions.**

1. Disconnect the negative battery cable, then drain the engine oil. Remove the engine from the vehicle and mount it on a suitable work stand.

2. Tag and disconnect the ignition wires from the spark plugs, then remove the distributor cap and ignition wires as an assembly. Remove the spark plugs.

3. On Taurus Police vehicles, remove the oil pan baffle.

4. Remove the oil pan and oil pickup tube.

5. Remove the front cover and water pump as an assembly.

6. Remove the distributor drive gear,.

7. Remove the camshaft and crankshaft sprockets and the timing chain. To do this: pull back on the ratcheting mechanism of the timing chain vibration damper, then install the pin through the hole to relieve the tension against the chain.

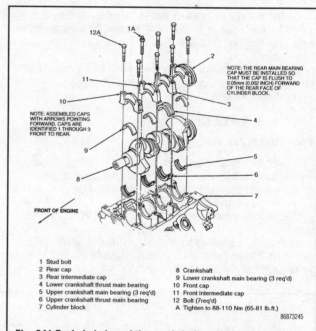

1 Stud bolt
2 Rear cap
3 Rear intermediate cap
4 Lower crankshaft thrust main bearing
5 Upper crankshaft main bearing (3 req'd)
6 Upper crankshaft thrust main bearing
7 Cylinder block
8 Crankshaft
9 Lower crankshaft main bearing (3 req'd)
10 Front cap
11 Front intermediate cap
12 Bolt (7req'd)
A Tighten to 88-110 Nm (65-81 lb.ft.)

86873245

**Fig. 241 Exploded view of the crankshaft, main bearing caps and bearings—3.8L engine**

8. Remove the flywheel and the engine rear cover.

9. Remove the connecting rod bearing nuts and caps. Identify each bearing cap to insure that they are installed in their original positions. Push the pistons up into the cylinder and put pieces of rubber hose on the connecting rod bolts so the crankshaft journals do not get damaged.

10. Inspect all the machined surfaces on the crankshaft for nicks, scratches, scores, etc., which could cause premature bearing wear.

➡**Because the engine crankshaft incorporates deep rolling of the main journal fillets, journal refinishing is limited to 0.25mm undersize. Further refinishing may result in fatigue failure of the crankshaft. Ensure the bearing inserts and the bearing bores are clean. Foreign material under the inserts will distort the bearing and cause a failure.**

11. Remove the main bearing caps and identify each bearing cap to insure that they are installed in their original positions.

12. Carefully lift the crankshaft out of the block to prevent damage to bearing surfaces. Remove rear oil seal and discard. Before installation, lightly oil all bolt and stud threads.

**To install:**

13. Make sure all crankshaft bearing journals and bearing caps are clean. Contaminants under a bearing will cause distortion. Contaminants on the bearing surface will cause damage to the bearing journals.

14. If the crankshaft journals have been refinished to a definite undersize, make sure the proper undersize is being used.

15. Install the used main bearings to their original positions. If using new ones, install the tabs on the bearings into the slots in the cap and the block.

16. Carefully lower crankshaft into position in the cylinder block. Be careful not to damage the thrust bearing surfaces.

17. Apply a 3mm bead of Silicone Sealer part No. D6AZ-19562-A or equivalent to the rear main bearing cap-to-cylinder block parting line.

18. Lubricate the bearing surfaces and journals with Oil Conditioner part No. D9AZ-19579-CF or equivalent heavy engine oil 50 SAE weight.

19. Install the main bearing caps in the proper direction. Tighten the retaining bolts as follows:

    a. Do NOT jam the pry bar into position. Carefully tap on the pry bar until it holds the crankshaft toward the front of the engine. Wedge a pry bar between the cylinder block web and crankshaft cheek in front of the No. 3 crankshaft main bearing.

    b. Tighten the main bearing cap retaining bolts to 65–81 ft. lbs. (88–110 Nm), then remove the prybar.

20. Check crankshaft end-play. If the end play exceeds specification, replace the upper and lower thrust bearings. If the end play is less than specification, inspect the thrust bearing faces for damage, dirt or improper alignment. Install the thrust bearing and align the faces. Recheck the end play.

21. Install a new crankshaft rear oil seal.

22. Install the used connecting rod bearings to their original positions. If using new ones, install the tabs on the bearings into the slots in the cap and the rod.

23. Rotate the crankshaft as necessary to bring each throw to the lowest point of travel. Pull the piston downward until the connecting rod seats on the crank throw. Install the connecting rod caps and torque in three steps:

    a. Tighten retaining nuts to 31–36 ft. lbs. (42–49 Nm).

    b. Loosen the nuts 2–3 turns.

    c. Final tighten the nuts to 31–36 ft. lbs. (42–49 Nm).

24. Install the timing chain assembly, distributor gear, oil pan baffle, oil pan, rear cover and flywheel, and spark plugs.

25. Install the distributor cap, then connect the ignition wires as tagged during removal.

26. Install the engine in the vehicle. Connect the negative battery cable, then fill the crankcase with the correct amount and type of engine oil.

## CLEANING & INSPECTION

▶ **See Figures 242, 243 and 244**

1. Clean the crankshaft with solvent and a brush. Clean the oil passages with a suitable brush, then blow them out with compressed air.

2. Inspect the crankshaft for obvious damage or wear. Check the main and connecting rod journals for cracks, scratches, grooves or scores. Inspect the crankshaft oil seal surface for nicks, sharp edges or burrs that could damage the oil seal or cause premature seal wear.

3. If the crankshaft passes a visual inspection, check journal run-out using a dial indicator. Support the crankshaft in V-blocks as shown in the figure and check the run-out as shown. Compare to specifications.

4. Measure the main and connecting rod journals for wear, out-of-roundness or taper, using a micrometer. Measure in at least 4 places around each journal and compare your findings with the journal diameter specifications.

5. If the crankshaft fails any inspection for wear or damage, it must be reground or replaced.

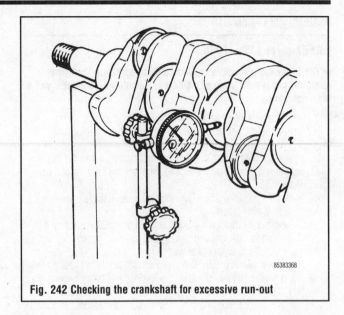

**Fig. 242 Checking the crankshaft for excessive run-out**

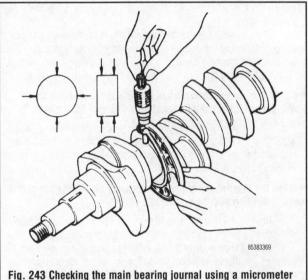

**Fig. 243 Checking the main bearing journal using a micrometer**

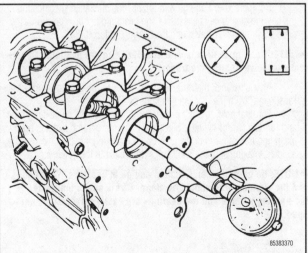

**Fig. 244 Checking main bearing bore diameter with the bearings installed**

## BEARING REPLACEMENT

▶ **See Figures 245 and 246**

➡ **The following procedure requires the use of Plastigage® or a micrometer set consisting of inside and outside micrometers, and a dial indicator.**

1. Inspect the bearings for scoring, chipping or other wear.
2. Inspect the crankshaft journals as detailed in the Cleaning and Inspection procedure.
3. If the crankshaft journals appear usable, clean them and the bearing shells until they are completely free of oil. Blow any oil from the oil hole in the crankshaft.
4. To check the crankshaft/rod bearing clearances using a micrometer, perform the following procedures:

   a. Set the crankshaft on V-blocks. Using a dial indicator set on the center bearing journal, check the crankshaft run-out. Repair or replace the crankshaft if out of specification.

   b. Using an outside micrometer, measure the crankshaft bearing journals for diameter and out-of-round conditions; if necessary, regrind the bearing journals.

   c. Install the bearings and caps, then torque the nuts/bolts to specifications. Using an inside micrometer, check the bearing bores in the engine block. If out of specification, regrind the bearing bores to the next largest oversize.

   d. The difference between the two readings is the bearing clearance. If out of specification, inspect for the cause and repair as necessary.

5. To inspect the main bearing surfaces, using the Plastigage® method, perform the following procedures:

➡ **NOTE: The journal surfaces and bearing shells must be completely free of oil to get an accurate reading with Plastigage®.**

   a. Place a strip of Plastigage® or equivalent gauging material, lengthwise along the bottom center of the lower bearing shell, then install the cap with the shell and torque the connecting rod nuts or main cap bolts to specification.

➡ **When the Plastigage® material is installed on the bearing surfaces, DO NOT rotate the crankshaft.**

   b. Remove the bearing cap with the shell. The flattened Plastigage® will either be sticking to the bearing shell or the crankshaft journal.

   c. Using the printed scale on the Plastigage® package, measure the flattened material at its widest point. The number on the scale that most closely corresponds to the width of the Plastigage® indicates the bearing clearance in thousandths of an inch or hundredths of a millimeter.

   d. Compare your findings with the bearing clearance specification. If the bearing clearance is excessive, the bearing must be replaced or the crankshaft must be ground and the bearing replaced.

➡ **NOTE: Bearing shell sets over standard size are available to correct excessive bearing clearance.**

   e. After clearance measurement is completed, be sure to remove the Plastigage® from the crankshaft and/or bearing shell.

   f. For final bearing shell installation, make sure the connecting rod and rod cap and/or cylinder block and main cap bearing saddles are clean and free of nicks or burrs. Install the bearing shells in the bearing saddles, making sure the shell tangs are seated in the notches.

➡ **NOTE: Be careful when handling any plain bearings. Your hands and the working area should be clean. Dirt is easily embedded in the bearing surface and the bearings are easily scratched or damaged.**

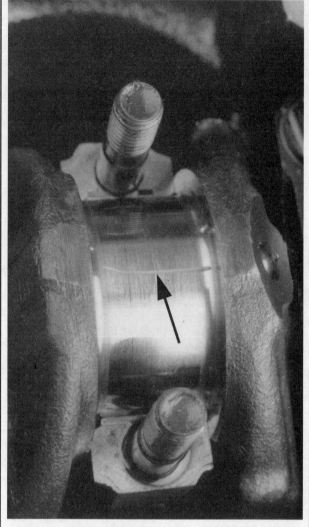

TCCS3243

**Fig. 245 Apply a strip of gauging material to the bearing, then install and tighten the cap**

TCCS3244

**Fig. 246 As with the connecting rod bearings, remove the cap and compare the gauging material to the provided scale**

## CRANKSHAFT END-PLAY/CONNECTING ROD SIDE PLAY

1. Place a prybar between a main bearing cap and crankshaft casting taking care not to damage any journals. Pry backward and forward, measure the distance between the thrust bearing and crankshaft with a feeler gauge.

2. Compare reading with specifications, 0.10-0.20mm. If too great a clearance is determined, a main bearing with a larger thrust surface or crank machining may be required. Check with an automotive machine shop for their advice.

3. Connecting rod clearance between the rod and crankthrow casting can be checked with a feeler gauge. Pry the rod carefully on one side as far as possible and measure the distance on the other side of the rod. Check the crankshaft and connecting rod specification table.

## Flywheel/Flexplate

▶ **See Figures 247 and 248**

### REMOVAL & INSTALLATION

1. For all vehicles except 1991–95 3.0L engines, remove the transaxle from the vehicle.
2. For the 1991–95 3.0L engine, remove the engine from the vehicle.
3. Remove the flywheel/flexplate attaching bolts and the flywheel.
4. The rear cover plate can be removed (manual transmission only).
**To install:**

➡**All major rotating components including the flexplate/flywheel are individually balance to zero. Engine assembly balancing is not required. Balance weights should not be installed on new flywheels.**

5. Install the rear cover plate, if removed.
6. Position the flywheel on the crankshaft and install the attaching bolts.

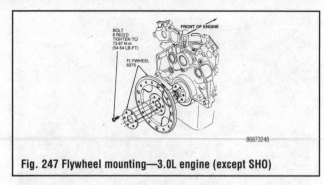

**Fig. 247 Flywheel mounting—3.0L engine (except SHO)**

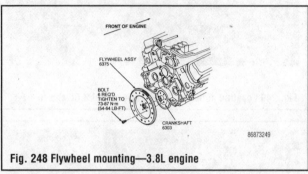

**Fig. 248 Flywheel mounting—3.8L engine**

For all engines except the SHO, tighten the attaching bolts to 54–64 ft. lbs. (73–87 Nm), using the standard cross-tightening sequence. For the SHO engines, tighten the bolts in two steps:
  a. Step 1: 29–39 ft. lbs. (39–53 Nm)
  b. Step 2: 51–58 ft. lbs. (69–79 Nm)
7. If removed, install the transaxle.

# EXHAUST SYSTEM

▶ **See Figures 249 thru 252**

## General Information

Two types of pipe connections are used on most exhaust systems; they are: the ball joint (to allow angular movement for alignment purposes) and the slip joint. Gaskets are used only with the ball joint type connections.

The system is supported by free hanging rubber mountings which permit some movement of the exhaust system but do not allow the transfer of noise and vibration into the passenger compartment. Any noise vibrations or rattles in the exhaust system are usually caused be damage or misalignment of the parts.

### ※ CAUTION

**Before performing any operations on the exhaust system, be sure to allow it sufficient time to cool.**

As with many areas of service on your car, the exhaust system presents its own dangers. Always follow safety precautions carefully during exhaust system service.

## Safety Precautions

➡**Safety glasses should be worn at all times when working on or near the exhaust system. Older exhaust systems will almost always be covered with loose rust particles which will shower you when disturbed. These particles are more than a nuisance and could injure your eye.**

Whenever working on the exhaust system, always follow these safety precautions:
• Support the car extra securely. Not only will you often be working directly under it, but you'll frequently be using a lot of force, say, heavy hammer blows, to dislodge rusted parts. This can cause a car that's improperly supported to shift and possibly fall.

• Wear goggles. Exhaust system parts are always rusty. Metal chips can be dislodged, even when you're only turning rusted bolts. Attempting to pry pipes apart with a chisel makes the chips fly even more frequently.

• If you're using a cutting torch, keep it a great distance from either the fuel tank or lines. Stop what you're doing and feel the temperature of the fuel bearing pipes on the tank frequently. Even slight heat can expand and/or vaporize fuel, resulting in accumulated vapor, or even a liquid leak, near your torch.

• Watch where your hammer blows fall and make sure you hit squarely. You could easily tap a brake or fuel line when you hit an exhaust system part with a glancing blow. Inspect all lines and hoses in the area where you've been working.

### ※ CAUTION

**Be very careful when working on or near the catalytic converter. External temperatures can reach 1,500°F (816°C) and more, causing severe burns. Removal or installation should be performed only on a cold exhaust system.**

• Inspect inlet pipes, outlet pipes and mufflers for cracked joints, broken welds and corrosion damage that would result in a leaking exhaust system. It is normal for a certain amount of moisture and staining to be present around the muffler seams. The presence of soot, light surface rust or moisture does not indicate a faulty muffler. Inspect the clamps, brackets and insulators for cracks and stripped or badly corroded bolt threads. When flat joints are loosened and/or disconnected to replace a shield pipe or muffler, replace the bolts and flange nuts if there is reasonable doubt that its service life is limited.

• Check the complete exhaust system for open seams, holes, loose connections, or other deterioration which could permit exhaust fumes to seep into the passenger compartment.

86873257

**Fig. 249 Location of the muffler—Early model 2.5L shown**

86873256

**Fig. 250 Location of the catalytic converter—early model 2.5L shown**

• The exhaust system, including brush shields, must be free of leaks, binding, grounding and excessive vibrations. These conditions are usually caused by loose or broken flange bolts, shields, brackets or pipes. If any of these conditions exist, check the exhaust system components and alignment. Align or replace as necessary. Brush shields are positioned on the underside of the catalytic converter and should be free from bends which would bring any part of the shield in contact with the catalytic converter or muffler. The shield should also be clear of any combustible material such as dried grass or leaves.

• Before removing any component of the exhaust system, ALWAYS squirt a liquid rust dissolving agent onto the fasteners for ease of removal. A lot of knuckle skin will be saved by following this rule.

• Coat all of the exhaust connections and bolt threads with anti-seize compound to prevent corrosion from making the next disassembly difficult.

### Special Tools

A number of special exhaust system tools can be rented from auto supply houses or local stores that rent special equipment. A common one is a tailpipe expander, designed to enable you to join pipes of identical diameter.

It may also be quite helpful to use solvents designed to loosen rusted bolts or flanges. Soaking rusted parts the night before you do the job can speed the work of freeing rusted parts considerably. Remember that these solvents are often flammable. Apply only to parts that have been allowed to cool!

### Resonator Assembly

#### REMOVAL & INSTALLATION

1. Raise and safely support the vehicle.
2. Remove the front resonator flange fasteners at the flex joint, then discard the flex joint gasket. Loosen the rear U-bolt connection.
3. Separate the resonator inlet and outlet connections, then remove the resonator.
   **To install:**
4. Loosely install the resonator to the muffler, then install a new flex joint gasket.
5. Install the resonator and muffler assembly to the converter outlet joint.
6. Align the exhaust system, making sure that the muffler and resonator are fully engaged.
7. Starting at the front of the exhaust system, tighten all nuts and bolts.

### Muffler

#### REMOVAL & INSTALLATION

1. Raise and safely support the vehicle.
2. Remove the U-bolt assembly and rubber insulators from the hanger brackets, then remove the muffler assembly. Slide the muffler rearward to disconnect it from the resonator or flexible pipe, as applicable.
3. Replace any damaged parts.
   **To install:**
4. Position the muffler assembly and slide it onto the resonator outlet pipe. Check the make sure the slot in the muffler and the tab on the resonator are fully engaged.
5. Install the rubber insulators on the hanger assemblies, then install the U-bolt and tighten it to 26–33 ft. lbs. (34–46 Nm).
6. Lower the vehicle. Start the engine and check for leaks.

### Catalytic Converter

Depending on your vehicle, the catalytic converter may be located underneath the car under the oil pan or located in the engine compartment.

#### REMOVAL & INSTALLATION

1. Raise and safely support the vehicle. As required, remove the transmission to converter support brace.
2. Remove the front catalytic converter flange fasteners at the flex joint and discard the flex joint gasket, remove the rear U-bolt connection.
3. Separate the catalytic converter inlet and outlet connections. Remove the converter.
4. Installation is the reverse of the removal procedure. Be sure to use new retaining clamps.
5. Lower the vehicle. Start the engine and check for leaks.

### Tailpipe

#### REMOVAL & INSTALLATION

1. Raise and safely support the vehicle. Remove the tailpipe retaining clamp from the tailpipe to the frame, if equipped.
2. Remove the retaining clamp holding the tailpipe to the muffler or resonator.
3. Using the proper tool separate the tailpipe from the muffler or resonator.
4. Carefully remove the tailpipe from the vehicle.
5. Installation is the reverse of the removal procedure. Be sure to use new retaining clamps.
6. Lower the vehicle. Start the engine and check for leaks.

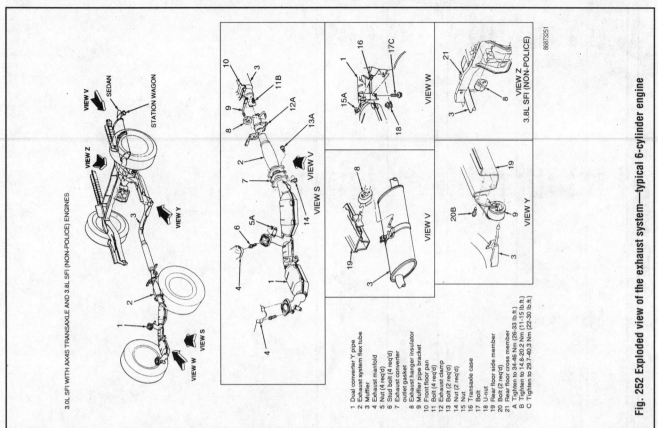

1 Dual converter Y pipe
2 Exhaust system flex tube
3 Muffler
4 Exhaust manifold
5 Nut (4 req'd)
6 Stud bolt (4 req'd)
7 Exhaust converter outlet gasket
8 Exhaust hanger insulator
9 Muffler pipe bracket
10 Front floor pan
11 Bolt (4 req'd)
12 Exhaust clamp
13 Bolt (2 req'd)
14 Nut (2 req'd)
15 Nut
16 Transaxle case
17 Bolt
18 U-nut
19 Rear floor side member
20 Bolt (2 req'd)
21 Rear floor cross member
A Tighten to 34-46 Nm (26-33 lb.ft.)
B Tighten to 14.8-20.2 Nm (11-15 lb.ft.)
C Tighten to 29.7-40.3 Nm (22-30 lb.ft.)

**Fig. 252 Exploded view of the exhaust system—typical 6-cylinder engine**

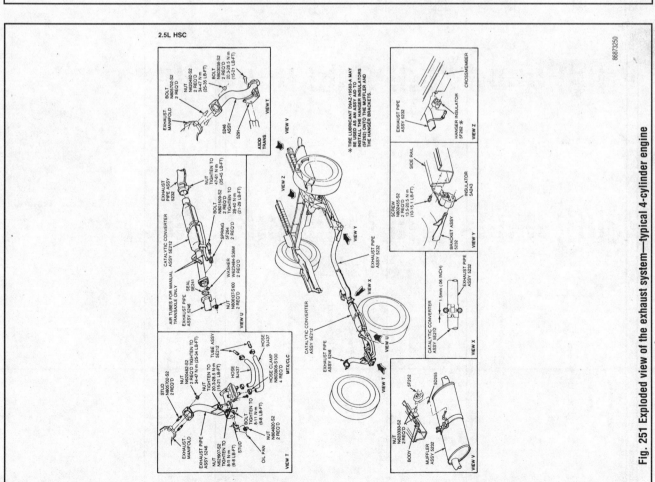

**Fig. 251 Exploded view of the exhaust system—typical 4-cylinder engine**

## TORQUE SPECIFICATIONS

| Component | | US | Metric |
|---|---|---|---|
| Cylinder Head | 2.5L (in two steps) | 52-59 ft. lbs. | 70-80 Nm |
| | 3.0L (in two steps) | 70-76 ft. lbs. | 95-103 Nm |
| | | 37 ft. lbs. | 50 Nm |
| | | 68 ft. lbs. | 92 Nm |
| | 3.0L/3.2L SHO (in two steps) | 36-51 ft. lbs. | 49-69 Nm |
| | | 62-69 ft. lbs. | 83-93 Nm |
| | 3.8L 1988-94 (in four steps) | 37 ft. lbs. | 50 Nm |
| | | 45 ft. lbs. | 60 Nm |
| | | 52 ft. lbs. | 70 Nm |
| | | 59 ft. lbs. | 80 Nm |
| | 1995 (in three steps) | 15 ft. lbs. | 20 Nm |
| | | 29 ft. lbs. | 40 Nm |
| | | 37 ft. lbs. | 50 Nm |
| Engine Coolant Temperature (ECT) Sensor | | 12-17 ft. lbs. | 16-23 Nm |
| Exhaust Manifold | 2.5L (in two steps) | 5-7 ft. lbs. | 7-10 Nm |
| | | 20-30 ft. lbs. | 27-41 Nm |
| | 3.0L | 15-22 ft. lbs. | 20-30 Nm |
| | 3.0L/3.2L SHO Left Side | 26-36 ft. lbs. | 35-52 Nm |
| | Right Side | 15-24 ft. lbs. | 20-32 Nm |
| | 3.8L | 15-22 ft. lbs. | 20-30 Nm |
| Intake Manifold | 2.5L | 15-22 ft. lbs. | 20-30 Nm |
| | 3.0L 1986-91 (in two steps) | 11 ft. lbs. | 15 Nm |
| | | 21 ft. lbs. | 28 Nm |
| | 1992-95 (in two steps) | 15-22 ft. lbs. | 20-30 Nm |
| | | 19-24 ft. lbs. | 26-32 Nm |
| | 3.0L/3.2L SHO | 11-17 ft. lbs. | 15-23 Nm |
| | 3.8L 1988-91 (in three steps) | 8 ft. lbs. | 11 Nm |
| | | 15 ft. lbs. | 20 Nm |
| | | 24 ft. lbs. | 32 Nm |
| | 1992-93 (in three steps) | 8 ft. lbs. | 11 Nm |
| | | 15 ft. lbs. | 20 Nm |
| | | 13 ft. lbs. | 18 Nm |
| | 1994-95 (in two steps) | 16 ft. lbs. | 22 Nm |
| Knock Sensor | | 21-29 ft. lbs. | 29-39 Nm |
| Oil Pan | 2.5L Oil Pan-to-Transaxle | 30-39 ft. lbs. | 41-53 Nm |
| | Pan Flange Bolts | 6-8 ft. lbs. | 8-11 Nm |
| | 3.0L (torque, then back-off and retighten) | 8 ft. lbs. | 11 Nm |
| | 3.0L/3.2L SHO | 11-17 ft. lbs. | 15-23 Nm |
| | 3.8L | 7-9 ft. lbs. | 9-12 Nm |
| Oil Pump | 2.5L | 15-22 ft. lbs. | 20-30 Nm |
| | 3.0L | 35 ft. lbs. | 48 Nm |

86873500

## TORQUE SPECIFICATIONS

| Component | | US | Metric |
|---|---|---|---|
| Oil Pump | 3.0L/3.2L SHO | 11-17 ft. lbs. | 15-23 Nm |
| | 3.8L 4 Large Bolts | 17-23 ft. lbs. | 23-32 Nm |
| | All Other Bolts | 6-8 ft. lbs. | 8-11 Nm |
| Rocker Arm/Valve Cover | 2.5L | 6-9 ft. lbs. | 8-12 Nm |
| | 3.0L 1986-90 | 9 ft. lbs | 12 Nm |
| | 1991-95 | 8-10 ft. lbs. | 10-14 Nm |
| | 3.0L/3.2L SHO | 7-12 ft. lbs. | 9.5-16 Nm |
| | 3.8L | 80-106 inch lbs. | 9-12 Nm |
| Rocker Arms | 2.5L (in two steps) | 6-8 ft. lbs. | 8-11 Nm |
| | | 20-26 ft. lbs. | 27-35 Nm |
| | 3.0L (in two steps) | 5-11 ft. lbs. | 7-15 Nm |
| | | 19-28 ft. lbs. | 26-38 Nm |
| Starter | | 44 inch lbs. | 5 Nm |
| Thermostat | 3.8L (in two steps) | 19-25 ft. lbs. | 25-35 Nm |
| | | 15-20 ft. lbs. | 20-27 Nm |
| | 2.5L | 12-18 ft. lbs. | 16-24 Nm |
| | 3.0L | 8-10 ft. lbs. | 10-14 Nm |
| | 3.0L/3.2L SHO | 5-8 ft. lbs. | 7-11 Nm |
| | 3.8L | 15-22 ft. lbs. | 20-30 Nm |
| Water Pump | 2.5L | 15-22 ft. lbs. | 20-30 Nm |
| | 3.0L | 15-22 ft. lbs. | 20-30 Nm |
| | Bolts 4, 5, 6, 7, 8, 9, 10 | 71-106 inch lbs. | 8-12 Nm |
| | Bolts 11, 12, 13, 14, 15 | 12-17 ft. lbs. | 16-23 Nm |
| | 3.0L/3.2L SHO | | |
| | 3.8L | 16 ft. lbs. | 21 Nm |

86873501

## ENGINE REBUILDING SPECIFICATIONS

| Component | | US | Metric |
|---|---|---|---|
| **Bore x Stroke** | | | |
| 2.5L | | 3.70 x 3.60 in. | 93.9 x 91.4 mm |
| 3.0L | | 3.50 x 3.15 in. | 88.9 x 80.0 mm |
| 3.0L SHO | | 3.50 x 3.15 in. | 88.9 x 80.0 mm |
| 3.2L SHO | | 3.62 x 3.15 in. | 91.8 x 80.0 mm |
| 3.8L | | 3.81 x 3.39 in. | 96.8 x 86.1 mm |
| **Camshaft End Play** | | | |
| 2.5L | | | |
| **Camshaft Journal-to-Bearing Clearance** | | | |
| 2.5L | | 0.0010-0.0030 in. | 0.0254-0.0762 mm |
| 3.0L | | 0.0010-0.0030 in. | 0.0254-0.0762 mm |
| 3.0L/3.2L SHO | | 0.0010-0.0026 in. | 0.0254-0.0660 mm |
| 3.8L | | 0.0010-0.0030 in. | 0.0254-0.0762 mm |
| **Camshaft Journal Diameter** | | | |
| 2.5L | | 2.0060-2.0080 in. | 20.095-51.003 mm |
| 3.0L | | 2.0074-2.0084 in. | 50.988-51.013 mm |
| 3.0L/3.2L SHO | | 1.2189-1.2195 in. | 30.960-30.975 mm |
| 3.8L | | 2.0505-2.0515 in. | 52.082-52.108 mm |
| **Camshaft Lobe Lift** | | | |
| 2.5L | Intake | 0.249 in. | 6.324 mm |
| | Exhaust | 0.239 in. | 6.070 mm |
| 3.0L | | | |
| 1986-91 | Intake | 0.260 in. | 6.604 mm |
| | Exhaust | 0.260 in. | 6.604 mm |
| 1992-95 | Intake | 0.2550-0.2600 in. | 6.477-6.604 mm |
| | Exhaust | 0.2550-0.2600 in. | 6.477-6.604 mm |
| 3.0L SHO | Intake | 0.3550 in. | 9.017 mm |
| | Exhaust | 0.3150 in. | 8.001 mm |
| 3.2L SHO | Intake | 0.3150 in. | 8.001 mm |
| | Exhaust | 0.3150 in. | 8.001 mm |
| 3.8L | Intake | 0.2400-0.2450 in. | 6.096-6.223 mm |
| | Exhaust | 0.2540-0.2590 in. | 6.452-6.579 mm |
| **Connecting Rod Oil Clearance** | | | |
| 2.5L | | 0.0008-0.0014 in. | 0.0203-0.0355 mm |
| 3.0L | | 0.0010-0.0014 in. | 0.0254-0.0355 mm |
| 3.0L/3.2L SHO | | 0.0009-0.0022 in. | 0.0229-0.0559 mm |
| 3.8L | | 0.0010-0.0014 in. | 0.0254-0.0355 mm |
| **Connecting Rod-to-Crankshaft Side Clearance** | | | |
| 2.5L | | 0.0035-0.0105 in. | 0.0889-0.2667 mm |
| 3.0L | | 0.0060-0.0140 in. | 0.1524-0.3556 mm |
| 3.0L SHO | | | |
| 1989-92 | | 0.0063-0.0123 in. | 0.1600-0.3124 mm |
| 1993-95 | | 0.0063-0.0138 in. | 0.1600-0.3505 mm |
| 3.2L SHO | | 0.0063-0.0138 in. | 0.1600-0.3505 mm |
| 3.8L | | 0.0047-0.0140 in. | 0.1194-0.3556 mm |

86873502

## ENGINE REBUILDING SPECIFICATIONS

| Component | US | Metric |
|---|---|---|
| **Connecting Rod Journal Diameter** | | |
| 2.5L | 2.1232-2.1240 in. | 53.929-53.949 mm |
| 3.0L | 2.1240 in. | 53.949 mm |
| 1986-87 | 2.1253-2.1261 in. | 53.982-54.002 mm |
| 1988-95 | 2.0463-2.0472 in. | 51.976-51.998 mm |
| 3.0L/3.2L SHO | | |
| 3.8L | 2.3103-2.3111 in. | 58.681-58.701 mm |
| **Crankshaft Endplay** | | |
| 2.5L | 0.0040-0.0080 in. | 0.1016-0.2032 mm |
| 3.0L | 0.0040-0.0080 in. | 0.1016-0.2032 mm |
| 3.0L/3.2L SHO | 0.0008-0.0087 in. | 0.0203-0.2209 mm |
| 3.8L | 0.0040-0.0080 in. | 0.1016-0.2032 mm |
| **Cylinder Bore Diameter** | | |
| 2.5L | 3.6790-3.6830 in. | 93.446-93.548 mm |
| 3.0L | 3.504 in. | 89.002 mm |
| 3.0L SHO | 3.5039-3.5051 in. | 88.999-89.029 mm |
| 3.2L SHO | 3.6220-3.6232 in. | 91.998-92.029 mm |
| 3.8L | 3.810 in. | 96.774 mm |
| **Cylinder Bore Max Taper** | | |
| 2.5L | 0.0100 in. | 0.2540 mm |
| 3.0L | 0.0020 in. | 0.5588 mm |
| 3.0L/3.2L SHO | 0.0008 in. | 0.0203 mm |
| 3.8L | 0.0020 in. | 0.0508 mm |
| **Cylinder Bore Out-Of-Round (Max.)** | | |
| 2.5L | 0.0048 in. | 0.1219 mm |
| 3.0L | 0.0020 in. | 0.0508 mm |
| 3.0L/3.2L SHO | 0.0008 in. | 0.0203 mm |
| 3.8L | 0.0020 in. | 0.0508 mm |
| **Main Bearing Journal Diameter** | | |
| 2.5L | 2.2489-2.2490 in. | 57.122-51.125 mm |
| 3.0L | 2.5190-2.5198 in. | 63.983-64.003 mm |
| 3.0L/3.2L SHO | 2.5187-2.5197 in. | 63.975-64.000 mm |
| 3.8L | 2.5190-2.5198 in. | 63.983-64.003 mm |
| **Main Bearing Clearance** | | |
| 2.5L | 0.0008-0.0015 in. | 0.0203-0.0381 mm |
| 3.0L | 0.0010-0.0014 in. | 0.0254-0.0356 mm |
| 3.0L/3.2L SHO | 0.0011-0.0022 in. | 0.0279-0.0559 mm |
| 3.8L | 0.0010-0.0014 in. | 0.0254-0.0356 mm |
| **Main Bearing Journal Runout (Max.)** | | |
| 2.5L | 0.0002 in. | 0.0050 mm |
| 3.0L | 0.0020 in. | 0.0508 mm |
| 3.0L/3.2L SHO | 0.0024 in. | 0.0609 mm |
| 3.8L | 0.0020 in. | 0.0508 mm |
| **Main Bearing Journal Taper (Max.)** | | |
| 2.5L | 0.0003 in. | 0.0076 mm |
| 3.0L | 0.0006 in. | 0.0152 mm |
| 3.0L/3.2L SHO | 0.0008 in. | 0.0203 mm |
| 3.8L | 0.0003 in. | 0.0076 mm |
| **Piston-to-Bore or Liner Clearance** | | |
| 2.5L | 0.0012-0.0022 in. | 0.0305-0.0559 mm |

86873503

## ENGINE REBUILDING SPECIFICATIONS

| Component | | US | Metric |
|---|---|---|---|
| Piston-to-Bore or Liner Clearance (cont.) | | | |
| 3.0L | | 0.0014-0.0022 in. | 0.0356-0.0559 mm |
| 3.0L/3.2L SHO | | 0.0012-0.0020 in. | 0.0305-0.0508 mm |
| 3.8L | | 0.0014-0.0032 in. | 0.0356-0.0813 mm |
| Piston Pin Diameter | | | |
| 2.5L | | 0.9124-0.9127 in. | |
| 3.0L | | 0.9119-0.9124 in. | |
| 3.0L SHO | | 0.8267-0.8271 in. | |
| 3.2L SHO | | 0.8660-0.8665 in. | |
| 3.8L | | 0.9122-0.9128 in. | |
| Piston Pin-to-Bore Clearance | | | |
| 2.5L | | 0.0002-0.0005 in. | 0.0050-0.0127 mm |
| 3.0L | | 0.0002-0.0005 in. | 0.0050-0.0127 mm |
| 3.0L/3.2L SHO | | -0.0002-0.00004 in. | -0.0050-0.0010 mm |
| 3.8L | | 0.0002-0.0005 in. | 0.0002-0.0005 mm |
| Piston Ring End Gap | | | |
| 2.5L | Top | 0.008-0.016 in. | 0.203-0.406 mm |
| | Bottom | 0.008-0.016 in. | 0.203-0.406 mm |
| | Oil | 0.015-0.055 in. | 0.381-1.397 mm |
| 3.0L | Top | 0.010-0.020 in. | 0.254-0.508 mm |
| | Bottom | 0.010-0.020 in. | 0.254-0.508 mm |
| | Oil | 0.010-0.049 in. | 0.254-1.245 mm |
| 3.0L SHO | Top | 0.012-0.018 in. | 0.305-0.457 mm |
| | Bottom | 0.012-0.018 in. | 0.305-0.457 mm |
| | Oil | 0.008-0.020 in. | 0.203-0.508 mm |
| 3.2L SHO | Top | 0.012-0.018 in. | 0.305-0.457 mm |
| | Bottom | 0.018-0.024 in. | 0.457-0.609 mm |
| | Oil | 0.008-0.020 in. | 0.203-0.508 mm |
| 3.8L | Top | 0.011-0.012 in. | 0.279-0.305 mm |
| | Bottom | 0.010-0.020 in. | 0.254-0.508 mm |
| | Oil | 0.015-0.058 in. | 0.381-1.473 mm |
| Piston Ring Side Clearance | | | |
| 2.5L | Top | 0.0020-0.0040 in. | 0.0508-0.1016 mm |
| | Bottom | 0.0020-0.0040 in. | 0.0508-0.1016 mm |
| 3.0L | Top | 0.0012-0.0031 in. | 0.0305-0.0787 mm |
| | Bottom | 0.0012-0.0031 in. | 0.0305-0.0787 mm |
| 3.0L SHO | Top | 0.0008-0.0024 in. | 0.0203-0.0609 mm |
| | Bottom | 0.0006-0.0022 in. | 0.0152-0.0559 mm |
| | Oil | 0.0024-0.0059 in. | 0.0609-0.1499 mm |
| 3.2L SHO | Top | 0.0016-0.0031 in. | 0.0406-0.0787 mm |
| | Bottom | 0.0008-0.0024 in. | 0.0203-0.0609 mm |

86873504

## ENGINE REBUILDING SPECIFICATIONS

| Component | | US | Metric |
|---|---|---|---|
| Piston Ring Side Clearance (cont.) | | | |
| 3.2L SHO | Oil | 0.0024-0.0059 in. | 0.0609-0.1499 mm |
| 3.8L | Top | 0.0016-0.0034 in. | 0.0406-0.0863 mm |
| | Bottom | 0.0016-0.0034 in. | 0.0406-0.0863 mm |
| Valve Face Angle | | | |
| 2.5L | | 45 degrees | |
| 3.0L | | 44 degrees | |
| 3.0L/3.2L SHO | | 45.5 degrees | |
| 3.8L | | 45.8 degrees | |
| Valve Seat Angle | | | |
| 2.5L | | 45 degrees | |
| 3.0L | | 45 degrees | |
| 3.0L/3.2L SHO | | 45 degrees | |
| 3.8L | | 44.5 degrees | |
| Valve Seat Runout | | | |
| 2.5L | | 0.0012 in. | 0.0305 mm |
| 3.0L | | 0.0010 in. | 0.0254 mm |
| 3.8L | | 0.0030 in. | 0.0762 mm |
| Valve Spring Pressure (closed) | | | |
| 2.5L | | 182 lbs. @ 1.13 in. | 82 kg @ 28.7 mm |
| 3.0L | 1986-87 | 185 lbs. @ 1.11 in. | 84 kg @ 28.2 mm |
| | 1988-95 | 180 lbs. @ 1.16 in. | 82 kg @ 29.5 mm |
| 3.0L/3.2L SHO | | 121 lbs. @ 1.19 in. | 55 kg @ 30.2 mm |
| 3.8L | | 220 lbs. @ 1.18 in. | 99 kg @ 29.9 mm |
| Valve Spring Free Length | | | |
| 2.5L | | 1.76 in. | 44.70 mm |
| 3.0L | | 1.84 in. | 46.74 mm |
| 3.0L/3.2L SHO | | 1.76 in. | 44.70 mm |
| 3.8L | | 1.97 in. | 50.04 mm |
| Valve Spring Installed Height | | | |
| 2.5L | | 1.49 in. | 37.85 mm |
| 3.0L | | 1.58 in. | 40.13 mm |
| 3.8L | | 1.97 in. | 50.04 mm |
| Valve Stem-to-Guide Clearance | | | |
| 2.5L | Intake | 0.0018 in. | 0.0457 mm |
| | Exhaust | 0.0023 in. | 0.0584 mm |
| 3.0L | Intake | 0.0001-0.0028 in. | 0.0025-0.0711 mm |
| | Exhaust | 0.0015-0.0033 in. | 0.0381-0.0838 mm |
| 3.0L/3.2L SHO | Intake | 0.0010-0.0023 in. | 0.0254-0.0584 mm |
| | Exhaust | 0.0012-0.0025 in. | 0.0304-0.0635 mm |
| 3.8L | Intake | 0.0010-0.0028 in. | 0.0254-0.0711 mm |
| | Exhaust | 0.0015-0.0033 in. | 0.0381-0.0838 mm |

86873505

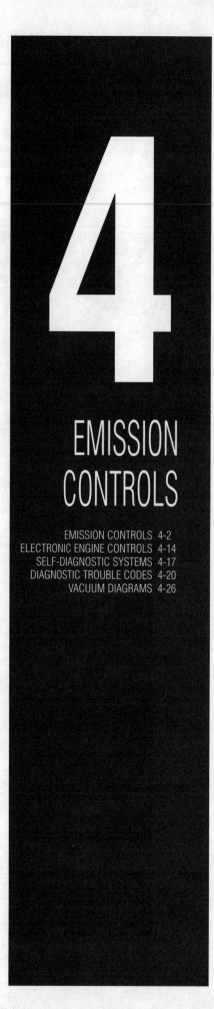

# 4

# EMISSION
# CONTROLS

## EMISSION CONTROLS

**See Figure 1**

There are three sources of automotive pollutants: crankcase fumes, exhaust gases and gasoline evaporation. The pollutants formed from these substances can be grouped into three categories: unburned hydrocarbons (HC), carbon monoxide (CO) and oxides of nitrogen ($NO_x$). The equipment that is used to limit these pollutants is commonly called emission control equipment.

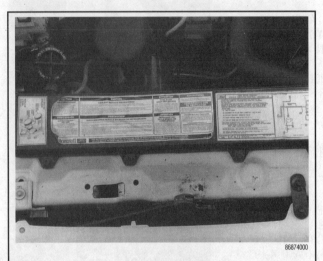

Fig. 1 The vehicle emission control information label includes instructions for engine control system adjustment

## Positive Crankcase Ventilation (PCV) System

### OPERATION

▶ **See Figures 2 and 3**

The Positive Crankcase Ventilation (PCV) system is used on all vehicles covered by this manual. The PCV system vents harmful combustion blow-by fumes from the engine crankcase into the engine air intake for burning with the fuel and air mixture. The PCV system maximizes oil cleanliness by venting moisture and corrosive fumes from the crankcase.

All of the vehicles covered by this manual, except for the 3.0L and the 3.2L SHO engines, utilize a PCV valve. The PCV valve limits the fresh air intake to suit the engine demand and also serves to prevent combustion backfiring into the crankcase. The PCV valve controls the amount of blow-by vapors pulled into the intake manifold from the crankcase. It also acts as

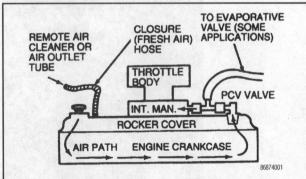

Fig. 2 Typical Taurus Positive Crankcase Ventilation (PCV) system schematic

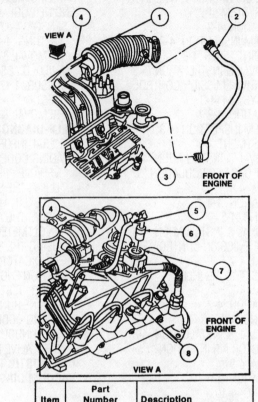

| Item | Part Number | Description |
|------|-------------|-------------|
| 1 | 9B659 | Air Cleaner Outlet Tube |
| 2 | 6853 | Crankcase Ventilation Hose |
| 3 | 6582 | Valve Cover |
| 4 | 9E926 | Throttle Body |
| 5 | 6853 | Crankcase Ventilation Hose |
| 6 | 6A666 | Positive Crankcase Ventilation Valve |
| 7 | 6A892 | Crankcase Ventilation Grommet |
| 8 | 9E926 | Throttle Body |

Fig. 3 PCV system components—3.0L shown (others similar)

a one-way check valve that prevents air from entering the crankcase in the opposite direction.

The PCV system on the SHO vehicles is unique because is does not use a PCV valve. Instead, the crankcase gases flow through an oil separator to three ports in the throttle body. Fresh air for the PCV system is supplied from another port on the throttle body to the cylinder head cover. Under various throttle conditions, the air and crankcase gases flow differently through the ports in the throttle body.

On some engine applications, the PCV system is connected with the evaporative emission system. Do not remove the PCV system from the engine, as doing so will adversely affect fuel economy and engine ventilation, with resultant shortening of engine life.

The components used in the PCV valve system consist of the PCV valve (or tube as in SHO applications), the rubber mounting grommet in the valve cover, the nipple in the air intake system and the necessary connecting hoses.

### SYSTEM INSPECTION

1. Visually inspect the components of the PCV system. Check for rough idle, slow starting, high oil consumption and loose, leaking, clogged or damaged hoses.

2. Check the fresh air supply hose and the PCV hose for air leakage or flow restriction caused by loose engagement, hose splitting, cracking, kinking, nipple damage, poor rubber grommet fit or any other damage.

3. If a component is suspected as the obvious cause of a malfunction, correct the cause before proceeding to the next step.

4. If all checks are okay, proceed to the pinpoint tests.

## PINPOINT TESTS

1. Remove the PCV valve from the valve cover grommet and shake the valve. If the valve rattles when shaken, reinstall and proceed to Step 2. If the valve does not rattle, it is sticking and should be replaced.

2. Start the engine and bring to normal operating temperature.

3. On the 2.5L engine, remove the corrugated hose from the oil separator nipple. On all other engines, disconnect the hose from the remote air cleaner or air outlet tube.

4. Place a stiff piece of paper over the nipple or hose end and wait 1 minute. If vacuum holds the paper in place, the system is okay; reconnect the hose. If the paper is not held in place, the system is plugged or the evaporative emission valve, if so equipped, is leaking. If the evaporative emission valve is suspected of leaking, proceed to Step 5.

5. Disconnect the evaporative hose, if equipped, and cap the connector.

6. Place a stiff piece of paper over the hose/nipple, as in Step 4 and wait 1 minute. If vacuum holds the paper in place, proceed to evaporative emission system testing. If the paper is not held in place, check for vacuum leaks/obstruction in the system: oil cap, PCV valve, hoses, cut grommets, the oil separator on the 2.5L engine and valve cover for bolt torque/gasket leak.

## REMOVAL & INSTALLATION

1. Remove the PCV valve from the mounting grommet in the valve cover.

2. Disconnect the valve from the PCV hose and remove the valve from the vehicle.

3. Installation is the reverse of the removal procedure.

## Evaporative Emission Control (EEC) System

▶ **See Figure 4**

### OPERATION

The evaporative emission control system prevents the escape of fuel vapors to the atmosphere under hot soak and engine off conditions by storing the vapors in a carbon canister. Then, with the engine warm and running, the system controls the purging of stored vapors from the canister to the engine, where they are efficiently burned.

Evaporative emission control components consist of the carbon canister, purge valve(s), vapor valve, rollover vent valve, check valve and the necessary lines. All vehicles may not share all components.

The carbon canister contains vapor absorbent material to facilitate the storage of fuel vapors. Fuel vapors flow from the fuel tank to the canister, where they are stored until purged to the engine for burning.

The purge valves control the flow of fuel vapor from the carbon canister to the engine. Purge valves are either vacuum or electrically controlled. When electrically controlled, a purge valve is known as a purge solenoid. A vehicle may be equipped with a vacuum purge valve or purge solenoid or a combination of the two. Purging occurs when the engine is at operating temperature and off idle.

The vapor valve is located on or near the fuel tank. Its function is to prevent fuel from flooding the carbon canister. The vapor valve incorporates the rollover valve. In the event of a vehicle rollover, the valve blocks the vapor line automatically to prevent fuel leakage.

The check valve is located in the fuel filler cap or on the underside of the vehicle. Its function is to protect the fuel tank from heat build-up rupture and cool-down collapse by allowing air to pass in or out of the tank to equalize pressure. On cool-down, air enters either at the carbon canister vent or at the check valve.

## SYSTEM INSPECTION

1. Visually inspect the components of the evaporative emission system. Check for the following, as applicable:
- Discharged battery
- Damaged connectors
- Damaged insulation
- Malfunctioning ECU
- Damaged air flow meter or speed sensor
- Inoperative solenoids
- Fuel odor or leakage
- Damaged vacuum or fuel vapor lines
- Loose or poor line connections
- Poor driveability during engine warm-up

2. Check the wiring and connectors for the solenoids, vane air flow meter, speed sensor and ECU, as applicable, for looseness, corrosion, damage or other problems. This must be done with the engine fully warmed up so as to activate the purging controls.

3. Check the fuel tank, fuel vapor lines, vacuum lines and connections for looseness, pinching, leakage, damage or other obvious cause for malfunction.

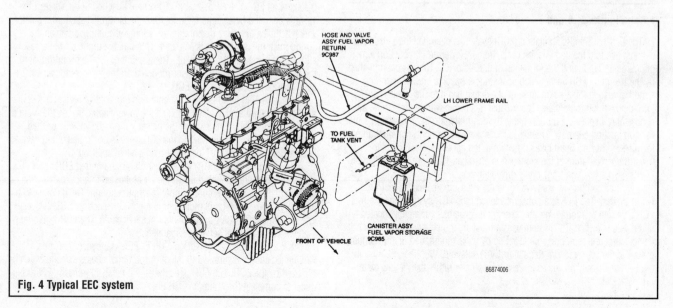

HOSE AND VALVE ASSY FUEL VAPOR RETURN 9C987

LH LOWER FRAME RAIL

TO FUEL TANK VENT

CANISTER ASSY FUEL VAPOR STORAGE 9C985

FRONT OF VEHICLE

86874006

**Fig. 4 Typical EEC system**

4. If fuel line, vacuum line or orifice blockage is suspected as the obvious cause of an observed malfunction, correct the cause before proceeding further.

## ADJUSTMENT

### Carbon Canister

There are no moving parts and nothing to wear in the canister. Check for loose, missing cracked or broken connections and parts. There should be no liquid in the canister.

## REMOVAL & INSTALLATION

### Carbon Canister

1. Disconnect the negative battery cable.
2. Detach the vapor hoses from the carbon canister.
3. Remove the canister mounting bolts and/or retaining straps, then remove the canister. The 3.0L Flexible Fuel engine uses four canisters mounted under the rear floor pan.
4. Installation is the reverse of the removal procedure.

### Purge Valves

1. Disconnect the negative battery cable.
2. Disconnect the vacuum hose or the electrical connector from the purge valve.
3. Disconnect the vapor hoses and remove the purge valve from the vehicle.
4. Installation is the reverse of the removal procedure.

### Vapor Valve

1. Disconnect the negative battery cable.
2. Raise and safely support the vehicle. Remove the fuel tank to gain access to the vapor valve.
3. Disconnect the vapor hoses from the vapor valve.
4. Remove the vapor valve mounting screws and the vapor valve from the underside of the vehicle, or remove the vapor valve from the fuel tank, as necessary.
5. Installation is the reverse of the removal procedure.

## Exhaust Gas Recirculation System

### OPERATION

#### ♦ See Figures 5, 6 and 7

The Exhaust Gas Recirculation (EGR) system is designed to reintroduce exhaust gas into the combustion cycle, thereby lowering combustion temperatures and reducing the formation of nitrous oxide. This is accomplished by the use of an EGR valve which opens under specific engine operating conditions, to admit a small amount of exhaust gas into the intake manifold, below the throttle plate. The exhaust gas mixes with the incoming air charge and displaces a portion of the oxygen in the air/fuel mixture entering the combustion chamber. The exhaust gas does not support combustion of the air/fuel mixture but it takes up volume, the net effect of which is to lower the temperature of the combustion chamber. There are a few different EGR systems used on front wheel drive vehicles.

The most commonly used system is the Pressure Feedback Electronic (PFE) system. The PFE is a subsonic closed loop EGR system that controls EGR flow rate by monitoring the pressure drop across a remotely located sharp-edged orifice. The system uses a pressure transducer as the feedback device and controlled pressure is varied by valve modulation using vacuum output of the EGR Vacuum Regulator (EVR) solenoid. With the PFE system, the EGR valve only serves as a pressure regulator rather than a flow metering device.

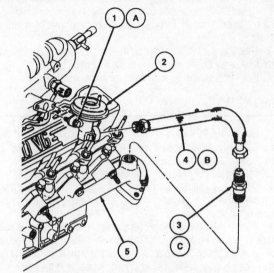

| Item | Part Number | Description |
|------|-------------|-------------|
| 1A | N804073-S8 | Bolt (2 Req'd) |
| 2 | 9D475 | EGR Valve |
| 3C | 9F485 | EGR Valve Tube to Manifold Connector |
| 4B | 9D477 | EGR Valve to Exhaust Manifold Tube |
| 5 | 9430 | Exhaust Manifold |
| A | | Tighten to 20-30 N·m (15-22 Lb-Ft) |
| B | | Tighten to 35-45 N·m (26-33 Lb-Ft) |
| C | | Tighten to 45-65 N·m (33-48 Lb-Ft) |

86874024

**Fig. 5 EGR system and related components for the 3.0L engine (except SHO)**

The Differential Pressure Feedback Electronic (DPFE) EGR system operates in the same manner except it directly monitors the pressure drop across the metering orifice. This allows for a more accurate assessment of EGR flow requirements.

The Electronic EGR (EEGR) valve system is used on some vehicles equipped with the 2.5L engine. An electronic EGR valve is required in EEC systems where EGR flow is controlled according to computer demands by means of an EGR Valve Position (EVP) sensor attached to the valve. The valve is operated by a vacuum signal from the electronic vacuum regulator which actuates the valve diaphragm. As supply vacuum overcomes the spring load, the diaphragm is actuated. This lifts the pintle off of its seat allowing exhaust gas to recirculate. The amount of flow is proportional to the pintle position. The EVP sensor mounted on the valve sends an electrical signal of its position to the ECU.

The ported EGR valve is the most common form of EGR valve. It is operated by a vacuum signal which actuates the valve diaphragm. As the vacuum increases sufficiently to overcome the power spring, the valve is opened allowing EGR flow. The vacuum to the EGR valve is controlled using devices such as the EVR or the BVT, depending on system application.

The Electronic EGR (EEGR) valve is similar to the ported EGR valve. It is also vacuum operated, lifting the pintle off of its seat to allow exhaust gas to recirculate when the vacuum signal is strong enough. The difference lies in the EVP sensor, which is mounted on top of the electronic EGR valve. The electronic EGR valve assembly is not serviceable. The EVP sensor and the EGR valve must be serviced separately.

The Pressure Feedback Electronic (PFE) EGR Transducer converts a varying exhaust pressure signal into a proportional analog voltage which is digitized by the ECU. The ECU uses the signal received from the PFE transducer to complete the optimum EGR flow.

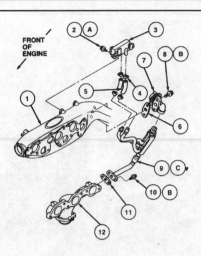

| Item | Part Number | Description |
|------|-------------|-------------|
| 1 | 9424 | Intake Manifold |
| 2A | 90105-06531 | Bolt (2 Req'd) |
| 3 | 9J460 | EGR Pressure Valve Sensor |
| 4 | — | Clamp (4 Req'd) (Part of 9P761) |
| 5 | 9P761 | EGR Pressure Valve Sensor Hose (2 Req'd) |
| 6 | 9D476 | EGR Valve Gasket |
| 7 | 9D475 | EGR Valve |
| 8B | 90119-08151 | Bolt (2 Req'd) |
| 9C | 9D477 | EGR Valve to Exhaust Manifold Tube |
| 10B | 90119-08146 | Bolt (2 Req'd) |
| 11 | 9F470 | EGR Valve Tube Inlet Gasket |
| 12 | 9430 | Exhaust Manifold |
| A | | Tighten to 2-3 N·m (18-27 Lb-In) |
| B | | Tighten to 15-23 N·m (11-17 Lb-Ft) |
| C | | Tighten to 45-65 N·m (33-48 Lb-Ft) |

86874025

**Fig. 6 Exploded view of the EGR valve and related components—3.0L and 3.2L SHO engines**

| Item | Part Number | Description |
|------|-------------|-------------|
| 1 | 9J460 | EGR Pressure Valve Sensor |
| 2 | 9D475 | EGR Valve |
| 3 | 9430 | Exhaust Manifold |
| 4A | 9F485 | EGR Valve Tube to Manifold Connector |
| 5B | 9D477 | EGR Valve to Exhaust Manifold Tube |
| A | | Tighten to 45-65 N·m (33-48 Lb-Ft) |
| B | | Tighten to 35-45 N·m (26-33 Lb-Ft) |

86874026

**Fig. 7 View of the EGR system components—late model 3.8L engine shown**

The EGR Valve Position (EVP) sensor provides the ECU with a signal indicating the position of the EGR valve. The Back pressure Variable Transducer (BVT) controls the vacuum input to the EGR valve based on the engine operating condition.

The EGR Vacuum Regulator (EVR) is an electromagnetic device which controls vacuum output to the EGR valve. The EVR replaces the EGR solenoid vacuum vent valve assembly. An electric current in the coil induces a magnetic field in the armature. The magnetic field pulls the disk back, closing the vent and increasing the vacuum level. The vacuum source is either manifold or vacuum. As the duty cycle is increased, an increased vacuum signal goes to the EGR valve.

### TESTING

#### Back pressure Variable Transducer (BVT)

1. Make sure all vacuum hoses are correctly routed and securely attached. Replace cracked, crimped or broken hoses.
2. Make sure there is no vacuum to the EGR valve at idle with the engine at normal operating temperature.
3. Connect a suitable tachometer.
4. Detach the idle air bypass valve electrical connector.
5. Remove the vacuum supply hose from the EGR valve nipple and plug the hose.
6. Start the engine and let it idle with the transaxle selector lever in Neutral. Check the engine idle speed and adjust to the proper specification, if necessary.
7. Slowly apply 5–10 in. Hg (17–34 kPa) of vacuum to the EGR valve vacuum nipple using a suitable hand vacuum pump.
8. When vacuum is fully applied to the EGR valve, check for the following:

   a. If idle speed drops more than 100 rpm or if the engine stalls, perform the next step. Otherwise, check for a vacuum leak at the EGR valve, and, if a leak is found, replace the valve.

   b. If the EGR passages are blocked, clean the EGR valve using a suitable cleaner.

   c. Remove the vacuum from the EGR valve. If the idle speed does not return to normal specifications (or within 25 rpm), check for contamination; clean the valve.

   d. If the symptom still exists, replace the EGR valve.

9. Attach the idle air bypass valve electrical connector.
10. Unplug and reconnect the EGR vacuum supply hose.
11. Disconnect the vacuum connection at the BVT.
12. Gently blow into the hose to port C until the relief valve closes and at the same time apply 5–10 in. Hg (17–34 kPa) of vacuum to port E with the hand vacuum pump. Port E should hold vacuum as long as there is pressure on port C.
13. Apply a minimum of 5–10 in. Hg (17–34 kPa) of vacuum to ports B and C using the hand vacuum pump. Ports B and C should hold vacuum.
14. Replace the BVT if any of the ports do not hold vacuum.
15. Reconnect the vacuum at the BVT.
16. If neither the EGR valve nor the BVT were replaced, the system is okay.

### REMOVAL & INSTALLATION

#### Ported EGR Valve

1. Disconnect the negative battery cable.
2. Detach the vacuum line(s) and/or electrical connector(s) from the EGR valve.
3. Unfasten the mounting bolts, then remove the EGR valve. Remove all old gasket material.

**To install:**

4. Using a new gasket, install the EGR valve, then secure using the retaining bolts.

5. Attach any vacuum lines or electrical connectors disengaged during removal.

6. Connect the negative battery cable.

### Electronic EGR (EEGR) Valve

▶ **See Figures 8 thru 13**

1. Disconnect the negative battery cable.
2. Disengage the the electrical connector from the EVP sensor.
3. Disconnect the vacuum line from the EGR valve.
4. Remove the mounting bolts and remove the EGR valve.
5. Remove the EVP sensor from the EGR valve.
6. Remove all old gasket material from the mating surfaces.

**To install:**

7. Install the EVP sensor to the EGR valve.
8. Using a new gasket, install the EGR valve in the vehicle, then secure using the retaining bolts.
9. Connect the vacuum line to the EGR valve, then engage the electrical connector.
10. Connect the negative battery cable.

Fig. 10 Disconnect the mounting bolts from the EGR valve

Fig. 8 Disengage the electrical connector from the EVP sensor—early model 2.5L engine

Fig. 11 Remove the mounting bolts from the EGR valve

Fig. 9 Disconnect the vacuum line from the EGR valve

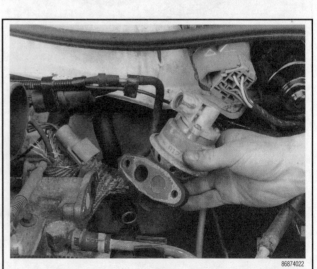

Fig. 12 Remove the EGR valve from the vehicle—early model engine shown

**Fig. 13 When installing the EGR valve, be sure to remove the old gasket and install a new one**

## Pressure Feedback Electronic (PFE) EGR Transducer

1. Disconnect the negative battery cable.
2. Separate the electrical connector and the exhaust pressure line from the transducer.
3. Remove the transducer from the vehicle.

**To install:**

4. Install the transducer, then engage the electrical connector and connect the exhaust pressure line to the transducer.
5. Connect the negative battery cable.

## EGR Valve Position (EVP) Sensor

▶ **See Figure 14**

1. Disconnect the negative battery cable.
2. Disengage the electrical connector from the sensor.
3. Disconnect the sensor mounting nuts, then remove the sensor from the EGR valve.

**To install:**

4. Install the sensor on the EGR valve, then secure using the mounting nuts.
5. Engage the electrical connector to the sensor, then connect the negative battery cable.

## Back pressure Variable Transducer (BVT)

1. Disconnect the negative battery cable.
2. Disconnect the vacuum lines from the BVT.
3. Remove the BVT from its mounting position, then remove it from the vehicle.

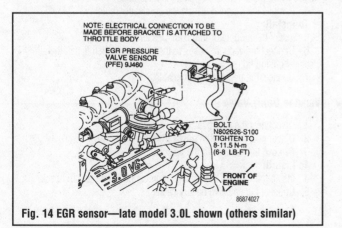

**Fig. 14 EGR sensor—late model 3.0L shown (others similar)**

**To install:**

4. Install the BVT in its mounting position.
5. Connect the vacuum lines to the BVT, then connect the negative battery cable.

## EGR Vacuum Regulator (EVR)

▶ **See Figure 15**

1. Disconnect the negative battery cable.
2. Disengage the electrical connector and the vacuum lines from the regulator.
3. Remove the regulator mounting bolts, then remove the regulator from the vehicle.

**To install:**

4. Install the regulator in the vehicle, then secure using the retaining bolts.
5. Connect the vacuum lines, then engage the electrical connector to the regulator.
6. Connect the negative battery cable.

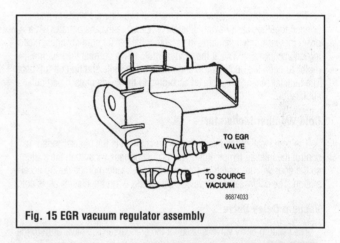

**Fig. 15 EGR vacuum regulator assembly**

## Exhaust Emission Control System

The exhaust emission control system begins at the air intake and ends at the tailpipe. Most vehicles are equipped with a thermostatic air inlet system, exhaust catalyst, and either a thermactor air injection system or pulse air injection system.

## Thermostatic Air Inlet System

▶ **See Figure 16**

### OPERATION

Most of the engines covered by this manual utilize the thermostatic air inlet system. The thermostatic air inlet system regulates the air inlet temperature by drawing in air from a cool air source, as well as heated air from a heat shroud which is mounted on the exhaust manifold. The system consists of the following components: duct and valve assembly, heat shroud, bimetal sensor, cold weather modulator, vacuum delay valve and the necessary vacuum lines and air ducts. All vehicles do not share all components.

### Duct and Valve Assembly

The duct and valve assembly which regulates the air flow from the cool and heated air sources is located either inside the air cleaner or mounted on the air cleaner. The flow is regulated by means of a door that is operated by a vacuum motor. The operation of the motor is controlled by delay valves, temperature sensors and other vacuum control systems. All vary with each application and engine calibration.

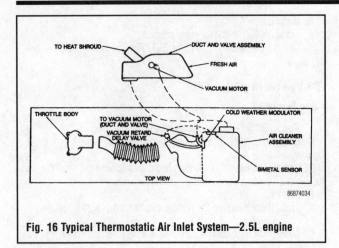

**Fig. 16 Typical Thermostatic Air Inlet System—2.5L engine**

### Bimetal Sensor

The core of the bimetal sensor is made of two different types of metals bonded together, each having different temperature expansion rates. At a given increase in temperature, the shape of the sensor core changes, bleeding off vacuum available at the vacuum motor. This permits the vacuum motor to open the duct door to allow fresh air in while shutting off full heat. The bimetal sensor is calibrated according to the needs of each particular application.

### Cold Weather Modulator

The cold weather modulator is used in addition to the bimetal sensor to control the inlet air temperature. The modulator traps vacuum in the system, so the door will not switch to cold air when the vacuum drops during acceleration. The cold weather modulator only works when the outside air is cold.

### Vacuum Delay Valve

The vacuum delay valve is used for the gradual release of vacuum to the vacuum motor.

## TESTING

### Duct and Valve Assembly

1. If the duct door is in the closed to fresh air position, remove the hose from the air cleaner vacuum motor.
2. The door should go to the open to fresh air position. If it sticks or binds, service or replace, as required.
3. If the door is in the open to fresh air position, check the door by applying 8 in. Hg (27 kPa) or greater of vacuum to the vacuum motor.
4. The door should move freely to the closed to fresh air position. If it binds or sticks, service or replace, as required.

➡Make sure the vacuum motor is functional before changing the duct and valve assembly.

### Bimetal Sensor

1. Bring the temperature of the bimetal sensor below 75°F (24°C) and apply 16 in. Hg (54 kPa) of vacuum with a vacuum pump at the vacuum source port of the sensor.
2. The duct door should stay closed. If not, replace the bimetal sensor.
3. The sensor will bleed off vacuum to allow the duct door to open and let in fresh air at or above the following temperatures:
   a. Brown: 75°F (24°C)
   b. Pink, black or red: 90°F (32.2°C)
   c. Blue, yellow or green: 105°F (40.6°C)

➡Do not cool the bimetal sensor while the engine is running.

### Cold Weather Modulator

A 16 in. Hg (54 kPa) vacuum applied to the motor side of the modulator holds or leaks as follows:
- Black: holds below 20°F (&minus;6.7°C) and leaks above 35°F (1.7°C)
- Blue: holds below 40°F (4.4°C) and leaks above 55°F (12.8°C)
- Green: holds below 50°F (10°C) and leaks above 76°F (24.4°C)
- Yellow: holds above 65°F (18.3°C) and leaks below 50°F (10°C)

### Vacuum Delay Valve

1. Connect a hand vacuum pump to the vacuum delay valve.
2. Valves with 1 side black or white and the other side colored are good if vacuum can be built up in 1 direction but not the other direction and if that built up vacuum can be seen to slowly decrease.
3. Valves with both sides the same color are good if vacuum can be built up in both directions before visibly decreasing.

➡Be careful in order to prevent oil or dirt from getting into the valve.

## REMOVAL & INSTALLATION

### Duct and Valve Assembly

1. Disconnect the negative battery cable.
2. Disconnect the vacuum hose from the vacuum motor.
3. Separate the vacuum motor from the vacuum operated door and remove the vacuum motor.
   **To install:**
4. Install the motor to the vacuum operated door.
5. Connect the vacuum hose to the vacuum motor.
6. Connect the negative battery cable.

### Bimetal Sensor

1. Disconnect the negative battery cable.
2. Remove the air cleaner housing lid to gain access to the sensor.
3. Disconnect the vacuum hoses from the sensor. It may be necessary to move the air cleaner housing to accomplish this.
4. Remove the sensor from the air cleaner housing.
   **To install:**
5. Install the sensor in the air cleaner housing.
6. Connect the vacuum hoses to the sensor, then install the air cleaner housing lid.
7. Connect the negative battery cable.

### Cold Weather Modulator

1. Disconnect the negative battery cable.
2. Remove the air cleaner housing lid to gain access to the modulator.
3. Disconnect the vacuum hoses from the modulator. It may be necessary to move the air cleaner housing to accomplish this.
4. Remove the modulator from the air cleaner housing.
   **To install:**
5. Install the modulator in the air cleaner housing.
6. Connect the vacuum hoses to the modulator, then install the air cleaner housing lid.
7. Connect the negative battery cable.

### Vacuum Delay Valve

1. Disconnect the negative battery cable.
2. Disconnect the vacuum hoses from the delay valve.
3. Remove the valve from the vehicle.
   **To install:**
4. Install the valve in the vehicle, then connect the vacuum hoses.
5. Connect the negative battery cable.

## Thermactor Air Injection System

### OPERATION

**▶ See Figures 17 and 18**

A conventional thermactor air injection system is used on some vehicles equipped with the 3.8L engine. The system reduces hydrocarbon and carbon monoxide content of the exhaust gases by continuing the combustion of unburned gases after they leave the combustion chamber. This is done by injecting fresh air into the hot exhaust stream leaving the exhaust ports, or into the catalyst. At this point, the fresh air mixes with hot exhaust gases to promote further oxidation of both the hydrocarbons and carbon monoxide, thereby reducing their concentration, and converting some of them into harmless carbon dioxide and water. During highway cruising and WOT operation, the thermactor air is dumped to atmosphere to prevent overheating in the exhaust system.

A typical air injection system consists of an air supply pump and filter, air bypass valve, check valves, air manifold, air hoses and air control valve.

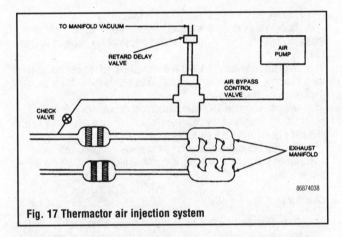

**Fig. 17 Thermactor air injection system**

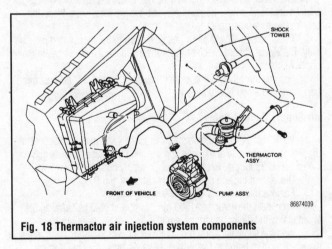

**Fig. 18 Thermactor air injection system components**

### Air Supply Pump

The air supply pump is a belt-driven, positive displacement, vane-type pump that provides air for the thermactor system. It is available in 19 and 22 cu. in. (311.35 and 360.5cc) sizes, either of which may be driven with different pulley ratios for different applications. The pump receives air from a remote silencer filter on the rear side of the engine air cleaner attached to the pump's air inlet nipple or through an impeller-type centrifugal filter fan.

### Air Bypass Valve

The air bypass valve supplies air to the exhaust system with medium and high applied vacuum signals when the engine is at normal operating temperature. With low or no vacuum applied, the pumped air is dumped through the silencer ports of the valve or through the dump port.

### Air Check Valve

**▶ See Figure 19**

The air check valve is a one-way valve that allows thermactor air to pass into the exhaust system while preventing exhaust gases from passing in the opposite direction.

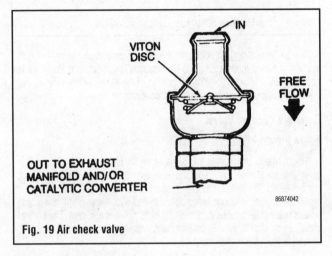

**Fig. 19 Air check valve**

### Air Supply Control Valve

**▶ See Figure 20**

The air supply control valve directs air pump output to the exhaust manifold or downstream to the catalyst system, depending upon the engine control strategy. It may also be used to dump air to the air cleaner or dump silencer.

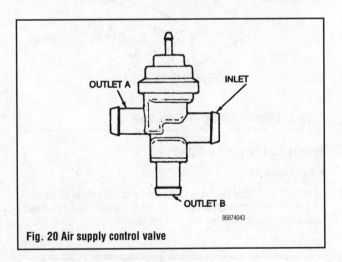

**Fig. 20 Air supply control valve**

### Combination Air Bypass/Air Control Valve

**▶ See Figure 21**

The combination air control/bypass valve combines the secondary air bypass and air control functions. The valve is located in the air supply line between the air pump and the upstream/downstream air supply check valves.

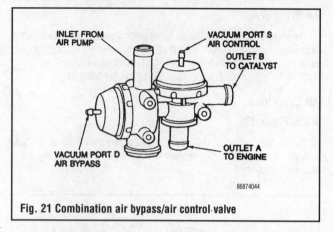

Fig. 21 Combination air bypass/air control valve

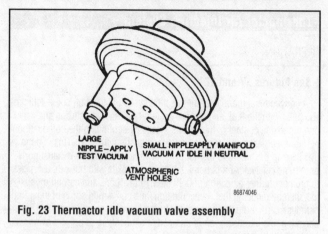

Fig. 23 Thermactor idle vacuum valve assembly

The air bypass portion controls the flow of thermactor air to the exhaust system or allows thermactor air to be bypassed to atmosphere. When air is not being bypassed, the air control portion of the valve switches the air injection point to either an upstream or downstream location.

### Solenoid Vacuum Valve

▶ See Figure 22

The normally closed solenoid valve assembly consists of 2 vacuum ports with an atmospheric vent. The valve assembly can be with or without control bleed. The outlet port of the valve is opened to atmospheric vent and closed to the inlet port when de-energized. When energized, the outlet port is opened to the inlet port and closed to atmospheric vent. The control bleed is provided to prevent contamination entering the solenoid valve assembly from the intake manifold.

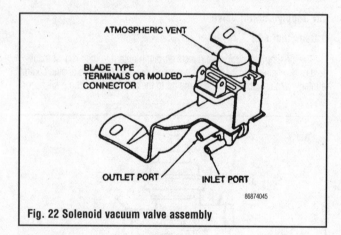

Fig. 22 Solenoid vacuum valve assembly

### Thermactor Idle Vacuum (TIV) Valve

▶ See Figure 23

The TIV valve vents the vacuum signal to the atmosphere when the preset manifold vacuum or pressure is exceeded. It is used to divert thermactor airflow during cold starts to control exhaust backfire.

## TESTING

### Air Supply Pump

1. Check belt tension and adjust if needed.

➡ Do not pry on the pump to adjust the belt. The aluminum housing is likely to collapse.

2. Disconnect the air supply hose from the bypass control valve.

3. The pump is operating properly if airflow is felt at the pump outlet and the flow increases as engine speed increases.

### Air Bypass Valve

1. Disconnect the air supply hose at the valve outlet.
2. Remove the vacuum line to check that a vacuum signal is present at the vacuum nipple. There must be vacuum present at the nipple before proceeding.
3. With the engine at 1500 rpm and the vacuum line connected to the vacuum nipple, air pump supply air should be heard and felt at the air bypass valve outlet.
4. With the engine at 1500 rpm, disconnect the vacuum line. Air at the outlet should be significantly decreased or shut off. Air pump supply air should be heard or felt at the silencer ports or at the dump port.
5. If the air bypass valve does not successfully complete these tests, check the air pump. If the air pump is operating properly, replace the air bypass valve.

### Check Valve

1. Visually inspect the thermactor system hoses, tubes, control valve(s) and check valve(s) for leaks that may be due to the backflow of exhaust gas. If holes are found and/or traces of exhaust gas products are evident, the check valve may be suspect.
2. Check valves should allow free flow of air in the incoming direction only. The valves should check or block the free flow of exhaust gas in the opposite direction.
3. Replace the valve if air does not flow as indicated or if exhaust gas backflows in the opposite direction.

### Air Supply Control Valve

1. Verify that airflow is being supplied to the valve inlet by disconnecting the air supply hose at the inlet and verifying the presence of airflow with the engine at 1500 rpm. Reconnect the air supply hose to the valve inlet.
2. Disconnect the air supply hose at outlets A and B.
3. Remove the vacuum line at the vacuum nipple.
4. Accelerate the engine to 1500 rpm. Airflow should be heard and felt at outlet B with little or no airflow at outlet A.
5. With the engine at 1500 rpm, connect a direct vacuum line from any manifold vacuum fitting to the air control valve vacuum nipple. Airflow should be heard and felt at outlet A with little or no airflow at outlet B.
6. If airflow is noted in Steps 4 and 5, the valve is okay. Reinstall the clamps and hoses. If the valve does not pass Step 4 and/or 5, replace the valve.

### Combination Air Bypass/Air Control Valve

1. Disconnect the hoses from outlets A and B.
2. Disconnect and plug the vacuum line to port D.
3. With the engine operating at 1500 rpm, airflow should be noted coming out of the bypass vents.

4. Reconnect the vacuum line to port D, then disconnect and plug the vacuum line to port S. Make sure vacuum is present in the line to vacuum port D.

5. With the engine operating at 1500 rpm, airflow should be noted coming out of outlet B and no airflow should be detected at outlet A.

6. Apply 8–10 in. Hg (27–34 kPa) of vacuum to port S. With the engine operating at 1500 rpm, airflow should be noted coming out of outlet A.

7. If the valve is the bleed type, some lesser amount of air will flow from outlet A or B and the main discharge will change when vacuum is applied to port S.

### Solenoid Vacuum Valve Assembly

1. The ports should allow air to flow when the solenoid is energized.

2. Check the resistance at the solenoid terminals with an ohmmeter. The resistance should be 51–108 ohms.

3. If the resistance is not as specified, replace the solenoid.

➡**The valve can be expected to have a very small leakage rate when energized or de-energized. This leakage is not measurable in the field and is not detrimental to valve function.**

### Thermactor Idle Vacuum Valve

The following applies to TIV valves with the code words ASH or RED on the decal.

1. Apply the parking brake and block the drive wheels. With the engine at idle, and the transaxle selector lever in **N** on automatic transaxle equipped vehicles or Neutral on manual transaxle equipped vehicles, apply vacuum to the small nipple and place fingers over the TIV valve atmospheric vent holes. If no vacuum is sensed, the TIV is damaged and must be replaced.

2. With the engine still idling and the transaxle selector lever remaining in **N** or Neutral, apply 1.5–3.0 in. Hg (5–10 kPa) of vacuum to the large nipple of the ASH TIV valve or 3.5–4.5 in. Hg (12–15 kPa) of vacuum to the large nipple of the RED TIV valve from a test source. If vacuum is still sensed when placing fingers over the vent holes, the TIV is damaged and must be replaced.

3. If the TIV valve meets both requirements, disconnect the TIV valve small nipple from the manifold vacuum and the TIV valve large nipple from the test vacuum. Reconnect the TIV valve to the original hoses or connectors.

### REMOVAL & INSTALLATION

### Air Supply Pump

1. Disconnect the negative battery cable.
2. Remove the drive belt from the air pump pulley.
3. Disconnect the air hose(s) from the air pump.
4. Remove the mounting bolts and, if necessary, the mounting brackets.
5. Remove the air pump from the vehicle.
**To install:**
6. Install the air pump in the vehicle, then secure using the mounting bolts and/or brackets.
7. Connect the air hose to the air pump, then install the belt on the air pump pulley.
8. Connect the negative battery cable.

### Air Bypass Valve

1. Disconnect the negative battery cable.
2. Tag and disconnect the air inlet hose, the outlet hose and the vacuum hose from the bypass valve.
3. Remove the bypass valve from the vehicle.
**To install:**
4. Install the bypass valve in the vehicle.
5. Connect the vacuum hose, the outlet hose and the air inlet hose to the bypass valve, as tagged during removal.
6. Connect the negative battery cable.

### Check Valve

▶ **See Figure 19**

1. Disconnect the negative battery cable.
2. Disconnect the input hose from the check valve.
3. Remove the check valve from the connecting tube.
**To install:**
4. Fasten the check valve to the connecting tube.
5. Connect the input hose to the check valve.
6. Connect the negative battery cable.

### Air Supply Control Valve

▶ **See Figure 20**

1. Disconnect the negative battery cable.
2. Disconnect the air hoses and the vacuum line from the air control valve.
3. Remove the air control valve from the vehicle.
**To install:**
4. Install the control valve in the vehicle.
5. Connect the vacuum line and the air hoses to the air control valve.
6. Connect the negative battery cable.

### Combination Air Bypass/Air Control Valve

▶ **See Figure 21**

1. Disconnect the negative battery cable.
2. Disconnect the air hoses and vacuum lines from the valve.
3. Remove the valve from the vehicle.
**To install:**
4. Install the valve in the vehicle.
5. Connect the vacuum lines and the air hoses to the valve.
6. Connect the negative battery cable.

### Solenoid Vacuum Valve Assembly

▶ **See Figure 22**

1. Disconnect the negative battery cable.
2. Detach the electrical connector and the vacuum lines from the solenoid valve.
3. Unfasten the mounting bolts and remove the solenoid valve.
**To install:**
4. Install the solenoid valve, then secure using the mounting bolts.
5. Connect the vacuum lines, then engage the electrical connector to the solenoid valve.
6. Connect the negative battery cable.

### Thermactor Idle Vacuum Valve

▶ **See Figure 23**

1. Disconnect the negative battery cable.
2. Disconnect the vacuum lines from the TIV valve, then remove the valve from the vehicle.
**To install:**
3. Install the TIV valve in the vehicle, then connect the vacuum lines to the valve.
4. Connect the negative battery cable.

## Pulse Air Injection System

▶ **See Figure 24**

### OPERATION

The pulse air injection system is used on some vehicles equipped with the 2.5L engine.

The pulse air injection system does not use an air pump. Instead the

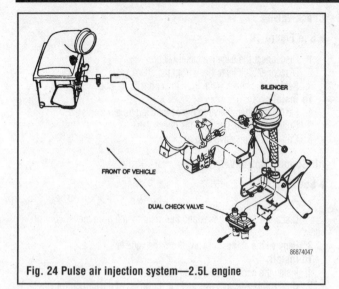

Fig. 24 Pulse air injection system—2.5L engine

system uses natural pulses present in the exhaust system to pull air into the catalyst through a pulse air valve. The pulse air valve is connected to the catalyst with a long tube and to the air cleaner and silencer with hoses.

## Pulse Air Valve

▶ See Figure 25

The pulse air control valve is normally closed. Without a vacuum signal from the solenoid, the flow of air is blocked.

## Air Silencer/Filter

The air silencer is a combustion silencer and filter for the pulse air system. The air silencer is mounted in a convenient position in the engine compartment and is connected to the pulse air valve inlet by means of a flexible hose.

## Check Valve

The air check valve is a one-way valve that allows air to pass into the exhaust system while preventing exhaust gases from passing in the opposite direction.

## Solenoid Vacuum Valve Assembly

The normally closed solenoid valve assembly consists of 2 vacuum ports with an atmospheric vent. The valve assembly can be with or without control bleed. The outlet port of the valve is opened to atmospheric vent and closed to the inlet port when de-energized. When energized, the outlet port is opened to the inlet port and closed to atmospheric vent. The control

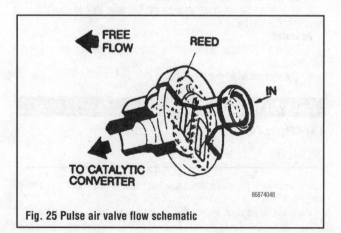

Fig. 25 Pulse air valve flow schematic

bleed is provided to prevent contamination entering the solenoid valve assembly from the intake manifold.

## TESTING

### Pulse Air Valve

1. Visually inspect the system hoses, tubes, control valve(s) and check valve(s) for leaks that may be due to backflow of exhaust gas. If holes are found and/or traces of exhaust gas products are evident, the check valve may be suspect.
2. The valve should allow free flow of air in one direction only. The valve should check or block, the free flow of exhaust gas in the opposite direction.
3. Replace the valve if air does not flow as indicated or if exhaust gas backflows in the wrong direction.
4. Remove the inlet hose.
5. Apply the parking brake and block the drive wheels. With the engine idling at normal operating temperature and the transaxle selector lever in **N** on automatic transaxle equipped vehicles or Neutral on manual transaxle equipped vehicles, air should be drawn into the valve.
6. Remove the vacuum line; the air flow should stop.
7. If these conditions are met, the valve is operating properly.
8. If these conditions are not met, verify that vacuum is present at the valve. Check the solenoid valve if vacuum is not present.
9. If vacuum is present but no air flows, check the pulse air check valve, silencer filter and air cleaner for blocked or restricted passages.
10. If vacuum is present and no blocked or restricted passages are found, replace the valve.

### Air Silencer/Filter

1. Inspect the hoses and air silencer for leaks.
2. Disconnect the hose from the air silencer outlet, remove the silencer and visually inspect for plugging.
3. The air silencer is operating properly, if no plugging or leaks are encountered.

### Check Valve

1. Visually inspect the system hoses, tubes, control valve(s) and check valve(s) for leaks that may be due to the backflow of exhaust gas. If holes are found and/or traces of exhaust gas products are evident, the check valve may be suspect.
2. Check valves should allow free flow of air in the incoming direction only. The valves should check or block, the free flow of exhaust gas in the opposite direction.
3. Replace the valve if air does not flow as indicated or if exhaust gas backflows in the opposite direction.

### Solenoid Vacuum Valve Assembly

1. The ports should flow air when the solenoid is energized.
2. Check the resistance at the solenoid terminals with an ohmmeter. The resistance should be 51–108 ohms.
3. If the resistance is not as specified, replace the solenoid.

➡The valve can be expected to have a very small leakage rate when energized or de-energized. This leakage is not measurable in the field and is not detrimental to valve function.

## REMOVAL & INSTALLATION

### Pulse Air Valve

1. Disconnect the negative battery cable.
2. Disconnect the air hose(s) from the pulse air valve.
3. Disconnect the vacuum line, if necessary.
4. Remove the pulse air valve.

**To install:**
5. Install the pulse air valve, then, if removed, connect the vacuum line.
6. Connect the air hose(s) from the pulse air valve.
7. Connect the negative battery cable.

### Air Silencer/Filter

1. Disconnect the negative battery cable.
2. Disconnect the hose from the silencer.
3. Remove the silencer from the vehicle.

**To install:**
4. Install the silencer, then connect the hose.
5. Connect the negative battery cable.

### Check Valve

1. Disconnect the negative battery cable.
2. Disconnect the input hose from the check valve.
3. Remove the check valve from the connecting tube.

**To install:**
4. Fasten the check valve to the connecting tube.
5. Connect the input hose to the check valve.
6. Connect the negative battery cable.

### Solenoid Vacuum Valve Assembly

1. Disconnect the negative battery cable.
2. Disengage the electrical connector, then disconnect the vacuum lines from the solenoid valve.
3. Remove the mounting bolts, then remove the solenoid vacuum valve.

**To install:**
4. Install the solenoid valve, then fasten using the mounting bolts.
5. Connect the vacuum lines, then engage the electrical connector to the solenoid valve.
6. Connect the negative battery cable.

## Catalytic Converters

Engine exhaust consists mainly of Nitrogen ($N_2$), however, it also contains Carbon Monoxide (CO), Carbon Dioxide ($CO_2$), Water Vapor ($H_2O$), Oxygen ($O_2$), Nitrogen Oxides (NOx) and Hydrogen (H), as well as various unburned Hydrocarbons (HC). Three of these exhaust components, CO, NOx and HC, are major air pollutants, so their emission to the atmosphere has to be controlled.

The catalytic converter, mounted in the engine exhaust stream, plays a major role in the emission control system. The converter works as a gas reactor whose catalytic function is to speed up the heat producing chemical reaction between the exhaust gas components in order to reduce the air pollutants in the engine exhaust. The catalyst material, contained inside the converter, is made of a ceramic substrate that is coated with a high surface area alumina and impregnated with catalytically active, precious metals.

All vehicles use a 3-way catalyst and some also use with a conventional oxidation catalyst. The conventional oxidation catalyst, containing Platinum (Pt) and Palladium (Pd), is effective for catalyzing the oxidation reactions of HC and CO. The 3-way catalyst, containing Platinum (Pt) and Rhodium (Rh) or Palladium (Pd) and Rhodium (Rh), is not only effective for catalyzing the oxidation reactions of HC and CO, but it also catalyzes the reduction of NOx.

The catalytic converter assembly consists of a structured shell containing a monolithic substrate; a ceramic, honeycomb construction. In order to maintain the converter's exhaust oxygen content at a high level to obtain the maximum oxidation for producing the heated chemical reaction, the oxidation catalyst usually requires the use of a secondary air source. This is provided by the pulse air or thermactor air injection systems.

The catalytic converter is protected by several devices that block out the air supply from the air injection system when the engine is laboring under one or more of the following conditions:
- Cold engine operation with rich choke mixture
- Abnormally high engine coolant temperatures above 225°F (107°C),

which may result from a condition such as an extended, hot idle on a hot day
- Wide-open throttle
- Engine deceleration
- Extended idle operation

## Service Interval Reminder Lights

### RESETTING

Approximately every 5,000 or 7,500 miles (8,000 or 12,000 km), depending on engine application, the word SERVICE will appear on the electronic display for the first 1.5 miles (2.4 km) to remind the driver that is is time for the regular vehicle service interval maintenance (for example, an oil change).

To reset the service interval reminder light for another interval, proceed as follows.
1. With the engine running, press the ODO SEL and TRIP RESET buttons.
2. Hold the buttons down until the SERVICE light disappears from the display and 3 audible beeps are heard to verify that the service reminder has been reset.

➡**Do not confuse the service interval reminder light with the CHECK ENGINE or SERVICE ENGINE SOON Malfunction Indicator Light (MIL). An illuminated MIL likely indicates the presence of a self-diagnostic trouble code. Information on reading such trouble codes appears later in this section.**

## Oxygen Sensor

▶ **See Figures 26 and 27**

The oxygen sensor or Heated Exhaust Gas Oxygen (HEGO) sensor supplies the ECU with a signal which indicates a rich or lean condition during engine operation. This input information assists the ECU in determining the proper air/fuel ratio. The oxygen sensor is threaded into the exhaust manifold on all vehicles.

### TESTING

#### Except Engines Equipped With MAF Sensor

1. Disconnect the oxygen sensor from the vehicle harness.
2. Connect a voltmeter between the HEGO signal terminal of the oxygen sensor connector and the negative battery terminal.

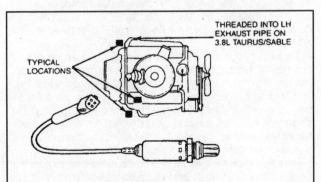

THREADED INTO CENTER REAR OF EXHAUST MANIFOLD ON 2.3L HSC, 2.5L
THREADED INTO Y-PIPE JUNCTURE OF CATALYST INLET ON 3.0L EFI/
2.9L TRUCK

86874051

**Fig. 26 Heated Exhaust Gas Oxygen (HEGO) sensor assembly**

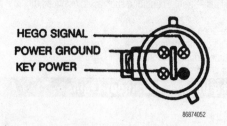

HEGO SIGNAL
POWER GROUND
KEY POWER

86874052

**Fig. 27 Oxygen sensor (HEGO) assembly electrical connector**

3. Disconnect and plug the vacuum line at the MAP sensor and set the voltmeter on the 20 volt scale.

4. Apply 10–14 in. Hg (34–47 kPa) of vacuum to the MAP sensor.

## ELECTRONIC ENGINE CONTROLS

### General Information

The fuel injection system (CFI, EFI or SFI), is operated along with the ignition system to obtain optimum performance and fuel economy while producing a minimum of exhaust emissions. The various sensors described in this section are used by the computer control module for feedback to determine proper engine operating conditions. As the Taurus and Sable changed through the years, so did the name of the computer control module. Depending on the year of the vehicle it was called the EEC-IV Processor, Electronic Control Assembly (ECA), Electronic Control Unit (ECU) or Powertrain Control Module (PCM). Keep in mind, that even though the name of the component may have changed, its function did not.

When dealing with the electronic engine control system, keep in mind that the system is sensitive to improperly connected electrical and vacuum circuits. The condition and connection of all hoses and wires should always be the first step when attempting to diagnose a driveability problem. Worn or deteriorated hoses and damaged or corroded wires may well make a good component appear faulty.

➡️ **When troubleshooting the system, always check the electrical and vacuum connectors which may cause the problem before testing or replacing a component.**

### Computer Control Module

▶ **See Figures 28 and 29**

The heart of the electronic control system which is found on vehicles covered by this manual is a computer control module. Depending on the year of the vehicle, this module was called the EEC-IV Processor, Electronic Control Assembly (ECA), Electronic Control Unit (ECU) or Powertrain Control Module (PCM).

The computer control module is a microprocessor that receives data from sensors, switches, relays and other electronic components, then uses this information to control fuel supply and engine emission systems. The module contains a specific calibration for optimizing emissions, fuel economy and driveability. Based on information received and programmed into it's memory, the module generates output signals to control the fuel injection system. On the vehicles covered by this manual, the computer control module is located ahead of the glove box.

Regardless of the name, all computer control modules are serviced in a similar manner. Care must be taken when handling these expensive components in order to protect them from damage. Carefully follow all instructions included with the replacement part. Avoid touching pins or connectors to prevent damage from static electricity.

### ✳️✳️ CAUTION

**To prevent the possibility of permanent control module damage, the ignition switch MUST always be OFF when disconnecting**

5. Start the engine and run it at approximately 2000 rpm for 2 minutes.

6. If the voltmeter does not indicate greater than 0.5 volts within 2 minutes, replace the sensor.

### REMOVAL & INSTALLATION

1. Disconnect the negative battery cable.

2. Disengage the oxygen/heated exhaust gas oxygen sensor electrical connector.

3. Remove the sensor from the exhaust manifold or exhaust pipes, as applicable.

**To install:**

4. Install the sensor in the exhaust manifold or pipe.

5. Engage the sensor electrical connector.

6. Connect the negative battery cable.

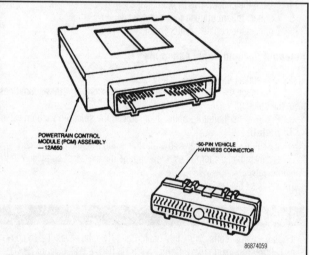

POWERTRAIN CONTROL MODULE (PCM) ASSEMBLY — 12A650

60-PIN VEHICLE HARNESS CONNECTOR

86874059

**Fig. 28 View of the computer control module—Powertrain Control Module (PCM) shown (other modules are basically identical)**

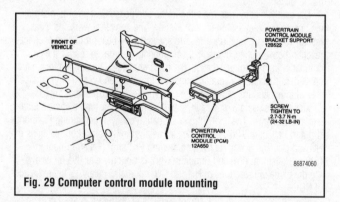

FRONT OF VEHICLE

POWERTRAIN CONTROL MODULE BRACKET SUPPORT 12B522

SCREW TIGHTEN TO 2.7-3.7 N·m (24-32 LB-IN)

POWERTRAIN CONTROL MODULE (PCM) 12A650

86874060

**Fig. 29 Computer control module mounting**

**power from or reconnecting power to the module. This includes unplugging the module connector, disconnecting the negative battery cable, removing the module fuse or even attempting to jump you dead battery using jumper cables.**

### REMOVAL & INSTALLATION

1. Disconnect the negative battery cable.

2. If necessary, remove the glove box or kick panel.

3. Loosen the engine control sensor wiring to the computer control module connector retaining bolt. Remove the wiring connector from the module.

4. Loosen the module bracket support screw, located forward of the glove compartment. Remove the bracket, then remove the computer control module.

5. Installation is the reverse of the removal procedure. Tighten the module retaining screw to 24–32 inch lbs. (2.7–3.7 Nm). Tighten the engine control sensor wiring connector retaining bolt to 32 inch lbs. (3.7 Nm).

## Mass Air Flow (MAF) Sensor

▶ See Figure 30

The Mass Air Flow (MAF) sensor directly measures the mass of the air flowing into the engine. The sensor output is an analog signal ranging from about 0.5–5.0 volts. The signal is used by the ECU to calculate the injector pulse width. The sensing element is a thin platinum wire wound on a ceramic bobbin and coated with glass. This "hot wire" is maintained at 11°F (200°C) above the ambient temperature as measured by a constant "cold wire". The MAF sensor is located in the outlet side of the air cleaner lid assembly.

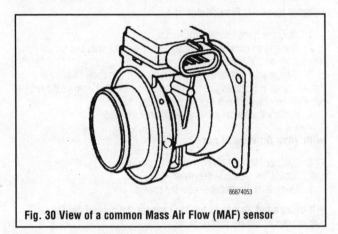

86874053

**Fig. 30 View of a common Mass Air Flow (MAF) sensor**

### TESTING

1. Make sure the ignition key is **OFF**.
2. Connect Breakout Box T83L-50EEC-IV or equivalent, to the computer control module harness, then connect the control module.
3. Start the engine and let it idle.
4. Use a voltmeter to measure the voltage between test pin **50** of the breakout box and the battery negative post.
5. Replace the MAF sensor if the voltage is not 0.36–1.50 volts.

### REMOVAL & INSTALLATION

1. Disconnect the negative battery cable.
2. Remove the air intake tube.
3. Detach the MAF sensor electrical connector.
4. Unfasten the sensor attaching screws, then remove the sensor.

➡Inspect the MAF sensor-to-air cleaner lid gasket for any signs of deterioration. Replace the gasket, as necessary. If scraping is necessary, be careful not to damage the air cleaner lid or the MAF sensor gasket surfaces.

5. Installation is the reverse of the removal procedure.

## Idle Air Bypass Valve

▶ See Figure 31

The idle air bypass valve is used to control engine idle speed and is operated by the computer control module, or in response to engine coolant temperature change, depending upon vehicle application. The valve allows

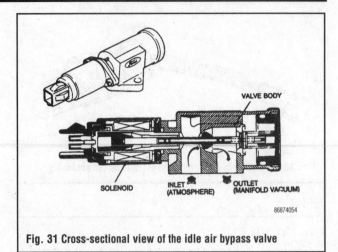

86874054

**Fig. 31 Cross-sectional view of the idle air bypass valve**

air to flow into the intake air stream to control cold engine fast idle, no touch start, dashpot, over temperature idle boost and engine idle load correction. The air bypass valve, which is used on all EFI and SEFI systems, is located on the throttle body housing.

### TESTING

1. Make sure the ignition is in the **OFF** position.
2. Disconnect the air bypass valve.
3. Use an ohmmeter to measure the resistance between the terminals of the valve solenoid.

➡**Due to the diode in the solenoid, place the ohmmeter positive lead on the VPWR pin and the negative lead on the ISC pin.**

4. If the resistance is not between 7–13 ohms, replace the air bypass valve.

### REMOVAL & INSTALLATION

1. Disconnect the negative battery cable.
2. Disengage the idle air bypass valve electrical connector from the wiring harness.
3. Remove the two retaining screws, then remove the idle air bypass valve and gasket assembly from the vehicle.

➡**If scraping is necessary to clean the gasket mating surfaces, be careful not to damage the air bypass valve or throttle body gasket surfaces or drop any material into the throttle body.**

**To install:**

4. Make sure the gasket mating surfaces are clean. Install a new gasket on the throttle body surface, then mount the valve assembly. Secure using the two retaining screws tightening them to 84 inch lbs. (9.5 Nm).

5. Engage the idle air bypass valve electrical connector to the wiring harness, then connect the negative battery cable.

## Idle Speed Control (ISC) Motor

▶ See Figure 32

The Idle Speed Control (ISC) motor, which is used in the CFI system, controls idle speed by moving the throttle lever. It regulates airflow to maintain the desired engine rpm for both warm and cold engine idles. An idle tracking switch, integral to the motor, is utilized to determine when the throttle lever has contacted it, thereby signalling the need to control engine rpm. The motor extends or retracts a linear shaft through a gear reduction system. The motor direction is determined by the polarity of the applied voltage.

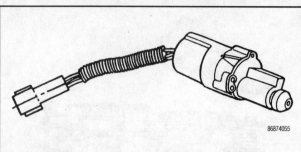

**Fig. 32 View of an Idle Speed Control (ISC) motor assembly**

## TESTING

#### ▶ See Figure 33

1. Connect Breakout Box T83L-50EEC-IV, or equivalent, to the ECU wiring harness.
2. Use a jumper wire to connect the positive circuit of the ISC motor, test pin **21**, to the positive battery terminal and connect another jumper wire between the negative circuit of the motor, test pin **41**, to battery ground for 4 seconds.

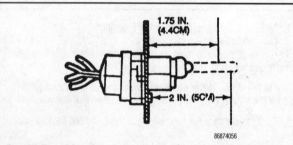

**Fig. 33 The ISC motor shaft should extend to greater than 2 in. (51mm) or retract to less than 1.75 in. (44.5mm) from the mounting bracket**

3. Reverse the jumper wires, connecting the positive circuit of the ISC motor to battery ground and the negative circuit to battery positive for 4 seconds.
4. The ISC motor shaft should extend to greater than 2 in. (51mm) or retract to less than 1.75 in. (44.5mm) from the mounting bracket. If it does not, replace the ISC motor.

## REMOVAL & INSTALLATION

1. Disconnect the negative battery cable.
2. Detach the electrical connector from the ISC motor.
3. Unfasten the ISC motor mounting screws and remove the ISC motor.
4. Installation is the reverse of the removal procedure.

## Throttle Position (TP) Sensor

The Throttle Position (TP) sensor is mounted to the throttle shaft and is used to supply a voltage output change proportional to the change in the throttle position. The TP sensor is used by the ECU to determine engine operation mode: closed throttle, part throttle and wide-open throttle. The proper fuel mixture, spark and EGR will be output only when the operation mode has been determined correctly.

## REMOVAL & INSTALLATION

1. Disconnect the negative battery cable.
2. Detach the electrical connector from the TP sensor.

3. Unfasten the TP sensor mounting screws and remove the TP sensor.
4. Installation is the reverse of the removal procedure.
5. Adjust the sensor, if necessary.

## Air Charge Temperature (ACT) Sensor

#### ▶ See Figures 34 and 35

The Air Charge Temperature (ACT) sensor in systems with vane air flow meters is used to measure the temperature of the incoming air and send the information to the computer control module. In all other systems, the sensor provides the computer control module with mixture, fuel and air temperature information.

The air temperature sensor is located in the meter in vane air flow meter systems. Otherwise, it is located in the air cleaner assembly or in the side of the throttle body.

## TESTING

#### Without Vane Air Flow Meter

1. Disconnect the temperature sensor.
2. Connect an ohmmeter between the sensor terminals and set the ohmmeter scale on 200,000 ohms.
3. Measure the resistance with the engine off and cool. Then measure the resistance with the engine running and warmed up. Compare the resistance values obtained with the accompanying chart.
4. Replace the sensor if the readings are incorrect.

#### With Vane Air Flow Meter

1. Unfasten the vane air flow meter connector.
2. Access the sensor in the meter.
3. Monitor the temperature near the sensor.

➡**If using a hot air gun to heat the sensor, be careful not to melt any plastic or rubber components.**

4. Measure and record the resistance between the meter **VAT** terminal and the meter Signal Return (**SIGRTN**) terminal.
5. Compare the resistance readings with the accompanying chart. If the readings are incorrect, replace the sensor.

## REMOVAL & INSTALLATION

#### Without Vane Air Flow Meter

1. Disconnect the negative battery cable.
2. Disengage the electrical connector from the air temperature sensor.

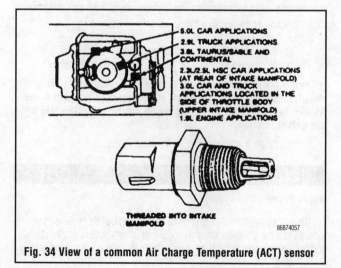

**Fig. 34 View of a common Air Charge Temperature (ACT) sensor**

| Temperature | | Engine Coolant/Air Charge Temperature Sensor Values | |
|---|---|---|---|
| °F | °C | Voltage (volts) | Resistance (K ohms) |
| 248 | 120 | .27 | 1.18 |
| 230 | 110 | .35 | 1.55 |
| 212 | 100 | .46 | 2.07 |
| 194 | 90 | .60 | 2.80 |
| 176 | 80 | .78 | 3.84 |
| 158 | 70 | 1.02 | 5.37 |
| 140 | 60 | 1.33 | 7.70 |
| 122 | 50 | 1.70 | 10.97 |
| 104 | 40 | 2.13 | 16.15 |
| 86 | 30 | 2.60 | 24.27 |
| 68 | 20 | 3.07 | 37.30 |
| 50 | 10 | 3.51 | 58.75 |

86874058

**Fig. 35 ACT and ECT temperature sensor value chart**

3. Remove the sensor.
4. Installation is the reverse of the removal procedure.

### With Vane Air Flow Meter

The air charge temperature sensor is an integral component of the vane air flow meter. If the temperature sensor is defective, the vane air flow meter must be replaced.

## Engine Coolant Temperature (ECT) Sensor

♦ **See Figure 35**

The Engine Coolant Temperature (ECT) sensor detects the temperature of engine coolant and supplies that information to the computer control module. The ECT sensor is located on the cylinder head or on the intake manifold. The sensor signal is used to modify ignition timing, EGR flow and air/fuel ratio as a function of engine coolant temperature.

## SELF-DIAGNOSTIC SYSTEMS

### General Information

All vehicles covered by this manual have self-diagnostic capabilities. Malfunctions in the engine control system are found through the Self-Test procedure. The vehicles covered by this manual use the Electronic Engine Control-IV (EEC-IV) system, which utilizes a Self-Test divided into 3 specialized tests: Key On Engine Off Self-Test, Engine Running Self-Test and Continuous Self-Test. The Self-Test is not a conclusive test by itself, but is used as a part of a functional Quick Test diagnostic procedure. The computer control module stores the Self-Test program in its permanent memory. When activated, it checks the EEC-IV system by testing its memory integrity and processing capability, then verifies that various sensors and actuators are connected and operating properly. The Key On Engine Off and Engine Running Self-Tests are functional tests which only detect faults present at the time of the Self-Test. Continuous Self-Test is an ongoing test that stores fault information in Keep Alive Memory (KAM) for retrieval at a later time.

Fault information is communicated through the Self-Test service codes. These service codes are 2-digit or 3-digit numbers representing the results of the Self-Test. The service codes are transmitted on the Self-Test output

## TESTING

1. Disconnect the temperature sensor.
2. Connect an ohmmeter between the sensor terminals and set the ohmmeter scale on 200,000 ohms.
3. Measure the resistance with the engine off and cool. Then, measure with the engine running and warmed up. Compare the resistance values obtained with the chart.
4. Replace the sensor if the readings are incorrect.

## REMOVAL & INSTALLATION

1. Disconnect the negative battery cable.
2. Drain the cooling system to a level below the sensor.
3. Disengage the electrical connector from the ECT sensor.
4. Remove the ECT sensor.
5. Installation is the reverse of the removal procedure. Properly refill and bleed the cooling system.

## Manifold Absolute Pressure (MAP) Sensor

The MAP sensor measures manifold vacuum using a frequency. This gives the computer control module information on engine load. It is used as a barometric sensor for altitude compensation, updating the control module during key ON, engine OFF and every wide-open throttle. The ECU uses the MAP sensor for spark advance, EGR flow and air/fuel ratio.

## TESTING

1. Disconnect the vacuum supply hose from the MAP sensor.
2. Connect a suitable vacuum pump to the MAP sensor and apply 18 in. Hg (61 kPa) of vacuum.
3. If the MAP sensor does not hold vacuum, it must be replaced.

## REMOVAL & INSTALLATION

1. Disconnect the negative battery cable.
2. Disengage the electrical connector and the vacuum line from the sensor.
3. Unfasten the sensor mounting bolts, then remove the sensor.
4. Installation is the reverse of the removal procedure.

line found in the vehicle Self-Test connector. They are in the form of timed pulses and can be read on a voltmeter, STAR or SUPER STAR II tester and the malfunction indicator light.

### Reading Codes

#### VEHICLE PREPARATION

1. Apply the parking brake, place the transaxle shift lever firmly into **P** on automatic transaxle or Neutral on manual transaxles, and block the drive wheels.
2. Turn all electrical loads (radio, lights, blower fan, etc.) **OFF**.

#### USING THE STAR OR SUPER STAR II TESTER

♦ **See Figures 36 and 37**

➡**The STAR tester cannot be used to read 3-digit service codes. If the STAR tester is used on a 3-digit service code application, the**

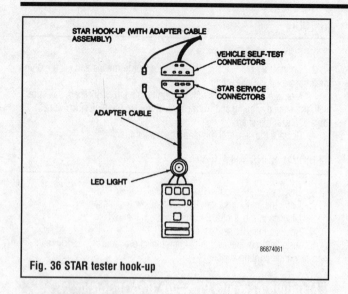

**Fig. 36 STAR tester hook-up**

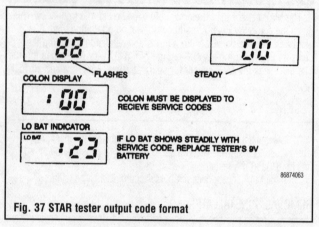

**Fig. 37 STAR tester output code format**

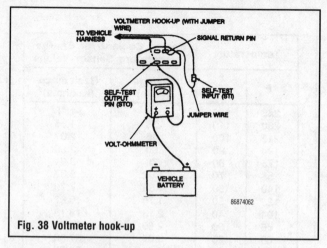

**Fig. 38 Voltmeter hook-up**

display will be blank. The SUPER STAR II tester must be used to read 3-digit service codes.

After hooking up the STAR tester and turning on its power switch, the tester will run a display check and the numerals **88** will begin to flash in the display window. A steady **00** will then appear, indicating that the STAR tester is ready. To receive service codes, press the button on the front of the STAR tester. The button will latch down and a colon will appear in the display window in front of the **00** numerals. The colon must be displayed to receive the service codes.

If it is desired to clear the display window during the Self-Test, turn **OFF** the vehicle's engine, press the tester's button once to unlatch it, then press the button again to latch down the button.

Connect the STAR or SUPER STAR II tester as follows:
1. Turn the ignition **OFF**.
2. Connect the color coded adapter cable to the STAR tester.
3. Connect the adapter cable leads to the proper Self-Test connectors.
4. Ground the adapter cable for vehicles using the SUPER STAR II tester.
5. Slide the SUPER STAR II tester switch to the MECS or EEC-IV position, according to the vehicle system.

## USING THE ANALOG VOLTMETER

▶ **See Figures 38 and 39**

Service codes will be represented by pulsing or sweeping movements of the voltmeter's needle across the dial face of the voltmeter. Therefore, a single number of 3 will be reported by 3 needle sweeps. However, a service code is represented by a 2-digit or 3-digit number, such as 23. As a

result, the Self-Test service code of 23 will appear on the voltmeter as 2 needle sweeps, then after a 2 second pause, the needle will sweep 3 times.
Connect the analog voltmeter as follows:
1. Turn the ignition **OFF**.
2. Set the voltmeter on a DC voltage range to read from 0–20 volts.
3. On all EEC-IV vehicles, connect the voltmeter from the battery positive post to the Self-Test Output (STO) pin of the large Self-Test connector. On all other vehicles, connect the positive voltmeter lead to the EEC STO line and the negative lead to engine ground, then jumper the EEC Self-Test Input (STI) to ground.

## USING THE MALFUNCTION INDICATOR LIGHT (MIL)

During the Self-Test, a service code is reported by the malfunction indicator light. It will represent itself as a flash on the CHECK ENGINE or SERVICE ENGINE SOON light on the dash panel. A single digit number of 3 will be reported by 3 flashes. However, a service code is represented by a 2-digit or 3-digit number, such as 23. As a result, the Self-Test service code of 23 will appear on the MIL light as 2 flashes, then, after a 2 second pause, the light will flash 3 times.

## KEY ON ENGINE OFF SELF-TEST

Start the engine and let it run until it reaches normal operating temperature. Turn the engine **OFF** and activate the Self-Test.
1. If using the STAR tester, proceed as follows:
   a. Latch the center button in the down position.
   b. Place the ignition key in the **ON** position.
   c. Record all service codes displayed.
2. If using the SUPER STAR II tester, proceed as follows:
   a. Latch the center button in the **TEST** position.
   b. Turn the ignition key **ON**.
   c. Turn the tester **ON**; the tester will sound and **888** will be displayed for 2 seconds.
   d. Unlatch and relatch the center test button. After all codes are received, unlatch the center button to review all codes retained in tester memory.

➡The SUPER STAR II tester has a mode switch. The tester will only display 3-digit service codes in fast code mode. If slow code mode is used on 3-digit service code applications, the display will be blank.

3. If using the analog voltmeter, jumper the Self-Test Input (STI) to the Signal Return (SIG RTN) at the Self-Test connectors, then, turn the ignition key and the voltmeter **ON**. Observe the needle for any code indications and record.
4. If using the malfunction indicator light; connect the jumper wire from STI to the SIG RTN at the Self-Test connectors and turn the ignition switch **ON**. Service codes will be flashed on the MIL.

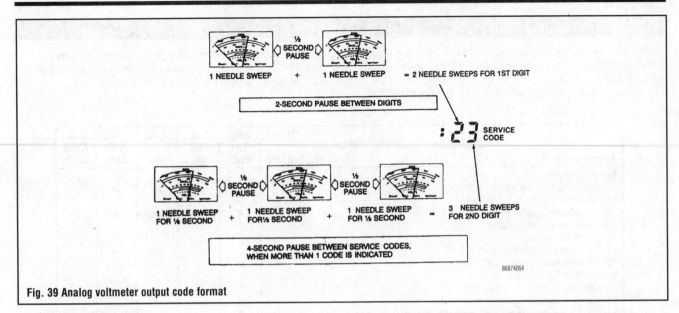

**1 NEEDLE SWEEP** + **1 NEEDLE SWEEP** = **2 NEEDLE SWEEPS FOR 1ST DIGIT**

½ SECOND PAUSE

2-SECOND PAUSE BETWEEN DIGITS

:23 SERVICE CODE

**1 NEEDLE SWEEP FOR ½ SECOND** + **1 NEEDLE SWEEP FOR½ SECOND** + **1 NEEDLE SWEEP FOR ½ SECOND** = **3 NEEDLE SWEEPS FOR 2ND DIGIT**

½ SECOND PAUSE

4-SECOND PAUSE BETWEEN SERVICE CODES, WHEN MORE THAN 1 CODE IS INDICATED

86874064

**Fig. 39 Analog voltmeter output code format**

## ENGINE RUNNING SELF-TEST

1. Deactivate the Self-Test.
2. Start and run the engine at 2000 rpm for 2 minutes.
3. Turn the engine **OFF** and wait 10 seconds.
4. Activate the Self-Test.
5. Start the engine.
6. Record all service codes displayed.

➡**Engine identification codes are issued at the beginning of the Engine Running Self-Test and are 1-digit numbers represented by the number of pulses sent out. The engine identification code is equal to ½ the number of engine cylinders. Two pulses equals 4 cylinders. The identification codes are used to verify that the proper processor is installed and that the Self-Test has been entered.**

## Clearing Codes

## CONTINUOUS MEMORY

➡**Do not disconnect the battery to clear continuous memory codes. This will erase the Keep Alive Memory (KAM) information which may cause a driveability concern.**

1. Run the Key On Engine Off Self-Test.
2. When the service codes begin to be displayed, deactivate the Self-Test as follows:
   a. STAR tester: unlatch the center button to the UP position.
   b. Analog voltmeter and MIL: remove the jumper wire from between the Self-Test Input (STI) connector and the signal return pin of the Self-Test connector.
   c. The continuous memory codes will be erased from the ECU memory.

## KEEP ALIVE MEMORY (KAM)

The computer control module stores information regarding vehicle operating conditions and uses this information to compensate for component tolerances. Whenever an emission related component is replaced, the Keep Alive Memory (KAM) should be cleared to erase the information stored by the control module from the original component.

To clear KAM, disconnect the negative battery cable for at least five minutes. After the KAM has been cleared, the vehicle may exhibit certain driveability concerns. If this is the case, it will be necessary to drive the vehicle at least 10 miles (16 km) for the computer to relearn the values for optimum driveability and performance.

## DIAGNOSTIC TROUBLE CODES

Listings of the Diagnostic Trouble Codes (DTCs) for the various engine control systems covered in this manual are located in this section. When using these codes, remember that a code only points to the faulty circuit, NOT necessarily to a faulty component. Loose, damaged or corroded connections may contribute to a fault code on a circuit when the sensor or component it operating properly. Be sure that components are faulty before replacing them, especially the expensive ones.

| Service Codes | ENGINE (Liters) FUEL SYSTEM | Quick Test Mode | 2.5L FLC CFI | 3.0L EFI | 3.0L SHO SEFI | 3.8L AXOD SEFI |
|---|---|---|---|---|---|---|
| 11—System pass | | O/R/C | ✓ | ✓ | ✓ | ✓ |
| 12—Rpm unable to reach upper test limit | | R | ✓ | ✓ | ✓ | ✓ |
| 13—DC motor movement not detected | | O | ✓ | | | |
| 13—Rpm unable to achieve lower test limit | | R | ✓ | | ✓ | ✓ |
| 13—DC motor did follow dashpot | | C | ✓ | | | |
| 14—PIP circuit failure | | C | ✓ | ✓ | ✓ | ✓ |
| 15—ECA read only memory test failed | | O | ✓ | ✓ | ✓ | ✓ |
| 15—ECA keep alive memory test failed | | C | ✓ | ✓ | ✓ | ✓ |
| 16—Idle rpm high with ISC off | | R | ✓ | | | |
| 16—Idle too low to perform EGO test | | R | | | | |
| 17—Idle rpm low with ISC off | | R | ✓ | | | |
| 18—SPOUT circuit open or spark angle word failure | | R | ✓ | ✓ | | ✓ |
| 18—IDM circuit failure or SPOUT circuit grounded | | C | | ✓ | ✓ | ✓ |
| 19—Failure in ECA internal voltage | | O | | ✓ | | |
| 19—CID circuit failure | | C | | ✓ | | |
| 19—Rpm dropped too low in ISC off test | | R | | | | |
| 19—Rpm for EGR test not achieved | | R | | | | |
| 21—ECT out of self-test range | | O/R | ✓ | ✓ | ✓ | ✓ |
| 22—BP sensor out of self-test range | | O/C | | | ✓ | |
| 22—BP or MAP out of self-test range | | O/R/C | ✓ | ✓ | | ✓ |
| 23—TP out of self-test range | | O/R | | ✓ | ✓ | ✓ |
| 23—TP out of self-test range | | O/R/C | ✓ | | | |
| 24—ACT sensor out of self-test range | | O/R | ✓ | ✓ | ✓ | ✓ |
| 25—Knock not sensed during dynamic test | | R | | | ✓ | |
| 26—VAF/MAF out of self-test range | | O/R | | | ✓ | |
| 28—VAT out of self-test range | | O/R | | | | |
| 29—Insufficient input from vehicle speed sensor | | C | ✓ | ✓ | ✓ | ✓ |
| 31—PFE, EVP or EVR circuit below minimum voltage | | O/R/C | ✓ | ✓ | ✓ | ✓ |
| 32—EPT circuit voltage low (PFE) | | R/C | | ✓ | ✓ | ✓ |
| 32—EVP voltage below closed limit | | O/R/C | ✓ | | | |
| 32—EGR not controlling | | R | | | | |
| 33—EGR valve opening not detected | | R/C | ✓ | ✓ | ✓ | ✓ |
| 33—EGR not closing fully | | R | | | | |
| 34—Defective PFE sensor or voltage out of range | | O | | ✓ | ✓ | ✓ |
| 34—EPT sensor voltage high (PFE) | | R/C | | ✓ | ✓ | ✓ |
| 34—EVP voltage above closed limit | | O/R/C | ✓ | | | |
| 34—EGR opening not detected | | R | | | | |
| 35—PFE or EVP circuit above maximum voltage | | O/R/C | ✓ | ✓ | ✓ | ✓ |
| 35—Rpm too low to perform EGR test | | R | | | | |
| 38—Idle tracking switch circuit open | | C | ✓ | | | |
| 39—AXOD lock up failed | | C | | ✓ | | |
| 41—HEGO sensor circuit indicates system lean | | R | ✓ | ✓ | ✓[4] | ✓[2] |
| 41—No HEGO switching detected | | R | ✓ | ✓ | ✓[4] | ✓[2] |
| 42—HEGO sensor circuit indicates system rich | | R | ✓ | ✓ | ✓[4] | ✓[2] |
| 42—No HEGO switching detected—reads rich | | C | | | | |
| 43—HEGO lean at wide open throttle | | C | | | | |
| 44—Thermactor air system inoperative—ride side | | R | | | | |
| 45—Thermactor air upstream during self-test | | R | | | ✓ | |
| 45—Coil 1 primary circuit failure | | C | | | ✓ | |
| 46—Thermactor air not bypassed during self-test | | R | | | ✓ | |
| 46—Coil 2 primary circuit failure | | C | | | ✓ | |
| 47—Measured airflow low at base idle | | R | | | | |
| 48—Coil 3 primary circuit failure | | C | | | ✓ | |
| 48—Measured airflow high at base idle | | R | | | | |
| 49—SPOUT signal defaulted to 10°BTDC or SPOUT open | | C | | | ✓ | |
| 51—ECT/ACT reads −40°F or circuit open | | O/C | ✓ | ✓ | | ✓ |
| 52—Power steering pressure switch circuit open | | O | ✓ | ✓ | ✓ | ✓ |
| 52—Power steering pressure switch always open or closed | | R | ✓ | ✓ | ✓ | ✓ |

**Top table (codes 81–99)**

| Service Codes | Quick Test Mode | 2.5L FLC CFI | 3.0L EFI | 3.0L SHO SEFI | 3.8L AXOD SEFI |
|---|---|---|---|---|---|
| 81—IAS circuit failure | O | | | | ✓ |
| 81—Air management 2 circuit failure | O | | | ✓ | ✓ |
| 82—Air management 1 circuit failure | O | | | ✓ | ✓ |
| 82—Supercharger bypass circuit failure | O/C | | | | ✓ |
| 83—High speed electro drive fan circuit failure | O/R | | | | ✓ |
| 84—Low speed fuel pump circuit failure | O/R | | | | ✓ |
| 84—EGR vacuum solenoid circuit failure | O/R | | | | ✓ |
| 85—Canister purge circuit failure | C | | ✓ | ✓ | ✓ |
| 85—Canister purge solenoid circuit failure | C | | | | ✓ |
| 86—Adaptive fuel lean limit reached | C | | ✓ | ✓ | ✓ |
| 86—3-4 shift solenoid circuit failure | C | | | | ✓ |
| 87—Adaptive fuel rich limit reached | O/C | | | | ✓ |
| 87—Fuel pump primary circuit failure | O/C/R | ⊕ | ⊖ | ⊖ | ✓ |
| 87—Fuel pump primary circuit failure | O | | | | ✓ |
| 87—Fuel pump primary circuit failure | O | | | | ✓ |
| 88—Electro drive fan circuit failure | O | | | | ✓ |
| 89—Converter clutch override circuit failure | O | | | | ✓ |
| 89—Lock-up solenoid circuit failure | O | | | | ✓ |
| 91—HEGO sensor indicates system lean | R | | | ⊕ | ⊕ |
| 91—No HEGO switching detected | C | | | ⊖ | ⊖ |
| 92—HEGO sensor indicates system rich | R | | | ⊖ | ⊖ |
| 93—TP sensor input low at maximum motor travel | R | | | | ✓ |
| 94—Thermactor air system inoperative-left side | O | | | | ✓ |
| 95—Fuel pump secondary circuit failure—ECA to ground | R | | | | ✓ |
| 96—Fuel pump secondary circuit failure—Battery to ECA | O/C | ✓ | ✓ | ✓ | ✓ |
| 96—High speed fuel pump circuit open | O/C | | | | ✓ |
| 98—Hard fault present | O/C | | | | ✓ |
| 99—EEC has not learned to control idle; ignore codes 12 & 13 | R | ✓ | ✓ | ✓ | ✓ |

No Codes: Cannot begin self-test or cannot transmit codes
Codes Not Listed: Do not apply to vehicle being tested
O—Key on, engine off test
R—Key on, engine running test
C—Continuous memory
⊕ Front HEGO
⊖ Right HEGO
① Left HEGO
② Rear HEGO

86874067

**Bottom table (codes 53–79)**

| Service Codes | Quick Test Mode | 2.5L FLC CFI | 3.0L EFI | 3.0L SHO SEFI | 3.8L AXOD SEFI |
|---|---|---|---|---|---|
| 53—TP circuit above maximum voltage | O/C | ✓ | ✓ | ✓ | ✓ |
| 54—ACT sensor circuit open | O/C | ✓ | ✓ | ✓ | ✓ |
| 55—Keypower circuit open | R | ✓ | | | |
| 56—VAF or MAF circuit above maximum voltage | O/C | ✓ | | ✓ | |
| 56—MAF circuit above maximum voltage | O/R/C | | | | ✓ |
| 57—Octane adjust service pin in use | O | | | | |
| 57—AXOD neutral pressure switch circuit failed open | C | | | | ✓ |
| 58—Idle tracking switch circuit open | C | ✓ | | | |
| 58—Idle tracking switch closed/circuit grounded | R | | | | |
| 58—VAT reads −40°F or circuit open | O/C | | | | |
| 59—Idle adjust service pin in use | C | | | | |
| 59—AXOD 4/3 pressure switch circuit failed open | C | | | | ✓ |
| 59—Low speed fuel pump circuit open—Battery to ECA | O/C | ✓ | ✓ | ✓ | ✓ |
| 59—AXOD 4/3 pressure switch failed closed | O/C | | | | ✓ |
| 61—ECT reads 254°F or circuit grounded | O | ✓ | ✓ | ✓ | ✓ |
| 62—AXOD 4/3 or 3/2 pressure switch circuit grounded | O/C | | | | ✓ |
| 63—TP circuit below minimum voltage | O/C | ✓ | ✓ | ✓ | ✓ |
| 64—ACT sensor input below minimum voltage | O/C | ✓ | ✓ | ✓ | ✓ |
| 65—Never went to closed loop fuel control | C | ✓ | ✓ | ✓ | ✓ |
| 66—MAF sensor input below minimum voltage | C | | | | ✓ |
| 66—VAF sensor below minimum voltage | O/C | ✓ | | ✓ | |
| 66—MAF circuit below minimum voltage | R/C | | | | |
| 67—Neutral/drive switch open or A/C on | O | ✓ | ✓ | | |
| 67—Clutch switch circuit failure | C | | | ✓ | |
| 67—Neutral/drive switch open or A/C on | O/R | | | | ✓ |
| 68—Idle tracking switch closed or circuit grounded | R | | | | |
| 68—Idle tracking switch circuit open | O | | | | |
| 68—AXOD transmission temperature switch failed open | O/R/C | | | | ✓ |
| 68—VAT reads 254°F or circuit grounded | O/C | | | | |
| 69—AXOD 3/2 pressure switch circuit failed closed | O | | | | ✓ |
| 69—AXOD 3/4 pressure switch circuit failed open | C | | | | |
| 70—ECA DATA communications link circuit failure | C | | | ✓ | |
| 71—Software re-initialization detected | C | | | ✓ | |
| 71—Idle tracking switch shorted to ground | C | ✓ | ✓ | | |
| 71—Cluster control assembly circuit failed | C | | | | |
| 72—Insufficient MAF/MAP change during dynamic test | R | | | | ✓ |
| 72—Power interrupt or re-initialization detected | C | | | ✓ | |
| 72—Message center control assembly circuit failed | C | | | | |
| 73—Insufficient throttle position change | C | ✓ | ✓ | ✓ | ✓ |
| 73—Insufficient TP change during dynamic test | R | | | | |
| 74—Brake on/off switch failure or not actuated | R | | | ✓ | |
| 75—Brake on/off switch circuit closed or ECA input open | R | | | ✓ | |
| 76—Insufficient VAF change during dynamic test | R | ✓ | ✓ | | |
| 77—No WOT seen in self-test or operator error | R | ✓ | ✓ | ✓ | ✓ |
| 79—A/C or defrost on during self-test | O | | | | ✓ |

86874066

## Service Codes (Table 1 — Codes 111–179)

| Service Codes | Quick Test Mode | 2.5L AXODE SEFI | 3.0L EFI | 3.0L AXODE SEFI | 3.8L AXODE SEFI |
|---|---|---|---|---|---|
| 111—System pass | O/R/C | ✓ | ✓ | ✓ | ✓ |
| 112—ACT sensor circuit grounded or reads 254°F | O/C | | ✓ | ✓ | ✓ |
| 112—ACT sensor circuit grounded | O/R | ✓ | | | |
| 113—ACT sensor circuit open | O/R | ✓ | | | |
| 113—ACT sensor circuit open or reads −40°F | O/C | | ✓ | ✓ | ✓ |
| 114—ACT outside test limits during KOEO or KOER tests | O/R | ✓ | ✓ | ✓ | ✓ |
| 116—ECT outside test limits during KOEO or KOER tests | O/R | ✓ | ✓ | ✓ | ✓ |
| 117—ECT sensor circuit grounded | O/C | ✓ | ✓ | ✓ | ✓ |
| 118—ECT sensor circuit above maximum voltage or reads −40°F | O/C | | ✓ | ✓ | ✓ |
| 118—ECT sensor circuit open | O/C | ✓ | | | |
| 121—Closed throttle voltage higher or lower than expected | O/R/C | ✓ | ✓ | ✓ | ✓ |
| 122—TP sensor circuit below minimum voltage | O/C | ✓ | ✓ | ✓ | ✓ |
| 123—TP sensor circuit above maximum voltage | O/C | ✓ | ✓ | ✓ | ✓ |
| 124—TP sensor voltage higher than expected, in range | C | ✓ | ✓ | ✓ | ✓ |
| 125—TP sensor voltage lower than expected in range | C | ✓ | ✓ | ✓ | ✓ |
| 126—BP or MAP sensor higher or lower than expected | O/R/C | ✓ | ✓ | ✓ | ✓ |
| 129—Insufficient MAF change during Dynamic Response test | R | | ✓ | ✓ | ✓ |
| 136—HEGO shows system always lean (front) | R | | ✓ | ✓ | |
| 136—HEGO shows system always lean (left) | R | | | | ✓ |
| 137—HEGO shows system always rich (front) | R | | ✓ | ✓ | |
| 137—HEGO shows system always rich (left) | R | | | | ✓ |
| 139—No HEGO switching (front) | C | | ✓ | ✓ | |
| 139—No HEGO switching (left) | C | | | | ✓ |
| 144—No HEGO switching (rear) | C | | ✓ | ✓ | |
| 144—No HEGO switching (right) | C | | | | ✓ |
| 144—No HEGO switching detected | C | ✓ | | | |
| 157—MAF sensor circuit below minimum voltage | C | ✓ | ✓ | ✓ | ✓ |
| 158—MAF sensor circuit above maximum voltage | C | ✓ | | | |
| 158—MAF sensor circuit above maximum voltage | O/C | | ✓ | ✓ | ✓ |
| 159—MAF higher or lower than expected during KOEO and KOER test | O/R/C | ✓ | ✓ | ✓ | ✓ |
| 167—Insufficient TP change during Dynamic Response test | R | | ✓ | ✓ | ✓ |
| 171—Fuel system at adaptive limit, HEGO unable to switch | C | ✓ | | | |
| 171—Fuel system at adaptive limit, HEGO unable to switch (right) | C | | | | ✓ |
| 171—No HEGO switching; system at adaptive limit (rear) | C | | ✓ | ✓ | |
| 172—HEGO shows system always lean (rear) | R/C | | ✓ | ✓ | |
| 172—No HEGO switching seen; indicates lean | R/C | ✓ | | | |
| 172—No HEGO switching seen; indicates lean (right) | R/C | | | | ✓ |
| 173—HEGO shows system always rich (rear) | R/C | | ✓ | ✓ | |
| 173—No HEGO switching seen; indicates rich | R/C | ✓ | | | |
| 173—No HEGO switching seen; indicates rich (right) | R/C | | | | ✓ |
| 174—HEGO switching time is slow (right) | R/C | | | | ✓ |
| 175—No HEGO switching; system at adaptive limit (front) | C | | ✓ | ✓ | |
| 175—No HEGO switching; system at adaptive limit (left) | C | | | | ✓ |
| 176—HEGO shows system always lean (front) | C | | ✓ | ✓ | |
| 176—HEGO shows system always lean (left) | C | | | | ✓ |
| 177—HEGO shows system always rich (front) | C | | ✓ | ✓ | |
| 177—HEGO shows system always rich (left) | C | | | | ✓ |
| 178—HEGO switching time is slow (left) | C | | | | ✓ |
| 179—Fuel at lean adaptive limit at part throttle; system rich | C | ✓ | | | |
| 179—System at lean adaptive limit at part throttle; system rich (rear) | C | | ✓ | ✓ | |
| 179—System at lean adaptive limit at part throttle; system rich (right) | C | | | | ✓ |

86874068

## Service Codes (Table 2 — Codes 181–519)

| Service Codes | Quick Test Mode | 2.5L AXODE SEFI | 3.0L EFI | 3.0L AXODE SEFI | 3.8L AXODE SEFI |
|---|---|---|---|---|---|
| 181—Fuel at rich adaptive limit at part throttle, system lean | C | ✓ | | | |
| 181—System at rich adaptive limit at part throttle; system lean (rear) | C | | ✓ | ✓ | |
| 181—System at rich adaptive limit at part throttle, system lean (right) | C | | | | ✓ |
| 182—Fuel at lean adaptive limit at idle; system rich | C | ✓ | | | |
| 182—System at rich adaptive limit at idle; system rich (rear) | C | | ✓ | ✓ | |
| 182—System at rich adaptive limit at idle; system rich (right) | C | | | | ✓ |
| 183—Fuel at rich adaptive limit at idle; system lean | C | ✓ | | | |
| 183—System at rich adaptive limit at idle; system lean (rear) | C | | ✓ | ✓ | |
| 184—MAF higher than expected | C | ✓ | ✓ | ✓ | ✓ |
| 185—MAF lower than expected | C | ✓ | ✓ | ✓ | ✓ |
| 186—Injector pulse width higher than expected | C | ✓ | ✓ | ✓ | ✓ |
| 187—Injector pulse width lower than expected | C | ✓ | ✓ | ✓ | ✓ |
| 188—System at lean adaptive limit at part throttle; system rich (front) | C | | ✓ | ✓ | |
| 188—System at lean adaptive limit at part throttle; system rich (left) | C | | | | ✓ |
| 189—System at rich adaptive limit at part throttle; system lean (front) | C | | ✓ | ✓ | |
| 189—System at rich adaptive limit at part throttle; system lean (left) | C | | | | ✓ |
| 191—System at lean adaptive limit at idle; system rich (front) | C | | ✓ | ✓ | |
| 191—System at lean adaptive limit at idle; system rich (left) | C | | | | ✓ |
| 192—System at rich adaptive limit at idle; system lean (front) | C | | ✓ | ✓ | |
| 192—System at rich adaptive limit at idle; system lean (left) | C | | | | ✓ |
| 211—PIP circuit fault | C | ✓ | ✓ | ✓ | ✓ |
| 212—Loss of IDM input to ECA or SPOUT circuit grounded | R | | | | ✓ |
| 213—SPOUT circuit open | R | ✓ | ✓ | ✓ | ✓ |
| 214—Cylinder identification circuit failure | C | | | | ✓ |
| 215—EEC processor detected Coil 1 primary circuit failure | O | | | | ✓ |
| 216—EEC processor detected Coil 2 primary circuit failure | O | | | | ✓ |
| 218—Loss of IDM signal, left side | C | | | | ✓ |
| 219—Spark timing defaulted to 10°BTDC or SPOUT circ. open | C | ✓ | ✓ | ✓ | ✓ |
| 222—Loss of IDM signal, right side | C | | | | ✓ |
| 223—Loss of dual plug inhibit control | C | | | | ✓ |
| 224—Erratic IDM input to processor | R/C | | | | ✓ |
| 225—Knock not sensed during Dynamic Response test | O/R/C | ✓ | ✓ | ✓ | ✓ |
| 311—Thermactor air system inoperative (right) | O/R/C | | | | ✓ |
| 313—Thermactor air not bypassed during self-test | R | | | | ✓ |
| 314—Thermactor air system inoperative (left) | R | | | | ✓ |
| 326—PFE or DPFE circuit voltage lower than expected | R | ✓ | ✓ | ✓ | ✓ |
| 327—EVP or DPFE circuit below minimum voltage | R/C | ✓ | ✓ | ✓ | ✓ |
| 328—EGR closed voltage lower than expected | O/R/C | ✓ | ✓ | ✓ | ✓ |
| 332—Insufficient EGR flow detected | R/C | ✓ | ✓ | ✓ | ✓ |
| 334—EGR closed voltage higher than expected | O | ✓ | ✓ | ✓ | ✓ |
| 335—PFE or DPFE sensor voltage out of self-test range | O | ✓ | ✓ | ✓ | ✓ |
| 336—PFE sensor voltage higher than expected | R/C | ✓ | ✓ | ✓ | ✓ |
| 337—EVP or DPFE circuit above maximum voltage | O | ✓ | ✓ | ✓ | ✓ |
| 341—Octane adjust service pin in use | O | ✓ | ✓ | ✓ | ✓ |
| 411—Cannot control rpm during KOEO low rpm check | R | ✓ | ✓ | ✓ | ✓ |
| 412—Cannot control rpm during KOER high rpm check | R | ✓ | ✓ | ✓ | ✓ |
| 452—Insufficient input from vehicle speed sensor | O | ✓ | ✓ | ✓ | ✓ |
| 511—EEC processor ROM test failed | O | ✓ | ✓ | ✓ | ✓ |
| 512—EEC processor Keep Alive Memory test failed | O | ✓ | ✓ | ✓ | ✓ |
| 512—EEC processor Keep Alive Memory test failed | O | ✓ | ✓ | ✓ | ✓ |
| 513—Failure in EEC processor internal voltage | O | ✓ | ✓ | ✓ | ✓ |
| 519—Power steering pressure switch circuit open | O | ✓ | ✓ | ✓ | ✓ |

86874069

| DIAGNOSTIC TROUBLE CODES | DEFINITIONS |
|---|---|
| 111 | System Pass |
| 112 | Intake Air Temp (IAT) sensor circuit below minimum voltage / 254°F indicated |
| 113 | Intake Air Temp (IAT) sensor circuit above maximum voltage / -40°F indicated |
| 114 | Intake Air Temp (IAT) sensor circuit voltage higher or lower than expected |
| 116 | Engine Coolant Temp (ECT) sensor circuit voltage higher or lower than expected |
| 117 | Engine Coolant Temp (ECT) sensor circuit below minimum voltage / 254°F indicated |
| 118 | Engine Coolant Temp (ECT) sensor circuit above maximum voltage / -40°F indicated |
| 121 | Closed throttle voltage higher or lower than expected |
| 121 | Throttle position voltage inconsistent with the MAF sensor |
| 122 | Throttle Position (TP) sensor circuit below minimum voltage |
| 123 | Throttle Position (TP) sensor circuit above maximum voltage |
| 124 | Throttle Position (TP) sensor voltage higher than expected |
| 125 | Throttle Position (TP) sensor voltage lower than expected |
| 126 | MAP / BARO sensor circuit voltage higher or lower than expected |
| 128 | MAP sensor vacuum hose damaged / disconnected |
| 129 | Insufficient MAP / Mass Air Flow (MAF) change during dynamic response test KOER |
| 136 | Lack of Heated Oxygen Sensor (HO2S-2) switch during KOER, indicates lean (Bank #2) |
| 137 | Lack of Heated Oxygen Sensor (HO2S-2) switch during KOER, indicates rich (Bank #2) |
| 139 | No Heated Oxygen Sensor (HO2S-2) switches detected (Bank #2) |
| 141 | Fuel system indicates lean |
| 144 | No Heated Oxygen Sensor (HO2S-1) switches detected (Bank #1) |
| 157 | Mass Air Flow (MAF) sensor circuit below minimum voltage |
| 158 | Mass Air Flow (MAF) sensor circuit above maximum voltage |
| 159 | Mass Air Flow (MAF) sensor circuit voltage higher or lower than expected |
| 167 | Insufficient throttle position change during dynamic response test KOER |
| 171 | Fuel system at adaptive limits, Heated Oxygen Sensor (HO2S-1) unable to switch (Bank #1) |
| 172 | Lack of Heated Oxygen Sensor (HO2S-1) switches, indicates lean (Bank #1) |
| 173 | Lack of Heated Oxygen Sensor (HO2S-1) switches, indicates rich (Bank #1) |
| 175 | Fuel system at adaptive limits, Heated Oxygen Sensor (HO2S-2) unable to switch (Bank #2) |
| 176 | Lack of Heated Oxygen Sensor (HO2S-2) switches, indicates lean (Bank #2) |
| 177 | Lack of Heated Oxygen Sensor (HO2S-2) switches, indicates rich (Bank #2) |
| 179 | Fuel system at lean adaptive limit at part throttle, system rich (Bank #1) |
| 181 | Fuel system at rich adaptive limit at part throttle, system lean (Bank #1) |
| 184 | Mass Air Flow (MAF) sensor voltage higher than expected |
| 185 | Mass Air Flow (MAF) sensor voltage lower than expected |
| 186 | Injector pulsewidth higher than expected (with BARO sensor) |
| 166 | Injector pulsewidth higher or mass air flow lower than expected (without BARO sensor) |
| 187 | Injector pulsewidth lower than expected (with BARO sensor) |
| 187 | Injector pulsewidth lower or mass air flow higher than expected (without BARO sensor) |
| 188 | Fuel system at lean adaptive limit at part throttle, system rich (Bank #2) |
| 189 | Fuel system at rich adaptive limit at part throttle, system lean (Bank #2) |
| 193 | Flexible Fuel (FF) sensor circuit failure |

86874071

| Service Codes | Quick Test Mode | 2.5L AXODE SEFI | 3.0L EFI | 3.0L AXODE SEFI | 3.8L AXODE SEFI |
|---|---|---|---|---|---|
| 519—Power steering pressure switch did not change state | R | ✓ | ✓ | ✓ | ✓ |
| 522—Vehicle not in Park or Neutral during KOEO test | O | ✓ | ✓ | ✓ | ✓ |
| 525—Vehicle in gear or A/C on during self-test | O | | | | |
| 528—Clutch switch circuit failure | C | ✓ | ✓ | ✓ | ✓ |
| 536—Brake On/Off circuit failure/not actuated during KOER test | R/C | ✓ | ✓ | ✓ | ✓ |
| 538—Insufficient rpm change during KOER Dynamic Response test | R | ✓ | ✓ | | |
| 539—A/C on or Defroster on during KOEO test | O | ✓ | ✓ | ✓ | ✓ |
| 542—Fuel pump secondary circuit failure: ECA to ground | O/C | ✓ | ✓ | ✓ | ✓ |
| 543—Fuel pump secondary circuit failure: Batt to ECA | O/C | ✓ | ✓ | ✓ | ✓ |
| 552—Air management 1 circuit failure | O | | | | |
| 556—Fuel pump primary circuit failure | O/C | ✓ | ✓ | ✓ | ✓ |
| 558—EGR vacuum regulator circuit failure | O | | | | |
| 563—High speed electro-drive fan circuit failure | O | ✓ | ✓ | ✓ | ✓ |
| 564—Electro-drive fan circuit failure | O | ✓ | ✓ | ✓ | ✓ |
| 565—Canister purge circuit failure | O | ✓ | ✓ | ✓ | ✓ |
| 566—3-4 shift solenoid circuit failure | O | ✓ | | ✓ | ✓ |
| 621—Shift solenoid 1 circuit failure | O | ✓ | | ✓ | ✓ |
| 622—Shift solenoid 2 circuit failure | O | ✓ | | ✓ | ✓ |
| 624—EPC solenoid or driver circuit failure | O/C | ✓ | | ✓ | ✓ |
| 625—EPC driver open in ECA | O | ✓ | | ✓ | ✓ |
| 628—Lock-up solenoid failure, excessive clutch slippage | C | ✓ | | ✓ | ✓ |
| 629—Converter clutch control circuit failure | O | ✓ | | ✓ | ✓ |
| 629—Lock-up solenoid failure | O | ✓ | | ✓ | ✓ |
| 634—MLP sensor voltage out of self-test range | C | ✓ | | ✓ | ✓ |
| 636—TOT sensor voltage out of self-test range | O/R | ✓ | | ✓ | ✓ |
| 637—TOT sensor circuit above maximum voltage | O/C | ✓ | | ✓ | ✓ |
| 638—TOT sensor circuit below maximum voltage | O/C | ✓ | | ✓ | ✓ |
| 639—Insufficient input from turbine speed sensor | R/C | ✓ | | ✓ | ✓ |
| 641—Shift solenoid 3 circuit failure | C | ✓ | | ✓ | ✓ |
| 645—Incorrect gear ratio obtained for 1st gear | C | ✓ | | ✓ | ✓ |
| 646—Incorrect gear ratio obtained for 2nd gear | C | ✓ | | ✓ | ✓ |
| 647—Incorrect gear ratio obtained for 3rd gear | C | ✓ | | ✓ | ✓ |
| 648—Incorrect gear ratio obtained for 4th gear | C | ✓ | | ✓ | ✓ |
| 649—EPC range failure | C | ✓ | | ✓ | ✓ |
| 651—EPC range failure | C | ✓ | | ✓ | ✓ |
| 998—Hard fault present | R | ✓ | ✓ | ✓ | ✓ |

Codes Not Listed: Do not apply to vehicle being tested
No Codes: Cannot begin self-test or cannot transmit codes
O—Key on, engine off test
R—Key on, engine running test
C—Continuous memory

86874070

| DIAGNOSTIC TROUBLE CODES | DEFINITIONS |
|---|---|
| 211 | Profile Ignition Pickup (PIP) circuit failure |
| 212 | Loss of Ignition Diagnostic Monitor (IDM) input to PCM / SPOUT circuit grounded |
| 213 | SPOUT circuit open |
| 214 | Cylinder Identification (CID) circuit failure |
| 215 | PCM detected coil 1 primary circuit failure (EI) |
| 216 | PCM detected coil 2 primary circuit failure (EI) |
| 217 | PCM detected coil 3 primary circuit failure (EI) |
| 218 | Loss of Ignition Diagnostic Monitor (IDM) signal-left side (dual plug EI) |
| 219 | Spark timing defaulted to 10 degrees-SPOUT circuit open (EI) |
| 221 | Spark timing error (EI) |
| 222 | Loss of Ignition Diagnostic Monitor (IDM) signal-right side (dual plug EI) |
| 223 | Loss of Dual Plug Inhibit (DPI) control (dual plug EI) |
| 224 | PCM detected coil 1, 2, 3 or 4 primary circuit failure (dual plug EI) |
| 225 | Knock not sensed during dynamic response test KOER |
| 226 | Ignition Diagnostic Module (IDM) signal not received (EI) |
| 232 | PCM detected coil 1, 2, 3 or 4 primary circuit failure (EI) |
| 238 | PCM detected coil 4 primary circuit failure (EI) |
| 241 | ICM to PCM IDM pulsewidth transmission error (EI) |
| 244 | CID circuit fault present when cylinder balance test requested |
| 311 | AIR system inoperative during KOER (Bank # 1 w / dual HO2S) |
| 312 | AIR misdirected during KOER |
| 313 | AIR not bypassed during KOER |
| 314 | AIR system inoperative during KOER (Bank # 2 w / dual HO2S) |
| 326 | EGR (PFE / DPFE) circuit voltage lower than expected |
| 327 | EGR (EGRP / EVP / PFE / DPFE) circuit below minimum voltage |
| 328 | EGR (EVP) closed valve voltage lower than expected |
| 332 | Insufficient EGR flow detected (EGRP / EVP / PFE / DPFE) |
| 334 | EGR (EVP) closed valve voltage higher than expected |
| 335 | EGR (PFE / DPFE) sensor voltage higher or lower than expected during KOEO |
| 336 | Exhaust pressure high / EGR (PFE / DPFE) circuit voltage higher than expected |
| 337 | EGR (EGRP / EVP / PFE / DPFE) circuit above maximum voltage |
| 338 | Engine Coolant Temperature (ECT) lower than expected (thermostat test) |
| 339 | Engine Coolant Temperature (ECT) higher than expected (thermostat test) |
| 341 | Octane adjust service pin open |
| 381 | Frequent A / C clutch cycling |
| 411 | Cannot control RPM during KOER low RPM check |
| 412 | Cannot control RPM during KOER high RPM check |
| 415 | Idle Air Control (IAC) system at maximum adaptive lower limit |
| 416 | Idle Air Control (IAC) system at upper adaptive learning limit |
| 452 | Insufficient input from Vehicle Speed Sensor (VSS) to PCM |
| 453 | Servo leaking down (KOER IVSC test) |
| 454 | Servo leaking up (KOER IVSC test) |
| 455 | Insufficient RPM increase (KOER IVSC test) |
| 456 | Insufficient RPM decrease (KOER IVSC test) |

86874072

| DIAGNOSTIC TROUBLE CODES | DEFINITIONS |
|---|---|
| 457 | Speed control command switch(s) circuit not functioning (KOEO IVSC test) |
| 458 | Speed control command switch(s) stuck / circuit grounded (KOEO IVSC test) |
| 459 | Speed control ground circuit open (KOEO IVSC test) |
| 511 | PCM Read Only Memory (ROM) test failure KOEO |
| 512 | PCM Keep Alive Memory (KAM) test failure |
| 513 | PCM internal voltage failure (KOEO) |
| 519 | Power Steering Pressure (PSP) switch circuit open KOEO |
| 519 | Power Steering Pressure (PSP) sensor circuit open |
| 521 | Power Steering Pressure (PSP) switch circuit did not change states KOER |
| 521 | Power Steering Pressure (PSP) sensor circuit did not change states KOER |
| 522 | Vehicle not in PARK or NEUTRAL during KOEO / PNP switch circuit open |
| 524 | Low speed fuel pump circuit open—battery to PCM |
| 525 | Indicates vehicle in gear / A / C on |
| 527 | Park / Neutral Position (PNP) switch circuit open—A / C on KOEO |
| 528 | Clutch Pedal Position (CPP) switch circuit failure |
| 529 | Data Communication Link (DCL) or PCM circuit failure |
| 532 | Cluster Control Assembly (CCA) circuit failure |
| 533 | Data Communication Link (DCL) or Electronic Instrument Cluster (EIC) circuit failure |
| 536 | Brake On / Off (BOO) circuit failure / not actuated during KOER |
| 538 | Insufficient RPM change during KOER dynamic response test |
| 538 | Invalid cylinder balance test due to throttle movement during test (SFI only) |
| 538 | Invalid cylinder balance test due to CID circuit failure |
| 539 | A / C on / Defrost on during Self-Test |
| 542 | Fuel pump secondary circuit failure |
| 543 | Fuel pump secondary circuit failure |
| 551 | Idle Air Control (IAC) circuit failure KOEO |
| 552 | Secondary Air Injection Bypass (AIRB) circuit failure KOEO |
| 553 | Secondary Air Injection Diverter (AIRD) circuit failure KOEO |
| 554 | Fuel Pressure Regulator Control (FPRC) circuit failure |
| 556 | Fuel pump relay primary circuit failure |
| 557 | Low speed fuel pump primary circuit failure |
| 558 | EGR Vacuum Regulator (EVR) circuit failure KOEO |
| 559 | Air Conditioning On (ACON) relay circuit failure KOEO |
| 563 | High Fan Control (HFC) circuit failure KOEO |
| 564 | Fan Control (FC) circuit failure KOEO |
| 565 | Canister Purge (CANP) circuit failure KOEO |
| 566 | 3-4 shift solenoid circuit failure KOEO (A4LD) |
| 567 | Speed Control Vent (SCVNT) circuit failure (KOEO IVSC test) |
| 568 | Speed Control Vacuum (SCVAC) circuit failure (KOEO IVSC test) |
| 569 | Auxiliary Canister Purge (CANP2) circuit failure KOEO |
| 571 | EGRA solenoid circuit failure KOEO |
| 572 | EGRV solenoid circuit failure KOEO |
| 578 | A / C pressure sensor circuit shorted |
| 579 | Insufficient A / C pressure change |

86874073

| DIAGNOSTIC TROUBLE CODES | DEFINITIONS |
|---|---|
| 667 | Transmission Range sensor circuit voltage below over minimum voltage |
| 668 | Transmission Range circuit voltage above maximum voltage |
| 675 | Transmission Range sensor circuit voltage out of range |
| 998 | Hard fault present—FMEM MODE |

86874075

| DIAGNOSTIC TROUBLE CODES | DEFINITIONS |
|---|---|
| 581 | Power to Fan circuit over current |
| 582 | Fan circuit open |
| 583 | Power to Fuel pump over current |
| 584 | VCRM Power ground circuit open (VCRM Pin 1) |
| 585 | Power to A/C clutch over current |
| 586 | A/C clutch circuit open |
| 587 | Variable Control Relay Module (VCRM) communication failure |
| 593 | Heated Oxygen Sensor Heater (HO2S HTR) circuit failure |
| 617 | 1-2 shift error |
| 618 | 2-3 shift error |
| 619 | 3-4 shift error |
| 621 | Shift Solenoid 1 (SS1) circuit failure KOEO |
| 622 | Shift Solenoid 2 (SS2) circuit failure KOEO |
| 623 | Transmission Control Indicator Lamp (TCIL) circuit failfire |
| 624 | Electronic Pressure Control (EPC) circuit failure |
| 625 | Electronic Pressure Control (EPC) driver open in PCM |
| 626 | Coast Clutch Solenoid (CCS) circuit failure KOEO |
| 627 | Torque Converter Clutch (TCC) solenoid circuit failure |
| 628 | Excessive converter clutch slippage |
| 629 | Torque Converter Clutch (TCC) solenoid circuit failure |
| 631 | Transmission Control Indicator Lamp (TCIL) circuit failure KOEO |
| 632 | Transmission Control Switch (TCS) circuit did not change states during KOER |
| 633 | 4x4L switch closed during KOEO |
| 634 | Transmission Range (TR) voltage higher or lower than expected |
| 636 | Transmission Fluid Temperature (TFT) higher or lower than expected |
| 637 | Transmission Fluid Temperature (TFT) sensor circuit above maximum voltage / -40°F (-40°C) indicated / circuit open |
| 638 | Transmission Fluid Temperature (TFT) sensor circuit below minimum voltage / 290°F (143°C) indicated / circuit shorted |
| 639 | Insufficient input from Turbine Shaft Speed Sensor (TSS) |
| 641 | Shift Solenoid 3 (SS3) circuit failure |
| 643 | Torque Converter Clutch (TCC) circuit failure |
| 645 | Incorrect gear ratio obtained for first gear |
| 646 | Incorrect gear ratio obtained for second gear |
| 647 | Incorrect gear ratio obtained for third gear |
| 648 | Incorrect gear ratio obtained for fourth gear |
| 649 | Electronic Pressure Control (EPC) higher or lower than expected |
| 651 | Electronic Pressure Control (EPC) circuit failure |
| 652 | Torque Converter Clutch (TCC) solenoid circuit failure |
| 653 | Transmission Control Switch (TCS) did not change states during KOER |
| 654 | Transmission Range (TR) sensor not indicating PARK during KOEO |
| 656 | Torque Converter Clutch continuous slip error |
| 657 | Transmission overtemperature condition occurred |
| 659 | High vehicle speed in park indicated |

86874074

## VACUUM DIAGRAMS

Following is a list of vacuum diagrams for most of the engine and emissions package combinations covered by this manual. Because vacuum circuits will vary based on various engine and vehicle options, always refer to the vehicle emission control information label. Should the label be missing, or should the vehicle be equipped with a different engine from the car's original equipment, refer to the diagrams below for the same or similar configuration.

If you wish to obtain a replacement emissions label, most manufacturers make the labels available for purchase. The labels can usually be ordered from a local dealer.

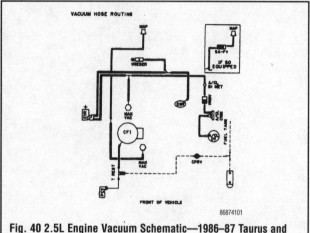

**Fig. 40 2.5L Engine Vacuum Schematic—1986–87 Taurus and Sable**

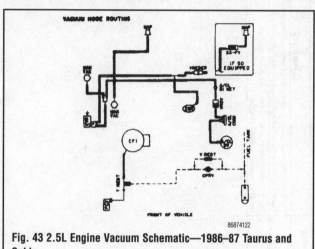

**Fig. 43 2.5L Engine Vacuum Schematic—1986–87 Taurus and Sable**

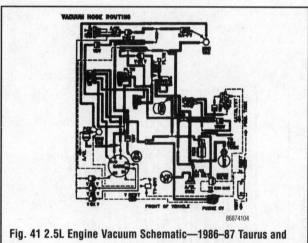

**Fig. 41 2.5L Engine Vacuum Schematic—1986–87 Taurus and Sable**

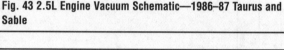
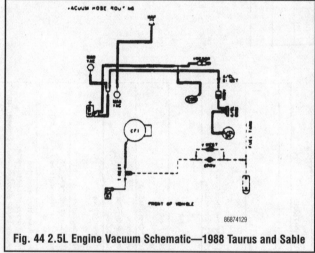

**Fig. 44 2.5L Engine Vacuum Schematic—1988 Taurus and Sable**

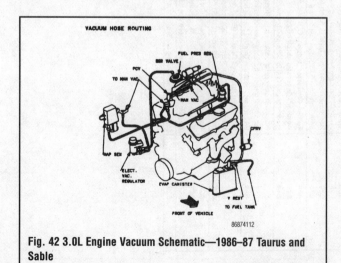

**Fig. 42 3.0L Engine Vacuum Schematic—1986–87 Taurus and Sable**

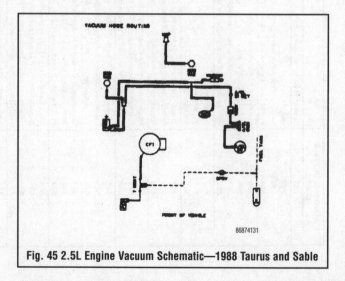

**Fig. 45 2.5L Engine Vacuum Schematic—1988 Taurus and Sable**

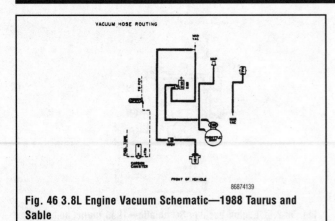

Fig. 46 3.8L Engine Vacuum Schematic—1988 Taurus and Sable

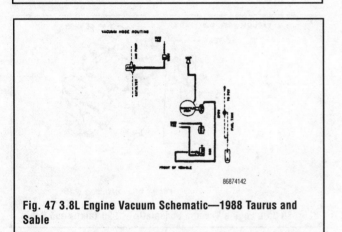

Fig. 47 3.8L Engine Vacuum Schematic—1988 Taurus and Sable

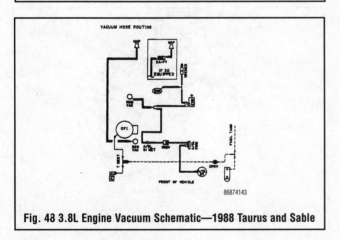

Fig. 48 3.8L Engine Vacuum Schematic—1988 Taurus and Sable

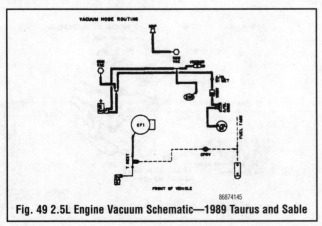

Fig. 49 2.5L Engine Vacuum Schematic—1989 Taurus and Sable

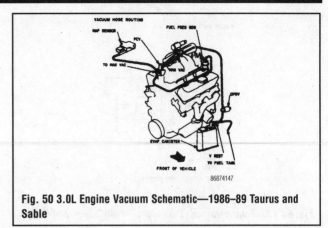

Fig. 50 3.0L Engine Vacuum Schematic—1986–89 Taurus and Sable

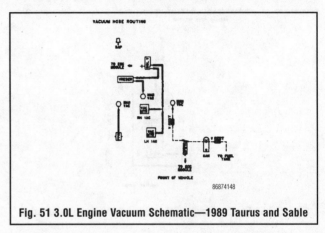

Fig. 51 3.0L Engine Vacuum Schematic—1989 Taurus and Sable

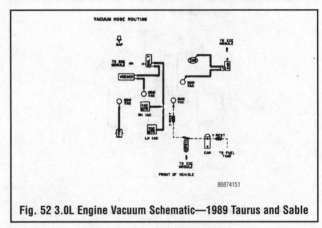

Fig. 52 3.0L Engine Vacuum Schematic—1989 Taurus and Sable

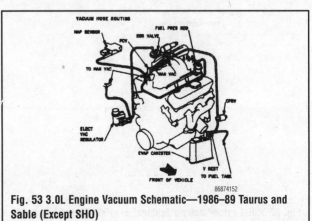

Fig. 53 3.0L Engine Vacuum Schematic—1986–89 Taurus and Sable (Except SHO)

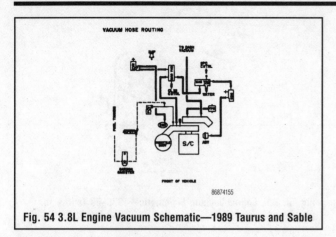

Fig. 54 3.8L Engine Vacuum Schematic—1989 Taurus and Sable

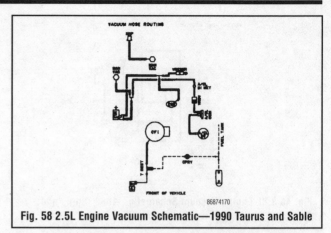

Fig. 58 2.5L Engine Vacuum Schematic—1990 Taurus and Sable

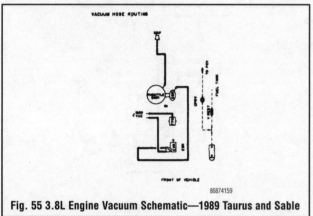

Fig. 55 3.8L Engine Vacuum Schematic—1989 Taurus and Sable

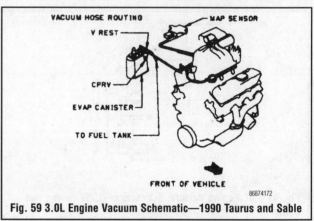

Fig. 59 3.0L Engine Vacuum Schematic—1990 Taurus and Sable

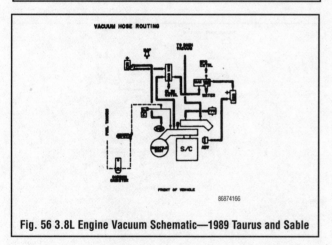

Fig. 56 3.8L Engine Vacuum Schematic—1989 Taurus and Sable

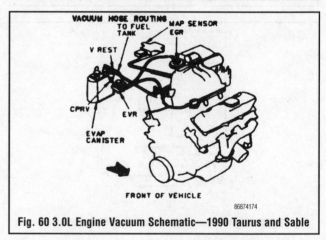

Fig. 60 3.0L Engine Vacuum Schematic—1990 Taurus and Sable

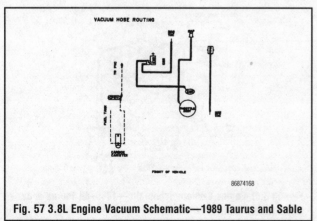

Fig. 57 3.8L Engine Vacuum Schematic—1989 Taurus and Sable

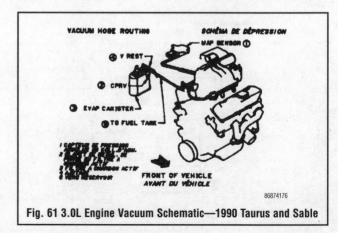

Fig. 61 3.0L Engine Vacuum Schematic—1990 Taurus and Sable

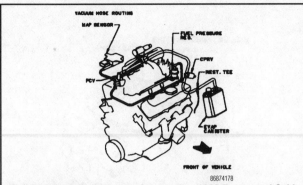

**Fig. 62 3.0L Engine Vacuum Schematic—1990 Taurus and Sable (Except SHO)**

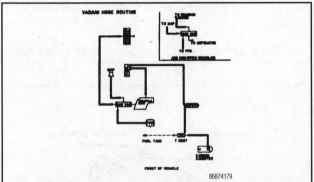

**Fig. 63 3.0L Engine Vacuum Schematic—1990 Taurus and Sable (Except SHO)**

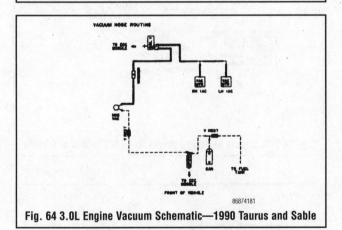

**Fig. 64 3.0L Engine Vacuum Schematic—1990 Taurus and Sable**

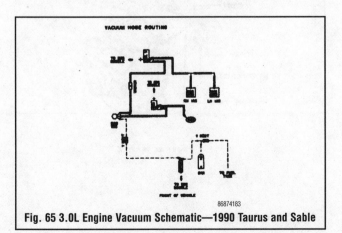

**Fig. 65 3.0L Engine Vacuum Schematic—1990 Taurus and Sable**

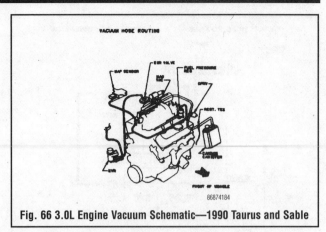

**Fig. 66 3.0L Engine Vacuum Schematic—1990 Taurus and Sable**

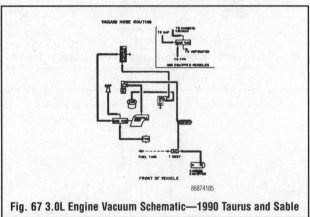

**Fig. 67 3.0L Engine Vacuum Schematic—1990 Taurus and Sable**

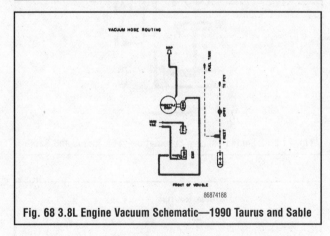

**Fig. 68 3.8L Engine Vacuum Schematic—1990 Taurus and Sable**

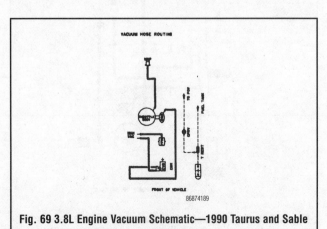

**Fig. 69 3.8L Engine Vacuum Schematic—1990 Taurus and Sable**

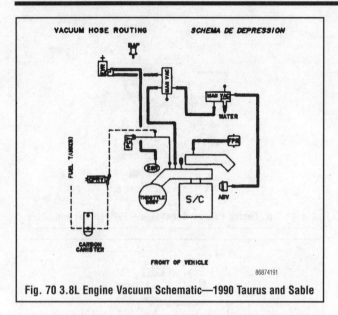

Fig. 70 3.8L Engine Vacuum Schematic—1990 Taurus and Sable

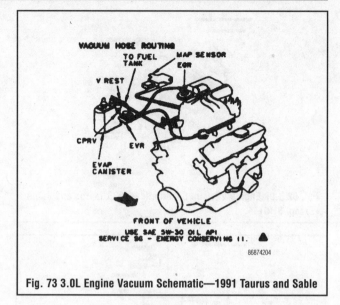

Fig. 73 3.0L Engine Vacuum Schematic—1991 Taurus and Sable

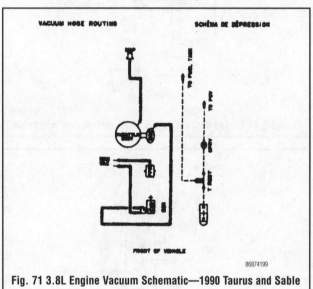

Fig. 71 3.8L Engine Vacuum Schematic—1990 Taurus and Sable

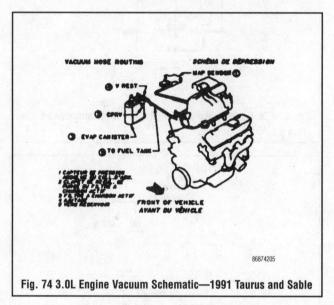

Fig. 74 3.0L Engine Vacuum Schematic—1991 Taurus and Sable

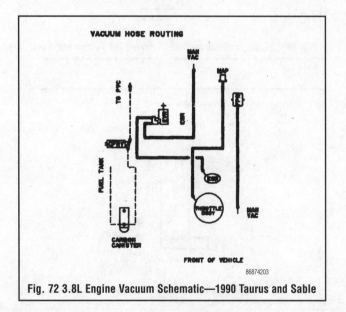

Fig. 72 3.8L Engine Vacuum Schematic—1990 Taurus and Sable

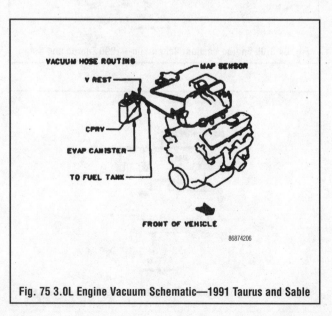

Fig. 75 3.0L Engine Vacuum Schematic—1991 Taurus and Sable

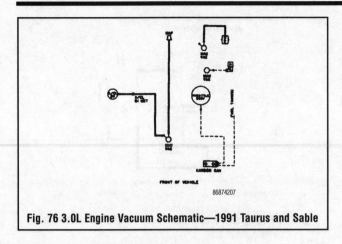

86874207

**Fig. 76 3.0L Engine Vacuum Schematic—1991 Taurus and Sable**

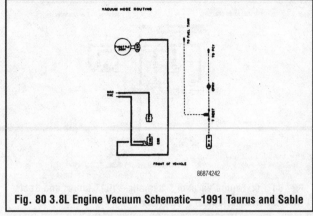

86874242

**Fig. 80 3.8L Engine Vacuum Schematic—1991 Taurus and Sable**

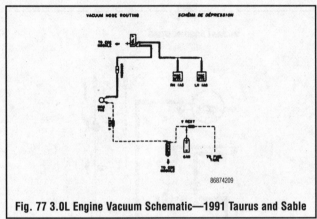

86874209

**Fig. 77 3.0L Engine Vacuum Schematic—1991 Taurus and Sable**

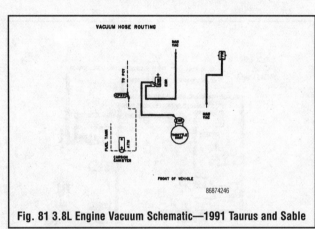

86874246

**Fig. 81 3.8L Engine Vacuum Schematic—1991 Taurus and Sable**

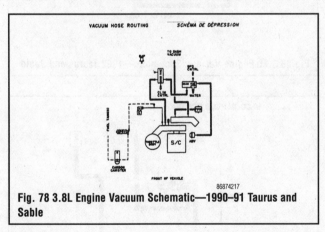

86874217

**Fig. 78 3.8L Engine Vacuum Schematic—1990–91 Taurus and Sable**

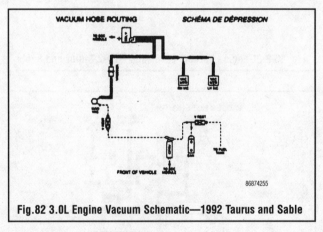

86874255

**Fig. 82 3.0L Engine Vacuum Schematic—1992 Taurus and Sable**

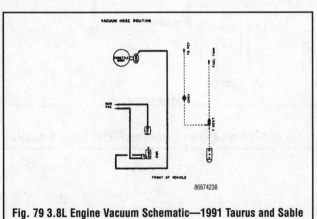

86874238

**Fig. 79 3.8L Engine Vacuum Schematic—1991 Taurus and Sable**

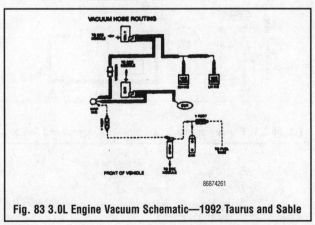

86874261

**Fig. 83 3.0L Engine Vacuum Schematic—1992 Taurus and Sable**

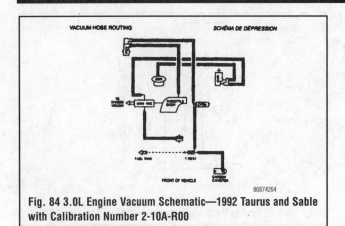

**Fig. 84 3.0L Engine Vacuum Schematic—1992 Taurus and Sable with Calibration Number 2-10A-R00**

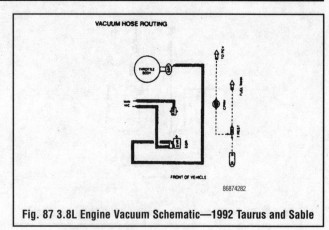

**Fig. 87 3.8L Engine Vacuum Schematic—1992 Taurus and Sable**

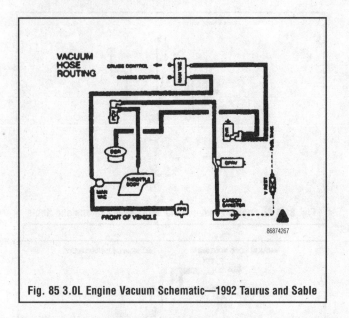

**Fig. 85 3.0L Engine Vacuum Schematic—1992 Taurus and Sable**

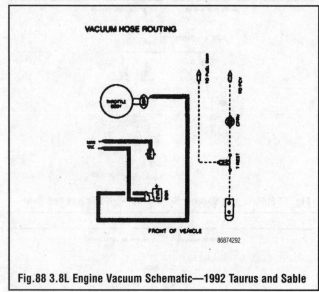

**Fig.88 3.8L Engine Vacuum Schematic—1992 Taurus and Sable**

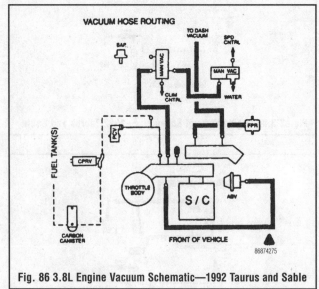

**Fig. 86 3.8L Engine Vacuum Schematic—1992 Taurus and Sable**

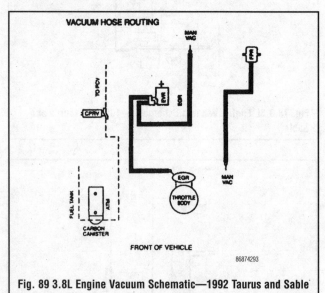

**Fig. 89 3.8L Engine Vacuum Schematic—1992 Taurus and Sable**

# 5

# FUEL SYSTEM

## BASIC FUEL SYSTEM DIAGNOSIS

When there is a problem starting or driving a vehicle, two of the most important checks involve the ignition and the fuel systems. The two questions that mechanics attempt to answer first, "is there spark?" and "is there fuel?" will often lead to solving most basic problems. For ignition system diagnosis and testing, please refer to Section 2 of this manual. If the ignition system checks out (there is spark), then you must determine if the fuel system is operating properly (is there fuel?).

### Precautions

Safety is the most important factor when performing not only fuel system maintenance, but any type of maintenance. Failure to conduct maintenance and repairs in a safe manner may result in serious personal injury or death. Maintenance and testing of the vehicle's fuel system components can be accomplished safely and effectively by adhering to the following rules and guidelines:

• To avoid the possibility of fire and personal injury, always disconnect the negative battery cable unless the repair or test procedure requires that battery voltage be applied.

• Always relieve the fuel system pressure prior to disconnecting any fuel system component (injector, fuel rail, pressure regulator, etc.), fitting or fuel line connection. Exercise extreme caution whenever relieving fuel system pressure to avoid exposing skin, face and eyes to fuel spray. Please be advised that fuel under pressure may penetrate the skin or any part of the body that it contacts.

• Always place a shop towel or cloth around the fitting or connection prior to loosening to absorb any excess fuel due to spillage. Ensure that all fuel spillage (should it occur) is quickly removed from engine surfaces. Ensure that all fuel soaked cloths or towels are deposited into a suitable waste container.

• Always keep a dry chemical (Class B) fire extinguisher near the work area.

• Do not allow fuel spray or fuel vapors to come into contact with a spark or open flame.

• Always use a backup wrench when loosening and tightening fuel line connection fittings. This will prevent unnecessary stress and torsion to fuel line piping. Always follow the proper torque specifications.

• Always replace worn fuel fitting O-rings with new ones. Do not substitute fuel hose or equivalent where fuel pipe is installed.

• Due to the possibility of a fire or explosion, never drain or store gasoline in an open container.

## CENTRAL FUEL INJECTION (CFI)

### General Description

▶ **See Figure 1**

The Central Fuel Injection (CFI) system is a single point, pulse time modulated injection system which was used on 1986–90 2.5L engines. Fuel is metered into the air intake stream according to engine demands by one or two solenoid injection valves, mounted in a throttle body on the intake manifold. Fuel is supplied from the fuel tank by a single low-pressure pump. The fuel is filtered and sent to the air throttle body, where a regulator keeps the fuel delivery pressure at a constant 39 psi (269 kPa) on high-pressure systems, or 14.5 psi (100 kPa) on low-pressure systems. One or two injector nozzles are mounted vertically above the throttle plates and connected in parallel with the fuel pressure regulator. Excess fuel supplied by the pump, but not needed by the engine, is returned to the fuel tank by a steel fuel return line.

The fuel charging assembly controls air/fuel ratio. It consists of a typical carburetor type throttle body, and has one or two bores without venturis. The throttle shaft and valves control engine air flow based on driver demand. The throttle body attaches to the intake manifold mounting pad.

A throttle position sensor is attached to the throttle shaft. It includes a potentiometer (or rheostat) that electrically senses throttle opening. A throttle kicker solenoid fastens opposite the throttle position sensor. During air conditioning operation, the solenoid extends to slightly increase engine idle speed.

Cold engine speed is controlled by an automatic kick-down vacuum motor. There is also an all-electric, bimetal coil spring which controls cold idle speed. The bimetal electric coil operates like a conventional carburetor choke coil, but the fuel injection system uses no choke. Fuel enrichment for cold starts is controlled by the computer and injectors.

The fuel pressure regulator controls critical injector fuel pressure. The regulator receives fuel from the electric fuel pump and then adjusts the fuel pressure for uniform fuel injection. The regulator sets fuel pressure at 39 psi (269 kPa) on high pressure systems, or 14.5 psi (100 kPa) on low pressure systems.

The fuel manifold (or fuel rail) evenly distributes fuel to each injector. Its main purpose is to equalize the fuel flow. One end of the fuel rail contains a relief valve for testing fuel pressure during engine operation.

The fuel injectors are electromechanical devices. The electrical solenoid operates a pintle or ball metering valve which always travels the same distance from closed to open to closed. Injection is controlled by varying the length of time the valve is open.

The computer, based on voltage inputs from the crank position sensor, operates each injector solenoid two times per engine revolution. When the injector metering valve unseats, fuel is sprayed in a fine mist into the intake manifold. The computer varies fuel enrichment based on voltage inputs from the exhaust gas oxygen sensor, barometric pressure sensor, manifold absolute pressure sensor, etc., by calculating how long to hold the injectors open. The longer the injectors remain open, the richer the mixture. This injector ON time is called pulse duration.

### Relieving Fuel System Pressure

▶ **See Figure 2**

1. Disengage the electrical connector from the inertia switch located on the left side of the storage compartment.
2. Crank the engine for 15 seconds.
3. Engage the electrical connector to the inertia switch located on the left side of the storage compartment.

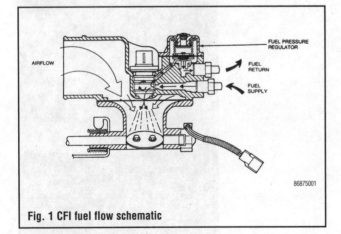

AIRFLOW

FUEL PRESSURE REGULATOR

FUEL RETURN

FUEL SUPPLY

86875001

**Fig. 1 CFI fuel flow schematic**

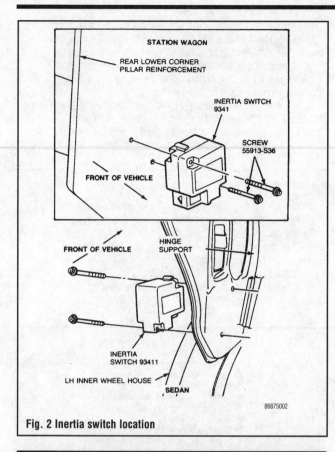

Fig. 2 Inertia switch location

## Electric Fuel Pump

### REMOVAL & INSTALLATION

▶ **See Figure 3**

1. Relieve the fuel system pressure. For details, please refer to the procedure located earlier in this section.
2. Disconnect the negative battery cable.
3. Remove the fuel from the fuel tank by pumping it out through the filler neck using Rotunda Fuel Storage Tanker 034-00002 and Adapter Hose 034-00011, or equivalent.
4. Raise and safely support the vehicle, then disconnect and remove the fuel filler tube.
5. Support the fuel tank, then remove the fuel tank support straps. Partially lower the fuel tank, then remove the fuel lines, electrical connectors and vent lines from the tank. Remove the fuel tank from the vehicle, then place it on a work bench. Remove any dirt around the fuel pump attaching flange, so it will not get into the fuel tank.
6. Using Fuel Tank Sender Wrench D84P-9275-A or equivalent, turn the fuel pump locking ring counterclockwise, then remove the lock ring.
7. Remove the fuel pump and bracket assembly from the fuel tank, then remove and discard the flange gasket.

   **To install:**
8. Clean the fuel pump mounting flange, along with the fuel tank mounting surface and seal ring groove.
9. Put a light coating of grease on the new seal gasket to hold it in place during assembly, then install the gasket in the fuel ring groove.
10. Carefully install the fuel pump and sender assembly, making sure that the filter is not damaged. Make sure that the locating keys are in the keyways and that the seal ring stays in place.
11. Hold the assembly in place, then install the lock ring finger-tight, making sure all locking tabs are under the tank lock ring tabs.
12. Tighten the lock ring using Fuel Tank Sender Wrench D84P-9275-A, by turning it clockwise until the the ring is up against the stops.

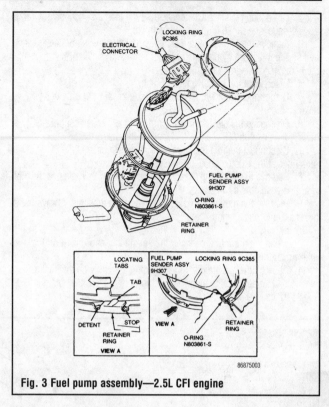

Fig. 3 Fuel pump assembly—2.5L CFI engine

13. Remove the fuel tank from the bench and support the tank while connecting the fuel lines, vent lines and electrical connectors to their proper locations.
14. Install the tank in the vehicle, then secure with the retaining straps. Carefully lower the vehicle.
15. Install the filler tube and tighten the retaining screws.
16. Fill the tank with at least 10 gallons of fuel, then check for leaks.
17. Connect the negative battery cable.
18. Connect a suitable fuel pressure gauge. Turn the ignition switch to the **ON** position 5–10 times, leaving it on for 3 seconds at a time, until the pressure gauge reads at least 30 psi (270 kPa). Check for leaks at the fittings.
19. Remove the pressure gauge, start the engine and recheck for leaks.

### TESTING

1. Ground the fuel pump lead of the self-test connector through a jumper wire at the FP lead.
2. Connect a suitable fuel pressure tester to the fuel pump outlet.
3. Turn the ignition key to the **RUN** position to operate the fuel pump.
4. Note the pressure reading. The fuel pressure should be 13–17 psi (90–117 kPa) for the CFI engine.

➡ **A safety inertia switch is installed to shut off the electric fuel pump in case of collision. The switch is located on the left-hand side (driver's side) of the car, behind the rearmost seat side trim panel, or inside the rear quarter shock tower access door. If the pump shuts off, or if the vehicle has been hit and will not start, check for leaks first, then reset the switch. The switch is reset by pushing down on the button provided.**

## Throttle Body/Fuel Charging Assembly

### REMOVAL & INSTALLATION

▶ **See Figure 4**

1. Remove the air tube clamp at the fuel charging/throttle body assembly air inlet.

2. Disengage the electrical connector at the inertia switch located on the left-hand side of the luggage compartment.

3. Remove the fuel cap and release the fuel tank pressure. Release the fuel system pressure by disengaging the inertia switch electrical connector, then cranking the engine for 15 seconds.

4. Disconnect the negative battery cable.

5. Disconnect the throttle cable and transmission throttle valve lever.

6. Disengage the electrical connector at the idle speed control (ISC), the throttle position (TP) sensor and the fuel injector.

7. Disconnect the fuel inlet and outlet connections, and the PCV vacuum lines at the throttle body assembly.

8. Remove fuel charging assembly retaining nuts, then remove the fuel charging assembly/throttle body.

9. Remove the mounting gasket from the intake manifold. Always use a new gasket for installation.

**To install:**

10. Clean the mounting surfaces, then position a new gasket on the intake manifold.

11. Position the throttle body/fuel charging assembly on the intake manifold, then secure with the two retaining nuts. Tighten the nuts to 15–25 ft. lbs. (20–34 Nm).

12. Engage the ISC, TP sensor and fuel injector electrical connectors.

13. Fasten the fuel inlet and outlet connections, then connect the PCV vacuum line at the throttle body/fuel charging assembly.

14. Connect the throttle cable and transaxle throttle valve lever.

15. Engage the electrical connector at the inertia switch. Install the air tube and clamp at the fuel charging assembly.

16. Connect the negative battery cable, then start the engine and check for leaks. Adjust the engine idle speed if necessary. Refer to the Engine/Emission Control Decal for idle speed specifications.

## INJECTOR REPLACEMENT

▶ **See Figure 5**

1. Remove the fuel injector retaining screw and retainer.

2. Remove the injector and the lower O-ring. Discard the O-ring.

**To install:**

3. Lubricate a new lower O-ring and the injector seat area with clean engine oil. Do NOT use transmission oil!

4. Install the lower O-ring on the injector.

5. Lubricate the upper O-ring, then clean and lubricate the throttle body O-ring seat.

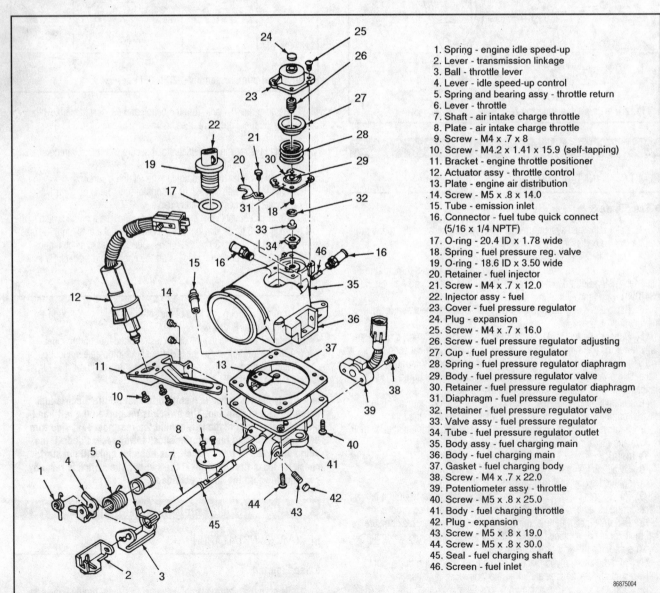

1. Spring - engine idle speed-up
2. Lever - transmission linkage
3. Ball - throttle lever
4. Lever - idle speed-up control
5. Spring and bearing assy - throttle return
6. Lever - throttle
7. Shaft - air intake charge throttle
8. Plate - air intake charge throttle
9. Screw - M4 x .7 x 8
10. Screw - M4.2 x 1.41 x 15.9 (self-tapping)
11. Bracket - engine throttle positioner
12. Actuator assy - throttle control
13. Plate - engine air distribution
14. Screw - M5 x .8 x 14.0
15. Tube - emission inlet
16. Connector - fuel tube quick connect (5/16 x 1/4 NPTF)
17. O-ring - 20.4 ID x 1.78 wide
18. Spring - fuel pressure reg. valve
19. O-ring - 18.6 ID x 3.50 wide
20. Retainer - fuel injector
21. Screw - M4 x .7 x 12.0
22. Injector assy - fuel
23. Cover - fuel pressure regulator
24. Plug - expansion
25. Screw - M4 x .7 x 16.0
26. Screw - fuel pressure regulator adjusting
27. Cup - fuel pressure regulator
28. Spring - fuel pressure regulator diaphragm
29. Body - fuel pressure regulator valve
30. Retainer - fuel pressure regulator diaphragm
31. Diaphragm - fuel pressure regulator
32. Retainer - fuel pressure regulator valve
33. Valve assy - fuel pressure regulator
34. Tube - fuel pressure regulator outlet
35. Body assy - fuel charging main
36. Body - fuel charging main
37. Gasket - fuel charging body
38. Screw - M4 x .7 x 22.0
39. Potentiometer assy - throttle
40. Screw - M5 x .8 x 25.0
41. Body - fuel charging throttle
42. Plug - expansion
43. Screw - M5 x .8 x 19.0
44. Screw - M5 x .8 x 30.0
45. Seal - fuel charging shaft
46. Screen - fuel inlet

86875004

**Fig. 4 Exploded view of the throttle body/fuel charging assembly—2.5L CFI engine**

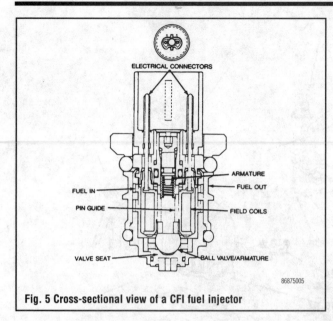

ELECTRICAL CONNECTORS

FUEL IN
PIN GUIDE

ARMATURE
FUEL OUT
FIELD COILS

VALVE SEAT          BALL VALVE/ARMATURE

86875005

**Fig. 5 Cross-sectional view of a CFI fuel injector**

6. Install the injector by centering and applying a steady downward pressure with a slight rotational force.

7. Install the injector and the injector retaining screw. Tighten the retaining screw to 18–22 inch lbs. (2.0–2.5 Nm).

## TESTING

1. Disengage the electrical connector from inertia switch on the left-hand side of the luggage compartment.

2. Crank the engine for 15 seconds to reduce fuel system pressure.

3. Disconnect the fuel supply line at the throttle body using Spring Lock Coupling Adapter D85L-9974-C or equivalent.

4. Connect a fuel pressure gauge that is suitable for reading 0–60 psi (0–300 kPa) to the adapter.

5. Connect the inertia switch in the luggage compartment.

6. Start the engine and check for fuel system pressure, then accelerate the engine. The pressure should remain stable throughout acceleration.

## Fuel Pressure Regulator

### REMOVAL & INSTALLATION

1. Relieve the fuel system pressure. For details, please refer to the procedure located earlier in this section.

## ELECTRONIC FUEL INJECTION (EFI)

### General Description

▸ **See Figures 6, 7, 8 and 9**

The Electronic Fuel Injection (EFI) system was used on 1991 2.5L, 1986–92 3.0L (except SHO) and 1988–92 3.8L engines. The EFI fuel system includes a high pressure (30–45 psi/209–310 kPa) tank-mounted electric fuel pump, throttle body, fuel charging manifold, pressure regulator, fuel filter, and both solid and flexible fuel lines. The fuel charging manifold includes six electronically controlled fuel injectors, each mounted directly above an intake port in the lower intake manifold. The Electronic Engine Control (EEC-IV) computer outputs a command to the fuel injectors to meter the appropriate quantity of fuel.

The fuel pressure regulator maintains a constant pressure drop across the injector nozzles. The regulator is referenced to intake manifold vacuum and is connected parallel to the fuel injectors and positioned on the far end

➥**The fuel pressure regulator cover is spring loaded. Apply downward pressure when removing it to avoid losing any of the components.**

2. Remove the four fuel pressure regulator retaining screws.

3. Remove the cover assembly, cup, spring, and diaphragm assembly, then remove the regulator valve seat.

**To install:**

4. Install the fuel pressure regulator valve seat.

5. Install the fuel pressure regulator diaphragm assembly, spring and spring cover.

6. While applying downward pressure to the cover, install the four retaining screws, then tighten them to 27–35 inch lbs. (3.1–3.9 Nm).

## Pressure Relief Valve

### REMOVAL & INSTALLATION

1. If the fuel charging assembly is mounted to the engine, remove the fuel tank gas cap.

2. Properly release the fuel system pressure. For details, please refer to the procedure located earlier in this section.

3. Using the proper wrench, remove the pressure relief valve from the fuel injection manifold.

**To install:**

4. Install the pressure relief valve to the fuel injection manifold. Tighten the valve to 4–6 inch lbs. (0.5–0.7 Nm).

5. Install the fuel tank gas cap.

## Throttle Position (TP) Sensor

### REMOVAL & INSTALLATION

1. Disconnect the negative battery cable.

2. Disconnect the Throttle Position (TP) sensor from the wiring harness.

3. Scribe a reference mark across the edge of the sensor where it meets the throttle body to ensure correct position during installation.

4. Unfasten the retaining screws, then remove the TP sensor.

**To install:**

5. Position the TP sensor according to the marks made during removal, then install the retaining screws. Tighten the the screws to 11–16 inch lbs. (1.2–1.8 Nm).

6. Connect the negative battery cable.

of the fuel rail. Any excess fuel supplied by the pump passes through the regulator and is returned to the fuel tank via a return line.

The fuel pressure regulator is a diaphragm operated relief valve in which one side of the diaphragm senses fuel pressure and the other side senses manifold vacuum. Normal fuel pressure is established by a spring preload applied to the diaphragm. Control of the fuel system is maintained through the Electronic Engine Control (EEC) power relay and the EEC-IV control unit, although electrical power is routed through the fuel pump relay and an inertia switch. The fuel pump relay is normally located on a bracket somewhere above the Electronic Control Assembly (ECA) and the inertia switch is located in the storage compartment. Tank-mounted pumps can be either high or low-pressure, depending on the model.

The inertia switch opens the power circuit to the fuel pump in the event of a collision. Once tripped, the switch must be reset manually by pushing the reset button on the assembly. Check to make sure that the inertia switch is reset before diagnosing power supply problems to the fuel pump circuit.

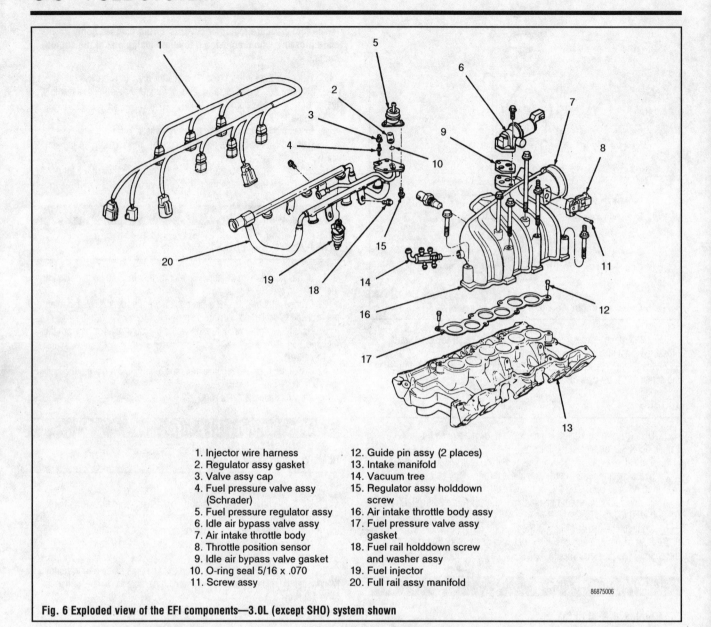

1. Injector wire harness
2. Regulator assy gasket
3. Valve assy cap
4. Fuel pressure valve assy (Schrader)
5. Fuel pressure regulator assy
6. Idle air bypass valve assy
7. Air intake throttle body
8. Throttle position sensor
9. Idle air bypass valve gasket
10. O-ring seal 5/16 x .070
11. Screw assy
12. Guide pin assy (2 places)
13. Intake manifold
14. Vacuum tree
15. Regulator assy holddown screw
16. Air intake throttle body assy
17. Fuel pressure valve assy gasket
18. Fuel rail holddown screw and washer assy
19. Fuel injector
20. Full rail assy manifold

86875006

**Fig. 6 Exploded view of the EFI components—3.0L (except SHO) system shown**

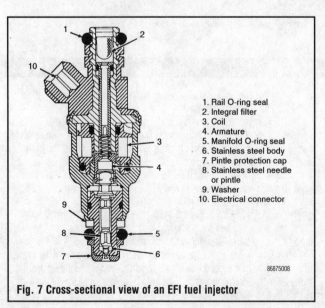

1. Rail O-ring seal
2. Integral filter
3. Coil
4. Armature
5. Manifold O-ring seal
6. Stainless steel body
7. Pintle protection cap
8. Stainless steel needle or pintle
9. Washer
10. Electrical connector

86875008

**Fig. 7 Cross-sectional view of an EFI fuel injector**

The fuel injectors used with the EFI system are an electromechanical (solenoid) type designed to meter and atomize fuel delivered to the intake ports of the engine. The injectors are mounted in the lower intake manifold and positioned so that their spray nozzles direct the fuel charge in front of the intake valves. The injector body consists of a solenoid actuated pintle and needle valve assembly. The control unit sends an electrical impulse that activates the solenoid, causing the pintle to move inward off the seat and allow the fuel to flow. The amount of fuel delivered is controlled by the length of time the injector is energized (pulse width), since the fuel flow orifice is fixed and the fuel pressure drop across the injector tip is constant. Correct atomization is achieved by contouring the pintle at the point where the fuel enters the pintle chamber.

➡**Exercise care when handling fuel injectors during service. Be careful not to lose the pintle cap and always replace old O-rings with new ones to assure a tight seal. Never apply direct battery voltage to test a fuel injector.**

The injectors receive high pressure fuel from the fuel manifold (fuel rail) assembly. The complete assembly includes a single, preformed tube with six injector connectors, a mounting flange for the fuel pressure regulator, mounting attachments which locate the fuel manifold assembly and provide

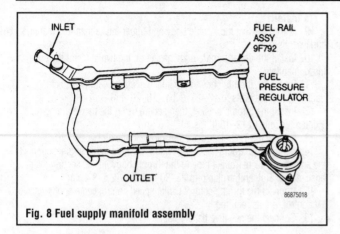

**Fig. 8 Fuel supply manifold assembly**

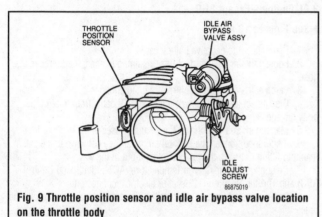

**Fig. 9 Throttle position sensor and idle air bypass valve location on the throttle body**

fuel injector retention and a Schrader® quick-disconnect fitting used to perform fuel pressure tests.

The fuel manifold is normally removed with fuel injectors and pressure regulator attached. Fuel injector electrical connectors are plastic and have locking tabs that must be released when disconnecting the wiring harness.

The air subsystem components include the air cleaner assembly, air flow (vane) meter, throttle air bypass valve and air ducts that connect the air system to the throttle body assembly. The throttle body regulates the air flow to the engine through a single butterfly-type throttle plate controlled by conventional accelerator linkage. The throttle body has an idle adjustment screw (throttle air bypass valve) to set the throttle plate position, a PCV fresh air source upstream of the throttle plate, individual vacuum taps for PCV and control signals, and a throttle position sensor that provides a voltage signal for the EEC-IV control unit.

The throttle air bypass valve is an electro-mechanical (solenoid) device whose operation is controlled by the EEC-IV control unit. A variable air metering valve controls both cold and warm idle air flow in response to commands from the control unit. The valve operates by bypassing a regulated amount of air around the throttle plate; the higher the voltage signal from the control unit, the more air is bypassed through the valve. In this manner, additional air can be added to the fuel mixture without moving the throttle plate. At curb idle, the valve provides smooth idle for various engine coolant temperatures, compensates for A/C load and compensates for transaxle load and no-load conditions. The valve also provides fast idle for start-up, replacing the fast idle cam, throttle kicker and anti-dieseling solenoid common to previous models.

There are no curb idle or fast idle adjustments. As in curb idle operation, the fast idle speed is proportional to engine coolant temperature. Fast idle kick-down will occur when the throttle is kicked. A time-out feature in the ECA will also automatically kick-down fast idle to curb idle after approximately 15–25 seconds once the coolant has reached approximately 160°F (71°C). The signal duty cycle from the ECA to the valve will be at 100% (maximum current) during the crank to provide maximum air flow, allowing no-touch starting at any time (engine cold or hot).

## Relieving Fuel System Pressure

1. Remove the fuel tank cap.
2. Remove the cap from the pressure relief Schrader valve on the fuel rail.
3. Attach pressure gauge tool T80L-9974-A or equivalent, to the fuel pressure relief valve.
4. Release the pressure from the system into a suitable container.
5. Remove the pressure gauge tool, then install the cap on the pressure relief valve. Install the fuel tank cap.

## Electric Fuel Pump

### REMOVAL & INSTALLATION

▶ **See Figure 10**

1. Disconnect the negative battery cable.
2. Relieve the fuel system pressure. For details, please refer to the procedure located earlier in this section.
3. Remove the fuel from the fuel tank by pumping it out through the filler neck using Rotunda Fuel Storage Tanker 034-00002 and Adapter Hose 034-00011, or equivalent.
4. Raise and safely support the vehicle, then disconnect and remove the fuel filler tube.
5. Support the fuel tank, then remove the fuel tank support straps. Partially lower the fuel tank, then detach the fuel lines, electrical connectors and vent lines from the tank. Remove the fuel tank from the vehicle, then place it on a work bench. Remove any dirt around the fuel pump attaching flange, so it will not get into the fuel tank.
6. Using Fuel Tank Sender Wrench D84P-9275-A or equivalent, turn the fuel pump lock ring counterclockwise, then remove the lock ring.
7. Remove the fuel pump and bracket assembly from the fuel tank, then remove and discard the flange gasket.

**To install:**

8. Clean the fuel pump mounting flange, as well as the fuel tank mounting surface and seal ring groove.

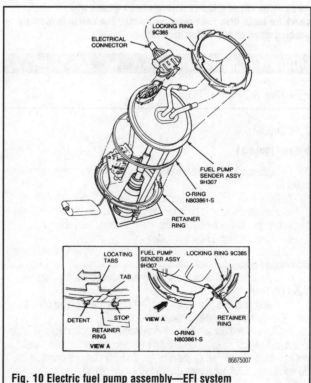

**Fig. 10 Electric fuel pump assembly—EFI system**

9. Put a light coating of grease on the new seal gasket to hold it in place during assembly, then install the gasket in the fuel ring groove.

10. Carefully install the fuel pump and sender assembly, making sure that the filter is not damaged. Make sure that the locating keys are in the keyways and that the seal ring stays in place.

11. Hold the assembly in place, then install the lock ring finger-tight, making sure all locking tabs are under the tank lock ring tabs.

12. Tighten the lock ring using Fuel Tank Sender Wrench D84P-9275-A or equivalent, by turning it clockwise until the ring is up against the stops.

13. Remove the fuel tank from the bench and support the tank while attaching the fuel lines, vent lines and electrical connectors to their proper locations.

14. Install the tank in the vehicle, then secure with the retaining straps. Carefully lower the vehicle.

15. Install the filler tube and tighten the retaining screws.

16. Fill the tank with at least 10 gallons of fuel, then check for leaks.

17. Connect the negative battery cable.

18. Connect a suitable fuel pressure gauge. Turn the ignition switch to the **ON** position 5–10 times, leaving it on for 3 seconds at a time, until the pressure gauge reads at least 30 psi (207 kPa). Check for leaks at the fittings.

19. Remove the pressure gauge, then start the engine and recheck for leaks.

## TESTING

1. Ground the fuel pump lead of the self-test connector through a jumper wire at the FP lead.

2. Connect a suitable fuel pressure tester to the fuel pump outlet.

3. Turn the ignition key to the **RUN** position to operate the fuel pump.

4. The fuel pressure should be 35–45 psi (241–310 kPa) for the 3.0L and 3.8L engines. For the 2.5L engine, the fuel pressure should be 45–60 psi (310–414 kPa).

➡**A safety inertia switch is installed to shut off the electric fuel pump in case of collision. The switch is located on the left-hand side (driver's side) of the car, behind the rearmost seat side trim panel, or inside the rear quarter shock tower access door. If the pump shuts off, or if the vehicle has been hit and will not start, check for leaks first, then reset the switch. The switch is reset by pushing down on the button provided.**

## Throttle Body

### REMOVAL & INSTALLATION

#### 2.5L Engine

▶ **See Figure 11**

1. Disconnect the negative battery cable. Remove the engine air cleaner outlet tube.

2. Relieve the fuel system pressure, as previously described.

3. Remove the throttle body retaining bolts. Be sure that the TPS electrical connector has been disengaged from the wiring harness.

4. Disconnect the air bypass hose.

5. Disconnect the throttle control cable. If equipped with speed control, disconnect the speed control cable.

6. If equipped with an automatic transaxle, disconnect the Throttle Valve (TV) control rod.

7. Disconnect and remove the throttle bracket. Carefully separate the throttle body from the upper intake manifold.

8. Remove and discard the gasket between the throttle body and upper intake manifold. If scraping is necessary to clean the surfaces, be careful not to damage the air bypass valve or throttle body gasket surfaces. Also, do not allow gasket material to drop into the throttle body.

**To install:**

9. Make sure that the throttle body and upper intake manifold mating surfaces are clean.

10. Install the upper throttle body gasket on the two studs of the upper intake manifold.

11. Retain the throttle body to the intake manifold with the attaching bolts. Tighten the bolts to 12–15 ft. lbs. (16–20 Nm).

12. Install the throttle bracket, then secure using the two retaining nuts. Tighten the nuts to 12–15 ft. lbs. (16–20 Nm).

13. Engage the TPS electrical connector and the air bypass hose.

14. If the fuel charging assembly is still mounted to the engine, connect the engine air cleaner outlet tube to the throttle body intake, securing with a hose clamp. Tighten the clamp to 23–30 inch lbs. (2.5–3.4 Nm).

15. Connect the throttle control cable, speed control cable and transaxle TV control rod, as required.

16. Connect the negative battery cable.

#### 3.0L Engine—Except SHO

▶ **See Figures 12 and 13**

1. Disconnect the negative battery cable.

2. Loosen the air cleaner duct hose retaining clamps, then remove the hose.

3. Remove the idle speed control solenoid shield.

4. Disconnect the throttle/accelerator and TV cable from the throttle body linkage.

5. Matchmark and disconnect the vacuum hoses at the vacuum tree.

6. If equipped, loosen the EGR tube nuts at the EGR valve and exhaust manifold fitting. Remove the tube or rotate it out of the way.

7. Disengage the Air Charge Temperature (ACT), Idle Speed Control (ISC) and Throttle Position (TP) sensor electrical connectors.

8. Remove the retaining nuts from the alternator brace, then remove the brace.

9. Note the location of the six throttle body retaining bolts, then loosen and remove the retaining bolts.

10. Lift and remove the throttle body assembly from the intake manifold, then discard the old gasket.

**To install:**

11. Lightly oil all bolt and stud threads. Clean and inspect the intake manifold and throttle body mating surfaces.

➡**Be careful when cleaning the gasket mating surfaces because aluminum gouges easily and may form leak paths.**

12. If available, position guide pins to aid in the alignment during installation.

13. Place a new gasket on the intake manifold.

14. Aligning the bolt holes, install the throttle body on the intake manifold. Install the one stud bolt and the five retaining bolts. Tighten the bolts to 15–22 ft. lbs. (20–30 Nm).

15. Install the alternator brace to the throttle body and alternator bracket. Tighten the nuts to 12 ft. lbs. (16 Nm).

16. Connect the PCV hose to the tube underneath the throttle body.

17. If equipped, install the EGR tube to the EGR valve and exhaust manifold fitting. Tighten to 37 ft. lbs. (50 Nm).

18. Connect the vacuum hoses to their proper locations as marked during removal.

19. Engage the electrical connectors to the ACT, ISC and TP sensors.

20. Connect the throttle and TV cables to the throttle body linkage.

21. Connect the air cleaner duct hose to the throttle body and air cleaner assembly. Tighten the clamp to 36 inch lbs. (4 Nm).

22. Connect the negative battery cable.

23. Start the engine and check for vacuum leaks. Check the engine idle.

➡**The Throttle Valve (TV) cable must be adjusted if the throttle body is removed for any reason and/or the throttle plate idle adjustment screw position is changed.**

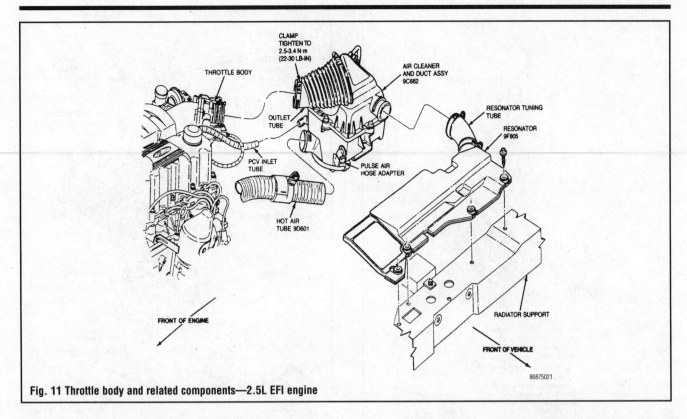

**Fig. 11 Throttle body and related components—2.5L EFI engine**

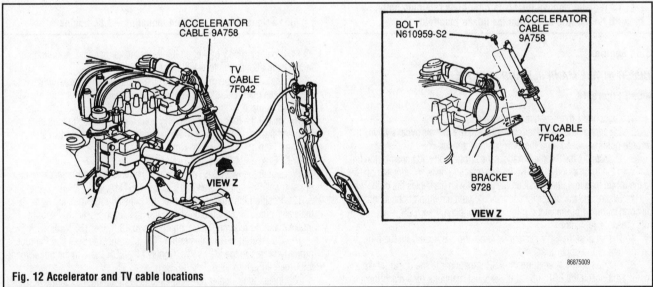

**Fig. 12 Accelerator and TV cable locations**

24. Adjust the TV cable as follows:

a. Connect the TV cable eye to the transaxle throttle control lever link, then attach the cable boot to the chain cover.

b. If equipped with the 3.0L engine, with the TV cable mounted in the engine bracket, make sure the threaded shank is fully retracted. To retract the shank, pull up on the spring rest with the index fingers and wiggle the top of the thread shank through the spring with the thumbs.

c. If equipped with the 3.8L engine, the TV cable must be unclipped from the right intake manifold clip. To retract the shank, span the crack between the two 180° segments of the adjuster spring rest with a suitable tool. Compress the spring by pushing the rod toward the throttle body with the right hand. While the spring is compressed, push the threaded shank toward the spring with the index and middle fingers of the left hand. Do not pull on the cable sheath.

d. Attach the end of the TV cable to the throttle body.

e. If equipped with the 3.8L engine, rotate the throttle body primary lever (the lever to which the TV-driving nail is attached) by hand to the wide-open-throttle position. The white adjuster shank must be seen to advance. If not, look for the cable sheath/foam hang-up on engine/body components. Attach the TV cable in the top position of the right intake manifold clip.

➡The threaded shank must show movement or "ratchet" out of the grip jaws. If there is no movement, inspect the TV cable system for broken or disconnected components, then repeat the procedure.

25. Install the shield onto the idle speed control solenoid, then tighten the bolts to 13 inch lbs. (1.4 Nm).

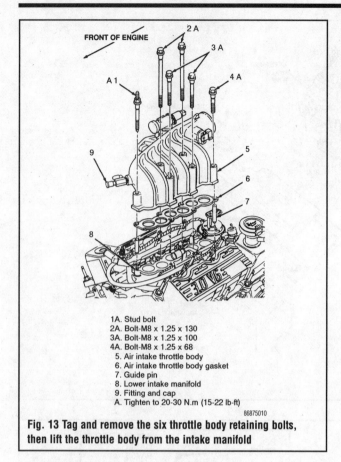

1A. Stud bolt
2A. Bolt-M8 x 1.25 x 130
3A. Bolt-M8 x 1.25 x 100
4A. Bolt-M8 x 1.25 x 68
5. Air intake throttle body
6. Air intake throttle body gasket
7. Guide pin
8. Lower intake manifold
9. Fitting and cap
A. Tighten to 20-30 N.m (15-22 lb-ft)

86875010

**Fig. 13 Tag and remove the six throttle body retaining bolts, then lift the throttle body from the intake manifold**

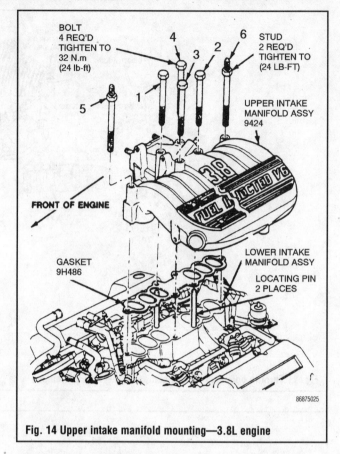

86875025

**Fig. 14 Upper intake manifold mounting—3.8L engine**

## 3.8L Engine

### UPPER INTAKE MANIFOLD AND THROTTLE BODY

▶ See Figure 14

1. Disconnect the negative battery cable.
2. Disengage the electrical connectors at the idle air bypass valve, throttle position sensor and the EGR position sensor.
3. Disconnect the throttle linkage at the throttle ball and transmission linkage from the throttle body. Remove the two retaining bolts securing the bracket to the intake manifold, then position the bracket with the cables out of the way.
4. Disengage the upper intake manifold vacuum fitting connections by disconnecting all of the vacuum lines to the vacuum tree, EGR valve and fuel pressure regulator.
5. Disconnect the PCV system by removing the hose from the fitting on the rear of the upper manifold.
6. Remove the nut retaining the EGR transducer to the upper intake manifold. Loosen the EGR tube at the exhaust manifold, then disconnect at the EGR valve.
7. Remove the two bolts retaining the EGR valve to the upper intake manifold, then remove the EGR valve and the EGR transducer as an assembly.
8. Remove the two canister purge lines from the fittings on the throttle body.
9. Remove the six upper intake manifold retaining bolts.
10. Remove the two retaining bolts on the front and rear edges of the upper intake manifold where the manifold support brackets are located.
11. Remove the nut retaining the alternator bracket to the upper intake manifold, then remove the two bolts retaining the alternator bracket to the water pump and alternator.
12. Remove the upper intake and throttle body as an assembly from the lower intake manifold.

**To install:**
13. Clean and inspect the mating surfaces of the lower and upper intake manifold.

14. Position a new gasket on the lower intake manifold mounting surface. Using alignment studs will make the job easier.
15. Install the upper intake manifold and throttle body assembly to the lower intake manifold. If alignment studs are not used, make sure the gasket stays in place.
16. Install the four center retaining bolts and two studs to the upper manifold and tighten to 8 ft. lbs. (10 Nm). Repeat, in sequence, in two steps:
    a. Step 1: 15 ft. lbs. (20 Nm).
    b. Step 2: 24 ft. lbs. (32 Nm).
17. Install the two bolts retaining the manifold support brackets to the upper manifold, then tighten to 19 ft. lbs. (25 Nm).
18. Position the alternator bracket, then install the two retaining bolts to the water pump and alternator. Install the alternator bracket to the upper intake manifold retaining nut, then tighten to 19 ft. lbs. (26 Nm).
19. Connect the EGR valve to the EGR tube, making sure that the tube is properly seated in the EGR valve. Connect the EGR valve to the upper manifold, then tighten to 19 ft. lbs. (26 Nm).
20. Install the canister purge lines to the fittings on the throttle body.
21. Connect the PCV hose to the rear of the upper manifold.
22. Connect the vacuum lines to the vacuum tree, EGR valve, and fuel pressure regulator.
23. Position the throttle linkage bracket with cables to the upper intake manifold. Install the two retaining bolts, then tighten them to 13 ft. lbs. (17 Nm). Connect the throttle cable and the transaxle cable to the throttle body.
24. Engage the air bypass valve, TP sensor and EGR position sensor electrical connectors.

➡️If the lower intake manifold was removed, fill and bleed the cooling system.

### AIR INTAKE THROTTLE BODY

▶ See Figure 15

1. Disconnect the negative battery cable.
2. Disengage the TP sensor and air bypass valve electrical connectors.

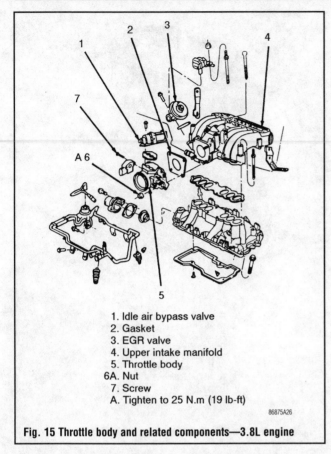

1. Idle air bypass valve
2. Gasket
3. EGR valve
4. Upper intake manifold
5. Throttle body
6A. Nut
7. Screw
A. Tighten to 25 N.m (19 lb-ft)

86875A26

**Fig. 15 Throttle body and related components—3.8L engine**

3. Remove the four throttle body retaining bolts. Remove the throttle body assembly, then remove and discard the gasket between the throttle body and the upper intake manifold.

4. If scraping is necessary, be careful not to damage the air bypass valve or throttle body gasket surfaces. Also, do not allow gasket material to drop into the throttle body.

**To install:**

5. Install the throttle body using a new gasket on the four studs of the upper intake manifold. Tighten the retaining nuts to 19 ft. lbs. (26 Nm).

6. Engage the throttle position sensor and the idle air bypass valve.

7. Connect the negative battery cable.

## Fuel Charging Assembly

### REMOVAL & INSTALLATION

#### 2.5L Engine

1. Disconnect the negative battery cable. Properly relieve fuel system pressure. Disconnect the air bypass connector from the EEC-IV harness. Disconnect the spring lock coupling. Remove the engine air cleaner outlet tube.

2. Disconnect and remove the accelerator and speed control cables from the accelerator mounting bracket and the throttle lever.

3. Detach the top manifold vacuum fitting by disconnecting the rear vacuum line to the dash panel vacuum tee, the vacuum line at the intake manifold, the MAP sensor vacuum line and the fuel pressure regulator vacuum line.

4. Disconnect the PCV system hoses. Disconnect the EGR vacuum line at the EGR valve.

5. Detach the EGR tube from the upper intake manifold by supporting the connector while loosening the compression nut.

6. Disconnect the upper support manifold bracket by removing only the top bolt. Leave the bottom bolts attached.

7. Disengage the electrical connectors at the main engine harness.

8. Remove the fuel supply and return lines. Remove the eight manifold retaining bolts.

9. Disconnect the lower support manifold bracket by removing only the top bolt. Leave the bottom bolts attached.

10. Remove the manifold along with the wiring harness and gasket.

**To install:**

11. Clean and inspect the mounting surfaces. Install a new gasket.

12. Install the manifold assembly and finger-tighten the retaining bolts.

13. Install the fuel return line. Tighten the manifold retaining bolts to 15–22 ft. lbs. (20–30 Nm).

14. Connect the upper and lower manifold support brackets. Tighten the retaining bolts to 15–22 ft. lbs. (20–30 Nm).

15. Install the EGR tube and connect the PCV system hoses. Fasten the rear manifold connections.

16. Connect the accelerator and speed control linkages. Connect the electrical wiring harness.

17. Connect the fuel supply line and the fuel return line. Install the spring lock coupling.

18. Use the EEC-IV self-test connector to check that the EEC-IV sensor is functioning properly.

19. Connect the negative battery cable.

20. Start the engine and check for fuel leaks. Adjust the idle speed, as required.

#### 3.0L Engine—Except SHO

1. With the ignition **OFF**, disconnect the negative battery cable.

2. Remove the fuel cap and release the pressure at the pressure relief valve on the fuel rail assembly using, Fuel Pressure Gauge part No. T80L-9974-B or equivalent.

3. Detach electrical connectors at the air bypass valve, throttle position sensor, EGR sensor and air charge temperature sensor (ACT).

4. Disconnect the fuel supply and return lines using Fuel Line Disconnect Tool part No. D87L-9280-A or equivalent.

5. Detach the wiring connectors from the fuel injectors.

6. Remove the snow/ice shield to expose the throttle linkage. Disconnect the throttle cable from the ball stud.

7. Remove the engine air cleaner outlet tube (between the air cleaner and air throttle body) by loosening the two clamps.

8. Disconnect and remove the accelerator and speed control cables, if so equipped, from the throttle lever.

9. Remove the transaxle Throttle Valve (TV) linkage from the throttle lever (automatic transaxle only).

10. Loosen the bolt which retains the A/C line at the upper rear of the upper manifold and disengage the retainer.

11. Remove the six retaining bolts and lift air intake throttle body assembly from the lower intake manifold assembly.

12. Clean and inspect the mounting faces of the lower and upper intake manifold.

**To install:**

13. Position a new gasket on the lower intake mounting face. The use of alignment studs may be helpful.

14. Install the upper intake manifold and throttle body assembly to the lower manifold, making sure the gasket remains in place (if alignment studs aren't used). Align EGR tube in valve.

15. Install the six upper intake manifold retaining bolts. Tighten to 15–22 ft. lbs. (20–30 Nm) in sequence as shown in the fuel charging assembly diagram in this section.

16. Engage the A/C line retainer cup and tighten the bolt to specification.

17. Tighten the EGR tube and flare fitting. Tighten the lower retainer nut at the exhaust manifold.

18. Install the canister purge line to the fitting.

19. Connect the PCV vacuum hose to the bottom of the upper manifold and the PCV closure hose to the throttle body.

20. Connect the vacuum lines to the vacuum tree, EGR valve, and fuel pressure regulator.

21. Connect the throttle cable to the throttle body and install snow/ice shield.

22. Attach the electrical connectors to the air bypass valve, TPS sensor, EGR sensor, and ACT sensor.

23. Connect the negative battery cable.

24. Install the fuel cap, start the engine and check for vacuum, fuel, or coolant leaks.

25. The transaxle TV linkage has to be readjusted after the fuel charging assembly has been serviced:

　a. With the ignition key **OFF** and shift selector in PARK.

　b. Reset the automatic transaxle TV linkage by holding the ratchet in the released position and pushing the cable fitting toward the accelerator control bracket.

　c. At the throttle body, reset the TV cable by rotating the throttle linkage to the wide-open throttle position by hand, then releasing it.

➡**If the lower intake manifold was removed, fill and bleed the cooling system.**

### 3.8L Engine

1. Disconnect the negative battery cable.

2. Drain the cooling system.

3. Remove the fuel cap at the tank.

4. Release the fuel pressure by attaching a Fuel Pressure Gauge part No. T80L-9974-B or equivalent to the pressure relief valve on the fuel rail assembly.

5. Detach the electrical connectors at the air bypass valve, throttle position sensor, and EGR position sensor.

6. Disconnect the throttle linkage at the throttle ball and the transaxle linkage from the throttle body.

7. Position the throttle and speed control linkage out of the way.

8. Disconnect the upper intake manifold vacuum fittings at the vacuum tree.

9. Remove the six upper intake manifold retaining bolts.

10. Remove the upper intake and throttle body assembly from the lower intake.

### To install:

11. Clean and inspect the mounting surfaces of the upper and lower intake manifolds. Be careful not to damage the mounting surfaces.

12. Install the new gasket and upper intake into position using the alignment studs. If alignment studs are not used, make sure the gasket stays in place.

13. Install the six manifold retaining bolts and tighten to 20–28 ft. lbs. (27–38 Nm).

14. Install the canister purge lines, PCV hose, and vacuum lines to the vacuum tree.

15. Install the throttle and speed control, if so equipped, to the upper intake manifold. Connect the TV cable to the throttle body.

16. The transaxle TV linkage has to be readjusted after the fuel charging assembly has been serviced. Proceed as follows:

　a. Turn the ignition key **OFF** and put the shift selector in PARK

　b. Reset the automatic transaxle TV linkage by holding the ratchet in the released position and pushing the cable fitting toward the accelerator control bracket.

　c. At the throttle body, reset the TV cable by rotating the throttle linkage to the wide-open throttle position by hand, then releasing it.

17. Refill the engine with coolant, then connect the negative battery cable. Start the engine and check for fuel, vacuum, and coolant leaks.

## Fuel Injection Wiring Harness

### REMOVAL & INSTALLATION

▶ **See Figure 16**

1. Make sure the ignition switch is in the **OFF** position, then release the fuel system pressure. For details, please refer to the procedure earlier in this section.

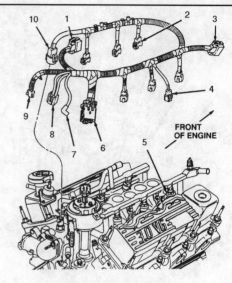

1. To throttle position sensor
2. Fuel injector wiring harness
3. To PFE transducer assy
4. To air charge temperature sensor
5. Fuel injector assy (6 req'd)
6. To harness assy
7. To oil pressure switch assy
8. To EGR vacuum regulator assy
9. To idle speed control
10. To engine coolant temperature sensor

86875011

**Fig. 16 View of the 3.0L EFI injector wiring harness**

2. Disconnect the negative battery cable.

3. Remove the throttle body and/or upper intake manifold. For details, please refer to the procedure earlier in this section.

4. Disengage the electrical connectors from the fuel injectors.

5. Disengage the electrical connectors from the main wiring harness and throttle position sensor, ACT sensor and the air bypass valve.

6. Remove the wiring assembly.

### To install:

7. Position the wiring harness alongside the fuel injectors.

8. Snap the electrical connectors into position on the injectors.

9. Install the throttle body. For details, please refer to the procedure earlier in this section.

10. Make sure that all of the electrical connectors are firmly in place.

11. Connect the negative battery cable.

## Fuel Injector Manifold/Rail Assembly

### REMOVAL & INSTALLATION

### 2.5L Engine

▶ **See Figure 17**

1. Remove the fuel tank cap, then release the fuel system pressure at the relief valve using Fuel Pressure Gauge T80L-9974-B or equivalent.

2. Remove the spring lock coupling. For details please refer to the procedure later in this section.

3. Disconnect the fuel supply and return lines.

4. Disconnect the wiring harness from the fuel injectors.

5. Remove the upper intake manifold.

6. Remove the two fuel injector manifold retaining bolts.

7. Carefully disengage the manifold from the fuel injectors.

8. Disconnect the vacuum line from the fuel pressure regulator valve, then remove the manifold.

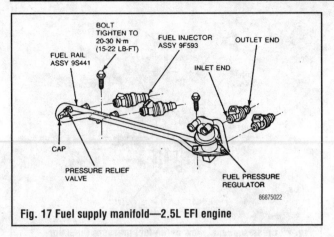

Fig. 17 Fuel supply manifold—2.5L EFI engine

## To install:

➡ **When installing the fuel rail assemblies, make sure the O-rings seat properly so that no fuel leaks will occur.**

9. Push the fuel rail down to be sure that all of the injector O-rings are fully seated in the fuel rail cups and intake manifold.

10. While holding the fuel rail down, install and tighten the retaining bolts to 15–22 ft. lbs. (20–30 Nm).

11. Install the spring lock coupling. For details, please refer to the procedure later in this section.

12. With the injector wiring still disconnected, turn the ignition to the **ON** position to allow the fuel pump to pressurize the system. Using a clean towel, check for fuel leaks.

13. Connect the fuel injector wiring harness.

14. Run the vehicle at idle for two minutes, then turn the engine **OFF** and check for fuel leaks.

### 3.0L Engine—Except SHO

▶ **See Figures 16 and 18**

1. Disconnect the negative battery cable.

2. Relieve the fuel system pressure. Remove the air intake throttle body.

3. On the 1992 engine, the distributor must be raised to allow the crossover tube to clear the distributor housing and lower intake manifold assembly.

4. Disconnect the fuel supply and return lines.

5. Carefully disconnect the wiring harness from the injectors.

6. Disconnect the vacuum line from the fuel pressure regulator valve.

7. Remove the four fuel injector manifold retaining bolts.

8. Carefully disengage the fuel rail assembly from the fuel injectors by lifting and gently rocking the rail.

9. Remove the injectors by lifting while gently rocking from side to side.

➡ **Place removed components in a clean container to keep clean and free of contamination.**

### ⁂ WARNING

**Be very careful when handling the fuel injectors and fuel rail to prevent damage to the sealing areas and sensitive fuel metering openings.**

## To install:

10. Lubricate new O-rings with engine oil and install 2 on each injector.

11. Make sure the injector cups are clean and undamaged.

12. Install the injectors in the fuel rail using a light twisting-pushing motion.

13. Carefully install the rail assembly and injectors into the lower intake manifold, 1 side at a time. Make sure the O-rings are seated by pushing down on the fuel rail.

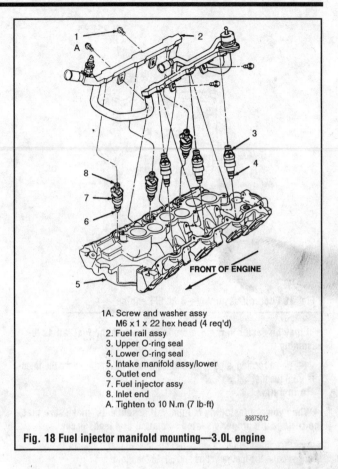

1A. Screw and washer assy
    M6 x 1 x 22 hex head (4 req'd)
2. Fuel rail assy
3. Upper O-ring seal
4. Lower O-ring seal
5. Intake manifold assy/lower
6. Outlet end
7. Fuel injector assy
8. Inlet end
A. Tighten to 10 N.m (7 lb-ft)

Fig. 18 Fuel injector manifold mounting—3.0L engine

14. While holding the fuel rail assembly in place, install the 2 retaining bolts and tighten to 7 ft. lbs. (10 Nm).

15. Connect the fuel supply and return lines.

16. Connect the negative battery cable.

17. Before connecting the fuel injector harness, turn the ignition switch to the **ON** position. This will pressurize the fuel system.

18. Using a clean paper towel, check for leaks where the injector connects to the fuel rail.

19. Install the air intake throttle body and connect the vacuum line to the fuel pressure regulator valve.

20. Connect the fuel injector harness, then start the engine and let it idle for 2 minutes.

21. Using a clean paper towel, check for leaks where the injector is installed into the intake manifold.

### 3.8L Engine

▶ **See Figure 19**

1. Disconnect the negative battery cable.

2. Remove the fuel cap and release tank pressure. Release the fuel system pressure. For details, please refer to the procedure earlier in this section.

3. Remove the upper intake manifold assembly. For details, please refer to the procedure earlier in this section.

4. Remove the spring lock coupling retaining clips from the fuel inlet and return fittings.

5. Using Spring Lock Coupling Disconnect Tool D87L-9280-A or equivalent, disconnect the inlet and outlet fuel lines from the fuel rail assembly.

6. Remove the four fuel rail assembly retaining bolts. There are two on each side.

7. Carefully disengage the fuel rail from the fuel injectors, then remove the rail.

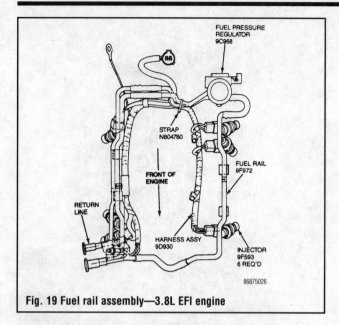

Fig. 19 Fuel rail assembly—3.8L EFI engine

➡It may be easier to remove the injectors with the fuel rail as an assembly.

8. Use a rocking, side-to-side motion while lifting to remove the injectors from the fuel rail.

**To install:**

➡When you are installing the fuel rail assemblies, make sure that the O-rings are properly seated so that no fuel leaks occur.

9. Push the fuel rail down to be sure that all of the injector O-rings are fully seated in the fuel rail clips and intake manifold.

10. While holding the fuel rail down, install the retaining bolts and tighten them to 7 ft. lbs. (10 Nm).

11. Install the spring lock coupling. For details please refer to the procedure later in this section.

12. With the injector wiring still disconnected, turn the ignition to the **RUN** position to allow the fuel pump to pressurize the system. Using a clean towel, check for fuel leaks.

13. Connect the fuel injector wiring harness.

14. Run the vehicle at idle for two minutes, then turn the engine **OFF** and check for leaks.

## Fuel Pressure Regulator

### REMOVAL & INSTALLATION

▶ **See Figures 20 and 21**

1. Disconnect the negative battery cable.

2. Remove the fuel tank cap and release the pressure from the fuel system at the Schrader (pressure relief) valve of the fuel rail assembly, using Fuel Pressure Gauge T80L-9974-B or equivalent.

3. For the 2.5L engine, remove the three bolts retaining the fuel supply manifold shield, then remove the shield.

4. Tag and remove the vacuum line(s) at the pressure regulator.

5. Remove the two fuel rail-to-lower intake manifold retaining bolts. Carefully lift the fuel rail (regulator side only) off of the injectors to gain access to the regulator retaining screws.

6. Remove the three Allen retaining screws from the regulator housing, then discard the screws.

7. Remove the pressure regulator assembly, gasket and O-ring. Discard the gasket and the O-ring.

➡If scraping is necessary, be careful not to damage the fuel pressure regulator or fuel rail gasket surfaces.

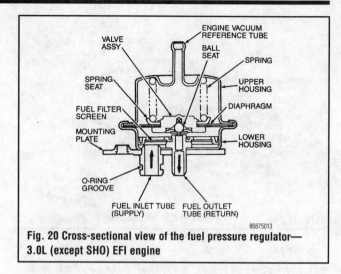

Fig. 20 Cross-sectional view of the fuel pressure regulator—3.0L (except SHO) EFI engine

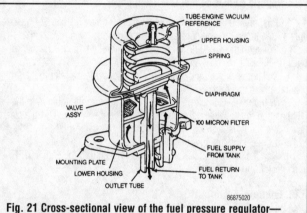

Fig. 21 Cross-sectional view of the fuel pressure regulator—2.5L and 3.8L EFI engine

**To install:**

8. Lubricate the new fuel pressure regulator O-ring with clean engine oil.

9. Ensure that the gasket surfaces of the fuel pressure regulator and fuel rail assembly are clean.

10. Install the new O-ring and new gasket on the regulator.

11. Using new Allen head retaining screws, install the fuel pressure regulator on the fuel rail assembly. Tighten the three retaining screws to 34 inch lbs. (4 Nm).

12. Carefully install the regulator side of the fuel rail to the injectors. If the injector(s) were completely disengaged from the fuel rail cup(s), lubricate the injector O-rings with clean engine oil prior to inserting in the fuel rail cups. Push the regulator side of the fuel rail down on the injectors, then tighten the retaining bolts to 7 ft. lbs. (10 Nm) while holding down the fuel rail.

13. Install the vacuum line(s) to the regulator.

14. For the 2.5L engine, install the fuel supply manifold shield, then tighten the retaining bolts to 15–22 ft. lbs. (20–30 Nm).

15. Connect the negative battery cable.

## Pressure Relief Valve

### REMOVAL & INSTALLATION

▶ **See Figures 22 and 23**

1. If the fuel rail assembly is mounted to the engine, remove the fuel tank cap, then release system pressure at the Schrader valve on the fuel injection manifold, using Fuel Pressure Gauge T80L-9974-B or equivalent.

➡The cap on the relief valve must be removed.

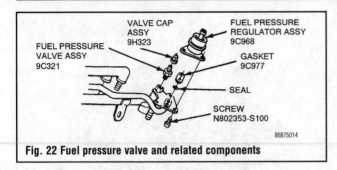

Fig. 22 Fuel pressure valve and related components

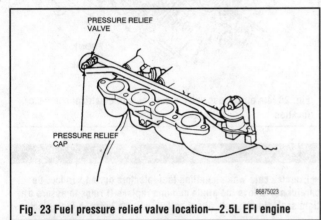

Fig. 23 Fuel pressure relief valve location—2.5L EFI engine

2. Using an open-end wrench or suitable deep well socket, remove the pressure relief valve from the fuel injection manifold.

**To install:**

3. Install the pressure relief valve and the cap. Tighten the valve to 66 inch lbs. (7.4 Nm) and the cap to 5.5 inch lbs. (0.6 Nm).

## Throttle Position (TP) Sensor

### REMOVAL & INSTALLATION

▶ See Figures 24 and 25

1. Disconnect the negative battery cable.
2. Disconnect the Throttle Position (TP) sensor from the wiring harness.
3. Unfasten the two retaining screws, then remove the throttle position sensor.

**To install:**

4. Install the throttle position sensor. Make sure that the rotary tangs on the sensor are properly aligned and that the red seal is inside the connector housing.

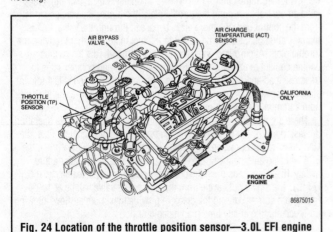

Fig. 24 Location of the throttle position sensor—3.0L EFI engine

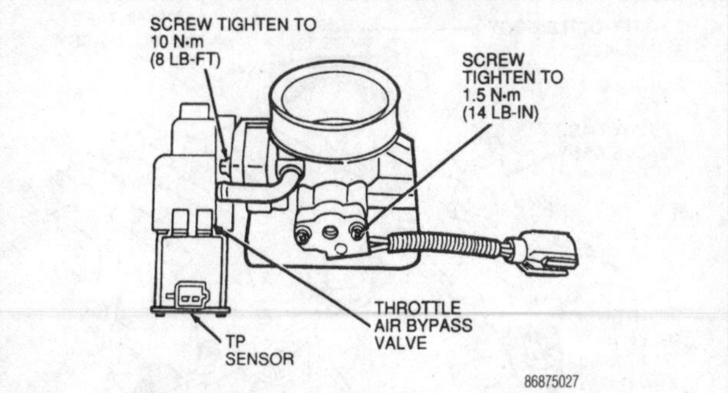

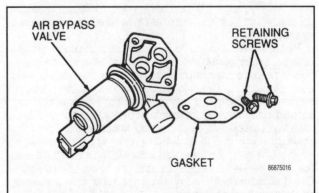

Fig. 25 Throttle position sensor and idle air bypass locations—3.8L EFI engine

➡️**Slide the rotary tangs into position over the throttle shaft blade, then rotate the TP sensor clockwise to its installed position. Failure to install the TP sensor in this manner may result in excessive idle speeds.**

5. Secure the sensor to the throttle body using the two retaining screws. Tighten the screws to 14 inch lbs. (1.5 Nm).

➡️**The Throttle Position (TP) sensor is NOT adjustable.**

6. Engage the sensor electrical connector to the wiring harness.
7. Connect the negative battery cable.

## Idle Air Bypass Valve

### REMOVAL & INSTALLATION

▶ See Figures 26, 27 and 28

1. Disconnect the negative battery cable.
2. Disengage the idle air bypass valve electrical connector from the wiring harness.
3. Remove the two idle air bypass retaining screws, then remove the idle air bypass valve and gasket.

➡️**If scraping is necessary to clean the mating surfaces, be careful not to damage the idle air bypass valve or throttle body gasket surfaces, or drop any gasket material or debris into the throttle body.**

**To install:**

4. Make sure that the throttle body and air bypass valve mating surfaces are clean.
5. Install the gasket on the throttle body surface, then mount the idle air bypass valve assembly, using the two retaining screws to secure it. Tighten the screws to 84 inch lbs. (9.5 Nm).
6. Engage the electrical connector to the idle air bypass valve.
7. Connect the negative battery cable.

Fig. 26 Idle air bypass valve—3.0L (except SHO) EFI engine

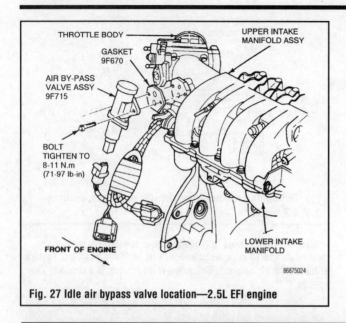

Fig. 27 Idle air bypass valve location—2.5L EFI engine

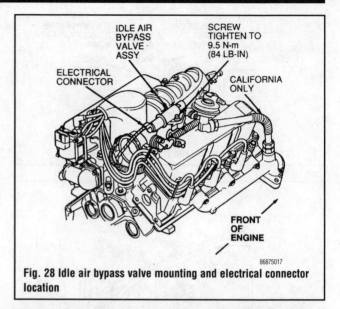

Fig. 28 Idle air bypass valve mounting and electrical connector location

## SEQUENTIAL ELECTRONIC FUEL INJECTION (SEFI)

### General Information

The Sequential Electronic Fuel Injection (SEFI) system is used on all Super High Output (SHO) vehicles, as well as on 1993 and later 3.0L and 3.8L engines. It is classified as a multi-point, pulse time, speed density control fuel injection system. The fuel is metered into the intake manifold port, in sequence, in accordance with the engine demand through the injectors mounted on a tuned intake manifold. The Electronic Engine Control (EEC-IV) computer outputs a command to the fuel injectors to meter the appropriate quantity of fuel. The remainder of the fuel system is basically the same as the EFI system installed on some earlier model 3.0L and 3.8L engines.

The SEFI fuel subsystem includes a high pressure (30-45 psi/209–310 kPa) tank-mounted electric fuel pump, fuel charging manifold, pressure regulator, fuel filter, and both solid and flexible fuel lines.

The fuel pressure regulator maintains a constant pressure drop across the injector nozzles. The regulator is referenced to intake manifold vacuum and is connected parallel to the fuel injectors and positioned on the far end of the fuel rail. Any excess fuel supplied by the pump passes through the regulator and is returned to the fuel tank via a return line.

The fuel pressure regulator is a diaphragm operated relief valve in which one side of the diaphragm senses fuel pressure and the other side senses manifold vacuum. Normal fuel pressure is established by a spring preload applied to the diaphragm. Control of the fuel system is maintained through the EEC-IV power relay and the EEC-IV control unit, although electrical power is routed through the fuel pump relay and an inertia switch. The fuel pump relay is normally located on a bracket somewhere above the Electronic Control Assembly (ECA) and the inertia switch is located in the storage compartment. Tank-mounted pumps can be either high or low pressure, depending on the model.

The fuel injectors used with the SEFI system are an electromechanical (solenoid) type designed to meter and atomize fuel delivered to the intake ports of the engine. The injectors are mounted in the lower intake manifold and positioned so that their spray nozzles direct the fuel charge in front of the intake valves. The injector body consists of a solenoid actuated pintle and needle valve assembly. The control unit sends an electrical impulse that activates the solenoid, causing the pintle to move inward off the seat, allowing the fuel to flow. The amount of fuel delivered is controlled by the length of time the injector is energized (pulse width), since the fuel flow orifice is fixed and the fuel pressure drop across the injector tip is constant. Correct atomization is achieved by contouring the pintle at the point where the fuel enters the pintle chamber.

➡ **Exercise care when handling fuel injectors during service. Be careful not to lose the pintle cap and replace O-rings to assure a tight seal. Never apply direct battery voltage to test a fuel injector.**

The injectors receive high pressure fuel from the fuel manifold (fuel rail) assembly. The complete assembly includes a single, preformed tube with six injector connectors, mounting flange for the pressure regulator, mounting attachments which locate the fuel manifold assembly and provide fuel injector retention, and a Schrader® quick-disconnect fitting used to perform fuel pressure tests.

The fuel manifold is normally removed with fuel injectors and pressure regulator attached. Fuel injector electrical connectors are plastic and have locking tabs that must be released when disconnecting the wiring harness.

The air subsystem components include the air cleaner assembly, air flow (vane) meter, throttle air bypass valve and air ducts that connect the air system to the throttle body assembly. The throttle body regulates the air flow to the engine through a single butterfly-type throttle plate controlled by conventional accelerator linkage. The throttle body has an idle adjustment screw (throttle air bypass valve) to set the throttle plate position, a PCV fresh air source upstream of the throttle plate, individual vacuum taps for PCV and control signals, and a throttle position sensor that provides a voltage signal for the EEC-IV control unit.

The throttle air bypass valve is an electro-mechanical (solenoid) device whose operation is controlled by the EEC-IV control unit. A variable air metering valve controls both cold and warm idle air flow in response to commands from the control unit. The valve operates by bypassing a regulated amount of air around the throttle plate; the higher the voltage signal from the control unit, the more air is bypassed through the valve. In this manner, additional air can be added to the fuel mixture without moving the throttle plate. At curb idle, the valve provides smooth idle for various engine coolant temperatures, adjusts for A/C load, and compensates for transaxle load and no-load conditions. The valve also provides fast idle for start-up, replacing the fast idle cam, throttle kicker and anti-dieseling solenoid common to previous models.

There are no curb idle or fast idle adjustments. As in curb idle operation, the fast idle speed is proportional to engine coolant temperature. Fast idle kick-down will occur when the throttle is kicked. A time-out feature in the ECA will also automatically kick-down fast idle to curb idle after approximately 15–25 seconds once the coolant has reached approximately 160°F (71°C). The signal duty cycle from the ECA to the valve will be at 100% (maximum current) during the crank to provide maximum air flow, allowing no-touch starting at any time (engine cold or hot).

### Relieving Fuel System Pressure

1. Remove the air cleaner assembly. For details, please refer to the procedure in Section 1 of this manual.
2. Connect EFI/CFI Fuel Pressure Gauge T80L-9974-B or equivalent to the fuel pressure relief valve on the fuel supply manifold.
3. Open the manual valve on the EFI/CFI fuel pressure gauge tool to relieve the fuel system pressure.

### Fuel Filter

#### REMOVAL & INSTALLATION

1. Disconnect the negative battery cable. Relieve the fuel system pressure.
2. Remove the push connect fittings at both ends of the fuel filter. This is accomplished by removing the hairpin clips from the fittings. Remove the hairpin clips by first bending and then breaking the shipping tabs on the clips. Then spread the 2 clip legs approximately ⅛ in. (3mm) to disengage the body and push the legs into the fitting. Pull on the triangular end of the clip and work it clear of the fitting.
3. Remove the filter from the mounting bracket by loosening the worm gear mounting clamp enough to allow the filter to pass through.

**To install:**

4. Install the filter in the mounting bracket, ensuring that the flow direction arrow is pointing forward. Locate the fuel filter against the tab at the lower end of the bracket.
5. Insert a new hairpin clip into any 2 adjacent openings on each push connect fitting, with the triangular portion of the clip pointing away from the fitting opening. Install the clip to fully engage the body of the fitting. This is indicated by the legs of the hairpin clip being locked on the outside of the fitting body. Apply a light coat of engine oil to the ends of the fuel filter and then push the fittings onto the ends of the fuel filter. When the fittings are engaged, a definite click will be heard. Pull on the fittings to ensure that they are fully engaged.
6. Tighten the worm gear mounting clamp to 15–25 inch lbs. (1.7–2.8 Nm).
7. Start the engine and check for leaks.

### Electric Fuel Pump

#### REMOVAL & INSTALLATION

#### Except 3.0L Flexible Fuel (FF) Vehicles

♦ **See Figure 29**

1. Disconnect the negative battery cable.
2. Relieve the fuel system pressure. For details, please refer to the procedure earlier in this section.
3. Drain the fuel from the fuel tank by inserting Rotunda Fuel Tanker Adapter Hose 034-00012 or equivalent into the fuel tank through the fuel tank filler pipe, then remove the fuel tank with Rotunda Fuel Storage Tanker 034-00002 or equivalent.
4. Remove the fuel tank filler pipe:
   a. Open the filler door to remove the three screws securing the fuel tank filler pipe to the pocket. Mark the fuel tank filler cap tether location.
   b. Raise and safely support the vehicle.
   c. Loosen the filler and vent hose on the fuel tank filler pipe.
   d. Remove the bolt securing the fuel tank filler pipe assembly to the underbody of the vehicle, then remove the fuel tank filler pipe.
5. Support the fuel tank, then remove the fuel tank straps. Partially lower the tank, then remove the fuel lines, electrical connectors and vent lines from the tank. Remove the fuel tank and place it on a work bench.
6. Remove any accumulated dirt from around the fuel pump retaining flange so that it will not enter the fuel tank during removal and installation.

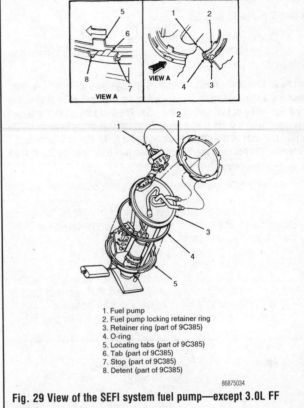

1. Fuel pump
2. Fuel pump locking retainer ring
3. Retainer ring (part of 9C385)
4. O-ring
5. Locating tabs (part of 9C385)
6. Tab (part of 9C385)
7. Stop (part of 9C385)
8. Detent (part of 9C385)

86875034

**Fig. 29 View of the SEFI system fuel pump—except 3.0L FF vehicles**

7. Turn the fuel pump locking ring counterclockwise using Fuel Tank Sender Wrench D84P-9275-A or equivalent, then remove the lock ring.
8. Remove the fuel pump from the fuel tank and discard the flange gasket.

**To install:**

9. Clean the fuel pump mounting flange and fuel tank mating surfaces and seal ring groove.
10. Put a light coating of grease on the new seal gasket to hold it in place during assembly and install it in the fuel ring groove.
11. Install the fuel pump and sender assembly carefully to be sure that the filter is not damaged. Make sure the locating keys are in the keyways and the seal gasket remains in place.
12. Hold the assembly in place and install the lock ring making sure all locking tabs are under the tank lock ring tabs. Tighten the lock ring by turning it clockwise using Fuel Tank Sender Wrench D84P-9275-A until it is up against the stops.
13. Remove the fuel tank from the bench and to the vehicle, then support the fuel tank while connecting the fuel lines, vent line and electrical connectors to the appropriate places. Install the fuel tank and secure it with the tank support straps.
14. Lower the vehicle.
15. Install the fuel tank filler pipe:
   a. Position the fuel tank filler pipe in the body location.
   b. Connect the hoses with clamps to the fuel tank filler pipe.
   c. Install the underbody fuel tank filler pipe assembly bolt, then tighten the bolt to 36–53 inch lbs. (4–6 Nm), then lower the vehicle.
   d. Install the fuel tank filler cap to the tether location, then install the three retaining screws.
16. Fill the tank with a minimum of 10 gallons of fuel, then check for leaks.
17. Connect the negative battery cable.
18. Connect a suitable fuel pressure gauge. Turn the ignition switch to the **ON** position 5–10 times, leaving it on for 3 seconds at a time, until the pressure gauge reads at least 30 psi (207 kPa). Check for leaks at the fittings.
19. Remove the pressure gauge, start the engine and recheck for leaks.

## 3.0L Flexible Fuel (FF) Engine

♦ **See Figures 30 thru 35**

1. Disconnect the negative battery cable.
2. Depressurize the fuel system. For details, please refer to the procedure earlier in this section.

➡️ The FF fuel tank cannot be drained through the fuel tank filler pipe because a special screen is installed in the fuel tank filler pipe to prevent siphoning of fuel through the pipe. The fuel tank on this vehicle is equipped with a drain tube connected to the fuel pump module on the right-hand side of the vehicle, which had a quick disconnect for this purpose. It is not necessary to lower the fuel tank to drain the system.

3. Drain the fuel tank:
   a. Remove the foam cover and protective rubber cover from the drain tube.
   b. Connect the drain tube quick disconnect fitting to the Rotunda Fuel Storage Tanker and Adapter Hose 034-00020, then drain the fuel from the tank into a suitable container.
4. Raise and safely support the vehicle.
5. Disconnect and remove the fuel filler pipe:
   a. Open the filler door to remove the three screws securing the fuel tank filler pipe to the pocket. Mark the fuel tank filler cap tether location.
   b. If not done already, raise and safely support the vehicle.
   c. Loosen the filler and vent hose on the fuel tank filler pipe.

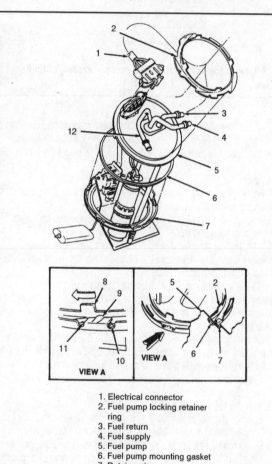

1. Electrical connector
2. Fuel pump locking retainer ring
3. Fuel return
4. Fuel supply
5. Fuel pump
6. Fuel pump mounting gasket
7. Retainer ring
8. Locating tabs
9. Tab
10. Stop
11. Detent
12. Fuel tank drain tube

86875028

**Fig. 30 Exploded view of the fuel pump and related components—3.0L Flexible Fuel (FF) engine**

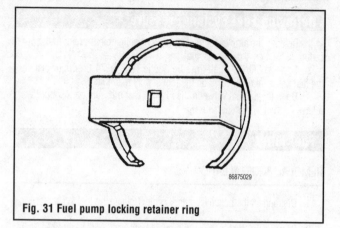

86875029

**Fig. 31 Fuel pump locking retainer ring**

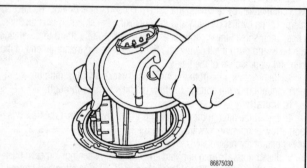

86875030

**Fig. 32 Lift fuel pump upward rotating left, while aligning the float wiper arm retainer and return line into the fuel tank location slots**

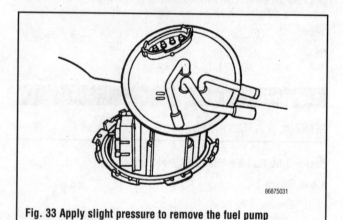

86875031

**Fig. 33 Apply slight pressure to remove the fuel pump**

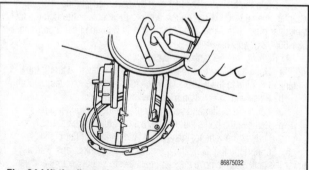

86875032

**Fig. 34 Lift the float wiper arm through the left-hand fuel tank slot and pass the pump motor retaining bracket through the right-hand fuel tank slot**

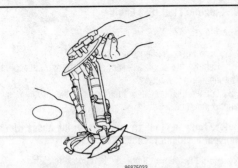

**Fig. 35 Remove the fuel pump while keeping the return line in the fuel tank slot. Lift the fuel pump inlet filter and then the sender arm float through the fuel tank opening**

d. Remove the bolt securing the fuel tank filler pipe assembly to the underbody of the vehicle, then remove the fuel tank filler pipe.

6. Support the fuel tank, then remove the fuel tank support straps. Partially lower the tank, then disconnect the fuel lines, electrical connectors and fuel vapor and vent lines from the fuel tank.

7. Remove the fuel tank and place it on a work bench. Remove any dirt that has accumulated around the fuel pump so that dirt does not enter the fuel tank during pump removal.

8. Remove the fuel pump locking retainer ring using Fuel Tank Locking Wrench D90P-9275-A, or equivalent.

9. Lift the fuel pump locating tabs from the fuel tank location slots.

10. Lift the fuel pump upward rotating left, while aligning the float wiper arm retainer and return line into the fuel tank location slots.

11. Apply light pressure to remove the fuel pump.

12. Lift the float wiper arm through the left-hand fuel tank slot, then pass the pump motor retaining bracket through the right-hand fuel tank slot.

13. Remove the fuel pump keeping return line in the fuel tank slot. Lift the fuel pump inlet filter then sender arm float through the fuel tank opening.

14. Remove and discard the fuel pump mounting gasket.

**To install:**

15. Position a new methanol compatible pump gasket on the fuel pump.

16. Install the fuel pump carefully to be sure that it is not damaged.

17. Hold the assembly in place and install the the fuel pump locking retainer finger tight. Make sure that all of the locking tabs are are under the fuel tank lock ring tabs.

18. Secure the unit with the fuel pump locking retainer ring using Fuel Tank Locking Wrench D90P-9275-A, or equivalent.

19. Remove the fuel tank from the bench to the vehicle, then support the fuel tank while connecting the fuel vapor and vent lines, electrical connectors and the fuel lines.

20. Install the fuel tank in the vehicle, then connect the support straps.

21. Install the fuel filler pipe:

a. Position the fuel tank filler pipe in the body location.

b. Connect the hoses with clamps to the fuel tank filler pipe.

c. Install the underbody fuel tank filler pipe assembly bolt, then tighten the bolt to 36–53 inch lbs. (4–6 Nm), then lower the vehicle.

d. Install the fuel tank filler cap to the tether location, then install the three retaining screws.

22. Insert Rotunda Fuel Tanker Adapter Hose 034-00020 or equivalent into the fuel tank through the fuel tank filler pipe.

23. Transfer the fuel from the Rotunda Fuel Storage Tanker 034-00002 or equivalent to the fuel tank.

24. Connect the negative battery cable, then check for fuel leaks.

## TESTING

1. Ground the fuel pump lead of the self-test connector through a jumper wire at the FP lead.

2. Connect a suitable fuel pressure tester to the fuel pump outlet.

3. Turn the ignition key to the **RUN** position to operate the fuel pump.

4. The fuel pressure should be 35–45 psi for all engines.

➡A safety inertia switch is installed to shut off the electric fuel pump in case of collision. The switch is located on the left hand side (driver's side) of the car, behind the rear most seat side trim panel, or inside the rear quarter shock tower access door. If the pump shuts off, or if the vehicle has been hit and will not start, check for leaks first then reset the switch. The switch is reset by pushing down on the button provided.

### Throttle Body

## REMOVAL & INSTALLATION

### 3.0L Engine—Except SHO and FF

▸ **See Figure 36**

1. Disconnect the negative battery cable. Loosen the air cleaner tube retaining clamps.

2. Disconnect the crankcase ventilation tube and aspirator hoses from the air cleaner outlet tube, then remove the air cleaner outlet tube.

3. Remove the idle speed control solenoid shield.

4. Remove the accelerator cable retaining bolt, then disconnect the accelerator cable from the throttle body lever.

5. Remove the two accelerator cable bracket retaining bolts from the side of the throttle body, then remove the accelerator cable bracket.

6. Tag and disconnect the vacuum hoses from the intake manifold vacuum outlet fitting and cap and the EGR valve.

7. Loosen the EGR valve to exhaust manifold tube nuts at the EGR valve and the EGR valve tube-to-manifold connector. Remove or rotate the tube to the side, out of the way.

8. Remove the PCV hose from the fitting under the throttle body.

9. Disengage the electrical connectors for the intake air temperature (IAT) sensor, idle control valve and the TP sensor.

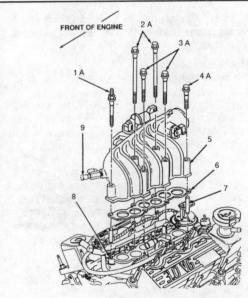

1. Stud bolt
2. Bolt (2 required)
3. Bolt (2 required)
4. Bolt
5. Throttle body
6. Intake manifold upper gasket
7. Guide pin (part of 9H486)
8. Intake manifold
9. Intake manifold vacuum outlet fitting and cap
A. Tighten to 20-30 N.m (15-22 lb-ft)

**Fig. 36 Throttle body assembly—3.0L SEFI engine (except SHO and FF)**

10. Remove the retaining bolts from the alternator brace, then remove the brace.

11. Loosen and remove the five throttle body retaining bolts and the one stud bolt. Make sure to note the location of the bolt to aid in installation.

12. Lift and remove the throttle body assembly from the manifold. Discard the intake manifold upper gasket.

**To install:**

13. Clean and inspect all gasket surfaces. When cleaning aluminum parts be careful not to gouge the surfaces. Lightly coat all bolts with clean engine oil prior to installation.

14. If available, install guide pins to guide the assembly onto its mounting. Place a new gasket on the manifold surface.

15. Aligning the bolt holes, install the throttle body on the intake manifold. Install the stud bolt and five retaining bolts then tighten to 15–22 ft. lbs. (20 –30 Nm).

16. Install the alternator brace to the throttle body mounting stud and alternator mounting bracket. Tighten the nuts to 9–15 ft. lbs. (12–20 Nm).

17. Connect the PCV hose to the fitting under the throttle body.

18. Install the EGR valve-to-exhaust manifold tube to the EGR valve and the EGR valve tube to manifold connector. Tighten to 26–48 ft. lbs. (35–65 Nm).

19. Connect the vacuum hoses to the intake manifold vacuum outlet fitting and cap and the EGR valve.

20. Engage the electrical connectors to the intake air temperature sensor, idle air control valve and the TP sensor.

21. Install the accelerator cable bracket to the side of the throttle body. Tighten the retaining bolts to 13 ft. lbs. (17 Nm).

22. Connect the accelerator cable to the throttle body lever, then install the retaining bolt and tighten to 13 inch lbs. (1.4 Nm).

23. Connect the air cleaner outlet tube to the throttle body and the air cleaner assembly. Tighten the clamp to 12–22 inch lbs. (1.4–2.5 Nm). Connect the crankcase tube and the aspirator hose.

24. Connect the negative battery cable. Start the engine and check for vacuum leaks.

➡**The Throttle Valve (TV) cable must be adjusted if the throttle body is removed for any reason and if the throttle plate idle adjustment screw position is changed.**

25. Adjust the TV cable as follows:

a. Connect the TV cable eye to the transaxle throttle control lever link, then attach the cable boot to the chain cover.

b. If equipped with the 3.0L engine, with the TV cable mounted in the engine bracket, make sure the threaded shank is fully retracted. To retract the shank, pull up on the spring rest with the index fingers and wiggle the top of the thread shank through the spring with the thumbs.

c. If equipped with the 3.8L engine, the TV cable must be unclipped from the right intake manifold clip. To retract the shank, span the crack between the two 180° segments of the adjuster spring rest with a suitable tool. Compress the spring by pushing the rod toward the throttle body with the right hand. While the spring is compressed, push the threaded shank toward the spring with the index and middle fingers of the left hand. Do not pull on the cable sheath.

d. Attach the end of the TV cable to the throttle body.

e. If equipped with the 3.8L engine, rotate the throttle body primary lever by hand, the lever to which the TV-driving nail is attached, to the wide-open-throttle position. The white adjuster shank must be seen to advance. If not, look for the cable sheath/foam hang-up on engine/body components. Attach the TV cable into the top position of the right intake manifold clip.

➡**The threaded shank must show movement or "ratchet" out of the grip jaws. If there is no movement, inspect the TV cable system for broken or disconnected components, then repeat the procedure.**

26. Check and adjust the engine idle speed as necessary. Adjust the transaxle TV cable. Install the idle speed control solenoid shield. Tighten the retaining bolts to 13 inch lbs. (1.5 Nm).

## 3.0L Flexible Fuel (FF) Engine

### ◆ See Figure 37

1. Disconnect the negative battery cable.

2. Remove the crankcase ventilation tube and the aspirator hoses from the air cleaner outlet tube.

3. Loosen the air cleaner tube clamp at the throttle body and the air cleaner outlet tube.

➡**Before relieving fuel pressure, cover the hoses with a shop cloth to prevent accidental fuel spray into eyes!**

4. Properly relieve the fuel system pressure.

5. Remove the snow shield from the idle air control valve.

6. Remove the accelerator cable retaining bolts, then disconnect the accelerator cable from the throttle body.

7. Remove the two accelerator cable bracket retaining bolts from the side of the throttle body, then remove the bracket.

8. Tag and disconnect the vacuum hoses attached to the intake manifold vacuum outlet fitting and cap and the EGR valve.

9. Disconnect the differential pressure feedback (DPFE) sensor hoses from the EGR valve-to-exhaust manifold tube.

10. Loosen the EGR valve-to-exhaust manifold tube nut at the EGR valve.

11. Remove the crankcase ventilation tube from the fitting on the throttle body.

12. Disengage the fuel charging wiring connections from the idle air control valve, differential pressure feedback and the throttle position sensors.

13. Remove the alternator brace retaining nuts from the alternator mounting bracket and throttle body stud, then remove the brace.

14. Note the location of the throttle body retaining bolts, then loosen and remove the five throttle body retaining bolts and the stud bolt.

15. Lift and remove the throttle body from the intake manifold, then discard the intake manifold upper gasket.

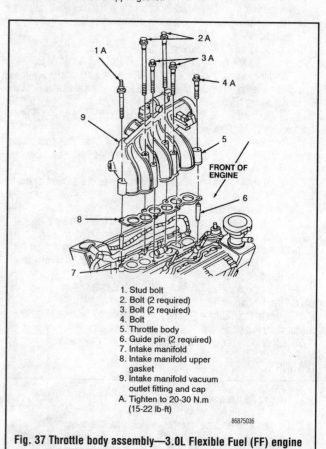

1. Stud bolt
2. Bolt (2 required)
3. Bolt (2 required)
4. Bolt
5. Throttle body
6. Guide pin (2 required)
7. Intake manifold
8. Intake manifold upper gasket
9. Intake manifold vacuum outlet fitting and cap
A. Tighten to 20-30 N.m (15-22 lb-ft)

86875036

**Fig. 37 Throttle body assembly—3.0L Flexible Fuel (FF) engine**

**To install:**

➡**For the FF vehicle, the throttle body is to be replaced as an assembly. If replacing the throttle body with a new one, reuse the original intake manifold vacuum outlet fitting and cap, EGR valve and EGR pressure sensor with the new throttle body.**

16. Carefully clean the intake manifold and throttle body gasket mating surfaces, being careful not the gouge the aluminum which will cause leaks, then inspect the mating surfaces for damage. Lightly coat all bolt and stud threads with oil.

17. If available, install guide pins in the front and rear bolt holes to aid in alignment.

18. Place a new intake manifold gasket on the intake manifold, using the guide pins if available.

19. Aligning the bolt holes, install the throttle body on the intake manifold. Install and hand-tighten the four center retaining bolts, then remove the guide pins if used. Install the stud bolt and the remaining retaining bolt. Tighten the bolts to 15–22 ft. lbs. (20–30 Nm).

20. Install the alternator brace to the throttle body mounting stud and alternator mounting bracket. Tighten the nuts to 9–15 ft. lbs. (12–20 Nm).

21. Install the EGR valve-to-exhaust manifold tube to the EGR valve and EGR valve tube to the manifold connector. Tighten the EGR valve-to-exhaust manifold tube nut to 26–48 ft. lbs. (35–65 Nm).

22. Connect the hoses from the EGR pressure sensor to the EGR valve-to-exhaust manifold tube. Check the condition of the hoses, and replace if damaged.

23. Connect the vacuum lines to their original locations on the intake manifold vacuum outlet fitting and cap, and EGR valve as tagged during removal. Check the condition of the hoses, and replace if damaged.

24. Engage the electrical connectors to the throttle position sensor, EGR pressure sensor and intake air temperature sensor.

25. Install the crankcase ventilation tube to the throttle body.

26. Install the accelerator cable bracket to the side of the throttle body, then tighten the retaining bolts to 13 ft. lbs. (17 Nm).

27. Connect the accelerator cable to the throttle body lever. Install the accelerator cable retaining bolt and tighten to 13 inch lbs. (1.4 Nm).

28. Install the air cleaner outlet tube to the throttle body. Tighten the tube clamps to 12–22 inch lbs. (1.4–2.5 Nm). Connect the crankcase ventilation tube and aspirator hose to their original locations.

29. Connect the negative battery cable, then start the engine and check for vacuum, exhaust and fuel leaks.

➡**The Throttle Valve (TV) cable must be adjusted if the throttle body is removed for any reason and if the throttle plate idle adjustment screw position is changed.**

30. Adjust the TV cable as follows:
   a. Connect the TV cable eye to the transaxle throttle control lever link, then attach the cable boot to the chain cover.
   b. If equipped with the 3.0L engine, with the TV cable mounted in the engine bracket, make sure the threaded shank is fully retracted. To retract the shank, pull up on the spring rest with the index fingers and wiggle the top of the thread shank through the spring with the thumbs.
   c. Attach the end of the TV cable to the throttle body.

➡**The threaded shank must show movement or "ratchet" out of the grip jaws. If there is no movement, inspect the TV cable system for broken or disconnected components, then repeat the procedure.**

31. Install the snowshield onto the idle air control valve, then tighten the retaining screw to 13 inch lbs. (1.4 Nm).

### 3.0L and 3.2L SHO Engines

▶ **See Figure 38**

1. Disconnect the negative battery cable.
2. Remove the fuel tank filler cap to relieve the fuel tank pressure, then properly relieve the fuel system pressure. There is a fuel pressure relief valve located on the fuel injection supply manifold for this purpose. For more details, please refer to the fuel pressure relief procedure located earlier in this section.
3. Remove the air cleaner outlet tube and accelerator cables.

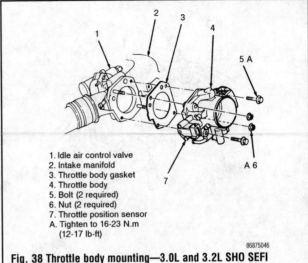

1. Idle air control valve
2. Intake manifold
3. Throttle body gasket
4. Throttle body
5. Bolt (2 required)
6. Nut (2 required)
7. Throttle position sensor
A. Tighten to 16-23 N.m (12-17 lb-ft)

86875046

**Fig. 38 Throttle body mounting—3.0L and 3.2L SHO SEFI engines**

4. Disconnect the fuel charging wiring connectors at the throttle position (TP) sensor and the idle air control valve.
5. Carefully relieve the cooling system pressure by releasing the pressure at the radiator cap, then remove the water bypass hoses.
6. Disconnect the crankcase ventilation tubes.
7. Remove the throttle body retaining bolts and nuts, then remove the throttle body from the vehicle. Discard the gasket.

**To install:**
8. Clean and inspect the throttle body and intake manifold mating surfaces. If scraping is necessary to clean the surfaces, be careful not to damage to gasket surfaces or allow and gasket and/or foreign material to enter the intake manifold.
9. Install a new throttle body gasket, then position the throttle body and secure using the retaining bolts. Tighten the bolts to 12–17 ft. lbs. (16–23 Nm).
10. Connect the crankcase ventilation tubes.
11. Connect the water bypass hoses, then refill the cooling system to the proper level. For details regarding this procedure, please refer to Section 1 of this manual.
12. Fasten the fuel charging wiring connectors at the throttle position (TP) sensor and idle air control valve.
13. Install the accelerator cables and the air cleaner outlet tube.
14. Install the fuel tank filler cap at the fuel tank.
15. Connect the negative battery cable, then check all of the connections at the fuel injection supply manifold, fuel injectors, push connect fittings, etc. to make sure they are all connected/fastened securely.
16. Turn the ignition switch **ON** and **OFF** several times without starting the engine to pressurize the fuel system.
17. Start the engine and run it until the engine reaches normal operating temperatures, then check for coolant leaks. Check the coolant level and add if necessary.

### 3.8L Engine

▶ **See Figure 39**

1. Disconnect the negative battery cable.
2. Remove the fuel tank filler cap to relieve the fuel tank pressure, then properly relieve the fuel system pressure. There is a fuel pressure relief valve located on the fuel injection supply manifold for this purpose. For more details, please refer to the fuel pressure relief procedure located earlier in this section.
3. Remove the air cleaner outlet tube from the throttle body, then disconnect the accelerator cable from the throttle body lever.
4. Disengage the fuel charging wiring connectors from the throttle position (TP) sensor and the idle air control valve.

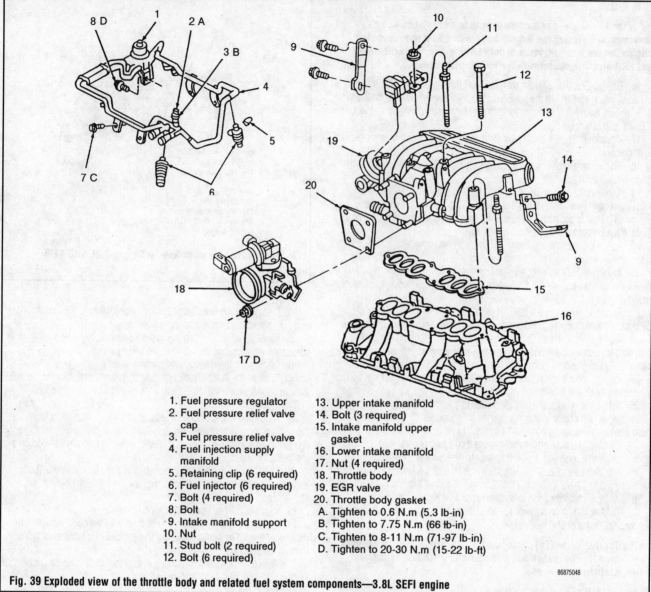

1. Fuel pressure regulator
2. Fuel pressure relief valve cap
3. Fuel pressure relief valve
4. Fuel injection supply manifold
5. Retaining clip (6 required)
6. Fuel injector (6 required)
7. Bolt (4 required)
8. Bolt
9. Intake manifold support
10. Nut
11. Stud bolt (2 required)
12. Bolt (6 required)
13. Upper intake manifold
14. Bolt (3 required)
15. Intake manifold upper gasket
16. Lower intake manifold
17. Nut (4 required)
18. Throttle body
19. EGR valve
20. Throttle body gasket
A. Tighten to 0.6 N.m (5.3 lb-in)
B. Tighten to 7.75 N.m (66 lb-in)
C. Tighten to 8-11 N.m (71-97 lb-in)
D. Tighten to 20-30 N.m (15-22 lb-ft)

**Fig. 39 Exploded view of the throttle body and related fuel system components—3.8L SEFI engine**

86875048

5. Remove the four throttle body retaining nuts, then remove the throttle body from the upper intake manifold and discard the throttle body gasket.

**To install:**

6. Clean and inspect the gasket mating surfaces. If scraping is required to clean the surface, be careful not the damage the gasket surfaces or allow any gasket material or foreign material to drop into the intake manifold.

7. Using a new throttle body gasket, install the throttle body in the four studs of the upper intake manifold, then tighten the retaining nuts to 15–22 ft. lbs. (20–30 Nm).

8. Engage the fuel charging wiring connectors to the throttle position sensor and idle air control valve.

9. Install the air cleaner outlet tube to the throttle body.

10. Install the fuel tank filler cap at the fuel tank.

11. Connect the negative battery cable, then check all of the connections at the fuel injection supply manifold, fuel injectors, push connect fittings, etc. to make sure they are all connected/fastened securely.

12. Turn the ignition switch **ON** and **OFF** several times without starting the engine to pressurize the fuel system.

## Fuel Charging Assembly

### REMOVAL & INSTALLATION

➡The fuel charging assembly consists of the air throttle body, and the upper and lower intake manifolds. Prior to service or removal of the fuel charging assembly, the following procedures must be taken.

1. Open the hood and install protective fender covers.
2. Disconnect the negative battery cable.
3. Remove the fuel cap at the tank.
4. Release the fuel pressure from the fuel system. Depressurize the fuel system by connecting a Fuel Pressure Gauge part No. T80L-9974-B or equivalent to the pressure relief valve on the fuel rail assembly.
5. Remove the intake air boot from the throttle body and airflow sensor and disconnect the throttle cable.
6. Disconnect the vacuum and electrical connectors from the throttle body.
7. Disconnect the coolant bypass hoses at the throttle body.

**⁂ WARNING**

The cooling system may be under pressure. Release the pressure at the radiator cap before removing the hoses. Also, allow the engine to cool down before performing any service.

8. Disconnect the EGR pipe from the EGR valve, if so equipped.

9. Remove the eight bolts at the intake manifold support brackets and remove the brackets.

10. Remove the bolt retaining the coolant hose bracket and disconnect the PCV hoses, if so equipped.

11. Remove the intake and throttle body assembly.

**To install:**

12. Clean and inspect the manifold mounting surfaces.

13. Position new intake manifold gaskets and install the manifold assembly onto the cylinder heads.

14. Install the 12 intake-to-head attaching bolts and tighten to 11–17 ft. lbs. (15–23 Nm).

15. Install the intake manifold support brackets and coolant hose bracket.

16. Connect all the coolant and vacuum hoses.

17. Connect the electrical connectors at the DIS module, vacuum switching valve, throttle position sensor, and the air bypass valve.

18. Install the throttle cable and intake air boot.

19. Connect the negative battery cable. Start the engine and check for fuel and coolant leaks.

## Fuel Injectors

### REMOVAL & INSTALLATION

▶ **See Figures 40, 41 and 42**

**3.0L Engine**

1. Disconnect the negative battery cable.

**⁂ CAUTION**

The fuel system is under high pressure. Use care when servicing the fuel system or personal injury may occur.

2. Remove the fuel tank filler cap to release the fuel tank pressure, then properly release the fuel system pressure.

3. Remove the fuel injection supply manifold. For details, please refer to the procedure located later in this section.

4. Carefully remove the fuel charging wiring connectors from the fuel injectors, as required.

5. Grasping the fuel injector body, pull up while gently rocking the fuel injector from side-to-side.

6. Inspect the fuel injector O-rings, there are two per injector, for signs of damage and/or deterioration and replace as necessary.

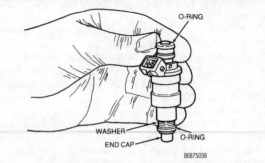

**Fig. 41 Inspect the injector O-rings, end cap, body and washer for signs of damage and/or deterioration, and replace worn components as necessary**

7. Inspect the fuel injector end cap, body and washer for signs of dirt and/or deterioration and replace as necessary.

**To install:**

8. Lubricate new O-rings with clean engine oil.

9. Install the fuel injectors using a light, twisting-pushing motion.

10. Install the fuel injection supply manifold. For details, please refer to the procedure later in this section.

11. Engage the fuel charging wiring connectors to the fuel injectors.

12. Install the fuel tank filler cap, then connect the negative battery cable.

13. Turn the ignition switch **ON** and **OFF** several times without starting the engine to pressurize the system, then check for fuel leaks.

**3.0L and 3.2L SHO Engines**

1. Disconnect the negative battery cable.

2. Remove the fuel tank filler cap, then properly relieve the fuel system pressure.

3. Remove the intake manifold as follows:

a. Properly drain the cooling system into a suitable container.

b. Remove the intake air tube from the throttle body and MAP sensor. Disconnect the throttle cables.

c. Disengage the electrical connectors at the TP sensor, air bypass valve, vacuum switching valve and DIS module.

d. Disconnect the coolant bypass hoses and vacuum lines.

e. Disconnect the EGR pipe from the EGR valve.

f. Remove the 8 bolts at the intake manifold support brackets, then remove the brackets.

1. Fuel injection supply manifold (2 required)
2. O-ring seal (6 required)
3. Fuel injector grommet (6 required)
4. Fuel injector (6 required)
5. Fuel injector gasket (6 required)
6. Cylinder head

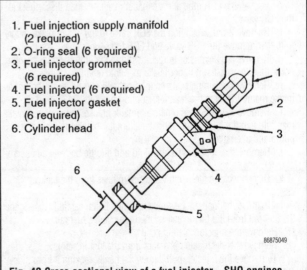

**Fig. 42 Cross-sectional view of a fuel injector—SHO engines**

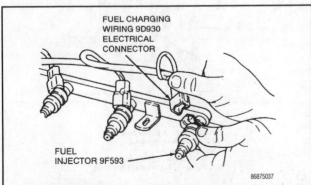

**Fig. 40 Removing the fuel charging wiring electrical connector(s) from the fuel injector(s)**

g. Remove the bolt retaining the coolant hose bracket, then disconnect the PCV hoses.

h. Remove the 12 manifold retaining bolts, then remove the intake manifold and throttle body assembly.

4. Disengage the electrical connectors at the fuel injectors.

5. Remove the fuel injection supply manifold/rail retaining bolts.

6. Raise and slightly rotate the fuel injection supply manifold/rail assembly, then remove the injectors.

**To install:**

7. Inspect the fuel injector O-ring seals and insulators for damage and/or deterioration, then replace as necessary.

8. Lubricate new O-rings with engine oil, then install them on the fuel injectors.

9. Install the injectors in the fuel injection supply manifold/rail by lightly twisting and pushing the injectors into position.

10. Install the fuel injection supply manifold/rail, making sure the injectors seat properly in the cylinder head.

11. Install the fuel injection supply manifold/rail retaining bolts, then tighten the bolts to 11–17 ft. lbs. (15–23 Nm).

12. Engage the electrical connectors at the fuel injectors.

13. Install the intake manifold by reversing the removal procedure.

14. Install the fuel tank filler cap, then connect the negative battery cable.

15. Then turn the ignition switch **ON** and **OFF** several times to pressurize the fuel system.

16. Start the engine and let it run until it reaches normal operating temperature, then check for leaks for fuel and/or coolant leaks. Check the coolant level and add if necessary.

### 3.8L Engine

1. Disconnect the negative battery cable.

2. Remove the fuel cap at the tank to release the fuel tank pressure.

3. Properly relieve the pressure from the fuel system. For details, please refer to the procedure located earlier in this section.

4. Remove the upper intake manifold and the fuel supply manifold as follows:

a. Disengage the electrical connectors at the air bypass valve, TP sensor and EGR position sensor.

b. Disconnect the throttle linkage at the throttle ball and the transmission linkage from the throttle body. Remove the 2 bolts securing the bracket to the intake manifold and position the bracket with the cables aside.

c. Disconnect the upper intake manifold vacuum fitting connections by disconnecting all vacuum lines to the vacuum tree, EGR valve and pressure regulator.

d. Disconnect the PCV hose and remove the nut retaining the EGR transducer to the upper intake manifold.

e. Loosen the EGR tube at the exhaust manifold, then disconnect at the EGR valve.

f. Remove 2 bolts retaining the EGR valve to the upper intake manifold, then remove the EGR valve and EGR transducer as an assembly.

g. Remove the 2 canister purge lines from the fittings on the throttle body, then remove the 6 upper intake manifold retaining bolts.

h. Remove 2 retaining bolts on the front and rear edges of the upper intake manifold where the manifold support brackets are located.

i. Remove the nut retaining the alternator bracket to the upper intake manifold and the 2 bolts retaining the alternator bracket to the water pump and alternator.

j. Remove the upper intake manifold and throttle body as an assembly.

k. Disconnect the fuel supply and return lines from the fuel rail assembly.

l. Remove the fuel rail assembly retaining bolts, carefully disengage the fuel rail from the fuel injectors, then remove the fuel rail.

5. Remove the injector retaining clips.

6. Remove the electrical connectors from the fuel injectors.

7. To remove the injector, pull it up while gently rocking it from side-to-side.

8. Inspect the injector O-rings, pintle protection cap (plastic hat) and washer for deterioration and replace, as required.

**To install:**

9. Lubricate new engine O-rings with engine oil and install 2 on each injector.

10. Install the injectors, using a light, twisting, pushing motion to install them.

11. Reconnect the injector retaining clips.

12. Install the fuel rail assembly.

13. Install the electrical harness connectors to the injectors.

14. Install the upper intake manifold by reversing the removal procedure.

15. Install the fuel cap at the tank.

16. Connect the negative battery cable.

17. Turn the ignition switch from **ON** to **OFF** position several times without starting the engine to check for fuel leaks.

## Fuel Injection Supply Manifold

### REMOVAL & INSTALLATION

#### 3.0L Engine—Except SHO

▶ See Figure 43

1. Disconnect the negative battery cable, then properly relieve the fuel system pressure.

2. Remove the throttle body. For details, please refer to the procedure located earlier in this section.

3. On unleaded gasoline vehicles only:

a. Scribe an alignment mark on the base of the distributor and the intake manifold.

b. Remove the hold down clamp, then lift the distributor enough to allow the fuel injection supply manifold to clear the distributor and intake manifold.

4. Disconnect the fuel supply and return lines.

5. Carefully disconnect the fuel charging wiring from the fuel injectors.

6. Disconnect the fuel charging wiring from the fuel pressure regulator.

7. Remove the four fuel injection supply manifold retaining bolts. There are two on each side.

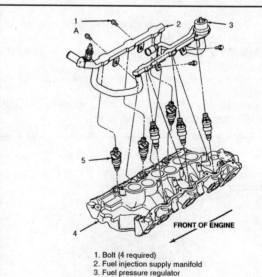

1. Bolt (4 required)
2. Fuel injection supply manifold
3. Fuel pressure regulator
4. Intake manifold
5. Fuel injector (6 required)
A. Tighten to 8-12 N.m (71-106 lb-in)

86875039

**Fig. 43 Fuel injection supply manifold—3.0L SEFI engine (except SHO)**

## ✳✴✳ WARNING

**The fuel injectors and supply manifold must be handled with extreme care to avoid damage to the sealing areas and sensitive fuel-metering orifices.**

8. Carefully disengage the fuel injection supply manifold from the fuel injectors by lifting and gently rocking the fuel injection supply manifold, then remove the fuel injectors by lifting while gently rocking from side-to-side.

9. Place the removed components in a clean container to avoid dirt of other contamination.

**To install:**

➡**When installing the manifold, make sure that the O-rings are properly seated to avoid leakage.**

10. Examine the fuel injector O-rings for deterioration, and install new ones if necessary.

➡**To avoid cutting the O-rings, do NOT try to install them if they are swollen. Allow them to dry out first.**

11. Using clean engine oil, lubricate the O-rings, then install two on each injector.

12. Make sure that the cups are clean and do not have any dirt or contamination.

13. Install the fuel injectors in the fuel injection supply manifold using a light, twisting-pushing motion.

14. On unleaded gasoline engines only:

   a. Lift the distributor enough to allow the fuel injection supply manifold to clear the distributor and intake manifold, then position the fuel injection manifold.

   b. Lower the distributor into position, then install the hold-down clamp and align the scribe marks made during removal. Tighten the clamp bolt to 18 ft. lbs. (24 Nm).

15. Carefully install the fuel injection supply manifold and fuel injectors into the intake manifold, one side at a time. Firmly push down on the fuel injection supply manifold to be sure that the injector O-rings are fully seated.

16. While holding the fuel injection manifold in place, install the retaining bolts, then tighten to 6–9 ft. lbs. (8–12 Nm).

17. Connect the fuel supply and return lines.

18. Connect the negative battery cable, then turn the ignition switch **ON** and **OFF** several times to pressurize the fuel system.

19. Using a clean paper towel and rubber gloves, check for leaks where the fuel injectors connect to the fuel injection supply manifold and intake manifold.

20. Connect the fuel charging wiring to the fuel injectors.

21. Connect the vacuum line to the fuel injectors.

22. Install the throttle body. For details, please refer to the procedure located earlier in this section.

23. Start the engine and allow it to idle, then check for fuel leaks and service as necessary.

### 3.0L and 3.2L SHO Engines

▶ **See Figure 44**

1. Disconnect the negative battery cable.

2. Remove the fuel tank filler cap to release the fuel tank pressure, then properly relieve the fuel system pressure. For details, please refer to the procedure located earlier in this section.

3. Remove the intake manifold. For details, please refer to the procedure located in Section 3 of this manual.

4. Disconnect the fuel line spring lock couplings. For details, please refer to the procedure located earlier in this section.

5. Disengage the connectors from the fuel charging wiring at the fuel injectors. Disconnect the vacuum hose at the fuel pressure regulator.

➡**The fuel injection supply manifolds are mounted on bushings. Keep the bushings for installation.**

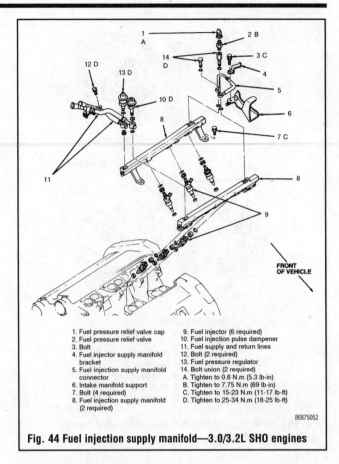

1. Fuel pressure relief valve cap
2. Fuel pressure relief valve
3. Bolt
4. Fuel injector supply manifold bracket
5. Fuel injection supply manifold connector
6. Intake manifold support
7. Bolt (4 required)
8. Fuel injection supply manifold (2 required)
9. Fuel injector (6 required)
10. Fuel injection pulse dampener
11. Fuel supply and return lines
12. Bolt (2 required)
13. Fuel pressure regulator
14. Bolt union (2 required)
A. Tighten to 0.6 N.m (5.3 lb-in)
B. Tighten to 7.75 N.m (69 lb-in)
C. Tighten to 15-23 N.m (11-17 lb-ft)
D. Tighten to 25-34 N.m (18-25 lb-ft)

86875052

**Fig. 44 Fuel injection supply manifold—3.0/3.2L SHO engines**

6. Remove the four fuel injection supply manifold retaining bolts, then remove the fuel injection supply manifold.

**To install:**

## ✳✴✳ WARNING

**ALWAYS use new gaskets when assembling the fuel injection supply manifold to avoid possible fire from fuel leakage!**

7. Using a new gasket, install the fuel injection supply manifolds, making sure that all of the injectors are properly seated.

8. Install the four fuel injection supply manifold retaining bolts, then tighten the bolts to 11–17 ft. lbs. (15–23 Nm).

9. Connect the fuel line spring couplings. For details, please refer to the procedure located later in this section.

10. Install the intake manifold. For details regarding this procedure, please refer to the intake manifold installation in Section 3 of this manual.

11. Connect the vacuum lines, then fasten the remaining fuel charging wiring connectors.

12. Install the cap on the fuel tank.

13. Connect the negative battery cable, then turn the ignition **ON** and **OFF** several times, without starting the engine, to pressurize the fuel system.

14. Start and run the engine, then check for leaks.

### 3.8L Engine

▶ **See Figure 45**

1. Disconnect the negative battery cable.

2. Remove the fuel tank filler cap to release the fuel tank pressure, then properly relieve the fuel system pressure. There is a fuel pressure relief valve located on the fuel injection supply manifold for this purpose. For more details, please refer to the procedure located earlier in this section.

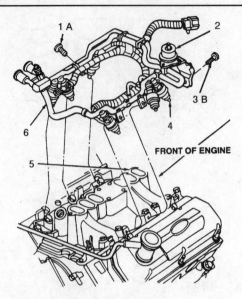

1. Bolt (4 required)
2. Fuel pressure regulator
3. Bolt
4. Fuel injector (6 required)
5. Lower intake manifold
6. Fuel injection supply manifold
A. Tighten to 8-11 N.m (71-97 lb-in)
B. Tighten to 20-30 N.m (15-22 lb-ft)

86875053

**Fig. 45 Fuel injection supply manifold and related components—3.8L SEFI engine**

3. Remove the upper intake manifold. For details regarding this procedure, please refer to the intake manifold removal procedure located in Section 3 of this manual.

4. Remove the spring lock coupling fittings from the fuel inlet and return fittings. For details, please refer to the procedure located later in this section.

5. Using Spring Lock Coupling Disconnect Tool D87L-9280-A (⅜ in.) or D87L-9280-B (½ in.) or equivalent, disconnect the inlet and outlet fuel lines from the fuel injection supply manifold.

6. Remove the four fuel injection supply manifold retaining bolts. There are two on each side. Remove the fuel pressure regulator bracket retaining bolt from the cylinder head.

➥It may be easier to remove the fuel injectors with the fuel injection supply manifold as an assembly.

7. Carefully disengage the fuel injection supply manifold from the fuel injectors, then remove the fuel injection supply manifold.

**To install:**

➥When installing the fuel injection supply manifold, make sure that the O-rings are properly seated so that there is no fuel leakage.

8. Push the fuel injector supply manifold down to be sure that all of the fuel injector O-rings are fully seated in the cylinder head pockets.

9. While holding the fuel injection supply manifold down, install the retaining bolts. Tighten the fuel injection supply manifold retaining bolts to the lower intake manifold to 6–8 inch lbs. (8–11 Nm). Tighten the fuel pressure regulator bracket retaining bolt to cylinder head to 15–22 ft. lbs. (20–30 Nm).

10. Install the spring lock coupling as described later in this section.

11. Install the fuel tank cap, then connect the negative battery cable.

12. With the fuel charging wiring still disconnected, turn the ignition switch **ON** and **OFF** several times. This allows the fuel pump to pressurize the system. Using a clean towel, check for fuel leaks.

13. Connect the fuel charging wiring.

14. Install the upper intake manifold. For details regarding this procedure, please refer to the upper intake manifold installation procedure in Section 3 of this manual.

15. Start the vehicle and let it run for two minutes, then turn the engine **OFF** and check for leaks.

## Fuel Pressure Regulator

REMOVAL & INSTALLATION

**3.0L Engine—Except SHO**

▶ See Figure 46

### ✷✷ WARNING

**Flexible Fuel vehicle pressure regulator components are strictly methanol compatible. Do NOT use components that are not specially designed for use with methanol fuel. The use of different parts or materials could produce an untested configuration that could result in fire, personal injury and/or engine damage.**

1. Disconnect the negative battery cable.

2. Remove the fuel tank filler cap to release the fuel tank pressure.

3. Properly release the fuel system pressure. There is a fuel pressure relief valve on the fuel injection supply manifold for this purpose. For more details, please refer to the fuel system relief procedure located earlier in this section.

4. Remove the vacuum line at the fuel pressure regulator.

5. Remove the two fuel injection supply manifold-to-intake manifold retaining bolts. Carefully lift the fuel injection supply manifold off of the fuel injectors to get to the fuel pressure regulator retaining screws.

6. Remove the Allen head retaining screws from the fuel pressure regulator housing and discard them.

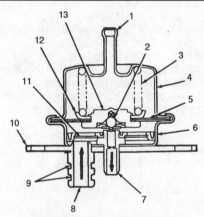

1. Engine vacuum reference tube (part of 9C968)
2. Ball seat (part of 9C968)
3. Spring (part of 9C968)
4. Upper housing (part of 9C968)
5. Diaphragm (part of 9C968)
6. Lower housing (part of 9C968)
7. Fuel outlet (return tube) (part of 9C968)
8. Fuel inlet (supply tube) (part of 9C968)
9. O-ring grooves (part of 9C968)
10. Mounting plate (part of 9C968)
11. Fuel filter screen (part of 9C968)
12. Spring seat (part of 9C968)
13. Valve assembly (part of 9C968)

86875040

**Fig. 46 Cross-sectional view of a fuel pressure regulator—3.0L SEFI engine (except SHO)**

7. Remove the fuel pressure regulator, return seal and O-rings, then discard the return seal and the O-rings.

**To install:**

8. Lubricate new regulator O-rings with clean engine oil, then make sure the mating surfaces of the regulator and fuel injection supply manifold are clean. If scraping is necessary, be careful not to damage the fuel pressure regulator or fuel injection supply manifold sealing surfaces.

9. Install the new fuel pressure regulator return seal and O-rings on the fuel pressure regulator.

10. Using new Allen head retaining screws, install the fuel pressure regulator on the fuel injection supply manifold. Tighten the screws to 34 inch lbs. (4 Nm).

11. Carefully install the fuel injection supply manifold to the fuel injectors. If the fuel injectors were completely disengaged from the fuel injection supply manifold, lubricate the fuel injector O-rings with clean engine oil before inserting them in the fuel supply manifold cups. Push the fuel injection supply manifold down on the fuel injector, then tighten the retaining bolts to 6–9 ft. lbs. (8–12 Nm) while holding down on the fuel injection supply manifold.

12. Install the fuel filler tank cap to the fuel tank.

13. Check all of the connections at the fuel injection supply manifold, fuel injectors, fuel line push connect fittings, etc. to make sure they are all fastened securely.

14. Connect the negative battery cable, then turn the ignition switch **ON** and **OFF** several times without starting the engine to pressurize the fuel system and check for fuel leaks.

15. Start the engine and allow it to warm up to normal operating temperature, then check for leaks.

### 3.0L and 3.2L SHO Engines

1. Disconnect the negative battery cable.

2. Remove the fuel tank filler cap to release the fuel tank pressure, the properly relieve the fuel system pressure. There is a pressure relieve valve located on the fuel injection supply manifold for this purpose. For details, please refer to the procedure located earlier in this section.

3. Disconnect the vacuum hose at the pressure regulator.

4. Remove the fuel pressure regulator from the fuel return lines and fuel injection supply manifold, then discard the sealing gaskets.

**To install:**

5. Install the fuel pressure regulator into the fuel return line and fuel injection supply manifold using new gaskets. Tighten the fuel pressure regulator to 18–25 ft. lbs. (25–34 Nm).

6. Connect the vacuum hose to the fuel pressure regulator.

7. Install the fuel tank cap, then connect the negative battery cable.

8. Check all of the fuel system connections to make sure they are all fastened/connected securely.

9. Turn the ignition switch **ON** and **OFF** without starting the engine and check for fuel leaks.

### 3.8L Engine

**♦ See Figure 47**

1. Disconnect the negative battery cable.

2. Remove the fuel tank filler cap to release the fuel tank pressure, the properly relieve the fuel system pressure. There is a pressure relieve valve located on the fuel injection supply manifold for this purpose. For details, please refer to the procedure located earlier in this section.

3. Remove the vacuum hose at the fuel pressure regulator.

4. Remove the Allen head retaining screw from the fuel pressure regulator housing.

5. Remove the fuel pressure regulator, return seal and the O-rings. Discard the return seal and the O-rings.

**To install:**

6. Make sure the mating surfaces of the fuel pressure regulator and fuel injection supply manifold are clean. If scraping is necessary, be careful not to damage the regulator or manifold.

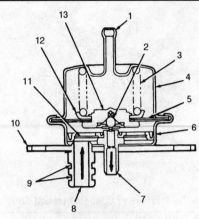

1. Engine vacuum reference tube (part of 9C968)
2. Ball seat (part of 9C968)
3. Spring (part of 9C968)
4. Upper housing (part of 9C968)
5. Diaphragm (part of 9C968)
6. Lower housing (part of 9C968)
7. Fuel outlet (return tube) (part of 9C968)
8. Fuel inlet (supply tube) (part of 9C968)
9. O-ring grooves (part of 9C968)
10. Mounting plate (part of 9C968)
11. Fuel filter screen (part of 9C968)
12. Spring seat (part of 9C968)
13. Valve assembly (part of 9C968)

86875054

**Fig. 47 Cross-sectional view of a fuel pressure regulator—3.8L SEFI engine**

7. Lubricate new O-rings with clean engine oil, then install a new return seal and O-rings on the fuel pressure regulator.

8. Install the fuel pressure regulator on the fuel injection supply manifold. Tighten the retaining screws to 34 inch lbs. (4 Nm).

9. Install the vacuum hose to the fuel pressure regulator.

10. Install the fuel tank cap, then connect the negative battery cable.

11. Check all of the fuel system connections to make sure they are all fastened/connected securely.

12. Turn the ignition switch **ON** and **OFF** without starting the engine and check for fuel leaks.

## Idle Air Control (IAC) Bypass Valve

### REMOVAL & INSTALLATION

### 3.0L (Except SHO) and 3.8L Engine

**♦ See Figures 48, 49 and 50**

1. Disconnect the negative battery cable. Properly relieve the fuel system pressure, as required.

2. Disengage the idle air control bypass valve assembly electrical connector from the wiring harness.

3. Remove the two IAC valve retaining screws, then remove the valve and gasket.

**To install:**

4. Clean the gasket mating surfaces. If scraping is necessary, be careful not to damage the idle air control valve or throttle body gasket surfaces. Also, do not allow gasket material to drop into the throttle body.

5. Install the gasket on the throttle body surface, then mount the IAC valve to its mounting and secure using the retaining screws. Tighten the screws to 84 inch lbs. (9.5 Nm).

6. Engage the air bypass valve electrical connector to the wiring harness.

7. Connect the negative battery cable.

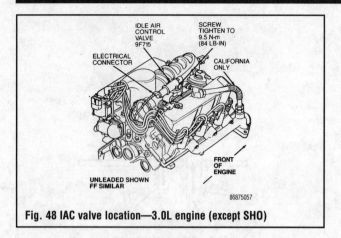

Fig. 48 IAC valve location—3.0L engine (except SHO)

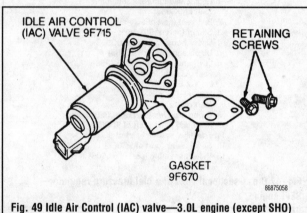

Fig. 49 Idle Air Control (IAC) valve—3.0L engine (except SHO)

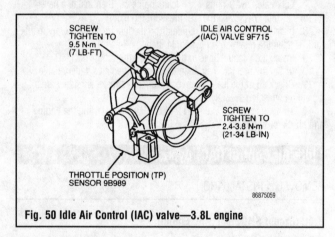

Fig. 50 Idle Air Control (IAC) valve—3.8L engine

### 3.0L and 3.2L SHO Engines

▶ **See Figure 51**

1. Disconnect the negative battery cable. Properly relieve the fuel system pressure, as required.

2. Disengage the idle air control bypass valve assembly electrical connector from the wiring harness.

3. Remove the IAC valve retaining bolts. Remove the top retaining bolt first and swing the valve upward to provide working clearance in order to remove the lower retaining bolt. Remove the valve and gasket.

**To install:**

4. Clean the gasket mating surfaces. If scraping is necessary, be careful not to damage the IAC valve or throttle body gasket surfaces. Also, do not allow gasket material to drop into the throttle body.

5. Install the gasket on the throttle body surface. Mount the air bypass valve to its mounting. Tighten the retaining bolts to 63–97 inch lbs. (7–11 Nm).

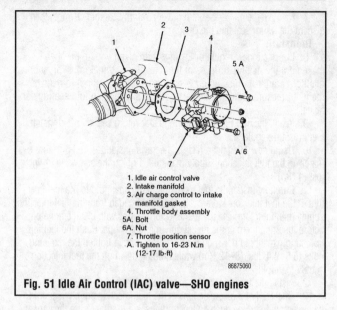

1. Idle air control valve
2. Intake manifold
3. Air charge control to intake manifold gasket
4. Throttle body assembly
5A. Bolt
6A. Nut
7. Throttle position sensor
A. Tighten to 16-23 N.m (12-17 lb-ft)

Fig. 51 Idle Air Control (IAC) valve—SHO engines

6. Engage the IAC valve electrical connector to the wiring harness.
7. Connect the negative battery cable.

## Fuel Pressure Relief Valve

### REMOVAL & INSTALLATION

▶ **See Figures 52, 53 and 54**

➡**Be sure to remove the cap from the fuel pressure relief valve!**

1. Disconnect the negative battery cable.

2. If the fuel injection supply manifold is mounted to the engine, remove the fuel tank filler cap. Release the fuel system pressure at the fuel pressure relief valve on the fuel injection supply manifold using EFI/CFI Fuel Pressure Gauge T80L-9974-B, or equivalent.

3. Using an open-end wrench or a suitable deep-well socket, remove the fuel pressure relief valve.

**To install:**

4. Install the fuel pressure relief valve and fuel pressure relief valve cap. Tighten the valve to 69 inch lbs. (7.75 Nm) and the cap to 5.3 inch lbs. (0.6 Nm).

5. Connect the negative battery cable.

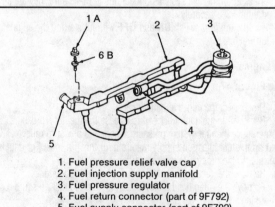

1. Fuel pressure relief valve cap
2. Fuel injection supply manifold
3. Fuel pressure regulator
4. Fuel return connector (part of 9F792)
5. Fuel supply connector (part of 9F792)
6. Fuel pressure relief valve
A. Tighten to 0.6 N.m (5.3 lb-in)
B. Tighten to 7.75 N.m (69 lb-in)

Fig. 52 Fuel pressure relief valve location—3.0L SEFI engine (except SHO)

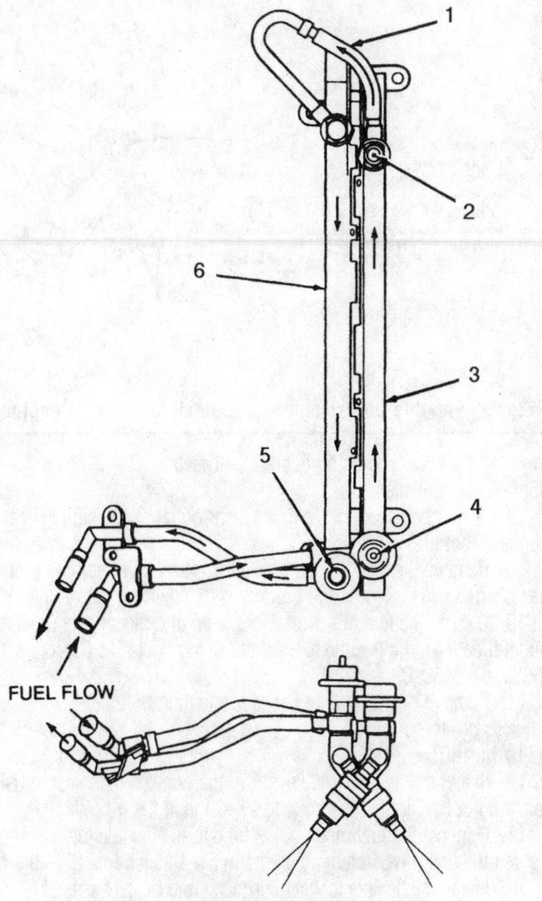

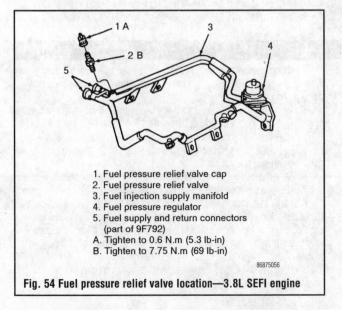

1. Fuel injection supply manifold connector hose
2. Fuel pressure relief valve
3. Fuel injection supply manifold, RH
4. Fuel injection pulse dampener, RH
5. Fuel pressure regulator
6. Fuel injection supply manifold, LH

86875055

**Fig. 53 Location of the fuel pressure relief valve—3.0L and 3.2L SHO engines**

1. Fuel pressure relief valve cap
2. Fuel pressure relief valve
3. Fuel injection supply manifold
4. Fuel pressure regulator
5. Fuel supply and return connectors (part of 9F792)
A. Tighten to 0.6 N.m (5.3 lb-in)
B. Tighten to 7.75 N.m (69 lb-in)

86875056

**Fig. 54 Fuel pressure relief valve location—3.8L SEFI engine**

## Throttle Position (TP) Sensor

### REMOVAL & INSTALLATION

#### 3.0L, 3.0L SHO and 3.2L SHO Engines

▶ **See Figures 55 and 56**

1. Disconnect the negative battery cable.
2. Disconnect the throttle position (TP) sensor from the fuel charging wiring.
3. Remove the two throttle position (TP) sensor retaining screw, then remove the sensor.

**To install:**

➡**Slide the rotary tangs into position over the throttle shaft blade, then rotate the throttle position sensor clockwise to the installed position only. Failure to install the TP sensor in this way may result in excessive idle speeds.**

4. Install the TP sensor, make sure that the rotary tangs on the sensor are in proper alignment and that the red seal is inside the connector.
5. Secure the TP sensor to the throttle body assembly with the two retaining screws, then tighten the screws as follows:
   a. For the 3.0L unleaded and flexible fuel vehicles, tighten the screws to 25–34 inch lbs. (2.8–3.8 Nm).
   b. For the 3.0L SHO and the 3.2L SHO, tighten the screws to 14 inch lbs. (1.5 Nm).
6. Connect the fuel charge wiring to the TP sensor, then connect the negative battery cable.

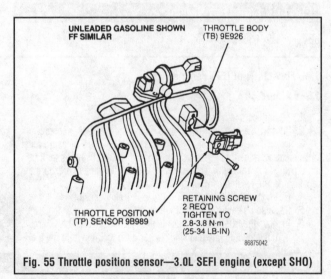

86875042

**Fig. 55 Throttle position sensor—3.0L SEFI engine (except SHO)**

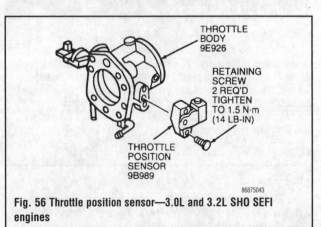

86875043

**Fig. 56 Throttle position sensor—3.0L and 3.2L SHO SEFI engines**

### 3.8L Engine

▶ See Figure 57

1. Disconnect the negative battery cable.
2. Disconnect the TP sensor from the engine control sensor wiring.
3. Remove the two throttle position sensor retaining screws, then remove sensor.

**To install:**

4. Install the TP sensor, then secure using the two retaining screws. Tighten the screws to 25–34 inch lbs. (2.8–3.8 Nm).
5. Connect the TP sensor to the engine control sensor wiring, then connect the negative battery cable.

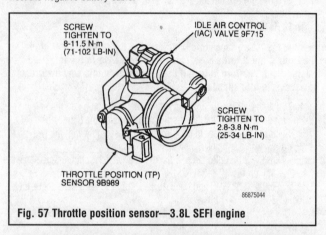

Fig. 57 Throttle position sensor—3.8L SEFI engine

## Flexible Fuel (FF) Sensor

REMOVAL & INSTALLATION

### 3.0L Flexible Fuel (FF) Vehicles

▶ See Figure 58

1. Disconnect the negative battery cable.
2. Remove the fuel filler tank cap to relieve the fuel tank pressure.
3. Properly relieve the fuel system pressure. There is a pressure relief valve located on the fuel injection supply manifold for this purpose. For more details regarding this procedure, please refer to the fuel pressure relief procedure located earlier in this section.
4. Disengage the flexible fuel sensor electrical connector.
5. Raise and safely support the vehicle.
6. Remove the front right-hand side tire and wheel assembly.
7. Remove the fuel line retaining clip, and the fuel line from the fuel

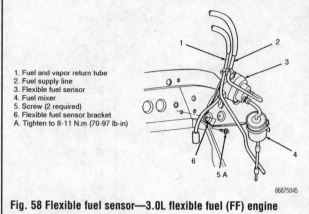

1. Fuel and vapor return tube
2. Fuel supply line
3. Flexible fuel sensor
4. Fuel mixer
5. Screw (2 required)
6. Flexible fuel sensor bracket
A. Tighten to 8-11 N.m (70-97 lb-in)

Fig. 58 Flexible fuel sensor—3.0L flexible fuel (FF) engine

mixer at the inlet hose using Fuel Lines Disconnect Tool (⅜ in.) T90T-9550-C, or equivalent.

8. Disconnect the flexible fuel sensor outlet hose using Fuel Line Disconnect Tool (⅜) T90T-9550-C.
9. Remove the flexible fuel bracket-to-frame rail retaining bolts and flexible fuel sensor/mixer and bracket assembly from the vehicle.
10. Loosen the fuel mixer retainer clamp and disconnect the fuel mixer outlet tube from the flexible fuel sensor using Fuel Line Disconnect Tool (⅜) T90T-9550-C.
11. Remove the flexible fuel sensor retaining bolts, then remove the sensor from the bracket.

**To install:**

12. Install the flexible fuel sensor to the bracket, then secure using the retaining bolts. Tighten the bolts to 27–34 inch lbs. (3–4 Nm).
13. Connect the fuel mixer outlet tube to the flexible fuel sensor, then tighten the fuel mixer retaining clamp to 51–82 inch lbs. (5.8–9.3 Nm).
14. Install the flexible fuel sensor/mixer and bracket assembly and secure with the retaining bolts. Tighten the bolts to 70–97 inch lbs. (8–11 Nm).
15. Connect the flexible fuel sensor outlet hose, then connect the fuel line to the fuel mixer and install the fuel line retaining clip.
16. Install the front right-hand wheel and tire assembly. Tighten the lug nuts to 85–105 ft. lbs. (115–142 Nm).
17. Carefully lower the vehicle.
18. Engage the flexible fuel sensor electrical connector.
19. Install the fuel tank filler cap at the fuel tank.
20. Connect the negative battery cable, then check all of the connections at the fuel injection supply manifold, fuel injectors, push connect fittings, etc. to make sure they are all properly connected/fastened.
21. Turn the ignition switch **ON** and **OFF** several times without starting the engine to pressurize the fuel system, then check for fuel leaks.

## FUEL LINE FITTINGS

### Spring Lock Coupling

▶ See Figure 59

The spring lock coupling is a fuel line coupling held together by a garter spring inside a circular cage. When the coupling is connected, the flared end of the female fitting slips behind the garter spring inside the cage of the male fitting. The garter spring and cage then prevent the flared end of the female fitting from pulling out of the cage. As a redundant locking feature, a horseshoe-shaped retaining clip is used to improve the retaining ability of the spring lock coupling.

REMOVAL & INSTALLATION

▶ See Figure 60

1. Disconnect the negative battery cable, then properly relieve the fuel system pressure. For details, please refer to the procedure covered in the appropriate fuel system in this section.

2. Using your hand only, remove the retaining clip from the spring lock coupling. Do NOT use any sharp tool or screwdriver because it may damage the coupling.
3. Twist the fitting to free it from any adhesion at the O-ring seals.
4. Fit Spring Lock Coupling Disconnect Tool D87L-9280-A (⅜ in.) or D87L-9280-B (½ in.), or equivalent, to coupling.
5. Close the tool and push into the open side of the cage to expand the garter spring and release the female fitting.
6. After the garter spring is expanded, pull the fittings apart.
7. Remove the tool from the disconnected coupling.
8. Make sure that the garter spring is in the cage of the male fitting. If the garter spring is missing, install a new spring by pushing it into the cage opening. If the garter spring is damaged, remove it from the cage with a small wire hook (do NOT use a screwdriver) and install a new spring.
9. Clean all dirt and/or foreign material from both pieces of the coupling.

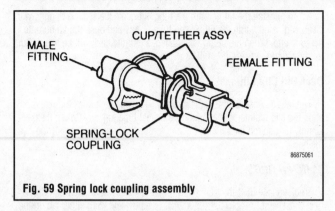

**Fig. 59 Spring lock coupling assembly**

➡**Flexible fuel vehicles use special Methanol compatible O-rings.**

10. Replace any missing or damaged O-rings. Only use the fuel resistant O-rings specified in the accompanying figure. For all vehicles except flexible fuel vehicles, lubricate the male fitting, O-rings and the inside of the female fitting with clean engine oil. For flexible fuel vehicles, lubricate with oil that has an API designation of Multi-Fuel Vehicles (MFV).

➡**Use only the specified (brown) O-rings because they are made of a special material. The use of other types of O-rings, may cause the connection to leak during engine operation.**

11. Fit the female fitting to the male fitting and push until the garter spring snaps over the flared end of the female fitting.

12. Make sure the coupling is engaged or fastened securely by pulling on the fitting and visually checking to make sure the garter spring is over the flared end of the female fitting.

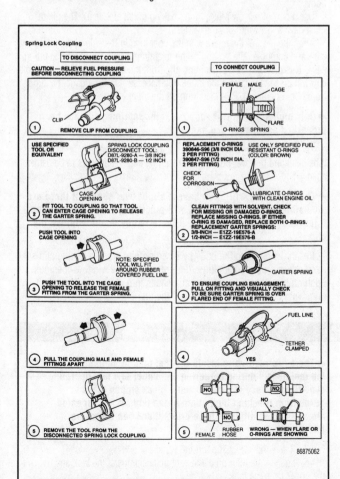

**Fig. 60 Disconnecting and connecting the spring lock coupling**

➡**All vehicles require the large black clip to be installed on the supply-side fuel line and the small grey clip to be installed on the return-side fuel line.**

13. Position the retaining clip over the metal portion of the spring lock coupling. Firmly push the retaining clip onto the spring lock coupling. Make sure that the horseshoe portion of the clip is over the coupling. Do not install the retaining clip over the rubber fuel line.

## Push Connect Fittings

◆ See Figures 61, 62, 63 and 64

Push connect fittings are designed with two different retaining clips. The fittings used with 8mm diameter tubing use a hairpin clip, while the fittings used with 6mm and 12.7mm diameter tubing use a "duck bill" clip. Each type of fitting requires different procedures for service.

➡**Push connect fitting disassembly must be accomplished prior to fuel component removal (filter, pump, etc.), except for the fuel tank, where removal is necessary for access to the push connect fittings.**

### REMOVAL & INSTALLATION

#### Hairpin Clip Fittings (5/16 in.)

1. Inspect the internal portion of the fitting for dirt accumulation. If more than a light coating of dust is present, clean the fitting before disassembly.

2. Remove the hairpin type clip from the fitting. This is done (using hands only) by spreading the two clip legs about 3mm each to disengage the body and pushing the legs into the fitting. Complete removal is accomplished by lightly pulling from the triangular end of the clip and working it clear of the tube and fitting.

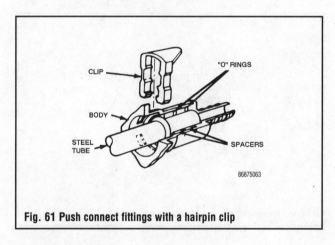

**Fig. 61 Push connect fittings with a hairpin clip**

➡**Do not use any tools.**

3. Grasp the fitting and hose assembly and pull in an axial direction to remove the fitting from the steel tube. Adhesion between sealing surfaces may occur. A slight twist of the fitting may be required to break this adhesion and permit effortless removal.

4. When the fitting is removed from the tube end, inspect clip to ensure it has not been damaged. If damaged, replace the clip. If undamaged, immediately reinstall the clip, insert the clip into any two adjacent openings with the triangular portion pointing away from the fitting opening. Install the clip to fully engage the body (legs of hairpin clip locked on outside of body). Piloting with an index finger is necessary.

5. Before installing the fitting on the tube, wipe the tube end with a clean cloth. Inspect the inside of the fitting to ensure it is free of dirt and/or obstructions.

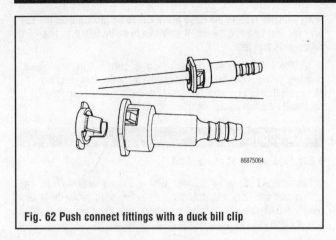

**Fig. 62 Push connect fittings with a duck bill clip**

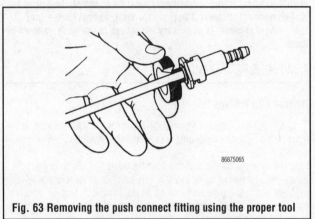

**Fig. 63 Removing the push connect fitting using the proper tool**

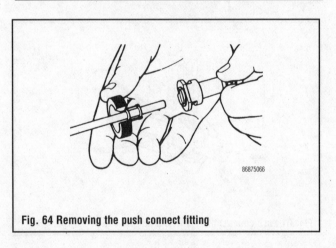

**Fig. 64 Removing the push connect fitting**

6. To reinstall the fitting onto the tube, lubricate the sealing O-rings with clean engine oil, align the fitting and tube axially and push the fitting onto the tube end. When the fitting is engaged, a definite click will be heard. Pull on the fitting to ensure it is fully engaged.

### Duck Bill Clip Fittings

The fitting consists of a body, spacers, O-rings and a duck bill retaining clip. The clip maintains the fitting to the steel tube juncture. When disassembly is required for service, be sure to use the appropriate following method.

#### ¼ IN. FITTINGS

To disengage the tube from the fitting, align the slot on the Push Connect Disassembly Tool T82L-9500-AH, or equivalent, with either tab on the clip (90° from slots on side of fitting), then insert the tool. This disengages the duck bill from the tube. Holding the tool and the tube with one hand, pull the fitting away from the tube.

➡**Only moderate effort is required if the tube has been properly disengaged. Use hands only. After disassembly, inspect and clean the tube sealing surface. Also inspect the inside of the fitting for damage to the retaining clip. If the retaining clip appears to be damaged, replace it. Some fuel tubes have a secondary bead which aligns with the outer surface of the clip. These beads can make tool insertion difficult. If there is extreme difficulty, use the following disassembly method.**

#### ½ IN. FITTING (AND ALTERNATE METHOD FOR ¼ IN. FITTING)

This method of disassembly disengages the retaining clip from the fitting body.

Use a pair of narrow pliers (6 in. locking pliers are ideal). The pliers must have a jaw width of 5mm or less.

Align the jaws of the pliers with the openings in the side of the fitting case and compress the portion of the retaining clip that engages the fitting case. This disengages the retaining clip from the case (often one side of the clip will disengage before the other. It is necessary to disengage the clip from both openings). Pull the fitting off the tube.

➡**Only moderate effort is required if the retaining clip has been properly disengaged. Use hands only.**

The retaining clip will remain on the tube. Disengage the clip from the tube bead and remove. Replace the retaining clip if it appears to be damaged.

➡**The clip's ring will often have a slight oval shape. If there are no visible cracks and the ring will pinch back to its circular configuration, it is not damaged. If there is any doubt, replace the clip.**

Install the clip into the body by inserting one of the retaining clip serrated edges on the duck bill portion into one of the window openings. Push on the other side until the clip snaps into place. Lubricate the O-rings with clean engine oil and slide the fuel line back into the clip.

## FUEL TANK

### Tank Assembly

♦ **See Figure 65**

REMOVAL & INSTALLATION

1. Disconnect the negative battery cable.
2. Relieve the fuel system pressure.
3. Siphon or pump the fuel from the fuel tank, through the filler neck, into a suitable container.

➡**There are reservoirs inside the fuel tank to maintain fuel near the fuel pickup during cornering and under low fuel operating conditions. These reservoirs could block siphon tubes or hoses from reaching the bottom of the tank. A few repeated attempts using different hose orientations can overcome this situation.**

4. Raise and safely support the vehicle.
5. Loosen the filler pipe and vent hose clamps at the tank and remove the hoses from the tank.
6. Place a safety support under the fuel tank and remove the bolts from

the rear of the fuel tank straps. The straps are hinged at the front and will swing aside.

7. Partially remove the tank. Remove the hairpin clips from the push connect fitting and disconnect the fuel lines. Disconnect the electrical connector from the fuel sender/pump assembly.

8. Remove the fuel tank from the vehicle.

**To install:**

➡**If the fuel pump has been removed, the O-ring seal on unleaded gasoline vehicles, or gasket on flexible fuel vehicles must be replaced.**

9. Before installing the fuel tank, check the following:

a. Check the fuel pump for leaks.

b. Make sure the evaporative emission valve is installed completely on the fuel tank top.

c. Make all of the required fuel line, fuel return line, vapor vent and electrical connections which will be inaccessible after the fuel tank is installed. Route lines through the clip on the fuel tank.

10. Raise the fuel tank into proper position in the vehicle.

11. Bring the fuel tank straps around the tank and start the retaining bolt. Align the tank as far forward in the vehicle as possible while securing the retaining bolts.

➡**If equipped with a heat shield, make sure it is installed with the straps and positioned correctly on the tank.**

12. Check the hoses and wiring mounted on the tank top, to make sure they are correctly routed and will not be pinched between the tank and the body.

13. Tighten the fuel tank strap retaining bolts to 22–30 ft. lbs. (29–41 Nm).

14. Install the fuel filler hoses which connect the fuel tank to the fuel tank filler pipe. Install the hose pipes, then tighten the clamps to 24–32 inch lbs. (2.7–3.7 Nm). Refill the fuel tank.

15. Check all connections for leaks, then connect the negative battery cable.

16. Start the engine, then recheck all of the connections for leaks.

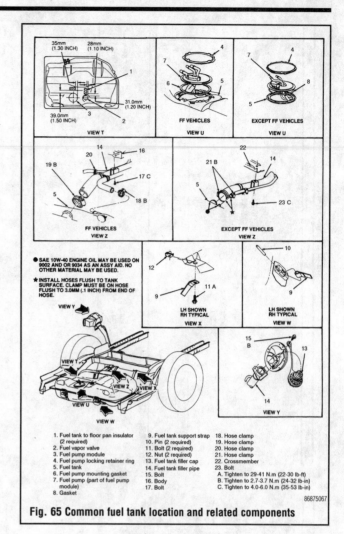

1. Fuel tank to floor pan insulator (2 required)
2. Fuel vapor valve
3. Fuel pump module
4. Fuel pump locking retainer ring
5. Fuel tank
6. Fuel pump mounting gasket
7. Fuel pump (part of fuel pump module)
8. Gasket
9. Fuel tank support strap
10. Pin (2 required)
11. Bolt (2 required)
12. Nut (2 required)
13. Fuel tank filler cap
14. Fuel tank filler pipe
15. Bolt
16. Body
17. Bolt
18. Hose clamp
19. Hose clamp
20. Hose clamp
21. Hose clamp
22. Crossmember
23. Bolt
A. Tighten to 29-41 N.m (22-30 lb-ft)
B. Tighten to 2.7-3.7 N.m (24-32 lb-in)
C. Tighten to 4.0-6.0 N.m (35-53 lb-in)

**Fig. 65 Common fuel tank location and related components**

## TORQUE SPECIFICATIONS

| Component | | US | Metric |
|---|---|---|---|
| Flexible Fuel (FF) Sensor | | | |
| 3.0L Flexible Fuel (FF) Engines only | | 27-34 inch lbs. | 3-4 Nm |
| Fuel Injection Supply Manifold | | | |
| SFI | | | |
| 3.0L (except SHO) | | 6-9 ft. lbs. | 8-12 Nm |
| 3.0L/3.2L SHO | | 11-17 ft. lbs. | 15-23 Nm |
| 3.8L | | 6-8 ft. lbs. | 8-11 Nm |
| Fuel Pressure Regulator | | | |
| CFI | | 27-35 inch lbs. | 3.1-3.9 Nm |
| EFI | | 34 inch lbs. | 3.8 Nm |
| SFI | | | |
| 3.0L (except SHO) and 3.8L | | 34 inch lbs. | 3.8 Nm |
| 3.0L/3.2L SHO | | 18-25 inch lbs. | 25-34 Nm |
| Fuel Pressure Relief Valve | | | |
| CFI | | 4-6 inch lbs. | 0.5-0.7 Nm |
| EFI | Valve | 66 inch lbs. | 7.4 Nm |
| | Cap | 5.5 inch lbs. | 0.6 Nm |
| SFI | Valve | 69 inch lbs. | 7.75 Nm |
| | Cap | 5.5 inch lbs. | 0.6 Nm |
| Fuel Rail Assembly | | | |
| EFI | | | |
| 2.5L | | 15-22 ft. lbs. | 20-30 Nm |
| 3.0L (except SHO) and 3.8L | | 7 ft. lbs. | 10 Nm |
| Fuel Tank | | | |
| Strap Retaining Bolts | | 22-30 ft. lbs. | 29-41 Nm |
| Hose Pipe Clamps | | 24-32 inch lbs. | 2.7-3.7 Nm |
| Idle Air Bypass Valve | | 84 inch lbs. | 9.5 Nm |
| Idle Air Control Valve | | | |
| 3.0L (except SHO) and 3.8L | | 84 inch lbs. | 9.5 Nm |
| 3.0L/3.2L SHO | | 63-97 inch lbs. | 7-11 Nm |
| Injector | | | |
| CFI | | 18-22 inch lbs. | 2.0-2.5 Nm |
| Throttle Body | | | |
| CFI | | | |
| 2.5L | | 15-25 ft. lbs. | 20-34 Nm |
| EFI | | | |
| 2.5L | | 12-15 ft. lbs. | 16-20 Nm |
| 3.0L (except SHO) | | 15-22 ft. lbs. | 20-30 Nm |

86875501

## TORQUE SPECIFICATIONS

| Component | | US | Metric |
|---|---|---|---|
| Throttle Body (cont.) | | | |
| EFI | | | |
| 3.8L | Step 1 | 8 ft. lbs. | 10 Nm |
| | Step 2 | 15 ft. lbs. | 20 Nm |
| | Step 3 | 24 ft. lbs. | 32 Nm |
| SFI | | | |
| 3.0L (except SHO) | | 15-22 ft. lbs. | 20-30 Nm |
| 3.0L/3.2L SHO | | 12-17 ft. lbs. | 16-23 Nm |
| 3.8L | | 15-22 ft. lbs. | 20-30 Nm |
| Throttle Position (TP) Sensor | | | |
| CFI | | 11-16 inch lbs. | 1.2-1.8 Nm |
| EFI | | 14 inch lbs. | 1.5 Nm |
| Throttle Position (TP) Sensor | | | |
| SFI | | | |
| 3.0L (except SHO) and 3.8L | | 25-34 inch lbs. | 2.8-3.8 Nm |
| 3.0L/3.2L SHO | | 14 inch lbs. | 1.5 Nm |

86875502

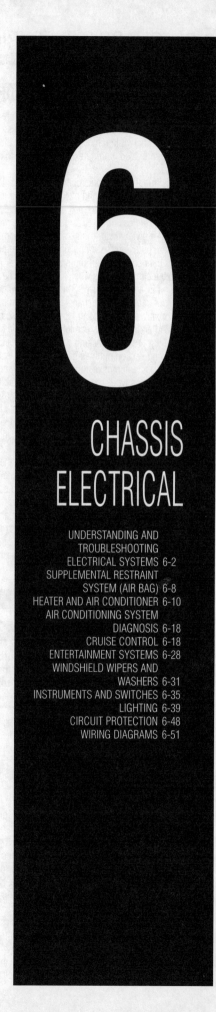

# 6

# CHASSIS ELECTRICAL

## UNDERSTANDING AND TROUBLESHOOTING ELECTRICAL SYSTEMS

Most new vehicles are equipped with one or more on-board computers, like the unit(s) installed on vehicles covered by this manual. These electronic components (with no moving parts) should theoretically last the life of the vehicle, provided nothing external happens to damage the circuits or memory chips.

While it is true that electronic components should never wear out, in the real world malfunctions can, and often do, occur. It is also true that any computer-based system is extremely sensitive to electrical voltages and cannot tolerate careless or haphazard testing or service procedures. An inexperienced individual can easily cause major damage looking for a minor problem by using the wrong kind of test equipment or connecting test leads or connectors under improper conditions. Always pay close attention to the circumstances when a test should be performed. NEVER disconnect an ECM connector with the ignition switch **ON**. When selecting test equipment, make sure the manufacturer's instructions state that the tester is compatible with whatever type of electronic control system is being serviced. Read all instructions carefully and double check all test points before installing probes or making any test connections.

The following section outlines basic diagnosis techniques for dealing with computerized automotive control systems. Along with a general explanation of the various types of test equipment available to aid in servicing modern electronic automotive systems, basic repair techniques for wiring harnesses and connectors are given. Read the basic information before attempting any repairs or testing any computerized system, to provide the background of information necessary in order to avoid the most common and obvious mistakes that can cost both time and money. Although the replacement and testing procedures are simple in themselves, the systems are not, and unless one has a thorough understanding of all components and their function within a particular computerized control system, the logical test sequence these systems demand cannot be followed. Minor malfunctions can make a big difference, so it is important to know how each component affects the operation of the overall electronic system in order to find the ultimate cause of a problem without replacing good components unnecessarily. It is not enough to use the correct test equipment; the test equipment must be used correctly.

### Safety Precautions

### ✳✳ WARNING

**Whenever working on or around any computer based microprocessor control system, always observe these general precautions to prevent the possibility of personal injury or damage to electronic components.**

- Never install or remove battery cables with the ignition switch **ON** or the engine running. Jumper cables should be connected with the key **OFF** to avoid power surges that can damage electronic control units. Engines equipped with computer controlled systems should avoid both giving and getting jump starts due to the possibility of serious damage to components from arcing in the engine compartment when connections are made with the ignition **ON**.
- Always remove the battery cables before charging the battery. Never use a high output charger on an installed battery or attempt to use any type of "hot shot" (24 volt) starting aid.
- Exercise care when inserting test probes into connectors to insure good connections without damaging the connector or spreading the pins. Always probe connectors from the rear (wire) side, NOT the pin side, in order to avoid accidental shorting of terminals during test procedures.
- Never remove or attach wiring harness connectors with the ignition switch **ON** unless the instructions specifically direct you to do so. NEVER disengage/engage the computer control module wiring connectors with the ignition **ON**.
- Do not drop any components during service procedures and never apply 12 volts directly to any component (like a solenoid or relay) unless instructed specifically to do so. Some component electrical windings are designed to safely handle only 4 or 5 volts and can be destroyed in seconds if 12 volts are applied directly to the connector.
- Remove the electronic control unit if the vehicle is to be placed in an environment where temperatures exceed approximately 176°F (80°C), such as a paint spray booth or when arc or gas welding near the control unit location in the car.

### ORGANIZED TROUBLESHOOTING

When diagnosing a specific problem, organized troubleshooting is a must. The complexity of a modern vehicle demands that you approach any problem in a logical, organized manner. There are certain troubleshooting techniques that are standard:

1. Establish when the problem occurs. Does the problem appear only under certain conditions? Were there any noises, odors, or other unusual symptoms?

2. Isolate the problem area. To do this, make some simple tests and observations; then, eliminate the systems that are working properly. Check for obvious problems such as broken wires, dirty connections, and split or disconnected vacuum hoses. ALWAYS check the obvious before assuming something complicated is the cause.

3. Test for problems systematically to determine the cause once the problem area is isolated. Are all the components functioning properly? Is there power going to electrical switches and motors? Is there vacuum at vacuum switches and/or actuators? Is there a mechanical problem such as bent linkage or loose mounting screws? Performing careful, systematic checks will often turn up most causes on the first inspection without wasting time checking components that have little or no relationship to the problem.

4. Test all repairs after the work is done to make sure that the problem is fixed. Some causes can be traced to more than one component, so a careful verification of repair work is important to pick up additional malfunctions that may cause a problem to reappear or a different problem to arise. A blown fuse, for example, is a simple problem that may require more than another fuse to repair. If you don't look for a problem that caused a fuse to blow, for example, a shorted wire may go undetected.

Experience has shown that most problems tend to be the result of a fairly simple and obvious cause, such as loose or corroded connectors or air leaks in the intake system; a careful inspection of components during testing is essential for quick and accurate troubleshooting. Special, hand held computerized testers designed specifically for diagnosing the system are available from a variety of aftermarket sources, as well as from the vehicle manufacturer, but care should be taken to assure that any test equipment being used is designed to diagnose that particular computer controlled system accurately without damaging the computer control module or other components being tested.

➡**Pinpointing the exact cause of trouble in an electrical system can sometimes only be accomplished by the use of special test equipment. The following describes commonly used test equipment and explains how to put it to best use in diagnosis. In addition to the information covered here, the manufacturer's instruction booklet provided with the tester should be read and clearly understood before attempting any test procedures.**

### TEST EQUIPMENT

#### Jumper Wires

Jumper wires are simple, yet extremely valuable, pieces of test equipment. Jumper wires are simply wires that are used to bypass sections of a circuit. The simplest type of jumper wire is merely a length of multi-strand wire with an alligator clip at each end. Jumper wires are usually fabricated from lengths of standard automotive wire and whatever type of connector (alligator clip, spade connector or pin connector) that is required for the particular vehicle being tested. The well equipped tool box will have several different styles of jumper wires in several different lengths. Some jumper wires are made with three or more terminals coming from a common splice for special purpose testing. In cramped, hard-to-reach areas it is advisable to have insulated boots over the jumper wire terminals in order to prevent accidental grounding, sparks, and possible fire, especially when testing fuel system components.

Jumper wires are used primarily to locate open electrical circuits, on either the ground (−) side of the circuit or on the hot (+) side. If an electrical component fails to operate, connect the jumper wire between the component and a good ground. If the component operates only with the jumper installed, the ground circuit is open. If the ground circuit is good, but the component does not operate, the circuit between the power feed and component is open. You can sometimes connect the jumper wire directly from the battery to the hot terminal of the component, but first make sure the component uses 12 volts in operation. Some electrical components, such as fuel injectors, are designed to operate on about 4 volts and running 12 volts directly to the injector terminals can burn out the wiring. By inserting an inline fuseholder between a set of test leads, a fused jumper wire can be used for bypassing open circuits. Use a 5 amp fuse to provide protection against voltage spikes. When in doubt, use a voltmeter to check the voltage input to the component and measure how much voltage is being applied normally. By moving the jumper wire successively back from the lamp toward the power source, you can isolate the area of the circuit where the open is located. When the component stops functioning, or the power is cut off, the open is in the segment of wire between the jumper and the point previously tested.

### ✳ CAUTION

**Never use jumpers made from wire that is of lighter gauge than used in the circuit under test. If the jumper wire is of too small a gauge, it may overheat and possibly melt. Never use jumpers to bypass high resistance loads (such as motors) in a circuit. Bypassing resistances, in effect, creates a short circuit which may, in turn, cause damage and fire. Never use a jumper for anything other than temporary bypassing of components in a circuit.**

### 12 Volt Test Light

The 12 volt test light is used to check circuits and components while electrical current is flowing through them. It is used for voltage and ground tests. Twelve volt test lights come in different styles but all have three main parts; a ground clip, a probe, and a light. The most commonly used 12 volt test lights have pick-type probes. To use a 12 volt test light, connect the ground clip to a good ground and probe wherever necessary with the pick. The pick should be sharp so that it can penetrate wire insulation to make contact with the wire, without making a large hole in the insulation. The wrap-around light is handy in hard to reach areas or where it is difficult to support a wire to push a probe pick into it. To use the wrap around light, hook the wire to be probed with the hook and pull the trigger. A small pick will be forced through the wire insulation into the wire core.

### ✳ WARNING

**Do not use a test light to probe electronic ignition spark plug or coil wires. Never use a pick-type test light to probe wiring on computer controlled systems unless specifically instructed to do so. Any wire insulation that is pierced by the test light probe should be taped and sealed with silicone after testing.**

Like the jumper wire, the 12 volt test light is used to isolate opens in circuits. But, whereas the jumper wire is used to bypass the open to operate the load, the 12 volt test light is used to locate the presence of voltage in a circuit. If the test light glows, you know that there is power up to that point; if the 12 volt test light does not glow when its probe is inserted into the wire or connector, you know that there is an open circuit (no power). Move the test light in successive steps back toward the power source until the light in the handle does glow. When it does glow, the open is between the probe and point previously probed.

➡**The test light does not detect that 12 volts (or any particular amount of voltage) is present; it only detects that some voltage is present. It is advisable before using the test light to touch its terminals across the battery posts to make sure the light is operating properly.**

### Self-Powered Test Light

The self-powered test light usually contains a 1.5 volt penlight battery. One type of self-powered test light is similar in design to the 12 volt test light. This type has both the battery and the light in the handle and pick-type probe tip. The second type has the light toward the open tip, so that the light illuminates the contact point. The self-powered test light is a dual purpose piece of test equipment. It can be used to test for either open or short circuits when power is isolated from the circuit (continuity test). A powered test light should NOT be used on any computer controlled system or component unless specifically instructed to do so. Many engine sensors can be destroyed by even this small amount of voltage applied directly to the terminals.

### Open Circuit Testing

To use the self-powered test light to check for open circuits, first isolate the circuit from the vehicle's 12 volt power source by disconnecting the battery or wiring harness connector. Connect the test light ground clip to a good ground and probe sections of the circuit sequentially with the test light. Start testing from either end of the circuit. If the light is out, the open is between the probe and the circuit ground. If the light is on, the open is between the probe and end of the circuit toward the power source.

### Short Circuit Testing

By isolating the circuit both from power and from ground, and using a self-powered test light, you can check for shorts to ground in the circuit. Isolate the circuit from power and ground. Connect the test light ground clip to a good ground and probe any easy-to-reach test point in the circuit. If the light comes on, there is a short somewhere in the circuit. To isolate the short, probe a test point at either end of the isolated circuit (the light should be on). Leave the test light probe connected and open connectors, switches, remove parts, etc., sequentially, until the light goes out. When the light goes out, the short is between the last circuit component opened and the previous circuit opened.

➡**The 1.5 volt battery in the test light does not provide much current. A weak battery may not provide enough power to illuminate the test light even when a complete circuit is made (especially if there are high resistances in the circuit). Always make sure that the test battery is strong. To check the battery, briefly touch the ground clip to the probe; if the light glows brightly the battery is strong enough for testing. Never use a self-powered test light to perform checks for opens or shorts when power is applied to the electrical system under test. The 12 volt vehicle power will quickly burn out the 1.5 volt light bulb in the test light.**

### Voltmeter

A voltmeter is used to measure voltage at any point in a circuit, or to measure the voltage drop across any part of a circuit. It can also be used to check continuity in a wire or circuit by indicating current flow from one end to the other. Voltmeters usually have various scales on the meter dial and a selector switch to allow the detection of different voltages. The voltmeter has a positive and a negative lead. To avoid damage to the meter, always connect the negative lead to the negative (−) side of circuit (to ground or nearest the ground side of the circuit) and connect the positive lead to the positive (+) side of the circuit (to the power source or nearest the power source). Note that the negative voltmeter lead will always be black and that the positive voltmeter will always be some color other than black (usually red). Depending on how the voltmeter is connected into the circuit, it has several uses.

A voltmeter can be connected either in parallel or in series with a circuit, and has a very high resistance to current flow. When connected in parallel, only a small amount of current will flow through the voltmeter current path; the rest will flow through the normal circuit current path and the circuit will work normally. When the voltmeter is connected in series with a circuit, only a small amount of current can flow through the circuit. The circuit will not work properly, but the voltmeter reading will show if the circuit is complete or not.

### ❋❋ WARNING

**Do not use a multimeter to probe electronic ignition spark plug or coil wires. Small pin holes in secondary ignition wires will allow high voltage to arc from the wire to a metal part, external to the secondary ignition circuit. This arcing may cause misfiring, leading to a driveability complaint.**

### Available Voltage Measurement

Set the voltmeter selector switch to the 20V position and connect the meter negative lead to the negative post of the battery. Connect the positive meter lead to the positive post of the battery and turn the ignition switch **ON** to provide a load. Read the voltage on the meter or digital display. A well charged battery should register over 12 volts. If the meter reads below 11.5 volts, the battery power may be insufficient to operate the electrical system properly. This test determines voltage available from the battery and should be the first step in any electrical trouble diagnosis procedure. Many electrical problems, especially on computer controlled systems, can be caused by a low state of charge in the battery. Excessive corrosion at the battery cable terminals can cause a poor contact that will prevent proper charging and full battery current flow.

Normal battery voltage is 12 volts when fully charged. When the battery is supplying current to one or more circuits it is said to be "under load". When everything is off the electrical system is under a "no-load" condition. A fully charged battery may show about 12.5 volts at no load, will drop to 12 volts under medium load, and will drop even lower under heavy load. If the battery is partially discharged, the voltage decrease under heavy load may be excessive, even though the battery shows 12 volts or more at no load. When allowed to discharge further, the battery's available voltage under load will decrease more severely. For this reason, it is important that the battery be fully charged during all testing procedures to avoid errors in diagnosis and incorrect test results.

### Voltage Drop

When current flows through a resistance, the voltage beyond the resistance is reduced (the larger the current, the greater the reduction in voltage). When no current is flowing, there is no voltage drop because there is no current flow. All points in the circuit which are connected to the power source are at the same voltage as the power source. The total voltage drop always equals the total source voltage. In a long circuit with many connectors, a series of small, unwanted voltage drops due to corrosion at the connectors can add up to a total loss of voltage which impairs the operation of the normal loads in the circuit.

### INDIRECT COMPUTATION OF VOLTAGE DROPS

1. Set the voltmeter selector switch to the 20 volt position.
2. Connect the meter negative lead to a good ground.
3. Probe all resistances in the circuit with the positive meter lead.
4. Operate the circuit in all modes and observe the voltage readings.

### DIRECT MEASUREMENT OF VOLTAGE DROPS

1. Set the voltmeter switch to the 20 volt position.
2. Connect the voltmeter negative lead to the ground side of the resistance load to be measured.

3. Connect the positive lead to the positive side of the resistance or load to be measured.
4. Read the voltage drop directly on the 20 volt scale.

Too high a voltage indicates too high a resistance. If, for example, a blower motor runs too slowly, you can determine if there is too high a resistance in the resistor pack. By taking voltage drop readings in all parts of the circuit, you can isolate the problem. Too low a voltage drop indicates too low a resistance. If, for example, a blower motor runs too fast in the MED and/or LOW position, the problem can be isolated in the resistor pack by taking voltage drop readings in all parts of the circuit to locate a possibly shorted resistor. The maximum allowable voltage drop under load is critical, especially if there is more than one high resistance problem in a circuit because all voltage drops are cumulative. A small drop is normal due to the resistance of the conductors.

### HIGH RESISTANCE TESTING

1. Set the voltmeter selector switch to the 4 volt position.
2. Connect the voltmeter positive lead to the positive post of the battery.
3. Turn on the headlights and heater blower to provide a load.
4. Probe various points in the circuit with the negative voltmeter lead.
5. Read the voltage drop on the 4 volt scale. Some average maximum allowable voltage drops are:

- FUSE PANEL — 0.7 volts
- IGNITION SWITCH — 0.5 volts
- HEADLIGHT SWITCH — 0.7 volts
- IGNITION COIL (+) — 0.5 volts
- ANY OTHER LOAD — 1.3 volts

➡**Voltage drops are all measured while a load is operating; without current flow, there will be no voltage drop.**

### Ohmmeter

The ohmmeter is designed to read resistance (ohms) in a circuit or component. Although there are several different styles of ohmmeters, all will usually have a selector switch which permits the measurement of different ranges of resistance (usually the selector switch allows the multiplication of the meter reading by 10, 100, 1000, and 10,000). A calibration knob allows the meter to be set at zero for accurate measurement. Since all ohmmeters are powered by an internal battery (usually 9 volts), the ohmmeter can be used as a self-powered test light. When the ohmmeter is connected, current from the ohmmeter flows through the circuit or component being tested. Since the ohmmeter's internal resistance and voltage are known values, the amount of current flow through the meter depends on the resistance of the circuit or component being tested.

The ohmmeter can be used to perform continuity tests for opens or shorts (either by observation of the meter needle or as a self-powered test light), and to read actual resistance in a circuit. It should be noted that the ohmmeter is used to check the resistance of a component or wire while there is no voltage applied to the circuit. Current flow from an outside voltage source (such as the vehicle battery) can damage the ohmmeter, so the circuit or component should be isolated from the vehicle electrical system before any testing is done. Since the ohmmeter uses its own voltage source, either lead can be connected to any test point.

➡**When checking diodes or other solid state components, the ohmmeter leads can only be connected one way in order to measure current flow in a single direction. Make sure the positive (+) and negative (−) terminal connections are as described in the test procedures to verify the one-way diode operation.**

In using the meter for making continuity checks, do not be concerned with the actual resistance readings. Zero resistance, or any resistance readings, indicate continuity in the circuit. Infinite resistance indicates an open in the circuit. A high resistance reading where there should be none indicates a problem in the circuit. Checks for short circuits are made in the same manner as checks for open circuits except that the circuit must be isolated from both power and normal ground. Infinite resistance indicates no continuity to ground, while zero resistance indicates a dead short to ground.

### RESISTANCE MEASUREMENT

The batteries in an ohmmeter will weaken with age and temperature, so the ohmmeter must be calibrated or "zeroed" before taking measurements. Many modern digital meters are self-zeroing and will require no adjustment. If your meter must be zeroed, be sure to check this each time it is used. To zero the meter, place the selector switch in its lowest range and touch the two ohmmeter leads together. Turn the calibration knob until the meter needle is exactly on zero.

➡️**All analog (needle) type ohmmeters must be zeroed before use, but most digital ohmmeter models are automatically calibrated when the switch is turned on. Self-calibrating digital ohmmeters do not have an adjusting knob, but it's a good idea to check for a zero readout before use by touching the leads together. All computer controlled systems require the use of a digital ohmmeter with at least 10 megohms impedance for testing. Before any test procedures are attempted, make sure the ohmmeter used is compatible with the electrical system, or damage to the on-board computer could result.**

To measure resistance, first isolate the circuit from the vehicle power source by disconnecting the battery cables or the harness connector. Make sure the ignition key is **OFF** when disconnecting any components or the battery. Where necessary, also isolate at least one side of the circuit to be checked to avoid reading parallel resistances. Parallel circuit resistances will always give a lower reading than the actual resistance of either of the branches. When measuring the resistance of parallel circuits, the total resistance will always be lower than the smallest resistance in the circuit. Connect the meter leads to both sides of the circuit (wire or component) and read the actual measured ohms on the meter scale. Make sure the selector switch is set to the proper ohm scale for the circuit being tested to avoid misreading the ohmmeter test value.

### ✳️✳️ WARNING

**Never use an ohmmeter with power applied to the circuit. Like the self-powered test light, the ohmmeter is designed to operate on its own power supply. The normal 12 volt automotive electrical system current could damage the meter.**

### Ammeters

An ammeter measures the amount of current flowing through a circuit in units called amperes or amps. Amperes are units of electron flow which indicate the speed at which electrons are flowing through the circuit. Since Ohm's Law dictates that current flow in a circuit is equal to the circuit voltage divided by the total circuit resistance, increasing voltage also increases the current level (amps). Likewise, any decrease in resistance will increase the amount of amps in a circuit. At normal operating voltage, most circuits have a characteristic amount of amperes, called "current draw" which can be measured using an ammeter. By referring to a specified current draw rating, measuring the amperes, and comparing the two values, one can determine what is happening within the circuit to aid in diagnosis. An open circuit, for example, will not allow any current to flow so the ammeter reading will be zero. More current flows through a heavily loaded circuit or when the charging system is operating.

An ammeter is always connected in series with the circuit being tested. All of the current that normally flows through the circuit must also flow through the ammeter; if there is any other path for the current to follow, the ammeter reading will not be accurate. The ammeter itself has very little resistance to current flow and therefore will not affect the circuit, but it will measure current draw only when the circuit is closed and electricity is flowing. Excessive current draw can blow fuses and drain the battery, while a reduced current draw can cause motors to run slowly, lights to dim and other components to not operate properly. The ammeter can help diagnose these conditions by locating the cause of the high or low reading.

### Multimeters

Different combinations of test meters can be built into a single unit designed for specific tests. Some of the more common combination test devices are known as Volt/Amp testers, Tach/Dwell meters, or Digital Multimeters. The Volt/Amp tester is used for charging system, starting system or battery tests and consists of a voltmeter, an ammeter and a variable resistance carbon pile. The voltmeter will usually have at least two ranges for use with 6, 12 and 24 volt systems. The ammeter also has more than one range for testing various levels of battery loads and starter current draw and the carbon pile can be adjusted to offer different amounts of resistance. The Volt/Amp tester has heavy leads to carry large amounts of current and many later models have an inductive ammeter pickup that clamps around the wire to simplify test connections. On some models, the ammeter also has a zero-center scale to allow testing of charging and starting systems without switching leads or polarity. A digital multimeter is a voltmeter, ammeter and ohmmeter combined in an instrument which gives a digital readout. These are often used when testing solid state circuits because of their high input impedance (usually 10 megohms or more).

The tach/dwell meter combines a tachometer and a dwell (cam angle) meter and is a specialized kind of voltmeter. The tachometer scale is marked to show engine speed in rpm and the dwell scale is marked to show degrees of distributor shaft rotation. In most electronic ignition systems, dwell is determined by the control unit, but the dwell meter can also be used to check the duty cycle (operation) of some electronic engine control systems. Some tach/dwell meters are powered by an internal battery, while others take their power from the vehicle battery in use. The internal battery powered testers usually require calibration much like an ohmmeter before testing.

### Special Test Equipment

A variety of diagnostic tools are available to help troubleshoot and repair computerized engine control systems. The most sophisticated of these devices are the console type engine analyzers that usually occupy a garage service bay, but there are several types of aftermarket electronic testers available that will allow quick circuit tests of the engine control system by plugging directly into a special connector located in the engine compartment or under the dashboard. Several tool and equipment manufacturers offer simple, hand held testers that measure various circuit voltage levels on command to check all system components for proper operation. Although these testers often cost about $300–$500, consider that the average computer control unit can cost just as much and the money saved by not replacing perfectly good sensors or components in an attempt to correct a problem could justify the purchase price of a special diagnostic tester the first time it's used.

These computerized testers can allow quick and easy test measurements while the engine is operating or while the vehicle is being driven. In addition, the on-board computer memory can be read to access any stored trouble codes, in effect allowing the computer to tell you "where it hurts" and aid trouble diagnosis by pinpointing exactly which circuit is malfunctioning. In the same manner, repairs can be tested to make sure the problem has been corrected. The biggest advantage these special testers have is their relatively easy hookups that minimize or eliminate the chances of making the wrong connections and getting false voltage readings or damaging the computer accidentally.

➡️**It should be remembered that these testers check voltage levels in circuits; they don't detect mechanical problems or failed components. Testers simply can inform you if the circuit voltage falls within the pre-programmed limits stored in the tester PROM unit. Also, most of the hand held testers are designed to work only on one or two systems made by a specific manufacturer.**

A variety of aftermarket testers are available to help diagnose different computerized control systems. Owatonna Tool Company (OTC), for example, markets a device called the OTC Monitor which plugs directly into the Assembly Line Diagnostic Link (ALDL). The OTC tester makes diagnosis a simple matter of pressing the correct buttons and, by changing the internal

PROM or inserting a different diagnosis cartridge, it will work on any model from full size to subcompact, over a wide range of years. An adapter is supplied with the tester to allow connection to all types of ALDL links, regardless of the number of pin terminals used. By inserting an updated PROM into the OTC tester, it can be easily updated to diagnose any new modifications of computerized control systems.

## Wiring Harnesses

The average vehicle contains about ½ mile (0.805 km) of wiring, with hundreds of individual connections. To protect the many wires from damage and to keep them from becoming a confusing tangle, they are organized into bundles, enclosed in plastic or taped together and called wiring harnesses. Different wiring harnesses serve different parts of the vehicle. Individual wires are color coded to help trace them through a harness where sections are hidden from view.

A loose or corroded connection or a replacement wire that is too small for the circuit will add extra resistance and an additional voltage drop to the circuit. A ten percent voltage drop can result in slow or erratic motor operation, for example, even though the circuit is complete. Automotive wiring or circuit conductors can be in any one of three forms:

1. Single-strand wire
2. Multi-strand wire
3. Printed circuitry

Single-strand wire has a solid metal core and is usually used inside such components as alternators, motors, relays and other devices. Multi-strand wire has a core made of many small strands of wire twisted together into a single conductor. Most of the wiring in an automotive electrical system is made up of multi-strand wire, either as a single conductor or grouped together in a harness. All wiring is color coded on the insulator, either as a solid color or as a colored wire with an identification stripe. A printed circuit is a thin film of copper or other conductor that is printed on an insulator backing. Occasionally, a printed circuit is sandwiched between two sheets of plastic for more protection and flexibility. A complete printed circuit, consisting of conductors, insulating material and connectors for lamps or other components is called a printed circuit board. Printed circuitry is used in place of individual wires or harnesses in places where space is limited, such as behind instrument panels.

### WIRE GAUGE

Since computer controlled automotive electrical systems are very sensitive to changes in resistance, the selection of properly sized wires is critical when systems are repaired. The wire gauge number is an expression of the cross-section area of the conductor. The most common system for expressing wire size is the American Wire Gauge (AWG) system.

Wire cross-section area is measured in circular mils. A mil is $\frac{1}{1000}$ in. (0.001 in. or 0.0254mm); a circular mil is the area of a circle one mil in diameter. For example, a conductor with ¼ in. (6.35mm) diameter is 0.250 in. or 250 mils. The circular mil cross-section area of the wire is 250 squared ($250^2$) or 62,500 circular mils. Imported vehicles usually use metric wire gauge designations, which is simply the cross-section area of the conductor in square millimeters ($mm^2$).

Gauge numbers are assigned to conductors of various cross-section areas. As gauge number increases, area decreases and the conductor becomes smaller. A 5 gauge conductor is smaller than a 1 gauge conductor and a 10 gauge is smaller than a 5 gauge. As the cross-section area of a conductor decreases, resistance increases and so does the gauge number. A conductor with a higher gauge number will carry less current than a conductor with a lower gauge number.

➡**Gauge wire size refers to the size of the conductor, not the size of the complete wire. It is possible to have two wires of the same gauge with different diameters because one may have thicker insulation than the other.**

12 volt automotive electrical systems generally use 10, 12, 14, 16 and 18 gauge wire. Main power distribution circuits and larger accessories usually use 10 and 12 gauge wire. Battery cables are usually 4 or 6 gauge, although 1 and 2 gauge wires are occasionally used. Wire length must also be considered when making repairs to a circuit. As conductor length increases, so does resistance. An 18 gauge wire, for example, can carry a 10 amp load for 10 feet without excessive voltage drop; however if a 15 foot wire is required for the same 10 amp load, it must be a 16 gauge wire.

### WIRING DIAGRAMS

An electrical schematic shows the electrical current paths when a circuit is operating properly. It is essential to understand how a circuit works before trying to figure out why it doesn't. Schematics break the entire electrical system down into individual circuits and show only one particular circuit. In a schematic, no attempt is made to represent wiring and components as they physically appear on the vehicle; switches and other components are shown as simply as possible. Face views of harness connectors show the cavity or terminal locations in all multi-pin connectors to help locate test points.

If you need to backprobe a connector while it is on the component, the order of the terminals must be mentally reversed. The wire color code can help in this situation, as well as a keyway, lock tab or other reference mark.

### WIRING REPAIR

Soldering is a quick, efficient method of joining metals permanently. Everyone who has the occasion to make wiring repairs should know how to solder. Electrical connections that are soldered are far less likely to come apart and will conduct electricity much better than connections that are only "pigtailed" together. The most popular (and preferred) method of soldering is with an electric soldering gun or iron. Soldering irons are available in many sizes and wattage ratings. Irons with higher wattage ratings deliver higher temperatures and recover lost heat faster. A small soldering iron rated for no more than 50 watts is recommended, especially on electrical systems where excess heat can damage the components being soldered.

There are three ingredients necessary for successful soldering; proper flux, good solder and sufficient heat. A soldering flux is necessary to clean the metal of tarnish, prepare it for soldering and to enable the solder to spread into tiny crevices. When soldering, always use a rosin flux or rosin core solder which is non-corrosive and will not attract moisture once the job is finished. Other types of flux (acid core) will leave a residue that will attract moisture and cause the wires to corrode. Tin is a unique metal with a low melting point. In a molten state, it dissolves and alloys easily with many metals. Solder is often made by mixing tin with lead. The most common proportions are 40/60, 50/50 and 60/40, with the percentage of tin listed first. Low priced solders usually contain less tin, making them very difficult for a beginner to use because more heat is required to melt the solder. A common solder is 40/60 which is well suited for all-around general use, but 60/40 melts easier, has more tin for a better joint and is preferred for electrical work.

#### Soldering Techniques

Successful soldering requires that the metals to be joined are heated to a temperature that will melt the solder—usually 360–460°F (182–238°C). Contrary to popular belief, the purpose of the soldering iron is not to melt the solder itself, but to heat the parts being soldered to a temperature high enough to melt the solder when it is touched to the work. Melting flux-cored solder on the soldering iron will usually destroy the effectiveness of the flux.

➡**Soldering tips are made of copper for good heat conductivity, but must be "tinned" regularly for quick transference of heat to the project and to prevent the solder from sticking to the iron. To "tin" the iron, simply heat it and touch the flux-cored solder to the tip; the solder will flow over the hot tip. Wipe the excess off with a clean rag, but be careful as the iron will be hot.**

After some use, the tip may become pitted. If so, simply dress the tip with a smooth file and "tin" the tip again. An old saying holds that "metals well cleaned are half soldered." Flux-cored solder will remove oxides but rust, bits of insulation and oil or grease must be removed with a wire brush or emery cloth. For maximum strength in soldered parts, the joint must start off clean and tight. Weak joints will result in gaps too wide for the solder to bridge.

If a separate soldering flux is used, it should be brushed or swabbed on only those areas that are to be soldered. Most solders contain a core of flux and separate fluxing is unnecessary. Hold the work to be soldered firmly. It is best to solder on a wooden board, because a metal vise will only rob the piece to be soldered of heat and make it difficult to melt the solder. Hold the soldering tip with the broadest face against the work to be soldered. Apply solder under the tip close to the work, using enough solder to give a heavy film between the iron and the piece being soldered, while moving slowly and making sure the solder melts properly. Keep the work level or the solder will run to the lowest part and favor the thicker parts, because these require more heat to melt the solder. If the soldering tip overheats (the solder coating on the face of the tip burns up), it should be retinned. Once the soldering is completed, let the soldered joint stand until cool. Tape and seal all soldered wire splices after the repair has cooled.

**Wire Harness and Connectors**

The on-board computer wire harness electrically connects the control unit to the various solenoids, switches and sensors used by the control system. Most connectors located in the engine compartment or which are otherwise exposed to the elements are protected against moisture and dirt which could create oxidation and deposits on the terminals. This protection is important because of the very low voltage and current levels used by the computer and sensors. All connectors have a lock which secures the male and female terminals together, with a secondary lock holding the seal and terminal into the connector. Both terminal locks must be released when disconnecting module connectors.

These special connectors are weather-proof and all repairs require the use of a special terminal and the tool required to service it. This tool is used to remove the pin and sleeve terminals. If removal is attempted with an ordinary pick, there is a good chance that the terminal will be bent or deformed. Unlike standard blade type terminals, these terminals cannot be straightened once they are bent. Make certain that the connectors are properly seated and all of the sealing rings in place when connecting leads. On some models, a hinge-type flap provides a backup or secondary locking feature for the terminals. Most secondary locks are used to improve the connector reliability by retaining the terminals if the small terminal lock tangs are not positioned properly.

Molded-on connectors require complete replacement of the connection. This means splicing a new connector assembly into the harness. All splices in on-board computer systems should be soldered to insure proper contact. Use care when probing the connections or replacing terminals in them as it is possible to short between opposite terminals. If this happens to the wrong terminal pair, it is possible to damage certain components. Always use jumper wires between connectors for circuit checking and never probe through weatherproof seals.

Open circuits are often difficult to locate by sight because corrosion or terminal misalignment can be hidden by the connectors. Merely wiggling a connector on a sensor or in the wiring harness may correct the open circuit condition. This should always be considered when an open circuit or a failed sensor is indicated. Intermittent problems may also be caused by oxidized or loose connections. When using a circuit tester for diagnosis, always probe connections from the wire side. Be careful not to damage sealed connectors with test probes.

All wiring harnesses should be replaced with identical parts, using the same gauge wire and connectors. When signal wires are spliced into a harness, use wire with high temperature insulation only. With the low voltage and current levels found in the system, it is important that the best possible connection at all wire splices be made by soldering the splices together. It is seldom necessary to replace a complete harness. If replacement is necessary, pay close attention to insure proper harness routing. Secure the harness with suitable plastic wire clamps to prevent vibrations from causing the harness to wear in spots or contact any hot components.

➡**Weatherproof connectors cannot be replaced with standard connectors. Instructions are provided with replacement connector and terminal packages. Some wire harnesses have mounting indicators (usually pieces of colored tape) to mark where the harness is to be secured.**

In making wiring repairs, it's important that you always replace damaged wires with wires that are the same gauge as the wire being replaced. The heavier the wire, the smaller the gauge number. Wires are color-coded to aid in identification and whenever possible the same color coded wire should be used for replacement. A wire stripping and crimping tool is necessary to install solderless terminal connectors. Test all crimps by pulling on the wires; it should not be possible to pull the wires out of a good crimp.

Wires which are open, exposed or otherwise damaged are repaired by simple splicing. Where possible, if the wiring harness is accessible and the damaged place in the wire can be located, it is best to open the harness and check for all possible damage. In an inaccessible harness, the wire must be bypassed with a new insert, usually taped to the outside of the old harness.

When replacing fusible links, be sure to use fusible link wire, NOT ordinary automotive wire. Make sure the fusible segment is of the same gauge and construction as the one being replaced and double the stripped end when crimping the terminal connector for a good contact. The melted (open) fusible link segment of the wiring harness should be cut off as close to the harness as possible, then a new segment spliced in as described. In the case of a damaged fusible link that feeds two harness wires, the harness connections should be replaced with two fusible link wires so that each circuit will have its own separate protection.

➡**Most of the problems caused in the wiring harness are due to bad ground connections. Always check all vehicle ground connections for corrosion or looseness before performing any power feed checks to eliminate the chance of a bad ground affecting the circuit.**

**Repairing Hard Shell Connectors**

Unlike molded connectors, the terminal contacts in hard shell connectors can be replaced. Replacement usually involves the use of a special terminal removal tool to depress the locking tangs (barbs) on the connector terminal and allow the connector to be removed from the rear of the shell. The connector shell should be replaced if it shows any evidence of burning, melting, cracks, or breaks. Replace individual terminals that are burnt, corroded, distorted or loose.

➡**The insulation crimp must be tight to prevent the insulation from sliding back on the wire when the wire is pulled. The insulation must be visibly compressed under the crimp tabs, and the ends of the crimp should be turned in for a firm grip on the insulation.**

The wire crimp must be made with all wire strands inside the crimp. The terminal must be fully compressed on the wire strands with the ends of the crimp tabs turned in to make a firm grip on the wire. Check all connections with an ohmmeter to insure a good contact. There should be no measurable resistance between the wire and the terminal when connected.

**Mechanical Test Equipment**

VACUUM GAUGE

Most gauges are graduated in inches of mercury (in. Hg), although a device called a manometer reads vacuum in inches of water (in. $H_2O$). The normal vacuum reading usually varies between 18 and 22 in. Hg (60.78–74.29 kPa) at sea level. To test engine vacuum, the gauge must be connected to a source of manifold vacuum. Many engines have a plug in the intake manifold which can be removed and replaced with an adapter fitting. Connect the vacuum gauge to the fitting with a suitable rubber hose or, if no manifold plug is available, connect the vacuum gauge to any device using manifold vacuum, such as EGR valves, etc. The vacuum gauge can be used to determine if enough vacuum is reaching a component to allow its actuation.

## HAND VACUUM PUMP

Small, hand-held vacuum pumps come in a variety of designs. Most have a built-in vacuum gauge and allow the component to be tested without removing it from the vehicle. Operate the pump lever or plunger to apply the correct amount of vacuum required for the test specified in the diagnosis routines. The level of vacuum in inches of Mercury (in. Hg) is indicated on the pump gauge. For some testing, an additional vacuum gauge may be necessary.

Intake manifold vacuum is used to operate various systems and devices on late model vehicles. To correctly diagnose and solve problems in vacuum control systems, a vacuum source is necessary for testing. In some cases, vacuum can be taken from the intake manifold when the engine is running, but vacuum is normally provided by a hand vacuum pump. These hand vacuum pumps have a built-in vacuum gauge that allows testing while the device is still attached to the component. For some tests, an additional vacuum gauge may be necessary.

# SUPPLEMENTAL RESTRAINT SYSTEM (AIR BAG)

## General Information

Introduced in 1990, a driver's side air bag became standard on Taurus and Sables. In 1992, an optional passenger side air bag was first offered on these vehicles, then in 1994, driver and passenger side air bags became standard equipment on the Taurus and Sable. The supplemental restraint system was designed to provide increased protection in the event of an accident for those in the front seat of the car, when used along with the safety belt system. The system **MUST** be disarmed before any work is performed on or around the supplemental air bag system.

## SERVICE PRECAUTIONS

• When performing service around the Supplemental Restraint System components or wiring, the system **MUST** be disabled. Failure to do so could result in possible air bag deployment, personal injury or unneeded system repairs.
• When carrying a live inflator module, make sure that the bag and trim cover are pointed away from you. Never carry the inflator module by the wires or connector on the underside of the module. In case of accidental deployment, the bag will then deploy with minimal chance of injury.
• When placing a live inflator on a bench or other surface, always face the bag and trim cover up, away from the surface.

## DISARMING THE SYSTEM

**1990–91 Vehicles**

▶ **See Figures 1 and 2**

1. Disconnect the negative battery cable.

➡**The backup power supply allows to air bag deployment if the battery or battery cables are damaged in an accident before the crash sensors close. The power supply is a capacitor that will leak down in approximately 15 minutes after the battery is disconnected or in 1 minute if the battery positive cable is grounded. The backup power supply must be disconnected before any air bag related service is performed.**

2. Open the glove compartment, then lower the door past its stops. Disconnect the backup power supply, located to the right of the glove compartment opening.

### ❊❊ CAUTION

**Whenever working near air bag system wiring or components, as an extra safety precaution, it is recommended that the air bag module also be disconnected and removed. Even with the negative battery cable and backup power supply disconnected, should voltage be inadvertently applied to the air bag system, the module could deploy.**

3. Remove the four nut and washer assemblies retaining the driver air module to the steering wheel.
4. Disengage the driver air bag module and place it out of the way on a sturdy, flat surface with the pad facing up.

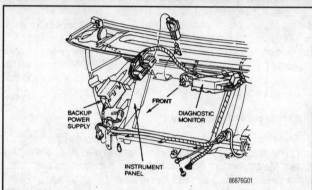

**Fig. 1 The backup power supply is accessible through the glove compartment opening**

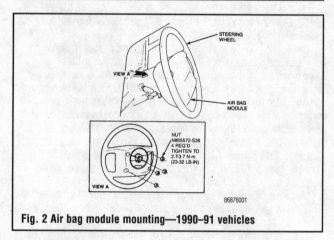

**Fig. 2 Air bag module mounting—1990–91 vehicles**

**1992–95 Vehicles**

▶ **See Figures 3 and 4**

1. Disconnect the negative, then the positive battery cables.
2. Wait one minute for the backup power supply in the diagnostic monitor to deplete its stored energy.

### ❊❊ CAUTION

**Whenever working near air bag system wiring or components, as an extra safety precaution, it is recommended that the air bag module(s) also be disconnected and removed. Even with the battery cables and backup power supply disconnected, should voltage be inadvertently applied to the air bag system, the module(s) could deploy.**

3. Remove the screw and washer assemblies retaining the driver air module to the steering wheel.
4. Disengage the driver air bag module and place it out of the way on a sturdy, flat surface with the pad facing up.

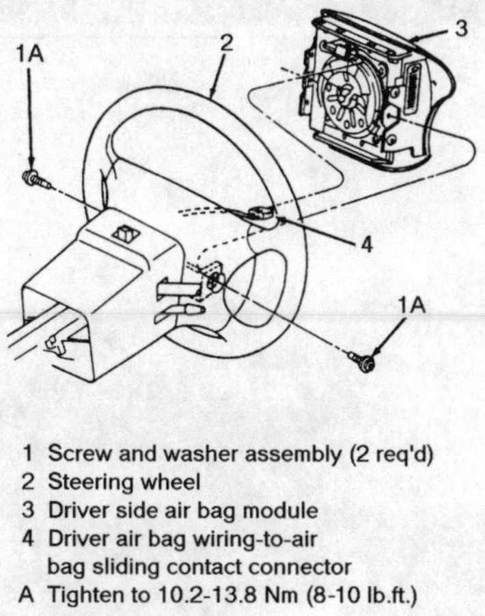

1A
2
3
4
1A
1 Screw and washer assembly (2 req'd)
2 Steering wheel
3 Driver side air bag module
4 Driver air bag wiring-to-air bag sliding contact connector
A Tighten to 10.2-13.8 Nm (8-10 lb.ft.)
86876003


**Fig. 3 Driver air bag module mounting—1995 vehicle shown**

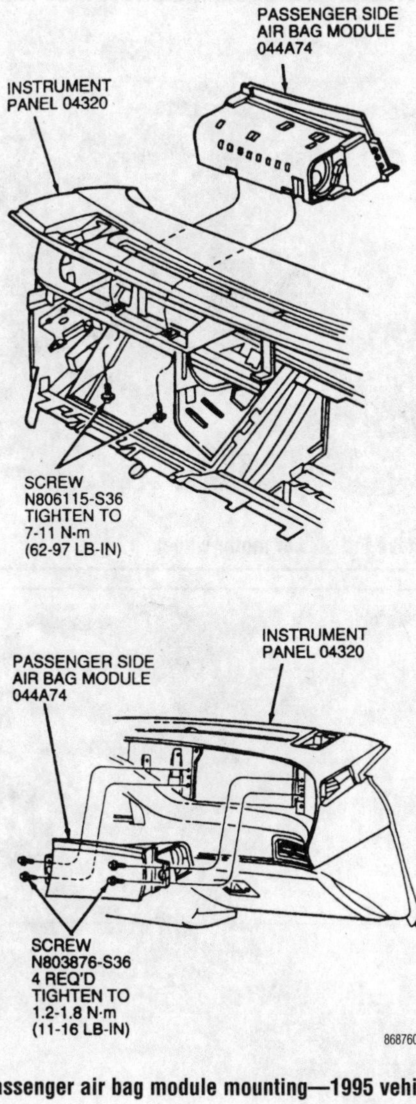

PASSENGER SIDE AIR BAG MODULE 044A74
INSTRUMENT PANEL 04320
SCREW N806115-S36 TIGHTEN TO 7-11 N·m (62-97 LB-IN)
INSTRUMENT PANEL 04320
PASSENGER SIDE AIR BAG MODULE 044A74
SCREW N803876-S36 4 REQ'D TIGHTEN TO 1.2-1.8 N·m (11-16 LB-IN)
86876006


**Fig. 4 Passenger air bag module mounting—1995 vehicle shown**

**➡If your vehicle is equipped with an optional passenger air bag, both the driver and passenger air bag modules must be disconnected for added safety.**

5. If equipped with a passenger air bag module, proceed as follows:
   a. Remove the right-hand and left-hand finish panels.
   b. Remove the instrument panel finish panel retaining spear clips.
   c. Open the glove compartment, press the side, then lower the glove compartment to the floor.
   d. Working through the glove compartment opening, remove the two lower air bag module retaining bolts.
   e. Remove the four remaining air bag module retaining screws from the side of the air bag cover.
   f. Disengage the electrical connector from the left side of the air bag, then remove the air bag module.

**⁂ CAUTION**

**When carrying a live air bag, make sure the bag and trim cover are pointed away from the body. In the unlikely event of an accidental deployment, the bag will then deploy with the minimal chance of injury. In addition, when placing a live air bag on a bench or other surface, always face the bag and trim cover up, away from the surface. This will reduce the motion of the unit if it is accidentally deployed.**

## ENABLING THE SYSTEM

### 1990–91 Vehicles

**See Figures 1 and 2**

1. If applicable, attach the air bag module connector, then position the module on the steering wheel. Secure the module with the 4 nut and washer assemblies.
2. If not already done, open the glove compartment, then lower the door past its stops. Connect the backup power supply located to the right of the glove compartment opening.
3. Connect the negative battery cable.
4. Verify operation of the air bag warning indicator lamp.

### 1992–95 Vehicles

**See Figures 3 and 4**

1. If applicable, connect the driver air bag module, then position it on the steering wheel and secure with the fasteners. Tighten to 8–10 ft. lbs. (10.2–13.8 Nm).
2. If equipped with a passenger side air bag module which was removed, proceed as follows:
   a. Engage the electrical connector to the passenger air bag module, then position the module in the instrument panel.
   b. Install the four upper retaining screws, then tighten the screws to 11–16 inch lbs. (1.2–1.8 Nm).
   c. Install the lower passenger air bag retaining screws, then tighten the screws to 62–97 inch lbs. (7–11 Nm).
   d. Return the glove compartment to the correct position.
   e. Install the instrument panel finish panel locator pin into the air bag bushing locator, align the spear clips, then press the finish panel into place.
3. Connect the positive, then the negative battery cables.
4. Turn the ignition switch from **OFF** to **RUN**, then visually check the air bag warning indicator light. The warning indicator should light continuously for about six seconds, then shut off. If an air bag system fault is detected, the air bag warning indicator will either fail to light, remain lighted continuously, or flash. If this problem occurs, take your vehicle to an authorized repair shop for service.

## HEATER AND AIR CONDITIONER

### Blower Motor

REMOVAL & INSTALLATION

▶ **See Figures 5 thru 12**

1. Disconnect the negative battery cable.
2. Open the glove compartment door, release the door retainers and lower the door.
3. Remove the screw attaching the recirculation duct support bracket to the instrument panel cowl.
4. Remove the vacuum connection to the recirculation door vacuum motor. Remove the screws attaching the recirculation duct to the heater assembly.
5. Remove the recirculation duct from the heater assembly, lowering the duct from between the instrument panel and the heater case.
6. Disconnect the blower motor electrical lead. Remove the blower motor wheel clip and remove the blower motor wheel.

86876009

**Fig. 7 Remove the blower motor wheel clip**

86876007

**Fig. 5 Release the glove compartment door retainers, then lower the door**

86876010

**Fig. 8 Remove the blower motor wheel**

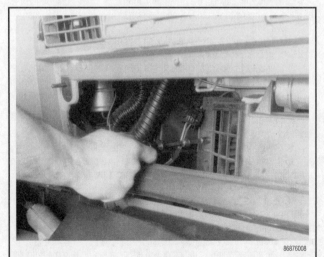

86876008

**Fig. 6 Remove the screws attaching the recirculation duct to the heater assembly, then remove the duct**

86876011

**Fig. 9 Disengage the electrical connector**

Fig. 10 Remove the blower motor retaining screws

Fig. 11 Remove the blower motor assembly from the vehicle

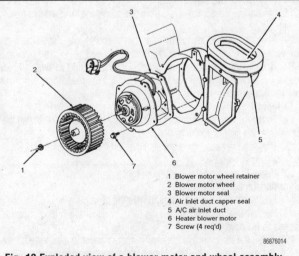

1 Blower motor wheel retainer
2 Blower motor wheel
3 Blower motor seal
4 Air inlet duct capper seal
5 A/C air inlet duct
6 Heater blower motor
7 Screw (4 req'd)

Fig. 12 Exploded view of a blower motor and wheel assembly—1995 vehicle shown

7. Remove the blower motor mounting plate screws and remove the blower motor from the evaporator case.
   **To install:**
8. Feed the blower motor electrical connector through the evaporator housing.
9. Position the blower motor into the evaporator housing. Install the retaining screws, making sure the mounting seal is in place.
10. Assembly to blower motor to the shaft aligning the flat on the shaft with the flat on the inside diameter of the blower wheel hub. Slide the blower motor wheel onto the blower motor shaft until the wheel is fully seated.
11. Install a new blower motor retainer on the blower shaft to retain the blower motor wheel.
12. Connect the blower motor electrical lead to the wiring harness.
13. Install the recirculation duct using the retaining screws.
14. Install the glove compartment door to its original closed position, then connect the negative battery cable.

## Blower Motor Resistor

### REMOVAL & INSTALLATION

♦ See Figure 13

1. Disconnect the negative battery cable.
2. Open the glove compartment door and release the glove compartment retainers so that the glove compartment hangs down.
3. Disengage the wire harness connector from the resistor assembly.
4. Remove the two resistor attaching screws and remove the resistor from the evaporator housing.
   **To install:**
5. Position the resistor assembly in the evaporator case opening and install the two attaching screws. Do not apply sealer to the resistor assembly mounting surface.
6. Engage the wire harness connector to the resistor.
7. Connect the negative battery cable, check the operation of the blower motor, then install the glove compartment to the retainers and close the door.

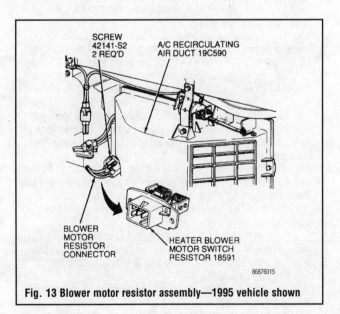

Fig. 13 Blower motor resistor assembly—1995 vehicle shown

## Heater Core

### REMOVAL & INSTALLATION

▶ **See Figures 14 and 15**

➡ **Be sure to consult the laws in your area before beginning any procedure which requires servicing the air conditioning system. In some states, it is illegal to perform repairs involving refrigerant unless the work is done by a certified technician.**

### ✳✳ CAUTION

**When draining the coolant, keep in mind that cats and dogs are attracted by the ethylene glycol antifreeze, and are quite likely to drink any that is left in an uncovered container or in puddles on the ground. This will prove fatal in sufficient quantity. Always drain the coolant into a sealable container. Coolant should be reused unless it is contaminated or several years old.**

➡ **When removing the instrument panel, it may be beneficial to have a friend or assistant help you.**

#### Without Air Conditioning

1. Disconnect the negative battery cable.
2. Remove the instrument panel on 1986–89 vehicles as follows:
   a. Remove the four screws retaining the steering column opening cover, then remove the cover.
   b. Remove the sound insulator under the glove compartment by removing the two push nuts securing the insulator to the studs on the climate control case.
   c. Remove the steering column trim shrouds, then tag and disengage all electrical connections from the steering column switches.
   d. Remove the four screws at the steering column bracket to remove the steering column.
   e. Remove the screws retaining the lower left and radio finish panels, then remove the panels by snapping them out.
   f. Remove the cluster opening finish panel retaining screws. On Taurus remove the jam nut behind the headlight switch and the screw behind the clock or clock cover. Remove the finish panel by rocking the upper edge toward the driver.
   g. Disconnect the speedometer cable by reaching up under the instrument panel and pressing on the flat surface of the plastic connector. The panel can be removed with the cluster installed.
   h. Release the glove compartment assembly by depressing the side of the glove compartment bin and swinging the door/bin down.
   i. Using the steering column, cluster and glove compartment openings and by reaching under the instrument panel, tag and disengage all electrical connections, vacuum hoses, heater control cables and the radio antenna cable.
   j. Tag and disengage all underhood electrical connectors of the main wire loom. Disengage the rubber grommet from the dash panel and push the wire and connectors into the instrument panel area.
   k. Remove the right and left speaker opening covers by snapping them out.
   l. Remove the two lower instrument panel-to-cowl side retaining screws from the right and left side. Remove the instrument panel brace retaining screw from under the radio area. On Sable, remove the defroster grille by snapping it out.
   m. Remove the three instrument panel upper retaining screws, then remove the instrument panel.
3. Remove the instrument panel on 1990–95 vehicles as follows:
   a. Position the front wheels in the straight-ahead position.
   b. Disconnect the positive battery cable.

c. Remove the ignition lock cylinder and, if equipped, remove the tilt lever.
   d. Remove the steering column trim shrouds. Tag and disengage all electrical connections from the steering column switches.
   e. Remove the four bolts and opening cover, and the two bolts and reinforcement from under the steering column.
   f. Disengage the insulator retainer and remove the insulator. Remove the four nuts and reinforcement from under the steering column.

➡ **Do not rotate the steering column shaft.**

g. Remove the four nuts retaining the steering column to the instrument panel, disconnect the shift indicator cable and lower the column on the front seat. Install the lock cylinder to make sure the steering column shaft does not turn.
   h. Remove bolt at the steering column opening attaching the instrument panel to the brace. Remove instrument panel brace retaining bolt from under the radio area.
   i. Remove the sound insulator under the glove compartment by removing the two push nuts that secure the insulator to the studs on the climate control case.
   j. Disconnect the wires of the main wire loom in the engine compartment. Disengage the rubber grommet from the dash panel, then feed the wiring through the hole in the dash panel into the passenger compartment.
   k. Remove the right and left cowl side trim panels. Disconnect the wires from the instrument panel at the right and left cowl sides.
   l. Remove screw each from the left and right side retaining the instrument panel. Pull up to unsnap the right and left speaker opening covers and remove.
   m. Release the glove compartment assembly by depressing the side of the glove compartment bin and swinging the door/bin down.
   n. Using the steering column and glove compartment openings and by reaching under the instrument panel, tag and disengage all electrical connections, vacuum hoses, heater control cables, speedometer cable and radio antenna cable.
   o. Close the glove compartment door, support the panel and remove the three screws attaching the top of the instrument panel to the cowl top and disconnect any remaining wires. Remove the panel from the vehicle.
4. Drain the coolant from the radiator.
5. Disconnect and plug the heater hoses at the heater core. Plug the heater core tubes.
6. Disconnect the vacuum supply hose from the inline vacuum check valve in the engine compartment. Remove the screw holding the instrument panel shake brace to the heater case and remove the shake brace.
7. Remove the floor register and rear floor ducts from the bottom of the heater case. Remove the three nuts attaching the heater case to the dash panel in the engine compartment.
8. Remove the two screws attaching the brackets to the cowl top panel. Pull the heater case assembly away from the dash panel and remove from the vehicle.
9. Remove the vacuum source line from the heater core tube seal and remove the seal from the heater core tubes.
10. Remove the four heater core access cover attaching screws and remove the access cover from the heater case. Lift the heater core and seals from the heater case.

#### To install:

11. Transfer the three foam core seals to the new heater core. Install the heater core and seals into the heater case.
12. Position the heater case access cover on the case, then install the four retaining screws.
13. Install the seal on the heater core tubes, then install the vacuum source line through the seal.
14. Position the heater case assembly to the dash panel and cowl top panel at the air inlet opening. Install the two screws to attach the support brackets to the cowl top panel.
15. Install the three nuts in the engine compartment to attach the heater case to the dash panel. Install the floor register and rear floor ducts on the bottom of the heater case.

16. Install the instrument panel shake brace and screw to the heater case.

17. Install the instrument panel by reversing the removal procedure.

18. Connect the heater hoses to the heater core. Connect the black vacuum supply hose to the vacuum check valve in the engine compartment.

19. Fill the radiator and bleed the cooling system.

20. Connect the negative battery cable and check the system for proper operation.

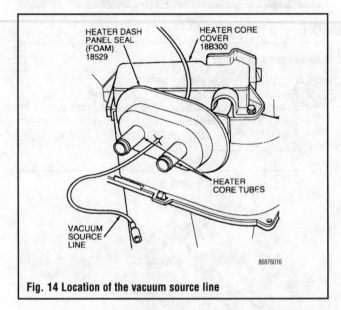

**Fig. 14 Location of the vacuum source line**

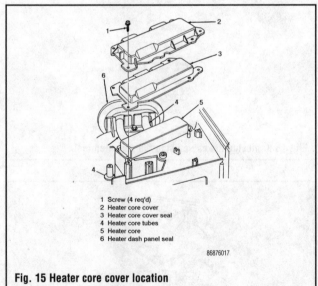

1 Screw (4 req'd)
2 Heater core cover
3 Heater core cover seal
4 Heater core tubes
5 Heater core
6 Heater dash panel seal

86876017

**Fig. 15 Heater core cover location**

### With Air Conditioning

> ※※ **CAUTION**
>
> **Some 1992–93 and all 1994–95 air conditioned vehicles covered by this manual are equipped with a new non-CFC (chlorofluorocarbon) refrigerant (R-134a). This new refrigerant is not available commercially in most areas, as it is usually illegal for do-it-yourselfers to service a vehicle with this refrigerant. If you have a Taurus or Sable that uses the new refrigerant, R-134a, the vehicle should be taken to a qualified technician for any repair requiring A/C system service.**

➡**It is necessary to remove the evaporator case in order to remove the heater core. Whenever an evaporator case is removed, it will be necessary to replace the suction accumulator/drier.**

1. Disconnect the negative battery cable.

2. Remove the instrument panel on 1986–89 vehicles as follows:

a. Remove the four screws retaining the steering column opening cover and remove the cover.

b. Remove the sound insulator under the glove compartment by removing the two push nuts securing the insulator to the studs on the climate control case.

c. Remove the steering column trim shrouds and disconnect all electrical connections from the steering column switches.

d. Remove the four screws at the steering column bracket to remove the steering column.

e. Remove the screws retaining the lower left and radio finish panels and remove the panels by snapping out.

f. Remove the cluster opening finish panel retaining screws. On Taurus remove jam nut behind the headlight switch and screw behind the clock or clock cover. Remove the finish panel by rocking the upper edge toward the driver.

g. Disconnect the speedometer cable by reaching up under the instrument panel and pressing on the flat surface of the plastic connector. The panel can be removed with the cluster installed.

h. Release the glove compartment assembly by depressing the side of the glove compartment bin and swinging the door/bin down.

i. Using the steering column, cluster and glove compartment openings and by reaching under the instrument panel, tag and disconnect all electrical connections, vacuum hoses, heater/air conditioner control cables and the radio antenna cable.

j. Disconnect all underhood electrical connectors of the main wire loom. Disengage the rubber grommet from the dash panel and push the wire and connectors into the instrument panel area.

k. Remove the right and left speaker opening covers by snapping out.

l. Remove the two lower instrument panel-to-cowl side retaining screws from the right and left side. Remove the instrument panel brace retaining screw from under the radio area. On Sable, remove the defroster grille by snapping out.

m. Remove the three instrument panel upper retaining screws and remove the instrument panel.

3. Remove the instrument panel on 1990–95 vehicles as follows:

a. Position the front wheels in the straight-ahead position.

b. Remove the ignition lock cylinder and, if equipped, remove the tilt lever.

c. Remove the steering column trim shrouds. Disconnect all electrical connections from the steering column switches.

d. Remove the four bolts and opening cover and the two bolts and reinforcement from under the steering column.

e. Disengage the insulator retainer and remove the insulator. Remove the four nuts and reinforcement from under the steering column.

➡**Do not rotate the steering column shaft.**

f. Remove the four nuts retaining the steering column to the instrument panel, disconnect the shift indicator cable and lower the column on the front seat. Install the lock cylinder to make sure the steering column shaft does not turn.

g. Remove bolt at the steering column opening attaching the instrument panel to the brace. Remove instrument panel brace retaining bolt from under the radio area.

h. Remove the sound insulator under the glove compartment by removing the two push nuts that secure the insulator to the studs on the climate control case.

i. Disconnect the wires of the main wire loom in the engine compartment. Disengage the rubber grommet from the dash panel, then feed the wiring through the hole in the dash panel into the passenger compartment.

j. Remove the right and left cowl side trim panels. Disconnect the wires from the instrument panel at the right and left cowl sides.

k. Remove one screw from each the left and right side retaining the instrument panel. Pull up to unsnap the right and left speaker opening covers and remove.

l. Release the glove compartment assembly by depressing the side of the glove compartment bin and swinging the door/bin down.

m. Using the steering column and glove compartment openings and by reaching under the instrument panel, tag and disconnect all electrical connections, vacuum hoses, heater/air conditioner control cables, speedometer cable and radio antenna cable.

n. Close the glove compartment door, support the panel and remove the three screws attaching the top of the instrument panel to the cowl top and disconnect any remaining wires. Remove the panel from the vehicle.

4. Drain the coolant from the radiator. Properly discharge the air conditioning system.

➡Be sure to consult the laws in your area before beginning any procedure which requires servicing the air conditioning system. In some states, it is illegal to perform repairs involving refrigerant unless the work is done by a certified technician.

5. Disconnect and plug the heater hoses at the heater core. Plug the heater core tubes.

6. Disconnect the vacuum supply hose from the inline vacuum check valve in the engine compartment.

7. Disconnect the air conditioning lines from the evaporator core at the dash panel. Cap the lines and the core to prevent entrance of dirt and moisture.

8. Remove the screw holding the instrument panel shake brace to the evaporator case and remove the shake brace.

9. Remove the two screws attaching the floor register and rear seat duct to the bottom of the evaporator case. Remove the three nuts attaching the evaporator case to the dash panel in the engine compartment.

10. Remove the two screws attaching the support brackets to the cowl top panel. Carefully pull the evaporator assembly away from the dash panel and remove the evaporator case from the vehicle.

11. Remove the vacuum source line from the heater core tube seal and remove the seal from the heater core tubes.

12. If equipped with automatic temperature control, remove the three screws attaching the blend door actuator to the evaporator case and remove the actuator.

13. Remove the four heater core access cover attaching screws and remove the access cover and seal from the evaporator case. Lift the heater core and seals from the evaporator case.

**To install:**

14. Transfer the seal to the new heater core, then install the heater core into the evaporator case.

15. Position the heater core access cover on the evaporator case and install the four attaching screws. If equipped with automatic temperature control, position the blend door actuator to the blend door shaft and install the three attaching screws.

16. Install the seal on the heater core tubes and install the vacuum source line through the seal.

17. Position the evaporator case assembly to the dash panel and cowl top panel at the air inlet opening. Install the two screws attaching the support brackets to the cowl top panel.

18. Install the three nuts in the engine compartment attaching the evaporator case to the dash panel. Install the floor register and rear seat duct to the evaporator case and tighten the two attaching screws.

19. Install the instrument panel shake brace and screw to the evaporator case. Install the instrument panel in the reverse order of removal.

20. Connect the air conditioning lines to the evaporator core and the heater hoses to the heater core.

21. Connect the black vacuum supply hose to the vacuum check valve in the engine compartment.

22. Fill and bleed the cooling system. Connect the negative battery cable.

23. Leak test, evacuate and charge the air conditioning system. Observe all safety precautions.

➡Some 1992–93 and all 1994–95 vehicles covered by this manual are equipped with R-134a NOT R-12 refrigerant. These two refrigerants are NOT compatible. Using the incorrect refrigerant in an R-134a system will lead to compressor failure, compressor oil sludge and/or poor air conditioning system performance.

24. Check the system for proper operation.

## Control Cables

### REMOVAL & INSTALLATION

▶ **See Figures 16 and 17**

1. Disconnect the negative battery cable.
2. Remove the instrument cluster opening finish panel.
3. Rotate the temperature control knob to the "COOL" position.
4. Disconnect the temperature control knob cable housing end retainer from the heater case bracket using Heater Control Cable Disconnect tool T83P-18532-AH, or equivalent.

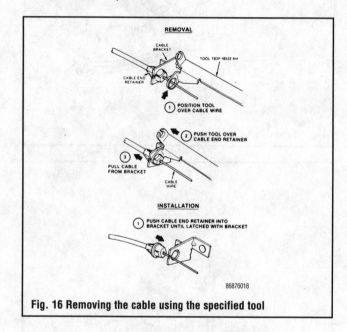

Fig. 16 Removing the cable using the specified tool

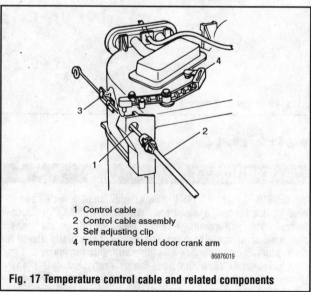

1 Control cable
2 Control cable assembly
3 Self adjusting clip
4 Temperature blend door crank arm

Fig. 17 Temperature control cable and related components

5. Disconnect the cable wire from the temperature door crank arm, using the proper tool.

6. Remove the retaining screws that secure the control assembly to the instrument panel. Pull the control assembly away from the instrument panel.

7. Disconnect the cable housing end retainer from the control assembly and the cable wire from the temperature control lever arm.

8. Remove the cable assembly from the vehicle through the control assembly opening in the instrument panel, being careful not to hook or damage the wiring or other cables.

**To install:**

9. Position the self-adjusting clip on the control cable.

10. Insert the cable through the control assembly opening of the instrument panel and over the left-hand duct to the left-hand side of the evaporator case.

11. Rotate the temperature control knob to the "COOL" position.

12. Insert the cable wire end into the hole in the temperature control arm. Connect the cable and retainer to the control assembly.

13. Position the control assembly to the instrument panel opening, then install the retaining screws.

14. Slide the cable housing and retainer into the heater case cable bracket, then push to secure the cable housing to the bracket.

15. Connect the self-adjusting clip at the temperature cable to the temperature door crank arm.

16. Connect the negative battery cable.

## Blower Switch

### REMOVAL & INSTALLATION

1. Disconnect the negative battery cable.

2. Remove the climate control assembly from the instrument panel. For details, please refer to the procedure located earlier in this section.

3. Remove the blower switch knob.

4. Disengage the blower switch electrical connector.

5. Remove the retaining screw, then remove the heater blower motor switch from the vehicle.

**To install:**

6. Install the blower switch, then secure using the retaining screw.

7. Engage the switch electrical connector.

8. Install the blower switch knob.

9. Install the climate control assembly to the instrument panel. For details, please refer to the procedure located earlier in this section.

10. Connect the negative battery cable, then check the switch for proper operation.

## Vacuum Selector Switch

### REMOVAL & INSTALLATION

1. Disconnect the negative battery cable.

2. Remove the control assembly from the instrument panel. For details, please refer to the procedure located earlier in this section.

3. Remove the knob from the function selector shaft.

4. Remove the screw attaching the vacuum switch to the control assembly, then remove the switch.

**To install:**

5. Rotate the function selector shaft to the OFF position.

6. Position the vacuum selector switch on the control assembly bracket.

7. Install the screw attaching the vacuum switch to the control assembly.

8. Connect the negative battery cable.

## Compressor

▶ See Figures 18 and 19

### ✳✳ CAUTION

**Please refer to Section 1 of this manual before discharging/recovering the A/C system or disconnecting the air conditioning lines. Damage to the air conditioning system or personal injury could result. Consult your local laws concerning refrigerant discharge and recycling. In many areas it may be illegal for anyone but a certified technician to service the A/C system. Always use an approved recovery station when discharging the air conditioning.**

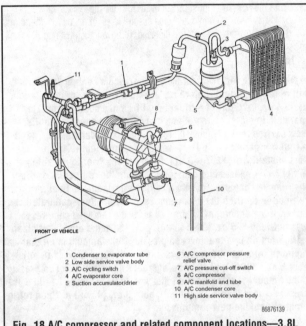

| | |
|---|---|
| 1 Condenser to evaporator tube | 6 A/C compressor pressure |
| 2 Low side service valve body | relief valve |
| 3 A/C cycling switch | 7 A/C pressure cut-off switch |
| 4 A/C evaporator core | 8 A/C compressor |
| 5 Suction accumulator/drier | 9 A/C manifold and tube |
| | 10 A/C condenser core |
| | 11 High side service valve body |

FRONT OF VEHICLE

86876139

**Fig. 18 A/C compressor and related component locations—3.8L engine shown**

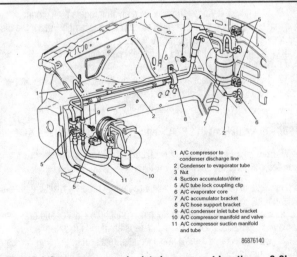

| | |
|---|---|
| 1 A/C compressor to | |
| condenser discharge line | |
| 2 Condenser to evaporator tube | |
| 3 Nut | |
| 4 Suction accumulator/drier | |
| 5 A/C tube lock coupling clip | |
| 6 A/C evaporator core | |
| 7 A/C accumulator bracket | |
| 8 A/C hose support bracket | |
| 9 A/C condenser inlet tube bracket | |
| 10 A/C compressor manifold and valve | |
| 11 A/C compressor suction manifold | |
| and tube | |

86876140

**Fig. 19 A/C compressor and related component locations—3.2L SHO shown**

## REMOVAL & INSTALLATION

### 1986–94 Vehicles—Except 3.8L Engine

➡**Whenever a compressor is replaced, it will be necessary to replace the suction accumulator/drier.**

1. Disconnect the negative battery cable and properly discharge the system.
2. Disconnect the compressor clutch wires at the field coil connector on the compressor.
3. Loosen and remove the drive belt and disconnect the hose assemblies from the condenser and suction line.
4. Remove the mounting bolts, then remove the compressor and manifold and tube assembly from the vehicle as a unit. The assembly will not clear the sub-frame and radio support if an attempt is made to remove the unit from the bottom. It must be removed from the top.
5. Remove the manifold and tube assembly as an on-bench operation.
6. If the compressor is to be replaced, remove the clutch and field coil assembly.

**To install:**

➡**New service replacement FS-6 compressors contain 10 oz. (300 ml) of refrigerant oil. Before replacement compressor installation, drain 4 oz. (120 ml) of refrigerant oil from the compressor. This will maintain the total system oil charge within the specified limits. New service replacement 10P15F compressors contain 8 oz. (240 ml) of refrigerant oil and new service replacement FX15 compressors contain 7 oz. (207 ml) of refrigerant oil. Prior to installing either type replacement compressor, drain the refrigerant oil from the removed compressor into a calibrated container. Then, drain the refrigerant oil from the new compressor into a clean calibrated container. If the amount of oil drained from the removed compressor was between 3–5 oz. (90–148 ml), pour the same amount of clean refrigerant oil into the new compressor. If the amount of oil that was removed from the old compressor is greater than 5 oz. (148 ml), pour 5 oz. (148 ml) of clean refrigerant oil into the new compressor. If the amount of refrigerant oil that was removed from the old compressor is less than 3 oz. (90 ml), pour 3 oz. (90 ml) of clean refrigerant oil into the new compressor.**

7. Install the manifold and tube assembly on the air conditioning compressor.
8. Install the compressor and manifold and tube assembly on the air conditioning mounting bracket.
9. Using new O-rings lubricated with clean refrigerant oil, connect the suction line to the compressor manifold and tube assembly. Attach the discharge line to the air conditioning condenser.
10. Connect the clutch wires to the field coil connector.
11. Install the drive belt.
12. Leak test, evacuate and charge the system according to the proper procedure. Observe all safety precautions.
13. Check the system for proper operation.

### 1988–95 Vehicles With 3.8L Engine; All 1995 Vehicles

➡**Whenever a compressor is replaced, it will be necessary to replace the suction accumulator/drier.**

1. Disconnect the negative battery cable and properly discharge the air conditioning system.
2. Position a suitable clean drain pan under the radiator and drain the coolant, keeping the coolant to refill the system during installation.
3. Disconnect and remove the integrated relay controller/constant control relay module.
4. Disconnect and remove the fan and shroud assembly.
5. Disconnect the upper and lower radiator hoses, then remove the radiator.
6. Disconnect the air conditioning compressor magnetic clutch wire at the field coil connector on the compressor.
7. Remove the top two compressor mounting bolts.
8. Raise and safely support the vehicle.
9. Loosen and remove the compressor drive belt.
10. Disconnect the HEGO sensor wire connector and remove the air conditioning muffler supporting strap bolt from the sub-frame.
11. Disconnect the air conditioning system hose from the condenser and suction accumulator/drier using the spring-lock coupling tool or equivalent. Immediately install protective caps on the open lines.
12. Make sure the compressor is properly supported, then remove the bottom two compressor mounting bolts.
13. Remove the compressor, manifold and tube assemblies from the vehicle as a unit. The assembly can be removed from the bottom using care not to scrape against the condenser.
14. Remove the manifold and tube assemblies from the compressor.
15. If the compressor is to be replaced, remove the clutch and field coil assembly.

**To install:**

➡**A new service replacement 10P15F compressor contains 8 oz. (240 ml) of refrigerant oil. Before installing a new compressor, drain 4 oz. (120 ml) of refrigerant oil from the compressor. This will maintain total system oil charge within specified limits.**

16. Using new O-rings, lubricated with clean refrigerant oil, install the manifold and tube assemblies onto the new compressor.
17. Install the compressor, manifold and tube assemblies onto the compressor mounting bracket.
18. Using new O-rings lubricated with clean refrigerant oil, connect the suction line to the compressor and manifold assembly.
19. Using new O-rings lubricated with clean refrigerant oil, connect the discharge line to the compressor and manifold assembly.
20. Install the muffler support onto the sub-frame and connect the HEGO sensor wire connector.
21. Install the compressor drive belt and lower the vehicle.
22. Install the radiator and connect the radiator hoses.
23. Install the fan and shroud assembly and connect the integrated relay connector.
24. Connect the negative battery cable and fill the radiator with the coolant that was saved.
25. Leak test, evacuate and charge the system according to the proper procedure. Check the system for proper operation.

## Condenser

➡**Refer to SECTION 1 for air conditioning system discharging information.**

### REMOVAL & INSTALLATION

▸ **See Figure 20**

➡**Whenever a condenser is replaced, it will be necessary to replace the suction accumulator/drier.**

1. Disconnect the negative battery cable and properly discharge the refrigerant from the air conditioning system. Observe all safety precautions.
2. Disconnect the two refrigerant lines at the fittings on the right side of the radiator. Perform the spring-lock coupling disconnect procedure located later in this section.
3. Remove the bolts or screws and washers attaching the condenser to the radiator support, then remove the condenser from the vehicle.

**To install:**

4. Add 1 oz. (30 ml) of clean refrigerant oil to a new replacement condenser.
5. Position the condenser assembly to the radiator support brackets, then install the attaching bolts or screws and washers.
6. Connect the refrigerant lines to the condenser assembly using new O-rings. Perform the spring-lock coupling connection procedure.

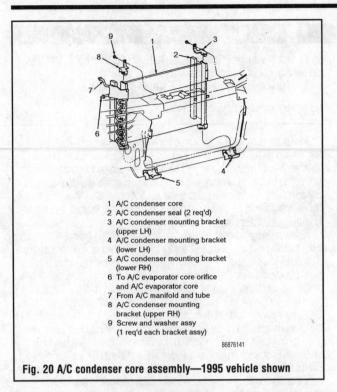

1 A/C condenser core
2 A/C condenser seal (2 req'd)
3 A/C condenser mounting bracket
   (upper LH)
4 A/C condenser mounting bracket
   (lower LH)
5 A/C condenser mounting bracket
   (lower RH)
6 To A/C evaporator core orifice
   and A/C evaporator core
7 From A/C manifold and tube
8 A/C condenser mounting
   bracket (upper RH)
9 Screw and washer assy
   (1 req'd each bracket assy)

86876141

**Fig. 20 A/C condenser core assembly—1995 vehicle shown**

7. Leak test, evacuate and charge the refrigerant system following the proper procedures. Observe all safety precautions.

## Control Panel

### REMOVAL & INSTALLATION

#### Manual Control Head

▶ **See Figure 21**

1. Disconnect the negative battery cable.
2. Remove the instrument panel finish applique.
3. Remove the four screws attaching the control assembly to the instrument panel. Pull the control head away from the instrument panel into a position which provides access to the rear connectors.
4. Disengage the two harness connectors from the control assembly by depressing the latches at the top of the connectors and pulling.
5. Disconnect the vacuum harness and temperature control cable from the control assembly. Discard the used pushnut from the vacuum harness.

**To install:**

6. Connect the temperature cable to the control assembly.
7. Engage the harness connectors and vacuum harness to the control assembly using new pushnuts.

➡**Push on the vacuum harness retaining nuts. Do not attempt to screw them onto the post.**

8. Position the control assembly to the instrument panel opening and install four attaching screws.
9. Install the instrument panel finish applique.
10. Connect the negative battery cable and check the system for proper operation.

#### Electronic Control Head

▶ **See Figure 22**

1. Disconnect the negative battery cable.
2. Perform the following:
   a. Pull out the lower left and lower right instrument panel snap-on finish panel inserts. Remove the eight screws retaining the upper finish panel.
   b. Pull the lower edge of the upper finish panel away from the instrument panel. It is best to grasp the finish panel from the lower left corner and pull the panel away by walking the hands around the panel in a clockwise direction.
3. Remove the four Torx® head screws retaining the control assembly. Pull the control assembly away from the instrument panel into a position which provides access to the rear connectors.
4. Disengage the two harness connectors from the control assembly by depressing the latches at the top of the connectors and pulling.
5. Remove the nuts retaining the vacuum harness to the control assembly. Pull the control assembly away from the instrument panel.

**To install:**

6. Engage the two electrical harness connectors to the control assembly. Push the keyed connectors in until a click is heard.
7. Attach the vacuum harness to the vacuum port assembly. Secure the harness by tightening the two nuts.
8. Position the control assembly into the instrument panel opening and install the four attaching Torx® head screws. Make sure, as the control is positioned, the locating posts are correctly aligned with their respective holes.
9. Carefully place the instrument panel applique into it's assembly position. Make sure the spring clips are aligned with their proper holes. Press the applique into place. Make sure all spring clips and screws are secure.
10. Install the eight screws retaining the upper finish panel. Insert the lower left and lower right instrument panel snap-on finish panel inserts.
11. If removed, install the left and right shelf mouldings.
12. Connect the negative battery cable, then check the system operation.

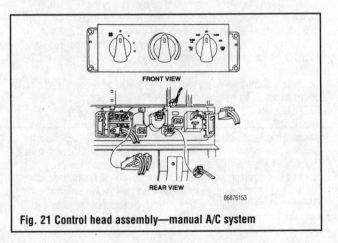

FRONT VIEW

REAR VIEW

86876153

**Fig. 21 Control head assembly—manual A/C system**

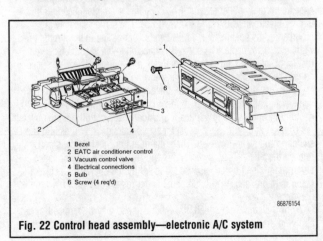

1 Bezel
2 EATC air conditioner control
3 Vacuum control valve
4 Electrical connections
5 Bulb
6 Screw (4 req'd)

86876154

**Fig. 22 Control head assembly—electronic A/C system**

## AIR CONDITIONING SYSTEM DIAGNOSIS

### Automatic Temperature Control System

#### DIAGNOSTIC PROCEDURE

1. Perform the Self Diagnostic Test. Record all error codes displayed during the test.
2. If error codes appear during the Self Diagnostic Test, follow the diagnostic procedures indicated in the Error Code Key.
3. If a malfunction exists but no error code appears during the Self Diagnostic Test, perform the Functional Test.

#### SELF-DIAGNOSTIC TEST

The control assembly will detect electrical malfunctions occurring during the self-test.
1. Make sure the coolant temperature is at least 120°F (49°C).
2. To display error codes, push the OFF and FLOOR buttons simultaneously and then the AUTOMATIC button within 2 seconds. The test may run as long as 20 seconds, during which time the display will be blank. If the display is blank for more than 20 seconds, consult the No Error Code Found Diagnosis and Testing chart.
3. The Self-Diagnostic Test can be initiated at any time with the resulting error codes being displayed. Normal operation of the system stops when the Self-Diagnostic Test is activated. To exit the self-test and restart the system, push the COOLER button. The self-test should be deactivated before powering the system down.

#### FUNCTIONAL TEST

The Functional Test is designed to catch those system failures that the self-test is unable to test.
1. Make sure the engine is cold.

2. The in-vehicle temperature should be greater than 50°F (10°C) for proper evaluation of system response.
3. Follow the instructions in each step of the Functional Test.

#### VACUUM SYSTEM DIAGNOSIS

To test the automatic temperature control vacuum system, start the engine and depress the function buttons slowly from one position to another. A momentary hiss should be heard as each button is depressed from one position to another, indicating that vacuum is available at the control assembly. A continuous hiss at the control assembly indicates a major leak somewhere in the system. It does not necessarily indicate that the leak is at the control assembly.

If a momentary hiss cannot be heard as each function button is depressed from 1 position to another, check for a kinked, pinched or disconnected vacuum supply hose. Also, inspect the check valve between the vacuum intake manifold and the vacuum reservoir to ensure it is working properly.

If a momentary hiss can be heard as each function button is depressed from one position to another, vacuum is available at the control assembly. Cycle the function buttons through each position with the blower on HI and check the location(s) of the discharge air. The airflow schematic and vacuum control chart shows the vacuum motors applied for each function selection along with an airflow diagram of the system. The airflow diagram shows the position of each door when vacuum is applied and their no-vacuum position. With this chart, airflow for each position of the control assembly can be determined. If a vacuum motor fails to operate, the motor can readily be found because the airflow will be incorrect.

If a vacuum motor is inoperative, check the operation of the motor with a vacuum tester. If the vacuum motor operates properly, the vacuum hose is probably kinked, pinched, disconnected or has a leak.

If the function system functions normally at idle, but goes to defrost during acceleration, a small leak exists in the system. The leak can best be located by shutting **OFF** the engine and using a gauge to check for vacuum loss while selectively blocking off vacuum hoses.

## CRUISE CONTROL

### General Description and Operation

The Integrated Vehicle Speed Control (IVSC) system consists of operator controls, servo (throttle actuator), brake light switch, speed sensor (not required for vehicles equipped with an electronic cluster), horn relay, vacuum dump valve, vacuum reservoir (called an aspirator on some models), check valve(s), wiring and hoses for vacuum. The vacuum reservoir or aspirator provides an additional vacuum signal when the engine is under heavy load to improve speed control performance. In the IVSC system, speed control amplifier assembly function has been integrated into the EEC-IV Electronic Control Assembly (ECA). The servo assembly is mounted in the engine compartment and is connected to the throttle linkage with an actuator cable. The servo is connected to the vacuum reservoir (aspirator) and to manifold vacuum through the check valve. The speed control sensor is located on the transmission or transaxle.

For the system to be activated, the engine must be running and the vehicle must be greater than approximately 25–35 mph (40–56 km/h), depending upon vehicle application. Under these conditions, the system is activated and is ready to accept a set speed signal by pressing the ON switch in the steering wheel. Then, the operator must depress and release the SET ACCEL switch. This will result in the current speed being maintained until a new speed is set by the operator, the brake pedal is depressed, the clutch pedal is depressed or the OFF switch is depressed.

To decrease the set speed, the vehicle speed may by reduced by applying the brake or clutch pedal and then resetting the speed using

the foregoing method or by depressing the COAST switch. When the vehicle has slowed to the desired speed, the COAST switch is released and the new speed is set automatically. If the vehicle speed is reduced below approximately 25–35 mph (40–60 km/h), depending upon vehicle application, the operator must manually increase the speed and reset the system.

To increase the set speed, the vehicle set speed may be manually increased at any time by depressing the accelerator until the higher speed is reached and stabilized, then depressing and releasing the SET ACCEL button. Speed may also be increased by depressing the SET ACCEL switch button, at speeds over approximately 25–35 mph (40–56 km/h), depending upon vehicle application, and holding it in that position. The vehicle will then automatically increase speed. When the desired rate of speed is attained and the button is released, that new set speed will be maintained.

The speed control system may be deactivated by depressing the brake or clutch pedal. To resume the set speed prior to deactivation, the RESUME switch is depressed and prior set speed may be re-established. The RESUME switch is hinged on the side closest to the SET ACCEL switch. Therefore, it should be depressed on the side farthest from the SET ACCEL switch. The resume feature will not function if the system is deactivated with the OFF switch, or if the vehicle speed has been reduced to below approximately 25–35 mph (40–56 km/h) depending upon vehicle application. In addition, when the ignition switch is turned **OFF**, the speed control memory is erased and the resume feature will not function.

## Actuator Cable

### REMOVAL & INSTALLATION

**Except 3.2L SHO**

▶ **See Figures 23, 24, 25 and 26**

1. Disconnect the negative battery cable.
2. Remove the servo assembly. For details, please refer to the procedure located later in this section.
3. Attach the new actuator cable assembly to the servo.

**To install:**

4. Install the complete actuator cable/servo assembly. For details, please refer to the servo procedure located later in this section.
5. Connect the negative battery cable.

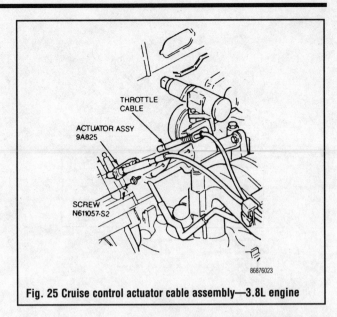

Fig. 25 Cruise control actuator cable assembly—3.8L engine

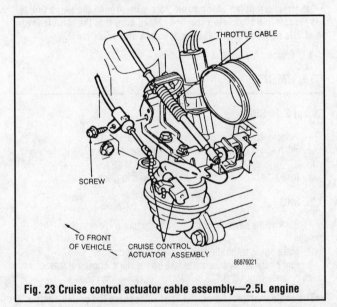

Fig. 23 Cruise control actuator cable assembly—2.5L engine

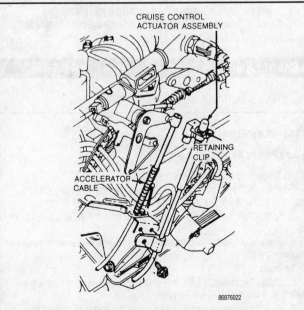

Fig. 24 Cruise control actuator cable assembly—3.0L engine except SHO

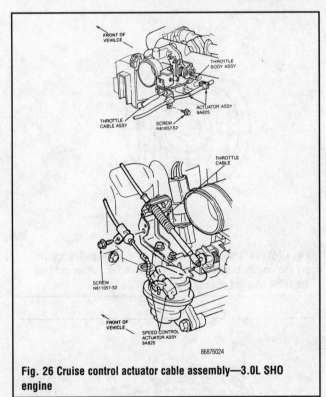

Fig. 26 Cruise control actuator cable assembly—3.0L SHO engine

**3.2L SHO Vehicles**

▶ **See Figures 27, 28 and 29**

1. Disconnect the negative battery cable.
2. Remove the screw attaching the actuator assembly cable to the accelerator shaft bracket.
3. Remove the actuator assembly cable from the throttle control.
4. Remove the actuator cable cap from the speed control servo by depressing the cap locking arm and rotating the cap counterclockwise.
5. Remove the cable slug from the servo pulley. Gently pry-up the arm **slightly** with a suitable small prytool, and at the same time push the cable slug out of the pulley slot.

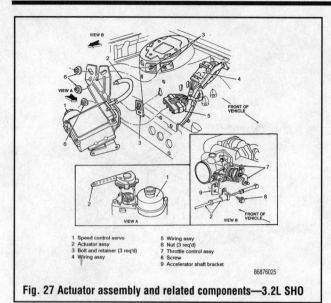

1 Speed control servo
2 Actuator assy
3 Bolt and retainer (3 req'd)
4 Wiring assy
5 Wiring assy
6 Nut (3 req'd)
7 Throttle control assy
8 Screw
9 Accelerator shaft bracket

86876025

**Fig. 27 Actuator assembly and related components—3.2L SHO**

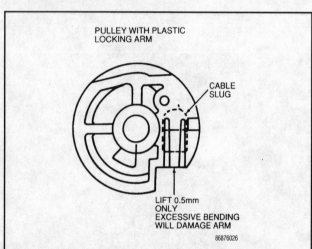

**Fig. 28 When removing the slug from the servo pulley, gently pry the arm up SLIGHTLY using a suitable tool, while pushing the cable slug out of the pulley slot—3.2L SHO**

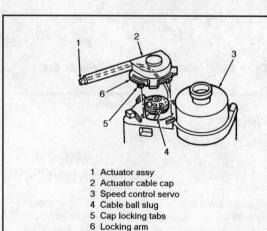

1 Actuator assy
2 Actuator cable cap
3 Speed control servo
4 Cable ball slug
5 Cap locking tabs
6 Locking arm

86876027

**Fig. 29 Align the cable cap tabs with the slots in the servo housing, then insert the cap into the speed control servo and rotate it until the locking arm engages—3.2L SHO**

➡**Excessive bending of the arm will cause it to break. DO NOT USE servos with damaged or missing locking arms.**

**To install:**

6. Make sure that the rubber seal is fully seated on the actuator cap.
7. Lock the cable ball slug into the servo pulley slot.
8. Pull on the throttle attachment end of the cable to draw the cable cap onto the servo pulley.
9. Align the cable cap tabs with slots in the servo housing. Insert the cap into the speed control servo and rotate it clockwise until the locking arm engages.
10. Snap the actuator assembly cable onto the throttle control, then install the screw at the accelerator shaft. Tighten to 27–35 inch lbs. (3–4 Nm).
11. Check the cable adjustment.
12. Make sure that the cable is routed properly, then position the retaining clips.

➡**Incorrect wrapping of the cable core wire around the servo pulley may result in a high idle condition. Make sure that the throttle lever is at idle position after cable installation and adjustment.**

13. Connect the negative battery cable.

## ADJUSTMENT

### Except 3.2L SHO

1. Remove speed control cable retaining clip.
2. Push speed control cable through adjuster until a slight tension is felt.
3. Insert the cable retaining clip and snap into place.

### 3.2L SHO

1. Remove the retaining clip from the actuator cable adjuster at the throttle.
2. Make sure the throttle is in a fully closed position.
3. Pull on the actuator cable to take up the slack. Loosen at least one notch so there is about 0.118 in. (3mm) of slack in the cable.

➡**The cable must not be pulled tight, otherwise the cruise control may not operate properly.**

4. Insert the cable retaining clip, then snap it into place.
5. Check to make sure that the throttle linkage operates freely and smoothly.

## Control Switches

### REMOVAL & INSTALLATION

#### 1986–89 Vehicles

▶ **See Figure 30**

1. Disconnect the negative battery cable.
2. Remove the steering wheel horn pad cover by removing the two retaining screws from the back of the steering wheel.
3. Disengage the electrical wiring connector from the slip ring terminal.
4. Remove the speed control switch assembly from the horn pad cover by removing the two attaching screws from each switch.

**To install:**

5. Install the control switches into the horn pad cover. Attach each switch with the two retaining screws.
6. Attach the control switch connector to the terminal on the slip ring.
7. Install the steering wheel horn pad cover. Snap latching hook in at the 12 o'clock position, then attach with the two retaining screws.
8. Connect the negative battery cable.

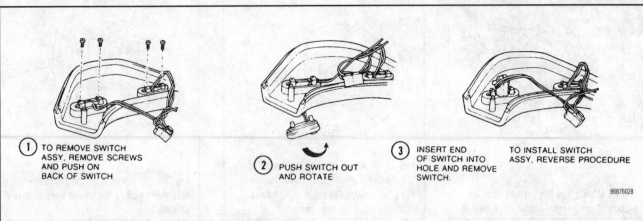

① TO REMOVE SWITCH ASSY, REMOVE SCREWS AND PUSH ON BACK OF SWITCH

② PUSH SWITCH OUT AND ROTATE

③ INSERT END OF SWITCH INTO HOLE AND REMOVE SWITCH.

TO INSTALL SWITCH ASSY, REVERSE PROCEDURE

86876028

**Fig. 30 Control switch removal—1986–89 vehicles**

### 1990–93 Vehicles

▶ See Figures 31 and 32

> ✳✳ **CAUTION**
>
> **Some vehicles are equipped with an inflatable restraint or air bag system. The air bag system must be disabled before performing service on or around the air bag, instrument panel components, or wiring. Failure to follow safety and disabling procedures could result in possible air bag deployment, personal injury or unnecessary air bag system repairs.**

1. Disconnect the negative battery cable and air bag back up power supply.
2. Remove the four nut and washer assemblies retaining the air bag module to the steering wheel.
3. Disengage the air bag electrical connector from the clockspring contact connector.
4. Remove the air bag module from the steering wheel. Place the module on the work bench with the trim cover facing upward.
5. Remove the horn buttons from the steering wheel by using a suitable small prytool.
6. Disengage the horn wiring electrical connector(s).
7. Remove the screws from the speed control switch assemblies.
8. Disconnect the speed control switches from the wiring harness, then remove the switches.
   **To install:**
9. Position the switches onto the steering wheel, then install the retaining screws.
10. Connect the wiring harness to the horn buttons, then install the horn buttons.

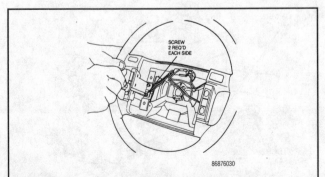

SCREW 2 REQ'D EACH SIDE

86876030

**Fig. 31 Remove the screws from the speed control switch assemblies; there are usually two on each side—1990–93 vehicles**

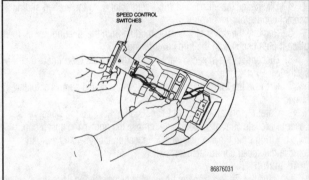

SPEED CONTROL SWITCHES

86876031

**Fig. 32 Disconnect the speed control switches from the wiring harness, then remove the switches—1990–93 vehicles**

11. Connect the speed control switches. Make sure the wires are positioned so that no interference is encountered when installing the air bag module.
12. Position the air bag module on the steering wheel so that the clockspring contact connector can be fastened to the air bag module.
13. Install the air bag module on the steering wheel, then install the four nut and washer assemblies behind the steering wheel. Tighten to 4–6 inch lbs. (36–53 Nm).
14. Connect the air bag back up power supply, then connect the negative battery cable.

### 1994–95 Vehicles

▶ See Figures 33, 34, and 35

> ✳✳ **CAUTION**
>
> **Some vehicles are equipped with an inflatable restraint or air bag system. The air bag system must be disabled before performing service on or around the air bag or instrument panel components or wiring. Failure to follow safety and disabling procedures could result in possible air bag deployment, personal injury or unnecessary air bag system repairs.**

1. Disconnect the negative battery cable.

➡ **Before any air bag component is serviced, the positive battery cable MUST be disconnected for one minute to de-energize the backup power supply.**

2. Disconnect the positive battery cable, then wait one minute for the backup power supply to deplete its stored energy.
3. Remove the two back cover plugs. Remove the two screw and

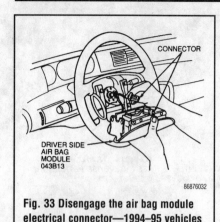

Fig. 33 Disengage the air bag module electrical connector—1994–95 vehicles

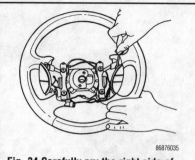

Fig. 34 Carefully pry the right side of the steering wheel back cover for clearance to remove the right hand speed control switch wiring, then . . .

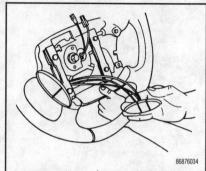

Fig. 35 . . . repeat on the left hand side and remove the speed control actuator switch

washer assemblies securing the driver side air bag module to the steering wheel .

4. Disengage the air bag electrical connector from the air bag sliding contact connector.

5. Remove the driver side air bag module from the steering wheel, then place it on a bench with the trim cover facing up.

6. Disconnect the speed control wire harness, then disconnect the horn switch wire.

7. Remove the four retaining screws from the speed control actuator switch.

8. Carefully pry away the right-hand side of the steering wheel back cover to provide enough clearance to remove the right-hand speed control switch wiring from the steering wheel. Repeat on the left-hand side, then remove the speed control actuator switch.

**To install:**

9. Carefully pry away the right-hand side of the steering wheel back cover to allow enough clearance to insert the right-hand aide of the speed control switch wiring into the steering wheel, then repeat the process on the left side.

10. Position the speed control actuator switch onto the steering wheel, then install the four retaining screws.

➡**Make sure that the wires are positioned so that no interference is encountered when installing the air bag module.**

11. Engage all of the harness connectors and route the wiring in the steering wheel cavity, then install the wire organizer.

12. Position the driver side air bag module on the steering wheel, then connect the air bag sliding contact.

13. Install the driver side air bag module on the steering wheel, then install the two screw and washer assemblies. Tighten to 8–10 ft. lbs. (10.2–13.8 Nm).

14. Install the two back cover plugs.

➡**Because battery voltage to the PCM was interrupted, performance may be affected until the PCM re-learns its driving strategy.**

15. Connect the positive, then the negative battery cables.

16. Check the operation of the speed control actuator switch, then make sure the air bag is operating properly by checking the air bag lamp in the dash panel.

## TESTING

1. Check to see that main fuse and stop lamp fuse are good. If so, detach 6-way connector at amplifier assembly.

2. Connect a voltmeter between light blue/black wire and ground. Depress ON button and check for battery voltage.

3. Connect an ohmmeter between light blue/black wire and ground.

4. Rotate steering wheel through its full range and make the following checks:

    a. Depress OFF button and check for a reading of 0–1 ohms.

    b. Depress SET/ACCEL button and check for a reading pf 714–646 ohms.

    c. Depress COAST button and check for a reading of 126–114 ohms.

    d. Depress RESUME button and check for a reading of 2090–2310 ohms.

5. If the resistance values are not as indicated, but the ohmmeter fluctuates, remove the steering wheel and clean the brushes and slip ring surface. Apply slip ring grease E1AZ-19590-A or equivalent, equally on the ring, approximately 0.02 in. (0.5mm) thick.

6. If the resistance values are greater than those specified above, check the switch assemblies and ground circuit.

7. Reconnect the 6-way connector at amplifier.

## Ground Brush/Clockspring Assembly/Air Bag Sliding Contact

### REMOVAL & INSTALLATION

**1986–89 Vehicles**

▶ See Figure 36

1. Disconnect the negative battery cable.

2. Remove the steering wheel hub horn pad cover by removing the two screws from the back of the steering wheel.

3. Remove and discard the steering wheel attaching bolt.

4. Remove the steering wheel from the upper shaft by grasping the rim of the steering wheel and pulling it off. Do not use a steering wheel puller.

5. Remove the tilt lever, if so equipped.

6. Remove the ignition lock cylinder and steering column lower trim shroud.

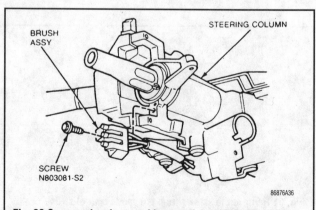

Fig. 36 Common brush assembly mounting—1986–89 vehicles

7. Separate the speed control brush wire harness at the connector and remove the wire harness retainers from the steering column.

8. Remove the screw securing the brush assembly to the upper steering column.

**To install:**

9. Position the brush assembly housing on the upper steering column and secure with the screw.

10. Install the wire harness into the steering column with the attached retainers. Connect the harness to the main wiring harness.

11. Attach the lower trim shroud to the upper shroud with the three retaining screws.

12. Install the ignition lock cylinder and tilt lever, if equipped.

13. Position the steering wheel on the end of the steering wheel shaft. Align the index mark on the wheel with the index mark on the shaft.

14. Install a new steering wheel bolt. Tighten to 23–33 ft. lbs. (31–45 Nm).

15. Install the steering wheel horn pad.

### 1990–95 Vehicles

▶ **See Figures 37, 38 and 39**

1. Set the steering wheel in the straight ahead position.
2. Disconnect the negative battery cable.
3. Remove the four nut and washer assemblies retaining the air bag module to the steering wheel.
4. Disengage the air bag electrical connector from the clockspring contact connector.
5. Remove the air bag module from the steering wheel.

### ✳✳ CAUTION

**Place the air bag module on the bench with the trim cover facing upward to prevent personal injury in the event of accidental deployment of the air bag.**

6. Disconnect the speed control switches and horn switches from the contact assembly.
7. Remove the steering wheel retaining bolt.
8. Using Steering Wheel Puller T67L-3600-A or equivalent suitable puller, remove the steering wheel.
9. If equipped, remove the tilt lever.
10. Remove the lower trim panel and lower steering column shroud.
11. Disconnect the contact assembly wiring harness.
12. Apply two pieces of tape across the contact assembly stator and rotor to prevent accidental rotation.
13. Remove the three contact assembly retaining screws, then lift the contact assembly off the steering column shaft.
14. Disengage the speed control brush wiring harness at the connector, then remove the wiring harness retainers from the steering column.

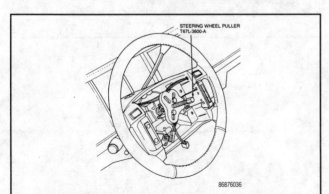

**Fig. 37 Using a suitable steering wheel puller, remove the steering wheel**

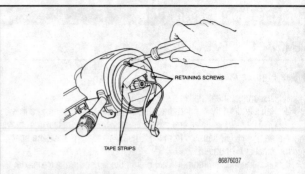

**Fig. 38 Apply two pieces of tape across the contact assembly stator and rotor to prevent accidental rotation, then remove the three contact assembly retaining screws**

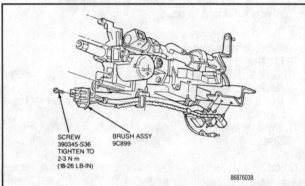

**Fig. 39 After unfastening the retaining screw, remove the brush and harness assembly**

15. Remove the screw retaining the brush assembly to the upper steering column. Remove the brush and harness assembly.

**To install:**

16. Position the brush assembly wire on the upper steering column and install the retaining screw. Tighten to 18–26 inch lbs. (2–3 Nm).

17. Install the wiring harness retainer into the steering column and connect the harness to the main wiring.

18. Align the contact assembly to the column shaft and mounting bosses and slide the contact assembly onto the shaft.

19. Install the three screws that retain the contact assembly, then tighten to 18–26 inch lbs. (2–3 Nm). Remove the tape from the contact assembly.

20. Route the contact assembly harness down the column and connect to the main wiring harness.

➡**If installing a new contact assembly, remove the lock mechanism.**

21. Install the steering column shroud.
22. Install the lower trim panel.
23. If equipped, install the tilt lever.

➡**Route the contact assembly wiring through the steering wheel as the wheel is being positioned.**

24. Position the steering wheel on the steering shaft and install a new steering wheel retaining bolt. Tighten to 23–33 ft. lbs. (31–45 Nm).

25. Connect the speed control and horn switches to the contact assembly.

26. Position the air bag module on the steering wheel so that the clockspring contact connector can be connected to the air bag module.

27. Install the air bag module on the steering wheel and install the four nut and washer assemblies.

28. Connect negative battery cable.

## Vehicle Speed Sensor (VSS)

### REMOVAL & INSTALLATION

◆ **See Figures 40 and 41**

1. Disconnect the negative battery cable.
2. Raise and safely support the vehicle. Remove the mounting clip.
3. On 1992–95 vehicles equipped with an automatic transaxle, remove the Y-pipe and HEGO sensors from the exhaust system. Remove the speed sensor exhaust heat shield.
4. Loosen the retaining nut/bolt holding the sensor in the transaxle. Remove the driven gear with the sensor from the transaxle.
5. Disconnect the electrical connector from the speed sensor.
6. Disconnect the speedometer cable by pulling it out of the speed sensor.

➡**Do not attempt to remove the spring retainer clip with the speedometer cable in the sensor.**

7. For 1992–95 vehicles equipped with and automatic transaxle, remove the driven gear retainer and driven gear from the speed sensor.

**To install:**

8. Position the driven gear to the speed sensor. Install the gear retainer.
9. Engage the electrical connector.
10. Make sure the internal O-ring is properly seated in the sensor housing. Snap the speedometer cable into the sensor housing.
11. Insert the sensor assembly into the transaxle housing. Tighten the retaining nut/bolt to 30–40 inch lbs. (3.4–4.5 Nm). Install the retaining clip.
12. On 1992–95 vehicles equipped with an automatic transaxle, install the Y-pipe and HEGO sensors to the exhaust system. Install the speed sensor exhaust heat shield.

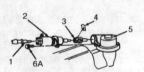

```
2      3    4         5
1   6A

1  Speed control cable and
   vehicle speed sensor
2  Vehicle speed sensor
3  Speedometer driven gear
4  Speedometer driven gear retainer
5  Speedometer cover
6  Bolt
A  Tighten to 3.4-4.5 Nm (31-39 lb.in.)
                          86876039
```

**Fig. 40 Vehicle speed sensor assembly—vehicles equipped with automatic transaxles**

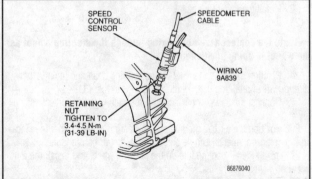

```
SPEED            SPEEDOMETER
CONTROL          CABLE
SENSOR

                 WIRING
                 9A839

RETAINING
NUT
TIGHTEN TO
3.4-4.5 N·m
(31-39 LB-IN)

              86876040
```

**Fig. 41 Vehicle speed sensor assembly—vehicles equipped with manual transaxles**

13. Carefully lower the vehicle.
14. Connect the negative battery cable, then check to make sure the speedometer and odometer are operating properly.

### TESTING

**Without Electronic Instrument Cluster**

1. Disconnect connector at speed sensor and connect an ohmmeter between wire connector terminals and speed sensor end. Reading should be 200–300 ohms.

➡**A reading of 0 ohms indicates a shorted coil and the speed sensor should be replaced. A maximum reading indicates an open coil and speed sensor should be replaced.**

2. If the ohmmeter reading is between 200–300 ohms, and speedometer operates properly within needle waver, speed sensor is probably functioning properly.
3. If available, a known good quality speed sensor can also be substituted in place of existing sensor to check for proper operation.

**With Electronic Instrument Cluster**

➡**Because AC and DC voltage measurements are required in the diagnosis of the speed control system on vehicles equipped with an electronic instrument cluster, a special diagnostic tool, Fluke 8022A or equivalent, should be used. Do not perform speed sensor testing on vehicles equipped with an electronic speedometer.**

1. Raise and safely support the vehicle drive wheels.
2. Bring vehicle speed to approximately 30 mph (48 km/h).
3. Connect an AC voltmeter to dark green/white wire and ground.
4. Back probe the amplifier connector. Voltmeter should read about 6–24 volts. If not, check speed sensor and related wiring. Repair and/or replace as necessary.
5. Lower the vehicle.

## Amplifier

### REMOVAL & INSTALLATION

On Integrated Vehicle Speed Control (IVSC) equipped vehicles, the amplifier assembly has been incorporated into the EEC-IV system Electronic Control Assembly (ECA).

**Non-IVSC Vehicles**

◆ **See Figure 42**

1. Disconnect the negative battery cable.
2. Disengage the two electrical connectors at the amplifier.

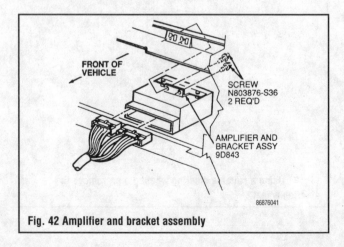

```
FRONT OF
VEHICLE

                    SCREW
                    N803876-S36
                    2 REQ'D

                    AMPLIFIER AND
                    BRACKET ASSY
                    9D843

                            86876041
```

**Fig. 42 Amplifier and bracket assembly**

3. Remove the two screws retaining the amplifier and bracket assembly.

4. Remove the amplifier and bracket assembly from the instrument panel.

5. Remove the two bolts and nuts retaining the amplifier assembly to the mounting bracket.

**To install:**

6. Place the amplifier assembly into position, then install the two bolts and nuts which secure the amplifier assembly to the mounting bracket.

7. Install the amplifier and bracket assembly to the instrument panel using the two retaining screws, then tighten to 45–61 inch lbs. (5–7 Nm).

8. Engage the two amplifier electrical connectors.

9. Connect the negative battery cable.

## TESTING

➡Do not use a test lamp to perform the amplifier tests as excessive current draw will damage electronic components inside the amplifier. Use a voltmeter of 5000 ohm/volt rating or higher.

### ON Circuit

1. With the ignition in the **RUN** position, connect a voltmeter between the white/pink wire and black wire (ground) in the 6-way connector at the amplifier. Voltmeter should read battery voltage.

2. Connect the voltmeter between light blue/black wire and black wire (ground) in the 6-way connector at the amplifier. Voltmeter should read battery voltage only when ON switch in steering wheel is depressed and held. If voltage is not present, perform control switch test.

3. Release ON button, voltmeter should read about 7.8 volts, this indicates that ON circuit is engaged. If voltmeter reads 0.0, check for a bad ground at amplifier.

4. If there is no ground at amplifier, check system ground connections and wiring. Also check the fuse.

5. If available, substitute a known good amplifier and check for proper circuit operation.

### Brake Circuit

1. Connect an ohmmeter between the red/light green wire on the 6-way connector and ground. Resistance should be less than 5 ohms.

2. If resistance is greater than indicated, check for improper wiring, burned out stop lamp lights or clutch malfunction, if equipped.

### OFF Circuit

1. With ignition in **RUN**, connect voltmeter between light blue/black wire of 6-way amplifier connector and ground. Depress OFF switch on steering wheel. Voltage on light blue/black wire should drop to 0 which indicates that ON circuit is not energized.

2. If voltage does not drop to 0, perform the control switch test. If control switch checks out good, install a good amplifier and recheck OFF circuit.

### SET/ACCEL Circuit

1. With ignition in **RUN**, connect voltmeter between light blue/black of 6-way amplifier connector and black wire (ground). Depress and hold SET/ACCEL button on steering wheel. Voltmeter should read about 4.5 volts.

2. Rotate steering wheel back and forth and watch voltmeter for fluctuations.

3. If voltage varies more than 0.5 volts, perform control switch test.

### COAST Circuit

1. With ignition in **RUN**, connect voltmeter between light blue/black of 6-way amplifier connector and ground. Depress and hold COAST button on steering wheel. Voltmeter should read about 1.5 volts.

2. If circuit checks out good, perform servo assembly test. If servo test checks out good, install a new amplifier and repeat tests. Do not substitute amplifier until after performing servo assembly test.

### RESUME Circuit

1. With ignition in **RUN**, connect voltmeter between light blue/black of 6-way amplifier connector and ground. Depress and hold RESUME button on steering wheel. Voltmeter should read about 6.5 volts.

2. If circuit checks out good, perform servo assembly test. If servo test checks out good, install a new amplifier and repeat tests. Do not substitute amplifier until after performing servo assembly test.

## Servo

### REMOVAL & INSTALLATION

#### Except 3.2L SHO

▸ **See Figures 43, 44, 45 and 46**

1. Disconnect the negative battery cable.

2. Remove the screw, then disconnect the speed control actuator cable from the accelerator cable bracket.

3. Disconnect the speed control actuator cable with the adjuster from the accelerator cable.

4. Remove the two vacuum hoses and electrical connector from the servo assembly.

5. Remove the two nuts attaching the servo to its mounting bracket.

6. Carefully remove the servo and cable assembly.

7. Remove the two nuts securing the cable cover to the servo.

8. Pull off the cover, then remove the cable assembly.

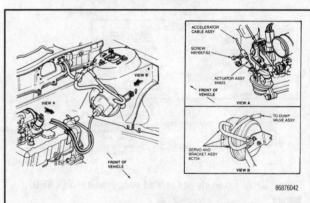

**Fig. 43 Servo assembly and related components—2.5L engine**

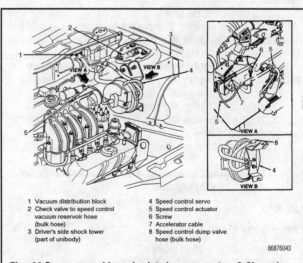

| 1 | Vacuum distribution block | 4 | Speed control servo |
| 2 | Check valve to speed control vacuum reservoir hose (bulk hose) | 5 | Speed control actuator |
| | | 6 | Screw |
| 3 | Driver's side shock tower (part of unibody) | 7 | Accelerator cable |
| | | 8 | Speed control dump valve hose (bulk hose) |

**Fig. 44 Servo assembly and related components—3.0L engine except SHO**

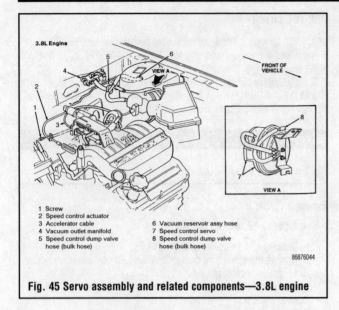

**Fig. 45 Servo assembly and related components—3.8L engine**

1 Screw
2 Speed control actuator
3 Accelerator cable
4 Vacuum outlet manifold
5 Speed control dump valve hose (bulk hose)
6 Vacuum reservoir assy hose
7 Speed control servo
8 Speed control dump valve hose (bulk hose)

86876044

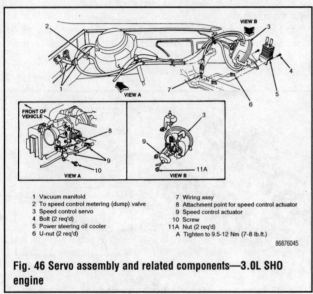

1 Vacuum manifold
2 To speed control metering (dump) valve
3 Speed control servo
4 Bolt (2 req'd)
5 Power steering oil cooler
6 U-nut (2 req'd)
7 Wiring assy
8 Attachment point for speed control actuator
9 Speed control actuator
10 Screw
11A Nut (2 req'd)
A Tighten to 9.5-12 Nm (7-8 lb.ft.)

86876045

**Fig. 46 Servo assembly and related components—3.0L SHO engine**

### To install:
9. Attach the cable to the servo.

10. Attach the cable cover to the servo with the two retaining nuts. For vehicles through 1993, tighten the nuts to 45–61 inch lbs. (5–7 Nm). For 1994–95 vehicles, tighten the nuts to 62–80 inch lbs. (7–9 Nm).

11. Attach the servo to the mounting bracket. For vehicles through 1993, tighten the retaining nuts to 45–61 inch lbs. (5–7 Nm). For 1994–95 vehicles, tighten the retaining nuts to 62–80 inch lbs. (7–9 Nm).

12. Feed the actuator cable under the air cleaner air duct.

13. Snap the actuator cable with the adjuster onto the accelerator cable bracket and install the screw.

14. Connect the actuator cable to the accelerator cable bracket and install the fastener.

15. Install the two vacuum hoses and electrical connector at the servo.

16. Connect negative battery cable.

### 3.2L SHO

♦ **See Figures 47, 48 and 49**

1. Disconnect the negative battery cable.
2. Remove the retaining clip from the actuator cable adjuster fitting.
3. Push the actuator tube out of the adjuster fitting attached to the throttle cable.

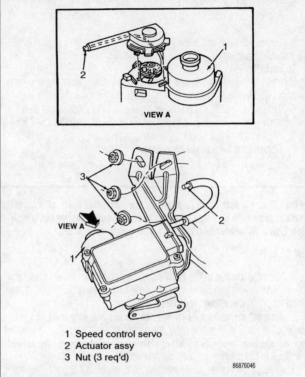

1 Speed control servo
2 Actuator assy
3 Nut (3 req'd)

86876046

**Fig. 47 Speed control servo assembly and related components—3.2L SHO engine**

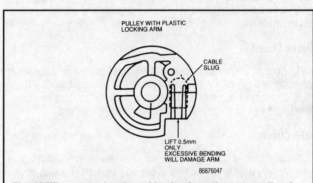

86876047

**Fig. 48 When removing the cable slug from the servo pulley, be careful when prying up the arm. Excessive bending will cause the arm to break.**

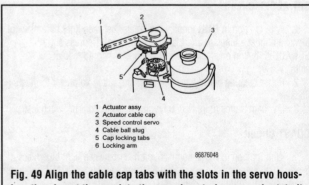

1 Actuator assy
2 Actuator cable cap
3 Speed control servo
4 Cable ball slug
5 Cap locking tabs
6 Locking arm

86876048

**Fig. 49 Align the cable cap tabs with the slots in the servo housing, then insert the cap into the speed control servo and rotate it clockwise until the locking arm engages the locking tab on the servo**

4. Disengage the harness connector at the speed control servo.

5. Remove the three nuts attaching the assembly to the vehicle.

6. Remove the actuator cable cap from the speed control servo by depressing the cap locking arm and rotating the cap counterclockwise.

7. Remove the cable slug from the servo pulley. Gently pry-up the arm **slightly** with a suitable small prybar and at the same time, push the cable slug out of the pulley slot.

➡**Excessive bending of the arm will cause it to break. DO NOT USE servos with damaged or missing locking arms.**

8. Remove the bracket from the speed control servo. Retain the bracket and three screws for reinstallation on the speed control servo.

**To install:**

9. Attach the bracket to the speed control servo with the three screws. Tighten the screw to 6–8 ft. lbs. (8–11 Nm).

10. Make sure that the rubber seal is fully seated on the actuator cap.

11. Lock the cable ball slug into the servo pulley slot.

12. Pull on the throttle attachment end of the cable to draw the cable cap onto the servo pulley.

13. Align the cable cap tabs with slots in the servo housing. Insert the cap into the speed control servo and rotate it clockwise until the locking arm engages the locking tab on the speed control servo.

14. Position the actuator cable and servo assembly in the vehicle. Tighten the mounting nuts to 45–61 inch lbs. (5–7 Nm).

15. Attach the harness connector to the speed control servo.

16. Adjust the actuator clip as outlined earlier in this section, then install the retaining clip.

➡**Incorrect wrapping of the cable core wire around the servo pulley may result in a high idle condition. Make sure that the throttle lever is at idle position after cable installation and adjustment.**

17. Connect the negative battery cable.

### TESTING

1. Disconnect 8-way amplifier connector. At connector, connect an ohmmeter between orange/yellow wire and grey/black wire. Resistance should be 40–125 ohms.

2. Connect an ohmmeter between orange/yellow wire and white/pink wire. Resistance should be 60–190 ohms.

3. Connect an ohmmeter between pink/light blue wire and brown/light green wire. Resistance should be 40,000–60,000 ohms.

4. Connect an ohmmeter between yellow/red wire and brown/light green wire. Resistance should be 20,000–30,000 ohms.

5. If proper reading is not obtained, check wiring and servo assembly separately for damage. Repair and/or replace as required.

6. Start engine and, with servo disconnected from amplifier, connect orange/yellow wire of servo to battery positive terminal. Connect white/pink wire of servo to ground.

7. Momentarily touch grey/black wire of servo to ground. Servo throttle actuator arm should pull in and engine speed should servo throttle actuator arm should hold in that position or slowly release.

8. When white/pink is removed from ground servo throttle actuator arm should release.

9. Replace servo assembly if it does not perform as indicated.

10. If orange/yellow wire is shorted to either white/pink wire or grey/black wire it may be necessary to replace amplifier assembly.

## Brake Light Switch and Circuit

### TESTING

This test is performed when brake pedal application will not disconnect the speed control system.

1. Check the brake light operation with maximum brake pedal effort of about 6 lbs. If more than about 6 lbs. is required, check brake actuation of brake light switch. Repair and/or replace as necessary.

2. If brake lights do not work, check fuse, bulbs and switch. Repair and/or replace as necessary.

3. If brake lights are working properly check for battery voltage at white/pink or pink/orange wire at 6-way electrical connector.

4. Depress brake pedal until tail lamps light. Check voltage on dark green/white wire at 6-way electrical connector.

5. Difference between the two voltage readings should not exceed 1.5 volts. If reading is higher, resistance in brake light circuit must be found and repaired.

6. There should be no voltage present on dark green/white wire with brake lights off.

7. Perform vacuum dump valve test.

## Vacuum Dump Valve

▶ **See Figure 50**

### ADJUSTMENT

Adjust the vacuum dump valve so that it is closed (no vacuum leak) when the brake pedal is up (brakes released) and open when the pedal is depressed.

### TESTING

The vacuum dump valve releases vacuum in the servo assembly whenever the brake pedal is depressed and thus acts as a redundant safety feature. The vacuum dump valve should be checked whenever brake application does not disconnect the speed control system.

1. Disconnect vacuum hose with the white stripe from the dump valve. Connect a vacuum pump to hose and apply vacuum.

2. If a vacuum cannot be obtained, hose or dump valve is leaking. Replace or repair defective components as required.

3. Step on the brake pedal, vacuum should be released. If not, adjust or replace dump valve.

4. The dump valve black housing must clear white plastic pad on brake pedal by 0.05–0.10 in. (1.3–2.5mm) with the brake pedal pulled to rearmost position.

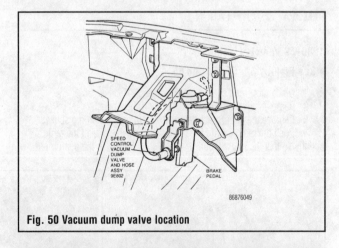

**Fig. 50 Vacuum dump valve location**

## Clutch Switch

### ADJUSTMENT

**Except 1995 3.0L SHO**

▶ **See Figure 51**

1. Prop the clutch pedal in a full-up position (pawl fully released from the sector).

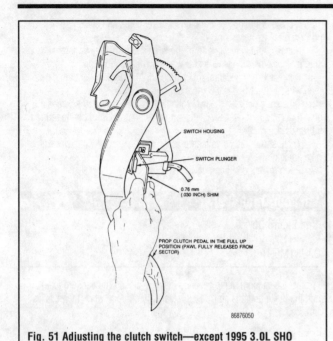

**Fig. 51 Adjusting the clutch switch—except 1995 3.0L SHO vehicles**

2. Loosen the switch retaining screw.
3. Slide the switch forward toward the clutch pedal until the switch plunger cap is 0.030 in. (0.76mm) from contacting the switch housing. Tighten the retaining screw.
4. Remove the prop from the clutch pedal, then test drive the vehicle to ensure that the clutch switch cancellation of cruise control operates properly.

## ENTERTAINMENT SYSTEMS

### Radio Receiver/Tape Player

REMOVAL & INSTALLATION

#### 1986–89 Vehicles

▶ **See Figures 52, 53, 54 and 55**

1. Disconnect the negative battery cable.
2. Remove the trim panel-to-center instrument panel.
3. Remove the radio/bracket-to-instrument panel retaining screws.
4. Push the radio toward the front, then raise the rear of the radio slightly so that the rear support bracket clears the clip in the instrument

### 1995 3.0L SHO

The clutch pedal position switch is self-adjusting. To adjust, press the clutch pedal to the floor to reset the clutch switch.

TESTING

#### Manual Transaxle

The speed control system is designed to disengage when the clutch pedal is depressed. This is accomplished with a clutch switch. The speed control system disengage function is operated by opening the circuit between the speed control module and the brake lamps. This prevents engine over speed when the clutch is depressed and the speed control system is engaged.

The disengagement switch is a plunger switch that operates when the clutch pedal is depressed and the pedal moves away from the switch plunger. The switch is adjustable and attaches to a mounting bracket on the clutch module assembly.

➡**Do not use a test light to perform the clutch switch test, as the light cannot properly indicate the condition of the switch. Do not use a strong magnet near the clutch switch, as it can be affected by magnetic fields.**

1. Disconnect clutch pigtail connector from speed control harness connector. Connect an ohmmeter to the two switch connector terminals.
2. With the clutch pedal in full up position, resistance should be less than 5 ohms.
3. With the clutch pedal depressed, the circuit should be open.
4. If switch does not perform as indicated, it must be replaced.

#### Automatic Transaxle

Vehicles equipped with automatic transmission use a shorting plug instead of a clutch switch. Make sure the plug is installed and has good contact.

panel. Slowly, pull the radio from the instrument panel.
5. Disengage the electrical connectors and the antenna cable from the radio.
**To install:**
6. Engage the wiring connectors and antenna cable to the radio.
7. Slide the radio into the instrument panel, keeping the rear of the radio slightly raised to engage the rear mounting bracket to clip in the instrument panel.
8. Install the four retaining screws, then torque the radio/bracket-to-instrument panel screws to 14–16 inch lbs. (1.6–1.8 Nm).
9. Install the center instrument trim panel.
10. Connect the negative battery cable, then test the radio/tape player for operation.

**Fig. 52 Remove the center instrument panel**

**Fig. 53 Remove the four screws retaining the radio and mounting bracket to the instrument panel**

**Fig. 54 Disconnect the antenna cable from the radio**

Fig. 55 Disengage the electrical connector from the radio

## Radio Receiver/CD Player

### REMOVAL & INSTALLATION

**1990–95 Vehicles**

▶ See Figures 56 and 57

1. Disconnect the negative battery cable.
2. Install Radio Removal Tool T87P-19061-A into the radio or CD player face plate. Push the tool in about 1 in. (25mm) in order to release the retaining clips.

➡**Do not use excessive force when installing the special tool because this will cause damage to the retaining clips.**

3. Apply a light spreading force to the tool, then pull the assembly out from the instrument panel.
4. Disengage the electrical wiring connectors and the antenna wire from the assembly, then remove the radio or CD player from the vehicle.
**To install:**
5. Engage the electrical wiring connectors, then connect the antennal cable to the radio or CD player assembly.

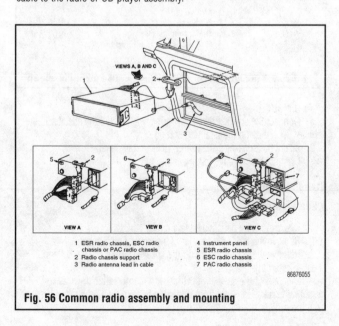

1 ESR radio chassis, ESC radio chassis or PAC radio chassis
2 Radio chassis support
3 Radio antenna lead in cable
4 Instrument panel
5 ESR radio chassis
6 ESC radio chassis
7 PAC radio chassis

Fig. 56 Common radio assembly and mounting

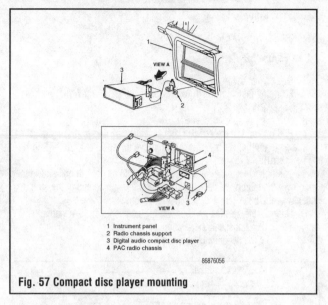

1 Instrument panel
2 Radio chassis support
3 Digital audio compact disc player
4 PAC radio chassis

Fig. 57 Compact disc player mounting

6. Slide the assembly into the instrument panel, making sure that the rear radio or CD player assembly support is engaged on the upper support rail.
7. Push the radio or CD player assembly inward until the retaining clips are fully engaged.
8. Connect the negative battery cable. Test the radio and/or CD player for operation.

## Speakers

### REMOVAL & INSTALLATION

**Door Mounted**

▶ See Figure 58

1. Disconnect the negative battery cable.
2. Remove the front door trim panel.
3. Remove the screws retaining the speaker to its mounting bracket.
4. Pull the speaker away from the mounting bracket far enough to disconnect the speaker electrical wires.
5. Remove the speaker from the vehicle.
**To install:**
6. Connect the speaker electrical wires, then install the speaker to the mounting bracket using the retaining screws.
7. Install the front door trim panel.
8. Connect the negative battery cable.

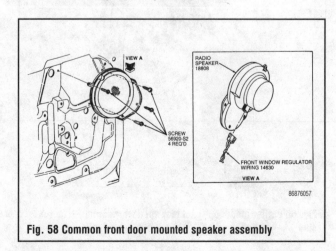

Fig. 58 Common front door mounted speaker assembly

### Rear Seat Mounted

#### STANDARD SPEAKER

▶ **See Figure 59**

1. Disconnect the negative battery cable.
2. From the inside of the trunk, disconnect the speaker wiring harness from the speaker.
3. Remove the speaker cover.
4. Pull one end of the speaker rubber retaining strap to disengage it from the tab on the package tray, then remove the speaker from the vehicle.

**To install:**

5. Position the speaker and strap assembly in place with one end of the strap over the tab on the package tray. Pull the opposite end of the strap to index over the other tab, securing the assembly.
6. Connect the speaker harness wiring, then connect the negative battery cable and check speaker operation.
7. Connect the negative battery cable.

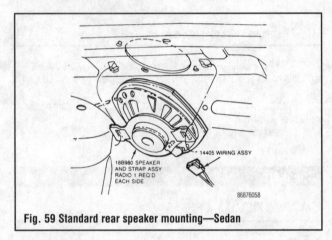

**Fig. 59 Standard rear speaker mounting—Sedan**

#### OPTIONAL SPEAKER

▶ **See Figures 60, 61 and 62**

1. Disconnect the negative battery cable.
2. Remove the speaker grille from the package tray panel.
3. Remove the speaker retaining screws.
4. Pull the speaker forward, then disconnect the speaker electrical wiring. Remove the speaker from the vehicle.

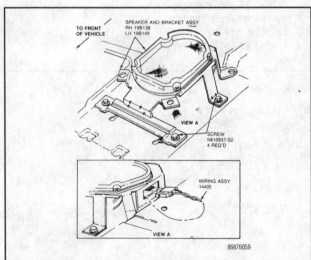

**Fig. 60 Earlier model optional rear speaker mounting—Taurus only**

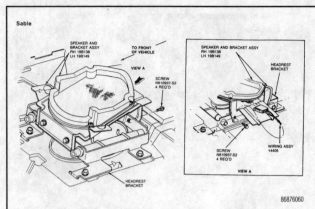

**Fig. 61 Earlier model optional rear speaker mounting—Sable only**

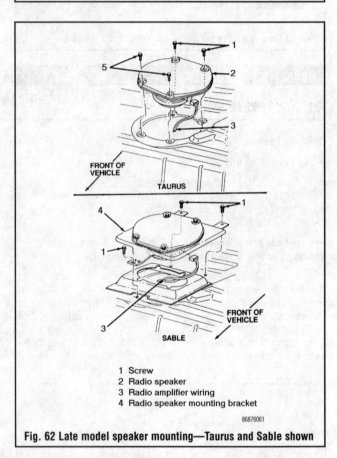

1 Screw
2 Radio speaker
3 Radio amplifier wiring
4 Radio speaker mounting bracket

**Fig. 62 Late model speaker mounting—Taurus and Sable shown**

**To install:**

5. Connect the speaker electrical wiring, then install the speaker in the vehicle. Secure using the retaining screws.
6. Install the speaker grille to the package tray panel.
7. Connect the negative battery cable.

### Station Wagon

▶ **See Figure 63**

1. Disconnect the negative battery cable.
2. Remove the inner rear corner of the upper finish panel.
3. Remove the screws retaining the speaker mounting bracket and speaker assembly.
4. Disconnect the speaker electrical wiring, then slide the speaker mounting bracket edge out from under the headlining. Remove the speaker from the vehicle.

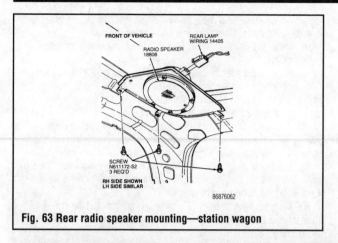

Fig. 63 Rear radio speaker mounting—station wagon

**To install:**

5. Position the speaker, then slide the speaker mounting bracket edge under the headlining and connect the speaker electrical wiring.

6. Install the speaker and mounting bracket retaining screws.

7. Install the inner rear corner of the upper finish panel.

8. Connect the negative battery cable.

## WINDSHIELD WIPERS AND WASHERS

### Windshield Wiper Blade and Arm

REMOVAL & INSTALLATION

▶ **See Figures 64 thru 69**

1. Turn the ignition switch to the ACC position. Turn the wiper switch ON. Allow the motor to move the pivot shafts 3 or 4 cycles, then turn off the switch. This operation will place the pivot shafts in the PARK position. Turn the ignition switch to the OFF position.

2. Disconnect the negative battery cable.

3. Remove the wiper arm and blade assembly by first applying downward pressure on the wiper arm head while holding the wiper arm. Then, lift the arm to the highest position and, using finger pressure only, grasp the slide latch tab and slide the latch out from under the arm head. Remove the arm and blade assembly.

4. To remove the blade assembly for vehicles through 1994, insert a screwdriver into the slot provided at the top of the blade frame, push down on the spring lock and pull the blade assembly from the wiper arm pin.

5. To remove the blade assembly for 1995 vehicles, depress the lock-

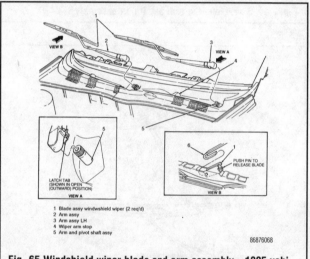

1 Blade assy windshield wiper (2 req'd)
2 Arm assy
3 Arm assy LH
4 Wiper arm stop
5 Arm and pivot shaft assy

Fig. 65 Windshield wiper blade and arm assembly—1995 vehicles

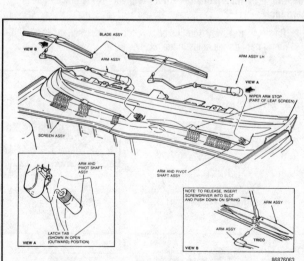

Fig. 64 Windshield wiper blade and arm assembly—Vehicles through 1994

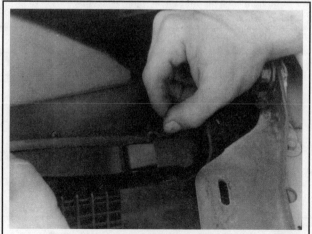

Fig. 66 Using finger pressure only, grasp the slide latch tab and slide the latch out from under the arm head, then . . .

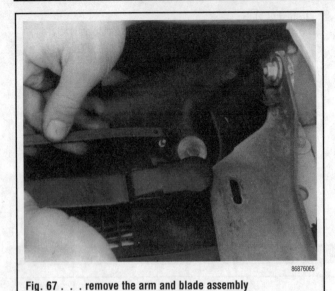

**Fig. 67 . . . remove the arm and blade assembly**

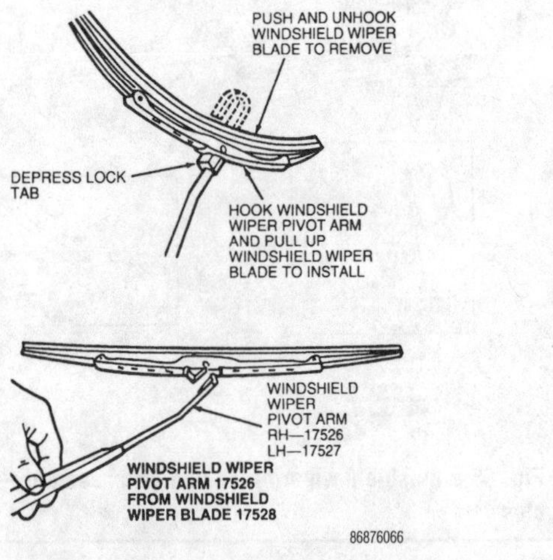

86876065

PUSH AND UNHOOK
WINDSHIELD WIPER
BLADE TO REMOVE

DEPRESS LOCK
TAB

HOOK WINDSHIELD
WIPER PIVOT ARM
AND PULL UP
WINDSHIELD WIPER
BLADE TO INSTALL

WINDSHIELD
WIPER
PIVOT ARM
RH—17526
LH—17527

WINDSHIELD WIPER
PIVOT ARM 17526
FROM WINDSHIELD
WIPER BLADE 17528

86876066

**Fig. 68 Removing the windshield wiper blade assembly—1995 vehicles**

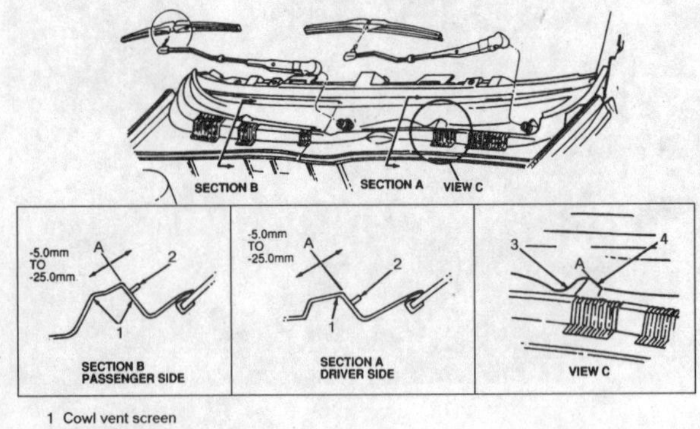

SECTION B    SECTION A    VIEW C

-5.0mm
TO
-25.0mm

-5.0mm
TO
-25.0mm

SECTION B
PASSENGER SIDE

SECTION A
DRIVER SIDE

VIEW C

1 Cowl vent screen
2 Windshield wiper pivot arm
3 Top surface
4 Park surface
A 5.0-25.0 mm (0.19-0.98 inches)

86876067

**Fig. 69 Specifications for installing the windshield wiper arm and blade assembly**

ing tab on the windshield wiper blade, then slide the blade downward away from the windshield wiper pivot arm and remove the blade.

6. Install the blade onto the new replacement wiper arm assembly.

**To install:**

7. Position the bottom surface of the wiper arm parallel with the top surface of the cowl screen louvers, making sure that arm rests against the top surface of the cowl screen. Install the arm onto the pivot shaft with the latch slide in the unlatched (outward position).

8. While applying downward pressure on the arm head to ensure full seating, raise the other end of the arm enough to allow the latch to slide under the pivot assembly to the latched position.

9. Lift the (latched) wiper arm and blade assembly away from the top surface of the cowl screen louvers and position the arm only on the rearward surface of the wiper arm stop.

10. Make sure the blade is fully seated on the arm and the arm is against (rearward of) the the wiper stop, before operating the wipers to verify the correction.

➡**If the blade does not touch the windshield, the slide latch is not completely in place.**

11. Connect the negative battery cable, then check for correct wiper operation.

## ADJUSTMENT

1. With the arm and blade assemblies removed from the pivot shafts, turn on the wiper switch and allow the motor to move the pivot shaft three or four cycles, then turn the wiper switch off. This will place the pivot shafts in the park position.

2. Install the arm and blade assemblies on the pivot shafts to the correct distance between the windshield lower molding or weatherstrip and the blade saddle centerline.

### Rear Window Wiper Blade and Arm

## REMOVAL & INSTALLATION

♦ **See Figures 70 and 71**

➡**To avoid scratching the glass and/or paint, do not pry the wiper mounting arm and pivot shaft from the pivot arm with a metal or sharp tool.**

1. Raise the arm away from the back window glass, then insert a 0.062 in. (1.6mm) pin into the holes in the retainer arm.

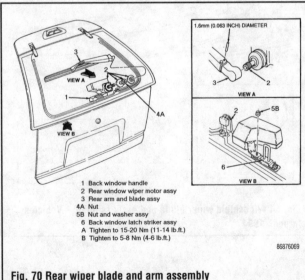

1.6mm (0.063 INCH) DIAMETER

VIEW A

VIEW A

VIEW B

VIEW B

1 Back window handle
2 Rear window wiper motor assy
3 Rear arm and blade assy
4A Nut
5B Nut and washer assy
6 Back window latch striker assy
A Tighten to 15-20 Nm (11-14 lb.ft.)
B Tighten to 5-8 Nm (4-6 lb.ft.)

86876069

**Fig. 70 Rear wiper blade and arm assembly**

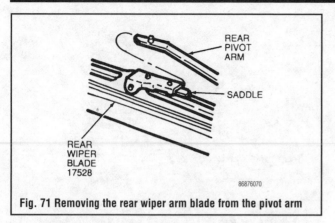

**Fig. 71 Removing the rear wiper arm blade from the pivot arm**

2. Lower the arm to the glass to relieve arm spring tension.
3. Lift the arm assembly off of the pivot shaft.
4. To remove the rear wiper blade, press down on the arm to unlatch the top stud, then pull the blade from the rear wiper pivot arm.

**To install:**

5. To install the rear wiper blade, slide the blade assembly on the the rear wiper pivot arm, then make sure that the top stud and bottom saddle are securely latched.
6. Push the main arm head over the pivot shaft. Be sure that the pivot shaft is in the park position.
7. Hold the main arm head on the pivot shaft while raising the blade end of the wiper arm and remove the 0.062 in. (1.6mm) pin.
8. Lower the blade to the glass.

## Windshield Wiper Motor

### REMOVAL & INSTALLATION

♦ **See Figures 72, 73, 74 and 75**

1. Disconnect the negative, then the positive battery cables.
2. Disconnect the power lead from the windshield wiper motor.
3. Remove the left windshield wiper pivot arm.
4. On 1991–95 vehicles, lift the water shield cover from the cowl on the passenger side.
5. On 1986–90 vehicles, remove the left cowl screen.
6. Remove the windshield wiper mounting arm and pivot shaft retaining clip from the operating arm on the motor by lifting the locking tab up, then pulling the clip away from the pin.

**Fig. 72 Disconnect the power lead from the windshield wiper motor**

7. Remove the attaching screws/bolts from the windshield motor and bracket assembly, then remove the assembly.

**To install:**

8. Position the windshield wiper motor, then install the retaining bolts/screws. Tighten to 60–80 inch lbs. (7–9 Nm).
9. Connect the power lead to the windshield wiper motor.
10. Install the retaining clip on the windshield wiper mounting arm.

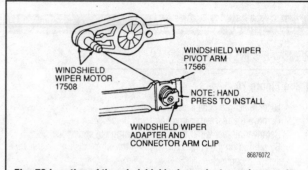

**Fig. 73 Location of the windshield wiper adapter and connector arm clip**

**Fig. 74 Remove the retaining bolts from the motor, then . . .**

**Fig. 75 . . . remove the windshield wiper motor assembly from the vehicle**

11. Install the windshield wiper mounting arm and pivot shaft on the windshield wiper motor. Make sure that the mounting arm and pivot shaft is securely attached to the windshield wiper motor. Install the mounting arm and pivot shaft by pulling until the clip snaps in place.

12. Install the left-hand watershield or cowl screen, as applicable.

13. Connect the positive, then the negative battery cables, then check the wiper operation through all of the modes.

14. Install the left-hand windshield wiper blade.

## Rear Window Wiper Motor

### REMOVAL & INSTALLATION

▶ **See Figure 76**

1. Disconnect the negative battery cable.
2. Remove the rear wiper pivot arm and blade.
3. Remove the rear wiper pivot arm retaining nut and spacers.
4. By pulling on the connector only, not the wires, disengage the wiper motor electrical connector.
5. Remove the nut retaining the rear wiper motor to the handle, then remove the motor.

**To install:**

6. Install the motor to the handle, then secure using the retaining nut.
7. Engage the wiper motor electrical connector.
8. Install the rear wiper pivot arm retaining nut and spacers.
9. Install the rear wiper arm and blade.
10. Connect the negative battery cable.

| | |
|---|---|
| 1 Back window handle | 6 Back window latch striker assy |
| 2 Rear window wiper motor cover | 7 1/16-inch diameter roll pin |
| 3 Rear arm and blade assy | 8 Rear windshield wiper motor |
| 4 Grommet and washer nut | A Tighten to 15-20 Nm (11-14 lb.ft.) |
| 5 Nut and washer assy (2 req'd) | B Tighten to 5-8 Nm (44-53 lb.in.) |

86876075

**Fig. 76 Rear window wiper motor mounting and related components**

## Internal Governor/Windshield Wiper Control Module

### REMOVAL & INSTALLATION

▶ **See Figure 77**

➡ **The internal governor is mounted on a bracket near the steering column support bracket.**

1. Disconnect the negative battery cable.
2. Disengage the electrical connector.
3. Remove the two retaining screws, then remove the component from the vehicle.

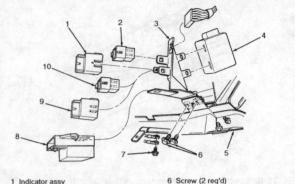

| | |
|---|---|
| 1 Indicator assy | 6 Screw (2 req'd) |
| 2 Relay assy horn | 7 Screw |
| 3 Bracket assy relay panel | 8 Safety belt warning chime assy |
| 4 Windshield wiper control module | 9 Rear window defroster timer (Sable) |
| 5 Instrument panel assy | 10 Relay assy fog lamps (SHO) |

86876076

**Fig. 77 View of the internal governor/windshield wiper control module**

**To install:**

4. Install the component in the vehicle, then secure using the retaining screws.
5. Engage the electrical connector.
6. Connect the negative battery cable, then check the wiper system for proper operation.

## Wiper Linkage

### REMOVAL & INSTALLATION

▶ **See Figure 78**

1. Disconnect the negative battery cable.
2. Remove the wiper pivot arm and blade assembly from the wiper mounting arm and pivot shafts.
3. Remove both the right and left cowl vent screens.
4. Disconnect the linkage drive arm/windshield wiper mounting arm and pivot shaft from the motor crank pin after removing the clip.
5. Remove the screws/bolts retaining the windshield wiper mounting arm and pivot shafts to the cowl. Remove the linkage/wiper mounting arm and pivot shafts from the cowl chamber.

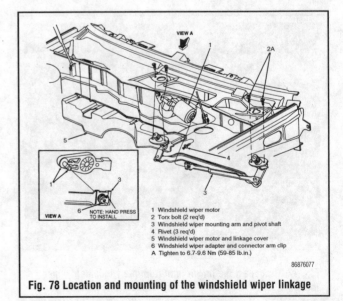

| | |
|---|---|
| 1 Windshield wiper motor | |
| 2 Torx bolt (2 req'd) | |
| 3 Windshield wiper mounting arm and pivot shaft | |
| 4 Rivet (3 req'd) | |
| 5 Windshield wiper motor and linkage cover | |
| 6 Windshield wiper adapter and connector arm clip | |
| A Tighten to 6.7-9.6 Nm (59-85 lb.in.) | |

86876077

**Fig. 78 Location and mounting of the windshield wiper linkage**

**To install:**

6. Install the linkage/wiper mounting arm and pivot shafts in the cowl chamber, then secure using the retaining screws/bolts.

7. Connect the linkage drive arm/wiper mounting arm and pivot shaft to the motor crank pin, then install the clip.

## INSTRUMENTS AND SWITCHES

## Instrument Cluster

### REMOVAL & INSTALLATION

#### Except Electronic Cluster

▶ **See Figures 79, 80, 81 and 82**

1. Disconnect the negative battery cable.

2. Remove the ignition lock cylinder to allow removal of the steering column shrouds.

3. Remove the steering column trim shrouds.

4. Remove the screws retaining the lower left-hand side instrument panel finish panels and radio finish panels, then remove the panels by snapping them out.

5. On the Taurus only, remove the clock assembly (or clock cover) to gain access to the finish panel screw behind the clock.

6. Remove the seven cluster opening finish panel retaining screws, and the jam nut behind the headlight switch. Remove the finish panel by rocking the upper edge toward the driver.

7. On column shift vehicles, disconnect the transaxle selector indicator from the column by removing the retaining screw and cable loop.

8. Disconnect the upper speedometer cable from the lower speedometer cable in the engine compartment.

9. Remove the four cluster-to-instrument panel retaining screws, then pull the cluster assembly forward.

10. Disengage the cluster electrical connector and the speedometer cable. Press the cable latch to disengage the cable from the speedometer head while pulling the cable away from the cluster. Remove the instrument cluster.

**To install:**

11. Position the cluster in front of the cluster opening.

12. Connect the speedometer cable, then engage the electrical connectors.

13. Install the cluster, then secure using the four cluster-to-instrument panel retaining screws.

14. Connect the upper speedometer cable to the lower speedometer cable in the engine compartment.

15. On column shift vehicles, connect the transaxle selector indicator.

16. Install the cluster opening finish panel.

17. On Taurus vehicles, install the clock assembly or clock cover.

18. Install the lower left and radio finish panels.

19. Install the steering column trim shrouds.

20. Install the ignition lock cylinder, then connect the negative battery cable.

8. Install the left and right side cowl vent screens.

9. Install the wiper pivot arm and blade assembly to the wiper arm mounting arm and pivot shafts.

10. Connect the negative battery cable.

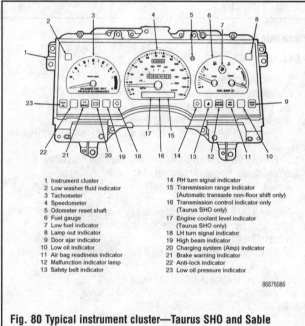

1. Instrument cluster
2. Low washer fluid indicator
3. Tachometer
4. Speedometer
5. Odometer reset shaft
6. Fuel gauge
7. Low fuel indicator
8. Lamp out indicator
9. Door ajar indicator
10. Low oil indicator
11. Air bag readiness indicator
12. Malfunction indicator lamp
13. Safety belt indicator
14. RH turn signal indicator
15. Transmission range indicator (Automatic transaxle non-floor shift only)
16. Transmission control indicator only (Taurus SHO only)
17. Engine coolant level indicator (Taurus SHO only)
18. LH turn signal indicator
19. High beam indicator
20. Charging system (Amp) indicator
21. Brake warning indicator
22. Anti-lock indicator
23. Low oil pressure indicator

86876086

**Fig. 80 Typical instrument cluster—Taurus SHO and Sable**

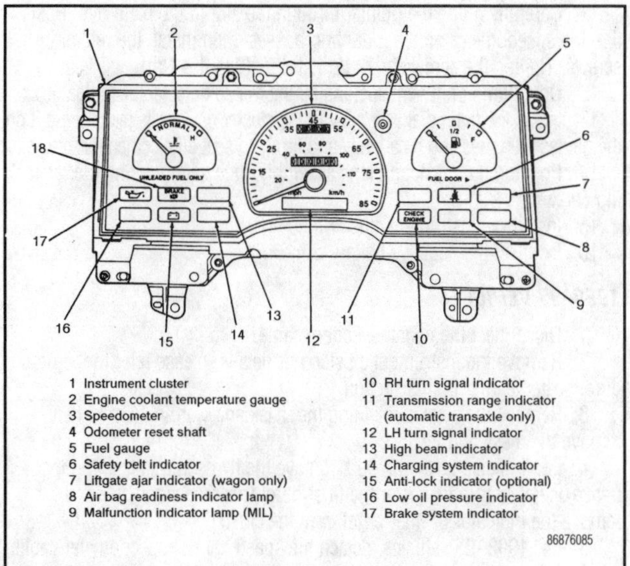

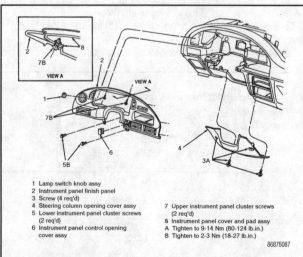

1. Lamp switch knob assy
2. Instrument panel finish panel
3. Screw (4 req'd)
4. Steering column opening cover assy
5. Lower instrument panel cluster screws (2 req'd)
6. Instrument panel control opening cover assy
7. Upper instrument panel cluster screws (2 req'd)
8. Instrument panel cover and pad assy
A. Tighten to 9-14 Nm (80-124 lb.in.)
B. Tighten to 2-3 Nm (18-27 lb.in.)

86876087

**Fig. 81 Exploded view of the instrument cluster mounting—late model Taurus shown**

1. Instrument cluster
2. Engine coolant temperature gauge
3. Speedometer
4. Odometer reset shaft
5. Fuel gauge
6. Safety belt indicator
7. Liftgate ajar indicator (wagon only)
8. Air bag readiness indicator lamp
9. Malfunction indicator lamp (MIL)
10. RH turn signal indicator
11. Transmission range indicator (automatic transaxle only)
12. LH turn signal indicator
13. High beam indicator
14. Charging system indicator
15. Anti-lock indicator (optional)
16. Low oil pressure indicator
17. Brake system indicator

86876085

**Fig. 79 Typical instrument cluster—Base Taurus model**

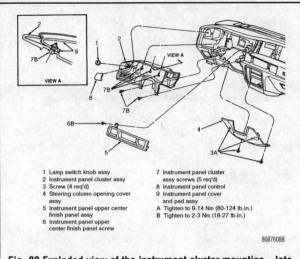

**Fig. 82 Exploded view of the instrument cluster mounting—late model Sable shown**

### Electronic Cluster

▶ **See Figure 83**

1. Disconnect the negative battery cable.
2. Remove the upper and lower steering column shrouds.
3. Remove the steering column cover, then disconnect the shift indicator cable from the cluster by removing the two retaining screws.
4. Disconnect the cluster message center switch module, then remove the cluster trim/finish panel.
5. Remove the cluster mounting screws, then pull the bottom of the instrument cluster toward the steering wheel.
6. Reaching behind and underneath the instrument cluster, disengage the three electrical connectors.
7. Swing the bottom of the cluster out to clear the top of the cluster from the crash pad, then remove the instrument cluster.

**To install:**

8. Insert the top of the cluster under the crash pad, leaving the bottom out.
9. Engage the three electrical connectors.
10. Properly seat the cluster, then install the retaining screws. Tighten the screws to 7–12 inch lbs. (0.8–1.4 Nm).
11. Connect the battery negative battery cable, then check the instrument cluster for proper operation.
12. Connect the shift indicator assembly to the cluster and secure with the retaining screw. Install the steering column cover.
13. Connect the cluster message center switch module to the cluster, then install the cluster trim/finish panel.
14. Install the lower and upper steering column shrouds.

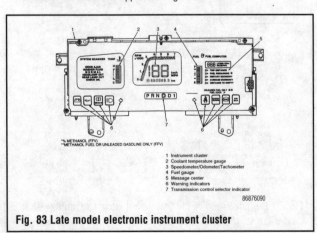

**Fig. 83 Late model electronic instrument cluster**

## Speedometer

### REMOVAL & INSTALLATION

#### Except Electronic Cluster

##### 1986–89 VEHICLES

1. Disconnect the negative battery cable.
2. Remove the instrument cluster finish panel retaining screws, then remove the finish panel. On Sable, remove the lower trim panel attaching screws, then remove the trim panel.
3. Remove the mask-and-lens mounting screws, then remove the mask and lens. If equipped, remove the lower floodlight bulb and socket assemblies.
4. Remove the entire dial assembly from the instrument cluster by carefully pulling it away from the cluster back plate.

➡**The speedometer, tachometer and gauges are mounted to the main dial and some effort may be required to pull the quick-connect electrical terminals from the clips.**

5. On column shift vehicles, remove the screws attaching the transaxle selector indicator to the main dial. Remove the transaxle selector indicator from the main dial/instrument cluster. On Sable and optional Taurus, remove the odometer drive jack shaft and remove the attachment clip at the odometer, slip the jack shaft out of the odometer bracket and speedometer bridge.
6. Pull the reset knob from the trip odometer, if equipped. To remove the speedometer from the main dial, manually rotate the speedometer pointer to align it with the slot in the dial. Remove the mounting screws and carefully pull the speedometer away from the dial, making sure to guide the pointer through the slot.
7. If necessary, remove the odometer assembly by pulling the reset knob from the lever.

**To install:**

8. Position the odometer on the mounting bosses, then install the retaining screws. Tighten the screws to 7–12 inch lbs. (0.8–1.4 Nm).
9. If removed, install the trip odometer reset knob.
10. Carefully position the speedometer pointer parallel to the rectangular raised portion of the speedometer dial.

### ✳✳ WARNING

**The speedometer is calibrated at the factory. Overly rough handling could disturb the calibration.**

11. Carefully guide the pointer through the slot in the main dial. Position the speedometer on the mounting bosses, then install the retaining screws. Tighten the screws to 7–12 inch lbs. (0.8–1.4 Nm).
12. On column shift vehicles, install the transaxle selector indicator.
13. Install the main dial assembly to the cluster back plate by aligning it on the guides then pressing it carefully and firmly to seat all electrical terminals.
14. Position the mask and lens assembly, then secure using the retaining screws.
15. Install the instrument cluster finish panel.
16. Connect the negative battery cable.

##### 1990–95 VEHICLES

1. Disconnect the negative battery cable.
2. Remove the instrument cluster. For details, please refer to the procedure located earlier in this section.
3. Remove the screws retaining the mask and warning lamp, then remove the mask and lens.
4. For vehicles through 1992, remove the two screws attaching the transaxle selector indicator or the filler bezel to the speedometer and remove the indicator or filler bezel from the cluster.
5. For 1993–95 vehicles, detach the speed control speedometer cable.
6. Lift the speedometer from the instrument cluster.

**To install:**

7. For 1993–95 vehicles, position the speedometer assembly to the

back plate, then attach the speed control speedometer cable, if removed, then install.

8. For 1990–92 vehicles, align the speedometer with the pins, then press carefully and firmly to seat the speedometer dial on the locators. Install the transmission selector indicator or filler bezel, and secure using the retaining screws.

9. Position the instrument cluster mask and instrument cluster warning lamp lens assembly to the back plate, then secure it using the retaining screws.

10. Install the instrument cluster. For details, please refer to the procedure located earlier in this section.

11. Connect the negative battery cable, then check for proper operation of the speedometer.

### Electronic Cluster

#### 1988–89 VEHICLES

1. Disconnect the negative battery cable.
2. Remove the instrument cluster assembly. For details, please refer to the procedure located earlier in this section.
3. Using a clean cloth to protect the lens, place the cluster face down on a bench.
4. Remove the five black hex head screws attaching the back plate to the mask assembly.
5. Carefully remove the speedometer and fuel computer flex circuit from their respective locating pins.
6. With even pressure on both sides of the back plate, lift up on the back plate to separate it from the mask assembly.

➡**The area near the gauge clips will cause the most resistance.**

7. Turn the cluster assembly over and disconnect the switch connector from the mask assembly by squeezing in on the retaining clips and pushing the connector through the hole in the mask.

8. Remove the four screws attaching the speedometer to the mask assembly, then remove the speedometer assembly.

**To install:**

9. Install the speedometer module with the flex circuit and switch connector toward the gauge side of the cluster.
10. Install the four speedometer retaining screws.
11. Push the switch connector through the hole in the mask.

➡**Make sure that the wires are routed to the top of the mask, out of the way of the gauges.**

12. Position the back plate onto the mask assembly making sure that the speedometer and fuel computer flex circuits are fed through their respective holes.

13. With the back plate properly aligned to the mask assembly, push down firmly on the gauge clips to seat the gauges properly into the clips.

14. Carefully position the speedometer and fuel computing flex circuits over their respective locating pins.

15. Install the five back plate-to-mask assembly screws.

16. Install the instrument cluster. For details regarding, please refer to the procedure located earlier in this section.

17. Connect the negative battery cable.

#### 1990–95 VEHICLES

The speedometer is part of a single electronic instrument cluster module and cannot be removed separately.

### Tachometer

## REMOVAL & INSTALLATION

### Except Electronic Cluster

1. Disconnect the negative battery cable.
2. Remove the instrument cluster.

3. Remove the cluster main lens and mask retaining screws, then remove the mask and lens.
4. Remove the tachometer from the gauge clips by pulling the tachometer from the instrument cluster back plate.

**To install:**

➡**The tachometer is calibrated at the factory. Excessive rough handling could disturb the calibration.**

5. Carefully position the tachometer over the gauge clips.
6. Being careful not the get fingerprints on the applique, press the tachometer into the gauge clips in the cluster back plate.
7. Install the cluster mask and lens using the retaining screws, then install the instrument cluster.
8. Connect the negative battery cable.

### Electronic Cluster

The tachometer is part of a single electronic instrument cluster module and cannot be removed separately.

### Fuel Gauge

## REMOVAL & INSTALLATION

1. Disconnect the negative battery cable.
2. Remove the instrument cluster finish panel retaining screws, then remove the finish panel.
3. On vehicles equipped with a tachometer, remove the lower trim panel retaining screws, then remove the lower trim panel.
4. Remove the mask and lens mounting screws, then remove the cluster mask and warning lamp lens.

➡**The lower flood lamp bulb filters are not secured and may fall out.**

5. On vehicles equipped with a tachometer, remove the two lower flood lamp bulb and socket assemblies.

➡**The gauges are mounted to the main dial, and some effort may be required to pull the quick connect electrical terminals from the clips.**

6. Lift the main dial assembly from the instrument cluster assembly back plate.
7. On column shift vehicles only, remove the two screws retaining the transmission range indicator to the main dial, them remove the transmission range indicator from the cluster.
8. Manually rotate the fuel gauge pointer to align it with the slot in the dial. Remove the mounting screws and carefully pull the fuel gauge away from the dial, guiding the pointer through the slot.

**To install:**

9. Carefully position the pointer parallel to the rectangular raised portion of the dial.
10. Guide the pointer carefully through the slot in the main dial. Then position the fuel gauge on mounting bosses, then install the mounting screws. Tighten the screw to 8–12 inch lbs. (0.8–1.4 Nm).
11. On column shift vehicles, install the transmission control selector indicator.
12. Install the main dial assembly to instrument cluster back plate by aligning it on the guides. Press carefully and firmly to seat all electrical terminals.
13. On vehicles equipped with a tachometer, install the two lower flood lamp bulb and socket assemblies.
14. Position the mask and lens assembly, then install the cluster mask and warning lamp lenses retaining screws.
15. Install the instrument finish panel.
16. Connect the negative battery cable.

## Engine Coolant Temperature Gauge

### REMOVAL & INSTALLATION

The engine coolant temperature gauge is integral to the fuel gauge. Refer to the fuel gauge removal and installation procedure for more information.

## Windshield Wiper Switch

### REMOVAL & INSTALLATION

The front windshield wiper switch is located deep inside the steering column assembly and is actuated by the multi-function lever on the left of the steering column. For details concerning removal and installation, please refer to the steering column procedures located in Section 8 of this manual.

## Rear Window Wiper Switch

### REMOVAL & INSTALLATION

#### 1986–89 Vehicles

1. Disconnect the negative battery cable.
2. Remove the four cluster opening finish panel retaining screws, then remove the finish panel by rocking the upper edge toward the driver.
3. Disengage the electrical wiring connector from the rear wiper switch.
4. Remove the wiper switch from the instrument panel. On Sable, the switch is retained with two screws.

**To install:**

5. Push the rear washer switch into the cluster finish panel until it snaps into place. On Sable, install the two retaining screws.
6. Engage the electrical wiring connector.
7. Install the cluster opening finish panel, then secure using the four retaining screws.
8. Connect the negative battery cable.

#### 1990–95 Vehicles

▶ See Figure 84

1. Disconnect the negative battery cable.
2. Remove the cluster opening finish panel as follows:
   a. Disconnect the positive battery cable.
   b. Engage the parking brake.
   c. Remove the ignition lock cylinder.
   d. If equipped with a tilt column, tilt the column to the full down position and remove the tilt lever.
   e. Remove the four bolts and the opening cover from under the steering column.

f. Remove the steering column trim shrouds. Disconnect all electrical connections from the multi-function switch.
   g. Remove the two screws retaining the multi-function switch, then remove the switch.
   h. Pull the gear shift lever to the full down position.
   i. Remove the cluster opening finish panel retaining screws. There are four retaining screws on the Taurus and five on the Sable.
   j. Remove the finish panel by pulling it toward the driver to unsnap the snap-in retainers and disconnect the wiring from the switches, clock and warning lights.
3. Disengage the electrical wiring connector from the rear wiper/washer switch.
4. Remove the washer switch from the cluster finish panel.

**To install:**

5. Push the rear washer switch into the cluster finish panel until it snaps into place.
6. Engage the wiring connector to the rear wiper/washer switch.
7. Install the cluster finish panel as follows:
   a. Engage the electrical wiring to the switches, clock and warning lights, then install the finish panel by snapping it into place.
   b. Install the cluster opening finish panel retaining screws.
   c. Place the gear shift lever to its original position.
   d. Install the multi-function switch by engaging the electrical connectors, then secure using the retaining screws.
   e. Install the steering column shrouds.
   f. Install the opening cover from under the steering column and secure using the retaining bolts.
   g. If removed, install the tilt lever, then return the column to its original position.
   h. Install the ignition lock cylinder.
   i. Disengage the parking brake, then connect the positive battery cable.
8. Connect the negative battery cable.

## Headlight Switch

### REMOVAL & INSTALLATION

#### 1986–89 Taurus

▶ See Figure 85

1. Disconnect the negative battery cable.
2. Pull off the headlight switch knob.
3. Remove the bezel retaining nut, then remove the bezel.
4. Remove the instrument cluster finish panel.
5. Remove the two screws retaining the headlight switch, then pull the switch out of the instrument panel, disengage the electrical connector, then remove the switch.

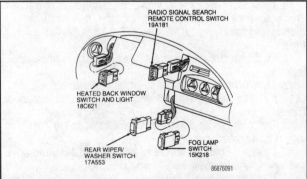

**Fig. 84 Location of the rear wiper/washer switch—Taurus shown, Sable similar**

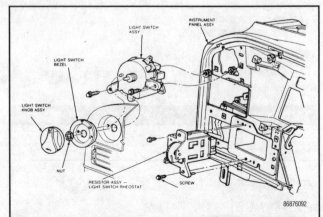

**Fig. 85 Taurus headlight switch location—1986–89 vehicles**

**To install:**

6. Position the switch, engage the electrical connector, then install the switch securing with the two retaining screws.

7. Install the instrument cluster finish panel.

8. Install the bezel, then secure using the retaining nut.

9. Fasten the headlight switch knob.

10. Connect the negative battery cable.

### 1986–89 Sable

▶ **See Figure 86**

1. Disconnect the negative battery cable.

2. Remove the lower left-hand finish panel.

3. Remove the two screws retaining the headlight switch to the finish panel, then disengage the electrical connector and remove the switch.

**To install:**

4. Position the switch, engage the electrical connector, then install the switch using the two retaining screws.

5. Install the lower left-hand finish panel.

6. Connect the negative battery cable.

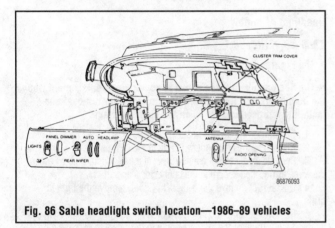

**Fig. 86 Sable headlight switch location—1986–89 vehicles**

### 1990–95 Vehicles

1. Disconnect the negative battery cable.

2. Pull off the headlight switch knob, then remove the retaining nut.

3. Remove the instrument cluster finish panel as follows:

a. Disconnect the negative battery cable.

b. Apply the parking brake.

c. Remove the ignition lock cylinder.

d. If equipped with a tilt column, tilt the column to the most downward position, then remove the tilt lever.

e. Remove the four bolts and opening cover from under the steering column.

f. Remove the steering column trim shrouds. Disengage all electrical connections from the steering column multi-function switch.

g. Remove the two screws retaining the multi-function switch, then remove the switch.

h. Pull the gear shift lever to the full down position.

i. Remove the four cluster opening finish panel retaining screws. Remove the finish panel by pulling it toward the driver to unsnap the snap-in retainers and disconnect the wiring from the switches, clock and warning lights.

4. Remove the two screws retaining the headlight switch to the instrument panel, pull the switch out of the instrument panel, disengage the electrical connector, then remove the switch.

**To install:**

5. Position the headlight switch, then engage the electrical connector. Install the switch in the instrument panel, then secure using the two retaining screws.

6. Install the cluster finish panel as follows:

a. Engage the electrical wiring to the switches, clock and warning lights, then install the finish panel by snapping it into place.

b. Install the cluster opening finish panel retaining screws.

c. Place the gear shift lever to its original position.

d. Install the multi-function switch by engaging the electrical connectors, then secure using the retaining screws.

e. Install the steering column shrouds.

f. Install the opening cover from under the steering column and secure using the retaining bolts.

g. If removed, install the tilt lever, then return the column to its original position.

h. Install the ignition lock cylinder.

i. Disengage the parking brake, then connect the positive battery cable.

7. Install the retaining nut, then connect the headlight switch knob.

8. Connect the negative battery cable.

## LIGHTING

### Headlights

#### REMOVAL & INSTALLATION

**Bulb Replacement**

▶ **See Figures 87, 88 and 89**

### ❋❋ CAUTION

**The replaceable Halogen headlamp bulb contains gas under pressure. The bulb may shatter if the glass envelope is scratched or the bulb is dropped. Handle the bulb carefully. Grasp the bulb ONLY by its plastic base. Avoid touching the glass envelope because the oils in your hand may cause the bulb to burst when turned on. Keep the bulb out of the reach of children.**

1. Disconnect the negative battery cable.

2. Check to see that the headlight switch is in the OFF position.

3. Raise the hood and locate the bulb and retainer installed in the rear of the headlight body.

4. Remove the electrical connector from the bulb by grasping the wires firmly and snapping the connector rearward.

5. Remove the bulb retaining ring by rotating it counterclockwise (when viewed from the rear) about ⅛ of a turn, then slide the ring off the plastic base.

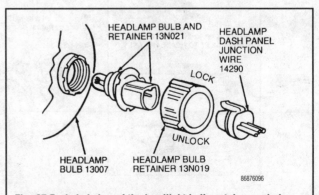

**Fig. 87 Exploded view of the headlight bulb, retainer and electrical connector**

**Fig. 88 On some vehicles, such as this early model Taurus, it it possible to remove the headlight bulb and electrical connector as an assembly**

**Fig. 89 After removing the bulb/connector assembly, gently pull the light bulb from the socket for replacement**

➡Keep the bulb retaining ring, since it will be reused with the new bulb.

6. Carefully remove the headlight bulb from its socket in the reflector by gently pulling it straight backward out of the socket. DO NOT rotate the bulb during removal.

**To install:**

7. With the flat side of the plastic base of the bulb facing upward, insert the glass envelope of the bulb into the socket. Turn the base slightly to the left or right, if necessary to align the grooves in the forward part of the plastic base with the corresponding locating tabs inside the socket. When the grooves are aligned, push the bulb firmly into the socket until the mounting flange on the base contacts the rear face of the socket.

8. Slip the bulb retaining ring over the rear of the plastic base against the mounting flange. Lock the ring into the socket by rotating the ring counterclockwise. A stop will be felt when the retaining ring is fully engaged.

9. Push the electrical connector into the rear of the plastic until it snaps and locks into position.

10. Turn the headlights on and check for proper operation.

11. Connect the negative battery cable.

**Headlight Assembly**

*1986–88 VEHICLES*

▶ **See Figures 90 thru 98**

➡The headlamps on these vehicles do not need replacement when the bulb burns out. Refer to bulb replacement for removal and installation procedures for when the bulb burns out.

1. Disconnect the negative battery cable.

2. Make sure the headlight switch is in the OFF position.

3. Remove the electrical connector from the headlight bulb by grasping the wires firmly, then snapping the connector rearward.

4. On Taurus, remove the grille. On Sable, remove the lighted grille.

5. Remove the lamp just outboard of the headlight; the side marker lamp on the Taurus, or the combination park/turn/side marker lamp on the Sable.

6. On the Taurus only, remove the park/turn lamp bulb and connector.

7. Remove the two bolts attaching the headlight housing to the fender.

8. Remove the three bolts (Taurus) or four bolts (Sable) attaching the headlight housing to the brackets.

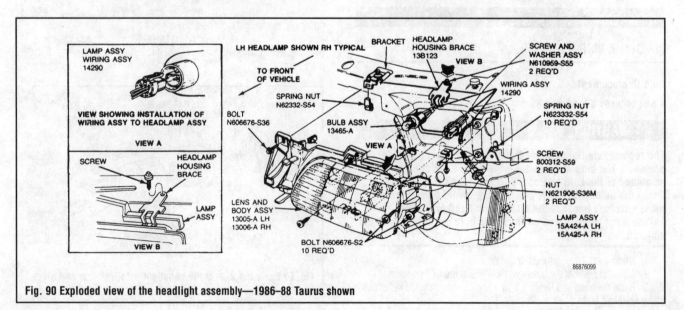

**Fig. 90 Exploded view of the headlight assembly—1986–88 Taurus shown**

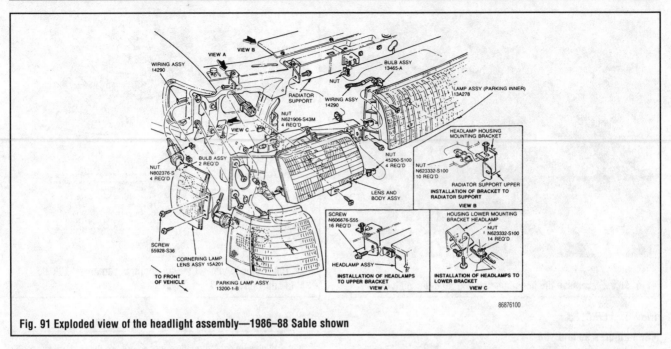

Fig. 91 Exploded view of the headlight assembly—1986–88 Sable shown

9. Remove the three screws attaching the lens and body assembly to the headlight housing, then remove the headlight housing.

**To install:**

10. Position the headlight housing, then install the three screws attaching lens and body assembly.

11. Depending upon vehicle application, install the three or four bolts attaching the headlight housing to the brackets.

12. Install the two bolts attaching the headlight housing to the fender.

13. On Taurus only, install the park/turn lamp bulb and connector.

14. Install the grille or lighted grille, as applicable.

15. Engage the headlight bulb electrical connector.

16. Connect the negative battery cable, then turn on the headlights to check for proper operation and aim if necessary.

Fig. 92 On Taurus, detach the grille retainers, then remove the grille

Fig. 93 Once the grille is removed, you can access the headlight assembly retaining bolts and screws

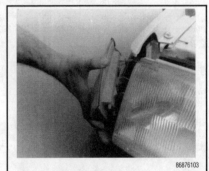

Fig. 94 Unfasten the retainers, then remove the side marker lamp (Taurus only)

Fig. 95 Remove the two bolts attaching the headlight housing to the fender

Fig. 96 When removing the retaining bolts, be careful not to drop any into the engine compartment

Fig. 97 Remove the headlight assembly retaining bolts, then . . .

Fig. 98 . . . remove the headlight housing from the vehicle

### 1989–95 VEHICLES

▶ See Figures 99 and 100

1. Disconnect the negative battery cable.
2. Make sure the headlight switch and the headlight time delay switch (if equipped) are in the OFF position.

➡ Use snapring pliers to spread the retainer.

3. Remove the headlight electrical connector from the headlight bulb and retainer by grasping the wires firmly, then snapping the connector rearward.
4. Remove the parking lamp miniature bulb and connector.
5. Remove the three retainers holding the headlight to the radiator grille opening panel reinforcement, then remove the headlight.

**To install:**

6. Install the headlight and secure using the three retainers.
7. Install the parking lamp miniature bulb and connector.
8. Engage the headlight electrical connector by pushing the connector until it snaps into position.
9. Connect the negative battery cable, then turn on the headlights to check for proper operation and aim if necessary.

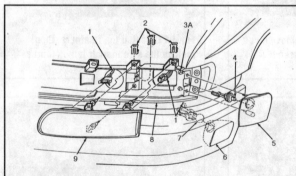

| | | |
|---|---|---|
| 1 Headlamp dash panel junction wire | 6 | Cornering lamp (part of bumper assy) |
| 2 Headlamp mounting clip (6 req'd) | 7 | Miniature bulb (2req'd) |
| 3 Nut (4 req'd) | 8 | Front bumper |
| 4 Front fender side lmap socket and wire (2 req'd) | 9 | Headlamp assy |
| 5 Front side marker lamp assy | A | Tighten to 5.2-7.2 Nm (47-63 lb.in.) |

86876108

Fig. 99 Exploded view of the headlight assembly—1989–95 Taurus, except SHO

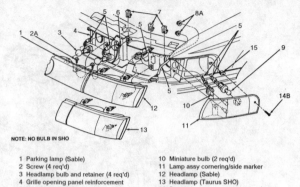

NOTE: NO BULB IN SHO

| | | |
|---|---|---|
| 1 Parking lamp (Sable) | 10 | Miniature bulb (2 req'd) |
| 2 Screw (4 req'd) | 11 | Lamp assy cornering/side marker |
| 3 Headlamp bulb and retainer (4 req'd) | 12 | Headlamp (Sable) |
| 4 Grille opening panel reinforcement | 13 | Headlamp (Taurus SHO) |
| 5 Headlamp dash panel junction wire | 14 | Screw |
| 6 Nut (4 req'd) (Sable) | 15 | Nut (2 req'd) |
| 7 Retainer/headlamp (6 req'd) | A | Tighten to 5.2-7.2 Nm (47-63 lb.in.) |
| 8 Nut (4 req'd) | B | Tighten to 0.8-1.7 Nm (7-15 lb.in.) |
| 9 Miniature bulb (2 req'd) | | |

86876109

Fig. 100 Exploded view of the headlight assembly—1989–95 Sable and Taurus SHO

## AIMING

The headlights must be properly aimed to provide the best, safest road illumination. The lights should be checked for proper aim and adjusted as necessary. Certain state and local authorities have requirements for headlight aiming; these should be checked before adjustment is made.

Headlight adjustment may be temporarily made using a wall, or on the rear of another vehicle. When adjusted, the lights should not glare in oncoming car or truck windshields, nor should they illuminate the passenger compartment of vehicles driving in front of you.

To aim the headlights in these vehicles, you must use Rotunda Aiming Kit 107-00001 with Adapter Kit 107-00011, or equivalent. All adjustments should be made with at least a half tank of gas in the fuel tank, an empty trunk except for the spare tire and jack and the correct tire pressures. The equipment in the aiming kit can be calibrated to accommodate a slight floor slope, but the floor should be reasonably flat. Set up and use the equipment as described in the instructions included in the headlight aiming kit.

## Signal and Marker Lights

### REMOVAL & INSTALLATION

#### Parking/Front Turn Signal Light Combination

The parking and turn signal lights share the same dual filament bulb. The parking/turn signal lamp assembly is part of the headlight assembly. To remove the parking/turn signal housing, please refer to the headlight assembly removal and installation procedure. The following procedures are for bulb replacement only.

### EXCEPT 1986–88 SABLE

▶ See Figures 101 and 102

1. Disconnect the negative battery cable.
2. Using the access hole in the radiator support, rotate the bulb socket counterclockwise to disengage it from the light housing, then remove the bulb.

**To install:**

3. Using the access hole in the radiator support, rotate the bulb socket clockwise to engage the socket into the housing.
4. Connect the negative battery cable.

Fig. 101 Using the access hole in the radiator support, rotate the bulb socket counterclockwise to disengage it from the light housing then . . .

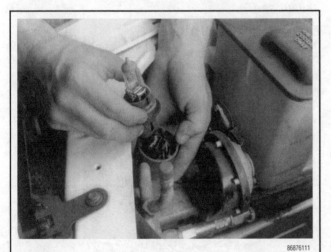

Fig. 102 . . . remove the bulb by pulling it straight out from the socket

### 1986–88 SABLE

1. Disconnect the negative battery cable.
2. Remove the two screws attaching the parking lamp assembly, then pull it forward.
3. Remove the bulb socket by twisting, then remove the bulb.

**To install:**

4. Install the bulb in the socket, then install the socket in the lamp assembly by twisting.
5. Position the parking lamp in place, then install the retaining screws.
6. Connect the negative battery cable.

### Side Marker Lights

#### TAURUS

◆ See Figures 103, 104, 105, 106 and 107

1. Disconnect the negative battery cable.
2. Remove the nut(s) and washer(s) from the attaching stud at the top of the lamp assembly.

3. Rotate the top outboard until the stud tip has cleared the slot in the housing.
4. Lift the lamp to clear the two lower tabs (on the headlamp) from the headlamp housing.
5. Remove the socket by twisting it counterclockwise, then pull the bulb from the socket.

**To install:**

6. Install the bulb into the socket, and install the socket by twisting it clockwise.
7. Position the lamp in place by lowering the two tabs on the lamp into the two slots on the headlamp housing.
8. Rotate the lamp inboard to allow the stud to enter the upper slot in the housing.
9. Install the nut and washer to the attaching stud, and secure |them.
10. Connect the negative battery cable.

**Side Marker Lamp, Front**
**Taurus**

**Removal**

1. Remove one nut and washer from attaching stud at top of lamp assembly.
2. Rotate top of lamp outboard until stud tip has cleared slot in grille opening reinforcement.
3. Lift lamp to clear lower tab from grille opening panel reinforcement.
4. Remove bulb socket by twisting

**Installation**

1. Install bulb, if removed, and install bulb socket by twisting clockwise.
2. Position lamp in place by inserting tab on bottom of lamp lowering tab into slot on grille opening panel reinforcement.
3. Rotate lamp inboard to allow stud to enter upper slot in grille opening reinforcement.

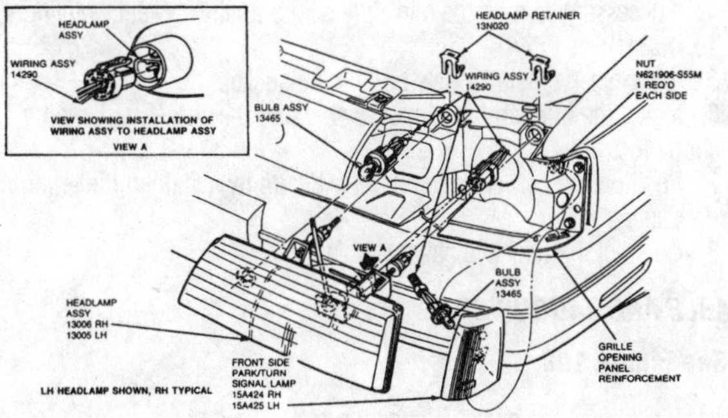

Fig. 103 Exploded view of the side marker light and related components—1989 Taurus shown

Fig. 104 Remove the nut and washer from the attaching stud at the top of the lamp assembly

**Fig. 105 Remove the lamp to clear the tab(s) on the headlamp housing**

**Fig. 106 Remove the socket by twisting it counterclockwise**

**Fig. 107 If the bulb needs to be replaced, remove it by pulling it straight out from the socket**

### Cornering Lights

#### 1990–95 TAURUS—EXCEPT SHO

1. Disconnect the negative battery cable.
2. Remove the cornering lamp retaining nuts/screws, then lift the cornering lamp from its mounting.
3. Remove the bulb and socket assembly by twisting counterclockwise, then remove the cornering lamp from the vehicle.
4. If necessary, remove the miniature bulb from the socket by pulling it out.

**To install:**

5. If necessary, install a new bulb in the socket.
6. Install the bulb and socket assembly into the cornering lamp by twisting clockwise.
7. Position the cornering lamp, then secure by installing the retaining screws/nuts.
8. Connect the negative battery cable.

#### SABLE AND TAURUS SHO

▶ See Figure 108

1. Disconnect the negative battery cable.
2. Remove the two screws attaching the cornering lamp assembly and lift it out.
3. Remove the bulb by twisting it counterclockwise.

**To install:**

4. Install the bulb, if removed, then install the socket by turning it clockwise.

**Fig. 108 Cornering lamp assembly—earlier model Sable shown**

5. Position the cornering light back in place, and install the two screws.
6. Connect the negative battery cable.

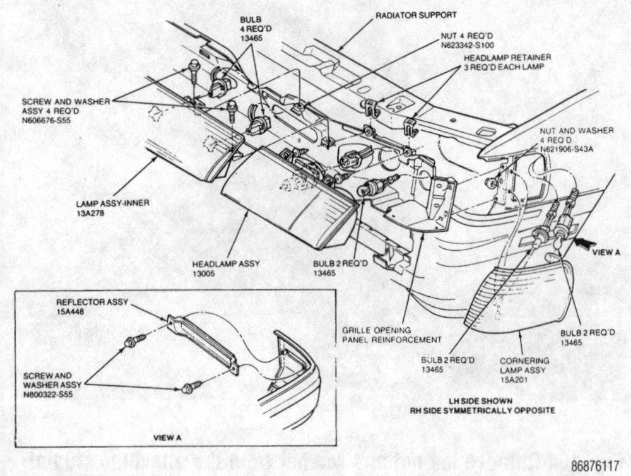

### Auxiliary Headlight Assembly

#### TAURUS SHO

▶ See Figure 109

1. Disconnect the negative battery cable.
2. Remove the headlight assembly.
3. Remove the two screws attaching the auxiliary headlight to the headlight assembly.

**To install:**

4. Connect the auxiliary headlight assembly using the two attaching screws.
5. Install the headlight assembly.
6. Connect the battery cable.

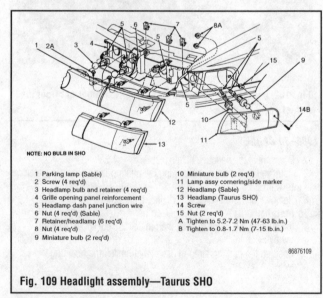

NOTE: NO BULB IN SHO

1 Parking lamp (Sable)
2 Screw (4 req'd)
3 Headlamp bulb and retainer (4 req'd)
4 Grille opening panel reinforcement
5 Headlamp dash panel junction wire
6 Nut (4 req'd) (Sable)
7 Retainer/headlamp (6 req'd)
8 Nut (4 req'd)
9 Miniature bulb (2 req'd)

10 Miniature bulb (2 req'd)
11 Lamp assy cornering/side marker
12 Headlamp (Sable)
13 Headlamp (Taurus SHO)
14 Screw
15 Nut (2 req'd)
A Tighten to 5.2–7.2 Nm (47–63 lb.in.)
B Tighten to 0.8–1.7 Nm (7–15 lb.in.)

**Fig. 109 Headlight assembly—Taurus SHO**

### Rear Turn Signal/Brake Lights

#### SEDAN

▶ See Figures 110, 111, 112 and 113

Bulbs can be serviced from the inside of the luggage compartment by removing the luggage compartment rear trim panel, if so equipped.

1. Disconnect the negative battery cable.
2. From inside the trunk, remove the lower back panel trim cover.

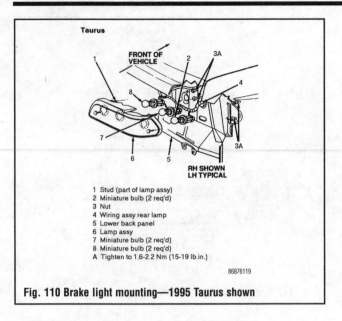

1 Stud (part of lamp assy)
2 Miniature bulb (2 req'd)
3 Nut
4 Wiring assy rear lamp
5 Lower back panel
6 Lamp assy
7 Miniature bulb (2 req'd)
8 Miniature bulb (2 req'd)
A Tighten to 1.6-2.2 Nm (15-19 lb.in.)

86876119

Fig. 110 Brake light mounting—1995 Taurus shown

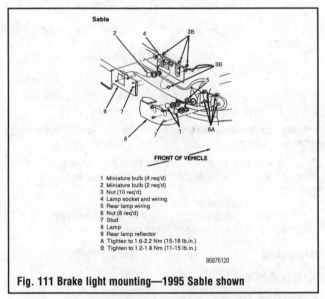

1 Miniature bulb (4 req'd)
2 Miniature bulb (2 req'd)
3 Nut (10 req'd)
4 Lamp socket and wiring
5 Rear lamp wiring
6 Nut (8 req'd)
7 Stud
8 Lamp
9 Rear lamp reflector
A Tighten to 1.6-2.2 Nm (15-19 lb.in.)
B Tighten to 1.2-1.8 Nm (11-15 lb.in.)

86876120

Fig. 111 Brake light mounting—1995 Sable shown

86876121

Fig. 112 To access the rear lights, the lower back panel trim cover must be removed

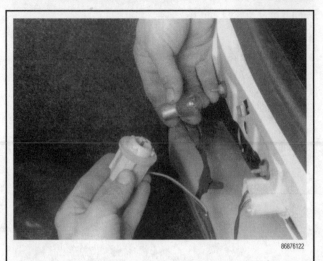

86876122

Fig. 113 Pull the bulb straight out to remove it from the socket assembly

3. Remove the nuts securing the rear lamp to the lower back panel, then pull the rear lamp away from the vehicle.

4. Remove the socket(s) from the lamp body and replace the bulb(s), if necessary.

**To install:**

5. Install the bulb, if necessary, then install the socket(s) in the lamp body.

6. Install the lamp and use the retaining screws to secure it.

7. Install the trim cover, then connect the negative battery cable.

### STATION WAGON

♦ **See Figure 114**

1. Disconnect the negative battery cable.

2. Remove the two screws securing the rear lamp to the quarter panel.

3. Remove the lamp socket and wiring from the lamp, then remove the lamp from the vehicle.

4. If necessary, replace the bulb.

**To install:**

5. Install the lamp socket and wiring to the rear lamp.

6. Position the rear lamp to the quarter panel, then secure using the two retaining screws.

7. Connect the negative battery cable.

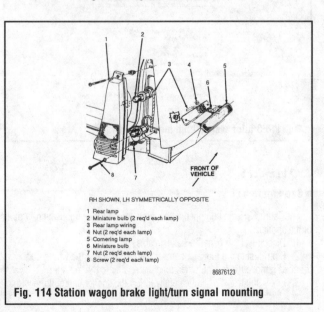

RH SHOWN, LH SYMMETRICALLY OPPOSITE

1 Rear lamp
2 Miniature bulb (2 req'd each lamp)
3 Rear lamp wiring
4 Nut (2 req'd each lamp)
5 Cornering lamp
6 Miniature bulb
7 Nut (2 req'd each lamp)
8 Screw (2 req'd each lamp)

86876123

Fig. 114 Station wagon brake light/turn signal mounting

**High Mount Brake Light**

*EXCEPT SHO*

▶ **See Figures 115 and 116**

1. Disconnect the negative battery cable.
2. On the sedan, remove the two covers and screws that retain the lamp assembly to the retainer, then disengage the electrical connector.
3. On the wagon, remove the lamp assembly trim cover at the top of the liftgate frame. Remove the two plugs, then remove the four retaining nuts retaining the lamp trim cover.
4. Remove the lamp assembly from its mounting.
5. Installation is the reverse of the removal procedure.

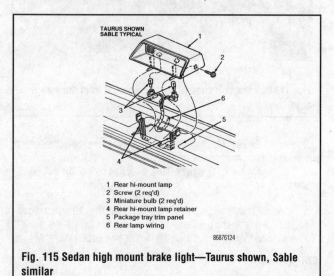

1 Rear hi-mount lamp
2 Screw (2 req'd)
3 Miniature bulb (2 req'd)
4 Rear hi-mount lamp retainer
5 Package tray trim panel
6 Rear lamp wiring

86876124

**Fig. 115 Sedan high mount brake light—Taurus shown, Sable similar**

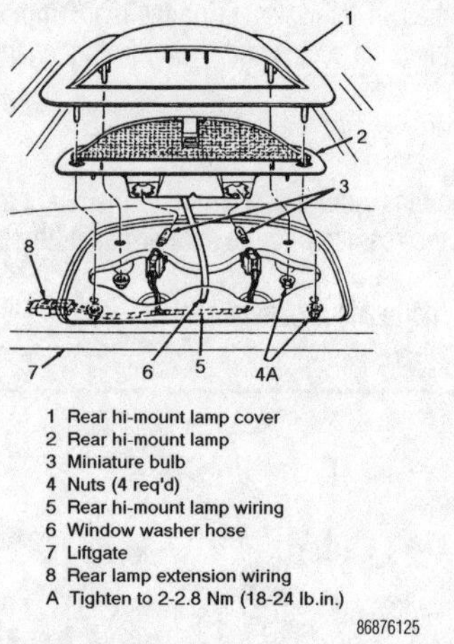

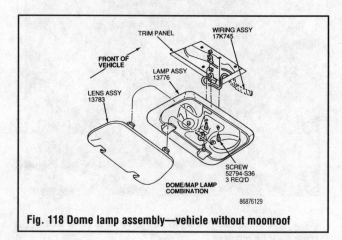

1 Rear hi-mount lamp cover
2 Rear hi-mount lamp
3 Miniature bulb
4 Nuts (4 req'd)
5 Rear hi-mount lamp wiring
6 Window washer hose
7 Liftgate
8 Rear lamp extension wiring
A Tighten to 2-2.8 Nm (18-24 lb.in.)

86876125

**Fig. 116 Station wagon high mount brake light**

*SHO VEHICLES*

▶ **See Figure 117**

The Taurus SHO is equipped with a high-mount brake light which is part of the spoiler.

1. Disconnect the negative battery cable.
2. From inside the luggage compartment, disengage the wiring connector, then remove the five nuts retaining the spoiler to the trunk lid.
3. Lower the trunk lid and carefully lift up the spoiler and pull the wiring

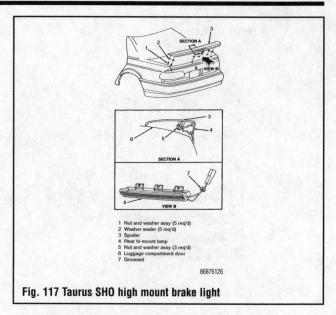

1 Nut and washer assy (5 req'd)
2 Washer sealer (5 req'd)
3 Spoiler
4 Rear hi-mount lamp
5 Nut and washer assy (3 req'd)
6 Luggage compartment door
7 Grommet

86876126

**Fig. 117 Taurus SHO high mount brake light**

grommet out of the luggage compartment door, then remove the spoiler from the trunk lid.
4. Turn the spoiler over, then lay it on a protective surface to avoid scratching it.
5. Remove the three nuts retaining the rear high-mount brake light to the spoiler, then remove the light from the spoiler.

**To install:**

6. Position the rear-high mount lamp to the spoiler, then install the three retaining nuts and tighten the lamp securely to the spoiler.

➡ **Make sure the sealer washers are on the five studs before setting it on the trunk lid.**

7. Align the studs on the spoiler to the holes in the luggage compartment door, route the wiring through hole in the trunk lid, then install the grommet.
8. Engage the electrical wiring connector.
9. Connect the negative battery cable, then depress the brake pedal to make sure the rear hi-mount lamp is functioning properly.

**Dome Light**

*WITHOUT MOONROOF*

▶ **See Figure 118**

1. Disconnect the negative battery cable.
2. Carefully squeeze the lens inward to release the locking tabs.

**Fig. 118 Dome lamp assembly—vehicle without moonroof**

3. Remove the lens from the lamp body. If necessary, replace the defective bulb.

4. Installation is the reverse of the removal procedure.

### WITH MOONROOF

◆ **See Figure 119**

1. Disconnect the negative battery cable.
2. Use a thin bladed tool and carefully pry out and unsnap the lens.
3. Replace the defective bulb.
4. Installation is the reverse of the removal procedure.

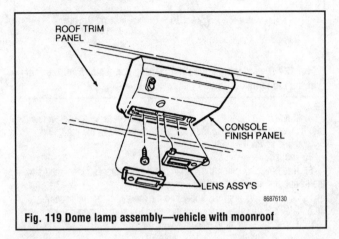

**Fig. 119 Dome lamp assembly—vehicle with moonroof**

### License Plate Lights

◆ **See Figures 120 and 121**

1. Disconnect the negative battery cable.
2. Remove the two lamp body plastic retaining rivets.
3. Remove the lamp assembly.
4. Remove the socket and bulb assembly from the rear of the lamp assembly. If necessary, replace the defective bulb.

**To install:**

5. Install the socket and bulb assembly to the lamp assembly.
6. Install the lamp assembly, then secure using the plastic rivets.
7. Connect the negative battery cable.

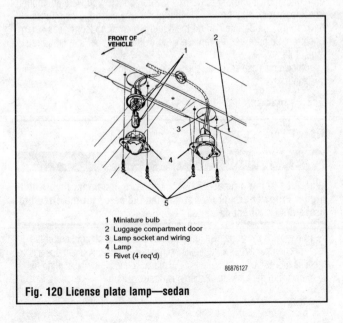

1 Miniature bulb
2 Luggage compartment door
3 Lamp socket and wiring
4 Lamp
5 Rivet (4 req'd)

86876127

**Fig. 120 License plate lamp—sedan**

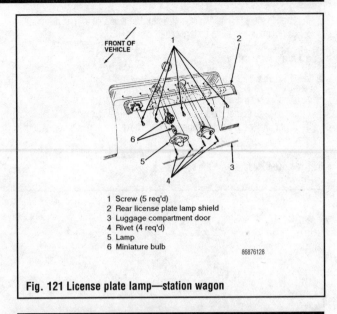

1 Screw (5 req'd)
2 Rear license plate lamp shield
3 Luggage compartment door
4 Rivet (4 req'd)
5 Lamp
6 Miniature bulb

86876128

**Fig. 121 License plate lamp—station wagon**

---

### Fog/Driving Lights

The Taurus SHO is the only vehicle covered by this manual which is equipped with fog lamps.

REMOVAL & INSTALLATION

**Fog Lamp Bulb**

◆ **See Figure 122**

➡ **If you are only replacing the bulb, you don't have to remove the fog lamp mounting bracket or fog lamp assembly.**

1. Disconnect the negative battery cable.
2. Disengage the electrical wiring connector from the fog lamp miniature bulb.

➡ **Do NOT touch the glass part of the fog lamp bulb. Grasp the bulb by its plastic base only.**

3. By grasping the bulb and socket by the plastic base only, rotate the miniature bulb and socket, then remove the bulb from the fog lamp.

**To install:**

4. Install the bulb to the socket assembly. The socket assembly is indexed, and can only be installed in one way.

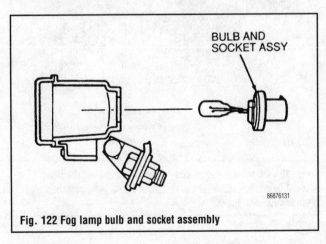

**BULB AND SOCKET ASSY**

86876131

**Fig. 122 Fog lamp bulb and socket assembly**

5. Engage the electrical wiring connector to the fog lamp miniature bulb.
6. Connect the negative battery cable.

**Fog Lamp Assembly**

▶ See Figures 123 and 124

1. Disconnect the negative battery cable.
2. Disengage the fog lamp electrical wiring connector.
3. From under the front bumper cover, remove nut(s) retaining the fog lamp to the mounting bracket.
4. Slide the fog lamp out of the fog lamp mounting bracket assembly, then remove the lamp from the vehicle.

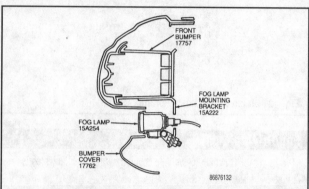

Fig. 123 Cross-sectional view of the fog lamp assembly—Taurus SHO only

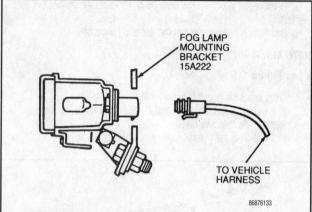

Fig. 124 Disengage the electrical wiring connector from the rear of the fog lamp assembly

5. If replacing the fog lamp mounting bracket, remove the screw retaining the mounting bracket to the front bumper, then keep the mounting bracket and screw for the transfer of parts.

**To install:**

6. If removed, position the fog lamp mounting bracket, then secure to the front bumper using the retaining screw.
7. Slide the fog lamp assembly into the mounting bracket assembly, then install the nut(s) retaining the fog lamp to the mounting bracket.
8. Engage the fog lamp electrical wiring connector.
9. Connect the negative battery cable.

## CIRCUIT PROTECTION

### Fuse Panel and Fuses

▶ See Figure 125

The fuse panel or block on most vehicles covered by this manual is located to the left of the steering column tube, and is hung from the instrument panel. To gain access the fuses, pull the release bar up with the right hand, pull the fuse panel down with the left hand, then remove the cover.

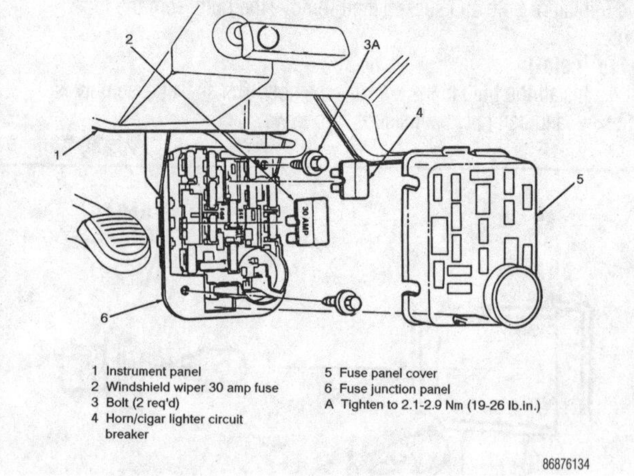

Fuses are a one-time circuit protection. If a circuit is overloaded or shorts, the fuse will blow thus protecting the circuit. A fuse will continue to blow until the circuit is repaired.

Each fuse block uses miniature fuses (normally cartridge-type for these vehicles) which are designed for increased circuit protection and greater reliability. The cartridge-type design allows for fingertip removal and replacement.

Although most fuses are interchangeable in size, the amperage values are not. Should you install a fuse with too high a value, damaging current could be allowed to destroy the component you were attempting to protect by using a fuse in the first place. The cartridge-type fuses have a bolt number molded on them and are color coded for easy identification. Be sure to only replace a fuel with the proper amperage rated substitute.

A blown fuse can easily be checked by visual inspection or by continuity checking.

REPLACEMENT

▶ See Figure 126

### ✳✳ WARNING

**When replacing a fuse, NEVER install a replacement fuse with a higher or lower amperage rating than indicated for the circuit to prevent component damage!**

To remove a cartridge fuse, grip the fuse and pull it straight out of the fuse junction panel/block. If the fuse cannot be gripped, you can use a non-metallic tool to pull the fuse out of the block. To install the fuse, align the terminals with the fuse panel, then push into position.

1 Instrument panel
2 Windshield wiper 30 amp fuse
3 Bolt (2 req'd)
4 Horn/cigar lighter circuit breaker
5 Fuse panel cover
6 Fuse junction panel
A Tighten to 2.1-2.9 Nm (19-26 lb.in.)

Fig. 125 On most vehicles covered by this manual, the fuse panel is located to the left of the steering column, attached to the instrument panel

86876135

**Fig. 126 Fuse panel/block location—Early model Taurus shown**

## Fusible Links

### REPLACEMENT

Fusible links are used to prevent major wire harness damage in the event of a short circuit or an overload condition in the wiring circuits that are normally not fused, due to carrying high amperage loads or because of their locations within the wiring harness. Each fusible link is of a fixed value for a specific electrical load and should a fusible link fail, the cause of the failure must be determined and repaired prior to installing a new fusible link of the same value. Please be advised that the color coding of replacement fusible links may vary from the production color coding that is outlined in the text that follows.

#### Taurus and Sable

• **Gray 12 Gauge Wire**—located in left side of engine compartment at starter relay; used to protect battery to alternator circuit on all except 3.0L SHO engine.
• **Green 14 Gauge Wire**—located in left side of engine compartment at starter relay; used to protect battery to alternator circuit if with 3.0L SHO engine.
• **Green 14 Gauge Wire**—located in left side of engine compartment at starter relay; used to protect anti-lock brake system power relay circuit.
• **Black 16 Gauge Wire**—located on the left shock tower; used to protect the battery feed to headlight switch and fuse panel circuits.
• **Black 16 Gauge Wire**—located on the left shock tower; used to protect the battery feed to ignition switch and fuse panel circuits.
• **Black 16 Gauge Wire**—located in left side of engine compartment at starter relay; used to protect rear window defrost circuit on 1986–90 vehicles and 1991 2.5L engine vehicles.
• **Brown 18 Gauge Wire**—located in left side of engine compartment at starter relay; used to protect rear window defrost circuit on 1991–95 vehicles, except 2.5L engine.
• **Brown 18 Gauge Wire**—located in right front of engine compartment at alternator output control relay; used to protect the alternator output control relay to heated windshield circuit.
• **Blue 20 Gauge Wire**—located on the left shock tower; used to protect the ignition coil, ignition module and cooling fan controller circuits.
• **Blue 20 Gauge Wire**—located in left rear of engine compartment; used to protect ignition switch to anti-lock brake system circuit.

## Circuit Breakers

### REPLACEMENT

Circuit breakers are used to protect electrical circuits by interrupting the current flow. A circuit breaker conducts current through an arm made of two types of metal bonded together. If the arm starts to carry too much current, it heats up. As one metal expands faster than the other, the arm bends, opening the contacts and interrupting the current flow.

• **Station Wagon Rear Window Wiper/Washer**—One 4.5 amp circuit breaker located on the instrument panel brace, on the left side of the steering column on Taurus or on the left instrument panel end panel on Sable.
• **Windshield Wipers and Washer Pump**—One 6 amp circuit breaker located on the fuse panel, on 1988 vehicles.
• **Windshield Wipers and Washer Pump**—One 8.25 amp circuit breaker located on the fuse panel, on 1989–95 vehicles.
• **Cigar Lighters, Horn Relay and Horns**—One 20 amp circuit breaker located on the fuse panel.
• **Power Windows, Power Locks and Power Seats**—One 20 amp circuit breaker located near the starter relay, on 1986–89 vehicles.
• **Power Windows, Power Locks and Power Seats**—One 20 amp circuit breaker located on the fuse panel, on 1990–92 vehicles.
• **Headlights**—One 22 amp circuit breaker incorporated in the headlight switch.

## Relays

### REPLACEMENT

Various relays are used in conjunction with the vehicle's electrical components. If a relay should fail it must be replaced with one of equal value. Replacement is simply a matter of disengaging the electrical connector and sliding the relay from its mounting. Depending on a vehicle's equipment, it may contain several of the following relays.

• **Alternator Output Control Relay**—located between the right front inner fender and fender splash shield (if equipped with 3.0L or 3.8L engines and a heated windshield.
• **Anti-lock Motor Relay**—located in lower left front of engine compartment (if equipped with anti-lock brakes).
• **Anti-lock Power Relay**—located in left rear corner of engine compartment (if equipped with anti-lock brakes).
• **Autolight Dual Coil Relay**—located behind the center of the instrument panel on the instrument panel brace (if equipped with automatic headlights).
• **Fog Light Relay**—located behind the center of the instrument panel on the instrument panel brace.
• **Horn Relay**—located behind the center of the instrument panel on the instrument panel brace.
• **LCD Dimming Relay**—located behind the center of the instrument panel on the instrument panel brace (if equipped with automatic headlights).
• **Low Oil Level Relay**—located behind the center of the instrument panel on the instrument panel brace.
• **Moonroof Relay**—located behind the right side of the instrument panel (if equipped with a moonroof).
• **Police Accessory Relay**—located behind the center of the instrument panel on police models.
• **Starter Relay**—located on the left fender apron, in front of the strut tower.
• **Window Safety Relay**—located behind the right side of the instrument panel (if equipped with power windows).

## Computers

### LOCATION

- **Electronic Engine Control Module**—located on the passenger side of the firewall.
- **Anti-lock Brake Control Module**—located at the front of the engine compartment next to the passenger side fender, except on Taurus SHO, where it is located at the front of the engine compartment on the driver's side.
- **Automatic Temperature Control Module**—located behind the center of the instrument panel.
- **Heated Windshield Control Module**—located behind the left side of the instrument panel, to the right of the steering column.
- **Integrated Control Module**—located at the front of the engine compartment, on the upper radiator support.
- **Air Bag Diagnostic Module**—located behind the right side of the instrument panel, above the glove box.

## Flashers

### REPLACEMENT

▶ **See Figure 127**

An electronic combination turn signal and emergency warning flasher is attached to the lower left instrument panel reinforcement above the fuse panel.

The turn signal unit is located on the LH side of the instrument panel. The combination turn signal and hazard flasher can be removed by pressing the plastic retaining clip and pulling straight rearward. One phillips® head or regular screw has to be removed from the retaining bracket.

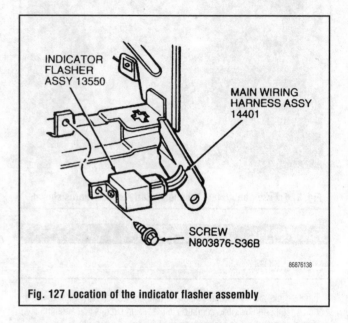

INDICATOR FLASHER ASSY 13550

MAIN WIRING HARNESS ASSY 14401

SCREW N803876-S36B

86876138

**Fig. 127 Location of the indicator flasher assembly**

## WIRING DIAGRAMS

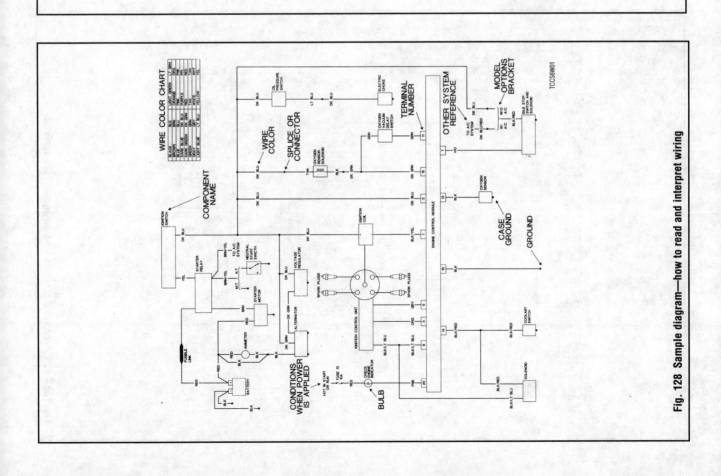

Fig. 129 Common wiring diagram symbols

Fig. 128 Sample diagram—how to read and interpret wiring

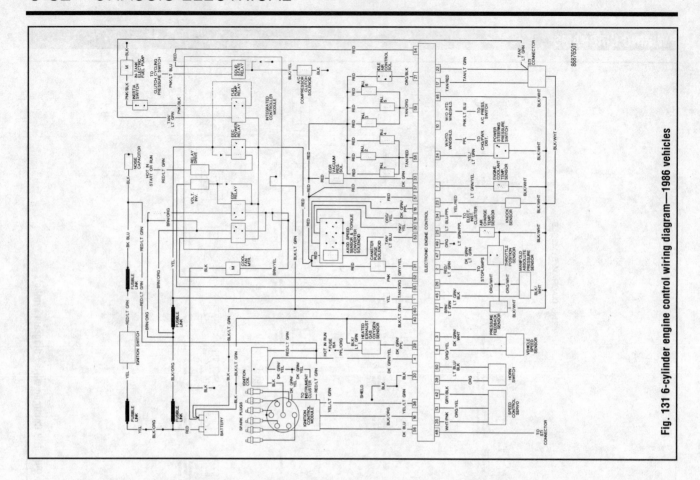

Fig. 131 6-cylinder engine control wiring diagram—1986 vehicles

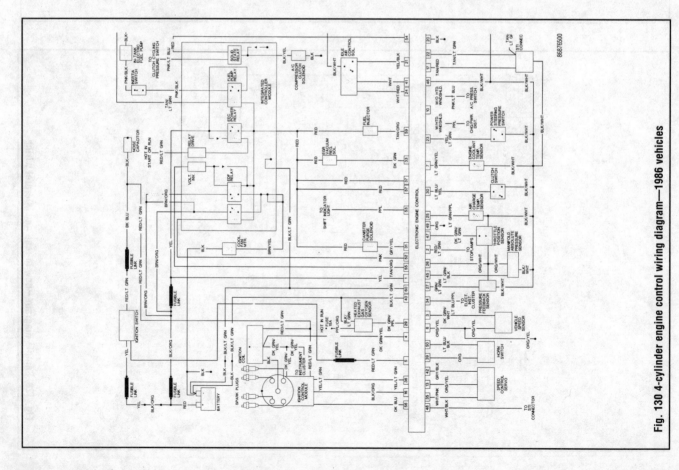

Fig. 130 4-cylinder engine control wiring diagram—1986 vehicles

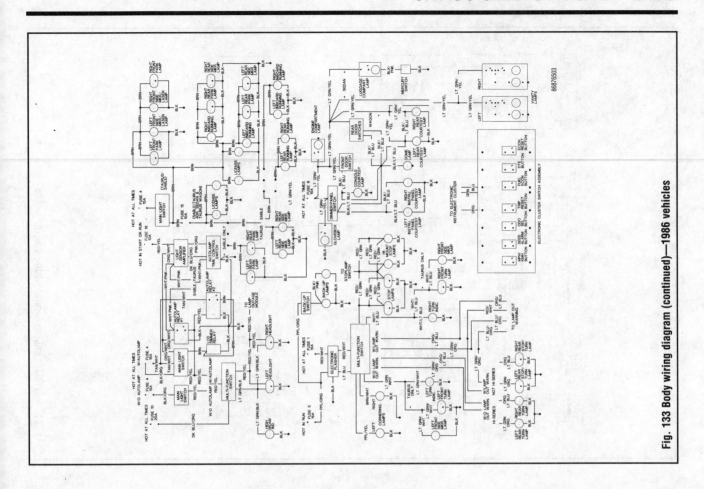

Fig. 133 Body wiring diagram (continued)—1986 vehicles

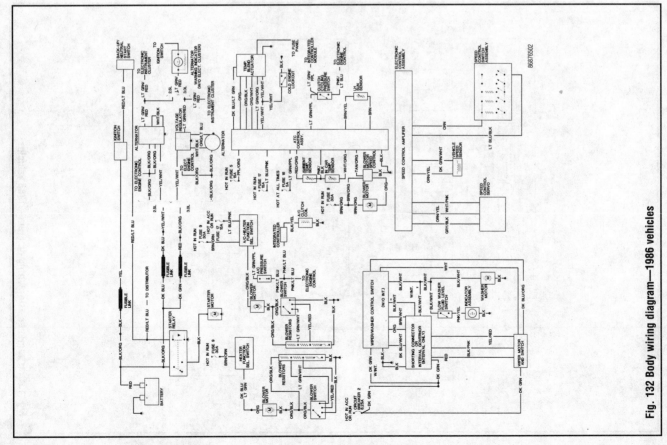

Fig. 132 Body wiring diagram—1986 vehicles

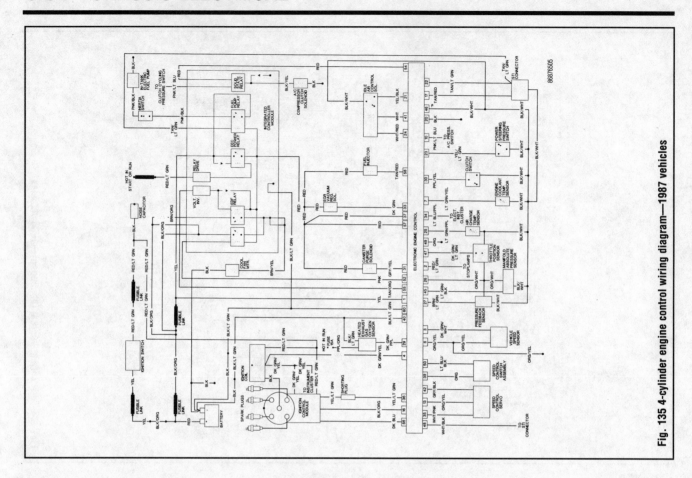

Fig. 135 4-cylinder engine control wiring diagram—1987 vehicles

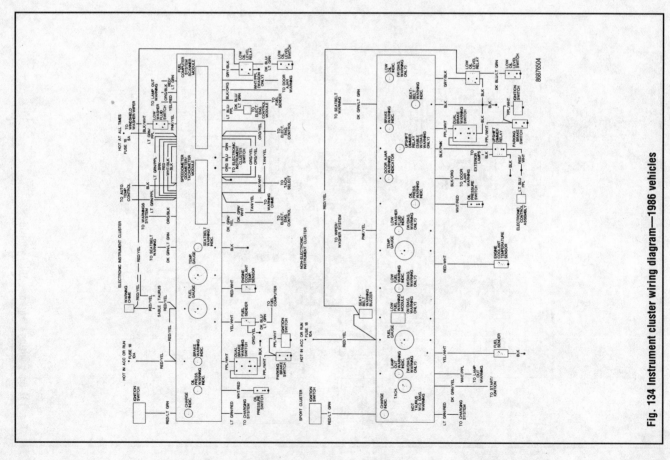

Fig. 134 Instrument cluster wiring diagram—1986 vehicles

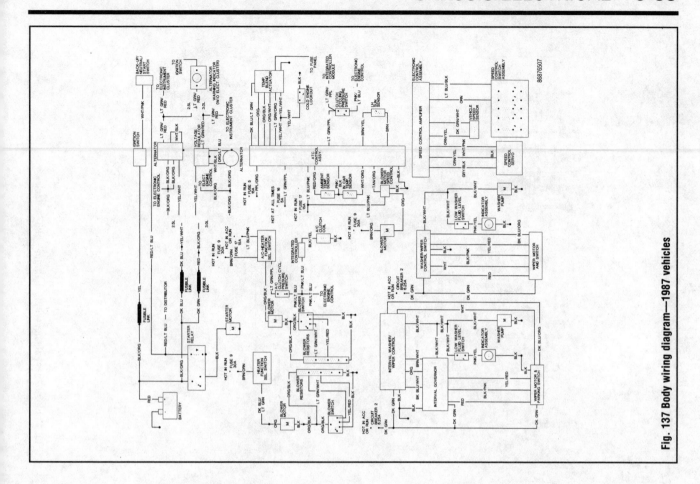

Fig. 137 Body wiring diagram—1987 vehicles

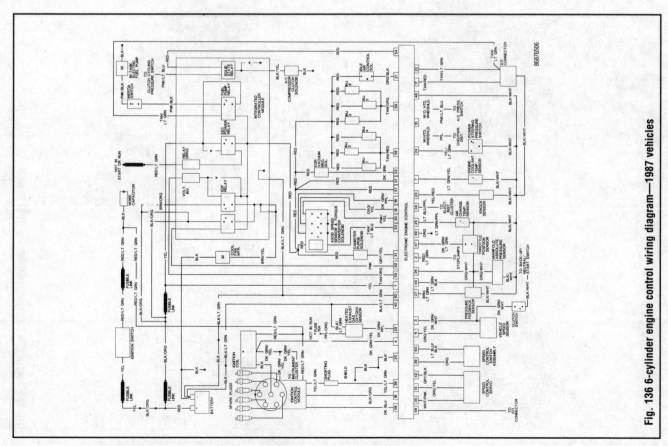

Fig. 136 6-cylinder engine control wiring diagram—1987 vehicles

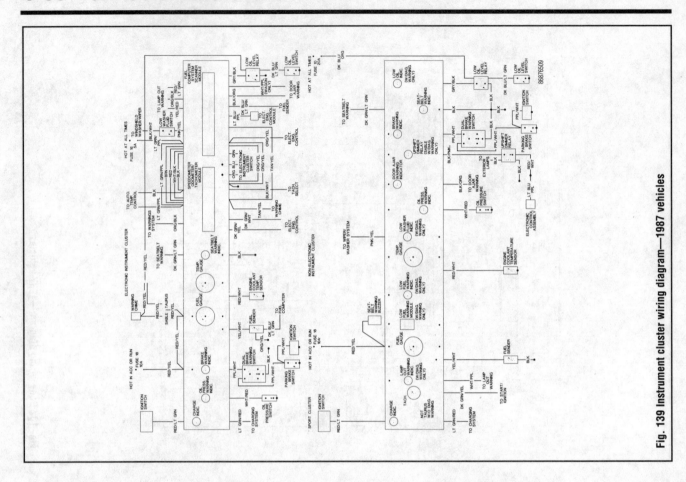

Fig. 139 Instrument cluster wiring diagram—1987 vehicles

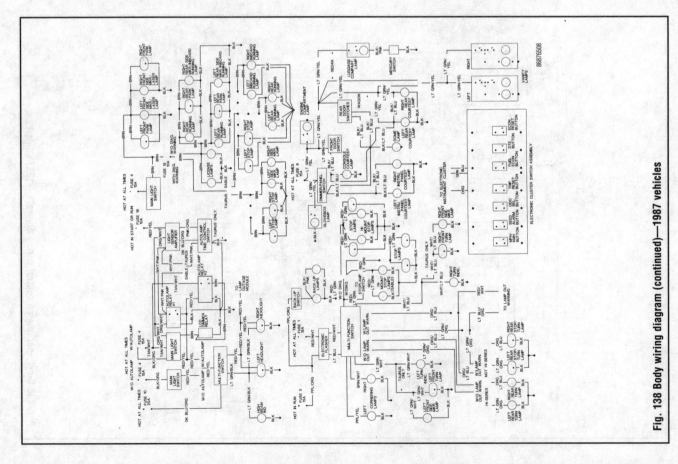

Fig. 138 Body wiring diagram (continued)—1987 vehicles

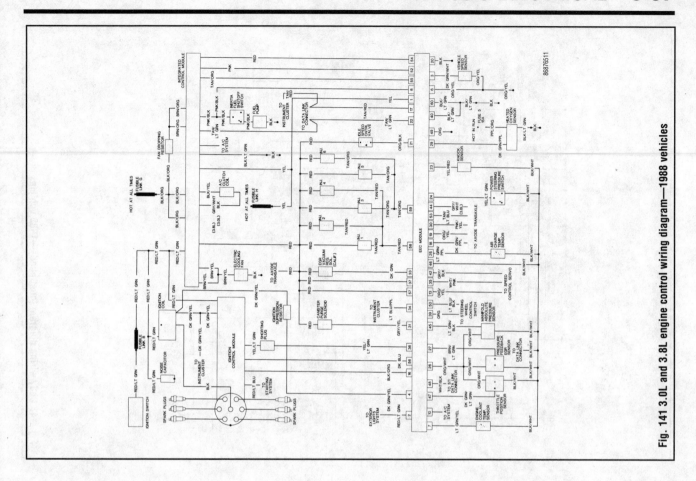

Fig. 141 3.0L and 3.8L engine control wiring diagram—1988 vehicles

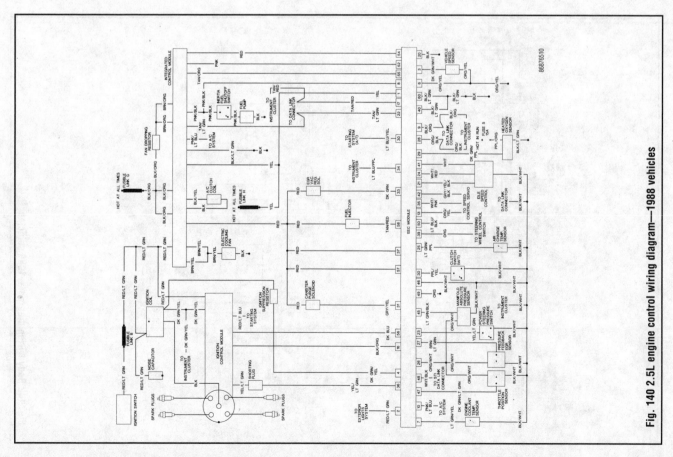

Fig. 140 2.5L engine control wiring diagram—1988 vehicles

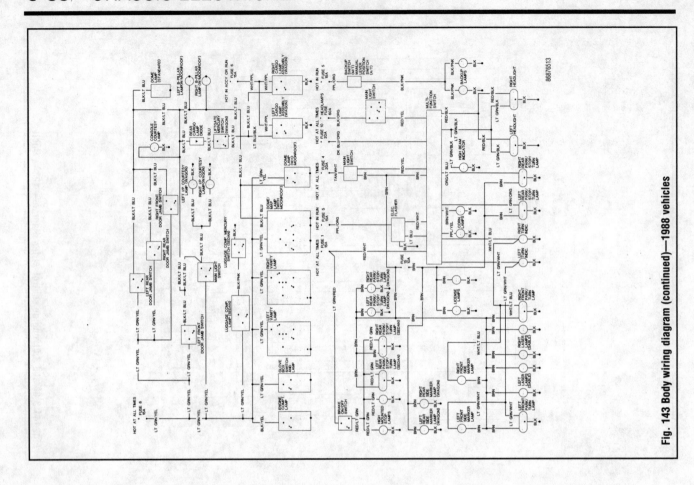

Fig. 143 Body wiring diagram (continued)—1988 vehicles

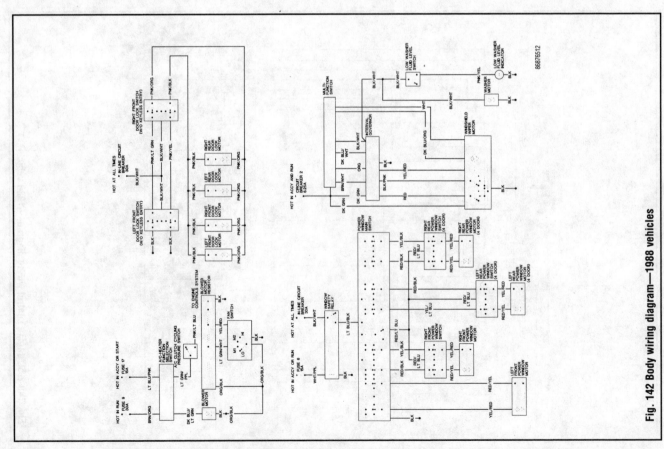

Fig. 142 Body wiring diagram—1988 vehicles

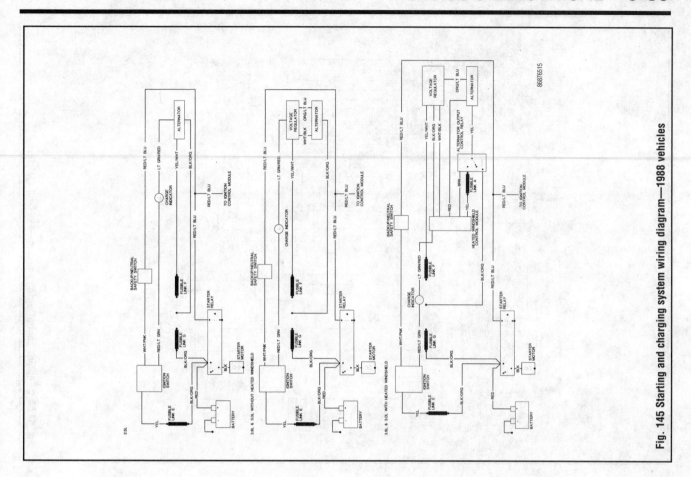

Fig. 145 Starting and charging system wiring diagram—1988 vehicles

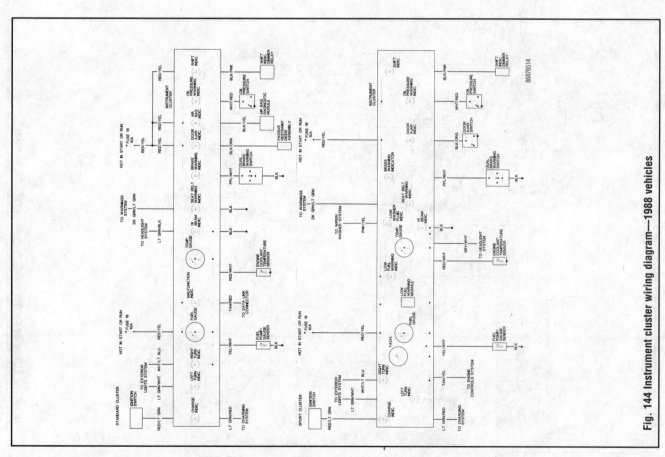

Fig. 144 Instrument cluster wiring diagram—1988 vehicles

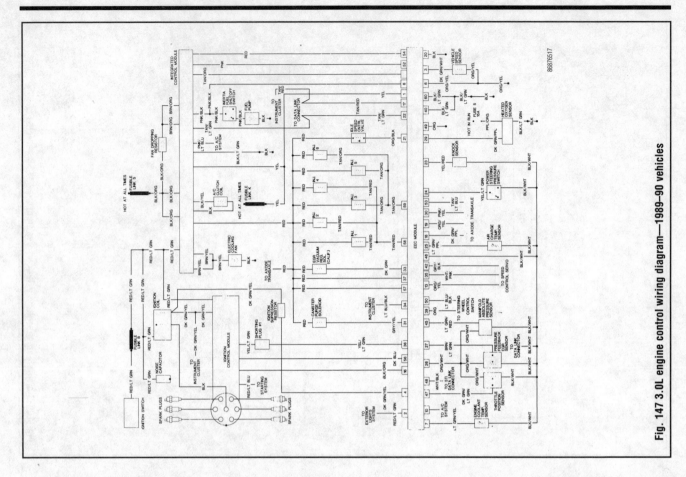

Fig. 147 3.0L engine control wiring diagram—1989–90 vehicles

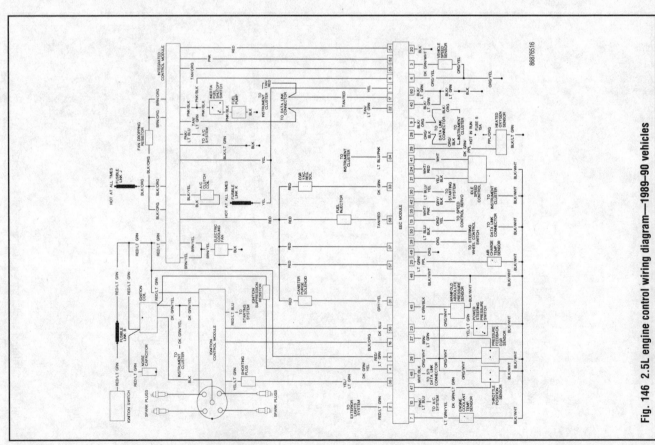

Fig. 146 2.5L engine control wiring diagram—1989–90 vehicles

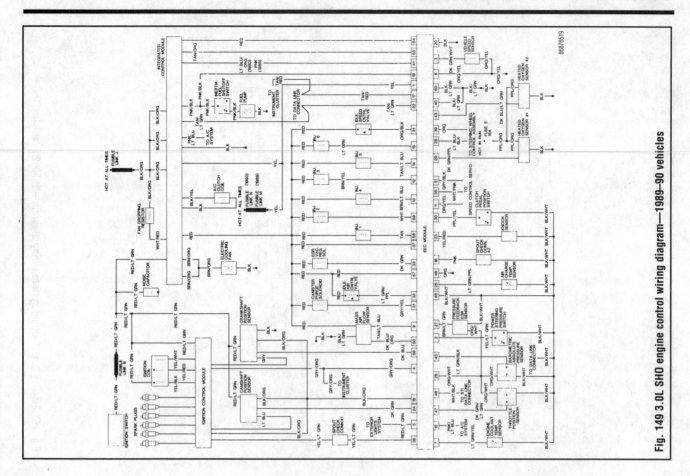

Fig. 149 3.0L SHO engine control wiring diagram—1989–90 vehicles

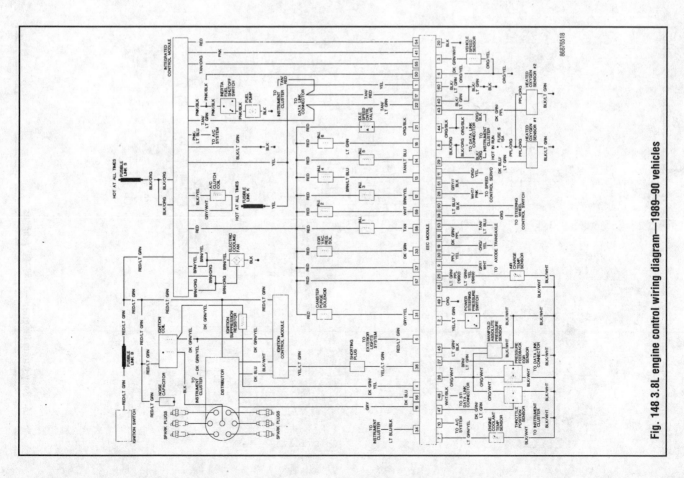

Fig. 148 3.8L engine control wiring diagram—1989–90 vehicles

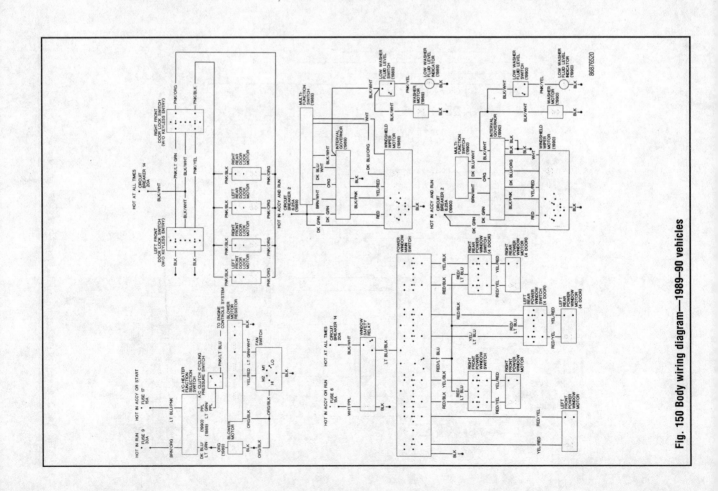

Fig. 151 Starting and charging system wiring diagram—1989–90 vehicles

Fig. 150 Body wiring diagram—1989–90 vehicles

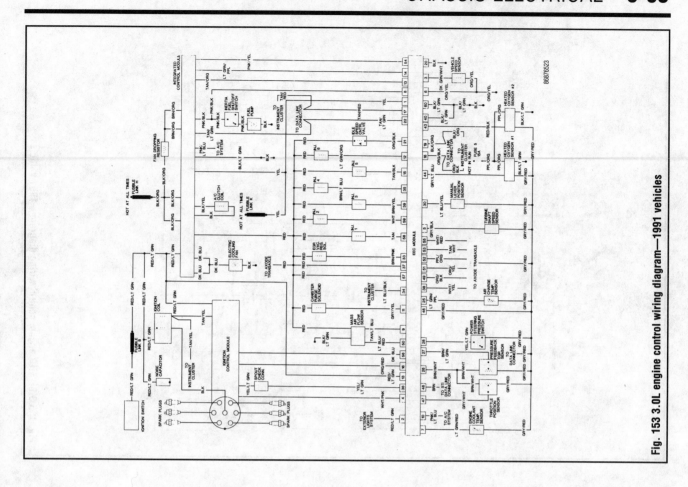

Fig. 153 3.0L engine control wiring diagram—1991 vehicles

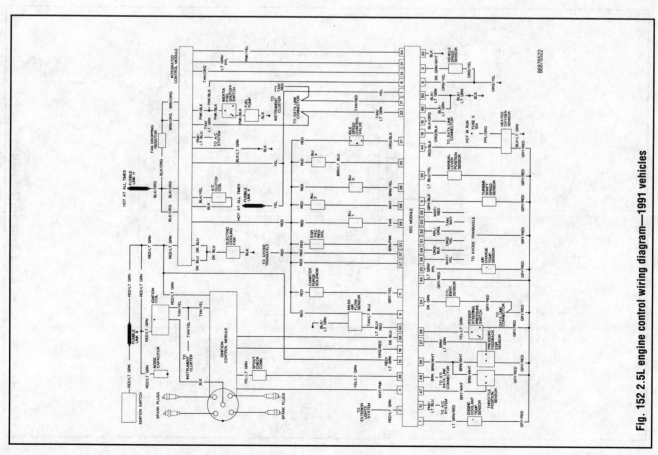

Fig. 152 2.5L engine control wiring diagram—1991 vehicles

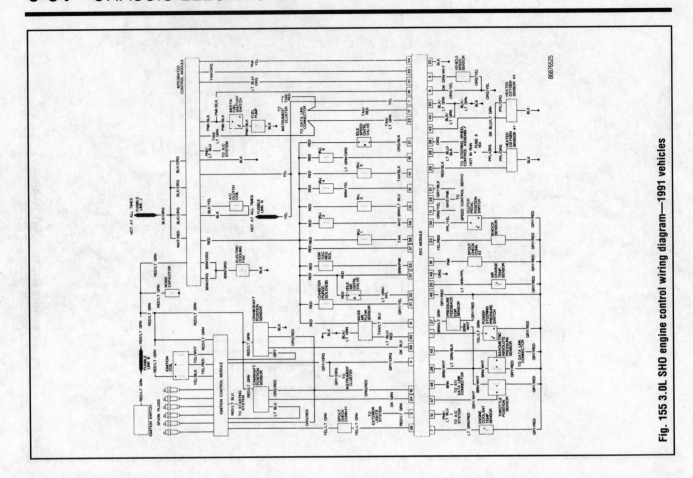

Fig. 155 3.0L SHO engine control wiring diagram—1991 vehicles

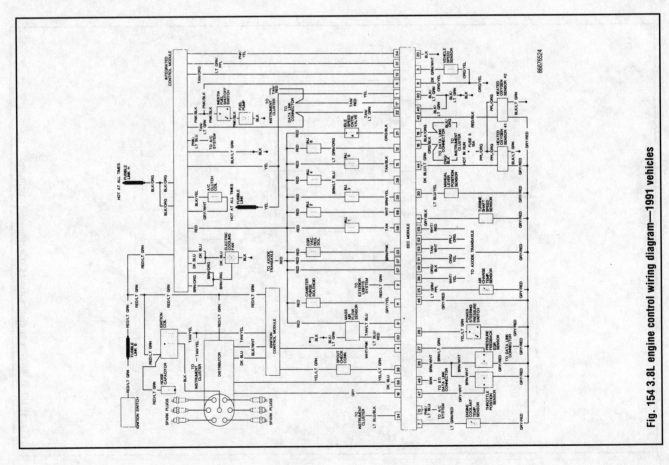

Fig. 154 3.8L engine control wiring diagram—1991 vehicles

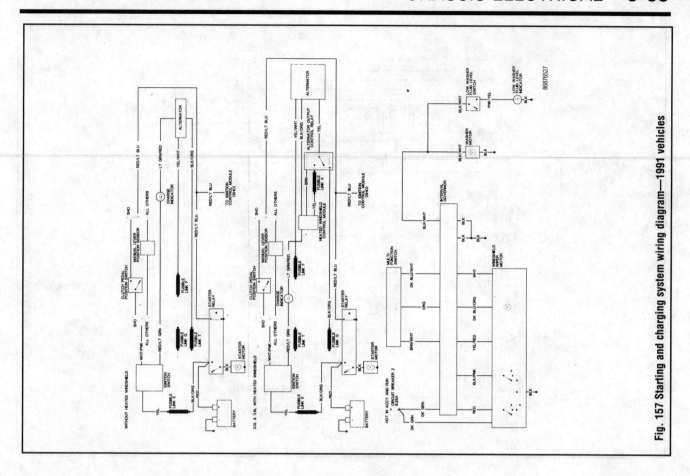

Fig. 157 Starting and charging system wiring diagram—1991 vehicles

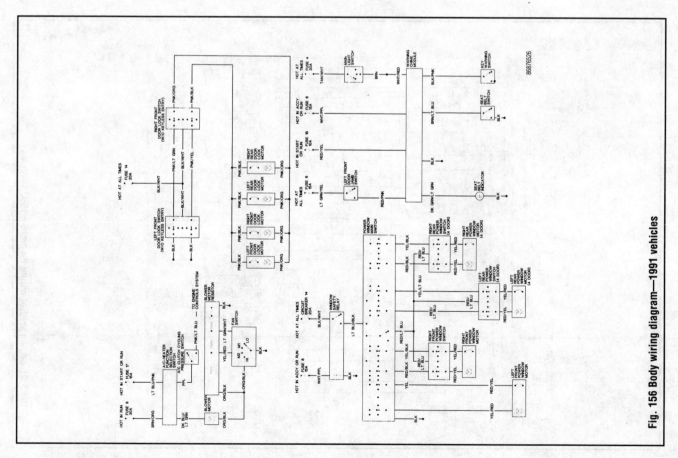

Fig. 156 Body wiring diagram—1991 vehicles

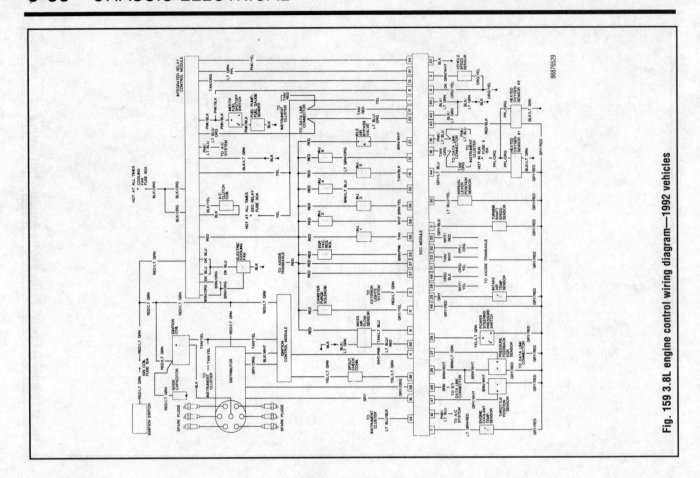

Fig. 159 3.8L engine control wiring diagram—1992 vehicles

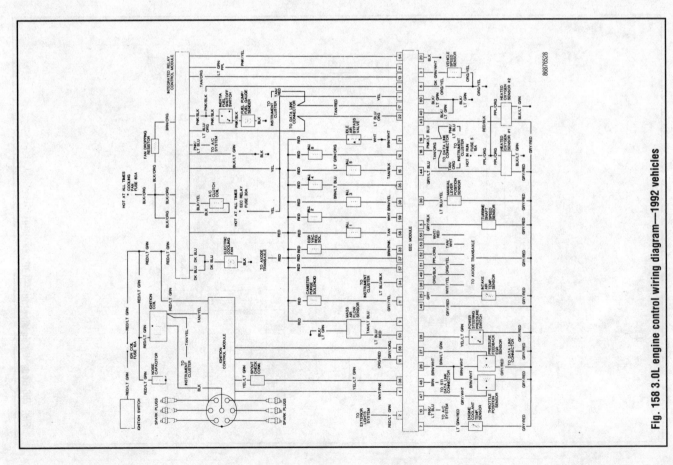

Fig. 158 3.0L engine control wiring diagram—1992 vehicles

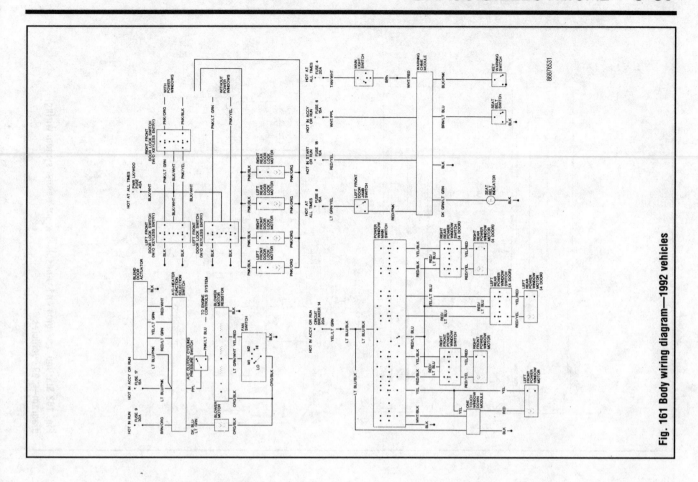

**Fig. 161 Body wiring diagram—1992 vehicles**

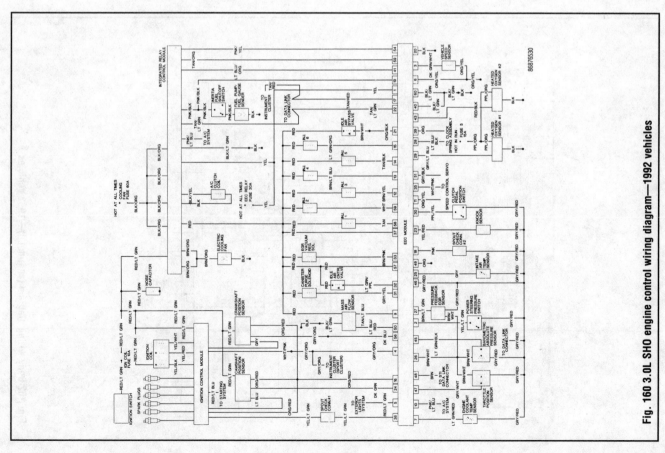

**Fig. 160 3.0L SHO engine control wiring diagram—1992 vehicles**

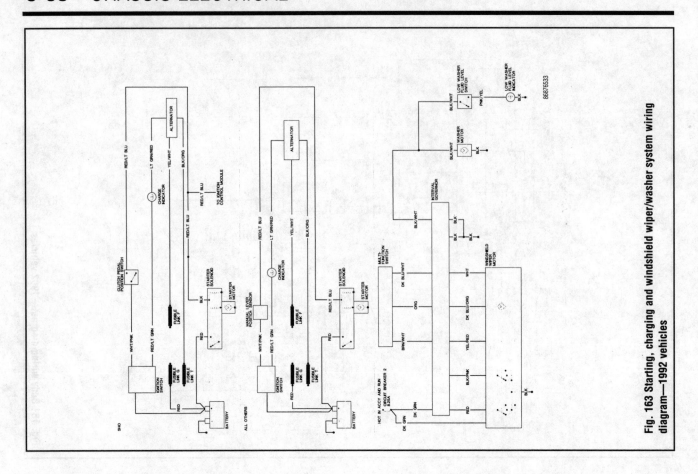

**Fig. 163 Starting, charging and windshield wiper/washer system wiring diagram—1992 vehicles**

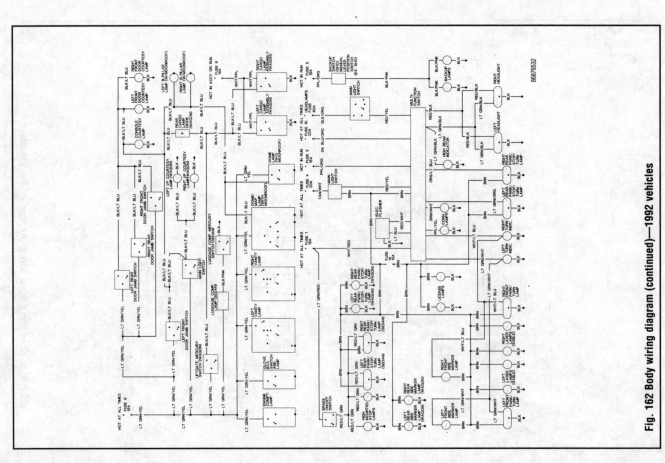

**Fig. 162 Body wiring diagram (continued)—1992 vehicles**

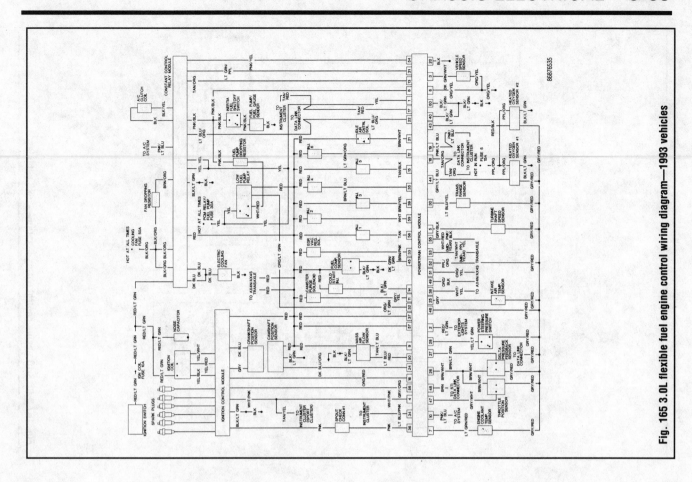

Fig. 165 3.0L flexible fuel engine control wiring diagram—1993 vehicles

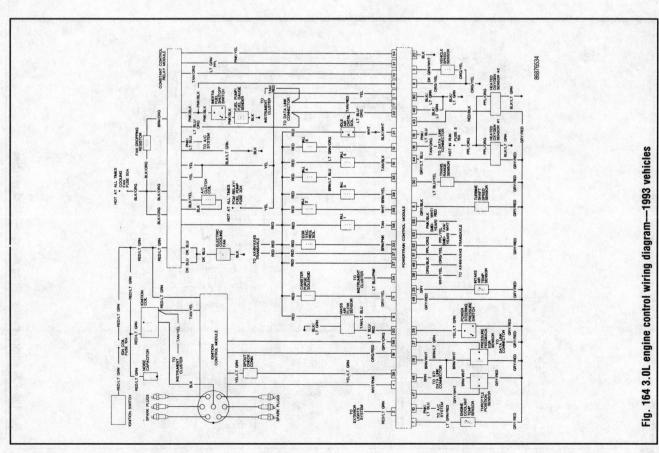

Fig. 164 3.0L engine control wiring diagram—1993 vehicles

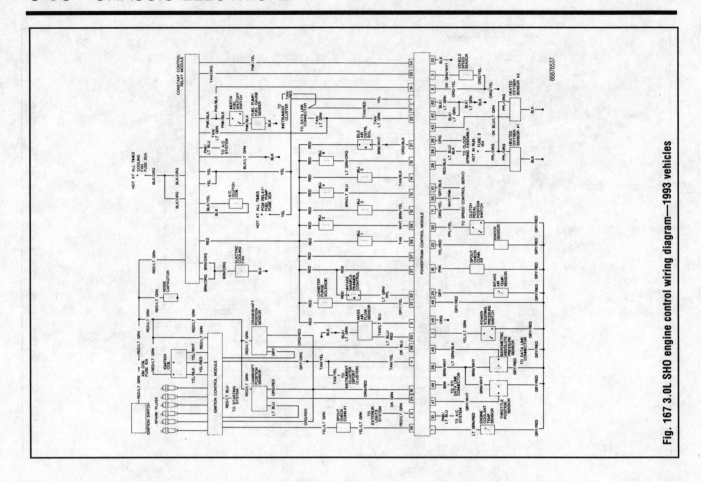

Fig. 167 3.0L SHO engine control wiring diagram—1993 vehicles

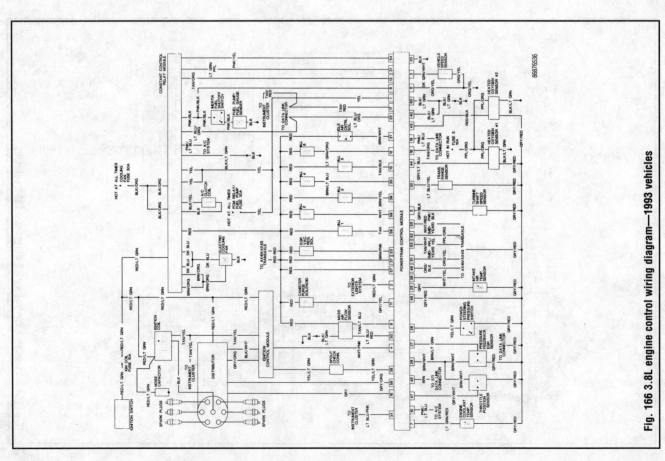

Fig. 166 3.8L engine control wiring diagram—1993 vehicles

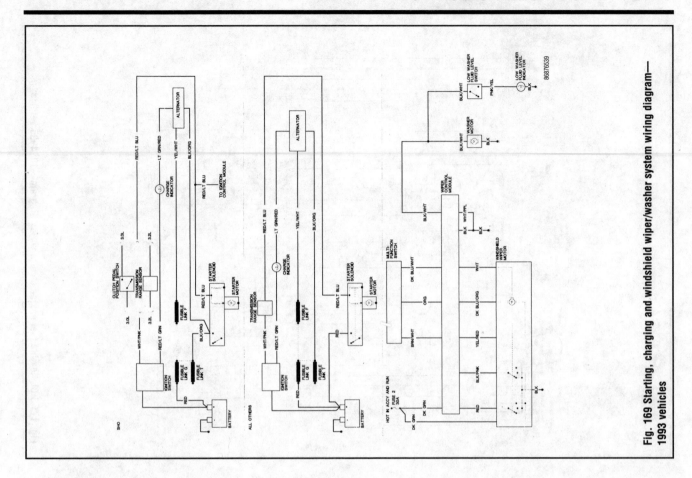

Fig. 169 Starting, charging and windshield wiper/washer system wiring diagram—1993 vehicles

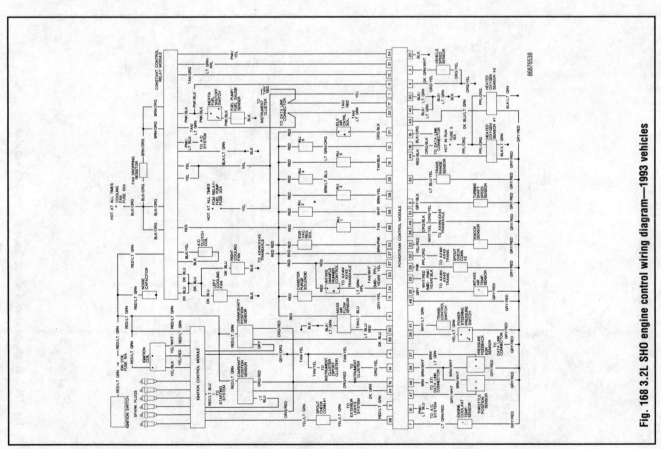

Fig. 168 3.2L SHO engine control wiring diagram—1993 vehicles

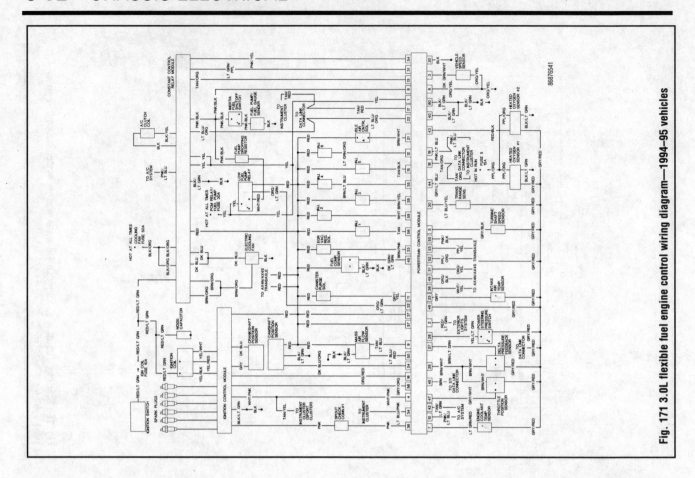

Fig. 171 3.0L flexible fuel engine control wiring diagram—1994–95 vehicles

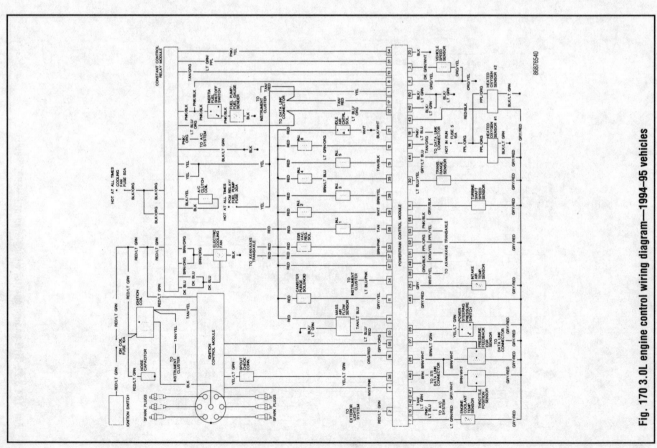

Fig. 170 3.0L engine control wiring diagram—1994–95 vehicles

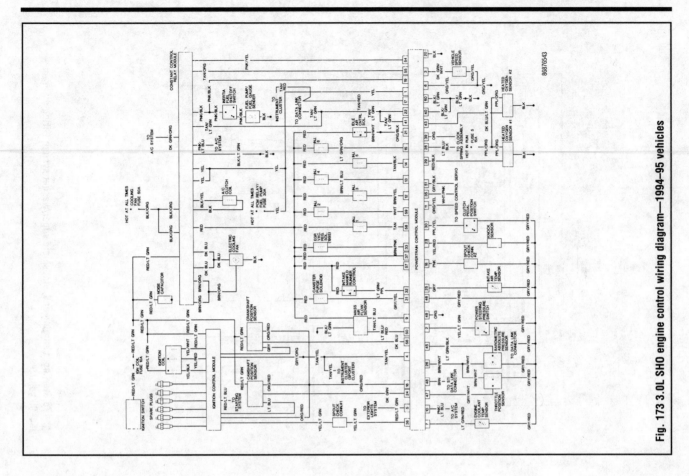

Fig. 173 3.0L SHO engine control wiring diagram—1994–95 vehicles

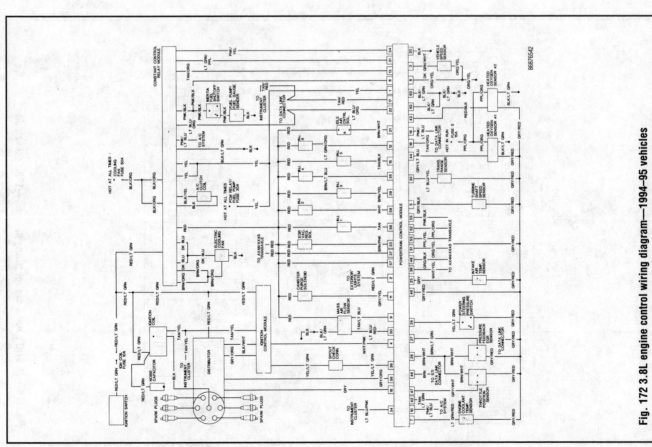

Fig. 172 3.8L engine control wiring diagram—1994–95 vehicles

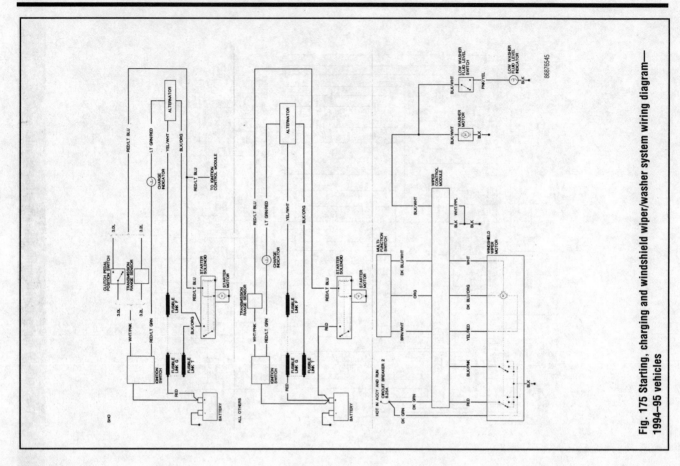

Fig. 175 Starting, charging and windshield wiper/washer system wiring diagram—1994–95 vehicles

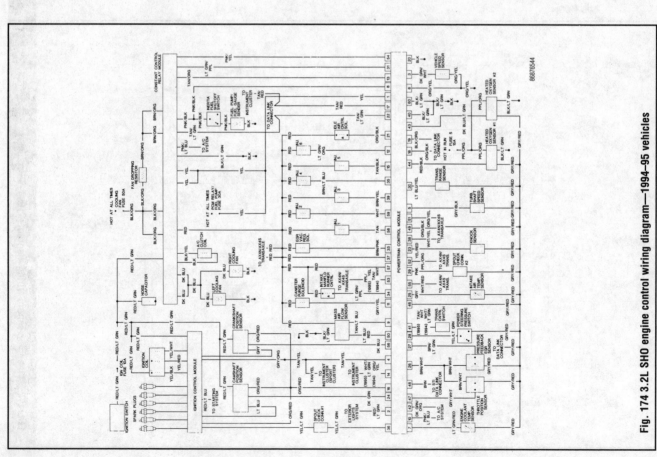

Fig. 174 3.2L SHO engine control wiring diagram—1994–95 vehicles

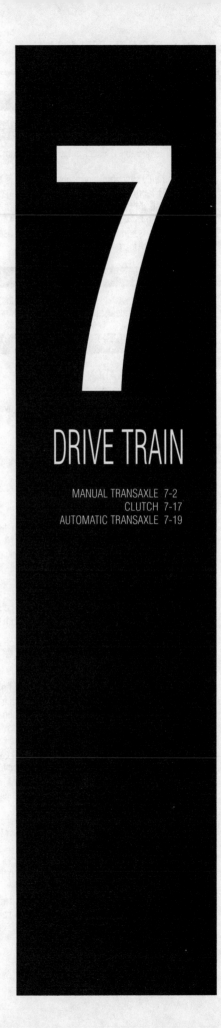

7

DRIVE TRAIN

## MANUAL TRANSAXLE

### Identification

Your Taurus or Sable uses a front wheel drive transmission called a transaxle.

A 5-speed fully synchronized manual transaxle is available on the 2.5L and 3.0L SHO Taurus/Sable models. An internally-gated shift mechanism and a single rail shift linkage eliminate the need for periodic shift linkage adjustments. The MTX transaxle is designed to use Type F or Dexron®II automatic transmission fluid as a lubricant. Never use gear oil (GL) in the place of Type F or Dexron®II.

### Adjustments

The manual shift mechanism and cables incorporate no adjustable features, therefore adjustments are neither possible or necessary.

### Shift Linkage

#### REMOVAL & INSTALLATION

1. Disconnect the negative battery cable. Remove the console, shift knob and boot.
2. Fold the carpet back from the dash panel to expose the shift cables and cable sealing grommets.
3. Remove the rear seat heating duct. Loosen the two screws and remove the cable bracket.
4. Pull the cable sealing grommets loose from the floorpan and dash panel.
5. Raise and support the vehicle safely.
6. Remove the two retaining screws that retain the cables to the bracket assembly.
7. Pry the cable sockets off the clamp assembly pivot balls and slide the cable insulators out of the bracket slots.
8. Loosen the two bolts retaining the bracket assembly to the transaxle case. Remove the bracket assembly.
9. Lower the vehicle. From inside the vehicle pull the shift cables through the sheet metal holes and remove them from the vehicle.
**To install:**
10. From inside the vehicle push the shift cables through the sheet metal holes. The crossover cable goes through the dash panel hole and the selector cable goes through the tunnel hole.
11. Seat the cable grommets in the sheet metal holes. Install the cable bracket. Tighten the retaining screws to 17–22 inch lbs. (1.9–2.5 Nm).
12. Make sure the crossover cable is secured under the hook on the bracket. A white alignment mark on the cable will assist in where to clip the cable under the hook.
13. Install the rear seat heat duct. Fold back the carpet over the cables.
14. Install the shifter, shift knob, boot and console.
15. Raise and support the vehicle safely. Install the clamp assembly onto the transaxle input shift shaft. Tighten the retaining nut to 6–10 ft. lbs. (8–14 Nm).
16. Install the bracket assembly to the transaxle case. Tighten the M12 retaining bolt to 22–35 ft. lbs. (30–47 Nm) and the M10 bolt to 16–24 ft. lbs. (22–33 Nm).
17. Feed the shift cables into the slots of the bracket assembly. Retain the cables with two retainers and four bolts. Tighten the bolts 6–10 ft. lbs. (8–14 Nm).
18. Snap the crossover cable socket onto the clamp assembly pivot ball. Position the selector cable rod end with the yellow painted side down. Snap the rod end onto the clamp assembly post.

### Shift Handle

#### REMOVAL & INSTALLATION

1. Disconnect the negative battery cable.
2. Remove the leather wrapped knob by rotating the knob counter-clockwise.
3. Remove the console trim surrounding the shift boot by sliding the boot assembly off the shift lever, in order to expose the four screws which connect the boot to the top of the console.
4. Remove the console to expose the shifter assembly. Remove the four bolts retaining the shifter to the floorpan.
5. Pry the two clips holding the shift cables to control assembly and pry the cable sockets off the control assembly pivot balls.
6. Do not bend or kink the cable core rods.
**To install:**
7. Feed the loose ends of the cables into the control assembly slots. A green painted mark on the shifter and crossover cable will aid in proper alignment.
8. Attach the control assembly to the floorpan J-nuts with four bolts. Tighten the bolts to 49–70 inch lbs. (5.5–7.8 Nm).
9. Seat the cable insulators into the shifter slots. Install new U-clips. Snap the cable sockets onto the shifter pivot balls. Install the console.
10. Slide the boot assembly over the shift lever. Attach it to the console and tighten the retaining screws to 14–21 inch lbs. (1.6–2.3 Nm).
11. Attach the shift knob to the shift lever.
12. Connect the negative battery cable.

### Back-Up Light Switch

#### REMOVAL & INSTALLATION

♦ **See Figure 1**

The back-up lamp switch is located on the top left side of the transaxle.

1. Disconnect the negative battery cable.

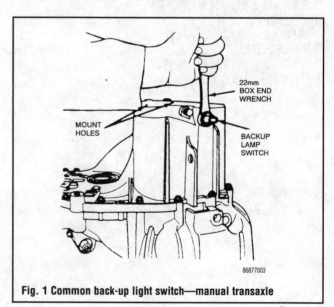

22mm BOX END WRENCH

BACKUP LAMP SWITCH

MOUNT HOLES

86877003

**Fig. 1 Common back-up light switch—manual transaxle**

2. Disengage the switch electrical connector.

3. Using a 22mm box-end wrench, remove the switch.

**To install:**

4. Apply Pipe Sealant with Teflon® part No. D8AZ-19554-A or equivalent to the threads of the switch. Turn the switch into the transaxle case clockwise and tighten to 12–15 ft. lbs. (16–20 Nm).

5. Engage the electrical connector.

6. Connect the negative battery cable.

## Transaxle

### REMOVAL & INSTALLATION

▶ **See Figures 2 thru 11**

**1986–88 Vehicles**

1. Disconnect the negative battery cable.

2. Wedge a wood block about 7 in. (178mm) long under the clutch pedal to hold the pedal up slightly beyond its normal position.

3. Grasp the clutch cable and pull it forward, disconnecting it from the clutch release shaft assembly. Remove the clutch cable casing from the rib on the top surface of the transaxle case.

4. Using a 13mm socket, remove the 2 top transaxle-to-engine mounting bolts.

5. Raise and safely support the vehicle.

6. Using a 15mm socket, remove the nut and bolt that secures the lower control arm ball joint to the steering knuckle assembly. Discard the nut and bolt. Repeat this procedure on the opposite side.

7. Using Tool D83P-4026-A, or equivalent, carefully pry the lower control arm away from the knuckle.

➡**Be careful not to damage or cut the ball joint boot. The prybar must not contact the lower arm.**

8. Using a large prybar, pry the left inboard CV-joint assembly from the transaxle.

➡**Plug the seal opening to prevent lubricant leakage.**

9. Remove the inboard CV-joint from the transaxle by grasping the left-hand steering knuckle and swinging the knuckle and halfshaft outward from the transaxle. If the CV-joint assembly cannot be pried from the transaxle, insert differential rotator tool T81P-4026-A or equivalent, through the left side and tap the joint out. The tool can be used from either side of transaxle.

10. Wire the halfshaft assembly in a near level position to prevent damage to the assembly during the remaining operations. Repeat this procedure on the opposite side.

11. Disengage the locking tabs using a small screwdriver, then remove the backup light switch connector from the transaxle backup light switch.

12. Using a deep well socket, remove the starter stud bolts.

13. Remove the shift mechanism to shift shaft attaching nut and bolt and control selector indicator switch arm. Remove from the shift shaft.

14. Remove the bolts attaching the shift cable and bracket assembly to the transaxle.

15. Using a crowfoot wrench, remove the speedometer cable from the transaxle.

16. Remove the stiffener brace attaching bolts from the lower position of the clutch housing.

17. Remove the subframe.

18. Position a suitable jack under the transaxle.

19. Lower the transaxle support jack.

20. Remove the lower engine to transaxle attaching bolts.

21. Remove the transaxle from the rear face of the engine and lower it from the vehicle.

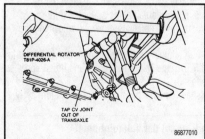

**Fig. 2 Wedge a wood block about 7 in. (178mm) long under the clutch pedal to hold the pedal up slightly beyond its normal position**

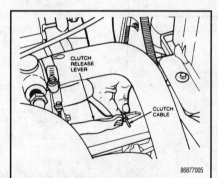

**Fig. 3 Remove the clutch cable casing from the rib on the top surface of the transaxle case**

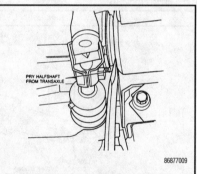

**Fig. 4 Using a large prybar, carefully pry the left inboard CV-joint assembly from the transaxle**

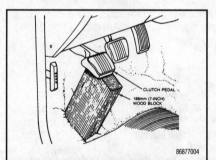

**Fig. 5 If the CV-joint assembly cannot be pried from the transaxle, insert Differential Rotator tool T81P-4026-A, or equivalent, through the left side and tap the joint out**

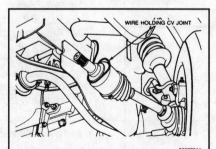

**Fig. 6 Wire the halfshaft assembly in a near level position to prevent damage to the assembly during the remainder of the procedure**

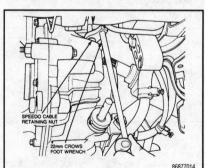

**Fig. 7 Using a crowfoot wrench, remove the speedometer cable from the transaxle**

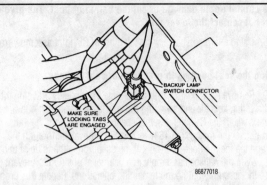

**Fig. 8 Attach the back-up lamp switch connector to the transaxle switch**

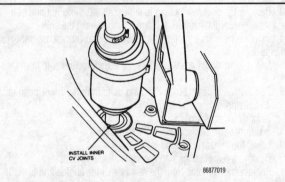

**Fig. 9 After removing the plugs, install the inner CV-joints into the transaxle**

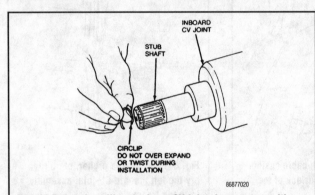

**Fig. 10 Before installing the inner CV-joint, be sure to position new circlips**

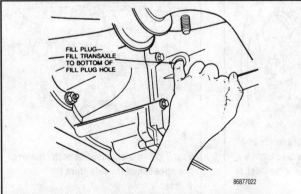

**Fig. 11 Fill the transaxle to the bottom of the fill plug hole**

**To install:**

22. Raise the transaxle into position with the support jack. Engage the input shaft spline into the clutch disc and work the transaxle onto the dowel sleeves. Make sure the transaxle assembly is flush with the rear face of the engine prior to installation of the attaching bolts.

23. Install the lower engine to transaxle attaching bolts and tighten them to 28–31 ft. lbs. (38–42 Nm).

24. Install the speedometer cable. Be careful when threading the cable nut onto the retainer to avoid crossthreading.

25. Install the 10M and 12M bolts attaching the the shift cable and bracket to the transaxle. Tighten the 10M bolt to 16–22 ft. lbs. (22–30 Nm) and the 12M bolt to 22–35 ft. lbs. (30–47 Nm).

26. Install the bolt attaching the shift mechanism-to-shift shaft and tighten to 7–10 ft. lbs. (9–14 Nm).

27. Install the 2 bolts that attach the stiffener brace to the lower portion of the clutch housing and tighten to 15–21 ft. lbs. (21–28 Nm).

28. Install the starter stud bolts, then tighten to 30–40 ft. lbs. (41–54 Nm).

29. Install the backup light switch connector to the transaxle switch.

30. Remove the seal plugs, then install the inner CV-joints into transaxle.

31. Install the center bearing to the bracket on the right-side halfshaft.

➡**New circlips are required on both inner CV-joints prior to installation. Make sure both CV-joints are seated in the transaxle.**

32. Attach the subframe and the lower ball joint to the steering knuckle. Insert a new service pinch bolt and a new nut. Tighten the nut to 37–44 ft. lbs. (50–60 Nm) but do not tighten the bolt.

33. Fill the transaxle with the proper type and quantity of transmission fluid.

34. Install the top transaxle to engine mounting bolts and tighten to 28–31 ft. lbs. (38–42 Nm).

35. Connect the clutch cable to the clutch release shaft assembly.

36. Remove the wood block from under the clutch pedal. Before starting the engine, set the hand brake, then pump the clutch pedal at least 2 times to ensure proper clutch adjustment.

### 1989–95 Vehicles

▶ **See Figures 2 thru 12**

1. Disconnect the negative battery cable.

2. Wedge a 7 in. (178mm) block of wood under the clutch pedal to hold the pedal up beyond it's normal position.

3. Remove the air cleaner hose.

4. Grasp the clutch cable and pull it forward, disconnecting it from the clutch release shaft assembly.

5. Disconnect the clutch cable casing from the rib on top of the transaxle case.

6. Install engine lifting eyes.

7. Tie up the wiring harness and power steering cooler hoses.

8. Disconnect the speedometer cable and speed sensor wire.

9. Support the engine using a suitable engine support fixture.

10. Raise the vehicle and support it safely. Remove the wheel and tire assemblies.

11. Remove the nut and bolt retaining the lower control arm ball joint to the steering knuckle assembly. Discard the removed nut and bolt. Repeat the procedure on the opposite side.

12. Using a suitable halfshaft remover, pry the lower control arm away from the knuckle.

➡**Be careful not to damage or cut the ball joint boot.**

13. Remove the upper nut from the stabilizer bar and separate the stabilizer bar from the knuckle.

14. Remove the tie rod nut and separate the tie rod end from the knuckle.

15. Disconnect the heated oxygen sensor.

16. Remove the catalytic converter assembly.

17. Disconnect the power steering cooler from the subframe and place it aside.

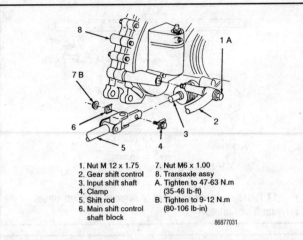

1. Nut M 12 x 1.75
2. Gear shift control
3. Input shift shaft
4. Clamp
5. Shift rod
6. Main shift control shaft block
7. Nut M6 x 1.00
8. Transaxle assy
A. Tighten to 47-63 N.m (35-46 lb-ft)
B. Tighten to 9-12 N.m (80-106 lb-in)

86877031

**Fig. 12 Unfasten the shift mechanism stabilizer bar-to-transaxle retaining bolt. Remove the shift rod-to-shift shaft retaining nut and bolt, then remove the rods from the transaxle**

18. Disconnect the battery cable bracket from the subframe.
19. Using a suitable prybar, pry the left inboard CV-joint assembly from the transaxle. Install a plug into the seal to prevent fluid leakage. Remove the CV-joint from the transaxle by grasping the left steering knuckle and swinging the knuckle and halfshaft outward from the transaxle. Repeat the procedure on the right side.

➡️**If the CV-joint assembly cannot be pried from the transaxle, insert a suitable tool through the left side and tap the joint out. The tool can be used from either side of the transaxle.**

20. Support the halfshaft assembly with wire in a near level position to prevent damage to the assembly during the remaining operations. Repeat the procedure on the opposite side.
21. Remove the retaining bolts from the center support bearing and remove the right halfshaft from the transaxle.
22. Remove the 2 steering gear retaining nuts from the subframe. Support the steering gear by wiring up the tie rod ends to the coil springs.
23. Remove the transaxle-to-engine retaining bolts.
24. Unfasten the shift mechanism stabilizer bar-to-transaxle retaining bolt. Remove the shift rod-to-shift shaft retaining nut and bolt, then remove the rods from the transaxle.
25. Remove the engine mount bolts.
26. Position jacks under the body mount positions and remove the 4 bolts, lower the subframe and position it aside.
27. Remove the starter mounting bolts, then remove the starter motor assembly.
28. Remove the left engine vibration dampener lower bracket.
29. Using a small screwdriver, remove the backup light switch connector from the transaxle backup light switch, located on top of the transaxle.
30. Position a suitable support jack and adapter under the transaxle.
31. Lower the transaxle, remove it from the engine and lower it from the vehicle.
**To install:**
32. Raise the transaxle into position. Engage the input shaft spline into the clutch disc and work the transaxle onto the dowel sleeves. Make sure the transaxle assembly is flush with the rear face of the engine before installation of the retaining bolts.
33. Install the engine to transaxle retaining bolts. Tighten to 28–31 ft. lbs. (38–42 Nm).
34. Engage the backup light switch electrical connector.
35. Install the starter motor. Tighten the retaining bolts to 30–40 ft. lbs. (41–54 Nm).
36. Using jacks, position the subframe and raise it into position. Install the 4 bolts and tighten to 65–85 ft. lbs. (88–115 Nm).
37. Install the left vibration dampener lower bracket.

38. Install the engine mount bolts and tighten to 40–55 ft. lbs. (54–75 Nm).
39. Connect the shift cables to the transaxle.
40. Install the engine to transaxle bolts and tighten to 28–31 ft. lbs. (38–42 Nm).
41. Install the steering gear retaining nuts and tighten to 85–100 ft. lbs. (115–135 Nm).
42. Install the center support bearing retaining bolts and tighten to 85–100 ft. lbs. (115–135 Nm).
43. Install the right halfshaft into the transaxle.
44. Install the left inboard CV-joint assembly into the transaxle.
45. Connect the battery cable bracket to the subframe.
46. Connect the power steering cooler to the subframe.
47. Position the catalytic converter, then install retaining bolts and tighten to 25–34 ft. lbs. (34–47 Nm).
48. Connect the heated oxygen sensor.
49. Install the tie rod end in the knuckle and the tie rod retaining nut. Tighten to 35–47 ft. lbs. (47–64 Nm).
50. Position the stabilizer bar to the knuckle, then install the nut.
51. Install the lower control arm ball joint to steering knuckle assembly. Install a new retaining nut and bolt, then tighten to 37–44 ft. lbs. (50–60 Nm).
52. Install the wheel and tire assemblies.
53. Apply Pipe Sealant with Teflon® D8AZ-19554-A or equivalent, to the transaxle fill plug threads, in a clockwise direction, then check the transaxle fluid level. Add the correct type of fluid (Motorcraft MERCON® Multi-Purpose Automatic Transmission Fluid or equivalent) to the bottom of the fill plug hole, then install the fill plug.
54. Carefully lower the vehicle.
55. Remove the engine support tool.
56. Using a crows foot wrench, install the speedometer cable. Connect the speedometer cable and speed sensor wire.
57. Remove the engine lifting eyes.
58. Connect the clutch cable to the clutch release lever.
59. Install the air cleaner hose, then remove the wood block from the clutch pedal.
60. Connect the negative battery cable, then check the transaxle for fluid leaks.

## Halfshafts

When removing both the left and right halfshafts, install suitable shipping plugs to prevent dislocation of the differential side gears. Should the gears become misaligned, the differential will have to be removed from the transaxle to re-align the side gears.

➡️**Do not begin this procedure unless you have the following parts: a new front axle wheel hub retainer, a new lower control arm-to-steering knuckle retaining retaining bolt and nut, a new driveshaft bearing retainer circlip and a new interconnecting shaft driveshaft bearing retainer circlip. Once these parts are removed, they CANNOT be reused. Their torque holding ability or retention capability is reduced during removal.**

➡️**Due to the automatic transaxle case configuration, the right halfshaft assembly must be removed first. Differential Rotator T81P-4026-A or equivalent, is then inserted into the transaxle to drive the left inboard CV-joint assembly from the transaxle. If only the left halfshaft assembly is to be removed for service, remove only the right halfshaft assembly from the transaxle. After removal, support it with a length of wire. Then, drive the left halfshaft assembly from the transaxle.**

REMOVAL & INSTALLATION

▶ **See Figures 13 thru 26**

1. Disconnect the negative battery cable.
2. Remove the wheel cover/hub cover from the wheel and tire assembly, then loosen the lug nuts.
3. Raise and safely support the vehicle, then remove the wheel and tire

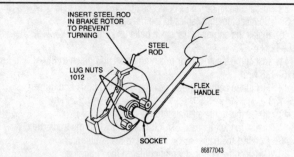

**Fig. 13** After the vehicle is safely raised, remove the wheel and tire assembly, then remove the axle wheel hub retainer, it is helpful to use a steel rod in the brake rotor to keep it from turning

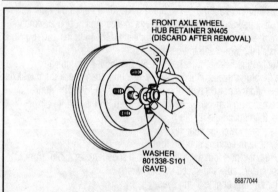

**Fig. 14** After removing the front axle wheel hub retainer, discard and replace it with a new one during installation

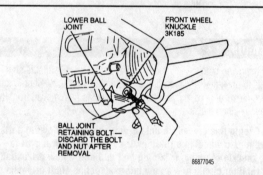

**Fig. 15** After removing the ball joint retaining bolt and nut, discard them since they lose their torque retaining quality and cannot be reused

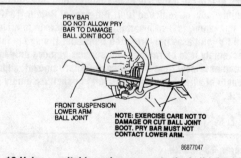

**Fig. 16** Using a suitable prybar, separate the ball joint from the steering knuckle. Position the end of the prybar outside of the bushing pocket to avoid damage to the bushing, being careful not to damage the ball joint boot

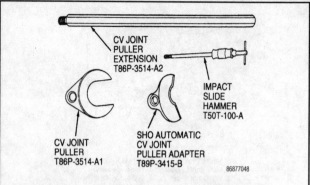

**Fig. 17** These tools are required to remove the front wheel driveshaft and joints

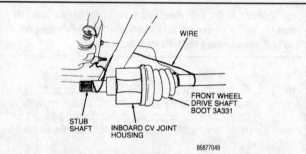

**Fig. 18** Support the end of the right-side front wheel driveshaft and joint by suspending it from a convenient underbody component with a piece of wire. Do NOT allow it to hang unsupported, as damage to the joint may occur

assembly. Insert a steel rod in the rotor to prevent it from turning, then remove the hub nut and washer. Discard the old hub nut.

4. Remove the nut from the ball joint to steering knuckle attaching bolts.

5. Drive the bolt out of the steering knuckle using a punch and hammer. Discard this bolt and nut after removal.

6. If equipped with anti-lock brakes, remove the anti-lock brake sensor and position it aside. If equipped with air suspension, remove the height sensor bracket retaining bolt and wire sensor bracket to inner fender. Position the sensor link aside.

7. Separate the ball joint from the steering knuckle using a suitable prybar. Position the end of the prybar outside of the bushing pocket to avoid damage to the bushing. Use care to prevent damage to the ball joint boot. Remove the stabilizer bar link at the stabilizer bar.

8. The following removal procedure applies to the right-side halfshaft/link shaft for all manual transaxles and for the 1986–90 2.5L engine Taurus with automatic transaxles.

   a. Remove the bolts attaching the bearing support to the bracket. Slide the link shaft out of the transaxle. Support the end of the shaft by suspending it from a convenient underbody component with a piece of wire. Do not allow the shaft to hang unsupported, damage to the outboard CV-joint may occur.

   b. Separate the outboard CV-joint from the hub using front hub remover tool T81P-1104-C or equivalent and metric adapter tools T83P-1104-BH, T86P-1104-AI and T81P-1104-A or equivalent.

➡ **Never use a hammer to separate the outboard CV-joint stub shaft from the hub. Damage to the CV-joint threads and internal components may result. The right-side link shaft and halfshaft assembly is removed as a complete unit.**

9. The following removal procedure applies to the right and left-side halfshafts of the automatic transaxle, except for 1986–90 Tauruses with a 2.5L engine and to left halfshaft for all manual transaxles.

   a. Install the CV-joint puller tool T86P-3514-A1 or equivalent,

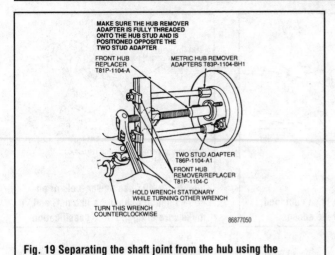

Fig. 19 Separating the shaft joint from the hub using the required tools

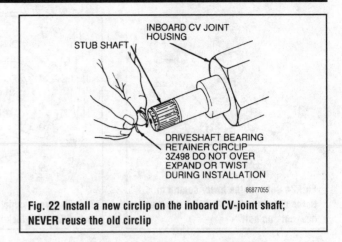

Fig. 22 Install a new circlip on the inboard CV-joint shaft; NEVER reuse the old circlip

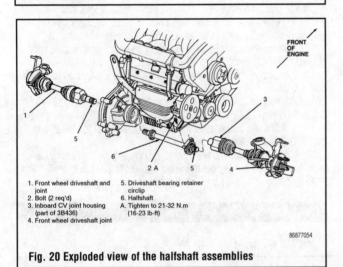

1. Front wheel driveshaft and joint
2. Bolt (2 req'd)
3. Inboard CV joint housing (part of 3B436)
4. Front wheel driveshaft joint
5. Driveshaft bearing retainer circlip
6. Halfshaft
A. Tighten to 21-32 N.m (16-23 lb-ft)

Fig. 20 Exploded view of the halfshaft assemblies

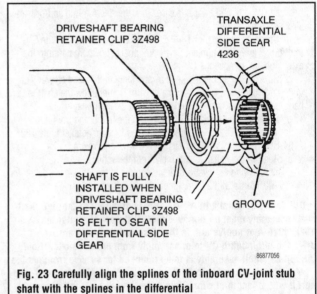

Fig. 23 Carefully align the splines of the inboard CV-joint stub shaft with the splines in the differential

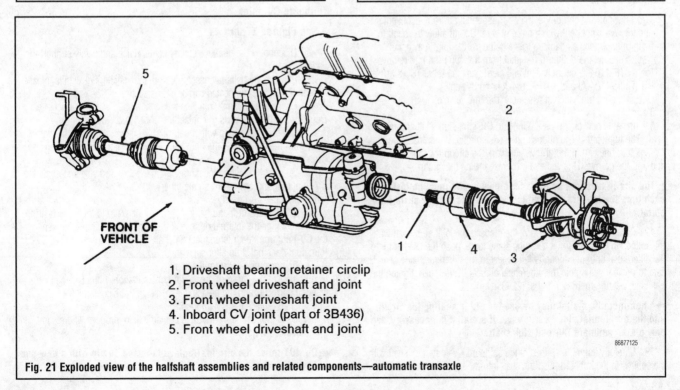

1. Driveshaft bearing retainer circlip
2. Front wheel driveshaft and joint
3. Front wheel driveshaft joint
4. Inboard CV joint (part of 3B436)
5. Front wheel driveshaft and joint

Fig. 21 Exploded view of the halfshaft assemblies and related components—automatic transaxle

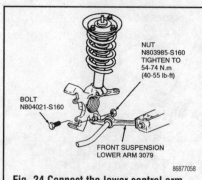

Fig. 24 Connect the lower control arm to the steering wheel knuckle using a new nut and bolt

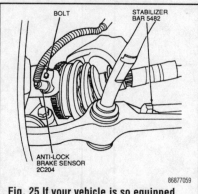

Fig. 25 If your vehicle is so equipped, install the anti-lock brake sensor

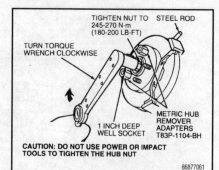

Fig. 26 Do NOT use power tools or an impact gun to tighten the hub nut, and make sure to tighten it to specification

between CV-joint and transaxle case. Turn the steering hub and/or wire strut assembly aside.

b. Screw extension tool T86P-3514-A2 or equivalent, into the CV-joint puller and hand tighten. Screw an impact slide hammer onto the extension and remove the CV-joint.

c. Support the end of the shaft by suspending it from a convenient underbody component with a piece of wire. Do not allow the shaft to hang unsupported, damage to the outboard CV-joint may occur.

d. Separate the outboard CV-joint from the hub using front hub remover tool T81P-1104-C or equivalent and metric adapter tools T83P-1104-BH, T86P-1104-Al and T81P-1104-A or equivalent.

e. Remove the halfshaft assembly from the vehicle.

10. The following removal procedure applies to the left-side halfshaft for the 1986–90 Taurus with 2.5L engine automatic transaxle:

➡**Due to the automatic transaxle case configuration, the right half-shaft assembly must be removed first. Differential rotator tool T81P-4026-A or equivalent, is then inserted into the transaxle to drive the left inboard CV-joint assembly from the transaxle. If only the left halfshaft assembly is to be removed for service, remove the right halfshaft assembly from the transaxle first. After removal, support it with a length of wire. Then drive the left halfshaft assembly from the transaxle.**

a. Support the end of the shaft by suspending it from a convenient underbody component with a piece of wire. Do not allow the shaft to hang unsupported as damage to the outboard CV-joint may occur.

b. Separate the outboard CV-joint from the hub front hub remover tool T81P-1104-C or equivalent and metric adapter tools T83P-1104-BH, T86P-1104-Al and T81P-1104-A or equivalent.

c. Remove the halfshaft assembly from the vehicle.

**To install:**

11. Install a new circlip on the inboard CV-joint stub shaft and/or link shaft. The outboard CV-joint does not have a circlip. When installing the circlip, start one end in the groove and work the circlip over the stub shaft end into the groove. This will avoid overexpanding the circlip.

➡**The circlip must not be re-used. A new circlip must be installed each time the inboard CV-joint is installed into the transaxle differential.**

12. Carefully align the splines of the inboard CV-joint stub shaft with the splines in the differential. Exerting some force, push the CV-joint into the differential until the circlip is felt to seat in the differential side gear. Use care to prevent damage to the differential oil seal. If equipped, tighten the link shaft bearing to 16–23 ft. lbs. (22–31 Nm).

➡**A non-metallic mallet may be used to aid in seating the circlip into the differential side gear groove. If a mallet is necessary, tap only on the outboard CV-joint stub shaft.**

13. Carefully align the splines of the outboard CV-joint stub shaft with the splines in the hub and push the shaft into the hub as far as possible.

14. Temporarily fasten the rotor to the hub with washers and two wheel lug nuts. Insert a steel rod into the rotor and rotate clockwise to contact the knuckle to prevent the rotor from turning during the CV-joint installation.

15. Install the hub nut washer and a new hub nut. Manually thread the retainer onto the CV-joint as far as possible.

16. Connect the control arm to the steering knuckle, then install a new nut and bolt. Tighten the nut to 40–55 ft. lbs. (54–74 Nm).

17. If equipped, install the anti-lock brake sensor and/or the ride height sensor bracket.

18. Connect the stabilizer link to the stabilizer bar. Tighten to 35–48 ft. lbs. (47–65 Nm).

19. Install a new hub retainer nut, then tighten the nut to 180–200 ft. lbs. (245–270 Nm). Remove the steel rod.

20. Install the wheel and tire assembly, snugging the lug nuts by hand, then lower the vehicle. Tighten the wheel lug nuts to 80–105 ft. lbs. (108–142 Nm). Fill the transaxle to the proper level with the specified fluid.

## CV-Joint

### REMOVAL & INSTALLATION

#### Outboard CV-Joint

▶ **See Figures 27 thru 49**

1. Disconnect the negative battery cable. Raise and safely support the vehicle.

2. Remove the halfshaft assembly from the vehicle. For details, please refer to the procedure located earlier in this section.

3. Clamp the halfshaft in a vise that is equipped with soft jaw covers. Do not allow the vise jaws to contact the boot or boot clamp.

4. Cut the boot clamp with a pair of side cutters, then pull the clamp away from the boot. Slide the boot back over the shaft after the clamp has been removed.

5. Support the interconnecting shaft in a soft jawed vise and angle the CV-joint pointing downward so the inner bearing race is exposed.

6. Use a brass drift and hammer, give a sharp tap to the inner bearing race to dislodge the internal driveshaft bearing retainer circlip and separate the CV-joint from the interconnecting shaft. Make sure to secure the CV-joint so it does not drop after separation.

7. Remove the boot from the shaft.

8. Inspect the CV-joint grease for contamination. If the CV-joints are working correctly, and the grease doesn't seem to be contaminated, add grease, then replace the CV-joint boot.

9. If the lubricant appears to be contaminated, proceed with a complete CV-joint disassembly.

➡**Do NOT reuse the circlip. Replace the used circlip with a new one before assembly.**

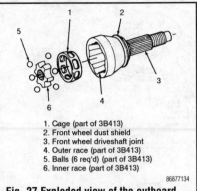

1. Cage (part of 3B413)
2. Front wheel dust shield
3. Front wheel driveshaft joint
4. Outer race (part of 3B413)
5. Balls (6 req'd) (part of 3B413)
6. Inner race (part of 3B413)

86877134

**Fig. 27 Exploded view of the outboard CV-joint assembly**

TCCS7030

**Fig. 28 Before removal, check the CV-boot for wear or damage**

TCCS7034

**Fig. 29 Clean the CV-joint prior to removing the boot, but be careful not to damage anything**

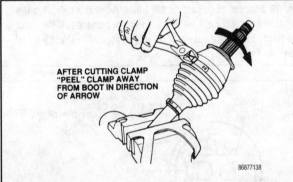

AFTER CUTTING CLAMP "PEEL" CLAMP AWAY FROM BOOT IN DIRECTION OF ARROW

86877138

**Fig. 30 Cut the boot clamp with a pair of side cutters, then pull the clamp away from the boot**

86877139

**Fig. 31 Slide the boot back over the shaft once the clamp has been removed**

10. Remove and discard the circlip located near the end of the interconnecting shaft. The stop ring, located just below the circlip should be removed and replaced only if damaged or worn.

➡ The vise must be equipped with soft jaw covers to avoid damaging the shaft splines.

11. Clamp the CV-joint in a vise with soft jaw covers, with the outer face pointing upward. Be careful not to damage the dust shield.
12. Press down on the inner race until it tilts enough to permit removal of the ball. A tight assembly can be tilted by tapping the inner race with a wooden dowel and hammer, but do not hit the cage.

### ✳✳ WARNING

**Be careful not to scratch or damage the inner race or cage spheres.**

13. With the cage sufficiently tilted, remove the ball from the cage. Repeat this until all of the balls are removed. If the balls are tight in the cage, use a blunt edged prytool to pry the balls from the cage.
14. Pivot the cage and inner race assembly until it is straight up and down in the outer race. Align the cage windows with the outer race lands while pivoting the bearing cage.
15. With the cage pivoted and aligned, lift the assembly from the outer race. Rotate the inner race up and out of the cage.

**To install:**

16. Apply a light coating of Ford High Temperature Constant Velocity Joint Grease E43Z-19590-A or equivalent, on the inner and outer ball races.
17. Install the inner race in the bearing cage.
18. Install the inner race and cage assembly in the outer race. Install the assembly vertically, then pivot 90° into position.
19. Align the bearing cage and inner race with the outer race. Tilt the inner race and cage, then install a ball. Repeat until all balls are installed.

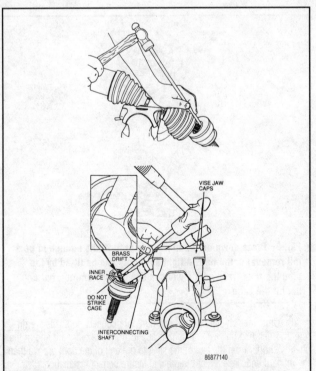

VISE JAW CAPS

BRASS DRIFT

INNER RACE

DO NOT STRIKE CAGE

INTERCONNECTING SHAFT

86877140

**Fig. 32 Using a brass drift and hammer, give a sharp tap to the inner bearing race to dislodge the internal driveshaft bearing retainer circlip and separate the CV-joint from the interconnecting shaft. Make sure to secure the CV-joint so it does not drop after separation. The boot cannot be removed from the shaft**

Fig. 33 Check the CV-joint grease for contamination or foreign debris by visually inspecting it and rubbing it with fingers. Any grittiness indicates contamination

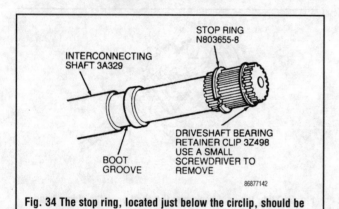

Fig. 34 The stop ring, located just below the circlip, should be removed and replaced only if damaged or worn

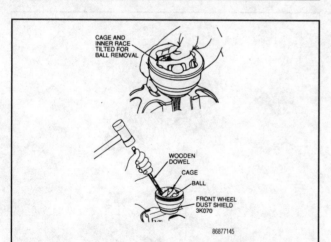

Fig. 35 Press down on the inner race until it tilts enough to permit removal of the ball. A tight assembly can be tilted by tapping the inner race with a wooden dowel and hammer, but do not hit the cage

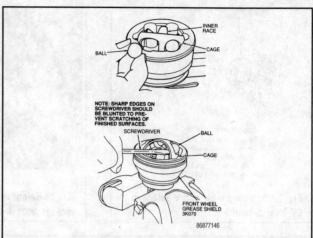

Fig. 36 With the cage sufficiently tilted, remove a ball from the cage. Repeat this until all of the balls are removed. If the balls are tight in the cage, use a blunt edged prytool to pry the balls from the cage

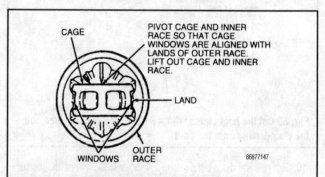

Fig. 37 Pivot the cage and inner race assembly until it is straight up and down in the outer race. Align the cage windows with the outer race lands while pivoting the bearing cage

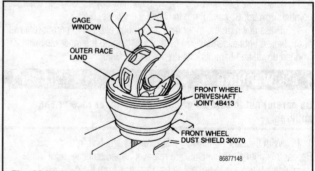

Fig. 38 With the cage pivoted and aligned, lift the assembly from the outer race. Rotate the inner race up and out of the cage

20. On some vehicles, the left and right interconnecting shafts are different, depending on year and vehicle application. The outboard end of the shaft is shorter from the end of the shaft to the end of the boot groove than the inboard end. Take a measurement to insure correct installation.

21. If removed, install the CV-joint boot after removing the stop ring. Make sure the CV boot is seated in its groove and the clamp is in position using Boot Clamp Installer T95P-3514-A or equivalent. Tighten the tool through the bolt until it's in a closed position, then remove the tool.

22. If removed, install the stop ring. If not removed, make sure the ring is properly seated in its groove.

23. Install a new circlip in the groove nearest the end of the shaft by starting one end in the groove, then work the circlip over the inboard CV joint stub shaft pilot bearing housing end and into the groove. This will avoid overexpanding the circlip.

24. Before positioning the boot over the CV-joint, pack the joint and boot with Ford High Temperature Constant Velocity Joint Grease E43Z-19590-A or equivalent. Pack the joint with grease. Any remaining grease in the tube is to be spread evenly inside of the boot.

25. With the front wheel driveshaft joint boot held back, position the CV-joint on the shaft and tap into position using a plastic tipped hammer.

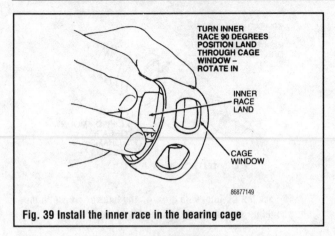

Fig. 39 Install the inner race in the bearing cage

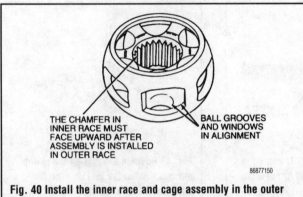

Fig. 40 Install the inner race and cage assembly in the outer race. Install the assembly vertically, then pivot 90° into position

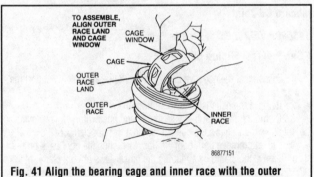

Fig. 41 Align the bearing cage and inner race with the outer race. Tilt the inner race and cage, then install a ball. Repeat until all balls are installed

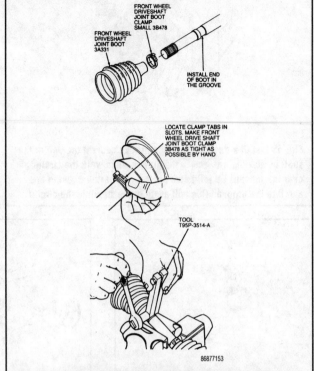

Fig. 43 Make sure the CV boot is seated in its groove and the clamp is in position using Boot Clamp Installer T95P-3514-A or equivalent. Tighten the tool through the bolt until it's in a closed position, then remove the tool

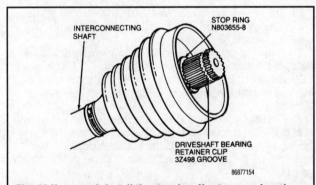

Fig. 44 If removed, install the stop ring. If not removed, make sure the ring is properly seated in its groove

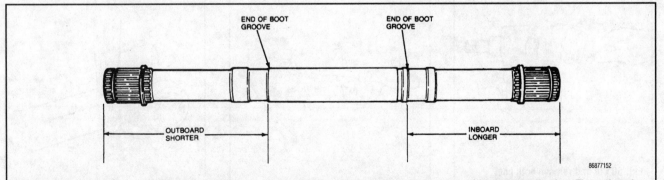

Fig. 42 On some vehicles, the left and right interconnecting shafts are different, depending on year and vehicle application. The outboard end of the shaft is shorter from the end of the shaft to the end of the boot groove than the inboard end. Take a measurement to insure correct installation

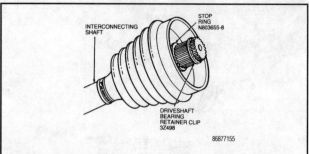

**Fig. 45 Install a new circlip in the groove nearest the end of the shaft by starting one end in the groove, then work the circlip over the inboard CV joint stub shaft pilot bearing housing end and into the groove. This will avoid overexpanding the circlip**

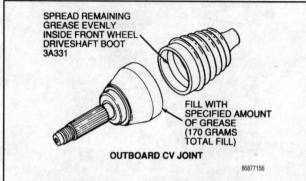

**Fig. 46 Pack the CV-joint with grease. Any leftover grease in the tube should be spread evenly inside of the boot**

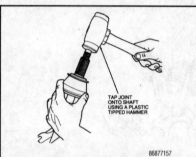

**Fig. 47 With the front wheel driveshaft joint boot held back, position the CV-joint on the shaft and tap into position using a plastic tipped hammer**

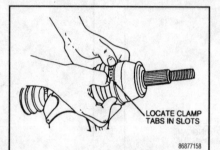

**Fig. 48 Make sure the boot is seated in its groove and the clamp is in position, using Boot Clamp Installer T95P-3514-A or equivalent**

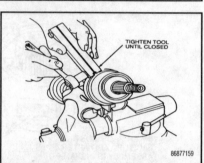

**Fig. 49 Position the tool on the clamp ear and tighten the tool through the bolt, until it is in the closed position, then remove the tool**

26. The CV-joint is fully seated when the circlip locks in the groove cut into the CV-joint inner race. Check for seating by trying to pull the joint away from the shaft.

27. Remove all excess grease from the CV-joint external surfaces and mating boot surface. Position the boot over the joint.

28. Before installing the boot clamp, make sure all air pressure that may have built up in the boot is removed. Pry up on the boot lip to allow the air to escape.

29. Position the boot over the joint, then make sure the boot is seated in its groove and the clamp is in position using Boot Clamp Installer T95P-3514-A or equivalent. Position the tool on the clamp ear, then tighten the tool through the bolt, until it is in the closed position. Remove the tool.

30. Install the halfshaft assembly and lower the vehicle. Connect the negative battery cable.

### Inboard CV-Joint

#### 1986–92 VEHICLES

#### ♦ See Figures 50 thru 55

1. Disconnect the negative battery cable. Raise and safely support the vehicle.

2. Remove the halfshaft assembly from the vehicle.

3. Clamp the halfshaft in a vise that is equipped with soft jaw covers. Do not allow the vise jaws to contact the boot or boot clamp.

4. Cut and remove both boot clamps, then slide the boot back on the shaft. Remove the clamp by engaging the pincer jaws of boot clamp pliers D87P-1090-A or equivalent, in the closing hooks on the clamp and draw together. Disengage the windows and locking hooks, then remove the clamp.

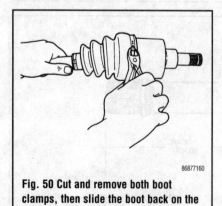

**Fig. 50 Cut and remove both boot clamps, then slide the boot back on the shaft**

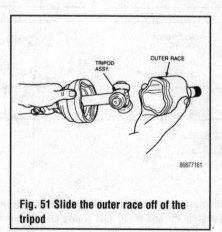

**Fig. 51 Slide the outer race off of the tripod**

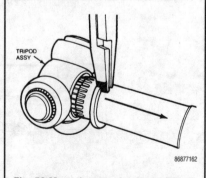

**Fig. 52 Move the stop ring back on the shaft using snapring pliers, then . . .**

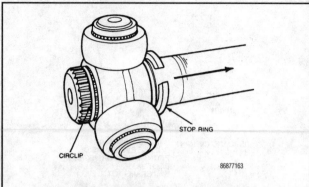

**Fig. 53 . . . move the tripod assembly back on the shaft to allow access to the circlip**

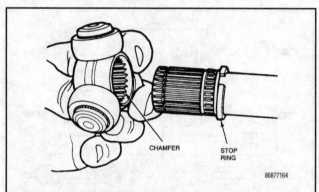

**Fig. 54 Install the tripod assembly with its chamfered side toward the stop ring**

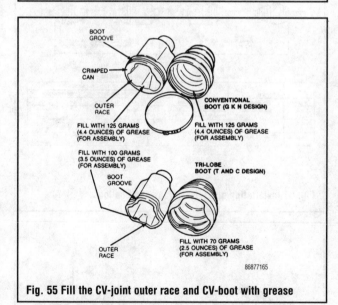

**Fig. 55 Fill the CV-joint outer race and CV-boot with grease**

5. Mark the position of the outer race in relation to the shaft, then remove the outer race from the tripod.

6. Move the stop ring back on the shaft using snapring pliers. Move the tripod assembly back on the shaft to allow access to the circlip.

7. Remove and discard the circlip from the shaft, then replace with a new one during installation. Mark the position of the tripod on the shaft and remove the tripod assembly. Remove the boot.

8. Check the CV-joint grease for contamination. If the CV-joints are operating properly and the grease is not contaminated, add grease and

replace the boot. If the grease appears contaminated, disassemble the CV-joint and clean or replace, as necessary.

**To install:**

9. Install the CV-joint boot. Make sure the boot is seated in the boot groove on the shaft. Tighten the clamp using crimping pliers, but do not tighten to the point where the clamp bridge is cut or the boot is damaged.

10. Install the tripod assembly with chamfered side toward the stop ring. If the tripod is being reused, align the marks that were made during the removal procedure.

11. Install a new circlip. Compress the circlip and slide the tripod assembly forward over the circlip to expose the stop ring groove.

12. Move the stop ring into the groove using snapring pliers, making sure it is fully seated in the groove.

13. Fill the CV-joint outer race and CV-boot with grease. Install the outer race over the tripod assembly, aligning the marks made during the removal procedure.

14. Remove all excess grease from the CV-joint external surfaces and mating boot surface. Position the boot over the CV-joint making sure the boot is seated in the groove. Move the CV-joint in and out, as necessary, to adjust the length to the following specifications:

- Automatic transaxle left halfshaft, except 1986–90 Taurus with 2.5L engine—18.27 in. (464mm)
- Automatic transaxle right halfshaft, except 1986–90 Taurus with 2.5L engine—23.58 in. (599mm)
- Automatic transaxle left halfshaft, 1986–90 Taurus with 2.5L engine—22.80 in. (579mm)
- Automatic transaxle right halfshaft, 1986–90 Taurus with 2.5L engine—20.09 in. (510mm)
- Manual transaxle left halfshaft—21.24 in. (539.5mm)
- Manual transaxle right halfshaft—21.63 in. (549.5mm)

15. Before installing the boot clamp, make sure any air pressure that may have built up in the boot is relieved. Insert a small prybar between the boot and outer race to allow the trapped air to escape. Release the air only after adjusting the length dimension.

16. Seat the boot in the groove and clamp in position using crimping pliers D87P-1098-A or equivalent. Install the clamp as follows:

    a. With the boot seated in the groove, place the clamp over the boot.

    b. Engage hook C in the window.

    c. Place the pincer jaws of the crimping pliers in closing hooks A and B.

    d. Secure the clamp by drawing the closing hooks together. When windows 1 and 2 are above locking hooks D and E, the spring tab will press the windows over the locking hooks and engage the clamp.

17. Install the halfshaft and lower the vehicle. Connect the negative battery cable.

### 1993–95 VEHICLES EXCEPT 3.2L SHO

▶ See Figures 56 thru 62

On this design, the tripod assembly cannot be removed from the interconnecting shaft. If a tripod assembly, or interconnecting shaft is required, a driveshaft and joint assembly must be used. But if CV-joint boots or boot clamps are needed, they are available separately.

1. Disconnect the negative battery cable. Raise and safely support the vehicle.

2. Remove the halfshaft assembly from the vehicle.

3. Clamp the halfshaft in a vise that is equipped with soft jaw covers. Do not allow the vise jaws to contact the boot or boot clamp.

4. Cut and remove both boot clamps, then slide the boot back on the shaft. Remove the clamp by engaging the pincer jaws of boot clamp pliers D87P-1090-A or equivalent, in the closing hooks on the clamp and draw together. Disengage the windows and locking hooks, then remove the clamp.

5. Slide the inboard CV-joint housing off of the tripod.

6. When replacing damaged boots, the grease should be checked for contamination. If the CV-joints are operating satisfactorily, and the grease does not seem to be contaminated, add grease, then replace the boot. If the

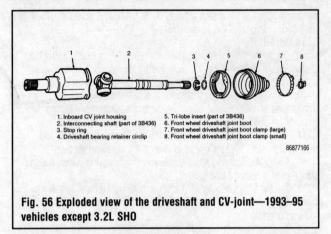

Fig. 56 Exploded view of the driveshaft and CV-joint—1993–95 vehicles except 3.2L SHO

1. Inboard CV joint housing
2. Interconnecting shaft (part of 3B436)
3. Stop ring
4. Driveshaft bearing retainer circlip
5. Tri-lobe insert (part of 3B436)
6. Front wheel driveshaft joint boot
7. Front wheel driveshaft joint boot clamp (large)
8. Front wheel driveshaft joint boot clamp (small)

86877166

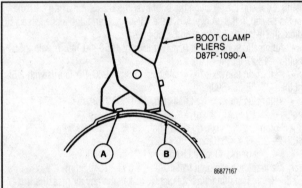

BOOT CLAMP PLIERS
D87P-1090-A

86877167

Fig. 57 Removing the clamp using Boot Clamp Pliers D87P-1090-A

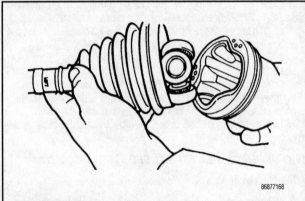

86877168

Fig. 58 Slide the inboard CV-joint housing off of the tripod

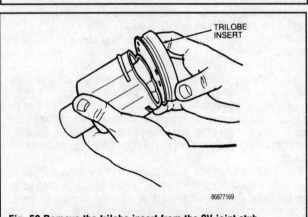

TRILOBE INSERT

86877169

Fig. 59 Remove the trilobe insert from the CV-joint stub

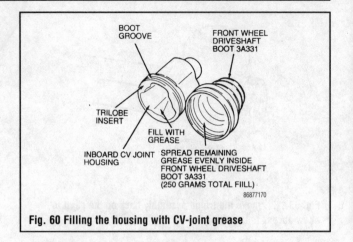

BOOT GROOVE

FRONT WHEEL DRIVESHAFT BOOT 3A331

TRILOBE INSERT

FILL WITH GREASE

INBOARD CV JOINT HOUSING

SPREAD REMAINING GREASE EVENLY INSIDE FRONT WHEEL DRIVESHAFT BOOT 3A331 (250 GRAMS TOTAL FILL)

86877170

Fig. 60 Filling the housing with CV-joint grease

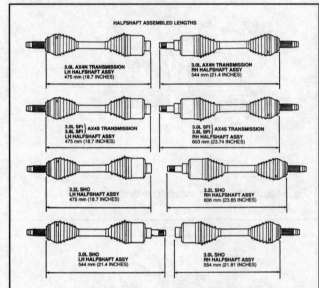

HALFSHAFT ASSEMBLED LENGTHS

3.0L AX4N TRANSMISSION LH HALFSHAFT ASSY 475 mm (18.7 INCHES)

3.0L AX4N TRANSMISSION RH HALFSHAFT ASSY 544 mm (21.4 INCHES)

3.0L SFI 3.8L SFI AX4S TRANSMISSION LH HALFSHAFT ASSY 475 mm (18.7 INCHES)

3.0L SFI 3.8L SFI AX4S TRANSMISSION RH HALFSHAFT ASSY 603 mm (23.74 INCHES)

3.2L SHO LH HALFSHAFT ASSY 475 mm (18.7 INCHES)

3.2L SHO RH HALFSHAFT ASSY 606 mm (23.85 INCHES)

3.0L SHO LH HALFSHAFT ASSY 544 mm (21.4 INCHES)

3.0L SHO RH HALFSHAFT ASSY 554 mm (21.81 INCHES)

LUBRICANT SPECIFICATIONS—HALFSHAFT ASSEMBLIES

| POWERTRAIN | | | TOTAL FILL AMOUNT | | | |
| | | | INBOARD CV | | OUTBOARD CV | |
| Engine | Transmission | Lubricant | LH | RH | LH | RH |
| --- | --- | --- | --- | --- | --- | --- |
| 3.2L | SHO Automatic | ESP-M1C207-A (E43Z-19590-A) | 490 g 17.3 oz | 490 g 17.3 oz | 170 g 6.0 oz | 170 g 6.0 oz |
| 3.2L | SHO Manual Transaxle | ESP-M1C207-A (E43Z-19590-A) | 250 g 8.8 oz | 250 g 8.8 oz | 170 g 6.0 oz | 170 g 6.0 oz |
| 3.0L / 3.8L | AX4S / AX4N | ESP-M1C207-A (E43Z-19590-A) | 250 g 8.8 oz | 250 g 8.8 oz | 170 g 6.0 oz | 170 g 6.0 oz |

86877171

Fig. 61 Installation and lubrication specifications

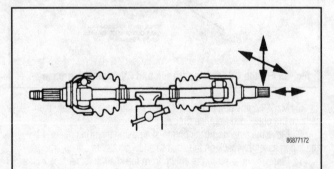

86877172

Fig. 62 Work the CV-joint through its full range of travel at various angles. The joint should flex, extend and compress smoothly

grease is contaminated, you will have to proceed with a complete CV-joint disassembly and inspection.

7. If further disassembly is required, remove the outboard CV-joint and boot as described earlier in this section.

8. Remove the driveshaft joint stop ring and bearing retainer circlip.

9. Slide the inboard boot off of the interconnecting shaft.

10. Remove the trilobe insert from the CV-joint stub. Remove the grease from the outer race, then inspect the outer race and tripod assembly.

**To install:**

11. Install the boot on the interconnecting halfshaft. Position the boot to allow for the CV-joint housing installation.

12. Install the trilobe insert on the CV-joint housing positioning in the groove on the outer race.

13. Fill the CV-joint housing with Ford High Temperature Constant Velocity Grease E43Z-19590-A or equivalent, and spread remaining grease evenly inside of the joint boot. The total fill amount is 9 oz. (250 grams).

14. Install the CV-joint on the tripod assembly.

15. Before installing the boot clamp, make sure any air pressure that may have built up in the boot is relieved. Insert a small prybar between the boot and outer race to allow the trapped air to escape. Release the air only after adjusting the length dimension.

16. Remove all excess grease from the CV-joint external surfaces and mating boot surface. Position the boot over the CV-joint making sure the boot is seated in the groove. Move the CV-joint in and out, as necessary, to adjust the length to the specifications in the accompanying figure.

➡All vehicles, except SHO vehicles, require a reusable low profile large front CV-joint boot clamp on the right-hand side inboard CV-joint.

17. Seat the boot in the grooves, then clamp in position using Boot Clamp Installer T94P-3514-A or equivalent, on the left CV-joint housing.

18. Install the large low profile right-hand boot clamp as follows:
   a. With the boot seated in the groove, place the clamp over the boot.
   b. Engage hook C in the window.
   c. Place the pincer jaws of the crimping pliers in closing hooks A and B.
   d. Secure the clamp by drawing the closing hooks together. When windows 1 and 2 are above locking hooks D and E, the spring tab will press the windows over the locking hooks and engage the clamp.

19. Position Boot Clamp Installer Tool T95P-3514-A or equivalent, on the clamp ears, then tighten the tool through the bolt until the tool is in the closed position. Remove the tool.

➡Do not overexpand or twist the circlip during installation. ALWAYS replace the circlip with a new one during installation.

20. On the right-hand side inboard CV-joint housing, install a new circlip, in the groove nearest the end of the shaft by starting one end in the groove, then working the circlip over the stub shaft and into the groove.

21. Work the CV-joint through its full range of travel at various angles. The joint should flex, extend and compress smoothly.

22. Install the halfshaft assembly, then carefully lower the vehicle.

23. Connect the negative battery cable.

### 3.2L SHO

▶ **See Figures 63 thru 71**

The inboard CV-joint assembly on these vehicles is permanently retained to the interconnecting shaft. The service CV-joint includes the shaft and CV-joint boot. The boot or driveshaft and joint replacement will necessitate removal of the CV-joint and boot.

1. Disconnect the negative battery cable. Raise and safely support the vehicle.

2. Remove the halfshaft assembly from the vehicle.

3. Clamp the halfshaft in a vise that is equipped with soft jaw covers. Do not allow the vise jaws to contact the boot or boot clamp.

4. Cut and remove both of the CV-joint boot clamps.

5. Slide the boot back on the shaft, then wipe the grease away from the CV-joint.

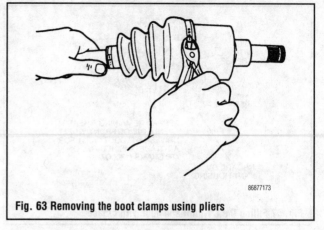

**Fig. 63 Removing the boot clamps using pliers**

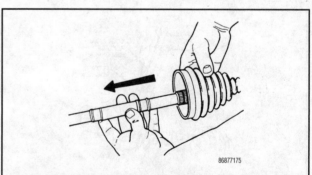

**Fig. 64 After sliding the boot back on the shaft, wipe away the grease from the CV-joint**

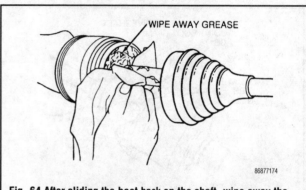

**Fig. 65 Installing the CV-joint boot on the interconnecting shaft; make sure to position the boot to allow for CV-joint housing installation**

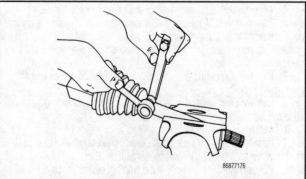

**Fig. 66 Using the boot clamp installer to fasten the small boot clamp**

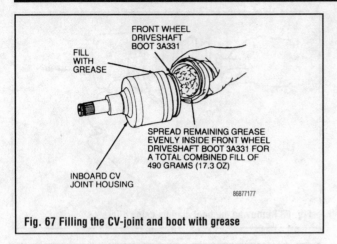

Fig. 67 Filling the CV-joint and boot with grease

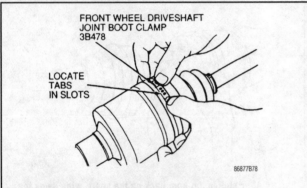

Fig. 68 After positioning the clamp tabs in the slots, make the clamps as tight as possible by hand

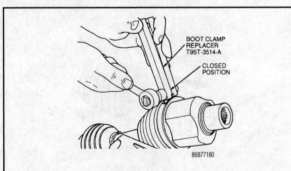

Fig. 69 Position the Boot Clamp Replacer T95T-3514-A or equivalent, on the clamp ear, then tighten the tool through the bolt until the tool is in a closed position

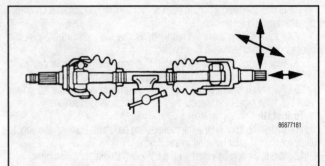

Fig. 70 Work the CV-joint through its full range of travel at various angles. The joint should flex, extend and compress smoothly

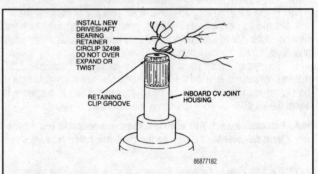

Fig. 71 Do not overexpand or twist the circlip during installation. ALWAYS replace the circlip with a new one during installation

6. When replacing damaged boots, the grease should be checked for contamination. If the CV-joints are operating satisfactorily, and the grease does not seem to be contaminated, add grease, then replace the boot. If the grease is contaminated, you will have to proceed with a complete CV-joint disassembly and inspection.

7. If further disassembly is required, remove the driveshaft and CV-joint, and the boot.

8. Remove the driveshaft stop ring and bearing retainer circlip, the slide the joint boot off of the interconnecting shaft.

**To install:**

9. Install the CV-joint boot on the interconnecting shaft. Position the boot to allow for inboard CV-joint housing installation.

10. Position the CV-joint boot in the small boot groove. Using Boot

Clamp Installer T95P-3514-A or equivalent, move the small boot clamp in position. Tighten the tool through the bolt until the tool is in the closed position.

11. Using Ford High Temperature Constant Velocity Grease E43Z-19590-A or equivalent, fill the inboard CV-joint with grease, then spread the remaining grease evenly inside of the boot.

12. Before installing the boot clamp, make sure any air pressure that may have built up in the boot is relieved. Insert a small prybar between the boot and outer race to allow the trapped air to escape. Release the air only after adjusting the length dimension.

13. Remove all excess grease from the external CV-joint surfaces, and boot sealing surfaces. Slide the CV-joint boot into position on the inboard CV-joint housing. Move the CV-joint in and out, as necessary, to adjust to the specified length shown in the accompanying figure.

14. Locate the clamp tabs in the slots, then make the clamps as tight as possible by hand.

15. Make sure the boot is seated in its groove and the clamp is in position. Position the Boot Clamp Replacer T95T-3514-A or equivalent on the clamp ear, then tighten the tool through the bolt until the tool is in a closed position.

16. Work the CV-joint through its full range of travel at various angles. The joint should flex, extend and compress smoothly.

➡**Do not overexpand or twist the circlip during installation. ALWAYS replace the circlip with a new one during installation.**

17. Install a new circlip, in the groove nearest the end of the shaft by starting one end in the groove, then working the circlip over the stub shaft and into the groove.

18. Install the halfshaft assembly, then carefully lower the vehicle.

19. Connect the negative battery cable.

## CLUTCH

### ✳✳ CAUTION

**The clutch driven disc may contain asbestos, which has been determined to be a cancer causing agent. Never clean clutch surfaces with compressed air! Avoid inhaling any dust from any clutch surface! When cleaning clutch surfaces, use a commercially available brake cleaning fluid**

### Adjustments

#### PEDAL HEIGHT/FREE-PLAY

The free-play in the clutch is adjusted by a built in mechanism that allows the clutch controls to be self-adjusted during normal operation. The self-adjusting feature should be checked every 5,000 miles (8,052 km). This is accomplished by insuring that the clutch pedal travels to the top of its upward position. Grasp the clutch pedal by hand or put a foot under the clutch pedal; pull up on the pedal until it stops. Very little effort is required (about 10 lbs.). During the application of upward pressure, a click may be heard which means an adjustment was necessary and has been accomplished.

### Driven Disc and Pressure Plate

#### REMOVAL & INSTALLATION

▶ **See Figures 72 thru 79**

1. Disconnect the negative battery cable, then raise and safely support the vehicle.

2. Remove the transaxle. For details, please refer to the procedure located earlier in this section.

3. Loosen the six clutch pressure plate cover retaining bolts evenly to release the spring tension gradually, and to avoid distorting the cover. If the same clutch pressure plate and cover are to be installed, mark the cover and the flywheel so the pressure plate can be installed in its original position.

4. Remove the pressure plate and clutch disc from the flywheel.

5. Inspect the flywheel, clutch disc, pressure plate, throwout bearing and the clutch fork for wear. Replace parts as required. If the flywheel shows any signs of overheating (blue discoloration) or if it is badly grooved or scored, it should be refaced or replaced.

**To install:**

➡**Avoid touching the clutch disc face, dropping parts or contaminating parts with oil or grease.**

6. The clutch disc must be assembled so that the stamped notation is facing toward the engine. The three flywheel-to-clutch pressure plate dowels must be properly aligned with the clutch pressure plate. (Bent, damaged or missing dowels must be replaced.)

7. Clean the pressure plate and flywheel surfaces thoroughly.

8. Position the disc and pressure plate on the flywheel, then insert the cover retaining bolts, but do not tighten them at this time.

9. Align the clutch disc using Clutch Arbor/Aligner Tool T81P-7550-A or equivalent, inserted in the crankshaft. To avoid clutch pressure plate cover distortion, alternately tighten the cover bolts until the cover is fully seated, then tighten to 24 ft. lbs. (33 Nm) for 1993–95 vehicles. For 1986–92 vehicles, alternately tighten the cover bolts to 12–24 ft. lbs. (16–33 Nm). Remove the alignment tool.

10. Install the transaxle. For details, please refer to the procedure earlier in this section.

11. Connect the negative battery cable.

**Fig. 72 Installing the clutch arbor/alignment tool—this can be done before removal, or during installation**

**Fig. 73 Once the transaxle is removed, the clutch pressure plate cover is visible**

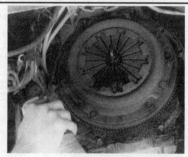

**Fig. 74 If the pressure plate cover is dirty or dusty, clean it with a commercially available spray cleaner**

**Fig. 75 Loosen the six pressure plate retaining bolts evenly to release the tension gradually**

**Fig. 76 After all of the retaining bolts are removed, you can remove the pressure plate and clutch disc from the flywheel**

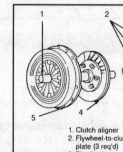

1. Clutch aligner
2. Flywheel-to-clutch pressure plate (3 req'd)
3. Flywheel
4. Clutch disc
5. Clutch pressure plate

**Fig. 77 View of a common clutch disc and pressure plate mounting**

Fig. 78 Exploded view of the location of the clutch disc, pressure plate and related components

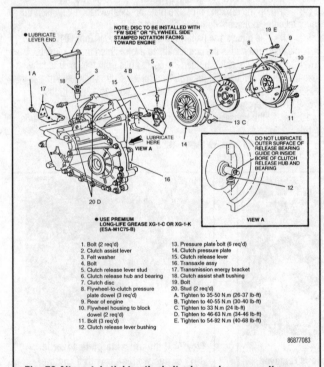

NOTE: DISC TO BE INSTALLED WITH "FW SIDE" OR "FLYWHEEL SIDE" STAMPED NOTATION FACING TOWARD ENGINE

LUBRICATE LEVER END

LUBRICATE HERE
VIEW A

DO NOT LUBRICATE OUTER SURFACE OF RELEASE BEARING GUIDE OR INSIDE BORE OF CLUTCH RELEASE HUB AND BEARING

VIEW A

USE PREMIUM LONG-LIFE GREASE XG-1-C OR XG-1-K (ESA-M1C75-B)

1. Bolt (2 req'd)
2. Clutch assist lever
3. Felt washer
4. Bolt
5. Clutch release lever stud
6. Clutch release hub and bearing
7. Clutch disc
8. Flywheel-to-clutch pressure plate dowel (3 req'd)
9. Rear of engine
10. Flywheel housing to block dowel (2 req'd)
11. Bolt (3 req'd)
12. Clutch release lever bushing

13. Pressure plate bolt (6 req'd)
14. Clutch pressure plate
15. Clutch release lever
16. Transaxle assy
17. Transmission energy bracket
18. Clutch assist shaft bushing
19. Bolt
20. Stud (2 req'd)
A. Tighten to 35-50 N.m (26-37 lb-ft)
B. Tighten to 40-55 N.m (30-40 lb-ft)
C. Tighten to 33 N.m (24 lb-ft)
D. Tighten to 46-63 N.m (34-46 lb-ft)
E. Tighten to 54-92 N.m (40-68 lb-ft)

Fig. 79 Alternately tighten the bolts, in a crisscross pattern, until the cover is fully seated to avoid cover distortion, then tighten the bolts to specification

## Clutch Cable

### REMOVAL & INSTALLATION

♦ See Figures 80 and 81

➡ Whenever the clutch cable is disconnected for any reason, such as transaxle removal or clutch/clutch pedal/clutch cable replacement, the proper method for installing the clutch cable must be followed.

1. Disconnect the negative battery cable.
2. Position the clutch shield away from the mounting plate bracket/clutch release plate by removing the rear retaining screw. Loosen the front retaining screw located near the toe board, then rotate the clutch

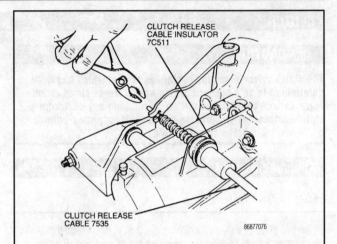

Fig. 80 Grasp the end of the clutch cable (not the wire strand part of the inner cable) with pliers, then unhook the clutch cable from the clutch lever

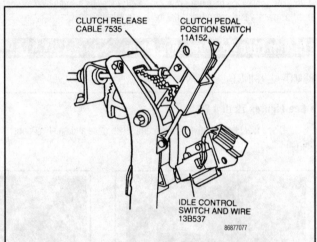

Fig. 81 With the quadrant at the window stop position, push the cable through the insulator on the bumper bracket and through the recess between the pedal and quadrant

pedal shield aside. Secure by tightening the front screw. (The rear retaining screw is closest the the instrument panel.)

3. Prop up the clutch pedal to lift the pawl free of the quadrant which is part of the self-adjuster mechanism.

➡ Do NOT allow the clutch pedal adjuster quadrant to snap back.

4. With the clutch pedal lifted up to release the clutch pedal quadrant adjuster pawl, rotate the clutch pedal adjuster quadrant forward. Unhook the clutch cable from the quadrant. Allow the quadrant to swing rearward.

5. Remove the air cleaner assembly to gain access to the clutch cable.

6. Grasp the end of the clutch cable using pliers, then unhook the clutch cable from the clutch bearing release lever.

➡ Do not grasp the wire strand portion of the inner cable since this might cut the wires and result in cable failure.

7. Disconnect the cable from the insulator that is located on the rib of the transaxle.

8. Pull the cable out through the recess between the pedal and the quadrant, and from the insulator on the pedal assembly.

9. Remove the cable by withdrawing it through the engine compartment.

**To install:**

➥The clutch pedal must be lifted to disengage the adjusting mechanism during cable installation. Failure to do so will result in damage to the self-adjuster mechanism. A prying instrument must never be used to install the cable into the quadrant.

10. Insert the clutch cable assembly from the engine or passenger compartment (if the clutch pedal was removed) through the dash panel and dash panel grommet. Make sure the cable is routed inboard of the brake lines and not trapped at the spring tower by the brake lines.

11. With the quadrant at the window stop position, push the clutch cable through the insulator on the stop bracket and through the recess between the pedal and the gear quadrant.

12. With the clutch pedal lifted up to release the pawl, rotate the gear quadrant forward. Hook the cable into the gear quadrant.

13. Secure the clutch shield on the clutch mounting/release plate.

14. Using a piece of wire, cord or other suitable device, secure the pedal in the upmost position.

15. Install the clutch cable in the insulator on the rib of the transaxle.

16. Hook the cable into the clutch release lever in the engine compartment.

17. Remove the device that was used to temporarily secure the pedal against its stop.

18. Adjust the clutch by pressing the clutch pedal down several times.

19. Install the air cleaner, then connect the negative battery cable.

## Clutch Interlock/Pedal Position Switch

### REMOVAL & INSTALLATION

▶ **See Figure 82**

1. Disconnect the negative battery cable.
2. Disengage the switch electrical connector.
3. Remove the retaining screw and hairpin clip, then remove the switch from the vehicle.

## AUTOMATIC TRANSAXLE

### Identification

Four automatic transaxle units are available. The ATX (automatic transaxle) model which is used with the 2.5L engine, and the AXOD (automatic transaxle overdrive) which is used with the 3.0L and 3.8L engine. Beginning in 1991 some vehicles were equipped with the AXOD-E transaxle which is basically the same as the AXOD with the addition of electronic transaxle controls. Beginning in 1993, some vehicles came equipped with the AX4S (automatic transaxle four-speed) or AX4N (automatic transaxle four-speed non-synchronized) transaxle. The AX4S was formerly the AXOD and is basically the same as the AXOD-E. And the AX4N which is also very similar, but is non-synchronized, hence the N in the name.

The ATX automatic transaxle is a 3-speed unit. A unique feature is a patented split path torque converter. The engine torque in second and third gears is divided, so that part of the engine torque is transmitted hydrokinetically through the torque converter, and part is transmitted mechanically by direct connection of the engine and transaxle. In the third gear, 93% of the torque is transmitted mechanically, making the ATX highly efficient. Torque splitting is accomplished through a splitter gear set. A conventional compound gear set is also used.

Only one band is used in the ATX. In service fluid additions, or fluid changes may be made with **Motorcraft Type H** automatic transmission fluid.

The AXOD, AXOD-E, AX4S and AX4N automatic transaxles are 4-speed units. They all have two planetary gear sets and a combination planetary/differential gear set. Four multiple plate clutches, two band assemblies, and two one-way clutches act together for proper operation of the planetary gear sets.

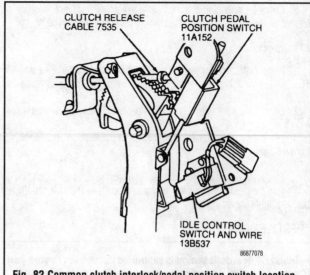

Fig. 82 Common clutch interlock/pedal position switch location

**To install:**

➥Always install the switch with the self adjusting clip about 1 in. (25mm) from the end of the rod. Be sure that the clutch pedal is in the full up position or the switch will be improperly adjusted.

4. Insert the eyelet end of the rod over the pin on the clutch pedal, then secure with the retaining clip.

5. Align the mounting boss with the corresponding hole in the bracket, then install the screw. Tighten the screw to 80–115 inch lbs. (9–13 Nm).

6. Reset the switch by pressing the clutch pedal to the floor.

7. Engage the switch electrical connector, then connect the negative battery cable.

A lock-up torque converter is coupled to the engine crankshaft and transmits engine power to the gear train by means of a drive link assembly (chain) that connects the drive and the driven sprockets. The application of the converter clutch is controlled through an electronic control integrated in the on-board EEC-IV system computer. These controls, along with the hydraulic controls in the valve body, operate a piston plate clutch in the torque converter to provide improved fuel economy by eliminating converter slip when applied.

In-service fluid additions, or fluid changes, may be made with **Motorcraft Type H** automatic transmission fluid.

The AXOD-E uses a turbine speed sensor in conjunction with a vehicle electronic control system. These components send operational signals to the EEC-IV microprocessor.

## Adjustments

### SHIFT LINKAGE

#### AXOD and AXOD-E Transaxle

1. Position the selector lever in the **OD** position against the rearward stop. The shift lever must be held in the rearward position using a constant force of 3 lbs. (1.4 Kg) while the linkage is being adjusted.

2. Loosen the manual lever-to-control cable retaining nut.

3. Move the transaxle manual lever to the **OD** position, second detent from the most rearward position.

4. Tighten the retaining nut to 11–19 ft. lbs. (15–26 Nm).

5. Check the operation of the transaxle in each selector lever position. Make sure the park and neutral start switch are functioning properly.

## ATX Transaxle

1. Position the selector lever in the **D** position against the drive stop. The shift lever must be held in the **D** position while the linkage is being adjusted.
2. Loosen the transaxle manual lever-to-control cable adjustment trunnion bolt.
3. Move the transaxle manual lever to the **D** position, second detent from the most rearward position.
4. Tighten the adjustment trunnion bolt to 12–20 ft. lbs. (16–27 Nm).
5. Check the operation of the transaxle in each selector lever position. Make sure the neutral start switch functions properly in **P** and **N** and the back-up lights are on in **R**.

## THROTTLE CABLE

➡Transaxle downshift control is controlled through the throttle position switch on 1991–95 vehicles equipped with the electronic automatic overdrive transaxle.

### 1986–90 3.0L and 3.8L Engines

▶ See Figures 83 and 84

The Throttle Valve (TV) cable normally does not need adjustment. The cable should be adjusted only if one of the following components is removed for service or replacement:
- Main control assembly
- Throttle valve cable
- Throttle valve cable engine mounting bracket
- Throttle control lever link or lever assembly
- Engine throttle body
- Transaxle assembly

1. Connect the TV cable eye to the transaxle throttle control lever link, then attach the cable boot to the chain cover.
2. If equipped with the 3.0L engine, with the TV cable mounted in the engine bracket, make sure the threaded shank is fully retracted. To retract the shank, pull up on the spring rest with the index fingers and wiggle the top of the thread shank while pressing the shank through the spring with the thumbs.
3. If equipped with the 3.8L engine, the TV cable must be unclipped from the right intake manifold clip. To retract the shank, span the crack

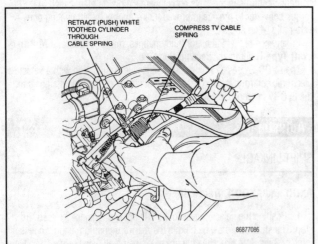

Fig. 83 While the spring is compressed, push the threaded shank toward the spring with the index and middle fingers of the left hand. Do not pull on the cable sheath

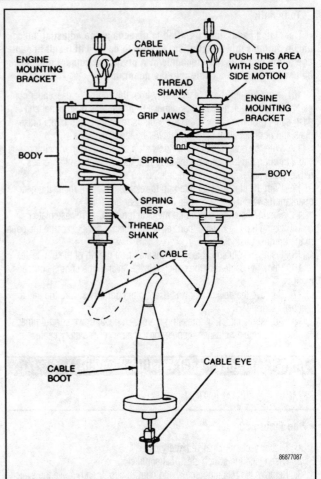

Fig. 84 The threaded shank must show movement or "ratchet" out of the grip jaws. If there is no movement, inspect the TV cable system for broken or disconnected components, then repeat the procedure

between the two 180 degree segments of the adjuster spring rest with a suitable tool. Compress the spring by pushing the rod toward the throttle body with the right hand. While the spring is compressed, push the threaded shank toward the spring with the index and middle fingers of the left hand. Do not pull on the cable sheath.
4. Attach the end of the TV cable to the throttle body.
5. If equipped with the 3.8L engine, rotate the throttle body primary lever by hand, the lever to which the TV-driving nailhead is attached, to the wide-open-throttle position. The white adjuster shank must be seen to advance. If not, look for cable sheath/foam hang-up on engine/body components. Attach the TV cable into the top position of the right intake manifold clip.

➡The threaded shank must show movement or "ratchet" out of the grip jaws. If there is no movement, inspect the TV cable system for broken or disconnected components, then repeat the procedure.

## THROTTLE VALVE CONTROL LINKAGE

### ATX Transaxle

The Throttle Valve (TV) Control Linkage System consists of a lever on the throttle body of the injection unit, linkage shaft assembly, mounting bracket assembly, control rod assembly, a control lever on the transaxle and a lever return spring.

The coupling lever follows the movement of throttle lever and has an adjustment screw that is used for setting TV linkage adjustment when a line pressure gauge is used. If a pressure gauge is not available, a manual adjustment can be made.

A number of shift troubles can occur if the throttle valve linkage is not in adjustment. Some are:

• **Symptom:** Excessively early and/or soft upshift with or without slip-bump feel. No forced downshift (kickdown) function at appropriate speeds.
• **Cause:** TV control linkage is set too short.
• **Remedy:** Adjust linkage.
• **Symptom:** Extremely delayed or harsh upshifts and harsh idle engagement.
• **Cause:** TV control linkage is set too long.
• **Remedy:** Adjust linkage.
• **Symptom:** Harsh idle engagement after the engine is warmed up. Shift clunk when throttle is backed off after full or heavy throttle acceleration. Harsh coasting downshifts (automatic 3–2, 2–1 shift in D range). Delayed upshift at light acceleration.
• **Cause:** Interference due to hoses, wires, etc. prevents return of TV control rod or TV linkage shaft. Excessive friction caused by binding grommets prevents the TV control linkage to return to its proper location.
• **Remedy:** Correct the interference area, check for bent or twisted rods, levers. or damaged grommets. Repair or replace whatever is necessary. Check and adjust linkage is necessary.
• **Symptom:** Erratic/delayed upshifts, possibly no kickdown, harsh engagement.
• **Cause:** Clamping bolt on trunnion at the upper end of the TV control rod is loose.
• **Remedy:** Reset TV control linkage.
• **Symptom:** No upshift and harsh engagements.
• **Cause:** TV control rod is disconnected or the linkage return spring is broken or disconnected.
• **Remedy:** Reconnect TV control rod, check and replace the connecting grommet if necessary, reconnect or replace the TV return spring.

The TV control linkage is adjusted at the sliding trunnion block.

1. Operate the engine until normal operating temperature is reached. Adjust the curb idle speed to specification.
2. After the curb idle speed has been set, shut off the engine. Make sure the choke is completely opened. Check the throttle lever to make sure it is against the hot engine curb idle stop.
3. Set the coupling lever adjustment screw at its approximate midrange. Make sure the TV linkage shaft assembly is fully seated upward into the coupling lever.

### ✷✷ CAUTION

**If adjustment of the linkage is necessary, allow the EGR valve to cool so you won't get burned.**

4. To adjust, loosen the bolt on the sliding block on the TV control rod a minimum of one turn. Clean any dirt or corrosion from the control rod, free-up the trunnion block so that it will slide freely on the control rod.
5. Rotate the transaxle TV control lever up using a finger and light force, to insure that the TV control lever is against its internal stop. With reducing the pressure on the control lever, tighten the bolt on the trunnion block.
6. Check the throttle lever to be sure it is still against the hot idle stop. If not, repeat the adjustment steps.

## TRANSAXLE CONTROL LEVER

### ATX Transaxle

1. Position the selector lever in DRIVE against the rear stop.
2. Raise the car and support it safely on jackstands. Loosen the manual lever to control lever nut.
3. Move the transaxle lever to the Drive position, second detent from

the rear most position. Tighten the attaching nut. Check the operation of the transaxle in each selector position. Readjust if necessary. Lower the car.

### AXOD and AXOD-E Transaxles

1. Position the selector lever in the OVERDRIVE position against the rearward stop.
2. If the vehicle is equipped with a floor shift selector the shift lever must be held in the rearward position using a constant force of about 3 lbs. as the linkage is being adjusted.
3. Loosen the manual lever to control cable retaining nut. Be sure that the transaxle lever is in the OVERDRIVE position. Tighten the retaining nut to 11–19 ft. lbs. (15–26 Nm).
4. Check operation of the transaxle in each range. Be sure that the park switch and neutral safety switch are working properly.

## Neutral Safety Switch/Back-Up Light Switch

The neutral start and backup switch are one unit mounted on the top left end of the transaxle. The neutral start portion of the switch allows electrical current to travel to the ignition system when the shift selector is in park or neutral only. The vehicle will not start when the selector is in any other gear. The backup portion operates the rear backup lamps when selector is in reverse gear.

### REMOVAL & INSTALLATION

▶ **See Figures 85 and 86**

1. Make sure the shift selector in the **Park** position, then apply the emergency brake.
2. Disconnect the negative battery cable.
3. Disengage the neutral start switch electrical connector, then remove the shift control lever on top of the switch.
4. Remove the two neutral switch attaching bolts, then remove the switch.
**To install:**
5. Install the switch on the manual shaft.
6. Loosely install the two attaching bolts and washers.
7. Insert a No. 43 drill (0.089 in.) through the hole.
8. Tighten the attaching bolts to 7–9 ft. lbs. (9–12 Nm), then remove the drill.
9. Engage the switch electrical connector, then connect the negative battery cable.

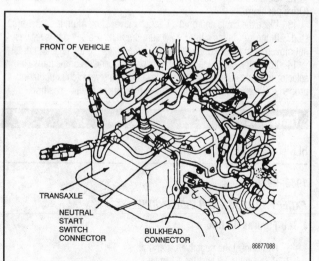

FRONT OF VEHICLE

TRANSAXLE

NEUTRAL START SWITCH CONNECTOR

BULKHEAD CONNECTOR

86877088

**Fig. 85 Neutral safety switch location—vehicles equipped with automatic transaxle**

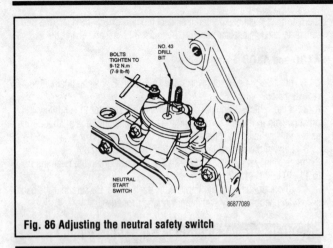

**Fig. 86 Adjusting the neutral safety switch**

## Shift Lever Cable

### REMOVAL AND INSTALLATION

1. Remove the shift knob, locknut, console, bezel assembly, control cable clip and cable retaining pin.

2. Disengage the rubber grommet from the floor pan by pushing it into the engine compartment.

3. Raise the car and safely support it on jackstands.

4. Remove the retaining nut and control cable assembly from the transaxle lever.

5. Remove the control cable bracket bolts. Pull the cable through the floor. To install:

6. To install the cable, feed the round end through the floor board. Press the rubber grommet into its mounting hole.

7. Position the control cable assembly in the selector lever housing and install the spring clip.

8. Install the bushing and control cable assembly on the selector lever and housing assembly shaft and secure it with the retaining pin.

9. Install the bezel assembly, console, locknut and shift knob.

10. Position the selector lever in the Drive position. The selector lever must be held in this position while attaching the other end of the control cable.

11. Position the control cable bracket on the retainer bracket and secure the two mounting bolts.

12. Shift the control lever into the second detent from full rearward (Drive position).

13. Place the cable end on the transaxle lever stud. Align the flats on the stud with the slot in the cable. Make sure the transaxle selector lever has not moved from the second detent position and tighten the retaining nut.

14. Lower the car to the ground. Check the operation of the transaxle selector in all positions. Make sure the neutral safety switch is operating properly. The engine should start only in the Park or Neutral position.

## Transaxle

### REMOVAL & INSTALLATION

#### 1986–90 Vehicles

#### *EXCEPT TAURUS WITH 2.5L ENGINE*

♦ See Figures 87 thru 94

1. Disconnect the negative battery cable.
2. Remove the air cleaner assembly.
3. Remove the bolt retaining the shift cable and bracket assembly to the transaxle.

➥Hold the bracket with a prybar in the slot to prevent the bracket from moving.

4. Remove the shift cable bracket bolts and bracket from the transaxle.

5. Disengage the electrical connector from the neutral safety switch.

6. Detach the electrical bulkhead connector from the rear of the transaxle.

7. Remove the oil dipstick.

8. For 3.8L engines, remove the throttle valve cable cover. Unsnap the throttle valve cable from the throttle body lever. Remove the throttle valve cable from the transaxle case.

9. Carefully pull up on the throttle valve cable and disconnect the throttle valve cable from the TV link.

➥Pulling too hard on the throttle valve may bend the internal TV bracket.

10. Install engine lifting brackets.

11. Disconnect the power steering pump pressure and return line bracket.

12. Remove the converter housing bolts from the top of the transaxle.

13. Install a suitable engine support fixture.

14. Raise the and safely support the vehicle.

15. Remove both front wheels. Remove the left-side outer tie rod end.

16. Remove the lower ball joint attaching nuts and bolts. Remove the lower ball joints and remove the lower control arms from each spindle. Remove stabilizer bar bolts.

17. Remove the nuts securing the steering rack to the subframe.

18. For 3.8L engines, disengage the oxygen sensor electrical connection, then remove the exhaust pipe, converter assembly and mounting bracket.

19. Remove the two 15mm bolts from the transaxle mount. Remove the four 15mm bolts from the left engine support, then remove the bracket.

20. Position a suitable subframe removal tool.

21. Remove the steering gear from the subframe and secure to the rear of the engine compartment. Remove the subframe-to-body retaining bolts, then remove the subframe.

22. Remove the dust cover retaining bolt and the starter retaining bolts then position the starter out of the way. Remove the dust cover.

23. Rotate the engine by the crankshaft pulley bolt to align the torque

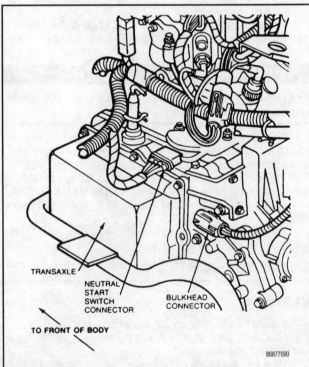

**Fig. 87 Detach the connectors from the neutral safety switch and the bulkhead connector**

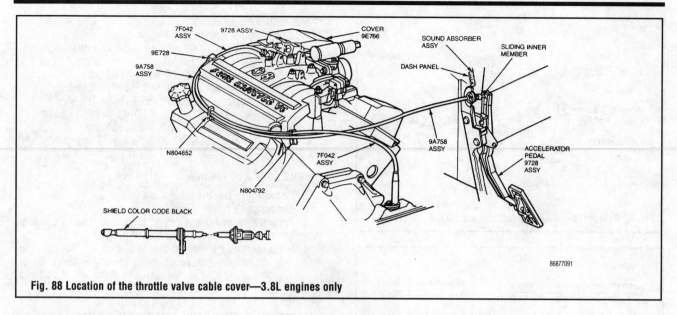

Fig. 88 Location of the throttle valve cable cover—3.8L engines only

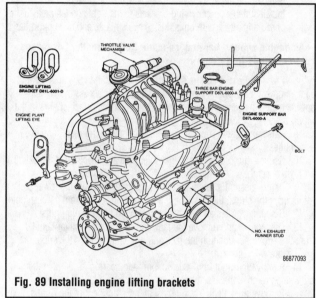

Fig. 89 Installing engine lifting brackets

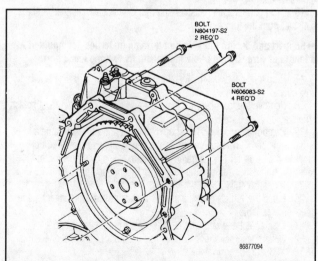

Fig. 90 Remove the four torque converter housing bolts from the top of the transaxle

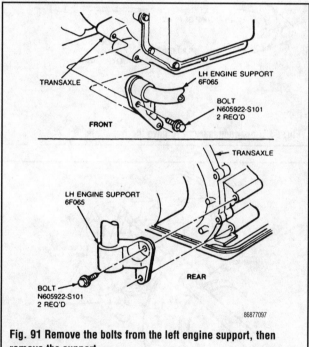

Fig. 91 Remove the bolts from the left engine support, then remove the support

converter bolts with the starter drive hole. Remove the torque converter-to-flywheel retaining nuts.

24. Remove the transaxle cooler line fitting retaining clips. Using Cooler Line Disconnect Tool T86P-77265-AH or equivalent, disconnect the transaxle cooler lines.

25. Remove the engine-to-transaxle retaining bolts.

26. Remove the speedometer sensor heat shield.

27. Remove the vehicle speed sensor from the transaxle.

➡Vehicles with electronic instrument clusters do not use a speedometer cable.

28. Position a suitable transaxle jack.

29. Remove the halfshafts as follows:

    a. Screw Extension T86P-3514-A2 into CV Joint Puller T86P-3514-A1, and insert Slide Hammer D79P-100-A or equivalent into the extension.

    b. Position the puller behind the CV joint, then remove the joint.

    c. Install shipping plugs.

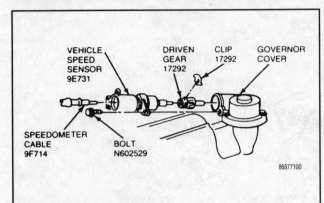

**Fig. 92 Remove the vehicle speed sensor from the transaxle**

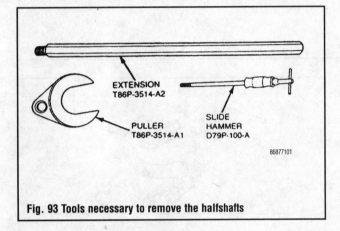

**Fig. 93 Tools necessary to remove the halfshafts**

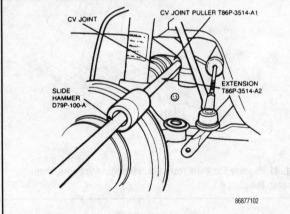

**Fig. 94 Position the puller behind the CV-joint, then remove the joint**

30. Remove the two remaining torque converter housing bolts.

31. Separate the transaxle from the engine, then carefully lower the transaxle from the vehicle.

**To install:**

32. Installation is the reverse of the removal procedure. During installation be sure to observe the following:

   a. Clean the transaxle oil cooler lines.

   b. Install new circlips on the CV-joint seals.

   c. Carefully install the halfshafts in the transaxle by aligning the splines of the CV-joint with the splines of the differential.

   d. Attach the lower ball joint to the steering knuckle with a new nut and bolt. Tighten the nut to 37–44 ft. lbs.

   e. When installing the transaxle to the engine, verify that the con-

verter-to-transaxle engagement is maintained. Prevent the converter from moving forward and disengaging during installation.

   f. Adjust the TV and manual linkages. Check the transaxle fluid level.

   g. Tighten the following bolts to the torque specifications listed:

- Transaxle-to-engine bolts: 41–50 ft. lbs. (55–68 Nm)
- Control arm-to-knuckle bolts: 36–44 ft. lbs. (49–60 Nm)
- Stabilizer U-clamp-to-bracket bolts: 60–70 ft. lbs. (81–95 Nm)
- Tie rod-to-knuckle nut: 23–35 ft. lbs. (31–47 Nm)
- Starter-to-transaxle bolts: 30–40 ft. lbs. (41–54 Nm)
- Converter-to-flywheel bolts: 23–39 ft. lbs. (31–53 Nm)
- Insulator-to-bracket bolts: 55–70 ft. lbs. (75–95 Nm)

### TAURUS WITH 2.5L ENGINE

1. Disconnect the negative battery cable.

2. Remove the air cleaner assembly.

3. Position the engine control wiring harness away from the transaxle converter housing area.

4. Disconnect the TV linkage and manual lever cable at the respective levers. Failure to disconnect the linkage during transaxle removal and allowing the transaxle to hang will fracture the throttle valve cam shaft joint (located under the transaxle cover).

5. Remove the power steering hose brackets.

6. Remove the upper transaxle-to-engine attaching bolts.

7. Install suitable engine lifting brackets to the right and left areas of the cylinder head and attach with bolts. Install two suitable engine support bars.

➡**An engine support bar may be made from a length of 4x4 wood cut to about 57 in. (1.45m).**

8. Place one of the engine support bars across the vehicle in front of each engine shock tower. Place another support bar across the vehicle approximately between the alternator and valve cover. Attach chains to the lifting brackets.

9. Raise and safely support the vehicle. Remove the wheel and tire assemblies.

10. Remove the catalytic converter inlet pipe and disconnect the exhaust air hose assembly.

11. Remove each tie rod end from it's spindle. Separate the lower ball joints from the struts, then remove the lower control arm from each spindle.

12. Disconnect the stabilizer bar by removing the retaining nuts.

13. Disconnect and remove the rack and pinion and auxiliary cooler from the subframe. Position the rack and pinion away from the subframe and secure with wire.

14. Remove the right front axle support and bearing assembly retaining bolts, then remove the assembly.

15. Remove the halfshaft and link shaft assembly out of the right side of the transaxle.

16. Disengage the left halfshaft from the differential side gear. Pull the halfshaft from the transaxle.

➡**Support and secure the halfshaft from an underbody component with a length of wire. Do not allow the halfshafts to hang unsupported.**

17. Plug the seal holes, by installing Shipping Plugs T81P-1177-B or equivalent.

18. Remove the front support insulator and position the left front splash shield aside.

19. Position a workbench or shop table to support the subframe after it is disconnected. Lower the vehicle to the bench table surface. Position blocks or support for the subframe, as required. Remove the subframe retaining bolts, then remove the subframe. Disconnect the neutral start switch wire assembly.

20. Raise the vehicle after the subframe is removed. Disconnect the speedometer cable.

21. Disconnect and remove the shift cable from the transaxle.

22. Disconnect the oil cooler lines using Cooler Line Disconnect Tool T86P-77265-AH or equivalent.

23. Disconnect the starter mounting bolts, then remove the starter.

24. Remove the dust cover from the torque converter housing and remove the torque converter-to-flywheel housing nuts.

25. Position a suitable transaxle jack under the transaxle.
26. Remove the remaining transaxle-to-engine retaining bolts.

➡ **Before the transaxle can be lowered from the vehicle, the torque converter studs must be clear of the flywheel. Insert a suitable tool between the flywheel and converter, then carefully guide the transaxle and converter away from the engine.**

27. Lower the transaxle from the engine.

**To install:**

28. Installation is the reverse of the removal procedure. During installation be sure to observe the following:

a. Clean the transaxle oil cooler lines using Rotunda Torque Converter Cleaner 014-00028 or equivalent.

b. Install new circlips on the CV-joint seals.

c. Carefully install the halfshafts in the transaxle by aligning the splines of the CV-joint with the splines of the differential.

d. Attach the lower ball joint to the steering knuckle with a new nut and bolt. Tighten the nut to 37–44 ft. lbs. (50–60 Nm). DO NOT tighten the bolt!

e. When installing the transaxle to the engine, make sure that the converter-to-transaxle engagement is maintained. Prevent the converter from moving forward and disengaging during installation.

f. Adjust the TV and manual linkages. Check the transaxle fluid level.

g. Tighten the following bolts to the torque specifications listed:

- Transaxle-to-engine bolts: 25–33 ft. lbs. (34–45 Nm)
- Control arm-to-knuckle bolts: 36–44 ft. lbs. (50–60 Nm)
- Stabilizer U-clamp-to-bracket bolts: 60–70 ft. lbs. (81–95 Nm)
- Tie rod-to-knuckle nut: 23–35 ft. lbs. (31–47 Nm)
- Starter-to-transaxle bolts: 30–40 ft. lbs. (41–54 Nm)
- Converter-to-flywheel bolts: 23–39 ft. lbs. (31–53 Nm)
- Insulator-to-bracket bolts: 55–70 ft. lbs. (75–90 Nm)

### 1991–95 Vehicles

♦ **See Figures 95 thru 100**

1. Disconnect the battery cables, then remove the battery and battery tray.

2. Place a drain pan under the transaxle, then properly drain the fluid into a suitable container.

3. Remove the air cleaner assembly, hoses and tubes.

4. Disengage the electrical connectors from the engine, then remove the bolt retaining the main wiring harness bracket.

5. Remove the shift lever.

6. Remove the EGR bracket and throttle body bracket retaining bolts.

7. On the 3.0L engine, install engine lifting eyes D81L-6001-D to the left rear cylinder with a bolt. The engine plant lifting eye should still be on the right front cylinder. If not, install second lifting eye. On the 3.2L SHO, remove the bracket on the back of the engine that retains the wiring harness and coolant line and attach Engine Lifting Eyes to the alternator bracket. On the 3.8L engine, install engine lifting eyes to the left front exhaust manifold stud and right rear exhaust manifold stud.

8. Secure the wiring harness aside and remove the radiator sight shield.

9. Position a suitable engine support fixture.

10. Position Three Bar Engine Support D88L-6000-A or equivalent.

11. If equipped with air suspension, turn the air suspension switch located in the luggage compartment to the **OFF** position.

12. Remove the oil level dipstick and disconnect the power steering pump pressure and return line bracket.

13. Remove the four torque converter housing bolts from the top of the transaxle.

14. Raise and safely support the vehicle. Remove the front wheel and tire assemblies.

15. Disconnect the left outer tie rod end. Remove the suspension height sensor, if equipped. Disconnect the brake line support brackets.

16. Remove the retaining bolts from the front stabilizer bar assembly. Disconnect the right and left lower arm assemblies.

17. Remove the steering gear retaining nuts from the subframe. Remove

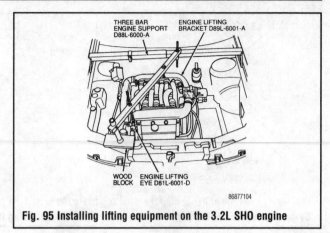

**Fig. 95 Installing lifting equipment on the 3.2L SHO engine**

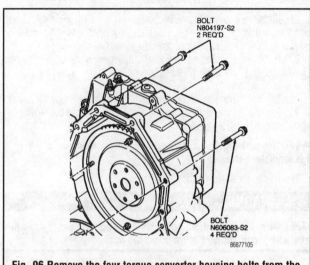

**Fig. 96 Remove the four torque converter housing bolts from the top of the transaxle**

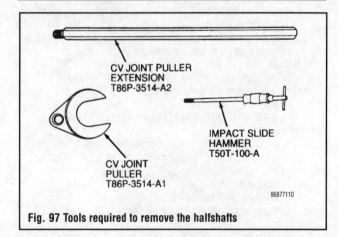

**Fig. 97 Tools required to remove the halfshafts**

the front heated oxygen sensor, exhaust pipe, converter assembly and mounting bracket.

18. Remove the two bolts from the engine mount and the four bolts from the left engine support, then remove the support.

19. Position Rotunda Subframe Removal Kit 014-00751, or equivalent. Remove the steering gear from the subframe and secure it to the rear of the engine compartment. Remove the subframe-to-body bolts, then lower the subframe.

20. Remove the two starter retaining bolts, then position the starter out of the way.

21. Remove the dust cover.

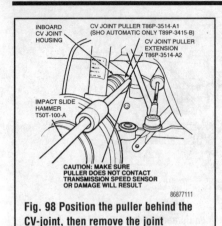

**Fig. 98 Position the puller behind the CV-joint, then remove the joint**

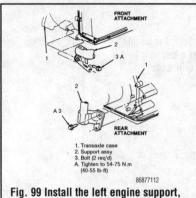

1. Transaxle case
2. Support assy
3. Bolt (2 req'd)
A. Tighten to 54–75 N.m (40–55 lb-ft)

**Fig. 99 Install the left engine support, then secure using the retaining bolts**

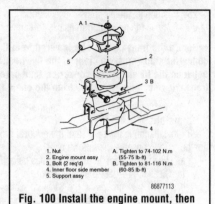

1. Nut
2. Engine mount assy
3. Bolt (2 req'd)
4. Inner floor side member
5. Support assy

A. Tighten to 74–102 N.m (55–75 lb-ft)
B. Tighten to 81–116 N.m (60–85 lb-ft)

**Fig. 100 Install the engine mount, then tighten to specification**

22. Rotate the engine with a ½ in. drive ratchet and ⅞ in. deep well socket on the crankshaft pulley bolt to align the torque converter bolts with the starter drive hole. Remove the four torque converter-to-flywheel retaining nuts.

23. Remove the transaxle cooler line fitting retaining clips. Using Cooler Line Disconnect Tool T86P-77265-AH or equivalent, disconnect the transaxle cooler lines.

24. Remove the engine-to-transaxle retaining bolts.

25. Remove the speedometer sensor heat shield. Remove the vehicle speed sensor from the transaxle.

➡ **Vehicles with electronic instrument clusters do not use a speedometer cable.**

26. Position a suitable transaxle jack.

### ❊❊ WARNING

**Make sure the puller does not contact the speed sensor or damage will occur. Do NOT pry against the case.**

27. Remove the halfshafts as follows:
   a. Screw Extension T86P-35140A2 into the CV-Joint Puller and install Impact Slide Hammer D79P-100-A or equivalent into the extension.
   b. Position the puller behind the CV-joint, then remove the joint.
   c. Install shipping plugs.

28. Remove the last two torque converter housing bolts, carefully separate the transaxle from the engine and lower out of the vehicle.

**To install:**

29. Place the transaxle assembly on the jack, and raise to the engine.

30. Position the transaxle to the engine, then align the torque converter bolts to the flywheel.

31. Install the transaxle housing bolts, then tighten to 41–50 ft. lbs. (55–68 Nm).

32. Install the four torque converter bolts through the starter drive hole by rotating the engine at the crankshaft pulley bolt with a ⅞ in. deep well socket and ½ in. drive ratchet. Tighten to 23–39 ft. lbs. (31–53 Nm).

33. Remove the transaxle jack.

34. Install the halfshaft assemblies.

35. Install the vehicle speed sensor, then tighten to 31–39 inch lbs. (3.4–4.5 Nm).

36. Install the transaxle cooler lines. At the transaxle, tighten to 18–23 ft. lbs. (24–31 Nm). At the oil cooler, tighten to 8–12 ft. lbs. (11–16 Nm).

37. Install the dust cover, then tighten to 7–9 ft. lbs. (9–12 Nm).

38. Install the starter, then tighten the mounting bolts to 30–40 ft. lbs. (41–50 Nm).

39. Raise the subframe and install the retaining bolts, then tighten the bolts to 55–75 ft. lbs. (75–102 Nm). Remove the subframe removal kit.

40. Install the left engine support. Tighten the four bolts to 40–55 ft. lbs. (54–75 Nm).

41. Install the engine mount, then tighten to 60–85 ft. lbs. (81–116 Nm).

42. Install the front exhaust pipe, converter assembly and mounting bracket. Connect the heated oxygen sensor.

43. Install the power steering gear assembly and retaining nuts, then tighten the nuts to 85–100 ft. lbs. (115–135 Nm).

44. Install the left and right lower arm assembly, Insert a new pinch bolt and nut, then tighten to 40–53 ft. lbs. (53–72 Nm).

45. Install the stabilizer retaining bolts, then tighten to 23–29 ft. lbs. (30–40 Nm).

46. Install the brake line support brackets, then tighten to 8 ft. lbs. (11 Nm).

47. Install the left and right tie rod retaining nuts. Tighten to 23–35 ft. lbs. (31–47 Nm). Tighten to the minimum specified torque, then continue tightening to the nearest cotter pin slot, then install a new cotter pin.

48. Install the front wheel and tire assemblies, then tighten the lug nuts to 85–105 ft. lbs. (115–142 Nm). Carefully lower the vehicle.

49. Install the power steering pump pressure and return bracket, then tighten to 40–50 inch lbs. (4.5–5.7 Nm).

50. Remove the Three Bar Engine Support. Install the radiator sight shield.

51. Remove all of the engine support equipment.

52. Install the shift lever.

53. Fasten the main wiring harness bracket, then engage the electrical connectors to the engine.

54. Install the battery tray and battery, then connect the positive and negative battery cables.

55. Install the air cleaner assembly, hoses and tubes.

56. Fill the transaxle with the specified quantity and type of oil. Start the engine, then move the transaxle selector lever through all of the ranges and check for leaks.

### Halfshafts

The halfshafts of automatic transaxles are serviced the same way as manuals. Please refer to the procedures earlier in this section.

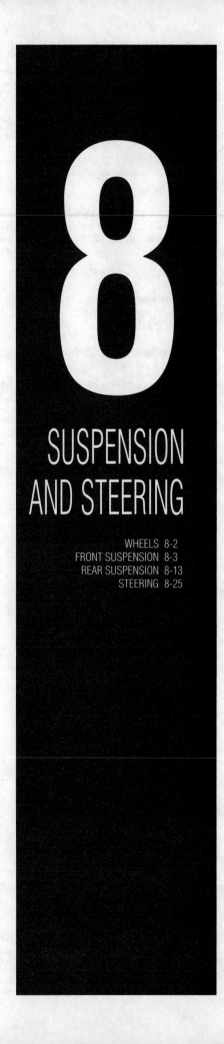

# 8

# SUSPENSION AND STEERING

# WHEELS

## Wheels

### REMOVAL & INSTALLATION

▶ **See Figure 1**

➡ **All vehicles use Metric (M-12) lug nuts. Replacement lug nuts must be of the same type and thread size. Metric lug nuts are identified by the word "Metric" stamped in the top surface of the nut.**

1. Position the vehicle on a level surface. Apply the emergency brake.
2. If equipped with automatic transaxle, be sure that the selector lever is in the PARK position.
3. If equipped with manual transaxle, be sure that the selector lever is gear.
4. Using the tapered end of the lug nut wrench, remove the hub cap from the wheel and tire assembly.

➡ **Aluminum wheels require a special bulge-type lug nut with an enlarged chamfer to prevent distortion of the wheel hub bolt nut seat.**

5. Using the proper size lug nut wrench, loosen, but do not remove, the lug nuts from the wheel and tire assembly.
6. Raise and properly support the vehicle.
7. Finish loosening, then remove the lug nuts from the wheel and tire assembly.

8. Remove the wheel and tire assembly from its mounting.

**To install:**

9. Install the tire and wheel assembly to the brake rotor or drum.
10. Install the lug nuts, then finger-tighten then is a crisscross pattern. Lower the vehicle to the ground.
11. Cross-tighten the lug nuts to 85–105 ft. lbs. (115–142 Nm).
12. Align the hub cap/wheel cover with the tire valve and cap extension, matching the hole in the cover (also identified on the backside of the wheel cover with the valve stem logo). With the palm of your hand, hit on the outside edges of the cover until it is snapped in place all the way around.

### INSPECTION

Replace wheels if they are bent, dented, heavily rusted, have air leaks, elongated bolt holes or excessive lateral and radial run-out.

Also inspect wheel lug nuts and be sure that they are tightened to specification.

## Wheel Lug Studs/Hub Bolts

### REPLACEMENT

▶ **See Figure 2**

1. Raise and safely support the vehicle.
2. Remove the wheel and tire assembly.

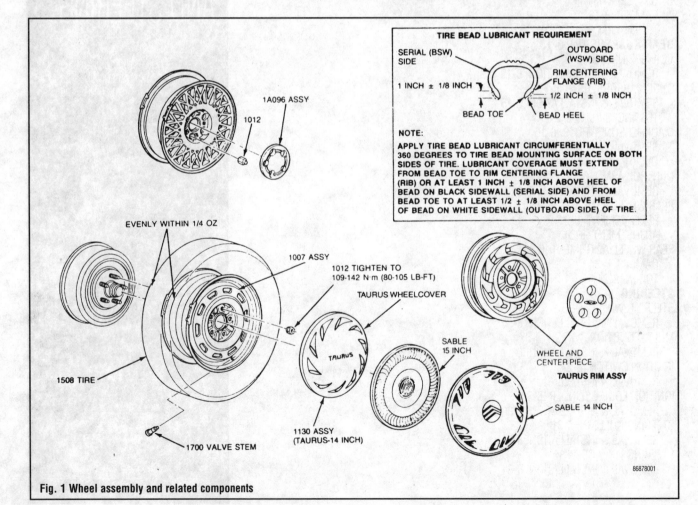

**TIRE BEAD LUBRICANT REQUIREMENT**

SERIAL (BSW) SIDE
OUTBOARD (WSW) SIDE
RIM CENTERING FLANGE (RIB)
1 INCH ± 1/8 INCH
1/2 INCH ± 1/8 INCH
BEAD TOE
BEAD HEEL

**NOTE:**
APPLY TIRE BEAD LUBRICANT CIRCUMFERENTIALLY 360 DEGREES TO TIRE BEAD MOUNTING SURFACE ON BOTH SIDES OF TIRE. LUBRICANT COVERAGE MUST EXTEND FROM BEAD TOE TO RIM CENTERING FLANGE (RIB) OR AT LEAST 1 INCH ± 1/8 INCH ABOVE HEEL OF BEAD ON BLACK SIDEWALL (SERIAL SIDE) AND FROM BEAD TOE TO AT LEAST 1/2 ± 1/8 INCH ABOVE HEEL OF BEAD ON WHITE SIDEWALL (OUTBOARD SIDE) OF TIRE.

1A096 ASSY
1012
EVENLY WITHIN 1/4 OZ
1007 ASSY
1012 TIGHTEN TO 109-142 N·m (80-105 LB-FT)
TAURUS WHEELCOVER
1508 TIRE
TAURUS
SABLE 15 INCH
WHEEL AND CENTER PIECE
**TAURUS RIM ASSY**
SABLE 14 INCH
1130 ASSY (TAURUS-14 INCH)
1700 VALVE STEM

86878001

**Fig. 1 Wheel assembly and related components**

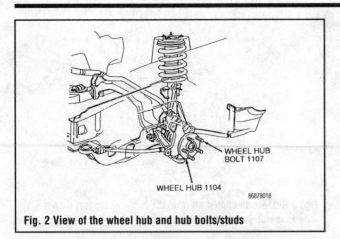

Fig. 2 View of the wheel hub and hub bolts/studs

3. Remove the caliper and rotor. For details, please refer to the procedures located in Section 9 of this manual.

4. Position the wheel hub bolt/stud to clear the steering knuckle.

5. Remove the bolt/stud from the wheel hub.

**To install:**

6. Install the bolt/stud into the wheel hub.

7. Using a lug nut, seat the bolt/stud into the wheel hub.

8. Install the caliper and rotor.

9. Install the wheel and tire assembly, then carefully lower the vehicle.

## FRONT SUSPENSION

### MacPherson Struts

#### REMOVAL & INSTALLATION

▶ **See Figures 3 thru 11**

1. Place the ignition switch in the **OFF** position and the steering column in the **UNLOCKED** position.

2. Remove the hub nut.

3. Loosen the 3 top mount-to-shock tower nuts; but do not remove the nuts at this time.

4. Raise and safely support the vehicle.

➡ **When raising the vehicle, do not lift by using the lower control arms.**

5. Remove the tire and wheel assembly.

6. Remove the brake caliper, then support it on a wire, out of the way. Remove the rotor.

7. At the tie rod end, remove the cotter pin and the castle nut. Discard the cotter pin and nut, and replace with new ones during installation.

8. Using tie rod end remover tool 3290-D and the tie rod remover adapter tool T81P-3504-W or equivalents, separate the tie rod from the steering knuckle.

#### ✷✷ WARNING

**Use extreme care not to damage the link ball joint boot seal.**

9. Unfasten the stabilizer bar link nut, then remove the stabilizer bar link from the strut.

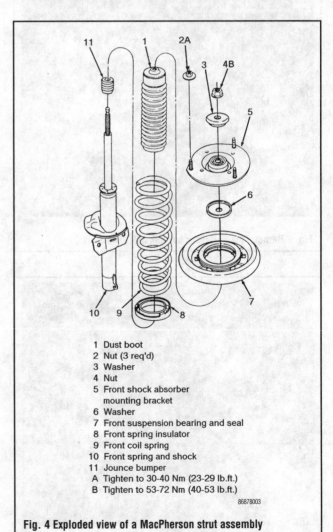

1 Dust boot
2 Nut (3 req'd)
3 Washer
4 Nut
5 Front shock absorber
  mounting bracket
6 Washer
7 Front suspension bearing and seal
8 Front spring insulator
9 Front coil spring
10 Front spring and shock
11 Jounce bumper
A Tighten to 30-40 Nm (23-29 lb.ft.)
B Tighten to 53-72 Nm (40-53 lb.ft.)

Fig. 4 Exploded view of a MacPherson strut assembly

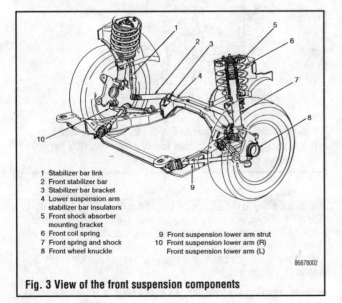

1 Stabilizer bar link
2 Front stabilizer bar
3 Stabilizer bar bracket
4 Lower suspension arm
  stabilizer bar insulators
5 Front shock absorber
  mounting bracket
6 Front coil spring
7 Front spring and shock
8 Front wheel knuckle
9 Front suspension lower arm strut
10 Front suspension lower arm (R)
   Front suspension lower arm (L)

Fig. 3 View of the front suspension components

Fig. 5 Loosen, but do not remove, the 3 top mount-to-shock tower nuts

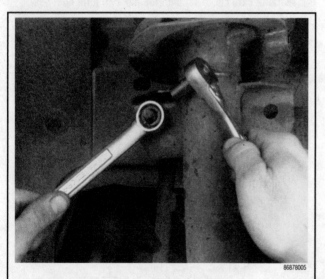

Fig. 6 Remove the stabilizer bar link nut, then . . .

Fig. 7 . . . remove the stabilizer bar link from the strut

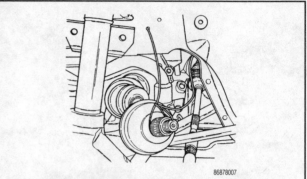

Fig. 8 Remove the halfshaft from the hub and support it on a wire to maintain a level position

Fig. 9 After removing the 3 top mount-to-shock tower nuts, remove the strut and spring assembly from the vehicle

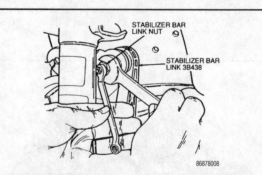

Fig. 10 Install the stabilizer link to the strut, making sure the link is positioned properly, then install a new stabilizer bar link nut. Tighten to 57–75 ft. lbs. (77–102 Nm).

10. Remove the lower arm-to-steering knuckle pinch bolt and nut; it may be necessary to use a drift punch to remove the bolt. Using a suitable tool, spread the knuckle-to-lower arm pinch joint, then remove the lower arm from the steering knuckle. Discard the pinch nut/bolt and replace with a new one during installation.

11. Remove the halfshaft from the hub and support it with a wire to maintain a level position.

➡When removing the halfshaft, do not allow it to move outward as the internal parts of the tripod CV-joint could separate, causing failure of the joint.

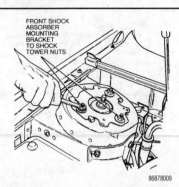

FRONT SHOCK
ABSORBER
MOUNTING
BRACKET
TO SHOCK
TOWER NUTS

86878009

**Fig. 11 Tighten the 3 top mount-to-shock tower nuts to 23–29 ft. lbs. (31–40 Nm)**

12. Remove the strut-to-steering knuckle pinch bolt. Using a small pry-bar, spread the pinch bolt joint and separate the strut from the steering knuckle. Remove the steering knuckle/hub assembly from the strut.

13. Remove the 3 top mount-to-shock tower nuts, then remove the strut and coil spring assembly from the vehicle.

**To install:**

14. Install the strut and coil spring assembly and the 3 top mount-to-shock tower nuts.

15. Install the steering knuckle and hub assembly to the strut.

16. Install a new strut-to-steering knuckle pinch bolt. Tighten the bolt to 73–97 ft. lbs. (98–132 Nm).

17. Install the halfshaft into the hub.

18. Install the lower arm to the steering knuckle, making sure the ball stud groove is properly positioned. Be very careful not to damage the ball joint seal. Fasten using a new pinch bolt and nut. Tighten to 40–53 ft. lbs. (54–72 Nm).

➡The letters "Top LH" and "Top RH" are moulded into the stabilizer bar link for correct assembly to the strut.

19. Install the stabilizer link to the strut, making sure the link is positioned properly, then install a new stabilizer bar link nut. Tighten to 57–75 ft. lbs. (77–102 Nm).

20. Using a new castle/slotted nut, install the tie rod end onto the knuckle. Tighten the nut to 23–35 ft. lbs. (31–47 Nm) for vehicles through 1994. For 1995 vehicles, tighten the nut to 35–46 ft. lbs. (47–63 Nm). Retain the castle/slotted nut with a new cotter pin.

21. Install the disc brake rotor, caliper and tire/wheel assembly. Tighten the wheel lug nuts to 85–105 ft. lbs. (115–142 Nm).

22. Tighten the 3 top mount-to-shock tower nuts to 23–29 ft. lbs. (31–40 Nm).

23. Lower the vehicle, then tighten the hub nut to 170–203 ft. lbs. (230–275 Nm).

24. Depress the brake pedal a few times before moving the vehicle.

OVERHAUL

▶ See Figures 12 thru 18

### ✳✳ CAUTION

**Never attempt to disassemble the spring or top mount without first compressing the spring using Strut Compressor Tool No. D85P-7178-A, Rotunda Spring Compressor 086-00029B or equivalent. Failure to properly compress the spring before disassembly can result in serious injury or death.**

The following procedure is performed with the strut assembly removed from the car.

➡A MacPherson Strut compression tool is required for the disassembly of the strut, a cage type tool such as part No. D85P-7178-A or equivalent is required.

86878011

**Fig. 12 Carefully compress the spring using a suitable spring compressor tool**

86878012

**Fig. 13 Place a 10mm box wrench on top of the shock strut shaft and hold while loosening the top shaft mounting nut with a 21mm 6-point crow's foot wrench and ratchet, then . . .**

86878013

**Fig. 14 . . . remove the mounting nut**

Fig. 15 After loosening the spring compressor tool, remove the washer, then . . .

Fig. 16 . . . remove the mounting bracket and bearing plate assembly

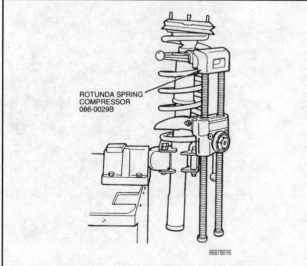

ROTUNDA SPRING COMPRESSOR 086-0029B

Fig. 17 Compress the coil spring using the proper tool

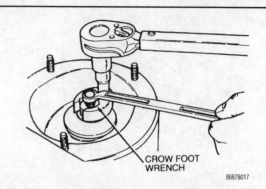

CROW FOOT WRENCH

Fig. 18 Place a 10mm box end wrench on top of the shock strut shaft, and hold while tightening the top shaft mounting nut with a 21mm 6-point crow's foot wrench and ratchet. Tighten to 40–53 ft. lbs. (53–72 Nm)

1. Compress the spring with the coil spring compressor part No. D85P-7178-A or equivalent.

2. Place a 10mm box wrench on top of the shock strut shaft and hold while removing the top shaft mounting nut with a 21mm 6-point crow's foot wrench and ratchet.

➡️It is important that the mounting nut be turned and the rod held still to prevent fracture of the rod at the base of the hex.

3. Loosen the spring compressor tool, then remove the top mounting bracket assembly, bearing plate assembly and spring.

**To assemble:**

➡️Ensure that the correct assembly sequence and proper positioning of the bearing and seat assembly are followed. The bearing and seat assembly is press-fit onto the upper mount. The mount washers must be installed with the correct orientation.

4. Install the spring compressor tool part No. D85P-7178-A or equivalent.

5. Install the spring, bearing plate assembly, lower washer and top mount bracket assembly.

6. Compress the spring with the coil spring compressor tool.

7. Install the upper washer and nut on the shock strut shaft.

8. Place a 10mm box end wrench on the top of the shock strut shaft and hold while tightening the top shaft mounting nut with a 21mm 6-point crow's foot wrench and a ratchet. Tighten to 40–53 ft. lbs. (53–72 Nm).

9. The strut assembly may now be installed in the vehicle. For details, please refer to the procedure located earlier in this section.

## Lower Ball Joint

### INSPECTION

1. Disconnect the negative battery cable.

2. Raise and safely support the vehicle so the wheels fall to the full-down position.

3. Have an assistant grasp the lower edge of the tire, then move the wheel and tire assembly in and out.

4. Observe the lower end of the knuckle and the lower control arm as the wheel is being moved in and out. Any movement indicates abnormal ball joint wear.

5. If there is any movement, install a new lower control arm assembly.

6. Lower the vehicle, then connect the negative battery cable.

### REMOVAL & INSTALLATION

Ball joints are integral parts of the lower control arms. If inspection reveals an unsatisfactory ball joint, the entire lower control arm assembly must be replaced.

## Stabilizer Bar

### REMOVAL & INSTALLATION

▶ **See Figures 19 and 20**

1. Raise and safely support the vehicle. Support the vehicle with jackstands behind the front subframe.

➡️ **Do NOT raise or support the vehicle by the front control arms.**

2. Remove the stabilizer bar link-to-stabilizer bar nut, the stabilizer bar link-to-strut nut and the link from the vehicle with an 8mm closed-end wrench and an 18mm open-end wrench. Discard the nuts, and replace with new ones during installation.

➡️ **Be very careful not to damage the line ball joint boot seal.**

3. Remove the steering gear-to-subframe nuts, then move the gear from the subframe.

4. Position another set of jackstands under the front subframe, then remove the rear subframe-to-frame bolts. Lower the rear or the subframe to access the stabilizer bar brackets.

5. Remove the stabilizer bar U-bracket bolts and the stabilizer bar from the vehicle.

➡️ **When removing the stabilizer bar, replace the insulators and the U-bracket bolts with new ones.**

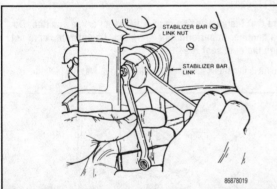

**Fig. 19 Remove the stabilizer bar link-to-stabilizer bar nut, the stabilizer bar link-to-strut nut and the link from the vehicle with an 8mm closed-end wrench and an 18mm open-end wrench. Discard the nuts, and replace with new ones during installation**

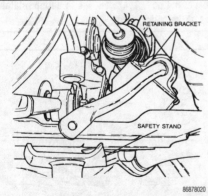

**Fig. 20 Position another set of jackstands under the front subframe, then remove the rear subframe-to-frame bolts. Lower the rear or the subframe to access the stabilizer bar brackets**

**To install:**

6. Clean the stabilizer bar to remove dirt and debris.

7. To install, reverse the removal procedure. Tighten the bolts to the following torque specifications:
- U-bracket-to-subframe 23–29 ft. lbs. (30–40 Nm)
- Subframe-to-steering gear 85–100 ft. lbs. (115–135 Nm)
- Stabilizer bar-to-stabilizer bar link 35–48 ft. lbs. (47–65 Nm)
- Stabilizer bar-to-strut 55–75 ft. lbs. (75–101 Nm)

8. Prior to assembly, coat the inside diameter of the new insulators with No. E25Y-19553-A or equivalent lubricant. Do not use any mineral or petroleum base lubricants, as they will cause deterioration of the rubber insulators.

## Lower Control Arm

### REMOVAL & INSTALLATION

▶ **See Figure 21**

1. Disconnect the negative battery cable.
2. Raise and safely support the vehicle.
3. Remove the wheel and tire assembly.
4. Remove and discard the tension strut-to-control arm nut, then pull off the dished washer.

➡️ **When separating the control arm from the steering knuckle, do not use a hammer. Be careful not to damage the ball joint boot seal.**

5. Remove and discard the control arm-to-steering knuckle pinch bolt. Using a small prybar, spread the pinch joint slightly, then separate the control arm from the steering knuckle. A drift punch may be used to remove the bolt, but be very careful not to damage the ball joint boot seal.

➡️ **Do not allow the halfshaft to move outward, or the tripod CV-joint internal parts could separate, causing failure of the joint.**

6. Remove and discard the lower control arm inner pivot bolt and nut.
7. Remove the lower control arm from the frame and the tension strut.

**To install:**

➡️ **Make sure the front washer is at the strut-to-lower control arm attachment.**

8. Insert the strut into the inner bushing.
9. Position the lower control arm into the subframe bracket, using a new nut and bolt. Tighten to 73–97 ft. lbs. (98–132 Nm).

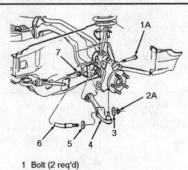

1 Bolt (2 req'd)
2 Nut (2 req'd)
3 Washer (2 req'd)
4 Front suspension lower arm
5 Washer (2 req'd)
6 Front suspension lower arm strut
7 Nut (2 req'd)
A Tighten to 53-72 Nm (40-53 lb.ft.)

**Fig. 21 Exploded view of the lower control arm and related components**

10. Assemble the lower control arm ball joint stud to the steering knuckle, making sure the ball stud groove is positioned properly. Be very careful not to damage the lower control arm seal.

11. Insert a new pinch bolt and nut, then tighten to 40–53 ft. lbs. (53–72 Nm).

12. Clean the strut threads to remove dirt and/or debris.

13. Install the dished washer, with its dished side away from the control arm bushing. Install a new nut on the strut and tighten to 73–97 ft. lbs. (98–132 Nm).

14. Install the wheel and tire assembly, tightening the lug nuts to 85–105 ft. lbs. (115–142 Nm), then carefully lower the vehicle.

## BUSHING REPLACEMENT

### Inner Pivot Bushing

1. Remove the lower control arm from the vehicle.

2. Using bushing removal tools T86P-5493-A3 and T86P-5493-A2, or equivalents, and a C clamp assembly, remove the old bushings from the control arm assembly.

**To install:**

3. Use the bushing removal tool and press new bushings in place on the lower control arm assembly.

4. Be sure that the bushing flange is at the front of the arm.

5. Install the lower control arm on the vehicle.

### Control Arm/Tension Strut Bushing

▶ **See Figure 22**

1. Remove the lower control arm from the vehicle.

2. Using bushing removal tools T86P-5493-A5 and T86P-5493-A, or equivalents, and a C clamp assembly, remove the old bushings from the control arm assembly. Be sure that the C clamp is positioned tightly in a bench vise.

**To install:**

3. Before installing the new bushing, saturate it in vegetable oil, as this will aid in the installation process. Use only vegetable oil; do NOT use mineral or petroleum based oil, as these will deteriorate the rubber.

4. Use the bushing removal tool and install new bushings in place on the lower control arm assembly. Stop tightening the C clamp when the bushing pops in place.

5. Install the lower control arm on the vehicle.

### Tension Strut/Sub Frame Insulators

1. Remove the lower control arm from the vehicle.

2. Remove and discard the nut, washer and insulator from the front of the tension strut. Pull the strut rearward to remove it from the subframe.

3. Remove and discard the insulator from the tension strut.

**To install:**

4. Install a new insulator on the tension strut end and insert it into the subframe.

5. Install a new front insulator. Clean the tension strut threads. Install a new washer and nut. Tighten to 70–95 ft. lbs. (95–129 Nm).

6. Install the lower control arm on the vehicle.

## Knuckle and Spindle

### REMOVAL & INSTALLATION

▶ **See Figures 23, 24 and 25**

1. Turn the ignition switch to the **OFF** position. Position the steering wheel in the unlocked position.

2. Remove the hub nut.

3. Raise and safely support the vehicle, then remove the tire and wheel assembly.

4. Remove the cotter pin from the tie rod end stud, then remove the slotted nut. Discard the cotter pin and nut.

5. Using Tie Rod End Remover TOOL-3290-D or equivalent, remove the tie rod end from the steering knuckle.

6. Remove the stabilizer bar link assembly from the strut.

7. Remove the brake caliper, then wire it aside in order to gain working clearance. Remove the brake rotor.

8. Loosen, but do not remove, the three top retaining nuts from the top of the shock tower.

9. Remove and discard the lower arm to steering knuckle pinch bolt and nut. A drift may be used to remove the bolt. Using a small prybar, spread the knuckle-to-lower arm pinch joint. Remove the lower arm from the steering knuckle.

➡ **Be sure that the steering column is in the unlocked position. Do not use a hammer to perform this operation. Use extreme care not to damage the boot seal.**

10. Remove the shock absorber strut-to-steering knuckle pinch bolt.

**Fig. 23 Loosen, but do not remove, the three top retaining nuts from the top of the shock tower**

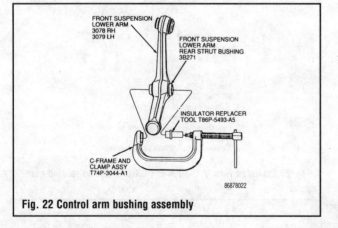

**Fig. 22 Control arm bushing assembly**

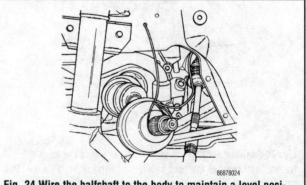

**Fig. 24 Wire the halfshaft to the body to maintain a level position**

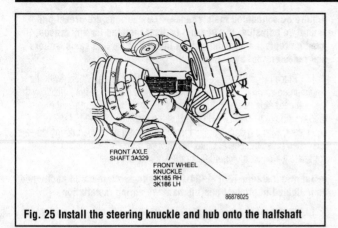

**Fig. 25 Install the steering knuckle and hub onto the halfshaft**

➡ **Do not allow the halfshaft to move outboard. Overextension of the CV joint could result in separation of internal parts, causing failure of the joint.**

11. Press the halfshaft from the hub. Wire the halfshaft to the body to maintain a level position.

12. If equipped, remove the rotor splash shield from the steering knuckle.

13. Remove the steering knuckle and hub assembly from the shock absorber strut.

14. Position the assembly on a workbench, then remove the hub retainer ring and front wheel bearing.

**To install:**

15. If equipped, install the rotor splash shield using new rivets and Heavy Duty Riveter D80L-23200-A or equivalent.

16. Install the front wheel bearing, retainer ring and hub. If necessary, replace the seal on the outboard CV-joint.

17. Install the steering knuckle onto the shock absorber strut, then loosely install a new pinch bolt in the knuckle to retain the strut.

18. Install the steering knuckle and hub onto the halfshaft.

19. Install the lower control arm to the knuckle, making sure that the ball stud groove is properly positioned. Install a new nut and bolt, then tighten to 40–53 ft. lbs. (53–72 Nm). Tighten the strut-to-knuckle pinch bolt to 73–97 ft. lbs. (98–132 Nm).

20. Install the rotor and brake caliper. For vehicles equipped with caliper retaining pins, tighten them to 18–25 ft. lbs. (24–34 Nm). For vehicles equipped with caliper retaining bolts, tighten them to 85 ft. lbs. (115 Nm).

21. Position the tie rod into the knuckle, then install a new slotted nut and tighten. If necessary, advance the nut to align a slot, then install a cotter pin. Tighten the nut to 23–35 ft. lbs. (31–47 Nm) for vehicles through 1994. For 1995 vehicles, tighten the nut to 35–46 ft. lbs. (47–63 Nm).

22. Install the stabilizer link bar assembly to the front shock absorber assembly. Tighten to 57–75 ft. lbs. (77–103 Nm).

23. Install the tire and wheel assembly, tightening the lug nuts to 85–105 ft. lbs. (115–142 Nm).

24. Carefully lower the vehicle.

25. Install the three top mount shock tower retaining bolts, and tighten to 23–29 ft. lbs. (30–40 Nm).

26. Tighten the hub nut to 170–203 ft. lbs. (230–275 Nm).

27. Pump the brake pedal prior to moving the vehicle, in order to reposition the brake linings.

## Front Hub and Bearing

### REMOVAL & INSTALLATION

▶ **See Figures 26 thru 32**

➡ **Do NOT start this procedure unless a new wheel hub retainer and washer as well as a new inboard CV-joint circlip are available. These components cannot be reused because their holding or retention ability is decreased during removal.**

1. Remove the wheel cover/hub cover and loosen the wheel nuts.

2. Remove the hub nut retainer and washer by applying sufficient torque to the nut to overcome the prevailing torque feature of the crimp in the nut collar. Do not use an impact-type tool to remove the hub nut retainer. The hub nut retainer is not reusable and must be discarded after removal.

3. Raise and safely support the vehicle. Remove the wheel and tire assembly.

4. If equipped with caliper locating pins, remove the brake caliper by loosening the pins and rotating the caliper off of the rotor, starting from the lower end of the caliper and lifting upwards. Do not remove the pins from the caliper assembly. If equipped with bolted-on calipers, remove the caliper by loosening, then rotating the mounting bolts. Lift the caliper off of the rotor. Once the caliper is free of the rotor, support it with a length of wire. Do not allow the caliper to hang from the brake hose.

5. Remove the rotor from the hub by pulling it off of the hub bolts. If the rotor is difficult to remove, strike it sharply between the studs with a rubber or plastic hammer. If the rotor will not pull off, apply a suitable rust penetrator to the inboard and outboard rotor hub mating surfaces. Install a suitable 3-jaw puller and remove the rotor by pulling on the rotor outside diameter and pushing on the hub center. If excessive force is required to remove the rotor, check it for lateral run-out prior to installation. Lateral run-out must be checked with the nuts clamping the stamped hat section of the rotor.

6. Remove the rotor splash shield.

7. Disconnect the lower control arm and tie rod from the knuckle, but leave the strut attached. Loosen the two strut top mount-to-apron nuts.

8. Loosen the three shock/strut top retaining nuts.

9. Install Front Hub Replacer T81P-1104-A with Front Hub Remover/Replacer T81P-1104-C and Metric Hub Remover Adapters T83P-1104-BH1

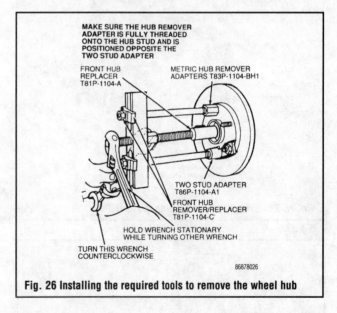

**Fig. 26 Installing the required tools to remove the wheel hub**

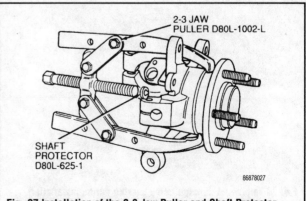

**Fig. 27 Installation of the 2-3 Jaw Puller and Shaft Protector**

and Two Stud Adapter T86P-1104-A1 or equivalents, then remove the wheel hub, bearing and knuckle assembly by pushing out the CV-joint outer shaft until it is free of the assembly.

10. Support the knuckle with a length of wire, remove the strut bolt and slide the hub/bearing/knuckle assembly off of the strut. Remove the support wire and carry the hub/bearing/knuckle assembly to a bench.

11. Install 2-3 Jaw Puller D80L-1002-L and Shaft Protector D80L-625-1 or equivalent, with the jaws of the puller on the knuckle bosses. Make sure the shaft protector is centered, clears the bearing inside diameter, and rests on the end face of the hub journal. Remove the hub.

12. Using snapring pliers, remove the snapring that retains the bearing in the knuckle assembly, then discard the ring.

13. Using a suitable hydraulic press, place Front Bearing Spacer T86P-1104-A2, or equivalent, on the press plate with the step side facing up, then position the knuckle with the outboard side up on the spacer. Install Front Bearing Remover/Replacer T83P-1104-AH2 or equivalent, centered on the bearing inner race, then press the bearing out of the knuckle and discard.

**To install:**

14. Remove all foreign material from the knuckle bearing bore and hub bearing journal to be sure of correct seating of the new bearing.

➡**If the hub bearing journal is scored or damaged, it must be replaced. The front wheel bearings are pre-greased and sealed, and**

require no scheduled maintenance. The bearings are preset and cannot be adjusted. If a bearing is disassembled for any reason, it must be replaced as a unit, since individual service seals, rollers and races are not available.

15. Place Front Bearing Spacer T86P-1104-A2 or equivalent, with the step side down on the hydraulic press plate, then position the knuckle with the outboard side down on the spacer. Position a new bearing in the inboard side of the knuckle. Install Bearing Installer T86P-1104-A3 or equivalent, with the undercut side facing the bearing, on the bearing outer race, then press the bearing into the knuckle. Make sure the bearing seats completely against the shoulder of the knuckle bore.

➡**Bearing installer T86P-1104-A3 or equivalent, must be positioned as indicated to prevent bearing damage during installation.**

16. Install a new snapring (part of the bearing kit) in the knuckle groove using snapring pliers.

17. Place Front Bearing Spacer T86P-1104-A2 or equivalent, on the press plate, then position the hub on the tool with the lugs facing downward. Position the knuckle assembly with the outboard side down on the hub barrel. Place Bearing Remover T83P-1104-AH2 or equivalent, with its flat side down, centered on the inner race of the bearing, then press down on the tool until the bearing is fully seated onto the hub. Make sure the hub rotates freely in the knuckle after installation.

18. Prior to hub/bearing/knuckle installation, replace the bearing dust seal on the outboard CV-joint with a new seal from the bearing kit. Make sure the seal flange faces outboard toward the bearing. Use Drive Tube T83T-3132-A1 and Front Bearing Dust Seal Installer T86P-1104-A4 or equivalent.

19. Suspend the hub/bearing/knuckle assembly on the vehicle with wire, then attach the strut loosely to the knuckle. Lubricate the CV-joint stub

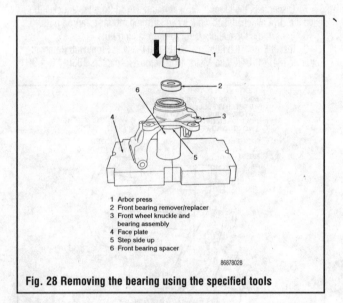

1 Arbor press
2 Front bearing remover/replacer
3 Front wheel knuckle and
   bearing assembly
4 Face plate
5 Step side up
6 Front bearing spacer

86878028

**Fig. 28 Removing the bearing using the specified tools**

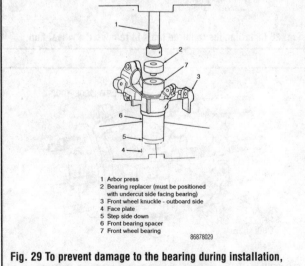

1 Arbor press
2 Bearing replacer (must be positioned
   with undercut side facing bearing)
3 Front wheel knuckle - outboard side
4 Face plate
5 Step side down
6 Front bearing spacer
7 Front wheel bearing

86878029

**Fig. 29 To prevent damage to the bearing during installation, the replacer tool must be positioned as shown**

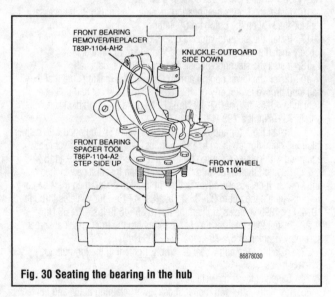

FRONT BEARING
REMOVER/REPLACER
T83P-1104-AH2

KNUCKLE-OUTBOARD
SIDE DOWN

FRONT BEARING
SPACER TOOL
T86P-1104-A2
STEP SIDE UP

FRONT WHEEL
HUB 1104

86878030

**Fig. 30 Seating the bearing in the hub**

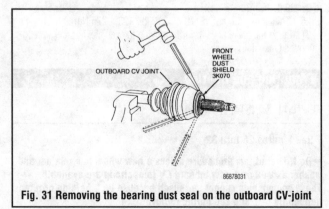

OUTBOARD CV JOINT

FRONT
WHEEL
DUST
SHIELD
3K070

86878031

**Fig. 31 Removing the bearing dust seal on the outboard CV-joint**

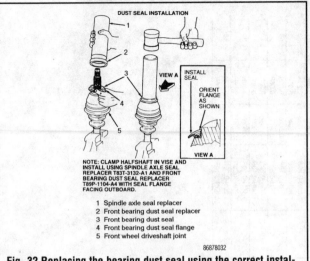

DUST SEAL INSTALLATION

VIEW A

INSTALL SEAL

ORIENT FLANGE AS SHOWN

VIEW A

NOTE: CLAMP HALFSHAFT IN VISE AND INSTALL USING SPINDLE AXLE SEAL REPLACER T83T-3132-A1 AND FRONT BEARING DUST SEAL REPLACER T89P-1104-AA WITH SEAL FLANGE FACING OUTBOARD.

1  Spindle axle seal replacer
2  Front bearing dust seal replacer
3  Front bearing dust seal
4  Front bearing dust seal flange
5  Front wheel driveshaft joint

86878032

**Fig. 32 Replacing the bearing dust seal using the correct installation tools**

shaft with SAE 30 weight motor oil, then using hand pressure only, insert the shaft into the hub splines as far as possible. Make sure the splines are properly engaged.

20.  Temporarily secure the rotor to the hub with washers and two wheel lug nuts. Insert a steel rod into the rotor diameter, then rotate clockwise to contact the knuckle.

21.  Install the hub nut washer and a new hub nut retainer. Rotate the nut clockwise to seat the CV-joint. Tighten the nut to 170–203 ft. lbs. (230–275 Nm). Remove the steel rod, washers and lug nuts.

➡ **Do not use power or impact tools to tighten the hub nut.**

22.  Install the remainder of the front suspension components.
23.  Install the brake rotor splash shield.

➡ **Apply a small amount of Disc Brake Caliper Slide Grease D7AZ-19590-A or equivalent, to the pilot diameter of the rotor.**

24.  Install the disc brake rotor and caliper. Make sure the outer brake pad spring hook is seated under the upper arm of the knuckle.

25.  Install the wheel and tire assembly, then finger-tighten the wheel nuts.

26.  Carefully lower the vehicle, then block the wheels to prevent the car from rolling. Tighten the wheel lug nuts to 85–105 ft. lbs. (115–142 Nm). Install the wheel cover/hub cover, then remove the wheel blocks.

## Upper Mount and Bearing Assembly

REMOVAL & INSTALLATION

### ✴✴ CAUTION

**When servicing the front suspension, keep in mind that brake shoes may contain asbestos which has been determined to be a cancer causing agent. Never clean the brake surfaces with compressed air! Avoid inhaling any dust from any brake surface! When cleaning brake surfaces, use a commercially available brake cleaning fluid.**

1.  Place the ignition switch in the **OFF** position and the steering column in the unlocked position.

2.  Remove the hub nut. Loosen, but do not remove, the strut-to-fender apron nuts.

3.  Raise and safely support the front of the vehicle on jackstands. Remove the wheel and tire assembly.

➡ **When raising the vehicle, do not lift it by the lower control arms.**

4.  Remove the brake caliper (support it by a wire) and the rotor.

5.  At the tie rod end, remove the cotter pin and the castle nut. Discard the cotter pin and replace it with a new one during installation.

6.  Using Tie-Rod End Remover tool No. 3290-C and the Tie Rod Remover Adapter tool No. T81P-3504-W, or equivalent, separate the tie rod from the steering knuckle.

7.  Remove the stabilizer bar link nut and the link from the strut.

8.  Remove the lower arm-to-steering knuckle pinch bolt and nut; it may be necessary to use a drift punch to remove the bolt. Using a small prybar, slightly spread the knuckle-to-lower arm pinch joint and remove the lower arm from the steering knuckle.

9.  Remove the halfshaft from the hub, then support it by a wire.

➡ **When removing the halfshaft, DO NOT allow it to move outward, as the tripod CV-joint could separate from the internal parts, causing failure of the joint.**

10.  Remove the strut-to-steering knuckle pinch bolt. Using a small pry bar, spread the pinch bolt joint and separate the strut from the steering knuckle. Remove the steering knuckle/hub assembly from the strut assembly.

11.  Remove the strut-to-fender apron nuts and the strut assembly from the vehicle.

### ✴✴ CAUTION

**Never attempt to disassemble the spring or top mount without first compressing the spring using a Universal MacPherson Strut Spring Compressor D85P-7178-A or a Rotunda Spring Compressor 086–00029 or equivalent. Failure to properly compress the spring before disassembly can result in serious injury or death.**

12.  Place a 10mm box-end wrench on top of the shock strut shaft and hold while removing the top shaft mounting nut with a 21mm 6-point crow foot wrench and ratchet.

13.  Loosen the MacPherson Strut Spring Compressor slowly. Remove the top mount bracket assembly, bearing plate and spring.

➡ **When servicing the shock absorber strut, check the spring insulator for damage before assembly. If the outer metal splash shield is bent or damaged, it must be bent back carefully so that it does not touch the locator tabs on the bearing and seal assembly.**

**To install:**

14.  Place the MacPherson Strut Spring Compressor on the base of the strut.

15.  Install the upper mount and bearing assembly on top of the strut and tighten the spring compressor far enough to install the shaft mounting nut.

16.  Install the washer and nut on the shock strut shaft, then tighten with the 10mm box-end and the 21mm 6-point crow's foot wrench and ratchet.

17.  Install the "MacPherson Strut", as previously outlined.

## Front End Alignment

CASTER

Caster is a measurement of the angle between the steering axis and vertical, as viewed from the side of the vehicle when the wheels are in the straight ahead position. Stated another way, it is the tilting of the front steering axis either forward or backward from the vertical. A backward tilt is said to be positive (+) and a forward tilt is said to be negative (-).

Although it is measured using a special instrument, it can usually be seen by observing the location of the upper and lower control arm ball joints. A line drawn through the center of these two points represents the steering axis. When looking straight downward from the top of the upper control arm, you can see if the ball joints are not aligned, indicating that the caster angle is more or less than 0 degrees. If the vehicle has positive caster, the lower ball joint would be located behind the upper joint center line. If the vehicle has negative caster, the lower ball joint would be located in front of the upper joint center line.

## WHEEL ALIGNMENT (1992–1995)

| Year | Model | | | Caster Range (deg.) | Caster Preferred Setting (deg.) | Camber Range (deg.) | Camber Preferred Setting (deg.) | Toe-in (in.) | Steering Axis Inclination (deg.) |
|---|---|---|---|---|---|---|---|---|---|
| 1992 (cont.) | Sable | F | 2 | 2 11/16P-4 11/16P | 3 11/16P | 1N-1/4P | 3/8N | 3/32N | 15 1/2 |
| | | R | 2 | | | 1 5/8N-7/32N | 15/16N | 1/16P | |
| 1993 | Taurus | F | 1 | 2 13/16P-5 13/16P | 2 13/16P | 1 1/8N-1/8P | 1/2N | 3/32N | 15 1/2 |
| | | R | 1 | | | | | 1/16P | |
| | Sable | F | 2 | 2 11/16P-4 11/16P | 3 11/16P | 1N-1/4P | 3/8N | 3/32N | 15 1/2 |
| | | R | 2 | | | 1 5/8N-7/32N | 15/16N | 1/16P | |
| | Taurus | F | 1 | 2 13/16P-5 13/16P | 2 13/16P | 1 1/8N-1/8P | 1/2N | 3/32N | 15 1/2 |
| | | R | 1 | | | 1 5/8N-7/32N | 15/16N | 1/16P | |
| | Sable | F | 2 | 2 11/16P-4 11/16P | 3 11/16P | 1N-1/4P | 3/8N | 3/32N | 15 1/2 |
| | | R | 2 | | | 1 5/8N-7/32N | 15/16N | 1/16P | |
| 1994 | Taurus | F | 1 | 2.81P-4.81P | 3.81P | 1.13N-0.13P | 0.50N | 0.09N | 15.50 |
| | | R | 2 | | | 1.60N-0.20N | 0.90N | 0.06P | |
| | Taurus | F | 2 | 2.70P-4.70P | 3.70P | 1.90N-0.10P | 0.40N | 0.20N | 15.50 |
| | | R | 2 | | | 1.60N-0.20N | 0.90N | 0.06P | |
| | Sable | F | 1 | 2.80P-4.80P | 3.80P | 1.10N-0.10P | 0.50N | 0.20N | 15.50 |
| | | R | 2 | | | 1.60N-0.20N | 0.90N | 0.06P | |
| | Sable | F | 2 | 2.70P-4.70P | 3.70P | 1.90N-0.10P | 0.40N | 0.20N | 15.50 |
| | | R | 2 | | | 1.60N-0.20N | 0.90N | 0.06P | |
| 1995 | Taurus | F | 1 | 2.80P-4.80P | 3.80P | 1.10N-0.10P | 0.50N | 0.20N | 15.50 |
| | | R | 2 | | | 1.60N-0.20N | 0.90N | 0.06P | |
| | Taurus | F | 2 | 2.70P-4.70P | 3.70P | 1.90N-0.10P | 0.40N | 0.20N | 15.50 |
| | | R | 1 | | | 1.10N-0.10P | 0.90N | 0.06P | |
| | Sable | F | 2 | 2.80P-4.80P | 3.80P | 1.60N-0.20N | 0.50N | 0.20N | 15.50 |
| | | R | 2 | | | 1.00N-0.20N | 0.90N | 0.06P | |
| | Sable | F | 1 | 2.70P-4.70P | 3.70P | 1.90N-0.10P | 0.40N | 0.20N | 15.50 |
| | | R | 2 | | | 1.60N-0.20N | 0.90N | 0.06P | |

P - Positive
N - Negative
F - Front
R - Rear
1 Sedan
2 Wagon

86878501

## WHEEL ALIGNMENT (1986–1992)

| Year | Model | | | Caster Range (deg.) | Caster Preferred Setting (deg.) | Camber Range (deg.) | Camber Preferred Setting (deg.) | Toe-in (in.) | Steering Axis Inclination (deg.) |
|---|---|---|---|---|---|---|---|---|---|
| 1986 | Taurus | F | | 3P-6P | 4P | 1 3/32N-3/32P | 1/2N | 3/32N | 15 3/8 |
| | | R | | | | 1 5/8N-1/4N | 15/16N | 1/16P | |
| | Sable | F | 1 | 3P-6P | 4P | 1 3/32N-3/32P | 1/2N | 3/32N | 15 3/8 |
| | | R | 1 | | | 1 5/8-1/4N | 15/16N | 1/16N | |
| | Sable | F | 2 | 3P-6P | 4P | 1 3/32N-3/32P | 12N | 3/32N | 15 3/8 |
| | | R | 2 | | | 1 5/16-1/16N | 5/8N | 1/16P | |
| 1987 | Taurus | F | 1 | 3P-6P | 4P | 1 3/32N-3/32P | 1/2N | 3/32N | 15 3/8 |
| | | R | 1 | | | 1 5/8N-1/4N | 15/16N | 1/16P | |
| | Sable | F | 1 | 3P-6P | 4P | 1 3/32N-3/32P | 1/2N | 3/32N | 15 3/8 |
| | | R | 1 | | | 1 5/8-1/4N | 15/16N | 1/16N | |
| | Sable | F | 2 | 3P-6P | 4P | 1 1/32-3/32P | 1/2N | 3/32N | 15 3/8 |
| | | R | 2 | | | 1 5/8-1/4N | 5/8N | 1/16P | |
| 1988 | Taurus | F | | 3P-6P | 4P | 1 3/32P-3/32P | 1/2N | 3/32N | 15 3/8 |
| | | R | | | | 1 5/8-1/4N | 15/16N | 1/16P | |
| | Sable | F | 1 | 3P-6P | 4P | 1 1/32-3/32P | 1/2N | 3/32N | 15 3/8 |
| | | R | 1 | | | 1 5/8-1/16N | 5/8N | 1/16N | |
| | Sable | F | 2 | 3P-6P | 4P | 1 3/32N-3/32P | 1/2N | 3/32N | 15 3/8 |
| | | R | 2 | | | 1 5/16-1/16N | 5/8N | 1/16P | |
| 1989 | Taurus | F | 1 | 2 13/16P-5 13/16P | 3 13/16P | 1/8N-1/8P | 15/16N | 3/16N | 15 1/2 |
| | | F | 2 | 2 11/16P-5 11/16P | 3 11/16P | 1 7/8P-1/8N | 7/8N | 3/16N | 15 1/2 |
| | | R | | | | 1 5/8N-7/32N | 15/16N | 1/16P | |
| | Sable | F | 1 | 2 13/16P-5 13/16P | 3 13/16P | 1/8N-1/8P | 15/16N | 3/16N | 15 1/2 |
| | | R | 1 | | | 1 5/8N-7/32N | 15/16N | 1/16P | |
| | Sable | F | 2 | 2 13/16P-5 13/16P | 3 13/16P | 1 7/8N-1/8N | 7/8N | 3/32N | 15 1/2 |
| | | R | 2 | | | 1 5/8N-7/32N | 15/16N | 1/16P | |
| 1990 | Taurus | F | 1 | 2 13/16P-5 13/16P | 2 13/16P | 1 1/8N-1/8P | 1/2N | 3/32N | 15 1/2 |
| | | F | 2 | 2 5/8P-4 5/8P | 3 5/8P | 1 1/16N-3/16P | 7/16N | 3/32N | |
| | Sable | R | | | | 1 1/8N-1/8P | 1/2N | 1/16P | 15 1/2 |
| | | F | | 2 13/16P-5 13/16 P | 2 13/16P | 1 5/8N-7/32N | 15/16N | 3/32N | |
| | Sable | F | | 2 5/8P-4 5/8P | 3 5/8P | 1 1/8N-3/16P | 7/8N | 1/16P | 15 1/2 |
| | | R | | | | 1 5/8N-7/32N | 15/16N | 1/16P | |
| 1991 | Taurus | F | 1 | 2 13/16P-5 13/16P | 2 13/16P | 1 1/8N-1/8P | 1/2N | 3/32N | 15 1/2 |
| | | F | 2 | 2 5/8P-4 5/8P | 3 5/8P | 1 1/16N-3/16P | Front | 3/32N | |
| | Sable | R | | | | 1 5/8N-3/16P | 15/16N | 1/16P | 15 1/2 |
| | | F | 1 | 2 13/16P-5 13/16 P | 2 13/16P | 1 1/8N-1/8P | 1/2N | 3/32N | |
| | Sable | F | 2 | 2 5/8P-4 5/8P | 3 5/8P | 1 1/6N-3/16P | 15/16N | 1/16P | 15 1/2 |
| | | R | | | | 1 5/8N-7/32N | 15/16N | 3/32N | |
| 1992 | Taurus | F | 1 | 2 31/16P-5 13/16P | 2 13/16P | 1 1/8N-1/8P | 1/2N | 3/32N | 15 1/2 |
| | | F | 2 | 2 11/16P-4 11/16P | 3 11/16P | 1N-1/4P | 3/8N | 3/32N | 15 1/2 |
| | Sable | R | | | | 1 5/8N-7/32N | 15/16N | 1/16P | |
| | | R | 1 | 2 13/16P-5 13/16 P | 2 13/16P | 1 1/8N-1/8P | 1/2N | 3/32N | 15 1/2 |
| | | | | | | 1 5/8N-7/32N | 15/16N | 1/16P | |

86878500

## CAMBER

Camber is a measurement of the wheel tilt from the vertical direction, when the wheel is viewed from the rear of the vehicle. Camber is negative when the top of the wheel is inboard and positive when the top is outboard. Always check for bent, damaged or worn suspension components before determining that adjustment is necessary. The amount of tilt is measured in degrees from the vertical, and this measurement is called the camber angle.

## TOE-IN

Toe is a measurement of how far a wheel is turned in or out from the straight ahead direction. When the front of the wheel is turned in, the toe is positive. When the front of the wheel is turned out, the toe is negative. An incorrect toe setting can affect steering feel and cause excessive tire wear.

Stated another way, toe-in is the amount that the front of the wheels are closer together than the backs of the same wheels. The actual amount of toe-in is normally only a fraction of a degree.

# REAR SUSPENSION

## Coil Springs

### REMOVAL & INSTALLATION

**Station Wagon Only**

▶ **See Figures 33 thru 44**

1. Raise the rear of the vehicle and support safely on the pads of the underbody forward of the tension strut bracket. Position a floor jack under the lower suspension arm and raise the lower arm to normal curb height.
2. Remove the wheel and tire assembly.
3. Locate the bracket retaining the flexible brake hose to the body. Remove the bracket retaining bolt and bracket from the body.
4. Remove the stabilizer bar U-bracket from the lower suspension arm and bushing.
5. Remove and discard the nuts attaching the shock absorber to the lower suspension arm and bushing.
6. Disconnect and remove the parking brake cable and clip from the lower suspension arm and bushing.
7. If equipped with rear disc brakes, remove the ABS cable from the clips on the lower suspension arm.
8. Remove and discard the bolt and nut attaching the tension strut and bushing to the lower suspension arm.
9. Suspend the spindle and upper suspension arms from the body with a piece of wire to prevent them from dropping down.
10. Remove the nut, bolt, washer and adjusting cam that retain the lower suspension arm to the spindle. Discard the nut, bolt and washer and replace with new ones during installation, then set the cam aside.
11. With the floor jack, slowly lower the suspension arm until the spring, lower and upper insulators can be removed. Replace the spring and insulators as required.

**To install:**

12. Position the spring center mounting insulator on the lower suspension arm, then press the insulator downward into place. Make certain the insulator is properly seated.
13. Position the upper insulator on top of the spring. Install the spring on the lower suspension arm. Make certain the spring is properly seated.
14. With the floor jack, slowly raise the suspension arm. Guide the upper spring insulator onto the upper spring underbody seat.
15. Position the rear wheel spindle in the lower suspension arm and bushing, with a new bolt, washer, nut, and the existing cam. Install the bolt with its head toward the front of the vehicle, but do NOT tighten the bolt at this time.
16. Remove the wire supporting the spindle and suspension arms.
17. Install the tension strut and bushing in the lower suspension arm using a new nut and bolt; but do NOT tighten at this time.
18. Attach the parking brake cable and clip to the lower suspension arm.
19. If equipped with rear disc brakes, install the ABS cable into the clips on the lower suspension arm.
20. Position the shock absorber on the lower suspension arm, then

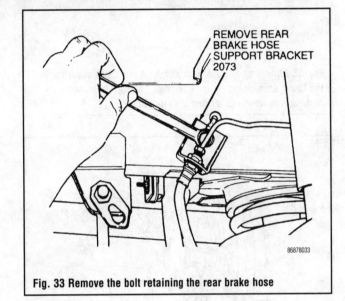

**Fig. 33 Remove the bolt retaining the rear brake hose**

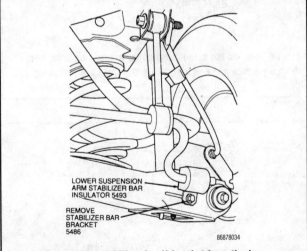

**Fig. 34 Remove the stabilizer bar U-bracket from the lower suspension arm and bushing**

install two new nuts. Tighten the nuts to 15–19 ft. lbs. (20–26 Nm).

21. Attach the stabilizer U-bracket to the lower suspension arm using a new bolt. Tighten the bolt to 23–30 ft. lbs. (31–40 Nm).
22. Attach the flexible brake hose bracket to the body, then tighten the retaining bolt to 8–12 ft. lbs. (11–16 Nm).
23. With the floor jack, raise the lower suspension to normal curb height. Tighten the lower suspension arm to 40–52 ft. lbs. (54–71 Nm). Tighten the bolt that attaches the tension strut to the body bracket to 40–52 ft. lbs. (54–71 Nm).

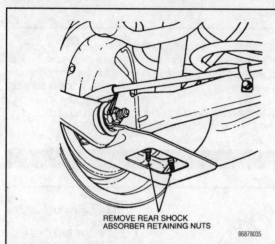

Fig. 35 After removing the nuts attaching the shock absorber to the lower suspension arm and bushing, discard them and replace with new ones during installation

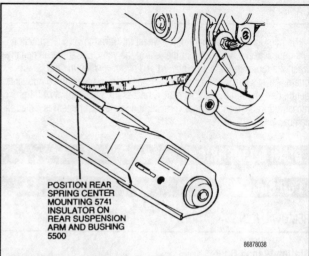

Fig. 38 Installing the center mounting insulator on the lower suspension arm

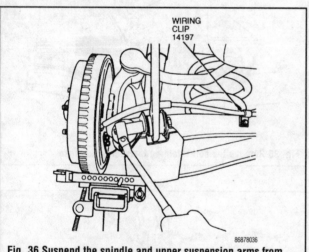

Fig. 36 Suspend the spindle and upper suspension arms from the body with a piece of wire to prevent them from dropping down

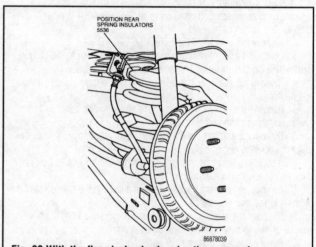

Fig. 39 With the floor jack, slowly raise the suspension arm. Guide the upper spring insulator onto the upper spring under-body seat

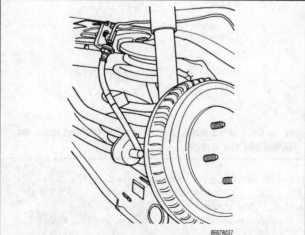

Fig. 37 With the floor jack, slowly lower the suspension arm until the spring, lower and upper insulators can be removed. Replace the spring and insulators as required

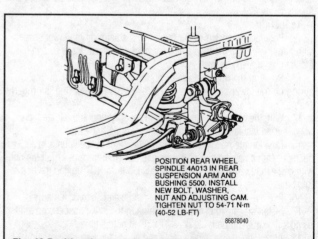

Fig. 40 Position the rear wheel spindle in the lower suspension arm and bushing, using a new bolt, nut washer, and the existing cam. Install the bolt with the head of the bolt toward the front of the vehicle, but do NOT tighten the bolt at this time

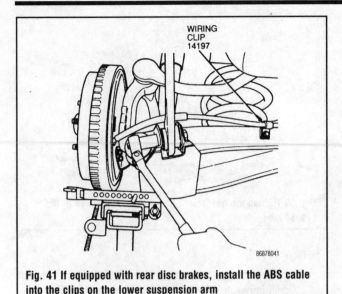

**Fig. 41 If equipped with rear disc brakes, install the ABS cable into the clips on the lower suspension arm**

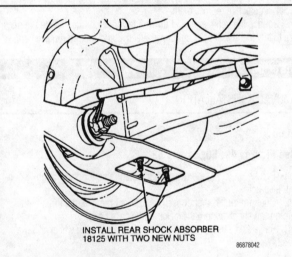

**Fig. 42 When installing the shock absorber on the lower arm, install new retaining nuts**

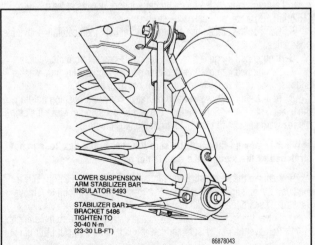

**Fig. 43 Attach the stabilizer U-bracket to the lower suspension arm using a new bolt. Tighten the bolt to 23–30 ft. lbs. (31–40 Nm)**

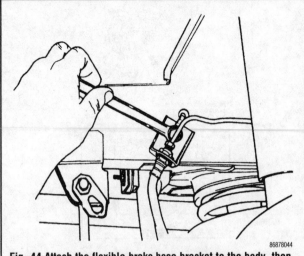

**Fig. 44 Attach the flexible brake hose bracket to the body, then tighten the retaining bolt to 8–12 ft. lbs. (11–16 Nm)**

24. Install the wheel and tire assembly. Remove the floor jack, then carefully lower the vehicle.

## Shock Absorbers

### REMOVAL & INSTALLATION

**Station Wagon Only**

▶ **See Figures 45, 46, 47 and 48**

1. Raise and safely support the vehicle.
2. Remove the wheel and tire assembly.
3. Position a jackstand under the lower suspension arm.
4. Slightly lower the vehicle to put the suspension at the normal position, then remove the two nuts retaining the shock absorber to the lower suspension arm.
5. From inside the vehicle, remove the rear compartment access panels.

➡**If the shock absorber is to be reused, do not grip the shaft with pliers or vise grips. Gripping the shaft in this manner will damage the shaft surface finish and will result in severe oil leakage.**

6. Remove and discard the top shock absorber attaching nut using a crow's foot wrench and ratchet, while holding the shock absorber shaft stationary with an open-end wrench.
7. Remove the rubber insulator from the shock, then remove the shock from the vehicle.

➡**The shock absorbers are gas filled. It may require extra effort to remove the shock from the lower arm.**

**To install:**

8. Install a new washer and insulator assembly on the upper shock absorber rod.
9. Maneuver the upper part of the shock absorber into the shock tower opening in the body. Push slowly on the lower part of the shock absorber until the mounting studs are aligned with the mounting holes in the lower suspension arm.
10. Install new lower attaching nuts, but do not tighten at this time.
11. Install a new shock absorber bushing repair kit, washer and nut on top of the shock absorber. Tighten the nut to 19–25 ft. lbs. (26–34 Nm).
12. Install the rear compartment access panel.
13. Tighten the two lower attaching nuts to 15–19 ft. lbs. (19–30 Nm).
14. Install the wheel and tire assembly. Remove the safety stand supporting the lower suspension arm, then carefully lower the vehicle.

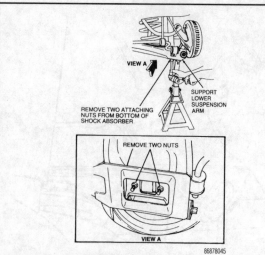

Fig. 45 Removing the two shock absorber-to-lower suspension arm retaining nuts

Fig. 46 Remove and discard the top shock absorber attaching nut using a crow's foot wrench and ratchet, while holding the shock absorber shaft stationary with an open end wrench

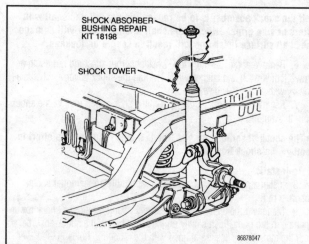

Fig. 47 Install a new shock absorber bushing repair kit, washer and nut on top of the shock absorber. Tighten the nut to 19–25 ft. lbs. (26–34 Nm)

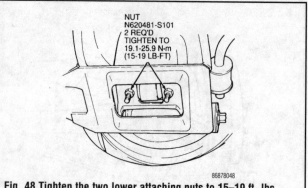

Fig. 48 Tighten the two lower attaching nuts to 15–19 ft. lbs. (19–30 Nm)

## TESTING

1. Visually inspect the shock absorber for signs of leakage.
2. If one shock absorber is leaking, replace both shock absorbers.
3. Stand back and look at the vehicle. If it sags on one end check the shocks; if defective replace them.
4. Bounce the vehicle up and down a few times; if the vehicle bounces more that twice, the shocks could be defective and require replacement.

## MacPherson Struts

### REMOVAL & INSTALLATION

#### Sedan

▶ See Figures 49, 50, 51 and 52

1. Position a jack under the vehicle, then raise it only enough to contact the vehicle.
2. Open the trunk, then loosen, but do not remove, the three nuts retaining the shock absorber bracket to the car's body.
3. Raise and safely support the vehicle. Remove the wheel and tire assembly.

➡ Do not raise or support the vehicle using the tension struts.

4. Remove the bolt retaining the brake differential control valve/brake load sensor proportioning valve to the control arm. Using a wire, secure the control arm to the body to ensure proper support, leaving at least 6 in. (152mm) clearance to assist in the strut removal.
5. Remove the brake hose-to-strut bracket clip, then carefully move the hose aside.
6. If equipped, remove the stabilizer bar U-bracket from the vehicle.
7. If equipped, remove the stabilizer bar-to-stabilizer link nut, washer and insulator, then separate the stabilizer bar from the link.
8. Remove the nut, washer and rear strut body end-bushing holding the tension strut and the bushing to the rear wheel spindle. Move the spindle rearward enough to separate it from the tension strut.

➡ When removing the strut, be sure the rear brake flex hose is not stretched or the steel brake tube is not bent.

9. Remove the shock strut-to-spindle pinch bolt. If necessary, use a medium prybar, slightly spread the strut-to-spindle pinch joint to remove the strut. Discard the bolt and replace it during installation.
10. Lower the jackstand, then separate the shock strut from the spindle.
11. Remove the nut, washer and lower suspension arm stabilizer bar

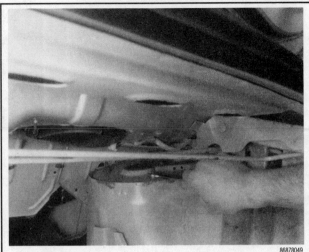

**Fig. 49 Open the trunk, then loosen, but do not remove, the three shock retaining nuts**

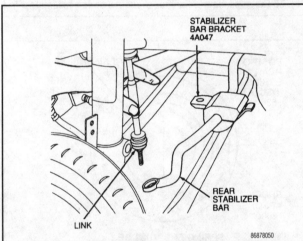

**Fig. 50 If equipped, remove the stabilizer bar-to-stabilizer link nut, washer and insulator, then separate the stabilizer bar from the link**

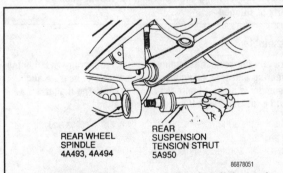

**Fig. 51 Move the spindle rearward, then install the tension strut and bushing into the spindle. Install the insulator, washer and nut on the tension strut**

insulator attaching the link to the rear shock absorber, then remove the stabilizer bar link.

12. From inside the trunk, remove and discard the three upper mount-to-body nuts. Be careful that the shock absorber does not drop when removing the three nuts, then remove the shock absorber from the vehicle.

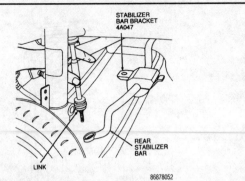

**Fig. 52 Position the link into the stabilizer bar, then install the insulator, washer and nut on the link**

**To install:**
13. Position the stabilizer bar link in the strut bracket. Install the insulator, washer and nut, then tighten to 5–7 ft. lbs. (7–9.5 Nm).

14. Insert the three upper mount studs into the strut tower in the apron, then hand-start three new nuts. Do not tighten the nuts at this time.

15. Partially raise the vehicle.

16. Install the strut into the spindle pinch joint. Install a new pinch bolt into the spindle and through the strut bracket. Tighten the bolt to 50–68 ft. lbs. (68–92 Nm).

17. Move the spindle rearward, then install the tension strut and bushing into the spindle. Install the insulator, washer and nut on the tension strut. Tighten the nut to 35–46 ft. lbs. (47–63 Nm).

18. Position the link into the stabilizer bar. Install the insulator, washer and nut on the link. Tighten to 5–7 ft. lbs. (7–9.5 Nm).

19. Position the stabilizer bar U-bracket on the body. Install the bolt, then tighten to 25–33 ft. lbs. (34–46 Nm).

20. Install the brake hose to the strut bracket.

21. Install the brake control differential valve/brake load sensor proportioning valve on the control arm, then remove the retaining wire.

22. In the trunk, tighten the top mount-to-body nuts to 19–25 ft. lbs. (25–34 Nm).

23. Install the wheel and tire assembly, then carefully lower the vehicle.

## OVERHAUL

♦ **See Figures 53, 54, 55, 56 and 57**

The following procedure is performed with the strut assembly removed from the car. A MacPherson Strut compression tool is required for the disassembly of the strut; use a cage type tool such as the No. D85P–7181–A, Rotunda Spring Compressor 086-0029B, or equivalent is required.

**❊❊ CAUTION**

**Never attempt to disassemble the spring or top mount without first compressing the spring using the strut compressor tool No. D85P–7178–A or equivalent. If a strut spring compressor is not used, the assembly could fly apart by the force of the spring tension, resulting in serious injury or death.**

➡**Before compressing the spring, mark the location of the insulator to the top mount using a grease pencil.**

1. Remove the rear shock and spring assembly, as outlined in the procedure located earlier in this section.

2. Compress the spring with the coil spring compressor D85P-7178-A, 086-0029B or equivalent.

3. Place a 10mm box wrench on top of the shock strut shaft, and hold while removing the top shaft mounting nut with a 21mm 6-point crow's foot wrench and ratchet.

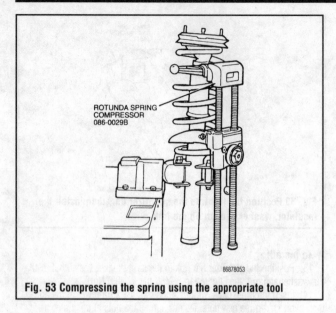

ROTUNDA SPRING COMPRESSOR 086-0029B

86878053

**Fig. 53 Compressing the spring using the appropriate tool**

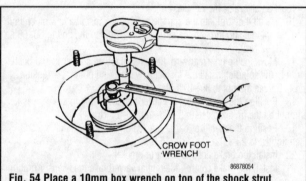

CROW FOOT WRENCH

86878054

**Fig. 54 Place a 10mm box wrench on top of the shock strut shaft, and hold while removing the top shaft mounting nut with a 21mm 6-point crow's foot wrench and ratchet**

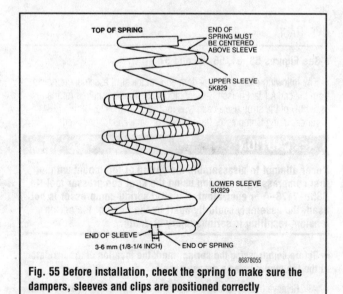

TOP OF SPRING

END OF SPRING MUST BE CENTERED ABOVE SLEEVE

UPPER SLEEVE 5K829

LOWER SLEEVE 5K829

END OF SLEEVE
3-6 mm (1/8-1/4 INCH)        END OF SPRING

86878055

**Fig. 55 Before installation, check the spring to make sure the dampers, sleeves and clips are positioned correctly**

➡**It is important that the mounting nut be turned and the rod held still to prevent fracture of the rod at the base of the hex.**

4. Loosen the spring compressor tool, then remove the top mounting bracket assembly, bearing plate assembly and spring.

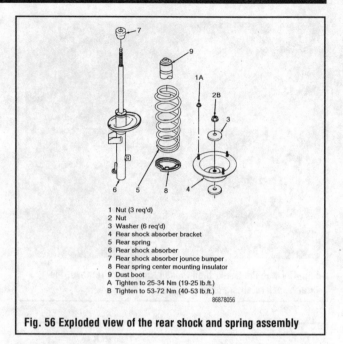

1 Nut (3 req'd)
2 Nut
3 Washer (6 req'd)
4 Rear shock absorber bracket
5 Rear spring
6 Rear shock absorber
7 Rear shock absorber jounce bumper
8 Rear spring center mounting insulator
9 Dust boot
A Tighten to 25-34 Nm (19-25 lb.ft.)
B Tighten to 53-72 Nm (40-53 lb.ft.)

86878056

**Fig. 56 Exploded view of the rear shock and spring assembly**

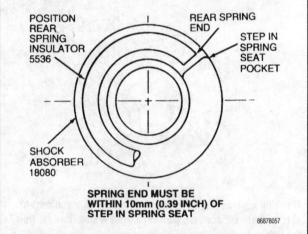

POSITION REAR SPRING INSULATOR 5536

REAR SPRING END

STEP IN SPRING SEAT POCKET

SHOCK ABSORBER 18080

**SPRING END MUST BE WITHIN 10mm (0.39 INCH) OF STEP IN SPRING SEAT**

86878057

**Fig. 57 Make sure the spring is correctly located in the upper mount and lower spring seat, and that the mount washers are properly positioned**

**To assemble:**

➡**Ensure that the correct assembly sequence and proper positioning of the bearing and seat assembly are followed. The bearing and seat assembly is press-fit onto the upper mount. The mount washers must be installed with the proper orientation.**

5. Inspect the spring to ensure that the dampers, sleeves and clips are properly positioned.

6. Install the spring compressor tool No. D85P-7178-A, 086-0029B or equivalent.

7. Install the spring, insulator, bottom washer (if equipped), top mount bracket assembly, upper washer and nut.

8. Compress the spring with the coil spring compressor tool. Be certain that the spring is properly located in the upper and lower spring seats and that the mount washers are oriented correctly.

9. Place a 10mm box-end wrench on the top of the shock strut shaft and hold while tightening the top shaft mounting nut with a 21mm 6-point crow's foot wrench and a ratchet. Tighten the nut to 40–53 ft. lbs. (53–72 Nm).

10. The strut assembly may now be installed in the vehicle.

## Control Arms

### REMOVAL & INSTALLATION

#### Sedan

▶ **See Figure 58**

1. Raise and safely support the vehicle.

➡ **Do not raise the vehicle by the tension strut.**

2. For vehicles through 1993, disconnect the brake load sensor proportioning valve(s) from the left side front control arm. For 1994–95 vehicles, disconnect the brake load sensor proportioning valve(s) from the rear arm and bushing.

3. Disconnect the parking brake cable from the front control arms on vehicles through 1993. For 1994–95 vehicles, disconnect the parking brake cable from the rear arm and bushings.

4. Remove and discard the arm-to-spindle bolt, washer and nut.

5. Remove and discard the arm-to-body bolt and nut.

6. Remove the lower control arm from the vehicle.

**To install:**

➡ **When installing new control arms, the offset on all arms must face up. The arms are stamped "bottom" on the lower edge. The flange edge of the right side rear arm stamping must face the front of the vehicle. The other 3 must face the rear of the vehicle. The rear control arms have two adjustment cams that fit inside the bushings at the arm-to-body attachment. The cam is installed from the rear on the left arm and from the front on the right arm.**

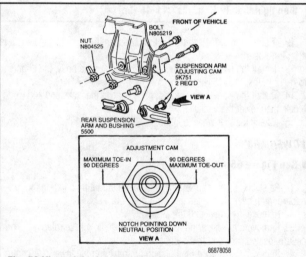

**Fig. 58 View of the lower control (suspension) arm mounting—sedan only**

7. Position the arm and cam where required, at the center of the vehicle. Insert a new bolt and nut, but do not tighten at this time.

8. Move the arm end up to the spindle, then insert a new bolt, washer and nut. Tighten the nut to 44–59 ft. lbs. (59–81 Nm).

9. Tighten the arm-to-body nut to 50–68 ft. lbs. (68–92 Nm).

10. Attach the parking brake cable to the front arms or rear arm, as applicable.

11. Connect the brake load sensor proportioning valve to the left side front arm or rear arm as applicable.

12. Carefully lower the vehicle, then have the alignment checked by a reputable repair shop.

#### Wagon

##### *UPPER ARM*

▶ **See Figures 59 thru 65**

1. Raise and safely support the vehicle, then place a jackstand and wood block under the rear lower control arm to support it so the suspension is at normal curb height, as shown in the accompanying figure.

2. Remove the wheel and tire assembly.

3. Remove the brake line flexible hose bracket from the body.

4. Loosen, but do not remove, the nut attaching the rear wheel spindle to the front and rear upper control arms.

5. Loosen, but do not remove, the nut attaching the rear wheel spindle to the rear lower control arm.

6. Remove and discard the nuts and bolts attaching the front and rear upper suspension arms to the body brackets. Make sure the spindle does not fall outward.

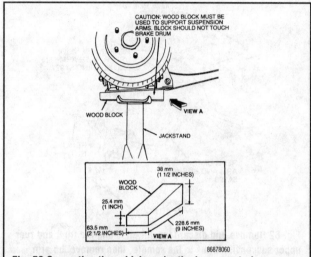

**Fig. 59 Supporting the vehicle under the lower control arm so the suspension is at normal curb height**

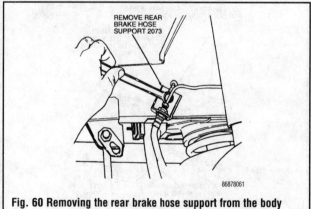

**Fig. 60 Removing the rear brake hose support from the body**

7. Carefully tilt the top of the spindle outward, letting it pivot on the lower suspension arm attaching bolt until the ends of the upper suspension arms are clear of the body bracket. Support the spindle with wire in this position.

8. Remove and discard the nut attaching the rear suspension front and rear upper suspension arms to the spindle, then remove the arm from the vehicle.

**To install:**

9. Install the rear suspension front and rear upper control arms on the spindle, then install a new nut, but do not tighten the nut yet.

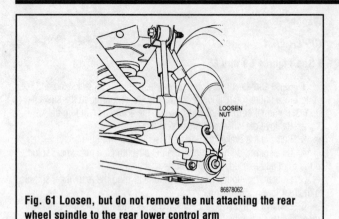

Fig. 61 Loosen, but do not remove the nut attaching the rear wheel spindle to the rear lower control arm

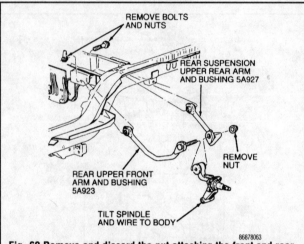

Fig. 62 Remove and discard the nut attaching the front and rear upper suspension arms to the spindle, then remove the arm from the vehicle

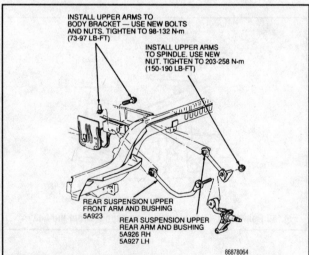

Fig. 63 Installing the rear upper control arm—station wagon only

10. Position the upper control arm ends to the body bracket, then install new nuts and bolts. Tighten to 73–97 ft. lbs. (98–132 Nm). Remove the wire from the rear wheel spindle.

11. Tighten the nut attaching the upper suspension arms to the spindle to 150–190 ft. lbs. (203–258 Nm).

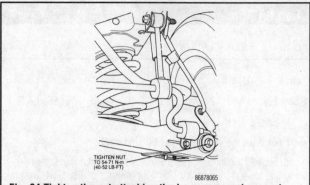

Fig. 64 Tighten the nut attaching the lower suspension arm to the spindle to 40–52 ft. lbs. (54–71 Nm)

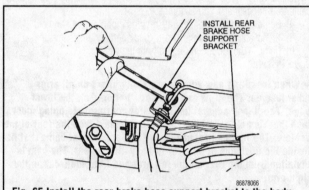

Fig. 65 Install the rear brake hose support bracket to the body, then tighten to 8–12 ft. lbs. (11–16 Nm)

12. Tighten the nut attaching the lower suspension arm to the spindle to 40–52 ft. lbs. (54–71 Nm).

13. Install the rear brake hose support bracket to the body, then tighten to 8–12 ft. lbs. (11–16 Nm).

14. Install the wheel and tire assembly, remove the jackstand and wood block, then lower the vehicle.

15. Check the rear wheel alignment.

### LOWER ARM

♦ See Figure 66

1. Raise and safely support the vehicle, on the lifting pads on the underbody forward of the tension strut body bracket.

2. Remove the wheel and tire assembly.

3. Remove the rear spring assembly. For details, please refer to the procedure located earlier in this section.

4. Remove and discard the bolt and nut retaining the lower rear control arm and bushing to the center body bracket, then remove the lower control arm and bushing assembly.

**To install:**

5. Position the rear lower control arm and bushing to the center body bracket, then install a new bolt and nut. Install the bolt with the bolt head toward the front of the vehicle, but do not tighten the bolt at this time.

6. Install the rear spring assembly. For details, please refer to the procedure located earlier in this section.

7. Support the control arm and bushing in the normal position when the vehicle is at curb height. Tighten the nut securing the arm to the body bracket to 40–52 ft. lbs. (54–71 Nm).

➡After rear control arm and bushing replacement, it is necessary to have the vehicle's rear alignment checked and/or adjusted by a reputable repair shop.

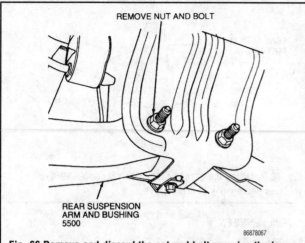

REMOVE NUT AND BOLT

REAR SUSPENSION
ARM AND BUSHING
5500

86878067

**Fig. 66 Remove and discard the nut and bolt securing the lower rear control arm and bushing to the center body bracket, then remove the lower control arm and bushing assembly**

8. Tighten the nut securing the lower control arm to the wheel spindle to 40–52 ft. lbs. (54–71 Nm).

9. Remove the jackstands, then carefully lower the vehicle.

## Rear Wheel Bearings

### REPLACEMENT

#### Drum Brakes

##### 1986–89 VEHICLES

▶ **See Figures 67, 68, 69 and 70**

1. Raise the vehicle and support it safely. Remove the wheel from the hub and drum.

2. Remove the grease cap from the hub, being careful not to damage the cap. Remove the cotter pin, nut retainer, adjusting nut and keyed flat washer from the spindle. Discard the cotter pin.

➡**Styled steel wheels and aluminum wheels require the removal of the wheel and tire assembly to remove the dust cover.**

3. Being careful not to drop the outer bearing assembly, pull the hub and drum assembly off of the spindle. Remove the outer bearing assembly.

4. Using Seal Remover tool 1175-AC or equivalent, remove and discard the grease seal. Remove the inner bearing assembly from the hub.

5. Wipe all lubricant from the spindle and inside of the hub. Cover the spindle with a clean cloth and vacuum all loose dust and dirt from the brake assembly. Carefully remove the cloth to prevent dirt from falling on the spindle.

6. Clean both bearing assemblies and cups using a suitable solvent. Inspect the bearing assemblies and cups for excessive wear, scratches, pits or other damage, then replace as necessary.

7. If the cups are to be replaced, remove them with Impact Slide Hammer T50T-100-A and Bearing Cup Puller T77F-1102-A or equivalents.

**To install:**

8. If the inner and outer bearing cups were removed, install the replacement cups using Driver Handle T80T-4000-W and Bearing Cup Replacers T73T-1217-A and T77F-1217-A or equivalents. Support the drum hub on a block of wood to prevent damage. Make sure the cups are properly seated in the hub.

➡**Do not use the cone and roller assembly to install the cups. This will result in damage to the bearing cup and the cone and roller assembly.**

9. Make sure all of the spindle and bearing surfaces are clean.

➡**Allow the cleaning solvent to dry before repacking the bearings. Do NOT spin the bearings dry with compressed air!**

10. Using a bearing packer, pack the bearing assemblies with Long-Life Lubricant C1AZ-19590-BA or equivalent suitable wheel bearing grease. If a packer is not available, work in as much grease as possible between the rollers and cages. Grease the cup surfaces.

11. Position the inner bearing cone and roller assembly in the inner cup. Apply a light film of grease to the lips of a new grease seal and install the seal with Rear Hub Seal Replacer T56T-4676-B or equivalent. Make sure the retainer flange is seated all around.

12. Apply a light film of grease on the spindle shaft bearing surfaces. Install the hub and drum assembly on the spindle. Keep the hub centered on the spindle to prevent damage to the grease seal and spindle threads.

13. Install the outer bearing assembly and the keyed flat washer on the spindle. Install the adjusting nut, then adjust the wheel bearings as outlined later in this section. Install a new cotter pin, then install the grease cap. Replace with a new grease cap if there is any corrosion on the inner surfaces of the cap.

14. Place the wheel and tire assembly on the drum. Install the lug nuts,

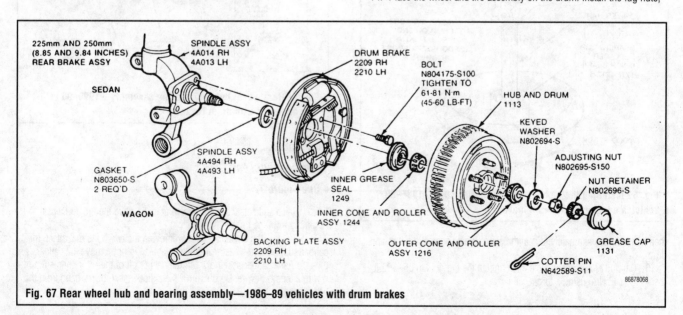

225mm AND 250mm
(8.85 AND 9.84 INCHES)
REAR BRAKE ASSY

SEDAN

GASKET
N803650-S
2 REQ'D

WAGON

SPINDLE ASSY
4A014 RH
4A013 LH

SPINDLE ASSY
4A494 RH
4A493 LH

DRUM BRAKE
2209 RH
2210 LH

BOLT
N804175-S100
TIGHTEN TO
61-81 N·m
(45-60 LB-FT)

INNER GREASE
SEAL
1249

INNER CONE AND ROLLER
ASSY 1244

BACKING PLATE ASSY
2209 RH
2210 LH

OUTER CONE AND ROLLER
ASSY 1216

HUB AND DRUM
1113

KEYED
WASHER
N802694-S

ADJUSTING NUT
N802695-S150

NUT RETAINER
N802696-S

GREASE CAP
1131

COTTER PIN
N642589-S11

86878068

**Fig. 67 Rear wheel hub and bearing assembly—1986–89 vehicles with drum brakes**

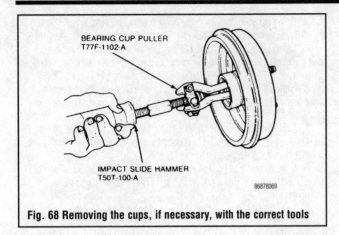

Fig. 68 Removing the cups, if necessary, with the correct tools

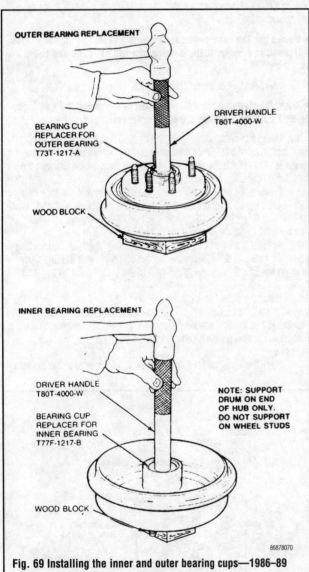

Fig. 69 Installing the inner and outer bearing cups—1986–89 vehicles equipped with drum brakes

then hand-tighten alternately to seal the wheel evenly against the hub and drum.

15. Carefully lower the vehicle, then tighten the lug nuts to 85–105 ft. lbs. (115–142 Nm) using a torque wrench.

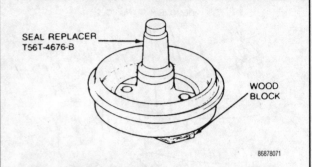

Fig. 70 Installing the grease seal in the rear hub—1986–89 vehicles equipped with drum brakes

### 1990–95 VEHICLES

▶ See Figure 71

1. Raise and safely support the vehicle.
2. Remove the wheel and tire assembly.
3. Remove the two pushnuts retaining the drum to the hub, then remove the drum.
4. Remove the rear hub cap grease seal from the hub assembly, then discard it.
5. Remove and discard the hub retainer, then remove the bearing and hub assembly from the spindle.

**To install:**

6. Position the hub on the spindle.
7. Install a new wheel hub retainer, then tighten to 188–254 ft. lbs. (255–345 Nm).
8. Install the new hub cap grease seal using Shaft Protector for Coil Removal T89P-19623-FH. Tap on the tool to make sure the grease cap is fully seated.
9. Install the brake drum on the hub, then install the two pushnuts that retain the brake drum.
10. Install the wheel and tire assembly, then carefully lower the vehicle.

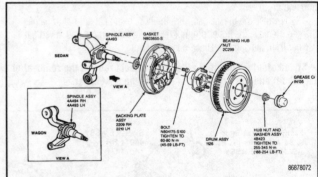

Fig. 71 Rear wheel hub and bearing assembly—1990–95 vehicles equipped with drum brakes

### Disc Brakes

### 1986–89 VEHICLES

▶ See Figure 72

1. Raise and safely support the vehicle. Remove the tire and wheel assembly from the hub.
2. Remove the brake caliper by removing the two bolts that attach the caliper support to the cast iron brake adapter. Do not remove the caliper pins from the caliper assembly. Lift the caliper off of the rotor, then support it with a length of wire. Do not allow the caliper assembly to hang from the brake hose.

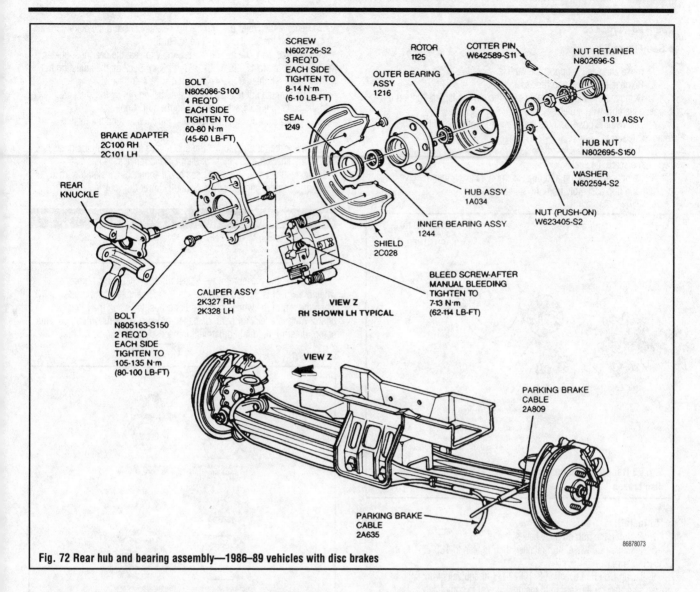

**Fig. 72 Rear hub and bearing assembly—1986–89 vehicles with disc brakes**

3. Remove the rotor from the hub by pulling it off the hub bolts. If the rotor is difficult to remove, strike the rotor sharply between the studs with a rubber or plastic hammer.

4. Remove the grease cap from the hub. Remove the cotter pin, nut retainer, adjusting nut and keyed flat washer from the spindle. Discard the cotter pin.

5. Pull the hub assembly off of the spindle. Remove the outer bearing assembly.

6. Using Seal Remover Tool 1175-AC or equivalent, remove and discard the grease seal. Remove the inner bearing assembly from the hub.

7. Wipe all of the lubricant from the spindle and inside of the hub. Cover the spindle with a clean cloth and vacuum all of the loose dust and dirt from the brake assembly. Carefully remove the cloth to prevent dirt from falling on the spindle.

8. Clean both bearing assemblies and cups using a suitable solvent. Inspect the bearing assemblies and cups for excessive wear, scratches, pits or other damage and replace as necessary.

9. If the cups are being replaced, remove them with Impact Slide Hammer Tool T50T-100-A and Bearing Cup Puller Tool T77F-1102-A or equivalents.

**To install:**

10. If the inner and outer bearing cups were removed, install the replacement cups using Driver Handle Tool T80T-4000-W and Bearing Cup Replacer Tools T73F-1217-A and T77F-1217-B or equivalents. Support the hub on a block of wood to prevent damage. Make sure the cups are properly seated in the hub.

➡ **Do not use the cone and roller assembly to install the cups. This will result in damage to the bearing cup as well as the cone and roller assembly.**

11. Make sure all of the spindle and bearing surfaces are clean.

12. Pack the bearing assemblies with a suitable wheel bearing grease using a bearing packer. If a packer is not available, work in as much grease as possible between the rollers and the cages. Grease the cup surfaces.

➡ **Allow all of the cleaning solvent to dry before repacking the bearings. Do not spin-dry the bearings with air pressure.**

13. Place the inner bearing cone and roller assembly in the inner cup. Apply a light film of grease to the lips of a new grease seal and install the seal with Rear Hub Seal Replacer Tool T56T-4676-B or equivalent. Make sure the retainer flange is seated all around.

14. Apply a light film of grease on the spindle shaft bearing surfaces. Install the hub assembly on the spindle. Keep the hub centered on the spindle to prevent damage to the grease seal and spindle threads.

15. Install the outer bearing assembly and keyed flat washer on the spindle. Install the adjusting nut and adjust the wheel bearings. Install a new cotter pin and the grease cap.

16. Install the disc brake rotor to the hub assembly. Install the disc brake caliper over the rotor.

17. Install the wheel and tire assembly, then carefully lower the vehicle.

### 1990–95 VEHICLES

▶ See Figure 73

1. Raise and safely support the vehicle.
2. Remove the wheel and tire assembly.
3. Remove the caliper assembly from the brake adapter. Support the caliper assembly with a piece of wire.
4. Remove the push-on nuts that retain the rotor to the hub, then remove the rotor.
5. Remove the hub cap grease seal from the bearing and hub assembly, then discard the seal.
6. Remove the bearing and hub assembly retainer, then remove the bearing and hub assembly from the spindle.

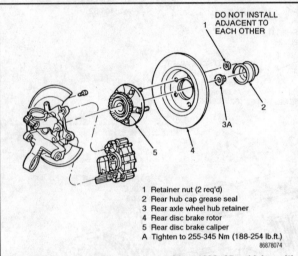

1 Retainer nut (2 req'd)
2 Rear hub cap grease seal
3 Rear axle wheel hub retainer
4 Rear disc brake rotor
5 Rear disc brake caliper
A Tighten to 255-345 Nm (188-254 lb.ft.)

86878074

**Fig. 73 Rear hub and bearing assembly—1990–95 vehicles with disc brakes**

**To install:**

7. Position the hub on the wheel spindle.
8. Install a new wheel hub retainer, then tighten to 188–254 ft. lbs. (255–345 Nm).
9. Using Coil Remover T89P-19623-FH or equivalent, install a new grease seal. Tap on the tool until the grease seal is completely seated.
10. Install the rotor on the hub. Install the two retaining push-on nuts that hold the rotor on the hub.
11. Install the brake caliper to the brake adapter.
12. Install the wheel and tire assembly, then carefully lower the vehicle.

### ADJUSTMENT

#### 1986–89 Vehicles

▶ See Figure 74

The following procedure applies only to 1986–89 vehicles. Adjustment is not possible on 1990–95 vehicles. This procedure should be performed whenever the wheel is excessively loose on the spindle or it does not rotate freely.

➡The rear wheel uses a tapered roller bearing which may feel loose when properly adjusted; this condition should be considered normal.

1. Raise and safely support the vehicle until tires clear the floor.
2. Remove the wheel cover or the ornament and nut cover. Remove the hub grease cap, being careful not the damage the cap.

➡If the vehicle is equipped with styled steel or aluminum wheels, the wheel/tire assembly must be removed to access the dust cover.

3. Remove the cotter pin and the nut retainer. Discard the cotter pin.
4. Back off the adjusting nut one full turn.
5. While rotating the hub/drum assembly to seat the bearings, tighten the adjusting nut to 17–25 ft. lbs. (23–24 Nm). Back off the adjusting nut ½ turn, then retighten it to 24–28 inch lbs. (2.7–3.2 Nm).
6. Position the nut retainer over the adjusting nut so the slots are in line with the cotter pin hole, without rotating the adjusting nut.
7. Install a new cotter pin, then bend the ends around the retainer flange.
8. Check the hub rotation. If the hub rotates freely, install the grease cap. If not, check the bearings for damage and replace, as necessary.
9. Install the wheel and tire assembly. If applicable, install the wheel cover or ornament and nut cover. Carefully lower the vehicle.

## Rear Wheel Alignment

### CAMBER

Camber is the measure of the wheel tilt from the vertical direction, when the wheel is viewed from the rear of the vehicle. Camber is negative when the top of the wheel is inboard and positive when the top is outboard. Always check for bent, damaged or worn suspension components before determining that adjustment is necessary. The amount of tilt is

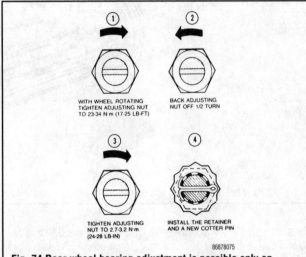

86878075

**Fig. 74 Rear wheel bearing adjustment is possible only on 1986–89 vehicles**

measured in degrees from the vertical and this measurement is called the camber angle.

Camber is not adjustable on the Sedan. On the Wagon camber is adjustable, but requires special equipment and procedures. If you suspect an alignment problem, have it checked by a qualified repair shop.

### TOE-IN

Toe is a measurement of how far a wheel is turned in or out from the straight ahead direction. When the front of the wheel is turned in, the toe is positive. When the front of the wheel is turned out, toe is negative. An incorrect toe setting can affect steering feel and cause excessive tire wear.

Stated another way, toe-in is the amount that the front of the wheels are closer together than the backs of the same wheels. The actual amount of toe-in is normally only a fraction of a degree.

Rear toe is adjustable, but requires special equipment and procedures. If you suspect an alignment problem, have it checked by a qualified repair shop.

## STEERING

## Steering Wheel

REMOVAL & INSTALLATION

### ✳✳ CAUTION

**If equipped with an air bag, the negative battery cable must be disconnected before working on the system. On 1990–95 vehicles, the backup power supply must also be disconnected. Failure to do so may result in deployment of the air bag and possible personal injury. Always wear safety glasses when servicing an air bag vehicle and when handling an air bag.**

**1986–89 Vehicles**

▶ **See Figures 75 thru 80**

1. Disconnect the negative battery cable.
2. Unfasten the two screws from the back of the steering wheel, then remove the steering wheel horn pad cover. Disengage the electrical connector. If equipped with cruise control, disengage the connector from the slip ring terminal.
3. Remove and discard the steering wheel retaining bolt/nut.
4. Remove the steering wheel from the upper shaft by grasping the rim of the steering wheel and pulling it off. A steering wheel puller is not required.

**To install:**

5. Position the steering wheel on the end of the shaft. Align the mark on the steering wheel with the mark on the shaft to ensure that the straight-ahead steering wheel position corresponds to the straight-ahead position of the front wheels.

➡**The combination switch lever must be in the middle (neutral) position before installing the steering wheel or damage to the switch cam may result.**

6. Install a new steering wheel retaining bolt, then tighten it to 23–33 ft. lbs. (31–45 Nm).
7. If equipped with cruise control, engage the connector to the slip ring terminal.
8. Install the steering wheel horn pad cover with the two retaining screws. Tighten to 5–10 inch lbs. (0.5–1.1 Nm).
9. Connect the negative battery cable, then check the steering wheel for proper operation.

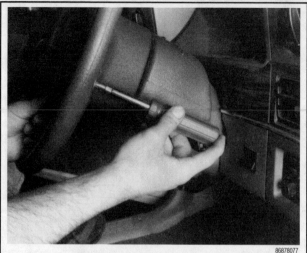
Fig. 76 Remove the two steering wheel horn pad cover retaining screws from the back of the steering wheel, then . . .

Fig. 77 . . . disengage the electrical connector and remove the steering wheel horn pad cover

Fig. 75 Steering wheel assembly—1986 Taurus shown

Fig. 78 Unfasten the wheel retaining nut, then . . .

Fig. 79 . . . remove the steering wheel by grasping the rim and pulling it off

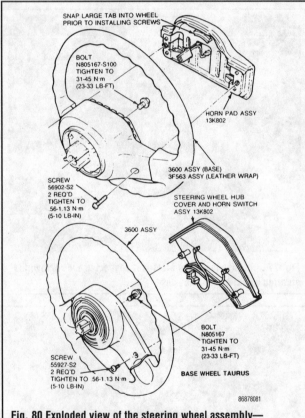

Fig. 80 Exploded view of the steering wheel assembly— 1986–89 vehicles

## 1990–95 Vehicles

▶ **See Figures 81 and 82**

1. Center the front wheels in the straight-ahead position.
2. Disconnect the negative battery cable. Lower the glove compartment past its stops, then disconnect the air bag backup power supply.
3. For 1990–93 vehicles except SHO, remove the four air bag module retaining nuts and lift the module from the wheel. Disconnect the air bag wire harness from the air bag module, then remove the module from the steering wheel.

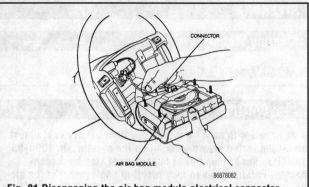

Fig. 81 Disengaging the air bag module electrical connector— 1992 vehicles shown

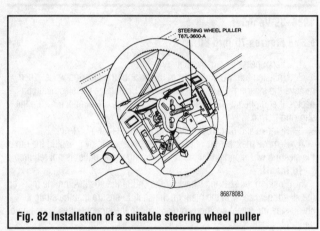

Fig. 82 Installation of a suitable steering wheel puller

4. For 1994–95 vehicles and SHO vehicles only, remove the two steering wheel back cover plugs. Remove the two air bag module retaining bolts, then lift the module off of the steering wheel. Disconnect the air bag wire harness from the air bag module, then remove the module from the steering wheel.

### ❋❋ CAUTION

**When carrying a live air bag, make sure the bag and trim cover are pointed away from the body. In the unlikely event of an accidental deployment, the bag will then deploy with minimal chance of injury. In addition, when placing a live air bag on a bench or other surface, always face the bag and trim cover up, away from the surface. This will reduce the chance of personal injury if it is accidentally deployed.**

5. Disconnect the cruise control wire harness from the steering wheel. Remove and discard the steering wheel retaining bolt.
6. Install Steering Wheel Puller T67L-3600-A or equivalent, and remove the steering wheel. Route the contact assembly wire harness through the steering wheel as the wheel is lifted off the shaft.

**To install:**

7. Make sure the vehicle's front wheels are in the straight-ahead position.
8. Route the contact assembly wire harness through the steering wheel opening at the 3 o'clock position and install the steering wheel on the shaft. The steering wheel and shaft alignment marks should be aligned. Make sure the air bag contact wire is not pinched.
9. Install a new steering wheel retaining bolt, then tighten to 23–33 ft. lbs. (31–45 Nm).

➡**Be sure the wiring does not get trapped between the steering wheel and the contact assembly.**

10. Connect the cruise control wire harness to the wheel, then snap the connector assembly into the steering wheel clip.

11. Connect the air bag wire harness to the air bag module, then install the module to the steering wheel. For 1990–93 vehicles except SHO, tighten the module retaining nuts to 36–47 inch lbs. (4–5.4 Nm). For 1994 vehicles and 1990–94 SHO vehicles, tighten the retaining screws to 7.5–10 ft. lbs. (10–14 Nm), then install the back cover plugs. For 1995 vehicles, tighten the retaining screws to 36–47 inch lbs. (4–5 Nm).

12. Connect the air bag backup power supply and the negative battery cable. Check the air bag warning indicator.

## Multi-Function Switch

The multi-function switch incorporates the turn signal, headlight dimmer, headlight flash-to-pass, hazard warning, cornering lights and windshield washer/wiper functions.

### REMOVAL & INSTALLATION

▶ **See Figure 83**

1. Disconnect the negative battery cable.

2. If equipped with a tilt steering column, set the tilt column to its lowest position, then remove the tilt lever by removing the Allen head retaining screw.

3. Remove the ignition lock cylinder.

4. Remove the steering column shroud screws, then remove the upper and lower shrouds.

5. For vehicles through 1989, unfasten the wiring harness retainer, then disengage the three electrical connectors.

6. Remove the self-tapping screws attaching the switch to the steering column, then disengage the switch from the steering column casting.

7. For 1990–95 vehicles, disengage the two or three electrical connectors, depending upon vehicle application.

**To install:**

8. For 1990–95 vehicles, engage the electrical connectors.

9. Align the turn signal switch mounting holes with the corresponding holes in the steering column and install self-tapping screws. Tighten the screws to 17–26 inch lbs. (2–3 Nm).

10. For vehicles through 1989, engage the electrical connectors, then install the wiring harness retainer.

11. Install the upper and lower steering column shroud and shroud retaining screws; tighten the screws to 6–10 inch lbs. (0.7–1.1 Nm).

12. Install the ignition lock cylinder.

13. Attach the tilt lever, if removed, then tighten the tilt lever Allen head retaining screw to 6–9 inch lbs. (0.7–1.0 Nm).

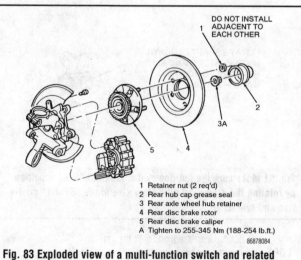

**Fig. 83 Exploded view of a multi-function switch and related components**

DO NOT INSTALL ADJACENT TO EACH OTHER

1 Retainer nut (2 req'd)
2 Rear hub cap grease seal
3 Rear axle wheel hub retainer
4 Rear disc brake rotor
5 Rear disc brake caliper
A Tighten to 255-345 Nm (188-254 lb.ft.)

86878084

14. Connect the negative battery cable. Check the switch and the steering column for proper operation.

## Ignition Switch

### REMOVAL & INSTALLATION

#### 1986–89 Vehicles

▶ **See Figures 84 thru 96**

1. Disconnect the negative battery cable.

2. Turn the ignition lock cylinder to the **RUN** position. Depress the lock cylinder retaining pin through the access hole in the shroud with a ⅛ diameter punch, then remove the lock cylinder.

3. If equipped with tilt columns, remove the tilt release lever after unfastening the retaining screw.

4. Remove the instrument panel lower cover and the steering column shroud after removing the retaining screws.

5. Remove the four nuts attaching the steering column to the support bracket, then lower the column.

6. Disengage the ignition switch electrical connector.

7. Remove the lock actuator cover plate by removing the Torx® head bolt. The lock actuator assembly will slide freely out of the lock cylinder housing when the ignition switch is removed.

8. Remove the ignition switch and cover after unfastening the two bolts with Torx® Driver D83L-2100-A or equivalent.

**To install:**

9. Make sure the ignition switch is in the **RUN** position by rotating the driveshaft fully clockwise to the **START** position and releasing.

10. Install the lock actuator assembly at a depth of 0.46–0.52 in. (11.75–13.25mm) from the bottom of the actuator assembly to the bottom of the lock cylinder housing.

TILT RELEASE LEVER

SOCKET HEAD CAP SCREW

86878086

**Fig. 84 Remove the tilt steering wheel lever by removing the socket head capscrew**

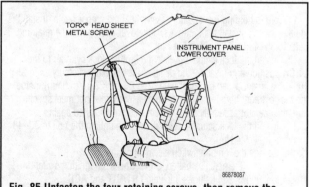

TORX® HEAD SHEET METAL SCREW

INSTRUMENT PANEL LOWER COVER

86878087

**Fig. 85 Unfasten the four retaining screws, then remove the instrument panel lower cover**

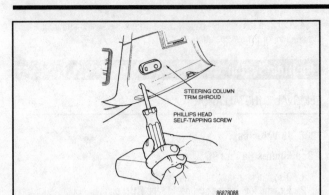

**Fig. 86 Unfasten the three self-tapping screws, then remove the steering column shroud**

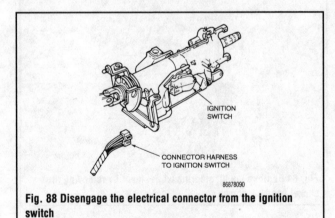

**Fig. 87 Lower the steering column by removing the four nuts attaching the column to the support bracket**

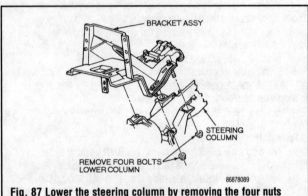

**Fig. 88 Disengage the electrical connector from the ignition switch**

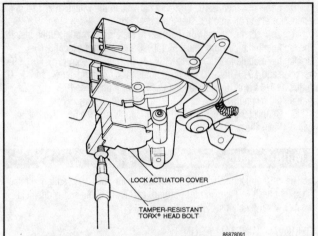

**Fig. 89 Remove the lock actuator cover plate by removing the Torx® head bolt. The lock actuator assembly will slide freely out of the lock cylinder housing when the ignition switch is removed**

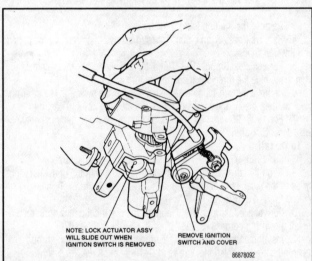

**Fig. 90 Remove the ignition switch and cover by removing the two bolts with Torx® Driver D83L-2100-A or equivalent**

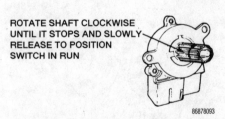

**Fig. 91 Make sure the ignition switch is in the "RUN" position by rotating the driveshaft fully clockwise to the "START" position and releasing**

11. While holding the actuator assembly at the proper depth, install the ignition switch. Install the ignition switch cover and tighten the retaining bolts to 30–48 inch lbs. (3.4–5.4 Nm).

12. Install the lock cylinder. Rotate the ignition lock cylinder to the **LOCK** position and measure the depth of the actuator assembly as in Step 10. The actuator assembly must be 0.92–1.00 in. (23.5–25.5mm) inside the lock cylinder housing. If the depth measured does not meet specification, the actuator assembly must be removed and installed again.

13. Install the lock actuator cover plate, then tighten the bolt to 30–48 inch lbs. (3.4–5.4 Nm).

14. Engage the ignition switch electrical connector.

15. Connect the negative battery cable. Check the ignition switch for proper function in all positions, including **START** and **ACC**.

16. Check the column function as follows:

a. With the column shift lever in the **P** position or with the floor shift key release button depressed, and with the ignition lock cylinder in the **LOCK** position, make certain the steering column locks.

b. Position the column shift lever in the **D** position or the floor shift key release button fully extended, and rotate the cylinder lock to the

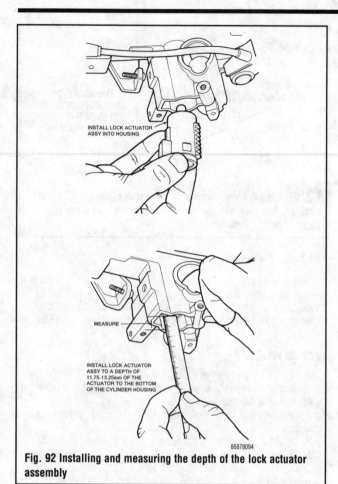

Fig. 92 Installing and measuring the depth of the lock actuator assembly

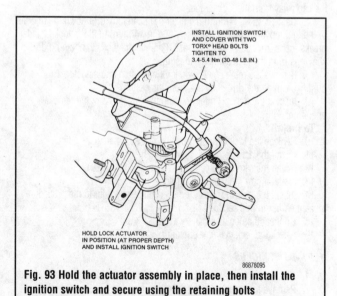

Fig. 93 Hold the actuator assembly in place, then install the ignition switch and secure using the retaining bolts

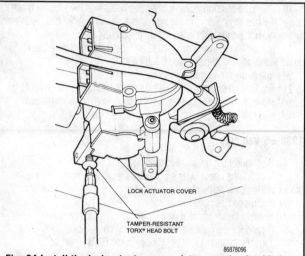

Fig. 94 Install the lock actuator cover plate, securing it with the Torx® head bolt

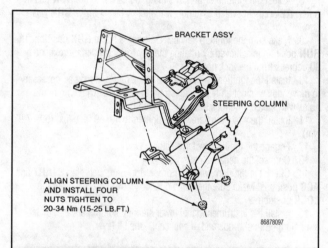

Fig. 95 Align the steering column mounting holes with the support bracket, center the steering column in the instrument panel opening, then install the four retaining nuts

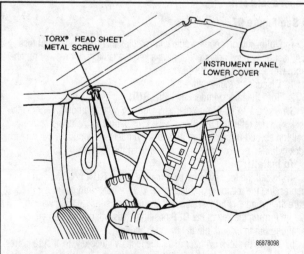

Fig. 96 Install the instrument panel lower cover, then secure using the four retaining screws

**RUN** position. Continue to rotate the cylinder toward the **LOCK** position until it stops. In this position, make certain the engine and all electrical accessories are **OFF** and that the steering shaft does not lock.

  c. Turn the radio power button **ON**. Rotate the cylinder counterclockwise to the **ACC** position to verify that the radio is energized.

  d. Place the shift lever in **P** and rotate the cylinder clockwise to the **START** position to verify that the starter energizes.

17. Remove the ignition lock cylinder.

18. Align the steering column mounting holes with the support bracket, center the steering column in the instrument panel opening, then install the four nuts. Tighten the nuts to 15–25 ft. lbs. (20–34 Nm).

19. Install the column trim shrouds and the instrument panel lower cover. Install the tilt release lever, if equipped.

20. Install the ignition lock cylinder.

21. For vehicle equipped with tilt columns, check the tilt travel to be sure there is no interference between the column and the instrument panel.

### 1990–95 Vehicles

1. Disconnect the negative battery cable.

2. Remove the upper steering column shroud after removing the four or five self-tapping screws.

3. If equipped, remove the tilt lever.

4. Remove the instrument panel lower steering column cover.

5. Disengage the ignition switch electrical connector.

6. Turn the ignition key lock cylinder to the **RUN** position.

7. Remove the two screws attaching the ignition switch, then disengage the switch from the actuator pin.

**To install:**

8. Adjust the ignition switch by sliding the carrier to the **RUN** position. A new replacement switch assembly will already be set in the **RUN** position.

9. Make sure the ignition key lock cylinder is in the **RUN** position. The **RUN** position is achieved by rotating the key lock cylinder approximately 90 degrees from the lock position.

10. Install the ignition switch into the actuator pin. It may be necessary to move the switch slightly back and forth to align the switch mounting holes with the column lock housing threaded holes.

11. Install the attaching screws and tighten to 50–69 inch lbs. (5.6–7.9 Nm).

12. Engage the ignition switch electrical connector.

13. Connect the negative battery cable.

14. Check the ignition switch for proper function, including **START** and **ACC** positions. Make sure the column is locked with the switch in the **LOCK** position.

15. Install the instrument panel lower steering column cover, the steering column trim shrouds and, if applicable, the tilt lever.

### Ignition Lock Cylinder

## REMOVAL & INSTALLATION

### Functional Lock

▶ See Figure 97

The following procedure applies to vehicles that have functional lock cylinders. Such cylinders either have a key available or known key numbers from which a key can be made.

1. Disconnect the negative battery cable.

2. Turn the lock cylinder key to the **RUN** position.

3. Using a ⅛ in. (3mm) diameter wire pin or a small drift, depress the lock cylinder retaining pin through the access hole in the upper steering column shroud (under the ignition lock cylinder) while pulling out on the lock cylinder. Remove the lock cylinder from the column.

**To install:**

4. Install the lock cylinder by turning it to the **RUN** position and depressing the retaining pin. Insert the lock cylinder into its housing. Make sure the cylinder is fully seated and aligned in the interlocking washer before turning the key to the **OFF** position. This will permit the cylinder retaining pin to extend into the cylinder housing.

5. Rotate the lock cylinder using the lock cylinder key, to ensure correct mechanical operation in all positions.

6. Connect the negative battery cable.

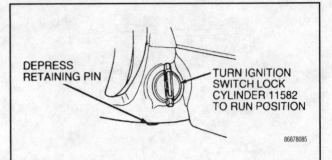

Fig. 97 Using the key, turn the ignition lock cylinder to the RUN position, then depress the retaining pin using a wire pin or small drift

### Non-Functional Lock

The following procedure applies to vehicles in which the ignition lock is inoperative and the lock cylinder cannot be rotated due to a lost or broken key, unknown key number or a lock cylinder cap that has been damaged and/or broken to the extent that the lock cylinder cannot be rotated.

#### 1986–90 VEHICLES

1. Disconnect the negative battery cable.

2. Remove the steering wheel. For details, please refer to the procedure located earlier in this section.

3. Remove the two trim shroud halves after removing the three attaching screws.

4. Disengage the electrical connector from the key warning switch.

5. Using a ⅛ in. (3mm) diameter drill, carefully drill out the retaining pin, being careful not to drill deeper than ½ in. (13mm).

6. Place a suitable chisel at the base of the ignition lock cylinder cap, then, using a suitable hammer, strike the chisel with sharp blows to break the cap away from the lock cylinder.

7. Using a ⅜ in. (10mm) diameter drill, carefully drill down the middle of the ignition key slot approximately 1¾ in. (44mm) until the lock cylinder breaks loose from its breakaway base. Remove the lock cylinder and drill shavings from the lock cylinder housing.

8. Remove the retainer, washer, ignition switch and actuator. Thoroughly clean all the drill shavings from the casting.

9. Inspect the lock cylinder housing for damage from the removal operation.

**To install:**

10. Replace the lock cylinder housing if it was damaged.

11. Install the actuator and ignition switch.

12. Install the trim and electrical parts.

13. Install a new ignition lock cylinder.

14. Install the steering wheel. For details, please refer to the procedure located earlier in this section.

15. Connect the negative battery cable.

16. Check the lock cylinder operation.

#### 1991–95 VEHICLES

1. Disconnect the negative battery cable.

2. Remove the steering wheel.

3. Using locking pliers, twist the cylinder cap until it separates from the lock cylinder.

4. Using a ⅜ in. (10mm) diameter drill bit, drill down the middle of the ignition lock key slot approximately 1¾ in. (44mm) until the lock cylinder releases from its breakaway base. Remove the lock cylinder and drill shavings from the lock cylinder housing.

5. Remove the retainer, washer, ignition switch and actuator. Thoroughly clean all drill shavings and other foreign materials from the casting.

6. Inspect the lock cylinder housing for damage from the removal operation. If the housing is damaged, it must be replaced.

**To install:**

7. Replace the lock cylinder housing, if damaged.
8. Install the actuator and ignition switch.
9. Install the trim and electrical parts.
10. Install the ignition lock cylinder.
11. Install the steering wheel.
12. Connect the negative battery cable, then check the lock cylinder operation.

## Steering Column

### REMOVAL & INSTALLATION

**1986–89 Vehicles**

▶ **See Figures 98 thru 105**

1. Disconnect the negative battery cable.
2. Remove the four self-tapping screws, then remove the steering column cover from the lower portion of the instrument panel.
3. Unfasten the retaining screw, then remove the tilt release lever.
4. Remove the ignition lock cylinder.
5. Remove the 3 self-tapping screws from the bottom of the lower shroud, then remove the steering column trim shrouds. Remove the horn pad and steering wheel assembly.
6. If equipped with column shift, perform the following:
   a. Disconnect the shift position indicator cable from the lock cylinder housing by removing the retaining screw.
   b. Disconnect the shift position indicator cable from the shift socket.
   c. Remove the shift position indicator cable from the retaining hook on the bottom of the lock cylinder housing.
7. Using a punch, remove the shift lever-to-shift socket retaining pin, then remove the shift lever.
8. Disengage the cruise control/horn brush wiring connector from the main wiring harness.
9. Remove the multi-function/combination switch wiring harness retainer from the lock cylinder housing by squeezing the end of the retainer and pushing out. Disengage the multi-function/combination switch connector, then unfasten the two self-tapping retaining screws and remove the multi-function/combination switch.
10. Disengage the key warning buzzer switch wiring connector from the main wiring harness and the wiring connector from the ignition switch.
11. Disconnect the steering shaft from the intermediate shaft after removing the two nuts and U-clamp. If equipped with an air bag, wire the lower end of the steering shaft to the column housing to prevent rotation of the steering shaft.

➡**Rotating the steering shaft could damage the air bag contact clockspring if the steering wheel is attached to the column.**

12. If equipped with column shift, perform the following:
   a. Remove the shift cable plastic terminal from the column selector lever pivot ball using a small prybar and prying between the plastic terminal and the selector lever. Be careful not to damage the cable during or after assembly.
   b. Remove the shift cable bracket, with shift cable still attached, from the lock cylinder housing by removing the two retaining screws.
13. If equipped with an automatic parking brake release mechanism, remove the vacuum hoses from the parking brake release switch.
14. Remove the two nuts retaining the rear column assembly. Loosen the two nuts retaining the front column assembly to the end of the studs, but do not remove them at this time.
15. Use a downward force to disengage the column assembly push-on clips from the rear attachments, then remove the two remaining nuts.

➡**When forcing downward, be careful to avoid damaging the safety slip-clips on the steering column.**

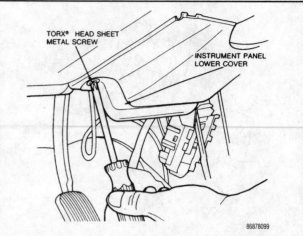

**Fig. 98 Remove the four self-tapping screws, then remove the steering column cover from the lower portion of the instrument panel**

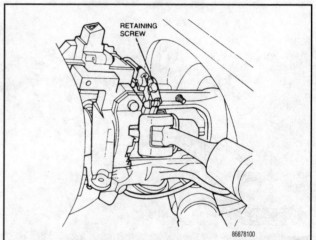

**Fig. 99 If equipped with column shift, disconnect the shift position indicator cable from the lock cylinder housing by removing the retaining screw**

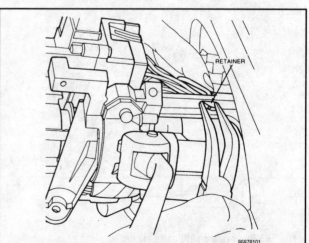

**Fig. 100 Remove the multi-function/combination switch wiring harness retainer from the lock cylinder housing by squeezing the end of the retainer and pushing out**

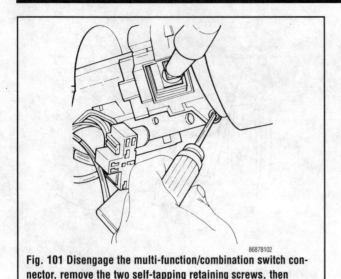

Fig. 101 Disengage the multi-function/combination switch connector, remove the two self-tapping retaining screws, then remove the multi-function/combination switch

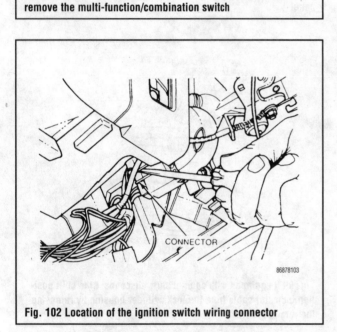

Fig. 102 Location of the ignition switch wiring connector

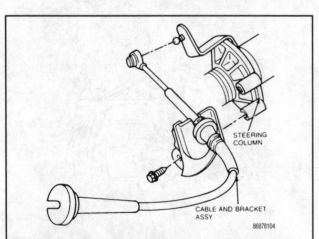

Fig. 103 Remove the shift cable plastic terminal from the column selector lever pivot ball using a small prybar between the plastic terminal and the selector lever. Be careful not to damage the cable during or after assembly

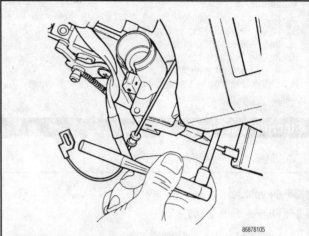

Fig. 104 Use a downward force to disengage the column assembly push-on clips from the rear attachments, then remove the two remaining nuts

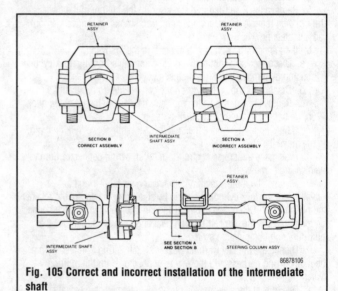

Fig. 105 Correct and incorrect installation of the intermediate shaft

16. Carefully lower the steering column assembly, then remove it from the vehicle.

**To install:**

17. Raise the steering column assembly into position, and align the four mounting holes over the four support bracket studs. Hand-start the 4 retaining nuts.

18. Center the column assembly in the instrument panel opening, then tighten the four nuts to 15–25 ft. lbs. (21–33 Nm).

19. If equipped with an automatic parking brake release mechanism, install the vacuum hoses on the parking brake release switch.

20. If equipped with column shift, perform the following:

a. Attach the cable shift bracket, with the shift cable attached, to the lock cylinder housing, then tighten the retaining screws to 5–7 ft. lbs. (7–9 Nm).

b. Snap the transaxle shift cable terminal to the selector lever pivot ball on the steering column.

21. Apply a generous amount of grease to the V-shaped steering shaft yoke. Connect the steering shaft to the intermediate shaft with the U-clamp and the two hex nuts. When installing the steering column to the intermediate shaft, connect the intermediate shaft to the steering column with the retainer assembly and two nuts.

➡️Make sure the V-angle of the intermediate shaft fits correctly into the V-angle of the mating steering column yoke. If the V-angle is misaligned and the retainer is tightened, the retainer plate will be bent, necessitating replacement.

22. After correctly installing the steering column to the intermediate shaft, tighten the nuts to 15–25 ft. lbs. (21–33 Nm).

➡️Tilt columns must be in the middle tilt position before the nuts are tightened.

23. Engage the main wiring harness connector to the ignition switch, and the key warning buzzer switch wiring connector to the main harness. Attach the steering sensor wire connector to the sensor lead connector.

24. Install the combination switch, then tighten the two self-tapping screws to 18–26 inch lbs. (2.0–2.9 Nm). Install the combination switch wiring harness retainer over the shroud mounting boss, and snap it into the slot in the lock cylinder housing.

25. Engage the cruise control/horn brush wiring connector to the main wiring harness.

26. If equipped with column shift, install the shift position indicator cable into the retaining hook on the lock cylinder housing, connect the cable to the shift socket and loosely install the cable onto the lock cylinder housing with the screw. Adjust the shift position indicator cable as follows:

a. Place the shift lever in **D** on Taurus equipped with the 2.5L engine. On all others, place the shift lever in **OD**. A weight of 8 lbs. (4 kg) should be hung on the shift selector lever to make sure the lever is firmly against the **D** or **OD** drive detent.

b. Adjust the cable until the indicator pointer completely covers the **D** or **OD**, then tighten the screw to 18–30 inch lbs. (2.0–3.4 Nm).

c. Cycle the shift lever through all positions and check that the shift position indicator completely covers the proper letter or number in each position.

27. Install the shift lever into the shift lever socket, then insert a new shift lever retaining pin. Use care to avoid damaging the shift position indicator post on the shift socket.

28. Place the combination switch in the middle position, then install the steering wheel and horn pad assembly.

29. Install the shrouds with the retaining screws. Tighten to 6–10 inch lbs. (0.7–1.1 Nm). If equipped with a tilt column, install the tilt release lever and tighten the screw to 6.5–9.0 ft. lbs. (8.8–12 Nm).

30. Install the ignition lock cylinder. Install the steering column cover on the lower portion of the instrument panel with 4 self-tapping screws.

31. Connect the negative battery cable. Check the column function as follows:

a. With the column shift lever in **P** position or the floor shift key release button depressed, and with the ignition switch in the **LOCK** position, make sure the steering column locks.

b. With the column shift lever in **D** or with the floor shift key release button extended, and with the ignition switch in the **RUN** position, rotate the ignition switch toward the **LOCK** position until it stops. In this position, make sure that there is no power to the engine and/or accessories and that the steering shaft does not lock.

c. On tilt columns, check column tilt travel through its entire range to make sure there is no interference between the column and instrument panel.

d. Cycle the combination switch through all of its functions.

### 1990–95 Vehicles

♦ See Figures 106, 107, 108, 109 and 110

1. Disconnect the negative battery cable. Lower the glove compartment past its stops and disconnect the air bag backup power supply.

2. Make sure the vehicle's front wheels are in the straight-ahead position. Remove the steering wheel.

3. Remove the left and right lower mouldings from the instrument panel by pulling up and snapping out of the retainers.

4. Remove the instrument panel lower trim cover and the lower steering column shroud.

5. Disconnect the air bag clockspring contact assembly wire harness.

Apply two strips of tape across the contact assembly stator and rotor to prevent accidental rotation. Remove the three contact assembly retaining screws, then pull the contact assembly off the steering column shaft.

6. Remove the tilt lever by unscrewing it from the column, then remove the four screws.

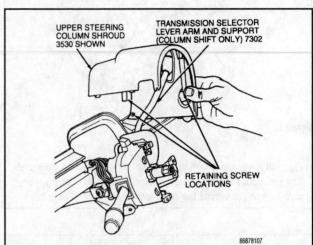

**Fig. 106 Remove the four retaining screws from the lower steering column shroud, then remove the lower and upper steering column shrouds**

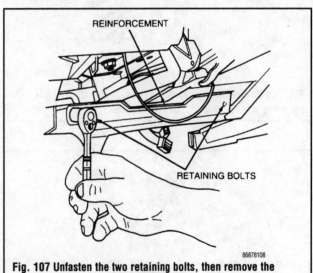

**Fig. 107 Unfasten the two retaining bolts, then remove the instrument panel reinforcement brace**

7. Rotate the ignition lock cylinder to the **RUN** position. Using a ⅛ in. (3mm) drift, depress the lock cylinder retaining pin through the access hole, then remove the lock cylinder.

8. Remove the four retaining screws from the lower steering column shroud, then remove the lower and upper steering column shrouds.

9. Remove the two instrument panel reinforcement brace retaining bolts, then remove the reinforcement.

10. If equipped with column shift, disconnect the shift position indicator cable from the actuator housing by removing the screw, then disconnect the cable loop from the shift tube hook. If equipped with console shift, remove the interlock cable retaining screws, then remove the cable.

11. Remove the two multi-function/combination switch retaining screws, then set the switch aside.

12. Disengage the wiring connector from the ignition switch.

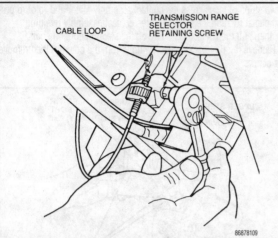

**Fig. 108 If equipped with column shift, disconnect the shift position indicator cable from the actuator housing by removing the screw, then disconnect the cable loop from the shift tube hook**

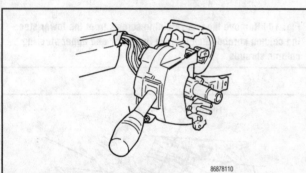

**Fig. 109 Remove the two multi-function/combination switch retaining screws, then set the switch aside**

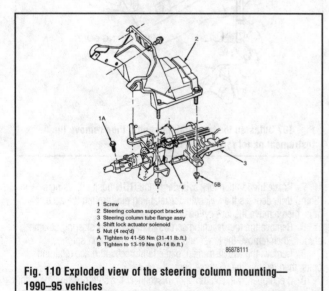

1 Screw
2 Steering column support bracket
3 Steering column tube flange assy
4 Shift lock actuator solenoid
5 Nut (4 req'd)
A Tighten to 41-56 Nm (31-41 lb.ft.)
B Tighten to 13-19 Nm (9-14 lb.ft.)

**Fig. 110 Exploded view of the steering column mounting—1990–95 vehicles**

13. Remove the four nuts securing the column skid plate, then remove the plate.

14. Remove the pinch bolt from the steering column lower yoke.

15. While supporting the steering column, remove the four steering col-

umn tube retaining nuts. Lower the steering column, then disconnect hoses at the parking brake release switch or remove the vacuum release assembly.

16. Disconnect the shift cable and bracket from the transmission column shift selector tube lever pivot.

17. For vehicles equipped with console shift, remove the two shift lock actuator cable retaining screws, then remove the actuator.

18. Remove the column from the vehicle.

**To install:**

19. Place the steering column in the vehicle, then align the column lower yoke to the lower steering column shaft. Install the bolt, then tighten to 31–41 ft. lbs. (41– 56 Nm).

20. Connect the parking brake release vacuum hoses.

21. For console shift, position the shift lock actuator, then install the two retaining screws.

22. Position the steering column assembly to the column support bracket. Install the four retaining nuts, then tighten to 9–13 ft. lbs. (13–17 Nm).

23. Position the shift cable bracket, with the shift cable attached, to the lower two screws of the column. Tighten to 5–8 ft. lbs. (7–11 Nm). Snap the shift cable onto the shift selector pivot ball.

24. Position the multi-function/combination switch, then install the two retaining screws. Tighten to 18–26 inch lbs. (2–3 Nm). Engage all electrical connectors.

25. Fasten the transmission shift cable and bracket loop on the shift selector hook, then install the transmission range selector cable bracket to the steering actuator housing. Install the retaining screw and tighten to 5–8 ft. lbs. (7–11 Nm).

26. Connect the steering column-to-parking brake control shake brace.

27. Install the instrument panel reinforcement brace, then secure with the two retaining bolts.

28. Attach the upper and lower steering column shrouds.

29. Install the ignition switch lock cylinder.

30. Connect the tilt steering column lock lever onto the steering column flange tube.

31. Attach the air bag sliding contact with the three retaining screws, then tighten the screws to 18–26 inch lbs. (2–3 Nm).

➡**If a new contact assembly is being installed, remove the plastic lock mechanism after the contact assembly is secured to the column.**

32. Install the steering wheel onto the steering gear input worm gear and rack, using a new bolt. Tighten the new bolt to 22–33 ft. lbs. (31–48 Nm).

33. Position the drivers side air bag module to the steering wheel. Install the two retaining screws, then tighten to 36–47 inch lbs. (4–5 Nm).

34. Connect the air bag backup power supply and the negative battery cable. Verify the air bag warning indicator.

## Steering Linkage

### REMOVAL & INSTALLATION

#### Tie Rod Ends

1. Remove and discard the cotter pin and nut from the worn tie rod end ball stud.

2. Disconnect the tie rod end from the steering knuckle, using Tie Rod End Remover tool 3290–D or equivalent.

3. Hold the tie rod end with a wrench, then loosen the tie rod jam nut.

4. Note the depth to which the tie rod is located by using the jam nut as a marker, then grip the tie rod with a pair of suitable pliers and remove the tie rod end assembly from the tie rod.

**To install:**

5. Clean the tie rod threads. Thread the new tie rod end onto the tie rod to the same depth as the removed tie rod end.

6. Make sure the front wheels are pointed straight-ahead, then place the tie rod end stud into the steering spindle.

7. Install a new nut on the tie rod end stud. Tighten the nut to 35 ft. lbs.

(48 Nm), then continue tightening until the next castellation on the nut is aligned with the cotter pin hole in the stud. Install a new cotter pin.

8. Set the toe to specification. Tighten the jam nut to 35–50 ft. lbs. (47–68 Nm).

## Power Steering Rack

### ADJUSTMENTS

**Except 1990–92 Taurus and Sable LX with 3.8L Engine, 1993–95 Taurus GL (high series only), LX and SHO models, and Sables**

#### *RACK YOKE PLUG CLEARANCE*

➡The rack yolk clearance adjustment is not a normal service adjustment. It is only required when the input shaft and valve assembly is removed.

1. Remove the steering gear from the vehicle. Clean the exterior of the steering gear thoroughly.

2. Install the steering gear in a suitable holding fixture. Do not remove the external transfer tubes unless they are leaking or damaged. If these lines are removed, they must be replaced with new ones.

3. Drain the power steering fluid by rotating the input shaft lock-to-lock twice, using a suitable tool. Cover the ports on the valve housing with a shop cloth while draining the gear to avoid possible oil spray.

4. Insert an inch pound torque wrench with a maximum capacity of 60 inch lbs. (6.77 Nm) into the Pinion Shaft Torque Adapter T74P-3504-R or equivalent. Position the adapter and wrench on the input shaft splines.

5. Loosen the yoke plug locknut and then the yoke plug.

6. Clean the threads of the yoke plug before tightening, to prevent a false reading. With the rack at the center of travel, tighten the yoke plug to 45–50 inch lbs. (5.0–5.6 Nm).

7. Back off the yoke plug approximately ⅛ turn (44–54 degrees) until the torque required to initiate and sustain rotation of the input shaft is 7–18 inch lbs. (0.78–2.03 Nm).

8. Place a suitable wrench on the yoke plug locknut. While holding the yoke plug, tighten the locknut to 44–66 ft. lbs. (60–89 Nm). Do not allow the yoke plug to move while tightening or preload will be affected. Check the input shaft torque as in step 7 after tightening the locknut.

9. Install the steering gear.

### REMOVAL & INSTALLATION

**Except 1990–92 Taurus and Sable LX with 3.8L Engine, 1993–95 Taurus GL (high series only), LX and SHO models, and Sables**

◆ See Figures 111, 112 and 113

1. Disconnect the negative battery cable. Working from inside the vehicle, remove the nuts retaining the steering shaft weather boot to the dash panel.

2. Remove the bolts retaining the intermediate shaft to the steering column shaft. Set the weather boot aside.

3. Remove the pinch bolt at the steering gear input shaft, then remove the intermediate shaft. Raise the vehicle and support safely.

4. Remove the left front wheel and tire assembly. Remove the steering shaft U-joint/heat shield. Cut the bundling strap retaining the lines to the gear.

5. Remove the tie rod ends from the spindles. Place a drain pan under the vehicle, then remove the hydraulic pressure and return lines from the steering gear.

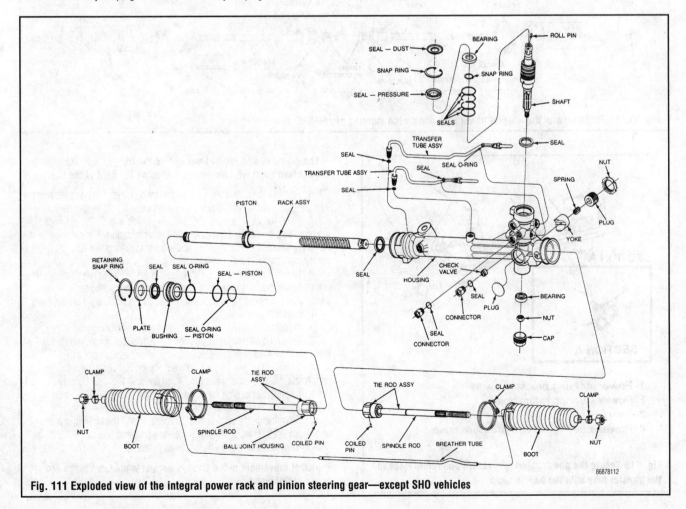

Fig. 111 Exploded view of the integral power rack and pinion steering gear—except SHO vehicles

86878112

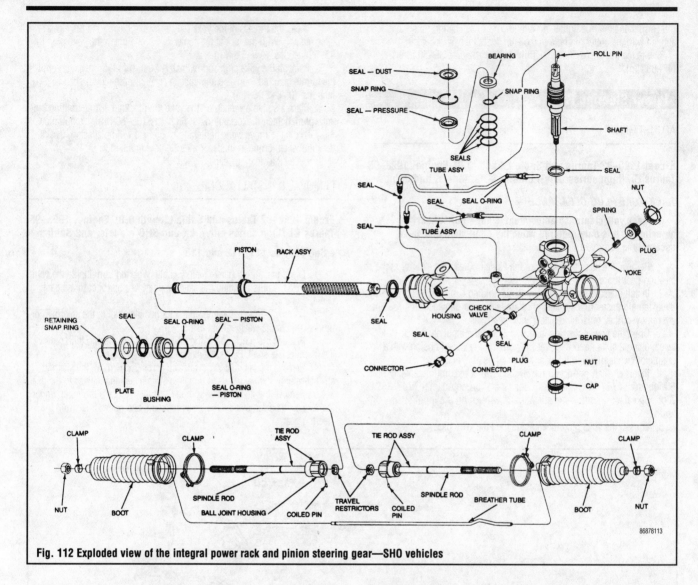

Fig. 112 Exploded view of the integral power rack and pinion steering gear—SHO vehicles

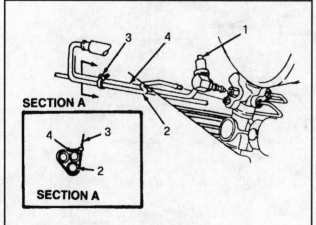

**SECTION A**

**SECTION A**

1 Power steering pressure switch
2 Power steering return hose
3 Strap
4 Power steering left turn pressure hose

86878114

Fig. 113 Secure the power steering pressure and return lines to the transfer tube with the bundle strap

➡The pressure and return lines are on the front of the housing. Do not confuse them with the transfer lines on the side of the valve.

6. Remove the nuts from the gear mounting bolts. The bolts are pressed into the gear housing and should not be removed during gear removal.

7. Push the weather boot end into the vehicle and lift the gear out of the mounting holes. Rotate the gear so the input shaft will pass between the brake booster and the floor pan. Carefully start working the steering gear out through the left fender apron opening.

8. Rotate the input shaft so it clears the left fender apron opening, then complete removal of the steering gear. If the steering gear seems to be stuck, check the right tie rod to ensure the stud is not caught on anything.

**To install:**

9. Install new plastic seals on the hydraulic line fittings.

10. Insert the steering gear through the left fender apron. Rotate the input shaft forward to completely clear the fender apron opening.

11. To allow the gear to pass between the brake booster and the floorpan, rotate the input shaft rearward. Align the steering gear bolts to the bolt holes. Install the mounting nuts and tighten them to 85–100 ft. lbs. (115–135 Nm). Lower the vehicle.

12. From inside the engine compartment, install the hydraulic pressure and return lines. Tighten the power steering pressure line to 15–25 ft. lbs. (20–35 Nm) and the return line to 15–25 ft. lbs. (20–35 Nm).

➡Swivel movement of the lines is normal when the fittings are properly tightened.

13. Raise and safely support the vehicle. Secure the power steering pressure and return lines to the transfer tube with the bundle strap. Install the steering shaft U-joint/heat shield.

14. Install the tie rod ends to spindles. Tighten the castle nuts to 35 ft. lbs. (48 Nm) and, if necessary, tighten the nuts a little bit more to align the slot in the nut for the cotter pin. Install the cotter pin.

15. Install the left front wheel and tire assembly, then carefully lower the vehicle. Working from inside the vehicle, pull the weather boot end out of the vehicle and install it over the valve housing. Install the intermediate shaft to the steering gear input shaft. Install the inner weather boot to the floor pan.

16. Install the intermediate shaft to the steering column shaft. Fill the power steering system.

17. Connect the negative battery cable. Check the system for leaks and proper operation. Adjust the toe setting as necessary.

### 1990–92 Taurus LX and Sable with 3.8L Engine, 1993–95 Taurus GL (high series only), LX and SHO models, and Sables

▶ See Figures 114 thru 120

The Variable Assist Power Steering (VAPS) system used on these vehicles consists of a micro-processor based module, a power rack and pinion steering gear, an actuator valve assembly, hose assemblies and a high efficiency power steering pump.

1. Disconnect the negative battery cable.

2. From inside the vehicle, remove the nuts securing the steering column tube boot to the cowl panel.

3. Remove the two bolts retaining the steering column gear input shaft coupling to the power steering gear shaft and yoke assembly.

4. Set the steering column tube boot aside. Remove the pinch bolt at the power steering gear shaft and yoke assembly, then remove the steering column gear input shaft coupling.

5. Raise the vehicle and support safely. Remove the front wheel and tire assemblies. Support the vehicle under the rear edge of the subframe with jack stands.

6. Remove the tie rod cotter pins and nuts. Remove the left and right-side tie rod ends from the steering knuckle.

7. Mark the position of the jam nut (to maintain the alignment), then remove the tie rod ends from the spindle tie rod.

8. Remove the nuts from the gear-to-subframe attaching bolts.

9. Remove the rear subframe-to-body attaching bolts.

10. Remove the exhaust pipe-to-catalytic converter attachment.

11. Lower the vehicle carefully until the subframe separates from the body approximately 4 in. (102mm).

12. Remove the heat shield band, then fold the shield down.

13. Disengage the VAPS electrical connectors from the actuator assembly.

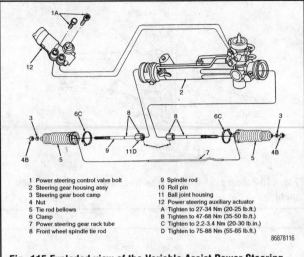

1 Power steering control valve bolt
2 Steering gear housing assy
3 Steering gear boot camp
4 Nut
5 Tie rod bellows
6 Clamp
7 Power steering gear rack tube
8 Front wheel spindle tie rod
9 Spindle rod
10 Roll pin
11 Ball joint housing
12 Power steering auxiliary actuator
A Tighten to 27-34 Nm (20-25 lb.ft.)
B Tighten to 47-68 Nm (35-50 lb.ft.)
C Tighten to 2.2-3.4 Nm (20-30 lb.in.)
D Tighten to 75-88 Nm (55-65 lb.ft.)

**Fig. 115 Exploded view of the Variable Assist Power Steering (VAPS) system**

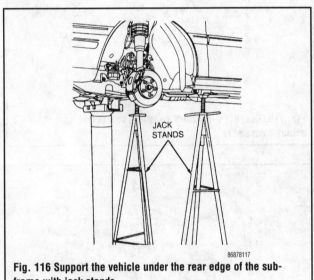

**Fig. 116 Support the vehicle under the rear edge of the subframe with jack stands**

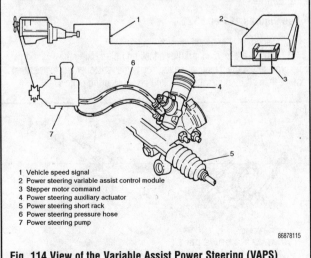

1 Vehicle speed signal
2 Power steering variable assist control module
3 Stepper motor command
4 Power steering auxiliary actuator
5 Power steering short rack
6 Power steering pressure hose
7 Power steering pump

**Fig. 114 View of the Variable Assist Power Steering (VAPS) system components**

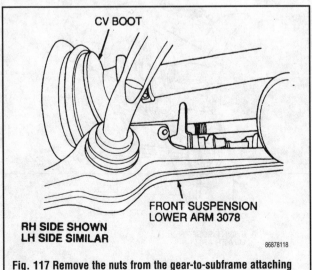

CV BOOT

RH SIDE SHOWN
LH SIDE SIMILAR

FRONT SUSPENSION
LOWER ARM 3078

**Fig. 117 Remove the nuts from the gear-to-subframe attaching bolts**

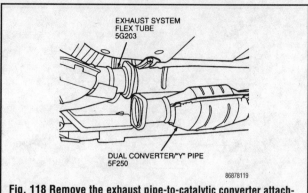

**Fig. 118 Remove the exhaust pipe-to-catalytic converter attachment**

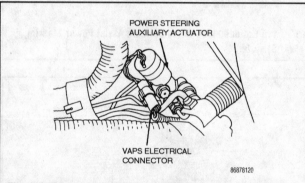

**Fig. 119 Disengage the VAPS electrical connectors from the actuator assembly**

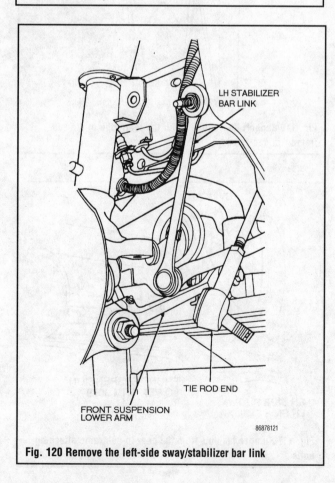

**Fig. 120 Remove the left-side sway/stabilizer bar link**

14. Rotate the gear to clear the bolts from the subframe and pull to the left to facilitate line fitting removal.

15. Position a suitable drain pan under the vehicle, then remove the line fittings. Remove the O-rings from the fitting connections, then replace with new ones during installation.

16. Remove the left-hand side sway/stabilizer bar link.

17. Remove the steering gear assembly through the left wheel well.

**To install:**

18. Install new Teflon® O-rings into the line fittings.

19. Place the gear attachment bolts in the gear housing.

20. Install the steering gear assembly through the left wheel well.

21. Connect and tighten the line fittings to the steering gear assembly.

22. Engage the VAPS electrical connectors.

23. Position the steering gear into the subframe.

24. Install the tie rod ends onto the front wheel spindle tie rod.

25. Install the heat shield band.

26. Attach the tie rod ends onto the knuckle. Install the nuts and secure with new cotter pins.

27. Attach the sway/stabilizer bar link.

28. Raise the vehicle until the subframe contacts the body. Install the rear subframe attaching bolts.

29. Install the gear-to-front subframe nuts, then tighten to 85–100 ft. lbs. (115–135 Nm).

30. Attach the exhaust pipe to the catalytic converter.

31. Install the wheels, then remove the jackstands and carefully lower the vehicle. Tighten the lug nuts to 85–105 ft. lbs. (115–142 Nm).

32. From inside the vehicle, push the steering column tube boot end out of the vehicle, then install over the steering gear housing.

33. Install the steering column gear input shaft coupling to the power steering gear shaft and yoke assembly. Tighten the bolt to 30–38 ft. lbs. (41–51 Nm).

34. Install the inner steering column tube boot to the cowl panel.

35. Install the input shaft coupling to the steering gear shaft and yoke assembly.

36. Fill the power steering system with Premium Power Steering Fluid E6AZ-19582-AA or equivalent.

37. Bleed the power steering system. For details, please refer to the procedure located later in this section.

38. Connect the negative battery cable, then check the system for leaks and proper operation.

39. If necessary, have the alignment checked by a reputable repair shop.

## Power Steering Pump

### REMOVAL & INSTALLATION

**2.5L Engines**

▶ **See Figures 121 and 122**

1. Disconnect the negative battery cable.

2. Loosen the tensioner pulley attaching bolts. Using the ½ in. drive hole provided in the tensioner pulley, rotate the tensioner clockwise, then remove the belt from the alternator and power steering pulley.

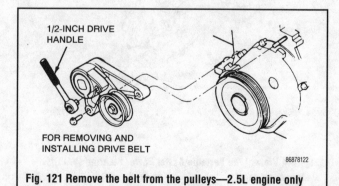

**Fig. 121 Remove the belt from the pulleys—2.5L engine only**

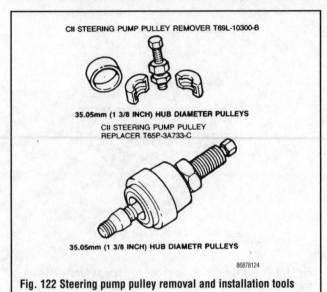

CII STEERING PUMP PULLEY REMOVER T69L-10300-B

35.05mm (1 3/8 INCH) HUB DIAMETER PULLEYS

CII STEERING PUMP PULLEY
REPLACER T65P-3A733-C

35.05mm (1 3/8 INCH) HUB DIAMETR PULLEYS

86878124

**Fig. 122 Steering pump pulley removal and installation tools**

3. Position a drain pan under the power steering pump beneath the vehicle. Disconnect the hydraulic pressure and return lines.

4. Remove the pulley from the pump shaft using Steering Pump Pulley Tool T69L–10300–B or equivalent.

5. Remove the three bolts retaining the pump to the bracket, then remove the power steering pump.

**To install:**

6. Install the pump on the mounting bracket, then install the three pump-to-bracket retaining bolts.

➡**To install the power steering pump pulley, use steering pump pulley replacer T65P–3A733–C or equivalent. When using this tool, the small diameter threads must be fully engaged in the pump shaft before pressing on the pulley. Hold the screw head and turn the nut to install the pulley. Install the pulley face flush with the pump shaft or within 0.100 in. (0.25mm).**

7. Install the pulley on the pump shaft using Steering Pump Pulley Replacer T65P-3A733-C or equivalent.

8. Connect the hydraulic pressure and return lines.

9. Position the belt over the alternator and power steering pulleys, then, using the ½ in. drive hole in the tensioner pulley, rotate the tensioner counterclockwise to install the belt.

10. Connect the negative battery cable, then fill to the correct level with the proper type of fluid and check operation. Remove the drain pan.

### 3.0L Engine—Except SHO

♦ **See Figure 123**

1. Disconnect the negative battery cable.

2. Loosen the idler pulley, then remove the power steering belt.

3. For vehicles through 1993 remove the pulleys from the hub as follows:

a. Remove the radiator overflow bottle in order to gain access to the 3 screws/bolts attaching the pulleys to the pulley hub.

b. Matchmark both pulley-to-hub positions with a grease pencil or dot of paint for installation purposes.

c. Remove the bolts and pulleys from the pulley hub.

4. For 1994–95 vehicles remove the pulley from the hub using Steering Pump Pulley Remover T69L-10300-B or equivalent.

5. Position a drain pan under the pump, then remove the return line from the pump. Be prepared to catch any spilled fluid in a suitable container.

6. Back off the pressure line attaching nut completely. The line will separate from the pump connection when the pump is removed.

7. Remove the three pump mounting bolts, then remove the pump.

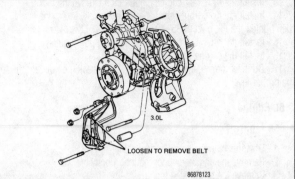

3.0L

LOOSEN TO REMOVE BELT

86878123

**Fig. 123 Removing the power steering belt—3.0L engine except SHO**

**To install:**

8. Install the pump on the mounting bracket. Guide the pressure hose into the pump outlet fitting while installing the pump.

9. Install the pressure and return lines to the pump.

10. For vehicles through 1993, install the pulley on the hub as follows:

a. Install the pulleys on the hub, aligning the marks made during removal.

b. Install the three bolts, then tighten to 15–24 ft. lbs. (21–32 Nm).

c. Install the radiator overflow bottle.

11. For 1994–95 vehicles, install the pulley on the hub using Steering Pump Pulley Replacer T65P-3A733-C or equivalent. The small diameter threads must be fully engaged in the pump shaft before pressing on the pulley. Screw the tool into the threads in the end of the pump shaft. Hold the small nut on the end of the tool, then turn the large nut to install the pulley on the shaft. Install the pulley face flush with the pump shaft or within 0.010 in. (0.25mm).

12. Install the power steering belt.

13. Connect the negative battery cable. Fill with the proper type of fluid and check for proper operation.

### 3.0L and 3.2L SHO Engines

1. Disconnect the negative battery cable.

2. Remove the engine damper strut.

3. Remove the power steering belt.

4. Raise and safely support the vehicle.

5. Remove the front right-side wheel and tire assembly.

6. Position a suitable jack under the engine, then remove the right rear engine mount.

7. Remove the power steering pump pulley as follows:

a. Loosen the idler pulley, then remove the drive belt.

b. Remove the power steering pump pulley from the power steering pump shaft using Steering Pump Pulley Remover T69L-10300-B or equivalent.

8. Place a drain pan under the pump, then remove the pressure and return lines from the pump.

9. Remove the four pump retaining bolts (three in the front and one in the rear), then remove the pump.

**To install:**

10. Position the pump, then install the retaining bolts. Tighten to 15–24 ft. lbs. (20–33 Nm).

11. Install the power steering pressure and return hoses to the power steering pump, then remove the drain pan.

12. Install the power steering pump pulley as follows:

a. Install the pulley to the pump using Steering Pump Pulley Replacer T65P-3A733-C or equivalent. The small diameter threads must be fully engaged in the pump shaft before pressing on the pulley. Screw the tool into the threads in the end of the pump shaft. Hold the small nut on the end of the tool, then turn the large nut to install the pulley on the shaft. Install the pulley face flush with the pump shaft or within 0.010 in. (0.25mm).

13. Install the right rear engine mount, then remove the jack.

14. Install the right front wheel and tire assembly. Lower the vehicle, then tighten the lug nuts to 85–105 ft. lbs. (115–142 Nm).

15. Install the drive belt to the power steering pump pulley.

16. Install the engine damper strut.

17. Connect the negative battery cable, then check the fluid and fill to the proper level.

### 3.8L Engine

▶ See Figure 124

1. Disconnect the negative battery cable.
2. Remove the engine damper mounting body bracket.
3. Remove the power steering drive belt.
4. Raise and safely support the vehicle.
5. Remove the right-side wheel and tire assembly.
6. Position a suitable jack under the engine. Remove the right rear engine mount.
7. Remove the power steering pump pulley from the power steering pump shaft using Steering Pump Pulley Remover T69L-10300-B or equivalent.
8. Position a suitable drain pan under the vehicle. Remove the pressure and return hoses from the pump, and allow it to drain into the pan.
9. Remove the four pump retaining bolts (three in front, one in rear), then remove the pump.

**To install:**

10. Position the power steering pump, then install the retaining bolts. Tighten the bolts to 15–24 ft. lbs. (20–33 Nm).

11. Install the pulley to the pump using Steering Pump Pulley Replacer T65P-3A733-C or equivalent. The small diameter threads must be fully engaged in the pump shaft before pressing on the pulley. Screw the tool into the threads in the end of the pump shaft. Hold the small nut on the end of the tool, then turn the large nut to install the pulley on the shaft. Install the pulley face flush with the pump shaft or within 0.010 in: (0.25mm).

12. Install the right rear engine mount, then remove the jack.

13. Install the right front wheel and tire assembly. Lower the vehicle, then tighten the lug nuts to 85–105 ft. lbs. (115–142 Nm).

14. Install the power steering pump belt to the pulley.

15. Install the engine damper mounting body bracket.

16. Connect the negative battery cable, then fill the power steering reservoir to the proper level with the correct type of fluid.

### BLEEDING

If air bubbles are present in the power steering fluid, bleed the system by performing the following:

1. Fill the reservoir to the proper level.

2. Operate the engine until the fluid reaches normal operating temperature of 165–175°F (74–79°C).

3. Turn the steering wheel all the way to the left, then all the way to the right several times. Do not hold the steering wheel in the far left or far right position stops.

4. Check the fluid level and recheck the fluid for the presence of trapped

STEERING PUMP PULLEY REMOVER T69L-10300-B

35.05 mm (1 3/8 INCHES) HUB DIAMETER PULLEYS

STEERING PUMP PULLEY REPLACER T65P-3A733-C

35.05 mm (1 3/8 INCHES) HUB DIAMETER PULLEYS

86878125

**Fig. 124 Power steering pump pulley removal and installation tools**

air. If it is apparent that air is still in the system, fabricate or obtain a vacuum tester and purge the system as follows:

a. Remove the pump dipstick cap assembly.

b. Check and fill the pump reservoir with fluid to the **COLD FULL** mark on the dipstick.

c. Disconnect the ignition wire, then raise the front of the vehicle and support safely.

d. Crank the engine with the starter and check the fluid level. Do not turn the steering wheel at this time.

e. Fill the pump reservoir to the **COLD FULL** mark on the dipstick. Crank the engine with the starter while cycling the steering wheel lock-to-lock. Check the fluid level.

f. Tightly insert a suitable size rubber stopper and air evacuator pump into the reservoir fill neck. Connect the ignition coil wire.

g. With the engine idling, apply a 15 in. Hg (51 kPa) vacuum to the reservoir for 3 minutes. As air is purged from the system, the vacuum will drop off. Maintain the vacuum on the system as required throughout the 3 minutes.

h. Remove the vacuum source. Fill the reservoir to the **COLD FULL** mark on the dipstick.

i. With the engine idling, reapply 15 in. Hg (51 kPa) vacuum source to the reservoir. Slowly cycle the steering wheel to lock-to-lock stops for approximately 5 minutes. Do not hold the steering wheel at the stops during cycling. Maintain the vacuum as required.

j. Release the vacuum and disconnect the vacuum source. Add fluid as required.

k. Start the engine and cycle the wheel slowly, then check for leaks at all connections.

l. Lower the front wheels.

5. In cases of severe aeration, repeat the procedure.

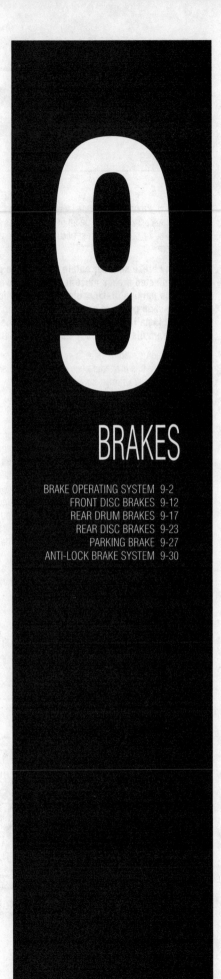

# 9

## BRAKES

# BRAKE OPERATING SYSTEM

## Adjustments

### DRUM BRAKES

▶ **See Figure 1**

The rear drum brakes on your Taurus/Sable are self-adjusting. The only adjustment necessary should be an initial one after new brake shoes have been installed or some type of service work has been done on the rear brake system.

➡**After any brake service, obtain a firm brake pedal before moving the car. Adjusted brakes must not drag. The wheel must turn freely. Be sure the parking brake cables are not too tightly adjusted. A special brake shoe gauge is necessary for making an accurate adjustment after installing new brake shoes. The special gauge measures both the drum diameter and the brake shoe setting.**

Since no adjustment is necessary except when service is performed on the rear brakes, this procedure begins with the car safely supported by jackstands and the rear drums removed.

1. Apply a small amount of Disc Brake Caliper Slide Grease D7AZ-19590-A or equivalent, to the points where the shoes contact the rear brake backing plate. Do NOT get grease on the linings!

2. Determine the inside diameter of the drum braking surface using Brake Adjustment Gauge D81L-1103-A or equivalent.

3. Adjust the brake shoes and linings diameter to fit the gauge. Align the brake shoes and linings vertically so that the flats on the bottom of the brake shoes and linings are about 0.05 in. (1.5mm) above the bottom of the brake shoe abutment plate BEFORE setting the gauge diameter. Hold the automatic brake shoe adjusting lever out of engagement while rotating the adjusting screw. Make sure the screw rotates freely. Lubricate if necessary.

4. Rotate the brake adjustment gauge around the brake shoes and linings to be sure of the proper setting.

5. Install the brake drum, as outlined later in this section.

6. Install the tire and wheel assembly. Install the wheel cover and nut covers, if applicable.

7. Finish the adjustment by pressing the brake pedal down several times with a minimum of 25 lbs. (111 N) of force.

8. After adjustment, check the brake operation by making several stops from various forward speeds.

### DISC BRAKES

Front disc brakes require no adjustment. Hydraulic pressure maintains the proper pad-to-disc contact at all times.

On vehicles equipped with rear disc brakes, the main difference is that the rear caliper houses the emergency brake actuator. The rear disc brakes are self-adjusting. Hydraulic pressure maintains the proper pad-to-disc contact at all times.

### BRAKE PEDAL FREE HEIGHT

1. Insert a slender sharp pointed rod through the carpet and sound deadener to dash panel metal.

2. Measure the distance to the center top of the brake pedal pad.

3. If the position of the pedal is not within specification, check the pedal for worn bushings, missing bushings and loose retaining bolts.

4. Repair defective components as required. Proper specification should be minimum 6.34 in. (161mm) pedal free height to maximum 7.09 in. (180mm) and maximum 2.34 in. (59.4mm) pedal travel.

5. If the measurement is still not within specification, check the brake pedal booster for proper adjustment.

## Brake Light Switch

### REMOVAL & INSTALLATION

▶ **See Figures 2 and 3**

The mechanical stop light switch assembly is installed on the pin of the brake pedal arm, so it straddles the master cylinder pushrod.

1. Disconnect the negative battery cable.

2. Disengage the wire harness at the connector from the switch.

➡**The locking tab must be lifted before the connector can be removed.**

3. Remove the hairpin retainer and white nylon washer. Slide the stop light switch and the pushrod away from the pedal. Remove the switch by sliding the it up or down.

➡**Since the switch side plate nearest the brake pedal is slotted, it is NOT necessary to remove the brake master cylinder pushrod**

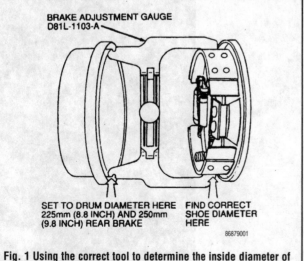

**SET TO DRUM DIAMETER HERE 225mm (8.8 INCH) AND 250mm (9.8 INCH) REAR BRAKE**    **FIND CORRECT SHOE DIAMETER HERE**

86879001

**Fig. 1 Using the correct tool to determine the inside diameter of the drum braking surface**

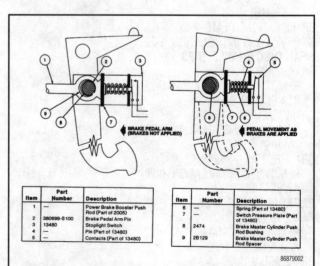

| Item | Part Number | Description |
|---|---|---|
| 1 | — | Power Brake Booster Push Rod (Part of 2005) |
| 2 | 380699-S100 | Brake Pedal Arm Pin |
| 3 | 13480 | Stoplight Switch |
| 4 | — | Pin (Part of 13480) |
| 5 | — | Contacts (Part of 13480) |

| Item | Part Number | Description |
|---|---|---|
| 6 | — | Spring (Part of 13480) |
| 7 | — | Switch Pressure Plate (Part of 13480) |
| 8 | 2474 | Brake Master Cylinder Push Rod Bushing |
| 9 | 2B129 | Brake Master Cylinder Push Rod Spacer |

86879002

**Fig. 2 Depressing the brake pedal compresses a spring which activates the brake light**

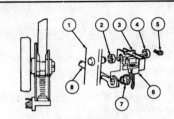

| Item | Part Number | Description |
|------|-------------|-------------|
| 1 | 2455 | Brake Pedal |
| 2 | — | Inside Nylon Washer (White) (Part of 13480) |
| 3 | 13480 | Stoplight Switch |
| 4 | — | Outer Nylon Washer (White) (Part of 13480) |
| 5 | — | Hairpin Retainer (Part of 13480) |
| 6 | — | Wire Harness Connector |
| 7 | — | Nylon Bushing (Black) (Part of 13480) |
| 8 | — | Master Cylinder Push Rod (Part of 2140) |

86879003

**Fig. 3 Exploded view of the brake light switch**

black bushing or the white spacer washer nearest the pedal arm from the brake pedal pin.

**To install:**

4. Position the switch so the U-shaped side is nearest the pedal and directly over/under the pin. The black bushing must be in position in the pushrod eyelet with the washer face on the side away from the brake pedal arm.

5. Slide the switch up/down, trapping the master cylinder pushrod and black bushing between the switch side plates. Push the switch and pushrod assembly firmly towards the brake pedal arm. Assemble the outside white plastic washer to the pin, then install the hairpin retainer to trap the whole assembly.

➡ **Do not substitute another type of pin retainer. Replace only with a production hairpin retainer.**

6. Attach the wire harness connector to the switch.

7. Check the stop light switch for proper operation. Stop lights should illuminate with less than 6 lbs. (27 N) of force applied to the brake pedal at the pad.

➡ **The stop light switch wire harness must have sufficient length to travel with the switch during full stroke at the pedal.**

8. Connect the negative battery cable.

## Brake Pedal

### REMOVAL & INSTALLATION

1. Disconnect the negative battery cable.

2. Disengage the brake light/stop light switch electrical connector.

3. Remove the pushrod retainer and master cylinder pushrod spacer (nylon washer). Slide the stop light switch outboard along the brake pedal pin just far enough for the outer hole of the switch frame to clear the pin.

4. Remove the switch by sliding it upward. Remove the master cylinder (black) bushing from the pushrod.

5. Loosen the four power brake booster retaining nuts at the pedal support bracket. Slide the pushrod and inner master cylinder nylon washer off the pedal pin if the vehicle does not have speed control.

6. Remove the locknut, then remove the pivot bolt, brake pedal, and brake master cylinder pushrod bushing from the pedal support. Remove the speed control adapter, if equipped by unlatching the locking tab.

**To install:**

7. Apply a light coating of clean engine oil to the clean bushings.

8. Position the brake pedal in the pedal support bracket, then install the pivot bolt. Install the locknut and tighten to 10–20 ft. lbs. (14–27 Nm).

➡ **The head of the brake master cylinder pushrod bushing must be on the side of the booster pushrod away from the brake pedal.**

9. Install the inner brake master cylinder pushrod spacer (or, if equipped, the speed control adapter), the master cylinder pushrod and the pushrod bushing on the brake pedal pin.

10. Do NOT oil the brake light switch. Position the brake light switch so that it straddles the pushrod with the slot on the pedal pin and the switch outer frame hole just clearing the pin. Slide the brake light switch down onto the pin and pushrod. Slide the assembly inboard toward the brake pedal arm. Install the outer brake master cylinder pushrod spacer and pushrod retainer. Lock the retainer securely.

11. Tighten the booster retaining nuts to 16–21 ft. lbs. (21–29 Nm).

12. Connect the brake light switch wiring to the brake light switch, then connect the negative battery cable.

## Master Cylinder

### REMOVAL & INSTALLATION

▶ **See Figures 4, 5, 6 and 7**

1. Disconnect the negative battery cable.

2. For vehicles equipped with ABS, apply the brake pedal a few times to eliminate all of the vacuum in the system.

3. Disengage the brake warning indicator electrical connector.

4. Disconnect the brake lines from the primary and secondary outlet ports of the master cylinder and the brake pressure control valve.

5. For vehicles equipped with ABS, disconnect the Hydraulic Control Unit (HCU) supply hose at the master cylinder, then secure in a position to prevent the loss of brake fluid.

6. Remove the nuts attaching the master cylinder to the brake booster assembly.

7. Slide the master cylinder forward and upward from the vehicle.

**To install:**

8. In order to ease installation, bench bleed the master cylinder before installation:

   a. Mount the master cylinder in a holding fixture, such as a soft jawed vise. Be careful not to damage the master cylinder housing.

   b. Fill the master cylinder with brake fluid.

   c. Place a suitable container under the master cylinder to catch the fluid being expelled from the outlet ports. Using a suitable tool inserted

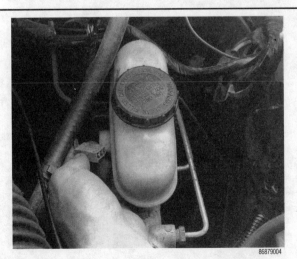

86879004

**Fig. 4 Disengage the electrical connector from the brake warning indicator**

**Fig. 5 Disconnect the brake lines from the primary and secondary outlet ports of the master cylinder**

**Fig. 6 Remove the retaining nuts attaching the master cylinder to the brake booster assembly, then . . .**

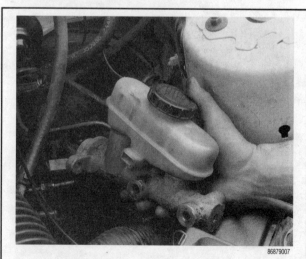

**Fig. 7 . . . slide the master cylinder assembly forward and upward from the vehicle**

into the booster pushrod cavity, push the master cylinder piston in slowly.

   d. Place a finger tightly over each outlet port, then allow the master cylinder piston to return.

   e. Repeat the procedure until only clear fluid is expelled from the master cylinder. Plug the outlet ports, then remove the master cylinder from the holding fixture.

  9. For vehicles equipped with ABS, install a new seal in the groove in the master cylinder mounting face.

  10. Mount the master cylinder over the booster pushrod and onto the two studs on the power brake booster assembly.

  11. Install the retaining nuts, then tighten them to 16–21 ft. lbs. (21–29 Nm).

  12. Attach the brake fluid lines to the master cylinder and the brake pressure control valve ports.

  13. For vehicles equipped with ABS, install the HCU supply hose to the master cylinder fitting, then secure it with the hose clamp.

  14. Connect the brake warning light wire.

  15. Fill the brake master cylinder with DOT 3 brake fluid to 0.16 in. (4.0mm) below the MAX lines on the side of the reservoir.

  16. Connect the negative battery cable, then bleed the brake system. For details, please refer to the procedure located later in this section.

  17. Operate the brakes several times, then check for external hydraulic leaks.

### OVERHAUL

▶ **See Figures 8 thru 15**

➡**Brake master cylinders on vehicles equipped with ABS cannot be overhauled. If service is required, the master cylinder must be replaced as an assembly.**

  1. Remove the master cylinder from the vehicle. Position the assembly in a suitable holding fixture. If mounting in a vise, clamp it to the vise by the flange to avoid damage to the bore or reservoir areas.

  2. Thoroughly clean the outside of the master cylinder assembly. Remove the cap, then drain and properly discard all old brake fluid.

  3. Depress the primary piston, then remove the snapring from the retaining groove at the open end of the bore.

  4. Remove the primary and secondary pistons from the master cylinder. Tap open the end of the master cylinder on the bench to remove the pistons. If the secondary piston does not come out readily, use low pressure compressed air to aid in removal.

  5. Remove the reservoir assembly.

  6. On the station wagon, remove the pressure control valve.

**Fig. 8 Depress the primary piston, then remove the snapring from the retaining groove at the open end of the**

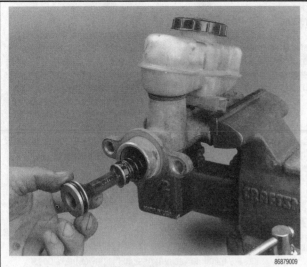

Fig. 9 Removing the primary piston from the master cylinder

Fig. 10 If the secondary piston does not come out readily, lightly tap the open end of the master cylinder on the bench, then the piston should slide out

Fig. 11 Remove the secondary piston, then . . .

Fig. 12 . . . remove the secondary piston spring

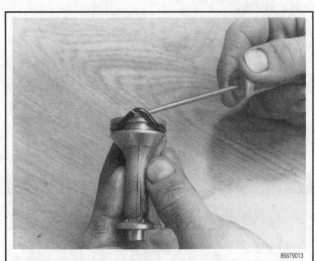

Fig. 13 Inspect all seals on the primary and secondary pistons, and replace if necessary

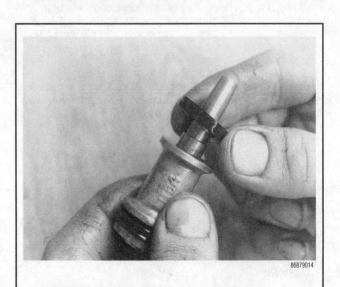

Fig. 14 Replacing a seal on the secondary piston

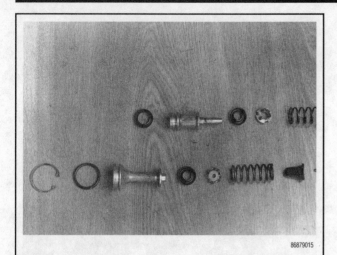

**Fig. 15 Exploded view of the internal components of the master cylinder**

**To assemble:**

7. Inspect all seals on the pistons for damage and replace as required. Inspect the master cylinder body, and replace if defective. Dip all parts in clean brake fluid before installation.

8. Install the secondary piston (smaller) assembly into the bore, spring end first.

9. Install the primary piston into the bore, spring end first.

10. Depress the primary piston, then install the snapring.

11. On the station wagon, install the brake pressure control valve.

12. Install the master cylinder reservoir assembly.

13. Fill and bleed the master cylinder, then put the securely cap the reservoir. Connect the negative battery cable.

## Power Brake Booster

### REMOVAL & INSTALLATION

▶ **See Figure 16**

1. Disconnect the negative battery cable, then remove the brake lines from the primary and secondary ports of the master cylinder.

2. Disconnect the manifold vacuum hose from the power brake booster check valve. For vehicles equipped with ABS, depress the brake pedal several times to eliminate all of the vacuum in the system.

3. Disengage the fluid level warning indicator electrical connector.

4. Unfasten the nuts securing the master cylinder to the power brake booster, then remove the master cylinder.

5. Working inside the vehicle, under the instrument panel, remove the brake light switch wiring connector from the switch. Remove the pushrod retainer and the master cylinder pushrod spacer (outer nylon washer) from the brake pin. Slide the brake light switch along the brake pedal pin, far enough for the outer hole to clear the pin.

6. Remove the switch by sliding it upward. Remove the booster-to-dash panel retaining nuts. Slide the booster pushrod and pushrod bushing off the brake pedal pin.

7. Working inside the engine compartment, remove the screws from the vacuum outlet manifold fitting at the dash panel, then position the vacuum fitting aside.

8. Position the wire harness aside. Remove the transaxle shift cable and bracket.

9. Move the power brake booster forward until the booster studs clear the dash panel, then remove the booster.

**To install:**

10. Align the pedal support bracket inside the vehicle, then place the

power brake booster in position on the dash panel and hand-start the retaining nuts.

11. Working inside the vehicle, install the master cylinder pushrod spacer or speed control dump valve, pushrod and master cylinder pushrod bushing onto the pedal pin and into the pushrod. The head of the bushing should be on the side of the pushrod away from the pedal arm. Tighten the booster-to-dash panel retaining nuts to 16–21 ft. lbs. (21–29 Nm).

12. Position the brake light switch so that is straddles the booster pushrod with the brake light switch slot toward the pedal blade and hole just clearing the pin. Slide the switch down onto the pin. Slide the assembly toward the pedal arm, being careful not to bend or deform the brake light switch. Install the master cylinder pushrod spacer on the pin, then secure all of the parts to the pin with the hairpin retainer. Make sure the retainer is fully installed and locked over the pedal pin. Attach the brake light switch wiring connector to the switch.

13. Position the speed control dump valve to the dash panel, then secure using the two retaining screws.

14. Move the wiring harness into position. Install the shift cable and bracket.

15. Connect the manifold vacuum hose to the power brake booster check valve.

16. Position the master cylinder assembly on the booster assembly studs.

17. Install the brake tube fittings into the master cylinder ports. Tighten to 10–17 ft. lbs. (14–24 Nm). Tighten the master cylinder nuts to 16–21 ft. lbs. (21–29 Nm).

18. Engage the fluid level warning indicator electrical connector.

19. Bleed the brake system. For details, please refer to the procedure later in this section.

20. Adjust the manual shift linkage.

21. Connect the negative battery cable, then start the engine and check the brake function.

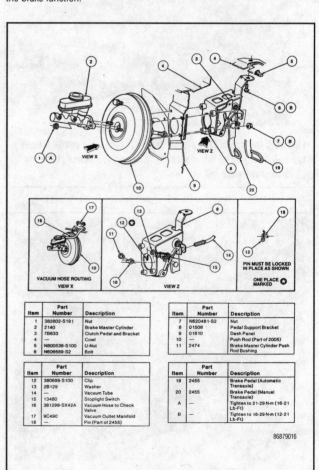

| Item | Part Number | Description |
|---|---|---|
| 1 | 382802-S191 | Nut |
| 2 | 2140 | Brake Master Cylinder |
| 3 | 7B633 | Clutch Pedal and Bracket |
| 4 | — | Cowl |
| 5 | N800538-S100 | U-Nut |
| 6 | N606689-S2 | Bolt |

| Item | Part Number | Description |
|---|---|---|
| 12 | 380699-S100 | Clip |
| 13 | 2B129 | Washer |
| 14 | — | Vacuum Tube |
| 15 | 13480 | Stoplight Switch |
| 16 | 381298-SX42A | Vacuum Hose to Check Valve |
| 17 | 9C490 | Vacuum Outlet Manifold |
| 18 | — | Pin (Part of 2455) |

| Item | Part Number | Description |
|---|---|---|
| 7 | N620481-S2 | Nut |
| 8 | 01508 | Pedal Support Bracket |
| 9 | 01610 | Dash Panel |
| 10 | — | Push Rod (Part of 2005) |
| 11 | 2474 | Brake Master Cylinder Push Rod Bushing |

| Item | Part Number | Description |
|---|---|---|
| 19 | 2455 | Brake Pedal (Automatic Transaxle) |
| 20 | 2455 | Brake Pedal (Manual Transaxle) |
| A | — | Tighten to 21-29 N·m (16-21 Lb-Ft) |
| B | — | Tighten to 16-29 N·m (12-21 Lb-Ft) |

**Fig. 16 Common power brake booster and related components**

## ADJUSTMENT

▶ **See Figures 17 and 18**

On vehicles without ABS, the power brake booster has an adjustable pushrod (output rod) which is used to compensate for dimensional variations in an assembled power brake booster. The pushrod length is adjusted after each booster unit has been assembled in production. A properly adjusted pushrod that remains assembled to the power brake booster with which it was matched during production should never require a service adjustment.

A power brake booster that is suspected of having an improper pushrod length will indicate either of the following:

• A pushrod that is too long will prevent the master cylinder piston from completely releasing hydraulic pressure and eventually cause the brakes to drag.

• A pushrod that is too short will have excessive brake pedal travel and cause a groaning noise to come from the power brake booster.

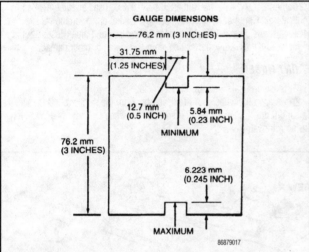

**Fig. 17 Power brake booster pushrod adjustment gauge dimensions**

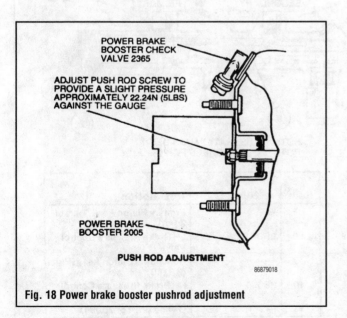

**Fig. 18 Power brake booster pushrod adjustment**

If necessary, pushrod length can be checked using a pushrod gauge and the following procedure.

1. Without disconnecting the brake lines, disconnect the master cylinder and set it away from the booster power unit.

➡**The master cylinder must be supported to avoid damaging the brake lines.**

2. With the engine running, check and adjust the pushrod length so that is it 0.230–0.245 in. (5.84–6.22mm), as indicated by the gauge shown. A force of approximately 5 lbs. (22 N) applied to the pushrod with the gauge will confirm that the pushrod is seated within the power booster. If adjustment is necessary, grip the rod only by the knurled area.

3. Install the master cylinder on the power booster. Gradually and alternately tighten the retaining nuts to 16–21 ft. lbs. (21–29 Nm).

## Proportioning Valve

### REMOVAL & INSTALLATION

The valve for the sedan is mounted to the floorpan near the left rear wheel. The valves for the station wagon are screwed into the master cylinder.

### Sedan

▶ **See Figure 19**

1. Raise and safely support the vehicle.
2. Note the position of the four brake tubes connected to the valve, then disconnect them from the valve assembly.

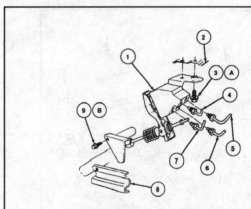

| Item | Part Number | Description |
|------|-------------|-------------|
| 1 | 2B547 | Brake Load Sensor Proportioning Valve |
| 2 | — | Body |
| 3 | N802191-S56 | Bolt |
| 4 | 2L568 | Brake Tube Assy |
| 5 | 2L569 | Brake Tube Assy |
| 6 | 2265 | Brake Tube Assy |
| 7 | 2B255 | Brake Tube Assy |
| 8 | 5500 | Rear Suspension Arm and Bushing |
| 9 | N804846-S56 | Bolt |
| 10 | — | Lower Adjusting Screw |
| 11 | — | Red Plastic Gauge (Not Shown) |
| A | — | Tighten to 11.4-15.6 N·m (8-12 Lb-Ft) |
| B | — | Tighten to 6-8 N·m (4-6 Lb-Ft) |

**Fig. 19 View of a common proportioning valve—sedan only**

3. Remove the screw retaining the valve bracket to the lower suspension arm.

4. Remove the two screws retaining the valve bracket to the underbody, then remove the assembly.

➡**The service replacement valve will have a red plastic gauge clip on the valve, which must not be removed until the valve is installed on the vehicle.**

**To install:**

5. Make sure the rear suspension is in the full rebound position.

6. Make sure the red plastic gauge clip is in position on the valve and that the operating rod lower adjustment screw is loose.

7. Position the valve assembly to the underbody, then install the two retaining screws.

8. Position the valve bracket to the lower suspension arm, then install one retaining screw. Tighten the screw to 4–6 ft. lbs. (6–8 Nm). Make sure the brake pressure differential valve adjuster sleeve is resting on the lower bracket, then tighten the setscrew.

9. Connect the brake lines in the same position as removed.

10. Bleed the rear brakes. For details, please refer to the procedure located later in this section.

11. Remove the red plastic gauge clip, then carefully lower the vehicle.

**Station Wagon**

▶ **See Figure 20**

1. Disconnect the primary or secondary brake line from the master cylinder, as necessary.

2. Loosen and remove the brake pressure control valve(s) from the master cylinder housing.

**To install:**

3. Install the brake pressure control valve(s) in the brake master cylinder housing port, then tighten to 10–16 ft. lbs. (13–22 Nm).

4. Install the brake tube, then tighten to 12–15 ft. lbs. (16–20 Nm).

5. Fill and bleed the brake system. For details, please refer to the procedure later in this section.

---

## Brake Hoses and Pipes

▶ **See Figures 21 and 22**

REMOVAL & INSTALLATION

### Flexible Hoses

Flexible hoses are usually installed between the frame-to-front calipers and the frame-to-rear differential, although they may be used elsewhere on some applications. Commonly, flexible hoses are used at points on the vehicle where suspension travel would damage or break a solid pipe. Hoses should be replaced if they show signs of softening, cracking or other damage.

***FRONT HOSE***

1. Raise and safely support the vehicle.

2. Remove the wheel and tire assembly from the rotor mounting face. Be careful not to damage or interfere with the wheel cylinder bleeder screw during removal.

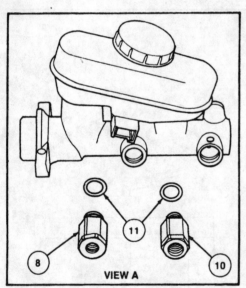
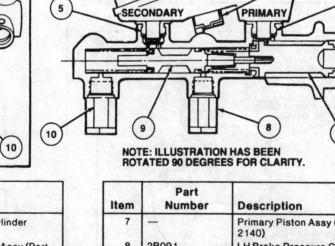

VIEW A

NOTE: ILLUSTRATION HAS BEEN ROTATED 90 DEGREES FOR CLARITY.

| Item | Part Number | Description |
|------|-------------|-------------|
| 1 | 2K478 | Brake Master Cylinder Reservoir |
| 2 | — | Cap and Gasket Assy (Part of 2K478) |
| 3 | — | Cap Vent Slot (2 places) |
| 4 | — | Reed Switch Assy (Part of 2K478) |
| 5 | — | Grommet (Part of 2K478) |
| 6 | — | Snap Ring |

| Item | Part Number | Description |
|------|-------------|-------------|
| 7 | — | Primary Piston Assy (Part of 2140) |
| 8 | 2B091 | LH Brake Pressure Control Valve |
| 9 | — | Secondary Piston Assy (Part of 2140) |
| 10 | 2B091 | RH Brake Pressure Control Valve |
| 11 | — | O-Ring (Part of 2B091) |

86879020

**Fig. 20 Location of the left and right-side brake pressure control valves—station wagon only**

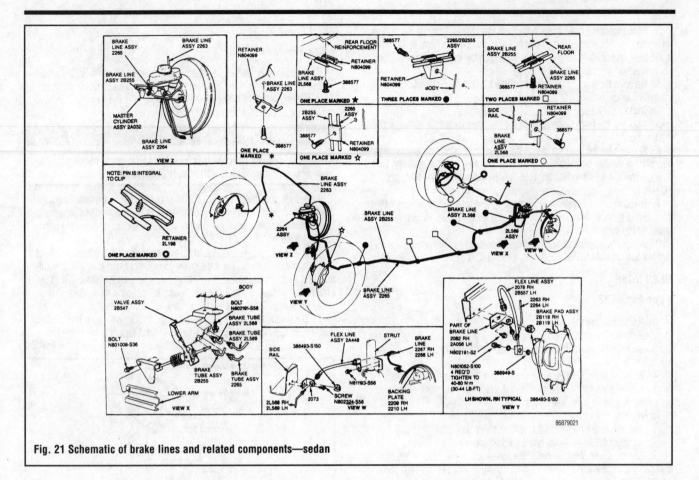

**Fig. 21 Schematic of brake lines and related components—sedan**

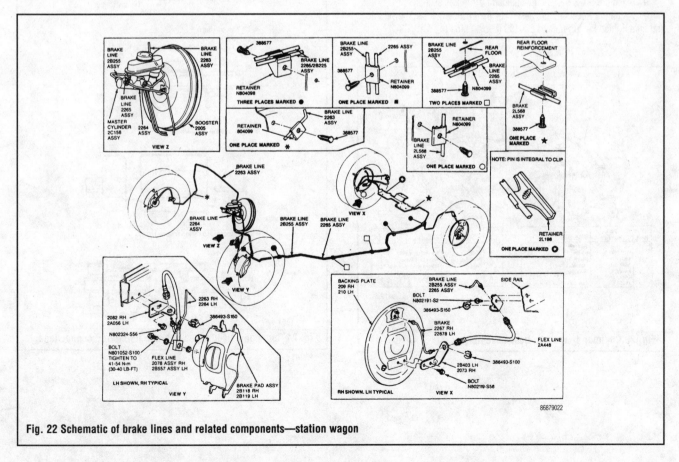

**Fig. 22 Schematic of brake lines and related components—station wagon**

3. Disconnect the front brake hose from the caliper. Remove the hollow retaining bolt that connects the hose fitting to the caliper. Remove the front brake hose assembly from the caliper, then plug the hose to avoid dirt or contamination from entering the hose.

4. Remove the front brake hose from the brake fluid distributor tube, then remove the brake hose clip and the brake hose.

**To install:**

5. Connect the front brake hose to the fluid distributor tube, then install the hose clip.

6. Remove the plugs, then install the brake hose on the caliper using a new copper washer on each side of the fitting outlet. Insert a retaining bolt through the washers and fittings, then tighten the bolts to 30–40 ft. lbs. (41–54 Nm).

7. Bleed the brake system. For details, please refer to the procedure later in this section. Make sure to replace the rubber bleed screw after bleeding the system.

8. Install the wheel and tire assembly, then carefully lower the vehicle. Tighten the lug nuts to 85–105 ft. lbs. (115–142 Nm).

### REAR HOSE

▶ **See Figure 23**

1. Raise and safely support the vehicle.
2. Remove the wheel and tire assembly.
3. Remove the rear wheel brake hose from the rear disc brake caliper assembly.
4. Remove the rear wheel brake hose from the rear shock absorber.
5. Remove the brake hose clip from the bracket, then remove the rear hose from the brake fluid distribution tube.

**To install:**

6. Seat the brake hose into the bracket, then install the hose clip.
7. Connect the hose to the brake fluid distributor tube.
8. Using new washers, connect the rear wheel brake hose to the rear disc caliper. Tighten the retaining bolt to 30–40 ft. lbs. (41–54 Nm).
9. Bleed the brake system, as outlined later in this section.
10. Install the wheel and tire assembly, then carefully lower the vehicle and final tighten the lug nuts to 85–105 ft. lbs. (115–142 Nm).

### Steel Pipes

▶ **See Figure 24**

When replacing steel brake pipes, always use the double-walled steel piping which is designed to withstand high pressure and resist corrosion. Also, it is important to make sure that the pipe is of the same size to assure both a proper fit and proper brake operation.

> **✳✳ CAUTION**
>
> **Never use copper tubing. It is subject to fatigue, cracking, and/or corrosion, which will result in brake line failure.**

Whenever possible, try to work with brake lines that are already cut to the length needed. These lines are available at most auto parts stores and have machine made flares, the quality of which is hard to duplicate with most of the available inexpensive flaring kits.

When the brakes are applied, there is a great deal of pressure developed in the hydraulic system. An improperly formed flare can leak with a resultant loss of stopping power. If you have never formed a double-flare, take time to familiarize yourself with the flaring kit; practice forming double-flares on scrap tubing until you are satisfied with the results.

1. Obtain the recommended bulk ³⁄₁₆ in. double wall steel brake tubing and the correct standard tube nuts for ³⁄₁₆ in. tubing.

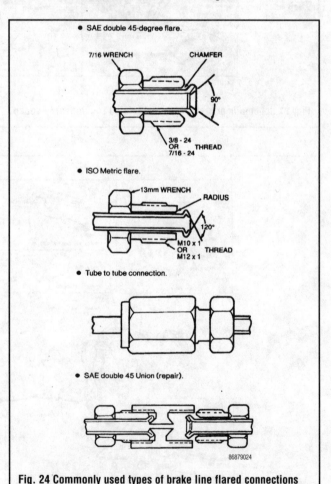

Fig. 24 Commonly used types of brake line flared connections

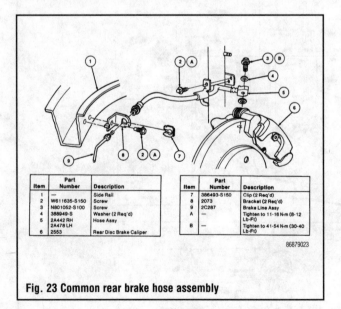

| Item | Part Number | Description |
|---|---|---|
| 1 | — | Side Rail |
| 2 | W611635-S150 | Screw |
| 3 | N801052-S100 | Screw |
| 4 | 388949-S | Washer (2 Req'd) |
| 5 | 2A442 RH 2A478 LH | Hose Assy |
| 6 | 2553 | Rear Disc Brake Caliper |

| Item | Part Number | Description |
|---|---|---|
| 7 | 386493-S150 | Clip (2 Req'd) |
| 8 | 2073 | Bracket (2 Req'd) |
| 9 | 2C287 | Brake Line Assy |
| A | — | Tighten to 11-16 N·m (8-12 Lb-Ft) |
| B | — | Tighten to 41-54 N·m (30-40 Lb-Ft) |

Fig. 23 Common rear brake hose assembly

➡The outside diameter of the line is used to specify size.

2. Using a tubing cutter, cut the tubing to the proper length. Clean burrs after cutting. The correct length may be determined by measuring the line to be replaced using a length of cord, then adding ⅛ in. (1.2mm) for each flare.

➡Make sure the fittings are installed and oriented correctly before flaring both ends of the line.

3. Place a tube nut onto the tube in the correct direction, then flare the tube with an SAE inverted flare or a metric ISO flare using Brake Line Flaring Tool D81L-2269-A, or equivalent. Carefully follow the instructions included with the tool. Repeat on the opposite end of the tube.

4. Bend the replacement tube to match the removed tube using a tubing bender. When the replacement brake tube is installed, maintain adequate clearance to metal edges and moving or vibrating parts.

5. Clean the brake tube by flushing with clean brake fluid. Install the brake tube, then tighten the tube nuts to specification using an inch lb. torque wrench.

6. Bleed the brake system.

## Bleeding

PROCEDURE

### Manual Bleeding

▶ See Figure 25

1. Clean all dirt from the master cylinder filler cap.

2. If the master cylinder is known or suspected to have air in the bore, it must be bled BEFORE any of the wheel cylinders or calipers. To bleed the master cylinder, loosen the upper secondary left front outlet fitting approximately ¾ of a turn.

3. Have an assistant depress the brake pedal slowly through its full travel. Close the outlet fitting and let the pedal return slowly to the fully released position. Wait 5 seconds and then repeat the operation until all air bubbles disappear.

4. Loosen the upper primary right-hand front outlet fitting about ¾ of a turn. Repeat Step 3 with the right-hand front outlet fitting.

5. To continue to bleed the brake system, remove the rubber dust cap from the wheel cylinder bleeder fitting or caliper fitting at the right rear side of the vehicle. Check to make sure the wheel cylinder bleeder screw is positioned at the upper half of the front caliper. If not, the caliper is located on the wrong side. Place a suitable box wrench on the bleeder fitting, then

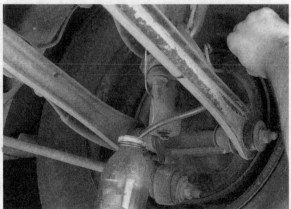

86879025

**Fig. 25 Submerge the free end of the brake tube in a container partly filled with clean brake fluid, then loosen the fitting about ¾ of a turn**

attach a rubber drain tube to the fitting. The end of the tube should fit snugly around the bleeder fitting.

6. Submerge the free end of the tube in a container partially filled with clean brake fluid, then loosen the fitting about ¾ of a turn.

7. Have an assistant push the brake pedal down slowly through its full travel. Close the bleeder fitting and allow the pedal to slowly return to its full release position. Wait 5 seconds, then repeat the procedure until no bubbles appear at the submerged end of the bleeder tube.

8. When the fluid is completely free of air bubbles, close the bleeder fitting, then remove the bleeder tube. Install the rubber dust cap on the bleeder fitting.

9. Repeat this procedure in the following sequence: left front, left rear and right front. Refill the master cylinder reservoir after each wheel cylinder or caliper has been bled, then install the master cylinder cover and gasket. When brake bleeding is completed, the fluid level should be filled to the maximum level indicated on the reservoir using clean brake fluid from a sealed container.

10. Always make sure the disc brake pistons are returned to their normal positions by depressing the brake pedal several times until normal pedal travel is established. If the pedal feels spongy, repeat the bleeding procedure.

### Pressure Bleeding

For pressure bleeding, use Rotunda Brake Bleeder 104-00064 or equivalent. Always bleed the longest line first. The bleeder tank should contain enough new brake fluid to complete the braking operation. Use only DOT 3 brake fluid from a new, sealed container. Never reuse brake fluid that has been drained from the hydraulic system. The pressure bleeder tank should be charged with 10–30 psi (69–206 kPa) of air pressure.

1. Clean all dirt from the reservoir filler cap and surrounding area.

➡NEVER exceed 50 psi (344 kPa) of air pressure to prevent system damage.

2. Remove the master cylinder filler cap, then fill the reservoir with fluid to the MAX fill line. Following the manufacturer's instructions, install the pressure bleeder adapter tool to the master cylinder reservoir, then attach the bleeder tank hose to the fitting on the adapter.

3. If all wheel cylinders are to be bled, start with the right-hand rear brake wheel cylinder. Remove the dust cap from the right rear caliper bleeder fitting. Attach a rubber drain tube to the fitting, making sure the tube fits snugly.

4. Open the valve on the bleeder tank to admit pressurized brake fluid to the master cylinder reservoir.

5. Submerge the free end of the tube in a container partly filled with clean brake fluid, then loosen the wheel cylinder bleeder screw.

6. When the air bubbles cease to appear in the fluid at the submerged end of the bleeder tube, close the wheel cylinder bleeder screw, then remove the tube. Tighten to 7.5–8.9 ft. lbs. (10–12 Nm). Replace the rubber dust cap on the wheel cylinder bleeder screw.

7. Repeat Steps 3–6 at the left front disc brake caliper.

8. Next, repeat Steps 4, 5 and 6 at the left rear wheel cylinder or caliper, and then the right front disc brake caliper.

9. When the bleeding procedure is finished, close the bleeder tank valve, then remove the hose from the adapter fitting.

10. After disc brake service, make sure the disc brake pistons are returned to their normal positions and that the brake shoe and lining assemblies are properly seated. This is accomplished by depressing the brake pedal a few times until normal pedal travel is established.

11. Remove the pressure bleeder adapter tool from the master cylinder. Fill the master cylinder reservoir to the proper level using clean brake fluid from a sealed container.

### Rear Brake Bleeding With a Fully Charged Accumulator

1. Remove the dust cap from the right rear caliper bleeder fitting. Attach a rubber drain tube to the fitting, making sure the tube fits snugly.

2. Turn the ignition switch to the RUN position. This will turn on the electric pump to charge the accumulator, as required.

3. Have an assistant hold the brake pedal in the applied position. Open the bleeder fitting for 10 seconds at a time until an air-free stream of brake fluid flow is observed.

### ✳✳ CAUTION

**To prevent possible injury, care must be used when opening the bleeder screws, due to the high pressures stored by a fully charged accumulator.**

## FRONT DISC BRAKES

### ✳✳ CAUTION

**Brake shoes may contain asbestos, which has been determined to be a cancer causing agent. Never clean the brake surfaces with compressed air! Avoid inhaling any dust from any brake surface! When cleaning brake surfaces, use a commercially available brake cleaning solvent.**

## Brake Pads

### REMOVAL & INSTALLATION

◆ **See Figures 26 thru 31**

1. Remove the master cylinder cap and check the fluid level in the reservoir. Remove the brake fluid until the reservoir is half full. Discard the removed fluid.

2. Raise and safely support the vehicle. Remove the wheel and tire assembly from the rotor mounting face, being careful not to damage or interfere with the caliper, rotor shield or the steering knuckle.

3. For vehicles through 1993, remove the caliper locating pins using Torx® Drive Bit D79P-2100-T40, or equivalent. For 1994–95 vehicles, remove the rear brake pin retainers.

➥**It is not necessary to disconnect the brake lines.**

4. Lift the caliper assembly from the integral knuckle, anchor plate and rotor using a rotating motion. Suspend the caliper inside the fender housing with wire. Do not allow the caliper to hang from the brake hose.

➥**Do not pry directly against the caliper piston or damage will result.**

4. Repeat the procedure at the left rear caliper.
5. Pump the brake pedal several times to complete the bleeding procedure.
6. Adjust the fluid level in the reservoir to the MAX mark with a fully charged accumulator.

➥**If the pump motor is allowed to run continuously for approximately 20 minutes, an internal thermal safety switch may shut the motor off to prevent it from overheating. If that happens, a 2–10 minute cool down period is typically required before normal operation can resume.**

5. Remove the inner and outer brake pads. Inspect the rotor braking surfaces for scoring and machine as necessary. Refer to the minimum rotor thickness specification when machining. If machining is not necessary, hand sand the glaze from the braking surfaces with medium grit sandpaper.
   **To install:**
6. Use a 4 in. (10cm) C-clamp and a wood block about 2¾ in. x 1 in. (7cm x 2.5cm) and about ¾ in. (19mm) thick to seat the caliper piston in its bore. This must be done to provide clearance for the caliper assembly with the new brake pads to fit over the rotor during installation. Care must

Fig. 27 View of an early model front disc brake assembly

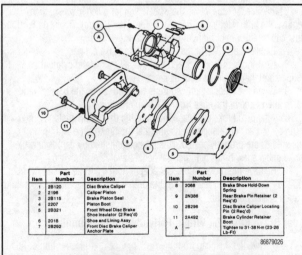

| Item | Part Number | Description |
|------|------|------|
| 1 | 2B120 | Disc Brake Caliper |
| 2 | 2196 | Caliper Piston |
| 3 | 2B115 | Brake Piston Seal |
| 4 | 2207 | Piston Boot |
| 5 | 2B321 | Front Wheel Disc Brake Shoe Insulator (2 Req'd) |
| 6 | 2018 | Shoe and Lining Assy |
| 7 | 2B292 | Front Disc Brake Caliper Anchor Plate |

| Item | Part Number | Description |
|------|------|------|
| 8 | 2068 | Brake Shoe Hold-Down Spring |
| 9 | 2N386 | Rear Brake Pin Retainer (2 Req'd) |
| 10 | 2B296 | Disc Brake Caliper Locating Pin (2 Req'd) |
| 11 | 2A492 | Brake Cylinder Retainer Boot |
| A | — | Tighten to 31-38 N·m (23-28 Lb-Ft) |

Fig. 26 Exploded view of the brake shoes and linings and related components—front disc brakes

Fig. 28 Lift the caliper assembly from the integral knuckle, anchor plate and rotor using a rotating motion

Fig. 29 Suspend the caliper inside the fender housing with wire. Do NOT let the caliper hang from the brake hose

Fig. 30 Remove the outer brake pad from the caliper assembly, then . . .

Fig. 31 . . . remove the inner brake pad

be taken during this procedure to prevent damage to the caliper piston. Do not allow metal or sharp objects to come into direct contact with the piston surface or damage will result.

7. Remove all rust buildup from the inside caliper legs (brake shoe contact area). Install the inner pad in the caliper piston. Do not bend the pad clips during installation in the piston or distortion and rattles can occur. Install the outer pad. Make sure the clips are properly seated.

8. Install the caliper over the rotor as outlined later in this section. Install the caliper locating pins or rear brake pin retainer, as applicable. Tighten the rear brake pin retainer to 25 ft. lbs. (34 Nm).

9. Install the wheel and tire assembly. Lower the vehicle, then, using a torque wrench, tighten the lug nuts to 85–105 ft. lbs. (115–142 Nm).

10. Pump the brake pedal prior to moving the vehicle to position the brake linings. Refill the master cylinder.

## INSPECTION

1. Remove the pads from the caliper.
2. Check both the inner and outer pads for excessive wear. Please refer to the specification chart in this section.
3. If only one pad is found to be defective, replace both of them on each side (complete axle set), not just the defective one.

## Brake Caliper

### REMOVAL & INSTALLATION

▶ See Figures 32, 33, 34 and 35

1. Raise and safely support the vehicle.
2. Remove the wheel and tire assembly, making sure not to damage the bleeder screw fitting during removal. Mark the caliper to ensure that it is reinstalled on the correct knuckle.
3. Disconnect the flexible brake hose from the caliper or rotor, depending upon application. Remove the hollow retaining bolt that connects the hose fitting to the caliper or rotor. Remove, then plug the hose assembly from the caliper or rotor.
4. For vehicles through 1993, remove the caliper locating pins using Torx® Drive Bit D79P-2100-T40, or equivalent. For 1994–95 vehicles, remove the two rear brake pin retainers.
5. Lift the caliper off of the rotor, integral knuckle and anchor plate using a rotating motion.
   **To install:**

➡Do not pry directly against the piston or damage to the piston will likely result.

6. Retract the piston fully into the piston bore. Position the caliper assembly above the rotor with the anti-rattle spring under the upper arm of the knuckle. Install the caliper over the rotor with a rotating motion. Make sure the inner and outer shoes are properly positioned and the outer anti-rattle spring is properly positioned. Make sure the clip-on insulators are attached to the brake shoe plate.

7. Lubricate the locating pins and the inside of the insulators with silicone grease. For vehicles through 1993, install the locating pins through the caliper insulators and hand-start the threads into the knuckle attaching holes. For 1994–95 vehicles, install the rear brake pin retainers through the caliper holes and into the caliper locating pins, then hand-start.

➡Make sure the correct caliper assembly, as marked during removal, is installed on the correct knuckle. The caliper bleed screw should be positioned on top of the caliper when assembled on the vehicle.

8. Tighten the locating pins to 18–25 ft. lbs. (24–34 Nm) or the rear brake pin retainers to 25 ft. lbs. (34 Nm).
9. Remove the plug and install the brake hose on the caliper using a new copper washer on each side of the fitting outlet. Insert the attaching bolt through the washers and fittings, then tighten to 30–40 ft. lbs. (41–54 Nm).

Fig. 32 Using a Torx® head tool to disconnect the caliper locating pins—vehicles though 1993

Fig. 33 Removing one of two caliper locating pins

Fig. 34 Lift the caliper off of the rotor using a rotating motion

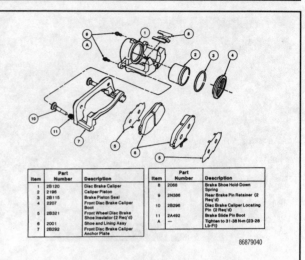

| Item | Part Number | Description |
|------|-------------|-------------|
| 1 | 2B120 | Disc Brake Caliper |
| 2 | 2196 | Caliper Piston |
| 3 | 2B115 | Brake Piston Seal |
| 4 | 2207 | Front Disc Brake Caliper Boot |
| 5 | 2B321 | Front Wheel Disc Brake Shoe Insulator (2 Req'd) |
| 6 | 2001 | Shoe and Lining Assy |
| 7 | 2B292 | Front Disc Brake Caliper Anchor Plate |

| Item | Part Number | Description |
|------|-------------|-------------|
| 8 | 2066 | Brake Shoe Hold-Down Spring |
| 9 | 2N386 | Rear Brake Pin Retainer (2 Req'd) |
| 10 | 2B296 | Disc Brake Caliper Locating Pin (2 Req'd) |
| 11 | 2A492 | Brake Slide Pin Boot |
| A | — | Tighten to 31-38 N·m (23-28 Lb-Ft) |

Fig. 35 Exploded view of a common caliper and related components

10. Bleed the brake system, filling the master cylinder as required; make sure to replace the rubber bleed screw cap after bleeding.

11. Install the wheel and tire assembly, then lower the vehicle. Final tighten the lug nuts, in a star pattern, to 85–105 ft. lbs. (115–142 Nm) using a torque wrench, not an impact tool. Pump the brake pedal prior to moving the vehicle to position the brake shoes and linings.

## OVERHAUL

▶ **See Figures 36, 37, 38, 39 and 40**

1. Remove the caliper assembly from the knuckle and rotor. Do not use a screwdriver or similar tool to pry the piston back into the cylinder bore. Use a C-clamp. Remove the outer shoe by pushing the shoe to move the "buttons" from the caliper housing and slipping down the caliper leg until the clip is disengaged. Remove the inner shoe by pulling it straight out of the piston.

➡**Inner shoe removal force may be as high as 10–20 lbs. (45–90 N)**

2. If further disassembly is required to service the piston, disconnect the caliper from the hydraulic system, then blow the piston out using air pressure. If the caliper piston is seized, and cannot be forced from the caliper, tap lightly around the piston while applying air pressure.

➡**Do not use a screwdriver or any similar tool to pry the piston out of the bore. It will result in damage to the piston. Cushion the piston's impact against the caliper when blowing it out of the bore by placing rags or a block of wood between the piston and the caliper bridge.**

3. Remove the dust seal from the caliper, then discard it and replace with a new one during assembly.

4. Remove the rubber piston seal from the caliper, then discard it and replace with a new one during assembly.

**To assemble:**

5. When assembling the caliper, examine the piston for surface irregularities or small chips and cracks. Replace the piston if damaged. Be sure to clean the foreign material from the piston surfaces and lubricate with brake fluid before inserting it into the caliper. Always install a new seal and dust boot.

6. When installing the piston back into its bore, use a wood block or another flat stock, like an old shoe lining assembly, between the C-clamp and piston. Do not apply the C-clamp directly to the piston surface. This can result in damage to the piston. Be sure the piston is not cocked.

7. Be certain the dust boot is tight in the boot groove on the piston and in the caliper.

8. To install the inner shoe with its attached three-finger clip into the piston, grab each end of the shoe, making it square with the piston. Push

Fig. 36 When removing the caliper assembly from the knuckle and rotor, do not use a screwdriver or other prytool to pry the piston back into the cylinder bore; use a C-clamp

Fig. 37 Blow the piston out of the caliper using air pressure, but be sure to put a piece of wood or rags between the piston and the caliper bridge first

Fig. 38 Remove the piston from the caliper

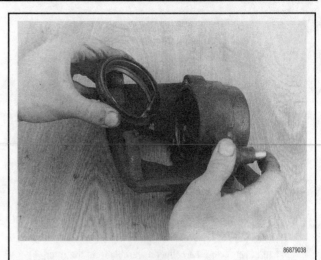

Fig. 39 Remove the dust seal from the caliper, then discard it and replace with a new one during assembly

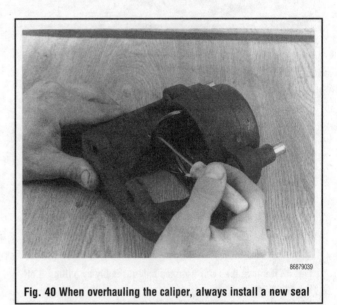

Fig. 40 When overhauling the caliper, always install a new seal

firmly until the shoe clip snaps into the piston. Do not allow the shoe or the clip tangs to cock during installation.

9.  Install the brake caliper as outlined earlier in this section.

## Brake Rotor

### REMOVAL & INSTALLATION

▶ **See Figures 41, 42, 43 and 44**

1.  Raise the vehicle and support it safely.
2.  Remove the wheel and tire assembly from the rotor face, being careful not to damage or interfere with the caliper bleeding screw fitting.

➡**Handle the rotor and caliper carefully as to prevent deformation, nicking, scratching and/or contamination of the rotor.**

3.  Remove the caliper anchor plate bolt, then remove the caliper assembly from the rotor. Position the caliper aside and support it with a length of wire. Do NOT allow the caliper to hang by the brake hose.
4.  Remove the rotor from the hub assembly by pulling it off the hub studs. If additional force is required to remove the rotor, apply rust penetrator on the front and rear rotor/hub mating surfaces, then strike the rotor

Fig. 41 After removing the caliper assembly from the rotor, position the caliper aside and support it with a length of wire. Do NOT allow the caliper to hang by the brake hose

Fig. 42 Remove the rotor from the hub assembly by pulling it off the hub studs

Fig. 43 View of the hub assembly with the rotor removed

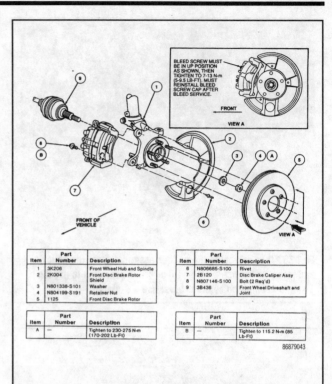

| Item | Part Number | Description |
|------|-------------|-------------|
| 1 | 3K206 | Front Wheel Hub and Spindle |
| 2 | 2K004 | Front Disc Brake Rotor Shield |
| 3 | N801338-S101 | Washer |
| 4 | N804199-S191 | Retainer Nut |
| 5 | 1125 | Front Disc Brake Rotor |

| Item | Part Number | Description |
|------|-------------|-------------|
| 6 | N806685-S100 | Rivet |
| 7 | 2B120 | Disc Brake Caliper Assy |
| 8 | N807146-S100 | Bolt (2 Req'd) |
| 9 | 3B436 | Front Wheel Driveshaft and Joint |

| Item | Part Number | Description |
|------|-------------|-------------|
| A | — | Tighten to 230-275 N·m (170-202 Lb-Ft) |

| Item | Part Number | Description |
|------|-------------|-------------|
| B | — | Tighten to 115.2 N·m (85 Lb-Ft) |

Fig. 44 Exploded view of the rotor assembly and related components

between the studs with a plastic hammer. If this does not work, attach a 3-jaw puller and remove the rotor.

➡ **If excessive force must be used to remove the rotor, it should be checked for lateral run-out before installation.**

**To install:**

5. Check the rotor for scoring and/or other wear. Machine or replace, as necessary. If machining, observe the minimum thickness specification.

6. If a new rotor is being installed, remove the protective coating from the rotor with Carburetor Tune-Up Cleaner D9AZ-19579-AA or equivalent before installation. If the old rotor is being installed, make sure the rotor braking and mounting surfaces are clean.

➡ **Failure to clean rust and foreign debris from the rotor and hub mounting faces when installing a new or used rotor, will result in high lateral run-out, which will speed up the development of brake roughness, shudder and/or vibration.**

7. Apply a small amount of Silicone Dielectric Compound D7AZ-19A331-A or equivalent to the pilot diameter of the rotor.

8. Install the rotor on the wheel hub assembly.

9. Install the caliper and caliper anchor bolts on the rotor, then tighten the bolts to 85 ft. lbs. (115 Nm).

10. Install the wheel and tire assembly, then hand-tighten the lug nuts.

11. Lower the vehicle, then final tighten the lug nuts to 85–105 ft. lbs. (115–142 Nm). Pump the brake pedal before moving the car to position the brake shoes and linings.

## INSPECTION

Check the disc brake rotor for scoring, cracks or other damage. Rotor run-out should be measured while the rotor is installed, but rotor thickness (or thickness variation) may be checked with the rotor installed or removed. Use a dial gauge to check the rotor run-out. Check the rotor thickness to make sure it is greater than the minimum allowable thickness, and check for thickness variations using a caliper micrometer.

## REAR DRUM BRAKES

### ✳✳ CAUTION

**Brake shoes may contain asbestos, which has been determined to be a cancer causing agent. Never clean the brake surfaces with compressed air! Avoid inhaling any dust from any brake surface! When cleaning brake surfaces, use a commercially available brake cleaning solvent.**

### Brake Drums

REMOVAL & INSTALLATION

**1986–89 Vehicles**

▶ See Figures 45 thru 52

1. Raise and safely support the vehicle.
2. Remove the wheel cover or nut covers, as required. Remove the wheel and tire assembly.
3. Remove the grease cap from the hub. Remove the cotter pin, nut lock, adjusting nut and keyed flat washer from the spindle. Remove the outer bearing and discard the cotter pin.
4. Remove the hub/drum assembly as a unit. Be careful not to damage the grease seal and inner bearing during removal. Make sure you don't drag the seal across the spindle threads during removal and installation.
5. Inspect the drum for scoring and/or other wear. Machine or replace, as necessary. If machining, observe the maximum permissible drum diameter specification.

**To install:**

6. Inspect and lubricate the bearings, as necessary. Replace the grease seal if any damage is visible.
7. Clean the spindle stem, then apply a thin coat of wheel bearing grease.
8. Install the hub and drum assembly on the spindle. Install the outer bearing in the hub on the spindle.
9. Install the keyed flat washer and adjusting nut, then finger-tighten the nut.
10. Adjust the wheel bearings. For details, please refer to the procedure in Section 8 of this manual.
11. Install the nut retainer and a new cotter pin. Install the grease cap, tapping lightly around the flange to seat the cap.

86871089

**Fig. 46 After removing the grease cap, unbend the cotter pin**

86871090

**Fig. 47 Grasp the cotter pin with needle-nose pliers and pull or pry it free of the spindle. Discard the cotter pin and replace it with a new one during installation**

86871088

**Fig. 45 After removing the wheel and tire assembly, pry the grease cap from the hub. Be careful not to distort or damage the flange**

86871091

**Fig. 48 Remove the adjusting nut from the spindle**

Fig. 49 Remove the keyed washer from the spindle

Fig. 51 Remove the hub and drum assembly from the spindle

12. Install the wheel and tire assembly. Install the wheel cover or nut covers, as required, then carefully lower the vehicle.

**1990–95 Vehicles**

▶ See Figures 53 and 54

1. Raise and safely support the vehicle.
2. Remove the wheel cover or nut covers, as required.
3. Remove the rear wheel and tire assembly.
4. Remove the two drum retaining nuts, then remove the drum.

➥If the drum will not come off, pry the rubber plug from the backing plate inspection hole. Remove the brake line-to-axle retention bracket. This will allow sufficient room to insert suitable brake tools through the inspection hole to disengage the adjusting lever and back off the adjuster.

5. Inspect the drum for scoring and/or other wear. Machine or replace, as necessary. If machining, observe the maximum permissible drum diameter specification.

**To install:**

6. Install the drum assembly on the rear hub, then secure using the two retaining nuts. Adjust the brakes as outlined earlier in this section.

Fig. 50 Remove the outer bearing assembly. Note that this can be done with the hub and drum on or off the vehicle

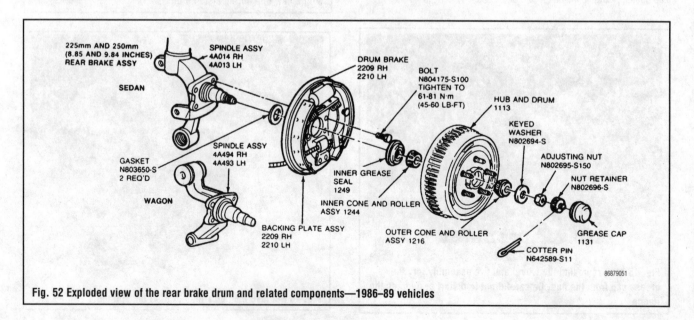

Fig. 52 Exploded view of the rear brake drum and related components—1986–89 vehicles

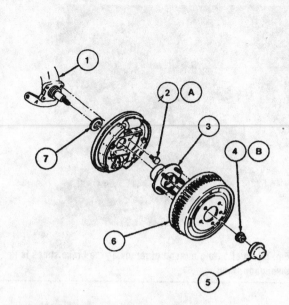

| Item | Part Number | Description |
|------|-------------|-------------|
| 1 | 4A013 | Rear Wheel Spindle |
| 2 | N804175-S100 | Bolt (4 Req'd Each Side) |
| 3 | 1104 | Wheel Hub |
| 4 | 4B477 | Rear Axle Wheel Hub Retainer (2 Req'd) |
| 5 | — | Rear Hub Cap Grease Seal |
| 6 | 1126 | Brake Drum |
| 7 | N803650-S | Gasket |
| A | — | Tighten to 60-80 N·m (45-60 Lb-Ft) |
| B | — | Tighten to 255-345 N·m (188-254 Lb-Ft) |

86879052

**Fig. 53 Exploded view of the brake drum and related components**

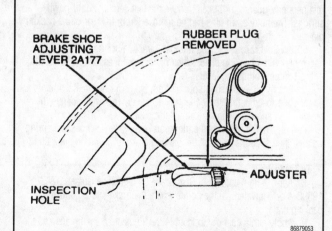

86879053

**Fig. 54 The brake shoe adjuster is accessible through an inspection hole in the backing plate**

7. Install the wheel and tire assembly.
8. Install the wheel cover or nut covers, as required, then carefully lower the vehicle.

## INSPECTION

Inspect the brake drums for excessive wear. Using a brake drum inspection gauge tool D81L–1103–A or equivalent, measure the drum inside diameter. If the drum is not within specification, it must be either cut or replaced. The maximum inside diameter of the drum is stamped on it. If this number exceeds the drum wear or refinishing specification, the drum must be replaced. For additional information on brake drum diameter, please refer to the specification chart later in this section.

## Brake Shoes

### INSPECTION

Inspect the brake shoes for excessive lining wear or shoe damage. If the lining is worn below $\frac{1}{32}$ in. (0.8mm) replace both shoes. Replace any lining that has become contaminated with brake fluid, oil or grease.

➡**Replace the brake shoe and lining in axle sets only. Never replace just one shoe of a brake assembly.**

Check the condition of the brake shoes and linings, retracting springs, hold-down springs and the brake drum for signs of overheating. If the shoes and linings have a slight blue coloring (indicating overheating), the retracting springs and hold-down springs should be replaced. If they're not replaced, the overheated springs will lose their tension and could allow new linings to drag and prematurely wear.

### REMOVAL & INSTALLATION

⬥ **See Figures 55 thru 60**

➡**Special brake tools are available from auto supply stores, which will ease removal and installation of the retracting springs and the shoe hold-down spring/anchor pin assembly.**

1. Raise and safely support the vehicle.
2. Remove the wheel and tire assembly, then remove the brake drum.
3. For 1993–95 vehicles, remove the parking brake cable and conduit from the parking brake lever. For vehicles though 1992, it may be easier to remove the parking brake cable after lifting the assembly off the backing plate.

86871094

**Fig. 55 Remove the rear hub and drum assembly from the spindle**

Fig. 56 Use an evaporative spray brake cleaner to remove brake dust from the components

Fig. 59 An alternate method of removing the brake shoes is to disengage, then . . .

Fig. 57 Use the brake tool to compress the hold-down spring and twist the plate to free the pin

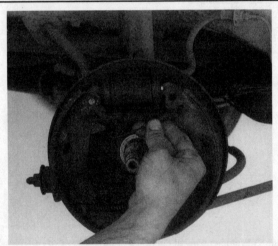

Fig. 60 . . . remove the adjuster screw retracting spring

Fig. 58 Once the pin is released, you can withdraw the spring from the backing plate

4. Using a suitable tool, depress and twist the two hold-down spring retainers one-quarter turn, then remove the retainers and hold-down springs. The hold-down pins can be removed from the rear of the backing plate.

5. Lift the brake shoes and linings, retracting springs, and adjuster assembly off the backing plate. When removing the assembly, be careful not to bend the adjusting lever.

6. Remove the retracting springs from the lower brake attachments and upper shoe-to-adjusting lever attachment points. This will separate the brake shoes and disengage the adjuster mechanism.

7. Remove the horseshoe parking brake lever pin retainer and spring washer, then slide the lever off the parking brake lever pin on the trailing shoe.

**To install:**

8. Apply a light coating of Disc Brake Caliper Slide Grease D7AZ-19590-A or equivalent, at the points where the brake shoes contact the backing plate.

9. Apply a thin coat of lubricant to the adjuster screw threads and the socket end of the adjusting screw. Install the stainless steel washer over the socket end of the adjusting screw and install the socket. Turn the adjusting nut all the way down on the screw, then back off ½ turn.

10. Assemble the parking brake lever to the trailing shoe by installing

the spring washer and a new horseshoe parking brake lever pin retainer. Crimp the clip until it retains the lever to the shoe securely.

11. Position the trailing shoe against the brake backing plate, then attach the parking brake cable.

12. For vehicles through 1992, attach the lower shoe retracting spring to the leading and trailing shoe, then install to the backing plate. It will be necessary to stretch the retracting spring as the shoes are installed downward over the anchor plate to the inside of the shoe retaining plate.

13. For 1993–95 vehicles, position the leading shoe on the rear brake backing plate, then attach the lower brake shoe retracting spring to the brake shoes.

14. Install the adjuster screw assembly between the leading shoe slot and the slot in the trailing shoe/parking brake lever assembly. The adjuster socket end slot must fit into the trailing shoe and parking brake lever.

15. Install the adjuster lever in the groove of the parking brake lever pin and into the slot of the adjuster socket that fits into the trailing shoe web.

➡The adjuster socket blade is marked R for the right-hand or L for the left-hand brake assemblies. The R or L adjuster blade must be installed with the letter R or L in the upright position, facing the wheel cylinder, on the correct side to ensure that the deeper of the 2 slots in the adjuster socket fits into the parking brake lever.

16. Attach the upper retracting spring to the leading shoe slot. Using a suitable spring tool, stretch the other end of the spring into the notch on the adjuster lever. If the adjuster lever does not contact the star wheel after installing the spring, it is possible that the adjuster socket is installed incorrectly.

17. Install the brake shoe hold-down spring pins, brake shoe hold-down springs and retainers. If installed, remove the brake cylinder clamp D81L-1103-B or equivalent. Attach the parking brake cable and conduit to the parking brake lever.

18. Adjust the brake shoes, as outlined earlier in this section.

19. Install the brake drum, then the wheel/tire assembly. Lower the vehicle.

## Wheel Cylinders

### REMOVAL & INSTALLATION

▶ See Figures 61 and 62

1. Raise and safely support the vehicle.
2. Remove the wheel and tire assembly.
3. Remove the brake drum, as outlined earlier in this section.

Fig. 61 Although you can clamp the brake lines to prevent fluid leakage during wheel cylinder removal, do NOT use locking pliers. There are special tools available for this purpose

Fig. 62 After removing the retaining bolts, remove the wheel cylinder from the backing plate

4. Remove the brake shoes, adjuster and retracting springs assembly from the brake backing plate, as previously outlined.

5. Disconnect and plug the brake line wheel cylinder, behind the backing plate.

6. Remove the wheel cylinder-to-backing plate bolts, then remove the wheel cylinder.

**To install:**

➡Before connecting, wipe the ends of the rear brake lines with a clean cloth to remove any foreign matter.

7. Position the wheel cylinder on the brake backing plate, then finger-tighten the brake line to the wheel cylinder.

### ✳✳ WARNING

**Do NOT allow brake fluid to come in contact with the brake shoes and linings or they must be replaced.**

8. Secure the wheel cylinder to the backing plate using the retaining bolts. Tighten the bolts to 8–10 ft. lbs. (10–14 Nm).

9. Using a tube nut wrench, install the tube nut fitting, then tighten to 11–15 ft. lbs. (15–20 Nm).

10. Install, then adjust the brakes, following the procedure earlier in this section.

11. Install the brake drum, followed by the tire and wheel assembly.

12. Bleed the brake system before attempting to drive the vehicle. For details, please refer to the procedure earlier in this section.

13. Lower and road test the vehicle.

### OVERHAUL

▶ See Figures 63 and 64

Wheel cylinders need not be rebuilt unless they are leaking or seized. To check the wheel cylinder for leakage, carefully pull the lower edge of the rubber end boot away from the cylinder. A slight amount of fluid in the boot is normal, but excessive brake fluid in the boot or running out of the boot (when the edges are pulled away from the cylinder) denotes leakage.

➡It is not necessary to remove the cylinder from the brake backing (mounting) plate to rebuild the cylinder, however removal makes the job easier.

1. Disengage and remove the rubber boots from both ends of the wheel cylinder. The piston should come out with the boot. If not, remove the piston by applying finger pressure inward on one piston; the piston on

**Fig. 63 Internal components of an early model wheel cylinder**

the opposite end should come out. Take care not to splash brake fluid all over yourself when the piston pops from the cylinder.

2. Remove the rubber cups, center expander and spring from the wheel cylinder. Remove the bleeder screw from the back of the cylinder.

3. Discard all rubber boots and cups. Wash the pistons and cylinder in denatured alcohol or clean brake fluid.

4. Inspect the pistons for scratches, scoring or other visible damage. Inspect the cylinder bore for score marks or rust. The cylinder may be honed (with a brake cylinder hone) if necessary. Do not hone more than 0.003 in. (0.076mm) beyond original diameter. If the scoring or pitting is deeper, replace the cylinder.

5. After honing the cylinder, wash again with alcohol or clean brake fluid. Check the bleeder screw hole to make sure it is opened. Wipe the cylinder bore with a clean cloth. Install the bleeder screw.

6. Never reuse the old rubber parts. Always use all of the parts supplied in the rebuilding kit.

7. Apply a light coating of brake fluid or the special lubricant (if supplied with the rebuilding kit) on the pistons, rubber cups and cylinder bore.

8. Insert the spring and expander assembly into the cylinder bore. Put the cups (facing inward) and the pistons into the cylinder. Install the boots and fit the outer lips into the retaining grooves on the outer edges of the wheel cylinder.

9. If removed, install the wheel cylinder onto the backing plate, then connect the brake line. Be sure that the inlet port (where the brake hose connects) is toward the rear of the car.

10. Install the brake shoes, drum and wheel assembly.

11. Adjust and bleed the brake system. Road test the car.

## Brake Backing Plate

### REMOVAL & INSTALLATION

▶ **See Figure 65**

1. Raise and safely support the vehicle. Remove the tire and wheel assembly.

2. Remove the brake drum, as well as the grease cap/seal. Remove and discard the retaining nut.

3. Remove the bearing hub unit from the spindle. Disconnect the brake line.

4. Remove the brake shoes, adjuster assemblies, wheel cylinder and parking brake cable from the backing plate.

5. Remove the backing plate-to-spindle retaining bolts, then discard them.

6. Remove the backing plate and foam gasket.

**To install:**

7. Install a new foam gasket on the rear wheel spindle.

8. Install the brake backing plate with new adhesive coated retaining bolts.

9. Install the wheel cylinder, then connect the brake line.

10. Install the brake shoe/lining and adjuster assemblies. Insert the parking brake lever through the backing plate. The prongs must be securely locked in place. Connect the parking brake cable to the lever.

11. Install the bearing and hub assembly on the spindle. Install the hub retainer, then tighten the nut to 188–254 ft. lbs. (255–345 Nm).

12. Install a new grease seal using a 1⅞ in. x ¾ in. drive socket.

13. Install the brake drum, then adjust the brakes, as previously outlined.

14. Bleed the brake system. Check the parking brake cable adjustment.

15. Install the tire and wheel assembly, then carefully lower the vehicle.

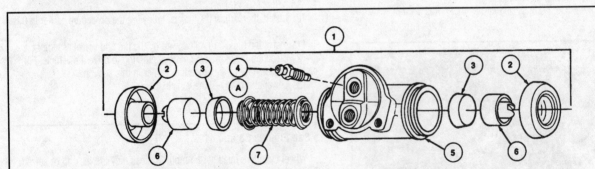

| Item | Part Number | Description |
|------|-------------|-------------|
| 1 | 2261 | Rear Wheel Cylinder |
| 2 | — | Boot (Part of 2261) |
| 3 | — | Cup (Part of 2261) |
| 4 | — | Wheel Cylinder Bleeder Screw (Part of 2261) |
| 5 | — | Cylinder Housing (Part of 2261) |

| Item | Part Number | Description |
|------|-------------|-------------|
| 6 | — | Piston (Part of 2261) |
| 7 | — | Return Spring and Cup Expander Assy (Part of 2261) |
| A | — | Tighten to 10-20 N·m (7.5-15 Lb-Ft) |

**Fig. 64 Exploded view of the wheel cylinder**

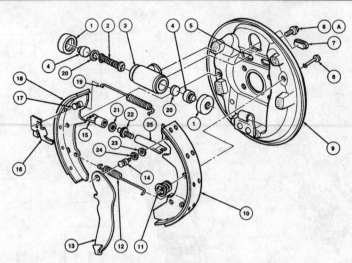

| Item | Part Number | Description |
|------|-------------|-------------|
| 1 | — | Boot (Part of 2261) |
| 2 | — | Spring Expander (Part of 2261) |
| 3 | 2261 | Rear Wheel Cylinder |
| 4 | — | Piston and Insert (Part of 2261) |
| 5 | — | Shoe Adjustment Access Hole |
| 6 | N801327 | Wheel Cylinder Retaining Screw (2 Req'd) |
| 7 | 2092 | Brake Adjusting Hole Cover |
| 8 | 2069 | Brake Shoe Hold Down Spring Pin |
| 9 | 2211 | Brake Backing Plate |
| 10 | — | Trailing Shoe and Lining (Part of 2200) |
| 11 | 2068 | Brake Shoe Hold-Down Spring |
| 12 | 2035 | Lower Brake Shoe Retracting Spring |
| 13 | 2A637 (RH) 2A638 (LH) | Parking Brake Lever |

| Item | Part Number | Description |
|------|-------------|-------------|
| 14 | 2107 | Parking Brake Lever Pin (Inner) |
| 15 | 2048 | Brake Shoe Adjusting Screw Socket |
| 16 | 2A177 (LH) 2A176 (RH) | Brake Shoe Adjusting Lever |
| 17 | 2107 | Parking Brake Lever Pin |
| 18 | — | Leading Shoe and Lining (Part of 2001) |
| 19 | 2049 | Brake Shoe Adjusting Screw Spring |
| 20 | — | Cup (Part of 2261) |
| 21 | 384373-S | Washer |
| 22 | — | Adjusting Screw (Part of 2261) |
| 23 | 356297-S2 | Washer |
| 24 | 2106 | Parking Brake Lever Pin Retainer |
| 25 | — | Adjusting Pivot Nut (Part of 2048) |
| A | — | Tighten to 10-14 N·m (8-10 Lb-In) |

86879074

**Fig. 65 Exploded view of the rear drum brake backing plate and related components**

## REAR DISC BRAKES

### ✳✳ CAUTION

**Brake shoes may contain asbestos, which has been determined to be a cancer causing agent. Never clean the brake surfaces with compressed air! Avoid inhaling dust from any brake surface! When cleaning brake surfaces, use a commercially available brake cleaning solvent.**

### Brake Pads

REMOVAL & INSTALLATION

▶ **See Figures 66, 67, 68 and 69**

1. Remove the master cylinder cap and check the fluid level in the reservoir. Remove brake fluid as necessary until the reservoir is half full. Discard the removed fluid.
2. Raise and safely support the vehicle.
3. Remove the wheel and tire assembly.
4. Remove the screw retaining the brake hose bracket to the shock absorber bracket. Remove the retaining clip from the parking brake cable at the caliper. Remove the cable end from the parking brake lever.
5. Hold the slider pin hex-head with an open-end wrench. Remove the upper rear brake pin retainer/pinch bolt. Rotate the caliper away from the rotor.
6. Remove the inner and outer brake pads from the rear disc support bracket/anchor plate.

**To install:**

7. Using Rear Caliper Piston Adjuster T87P-2588-A or equivalent, rotate the piston and adjuster clockwise until it is fully seated. Make sure one of the two slots in the piston face is positioned so it will engage the nib on the brake pad.
8. Install the inner and outer brake pads in the anchor plate/support bracket. Rotate the caliper assembly over the rotor into position on the anchor plate/support bracket. Make sure the brake pads are installed correctly.
9. Remove the residue from the rear brake pin retainers/pinch bolt threads, then apply one drop of Threadlock and Sealer E0AZ-19554-AA or equivalent to the threads. Install and tighten the retainers to 23–26 ft. lbs. (31–35 Nm) while holding the slider pins with an open-end wrench.
10. Attach the cable end to the parking brake lever. Install the cable retaining clip on the caliper assembly. Position the flexible brake hose and bracket assembly to the shock absorber bracket, then install the retaining screw. Tighten the screw to 8–11 ft. lbs. (11–16 Nm).
11. Install the wheel and tire assembly, then carefully lower the vehicle. Pump the brake pedal prior to moving the vehicle to position the brake linings. Refill the master cylinder.

### INSPECTION

The rear disc brakes can be inspected through an oval hole in the back of the brake caliper. Raise the rear of the vehicle, then remove the wheel and tire assembly to inspect the brake pads. If the brake lining thickness is less than 0.12 in. (3mm) the brake pads should be replaced.

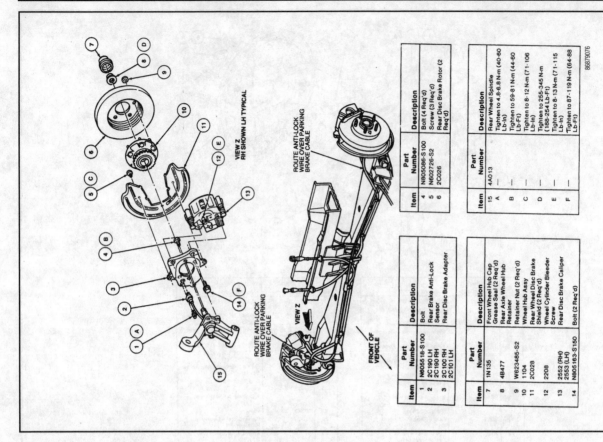

| Item | Part Number | Description |
|---|---|---|
| 1 | N805518-S100 | Bolt |
| 2 | 2C190 LH<br>2C190 RH | Rear Brake Anti-Lock Sensor |
| 3 | 2C100 RH<br>2C101 LH | Rear Disc Brake Adapter |

| Item | Part Number | Description |
|---|---|---|
| 4 | N805086-S100 | Bolt (4 Req'd) |
| 5 | N602726-S2 | Screw (3 Req'd) |
| 6 | 2C026 | Rear Disc Brake Rotor (2 Req'd) |

| Item | Part Number | Description |
|---|---|---|
| 7 | 1N135 | Front Wheel Hub Cap |
| 8 | 4B477 | Grease Seal (2 Req'd)<br>Rear Axle Wheel Hub |
| 9 | W623485-S2 | Retainer |
| 10 | 1104 | Wheel Hub Assy |
| 11 | 2C028 | Rear Wheel Disc Brake Shield (2 Req'd) |
| 12 | 2208 | Wheel Cylinder Bleeder Screw |
| 13 | 2552 (RH)<br>2553 (LH) | Rear Disc Brake Caliper |
| 14 | N805163-S150 | Bolt (2 Req'd) |

| Item | Part Number | Description |
|---|---|---|
| 15 | 4A013 | Rear Wheel Spindle |
| A | — | Tighten to 4.8-6.8 N·m (40-60 Lb-In) |
| B | — | Tighten to 59-81 N·m (44-60 Lb-Ft) |
| C | — | Tighten to 8-12 N·m (71-106 Lb-In) |
| D | — | Tighten to 255-345 N·m (188-254 Lb-Ft) |
| E | — | Tighten to 8-13 N·m (71-115 Lb-In) |
| F | — | Tighten to 87-119 N·m (64-88 Lb-Ft) |

**Fig. 67 Exploded view of the rear disc brake components—late model station wagon with ABS shown**

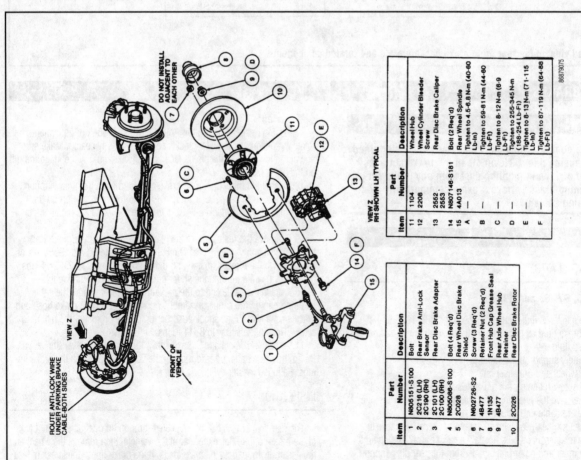

| Item | Part Number | Description |
|---|---|---|
| 1 | N805151-S100 | Bolt |
| 2 | 2C216 (LH)<br>2C190 (RH) | Rear Brake Anti-Lock Sensor |
| 3 | 2C101 (LH)<br>2C100 (RH) | Rear Disc Brake Adapter |
| 4 | N805086-S100 | Bolt (4 Req'd) |
| 5 | 2C028 | Rear Wheel Disc Brake Shield |
| 6 | N602726-S2 | Screw (3 Req'd) |
| 7 | 4B477 | Retainer Nut (2 Req'd) |
| 8 | 1N135 | Front Hub Cap Grease Seal |
| 9 | 4B477 | Retainer |
| 10 | 2C026 | Rear Disc Brake Rotor |

| Item | Part Number | Description |
|---|---|---|
| 11 | 1104 | Wheel Hub |
| 12 | 2208 | Wheel Cylinder Bleeder Screw |
| 13 | 2552<br>2553 | Rear Disc Brake Caliper |
| 14 | N807146-S181 | Bolt (2 Req'd) |
| 15 | 4A013 | Rear Wheel Spindle |
| A | — | Tighten to 4.5-6.8 N·m (40-60 Lb-In) |
| B | — | Tighten to 59-81 N·m (44-60 Lb-Ft) |
| C | — | Tighten to 8-12 N·m (6-9 Lb-Ft) |
| D | — | Tighten to 255-345 N·m (188-254 Lb-Ft) |
| E | — | Tighten to 8-13 N·m (71-115 Lb-In) |
| F | — | Tighten to 87-119 N·m (64-88 Lb-Ft) |

**Fig. 66 Exploded view of the rear disc brake components—late model sedan with ABS shown**

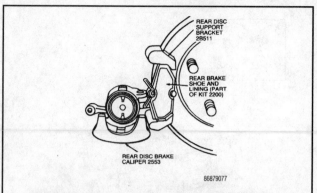

Fig. 68 After removing the upper rear brake pin retainers or pinch bolt (as applicable) rotate the caliper away from the rotor

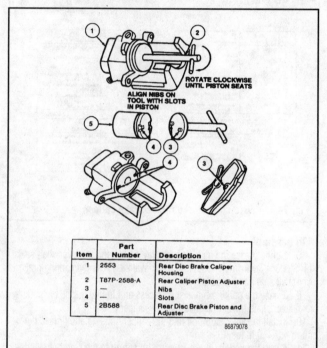

| Item | Part Number | Description |
|---|---|---|
| 1 | 2553 | Rear Disc Brake Caliper Housing |
| 2 | T87P-2588-A | Rear Caliper Piston Adjuster |
| 3 | — | Nibs |
| 4 | — | Slots |
| 5 | 2B588 | Rear Disc Brake Piston and Adjuster |

Fig. 69 Make sure one of the two slots in the piston face is positioned so it will engage the nib on the brake pad

## Brake Caliper

### REMOVAL & INSTALLATION

▶ See Figures 70, 71, 72 and 73

1. Raise and safely support the vehicle.
2. Remove the wheel and tire assembly.
3. Remove the brake hose from the caliper assembly.
4. Remove the retaining clip from the parking brake cable at the caliper. Disengage the parking brake cable end from the lever arm.
5. Depending on vehicle application, hold one of the slider pin hexheads with an open-end wrench, then remove the pinch bolt or pin retainer. Repeat for the other slider pin. Lift the caliper assembly away from the anchor plate. Remove the locating/slider pins and boots from the anchor plate/support bracket.

**To install:**

6. Apply Silicone Dielectric Compound or equivalent to the inside of the locating/slider pin boots and to the pins.
7. Position the slider pins and boots in the anchor plate. Position the

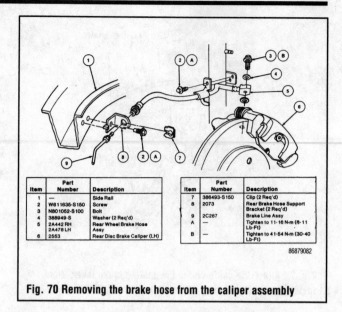

| Item | Part Number | Description |
|---|---|---|
| 1 | — | Side Rail |
| 2 | W611635-S150 | Screw |
| 3 | N801052-S100 | Bolt |
| 4 | 388949-S | Washer (2 Req'd) |
| 5 | 2A442 RH 2A478 LH | Rear Wheel Brake Hose Assy |
| 6 | 2553 | Rear Disc Brake Caliper (LH) |
| 7 | 386493-S150 | Clip (2 Req'd) |
| 8 | 2073 | Rear Brake Hose Support Bracket (2 Req'd) |
| 9 | 2C267 | Brake Line Assy |
| A | — | Tighten to 11-16 N·m (8-11 Lb-Ft) |
| B | — | Tighten to 41-54 N·m (30-40 Lb-Ft) |

Fig. 70 Removing the brake hose from the caliper assembly

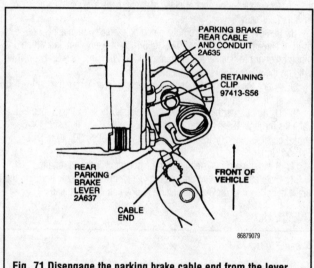

Fig. 71 Disengage the parking brake cable end from the lever arm

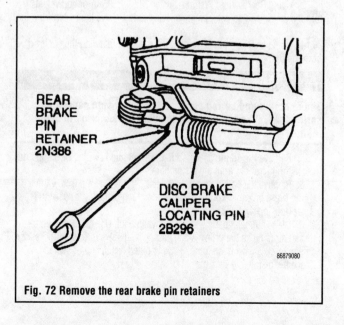

Fig. 72 Remove the rear brake pin retainers

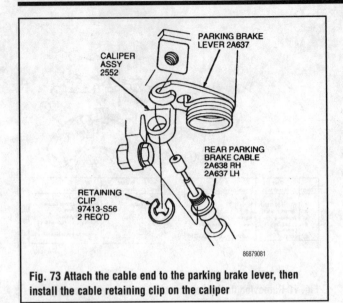

Fig. 73 Attach the cable end to the parking brake lever, then install the cable retaining clip on the caliper

caliper assembly on the anchor plate. Make sure the brake pads are installed correctly.

8. Remove the residue from the pinch bolt threads, then apply one drop of Threadlock and Sealer E0AZ-19554-AA or equivalent. Install the pinch bolts or pin retainers, then tighten to 23–26 ft. lbs. (31–35 Nm) while holding the slider pins with an open-end wrench.

9. Attach the cable end to the parking brake lever. Install the cable retaining clip on the caliper assembly.

10. Using new washers, connect the brake flex hose to the caliper. For vehicles through 1992, tighten the retaining bolt to 8–11 ft. lbs. (11–16 Nm). For 1993–95 vehicles, tighten the retaining bolt to 30–40 ft. lbs. (41–54 Nm).

11. Bleed the brake system, filling the master cylinder as required.

12. Install the wheel and tire assembly, then lower the vehicle. Pump the brake pedal prior to moving the vehicle to position the brake pads.

## OVERHAUL

▶ **See Figure 74**

1. Remove the caliper assembly from the vehicle following the procedure earlier in this section.

2. Mount the caliper in a vise with soft-jawed protectors.

3. Using Rear Caliper Piston Adjuster T87P–2588–A or equivalent, turn the piston and adjuster counterclockwise to remove the piston from the bore.

4. Using snapring pliers, remove the snapring retaining the pushrod from the caliper.

### ✳✳ CAUTION

**The snapring and spring cover are under tension caused by spring load. Be careful when removing the snapring to avoid injury.**

5. Remove the spring cover, spring, washer and key plate, then pull out the pushrod strut pin from the piston bore.

6. Remove the parking brake lever return spring, then unscrew the parking brake lever stop bolt and pull the parking brake lever out of the caliper housing.

7. Clean all metal parts with isopropyl alcohol. Use clean, dry compressed air to clean the grooves and passages. Inspect the caliper bores for damage or excessive wear. If the piston is pitted, scratched or scored replace the piston.

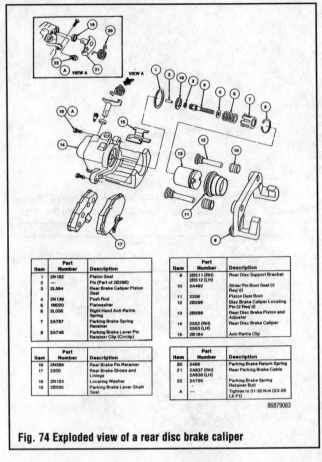

| Item | Part Number | Description |
|---|---|---|
| 1 | 2N182 | Piston Seal |
| 2 | — | Pin (Part of 2B296) |
| 3 | 2L594 | Rear Brake Caliper Piston Seal |
| 4 | 2N139 | Push Rod |
| 5 | 1N020 | Flatwasher |
| 6 | 2L035 | Right Hand Anti-Rattle Spring |
| 7 | 2A787 | Parking Brake Spring Retainer |
| 8 | 2A746 | Parking Brake Lever Pin Retainer Clip (Circlip) |

| Item | Part Number | Description |
|---|---|---|
| 16 | 2N386 | Rear Brake Pin Retainer |
| 17 | 2200 | Rear Brake Shoes and Linings |
| 18 | 2N183 | Locating Washer |
| 19 | 2B595 | Parking Brake Lever Shaft Seal |

| Item | Part Number | Description |
|---|---|---|
| 9 | 2B511 (RH) 2B512 (LH) | Rear Disc Support Bracket |
| 10 | 2A492 | Slider Pin Boot Seal (2 Req'd) |
| 11 | 2206 | Piston Dust Boot |
| 12 | 2B296 | Disc Brake Caliper Locating Pin (2 Req'd) |
| 13 | 2B588 | Rear Disc Brake Piston and Adjuster |
| 14 | 2552 (RH) 2553 (LH) | Rear Disc Brake Caliper |
| 15 | 2B164 | Anti-Rattle Clip |

| Item | Part Number | Description |
|---|---|---|
| 20 | 2456 | Parking Brake Return Spring |
| 21 | 2A637 (RH) 2A638 (LH) | Rear Parking Brake Cable |
| 22 | 2A795 | Parking Brake Spring Retainer Bolt |
| A | — | Tighten to 31-35 N·m (23-26 Lb-Ft) |

Fig. 74 Exploded view of a rear disc brake caliper

## To assemble:

8. Lightly grease the parking brake lever bore and the lever shaft seal with Silicone Dielectric Compound or equivalent. Press the parking brake lever shaft seal into the caliper bore.

9. Grease the parking brake shaft recess and lightly grease the parking brake lever shaft. Install the shaft into the caliper housing.

10. Install the lever stop bolt into the caliper housing and tighten the bolt to 4.5–7.0 ft. lbs. (6–9 Nm).

11. Attach the parking brake lever return spring to the stop bolt, then install the free end into the parking brake lever slot.

12. Install a new O-ring seal in the groove of the pushrod. Grease the pushrod end with Silicone Dielectric Compound or equivalent.

13. Position the strut pin in the caliper housing and in the recess of the parking brake lever shaft. Install the pushrod into the bore. Make sure the pin is positioned correctly between the shaft recess. Install the flat washer, pushrod, spring and spring cover, in that order.

### Brake Rotor

## REMOVAL & INSTALLATION

▶ **See Figure 75**

1. Raise and safely support the vehicle.

2. Remove the wheel and tire assembly.

3. Remove the caliper assembly from the rotor, then support it with a length of wire. Do NOT let the caliper hang from the brake line.

4. For 1993–95 vehicles, unfasten the upper and lower support bracket-to-rear disc brake adapter bolts, then remove the rear disc support bracket.

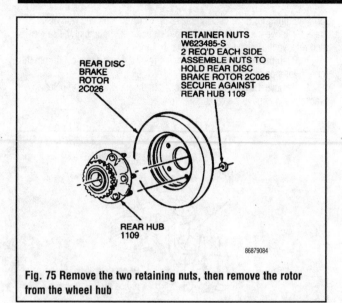

**Fig. 75 Remove the two retaining nuts, then remove the rotor from the wheel hub**

5. Remove the two rotor retaining nuts, then remove the rotor from the hub.

**To install:**

6. Check the rotor for scoring and/or other wear. Machine or replace, as necessary. If machining, observe the minimum thickness specification.

7. If the rotor is being replaced, remove the protective coating from the new rotor with Carburetor Tune-Up Cleaner D9AZ-19579-AA or equivalent.

8. Install the rotor on the hub, then fasten the two retaining nuts securely.

➡**The support brackets are interchangeable from right or left.**

9. For 1993–95 vehicles, install the support bracket. Position the bracket on the right or left-hand rear disc brake adapter, as applicable. Add one drop of Threadlock and Sealer E0AZ-19554-AA or equivalent to each bolt, then attach the bracket to the right or left-hand brake adapter. Tighten to 64–88 ft. lbs. (87–117 Nm).

10. Install the brake shoes and linings, then install the caliper assembly as outlined earlier in this section.

11. Install the wheel and tire assembly, then carefully lower the vehicle. Pump the brake pedal prior to moving the vehicle to position the brake pads.

## INSPECTION

Check the disc brake rotor for scoring, cracks or other damage. Rotor run-out should be measured while the rotor is installed, but rotor thickness or thickness variation may be checked with the rotor installed or removed. Use a dial gauge to check the rotor run-out. Check the rotor thickness to make sure it is greater than minimum thickness and check for thickness variations using a caliper micrometer. If the rotor is not within specification, either have it cut (if possible) or replace it.

## PARKING BRAKE

### Cable

#### REMOVAL & INSTALLATION

**Front Cable**

▶ **See Figures 76, 77 and 78**

1. Raise and safely support the vehicle.
2. Loosen the adjuster nut at the cable adjuster bracket.
3. Lower the vehicle.
4. Disconnect the front parking brake cable and conduit from the control assembly at the clevis using a ½ in. (13mm) box-end wrench to press the conduit retaining prongs, then remove the cable-end pronged fitting from the parking brake control.
5. Remove the left-hand cowl side trim panel, then pull the carpet back to expose the cable and conduit.
6. Raise and safely support the vehicle.
7. Disconnect the front cable from the rear cable at the cable connector.
8. Remove the cable and push-in prong retainer from the cable bracket, using a ½ in. (13mm) box-end wrench to depress the retaining prongs.
9. Pull the cable assembly down through the floorpan hole.

**To install:**

10. Start the front parking brake cable and conduit through the hole in the floor pan, then secure the grommet in place.

➡**The prongs must be securely locked into place.**

11. Position the cable and conduit through the front cable bracket at the inner floor side member. Push the prong into the bracket. Seat the cable seal into the hole in the front floorpan.
12. Connect the rear cable to the front cable.
13. Carefully lower the vehicle.
14. Push the prong retainer into the parking brake control housing until the prongs are secure, then connect the front parking brake cable and conduit to the parking brake control clevis.

15. Reinstall the carpet and the left-hand cowl side trim panel.
16. Raise and safely support the vehicle.
17. Adjust the parking brake, following the procedure located in this section, then lower the vehicle and check the parking brake operation.

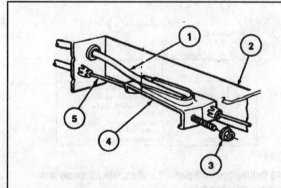

| Item | Part Number | Description |
|------|-------------|-------------|
| 1 | 2A635 | LH Parking Brake Rear Cable and Conduit |
| 2 | 10116 | Inner Floor Side Member |
| 3 | W5202A2-S60 | Adjuster Nut |
| 4 | 2K390 | Rear Parking Brake Cable Adjuster |
| 5 | 2A635 | RH Parking Brake Rear Cable and Conduit |

**Fig. 76 Remove the left-hand cowl side trim panel, then pull the carpet back to expose the cable and conduit**

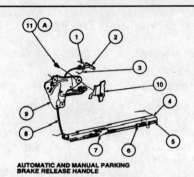

AUTOMATIC AND MANUAL PARKING
BRAKE RELEASE HANDLE

| Item | Part Number | Description |
|------|-------------|-------------|
| 1 | 391115-S411 | Clip |
| 2 | 2780 | Parking Brake Release Handle |
| 3 | 04320 | Instrument Panel |
| 4 | 11135 | Front Floor Pan |
| 5 | 2A635 | Parking Brake Rear Cable and Conduit |
| 6 | 2A709 | Cable Connector |
| 7 | 2K390 | Rear Parking Brake Cable Adjuster |
| 8 | 2853 | Front Parking Brake Cable and Conduit |
| 9 | 2780 | Parking Brake Control |
| 10 | 02344 | Cowl Side Trim Panel |
| 11 | N800377-S2 | Bolt (3 Req'd) |
| A | — | Tighten to 23-35 N·m (17-26 Lb-Ft) |

86879086

**Fig. 77 Front parking brake cable and related components**

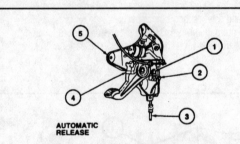

AUTOMATIC
RELEASE

| Item | Part Number | Description |
|------|-------------|-------------|
| 1 | — | Clevis (Part of 2780) |
| 2 | — | Cable End (Part of 2853) |
| 3 | 2853 | Front Parking Brake Cable and Conduit |
| 4 | 15A851 | Parking Brake Signal Switch and Bracket |
| 5 | 2780 | Parking Brake Control |

86879087

**Fig. 78 Pulling the front parking brake cable assembly down through the floorpan hole**

### Rear Cable

#### LEFT SIDE

♦ **See Figure 79**

1. Raise and safely support the vehicle.
2. Remove the parking brake cable adjusting nut.
3. Remove the rear cable end fitting from the front cable connector.
4. If equipped with drum brakes, remove the wheel and tire, then remove the brake drum.
5. Disconnect the cable from the parking brake actuating lever. On vehicles equipped with drum brakes, use a ½ in. (13mm) box-end wrench to depress the conduit retaining prongs, then remove the cable end

pronged fitting from the backing plate. On vehicles equipped with disc brakes, remove the E-clip from the conduit end of the fitting at the caliper, then remove the cable from the caliper.

6. Push the plastic snap-in grommet rearward to disconnect it from the inner floor side rail bracket.

7. Remove the pronged connector from the parking park adjuster bracket, then remove the cable assembly.

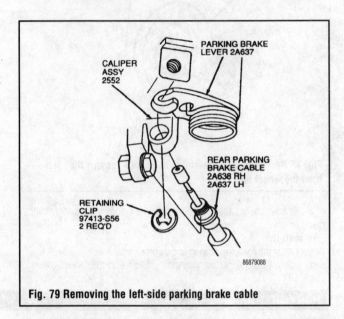

CALIPER ASSY 2552

PARKING BRAKE LEVER 2A637

REAR PARKING BRAKE CABLE 2A638 RH 2A637 LH

RETAINING CLIP 97413-S56 2 REQ'D

86879088

**Fig. 79 Removing the left-side parking brake cable**

**To install:**

8. Insert the cable through the inner floor side rail bracket and cable adjuster. Make sure the pronged connector is securely attached to the adjuster.

9. Seat the plastic snap-in grommet inside the inner floor side rail bracket.

➡**The left-side parking brake rear cable must be located over the right-side parking brake rear cable and conduit.**

10. For vehicles equipped with drum brakes, insert the parking brake and conduit end into the support plate, then push the pronged cable end into the parking brake support plate hole. Make sure the prongs are locked into place.

11. Connect the brake cable to the parking brake actuating lever.

12. For vehicles equipped with disc brakes, insert the parking brake rear cable and conduit end into the caliper, then install the E-clip.

13. Attach the parking brake rear cable and conduit end to the parking brake lever.

14. Attach the parking brake rear cable and conduit to the parking brake front cable and conduit.

15. If equipped with drum brakes, install the drum, followed by the wheel and tire assembly.

16. Install the parking brake cable adjusting nut. Adjust the parking brake, as described later in this section.

17. Lower the vehicle, then check the parking brake for proper operation.

#### RIGHT SIDE

1. Raise and safely support the vehicle.
2. Remove the parking brake cable adjuster nut.
3. Use a ½ in. (13mm) box wrench to remove the conduit retainer prongs, then remove the cable from the frame inner floor side rail bracket.
4. If equipped with drum brakes, remove the rear wheel and drum assembly.
5. Disconnect the brake cable from the parking brake actuating lever.

On drum brake vehicles, use a ½ in. (13mm) box end wrench to depress the conduit retaining prongs, then remove the cable end pronged fitting from the backing plate. On disc brake vehicles, remove the E-clip from the conduit end of the fitting at the caliper, then remove the cable and conduit from the caliper.

6. On Taurus/Sable sedans, perform the following:

   a. Remove the brake pressure control valve bracket at the control arm.

   b. Remove the cable retaining screw and clip from the lower control arm.

   c. Remove the screw from the cable bracket at the crossmember.

   d. Remove the entire right-side rear parking brake cable assembly.

7. On station wagons, perform the following:

   a. Remove the cable retaining clip and screw from each lower control arm.

   b. Remove the cable clip retaining screw from the lower control inner mounting bracket.

8. Remove the parking brake cable assembly from the vehicle.

**To install:**

9. Insert the cable and conduit into the opening in the inner floor side rail bracket and threaded end of the cable and conduit in the cable adjuster, then start the adjuster nut on the threads. Make sure the pronged fitting is pressed into the inner floor side rail bracket and securely locked into place.

10. Route the right-side parking brake rear cable and conduit under the left-side parking brake rear cable/conduit and rear control arm.

11. Secure the cable and conduit end into the parking brake lever.

12. For vehicles equipped with disc brakes, insert the parking brake cable and conduit end into the caliper, then install the E-clip.

13. For vehicles equipped with drum brakes, insert the cable and conduit end pronged fitting into the support plate, then lock securely into place.

14. Attach the brake hose clip, then install the nut and screw, then tighten to 6–8 ft. lbs. (8–11 Nm).

15. On station wagons, install the parking brake rear cable and conduit retaining clips to the rear suspension arm. On sedans, install the parking brake rear cable/conduit screw and clip, then tighten the screws to 6–8 ft. lbs. (8–11 Nm).

16. Position the cable and conduit assembly to the lower control arm, then tighten the retaining screw to 4–6 ft. lbs. (6–8 Nm).

17. On sedans, if applicable, fasten the brake load sensor proportioning valve to the control arm.

18. If equipped with drum brakes, install the rear wheel and drum assembly.

19. Install the parking brake cable adjuster nut.

20. Adjust the parking brake. following the procedure later in this section. Carefully lower the vehicle, then check the parking brake for proper operation.

## ADJUSTMENT

### Vehicles With Drum Brakes

1. Make sure the parking brake is fully released. Place the transaxle in the **N** position.

2. Raise and safely support the vehicle. Working in front of the left rear wheel, tighten the adjusting nut against the cable equalizer, causing a rear wheel brake drag. Then, loosen the adjusting nut until the rear brakes are fully released. There should be no brake drag. Refer to the accompanying figure for adjusting nut location.

3. If the brake cables were replaced, stroke the parking brake with about 100 lbs. (445 Nm) of pedal effort several times, then release the control and repeat Step 2.

4. Check for operation of the parking brake with the vehicle supported and the parking brake fully released. If there is any slack in the cables, or if the rear brakes drag when the wheels are turned, adjust as required.

5. Lower the vehicle.

### Vehicles With Disc Brakes

1. Make sure the parking brake is fully released.

2. Raise and safely support the vehicle.

3. Tighten the adjusting nut against the cable adjuster bracket until there is less than ¹⁄₁₆ in. (1.6mm) movement of either rear parking brake lever at the caliper. Refer to the accompanying figure for adjusting nut location.

4. If the brake cables were replaced, stroke the parking brake with about 100 lbs. (445 Nm) of pedal effort several times, then release the control and repeat Step 3.

5. Lower the vehicle, then check operation of the parking brake.

## Brake Pedal

### REMOVAL & INSTALLATION

♦ **See Figure 80**

1. Fully release the parking brake. Raise and safely support the vehicle.

2. Remove all tension from the rear cables by backing off the adjusting nut from the equalizer or adjuster.

3. Lower the vehicle. If equipped, disconnect the vacuum hose from the parking brake release control motor.

4. Disconnect the release cable from the parking brake control release arm. Remove the release cable grommet from the parking brake control.

5. Disengage the wiring connector from the parking brake warning indicator switch. Remove the cable from the clevis at the brake control.

6. Remove the push pin from the cowl side trim panel.

7. Remove the conduit retainer from the control assembly by using a ½ in. (13mm) box-end wrench to press the retaining prongs.

8. Remove the three bolts and one push pin retaining the control assembly to the cowl side panel. Remove the control assembly from the vehicle.

**To install:**

9. Position the control assembly in the vehicle. Fit the cable through its mounting hole, then press the pronged retainer in place. Make sure the prongs are locked securely into place.

10. Connect the cable to the control assembly. Install the retaining bolts and push pin. Tighten the retaining bolts to 17–26 ft. lbs. (23–35 Nm).

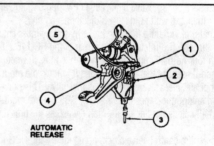

AUTOMATIC RELEASE

| Item | Part Number | Description |
|------|-------------|-------------|
| 1 | — | Clevis (Part of 2780) |
| 2 | — | Cable End (Part of 2853) |
| 3 | 2853 | Front Parking Brake Cable and Conduit |
| 4 | 15A851 | Parking Brake Signal Switch and Bracket |
| 5 | 2760 | Parking Brake Control |

86879090

**Fig. 80 Parking brake pedal control assembly**

11. If equipped, connect the vacuum hose to the parking brake release control motor.

12. Connect the release cable to the parking brake control release arm. Install the release cable grommet to the parking brake control.

13. Engage the wiring connector to the warning switch and bracket.

14. Raise and safely support the vehicle. Adjust the parking brake assembly, as outlined earlier in this section.

15. Carefully lower the vehicle, then check the parking brake assembly for proper operation.

## ANTI-LOCK BRAKE SYSTEM

### Description

Beginning in 1990, the Taurus and Sable (except 2.5L engine) were available with Anti-lock Braking System (ABS) as an option on vehicles with four wheel disc brakes. The system was standard on the Taurus SHO starting in 1990. The system prevents wheel lock-up by automatically modulating the brake pressure during emergency stopping. The system controls each front brake separately and the rear brakes as an axle set. During ABS operation, the driver will sense brake pedal pulsation, along with a slight up-and-down movement in the pedal height and a clicking sound; this is normal.

### Component Operation

The ABS system consists of the following major components.

#### POWER BRAKE BOOSTER

The power brake booster is a self-contained unit that is mounted on the engine compartment side of the dash panel and uses engine intake manifold vacuum and atmospheric pressure for its power. If it becomes damaged or stops functioning properly, it must be replaced as an assembly, except for the power brake booster check valve.

#### BRAKE MASTER CYLINDER

The brake master cylinder is a tandem master cylinder. The primary (rear) circuit feeds the right-hand front and left-hand rear brakes. The secondary (front) circuit feeds the left-hand front and right-hand rear brakes. The master cylinder is serviced as a complete assembly.

#### HYDRAULIC CONTROL UNIT

The anti-lock brake Hydraulic Control Unit (HCU) is located in the front of the engine compartment on the left-hand side of the vehicle. If consists of the brake pressure control valve block assembly, pump motor, and the master cylinder filler cap with fluid level indicator assembly.

During normal braking, fluid from the brake master cylinder enters the HCU reservoir through two inlet ports at the rear of the HCU. The fluid then passes through four normally open inlet valves, one to each wheel. If the ABS control module senses that a wheel is about to lock, the module activates the appropriate inlet valve which closes that valve. This prevents any more fluid from entering the affected brake. The ABS control module then opens the normally closed outlet valve which decreases the pressure trapped in the line.

The brake pressure control valve block, pump motor and HCU reservoir are serviced separately. Other than seals and gaskets, no internal parts can be serviced.

#### ANTI-LOCK BRAKE (ABS) CONTROL MODULE

The Anti-lock Brake System (ABS) control module is located on the front right-hand side, next to the windshield washer reservoir for all vehicles except the SHO. On the Taurus SHO, it is mounted on top of the front left brake anti-lock sensor.

It is an on-board diagnostic, non-serviceable unit consisting of two microprocessors and the necessary circuitry for their operation. The module monitors system operation during normal driving, as well as during anti-lock braking. Under normal driving conditions, the ABS control module produces short test pulses to the solenoid valves that check the electrical system without any mechanical reaction. Impending wheel lock conditions trigger signals from the ABS control module that open and close the appropriate solenoid valves. This results in moderate pulsations in the brake pedal.

If brake pedal travel exceeds a preset dimension determined by the anti-lock brake pedal sensor switch setting, the ABS control module will send a signal to the pump motor to turn on and provide high pressure to the brake system. Each time the vehicle is driven, as soon as the speed reaches 42 mph (70 km/h), the ABS control module turns on the pump motor for about ½ second (a mechanical noise will be heard; this is normal). When the pump motor starts to run, a gradual rise in brake pedal height will be noticed. The rise will continue until the sensor switch closes, and the pump motor will shut off until the brake pedal travel again exceeds the anti-lock brake pedal sensor switch setting.

Most malfunctions to the anti-lock braking system will be stored as a Diagnostic Trouble Code (DTC) in the keep-alive memory of the ABS control module.

#### ANTI-LOCK BRAKE SENSOR

Four sets of variable-reluctance brake anti-lock sensors and sensor indicators which determine the rotational speed of each wheel are used in the ABS system. The sensors operate on magnetic induction principle. As the teeth on the ABS sensor indicators rotate past the sensors, a signal proportional to the speed of rotation is generated and sent to the ABS control module.

The front brake anti-lock sensors are attached to the front wheel spindles. The front brake anti-lock sensor indicators are pressed into the outer CV-joints. The rear brake anti-lock sensors are attached to the right and left-hand rear disc brake adapters. The rear brake anti-lock sensor indicators are pressed into the wheel hub assemblies.

#### BRAKE PEDAL TRAVEL SWITCH

The brake pedal travel switch monitors brake pedal travel, then sends this information to the ABS control module through the wire harness. The brake pedal sensor switch adjustment is critical to pedal feel during ABS cycling. The switch is mounted in a hole in the right-hand side of the brake pedal support bracket, and to a pin on the speed control dump valve adapter bracket.

The switch is normally closed. When brake pedal travel exceeds the switch setting during an anti-lock stop, the ABS control module senses that the switch is open and grounds the pump motor relay coil. This energizes the relay and turns the pump motor on. When the pump motor is running, the HCU reservoir is filled with high pressure brake fluid, and the brake pedal will be pushed up until the brake pedal travel switch closes.

When the switch closes, the pump motor is turned off; the brake pedal will drop some with each ABS control cycle until the switch opens again and the pump motor is turned on again. This minimizes pedal feedback during ABS cycling. If the switch is not adjusted properly or is not electrically connected, it will result in objectionable pedal feel during ABS stops.

### Anti-Lock Brake System Service

#### PRECAUTIONS

Failure to observe the following precautions may result in system damage.

• Before servicing any high pressure component, be sure to discharge the hydraulic pressure from the system.

- Do not allow the brake fluid to contact any of the electrical connectors.
- Use care when opening the bleeder screws due to the high pressures available from the accumulator.

## RELIEVING SYSTEM PRESSURE

Before servicing any components which contain high pressure, it is mandatory that the hydraulic pressure in the system be discharged. To discharge the system, turn the ignition **OFF** and pump the brake pedal a minimum of 20 times until an increase in pedal force is clearly felt.

## Hydraulic Control Unit (HCU)

The anti-lock brake Hydraulic Control Unit (HCU) is located in the front of the engine compartment on the left-hand side of the vehicle. It attaches to a bracket that is mounted to the left-hand front inside rail inside the engine compartment. The battery and battery tray sit atop the hydraulic control bracket.

## REMOVAL & INSTALLATION

### ◗ See Figures 81 and 82

1. On all vehicles, except Taurus SHO, disconnect the battery cables, then remove the battery from the vehicle. Remove the battery tray. Remove the three plastic push pins holding the acid shield to the HCU mounting bracket, then remove the acid shield.
2. On Taurus SHO, it is only necessary to disconnect the negative battery cable and remove the electronic control unit and its mounting bracket from the top of the HCU mounting bracket.

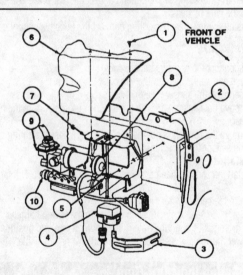

| Item | Part Number | Description |
|---|---|---|
| 1 | N805636S | Push Pin (3 Req'd) |
| 2 | 16138 | Radiator Support |
| 3 | 2C303 | Anti-Lock Brake Pump Bracket |
| 4 | — | Pump Relay (Part of 2C303) |
| 5 | N606688S56 | Bolt (3 Req'd) |
| 6 | 2C314 | Acid Shield |
| 7 | 2C304 | Anti-Lock Brake Hydraulic Control Bracket |
| 8 | 2C256 | Pump Motor |
| 9 | 2C246 | Hydraulic Control Unit Reservoir |
| 10 | 2C266 | Brake Pressure Control Valve Block |

86879091

**Fig. 81 HCU location and related components—except SHO vehicles**

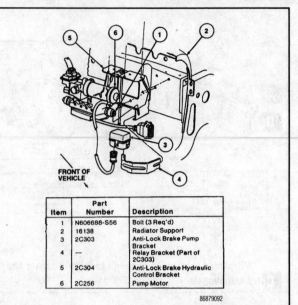

| Item | Part Number | Description |
|---|---|---|
| 1 | N606688-S56 | Bolt (3 Req'd) |
| 2 | 16138 | Radiator Support |
| 3 | 2C303 | Anti-Lock Brake Pump Bracket |
| 4 | — | Relay Bracket (Part of 2C303) |
| 5 | 2C304 | Anti-Lock Brake Hydraulic Control Bracket |
| 6 | 2C256 | Pump Motor |

86879092

**Fig. 82 HCU location and related components—SHO vehicles only**

3. Unfasten the 19-pin connector from the HCU to the wiring harness, then detach the 4-pin connector from the HCU to the pump motor relay.
4. Remove the two lines from the inlet ports and the four lines from the outlet ports of the HCU. Plug each port to prevent brake fluid from spilling onto the paint and wiring.

➡**The nut on the front of the HCU also retains the relay mounting bracket.**

5. Remove the three nuts retaining the HCU assembly to the mounting bracket, then remove the assembly from the vehicle.

**To install:**

➡**Attach the relay mounting bracket with the nut on the front of the hydraulic control unit reservoir.**

6. Position the HCU reservoir assembly into the mounting bracket, then secure using the three retaining nuts. Tighten the nuts to 12–18 ft. lbs. (16–24 Nm).
7. Connect the four lines to the outlet ports on the side of the HCU reservoir and the two tubes to the inlet ports on the rear of the HCU reservoir, then tighten to 10–18 ft. lbs. (14–24 Nm).
8. Fasten the 19-pin connector to the harness, then attach the 4-pin connector to the pump motor relay.
9. On all vehicles except SHO, install the acid shield and the three plastic push pins holding the acid shield to the HCU bracket. Install the battery tray, then install the battery and connect the cables.
10. On the SHO, install the anti-lock brake control module to the top of the anti-lock brake control module mounting bracket. Connect the negative battery cable.
11. Bleed the brake system, then check for fluid leaks.

## Wheel Sensors

## REMOVAL & INSTALLATION

### Front

### ◗ See Figure 83

1. Disconnect the negative battery cable.
2. Disengage the sensor connector located in the engine compartment.
3. For the right front sensor, remove the two plastic push studs to

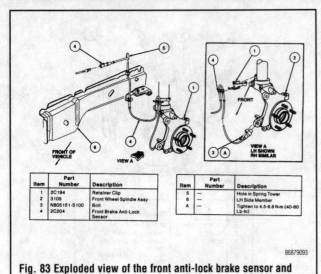

| Item | Part Number | Description |
|------|-------------|-------------|
| 1 | 2C194 | Retainer Clip |
| 2 | 3105 | Front Wheel Spindle Assy |
| 3 | N805151-S100 | Bolt |
| 4 | 2C204 | Front Brake Anti-Lock Sensor |

| Item | Part Number | Description |
|------|-------------|-------------|
| 5 | — | Hole in Spring Tower |
| 6 | — | LH Side Member |
| A | — | Tighten to 4.5-6.8 N·m (40-60 Lb-In) |

86879093

**Fig. 83 Exploded view of the front anti-lock brake sensor and related components**

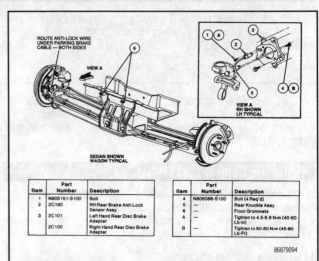

| Item | Part Number | Description |
|------|-------------|-------------|
| 1 | N805151-S100 | Bolt |
| 2 | 2C190 | RH Rear Brake Anti-Lock Sensor Assy |
| 3 | 2C101 | Left Hand Rear Disc Brake Adapter |
|  | 2C100 | Right Hand Rear Disc Brake Adapter |

| Item | Part Number | Description |
|------|-------------|-------------|
| 4 | N805086-S100 | Bolt (4 Req'd) |
| 5 | — | Rear Knuckle Assy |
| 6 | — | Floor Grommets |
| A | — | Tighten to 4.5-6.8 N·m (40-60 Lb-In) |
| B | — | Tighten to 60-80 N·m (45-60 Lb-Ft) |

86879094

**Fig. 84 Rear anti-lock brake sensor location—sedan shown, station wagon similar**

loosen the front section of the splash shield in the wheel well. For the left front sensor, remove the two plastic push studs to loosen the rear section of the splash shield.

4. Thread the sensor wire(s) through the holes in the fender apron. For the right front sensor, remove the two retaining clips behind the splash shield.

5. Raise and safely support the vehicle. Remove the wheel and tire assembly.

6. Disengage the sensor wire grommets at the height sensor bracket and from the retainer clip on the shock strut just above the spindle.

7. Loosen the sensor retaining screw, then remove the sensor assembly from the front knuckle.

**To install:**

8. Align the sensor with its mounting holes on the front wheel spindle. Tighten the retaining screws to 40–60 inch lbs. (4.5–6.8 Nm).

9. Install the grommets at the height sensor bracket, then install the retainer clip at the shock absorber.

10. Thread the wire through the holes in the fender apron. For the right-hand sensor only, install the retainer clips. Secure the splash shield with the plastic push studs.

11. Engage the sensor connector to the wiring harness from the engine compartment.

12. Connect the negative battery cable.

**Rear**

▶ See Figure 84

### EXCEPT STATION WAGON

1. Disconnect the negative battery cable.
2. Remove the rear seat and seat back insulation.
3. Disengage the sensor wire from the harness, then tie one end of a string or wire to the sensor connector and the other end to the rear seat sheet metal bracket.
4. Push the sensor wire grommet and connector through the floorpan, drawing the string or wire with the sensor connector.
5. Raise and safely support the vehicle.
6. Disconnect the string or wire from the sensor from underneath the vehicle.
7. Disconnect the routing clips from the suspension arms, then unfasten the sensor retaining bolts from the rear brake adapters and remove the sensor from the vehicle.

**To install:**

8. Insert the sensor into the hole in the right or left-hand rear disc

brake adapter, then install the retaining bolt. Tighten to 40–60 inch lbs. (4.6–6.8 Nm).

9. Install the sensor wire routing clips to the suspension arms.

10. Attach string or wire to the new sensor connector, then pull the sensor connector through the hole in the floor pan using the string or wire.

11. Install the sensor wire grommet into the hole in the floorpan.

12. Remove the string or wire, then connect the rear brake anti-lock sensor to the wire harness.

13. Install the rear seat back, then connect the negative battery cable.

### STATION WAGON

1. Disconnect the negative battery cable.
2. Raise and safely support the vehicle.
3. Disengage the sensor electrical connector from the harness.
4. Remove the sensor wire with the attached grommet from the hole in the floorpan.
5. Remove the routing clips, then unfasten the sensor retaining bolt and remove the sensor from the vehicle.

**To install:**

6. Install the sensor, then secure using the retaining bolt. Tighten the bolt to 40–60 inch lbs. (4.6–6.8 Nm).

7. Route the sensor wire, then install the clips.

8. Engage the sensor electrical connector to the wiring harness, then push the grommet through the hole in the floorpan and into position.

9. Lower the vehicle, then connect the negative battery cable.

## Rear Speed Indicator Ring

### REMOVAL & INSTALLATION

▶ See Figure 85

1. Raise and safely support the vehicle. Remove the tire and wheel assembly.

2. Remove the caliper, rotor and rear hub assemblies.

3. Position the hub assembly in an arbor press, then press the hub out of the speed sensor ring.

**To install:**

4. Position the rear speed sensor ring over the hub.

5. Using a flat piece of steel or similar tool, press the ring down until it is flush with the top of the hub.

6. Install the rear hub, rotor and caliper. Install the wheel and tire assembly, then carefully lower the vehicle.

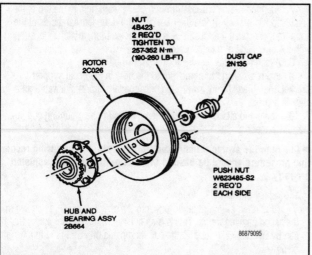

Fig. 85 After the hub assembly is removed, place it in an arbor press, then press the hub out of the speed sensor ring

## Front Speed Indicator Ring

REMOVAL & INSTALLATION

▶ **See Figures 86, 87, 88, and 89**

1. Raise and safely support the vehicle.
2. Remove the outboard CV-joint. For details, please refer to the procedure in Section 7 of this manual.
3. Position Front Sensor Ring Remover/Replacer T88P–20202–A or equivalent, in a press. Position the CV-joint on the tool.
4. With the CV-joint positioned on the tool, use the press ram to apply pressure to the joint, then remove the speed indicator ring.

**To install:**

5. With Front Sensor Ring Remover/Replacer T88P-20202-A or equivalent positioned on the press, place the sensor ring on the tool.
6. Position the CV-joint in the Front Sensor Remover/Replacer, then allow the joint to rest on the ring.

➡**Be very careful not to damage the sensor during installation. If the teeth on the sensor are damaged, brake performance will be affected.**

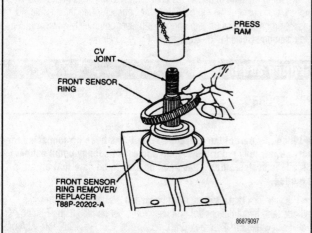

Fig. 86 With the CV-joint positioned on the tool, use the press ram to apply pressure to the joint, then remove the speed indicator ring

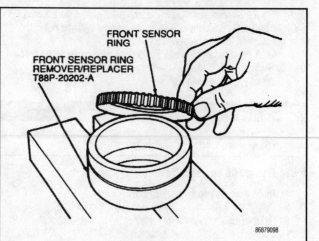

Fig. 87 With Front Sensor Ring Remover/Replacer T88P-20202-A or equivalent positioned on the press, place the sensor ring on the tool

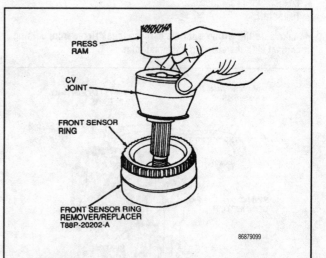

Fig. 88 Position the CV-joint in the Front Sensor Remover/Replacer, then allow the joint to rest on the ring

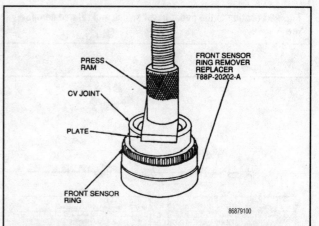

Fig. 89 With the CV-joint installed in the tool, place a steel plate across the CV-joint back face. Press the CV-joint until the joint bottoms out in the tool; at that point, the ring will be properly installed

7. With the CV-joint installed in the tool, place a steel plate across the CV-joint back face. Press the CV-joint until the joint bottoms out in the tool; the ring will then be properly installed.

8. Install the outboard CV-joint. For details, please refer to the procedure in Section 7 of this manual.

9. Carefully lower the vehicle.

## Pedal Travel Switch

### REMOVAL & INSTALLATION

▶ **See Figures 90 and 91**

1. Disconnect the negative battery cable.

2. Detach the wiring harness lead at the switch connector.

3. Using a suitable prytool, carefully pry the connector's locator pins from the holes in the brake pedal support.

4. Unsnap the switch hook from the pin on the dump valve adapter bracket.

5. Using needlenose pliers, squeeze the tabs on the switch mounting clip, then push the clip through the hole in the pedal support bracket.

6. Remove the switch by feeding the switch harness through the hole in the top of the pedal support bracket.

**To install:**

➡ **Make sure the wiring from the harness is restricted from coming in contact with the steering universal joint.**

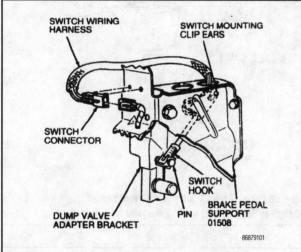

**Fig. 90 Location of the pedal travel switch and related components**

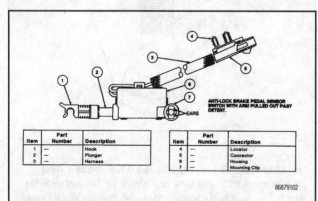

**Fig. 91 Pedal position switch with the arm pulled out**

7. Feed the switch harness through the forward hole in the top of the pedal support bracket. Route the harness around the left-hand side of the support, then install the locator pins to the holes in the brake pedal support with the open side of the connector facing the center of the vehicle.

8. Attach the switch connector to the wiring harness.

9. Insert a switch mounting clip to the hole in the pedal support bracket, then press firmly toward the brake pedal support sidewall until a click is heard.

10. Route and attach the switch, then make sure the mounting clip tabs are fully engaged.

➡ **Any time the switch it unhooked from the pin, the following resetting procedure should be used to make sure the switch is adjusted properly.**

11. Adjust the switch as follows:

a. Push the switch plunger fully into the switch housing as shown in the accompanying figure. This zeroes out the switch adjustment so that it can be automatically reset to the correct dimension during the following steps.

b. Slowly pull the arm back out of the switch housing past the detent point. At this point, it should be impossible to reattach the arm to the pin unless the brake pedal is forced down.

c. To complete the adjustment, press the brake pedal until the switch hook can be snapped onto the pin. Snap the hook onto the pin and pull the brake pedal back up to its normal at-rest position. This automatically sets the switch to the proper adjustment.

12. Connect the negative battery cable.

## Electronic Control Unit (ECU)/Anti-Lock Brake (ABS) Control Module

### REMOVAL & INSTALLATION

The ECU or ABS module is located on the front right side of the engine compartment next to the windshield washer bottle, except on Taurus SHO. On Taurus SHO it is mounted on the top of the front left brake anti-lock sensor.

1. Disconnect the negative battery cable.

2. Disengage the 55-pin connector from the ECU/ABS module. Unlock the connector by completely pulling up the lever. Move the top of the connector away from the ECU/ABS module until all terminals are clear, then pull the connector up out of the slots in the ECU/ABS module.

3. Remove the screws attaching the ECU/ABS module, then remove the ECU/ABS module from the vehicle.

4. Install in the reverse order of removal. Fasten the 55-pin connector by installing the bottom part of the connector into the slots in the ECU/ABS module and pushing the top portion of the connector into the module. To ensure proper installation, pull the locking lever completely down. Tighten the retaining screws to 15–20 inch lbs. (1.7–2.3 Nm).

## Filling and Bleeding

### PROCEDURE

➡ **When any part of the hydraulic system has been disconnected for service, air may enter the system and cause spongy pedal action. Bleed the system after it has been opened to be sure that all air is expelled.**

The anti-lock brake system must be bled in 2 steps; both the master cylinder and hydraulic control unit reservoir must be bled using Rotunda Anti-Lock Brake Breakout Box/Bleeding Adapter tool No. T90P–50–ALA or equivalent. If this procedure is not followed, air will be trapped in the hydraulic control unit, and will eventually lead to a spongy brake pedal.

1. Disconnect the 55-pin plug from the electronic control unit/ABS con-

trol module, then install Anti-Lock Brake Breakout Box/Bleeding Adapter tool No. T90P-50-ALA or equivalent to the wire harness 55-pin plug.

    a. Place the Bleed/Harness switch in the **BLEED** position.

    b. Turn the ignition to the **ON** position. At this point the red OFF light should come ON.

    c. Push the motor button on the adapter down to start the pump motor. The red OFF light will turn OFF, and the green ON light will turn ON. The pump motor will run for 60 seconds after the motor button is pushed. If the pump motor is to be turned off for any reason before the 60 seconds have elapsed, push the abort button to turn the pump motor off.

    d. After 20 seconds of pump motor operation, push and hold the valve button down. Hold the valve button down for 20 seconds, then release it.

    e. The pump motor will continue to run for an additional 20 seconds after the valve button is released.

2. The brake lines can now be bled in the normal fashion. Bleed the brake system by removing the rubber dust cap from the caliper fitting at the right rear of the vehicle. Place a suitable box wrench on the bleeder fitting and attach a rubber drain tube to the fitting. The end of the tube should fit snugly around the bleeder fitting. Submerge the other end of the tube in a container partially filled with clean brake fluid and loosen the fitting ¾ turn.

3. Have an assistant push the brake pedal down slowly through its full travel. Close the bleeder fitting and allow the pedal to slowly return to its full release position. Wait 5 seconds and repeat the procedure until no bubbles appear at the submerged end of the bleeder tube. Secure the bleeder fitting and remove the bleeder tube. Install the rubber dust cap on the bleeder fitting.

4. Repeat the bleeding procedure at the left front, left rear and right front (in that order). Refill the master cylinder reservoir after each caliper has been bled, and install the master cylinder cap and gasket. When brake bleeding is completed, the fluid level should be filled to the maximum level indicated on the reservoir.

5. Always make sure the disc brake pistons are returned to their normal positions by depressing the brake pedal several times until normal pedal travel is established. If the pedal feels spongy, repeat the bleeding procedure.

## Power Brake Booster

### REMOVAL & INSTALLATION

1. Disconnect the negative battery cable. Pump the brake pedal until all vacuum is removed from the booster. This will prevent the O-ring from being sucked into the booster during disassembly.

2. Disconnect the manifold vacuum hose from the booster check valve, and the electrical connector from the master cylinder reservoir cap.

3. Remove the brake lines from the primary and secondary outlet ports of the master cylinder, then remove the Hydraulic Control Unit (HCU) supply hose. Plug the ports and reservoir feed to prevent brake fluid from leaking onto paint and wiring.

4. Under the instrument panel, remove the stop light switch wiring connector from the switch. Disengage the pedal travel switch from the stud. Remove the hairpin retainer and outer nylon washer from the pedal pin. Slide the stop light switch off the brake pedal just far enough for the outer arm to clear the pin. Remove the switch.

5. Remove the booster-to-dash panel attaching nuts. Slide the bushing and booster pushrod off the brake pedal pin.

6. Move the booster forward until the booster studs clear the dash panel. Remove the booster and master cylinder assembly.

7. Place the booster and master cylinder assembly on a bench. Unfasten the 2 nuts attaching the master cylinder to the booster, then remove the master cylinder.

### To install:

8. Slide the master cylinder onto the booster studs. Make sure the O-ring is in place in the groove on the master cylinder and install the 2 attaching nuts. Tighten the nuts to 13–25 ft. lbs. (18–34 Nm).

9. Under the instrument panel, install the booster pushrod and bushing on the brake pedal pin. Fasten the booster to the dash panel with self-locking nuts. Tighten the nuts to 13–25 ft. lbs. (18–34 Nm).

10. Position the stop light switch so it straddles the booster pushrod with the switch slot towards the pedal blade, and with the hole just clearing the pin. Slide the switch completely onto the pin.

11. Install the outer nylon washer on the pin, then secure all parts to the pin with the hairpin retainer. Make sure the retainer is fully installed and locked over the pedal pin. Attach the stoplight switch wiring connector.

12. Install and adjust the pedal travel switch, as detailed earlier in this section.

13. Connect the brake lines to the master cylinder, then tighten to 10–18 ft. lbs. (14–24 Nm). Attach the HCU supply hose to the reservoir.

14. Connect the manifold vacuum hose to the booster check valve, then engage the electrical connector to the master cylinder reservoir cap.

15. Connect the negative battery cable, then bleed the brake system.

## BRAKE SPECIFICATIONS
All measurements in inches unless noted

| Year | Model | | Master Cylinder Bore | Brake Disc Original Thickness | Brake Disc Minimum Thickness | Brake Disc Maximum Runout | Brake Drum Diameter Original Inside Diameter | Brake Drum Diameter Max. Wear Limit | Brake Drum Diameter Maximum Machine Diameter | Minimum Lining Thickness Front | Minimum Lining Thickness Rear |
|---|---|---|---|---|---|---|---|---|---|---|---|
| 1986 | Taurus | 1 | 0.875 | NA | 0.896 | 0.002 | 8.86 | 8.93 | 8.92 | 0.125 | 0.030 |
| | Taurus | 2 | 0.875 | NA | 0.896 | 0.002 | 9.84 | 9.99 | 9.90 | 0.125 | 0.030 |
| | Sable | 1 | 0.875 | NA | 0.896 | 0.002 | 8.86 | 8.93 | 8.92 | 0.125 | 0.030 |
| | Sable | 2 | 0.875 | NA | 0.896 | 0.002 | 9.84 | 9.99 | 9.90 | 0.125 | 0.030 |
| 1987 | Taurus | 1 | 0.875 | NA | 0.896 | 0.002 | 8.86 | 8.93 | 8.92 | 0.125 | 0.030 |
| | Taurus | 2 | 0.875 | NA | 0.896 | 0.002 | 9.84 | 9.89 | 9.90 | 0.125 | 0.030 |
| | Sable | 1 | 0.875 | NA | 0.896 | 0.002 | 8.86 | 8.93 | 8.92 | 0.125 | 0.030 |
| | Sable | 2 | 0.875 | NA | 0.896 | 0.002 | 9.84 | 9.89 | 9.90 | 0.125 | 0.030 |
| 1988 | Taurus | 1 | 0.875 | NA | 0.896 | 0.002 | 8.86 | 8.93 | 8.92 | 0.125 | 0.030 |
| | Taurus | 2 | 0.875 | NA | 0.896 | 0.002 | 9.84 | 9.89 | 9.90 | 0.125 | 0.030 |
| | Sable | 1 | 0.875 | NA | 0.896 | 0.003 | 8.86 | 8.93 | 8.92 | 0.125 | 0.030 |
| | Sable | 2 | 0.875 | NA | 0.896 | 0.002 | 9.84 | 9.89 | 9.90 | 0.125 | 0.030 |
| 1989 | Taurus | 1 | 0.875 | NA | 0.896 | 0.002 | 8.86 | 8.93 | 8.92 | 0.125 | 0.030 |
| | Taurus | 2 | 0.875 | NA | 0.896 | 0.002 | 9.84 | 9.89 | 9.90 | 0.125 | 0.030 |
| | Taurus SHO | F | 0.875 | NA | 0.972 | 0.002 | - | - | - | 0.125 | 0.123 |
| | Taurus SHO | R | - | - | 0.900 | 0.002 | - | NA | - | - | 0.123 |
| 1990 | Sable | 1 | 0.875 | NA | 0.896 | 0.002 | 8.86 | 8.93 | 8.92 | 0.125 | 0.030 |
| | Sable | 2 | 0.875 | NA | 0.896 | 0.002 | 9.84 | 9.89 | 9.90 | 0.125 | 0.030 |
| | Taurus | 1 | 0.875 | NA | 0.972 | 0.002 | 8.86 | 8.93 | 8.92 | 0.125 | 0.030 |
| | Taurus SHO | 2 | 0.875 | NA | 0.972 | 0.002 | 9.84 | 9.89 | 9.90 | 0.125 | 0.030 |
| | Taurus SHO | R | - | - | 0.900 | 0.002 | - | - | - | 0.125 | 0.030 |
| 1991 | Sable | 1 | 0.875 | NA | 0.896 | 0.003 | 8.86 | 8.93 | 8.92 | 0.125 | 0.030 |
| | Taurus SHO | F | 1.000 | 1.024 | 0.997 | 0.002 | - | - | - | 0.125 | 0.123 |
| | Sable | R | - | 0.940 | 0.900 | 0.002 | - | 8 | - | - | 0.123 |
| 1992 | Sable | 1 | 0.875 | NA | 0.972 | 0.002 | 8.86 | 8.93 | 8.92 | 0.125 | 0.030 |
| | Taurus | 2 | 0.875 | NA | 0.972 | 0.002 | 9.84 | 9.89 | 9.90 | 0.125 | 0.030 |
| | Taurus SHO | 1 | 0.875 | NA | 0.972 | 0.002 | 8.86 | 8.93 | 8.92 | 0.125 | 0.030 |
| | Taurus SHO | 2 | 0.875 | NA | 0.972 | 0.002 | 9.84 | 9.89 | 9.90 | 0.125 | 0.030 |
| | Sable | F | 1.000 | 1.024 | 0.900 | 0.002 | - | - | - | 0.125 | 0.123 |
| | Sable | R | - | - | 0.900 | 0.002 | - | 8 | - | - | 0.123 |
| 1993 | Taurus | 1 | 0.875 | NA | 0.972 | 0.002 | 8.86 | 8.93 | 8.92 | 0.125 | 0.030 |
| | Taurus | 2 | 0.875 | NA | 0.972 | 0.002 | 9.84 | 9.89 | 9.90 | 0.125 | 0.030 |
| | Taurus SHO | 3 | 0.875 | NA | 0.972 | 0.002 | 8.86 | 8.93 | 8.92 | 0.125 | 0.030 |
| | Taurus SHO | 4 | - | - | 0.900 | 0.002 | - | - | - | 0.125 | 0.123 |
| | Sable | F | 1.000 | 1.024 | 0.974 | 0.003 | - | - | - | 0.125 | 0.030 |
| | Sable | R | - | - | 0.900 | 0.002 | - | 8 | - | - | 0.123 |
| 1994 | Taurus | | 1.000 | 0.940 | | 7 | | NA | 9 | 0.040 | 10 |
| | Taurus SHO | | 1.000 | | 6 | 7 | | NA | 9 | 0.040 | 0.123 |
| | Sable | F | 1.000 | 1.020 | 0.974 | 0.003 | - | 8 | 9 | 0.125 | 0.030 |

86879500

## BRAKE SPECIFICATIONS
All measurements in inches unless noted

| Year | Model | | Master Cylinder Bore | Brake Disc Original Thickness | Brake Disc Minimum Thickness | Brake Disc Maximum Runout | Brake Drum Diameter Original Inside Diameter | Brake Drum Diameter Max. Wear Limit | Brake Drum Diameter Maximum Machine Diameter | Minimum Lining Thickness Front | Minimum Lining Thickness Rear |
|---|---|---|---|---|---|---|---|---|---|---|---|
| 1994 | Sable | R | - | 0.940 5 | 0.900 | 0.002 | - | NA | - | 0.040 | 0.123 10 |
| 1995 | Taurus | | 1.000 | | | | 8 | NA | 8 | | |
| | Taurus SHO | | 1.000 | 0.940 5 | 0.900 6 | 0.002 7 | 7 | | | 0.040 | 0.123 9 |
| | Sable | R | - | | | | 8 | | | | 0.030 |
| | Sable | R | - | 0.940 | 0.900 | 0.002 | 8 | NA | 4 | - | 0.030 |

NOTE: Follow specifications stamped on rotor or drum if figures differ from those in this chart.

NA - Not Available
F - Front
R - Rear
1 — Sedan
2 — Wagon
3 — Except rear disc
4 — With rear disc
5 — Front: 1.020 / Rear: 0.940
6 — Front: 0.974 / Rear: 0.500
7 — Front: 0.003 / Rear: 0.002
8 — Sedan: 8.85 / Wagon: 9.84
9 — Sedan: 8.91 / Wagon: 9.90
10 — With disc brakes: 0.123 / With drum brakes: 0.030

86879501

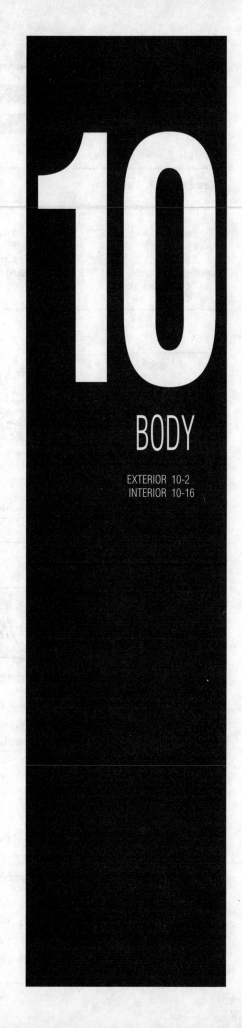

10

BODY

EXTERIOR 10-2
INTERIOR 10-16

## EXTERIOR

### Doors

#### REMOVAL & INSTALLATION

▶ **See Figures 1, 2 and 3**

1. Support the door using Rotunda Door Rack 103-00027 or an equivalent suitable tool.
2. Remove the hinge attaching bolts and nuts from the door, then remove the door.
3. If equipped, disengage the window regulator wiring harness connector from the door by removing the trim cap, loosening the screw, then separating the connector halves.

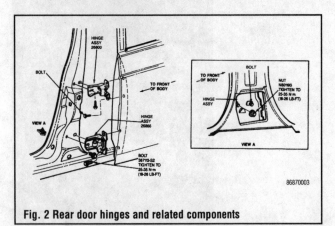

**Fig. 1 Front door hinges and related components**

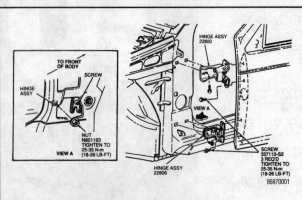

**Fig. 2 Rear door hinges and related components**

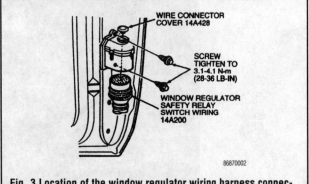

**Fig. 3 Location of the window regulator wiring harness connector and cover**

4. If the door is to be replaced, transfer the following components to the new door if they are in usable condition: trim panel, watershield, outside moldings, clips, window regulators and the door latch components.
   **To install:**
5. Position the door hinges, then partially tighten the bolts.
6. Align the door, then tighten the bolts securely to 18–26 ft. lbs. (25–35 Nm).
7. If disconnected, engage the wiring harness connector. Tighten the screw to 28–36 inch lbs. (3.1–4.1 Nm), then install the wire connector cover.

#### ADJUSTMENT

##### Door Alignment

▶ **See Figures 1 and 2**

The door hinges provide sufficient adjustment to correct most door misalignment conditions. The holes of the hinge and/or the hinge attaching points are enlarged or elongated to provide for hinge and door alignment.

➡ **Do not cover up a poor door alignment with a door latch striker plate adjustment.**

1. Determine which hinge bolts and nuts must be loosened to move the door in the desired direction.
2. Loosen the hinge bolts and nuts just enough to permit movement of the door with a padded pry bar.
3. Move the door the distance estimated to be necessary. Tighten the hinge bolts and nuts to 18–26 ft. lbs. (25–35 Nm), then check the door fit to make sure there is no bind or interference with the adjacent panel.
4. Repeat the operation until the desired fit is obtained, then check the striker plate alignment for proper door closing.

##### Door Latch Striker

▶ **See Figures 4 and 5**

➡ **Adjust the door latch striker after the door is properly aligned. Refer to the procedure located earlier in this section. Do not adjust the door latch striker to correct door sag.**

The latch striker is moved vertically and horizontally to align the striker and the latch. The striker will move 0.25 in. (6.3mm) in any direction on the B-pillar. The striker must be shimmed to move fore and aft to provide striker clearance.

The latch striker should be shimmed to attain the clearance shown between the striker and the latch. To check this clearance:

1. Clean the latch jaws and striker area, then apply a thin layer of dark grease to the striker.

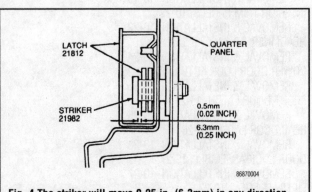

**Fig. 4 The striker will move 0.25 in. (6.3mm) in any direction on the B-pillar**

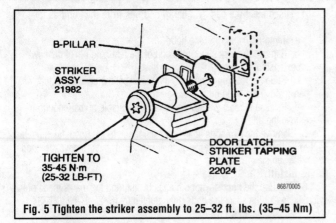

Fig. 5 Tighten the striker assembly to 25–32 ft. lbs. (35–45 Nm)

2. Open and close the door to produce a measurable pattern on the latch striker.

3. Using Torx® Drive Bit Set D79P-2100-T or equivalent, reposition the striker as required to ensure easy and secure door closure. Install no more than one shim between the striker and B-pillar to adjust fore and aft clearance.

4. Tighten the striker assembly to 25–32 ft. lbs. (35–45 Nm).

## Hood

### REMOVAL & INSTALLATION

▶ See Figures 6 thru 12

### ✳✳ CAUTION

**Do not heat or try to disassemble the hood gas supports. The supports are gas charged and will explode if heated or disassembled.**

➡ Due to its size and weight, hood removal and installation should be performed with an assistant.

1. Open and support the hood in the fully open position.
2. Mark the hood hinge locations on the hood for installation purposes.
3. Protect the body with covers to prevent damage to the paint.

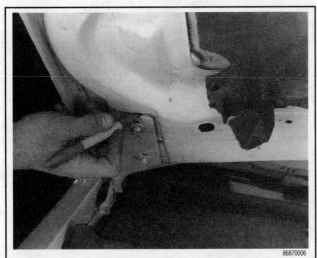

Fig. 6 Scribe the hood hinge locations on the hood for installation purposes

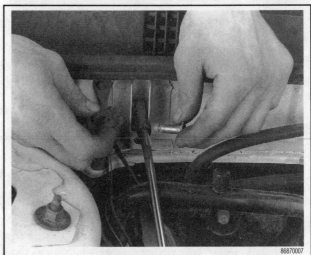

Fig. 7 Remove the lock clip on the end of the retaining pin at the cowl top extension, then . . .

Fig. 8 . . . remove the end of the hood lift

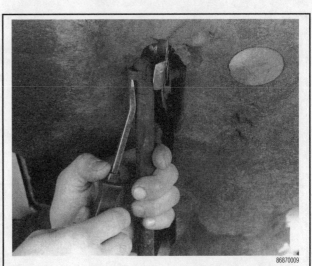

Fig. 9 Using a suitable pry bar, release the lock clip on the other end of the hood lift, then . . .

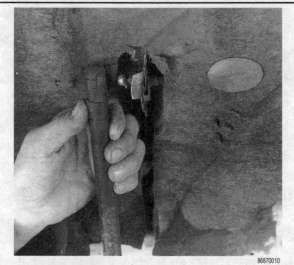

**Fig. 10 . . . remove the hood lift/gas cylinder from the hood**

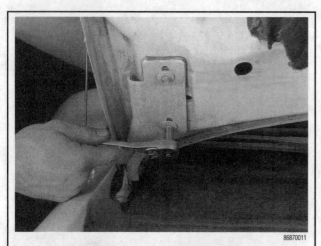

**Fig. 11 Unfasten the two hinge-to-hood bolts, being careful not to let the hood slip when the bolts are removed, then remove the hood from the vehicle**

4. Disconnect the gas cylinders/hood lifts from the hood as follows:

a. Temporarily support the hood.

b. Remove the lock clip on the end of the retaining pin at the cowl top extension.

c. Slide the retaining clip from the bracket at the cowl top extension, then remove the hood lift.

d. Release the lock clip by prying with a suitable prybar enough to remove the lift.

5. Remove the two bolts attaching each hinge to the hood, taking care not to let the hood slip when the bolts are removed, then remove the hood from the vehicle.

**To install:**

6. Position the hood-to-hood hinges by aligning the marks made previously. Install the attaching bolts, then tighten to 16–25 ft. lbs. (22–34 Nm). Remove the body covers.

7. Adjust the hood for even fit between the fenders and for a flush fit with the front of the fenders.

8. Adjust the hood for a flush fit with the top of the cowl and the fenders.

9. Install the gas cylinder/hood lifts to the hood as follows:

a. Position the hole at the end of the hood lift in the retaining bracket on the cowl top extension.

b. Insert the retaining pin, then install the lock clip on the end of the pin.

c. Make sure the lock clip is in place on the hood lift. Connect the opposite end of the hood lift to the ball stud on the hood.

10. Adjust the hood latch, if necessary.

## ADJUSTMENT

### Hood

♦ **See Figure 13**

The hood can be adjusted fore-and-aft and side-to-side by loosening two hood-to-hinge attaching bolts at each hinge. Then, reposition the hood as required and tighten the hood-to-hinge attaching bolts. A 0.10–0.22 in. (2.5–5.5 Nm) margin should be kept between the hood and front fenders. Always use protective fender covers.

To raise or lower the rear of the hood, loosen the hood hinge pivot nut. The pivot can now move up or down. Raise or lower the hood as necessary to obtain a flush condition at the rear of the hood with the front fenders. Then, tighten the hood hinge pivot nut to 17–25 ft. lbs. (22–34 Nm).

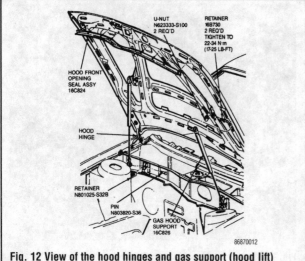

**Fig. 12 View of the hood hinges and gas support (hood lift) mountings**

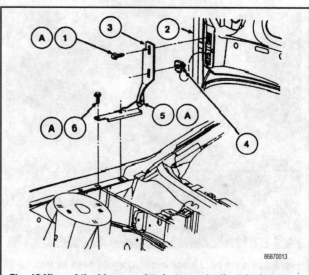

**Fig. 13 View of the hinge used to fasten and adjust the hood**

## Hood Latch

Before adjusting the hood latch mechanism, make certain that the hood is properly aligned. The hood latch can be moved from side-to-side to align with the opening in the hood inner panel.

Adjust the latch up and down to obtain a flush fit with the front fenders.

1. Loosen the hood latch attaching bolts in the radiator support until they are just loose enough to move the hood latch from side-to-side.

2. Move the latch from side-to-side to align it with the opening in the hood.

3. Loosen the locknuts on the two hood bumpers, then lower the bumpers.

4. Move the hood latch up and down as required to obtain a flush fit between the top of hood and the front fenders when upward pressure is applied to the front of the hood. Tighten the hood latch attaching screw to 7–10 ft. lbs. (9–14 Nm).

5. Raise the two hood bumpers to eliminate any looseness at the front of the hood when closed. Tighten the hood bumper locknuts.

6. Open and close the hood several times to check its operation.

## Hood Latch Control Cable

### REMOVAL & INSTALLATION

▶ **See Figures 14, 15 and 16**

1. From inside the vehicle, release the hood.
2. Remove the two bolts retaining the latch to the upper radiator support.
3. Remove the screw securing the cable end retainer to the latch assembly.
4. Disengage the cable by rotating it out of the latch return spring.
5. To ease installation of the cable, fasten a length of fishing line about 8 ft. (2.4m) long to the end of the cable.
6. From inside the vehicle, unseat the sealing grommet from the cowl side, remove the cable mounting bracket attaching screws and carefully pull the cable assembly out. Do not pull the "fishing line" out.

**To install:**

7. Using the previously installed fishing line, pull the new cable assembly through the retaining wall, seat the grommet securely, then install the cable mounting bracket attaching screws.
8. Thread the terminal end of cable into the hood latch return spring.
9. Route the cable through the V-slot on the latch and install the cable end retaining screw.
10. Install the two bolts securing the hood latch to the upper radiator support. Tighten to 7–10 ft. lbs. (9–14 Nm).
11. Check the hood latch cable release operation before closing the hood. Adjust if necessary, then close the hood.

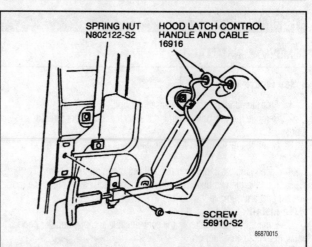

**Fig. 15 From inside the vehicle, unseat the sealing grommet from the cowl side, remove the cable mounting bracket attaching screws and carefully pull the cable assembly out**

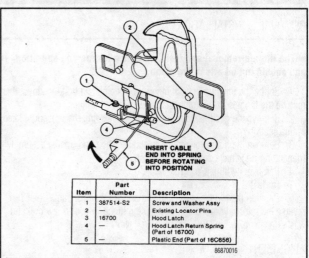

| Item | Part Number | Description |
|---|---|---|
| 1 | 387514-S2 | Screw and Washer Assy |
| 2 | — | Existing Locator Pins |
| 3 | 16700 | Hood Latch |
| 4 | — | Hood Latch Return Spring (Part of 16700) |
| 5 | — | Plastic End (Part of 16C656) |

**Fig. 16 Thread the terminal end of cable into the hood latch return spring**

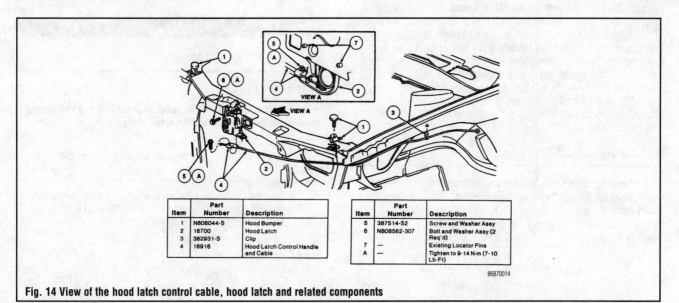

| Item | Part Number | Description |
|---|---|---|
| 1 | N806044-S | Hood Bumper |
| 2 | 16700 | Hood Latch |
| 3 | 382931-S | Clip |
| 4 | 16916 | Hood Latch Control Handle and Cable |
| 5 | 387514-S2 | Screw and Washer Assy |
| 6 | N808562-307 | Bolt and Washer Assy (2 Req'd) |
| 7 | — | Existing Locator Pins |
| A | — | Tighten to 9-14 N·m (7-10 Lb-Ft) |

**Fig. 14 View of the hood latch control cable, hood latch and related components**

## Hood Latch

### REMOVAL & INSTALLATION

▶ **See Figure 14**

1. From inside the vehicle, release the hood.
2. Remove the two bolts retaining the latch to the upper radiator support.
3. Remove the screw securing the cable end retainer to the hood latch assembly.
4. Disengage the cable by rotating it out of the return spring.
5. Remove the two bolts retaining the hood latch assembly to the radiator support and remove the latch.

**To install:**
6. Engage the hood latch to the control cable and position the hood latch to the radiator support.
7. Install the two attaching bolts.
8. Adjust the hood latch, then tighten the attaching bolts to 7–10 ft. lbs. (9–14 Nm).

## Liftgate

### REMOVAL & INSTALLATION

➡ **The liftgate removal and installation is a two-person operation and should not be attempted alone.**

1. Scribe the location of each hinge's roof frame and bolt locations, then remove the hinge-to-roof frame attachments at both hinges.
2. Remove the gas lifts/support cylinders, following the procedure later in this section.
3. Remove the hinge-to-roof frame screw or bolt and washer assembly (depending on vehicle application) at each hinge.
4. Remove the liftgate from the vehicle.

**To install:**
5. Position the hinges to the scribe marks on the roof frame, then reverse the removal procedures. Tighten the hinge-to-roof screw/bolt and washer assemblies to 3.8–5.0 ft. lbs. (5–7 Nm).

### ALIGNMENT

The station wagon liftgate latch has double-bolt construction, designed to be equivalent in function and load capacity to side door latches. The latch is non-adjustable. All movement for adjustment is accomplished in the striker which has a 0.22 in. (5.5mm) radial range. This latch system has a two-position latching system. The closing latch cycle consists of a secondary position which latches the liftgate, but does not seal the door to the liftgate weatherstrip. The primary position holds the liftgate door firmly against the weatherstrip. Water leaks and rattles may occur even though the liftgate appears closed, if it is only closed to the secondary (first) position. Be sure that positive primary engagement of the liftgate latch is achieved upon closing. To check it, use the following procedure:

### LATCH FUNCTION TEST

1. Close the liftgate to an assumed primary condition.
2. Insert the key into the key cylinder. Place your left hand on the liftgate glass above and left of the key cylinder. Press firmly on the glass with your left hand and slowly turn the key until the latch is released. Return the key

and release your left hand pressure. The liftgate should be in the secondary position.
3. If this test indicates that the liftgate will not close to the primary position, adjust the striker rearward (rear of the vehicle) so that a positive primary engagement is obtained upon closing the liftgate.

## Liftgate Support Cylinder/Gas Lift

### REMOVAL & INSTALLATION

▶ **See Figure 17**

1. Open and temporarily support the liftgate.
2. Using a small prybar, pry the locking spring out of the ball socket at both ends of the liftgate door hydraulic lift, just far enough to release the socket from the ball stud.
3. Remove the support cylinder.

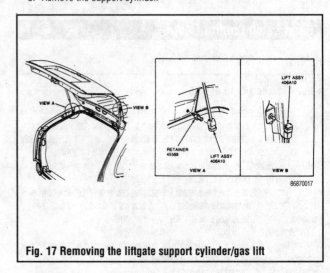

**Fig. 17 Removing the liftgate support cylinder/gas lift**

**To install:**
4. Make sure the locking spring is pressed into place on the door hydraulic lift.
5. Install the ball sockets of the hydraulic lift onto the ball stud at the bracket. Push the hydraulic lift at the ball socket until the lift snaps into place.
6. Close the liftgate. Check the support cylinder operation.

## Trunk Lid

### REMOVAL & INSTALLATION

▶ **See Figure 18**

➡ **The trunk lid removal and installation procedure is a two-person operation and should not be attempted alone.**

1. Matchmark the trunk lid to hinge locations.
2. Unfasten the four hinge-to-trunk lid screws, then remove the trunk lid from the vehicle.

**To install:**
3. Position the trunk lid to the hinges and install the four hinge-to-trunk lid retaining bolts. Tighten the bolts to 4–6 ft. lbs. (5.0–8.5 Nm).
4. Adjust for fit as outlined later in this section.

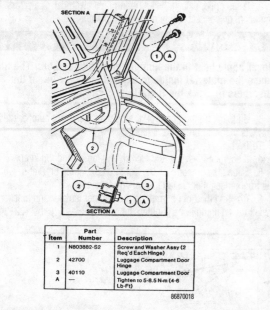

| Item | Part Number | Description |
|---|---|---|
| 1 | N803882-S2 | Screw and Washer Assy (2 Req'd Each Hinge) |
| 2 | 42700 | Luggage Compartment Door Hinge |
| 3 | 40110 | Luggage Compartment Door |
| A | — | Tighten to 5-8.5 N-m (4-6 Lb-Ft) |

86870018

**Fig. 18 Remove the four hinge-to-trunk lid screws, then remove the trunk lid from the vehicle**

## ALIGNMENT

The trunk lid door can be shifted fore-and-aft and from side-to-side on all models.

The trunk lid should be adjusted for an even and parallel fit with the opening. The trunk lid should also be adjusted up and down for a flush fit with the surrounding panels. Be careful not to damage the trunk lid or surrounding body panel.

Fore-and-aft and up-and-down adjustment of the trunk lid is achieved by loosening the hinge-to-trunk lid attaching screw(s) or bolt(s), shifting the trunk lid to the proper position, then tightening the fasteners to 7–10 ft. lbs. (9–14 Nm).

## TRUNK LID TORSION BAR LOADING

▶ **See Figure 19**

➡ **This procedure requires an assistant.**

1. Obtain the following materials:
   a. A round flexible cable, ¼ in. (6mm) in diameter by 4 ft. (1.2m) long.
   b. One ¼ in. (6mm) cable clamp.
   c. A water pipe, ½ in. (12.7mm) diameter by 2 in. (51mm) long.
   d. A piece of heater hose, ⅝ in. (16mm) diameter and 6 in. (153mm) long.

### ❊❊ CAUTION

**Safety glasses MUST be worn when performing the trunk lid torsion bar loading procedure!**

2. Properly assemble the materials as shown in the accompanying figure. Safety glasses **MUST** be worn when performing this operation.

3. Install the torsion bar by inserting one end into the hole provided in the luggage compartment door hinge and resting the other end in the upper groove of the opposite hinge support.

4. Install the homemade tool on the end of the torsion bar to be loaded.

5. With an assistant, place a long, flat prybar over the top of the torsion bar to be loaded. Pull on the torsion bar with the assistant holding the prybar, then guide the torsion bar down along the rear edge of the support, into the lower groove of the hinge support and lock it in the lowest adjustment notch.

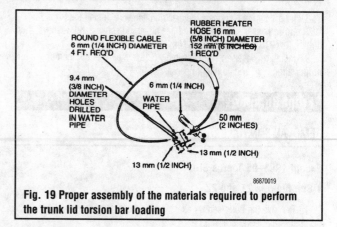

86870019

**Fig. 19 Proper assembly of the materials required to perform the trunk lid torsion bar loading**

6. Using the homemade tool, install the tool into the end of the torsion bar and unlock the bar by pulling toward yourself with the tool. Work the torsion bar into the second notch and release. If further adjustment is needed, proceed to step 7.

7. Using a ⅜ in. drive, ½ in. deep well socket and a 6 in. (153mm) extension, position the socket over the end of the torsion bar and unlock the bar. Reposition the torsion bar up the hinge support to the top notch, then release.

## Trunk Lid Latch and Lock

### REMOVAL & INSTALLATION

▶ **See Figure 20**

1. Open the trunk lid.

2. Remove the lever assembly and clip. If the clip breaks, replace with a new lever and clip assembly.

3. Remove the three latch attaching screws, then disconnect the electric latch wire, if so equipped.

4. Remove the luggage compartment latch and rod from the vehicle with the retainer and seal.

5. Remove the screw and washer retaining the trunk lid lock cylinder plate to the support, then remove the plate and support.

6. Remove the lock cylinder and rod.

**To install:**

7. Position the lock cylinder and seal into the hole in the trunk lid. Push the lock cylinder retainer into position until it is locked.

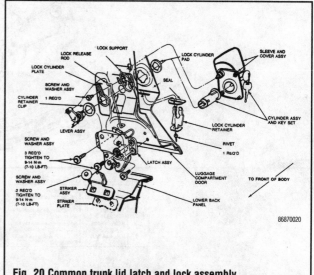

86870020

**Fig. 20 Common trunk lid latch and lock assembly**

8. If so equipped, connect the electric latch wire. Install the trunk lid latch and rod assembly. Install the three attaching screws and washers, then tighten to 7–10 ft. lbs. (9.5–13.6 Nm).

9. Install the lever and clip assembly. Close the trunk lid, then check for proper alignment and adjust, if necessary.

## Front Bumper

### REMOVAL & INSTALLATION

#### Except 1993–95 Taurus SHO

▶ See Figures 21 and 22

1. Remove the bolts/screws attaching the front bumper to the front bumper isolator and brackets.

2. If equipped, detach the cornering light electrical connectors. If equipped, disconnect and remove the fog lamps.

### ✳✳ WARNING

**Never apply heat to the bumper energy absorbers! The heat may cause the material inside to expand and flow out of the absorbers or crack the metal!**

3. Slide the front bumper off the right and left front bumper guide brackets mounted on the front fender.

**To install:**

4. If equipped, assemble the cornering lamps and fog lamps.

5. Slide the bumper onto the front bumper guide bracket mounted on the front fender, then install the parking lamps.

6. Position the front bumper to the bumper isolator and bracket, then install the retaining bolts. Tighten the bolts to 16–25 ft. lbs. (22–34 Nm).

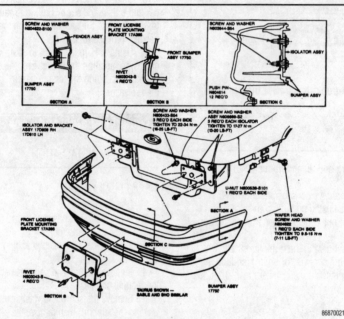

Fig. 21 Front bumper for 1986–91 vehicles—Taurus shown, Sable and SHO similar

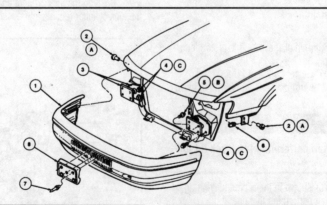

| Item | Part Number | Description |
|---|---|---|
| 1 | 17757 | Front Bumper |
| 2 | N804984-S102 | Bolt and Washer (1 Req'd Each Side) |
| 3 | 17754 RH<br>17755 LH | Front Bumper Isolator and Bracket |
| 4 | N606689-S2 | Bolt and Washer Assy (3 Req'd Each Isolator) |
| 5 | N803944-S301 | Bolt and Washer (3 Req'd Each Side) |

| Item | Part Number | Description |
|---|---|---|
| 6 | N800538-S101 | U-Nut (1 Req'd Each Side) |
| 7 | N806830-S100 | Rivet (3 Req'd) (Sable) |
| 8 | 17A385 | Front License Plate Mounting Bracket |
| A | — | Tighten to 9-21 N·m (7-15 Lb-Ft) |
| B | — | Tighten to 22-34 N·m (17-25 Lb-Ft) |
| C | — | Tighten to 17-27 N·m (13-19 Lb-Ft) |

Fig. 22 Front bumper for 1992–95 Taurus and Sable

**1993–95 Taurus SHO**

▶ **See Figures 23 and 24**

1. Remove the six push pins holding the front bumper cover to the top of the radiator grille opening panel reinforcement.

2. Remove the four push pins securing the front bumper cover to the bottom of the bumper. Remove the two push pins (there is one on each side) holding the bumper cover to the front fender wheel opening flange.

3. Remove the four nuts (two on each side) securing the bumper cover to the front fenders. Pull the ends of the bumper cover away from the front fenders to clear the retaining studs, then remove the cover.

4. If replacing the front cover, transfer the front license plate mounting bracket (if equipped).

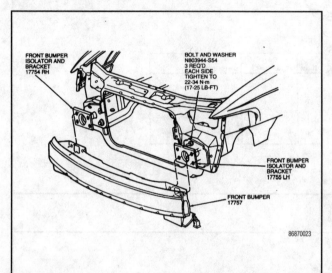

**Fig. 23 Removing the front bumper—SHO vehicles only**

5. Remove the bolts securing the front bumper to the front bumper isolator and bracket.

6. Slide the bumper off the right and left front bumper guide brackets mounted on the front fender.

7. If the front bumper is to be replaced, assemble the front valance panel for the front bumper.

8. To install, reverse the removal procedures. Tighten the front bumper or bumper isolator and bracket-to-front bumper bolts to 17–25 ft. lbs. (22–34 Nm).

### Rear Bumper

REMOVAL & INSTALLATION

▶ **See Figures 25, 26 and 27**

➥**Never apply heat to the bumper energy absorbers! The heat may cause the material inside to expand and flow out of the absorbers or crack the metal!**

1. Remove the bolts retaining the rear bumper to the rear bumper isolator and bracket.

2. With an assistant, slide the rear bumper off the right and left rear bumper isolator and brackets.

3. On the station wagon, remove the step pad and rear bumper stone deflector.

**To install:**

4. On the station wagon, assemble the step pad and rear bumper stone deflector.

5. To install the station wagon rear bumper step pad: starting at the center of the pad, carefully align the tabs to the rear bumper, then use a rubber mallet to impact the pad surface.

6. With an assistant, slide the rear bumper onto the rear bumper guide bracket mounted on the quarter panel.

7. Position the bumper to the bumper isolator and brackets, then install the retaining bolts. Tighten the bolts to 16–25 ft. lbs. (22–34 Nm).

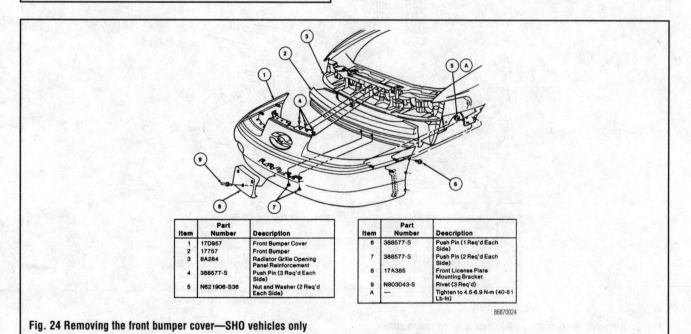

| Item | Part Number | Description |
|------|-------------|-------------|
| 1 | 17D957 | Front Bumper Cover |
| 2 | 17757 | Front Bumper |
| 3 | 8A284 | Radiator Grille Opening Panel Reinforcement |
| 4 | 388577-S | Push Pin (3 Req'd Each Side) |
| 5 | N621906-S36 | Nut and Washer (2 Req'd Each Side) |

| Item | Part Number | Description |
|------|-------------|-------------|
| 6 | 388577-S | Push Pin (1 Req'd Each Side) |
| 7 | 388577-S | Push Pin (2 Req'd Each Side) |
| 8 | 17A385 | Front License Plate Mounting Bracket |
| 9 | N803043-S | Rivet (3 Req'd) |
| A | — | Tighten to 4.5-6.9 N·m (40-61 Lb-In) |

**Fig. 24 Removing the front bumper cover—SHO vehicles only**

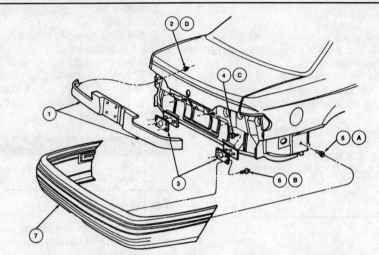

| Item | Part Number | Description |
|------|-------------|-------------|
| 1 | 423A42 | Panel |
| 2 | N621926-S36 | Nut and Washer (10 Req'd) |
| 3 | 17787 | Rear Bumper Isolator and Bracket |
| 4 | N606702-S36 | Bolt and Washer (2 Req'd Each Side) |
| 5 | N804984-S102 | Bolt and Washer (1 Req'd Each Side) |
| 6 | N805433-S301 | Bolt and Washer (3 Req'd Each Side) |

| Item | Part Number | Description |
|------|-------------|-------------|
| 7 | 17906 | Rear Bumper |
| A | — | Tighten to 9.5-15 N·m (8-11 Lb-Ft) |
| B | — | Tighten to 22-34 N·m (17-25 Lb-Ft) |
| C | — | Tighten to 35-55 N·m (26-40 Lb-Ft) |
| D | — | Tighten to 9-14 N·m (7-10 Lb-Ft) |

86870025

**Fig. 25 Rear bumper mounting—late model Taurus sedan shown**

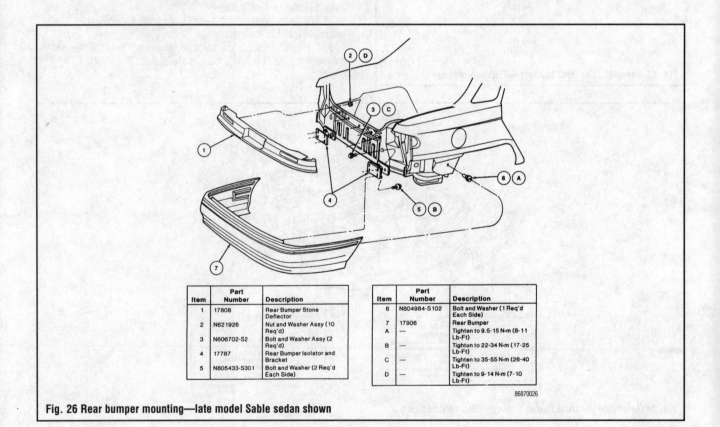

| Item | Part Number | Description |
|------|-------------|-------------|
| 1 | 17808 | Rear Bumper Stone Deflector |
| 2 | N621926 | Nut and Washer Assy (10 Req'd) |
| 3 | N606702-S2 | Bolt and Washer Assy (2 Req'd) |
| 4 | 17787 | Rear Bumper Isolator and Bracket |
| 5 | N805433-S301 | Bolt and Washer (2 Req'd Each Side) |

| Item | Part Number | Description |
|------|-------------|-------------|
| 6 | N804984-S102 | Bolt and Washer (1 Req'd Each Side) |
| 7 | 17906 | Rear Bumper |
| A | — | Tighten to 9.5-15 N·m (8-11 Lb-Ft) |
| B | — | Tighten to 22-34 N·m (17-25 Lb-Ft) |
| C | — | Tighten to 35-55 N·m (26-40 Lb-Ft) |
| D | — | Tighten to 9-14 N·m (7-10 Lb-Ft) |

86870026

**Fig. 26 Rear bumper mounting—late model Sable sedan shown**

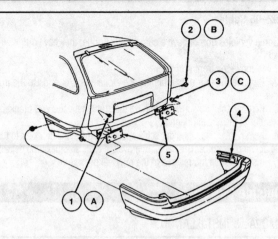

| Item | Part Number | Description |
|---|---|---|
| 1 | N606702-S36 | Screw and Washer Assy (2 Req'd) |
| 2 | N804984-S102 | Screw and Washer (1 Req'd Each Side) |
| 3 | N805433-S301 | Piloted Screw and Washer (3 Req'd Each Side) |
| 4 | 17906 | Rear Bumper |
| 5 | 17787 | Rear Bumper Isolator and Bracket |
| A | — | Tighten to 35-55 N·m (26-40 Lb-Ft) |
| B | — | Tighten to 9.5-15 N·m (8-11 Lb-Ft) |
| C | — | Tighten to 22-34 N·m (16-25 Lb-Ft) |

86870027

**Fig. 27 Rear bumper mounting—Station wagon shown**

## Grille

### REMOVAL & INSTALLATION

#### Vehicles Through 1992, Except 1992 Sable

▶ See Figure 28

1. Raise and support the hood.
2. Remove the two plastic retainers at the top corners with a cross-recessed prybar.
3. Depress the tabs on the spring clips attached to the grille at both lower corners and pull the grille assembly from the vehicle.

**To install:**

4. Position the bottom of the spring tabs in the slots in the grille opening reinforcement.
5. Rotate the top of the grille toward the rear of the vehicle until the upper tab slots line up with the holes in the grille opening.
6. Install the two plastic retainers through the holes in the grille and grille opening. The retainers can be tapped in.

#### 1993–95 Taurus

▶ See Figures 29 and 30

The conventional grille is not used on the 1993–95 Taurus. The grille is part of the front stone deflector.

1. Remove the four push pins securing the front bumper stone deflector to the radiator grille opening panel reinforcement.
2. Remove the two push pins (one on each side) holding the front bumper stone deflector to the front fenders.
3. Fold back the front half of the front fender splash shields.
4. Remove the four nuts (two on each side) securing the front bumper stone deflector to the front fenders.
5. Remove the front bumper stone deflector.
6. To install, reverse the removal procedure.

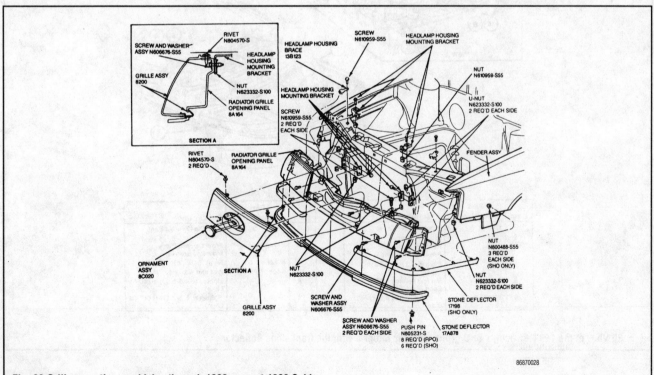

86870028

**Fig. 28 Grille mounting—vehicles through 1992, except 1992 Sable**

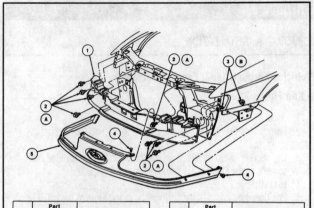

| Item | Part Number | Description |
|---|---|---|
| 1 | 8A284 | Radiator Grille Opening Panel Reinforcement |
| 2 | N606676-S55 | Screw and Washer Assy (8 Req'd) |
| 3 | N621906-S36 | Nut and Washer Assy (2 Req'd Each Side) |
| 4 | 388577-S | Push Pin (1 Req'd Each Side) |

| Item | Part Number | Description |
|---|---|---|
| 5 | 17779 | Front Bumper Stone Deflector |
| A | — | Tighten to 5.3-7.1 N·m (47-63 Lb-In) |
| B | — | Tighten to 4.5-6.9 N·m (40-61 Lb-In) |

86870029

**Fig. 29 View of the 1993–95 Taurus grille, which is integral with the front stone deflector**

### 1992–95 Sable

Some vehicles do not have a conventional grille; they have a lighted panel.

1. Remove the front bumper.
2. Remove the four nuts retaining the stone deflector ends to the front fender.
3. Remove the two screws retaining the stone deflector end bracket to the fender at the wheel opening.
4. Remove the nine shoulder screws retaining the stone deflector to the grille opening reinforcement panel. Remove the grille and the stone deflector.
5. Installation is the reverse of the removal procedure.

## Outside Mirrors

### REMOVAL & INSTALLATION

#### Standard Manual Type—Right-Hand Only

1. Remove the inside sail cover.
2. Unfasten the retaining nuts and washers, then lift the mirror off the door.

**To install:**

3. Position the mirror on the door.
4. Install, then tighten the retaining nuts and washers.
5. Install the inside sail cover.

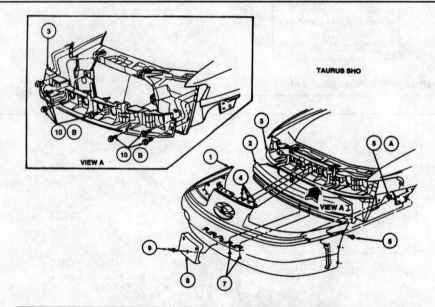

TAURUS SHO

| Item | Part Number | Description |
|---|---|---|
| 1 | 17D957 | Front Bumper Cover |
| 2 | 17757 | Front Bumper |
| 3 | 8A284 | Radiator Grille Opening Panel Reinforcement |
| 4 | 388577S | Push Pin (3 Req'd Each Side) |
| 5 | N621906-S36 | Nut and Washer (2 Req'd Each Side) |
| 6 | 388577-S | Push Pin (1 Req'd Each Side) |

| Item | Part Number | Description |
|---|---|---|
| 7 | 388577-S | Push Pin (2 Req'd Each Side) |
| 8 | 17A385 | Front License Plate Mounting Bracket |
| 9 | N803043-S | Rivet (3 Req'd) |
| 10 | N606676-S55 | Bolt and Washer |
| A | — | Tighten to 4.5-6.9 N·m (40-61 Lb-In) |
| B | — | Tighten to 5.3-7.1 N·m (47-63 Lb-In) |

86870030

**Fig. 30 View of the 1993–95 Taurus SHO grille, which is integral with the front stone deflector**

## Left-Hand Remote Control

**♦ See Figure 31**

1. Pull the knob assembly to remove it from the control shaft.
2. Unfasten the interior sail cover retainer screw, then remove the cover.
3. Loosen the setscrew retaining control assembly from the sail cover.
4. Remove the mirror attaching nuts, washers and grommet. Remove the mirror and the control assembly.

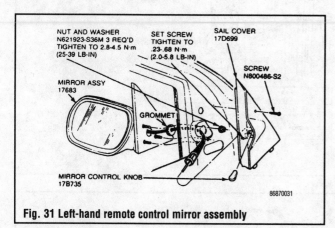

**Fig. 31 Left-hand remote control mirror assembly**

### To install:

5. Seat the grommet in the outer door panel and position the mirror to the door. Install the attaching nuts and washer, then tighten to 25–39 inch lbs. (2.8–4.5 Nm).
6. Route the control mechanism through the door, then position to the sail trim panel. Tighten the setscrew to 2–6 inch lbs. (0.23–0.68 Nm).
7. Position the sail cover to the door, then install the retaining screw.
8. Position the rubber knob onto the control shaft and push to install.

## Power Outside Mirrors

**♦ See Figure 32**

➡**Outside mirrors that are frozen must be thawed prior to adjustment. Do not attempt to free-up the mirror by pressing on the glass.**

1. Disconnect the negative battery cable.
2. Remove the screw retaining the mirror mounting hole cover, then remove the cover.
3. Remove the front door trim panel.
4. Disengage the mirror assembly wiring connector. Remove the necessary wiring guides.
5. Remove the mirror retaining nuts on the sail mirrors (three on sail mirrors, two on door mirrors). Remove the mirror while guiding the wiring and connector through the hole in the door.

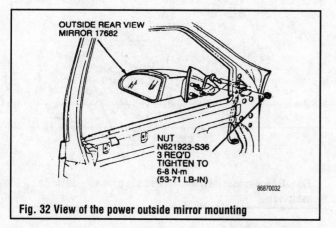

**Fig. 32 View of the power outside mirror mounting**

### To install:

6. Install the mirror assembly by routing the connector and wiring through the hole in the door. Attach with the three retaining nuts on the sail mirrors, or two on the door mirrors. Tighten the retaining nuts to 53–71 inch lbs. (6–8 Nm).
7. Engage the mirror electrical wiring connector, then install the wiring guides.
8. Position the mirror mounting hole cover, then install the retaining screw.
9. Install the door trim panel.
10. Connect the negative battery cable.
11. If a new mirror has been installed, snap on the new trim (Top Finish Panel, part no. 17D742-3 or equivalent).

## Antenna

### REMOVAL & INSTALLATION

**♦ See Figures 33, 34 and 35**

1. Push in on the sides of the glove compartment door and place the door in the hinged downward position.
2. Disconnect the antenna lead from the right-hand rear of the radio, then remove the cable from the heater or A/C cable retaining clips.

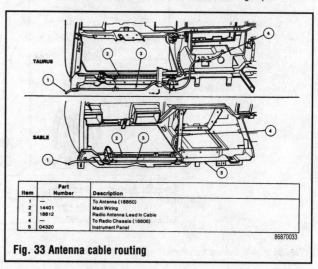

| Item | Part Number | Description |
|---|---|---|
| 1 | — | To Antenna (18850) |
| 2 | 14401 | Main Wiring |
| 3 | 18812 | Radio Antenna Lead In Cable |
| 4 | — | To Radio Chassis (18806) |
| 5 | 04320 | Instrument Panel |

**Fig. 33 Antenna cable routing**

3. Remove the right front fender liner/splash shield. Unplug the coaxial cable from the power antenna assembly or the manual antenna base assembly. If so equipped, unplug the power lead from the power antenna.

➡**The manual antenna mast is detachable from the base and cable assembly.**

4. Under the right front fender, pull the antenna cable through the hole in the door hinge pillar, then remove the antenna cable assembly from the wheel well area.
5. To remove the manual or power antenna base, remove the antenna nut and stanchion on the right front fender.
6. Remove the lower antenna base screw, then remove the antenna.
   **To install:**
7. Install the antenna assembly and base screw.
8. Install the antenna nut and stanchion on the right front fender. Tighten the antenna nut to 4 inch lbs. (0.45 Nm)
9. Pull the antenna cable through the hole in the door hinge pillar. Attach the antenna cable lead to the right-hand rear of the radio.
10. Attach the cable to the heater or A/C housing. Install the front fender liner/splash shield.
11. Return the glove compartment door to its normal position.

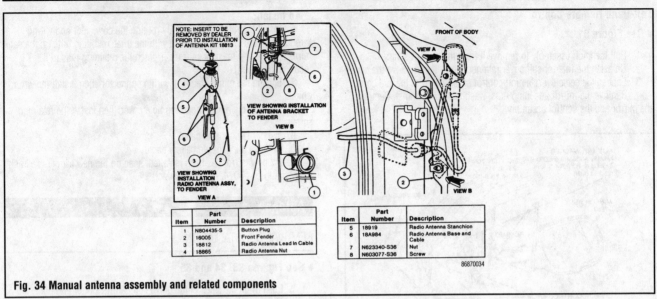

**Fig. 34 Manual antenna assembly and related components**

| Item | Part Number | Description |
|---|---|---|
| 1 | N804435-S | Button Plug |
| 2 | 16005 | Front Fender |
| 3 | 18812 | Radio Antenna Lead In Cable |
| 4 | 18865 | Radio Antenna Nut |

| Item | Part Number | Description |
|---|---|---|
| 5 | 18919 | Radio Antenna Stanchion |
| 6 | 18A984 | Radio Antenna Base and Cable |
| 7 | N623340-S36 | Nut |
| 8 | N603077-S36 | Screw |

86870034

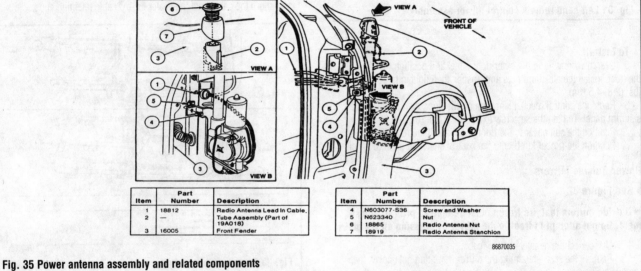

**Fig. 35 Power antenna assembly and related components**

| Item | Part Number | Description |
|---|---|---|
| 1 | 18812 | Radio Antenna Lead In Cable, Tube Assembly (Part of 19A018) |
| 2 | — | |
| 3 | 16005 | Front Fender |

| Item | Part Number | Description |
|---|---|---|
| 4 | N603077-S36 | Screw and Washer |
| 5 | N623340 | Nut |
| 6 | 18865 | Radio Antenna Nut |
| 7 | 18919 | Radio Antenna Stanchion |

86870035

## Fenders

### REMOVAL & INSTALLATION

#### 1986–88 Vehicles

▶ **See Figure 36**

1. Remove the pins securing the splash shield to the body.
2. Unfasten the screws securing the fender and splash shield to the body.
3. Remove the insulator assembly from the fender.
4. Unfasten the fender retaining bolts. Remove the fender and the splash shield from the vehicle.

**To install:**

5. Position the splash shield to the fender, then secure with the retaining screws.
6. Install the insulator assembly to the fender.
7. Position the splash shield and fender to the body of the vehicle. Secure with the retaining screws and pushpins.

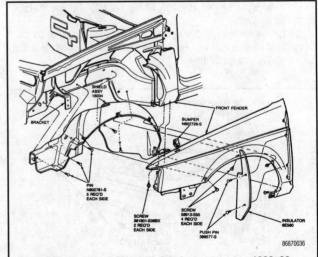

**Fig. 36 Fender assembly and related components—1986–88 vehicles**

86870036

**1989–95 Vehicles**

♦ **See Figure 37**

1. Remove the front bumper assembly.
2. Unfasten the two screws retaining the grille opening reinforcement panel to the fender.
3. Disconnect the screw retaining the upper front fender mounting bracket to the fender.
4. Remove the screw retaining the front fender mounting bracket to the fender.

7. Lift the front of the roof sliding panel headlining, slide it forward, then rotate 90° to remove.

**To install:**

8. With the roof sliding panel headlining at an angle, insert one roof sliding panel headlining rear tab into the channel at the rear of the roof panel opening. Insert the other rear tab and place the roof sliding panel headlining in position.
9. Slide the roof sliding panel opening shield forward, lifting it to clear the roof sliding panel headlining.

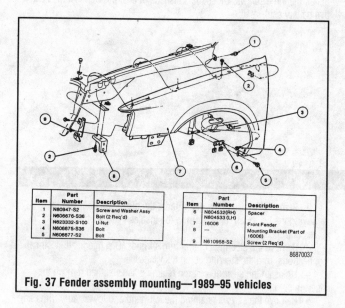

| Item | Part Number | Description |
|------|-------------|-------------|
| 1 | N80947-S2 | Screw and Washer Assy |
| 2 | N606676-S36 | Bolt (2 Req'd) |
| 3 | N623332-S100 | U-Nut |
| 4 | N606675-S36 | Bolt |
| 5 | N606677-S2 | Bolt |

| Item | Part Number | Description |
|------|-------------|-------------|
| 6 | N804532(RH) N804533 (LH) | Spacer |
| 7 | 16006 | Front Fender |
| 8 | — | Mounting Bracket (Part of 16006) |
| 9 | N610958-S2 | Screw (2 Req'd) |

86870037

**Fig. 37 Fender assembly mounting—1989–95 vehicles**

5. Unfasten the two screws retaining the lower rear fender to the side of the body.
6. Disconnect the two bolts retaining the upper and lower front fender. Remove the three retaining bolts from the "catwalk" area of the fender apron. Remove the fender from the vehicle.
7. Installation is the reverse of the removal procedure.

## Power Sunroof

### REMOVAL & INSTALLATION

#### Glass and Sunshade

♦ **See Figures 38, 39, 40 and 41**

1. Disconnect the negative battery cable.
2. To remove the outer glass panel, remove the roof sliding panel opening shield three front retaining screws.
3. Position the roof sliding panel opening shield (sunshade) fully rearward to expose the six glass retaining screws. There are three screws on each side.
4. To remove the sunshade, unfasten the glass's six retaining screws or bolts and washers.
5. Push the glass upward from inside the vehicle, then remove it, being careful not to scratch the glass or roof paint. Be sure to lift the roof sliding panel opening shield to clear the sunshade.
6. Push the roof sliding panel opening shield fully rearward. Slide the roof sliding panel headlining fully forward.

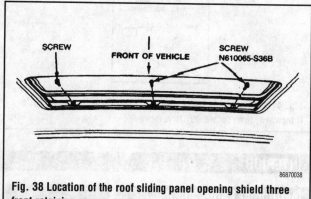

86870038

**Fig. 38 Location of the roof sliding panel opening shield three front retaining screws**

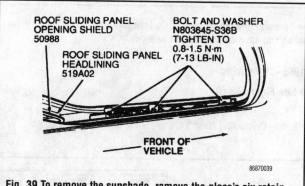

86870039

**Fig. 39 To remove the sunshade, remove the glass's six retaining screws or bolts and washers**

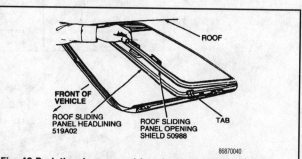

86870040

**Fig. 40 Push the glass upward from inside the vehicle, then remove it, being careful not to scratch the glass or roof paint. Be sure to lift the roof sliding panel opening shield to clear the sunshade.**

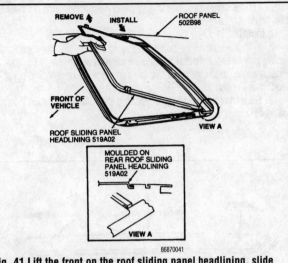

**Fig. 41 Lift the front on the roof sliding panel headlining, slide it forward, then rotate 90° to remove**

10. Lower the roof sliding panel opening shield onto the roof sliding panel headlining. The roof sliding panel opening shield must be outside of the rail or the roof panel will not work correctly.

11. Slide the roof sliding panel headlining and roof sliding panel opening shield fully rearward.

12. Install the roof sliding outer glass panel. Align with the holes for the bolts. Be careful not to push the lifter arm slide out of the track.

13. Install the glass retaining screws or bolts and washers, then tighten to 7–13 inch lbs. (0.8–1.5 Nm).

14. Position the roof sliding panel opening shield fully forward, then install the three screws. Close the sunshade, if desired. Connect the negative battery cable.

## INTERIOR

### Instrument Panel and Pad

#### REMOVAL & INSTALLATION

➡**Removal and installation of the instrument panel is much easier when you have an assistant to help you.**

**1986–89 Vehicles**

▸ **See Figure 42**

1. Disconnect the negative battery cable. Remove the four screws retaining the steering column opening cover, then remove the cover.

2. Remove the sound insulator under the glove compartment by removing the two push nuts securing the insulator to the studs on the climate control case.

3. Remove the steering column trim shrouds. Disengage all electrical connections from the steering column switches.

4. Unfasten the steering column retaining screws, then remove the steering column.

5. Remove the screws retaining the left-hand and lower radio trim panels. Remove the trim panels by snapping them out.

6. Remove the instrument cluster trim panel retaining screws, the jam-nut behind the headlight switch and the screw behind the clock. Remove the trim panel by rocking the upper edge toward the driver.

7. Disconnect the speedometer cable by reaching up under the instrument panel and pressing on the flat surface of the plastic connector. The cluster can be removed along with the panel.

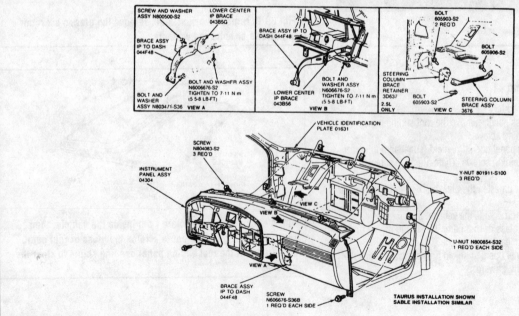

**Fig. 42 View of the instrument panel assembly and mounting bolt locations—1986–89 vehicles**

8. Release the glove compartment assembly by depressing the side of the glove compartment bin, and allow the compartment to hang open.

9. Using all openings, tag and remove all instrument panel electrical connections, air conditioning outlets, air conditioning control cables, antenna wires, and anything else that may interfere with panel removal.

10. Disengage the underhood electrical connectors at the main wire loom. Push the wires and grommets through to the instrument panel area.

11. Remove the right and left speaker covers by snapping them out. Unfasten the two lower instrument panel-to-cowl side retaining screws, and the instrument panel brace retaining screw.

12. Unfasten the three upper instrument panel retaining screws, then remove the instrument panel from the vehicle.

**To install:**

13. Push the instrument panel wiring harness and connector through the dash panel into the engine compartment, then install the grommet in the dash panel. Connect the speedometer cable to the speedometer head.

14. Position the instrument panel with the locating pin through the hole in the steering column reinforcement. Install the three upper panel retaining screws, then tighten to 12–20 inch lbs. (1.4–2.3 Nm).

15. Install the two instrument panel-to-side cowl retaining screws, then tighten to 5–8 ft. lbs. (7–11 Nm).

16. Install one brace-to-lower instrument panel retaining screw (located under the radio). Tighten the screw to 5–8 ft. lbs. (7–11 Nm). Install the radio speaker grilles.

17. From inside the engine compartment, engage the instrument panel wiring connectors to the engine compartment wiring. Using all necessary openings, engage all electrical connections, vacuum hoses, heater and A/C control cables, the radio antenna cable, and anything else that may have been removed.

18. Swing the glove compartment assembly back into place, then install by depressing the side tabs on the bin.

19. Install the instrument cluster finish panel in position, then install the retaining screws. Tighten the screws to 18–26 inch lbs. (2.0–2.9 Nm). Install the clock or cover plate.

20. Snap the lower left-hand and radio finish panels into position, then install the retaining screws (one each). Tighten the screws to 18–26 inch lbs. (2.0–2.9 Nm).

21. Raise the steering column into position. Install the four retaining screws at the support bracket.

22. Engage all electrical connections to the steering column switches. Install the steering column trim shrouds.

23. Position the steering column cover to the instrument panel, then install the four retaining screws. Position the sound insulator under the glove compartment, then install push nuts onto the two studs on the climate control case.

24. Connect the negative battery cable. Check for proper operation of all components.

### 1990–91 Vehicles

▶ See Figure 43

➡Some vehicles are equipped with air bags. Before attempting to service air bag equipped vehicles, be sure that the system is properly disarmed and all safety precautions are taken. Serious personal injury and vehicle damage could result if this note is disregarded.

1. Position the wheels in the straight ahead position. Disable the air bag system. For details, please refer to the procedure in Section 6 of this manual. Disconnect the negative battery cable.

2. Remove the ignition lock cylinder. If equipped, remove the tilt lever. Remove the steering column trim shrouds. Disengage all electrical connectors from the steering column switches.

3. Remove the two bolts and reinforcement from under the steering column. Disengage the insulator, then remove the insulator.

4. Remove the four nuts and the reinforcement from under the steering column. Do NOT rotate the steering column shaft.

5. Remove the four nuts retaining the steering column to the instrument panel, disconnect the PRNDL cable and lower the steering column on the front seat. Cover the front seat to protect it from damage.

6. Install the ignition lock cylinder to ensure that the steering column shaft does not turn. Remove the one bolt at the steering column opening attaching the instrument panel brace retaining bolt under the radio.

7. Remove the sound insulator from under the glove compartment by removing the two push nuts that secure the insulator to the studs on the climate control case assembly.

8. Disconnect the wires of the main wire loom inside the engine compartment. Disengage the rubber grommet from the dash panel, then feed the wiring through the hole in the dash panel into the passenger compartment.

9. Remove the right and left-hand cowl side trim panels. Remove the two screws (one on each side) retaining the instrument panel to the left and right side.

10. Remove both speaker covers by pulling upward on them. Open the glove compartment door and allow it to hang open.

11. Using all openings, tag and remove all instrument panel electrical connections, air conditioning outlets, air conditioning control cables, antenna wires, and anything else that may interfere with panel removal.

12. Close the glove compartment lid. Remove the three instrument panel screws at the top of the assembly. Disconnect any remaining electrical wires. Remove the instrument panel assembly from the vehicle.

13. If the panel is being replaced, transfer all components, wiring and hardware to the new instrument panel.

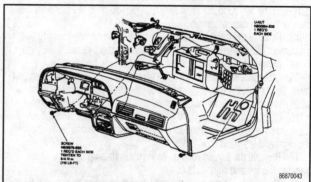

**Fig. 43 View of the instrument panel assembly and mounting bolt locations—1990–91 vehicles**

**To install:**

14. Position the instrument panel in place. Engage the underhood electrical connections. Install the instrument panel upper and lower retaining screws.

15. Install the lower brace and tighten the bolt to 5–8 ft. lbs. (6.8–10.8 Nm) Install the radio speaker grilles.

16. Using all necessary openings, engage all instrument panel electrical connections, air conditioning outlets, air conditioning control cables, antenna wires, and anything else that may have been removed.

17. Continue the installation in the reverse order of the removal procedure.

18. Connect the negative battery cable. Enable the air bag system following the procedure in Section 6 of this manual. Check for proper operation of the air bag indicator. Check for proper operation of all components.

### 1992–95 Vehicles

▶ See Figure 44

➡Some vehicles are equipped with air bags. Before attempting to service air bag equipped vehicles, be sure that the system is properly disarmed and that all safety precautions are taken. Serious personal injury and vehicle damage could result if this note is disregarded.

1. Position the wheels in the straight ahead position. Disconnect the negative and then the positive battery cables.

2. Remove the radio chassis and the instrument panel finish panel.

3. Disengage all electrical connections from the steering column switches.

4. Remove the four screws and instrument panel steering column cover from under the steering column tube.

5. Disengage the insulator retainer, then remove the insulator.

➡**Do NOT rotate the steering column shaft.**

6. Remove the four nuts and absorber assembly from under the steering column.

7. If equipped, detach the parking brake release control motor from the parking brake control and ignition switch lock cylinder wiring connector.

8. Cover the front seat to protect it from damage. Remove the four nuts retaining the steering column to the instrument panel, disconnect the PRNDL cable, then lower the steering column on the front seat.

9. Install the ignition lock cylinder to ensure that the steering column shaft does not turn.

10. Remove the four retaining screws from the instrument cluster, then disconnect the speed control cable and vehicle speed sensor (if equipped). Disconnect the wiring, then remove.

11. Remove the bolt at the steering column opening attaching the instrument panel to the instrument panel dash brace. Remove the one instrument panel dash brace retaining bolt from under the radio.

12. Remove the sound insulator from under the glove compartment by removing the two push nuts that secure the insulator to the studs on the climate control case assembly.

13. Remove the three screws retaining the glove compartment to the instrument panel, then remove the glove compartment door.

14. Remove the air cleaner assembly, battery and battery tray.

15. Disengage the wires of the main wire loom inside the engine compartment. Disconnect the rubber grommet from the dash panel, then feed the wiring through the hole in the dash panel into the passenger compartment.

16. Remove the retaining screws, then remove the right and left-hand cowl side trim panels. Disconnect the wires from the instrument panel at the right and left-hand cowl sides.

17. Remove the screws (one on each side) retaining the instrument panel to the left and right-side cowls.

18. Pull up to unsnap the right and left-side speaker covers, and the center cover assembly, then remove them upward. Open the glove compartment door and allow it to hang open.

19. Using all openings, tag and remove all instrument panel electrical connections, A/C outlets, A/C control cables, antenna wires, and anything else that may interfere with panel removal.

20. Support the instrument panel, then remove the three instrument panel screws at the top of the assembly. Disconnect any remaining electrical wires. Remove the instrument panel assembly from the vehicle.

21. If the panel is being replaced, transfer all components, wiring and hardware to the new instrument panel.

**To install:**

22. Position the instrument panel in place. Engage the underhood electrical connections. Install the instrument panel upper and lower screws.

23. Install the lower brace and tighten the bolt to 5–8 ft. lbs. (6.8–10.8 Nm). Install the radio speaker grilles.

24. Using all necessary openings, engage all instrument panel electrical connections, air conditioning outlets, air conditioning control cables, antenna wires, and anything else that may have been removed.

25. Continue the installation in the reverse order of the removal procedure.

26. Check for proper operation of the air bag indicator. Check for proper operation of all components.

## Console

### REMOVAL & INSTALLATION

#### Vehicles Through 1992

▶ **See Figure 45**

1. Disconnect the negative battery cable.

2. Remove the two plug buttons located at the base of the console assembly, in order to expose the console mounting screws. Remove the mounting screws.

3. Remove the gearshift opening panel by snapping it out, then remove the console floor bracket retaining screw(s). Manual transaxle equipped vehicles with a floor shifter, as well as automatic transaxle equipped models with a column shifter, have one screw; automatic transaxle equipped models with a floor shifter have two screws.

4. Remove the rear access panel by snapping it out, then remove the three console-to-floor bracket retaining screws.

5. Move the floor mounted shift lever to the rearward-most position. Slide the console rearward and up. Disengage the electrical connectors, then remove the console from the vehicle.

**To install:**

6. Position the console assembly in the vehicle. Engage the electrical connectors.

7. Install the rear access panel and the three console-to-floor bracket retaining screws.

8. Install the gearshift opening panel and console floor bracket retaining screws.

9. Install the retaining screws, then install the two plug buttons located at the base of the console assembly.

10. Connect the negative battery cable.

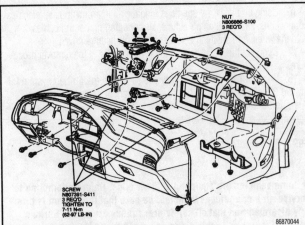

**Fig. 44 View of the instrument panel assembly and mounting bolt locations—1992–95 vehicles**

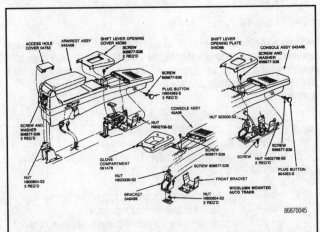

**Fig. 45 Floor console and related components—vehicles through 1992**

**1993–95 Vehicles**

▶ **See Figure 46**

1. Disconnect the negative battery cable.
2. Remove the console finish panel retaining screw.
3. Move the transaxle selector lever arm and support it rearward.
4. Remove the transaxle gear shift opening seal (it snaps out).
5. Remove the eight console panel-to-console panel bracket retaining screws. The two rear screws are under the the console glove compartment mat in the rear storage bin.
6. Disengage all necessary electrical connections, then remove the console panel.

**To install:**

7. Position the console panel, then engage the electrical connections. Install the eight retaining screws.
8. Install the transaxle gear shift opening seal by snapping it into place. Place the transaxle selector lever arm into its original position.
9. Install the console finish panel retaining screw. Connect the negative battery cable.

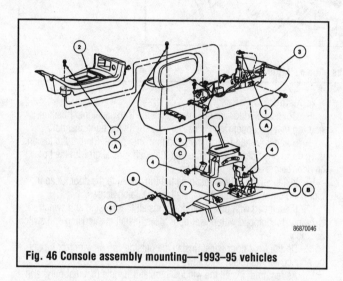

**Fig. 46 Console assembly mounting—1993–95 vehicles**

## Door Trim Panels

REMOVAL & INSTALLATION

**1986–88 Vehicles**

▶ **See Figures 47, 48 and 49**

1. Remove the window regulator handle by unsnapping the handle cover from the base to expose the attaching screw. Remove the screw, handle and wearplate.
2. Remove the door pull handle retaining screws and cover. Remove the handle.
3. Unfasten the upper trim panel retaining screws and remove the panel.
4. On Taurus vehicles, remove the trim panel opening panel cover.
5. Unfasten the retaining screw and remove the outside mirror's mounting hole cover assembly.
6. Remove all the screws retaining the door trim panel to the door, then using Trim Pad Removing Tool from Rotunda Moulding/Trim Kit 107-00401, or an equivalent door panel removing tool, pry the trim panel retaining push pins from the door inner panel.
7. If the trim panel is to be replaced, transfer all the push pins to the new panel. Replace any bent, broken or missing push pins.

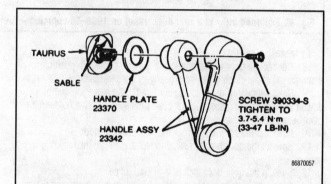

**Fig. 47 Remove the window regulator handle after unsnapping the handle cover from the base to expose the attaching screw**

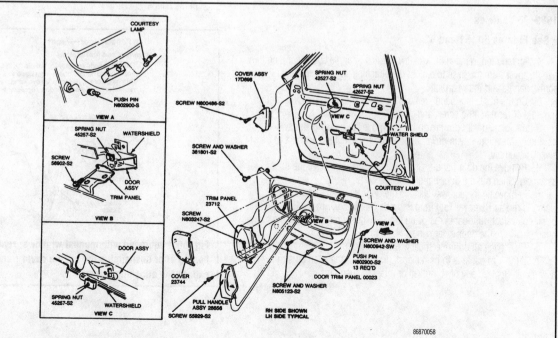

**Fig. 48 Exploded view of a front door panel on 1986–88 vehicles—Taurus shown, Sable similar**

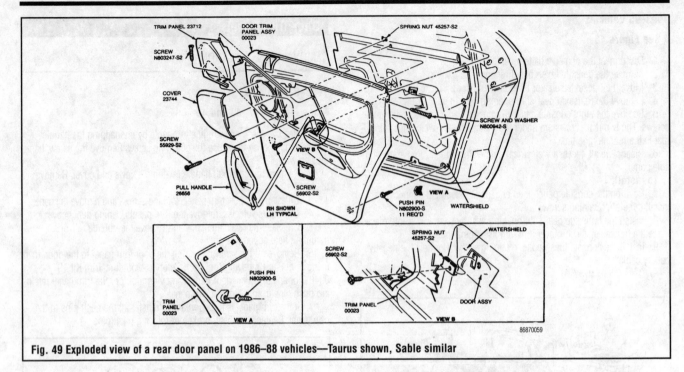

**Fig. 49 Exploded view of a rear door panel on 1986–88 vehicles—Taurus shown, Sable similar**

**To install:**

8. Connect all door wiring and install the trim panel into position, ensuring the upper ridge is seated properly in the door channel.

9. Snap the push pins in using your hand. Start at the top and move down the sides, making sure that the push pins align with the holes in the door before applying pressure.

10. Install all the screws retaining the trim panel-to-door.

11. Snap in the door handle retainer cover and install the retaining screws.

12. Snap in the front door lock control knob plate.

13. Install the outside rear view mirror mounting hole cover and retaining screw.

14. Install the window regulator handle (manual only) and snap in the handle cover.

**1989–95 Vehicles**

▶ **See Figures 50, 51 and 52**

1. As required, remove the window regulator handle by unsnapping the handle cover from the base to expose the attaching screw. Remove the screw, handle and the wearplate.

2. On the front door panel, remove the outside rear view mounting hole cover retaining screw and cover.

3. If equipped with power windows, remove the housing and switch assembly. If equipped with power door locks, remove the housing and switch assembly.

4. Remove the door handle filler retaining screw. Remove the filler assembly. Snap out the door handle retainer cover.

5. Remove all the screws retaining the door trim panel to the door. Using Trim Pad Removal Tool from Rotunda Moulding/Trim Kit 107-00401 or an equivalent door panel removing tool, pry the trim panel retaining push pins from the door inner panel.

6. Disengage all door electrical wiring connectors.

7. If the trim panel is to be replaced, transfer all the push pins to the new panel. Replace any bent, broken or missing push pins.

**To install:**

8. Connect all door wiring, then install the trim panel into position, ensuring that the upper ridge is seated properly in the door channel.

9. Using your hand, snap the push pins into place. Start at the top and move down the sides making sure that the push pins align with the holes in the door before applying pressure.

10. Install all the screws retaining the trim panel to the door. Snap in the door handle retainer cover, then install the retaining screws.

11. If equipped with power windows, install the housing and switch assembly. If equipped with power door locks, install the housing and switch assembly.

12. On the front door panel, install the outside rear view mirror mounting hole cover and retaining screw.

13. As required, install the window regulator handle (manual only) and snap in the handle cover.

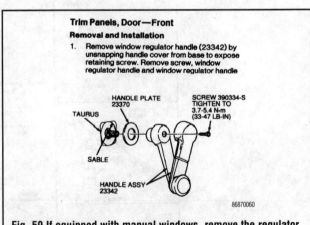

**Trim Panels, Door—Front**

**Removal and Installation**

1. Remove window regulator handle (23342) by unsnapping handle cover from base to expose retaining screw. Remove screw, window regulator handle and window regulator handle

**Fig. 50 If equipped with manual windows, remove the regulator handle after unsnapping the handle cover from the base to expose the attaching screw**

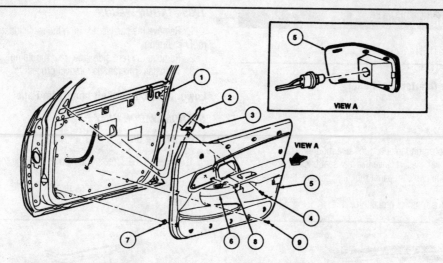

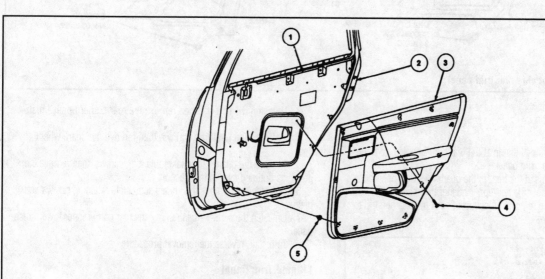

| Item | Part Number | Description |
|------|-------------|-------------|
| 1 | 20124 | Front Door |
| 2 | 17K709 | Rear View Mirror Mounting Hole Cover |
| 3 | N800486-S58 | Screw (1 Req'd Each Side) |
| 4 | N805621-S58 | Screw and Washer Assembly (1 Req'd Each Side) |
| 5 | 23942 | Front Door Trim Panel |

| Item | Part Number | Description |
|------|-------------|-------------|
| 6 | 14529 | Window Regulator Control Switch |
| 7 | N802900-S | Push Pin (14 Req'd Each Side) |
| 8 | 18B978 | Radio Speaker Grille Name Plate |
| 9 | N805621-S58 | Screw and Washer Assy (1 Req'd Each Door) |

86870061

**Fig. 51 Late model front door panel—vehicle equipped with power windows**

| Item | Part Number | Description |
|------|-------------|-------------|
| 1 | 237A04 | Rear Door Trim Water Shield Assy |
| 2 | 24631 | Rear Door |
| 3 | 27406 | Rear Door Trim Panel |
| 4 | N805621-S58 | Screw (1 Req'd Each Side) |
| 5 | N802900-S | Push Pin (11 Req'd Each Side) |

86870062

**Fig. 52 Late model rear door panel—vehicle equipped with power windows**

## Interior Trim Panels

### REMOVAL & INSTALLATION

**Roof Side Rear/Upper Quarter Trim Panel**

#### 1986–91 SEDANS

▶ See Figure 53

1. Remove the coat hooks and interior roof side mouldings.
2. For 1989 and later vehicles, remove the rear seat back assembly.
3. Remove the roof side rear trim panel retaining screws, then remove the panel.
4. To install, reverse the removal procedure.

#### 1995 STATION WAGON

1. Remove the screws retaining the roof side inner rear moulding to the roof headlining.
2. Remove the roof side inner rear moulding.
3. To install, reverse the removal procedure.

**Lower Rear Corner Left-hand Trim Panel**

#### STATION WAGON ONLY

▶ See Figure 55

1. Unfasten the screws, then remove the the roof side inner rear moulding.
2. Unfasten the screws, then remove the liftgate header rail garnish moulding.

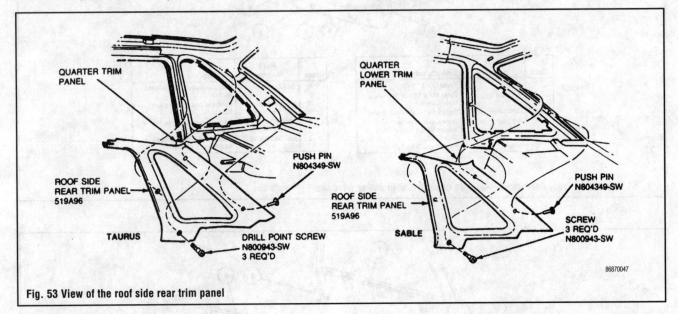

**Fig. 53 View of the roof side rear trim panel**

#### 1992–95 SEDANS

▶ See Figure 54

1. Remove the primary weatherstrip at the rear door opening from the headliner and roof side rear trim panel.
2. Remove the push pins at the front of the quarter window opening and at the rear to remove the roof side rear/upper quarter trim panel.
3. To install, reverse the removal procedure. Check the weatherstrip to be sure it is properly secured.

**Fig. 54 Location of the upper quarter trim panel—1995 sedan shown**

3. Unfasten the screws, then remove the rear corner upper finish panel.
4. Unfasten the retaining screws, then remove the spare wheel cover.
5. Remove the quarter trim panel retaining screws, then remove the panel, as outlined later in this section.
6. Unfasten the Remove the liftgate scuff plate retaining screws and plate.
7. Unfasten the screws, then remove the rear corner inner lower finish panel.
8. To install, reverse the removal procedure.

**Liftgate Trim Panel**

#### STATION WAGON ONLY

▶ See Figure 56

1. Disconnect the rear defroster wires.
2. Remove the liftgate window garnish moulding retaining crews and moulding.
3. Remove the liftgate assist handle retaining screws, then remove the handle.
4. Using the Trim Pad Removing Tool from Rotunda Moulding/Trim Kit 107-00401 or equivalent, pry out the push pins retaining the liftgate trim panel. Remove the panel.
5. To install, reverse the removal procedure. Replace any bent or damaged push pins.

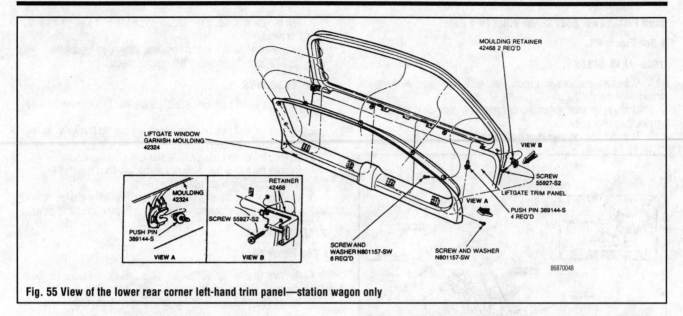

Fig. 55 View of the lower rear corner left-hand trim panel—station wagon only

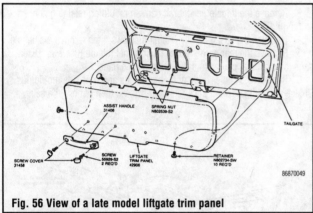

Fig. 56 View of a late model liftgate trim panel

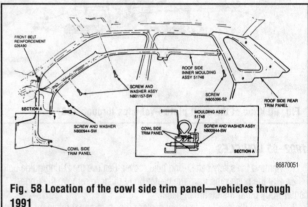

Fig. 58 Location of the cowl side trim panel—vehicles through 1991

## Cowl Side Trim Panel

### 1986–91 VEHICLES

▶ See Figures 57 and 58

1. Remove the center body pillar finish panels, as outlined later in this section.
2. Unfasten the retaining screw, then remove the coat hook.
3. Remove the interior roof side moulding retaining screws and moulding.
4. Remove the cowl side trim panel retaining screws, then remove the panel.
5. To install, reverse the removal procedure.

### 1992–95 VEHICLES

▶ See Figure 59

1. Remove the retaining screws at the front scuff plate to loosen the panel.
2. Remove the cowl side trim panel retaining screw and panel.
3. To install, reverse the removal procedure.

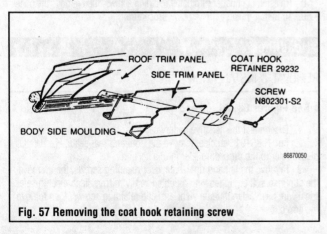

Fig. 57 Removing the coat hook retaining screw

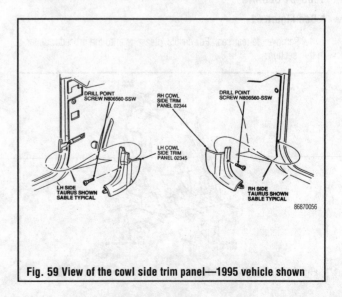

Fig. 59 View of the cowl side trim panel—1995 vehicle shown

**Scuff Plate/Lower Body Center Pillar Trim Panel**

▶ See Figure 60

### 1986–91 VEHICLES

1. Unfasten the upper center body pillar inside finish panel retaining screws, then remove the panel.
2. Unfasten the scuff plate/lower center pillar trim panel retaining screws, then remove the panel.
3. To install, reverse the removal procedure.

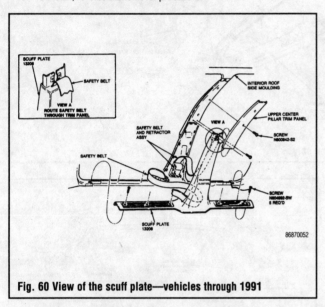

**Fig. 60 View of the scuff plate—vehicles through 1991**

### 1992–95 VEHICLES

1. Remove the safety belt D-ring/guide cover. Remove the D-ring/guide bolt.
2. Pry the push pins from the center body pillar to remove the upper center body pillar inside finish panel.
3. Remove the scuff plate/lower center pillar trim panel retaining screws and panel.
4. Remove the safety belt anchor bolt, then slide the safety belt through the lower center pillar trim panel slot.
5. To install, reverse the removal procedure. Position the safety belt anchor tab in its original position while feeding in the lower center pillar trim.

**Quarter Trim Panels**

### 1986–91 SEDANS

▶ See Figure 61

1. Remove the rear seat. For details, please refer to the procedure later in this section.

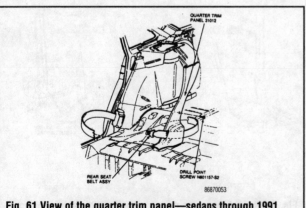

**Fig. 61 View of the quarter trim panel—sedans through 1991**

2. Remove the roof side trim panel. Remove the scuff plate/lower center pillar trim panel.
3. Unfasten the quarter trim panel retaining screw, then remove the panel.
4. Installation is the reverse of the removal procedure.

### 1992–95 SEDANS

1. Remove the rear seat. For details, please refer to the procedure later in this section.
2. Remove the roof side rear trim panel. Remove the screws at the rear scuff plate to loosen the panel.
3. Remove the quarter trim panel retaining push pin and panel.
4. Remove the bolt at the safety belt anchor tab, then slide the belt through the access slot in the quarter trim panel.
5. To install, reverse the removal procedure. Position the safety belt anchor tab in its original position while feeding in the quarter trim panel.

### STATION WAGON

▶ See Figure 62

1. Remove the rear seat. For details, please refer to the procedure later in this section.
2. Remove the roof side inner rear moulding retaining screws and moulding.
3. Remove the liftgate header rail garnish moulding retaining screws and moulding.
4. Unfasten the assist handle retaining screws, then remove the handle.
5. Remove the rear corner upper finish panel retaining screws. Disengage the electrical connectors, then remove the panel.
6. Remove the center body pillar mouldings and roof side mouldings. Unfasten the liftgate scuff plate retaining screws, then remove the scuff plate.

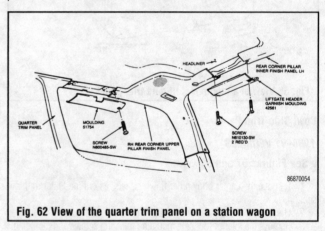

**Fig. 62 View of the quarter trim panel on a station wagon**

7. If equipped, remove the spare wheel cover retaining screws, then remove the cover.
8. Unfasten the quarter trim panel retaining screws, then remove the panel.
9. To install, reverse the removal procedure.

## Headliner

REMOVAL & INSTALLATION

▶ See Figures 63, 64, 65 and 66

1. Disconnect the negative battery cable.
2. For 1986–91 vehicles, remove the front and rear seats. For details, please refer to the procedure later in this section.
3. Remove the left and right-side visor retaining screws, then remove the sun visors. If equipped with a lighted vanity mirror, disconnect the electrical wires. Unfasten the sun visor arm clip retaining screws, then remove the arm clips.

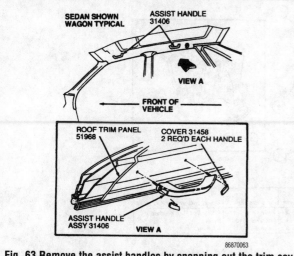

Fig. 63 Remove the assist handles by snapping out the trim covers, then removing the retaining screws

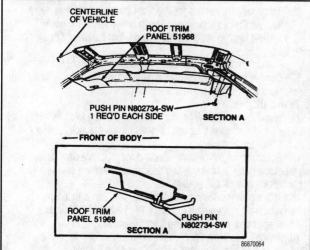

Fig. 64 Installing the headliner—vehicles without the roof sliding panel

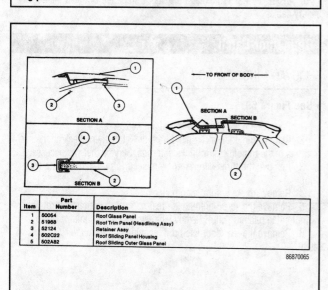

| Item | Part Number | Description |
|------|-------------|-------------|
| 1 | 50054 | Roof Glass Panel |
| 2 | 51968 | Roof Trim Panel (Headlining Assy) |
| 3 | 52124 | Retainer Assy |
| 4 | 502C22 | Roof Sliding Panel Housing |
| 5 | 502A82 | Roof Sliding Outer Glass Panel |

Fig. 65 Installing the headliner—sedans with the roof sliding panel

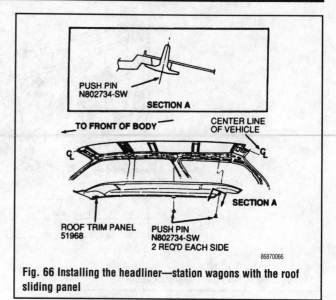

Fig. 66 Installing the headliner—station wagons with the roof sliding panel

4. If equipped, remove the roof console. Remove all dome and reading lights.

5. Snap out the assist strap trim covers. Remove the retaining screws (two screws each), then remove the straps from their mountings.

6. Remove the center body pillar inside finish panel.

7. If necessary, remove the weatherstrips at the door openings above the belt line. Remove the windshield side garnish moulding and front door scuff plate.

8. Remove the coat hook covers and coat hooks.

9. If equipped with a moonroof, remove the moonroof headlining retaining screws.

10. On sedans, remove the rear roof side trim panel.

11. On station wagons, remove the roof side inner moulding, the liftgate header rail garnish moulding, and the upper rear corner pillar finish panel.

12. Remove the quarter trim panel.

13. Remove the rear push pins, then remove the headliner from the vehicle.

**To install:**

➡The weatherstrip must overlap at the headlining and mouldings above the belt line.

14. Position the headliner assembly in the vehicle by aligning it at the front of the vehicle over the visor mounting holes, then loosely secure. Install the rear push pins.

15. Install the appropriate trim panels.

16. Install the coat hooks and covers. Install the assist straps.

17. Install all dome and reading lights.

18. If equipped, install the roof console.

19. Install the sun visors, connecting the electrical wiring, if applicable.

20. If removal was necessary, install the front and rear seats.

21. Connect the negative battery cable.

## Power Door Lock Actuator

### REMOVAL & INSTALLATION

♦ **See Figure 67**

1. Remove the door trim panel and watershield.

2. Using a letter **X** and ¼ in. (6mm) diameter drill bit, drill out the pop rivet attaching the actuator motor to the door. Disengage the wiring at the connector and the actuator rod at the latch assembly.

3. To install, attach the actuator motor rod to the door latch and engage the wire to the actuator connector.

4. Install the door actuator motor to the door with a pop rivet or equivalent fastener.

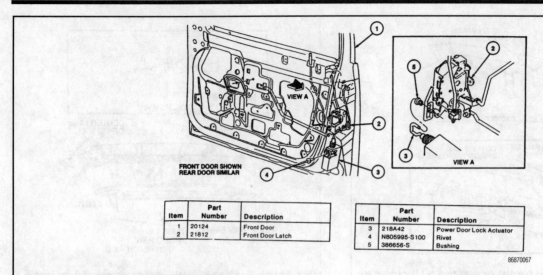

| Item | Part Number | Description |
|------|-------------|-------------|
| 1 | 20124 | Front Door |
| 2 | 21812 | Front Door Latch |

| Item | Part Number | Description |
|------|-------------|-------------|
| 3 | 218A42 | Power Door Lock Actuator |
| 4 | N805995-S100 | Rivet |
| 5 | 386656-S | Bushing |

86870067

Fig. 67 View of the power door lock actuator

## Front Door Latch

### REMOVAL & INSTALLATION

▶ **See Figure 68**

1. Disconnect the negative battery cable.
2. Remove the door trim panel and the watershield.
3. Check all connections of the remote control link and rod and service if necessary.
4. Remove the remote control assembly and the link clip.

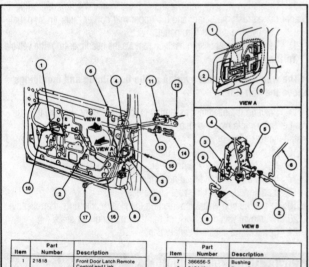

| Item | Part Number | Description |
|------|-------------|-------------|
| 1 | 21818 | Front Door Latch Remote Control and Link |
| 2 | 21940 | Front Door Latch Remote Control Link |
| 3 | 22134 | Front Door Latch Control Cylinder Rod |
| 4 | 22152 | Front Door Latch Actuating Rod |
| 5 | 21812 | Front Door Latch |
| 6 | 21850 | Door Latch Control Rod Knob |

| Item | Part Number | Description |
|------|-------------|-------------|
| 7 | 386656-S | Bushing |
| 8 | 218A42 | Power Door Lock Actuator |
| 9 | 386656-S | Bushing |
| 10 | N610128-S2 | Screw (1 Req'd Each Side) |
| 11 | 22404 | Door Handle |
| 12 | 391255-S102 | Rivet (2 Req'd Each Side) |
| 13 | 21985 | Door Lock Cylinder |
| 14 | 22023 | Door Lock Cylinder Retainer |
| 15 | N805653-S100 | Screw (3 Req'd Each Side) |
| 16 | N805995-S100 | Rivet |
| 17 | 377934-S | Grommet |

86870068

Fig. 68 Location of the front door latch and related components

5. Remove the clip attaching the control assembly and the link clip.
6. If so equipped, remove the clip from the actuator motor.
7. Remove the clip attaching the push button rod to the latch.
8. Remove the clip attaching the outside door handle rod to the latch assembly.
9. Remove the three screws attaching the latch assembly to the door.
10. Remove the latch assembly (with the remote control link lock cylinder rod) and anti-theft shield from the door cavity.

**To install:**

11. Install the new bushings and clips onto the new latch assembly. Install the anti-theft shield, remote control link and the lock cylinder rod onto the latch assembly levers.
12. Position the latch (with the link and rod) onto the door cavity, aligning the screw holes in the latch and door. Install the three screws and tighten to 35–70 inch lbs. (4–8 Nm).
13. Attach the outside door handle rod to the latch with a clip.
14. Attach the push button rod to the latch assembly with clip.
15. If equipped, remove the clip from the actuator motor.
16. Attach the lock cylinder rod to the lock cylinder with its clip.
17. Install the remote control assembly and the link clip.
18. Open and close the door to check the latch assembly operation.
19. Install the watershield and the door trim panel. Connect the negative battery cable.

## Rear Door Latch

### REMOVAL & INSTALLATION

▶ **See Figure 69**

1. Remove the door trim panel and the watershield.
2. Remove the door latch shield from the latch, then check all the connections of the remote control links and rods. Service them as necessary.
3. Remove the three screws or bolts securing the latch to the rear door.
4. Remove the rear door latch bellcrank.
5. Remove the screw holding the rear door latch remote control link (with the line retaining clip). Remove the remote control link.
6. Remove the rear door latch rod retaining clip from the rear door latch.

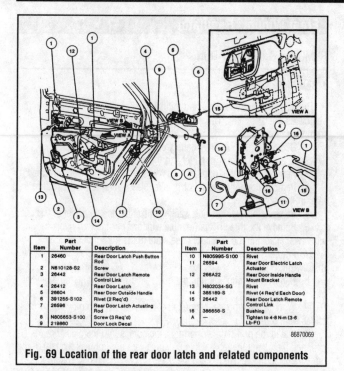

| Item | Part Number | Description |
|------|-------------|-------------|
| 1 | 26460 | Rear Door Latch Push Button Rod |
| 2 | N810128-S2 | Screw |
| 3 | 26442 | Rear Door Latch Remote Control Link |
| 4 | 26412 | Rear Door Latch |
| 5 | 26604 | Rear Door Outside Handle |
| 6 | 391255-S102 | Rivet (2 Req'd) |
| 7 | 26596 | Rear Door Latch Actuating Rod |
| 8 | N805853-S100 | Screw (3 Req'd) |
| 9 | 219860 | Door Lock Decal |

| Item | Part Number | Description |
|------|-------------|-------------|
| 10 | N805995-S100 | Rivet |
| 11 | 26594 | Rear Door Electric Latch Actuator |
| 12 | 266A22 | Rear Door Inside Handle Mount Bracket |
| 13 | N802034-SG | Rivet |
| 14 | 385189-S | Rivet (4 Req'd Each Door) |
| 15 | 26442 | Rear Door Latch Remote Control Link |
| 16 | 386656-S | Bushing |
| A | — | Tighten to 4–8 N·m (3-6 Lb-Ft) |

**Fig. 69 Location of the rear door latch and related components**

7. If equipped, remove the rivet from the rear door electric latch actuator, then disconnect the harness.

8. Remove the rear door latch, rear door electrical latch actuator, and rear door latch control rod as an assembly from the rear door.

9. If installing a new latch, transfer the bushings and retaining clips, along with the electric latch actuator and rear door latch control rod, to the new latch.

**To install:**

10. If so equipped, install the clip on the actuator motor.

11. Install the remote control slide links onto the latch assembly. Install the latch with the links in the door cavity.

12. Position the latch assembly to the door, aligning the screw holes in the latch and door. Install the three screws and tighten to 35–70 inch lbs. (4–8 Nm).

13. Install the door latch shield.

14. Install the bellcrank to the inner door panel. Install the bellcrank attaching rivet.

15. Open and close the door to check the latch component operation.

16. Install the watershield and door trim panel.

17. Connect the negative battery cable.

## Door Lock Assembly

### REMOVAL & INSTALLATION

▶ **See Figure 70**

➡ **When a lock cylinder must be replaced, replace both sides as a set to avoid carrying an extra set of keys.**

1. Remove the door trim panel and watershield.

2. Remove the clip attaching the lock cylinder rod to the lock cylinder.

3. Pry the lock cylinder out of the slot in the door.

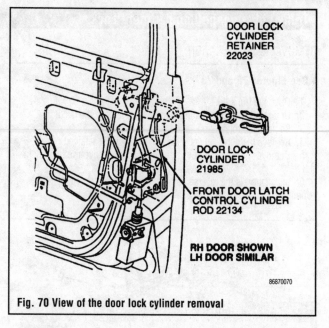

**Fig. 70 View of the door lock cylinder removal**

**To install:**

4. Work the lock cylinder assembly into the outer door panel.

5. Install the cylinder retainer into the slot and push the retainer onto the lock cylinder.

6. Connect the lock cylinder rod to the lock cylinder and install the clip. Lock and unlock the door to check for proper operation.

7. Install the watershield and door trim panel.

## Liftgate Lock

### REMOVAL & INSTALLATION

▶ **See Figure 71**

1. Remove the liftgate interior trim panel. Remove the latch rod from the control assembly lever.

2. Remove the screws retaining the latch assembly to the liftgate. Disengage the lock cylinder rod at the latch lever.

3. Remove the latch assembly from the liftgate.

4. Installation is the reverse of the removal procedure.

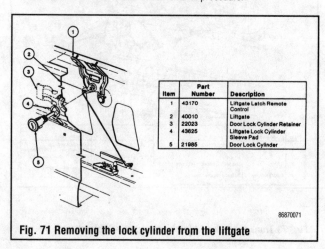

| Item | Part Number | Description |
|------|-------------|-------------|
| 1 | 43170 | Liftgate Latch Remote Control |
| 2 | 40010 | Liftgate |
| 3 | 22023 | Door Lock Cylinder Retainer |
| 4 | 43625 | Liftgate Lock Cylinder Sleeve Pad |
| 5 | 21985 | Door Lock Cylinder |

**Fig. 71 Removing the lock cylinder from the liftgate**

## Trunk Lid/Luggage Compartment Lock

### REMOVAL & INSTALLATION

▶ **See Figures 72 and 73**

1. Open the trunk lid.
2. Unfasten the latch retaining screws, then remove the latch.
3. Remove the retainer clip and the lock support.
4. Remove the pop rivet securing the lock cylinder retainer.
5. Remove the lock cylinder retainer as you remove the lock cylinder.

6. Installation is the reverse of the removal procedure. Tighten the retaining screws to 7–10 ft. lbs. (9–14 Nm).

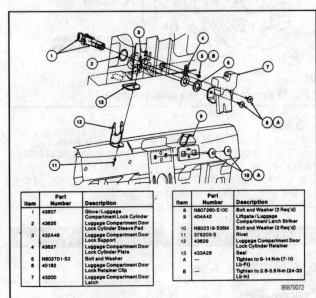

| Item | Part Number | Description | | Item | Part Number | Description |
|------|-------------|-------------|---|------|-------------|-------------|
| 1 | 43607 | Glove/Luggage Compartment Lock Cylinder | | 8 | N807260-S100 | Bolt and Washer (2 Req'd) |
| 2 | 43625 | Luggage Compartment Door Lock Cylinder Sleeve Pad | | 9 | 404A42 | Liftgate/Luggage Compartment Latch Striker |
| 3 | 432A48 | Luggage Compartment Door Lock Support | | 10 | N802319-S36M | Bolt and Washer (2 Req'd) |
| 4 | 43627 | Luggage Compartment Door Lock Cylinder Plate | | 11 | 375203-S | Rivet |
| 5 | N802701-S2 | Bolt and Washer | | 12 | 43629 | Luggage Compartment Door Lock Cylinder Retainer |
| 6 | 40182 | Luggage Compartment Door Lock Retainer Clip | | 13 | 433A28 | Seal |
| 7 | 43200 | Luggage Compartment Door Latch | | A | — | Tighten to 9-14 N·m (7-10 Lb-Ft) |
| | | | | B | — | Tighten to 2.6-3.8 N·m (24-33 Lb-In) |

86870072

**Fig. 72 Trunk lid lock and latch assembly—Taurus shown**

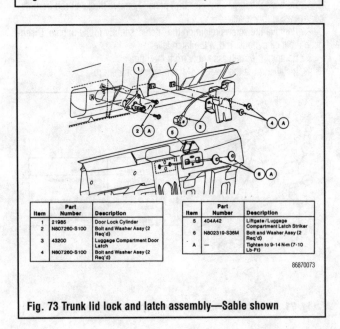

| Item | Part Number | Description | | Item | Part Number | Description |
|------|-------------|-------------|---|------|-------------|-------------|
| 1 | 21985 | Door Lock Cylinder | | 5 | 404A42 | Liftgate/Luggage Compartment Latch Striker |
| 2 | N807260-S100 | Bolt and Washer Assy (2 Req'd) | | 6 | N802319-S36M | Bolt and Washer Assy (2 Req'd) |
| 3 | 43200 | Luggage Compartment Door Latch | | A | — | Tighten to 9-14 N·m (7-10 Lb-Ft) |
| 4 | N807260-S100 | Bolt and Washer Assy (2 Req'd) | | | | |

86870073

**Fig. 73 Trunk lid lock and latch assembly—Sable shown**

## Front Window Regulator

### REMOVAL & INSTALLATION

▶ **See Figure 74**

The glass bracket assembly and regulator assembly are installed into the vehicle as one assembly. The glass bracket assembly may be disassembled from the regulator.

1. Disconnect the negative battery cable.
2. Remove the door trim panel and the watershield.
3. Remove the inside door belt weatherstrip and the glass stabilizer.
4. Remove the door glass. For details, please refer to the procedure later in this section.
5. Remove the two nuts and washers attaching the equalizer bracket.
6. Remove the three rivets (manual windows) or the four rivets (power windows) attaching the regulator base plate to the door inner panel.
7. For vehicles equipped with power windows, disconnect the body main wiring.
8. Remove the regulator and the glass bracket assembly from the vehicle.
9. Working on a bench, carefully bend the tab flat to remove the arm slides from the glass bracket C-channel.
10. Install the new regulator arm plastic guides into the glass bracket C-channel, then bend the tab back to 90° (use care not to break the tab). If the tab is cracked or broken, replace the glass bracket assembly. Ensure that the rubber bumper is installed properly on the new glass bracket, if a replacement is made.
11. For vehicles equipped with power windows, remove the bolts retaining the window regulator electric drive to the front door regulator.

➡ **If the regulator counterbalance spring must be removed or replaced for any reason, ensure that the regulator arms are in a fixed position prior to removal, to prevent possible injury during C-spring unwinding.**

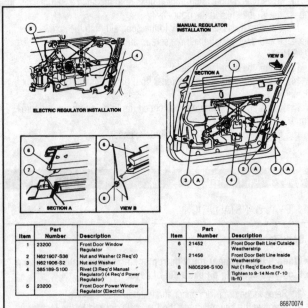

| Item | Part Number | Description | | Item | Part Number | Description |
|------|-------------|-------------|---|------|-------------|-------------|
| 1 | 23200 | Front Door Window Regulator | | 6 | 21452 | Front Door Belt Line Outside Weatherstrip |
| 2 | N621907-S36 | Nut and Washer (2 Req'd) | | 7 | 21456 | Front Door Belt Line Inside Weatherstrip |
| 3 | N621906-S2 | Nut and Washer | | 8 | N805296-S100 | Nut (1 Req'd Each End) |
| 4 | 385189-S100 | Rivet (3 Req'd Manual Regulator) (4 Req'd Power Regulator) | | A | — | Tighten to 9-14 N·m (7-10 lb-ft) |
| 5 | 23200 | Front Door Power Window Regulator (Electric) | | | | |

86870074

**Fig. 74 View of a manual and electric front window regulator installation**

**To install:**

12. Install the window channel bracket onto the front door window regulator.

13. For power windows, install the window regulator electric drive to the front door window regulator.

14. Install the regulator with the pre-assembled glass bracket into the vehicle. Set the regulator base plate to the door inner panel using the base plate locator tab as a guide.

15. Install the new pop rivets (385189–S100 or equivalent) to attach the regulator to the door inner panel.

16. Install the equalizer bracket.

17. Install the inside door belt weatherstrip and the glass stabilizer.

18. Lower the regulator arms to the access holes in the door inner panel. Install the door glass, as outlined later in this section.

19. If applicable, connect the body main wiring.

20. Adjust the glass to ensure proper alignment with the glass run. Cycle the glass for smooth operation.

21. Install the door trim panel and the watershield. Connect the negative battery cable.

## Rear Window Regulator

REMOVAL & INSTALLATION

▶ **See Figure 75**

1. Disconnect the negative battery cable.
2. Remove the door trim panel and the watershield.
3. Remove the rear door window, as outlined later in this section.
4. Remove the three rivets (manual windows) or four rivets (power windows) attaching the regulator mounting plate assembly to the door inner panel.

➡ **Use the access hole in the door inner panel for removal and installation.**

5. Slide the regulator arm plastic guides out of the C-channel.
6. For manual windows, remove the window regulator from door.
7. For vehicles equipped with power windows, disengage the wiring connector. Remove the electrical window regulator from the rear door.
8. For power windows, remove the bolts retaining the regulator electric drive to the regulator, then remove the electric drive.

**To install:**

9. For power windows, install the electric drive to the regulator.
10. Install the window regulator through the access hole in the rear door and slide the regulator arm plastic guides into the glass bracket C-channel.

11. Install new rivets (part No. 385189–S100 or equivalent) using Heavy Duty Riveter D80L–23200–A or equivalent, or ¼–20 x ½ in. screw and washer assemblies to secure the regulator mounting plate to the door inner panel.

12. For power windows, engage the electrical wiring connector.
13. Cycle the glass to check for smooth operation.
14. Install the watershield and the door trim panel. Connect the negative battery cable.

## Electric Window Motor

REMOVAL & INSTALLATION

▶ **See Figure 76**

1. Raise the window to the full up position, if possible. If the glass cannot be raised and is in a partially down or full down position, it must be supported so that it will not fall into the door well during motor removal.

2. Disconnect the negative battery cable.
3. Remove the door trim panel and watershield.

➡ **Before motor drive assembly removal, make sure that the regulator arm is in a fixed position to prevent dangerous counterbalance spring unwinding!**

4. Remove the two forward regulator mounting plate attaching rivets. Use a ¼ in. (6mm) drill bit, then carefully drill out the attaching rivets.

5. Remove the three window motor mounting screws.
6. Push the regulator mounting plate outboard sufficiently to remove the power window motor.

**To install:**

7. Position the motor and drive assembly to the power window regulator, then install the three retaining screws snug (NOT tight).

8. Attach the window regulator electric drive wires at the connector, then cycle the door window glass to be sure of gear engagement. After the gears are engaged, tighten the three motor mounting screws to 50–84 inch lbs. (5.6–9.6 Nm).

9. Install two new regulator mounting plate rivets (part No. 385189–S100 or equivalent) using Heavy Duty Riveter No. D80L–23200–A or equivalent.

10. Connect the negative battery cable.
11. Check the power window for proper operation.
12. Install the door trim panel and the watershield.

➡ **Verify that all the drain holes at the bottom of the doors are open to prevent water accumulation over the motor.**

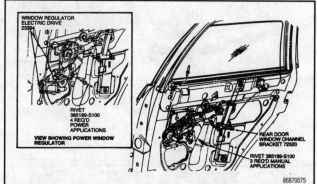

**Fig. 75 View of a manual and electric rear window regulator installation**

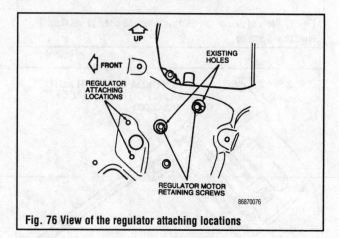

**Fig. 76 View of the regulator attaching locations**

## Windshield Glass

### REMOVAL & INSTALLATION

▶ See Figures 77, 78, 79 and 80

### ❋❋ CAUTION

**Safety glasses and gloves MUST be worn! Failure to do so may result in personal injury.**

1. Disconnect the negative battery cable. Remove the windshield wiper arms and blades.
2. Remove all windshield trim mouldings. Remove the cowl vent/leaf screen.
3. Using Rear View Mirror Remover T91T-17700-A or equivalent, remove the rear view mirror by pulling it upward to remove it from the windshield glass retainer.
4. If using the "Music Wire" method of removing the windshield:
   a. Using a three-foot length of single strand music wire (with the smallest available diameter), cut the urethane seal and rubber seal around the entire edge of the windshield.
   b. Force the music wire through the seal at the bottom of the windshield. With someone holding the wire inside the vehicle and the other person holding the wire outside the vehicle, move the wire along the bottom and then along the sides and top of the windshield to cut the seal.
5. If using the "Glass Adhesive Cutting Tool" method:
   a. Use Rotunda Knife with Offset Blade 107-R-1511, or Rotunda Interior Auto-Glass Cut-out Knife Kit 163-00001, or equivalent, to cut the sealer. When using this tool, follow the manufacturer's instructions.

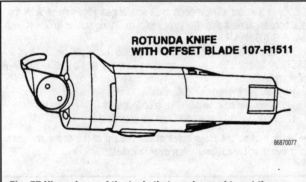

**Fig. 77 View of one of the tools that can be used to cut the windshield sealer**

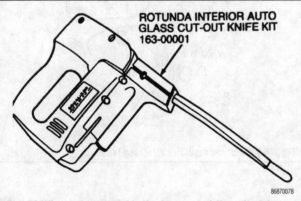

**Fig. 78 When using special tools, be sure to follow all of the manufacturer's instructions**

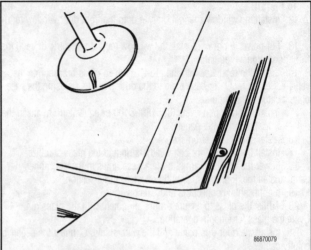

**Fig. 79 Use a suitable suction tool to remove the windshield glass from the vehicle**

6. Using tool D81T-33610-H, or another suitable glass holding suction tool, remove the windshield from the vehicle.

**To install:**

7. If the existing urethane remains on the windshield opening flange, the new urethane can be applied over it, but at no time should the thickness of the material be above 0.10 in. (2.5mm).
8. Using a clean brush, apply urethane metal primer ESB-M2G234-A or equivalent to any sheet metal that has been exposed along the windshield.
9. Apply about 4 in. (10cm) or vinyl foam tape (C6AZ-19627-A or equivalent that meets Ford Motor Company's specification ESB-M3G77-A) along the cowl and lower A pillars.
10. Allow the primer to dry for a minimum of about 30 minutes:
11. Be sure that the windshield is clean and free of any dirt or used material. Install the rear view mirror mounting bracket, as required.

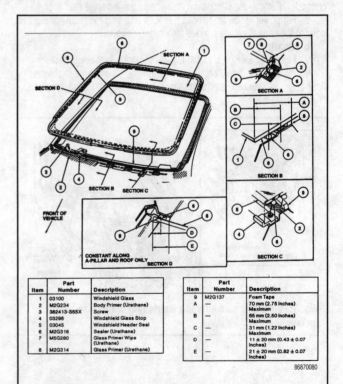

| Item | Part Number | Description |
|------|-------------|-------------|
| 1 | 03100 | Windshield Glass |
| 2 | M2G234 | Body Primer (Urethane) |
| 3 | 382413-S55X | Screw |
| 4 | 03296 | Windshield Glass Stop |
| 5 | 03045 | Windshield Header Seal |
| 6 | M2G316 | Sealer (Urethane) |
| 7 | M5G280 | Glass Primer Wipe (Urethane) |
| 8 | M2G314 | Glass Primer (Urethane) |

| Item | Part Number | Description |
|------|-------------|-------------|
| 9 | M2G137 | Foam Tape |
| A | — | 70 mm (2.75 inches) Maximum |
| B | — | 65 mm (2.50 inches) Maximum |
| C | — | 31 mm (1.22 inches) Maximum |
| D | — | 11 ± 20 mm (0.43 ± 0.07 inches) |
| E | — | 21 ± 20 mm (0.82 ± 0.07 inches) |

**Fig. 80 Installing the windshield glass**

12. Using a lint-free rag, wipe the inside edge of the windshield, 0.80 in. (20mm) along the top and 2.75 in. (70mm) along the sides and bottom with urethane glass wipe ESB–M5B280–A or equivalent. Wipe off immediately after application since this material will flash dry.

13. Install the windshield moulding. Position the glass on top of the lower glass stops. Center it top-and-bottom and side-to-side. Adjust the lower glass stops, as required.

14. Using crayon, make alignment marks at points on four sides of both the glass and the window opening.

15. Remove the window glass and the moulding assemblies from the vehicle.

16. Using a clean brush, apply urethane primer to the edge of the windshield, 0.80 in. (20mm) along the top and 2.75 in. (70mm) along the sides and bottom.

17. Apply an even bead of urethane ESB–M2G316–A around the entire sheet metal flange using an air pressure cartridge gun; air pressure should be about 40 psi (276 kPa). The bead should be triangular in shape, 0.55 in. (14mm) high and 0.33 in. (8mm) at the base.

18. Apply a double bead of urethane along the cowl top and bottom of the opening. Install the windshield, taking care to position the glass with the alignment marks. This must be done within 15 minutes of applying the urethane.

19. Install the wiper arms, wiper blades and leaf screen. Install the rear view mirror.

## Front Door Glass

### REMOVAL & INSTALLATION

▶ **See Figure 81**

1. Remove the door trim panel and the watershield. For details, please refer to the procedure earlier in this section.

2. Remove the inside door belt weatherstrip assembly.

3. Lower the glass to access the holes in the door inner panel. Remove the two rivets retaining the glass to the glass channel bracket.

➡ **Prior to removing the center pins from the rivets, it is recommended that a suitable block support be inserted between the door outer panel and glass bracket to stabilize the glass during rivet removal. Remove the center pin from each rivet using a drift punch. Using a ¼ in. (6mm) diameter drill, remove the remaining rivets. Use care when drilling out the rivets to prevent enlarging the bracket and spacer holes, and damaging the retainer.**

4. Loosen the nut and washer securing the door glass inner stabilizer.

5. Remove the glass by tipping it forward, then removing it from between the door belt opening to the outer side of door.

6. Remove the drill shavings and pins from the bottom of the door.
**To install:**

7. Snap the plastic retainer and spacer into the two glass retainer holes. Ensure that the metal washer within the retainer assembly is on the outer side of the glass.

8. Install the glass into the door at the belt. Ensure that the glass is set within the front and rear glass run retainers.

9. Position the glass to the glass bracket. Install two new rivets to secure the glass to the glass bracket.

➡ **Two ¼–20 x 1 in. bolts and two ¼–20 nuts and washers may be used as alternates for glass retention. However, their torque must not exceed 36–61 inch lbs. (4–7 Nm). Equivalent metric retainers may be used.**

10. Install the inside door belt weatherstrip assembly.

11. Raise the glass to within 3 in. (75mm) of the full–up position, then adjust glass as described in the following procedure.

12. Install the door trim panel and watershield, as outlined earlier in this section.

### ADJUSTMENT

▶ **See Figure 82**

1. Remove the door trim panel and the watershield.

2. Lower the door glass approximately 3 in. (75mm) from the full-up position.

3. Loosen the nut and washer assemblies **A** and **B** retaining the equalizer bracket to the door inner panel. Refer to the following door glass adjustment illustration.

4. Loosen the nut and washer assembly **C** retaining the door glass stabilizer.

5. With the door open, place your hands on each side of the glass and pull the glass fully into the door glass run assembly at the B-pillar.

6. Tighten the nut and washer **A**, then apply a downward pressure on the equalizer bracket and tighten the nut/washer **B** to 5–8 ft. lbs. (7–11 Nm).

7. Set the door glass stabilizer so that it is slightly touching the glass, then tighten the nut and washer assembly to 5–8 ft. lbs.

8. Cycle the door glass to ensure proper function and door fit.

9. Install the door trim panel and the watershield.

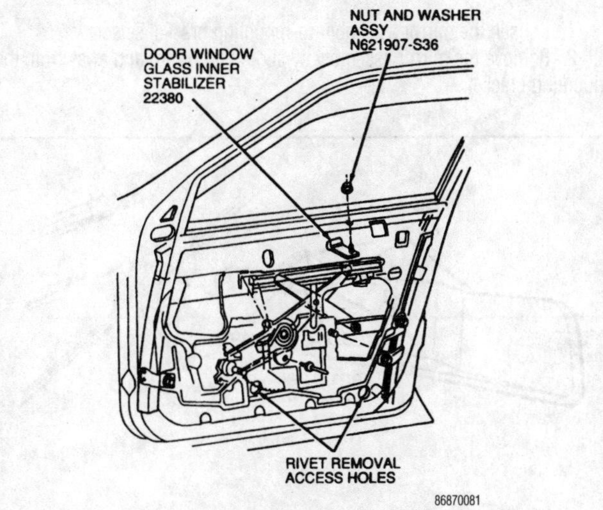

**Fig. 81 View of the front door glass removal and installation**

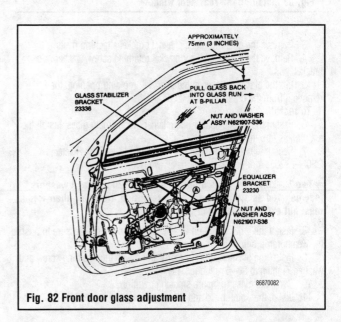

**Fig. 82 Front door glass adjustment**

## Rear Door Glass

### REMOVAL & INSTALLATION

▶ **See Figure 83**

1. Remove the door trim panel and the watershield.
2. Remove the inner door belt weatherstrip by gently pulling the weatherstrip from the door flange.

➡**Before removing the rivet center pins, a suitable block support should be inserted between the door outer panel and glass to stabilize the glass during rivet pin removal. Use a ¼ in. (6mm) diameter drill to drill out the remainder of the rivet, being careful not to enlarge the sheet metal holes or damage the plastic retainer and spacer.**

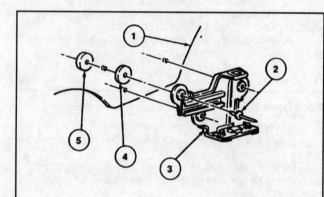

| Item | Part Number | Description |
|------|-------------|-------------|
| 1 | 25712 | Rear Door Window Glass |
| 2 | 385323-S102 | Rivet (3 Req'd) |
| 3 | 263A52 | Rear Door Glass Channel Front Bracket |
| 4 | 234A44 | Door Window Glass Bracket Spacer |
| 5 | 234A46 | Door Window Glass Channel Bracket Retainer |

86870083

**Fig. 83 Installing the rear door window**

3. Remove the glass-to-glass channel bracket attaching rivets.
4. Remove the glass stabilizer bracket retaining screw, washer and bracket.
5. Lift the glass up between the door belt molding opening, then remove it from the door.

**To install:**

6. Fasten the plastic spacer and retainers to the main glass. Install the main glass into the door.
7. Secure the glass-to-glass bracket using Heavy Duty Riveter D80L–23200–A or equivalent to install two rivets.

➡**Two ¼–20 x 1 in. bolts along with two ¼–20 nuts and washers may be used as alternates for glass retention. However, their torque must not exceed 36–61 inch lbs. (4–7 Nm).**

8. Install the inner door belt weatherstrip, using hand pressure to push the weatherstrip onto the door flange.
9. Install the glass stabilizer bracket along with the retaining screw and washer. Tighten to 36–61 inch lbs. (4–7 Nm).
10. Cycle the glass to insure smooth operation.
11. Install the watershield and the door trim panel.

### ADJUSTMENT

▶ **See Figure 84**

The rear door glass has in-and-out and fore-and-aft adjustments. The in-and-out adjustment may be accomplished by loosening the two screws in the lower glass bracket assembly and moving the glass in or out as required. The fore-and-aft adjustment is accomplished by loosening the tube run upper screw and washer assembly, as well as the lower nut and washer assembly attaching the rear door run and bracket assembly to the inner door panel, then adjusting the glass fore or aft as required.

When setting the glass to the window opening, lower the glass approximately 2 in. (50mm) from the full-up position with the four retention points loosely installed. Set the glass forward into the B-pillar and tighten the lower run nut and washer number one, followed by numbers two, three and four.

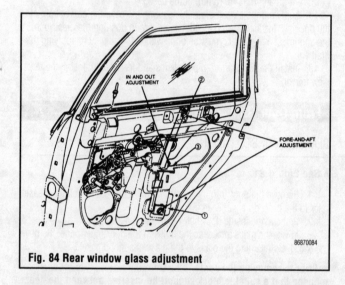

**Fig. 84 Rear window glass adjustment**

## Inside Rear View Mirror

### REPLACEMENT

**Except Electric Mirror**

▶ **See Figure 85**

1. Loosen the mirror assembly-to-mounting bracket setscrew.
2. Remove the mirror assembly by sliding it upward and away from the mounting bracket.

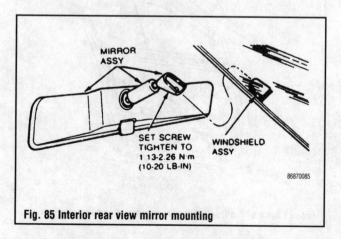

**Fig. 85 Interior rear view mirror mounting**

3. If the bracket vinyl pad remains on the windshield, apply low heat from an electric heat gun until the vinyl softens. Peel the vinyl off the windshield and discard.

**To install:**

4. Make sure the glass, bracket, and adhesive kit (Rear View Mirror Repair Kit D9AZ–19554–B or equivalent) are at least at a room temperature of 65–75°F (18–24°C).

5. Locate and mark the mirror mounting bracket location on the outside surface of the windshield with a wax pencil.

6. Thoroughly clean the bonding surfaces of the glass and the bracket to remove old adhesive. Use a mild abrasive cleaner on the glass and fine sandpaper on the bracket to lightly roughen the surface. Wipe it clean with the alcohol-moistened cloth.

7. Crush the accelerator vial (part of Rear View Mirror Repair Kit D9AZ–19554–B or equivalent), then apply the accelerator to the bonding surface of the bracket and windshield. Let it dry for three minutes.

8. Apply two drops of adhesive (Rear View Mirror Repair Kit D9AZ–19554–B or equivalent) to the mounting surface of the bracket. Using a clean toothpick or wooden match, quickly spread the adhesive evenly over the mounting surface of the bracket.

9. Quickly position the mounting bracket on the windshield. The ⅜ in. (10mm) circular depression in the bracket must be toward the inside of the passenger compartment. Press the bracket firmly against the windshield for one minute.

10. Allow the bond to set for five minutes. Remove any excess bonding material from the windshield with an alcohol-dampened cloth.

11. Attach the mirror to the mounting bracket and tighten the setscrew to 10–20 inch lbs. (1.13–2.26 Nm).

## Electric Mirror

1. Remove the grommet from the garnish moulding above the mirror assembly.

2. Pull the wire assembly away from the garnish moulding opening until the connector is exposed, then disconnect the wire.

3. Loosen the mirror assembly-to-mounting bracket setscrew and remove the mirror by sliding upward, away from the bracket.

**To install:**

4. If the mounting bracket on the windshield has to be serviced, refer to the following steps. Otherwise, installation is the reverse of removal.

5. If the bracket vinyl pad remains on the windshield, apply low heat from an electric heat gun until the vinyl softens. Peel the vinyl off the windshield and discard.

6. Make sure the glass, bracket, and adhesive kit (Rear view Mirror Repair Kit D9AZ–19554–B or equivalent) are at least at a room temperature of 65–75°F (18–24°C).

7. Locate and mark the mirror mounting bracket location on the outside surface of the windshield with a wax pencil.

8. Thoroughly clean the bonding surfaces of the glass and the bracket to remove old adhesive. Use a mild abrasive cleaner on the glass and fine sandpaper on the bracket to lightly roughen the surface. Wipe it clean with the alcohol-moistened cloth.

9. Crush the accelerator vial (part of Rear View Mirror Repair Kit D9AZ–19554–B or equivalent), then apply the accelerator to the bonding surface of the bracket and windshield. Let it dry for three minutes.

10. Apply two drops of adhesive (Rear View Mirror Repair Kit D9AZ–19554–B or equivalent) to the mounting surface of the bracket. Using a clean toothpick or wooden match, quickly spread the adhesive evenly over the mounting surface of the bracket.

11. Quickly position the mounting bracket on the windshield. The ⅜ in. (10mm) circular depression in the bracket must be toward the inside of the passenger compartment. Press the bracket firmly against the windshield for one minute.

12. Allow the bond to set for five minutes. Remove any excess bonding material from the windshield with an alcohol-dampened cloth.

13. Position the mirror assembly over the mounting bracket after it has dried.

14. Tighten the mounting bracket setscrew to 10–20 inch lbs. (1.13–2.26 Nm).

15. Engage the wire connector and push the wire back into the garnish moulding. Install the grommet to the garnish moulding.

**AIR/FUEL RATIO:** The ratio of air-to-gasoline by weight in the fuel mixture drawn into the engine.

**AIR INJECTION:** One method of reducing harmful exhaust emissions by injecting air into each of the exhaust ports of an engine. The fresh air entering the hot exhaust manifold causes any remaining fuel to be burned before it can exit the tailpipe.

**ALTERNATOR:** A device used for converting mechanical energy into electrical energy.

**AMMETER:** An instrument, calibrated in amperes, used to measure the flow of an electrical current in a circuit. Ammeters are always connected in series with the circuit being tested.

**AMPERE:** The rate of flow of electrical current present when one volt of electrical pressure is applied against one ohm of electrical resistance.

**ANALOG COMPUTER:** Any microprocessor that uses similar (analogous) electrical signals to make its calculations.

**ARMATURE:** A laminated, soft iron core wrapped by a wire that converts electrical energy to mechanical energy as in a motor or relay. When rotated in a magnetic field, it changes mechanical energy into electrical energy as in a generator.

**ATMOSPHERIC PRESSURE:** The pressure on the Earth's surface caused by the weight of the air in the atmosphere. At sea level, this pressure is 14.7 psi at 32°F (101 kPa at 0°C).

**ATOMIZATION:** The breaking down of a liquid into a fine mist that can be suspended in air.

**AXIAL PLAY:** Movement parallel to a shaft or bearing bore.

**BACKFIRE:** The sudden combustion of gases in the intake or exhaust system that results in a loud explosion.

**BACKLASH:** The clearance or play between two parts, such as meshed gears.

**BACKPRESSURE:** Restrictions in the exhaust system that slow the exit of exhaust gases from the combustion chamber.

**BAKELITE:** A heat resistant, plastic insulator material commonly used in printed circuit boards and transistorized components.

**BALL BEARING:** A bearing made up of hardened inner and outer races between which hardened steel balls roll.

**BALLAST RESISTOR:** A resistor in the primary ignition circuit that lowers voltage after the engine is started to reduce wear on ignition components.

**BEARING:** A friction reducing, supportive device usually located between a stationary part and a moving part.

**BIMETAL TEMPERATURE SENSOR:** Any sensor or switch made of two dissimilar types of metal that bend when heated or cooled due to the different expansion rates of the alloys. These types of sensors usually function as an on/off switch.

**BLOWBY:** Combustion gases, composed of water vapor and unburned fuel, that leak past the piston rings into the crankcase during normal engine operation. These gases are removed by the PCV system to prevent the buildup of harmful acids in the crankcase.

**BRAKE PAD:** A brake shoe and lining assembly used with disc brakes.

**BRAKE SHOE:** The backing for the brake lining. The term is, however, usually applied to the assembly of the brake backing and lining.

**BUSHING:** A liner, usually removable, for a bearing; an anti-friction liner used in place of a bearing.

**CALIPER:** A hydraulically activated device in a disc brake system, which is mounted straddling the brake rotor (disc). The caliper contains at least one piston and two brake pads. Hydraulic pressure on the piston(s) forces the pads against the rotor.

**CAMSHAFT:** A shaft in the engine on which are the lobes (cams) which operate the valves. The camshaft is driven by the crankshaft, via a belt, chain or gears, at one half the crankshaft speed.

**CAPACITOR:** A device which stores an electrical charge.

**CARBON MONOXIDE (CO):** A colorless, odorless gas given off as a normal byproduct of combustion. It is poisonous and extremely dangerous in confined areas, building up slowly to toxic levels without warning if adequate ventilation is not available.

**CARBURETOR:** A device, usually mounted on the intake manifold of an engine, which mixes the air and fuel in the proper proportion to allow even combustion.

**CATALYTIC CONVERTER:** A device installed in the exhaust system, like a muffler, that converts harmful byproducts of combustion into carbon dioxide and water vapor by means of a heat-producing chemical reaction.

**CENTRIFUGAL ADVANCE:** A mechanical method of advancing the spark timing by using flyweights in the distributor that react to centrifugal force generated by the distributor shaft rotation.

**CHECK VALVE:** Any one-way valve installed to permit the flow of air, fuel or vacuum in one direction only.

**CHOKE:** A device, usually a moveable valve, placed in the intake path of a carburetor to restrict the flow of air.

**CIRCUIT:** Any unbroken path through which an electrical current can flow. Also used to describe fuel flow in some instances.

**CIRCUIT BREAKER:** A switch which protects an electrical circuit from overload by opening the circuit when the current flow exceeds a predetermined level. Some circuit breakers must be reset manually, while most reset automatically.

**COIL (IGNITION):** A transformer in the ignition circuit which steps up the voltage provided to the spark plugs.

**COMBINATION MANIFOLD:** An assembly which includes both the intake and exhaust manifolds in one casting.

**COMBINATION VALVE:** A device used in some fuel systems that routes fuel vapors to a charcoal storage canister instead of venting them into the atmosphere. The valve relieves fuel tank pressure and allows fresh air into the tank as the fuel level drops to prevent a vapor lock situation.

**COMPRESSION RATIO:** The comparison of the total volume of the cylinder and combustion chamber with the piston at BDC and the piston at TDC.

**CONDENSER:** 1. An electrical device which acts to store an electrical charge, preventing voltage surges. 2. A radiator-like device in the air conditioning system in which refrigerant gas condenses into a liquid, giving off heat.

**CONDUCTOR:** Any material through which an electrical current can be transmitted easily.

**CONTINUITY:** Continuous or complete circuit. Can be checked with an ohmmeter.

**COUNTERSHAFT:** An intermediate shaft which is rotated by a mainshaft and transmits, in turn, that rotation to a working part.

**CRANKCASE:** The lower part of an engine in which the crankshaft and related parts operate.

**CRANKSHAFT:** The main driving shaft of an engine which receives reciprocating motion from the pistons and converts it to rotary motion.

**CYLINDER:** In an engine, the round hole in the engine block in which the piston(s) ride.

**CYLINDER BLOCK:** The main structural member of an engine in which is found the cylinders, crankshaft and other principal parts.

**CYLINDER HEAD:** The detachable portion of the engine, usually fastened to the top of the cylinder block and containing all or most of the combustion chambers. On overhead valve engines, it contains the valves and their operating parts. On overhead cam engines, it contains the camshaft as well.

**DEAD CENTER:** The extreme top or bottom of the piston stroke.

**DETONATION:** An unwanted explosion of the air/fuel mixture in the combustion chamber caused by excess heat and compression, advanced timing, or an overly lean mixture. Also referred to as "ping".

**DIAPHRAGM:** A thin, flexible wall separating two cavities, such as in a vacuum advance unit.

**DIESELING:** A condition in which hot spots in the combustion chamber cause the engine to run on after the key is turned off.

**DIFFERENTIAL:** A geared assembly which allows the transmission of motion between drive axles, giving one axle the ability to turn faster than the other.

**DIODE:** An electrical device that will allow current to flow in one direction only.

**DISC BRAKE:** A hydraulic braking assembly consisting of a brake disc, or rotor, mounted on an axle, and a caliper assembly containing, usually two brake pads which are activated by hydraulic pressure. The pads are forced against the sides of the disc, creating friction which slows the vehicle.

**DISTRIBUTOR:** A mechanically driven device on an engine which is responsible for electrically firing the spark plug at a predetermined point of the piston stroke.

**DOWEL PIN:** A pin, inserted in mating holes in two different parts allowing those parts to maintain a fixed relationship.

**DRUM BRAKE:** A braking system which consists of two brake shoes and one or two wheel cylinders, mounted on a fixed backing plate, and a brake drum, mounted on an axle, which revolves around the assembly.

**DWELL:** The rate, measured in degrees of shaft rotation, at which an electrical circuit cycles on and off.

**ELECTRONIC CONTROL UNIT (ECU):** Ignition module, module, amplifier or igniter. See Module for definition.

**ELECTRONIC IGNITION:** A system in which the timing and firing of the spark plugs is controlled by an electronic control unit, usually called a module. These systems have no points or condenser.

**END-PLAY:** The measured amount of axial movement in a shaft.

**ENGINE:** A device that converts heat into mechanical energy.

**EXHAUST MANIFOLD:** A set of cast passages or pipes which conduct exhaust gases from the engine.

**FEELER GAUGE:** A blade, usually metal, or precisely predetermined thickness, used to measure the clearance between two parts.

**FIRING ORDER:** The order in which combustion occurs in the cylinders of an engine. Also the order in which spark is distributed to the plugs by the distributor.

**FLOODING:** The presence of too much fuel in the intake manifold and combustion chamber which prevents the air/fuel mixture from firing, thereby causing a no-start situation.

**FLYWHEEL:** A disc shaped part bolted to the rear end of the crankshaft. Around the outer perimeter is affixed the ring gear. The starter drive engages the ring gear, turning the flywheel, which rotates the crankshaft, imparting the initial starting motion to the engine.

**FOOT POUND (ft. lbs. or sometimes, ft.lb.):** The amount of energy or work needed to raise an item weighing one pound, a distance of one foot.

**FUSE:** A protective device in a circuit which prevents circuit overload by breaking the circuit when a specific amperage is present. The device is constructed around a strip or wire of a lower amperage rating than the circuit it is designed to protect. When an amperage higher than that stamped on the fuse is present in the circuit, the strip or wire melts, opening the circuit.

**GEAR RATIO:** The ratio between the number of teeth on meshing gears.

**GENERATOR:** A device which converts mechanical energy into electrical energy.

**HEAT RANGE:** The measure of a spark plug's ability to dissipate heat from its firing end. The higher the heat range, the hotter the plug fires.

**HUB:** The center part of a wheel or gear.

**HYDROCARBON (HC):** Any chemical compound made up of hydrogen and carbon. A major pollutant formed by the engine as a byproduct of combustion.

**HYDROMETER:** An instrument used to measure the specific gravity of a solution.

**INCH POUND (inch lbs.; sometimes in.lb. or in. lbs.):** One twelfth of a foot pound.

**INDUCTION:** A means of transferring electrical energy in the form of a magnetic field. Principle used in the ignition coil to increase voltage.

**INJECTOR:** A device which receives metered fuel under relatively low pressure and is activated to inject the fuel into the engine under relatively high pressure at a predetermined time.

**INPUT SHAFT:** The shaft to which torque is applied, usually carrying the driving gear or gears.

**INTAKE MANIFOLD:** A casting of passages or pipes used to conduct air or a fuel/air mixture to the cylinders.

**JOURNAL:** The bearing surface within which a shaft operates.

**KEY:** A small block usually fitted in a notch between a shaft and a hub to prevent slippage of the two parts.

**MANIFOLD:** A casting of passages or set of pipes which connect the cylinders to an inlet or outlet source.

**MANIFOLD VACUUM:** Low pressure in an engine intake manifold formed just below the throttle plates. Manifold vacuum is highest at idle and drops under acceleration.

**MASTER CYLINDER:** The primary fluid pressurizing device in a hydraulic system. In automotive use, it is found in brake and hydraulic clutch systems and is pedal activated, either directly or, in a power brake system, through the power booster.

**MODULE:** Electronic control unit, amplifier or igniter of solid state or integrated design which controls the current flow in the ignition primary circuit based on input from the pick-up coil. When the module opens the primary circuit, high secondary voltage is induced in the coil.

**NEEDLE BEARING:** A bearing which consists of a number (usually a large number) of long, thin rollers.

**OHM:** (Ω) The unit used to measure the resistance of conductor-to-electrical flow. One ohm is the amount of resistance that limits current flow to one ampere in a circuit with one volt of pressure.

**OHMMETER:** An instrument used for measuring the resistance, in ohms, in an electrical circuit.

**OUTPUT SHAFT:** The shaft which transmits torque from a device, such as a transmission.

**OVERDRIVE:** A gear assembly which produces more shaft revolutions than that transmitted to it.

**OVERHEAD CAMSHAFT (OHC):** An engine configuration in which the camshaft is mounted on top of the cylinder head and operates the valve either directly or by means of rocker arms.

**OVERHEAD VALVE (OHV):** An engine configuration in which all of the valves are located in the cylinder head and the camshaft is located in the cylinder block. The camshaft operates the valves via lifters and pushrods.

**OXIDES OF NITROGEN (NOx):** Chemical compounds of nitrogen produced as a byproduct of combustion. They combine with hydrocarbons to produce smog.

**OXYGEN SENSOR:** Use with the feedback system to sense the presence of oxygen in the exhaust gas and signal the computer which can reference the voltage signal to an air/fuel ratio.

**PINION:** The smaller of two meshing gears.

**PISTON RING:** An open-ended ring with fits into a groove on the outer diameter of the piston. Its chief function is to form a seal between the piston and cylinder wall. Most automotive pistons have three rings: two for compression sealing; one for oil sealing.

**PRELOAD:** A predetermined load placed on a bearing during assembly or by adjustment.

**PRIMARY CIRCUIT:** the low voltage side of the ignition system which consists of the ignition switch, ballast resistor or resistance wire, bypass, coil, electronic control unit and pick-up coil as well as the connecting wires and harnesses.

**PRESS FIT:** The mating of two parts under pressure, due to the inner diameter of one being smaller than the outer diameter of the other, or vice versa; an interference fit.

**RACE:** The surface on the inner or outer ring of a bearing on which the balls, needles or rollers move.

**REGULATOR:** A device which maintains the amperage and/or voltage levels of a circuit at predetermined values.

**RELAY:** A switch which automatically opens and/or closes a circuit.

**RESISTANCE:** The opposition to the flow of current through a circuit or electrical device, and is measured in ohms. Resistance is equal to the voltage divided by the amperage.

**RESISTOR:** A device, usually made of wire, which offers a preset amount of resistance in an electrical circuit.

**RING GEAR:** The name given to a ring-shaped gear attached to a differential case, or affixed to a flywheel or as part of a planetary gear set.

**ROLLER BEARING:** A bearing made up of hardened inner and outer races between which hardened steel rollers move.

**ROTOR:** 1. The disc-shaped part of a disc brake assembly, upon which the brake pads bear; also called, brake disc. 2. The device mounted atop the distributor shaft, which passes current to the distributor cap tower contacts.

**SECONDARY CIRCUIT:** The high voltage side of the ignition system, usually above 20,000 volts. The secondary includes the ignition coil, coil wire, distributor cap and rotor, spark plug wires and spark plugs.

**SENDING UNIT:** A mechanical, electrical, hydraulic or electro-magnetic device which transmits information to a gauge.

**SENSOR:** Any device designed to measure engine operating conditions or ambient pressures and temperatures. Usually electronic in nature and designed to send a voltage signal to an on-board computer, some sensors may operate as a simple on/off switch or they may provide a variable voltage signal (like a potentiometer) as conditions or measured parameters change.

**SHIM:** Spacers of precise, predetermined thickness used between parts to establish a proper working relationship.

**SLAVE CYLINDER:** In automotive use, a device in the hydraulic clutch system which is activated by hydraulic force, disengaging the clutch.

**SOLENOID:** A coil used to produce a magnetic field, the effect of which is to produce work.

**SPARK PLUG:** A device screwed into the combustion chamber of a spark ignition engine. The basic construction is a conductive core inside of a ceramic insulator, mounted in an outer conductive base. An electrical charge from the spark plug wire travels along the conductive core and jumps a preset air gap to a grounding point or points at the end of the conductive base. The resultant spark ignites the fuel/air mixture in the combustion chamber.

**SPLINES:** Ridges machined or cast onto the outer diameter of a shaft or inner diameter of a bore to enable parts to mate without rotation.

**TACHOMETER:** A device used to measure the rotary speed of an engine, shaft, gear, etc., usually in rotations per minute.

**THERMOSTAT:** A valve, located in the cooling system of an engine, which is closed when cold and opens gradually in response to engine heating, controlling the temperature of the coolant and rate of coolant flow.

**TOP DEAD CENTER (TDC):** The point at which the piston reaches the top of its travel on the compression stroke.

**TORQUE:** The twisting force applied to an object.

**TORQUE CONVERTER:** A turbine used to transmit power from a driving member to a driven member via hydraulic action, providing changes in drive ratio and torque. In automotive use, it links the driveplate at the rear of the engine to the automatic transmission.

**TRANSDUCER:** A device used to change a force into an electrical signal.

**TRANSISTOR:** A semi-conductor component which can be actuated by a small voltage to perform an electrical switching function.

**TUNE-UP:** A regular maintenance function, usually associated with the replacement and adjustment of parts and components in the electrical and fuel systems of a vehicle for the purpose of attaining optimum performance.

**TURBOCHARGER:** An exhaust driven pump which compresses intake air and forces it into the combustion chambers at higher than atmospheric pressures. The increased air pressure allows more fuel to be burned and results in increased horsepower being produced.

**VACUUM ADVANCE:** A device which advances the ignition timing in response to increased engine vacuum.

**VACUUM GAUGE:** An instrument used to measure the presence of vacuum in a chamber.

**VALVE:** A device which control the pressure, direction of flow or rate of flow of a liquid or gas.

**VALVE CLEARANCE:** The measured gap between the end of the valve stem and the rocker arm, cam lobe or follower that activates the valve.

**VISCOSITY:** The rating of a liquid's internal resistance to flow.

**VOLTMETER:** An instrument used for measuring electrical force in units called volts. Voltmeters are always connected parallel with the circuit being tested.

**WHEEL CYLINDER:** Found in the automotive drum brake assembly, it is a device, actuated by hydraulic pressure, which, through internal pistons, pushes the brake shoes outward against the drums.

# MASTER INDEX